Fourth Edition

INTERNATIONAL BUSINESS

Alan M. Rugman
Kelley School of Business, Indiana University

Simon Collinson
Warwick Business School, The University of Warwick

Richard M. Hodgetts
(deceased)

FT Prentice Hall
FINANCIAL TIMES

An imprint of **Pearson Education**
Harlow, England • London • New York • Boston • San Francisco • Toronto
Sydney • Tokyo • Singapore • Hong Kong • Seoul • Taipei • New Delhi
Cape Town • Madrid • Mexico City • Amsterdam • Munich • Paris • Milan

Pearson Education Limited

Edinburgh Gate
Harlow
Essex CM20 2JE
England

and Associated Companies throughout the world

Visit us on the World Wide Web at:
http://www.pearsoned.co.uk

_____

First published by McGraw-Hill, Inc. 1995
Fourth edition 2006

ISBN 13: 978-0-273-70174-3
ISBN 10: 0-273-70174-6

British Library Cataloguing-in-Publication Data
A catalogue record for this book is available from the British Library.

Library of Congress Cataloging-in-Publication Data

Rugman, Alan M.
  International business / Alan M. Rugman, Simon Collinson, Richard M. Hodgetts.—4th ed.
    p. cm.
  Includes bibliographical references and index.
  ISBN 0-273-70174-6 (paperback)
  1. International business enterprises—Management. I. Collinson, Simon. II. Hodgetts,
Richard M. III. Title.

HD62.4.R843 2005
658'.049—dc22   2005054646

10 9 8 7 6 5 4 3 2
09 08 07 06

Typeset by 72 in 10/12.5 Minion
Printed by Mateu Cromo Artes Graficas, Spain

Contents in Brief

Contents

Part One

THE WORLD OF INTERNATIONAL BUSINESS

Chapter 3

The Triad and International Business | 67

Part Two

THE ENVIRONMENT OF INTERNATIONAL BUSINESS

Chapter 4

International Politics | 99

Chapter 5

International Culture | 127

Part Three

INTERNATIONAL BUSINESS STRATEGIES

Chapter 8

Multinational Strategy   225

Chapter 9

Organizing Strategy   252

Part Four

INTERNATIONAL BUSINESS STRATEGIES IN ACTION

Chapter 15

Corporate Strategy and National Competitiveness

Chapter 16

European Union

Chapter 20

Ethics and the Natural Environment 606

List of Figures, Tables, and Maps

Tables

Maps

Supporting resources

Visit www.pearsoned.co.uk/rugman to find valuable resources.

Companion Website for students
- Engaging interactivities to reinforce learning
- Video clips that illustrate core international business issues and stimulate discussion
- Multiple-choice questions to test understanding
- Extensive links to valuable resources on the web
- An online glossary to explain key terms
- Interactive online flashcards that allow the reader to check definitions against the key terms during revision

For instructors
- Complete, downloadable Instructor's Manual, including:
  - Chapter objectives, summaries, and outlines
  - Suggested class schedules and assignments
  - Answers to review and discussion questions
- PowerPoint slides that can be downloaded and used as OHTs
- Testbank of over 2,000 questions
- Extensive links to valuable resources on the web
- A gradebook function that allows you to create classes in which you can track and monitor your students' grades

Also: The Companion Website provides the following features:
- Search tool to help locate specific items of content
- Online help and support to assist with website usage and troubleshooting

For more information please contact your local Pearson Education sales representative or visit www.pearsoned.co.uk/rugman.

Preface

Major improvements were made to this Fourth Edition of one of the leading international business textbooks in Europe and Asia. We have retained the focus on the "triad" economies of the EU, Japan, and North America but also increased coverage of the non-triad economies, especially with a greatly increased emphasis on the role of China and India in Chapter 19. This chapter, along with Chapters 5, 13, and 17, was prepared by Simon Collinson of Warwick Business School. Simon joins us as co-author of the textbook, and he will take an even greater role in future editions. He represents a younger generation of teachers and scholars who use this book. The four chapters by Simon have been totally reorganized and rewritten to update the text.

The other major changes involve international financial management—Chapters 7 and 14—which have been prepared by Robert Grosse of Thunderbird. These also update and improve the text. Along with a greater theoretical emphasis in the first three chapters and in Chapter 20 on analytical frameworks for the field, these rewritten chapters serve to upgrade the analytical content of the book, as requested by many adopters.

Features of the Fourth Edition

- Chapter 19 was completely reworked with much new material in emerging Asian markets, including China and India, and adding the software industry and outsourcing.

- Chapter 20 was rewritten to increase its emphasis on corporate ethics and the natural environment.

- Of the 100 cases, approximately 40 new ones were developed, as indicated in the case list. All the other cases were updated.

- Chapter 5 on culture has been extensively revised and includes new materials such as John Mole's framework and insights from the GLOBE Research Program.

- The focus on regional activity is even greater, with additional firm level data on the world's 500 largest firms (in Chapters 1–3). Also new triad diagrams showing intraregional trade and FDI have been added to give an upfront focus on regional business.

- The basic integrative FSA/CSA matrix has been moved from Chapter 20 to Chapter 2, to serve as a synthesizing device. The Dunning eclectic model has been added as an appendix to Chapter 3.

- Chapters 7 and 14 were totally rewritten with more advanced material on international financial management and several new cases.

- The treatment of the transnational network has been extended with a three-part diagram in Chapter 9.

- Chapter 13 on political risk now focuses on country risk analysis and links this to investment appraisal and NPV final analysis.

- Chapter 17 on Japan was rewritten with an historical approach to explain the background of its current economic state. The Renault/Nissan case was entirely revised and moved to Chapter 17 from Chapter 6.

- All tables were updated.

- Photos were added, including logo pictures of MNEs.

We wish to thank several professors who made extremely helpful comments on earlier drafts of this Fourth Edition. Their names are given on page xxxii.

At Pearson we thank Editor Matthew Walker, Development Editors Stuart Hay and Paula Parish, and Production Editors Nicola Chilvers and Mary Lince. We also thank Helen Rugman and Melanie Hunter for proofreading the manuscript, and most of all, Cecilia Brain for excellent research assistance and contributions to the resources available on the companion website and Mildred Harris for exceptional dedication in the preparation of this book and its supporting materials.

Alan M. Rugman, Indiana
Simon Collinson, Warwick

Dr. Alan M. Rugman is L. Leslie Waters Chair of International Business at the Kelley School of Business, Indiana University, where he is also Professor of International Business and Professor of Business Economics and Public Policy. He is also Director of the IU CIBER. He was Thames Water Fellow in Strategic Management at Templeton College, University of Oxford from 1998–2001 where he remains an Associate Fellow. Previously he was Professor of International Business at the University of Toronto 1987–1998, Dalhousie University 1979–1987, and the University of Winnipeg 1970–1978. He has also been a visiting professor at Columbia Business School, London Business School, Harvard University, U.C.L.A., M.I.T., Warwick Business School, and the University of Paris-La Sorbonne.

Dr. Rugman has published over 200 articles dealing with the economic, managerial, and strategic aspects of multinational enterprises and with trade and investment policy. These have appeared in such leading refereed journals as *The American Economic Review, Strategic Management Journal, Journal of International Business Studies*, and *California Management Review*.

His 40 books include *Inside the Multinationals* (Columbia University Press, 1981); *Multinationals and Transfer Pricing* (co-author) (St. Martin's Press, 1985); *Administered Protection in America* (co-author) (Routledge, 1987); *Global Corporate Strategy and Trade Policy* (co-author) (Routledge, 1990); *Foreign Investment and North American Free Trade* (ed.) (University of South Carolina Press, 1994); *International Business* (co-author) (McGraw-Hill, 1985, 1995); *The Theory of multinational Enterprises* and *Multinational Enterprises and Trade Policy* (Elgar, 1996); *Environmental Regulations and Corporate Strategy* (co-author) (Oxford University Press, 1999); *Multinationals as Flagship Firms* (co-author) (Oxford University Press, 2000); *International Business* (FT/Prentice Hall, 2000, 2003); *The End of Globalization* (Random House, 2000; AMACOM 2001); *The Oxford Handbook of International Business* (co-ed) (Oxford University Press, 2001); and *The Regional Multinationals* (Cambridge University Press, 2005).

As a leading authority in international business, Dr. Rugman served as Vice-President of the Academy of International Business in 1989–1990 and was elected a Fellow of the Academy in 1991. He is now serving as President of AIB from 2004–2006. He is also a Fellow of the Royal Society of Arts, elected 1998. He serves on the Editorial Boards of *Strategic Management Journal, Management International Review, Journal of International Business Studies*, and several others.

In 1994 he received the Booz, Allen Hamilton Award as Eminent Scholar in International Management, Academy of Management. He was also honored at a special plenary session of the European International Business Association annual meetings, Slovenia, December 2004 for the 25th Anniversary of his 1979 book, *International Diversification and the Multinational Enterprise*.

Born in England in 1945, Dr. Rugman became a Canadian citizen in 1973 and a US resident in 2002. He earned his BA in economics from Leeds University in 1966, MSc in economic development from London University's School of Oriental and African Studies (SOAS) in 1967, and his PhD in economics from Simon Fraser University in 1974. He was elected to an MA (Oxon) in 1998.

He has been a consultant to major private-sector companies, research institutes, and government agencies. These include Exxon/Imperial Oil, Kodak, Royal Bank of Canada, Northern Telecom, the United Nations (UNCTAD), NAFTA's Commission on Environmental Co-operation, and the Organization for Economic Co-operation and Development (OECD). Dr. Rugman served as an outside advisor on free trade, foreign investment, and international competitiveness to two Canadian Prime Ministers over the 1986–1993 period.

Dr. Simon Collinson is Senior Lecturer in International Business at Warwick Business School, the University of Warwick, UK. He teaches International Business at Undergraduate, MBA, and Executive levels and previously held the post of Associate Dean (MBAs) at Warwick Business School, heading one of the largest and most highly-rated MBA programs in Europe. Dr. Collinson has had visiting positions as Senior Research Fellow at the Australian Graduate School of Management (AGSM) in Sydney and Visiting Professor at the Kelley School of Business, Indiana University. He is also an Associate at the Center for the Study of Globalization and Regionalization (CSGR), University of Warwick, and UK Representative for the Academy of Management (AOM) International Management Division.

Dr. Collinson was formerly Lecturer and Senior Research Fellow at Edinburgh University Management School and the Assistant Director of the Japanese–European Technology Studies (JETS) institute for seven years. During this period he was awarded a Royal Society Fellowship to study in Japan, hosted by the National Institute for Science and Technology Policy (NISTEP) in Tokyo.

His research interests include global innovation strategies, R&D, knowledge and intellectual asset management in multinational firms; the competitiveness of international UK firms; national systems of innovation and emerging economies; high-technology entrepreneurship, small firm networks, and regional development; Japan and China: local business practices and cross-cultural management, foreign direct investment, and economic change. Dr. Collinson has received research funding awards from the UK Economic and Social Research Council, the UK government's

Department of Trade and Industry, Japan's Science and Technology Agency, the British Royal Society, and DGXII of the European Union. He has research, consulting, and executive teaching experience with firms such as British Aerospace, Corus Steel, Diageo, HSBC, ICI, GKN, Jones Lang LaSalle, Kodak (Japan), Lloyd's Register, Nippon Steel, Philips, Prudential, and Sony.

In addition to numerous book chapters and a sole-authored book, *Small and Successful in Japan* (Ashgate Publishing, 1996), he has published in a range of refereed journals including *Organization Studies*, *International Journal of Technology Management*, *European Management Journal*, *R&D Management*, *Organization Dynamics*, and *Technology Analysis and Strategic Management*.

Born in Tanzania in 1964, Dr. Collinson earned a Joint-BA (Hons.) in geography and sociology at Leeds University and an MA in Human Geography at the University of Florida, Gainesville. He was awarded his DPhil from the Science Policy Research Unit (SPRU) at Sussex University in 1991.

In Memoriam: Richard M. Hodgetts

Richard M. Hodgetts passed away in November 2001, having battled cancer for several years. Richard was an enthusiastic, involved, and dedicated scholar who excelled in producing clearly written text that is relevant and readable for management students.

Richard Hodgetts was a Professor of Management in the Department of Management and International Business at Florida International University (FIU). He earned his BS at New York University in 1963, his MBA at Indiana University in 1964, and his PhD at the University of Oklahoma in 1968. He was at the University of Nebraska, Lincoln (1966–1975); Texas Tech University (1975–1976); and Florida International University (FIU) from 1976–2001. Dr. Hodgetts published over 125 articles and research papers. He was the author or co-author

of 50 different books. Overall, Richard Hodgetts sold one million copies of his textbooks.

Professor Hodgetts also served as a consultant for a wide variety of organizations and firms including Advanced Micro Systems, AT&T Technologies, Digital Equipment, Eastman Kodak, General Electric, General Motors, Hewlett Packard, Motorola, Procter & Gamble, Wal-Mart, and the US Federal Reserve System.

Professor Hodgetts was the recipient of a number of awards including the Outstanding Educator Award, Academy of Management (1999), the John F. Mee, Management Contribution Award, Management History Division, Academy of Management (1998), and the Professorial Excellence Program Award, FIU (1997).

Guide to the Case Studies

CHAPTER	TYPE OF CASE	ORGANIZATION/INDUSTRY	COUNTRY/ REGION	NEW?	PAGE
Chapter 1 Regional and Global Strategy	■ Active Learning Case	Coke goes worldwide with a local strategy	US		4
	■ International Business Strategy in Action	Amazon.com	US		14
	■ International Business Strategy in Action	The Italian tile industry	EU: Italy		20
	■ Real Case	Big oil gets bigger	US/EU/Japan		26
	■ Real Case	Wal-Mart	US	✔	27
Chapter 2 The Multinational Enterprise	■ Active Learning Case	Disneyland in Europe	US		37
	■ International Business Strategy in Action	Italian family firms	EU: Italy		44
	■ International Business Strategy in Action	Nestlé	EU/Emerging Economies	✔	48
	■ Real Case	Starbucks	US	✔	58
	■ Real Case	Sony	Japan	✔	59
Chapter 3 The Triad and International Business	■ Active Learning Case	Boeing versus Airbus	US/EU		68
	■ International Business Strategy in Action	Aflac	Japan/US		73
	■ International Business Strategy in Action	Lafarge and Cemex: concrete multinationals	US/Emerging Economies	✔	74
	■ Real Case	Matsushita and Philips	Japan/EU		88
	■ Real Case	Toys "Я" Us in Europe and Japan	US/EU/Japan	✔	89
Chapter 4 International Politics	■ Active Learning Case	How risky is investment in Russia?	Emerging Economies		100
	■ International Business Strategy in Action	Softwood lumber: not-so-free trade	US		104
	■ International Business Strategy in Action	Non-governmental organizations and political power	US/EU		112
	■ Real Case	How environmental regulations can be used as trade barriers	US/Emerging Economies		123
	■ Real Case	Embraer versus Bombardier	US/Emerging Economies: Brazil/US	✔	124
Chapter 5 International Culture	■ Active Learning Case	Culture clash at Pharmacia and Upjohn	EU: Sweden and Italy/US	✔	128
	■ International Business Strategy in Action	McDonald's	US	✔	133
	■ International Business Strategy in Action	Danone and Parmalat – going international, staying local	EU: Sweden and Italy/US		146

CHAPTER	TYPE OF CASE	ORGANIZATION/INDUSTRY	COUNTRY/ REGION	NEW?	PAGE
	■ Real Case	Do not throw your "meishi"!	EU: UK/Japan	✔	152
	■ Real Case	Cultural differences in international sport	EU/US		153
Chapter 6 International Trade	■ Active Learning Case	Trade of the Triad and China	US/EU/Japan/ Emerging Economies: China	✔	158
	■ International Business Strategy in Action	China's organic food exports	Emerging Economies: China	✔	166
	■ International Business Strategy in Action	The EU-US courier wars	US		171
	■ Real Case	Outsourcing to China	US	✔	180
	■ Real Case	Dumping on trade complaints			181
Chapter 7 International Financial Markets and Institutions	■ Active Learning Case	Barclays Bank international financial dealings	EU: UK	✔	192
	■ International Business Strategy in Action	The Wall Stret crash of 2001	US		203
	■ International Business Strategy in Action	AngloGold Ashanti	Emerging Economies: South Africa		212
	■ Real Case	HSBC	EU: UK		218
	■ Real Case	World financial crises	Emerging Economies		219
Chapter 8 Multinational Strategy	■ Active Learning Case	Vodafone and the triad telecom market	EU		226
	■ International Business Strategy in Action	Arthur Andersen, Accenture, and McKinsey	US		229
	■ International Business Strategy in Action	Fuji Xerox and Xerox	US/Japan		240
	■ Real Case	Mountain Equipment Co-op: a small business	Emerging Economies: Canada		247
	■ Real Case	Benetton	EU: Italy		248
Chapter 9 Organizing Strategy	■ Active Learning Case	Procter & Gamble	US	✔	253
	■ International Business Strategy in Action	Aventis	EU: France/ Germany	✔	257
	■ International Business Strategy in Action	Making matrix work	EU/US/Japan		263

CHAPTER	TYPE OF CASE	ORGANIZATION/INDUSTRY	COUNTRY/ REGION	NEW?	PAGE
	■ Real Case	LVMH: organizing luxury products in the international arena	EU		273
	■ Real Case	Command Alkon: a small software business	US		274
Chapter 10 Production Strategy	■ Active Learning Case	The GE production process and Six Sigma	US		279
	■ International Business Strategy in Action	When the rubber hits the road: Michelin, Ford, and Firestone	EU/US		284
	■ International Business Strategy in Action	Greening the supply chain	EU		289
	■ Real Case	Flextronics	Emerging Economies: Singapore	✔	305
	■ Real Case	Nike	US		306
Chapter 11 Marketing Strategy	■ Active Learning Case	Volkswagen in the United States	EU		311
	■ International Business Strategy in Action	Kola Real Group	Emerging Economies: Mexico	✔	318
	■ International Business Strategy in Action	IKEA in international markets	EU: Sweden		322
	■ Real Case	Citigroup in China	US/Emerging Economies: China		334
	■ Real Case	Brazilian soap operas: a world market	Emerging Economies: Brazil		335
Chapter 12 Human Resource Management Strategy	■ Active Learning Case	The Coca-Cola company thinks local	US		340
	■ International Business Strategy in Action	P&O cruise ships	EU		348
	■ International Business Strategy in Action	German management gets tough	EU		355
	■ Real Case	Outsourcing to India	US/Emerging Economies: India	✔	365
	■ Real Case	Executive search firms	EU		366
Chapter 13 Political Risk and Negotiation Strategy	■ Active Learning Case	Kodak in China: changing the rules of the game	US/Emerging Economies: China	✔	371
	■ International Business Strategy in Action	Political risk for De Beers	Emerging Economies: South Africa	✔	387
	■ International Business Strategy in Action	Dell goes to Brazil	US/Emerging Economies: Brazil	✔	391

CHAPTER	TYPE OF CASE	ORGANIZATION/INDUSTRY	COUNTRY/ REGION	NEW?	PAGE
	■ Real Case	Yukos and the Russian oligarchs	Japan/ Emerging Economies: Russia		398
	■ Real Case	Problems with ports	Japan/ Emerging Economies: Kenya	✔	400
Chapter 14 International Financial Management	■ Active Learning Case	British Airways	EU: UK/US		405
	■ International Business Strategy in Action	Tax havens	Emerging Economies		414
	■ International Business Strategy in Action	News Corp		✔	418
	■ Real Case	Skandia	EU: Sweden		435
	■ Real Case	Repsol's acquisition of YPF	EU: Spain/ Emerging Economies: Argentina	✔	436
Chapter 15 Corporate Strategy and National Competitiveness	■ Active Learning Case	Worldwide operations and local strategies of ABB	EU		442
	■ International Business Strategy in Action	Nokia and Ericsson	EU		449
	■ International Business Strategy in Action	Kodak	US	✔	455
	■ Real Case	There is no global beer, only local	US/EU		464
	■ Real Case	IBM	US/EU	✔	465
Chapter 16 European Union	■ Active Learning Case	France Telecom	EU: France		471
	■ International Business Strategy in Action	Ford and Volvo	US/EU: Sweden	✔	481
	■ International Business Strategy in Action	Kingfisher as a European retailer	EU: UK		488
	■ Real Case	Accor budget hotels	EU: France		497
	■ Real Case	Carrefour	EU: France	✔	498
Chapter 17 Japan	■ Active Learning Case	Doing business in Japan	Japan		502
	■ International Business Strategy in Action	Kirin beer goes international	Japan		516
	■ International Business Strategy in Action	Wal-Mart takes Seiyu	US/Japan	✔	525
	■ Real Case	Nissan-Renault: no pain, no gain	Japan EU: France	✔	532

CHAPTER	TYPE OF CASE	ORGANIZATION/INDUSTRY	COUNTRY/ REGION	NEW?	PAGE
	■ Real Case	Canon Group	Japan	✔	535
Chapter 18 North America	■ Active Learning Case	The free trade of the Americas builds on NAFTA	US/Emerging Economies: Mexico and Canada		541
	■ International Business Strategy in Action	Bombardier	Emerging Economies: Canada	✔	544
	■ International Business Strategy in Action	Mexico and NAFTA	US/Emerging Economies: Mexico	✔	558
	■ Real Case	Jumex	Emerging Economies: Mexico	✔	563
	■ Real Case	GlaxoSmithKline	US	✔	564
Chapter 19 Emerging Economies	■ Active Learning Case	Acer Taiwan goes international	Emerging Economies: Taiwan		569
	■ International Business Strategy in Action	From Oserian to Tesco: the Kenyan cut flower industry	Emerging Economies: Kenya	✔	581
	■ International Business Strategy in Action	Oxford Instruments in China	EU: UK/ Emerging Economies: China	✔	593
	■ Real Case	Korean chaebols: different paths for Hyundai and Samsung	Emerging Economies: Korea		599
	■ Real Case	The Indian IT, software, and services industry	Emerging Economies: India	✔	601
Chapter 20 International Business, Ethics and the Natural Environment	■ Active Learning Case	The environment, NGOs, and MNE	EU/US		607
	■ International Business Strategy in Action	3M	US		610
	■ International Business Strategy in Action	Is The Body Shop an ethical business?	EU: UK		621
	■ Real Case	Dell: B2C	US/Emerging Economies: China		627
	■ Real Case	Merck	US	✔	628

Guided Tour of the Book

Active Learning Case
A real-life case that is re-visited throughout the chapter to illustrate how the chapter relates to multinational enterprise strategy and activity. It provides a framework of learning for the chapter and comes with thought-provoking questions and weblinks. Answers to the questions appear throughout the chapter in the Active Learning Checks.

Chapter Objectives
Outline the core content of the chapter and explain how the chapter fits into the larger structure of the book. A mini-contents list aids navigation through the chapter.

Margin Notes
Provide easy-to-understand definitions of key terms highlighted within the text.

International Business Strategy in Action
Drawn from current literature that provides strategy applications for the material under discussion.

Real Cases
Drawn from recent newspaper and journal sources that allow the student to apply the chapter concepts to real-world situations.

Active Learning Check
Provides answers to the Active Learning Case questions throughout the chapter.

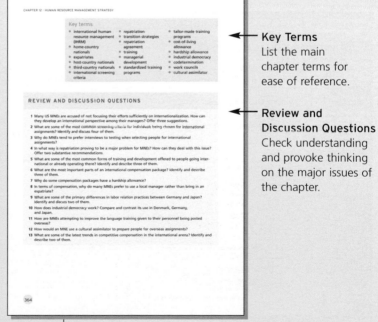

Key Terms
List the main chapter terms for ease of reference.

Review and Discussion Questions
Check understanding and provoke thinking on the major issues of the chapter.

Key Points
Revisit the main issues covered in the chapter.

Guided Tour of the Companion Website

Extra material has been prepared to help you study using *International Business*. This material can be found on the book's Companion Website at **www.pearsoned.co.uk/rugman**. You will find links to websites of interest, as well as a range of material including:

Video clips and other interactivities illustrate core international business issues and stimulate discussion.

Multiple-choice questions test understanding and provide immediate feedback.

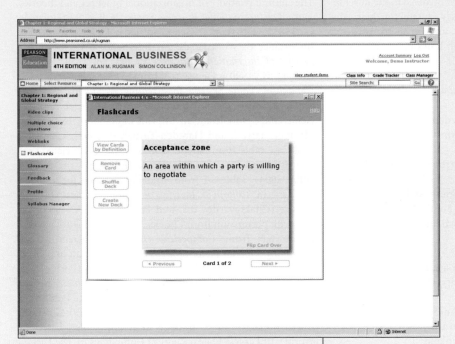

Flashcards are a valuable revision tool, enabling readers to check their knowledge of definitions and key terms.

An **online glossary** provides comprehensive definitions of key terms used in the book.

Acknowledgments

We would like to express thanks to the original reviewers and review panel members who have been involved in the development of this edition. We are extremely grateful for their valuable feedback on the Third Edition, and for their instructive comment on the drafts of this Fourth Edition.

Fourth Edition reviewers:
Jean Barclay, Sheffield Hallam University, UK
Alex Mohr, Bradford University, UK
Olivia Kang, Uppsala University, Sweden
Matthijs Wolters, Vrije Universiteit Amsterdam, The Netherlands
Pierre Le Roux, Nelson Mandela Metropolitan University, South Africa
Marcel Kohler, University of Natal, South Africa
Catherine Welch, University of New South Wales, Australia
Stanley Flax, St Thomas University, Miami, USA

Third Edition reviewers:
Mohammed Salisu, Lancaster University, UK
Hedley Bryers, Birmingham University, UK
Alex Mohr, Bradford University, UK
Lester Lloyd-Reason, Anglia Polytechnic University, UK
Debbie Holley, London Metropolitan University, UK
Taru Oksanen, Turku Polytechnic, Finland
Jerome Pascoe, Free University of Brussels, Belgium
Olivia Kang, Uppsala University, Sweden
Madan Annavarjula, Northern Illinois University, USA
Stanley Flax, St. Thomas University, Miami, USA
Kenneth Gray, Florida A&M University, USA

We are grateful to the following for permission to reproduce copyright material:

Appendix 1A, 1B, and 1C from *IMF Direction of Trade Statistics Yearbook*, International Monetary Fund (IMF, 2003), reproduced with permission of IMF via Copyright Clearance Center; Appendix 1D based on *IMF Direction of Trade Statistics Yearbook*, International Monetary Fund (IMF, 2003), reproduced with permission of IMF via Copyright Clearance Center; Appendix 1E and 1F based on *World Investment Report 2003*, United Nations Publications (2003). The United Nations is the author of the original material; Table 2.1 from *The Fortune Global 500*, Fortune (2004) by permission of Fortune; Table 2.2 from *World Investment Report 2001*, United Nations Publications (2001). The United Nations is the author of the original material; Table 3.2 based on "The world's top 100 non-financial TNCs" in *The Regional Multinationals*, Cambridge University Press (Rugman, A.M. 2005) and *World Investment Report 2000*, United Nations Publications (2000). The United Nations is the author of the original material; Figure 5.2 from The cultural relativity of organizational practices and theories, *Journal of International Business Studies*, Fall, p. 92 (Hofstede, G., 1983). Copyright © Geert Hofstede; Table 5.2 from The Importance of Work Goals: An International Perspective in *Journal of International Business Studies*, Vol 21, 1, Palgrave (Itzhak, H. 1990); Figure 5.5 from *The Seven Cultures of Capitalism: Value Systems for Creating Wealth in the United States, Britain, Japan, Germany, France, Sweden and the Netherlands*, Doubleday, an imprint of Random House, Inc. (Trompenaars, F. and Hamden-Turner, C. 1993); Chapter 6 Real Case table from Extended Mass Layoffs Associated with Domestic and Overseas Relocations; Tables 6.3, 6B, and 6C (BEA, 2004); Table 8.1 from Strategic Planning for a Global Business in *Columbia Journal of World Business*, Elsevier Science (Chakravarthy, B.S. and Perlmutter, H.V. 1985), pp. 5–6, with permission from Elsevier; Figure 8.1, Figure 8.3, and Figure 8.5 from *Competitive Advantage: Creating and Sustaining Superior Performance*, The Free Press, an imprint of Simon and Schuster Adult Publishing Group (Porter, M.E. 1985); Table 8.2 from *International Dimensions of Management, 2nd edition*, South-Western College Publishing, an imprint of Thomson Learning (Phatak, A. 1989); Chapter 9 International Business Strategy in Action table based on World's 10 Largest Pharmaceutical Companies in *The Fortune Global 500*, Fortune (2004) by permission of Fortune; Figure 9.8 from *Matrix Organizations of Complex Businesses*, The Conference Board (Janger, A.R. 1979); Figure 9.11 from *Comparative and Multinational Management*, John Wiley and Sons Inc. (Ronen, S. 1986) © John Wiley and Sons, Inc. Reprinted with permission of John Wiley & Sons, Inc; Table 10.1 from The New Competitors: They Think in Terms of "Speed-to-Market" in *Academy of Management Executive*, May, Academy of Management (Vesey, J.T. 1991), reproduced with permission of Academy of Management via Copyright Clearance Center; Figure 10.2 from Japan's Smart Secret Weapon in *Fortune*, 12 August 1991, Fortune (Worthy, F.S. 1991) by permissions of Fortune; Table 10.2 based on *Fortune*, 15 July 1991, Fortune (1991) by permission of Fortune; Figure 10.4 based on *World Investment Report 2002*, United Nations Publications (2002) © United Nations, reprinted by permission of the publisher; Figure 12.1 from Who Manages Multinational Enterprises? in *Columbia Journal of World Business* (Franko, L.G. 1973), p. 33, with permission from Elsevier; Table 12.1 from Expatriate Incentives: Beyond Tradition in *HRfocus*, Institute of Management and Administration (Latta, G.W. 1998); Figure 12.2 from Compensation of Overseas Personnel in *Handbook of Human Resource Administration*, 2nd edition, McGraw Hill (Reynolds, C. in ed. Famularo, J.J. 1986); Table 12.2 from The Culture

Assimilator: An Approach to Cross-Cultural Training in *Journal of Applied Psychology*, American Psychological Association (Fiedler, F.E., Mitchell, T. and Triandis, H.C. 1971); Figure 12.3 based on International Labour Organization in *World Labour Report*, International Labour Office (1997); Table 12.3 from *The Economist Intelligence Unit*, 22 June 2005 (EIU, 2005) by permission of Economist Intelligence Unit via Copyright Clearance Center; Table 12.4 from Competition and Change: Mapping the Indiana HRM Recipe Against Worldwide Patterns in Journal of World Business, Vol 32, 3, Elsevier Science (Sparrow, P.R. and Budhwar, P.S. 1997), p.233, with permission from Elsevier; Table 13.1 from *World Investment Report 2004: The Shift Towards Services*, United Nations Publications (2004). The United Nations is the author of the original material; Table 13.4 from The Influence of Culture on the Process of Business Negotiations: An Exploratory Study in *Journal of International Business Studies*, Palgrave (Graham, J.L. 1985); Figure 15.1 and 15.2 from *The Competitive Advantage of Nations*, The Free Press, an imprint of Simon and Schuster Adult Publishing Group (Porter, M.E. 1990); Figure 15.3 from *Fast Forward: Improving Canada's International Competitiveness*, Kodak Canada (Rugman, A.M. and D'Cruz, J.R. 1991); Figure 15.4 from "The Double Diamond" Model of International Competitiveness: The Canadian Experience in *Management International Review*, Vol 33, Special Issue 2, Management International Review (Rugman, A.M. and D'Cruz, J.R. 1993); Figure 15.6 from Porter's Diamond Framework in a Mexican Context in *Management International Review*, Vol 33, Special Issue 2, Management International Review (Hodgetts, R.M. 1993); Figure 15.7 based on Building and Managing the Transnational: The New Organizational Challenge in *Competition in Global Industries*, edited by M. E. Porter, Harvard Business School Publishing (Bartlett, C.A. 1986) and *Managing Across Borders: The Transnational Solution, 2nd edition*, Harvard Business School Publishing (Bartlett, C.A. and Ghoshal, S. 1998); Figure 16.2 from Europe 1992 and Competitive Strategies for North American Firms in *Business Horizons*, Kelley School of Business (Rugman, A.M. and Verbeke, A. 1991); Table 16.2 from the Bureau of Labor Statistics, US Department of Labor (2004); Table 16.3 from *World Competitiveness Report 1989* and *The World Competitiveness Yearbook 2005*, IMD International (IMD, 1989 and 2005); Table 16.7 from *Twenty-First Annual Report from the Commission to the European Parliament on the Communities' Anti-Dumping and Anti-Subsidy Activities*, Office for Official Publications of the European Communities (Commission of the European Communities, 2002); Table 17.3 from JETRO White Paper, 2003 (Japan External Trade Organization, 2003); Figure 17.3 from *JETRO Survey of Japanese Businesses* (Japan External Trade Organization, 2004); Figure 17.6 from *Modern Japan: A Concise Survey*, Palgrave (Cortazzi, Sir H. 1993); Table 17.6 from *JETRO White Paper on Foreign Direct Investment 2003*, Japan External Trade Organization (JETRO 2003); Figure 17.10 from M&A Integration Transforming the Corporate Landscape in *Invest Japan*, JETRO (Japan External Trade Organization, 2004); Table 19.1, Table 19.2, and Table 19.3 from *World Investment Report 2004*, United Nations Publications (2004). The United Nations is the author of the original material; Table 19.8 from *Forbes 2000 List* (2005); Figure 20.1 and Figure 20.2 from *Multinationals as Flagship Firms: Regional Business Networks*, Oxford University Press (Rugman, A.M. and D'Cruz, J.R. 2000) by permission of Oxford University Press http://www.oup.com.

Photographs: p. 4 Getty Images/AFP; p. 26 Getty Images/Michael St Maur Sheil; p. 48 Corbis/Swim Ink 2, LLC; p. 58 Getty Images/Spencer Platt; p. 60 Getty Images/AFP; p. 74 Corbis/Raymond Gehman; p. 89 Getty Images/Tim Boyle; p. 100 Getty Images/Royalty Free; p. 104 Getty Images/Alan Kearney; p. 146 Corbis/Lucas Schifres; p. 153 Getty Images/AFP/Javier Soriano; p. 166 Alamy/Pat Behnke; p. 171 Getty Images/Business Link; p. 212 Corbis/Reuters; p. 219 Corbis/Reuters; p. 226 Corbis/Reuters; p. 247 Getty/Melissa McManus; p. 257 Corbis/Vincent Kessler; p. 274 Corbis/Stephane Cardinale; p. 284 Getty Images/AFP/Jeff Kowalsky; p. 305 Corbis/Thomas White; p. 311 Corbis/Greg Smith; p. 322 Getty/Stephen Chernin; p. 348 Alamy/Tim Gardner; p. 355 Corbis/Adam Woolfitt; p. 371 Alamy/Royalty Free; p. 400 Getty Images/Pete Turner; p. 405 Getty Images/Ian Waldie; p. 414 Getty Images/Royalty Free; p. 455 Getty Images/Ian Waldie; p. 466 Getty Images/AFP/Jung Yeon-Je; p. 471 Getty Images/Pascal Le Segretain; p. 498 Getty Images/AFP/Omar Torres; p. 502 Getty Images/Junko Kimira; p. 516 Getty Images/John Chiasson; p. 541 Corbis/ Bettmann; p. 544 Corbis/Keith Dannemiller; p. 593 Simon Collinson; p. 600 Corbis/Reuters; p. 621 Getty/Time & Life Pictures/Forrest Anderson; p. 627 Getty Images/Business Wire.

In some instances we have been unable to trace the owners of copyright material, and we would appreciate any information that would enable us to do so.

Part One

THE WORLD OF INTERNATIONAL BUSINESS

Chapter 1

REGIONAL AND GLOBAL STRATEGY

Contents

Objectives of the chapter

In this chapter we are going to look at some of the challenges of conducting international business in the 21st century. We will begin by examining trade and foreign direct investment, as well as the emergence of the triad economic blocs of North America, the European Union (EU), and Japan. We will then examine some of the worldwide economic and political changes that are taking place and look at how technology is altering the way international business is conducted. We will also study some of the approaches being used by multinational enterprises both to establish and to maintain their competitive advantage. In the last part of the chapter, we will present the model that we are going to use in our study of international business.

The specific objectives of this chapter are to:

1 *Define* the terms *international business* and *multinational enterprise*.
2 *Discuss* the two primary ways in which international business occurs: trade and foreign direct investment.
3 *Examine* the impact of the triad on international trade and investment.
4 *Describe* the current state of world economies and the role of government and trade regulations in the conduct of international business.
5 *Discuss* the importance of technology and the role of small and medium-sized enterprises in the international business arena.
6 *Examine* how multinational enterprises use triad/regional strategies to compete effectively in the international marketplace.
7 *Discuss* the determinants of national competitive advantage.
8 *Present* the model that will be used in this text for studying international business.

Coke goes worldwide with a local strategy

Coca-Cola is the largest selling soft drink in the world, but sales vary by nation. For example, Americans consume almost 30 gallons of Coke annually, in contrast to Europeans who drink less than half this amount and in some countries, such as France, Italy, and Portugal, the average is in the range of 10 gallons. In the 1990s, Coke took a number of steps to increase its European sales.

One of these was to replace local franchisers who had become too complacent with more active, market-driven sellers. In France, for example, Pernod, a Coca-Cola franchisee, was forced to sell some of its operations back to Coke which, in turn, appointed a new marketing manager for the country. In addition, Coke's price was lowered and advertising was sharply increased. As a result, per capita consumption in France went up.

In England, Beecham and Grand Metropolitan used to be Coke's national bottlers but that was turned over to Cadbury Schweppes, most famous for its Schweppes mixers. The latter immediately began a series of marketing programs that resulted in sales tripling within three years.

In Germany the pace has been even faster. Beginning in the early 1990s Coke identified Germany as one of its primary targets and began building a distribution network there to both package and sell Coke locally. Meanwhile throughout the entire country the company has taken even bolder steps including the replacement of an inefficient bottling network and the institution of a new, well-financed marketing campaign. As a result, Germany became Coca-Cola's largest and most profitable market in Europe.

But all of this came at a price. For example, some government agencies and companies expressed concern about Coke's overriding emphasis on cost control and market growth and its willingness to push aside those who are unable to meet these goals. As a result, the European Union's Competition Department was asked to investigate possible anti-competitiveness tactics. Meanwhile, in the UK, the British Monopolies and Mergers Commission investigated Coke regarding its joint venture with Schweppes; and San Pellegrino, the mineral water company, filed a complaint with the Commission of the European Communities, contending that Coca-Cola abused its dominant position by giving discounts to Italian retailers who promised to stock only Coke.

Source: Getty Images/AFP

Yet none of these actions stopped Coca-Cola's efforts to establish a strong foothold in Europe. As the European Union eliminated all internal tariffs, it became possible for a chain store with operations in France, Germany, Italy, and the Netherlands to buy soft drinks from the lowest-cost supplier on the continent and not have to worry about paying import duties for shipping them to the retail stores. Low cost and rapid delivery were going to be key strategic factors for success. Coke believes that its current European strategy puts it in an ideal competitive position against competitors.

Recent developments shed some doubt on whether the company will be as successful as it is forecasting. Worldwide market growth has been flat and there has been a move away from carbonated drinks. In Eastern Europe, it is the market for bottled water that is booming. Between 1998 and 2004, per capita consumption of bottled water in Eastern Europe doubled. Although Coca-Cola water division is one of four major players, it is not the market leader and smaller, local competitors account for a large portion of the market. Other efforts to develop innovative, non-carbonated products have not proven very successful. The company knows that its future growth is going to depend heavily on its ability to supplement its current product line with new offerings such as vitamin-enriched drinks, and perhaps coffee and tea offerings. Worst of all perhaps, a few years ago the company began centralizing control and encouraging consolidation among its bottling partners. Coke believed that by making all key operating decisions in Atlanta, it could drive up profitability. Unfortunately, at the same time that it was pushing for this centralized type of operation, regional markets began demanding that the company be more responsive to local needs. In short, Coke was going global while the market wanted it to go local.

Coke is now trying to turn things around. In particular, the firm is now implementing three principles that are designed to make it more locally responsive. First, the company is instituting a strategy of "think local, act local" by putting increased decision making in the hands of local managers. Second, the firm is focusing itself as a pure marketing company and pushing its brands on a regional basis and local basis rather than on a worldwide basis. Third, Coke is now working to become a model citizen by reaching out to local communities and getting involved in civic and charitable activities.

Europe remains an important market for Coke, which derives about a quarter of its revenues from the region, about the same as the Asia-Pacific region. North America, though the dominant market, accounts for just under a third of Coke's revenues.

In the past, Coke succeeded as a multinational because of its understanding and appeal to global commonalities. Today, it is trying to hold its market share by better understanding and appealing to local differences.

Websites: www.coca-cola.com; www.cokecce.com; www.coca-colahbc.com; and www.cadburyschweppes.com.

Sources: Adapted from John Huey, "The World's Best Brand," *Fortune*, May 31, 1993; Dean Foust and Gerry Khermouch, "Repairing the Coke Machine," *Business Week*, March 19, 2001, pp. 86–88; Kerlin Hope, "Coke Bottler Boosts East European Presence with Purchase from Parent," *Financial Times*, July 28/29, 2001, p. 24; Alan Rugman and Richard Hodgetts, "The End of Global Strategy," *European Management Journal*, August 2001, p. 336; and "Competition, Coolers, Drive East European Water Sales," *Food and Drink Europe*, February 2, 2004.

1. Why did Coca-Cola engage in foreign direct investments in Europe?
2. How did Coke improve its factor conditions in Europe?
3. How is local rivalry helping to improve Coke's competitive advantage?
4. Is the Coca-Cola Company a multinational enterprise? Is it global? Why?

INTRODUCTION

International business is the study of transactions taking place across national borders for the purpose of satisfying the needs of individuals and organizations. These economic transactions consist of trade, as in the case of exporting and importing, and foreign direct investment, as in the case of companies funding operations in other countries. Over half of all world trade and approximately 80 per cent of all foreign direct investment is made by the 500 largest firms in the world. These companies, called **multinational enterprises (MNEs)**, are firms that are headquartered in one country but have operations in one or more other countries. Who are these firms? Some of them you know by name because you have used their products or seen their advertising. In order of annual revenue, here is a list of those MNEs that grossed more than $100 billion in 2003.

Wal-Mart (US)

BP (Britain)

Exxon Mobil (US)

Royal Dutch/Shell Group (Britain/Netherlands)

General Motors (US)

Ford (US)

DaimlerChrysler (Germany)

Toyota (Japan)

International business
The study of transactions taking place across national borders for the purpose of satisfying the needs of individuals and organizations

Multinational enterprises (MNEs)
A company headquartered in one country but having operations in other countries

General Electric (US)

Total (France)

Allianz (Germany)

ChevronTexaco (US)

AXA (France)

A close look at this list shows that each of these companies comes from one of three geographic locales: the United States, the EU, or Japan. We call this the core "triad." And of these 13 companies, six were from the United States, six from the EU, and one from Japan. The list helps point up an important fact and one that we will continue to emphasize throughout the book – companies from one of these three geographic areas account for most of the world's international business. The implications of this statement will be explained in greater detail in this next section where a brief overview of the world of international business is provided. We then elaborate on the triad theme in Chapter 3.

WORLD BUSINESS: A BRIEF OVERVIEW

There are thousands of multinational enterprises that collectively perform a wide range of operations and services.[1] However, if we were to examine what these companies are doing, we would discover that much of their activity could be classified into two major categories: (1) exports and imports and (2) foreign direct investment. International business operations are discussed in more detail in Chapter 2.

Exports and imports

International trade
The exchange of goods and services across international borders

Exports
Goods and services produced by a firm in one country and then sent to another country

Imports
Goods and services produced in one country and bought in by another country

International trade is the exchange of goods and services across international borders and is also known as exports and imports. Exports are goods and services produced by a firm in one country and then sent to another country. For example, many companies in China export clothing and other textile products to the United States. Imports are goods and services produced in one country and brought in by another country. Japan, for example, is a major importer of petroleum because it must rely on outside suppliers for all of its energy needs. For the UK, the City of London generates exports of financial services that are "invisibles" in the British balance of payments. (See the Appendix to Chapter 6 for further discussion of the balance of payments.)

In most cases people think of exports and imports as physical goods (clothes, oil, cars), but they also include services such as those provided by international airlines, cruise lines, reservation agencies, and hotels. Indeed, many international business experts now recognize that one of the major US exports is its entertainment and pop culture such as movies, television, and related offerings.

Table 1.1 provides a breakdown of worldwide trade in a recent year. The data show that the EU is the world's single largest exporter, followed by North America and then Asia. These data are for 2002, when there were 15 member countries in the EU. We call them the EU(15). The EU is also the largest importer, followed by Asia and North America. If you were to investigate further, you would find that the majority of this export and import activity involves manufactured goods such as industrial machinery, computers, cars, televisions, VCRs, and other electronic goods. However, as will be seen later, an increasing proportion of world trade is in services.

Information on exports and imports is important to the study of international business for a number of reasons. First, trade is the historical basis of international business and trade activities help us understand MNE practices and strategies. In 2002 the world's largest

Table 1.1 World trade, 2002

Country/Region	Imports		Exports	
	Billions of US $	% of total	Billions of US $	% of total
North America	1,487.5	23.2	1,175.3	17.7
United States	1,132.9	17.6	751.8	11.3
Canada	219.1	3.4	260.9	3.9
Mexico	135.5	2.1	162.7	2.5
European Union (15)	2,328.3	36.3	2,295.8	34.6
Asia including Japan	1,529.2	23.8	1,938.3	29.2
Japan	305.7	4.8	457.3	6.9
Other Asia	1,223.5	19.1	1,481.0	22.3
All others	1,073.6	16.7	1,227.5	18.5
Total	6,418.6	100.0	6,636.9	100.0

Note: Data for EU(15) includes intra-EU trade. Exports are calculated by including freight and insurance, whereas imports do not include freight and insurance.

Sources: Author's calculations and International Monetary Fund, *Direction of Trade Statistics Yearbook, 2003*. (Washington, DC: IMF, 2003).

importers and exporters were the United States, Germany, and China (see Appendixes 1A and 1B, 2002 data). Note that the world's top importers are also the world's largest exporters. Some of the major products that are traded by these countries include computers, farm machinery, machine tools, automobiles, and electronic goods. These countries sell and buy a large percentage of their goods and services from a small number of countries. (See also Appendixes 1A–1D at the end of the chapter for information on major exporters, importers, and the direction of world trade flows.)

Second, trade helps us better understand the impact of international business on world economies. For example, Japan imports all of its oil. So when the price of oil in the world market rises sharply, we can readily predict that the cost of manufacturing cars in Japan will rise and Japanese auto exports will decline. Conversely, if oil prices decline, we can predict that world imports of Japanese cars are likely to increase.

A third reason why exports and imports are important in the study of international business is that they are main drivers of international trade (FDI is another driver, which we discuss below and then in detail in Chapter 3). When worldwide exports and imports begin to slow down, this is a pretty good sign that world economies are going into a slump.

The US trade ties to Canada and Mexico reflect the triad effect, as these three countries are members of the North American Free Trade Agreement (NAFTA). Indeed, more than 50 per cent of the exports of the United States, Canada, and Mexico are intra-regional, that is, to each other.[2] A similar picture of regional trade concentrations appears in the EU, where just over 60 per cent of all the exports of the member states are with each other.[3] Similarly, over 50 per cent of Asian exports are to other Asian countries.[4] Table 1.2 reports that the majority of exports of these triad areas now occur within each region and that this intra-regional trade has increased significantly since 1980. The recent decrease in intra-regional trade in the Asian region is partly due to the emergence of China as a manufacturer for the US market.

Foreign direct investment

Foreign direct investment (FDI) is equity funds invested in other nations. It is different from portfolio (financial) investment in that FDI is undertaken by MNEs who exercise control of their foreign affiliates. Like exports and imports, FDI is a driver of international business and many companies use FDI to establish footholds in the world marketplace by setting up operations in foreign markets or by acquiring businesses there. Firms engage in FDI for a

Foreign direct investment (FDI)
Equity funds invested in other nations

Table 1.2 Intra-regional trade in the triad, 1980–2002

Year	Intra-regional exports (%)		
	EU	NAFTA	Asia
2002	61.0	56.0	50.0
2000	62.1	55.7	55.7
1997	60.6	49.1	53.1
1980	52.1	33.6	35.3
Cumulative Average Annual Change			
1980–2002	0.7	2.3	1.6
1997–2002	0.1	2.7	−1.2

Sources: Author's calculations and International Monetary Fund, *Direction of Trade Statistics Yearbook, 1983–2003* (Washington, DC: IMF, 2003). For an explanation of the methodology used in calculating these data on intra-regional trade and FDI stocks, see Alan M. Rugman, *The End of Globalization* (New York: Amacom, 2000), Chapter 7.

number of reasons: to increase sales and profits, to enter rapidly growing markets, to reduce costs, to gain a foothold in economic unions, to protect domestic markets, to protect foreign markets, and to acquire technological and managerial know-how. These will be discussed in more detail in Chapter 3.

When examined from an overall perspective, FDI data show that industrialized countries have invested very large amounts of money in other industrialized nations as well as smaller amounts in less developed countries (LDCs) such as those in Eastern Europe or newly industrialized countries (NICs) such as Korea and Singapore. However, most of the world's FDI is invested both by and within the three major groups we identified earlier: the United States, Western Europe, and Japan. The United States is an excellent example of a country that is a

Table 1.3a Foreign direct investment in the United States, 2002

Country/region	Millions of US $	% of total
All countries	1,347,994	100.0
Canada	92,041	6.8
Europe	1,006,530	74.7
France	170,619	12.7
Germany	137,036	10.2
Luxembourg	34,349	2.5
Netherlands	154,753	11.5
Switzerland	113,232	8.4
United Kingdom	283,317	21.0
Latin America and other Western Hemisphere	52,291	3.9
Bermuda	977	0.1
Mexico	7,857	0.6
Panama	5,668	0.4
United Kingdom Islands, Caribbean	25,502	1.9
Africa	2,344	0.2
Middle East	6,766	0.5
Asia and Pacific	188,023	13.9
Australia	24,470	1.8
Japan	152,032	11.3
Singapore	2,902	0.2

Note: Numbers might not add up due to rounding.

Sources: Author's calculations and US Department of Commerce, *Survey of Current Business*, May 2004.

major target of investment as well as a major investor in other countries. Its high GDP per capita and consumer spending make it an attractive market for foreign multinationals. Conversely, US firms have specialized capabilities that can be exploited in other countries.

By 2002 the United States had become such a major investment target that foreign holdings were over $1.3 trillion! (See Table 1.3a on stocks of FDI in the United States.) The largest investors have been the United Kingdom, Japan, the Netherlands, Germany, and Canada. Collectively these countries account for just over 66 per cent of the stock of all FDI in the United States. At the same time, as seen in Table 1.3b, American companies have substantial FDI in other countries and these total more than $1.5 trillion. The major areas for this FDI are the UK, Canada, the Netherlands, Switzerland, and Japan.

A close look at Tables 1.3a and 1.3b shows that Europe and Japan have larger FDI stocks in the United States than the United States has FDI stock in these two geographic areas. On the other hand, US businesses have more FDI in Latin America and the Western hemisphere relative to the Europeans or Japanese. US companies have put much more FDI into the UK and Australia than either of these two nations have FDI in the United States.

These recent data reveal two important trends. First, the United States is a prime site for FDI by both Japan and countries in Western Europe. Second, US firms have invested most heavily in Canada, Europe, Latin America and other Western Hemisphere, and Asia and Pacific. These four areas account for over 97.5 per cent of the stock of all US FDI. (For more on FDI see Appendixes 1E and 1F at the end of this chapter. We also discuss FDI and the role of MNEs in more detail in Chapter 2.)

Table 1.3b Foreign direct investment by the United States, 2002

Country/region	Millions of US $	% of total
All countries	1,529,965	100.0
Canada	152,522	10.0
Europe	796,913	52.1
United Kingdom	272,391	17.8
Netherlands	145,474	9.5
Germany	64,739	4.2
Switzerland	70,051	4.6
France	43,978	2.9
Ireland	41,635	2.7
Other	158,645	10.4
Latin America and other Western Hemisphere	272,363	17.8
Bermuda	68,856	4.5
Mexico	58,074	3.8
Brazil	31,715	2.1
United Kingdom Islands, Caribbean	29,252	1.9
Other	84,466	5.5
Africa	15,066	1.0
Middle East	14,154	0.9
Asia and Pacific	269,947	17.6
Japan	65,676	4.3
Australia	36,337	2.4
Hong Kong	35,764	2.3
Singapore	61,361	4.0
Other	70,809	4.6

Note: Numbers might not add up due to rounding.

Sources: Author's calculations and US Department of Commerce, *Survey of Current Business*, May 2004.

Active learning check

Review your answer to Active Learning Case question 1 and make any changes you like. Then compare your answer with the one below.

1 **Why did Coca-Cola engage in foreign direct investments in Europe?**

Coke made these investments in order to improve its market position. This is being done in three ways. First, the construction of new bottling plants is helping the company produce a low-cost product. Second, marketing expenditures are helping the firm gain the product recognition needed for growth. Third, direct investments in facilities closer to the market are reducing delivery time and eliminating associated expenses.

The triad

Triad
The three major trading and investment blocs in the international arena: the United States, the EU, and Japan

As we noted above, companies in the United States, Western Europe, and Japan conduct most of the world's trade and FDI. Of these companies, those located in Western Europe mainly come from nations that are members of the EU. The triad is a group of three major trading and investment blocs in the international arena: the United States, the EU, and Japan. Before looking more closely at the impact of the triad on international business, it is important to discuss the countries that are members of this group.

The first of these, the *United States*, has the largest economy in the world with a gross domestic product (GDP) of over $10 trillion![5] Sometimes when the United States is discussed as a member of the triad, Canada and Mexico are included. This is because these three countries implemented the North American Free Trade Agreement (NAFTA) in 1994, an international covenant that has resulted in the elimination of many trade and investment barriers between the three. We further discuss NAFTA in Chapter 18. In our discussions of the triad in the book, we will be talking only about the United States; if we intend to include Canada and Mexico we will indicate so by referring to them as members of NAFTA. The reason that our triad discussions will include only the United States is that the US economy is extremely large when compared with that of Canada and Mexico. As a result, if we were to talk about the 25 largest MNEs in NAFTA we would be discussing American firms only. Canadian or Mexican firms are not big enough to make this list of 25. Simply put, the US economy is so large that this one country constitutes an entire segment of the triad.

North American Free Trade Agreement (NAFTA)
A regional free trade agreement among Canada, the US, and Mexico

The second segment of the triad is the *European Union*. This group of nations, whose history and current developments will be discussed in Chapters 3 and 16, was formed by six countries in the late 1950s. Today there are 25 members of the EU. This includes the EU(15) – Austria, Belgium, Denmark, Finland, Germany, Greece, France, Ireland, Italy, Luxembourg, the Netherlands, Portugal, Spain, Sweden, and the UK – an additional 8 Eastern European countries that joined on May 1, 2004 – Czech Republic, Estonia, Latvia, Lithuania, Hungary, Poland, Slovenia, and Slovakia – as well as Cyprus and Malta. In this book, unless noted otherwise, data are for the EU(15). These are the largest countries in the group, accounting for 95 per cent of the GDP of the EU(25). Statistical information on the EU(25) is not yet generally available. Bulgaria and Romania are scheduled to become members of the EU in 2007 (see map, European Union timeline) while Turkey continues to negotiate its entry into the union. The collective GDP of the EU is greater than that of the United States or Japan, and a brief look at some of the economic data in this chapter helps show how important the EU is in the international arena. For example, in terms of imports and exports, as seen back in Table 1.1, the EU(15) accounts for more than 36 per cent of all imports and over 34 per cent of all world exports. Again, this includes 61 per cent intra-EU trade. And in terms of FDI, as seen in Table 1.3b, five EU countries (France, Germany,

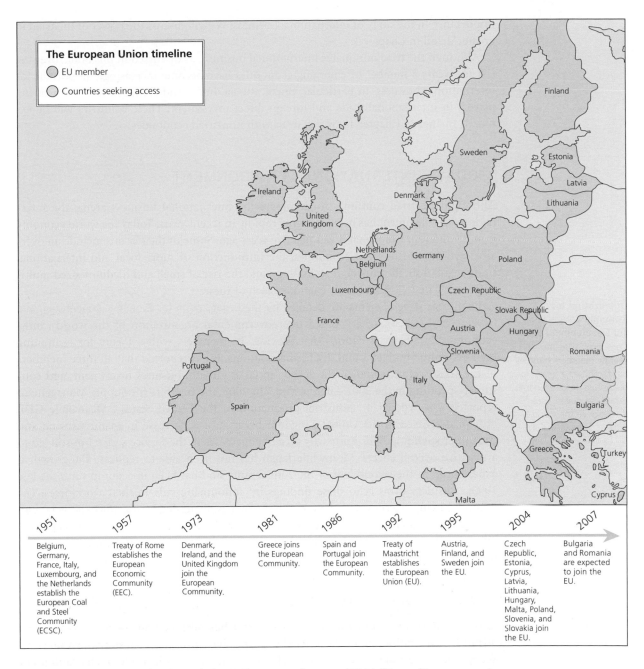

The European Union timeline
○ EU member
○ Countries seeking access

1951	1957	1973	1981	1986	1992	1995	2004	2007
Belgium, Germany, France, Italy, Luxembourg, and the Netherlands establish the European Coal and Steel Community (ECSC).	Treaty of Rome establishes the European Economic Community (EEC).	Denmark, Ireland, and the United Kingdom join the European Community.	Greece joins the European Community.	Spain and Portugal join the European Community.	Treaty of Maastricht establishes the European Union (EU).	Austria, Finland, and Sweden join the EU.	Czech Republic, Estonia, Cyprus, Latvia, Lithuania, Hungary, Malta, Poland, Slovenia, and Slovakia join the EU.	Bulgaria and Romania are expected to join the EU.

Luxembourg, the Netherlands, and the UK) account for over $780 billion of investment in the United States. Quite clearly, the EU is a worldwide economic force.

The third group in the core triad is *Japan*, which like the other two members plays a major role in international business. This is made particularly clear by looking at areas such as importing, exporting, and FDI. As seen in Appendixes 1A and 1B at the end of the chapter, Japan is the world's sixth largest importer and fourth largest exporter. At market prices it is the largest economy in Asia and it has by far the highest GDP per capita. Japan accounts for 4.8 per cent of all the imports and 6.9 per cent of all of the exports. Japan also accounts for 4.8 per cent of all outward stocks of FDI. (See Appendix 1F.)

In examining the current state of world business, the triad merits close attention. Every year companies from these three groups account for more trade and FDI than those of any other economic bloc. As a result, during the 21st century the triad will be of central importance in the study of international business. We will discuss the power of the triad in greater detail in Chapter 3.

Although the triad dominates international business, as discussed in this book, over the last few years a number of emerging economies have become increasingly important for international business. In particular, Brazil, Russia, India, and China (BRIC) are growing players in international trade and foreign direct investment. These countries will be explored further in Chapter 19, which deals with non-triad economies.

TODAY'S INTERNATIONAL ENVIRONMENT

Although the triad continues to dominate the international business arena, the international environment has been changing rapidly in recent years. Today the world economy is quite different from what it was just five years ago. Some of the reasons include an overall slowdown in the triad economies, the introduction of more local and international trade regulation, the impact of technology, and the rise of small and medium-sized multinationals. The following briefly examines each of these.

Organization for Economic Cooperation and Development (OECD)
A group of 30 relatively wealthy member countries that facilitates a forum for the discussion of economic, social, and governance issues across the world

Economic developments are detailed by the Organization for Economic Cooperation and Development (OECD), a Paris-based intergovernmental organization of the world's most economically advanced nations that provides its members with a forum for examining their economic problems and discussing solutions. It has reported that all three members of the triad were experiencing a decline in GDP growth, business investment, and consumer spending in the 2001–2003 period.[6] In 2005, the Institute for Supply Management reported a slowdown in industrial production in the United States.[7] Meanwhile GDP growth decreased in the United Kingdom because of a decrease in manufacturing and consumer spending. This was partly offset by increases in the service sector but still led to a negative overall effect.[8] Meanwhile Japan has not been able to replicate the growth it experienced in the second half of the 20th century and has been in a slump since the late 1990s. Business firms echo these findings by announcing cuts in their workforces. For example, many telecom and dot.com companies went under in the 2001–2003 period. Siemens is a case in point. In 2002 it cut 17,000 jobs and in 2003 it cut an additional 2,300 jobs.[9] In the automotive industry, GM cut 12,000 jobs in 2005 to offset heavy losses that reflected poor car sales.[10]

International trade regulation

World Trade Organization (WTO)
An international organization that deals with the rules of trade among member countries; one of its most important functions is to act as a dispute-settlement mechanism

General Agreement on Tariffs and Trade (GATT)
A major trade organization that has been established to negotiate trade concessions among member countries

Another important international business trend has been the emergence of trade and investment liberalization. Firms in triad countries have prospered in more open markets. Yet, at the same time, triad rivalry has led to some setbacks in trade liberalization. For example, Japan and China have been threatened with trade sanctions by the United States unless they allow US firms to sell products and services in their countries. There are also trade conflicts between the EU and the United States over biotech foods and crops, steel, beef hormones, and export subsidies.[11] Many such trade disputes, however, are handled not by countries but by international organizations set up to regulate international commerce. The main one is the World Trade Organization.

The World Trade Organization (WTO) was established on January 1, 1995, and it is now the umbrella organization that governs the international trading system. It is the successor to the General Agreement on Tariffs and Trade (GATT). The GATT was established in 1947. The purpose of the GATT was to liberalize trade and to negotiate trade concessions among member countries. Although the early years saw a great deal of progress in reducing tariffs, by the 1980s there was a trend toward protectionism by many countries. At the GATT's eighth round of negotiations in 1986 (called the Uruguay Round because this is where the group met), negotiations dragged on for years before culminating in a number of agreements including reductions on industrial goods and agricultural subsidies, the increased protection of intellectual property rights under the Agreement on Trade-Related Aspects of Intellectual Property Rights (TRIPS), the creation of the General Agreement on Trade in Services (GATS) and the creation of the World Trade Organization to implement the GATT agreement. Today the World Trade Organization is enforcing these agreements. Presently, the Doha Round of the WTO has opened the door for further trade negotiations.

When member nations have a dispute they can turn to the WTO to help resolve it. For example, the United States brought a case against the EU charging it with a discriminatory banana import policy and the WTO ruled in its favor. In another case the United States requested that Japan be instructed to reorganize its commercial economy so that Kodak could better compete in that market against Fuji, its major rival, but the WTO rejected the claim and ruled in Japan's favor. In recent years the United States, the EU, and Japan, in particular, have been using the WTO to help resolve trade disputes, and this bodes well for the future of the organization. The important thing to remember about the WTO is that it can enforce its decisions. Countries that refuse to comply can find themselves suffering severe consequences in the form of trade retaliation. Despite minor conflicts, international trade liberalization has arrived and this promises to help stimulate international business transactions.

Technology

Another major development that is changing the way MNEs do business is technology. Two areas, in particular, are having a major impact. One is communication technology that has advanced at such a rapid rate that all businesses now use computers and rely on the World Wide Web to both access and send information. In addition, thanks to cellular technology, individuals can now remain in constant contact with both their customers and their home office. Communication technology has advanced so much that the latest technology reports reveal that there now are more than 300 million mobile phone users in the EU(15), or 81 per cent of the population. In some EU countries, mobile users account for 90 per cent of the population![12] Over 55 per cent of the US population has access to the Internet.[13] The box **International Business Strategy in Action: Amazon.com** discusses the issues of fast growth of new service businesses.

The other major application of technology is for the production of goods and services. Modern factories can now produce goods in a shorter period of time and with fewer defects thanks to production process programs. One example is the introduction of "Six Sigma" – a statistical term that means 3.4 errors per million – that eliminates performance problems in the production process and encourages worker participation and innovation to create products that meet the needs and wants of consumers.[14] Since Motorola engineers introduced the concept into their production process in the 1980s, hundreds of MNEs, including GE, Coca-Cola, and Boeing, have adopted the process, reducing defects, lowering costs, and improving quality.[15] (See Chapter 10 for a discussion of Six Sigma and other production process programs.)

Small and medium-sized enterprises (SMEs)

Whenever MNEs are discussed, it is common to hear about large firms. In fact, the best known multinationals are companies that have become household words. In the auto industry everyone knows of Honda, General Motors, and Volkswagen. However, there are thousands of small and medium-sized enterprises (SMEs), many of whom are suppliers to

Small and medium-sized enterprises (SMEs) The definition of SMEs varies according to the nation. In the US, SMEs are companies with up to 500 employees. In the EU, SMEs have between 11 and 200 employees and sales of under US $40 billion. In Japan, SMEs in industry have up to 300 employees whereas those in wholesale and retail have up to 150 and 50 employees, respectively. Developing countries use the World Bank benchmark of 11 to 150 employees and sales of under US $5 billion

INTERNATIONAL BUSINESS STRATEGY *IN ACTION*

Amazon.com is only one-third of the way there

There are thousands of "global" businesses on the Internet. However, the best known of these may well be Amazon.com. Every day thousands of people go to the company's website to browse and purchase books. A novel that is reviewed on Sunday in the *New York Times Book Review* is likely to get a minimum of 10,000 hits within the next week, as readers read the comments of others, and check for price and availability. For example, when the *Times Book Review* gave a good review to *Nickel and Dimed*, a book which had to that date generated lukewarm sales and for which its publisher had little hope, thousands went to Amazon.com to place an order and within a few hours the current inventory was exhausted. The incident shows not only the impact of the *Times Book Review* but also that of Amazon.com. The first created the demand while the second facilitated its distribution.

Amazon.com was founded in 1995 by Jeff Bezos. In less than 10 years the company became one of the largest 1,000 US corporations according to *Fortune*. In 2004, sales were $5.3 billion. On the other hand, Amazon.com has consistently lost money. In 2000, for every dollar the company took in, it lost 51 cents. Losses continued through to 2003, when a small profit was first reported.

Amazon was initially created to change the way people buy books. The company wanted to offer buyers a virtual store where they could use their computer to place an order that would then be delivered to them by mail. Going to a bookstore was going to be a thing of the past. In addition to making it easy to buy books, Amazon's prices were lower than those at most bookstores – and even when shipping costs were added in, it was often less expensive to shop online with Amazon than it was to visit the local bookstore.

From the beginning, Bezos's strategy was to grow as fast as possible. He began recruiting highly skilled staff to design the e-commerce end of the business, as well as hiring less skilled workers to handle warehouse, distribution, and supply operations. Initially, all of the employees had a common vision regarding what the company wanted to do. However, in a few short years this rapid growth resulted in both confusion and internal problems. Among other things, some of the personnel filed lawsuits against the company for better compensation. Continued losses and the dot.com crash of 2000 severely reduced the price of its stock.

Today the biggest problem for Amazon.com is that it is not a global company – it is a US firm. The Internet is really only a tool for business and, in Amazon's case, a way to sell products that are produced by others. While the company now sells more than just books, it continues to be an American company. One reason is because books tend to sell most heavily in the market where they are published. A college text published in North America, for example, will not sell very much in Europe or Japan. Quite simply, triad and geographic region segment the market – and even within this grouping it can be difficult to sell to other countries. For example, Amazon generates only 21.6 per cent of its sales outside North America. But, even in Canada, the firm continually confronts a number of problems doing business including how to address Canadian sales taxes and how to deal with the threat by Canadian publishers of having the state-run postal service refuse to deliver "foreign" books. In fact, these problems have created such a headache for Canadian buyers that many of them now order their online books from Canadian suppliers such as Chapters and Borders rather than from Amazon. And in Europe, where Amazon operates through foreign subsidiaries, such as Amazon.co.uk, Amazon.fr, and Amazon.de, the company offers a totally different stock of books from those marketed in North America, and it targets a smaller, more affluent group of customers in this niche. The same marketing strategy is used in Asia. On both of these continents customers are finding that local book suppliers often do a better job of meeting their needs in terms of both the range of their offerings and the price of their products. In short, Amazon.com is finding that if it wants to be a global competitor it is going to have to formulate a strategy that helps it expand out of the US market and become much more competitive throughout the triad. At the present time, Amazon.com is only one-third of the way there.

Websites: www.amazon.com; www.amazon.co.uk; www.amazon.co.jp; www.amazon.fr; and www.amazon.de.

Sources: Amazon.com, *Annual Report*, 2003; Alan M. Rugman, *The End of Globalization* (London: Random House, 2001; New York: Amacom, 2000; Toronto: McGraw Hill Ryerson, 2001); Robert Spector, *Amazon.com Get Big Fast* (New York: HarperCollins, 2000; London: Random House, 2000); and *Fortune*, April 16, 2000, p. F 63.

these MNEs.[16] Most of these companies have annual sales of less than $5 million, but thanks to innovation, technology, and a well-trained workforce, they are able to compete effectively and perform functions that multinationals cannot do as efficiently. For example, some SMEs are able to provide their customers with two-day deliveries. In this way, their customers can keep a minimum amount of inventory on hand because the suppliers will replenish the stock every other day. And since these SMEs are small operations that focus heavily on cost control and quality, they are critical to the success of their customers. Result: SMEs are proving to be the backbone of many industries because of their efficiency and flexibility. In addition, a number of SMEs compete effectively against large companies in niche markets. In this book we will be studying a large number of international business concepts that are used not just by MNEs but also by SMEs. In particular, we discuss the strategies of some SMEs in cases like Command Alkon in Chapter 9 and Mountain Equipment Co-op in Chapter 8.

GLOBALIZATION AND STRATEGIC MANAGEMENT

At the end of each chapter in this book we use Real Cases to illustrate some of the ways MNEs use the ideas that have been presented. In this opening chapter we introduced the world of international business and showed the impact of the triad on international trade and investment. We also noted that the major world economics are beginning to slow down and this, of course, is putting increased pressure on multinational enterprises to maintain growth and profitability. In this section we want to address three areas that are important in understanding how companies are coping with this international environment. First, we are going to look at some of the misconceptions that people have about multinational enterprises and how they formulate their international strategies. Second, we are going to look at some of the criteria that are important to MNEs in achieving strategic competitive advantage. Third, we are going to examine some examples of MNEs that are using concepts that we have introduced in this chapter.

Regional triad strategies

There are a number of misconceptions that people have about the world of international business, and it is important to dispel these at the very start of this book. One is the belief that multinationals have far-flung operations and earn most of their revenues overseas. Nestlé is often cited as an example. This company sells over 8,500 products in more than 100 countries and earns more than 65 per cent of its revenues outside of Switzerland.[17] Although this is true, Nestlé is an exception to the rule. Most MNEs earn the bulk of their revenues either within their home country or by selling in nearby locales. In fact, recent research reports that:

> More than 85 per cent of all automobiles sold in North America are built in North American factories owned by General Motors, Ford, DaimlerChrysler, or European or Japanese MNEs; over 90 per cent of the cars produced in the EU are sold there; and more than 93 per cent of all cars registered in Japan are manufactured domestically.
>
> In the specialty chemicals sector over 90 per cent of all paint is made and used regionally by triad based MNEs and the same is true for steel, heavy electrical equipment, energy, and transportation.
>
> In the services sector, which now employs approximately 70 per cent of the work force in North America, Western Europe, and Japan, these activities are all essentially local or regional.[18]

To be successful, MNEs need to create strategies that are regional, not worldwide, in focus and they need to be responsive to local consumers as opposed to being global in nature and uniform throughout.

Another misunderstanding about MNEs is the belief that they are globally monolithic and excessively powerful in political terms. Actually, the latest research shows that, of the 500 largest MNEs, 203 are headquartered in North America, 153 are in the EU, and 123 are in Japan/Asia. We discuss this further in Chapter 2, Table 2.1. In short, these firms are not spread out around the world but are clustered in the triad. This relatively even distribution across the three regions of the triad implies not a dominant MNE culture but the interaction of different cultures in the international business arena. Recent research has also shown that the vast majority of MNEs have not been able to spread their marketing operations evenly across the world but depend on their own regions of the triad for over half of their revenue.[19] These companies are engaged not in global competition but in triad/regional competition; and this rivalry is so strong that it has effectively eliminated the possibility of their either achieving sustainable long-term profits or building strong, enduring political advantage. In fact, it is now common to find MNEs joining forces with local firms who can help them in their efforts to penetrate local markets. In recent years the strategic alliance, a business relationship in which two or more companies work together to achieve a collective advantage, has become extremely popular with MNEs who now realize that they need to develop strategies with a regional or local focus if they hope to succeed.

Strategic alliance
A business relationship in which two or more companies work together to achieve a collective advantage

A third misunderstanding is the belief that MNEs develop homogeneous products for the world market and through their efficient production techniques are able to dominate local markets everywhere. In fact, multinationals have to adapt their products for the local market. For example, there is no worldwide, global car. Rather, there are regionally based auto factories that are supported by local and regional suppliers who provide steel, plastic, paint, seats, tires, radios, and other necessary inputs for producing cars for that geographic region. Additionally, the car designs that are popular in one area of the world are typically rejected by buyers in other geographic areas. The Toyota Camry that dominates the American auto market is a poor seller in Japan and does even poorer in Europe.[20] And the Volkswagen Golf, which does extremely well in Europe, has not made much of an impact in North America. And pharmaceutical firms, which manufacture medicines that are often referred to as "universal products," have to modify their goods to satisfy national and state regulations, thus making centralized production and worldwide distribution economically difficult.[21]

In this book we are going to use examples throughout of what is happening in the international environment and show how an understanding of international business concepts can be useful to companies in addressing these developments. In many cases you will find that things you believed to be true are not. There is a great deal of misinformation about the world of international business. One of these misperceptions is that MNEs are giant corporations that are world dominant. In fact, their success comes most heavily from formulating and implementing strategies on a regional and local basis.

Maintaining economic competitiveness

During the 1980s US businesses saw some of their economic competitiveness eroded by Japanese and European competitors. By the mid-1990s, however, American firms had bounced back strongly and, despite a recession in the early 2000s, by 2004 the United States continued to be the most competitive nation in the world.[22] How did American companies manage to achieve and then maintain this international competitive advantage? One way was by continuing to be innovative. In the computer industry, for example, Intel's research and development (R&D) arm created a continuing flow of new-age computer chips – each more powerful than its predecessor. And at the upper end of this market, IBM's R&D

prowess helped it capture more and more of the business demand for powerful computers, while at the lower end Dell Computer dominated the field with its high-quality PCs that were sold at rock bottom prices. In other industries as well, from industrial equipment to financial services and from shipping to entertainment, American companies led the way thanks to their ability to innovate. In looking more closely at these developments, a likely question is: Why are some firms able to innovate consistently while others cannot? Michael Porter of Harvard University has provided one of the best answers to this question. After conducting a comprehensive study of 100 industries in 10 countries, Porter found that the success of nations in international competition is determined by four broad attributes that individually and interactively determine national competitive advantage: factor conditions, demand conditions, related and supporting industries, and the environment in which firms compete.[23] These four determinants are briefly discussed below.

Factor conditions

According to basic international trade theory, a nation will export those goods that make most use of the factor conditions with which it is relatively well endowed. These factor conditions include land, labor, and capital. As a result, if a country has a large, relatively uneducated workforce, it will seek to export goods that are highly labor-intensive. On the other hand, if the workforce is highly educated, the country will seek to produce goods and services that tap the intellectual abilities of these people. However, there is more to international trade theory than merely capitalizing on these basic factors. To maintain a competitive position, a country must continually upgrade or adjust its factor conditions. For example, Denmark has two hospitals that specialize in studying and treating diabetes; Denmark also is a world leader in the export of insulin. By creating specialized factors and then working to upgrade them, the country has maintained its premier position in the health-care field. Similarly, the Netherlands, the world's leading exporter of flowers, has created research institutes in the cultivation, packaging, and shipping of flowers. As a result, no one has been able to dislodge that country's foothold in the international flower industry.

Factor conditions
Land, labor, and capital

 Active learning check

Review your answer to Active Learning Case question 2 and make any changes you like. Then compare your answer with the one below.

2 How did Coke improve its factor conditions in Europe?

Coke's factor conditions include land, labor, and capital. The company is using land and capital to build new bottling plants that are more efficient and better suited to meet market demand. It is working to improve the effectiveness of the labor force by getting the personnel to become more market oriented and to sell the product more vigorously throughout Europe.

Demand conditions

Porter states that a nation's competitive advantage is strengthened if there is strong local demand for its goods and services. This demand provides a number of benefits. First, it helps the seller understand what buyers want. Second, if changes become necessary, such as customer desires for a product that is smaller, lighter, or more fuel efficient, the local seller has early warning and can adjust or innovate for the market before more distant competitors can respond. In fact, the more sophisticated the local buyers, the greater the advantage to the local seller. For example, one reason that Japanese firms pioneered small, quiet air-conditioning units is that many Japanese live in small houses and apartments where loud noise can be a problem. Japanese firms also developed units that were powered by energy-saving rotary compressors because customers complained that the price of energy was very high and they wanted a more fuel-efficient unit. Similarly, Sweden, long concerned with helping the disabled, has spawned a competitive industry that focuses on the special needs of these people, and Denmark's environmental concern has resulted in Danish companies developing highly effective water-pollution control equipment and windmills. In the United States, consumers helped to develop a highly efficient fast-food industry, and as the desire for this cuisine spread worldwide, US franchisors like McDonald's and Pizza Hut have been able to tap international demand for their products.

Related and supporting industries

Porter's third major determinant of national competitive advantage is the presence of related and supporting industries that are internationally competitive. When suppliers are located near the producer, these firms often provide lower-cost inputs that are not available to the producer's distant competitors. In addition, suppliers typically know what is happening in the industry environment and are in a position to both forecast and react to these changes. By sharing this information with the producer, they help the producer maintain its competitive position. The Italian shoe industry is an excellent example. Shoe producers interact on a regular basis with leather manufacturers, exchanging information that is useful to each in remaining competitive. This interaction is mutually beneficial to both parties.[24]

Firm strategy, structure, and rivalry

Porter's fourth broad determinant of national advantage is the context in which the firms are created, organized, and managed, as well as the nature of domestic rivalry. No one managerial system is universally appropriate. Nations tend to do well in industries where the management practices favored by the national environment are suited to their industries' sources of competitive advantage. In Italy, for example, successful firms typically are small or medium sized; operate in fragmented industries such as lighting, furniture, footwear, and packaging machines; are managed like extended families; and employ a focus strategy geared toward meeting the needs of small market niches. Germany, in contrast, tends to have hierarchical organizations that emphasize technical or engineering content (optics, chemicals, complicated machinery) that demand precision manufacturing, a careful development process, after-sale service, and a highly disciplined management structure. In Japan, successful firms are often those that require unusual cooperation across functional lines and that demand management of complex assembly operations. Auto production, television manufacturing, and computer assembly are examples of such industries.

National goals are also important. Some countries want rapid results. Others tend to do best in industries where long-term development is valued more. In the United States, for example, investors like fast financial returns. So US firms are more likely to invest in new industries such as software and biotechnology where success can come quickly. In Germany and Switzerland, investments are held for long-term appreciation and are rarely traded. These countries are more likely to invest in mature industries where ongoing investment in research and development and new facilities are important but return on investment is only moderate.

Another area of importance is domestic rivalry. Researchers have found that vigorous domestic rivalry and competitive advantage are related. Nations with leading world positions often have a number of strong, local rivals. For example, in Switzerland, the pharmaceutical firms Roche and Novartis help the country to maintain its internationally competitive edge. In Germany, BASF and Bayer help the country to keep ahead in chemicals.

Active learning check

Review your answer to Active Learning Case question 3 and make any changes you like. Then compare your answer with the one below.

3 How is local rivalry helping to improve Coke's competitive advantage?

Coke faces strong competition in Europe. Europeans do not drink as much Coke as do Americans; drinks like coffee and tea are more popular. As a result, Coke has had to modify its strategy to address this market. This includes the building of new bottling plants that can help drive down costs and make the company more price-competitive, and new marketing campaigns that are designed to draw customers away from competing products. Coke is also working to develop non-carbonated drinks to address local tastes. Finally, competition from locals who better understand their market is forcing Coke to "think local, act local."

Porter's determinants as a system

As noted earlier, each of Porter's determinants of international competitiveness often depends on the others. For example, even if a country has sophisticated buyers that can provide a company with feedback about how to modify or improve its product (demand conditions), this information will not be useful if the firm lacks personnel with the skills to carry out these functions (factor conditions). Similarly, if suppliers can provide the company with low-cost inputs and fresh ideas for innovation (related and supporting industries) but the firm clearly and easily dominates the industry (firm strategy, structure, and rivalry) and does not feel a need to upgrade the quality of its products and services, it will eventually lose this competitive advantage.

Research shows that of Porter's determinants of competitiveness, domestic rivalry/ geographic clustering is particularly important. Domestic rivalry promotes improvements in the other three determinants and geographic concentration magnifies the interaction of the four separate influences.[25] The box **International Business Strategy in Action: The Italian tile industry** illustrates how these influences helped Italy develop a premier position in the ceramic tile industry.

A firm's international abilities and competitiveness can also be described through a combination of firm-specific advantages (FSAs) and country-specific advantages (CSAs). This theoretical framework is developed in Chapter 2. The Porter country diamond framework, discussed in this section, is an excellent framework to capture the CSAs. In Chapter 2, we will start to discuss the FSAs of the MNE. The CSAs and FSAs can then be combined into the matrix of Chapter 2. This becomes the building block for the book. For example, the CSAs will be explored in more detail in part two of the book (Chapters 4, 5, 6, and 7), which deal respectively with political, cultural, trade, and financial issues. These are all issues affecting the environment of international business. Then, part three of the book looks into strategies of the MNEs. These include how the firm develops FSAs in production, marketing, human resource management, political risk negotiation, and international financial management.

Multinationals in action

In each chapter of this book we are going to provide examples of how MNEs are using the ideas that we have been presenting. In this first chapter we have examined the roles of importing, exporting, and FDI in international business, as well as discussing some of the things that MNEs have to do in order to create sustainable competitive advantage.

INTERNATIONAL BUSINESS STRATEGY *IN ACTION*

The Italian tile industry

The Italian ceramic tile industry is an excellent example of how regional manufacturers can gain national, and even international, prominence. The heart of this industry is in Sassuolo near Bologna in northern Italy. Tile has been produced here for over 700 years. So when Italy started rebuilding after World War II, the area began to flourish. Within 15 years the number of local tile companies had increased sevenfold and Sassuolo began to attract engineers and skilled workers.

At first the tile manufacturers had to import raw materials and machinery. There was no white clay in the region, so it was brought in from England. There were no tile equipment manufacturers, so kilns were purchased from Germany, the United States, and France; and presses for both forming and glazing tiles were bought overseas. However, the Italian tile producers soon learned how to modify the equipment to better fit their needs, and technicians began leaving the tile companies to set up their own equipment firms. By 1970 companies in the region were exporting tile kilns and presses. At the same time, the local equipment producers were competing fiercely for the business of the tile companies, thus keeping down the cost of making tile; and supporting companies began to establish businesses in the Sassuolo region to offer molds, packaging materials, glazes, and transportation services. Specialized consulting companies soon emerged to give advice to tile producers on plant design, logistics, and commercial, advertising, and fiscal matters. The ceramic tile industry association, Assopiastrelle, started offering services of common interest to the firms: bulk purchasing, foreign market research, and consulting on fiscal and legal matters. A consortium consisting of the University of Bologna, regional agencies, and the ceramic industry association was founded to conduct process research and product analysis.

While these developments occurred, Italian customers continued to give the manufacturers feedback on product quality and ideas for innovative designs and features. This led to intense rivalry in the form of product offerings. At the same time the tile companies began working to improve their equipment and to lower their production costs. One result was a rapid single-fire process for tile making. This system reduced the number of workers by 60 per cent and cut the cycle time by 95 per cent, so more tiles could be made by fewer people. This new equipment was also smaller and lighter than its predecessor and it found an eager international market. The manufacturers also developed a continuous, automated production system to replace the batch process and this, too, drove down costs and increased productivity.

Today the Italian ceramic tile industry is the world leader. In recent years Italy has accounted for 20 per cent of world production and 50 per cent of world exports.

Websites: **www.italiatiles.com** and **www.assopiastrelle.it**.

Sources: Adapted from Michael J. Enright and Paolo Tenti, "How the Diamond Works: The Italian Ceramic Tile Industry," *Harvard Business Review*, March–April 1990; **www.assopiastrelle.it/welcome.html**; and **www.itse.com/exhibitor_pages/467.html**.

Here are examples of how three multinationals are using some of these ideas in their operations.

Volkswagen

Volkswagen (VW) is well known in the auto market, although like most MNEs it does much better in its regional market (Europe, where it has 71 per cent of its sales) than it does in other areas of the triad. North America, VW's second largest market, accounts for just 17 per cent of total sales. The company's VW and Audi brand groups collectively hold 18.2 per cent of the Western European new passenger car market and 4.8 per cent of the US market. In the last decade VW's market share in both Europe and America has increased because the company has been doing a number of things well. One is the use of innovative design. The top selling VW brands in the United States, for example, all have innovative features such as dashboard instruments like the speedometer and clock that light up in red at night, while those items that the driver touches, such as the radio, are backlit in blue. Commenting on these design features, one auto researcher remarked, "It gives the vehicle some soul, which many of VW's competitors lack horribly."[26] A second factor accounting for VW's success is its commitment to using the most efficient technology in building its cars. Its Wolfsburg plant in Germany is one of the most innovative in the world. It has the largest state-of-the-art paint shop in Europe, which uses eco-friendly, water-based paints. A combination of human skill and automation allows VW to design each car to each customer's specifications. Yet VW is not counting on its present achievements in design and production processes to maintain its competitive advantage. It must continuously update these to keep at the top of the game.

Carrefour

Carrefour is the world's second largest retailer (behind Wal-Mart) and the largest in terms of number of stores and geographic coverage. In 2003, Carrefour had 87 per cent of its sales in Europe but it had almost 6,067 stores spread throughout 29 countries on four continents. What makes the company particularly successful is its ability to create a local strategy for each of its units. Carrefour has a knack for designing its stores to meet local tastes. At least 90 per cent of the goods that it sells in a store cater to the local market because the company believes that each unit should reflect the image of that country.[27] "You have to adapt your food and other products to the local culture," notes the company's chairman and chief executive officer; and this is done in a wide variety of ways.[28] For example, in Catholic Poland, the latest Carrefour hypermarket has a special religion section featuring Bibles, candles, and primers for children who are preparing for their first communion. In China, where many shoppers are superstitious, the company takes care to ensure that vegetables are chopped vertically – not laterally – so as not to bring bad luck to shoppers. And to make sure that it does not stumble badly by getting into countries where it truly does not know how to do business effectively, the company never sets up operations until it has researched the local market for at least one year so that it knows the dos and don'ts of doing business there. As a result, while Wal-Mart has had a wide variety of operating problems in markets such as China, Thailand, and Brazil, Carrefour's efforts in these countries have all worked out well.

Kawasaki and Suzuki

Competition in the international motorcycle marketplace today is greater than ever. Japan is a good example. In this market where Honda and Yamaha are the leaders and Kawasaki and Suzuki are the next largest competitors, the four firms have consistently led the world market with their technologically innovative sports bikes. The problem for all four, however, is that the high cost of R&D has resulted in very high prices for their bikes. And to make matters worse, international rivals such as Harley Davidson of the United States, Triumph of the UK, Ducati of Italy, and BMW of Germany have all been aggressively remodeling their own products, improving the quality and specifications of these machines, setting competitive prices, and stepping up their worldwide marketing efforts. To meet these challenges, Kawasaki and Suzuki have now created a strategic alliance.[29] This alliance, the first ever in the Japanese motorcycle industry, breaks the pattern of each company competing fiercely with the other three. In particular, the two firms are going to jointly develop new models and unify their parts procurement and production activities in order to cut costs. They also plan on developing and building off-road motorcycles and high-powered scooters. The alliance could not have come at a better time. Worldwide market demand for motorcycles is poor, and both companies have seen declining sales in all three of their market regions: Asia, Europe, and the United States. However, the biggest competition is in the large bike market, and Kawasaki and Suzuki intend to bypass this niche and focus instead on small bikes and scooters. The two believe that, if they can produce quality products at a competitive price, they can make major inroads in China. In the past this market has proved very difficult for Japanese motorcycle makers because Chinese companies have been able to pirate copies of their machines and then produce them in their own factories, without fear of any government intervention to stop such practices.[30] Under WTO rules this is something that China will have to do in the future or run the risk of severe economic retaliation. The decision by Kawasaki and Suzuki to form a strategic alliance and focus on China may prove to be a very profitable strategic move.

 Active learning check

Review your answer to Active Learning Case question 4 and make any changes you like. Then compare your answer with the one below.

4 Is the Coca-Cola Company a multinational enterprise? Is it global? Why?

Coke indeed is an MNE. The firm conducts production and distribution activities in nations other than its home country. And in terms of strategy and management orientation, Coca-Cola does three things that illustrate its multinational nature. First, the company modifies its operations to meet local needs. The firm markets on a country-by-country basis. Second, Coke has international partners who help to run the operation and do not report directly to the company on day-to-day matters. Third, the multinational relies heavily on teamwork by all involved parties and, to a large degree, serves more as a coordinator and cheerleader for the product than as an on-site manager.

Coke is a global company. Together, the United States and Canada account for just a third of its revenues. European and Asian operations are just as important for the company. No one region absolutely dominates. Unlike MNEs that depend predominantly on their home market, Coke has a global view and a global strategy.

THE STUDY OF INTERNATIONAL BUSINESS

As you have seen from the material in this chapter, the world of international business is undergoing a number of major changes. Quite clearly, international business is both an interesting and a challenging area! In this book we are going to study what international business is all about and what MNEs are now doing in order to compete effectively. In this section we examine the current state of the field of international business and then discuss the approach that will be used in this book in studying this field.

From general to strategic emphasis

The field of modern international business began to develop in the 1950s. At this time there was not a great number of MNEs and most of them were American. World War II had ended less than a decade before and many nations, including Japan and the European countries, were more concerned with rebuilding than with overseas investing. Early international business textbooks were often written by American professors and offered a general, descriptive approach to the field. There were few international research studies to provide substantive information. International companies that served as teaching examples were often those with international divisions, rather than true MNEs. And professors teaching international business were frequently educated in areas such as economics or general business and relied on an interdisciplinary approach to address the varied needs of the course. (Table 1.4 provides additional comparisons.)

During the 1970s and 1980s the field of international business changed greatly. The economic growth of Europe and Japan, coupled with great strides by newly industrialized countries, resulted in more and more attention being focused on international business. Professors were now becoming much more research oriented and the number of PhD-granting institutions offering at least a minor in international business began to increase. Articles and books by Canadian, European, and Asian professors started to appear and US

Table 1.4 Comparative differences in the study of international business, 1950–2010

Topic	1950–1969	1970–1989	1990–2010
Focus of interest	General information	Functional areas of development	Strategic emphasis
Approach to studying international business	Descriptive	Analytical	Integrative
Method of explanation	Heavily historical	Functional	Multidisciplinary
Research emphasis	Interdisciplinary	More quantitative research methods and overseas travel	Quantitative research methods, overseas travel, and international assignment
Enterprise viewpoint	US enterprises	Global enterprises	Multinational enterprises
Countries examined	Industrialized	Industrialized, NICs, and LDCs	Industrialized, NICs, and LDCs
Number of journals	Some	Many	Ever increasing
Journal emphasis	General international topics	Functional	Functional and strategic
Amount of joint research	Some	Much more	Ever increasing

research sophistication gained markedly. International economics and finance now became primary areas of interest and the general research approach of the 1950s and 1960s was supplanted by more rigorous quantitative and methodological designs. More and more research studies were conducted and the number of journals in the field rose sharply. In the latter part of the 1980s we also saw the beginning of efforts to bring together much of what was happening into a meaningful composite. How could we understand what was going on in the world of international business, when so much seemed to be occurring at the same time? It was becoming evident that many of the developments of the 1970s and 1980s were being studied in too micro a fashion and a more macro approach to the field was needed.

The 1990s saw the emergence of a strategic management focus for drawing together the field of international business. The descriptive ideas of the 1950s and 1960s and the analytical ideas of the 1970s and 1980s were now being combined into an integrative approach. Historical and quantitative research was now being incorporated into models for describing, explaining, and helping predict what was happening in the international business arena. The earlier interdisciplinary and functional approaches were being supplemented by a multidisciplinary approach that drew on information from a wide variety of disciplines that affected international business. New journals in the field were also taking a more strategic management view of developments. This theme of **strategic management**, managerial actions that include strategy formulation, strategy implementation, evaluation, and control, encompasses a wide range of activities, including environmental analysis of external and internal conditions and evaluation of organizational strengths and weaknesses. In this text strategic management will serve as the basis for our overall framework.

Strategic management
Managerial actions that include strategy formulation, strategy implementation, evaluation, and control and encompass a wide range of activities, including environmental analysis of external and internal conditions and evaluation of organizational strengths and weaknesses

FRAMEWORK FOR THIS BOOK

This book employs a strategic management approach to the study of international business. In each chapter we will first study international business concepts and then we will examine how MNEs integrate these concepts into their overall strategy.

There are four major parts in this text. Part One is an introduction and encompasses this chapter and Chapters 2 and 3. The focus of attention in this part of the book is on such areas as imports, exports, FDI, the nature of MNEs, and the role and importance of the triad. Part Two examines the environments of international business with particular attention on international politics, culture, trade, and finance. Part Three focuses on international business strategies from a functional standpoint with particular attention to global strategic planning, organizational structures, production strategy, marketing strategy, human resource management strategy, political risk, negotiation strategies, and international financial management and accounting. Part Four looks at the ways in which the information presented thus far in the book is being used by organizations to do business internationally. In this part, specific attention is given to strategic alliances, the flagship framework, and ways of doing business in the EU, Asia, North America, and emerging economies.

Figure 1.1 presents an illustration of the model that will be used throughout this book. The current chapter has set the stage for the study of international business. In Chapter 2 we will examine the key actor on this stage: the MNE.

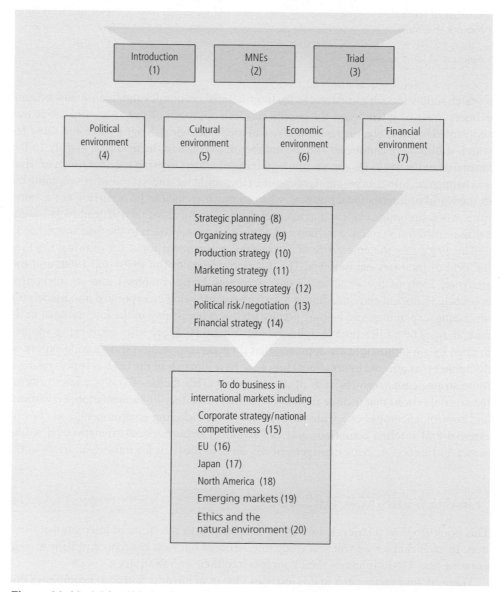

Figure 1.1 Model for this book

KEY POINTS

1 International business is the study of transactions taking place across national borders for the purpose of satisfying the needs of individuals and organizations. Two of the most common types of international business activity are export/import and foreign direct investment (FDI). In recent years both have been on the rise. Much of this is a result of large multinational enterprises (MNEs) that are headquartered in triad countries. In particular, triad members account for most of the worldwide trade and FDI. The majority of trade is intra-regional.

2 Small and medium-sized enterprises (SMEs) often function as the backbone of large multinational enterprises, efficiently providing goods and services that are integrated into the production process of large MNEs. SMEs also compete with MNEs in niche markets.

3 Trade regulation has become an important issue in international business. Today the World Trade Organization is the major group responsible for governing the international trading system.

4 Changes taking place in both communication and production technologies are transforming the way in which MNEs do business.

5 One way in which MNEs are competing is by drawing up strategies that focus on regions and geographic areas, thus ensuring that they are addressing the needs of their local customers. Another way is by continuing to be innovative. A third is by maintaining competitive position by addressing the determinants of national competitive advantage: (a) creating the necessary factor conditions; (b) having strong local demand for the goods and services that are being produced; (c) having related and supporting industries that are internationally competitive; and (d) having a suitable strategy and structure and domestic rivalry that encourages continued innovation.

Key terms

- international business
- multinational enterprise (MNE)
- international trade
- exports
- imports
- foreign direct investment (FDI)
- triad
- North American Free Trade Agreement (NAFTA)
- Organization for Economic Cooperation and Development (OECD)
- World Trade Organization (WTO)
- General Agreement on Tariffs and Trade (GATT)
- small and medium-sized enterprises (SMEs)
- strategic alliance
- factor conditions
- strategic management

REVIEW AND DISCUSSION QUESTIONS

1 What is international business all about? In your answer be sure to include a definition of the term.

2 What are the two primary ways in which world trade is conducted?

3 What does international trade consist of?

4 What is the difference between international business and international trade?

5 Will foreign direct investment increase or decrease in the current decade? Why?

6 How important are the triad areas in promoting international commerce? Explain.

7 What role does the World Trade Organization play in the international business arena? Is the WTO helpful to international trade or is it a hindrance? Why?

8 Multinational enterprises do not formulate worldwide strategies, but rather regional strategies. What does this statement mean and how does it help us better understand international business?

9 How do the four determinants of national competitive advantage help explain how companies can maintain their economic competitiveness? Be complete in your answer.

10 What are two of the advantages associated with using strategic alliances?

REAL CASE

Big oil gets bigger

Between 1998 and 2002 there were a series of mergers in the oil industry that resulted in a handful of private companies emerging as dominant players. In the United States the largest of these was Exxon Mobil, the result of a 1999 merger. In 2003 this company had sales of $222.9 billion (see table, "Rankings of oil MNEs, 2003" below).

In Europe mergers and acquisitions had created three dominant firms. BP, which recently overtook Exxon Mobil, is the largest with $232.6 billion in revenues. In 1998 BP and Amoco merged and subsequently the firm acquired a number of other companies, including Arco and Burmah Castrol.

With $201.7 billion in revenues, the next largest European firm in the oil industry is the Royal Dutch/Shell Group. In 2002, Royal Dutch/Shell purchased Pennzoil-Quaker State for $1.8 billion and consistently purchases

Source: Getty Images/Michael St Maur Shell

Rankings of oil MNEs, 2003

MNE	Country	US $ (billion)
BP	United Kingdom	232.6
Exxon Mobil	United States	222.9
Royal Dutch/Shell Group	UK/Netherlands	201.7
Total	France	118.4
ChevronTexaco	United States	112.9
Conoco Phillips	United States	99.5
ENI	Italy	59.3
Repsol YPF	Spain	42.0
Marathon Oil	United States	37.1
Petrobras	Brazil	30.8
Nippon Oil	Japan	28.6
Lukoil	Russia	19.3

Note: Revenues represent total revenues, including revenues from non-petroleum business.

Sources: Author's calculations and research and Fortune, *The Fortune Global 500*, July 26, 2004.

stakes on other companies. Unlike most of its competitors, however, Royal Dutch has remained clear of any major mergers with competitors and has instead opted to rely on restructuring of its operations to remain competitive.

The third largest European firm in the industry is Total, the result of a merger between Total Fina and Elf in 2000. Today the firm has revenues of $118.4 billion.

Texaco and Chevron merged in 2000 creating the world's fifth largest oil firm. In 2001, Oklahoma-based Phillips Petroleum acquired Tosco, a major oil refiner. Soon after, Phillips merged with Conoco. Conoco Phillips is the world's sixth largest oil firm.

This pattern of increasing company size through acquisitions has also been used in Asia. In 1999 Nippon Oil bought Mitsubishi Oil, creating Japan's largest oil company. In 2003 Nippon Mitsubishi Oil had revenues of $28.6 billion.

The largest oil state-owned enterprises, 2003

MNE	Country	US $ (billion)
Saudi Aramco	Saudi Arabia	55.0
Sinopec	China	51.3
Pemex	Mexico	49.2
China National Petroleum	China	47.0
PDVSA	Venezuela	46.0
Statoil	Norway	35.2
SK	South Korea	33.8
Petronas	Malaysia	25.7
Indian Oil	India	25.3
Bharat Petroleum	India	12.1

Note: Saudi Aramco's revenue was calculated using information from OPEC and EIA and only includes export revenues.

Sources: Author's calculations and research and Fortune, *The Fortune Global 500*, July 26, 2004.

Why are these oil companies merging? One of the main reasons is that the maturity of existing oil fields is forcing companies to search for new oil deposits in areas that are not easily accessible. Oil exploration in mountainous regions, the frigid Arctic, and ocean depths of more than one mile requires extremely large capital outlays and entails a great deal of risk. In addition, these firms have to invest millions of dollars in research and development and sometimes end up spending years negotiating with governments for the right to drill for oil in the country (or in offshore waters that are controlled by them) and to build refineries and pipelines there. Only large companies with enormous financial resources are able to do this. State-owned oil MNEs are major competitors (see table, "The largest oil state-owned enterprises, 2003") and often hold a privileged position when accessing their own country's reserves. Moreover, if a company has a major oil strike, it has to be able to take advantage of economies of scale in order to bring the oil to market at competitive prices. Again, this development favors large firms. This is why experts in the energy business predict that there will be continual mergers and acquisitions in the industry as the large firms jockey for position and acquire smaller rivals and others in complementary businesses such as chemicals and oil-related products.

Websites: www.exxon.com; www.bp.com; www.shell.com; www.totalfinaelf.com; www.chevron.com; www.texaco.com; www.chevrontexaco.com; www.eni.it; www.repsol-ypf.com; www.marathon.com; www.conoco.com; www.sk.com; www.nmoc.co.jp; www.phillips66.com; www.saudiaramco.com; www.pdvsa.com; www.sinopec.com.cn; www.petrobras.com.br; www.statoil.com; and www.iocl.com.

Sources: Adapted from Fortune, *The Fortune Global 500*, April 16, 2001; Raymond Colitt, "Brazil Seeks Energy Boost," *Financial Times*, June 18, 2001; "In Praise of Big Oil," *Economist*, October 19, 2000; "Hunting the Big One," *Economist*, October 19, 2000; "ChevronTexaco Merger Approved by US Regulator," **BBC.co.uk**, September 7, 2001; "Shell Buys Pennzoil-Quaker State," **CNN.com**, March 26, 2002.

1 Are companies such as Exxon Mobil, BP Amoco, and Royal Dutch/Shell MNEs? What criteria do they meet that makes them MNEs?

2 How important is an understanding of governmental regulation to success in this industry?

3 In terms of Porter's determinants of national competitive advantage, which one of these four determinants is most important for these oil companies? Why?

REAL CASE

Wal-Mart

In 2001, Wal-Mart became the world's biggest company in terms of sales revenues, a title it has kept to date; a breathtaking achievement for the company that Sam Walton started in Arkansas as recently as 1962. Indeed, with revenues of $256 billion for the year ending in 2003, Wal-Mart is now ahead of General Motors and Exxon Mobil. The second largest retailer, Carrefour, is only about one fourth the size of Wal-Mart.

Wal-Mart's success can be attributed to a scale strategy based on reduction of costs to steadily generate its "always low prices" formula and physical growth or market coverage. The United States offers the perfect landscape for Wal-Mart's expansion. Large, wealthy suburbs with vast, inexpensive land allow the firm to set up huge warehouse-style retail centers, reducing overall prices. This is complemented by an entrepreneurial culture in which store managers have a lot of decision-making power. Wal-Mart pushes its suppliers to provide the best product they can at the lowest possible price, making its products of better quality than those of other discount stores.

Presently, Wal-Mart commands an 8 per cent share of the retail sales in its home market and its growth shows no signs of slowing down any time soon. The firm's critics accuse it of exploiting its workers, destroying traditional retail stores, and eroding the manufacturing industry by importing from countries with low labor costs, among other things. Even those who sympathize with objectors, however, might not resist saving $100 for an appliance. The criticism can be argued both ways. Some traditional retail stores suffered as a result of Wal-Mart's expansion, but if Wal-Mart sets up shop in a run-down mall, neighboring stores benefit from the increased traffic. This might include dollar-stores, hair cutting places, and sportswear outlets, among others. Wal-Mart's bicycle section falls short of offering all the equipment, not to mention the service, of a traditional bicycle store. A mother buying her daughter her first bicycle might go to Wal-Mart, but a young woman looking for quality, accessories, service, and a knowledgeable salesperson might instead visit her local bike store. The same can be said for most product sections within the store. Large competitors have either stopped competing with Wal-Mart or sought to beat it in its own game. Indeed, Wal-Mart may be responsible for a more consumer-oriented retail service sector in the United States.

One main criticism of Wal-Mart is its dependence on imports from low-cost countries such as China. In 2003, the firm purchased approximately $15 billion in Chinese products, a fraction of revenues perhaps, but a sizeable amount just above the total revenues of McDonald's for the same year. Here, Wal-Mart had done nothing more than take advantage of the opportunities, available to all US retailers, that arose from the liberalization of China.

Those things that have helped Wal-Mart grow might be the same things that eventually will halt its growth. Low-cost laborers have a higher turnover. The firm hires approximately 600,000 new employees a year, and if it wants to reduce the costs of searching for personnel and training them, it might find that increased salaries and benefits are its only alternative. The firm has been constantly lowering the prices of its products, but this too will come to a stop when it exploits all available opportunities in low-cost areas and as China begins to see its production costs increase in the face of development. Finally, the entrepreneurial nature of Wal-Mart's decentralized business structure has meant that the organization lacks a coordinated bureaucracy with the power to impose corporate rules on store managers. For that reason, the firm is now being plagued with lawsuits, including a class action suit by its female employees for gender discrimination.

For future long-term growth, Wal-Mart has looked beyond its borders. However, while it has done extremely well in Canada, Mexico, and the United Kingdom, it has had a rough time in other markets, including Germany and Japan.

Wal-Mart's international expansion begun in 1992 when it entered into a joint venture with Cifra S.A., a successful Mexican retailer, in which it held 50 per cent interest in its partner's retail operations. In 1998, Wal-Mart acquired a controlling interest in Cifra and officially changed the company's name to Wal-Mart of Mexico in 2000. Wal-Mart entered Canada in 1994 when it acquired 122 Woolco stores. Since then, the firm has established itself successfully in the markets of its NAFTA partners. One reason for this success is that it can rely on suppliers for its US stores to deliver products for the Canadian and Mexican market. In addition, the landscape, culture, and economic situation in Canada are much like in the United States.

The group entered Europe in the late 1990s, by purchasing the Wertkauf and Interspar supermarkets in Germany. Here, Wal-Mart ran into some trouble. Competitors in Europe had emulated the company's most successful strategies in cost reduction and supply-chain management, reducing Wal-Mart's relative competitive advantage. In Germany, local competitors offer very low prices, and Wal-Mart is not big enough to achieve the local economies of scale required to compete on price alone. There was also a different cost structure. Real estate development, when possible, was more costly and wages were also higher. The scale effect does not work in Europe. When the company must source 90 per cent of its goods locally, which bargain or logistics savings can it cash in with so few stores? To top it all off, Wal-Mart's American managers had problems adapting to the culture and did not speak German.

Wal-Mart entered the British market by acquiring ASDA and retained the name. ASDA had already adopted a focus on low prices and so it had exactly the type of consumer that Wal-Mart was looking for. Even though it has done relatively well in England, a low-cost strategy was secondary to developing long-term relationships with suppliers of well-known, quality-oriented, differentiated brands.

Time, patient investment, and key expertise in each foreign market may help Wal-Mart to successfully expand its international operations to become a more international player. Until then, however, the firm remains extremely NAFTA focused.

Website: www.walmart.com.

Sources: Adapted from www.walmart.com; Wal-Mart, *Annual Report 2002*; Fortune, *The Fortune Global 500*, July 2002; Alan M. Rugman and Stephane Girod, "Retail Multinationals and Globalization: The Evidence Is Regional," *European Management Journal*, 21:1, 24–37; "How Big Can It Grow," *Economist*, April 15, 2004.

1 Is Wal-Mart a multinational enterprise? Why?

2 Why is Wal-Mart making foreign direct investments in Europe?

3 Using the Porter model, what are the determinants of Wal-Mart's competitive advantage?

4 Is Wal-Mart's competitiveness in Europe dependent on the same determinants listed in question 3? Why?

Endnotes

1 United Nations, *World Investment Report 2001* (Geneva: UNCTAD, 2001) stated that there are as many as 60,000 MNEs in the world. But most of them are small companies. The largest 500 MNEs account for over 80 per cent of all the sales of the MNEs. We focus on the 500 MNEs in this book.

2 See Alan M. Rugman, *The End of Globalization* (London: Random House, 2000), Chapter 7, pp. 120–137. These data were for 1999 and have been updated to 2002 for this book using the same sources.

3 Rugman (2000) n. 2 above, Chapter 7, pp. 120–129. These data were for 1999 and have been updated to 2002 for this book using the same sources.

4 Rugman (2000) n. 2 above, Chapter 7, pp. 120, 134–136. These data were for 1999 and have been updated to 2002 for this book using the same sources.

5 GDP is at purchasing power parity. CIA, *The World Factbook 2004*, www.cia.gov.

6 Joseph Kahn and Edmund L. Andrews, "World's Economy Slows to a Walk in Rare Lockstep," *New York Times*, August 20, 2001, pp. A1, A8 and Jean-Philippe Cotis, "Making the Most of the Recovery," *OECD Economic Outlook*, December 2003.

7 "Slowdown Hits US Factory Growth," *BBC.co.uk*, May 2, 2005.

8 "UK's Economic Growth in Slowdown," *BBC.co.uk*, April 22, 2005 and "Spending Slowdown Hits Retailers," *BBC.co.uk*, May 3, 2005.

9 "Siemens Cuts 2,300 Jobs," *BBC News*, July 30, 2003 and "Siemens Mulls 4,000 Extra Layoffs," *BBC News*, August 26, 2002.

10 "GM Loses $1.1bn as Car Sales Slow," *BBC.co.uk*, April 19, 2005.

11 Nancy Dunne, "US Sends Top Official to Help Solve Trade Dispute," *FT.com*, November 27, 2001; United States Department of Agriculture, "U.S. and Cooperating Countries File WTO Case Against the EU Moratorium on Biotech Foods and Crops," *USDA News Release*, May 13, 2003; Jagdish Bhagwati, "The Unwinnable War," *FT.com*, January 29, 2002; "EU Hits Back Against US Steel Duties," *BBC News*, March 7, 2002; Andrew Walker, "EU Says Science Backs Its Beef Ban," *BBC News*, October 15, 2003.

12 EUROSTAT, "International Roaming," *Press Release*, July 26, 2004.

13 International Telecommunications Union, www.itu.int.

14 Richard M. Hodgetts, *Measures of Quality and High Performance* (New York: American Management Association, 1998).

15 Debby Arkell, "Better, Faster, Cheaper – But Most of All, Better," *Boeing Frontiers*, vol. 2, no. 3, July 2003.

16 Also see Paul Ellis and Anthony Pecotich, "Social Factors Influencing Export Initiation in Small and Medium-Sized Enterprises," *Journal of Marketing Research*, February 2001, pp. 119–130.

17 UNCTD, *World Investment Report 2003* (New York: United Nations, 2003).

18 Alan Rugman and Richard Hodgetts, "The End of Global Strategy," *European Management Journal*, August 2001, pp. 333–343.

19 Alan M. Rugman, *The Regional Multinationals* (Cambridge: Cambridge UP, 2005).

20 Dan Lienert, "The Best-Selling Cars," *Forbes*, August 2, 2004.

21 Rugman (2005).

22 IMD, *World Competitiveness Yearbook*, 2004.

23 The following section is based on Michael Porter, *The Competitive Advantage of Nations* (New York: Free Press, Macmillan, 1990), especially Chapters 3 and 4.

24 Michael E. Porter, "The Competitive Advantage of Nations," *Harvard Business Review*, March/April 1990, pp. 80–81.

25 Porter, ibid., p. 83.

26 Christine Tierney et al., "Volkswagen," *Business Week*, July 23, 2001, p. 64.

27 Sarah Ellison, "Carrefour and Ahold Find Shoppers Like to Think Local," *Wall Street Journal*, August 31, 2001, p. A 5.

28 Richard Tomlinson, "Who's Afraid of Wal-Mart?" *Fortune*, June 26, 2000, p. 188.

29 David Ibison and Rpohit Jaggi, "Kawasaki Joins Suzuki in Search of an Easier Ride," *Financial Times*, August 30, 2001, p. 15.

30 "Kawasaki and Suzuki Join Forces," *BBC News*, August 29, 2001.

Additional bibliography

Beamish, Paul W. and Calof, Jonathan L. "International Business Education: A Corporate View," *Journal of International Business Studies*, vol. 20, no. 3 (Fall 1989).

Becker, Fred G. "International Business and Governments: Issues and Institutions," *Management International Review*, vol. 32, no. 4 (Fourth Quarter 1992).

Caves, Richard E. "Research on International Business: Problems and Prospects," *Journal of International Business Studies*, vol. 29, no. 1 (First Quarter 1998).

Daniels, John D. "Relevance in International Business Research: A Need for More Linkages," *Journal of International Business Studies*, vol. 22, no. 2 (Second Quarter 1991).

Dunning, John H. "The Study of International Business: A Plea for a More Interdisciplinary Approach," *Journal of International Business Studies*, vol. 20, no. 3 (Fall 1989).

Eden, Lorraine and Lenway, Stefanie. "Introduction to the Symposium Multinationals: The Janus Face of Globalization," *Journal of International Business Studies*, vol. 32, no. 3 (Fall 2001).

Gupta, Anil K. "Converting Global Presence into Global Competitive Advantage," *The Academy of Management Executive*, vol. 15, no. 2 (May 2001).

Hax, Arnoldo C. "Building the Firm of the Future," *Sloan Management Review*, vol. 30, no. 3 (Spring 1989).

Kline, John M. "Trade Competitiveness and Corporate Nationality," *Columbia Journal of World Business*, vol. 24, no. 3 (Fall 1989).

Lecraw, Donald J. "Review of World Investment Report 1992: Transnational Corporations as Engines of Growth," *Journal of International Business Studies*, vol. 24, no. 3 (Third Quarter 1993).

Mulligan, Thomas M. "The Two Cultures in Business Education," *Academy of Management Review*, vol. 12, no. 4 (October 1987).

Nehrt, Lee C. "The Internationalization of the Curriculum," *Journal of International Business Studies*, vol. 18, no. 1 (Spring 1987).

Rugman, Alan M. and Stanbury, William. *Global Perspective: Internationalizing Management Education* (Vancouver BC: Centre for International Business Studies, UBC, 1992).

Rugman, Alan M. and Verbeke, Alain. "Multinational Enterprises and Public Policy," *Journal of International Business Studies*, vol. 29, no. 1 (First Quarter 1998).

Yip, George S., Loewe, Pierre M. and Yoshino, Michael Y. "How to Take Your Company to the Global Market," *Columbia Journal of World Business*, vol. 23, no. 4 (Winter 1988).

APPENDIX TO CHAPTER 1

Table 1A The top 25 importers in the world, 2002

Rank	Country	Value of world imports (in millions of US $)
1	United States	1,132.9
2	Germany	489.0
3	China	468.9
4	United Kingdom	344.3
5	France	323.6
6	Japan	305.7
7	Italy	237.1
8	Netherlands	228.0
9	Canada	219.1
10	Belgium	178.9
11	Spain	164.0
12	Korea	141.5
13	Mexico	135.5
14	Singapore	111.9
15	Switzerland	94.8
16	Malaysia	77.1
17	Austria	70.6
18	Australia	68.0
19	Sweden	67.5
20	Thailand	58.6
21	Russia	57.3
22	Ireland	52.6
23	Brazil	50.7
24	Poland	50.2
25	India	46.3

Note: Reported at cif (cost, insurance, and freight).

Source: Adapted from International Monetary Fund, *Direction of Trade Statistics Yearbook, 2003* (Washington DC: IMF, 2003).

Table 1B The top 25 exporters in the world, 2002

Rank	Country	Value of world exports (in millions of US $)
1	United States	751.8
2	Germany	604.2
3	China, P.R.	547.7
4	Japan	457.3
5	France	308.5
6	United Kingdom	265.9
7	Canada	260.9
8	Italy	239.7
9	Netherlands	204.2
10	Korea	174.1
11	Belgium	167.5
12	Mexico	162.7
13	Spain	119.8
14	Russia	116.9
15	Malaysia	116.0
16	Switzerland	101.1
17	Singapore	96.9
18	Ireland	96.8
19	Sweden	82.0
20	Thailand	75.1
21	Australia	68.4
22	Austria	66.3
23	Brazil	66.2
24	Indonesia	64.7
25	Norway	57.1

Note: Reported at cif (cost, insurance, and freight).

Source: Adapted from International Monetary Fund, *Direction of Trade Statistics Yearbook, 2003* (Washington DC: IMF, 2003).

Table 1C Direction of world trade flows, 1993–2002

	With industrial countries		With developing countries		With other countries n.i.e.*		Total	
	Exports	Imports	Exports	Imports	Exports	Imports	Exports	Imports
Industrial Countries								
1993	1,803.6	1,793.7	726.3	708.2	1.1	0.9	2,558.2	2,529.0
1994	2,044.7	2,038.1	809.2	812.7	1.2	1.1	2,888.1	2,882.0
1995	2,416.3	2,398.1	976.8	966.9	1.6	1.3	3,425.9	3,392.1
1996	2,459.1	2,442.2	1,020.7	1,038.1	1.7	1.3	3,513.7	3,507.4
1997	2,507.5	2,483.9	1,077.5	1,107.1	1.8	1.4	3,618.2	3,622.2
1998	2,600.3	2,574.3	992.4	1,104.8	2.0	1.2	3,621.0	3,705.5
1999	2,755.1	2,724.2	988.8	1,210.3	1.9	1.1	3,761.8	3,954.2
2000	2,889.9	2,870.9	1,118.3	1,482.9	1.9	1.4	4,025.2	4,372.8
2001	2,806.0	2,759.9	1,079.4	1,427.3	2.9	1.2	3,910.3	4,218.6
2002	2,869.0	2,805.2	1,127.3	1,481.1	2.0	1.2	4,021.8	4,316.9
Developing Countries								
1990	571.0	572.4	335.4	335.8	2.3	1.4	936.6	927.4
1991	583.6	622.7	370.9	366.3	2.1	1.1	984.0	1,006.6
1992	640.4	720.4	429.0	423.6	1.9	2.2	1,102.3	1,162.8
1993	664.6	768.4	470.6	470.0	1.7	1.3	1,160.5	1,261.4
1994	755.8	856.8	569.5	549.4	1.7	1.4	1,356.5	1,431.6
1995	884.2	1,021.8	712.0	689.7	2.2	1.3	1,640.0	1,737.9
1996	954.5	1,085.0	782.4	759.2	2.5	1.9	1,784.0	1,873.8
1997	1,018.8	1,133.7	843.4	810.4	1.8	1.5	1,904.6	1,969.7
1998	1,004.7	1,063.9	735.9	725.9	1.8	1.4	1,773.2	1,814.5
1999	1,104.5	1,069.4	762.3	766.4	1.9	1.3	1,900.7	1,863.0
2000	1,344.8	1,202.6	950.6	961.0	3.2	1.3	2,334.7	2,212.7
2001	1,264.9	1,156.9	916.9	954.9	3.2	1.6	2,221.9	2,156.0
2002	1,327.1	1,203.3	1,023.4	1,060.1	2.7	1.6	2,394.3	2,314.9

* n.i.e. (not included elsewhere) refers to Cuba and North Korea.
Note: Numbers do not add up due to trade to non-identified countries and due to rounding.
Exports are calculated without including freight and insurance, whereas imports include freight and insurance costs.

Sources: Adapted from International Monetary Fund, *Direction of Trade Statistics Yearbook, 1996* (Washington DC: IMF, 1996); International Monetary Fund, *Direction of Trade Statistics Yearbook, 1996* (Washington DC: IMF, 1996); and International Monetary Fund, *Direction of Trade Statistics Yearbook, 2003* (Washington DC: IMF, 2003).

Table 1D World trade flows by major countries and regions, 2002

Countries/regions	2002 (in billion of US $)	% of world	Countries/regions	2002 (in billion of US $)	% of world
Exports to			**Imports from**		
World	5,265.8	100.0	World	5,401.0	100.0
Industrial countries	3,397.3	64.5	Industrial countries	3,531.7	65.4
Developing countries	1,782.7	33.9	Developing countries	1,813.7	33.6
Africa	97.1	1.8	Africa	110.6	2.0
Asia	974.6	18.5	Asia	978.6	18.1
Europe	288.5	5.5	Europe	259.5	4.8
Middle East	153.5	2.9	Middle East	194.9	3.6
Western hemisphere	269.0	5.1	Western hemisphere	270.2	5.0
Not included elsewhere	4.8	0.1	Not included elsewhere	3.2	0.1
Country not specified/special	82.3	1.6	Country not specified/special	53.9	1.0

Note: Numbers might not add up due to rounding.

Source: Adapted from International Monetary Fund, *Direction of Trade Statistics Yearbook, 2003* (Washington DC: IMF, 2003).

Table 1E Inward stocks of world foreign direct investment

Country/regions	2001 (in billion of US $)	% of total	2002* (in billion of US $)	% of total
Developed countries	4,277,195	64.7	4,594,850	64.5
North America	1,530,527	23.2	1,572,561	22.1
United States	1,321,063	20.0	1,351,093	19.0
Canada	209,464	3.2	221,468	3.1
Western Europe	2,544,445	38.5	2,779,857	39.0
EU	2,418,136	36.6	2,623,903	36.8
Austria	34,328	0.5	42,539	0.6
Belgium/Luxembourg	203,580	3.1	na	na
Denmark	65,830	1.0	71,784	1.0
Finland	26,267	0.4	35,509	0.5
France	289,015	4.4	401,305	5.6
Germany	413,556	6.3	451,589	6.3
Greece	12,006	0.2	12,056	0.2
Ireland	138,266	2.1	157,298	2.2
Italy	107,921	1.6	126,481	1.8
Netherlands	285,387	4.3	314,569	4.4
Portugal	32,921	0.5	43,962	0.6
Spain	164,754	2.5	217,769	3.1
Sweden	92,243	1.4	110,482	1.6
United Kingdom	552,062	8.4	638,561	9.0
Other Western Europe	126,309	1.9	155,954	2.2
Switzerland	89,269	1.4	118,139	1.7
Norway	32,580	0.5	33,452	0.5
Others	4,460	0.1	4,363	0.1
Other developed countries	202,224	3.1	242,432	3.4
Australia	105,391	1.6	128,696	1.8
Japan	50,319	0.8	24,762	0.3
Israel	25,111	0.4	59,646	0.8
New Zealand	21,402	0.3	29,328	0.4
Developing countries	2,173,769	32.9	2,339,632	32.8
Africa	157,823	2.4	170,876	2.4
Asia and the Pacific	1,310,200	19.8	1,406,527	19.7
Latin America and the Caribbean	705,746	10.7	762,229	10.7
Central and Eastern Europe	155,734	2.4	187,868	2.6
Least developed countries	40,867	0.6	46,099	0.6
Total	6,606,855	100.0	7,122,506	100.0
Addenda:				
Outwards stock	6,318,861		6,866,362	
Inward stock	6,606,855		7,122,506	
Difference	−287,994		−256,144	

* 2002 numbers are estimates.

Note: Numbers might not add up due to rounding.

Source: Adapted from United Nations, *World Investment Report 2003*.

Table 1F Outward stocks of world foreign direct investment

Country/regions	2001 (in billion of US $)	% of total	2002* (in billion of US $)	% of total
Developed countries	5,487,592	86.8	5,987,746	87.2
North America	1,626,312	25.7	1,775,134	25.9
United States	1,381,674	21.9	1,501,415	21.9
Canada	244,638	3.9	273,719	4.0
Western Europe	3,453,487	54.7	3,771,452	54.9
EU	3,171,860	50.2	3,434,297	50.0
Austria	28,511	0.5	40,220	0.6
Belgium/Luxembourg	181,460	2.9	na	na
Denmark	69,766	1.1	74,605	1.1
Finland	56,055	0.9	69,468	1.0
France	489,411	7.7	652,105	9.5
Germany	553,315	8.8	577,849	8.4
Greece	6,371	0.1	7,026	0.1
Ireland	33,748	0.5	36,453	0.5
Italy	182,375	2.9	194,498	2.8
Netherlands	329,383	5.2	355,652	5.2
Portugal	23,491	0.4	31,983	0.5
Spain	189,418	3.0	216,051	3.1
Sweden	122,053	1.9	145,382	2.1
United Kingdom	906,474	14.3	1,033,003	15.0
Other Western Europe	281,627	4.5	337,156	4.9
Switzerland	247,807	3.9	297,570	4.3
Norway	32,771	0.5	38,308	0.6
Others	1,049	0.0	1,278	0.0
Other developed countries	407,792	6.5	441,160	6.4
Australia	91,343	1.4	91,249	1.3
Japan	300,115	4.7	331,596	4.8
Others	16,334	0.3	18,315	0.3
Developing countries	806,524	12.8	849,464	12.4
Africa	43,066	0.7	43,574	0.6
Asia and the Pacific	595,552	9.4	632,702	9.2
Latin America and the Caribbean	167,906	2.7	173,187	2.5
Central and Eastern Europe	24,746	0.4	29,152	0.4
Least developed countries	3,147	0.0	3,223	0.0
Total	6,318,861	100.0	6,866,362	100.0

* 2002 numbers are estimates.

Note: Numbers might not add up due to rounding.

Source: Adapted from United Nations, *World Investment Report 2003*.

Chapter 2

THE MULTINATIONAL ENTERPRISE

Contents

Objectives of the chapter

Most of the best-known companies in the world are multinational enterprises, and many of their names are easily recognized because their products and services are so popular. This is true for US MNEs, such as General Motors, Exxon, and IBM, but for others as well. Consider, for example, some of the largest industrial multinationals headquartered in the European Union: Unilever (Britain/Netherlands), Fiat (Italy), Nokia (Finland), Volkswagen (Germany), Philips (Netherlands), Peugeot (France), and in Japan: Sony, Fuji, and Toyota. There are also MNEs from non-triad areas such as Samsung (South Korea), Codelco (Chile), AngloGold (South Africa), and Bombardier (Canada). The primary objective of this chapter is to examine the nature and operations of multinational enterprises.

The objectives of this chapter are to:

1 *Describe* the characteristics of multinational enterprises.
2 *Explain* the internationalization process.
3 *Explain* why firms become multinational enterprises.
4 *Discuss* the strategic philosophy of these firms.
5 *Introduce* a country/firm framework for examining a firm's competitiveness.
6 *Study* some of the ways in which these firms use strategic management.

Disneyland in Europe

Between 1988 and 1990 three $150 million amusement parks opened in France. By 1991 two of them were bankrupt and the third was doing poorly. Despite this, the Walt Disney Company went ahead with a plan to open Europe's first Disneyland in 1992. Far from being concerned about the theme park doing well, Disney executives were worried that Euro Disneyland would be too small to handle the giant crowds. The $4.4 billion project was to be located on 5,000 acres in Seine-et-Marne 20 miles east of Paris. And the city seemed to be an excellent location; there were 17 million people within a two-hour drive of Euro Disneyland, 41 million within a four-hour drive, and 109 million within six hours of the park. This included people from seven countries: France, Switzerland, Germany, Luxembourg, the Netherlands, Belgium, and Britain.

Disney officials were optimistic about the project. Their US parks, Disneyland and Disneyworld, were extremely successful, and Tokyo Disneyland was so popular that on some days it could not accommodate the large number of visitors. Simply put, the company was making a great deal of money from its parks. However, the Tokyo park was franchised to others—and Disney management felt that it had given up too much profit with this arrangement. This would not be the case at Euro Disneyland. The company's share of the venture was to be 49 per cent for which it would put up $160 million. Other investors put in $1.2 billion, the French government provided a low-interest $900 million loan, banks loaned the business $1.6 billion, and the remaining $400 million was to come from special partnerships formed to buy properties and to lease them back. For its investment and management of the operation, the Walt Disney Company was to receive 10 per cent of Euro Disney's admission fees, 5 per cent of food and merchandise revenues, and 49 per cent of all profits.

The location of the amusement park was thoroughly researched. The number of people who could be attracted to various locations throughout Europe and the amount of money they were likely to spend during a visit to the park were carefully calculated. In the end, France and Spain had proved to offer the best locations. Both countries were well aware of the park's capability for creating jobs and stimulating their economy. As a result, each actively wooed the company. In addition to offering a central location in the heart of Europe, France was prepared to provide considerable financial incentives. Among other things, the French government promised to build a train line to connect the amusement park to the European train system. Thus after carefully comparing the advantages offered by both countries, France was chosen as the site for the park.

At first things appeared to be off to a roaring start. Unfortunately, by the time the park was ready to open, a number of problems had developed, and some of these had a very dampening effect on early operations. One was the concern of some French people that Euro Disney was nothing more than a transplanting of Disneyland into Europe. In their view the park did not fit into the local culture, and some of the French press accused Disney of "cultural imperialism." Others objected to the fact that the French government, as promised in the contract, had expropriated the necessary land and sold it without profit to the Euro Disneyland development people. Signs reading "Don't gnaw away our national wealth" and "Disney go home" began appearing along roadways. These negative feelings may well have accounted for the fact that on opening day only 50,000 visitors showed up, in contrast to the 500,000 that were expected. Soon thereafter, operations at the park came under criticism from both visitors and employees. Many visitors were upset about the high prices. In the case of British tourists, for example, because of the Franc exchange rate, it was cheaper for them to go to Florida than to Euro Disney. In the case of employees, many of them objected to the pay rates and the working conditions. They also raised concerns about a variety of company policies ranging from personal grooming to having to speak English in meetings, even if most people in attendance spoke French. Within the first month 3,000 employees quit. Some of the other operating problems were a result of Disney's previous experiences. In the United States, for example, liquor was not sold outside of the hotels or specific areas. The general park was kept alcohol free, including the restaurants, in order to maintain a family atmosphere. In Japan, this policy was accepted and worked very well. However, Europeans were used to having outings with alcoholic beverages. As a result of these types of problems, Euro Disney soon ran into financial problems.

In 1994, after three years of heavy losses, the operation was in such bad shape that some people were predicting that the park would close. However, a variety of developments saved the operation. For one thing, a major investor purchased 24.6 per cent (reducing Disney's share to

39 per cent) of the company, injecting $500 million of much needed cash. Additionally, Disney waived its royalty fees and worked out a new loan repayment plan with the banks, and new shares were issued. These measures allowed Euro Disney to buy time while it restructured its marketing and general policies to fit the European market.

In October 1994, Euro Disney officially changed its name to "Disneyland Paris." This made the park more French and permitted it to capitalize on the romanticism that the word "Paris" conveys. Most importantly, the new name allowed for a new beginning, disassociating the park from the failure of Euro Disney. This was accompanied with measures designed to remedy past failures. The park changed its most offensive labor rules, reduced prices, and began being more culturally conscious. Among other things, alcohol beverages were now allowed to be served just about anywhere.

The company also began making the park more appealing to local visitors by giving it a "European" focus. Ninety two per cent of the park's visitors are from eight nearby European countries. Disney Tomorrowland, with its dated images of the space age, was jettisoned entirely and replaced by a gleaming brass and wood complex called Discoveryland, which was based on themes of Jules Verne and Leonardo da Vinci. In Disneyland food services were designed to reflect the fable's country of origin: Pinocchio's facility served German food, Cinderella's had French offerings, and at Bella Notte's the cuisine was Italian. The company also shot a 360-degree movie about French culture and showed it in the "Visionarium" exhibit.

These changes were designed to draw more visitors, and they seemed to have worked. Disneyland Paris reported a

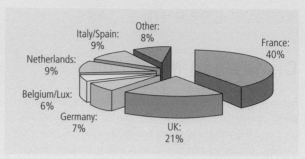

Geographic distribution of Disneyland Paris visitors, 2002

slight profit in 1996, and the park continued to make a modest profit through to the early 2000s. In 2002 and 2003, the company was once again making losses, and new deals had to be worked out with creditors. This time, however, it wasn't insensitivity to local customs but a slump in the travel and tourism industry, strikes and stoppages in France, and an economic downturn in many of the surrounding markets.

Websites: www.disneyinternational.com; www.disneylandparis.com; and www.disney.com.

Sources: Adapted from Euro Disney SCA, *Annual Report*, 2003; Steven Greenhouse, "Playing Disney in the Parisian Fields," *New York Times*, February 17, 1991, Section 3, pp. 1, 6; Stewart Toy and Paula Dwyer, "Is Disney Headed for the Euro-Trash Heap?," *Business Week*, January 4, 1994, p. 52; Theodore Stanger et al., "Mickey's Trip to Trouble," *Newsweek*, February 4, 1994, pp. 34–39; "Euro Disney Theme Park Cuts Loss, Shares Fall," *Yahoo News: Reuters*, April 22, 1998; Charles Fleming, "Euro Disney to Build Movie Theme Park Outside Paris," *Wall Street Journal*, September 30, 1999, pp. 18, 21; and Paulo Prada, "Euro Disney Does Nicely. So Why Are Investors Grumpy?" *Wall Street Journal*, September 6, 2000, p. A 20.

1. What are some of the characteristics of multinational enterprises that are displayed by the Walt Disney Company?

2. Why did Disney take an ownership position in the firm rather than simply licensing some other firm to build and operate the park and settling for a royalty on all sales?

3. In what way did Euro Disney reflect the strategic philosophy of Walt Disney as a multinational enterprise?

4. Did Disney management conduct an external environmental analysis before going forward with Euro Disney? Explain.

INTRODUCTION

Multinational enterprise (MNE)
A company headquartered in one country but having operations in other countries

A **multinational enterprise (MNE)** is a company that is headquartered in one country but has operations in one or more other countries. Sometimes it is difficult to know if a firm is an MNE because multinationals often downplay the fact that they are foreign held. For example, many people are unaware that Bayer, the drug company, is German owned; Nestlé, the chocolate manufacturer, is a Swiss company; Northern Telecom is Canadian; and Ford

Motor now owns Jaguar, the British-based auto maker. Similarly, approximately 25 per cent of banks in California are Japanese owned, but this is often not evident from their names. Simply put, many large MNEs have world holdings far beyond that what is known to the casual observer. A closer look at these MNEs will reveal the impact they have on international business and the world economy.

THE NATURE OF MULTINATIONAL ENTERPRISES

The United Nations has identified over 60,000 MNEs, but the largest 500 account for 80 per cent of the world's foreign direct investment.[1] Table 2.1 shows the distribution of the world's largest 500 MNEs. Of these, 424 are from the "triad." There are 189 from the United States, 153 from the EU, and 82 from Japan. The fact that over 80 per cent of the world's largest 500 MNEs are from the core triad is highly significant. It means that the triad is the basic unit of analysis for MNE strategy. Also, about 80–85 per cent of the world's top MNEs have been from the triad for the last 20–30 years.[2] Total annual sales of these 500 firms are in excess of $14.9 trillion.[3] These firms are engaged in a wide variety of operations including autos, chemicals, computers, consumer goods, financial services, industrial equipment, and oil and steel production.

The names of the largest triad-based MNEs, as well as those from non-triad countries, are listed in Appendixes 2A–2E. Students should become familiar with at least some of these MNEs as we proceed through this book. We provide the websites for all the MNEs we discuss in the case boxes.

Characteristics of multinational enterprises

One way of identifying the characteristics of MNEs is by looking at the environment in which they operate. Figure 2.1 shows some of the major forces in this environment. Notice that an MNE has two major areas of concern: the home country of its headquarters and the

Table 2.1 The world's largest 500 multinational enterprises, 2003

Country	Number of MNEs
United States	189
European Union	153
Japan	82
China	15
Canada	13
Switzerland	12
South Korea	11
Australia	7
India	4
Brazil	3
Russia	3
Norway	2
Venezuela	1
Mexico	1
Taiwan	1
Thailand	1
Singapore	1
Malaysia	1
Total	**500**

Source: Adapted from Fortune, *The Fortune Global 500*, July 26, 2004.

Home Country	Stakeholders	Host Countries
Competitors		Competitors
Customers	**Multinational**	Customers
Domestic affiliates	**enterprise**	Foreign affiliates
Suppliers		Suppliers
Government		Government
	Banks	

Figure 2.1 The multinational enterprise and its environment

host countries in which it does business. Stakeholders are not included within these two areas of Figure 2.1 because they can come from anywhere in the world. For example, an investor in Switzerland can purchase stock in Sears Roebuck even though the company does not do business in Switzerland.

One characteristic of MNEs is that their affiliates must be responsive to a number of important environmental forces, including competitors, customers, suppliers, financial institutions, and government (again see Figure 2.1). In some cases the same forces are at work in both the home and host-country environments. For example, many of General Motors' competitors in the US market are the same as those in Europe: BMW, Ford, DaimlerChrysler, Honda, and Volkswagen, among others. Similarly, MNEs often use the same suppliers overseas that they employ domestically, and it is common to find home-country-based suppliers following their MNE customer to other geographic locales in order to provide the same types of services worldwide. In other cases, however, these same environmental factors can be very different on each of the markets in which the firm operates.

A second characteristic of an MNE is that it draws on a common pool of resources, including assets, patents, trademarks, information, and human resources. Because the affiliates are all part of the same company, they have access to assets that are often not available to outsiders. For example, both Ford and General Motors compete vigorously in Europe and many of the design and styling changes developed for their European cars have now been introduced in US models. The flow of information and technology between European and US affiliates has led to success in the worldwide market for many MNEs. Similarly, if an affiliate needs expansion funds, an MNE will often help out by working with the affiliate to raise the money. If a loan is needed, the affiliate is likely to find many financial institutions that are willing to provide the money because the MNE will back the loan.

A third characteristic of an MNE is that it links together the affiliates and business partners with a common strategic vision. Simply put, all of the firms with whom the MNE works fit into the company's overall plan of what it wants to do and how it intends to go about implementing this strategy. General Motors (GM) is a good example. The auto giant has announced that it is now going to rely heavily on partnerships to help it grow.[4] GM realizes that no auto maker has all of the resources for achieving leadership in every region of the world or in every product segment. As a result, the company has formed a manufacturing partnership with Toyota to conduct research and development on fuel cell and gas-electric hybrid vehicles. GM also has created an alliance with Fuji Heavy Industries and its Subaru brand that allows GM to benefit from Fuji's strengths in small sport utility vehicles, continuously variable transmissions, and all-wheel-drive systems and, in turn, gives Fuji access to GM's vehicle platforms and other important manufacturing technologies. These types of arrangements are part of GM's new strategic vision—one that is not limited just to building cars. Today the company is looking into ways of providing customers with other auto-related services as seen by its Onstar communications program with wireless phone service that allows drivers to be in constant contact with someone who can give them information and assistance.

✔ Active learning check

Review your answer to Active Learning Case question 1 and make any changes you like. Then compare your answer with the one below.

1 **What are some of the characteristics of multinational enterprises that are displayed by the Walt Disney Company?**

One of the characteristics of a multinational enterprise is that ties of common ownership link affiliated firms. In this case the Walt Disney Company holds a substantial interest in Disneyland Paris, in addition to its ownership of Disneyland and Disneyworld in the United States. A second characteristic is that the MNE draws on a common pool of resources. One way Euro Disney does this is through the use of trademarks and characters (Mickey Mouse, Goofy, Donald Duck) and the experience of the Disney team in setting up and running similar theme parks in the United States. A third characteristic is that MNEs have a common strategy for linking together the affiliates. The Walt Disney Company does this through its overall plan such as the one it used for deciding where to set up Euro Disney and how to manage the park.

The internationalization process

Not all international business is done by MNEs. Indeed, setting up a wholly-owned subsidiary is usually the last stage of doing business abroad, as is shown in Figure 2.2.

Figure 2.2 outlines the typical process by which a firm producing a standardized product will seek to involve itself in a foreign market.[5] This, however, is a generalization as firms ultimately make decisions depending on their particular circumstances. The

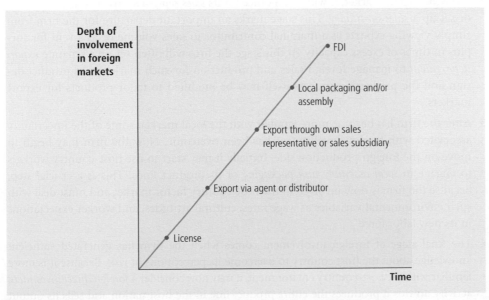

Figure 2.2 Entry into foreign markets: the internationalization process

process we illustrate here, however, is important because it is based on how the firm perceives risk and how it deals with it. In this internationalization process the firm regards foreign markets as risky due to the fact that, as these markets are unknown to it, the firm faces export marketing costs. To avoid such information costs and risk, its strategy is to go abroad at a slow and cautious pace, often using the services of specialists in international trade outside the firm. Over time, familiarity with the foreign environment will reduce the information costs and help to alleviate the perceived risk of foreign involvement. There is a "learning" effect as firms become familiar with a foreign market.[6]

Initially the firm may seek to avoid the risks of foreign involvement by arranging a joint venture or a license. A license is a contractual arrangement in which one firm, the licensor, provides access to some of its patents, trademarks, or technology to another firm, the licensee, in exchange for a fee or royalty. This fee often involves a fixed amount upon signing the contract and then a royalty of 2–5 per cent on sales generated by the agreement. A typical licensing contract will run from five to seven years and be renewable at the option of either or both parties. This strategy is most suitable for a standardized product where there is no risk of dissipation of the firm's technological or managerial advantages. Otherwise, licensing will be reserved for a much later stage of entry. Indeed, when it is important for the firm to retain control over its firm-specific advantage in technology (as in internalization theory),[7] licensing will be the last stage of entry. The firms involved in the process of internationalization, on the other hand, typically are not concerned about losing their firm-specific advantages. Rather, they want to avoid exposure to an uncertain foreign environment. Abstracting from the licensing option (and the more complex problem of joint ventures), the major types of foreign entry for a firm are as follows:

1 The firm sees potential extra sales by *exporting* and uses a *local agent or distributor* to enter a particular market. Often the firm uses exporting as a "vent" for its surplus production and may have no long-run commitment to the international market. If it does well abroad, however, it may then set up its own local sales representative or marketing subsidiary, in the hope of securing a more stable stream of export sales.

2 As exports come to represent a larger share of sales, the firm may increase its capacity to serve the export market. It will set an office for its *sales representative* in a major market, or set up a *sales subsidiary*. This stage marks an important departure for the firm from simply viewing exports as a marginal contributor to sales volume or as a vent for surplus in times of excess capacity. At this stage the firm will often set up a separate *export department* to manage foreign sales and production for such markets and product design and the production process itself may be modified to tailor products for export markets.

3 After the firm has become more familiar with the local market, some of the uncertainty associated with foreign involvement has been overcome. Now the firm may begin to move on the foreign production side. Initially it may start to use host-country workers to engage in *local assembly and packaging* of its product lines. This is a crucial step, because the firm is now involved in the host-country factor market and must deal with such environmental variables as wage rates, cultural attitudes, and worker expectations in its new labor force.

4 The final stage of foreign involvement comes when the firm has generated sufficient knowledge about the host country to overcome its perceptions of risk. Because it is more familiar with the host-country environment, it may now consider a *foreign direct investment* activity. In this it produces the entire product line in the host nation and sells its output

Internationalization
The process by which a company enters a foreign market

License
A contractual arrangement in which one firm (the licensor) provides access to some of its patents, trademarks, or technology to another firm in exchange for a fee or royalty

Licensor
A company that provides access to some of its patents, trademarks, or technology to another firm in exchange for a fee or royalty

Licensee
A firm given access to some of the patents, trademarks, or technology of another firm in exchange for a fee or royalty

there, or it may even be able to re-export back to the home country. These decisions depend on the relative country-specific costs; for example, if labor is inexpensive in the host nation (as in Southeast Asia), more exporting takes place than if it is expensive (as in Western Europe and the United States).

It has become clear that the internationalization process is more complicated than it seems at first glance. Like all generalizations, this schematic path of export commitment relies on simplifications. In reality, the process of foreign entry is sufficiently complicated to depend on a careful weighing of many firm-specific and country-specific factors. A framework to model these firm-specific advantages (FSAs) and country-specific advantages (CSAs) is developed in the next section.

✔ **Active learning check**

Review your answer to Active Learning Case question 2 and make any changes you like. Then compare your answer with the one below.

2 **Why did Disney take an ownership position in the firm rather than simply licensing some other firm to build and operate the park and settling for a royalty on all sales?**

Disney believed that the theme park was too lucrative a venture to settle for just a royalty on sales. The company felt that it would be giving up too much to simply "take the money and run" when by remaining and managing the operation it could garner a great deal more revenue. Moreover, not only is the revenue potential of the park extremely high, but Disney's initial investment of $160 million was extremely low given the amount of control it maintains and the fees and profits that would be generated should the park prove as highly attractive as company executives were forecasting. Disney also wanted to retain control over its brand name products and services in order to prevent imitation by substandard rivals, and this is best done with an ownership position.

Why firms become multinational enterprises

Companies become MNEs for a number of reasons. One is to *diversify* themselves against the risks and uncertainties of the domestic business cycle. By setting up operations in another country, multinationals can often diminish the negative effects of economic swings in the home country. This is a form of international diversification, and it has been widely used by Japanese MNEs, for example, which have found that, while their home economy has been in an economic slump since the 1990s, their US operations have done quite well.

A second reason is to tap the growing world market for goods and services. For example, many MNEs have targeted the United States because of its large population and high per capita income. It is the world's single largest market in terms of gross domestic product. And since Americans have both a desire for new goods and services and the money to buy them, the United States can be an ideal market. MNEs are also targeting China. Although per capita gross domestic product is not very high, the country's large population and growing economy make it very attractive to multinationals. In 2001, China entered the World Trade Organization, and this acceptance of international rules made China more attractive for MNEs.

Firms also become MNEs in response to increased foreign competition and a desire to protect their home market share. Using a "*follow the competitor*" strategy, a growing

INTERNATIONAL BUSINESS STRATEGY *IN ACTION*

Italian family firms

In Italy more than 90 per cent of all small and medium-sized companies and some of the largest enterprises are family owned. In the fashion industry, for example, Versace, Missoni, and Benetton are family-held firms. In addition, Italian families own important manufacturers and hold operating control of some of the major banks and transportation companies in the country. For example, the Fiat Group grosses more than $47.3 billion euros annually and employs more than 160,000 people. It does this through the Fiat Group, a conglomerate consisting of 777 firms with holdings in agricultural and construction equipment, automobiles, aviation, commercial vehicles, communications, insurance services, metallurgical products, production systems, and publishing.

Another large family-owned Italian company is Pirelli, which, in recent years, has had annual revenues of around $8.4 billion and employs about 36,000 people. Most of the firm's revenues are generated from its tire and cable businesses. Along with Benetton, Pirelli has bought a controlling interest in Olivetti, the giant Italian computer and telecommunications corporation. As a result of this acquisition, Pirelli now has a 27 per cent stake in Telecom Italia, a telecommunications, information, and communication technology company with annual revenues of $30 billion euros and a workforce of around 93,000 people. This acquisition has also brought both Benetton and Pirelli into the wireless telecommunications business.

These two examples, Fiat and Pirelli, are typical of the holdings and influence of large Italian families in the country. Through their vast holdings and political power, they have been able to maintain a tight rein on various sectors of the economy. In addition, these family firms are protected against foreign investment by a secretive banking system that is headed by the Milan Bank, Mediobanca. This bank has financed nearly all of the takeover deals in Italy during the last 35 years. The bank also holds board positions on many of the country's conglomerates.

On a macro basis, the Italian business system reflects the twin pressures of local family culture and the increasing demands of international business. Like their larger counterparts, small and medium-sized family businesses are now using their personal and business networks to create MNEs that are branching out into the EU, as well as putting together deals in both North America and Asia.

Websites: www.olivetti.com; www.versace.com; www.missoni.it; www.benetton.com; www.fiat.com; www.pirelli.com; www.montedison.it; and www.mediobanca.it.

Sources: Fred Kapner, "Pirelli Seeks Rumour Probe," *Financial Times*, September 11, 2000, p. 18; Paul Meller, "European Panel Approves Takeover of Montedison," *New York Times*, August 29, 2001, p. W 1; Richard Owen, Clive Mathieson, and Caroline Merrell, *London Times*, August 4, 2001, p. 43; "Flattering to Deceive," *Economist*, August 2, 2001; www.olivetti.com; Pirelli, *Annual Report*, 2000; and Juliana Ratner, Krishna Guha, and Fred Kapner, "Small Stake Won Control of Telecom Italia," *Financial Times*, July 31, 2001.

number of MNEs now set up operations in the home countries of their major competitors. This approach serves a dual purpose: (1) it takes away business from their competitors by offering customers other choices, and (2) it lets competitors know that, if they attack the MNE's home market, they will face a similar response. This strategy of staking out global market shares is particularly important when MNEs want to communicate the conditions under which they will retaliate.

A fourth reason why companies become an MNE is to reduce costs. By setting up operations close to the foreign customer, these firms can eliminate transportation expenses, avoid the overhead associated with having intermediaries handle the product, respond more accurately and rapidly to customer needs, and take advantage of local resources. This process, known as "*internalization*" of control within the MNE, can help to reduce overall costs.

A fifth reason is to overcome *protective* devices such as tariff and non-tariff barriers by serving a foreign market from within. The EU provides an excellent example. Firms outside the EU are subject to tariffs on goods exported to EU countries. Firms producing the goods within the EU, however, can transport them to any other country in the bloc without paying tariffs. The same is now occurring in North America, thanks to the North American Free Trade Agreement (NAFTA), which has eliminated tariffs among Canada, the United States, and Mexico.

A sixth reason for becoming an MNE is to take advantage of technological expertise by manufacturing goods directly (by FDI) rather than allowing others to do it under a license. Although the benefits of a licensing agreement are obvious, in recent years some MNEs have concluded that it is unwise to give another firm access to proprietary information such as patents, trademarks, or technological expertise, and they have allowed current licensing agreements to lapse. This has allowed them to reclaim their exclusive rights and then to manufacture and directly sell the products in overseas markets.

Firms become multinational enterprises for the same reasons they engage in FDI. The next chapter will provide a more detailed examination of some of the reasons introduced in this chapter.

The strategic philosophy of multinational enterprises

Multinational enterprises make decisions based on what is best for the overall company, even if this means transferring jobs to other countries and cutting back the local workforce. In the last decade IBM, ABB, and Sony, for example, have spent considerable sums of money to train and develop local managers to handle overseas operations because the companies are finding that these managers are often much more effective than those sent from the home country. MNEs also hire large numbers of non-managerial workers in overseas countries. For example, US-based GM employs 66,000 workers in Europe and 11,000 workers in the Asia-Pacific region; and European Siemens has 83,400 workers in North America and 46,000 in the Asia-Pacific region.[8]

As a result there is a great deal of economic interaction in the international arena, giving business firms headquartered in one country a significant impact on the economies of other countries. This is true both when things are going well as well as when they are not. For example, with the recent slowdown of the world economy more and more MNEs are now trimming their workforces. Alcatel, the giant French telecommunications equipment maker, announced plans to cut 29 per cent of its workforce and to reduce its factories to a dozen, using outsourcing to handle all other production needs.[9] Philips, the giant Dutch electronics firm, reacted to a severe slowdown in demand for mobile phones and semiconductors, and eliminated more than 7,000 jobs;[10] and Disney cut 4,000 positions, about 3 per cent of its worldwide workforce.[11] These decisions were made to improve the situation of the company as a unit.

This same worldwide approach to operations can be seen in the way MNEs team up to get things done. One example is Embraer of Brazil, the fourth largest airplane manufacturer in the world. The company teamed up with 22 of its main suppliers, many of which are Japanese, to introduce a new family of aircraft. Suppliers became risk investors and by funding Embraer's plan secured future contracts from the company.[12] For more on Embraer, see the Real Case in Chapter 4. Another example is provided by the production of the V2500 engine by a consortium led by US Pratt & Whitney and British Rolls Royce. Other partners are Japanese Aero Engines and Germany's MTU Aero Engines.[13] Simply put, MNEs make whatever agreements are in their best interests, even if this means bringing in firms from three or four different countries.

Active learning check

Review your answer to Active Learning Case question 3 and make any changes you like. Then compare your answer with the one below.

3 **In what way did Euro Disney reflect the strategic philosophy of Walt Disney as a multinational enterprise?**

One way in which Euro Disney reflects the strategic philosophy of the company as an MNE is that Disney is willing to modify the park to meet the preferences of local visitors by catering to their markets. Euro Disney is not identical to Disneyland in California. The focus on European roots and culture is now an integral part of the park. In addition, notice how the company used an international approach to funding the project. The monies were not all raised in France. The government helped, but so did banks, private investors, and Disney itself. And when the operation ran into trouble, the company was willing to reconfigure its arrangement and give up some ownership and some revenue in order to get things back on an even keel.

Table 2.2 The international expansion of four MNEs

	Number of majority-owned foreign affiliates		
MNE	**1970**	**1985**	**2000**
Ford (US)	65	140	270
Unilever (EU)	94	146	244
Siemens (EU)	84	165	416
Marubeni (Japan)	16	44	170

Source: United Nations, *World Investment Report 2001* (Geneva: United Nations Conference on Trade and Development, 2001).

Table 2.2 reports the geographical expansion between 1970 and 2000 of four of the world's largest MNEs, especially since 1985. The international scope of these MNEs is measured by the number of majority-owned foreign affiliates (subsidiaries) that they have.

STRATEGIC MANAGEMENT AND MULTINATIONAL ENTERPRISES

As noted earlier, one of the characteristics of MNE affiliates is that they are linked by a strategic plan. As a result, units that are geographically dispersed and/or have diverse product offerings all work in accord with a strategic vision. The formulation and implementation of strategy will be discussed in detail in Chapter 8. Here we will look at the basic nature of the strategic management process and how select MNEs use strategic planning in managing their far-flung enterprises.

Strategic management of MNEs: an introduction

The strategic management process involves four major functions: strategy formulation, strategy implementation, evaluation, and the control of operations. These functions encompass a wide range of activities, beginning with an environmental analysis of external and internal conditions and an evaluation of organizational strengths and weaknesses. These activities serve as the basis for a well-formulated strategic plan; and by carefully

Figure 2.3 The strategic management process in action

implementing and controlling this plan, the MNE is able to compete effectively in the international arena. Figure 2.3 illustrates the five specific steps in this overall process.

Steps in the strategic management process

Strategic planning typically begins with a review of the company's basic mission, which is determined by answering the questions: What is the firm's business? What is its reason for existence? By answering these questions, the company clearly determines the direction in which it wants to go. Shell Oil, BP Amoco, and Texaco, for example, see themselves as being in the energy business, not in the oil business, and this focus helps to direct their long-range thinking. AT&T, Sprint, and MCI view themselves as being in the communications business, not in the telephone business. Coca-Cola and PepsiCo see themselves in the food business, not in the soft-drink business. One of their strategic rivals is Nestlé.

In recent years a growing number of MNEs have revised their strategic plans because they realized that they had drifted too far away from their basic mission. Unilever, the giant Anglo-Dutch MNE, is a good example. After assessing its operations, the company concluded that it needed to adopt a "back to the core" strategy. As a result, it sold a wide range of peripheral operations, including transport, oil, milling, wallpaper, floor coverings, specialty chemicals, and turkey breeding. Today Unilever confines its business to consumer products goods: food, health and wellness products, personal care, and home care. The firm's strong research and development labs continue to develop new products in each of these areas, thus helping Unilever remain competitive in worldwide markets.[14]

After determining its mission, an MNE will evaluate the external and internal environment. The goal of external environmental analysis is to identify opportunities and threats that will need to be addressed. Based on opportunity analysis, for example, a number of MNEs have been moving into the former East Germany. Adidas-Salomon now produces a large portion of its textiles in this part of Germany. Metro, a German retailer, now has a large presence in Hungary, Poland, the Czech Republic, and Russia.[15] These companies all see the region as having tremendous financial potential.

However, these expansion decisions were made only after the companies had analyzed the potential pitfalls, and there were many of them. One is that eastern Germans lived in a centrally-planned bureaucracy for almost a half century. Could they adapt to a free-market economy? Would they be able to accept individual responsibility in a country where the state was no longer the major provider? Would they be able to upgrade their inefficient factories and improve the quality of output? Many MNEs believed that, with an influx of capital, the country's economy could be turned around. At the same time, their external environmental analysis showed that it would be necessary to increase worker productivity, improve the local infrastructure, and bring in qualified managers to run the operations until a local cadre could be developed.

The purpose of internal environmental analysis is to evaluate the company's financial and personnel strengths and weaknesses. Examining its financial picture will help the MNE

Basic mission
The reason that a firm is in existence

decide what it can afford to do in terms of expansion and capital investment. Examining its financial picture will also help it to identify areas where cost cutting or divestment is in order. By making an evaluation of its personnel, an MNE will be able to determine how well its current workforce can meet the challenges of the future and what types of people will have to be hired or let go. In addition, the firm might like to include in its internal

INTERNATIONAL BUSINESS STRATEGY *IN ACTION*

Nestlé

With 230,000 employees, 6,000 brands, and factories spread around the world, Nestlé is the world's largest food company. Nescafé instant coffee, Perrier water, and KitKat chocolate are just some of the products that the company produces and markets around the world.

A significant portion of Nestlé's revenues derives from developing countries. In 2002, developing nations in Latin America, Africa, and the Middle East accounted for 33.7 per cent of all sales. Nestlé's strategy in these nations consists of purchasing successful local brands, keeping their original names, and adding its own brand. In Peru, for instance, the company purchased ice cream and chocolate maker, D'Onofrio, and continued to market its products under the D'Onofrio brand, capitalizing on the reputation of this brand while adding the Nestlé logo as a parent brand to all packaging. Not a bad analogy to the entire Nestlé business where a "think local" philosophy is meshed together at the multinational level.

Entering third-world countries can be risky and unrewarding. For one thing, there is a currency risk. During 1998–2002, Nestlé's volume sales in Brazil rose by 10 per cent but because of the devaluation of Brazil's currency, revenues in Swiss francs fell by 30 per cent. Products must be adapted to the local tastes. In China, red bean and sesame-flavored chocolate ice cream cubes are two of the more than 100 flavors of ice cream that Nestlé markets in China alone. Political risk, in terms of expropriation or war, is also higher in developing countries.

Dealings with third-world countries may also affect a company's reputation in its large industrialized markets. In 2002, Nestlé demanded that the Ethiopian government deliver $6 million for a company that was expropriated in 1975 under a communist regime. Non-governmental organizations (NGOs) and concerned citizens were outraged. At the time, Ethiopia was undergoing a famine that threatened as many as 11 million citizens with starvation. The Ethiopian government offered $1 million, but Nestlé rejected the offer. Oxfam decried the company's stance claiming that one of the richest companies in the world was trying to squeeze out as much as it could from one of the poorest countries in the world. A spokesperson for the World Bank, which was brokering the

Source: Corbis/Swim Ink 2, LLC

deal, stated that the $1 million offer seemed reasonable and accused Nestlé of trying to get as much as it could. The backlash led Nestlé to accept $1.5 million in compensation and to donate the entire amount for famine relief in the country.

Website: www.nestle.com.

Sources: www.nestle.com; "Nestlé in Ethiopia Compensation Row," BBC.co.uk, December 18, 2002; "Selling to the Developing World," Economist.com, December 11, 2003.

environmental analysis the reputation of its products, the structure of its organization, and its relationship with suppliers.

Internal and external analyses will also help the MNE to identify both long-range goals (typically two to five years) and short-range goals (less than two years). The plan is then broken down into major parts, and each affiliate and department will be assigned goals and responsibilities. This begins the implementation process. Progress is then periodically evaluated and changes are made in the plan. For example, an MNE might realize that it must stop offering a particular good or service because the market is no longer profitable or it might create a new product in order to take advantage of an emerging demand. Figure 2.3 describes the strategic management process. External and internal environmental assessments are discussed in more detail in Chapter 8.

The box **International Business Strategy in Action: Nestlé** provides an example of some aspects of the strategic management process.

✔ Active learning check

Review your answer to Active Learning Case question 4 and make any changes you like. Then compare your answer with the one below.

4 **Did Disney management conduct an external environmental analysis before going forward with Euro Disney? Explain.**

The company conducted a thorough external environmental analysis. First, the location of the European population was examined to identify how far people would have to travel to visit the park. Second, the company examined the cost of building the park and identified potential sources of funds. Third, the firm determined how the park was to be built and where it would find the necessary contractors. Fourth, the company made a forecast regarding the number of visitors to the park each year, how much they would spend, and what the firm's profit would be on the venture.

However, the company failed in its examination of the cultural preferences of Europeans and the relative competitiveness of its European operation against its North American operation. In particular, Disney failed to take into consideration the effect of exchange rates on the affordability of traveling to France as opposed to Florida to visit its amusement park.

A FRAMEWORK FOR GLOBAL STRATEGIES: THE CSA-FSA MATRIX

Much of the material in this book can be synthesized within a single analytical framework.[16] We develop this here to help summarize our key points. There are two basic building blocks in an international business course, as illustrated in Figure 2.4. First, there is a set of firm-specific factors that determine the competitive advantage of an organization. We call these firm-specific advantages (FSAs). An FSA is defined as a unique capability proprietary to the organization. It may be built on product or process technology, marketing, or distributional skills. Second, there are country factors. These, of course, are unique to an international business course. They can lead to country-specific advantages (CSAs). The CSAs can be based on natural resource endowments (minerals, energy, forests) or on the labor force and associated cultural factors.

Managers of most MNEs use strategies that build on the interactions of CSAs and FSAs. They do this so that they can be positioned in a unique strategic space. The CSAs represent the natural factor endowments of a nation; they are based on the key variables in its

Firm-specific advantages (FSAs)
Strengths or benefits specific to a firm and a result of contributions that can be made by its personnel, technology, and/or equipment

Country-specific advantages (CSAs)
Strengths or benefits specific to a country that result from its competitive environment, labor force, geographic location, government policies, industrial clusters, etc.

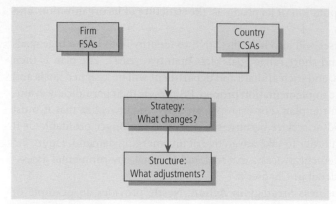

Figure 2.4 The basic components of international business

aggregate production function. For example, CSAs can consist of the quantity, quality, and cost of the major factor endowment, namely resources.

Using Porter's terminology, the CSAs form the basis of the global platform from which the multinational firm derives a home-base "diamond" advantage in global competition.[17] Tariff and non-tariff barriers to trade and government regulation also influence CSAs. Building on these CSAs, the firm makes decisions about the efficient global configuration and coordination between segments of its value chain (operations, marketing, R&D, and logistics). The skill in making such decisions represents a strong, managerial firm-specific advantage (FSA).

The FSAs possessed by a firm are based ultimately on its internalization of an asset, such as production knowledge, managerial or marketing capabilities, over which the firm has proprietary control. FSAs are thus related to the firm's ability to coordinate the use of the advantage in production, marketing, or the customization of services.

The competitive advantage matrix

To help formulate the strategic options of the MNE, it is useful to identify the relative strengths and weaknesses of the CSAs and FSAs they possess. Figure 2.5, the competitive advantage matrix, provides a useful framework for discussion of these issues. The "strength" or "weakness" of FSAs and CSAs is a relative notion, depending on the relevant market and the CSAs and FSAs of potential competitors. A strong FSA implies that, under identical CSAs, a firm has a potential competitive advantage over its rivals.

Quadrants 1, 2, and 3 correspond broadly to the three generic strategies suggested: cost leadership, differentiation, and focus.[18] Quadrant 1 firms are generally resource-based and/or mature, globally-oriented firms producing a commodity-type product. Given their late stage in the product life cycle, production FSAs flowing from the possession of intangible skills are less important than the CSAs of location and energy costs, which are the main sources of the firm's competitive advantage. Quadrant 2 firms represent inefficient, floundering firms with no consistent strategy, nor any intrinsic CSAs or FSAs. These firms are preparing to exit or to restructure. Quadrant 2 can also represent domestically-based small and medium-sized firms with little global exposure. Quadrant 3 firms generally can chose to follow any of the generic strategies listed above because of the strength of both their CSAs and FSAs.

Firms in quadrant 4 are generally differentiated firms with strong FSAs in marketing and customization. These firms follow basically a differentiation strategy. In quadrant 4 the FSAs dominate, so in world markets the home-country CSAs are not essential in the long run. Thus these firms are following low-cost and price competition strategies.

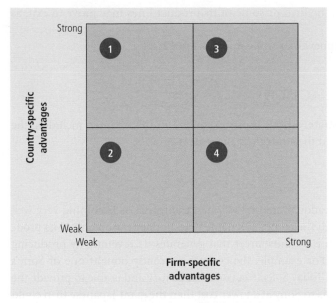

Figure 2.5 The competitive advantage matrix

In terms of business strategy, quadrants 3 and 2 are unambiguous in their implications. A quadrant 3 firm can benefit from strategies of both low cost and differentiation. Such a firm is constantly evaluating its production mix. As a product line matures and then declines it eventually graduates to quadrant 2. However, by adopting new product lines, developing dynamic organizational capabilities, and maintaining an effective strategy, the firm can maintain its overall position in quadrant 3. In quadrant 2 there is no alternative but to restructure or to eventually leave the market.

Quadrants 4 and 1 are credible positions for different types of firms. For instance, a quadrant 4 firm that has strong FSAs in marketing (customization) can operate globally without reliance on its home-market CSA, or the CSAs of the host nation. For such a firm, quadrant 4 does not signal a CSA weakness; the CSA is not relevant. In contrast, quadrant 1 has mature multinationals or product lines determined more by CSAs than by FSAs. By improving potential FSAs in marketing or product innovation and increasing value added through vertical integration, the quadrant 1 firm can move to quadrant 3, where its profitability should be enhanced.

Although quadrants 1, 3, and 4 represent appropriate strategic positioning for some firms, there exists an asymmetry between quadrants 4 and 1. A quadrant 4 strategic choice may be a stable one for some firms; however, quadrant 1 firms should be able to aim for quadrant 3. The reason for this asymmetry is rooted in the fact that CSAs are for the most part exogenous to the firm, whereas FSAs are not. Even to the extent that CSAs can be influenced by government protection, there is always increased uncertainty associated with such strategies. For the firm in quadrant 4 already following an efficiency-based strategy there is no incentive, nor need, to move to quadrant 3.

It is useful to note the following two points. First, if the firm has a conglomerate structure it would be more useful to situate each division or product line individually, recognizing that different units of the diversified firm would use different generic strategies. Second, changes in the trading environment—such as the EU 1992 single-market measures, or the EU 1999 single currency, or the United States–Canada Free Trade Agreement and NAFTA—will affect the relative CSAs of the firms. To the extent that CSAs are improved, the firms will tend to move to quadrant 3, and, to the extent that the CSAs are hampered, the firm or some of its product lines may move to exit, as in quadrant 2.

For a related theoretical framework see the Appendix to Chapter 3.

MULTINATIONALS IN ACTION

The following five firms illustrate various topics examined in this chapter, including the internationalization process and the strategic management process.

Solectron

The Solectron Corporation, headquartered in Milpitas, California, is becoming very well known internationally, although the company's name does not appear on any of its products. This is because Solectron is an outsourcer that generates its revenues by producing goods for other companies.[19] For example, the company recently bought one of Sony's manufacturing plants in Japan. Today Solectron runs that factory and is able to provide the same type of electronic products to Sony at a lower cost than the giant Japanese firm could do itself. Like many electronic companies that design, manufacture, and sell their own products, Sony's return on investment has been shockingly low because of the large amount of capital that is tied up in its factories. In a typical year Sony's return on equity is around 5 per cent. In contrast, Solectron is able to earn a return on equity in the range of 12 per cent. By focusing exclusively on such things as customized electronics technology, state-of-the-art manufacturing, and supply chain assistance, Solectron is able to achieve economies of scale that allow it to produce and deliver goods both quickly and inexpensively. As a result, its customer list is extensive. Large firms such as Cisco Systems, the giant Internet equipment company, rely on Solectron to handle a significant portion of their manufacturing needs. So too do smaller firms such as Handspring Inc., a California-based company that competes in the palm-size organizer market. In Handspring's case, the company realizes that its expertise is in designing and developing organizers as well as marketing them. As a result, it has turned over the production of these units to Solectron.

Today the cost of building new manufacturing plants is prohibitive for many firms. At the same time, the life cycle of products is becoming increasingly shorter. So if firms are going to reach their profit goals, they are going to have to find new ways to cut their expenses by outsourcing. This is good news for Solectron, which is becoming one of the fastest growing MNEs. (For more on contract manufacturing, see the Real Case: Flextronics, in Chapter 10.)

BMW

BMW is one of the world's best-known auto firms and for many years it has successfully produced and sold quality cars. As a result, the company has been able to capture and hold a solid share of the middle and upper-middle car market. BMW has 57 per cent of its sales in Europe and 32 per cent in North America, where its cars and SUVs sell well in the upper end of the market. Most recently, however, BMW has been turning its attention to the lower end of the market. One of its new objectives is to produce a small BMW and sell it at a premium price. This car line, which has been dubbed the 2 Series by the press, hit the market in 2004.[20]

Will BMW be successful in this venture? Some observers are quick to point out that small cars are a tempting but dangerous segment of the market. Profits are often elusive and competition is fierce. One of the big questions that is yet to be answered is how much of a premium buyers will be willing to pay for a small BMW. The company believes that there are customers who will pay a premium for value-added features and high perform-ance. One of the features in the 2 Series will be rear-wheel drive, not the front-wheel drive that is common in most small cars. While front-wheel drive offers better fuel economy, BMW believes that rear-wheel drive will provide better handling and give the driver a bet-ter feel for the road. In addition, the company intends to give the 2 Series the same dis-tinctive exterior look as its larger cars. As a result of these types of features, BMW feels that it will be able to attract buyers who are willing to pay a premium. In addition, the company is convinced that its name and reputation for quality will help it garner market share. In the past the firm has done exceptionally well and has consistently been one of the most profitable car makers in the world. However, this success has been in the upscale market. Making money in the small car market while charging a premium price is going to be an interesting challenge for it.

Levi Strauss

Bruce Springsteen wore a pair of Levi's jeans on the cover of his "Born in the USA" album, and James Dean and Madonna also did their part in marketing the brand. Levi's success at infiltrating itself into American pop culture is such that it pops up in the memory of many baby boomers remembering their school years: The "cool" kids wore Levi's.

In the mid-19th century denim was considered work wear, and Levi Strauss & Co. was a small dry goods store that sold functional items like clothing, linens, and bedding in California. Marketing of Levi's denim products borrowed from the American Western landscape featuring cowboys, fishermen, and mechanics, among others, at work in every-thing from their catalogues to the garment's tag. Durable, functional, and guaranteed were the pillars on which the firm built the reputation of its products.

By the start of the 20th century, the firm had expanded its product line to include children's clothing. At the same time, the firm's marketing became more "artistic," taking on the cultural trends of the times and marking a significant shift in philosophy that would turn the brand into an American icon and make jeans a fashion statement.

Being an American tradition, however, has not been enough to spare the firm from the challenges facing the industry around the world. Over the last two decades the firm has underperformed as a result of increased competition and changing consumer trends around the world. Protecting the brand name it so painstakingly built might never have been such a difficult task.

Levi Strauss was one of the last firms to hold on to domestic manufacturing. After all, the value of the brand was closely tied to American manufacturing quality. As competitors flocked to Asia in the mid-1990s, the firm remained hopeful that its brand would survive the price competition. By 1999, the strategy shifted as Levi Strauss announced it would turn itself into a marketing firm and shed the manufacturing side of its supply chain. This, it argued, would allow the firm to have a more flexible price structure. By 2004, all US-based factories had been closed. Newspapers were flocked with disappointed customers and nostalgia.[21]

Diesel, Guess, Buffalo, Silver, and Gap have also eroded the star power of Levi's jeans. Diesel jeans, for example, are considered a step above in terms of quality and design. While some competing brands might not be as durable as Levi's, they are less traditional in design, ac-commodating the ever-changing tastes of consumers who seasonally update their wardrobes.

In England, Levi went as far as suing Tesco, a major supermarket, for selling their prod-ucts at a discounted price. Levi's argued that Tesco's actions devalued the brand by selling jeans next to household products, groceries, and produce. Tesco had purchased Levi's jeans in the grey market—from distributors whose products originated from Levi's, because Levi refused to sell jeans directly to Tesco or other supermarkets. A European Union law prohibits branded products purchased abroad from being sold in the EU market without the consent of the brand owner. The ruling forbade Tesco from purchasing products outside the EU for sale in the UK, but allowed it to continue purchasing jeans in other EU countries.[22]

Winning the lawsuit did little to solve the erosion of its market by competitors, and the company continued to make losses. Realizing the potential of using these "discount" marketing channels, Levi's introduced a cheaper version of its jeans to be sold directly to supermarkets, including Tesco. Levi's "Signature" brand may solve the firm's problem of attracting as wide a customer base as possible while retaining the value of its original line of jeans.[23]

Levi Strauss is one of the few companies that pulled out of China during the mid-1990s because it felt that the government was guilty of pervasive human rights violations. The company stopped manufacturing jeans in China after it found evidence of child labor, forced labor, and a military presence at factories that were producing clothing for the firm. The company did not own any of these factories on the mainland; it relied on local subcontractors to perform the manufacturing. However, company guidelines prohibited the suppliers from using child labor, forced labor, or excessive work hours. So when Levi Strauss learned of these violations, the company concluded that its association with the contractors would damage its reputation, and it began a phased withdrawal from China.

Now Levi Strauss is coming back into the marketplace and even has plans to start a direct-marketing operation on the mainland. The firm has promised to monitor its new Chinese factories carefully to ensure that they comply with human rights guidelines. At the same time, however, Levi Strauss is glad to be back because, like many other MNEs, the company believes that China is a marketplace of the future.[24] One senior executive in the company put it this way, "You're nowhere in Asia without being in China."

Canon

Canon is one of the world's leading photo and printer firms, but this has not always been true. For many years Canon followed the leaders and worked to improve its technology. However, in recent years the company has taken the lead against firms such as Leica in cameras and Xerox in photocopiers.[25] It is a "global" firm with 32.7 per cent of its sales in North America, 30.3 percent in Asia, and 25.1 per cent in Europe.[26]

Today Canon is in the top three in all of its major business lines; and its original product, cameras, now accounts for less than 10 per cent of sales. However, the firm is the world leader in both single-lens reflexes and compacts, and earns almost one-third of its income from copiers. And to maintain its momentum, Canon has adopted a two-pronged strategy. First, it is seeking to maintain profits by cutting costs in its core business by making suppliers more efficient and by shifting work to factories in Taiwan, in order to reduce the high cost of building some of its products in Japan.

Second, Canon is moving into the digital age by cultivating alliances with companies that know the networking and computer world better than it does. For example, Canon has teamed with Hewlett-Packard, one of its major competitors, to build laser printers. The company is also looking into developing smart printers with personal computer-like abilities, including electronic mail, and printers that produce high-quality photo prints on plain paper. Quite clearly, Canon believes that its future rests with the continued development of innovative products that draw on its core competencies in the optical field.

Zara

Zara is the world's fastest-growing fashion retailer. Headquartered in northwestern Spain, the company has expanded rapidly in recent years, and by 2004 had over 600 stores in about 50 countries stretching from Copenhagen to Tokyo.[27] There are only a few Zara units in the United States, but the company's plans call for a rapid expansion there in the next couple of years.

There are two things that make Zara's implementation of its strategic plan so successful. One is that the company has created a lightning-speed production and distribution system. In an industry where competitors have their goods produced as much as five months in advance of delivery to stores, Zara's turnaround time is a mere three weeks. This means that the company can alter its designs and create new ones as the season moves along, thus allowing it to continually accommodate the changing tastes of its customers. Moreover, because Zara can change designs so quickly, none of its styles last more than four weeks. Coupled with this flexibility is a computerized inventory system that helps the firm minimize warehousing costs. Clothes are sorted in a single distribution center and then shipped out in pre-programmed lots directly to the stores. Twice a week each store receives deliveries that have been triggered by real-time inventory data that are collected through a network of computer handsets that feed information through the Internet into computers at headquarters. This system is so sophisticated and accurate that the company's inventory level is a mere 7 per cent of annual revenues, sharply lower than the 13 per cent of its main competitor.

The other thing that helps account for the firm's success in implementing its plan is the salespeople who act as grass-roots market researchers. Each person has a wireless organizer that is used to enter trends, customer comments, and orders. As a result, if an item does not sell well, it can be off the shelf within weeks. Conversely, if it is successful, company designers can quickly learn this and turn out a new version in a myriad of colors in record time. As an example, when Zara store personnel sold pink men's dress shirts they learned from the customers that they would have preferred a purple one. This information was conveyed to the company's in-house manufacturing team, which raced into action. Within two weeks Zara stores were selling purple shirts.

The company implements the same basic strategy worldwide. It does no advertising, and the products that it sells in Europe are similar to those in its stores in the United States. Inventory control is also given a strong emphasis with all US stores supplied by air from Spain. At the same time, however, Zara does try to create an image that fits local taste. For example, in one of its mid-Manhattan stores the company tore out the entire interior and put in marble-like floors and high-tech lights to create a stunning 10,000-square-foot emporium. Customers, most of whom are in their 20s, are attracted by the feeling of being in an upscale European boutique, even though the prices are sharply lower and are targeted to compete with those at Gap.[28]

Zara has been very effective in implementing its strategic plan as seen by the financial results. In an industry that has been seeing sluggish growth, Zara's sales have been rising by over 20 per cent annually, and in one recent year the company netted almost $200 million on sales of $2 billion. As a result the company is now increasing the number of stores in Europe, North America, and Asia, using the same basic approach for implementation that has proven successful thus far.

These examples of large MNEs sometimes give the misleading impression that MNEs are larger than some countries. This mistake is compounded by the simple listing of the sales of MNEs against the GDP of nations (see Table 2.3). In such a listing Wal-Mart appears 18th in the list and it is larger than Belgium. Altogether there are 16 MNEs in the top 50 and 39 in the top 100. There are two problems with this.

First, even the sales of GM at $263 billion are tiny in comparison with the size of the US GDP at $10,110 billion. Similarly, the European MNEs are small compared with the EU size (which is not recognized in Table 2.3—as the individual 15 members are included—but was estimated at more than $7.9 trillion in 2003). And the largest Japanese MNE, Toyota, at $153.1 billion is tiny compared with the GDP of Japan at $4,265.6 billion.[29]

Table 2.3 The Top 100 economies and MNEs, 2003

Rank	Country/company	Billions of US $	Rank	Country/company	Billions of US $
1	United States	10,110.1	51	Egypt Arab Rep.	97.6
2	Japan	4,265.6	52	ING	95.9
3	Germany	1,870.4	53	Citigroup	94.7
4	United Kingdom	1,486.2	54	Ireland	92.6
5	France	1,342.7	55	IBM	89.1
6	China	1,209.5	56	Singapore	86.1
7	Italy	1,097.9	57	Malaysia	86.0
8	Canada	700.5	58	Philippines	81.5
9	Mexico	596.7	59	AIG	81.3
10	Spain	594.1	60	Siemens	80.5
11	India	501.5	61	Colombia	80.1
12	Brazil	497.4	62	Carrefour	79.8
13	South Korea	473.0	63	Hitachi	76.4
14	Netherlands	386.8	64	HP	73.1
15	Australia	386.6	65	Honda	72.3
16	Russia	307.9	66	McKesson	69.5
17	Switzerland	274.2	67	US Postal Service	68.5
18	Wal-Mart	263.0	68	Verizon Communications	67.8
19	Belgium	239.9	69	Assicurazioni Generali	66.8
20	BP	232.6	70	Sony	66.4
21	Exxon Mobil	222.8	71	Chile	66.3
22	Sweden	221.5	72	Matsushita Elec. Ind.	66.2
23	Royal Dutch/Shell	201.7	73	Nissan Motor	65.8
24	General Motors	195.3	74	Nestlé	65.4
25	Austria	190.4	75	Home Depot	64.8
26	Poland	176.6	76	Berkshire Hathaway	63.9
27	Turkey	174.0	77	Nippon Life Insurance	63.8
28	Norway	171.8	78	Royal Ahold	63.5
29	Hong Kong, China	167.6	79	Deutsche Telekom	63.2
30	Ford	164.5	80	Peugeot	61.4
31	Denmark	162.7	81	Altria Group	60.7
32	DaimlerChrysler	156.6	82	Metro	60.7
33	Argentina	154.1	83	Aviva	59.7
34	Toyota	153.1	84	ENI	59.3
35	Indonesia	149.9	85	Pakistan	59.2
36	General Electric	134.2	86	Munich Re Group	59.1
37	Greece	123.9	87	Credit Suisse	59.0
38	Finland	122.2	88	State Grid	58.3
39	Thailand	122.2	89	HSBC Holdings	57.6
40	Total	118.4	90	BNP Paribas	57.3
41	Allianz	114.9	91	Vodafone	56.8
42	South Africa	113.5	92	Cardinal Health	56.8
43	ChevronTexaco	112.9	93	Czech Republic	56.7
44	Iran	112.1	94	Fortis	56.7
45	Axa	111.9	95	State Farm Insurance	56.1
46	Portugal	108.7	96	Sinopec	55.1
47	Venezuela	102.6	97	Peru	54.7
48	ConocoPhillips	99.5	98	Samsung Electronics	54.4
49	VW	98.6	99	Algeria	53.8
50	NTT	98.2	100	Kroger	53.8

Note: Data for countries is for 2002, the latest year available; data for companies is for 2003.

Sources: Adapted from World Bank, *World Development Report 2003* and Fortune, *The Fortune Global 500*, July 26, 2004.

Second, the measures are biased against the countries. The GDP is a "value-added" concept. It considers the final sales of goods and services. To develop a comparable measure for MNEs requires that only their value added be calculated, not the total sales. If this is done, then the "size" of the MNEs is reduced by 70–80 per cent. For example, in 2000, the value added of GM was only $46.2 billion, not the $176.6 billion reported as revenues.[30]

KEY POINTS

1   A multinational enterprise is a company that is headquartered in one country but has operations in two or more countries. There is a series of characteristics that are common to multinational enterprises. These include (a) affiliated firms that are linked by ties of common ownership, (b) a common pool of resources, and (c) a strategic vision that guides all the affiliates.

2   Multinationals, especially large industrial enterprises, account for a large percentage of world sales and employment. MNEs, large or small, also engage in a wide variety of business activities ranging from manufacturing to retailing to consulting services.

3   The internationalization process is one of going abroad at incremental stages, on the premise that foreign markets are risky. Thus, a typical process is: license, export, sales office, and, finally, FDI.

4   Companies become MNEs for a number of reasons, including (a) a desire to protect themselves from the risks and uncertainties of the domestic business cycle, (b) a growing world market for their goods or services, (c) a response to increased foreign competition, (d) a desire to internalize in order to reduce costs, (e) a desire to overcome tariff barriers, and (f) the chance to take advantage of technological expertise by manufacturing goods directly rather than allowing others to do it under a license agreement.

5   Multinational enterprises do not see themselves as an extension of their domestic roots. They hire, fire, and transfer personnel to meet global needs, even if this means laying off home-country employees. They also combine their talents with those of other MNEs in creating, financing, and managing joint ventures.

6   Successful MNEs rely on the strategic management process, which has five major phases: (a) identification of the firm's basic mission, (b) external and internal environmental analysis, (c) formulation of objectives and overall plans, (d) implementation of these plans, and (e) evaluation and control of operations.

7   Managers of most MNEs use strategies that build on firm-specific advantages (FSAs) and country-specific advantages (CSAs). CSAs are natural factor endowments of a nation. FSAs are based on the firm's internalization of an asset.

8   The key concepts in this book can be brought together in the framework of the CSA-FSA matrix. The multinational enterprises have FSAs that can be related to home and host CSAs.

Key terms

- multinational enterprise (MNE)
- internationalization
- license
- licensor
- licensee
- basic mission
- firm-specific advantages (FSAs)
- country-specific advantages (CSAs)

REVIEW AND DISCUSSION QUESTIONS

1 What is a multinational enterprise? Is it likely that the number of MNEs will increase during the next decade? Why?

2 What are the three common characteristics of an MNE? Identify and briefly describe each.

3 Why do firms become multinational enterprises? Identify and discuss four reasons.

4 How are CSAs different than FSAs?

5 How successful are the large industrial MNEs? What accounts for this?

6 What are the five basic steps in the strategic management process? Identify and briefly describe each.

7 How has Zara used the strategic management process to help it become a successful multinational?

8 How has Levi used the strategic management process to help it improve its competitiveness?

REAL CASE

Starbucks

From its first location in Seattle's Pike Place Market in 1971, Starbucks has grown into one of the largest coffee chains with 7,225 locations in markets across the world in 2003. The company purchases and roasts high-quality coffee beans that are then brewed and retailed in trendy designer coffee shops that cater to a loyal following of young urban professionals who appreciate the distinct taste of Starbucks' coffee.

The company's road to success began in 1985, when, after convincing the founders of Starbucks to test the coffee bar concept, the then director of retail operations, Howard Schultz, started his own coffee house to sell Starbucks coffee under the name Il Giornale. Within two years, Schultz purchased Starbucks and changed its company's name to Starbucks Corporation. Since then, the company has expanded rapidly, opening stores in key markets and creating a "corporate coffee culture" in each of the urban areas in which it settled. Coffee bars are located in high-traffic areas and include large bookstores, suburban malls, universities, and high-traffic intra-urban communities.

Popularity has not come without a price for Starbucks. Coffee prices fell considerably in the late 1990s and led to the displacement of thousands of farmers. The main reason for a fall in the price of coffee was the oversupply that arose from improved production techniques and from a crop boom in the 1990s. Although Starbucks only purchases approximately 1 per cent of the global supply of coffee, its high profile has made it a main target for protestors who accuse the coffee giant of not providing a fair price to coffee growers; this, despite Starbucks' policy of purchasing

Source: Getty Images/Spencer Platt

high-quality beans at premium market prices. To address the concerns of protestors, Starbucks introduced Fairtrade endorsed coffee to its coffee houses. While the amount of Fairtrade coffee sold by the company is insignificant, at 1 per cent of total sales, it is enough to portray the company as progressive and avert a consumer boycott.

The company directly operates 3,779 coffee houses in the United States in 2003. Unlike many coffee and fast-food chains, Starbucks does not franchise (license the right to operate one of its stores) to individuals in the United States. It does, however, negotiate licensing agreements with companies that have control over valuable retail space, such an airport or hospital. In 2003, there were 1,422 Starbucks stores operating under licenses.

With coffee houses in 28 countries, today Starbucks has a global presence. In contrast to its domestic operations, the vast majority of Starbucks' international operations are through licenses. Indeed, of 2,024 international stores in 2003, 1,257 were licensed.

Starbucks might have operations in far away countries like Australia, Oman, and China, but it is not global in its scope of operations. In 2003, 73.5 per cent of its stores were located in its home region of North America, including operations in Canada, Mexico, and Puerto Rico. An even larger portion of Starbucks' revenues and operating income are home-region oriented. The United States alone accounts for 85.2 per cent of revenues and 99 per cent of operating income. International operations, including those that are directly owned and operated by Starbucks, require a higher degree of administrative support to be responsive to country-specific regulatory requirements. In addition, because these are mainly new markets, economies of scale in marketing and production have not yet materialized.

Website: **www.starbucks.com.**

Sources: Adapted from Starbucks, *Annual Report*, 2002; Starbucks, *Annual Report*, 2003; **www.starbucks.com**; Nicholas Stein, "Crisis in a Coffee Cup," *Fortune*, December 4, 2002; "Mug Shot," *Economist*, September 19, 2002; and Janet Williams, "Starbucks Takes on its Critics," **BBC.co.uk**, February 27, 2002.

1 Why does Starbucks rely on licenses for most of its international operations? Does the firm risk the dissipation of its managerial or technological advantages?

2 Can you argue that Starbucks is a global company regardless of the strong dominance of its home region in terms of sales and locations? Please explain.

3 What accounts for the discrepancy between percentage of foreign locations and percentage of foreign net revenues?

4 What are some of the reasons why Starbucks chooses to retain operational control of its domestic operations?

REAL CASE

Sony

Very few companies can claim to be globally successful, but Sony, which brought us the Walkman and co-developed the CD and the DVD, has the numbers to prove it. In 2004, the company's $72 billion in revenues were evenly distributed across mainly three markets: Japan, the United States, and Europe.

Headquartered in Japan, Sony is best known for its high-quality consumer electronics, which account for 61 per cent of total revenues, but the firm also produces games, music, and pictures. Consumers might not own a Sony electronic system, but the movie they watched last night or the CD they listen to while jogging may be the intellectual property of a Sony company. Sony's strategy boils down to producing electrical gadgets and controlling the content that goes through them much in the same way as its successful PlayStation2 game console provides the hardware necessary for the firm to capture the games market.

In the 1980s, Sony's Betamax lost the VCR war to JVC's VHS. Both systems had been developed in the mid-1970s and initially, Sony's Betamax was the clear winner. Indeed, all movies were originally released in Betamax format. General wisdom argues that Betamax lost the

VCR war because it failed to license its software to rival manufacturers while Matsushita licensed to all. Today, the Betamax-VHS battle is often cited to argue the benefits of licensing new technology.

Yet, how could Sony have been so reckless as to ignore the benefits of licensing? The answer is that it did not. In 1974, a year before the Betamax release, Sony approached JVC and Matsushita seeking to reach an agreement on standards for the new product. In doing so, it freely disclosed Betamax patented specification and technology to its rivals. The VHS format developed by JVC used very similar technology, but, because of its different size, was incompatible with Betamax. Matsushita was asked to choose between Sony's and JVC's product. Its decision came down to cost. It was cheaper to produce the VHS format because it had fewer components. With this, the players for the market were defined. The Betamax was to be manufactured by Toshiba, Sanyo Electric, NEC, Aiwa, and Pioneer. Matsushita, Hitachi, Mitsubishi Electric, Sharp, and Akai Electric manufactured JVC's VHS.

Perhaps more important than the size of the VCR disks of the two formats, was that the VHS format allowed recording for two hours, twice that of Betamax. This would have allowed consumers to record an entire movie while away for the night. Sony was close to integrating technology into its format that would have increased the recording time to that of the VHS. If this was what tilted the balance, then all Sony would have needed is a bit of time. Potentially, at least, it could have bought itself some time if it owned the rights of the movies and refused to release them in anything but Betamax format. And so it is that Sony's latest technological bets, the CD and DVD, have Sony Music Entertainment Inc and Sony Pictures Entertainment to back them up.

In today's market, however, this type of vertical integration can hamper the ability of the consumer electronics division to develop the products that consumers want. Practically every major development in the consumer's electronic industry in recent years has been developed by, or with the help of, Sony. Yet, very recently, Apple introduced the iPod, a very small and light device that can store up to 10,000 music files. The iPod is based on a small hard drive equipped with an audio function. Since similar memory cards are available across product lines in the industry and no other firm has Sony's reputation in the audio market, why, then, did Sony not come up with its own version? One argument is that the conglomerate must now weigh the benefits of developing a product in one division that may increase piracy of its music in another division.

If that is so, Sony is walking a fine line. Its electronics branch has ceased to produce stand-alone products and is instead integrating new products with others, which is likely to make piracy even easier than it is now. Soon, Sony hopes, your computer will be able to communicate with your television, stereo, and DVD player wirelessly creating an integrated network of consumer electronics. And, if it all goes according to plan, Sony's media content will flow within these networks.

With PlayStation2, Sony's dominance in the market for games was assured, at least in the short term, because it managed to capture most of the market and a game console creates a barrier to other game marketers because of lack of compatibility and intellectual property owned by the firm. Other forms of entertainment, however, are not as easily monopolized. Indeed, most new products, like the iPod, are based on technology that is standardized or can be adapted to work with that of competitors. If

Source: Getty Images/AFP

products do not do this, they might suffer the fate of the Betamax.

Websites: www.sony.com and www.sony.net.

Sources: www.sony.net; www.sony.com; Sony, *Annual Report,* 2003; Jack Schofield, "Why VHS Was Better Than Betamax," *The Guardian,* January 25, 2003; and Economist, "The Complete Home Entertainer," *Economist.com,* February 27, 2003.

1   Is Sony a multinational enterprise?

2   If the vast majority of Sony's consumer electronics business is based and developed in Japan and the vast majority of Sony's music and movie business is based in the United States, does Sony make decisions that are best for the entire company regardless of location?

3   Why does Sony need to license its technology to competitors?

Endnotes

1 United Nations, *World Investment Report 2001* (Geneva: United Nations Conference on Trade and Development, 2001).

2 Alan M. Rugman, *The End of Globalization* (London: Random House, 2000), Chapter 7, especially p. 140.

3 *Fortune*, July 26, 2004.

4 Robyn Meredith, "In Policy Shift, G.M. Will Rely On Alliances," *New York Times*, January 18, 2000, pp. C 1, C 14.

5 This figure was first developed in Alan M. Rugman et al., *International Business: Firm and Environment* (New York: McGraw-Hill, 1985), pp. 89–93. It is based on the ideas in Alan M. Rugman, *Inside the Multinationals: The Economics of Internal Markets* (New York: Columbia Press, 1981).

6 Rugman (1981) n. 5 above.

7 Rugman (1981) n. 5 above.

8 GM, *Annual Report*, 2002 and Siemens, *Annual Report*, 2003.

9 Raphael Minder and Daniel Dombey, "Alcatel Cut Plans 'Stun' French," *Financial Times*, June 28, 2001, p. 21.

10 Suzanne Kapner, "Citing U.S. Slowdown, Philips Will Cut 7,000 Jobs," *New York Times*, April 18, 2001, p. W 1.

11 Bill Carter, "Disney Is Cutting 4,000 Jobs Worldwide," *New York Times*, March 28, 2001, pp. C 1, C 13.

12 Andrew Carey, "Embraer: High Hopes for the Future," *CNN.com*, April 5, 2004.

13 Pratt & Whitney, "Japan Air System Awards Three-Year Maintenance Agreement To Pratt & Whitney Joint Venture," *Press Release*, September 29, 2003.

14 Unilever, *Annual Report*, 2003.

15 Michael Freedman, "Sturm und Drung," *Forbes.com*, July 26, 2004.

16 Alan M. Rugman, *Inside the Multinationals: The Economics of Internal Markets* (New York: Columbia University Press, 1981); Alan M. Rugman (ed.), *International Business in Canada: Strategies for Management* (Toronto: Prentice-Hall Canada, 1989), Chapters 8, 13; Alan M. Rugman, *The Theory of Multinational Enterprises* (Cheltenham: Edward Elgar, 1996).

17 See Michael E. Porter, *The Competitive Advantage of Nations* (New York: Free Press, Macmillan, 1990).

18 See Michael E. Porter, *Techniques for Analyzing Industries and Competitors* (New York & London: Free Press, 1980).

19 Peter Landers, "Why Some Sony Gear Is Made in Japan—By Another Company," *Wall Street Journal*, June 14, 2001, pp. A 1, A 10 and Lucent Technologies, "Lucent Technologies closes agreement with Solectron for certain manufacturing assets in Massachusetts," *News Release*, May 31, 2002.

20 Scott Miller, "BMW Takes the High Road in Market for Small Cars," *Wall Street Journal*, August 3, 2000, p. A 11.

21 Malcom Mayhew, "Levi's fades as pop icon as last factory moves overseas," Fort Worth Star-Telegram, December 5, 2003.

22 BBC, "Tesco Defeated in Cheap Jeans Battle," *BBC News*, July 31, 2002.

23 BBC, "Levi Losses Trimmed as Sales Rise," *BBC News*, April 13, 2004.

24 Mark Landler, "Reversing Course, Levi Strauss Will Expand Its Output in China," *New York Times*, April 9, 1998, pp. 1, 5.

25 Edward W. Desmond, "Can Canon Keep Clicking?" *Fortune*, February 2, 1998, pp. 98–104.

26 Canon, *Annual Report*, 2003.

27 Richard Heller, "Galician Beauty," *Forbes*, May 28, 2001, p. 98.

28 William Echikson, "The Mark of Zara," *Business Week*, May 29, 2000, pp. 98, 100.

29 Alan M. Rugman, *The End of Globalization* (London: Random House, 2000), pp. 59–60.

30 Martin Wolf, "Countries Still Rule the World," *Financial Times*, February 6, 2002, p. 13.

Additional bibliography

Beamish, Paul W. and Banks, John C. "Equity Joint Ventures and the Theory of the Multinational Enterprise," *Journal of International Business Studies*, vol. 18, no. 2 (Summer 1987).

Birkinshaw, Julian and Hood, Neil. "Multinational Subsidiary Evolution: Capability and Charter Change in Foreign-Owned Subsidiary Companies," *Academy of Management Review*, vol. 23, no. 4 (October 1998).

Buckley, Peter J. "The Frontiers of International Business Research," *Management International Review*, vol. 31, Special Issue (1991).

Buckley, Peter J. and Casson, Mark C. "Models of the Multinational Enterprise," *Journal of International Business Studies*, vol. 29, no. 1 (First Quarter 1998).

Chernotsky, Harry I. "The American Connection: Motives for Japanese Foreign Direct Investment," *Columbia Journal of World Business*, vol. 22, no. 4 (Winter 1987).

Cho, Kang Rae. "The Role of Product-Specific Factors in Intra-Firm Trade of US Manufacturing Multinational Corporations," *Journal of International Business Studies*, vol. 21, no. 2 (Second Quarter 1990).

Devinney, Timothy M. "Multinationals as Flagship Firms," *Academy of Management Review*, vol. 26, no. 3 (July 2001).

Dunning, John H. *Global Capitalism at Bay?* (London: Routledge, 2001).

Dunning, John H. "The Eclectic Paradigm of International Production: A Restatement and Some Possible Extensions," *Journal of International Business Studies*, vol. 19, no. 1 (Spring 1988).

Hennart, Jean-François. "Can the New Forms of Investment Substitute for the Old Forms?: A Transaction Cost Perspective," *Journal of International Business Studies*, vol. 20, no. 2 (Summer 1989).

Kim, W. Chan and Hwang, Peter. "Global Strategy and Multinationals' Entry Mode Choice," *Journal of International Business Studies*, vol. 23, no. 1 (First Quarter 1992).

Kim, Wi Saeng and Lyn, Esmeralda O. "Foreign Direct Investment Theories, Entry Barriers, and Reverse Investments in US Manufacturing Industries," *Journal of International Business Studies*, vol. 18, no. 2 (Summer 1987).

Kimura, Yui. "Firm-Specific Strategic Advantage and Foreign Direct Investment Behaviour of Firms: The Case of Japanese Semiconductor Firms," *Journal of International Business Studies*, vol. 20, no. 2 (Summer 1989).

Madura, Jeff and Whyte, Ann Marie. "Diversification Benefits of Direct Foreign Investment," *Management International Review*, vol. 30, no. 1 (First Quarter 1990).

Moore, Karl and Lewis, David. "The First Multinationals," *Management International Review*, vol. 38, no. 2 (Second Quarter 1998).

Porter, Michael E. *Competitive Strategy: Techniques for Analyzing Industries and Competitors* (New York & London: Free Press, 1980).

Porter, Michael E. *The Competitive Advantage of Nations* (New York: Free Press, Macmillan, 1990).

Rugman, Alan M. *Inside the Multinationals: The Economics of Internal Markets* (New York: Columbia University Press, 1981).

Rugman, Alan M. "The Multinational Enterprise," in Ingo Walter (ed.), *Handbook of International Management* (New York: Wiley, 1988), pp. 1–18.

Rugman, Alan M. *The Theory of Multinational Enterprises* (Cheltenham: Elgar, 1996).

Rugman, Alan M. *The Regional Multinationals* (Cambridge: Cambridge University Press, 2005).

Rugman, Alan M. and Verbeke, Alain. "A Note on the Transnational Solution and the Transaction Cost Theory of Multinational Strategic Management," *Journal of International Business Studies*, vol. 23, no. 4 (Fourth Quarter 1992).

Sabi, Manijeh. "An Application of the Theory of Foreign Direct Investment to Multinational Banking in LDCs," *Journal of International Business Studies*, vol. 19, no. 3 (Fall 1988).

Yoshida, Mamoru. "Macro-Micro Analyses of Japanese Manufacturing Investments in the United States," *Management International Review*, vol. 27, no. 4 (Fourth Quarter 1987).

APPENDIX TO CHAPTER 2

Table 2A The 25 largest US MNEs, 2003

Rank	Company	Revenues (in million of US $)	% intra-regional sales
1	Wal-Mart	263,009.0	94.5
2	Exxon Mobil	222,833.0	37.5
3	General Motors	195,324.0	78.7
4	Ford	164,505.0	67.7
5	General Electric	134,187.0	59.8
6	ChevronTexaco	112,937.0	43.5
7	ConocoPhillips	99,468.0	74.4
8	Citigroup	94,713.0	70.0
9	IBM	89,131.0	42.7
10	American International Group	81,303.0	59.0
11	HP	73,061.0	41.6
12	McKesson	69,506.1	93.4
13	US Postal Service	68,529.0	97.0
14	Verizon Communications	67,752.0	96.2
15	Home Depot	64,816.0	100.0
16	Berkshire Hathaway	63,859.0	na
17	Altria Group	60,704.0	44.9
18	Cardinal Health	56,829.5	97.9
19	State Farm Insurance	56,064.6	100.0
20	Kroger	53,790.8	100.0
21	Fannie Mae	53,766.9	100.0
22	Boeing	50,458.0	66.7
23	AmerisourceBergen	49,657.3	100.0
24	Target	48,163.0	100.0
25	Bank of America Corporation	48,065.0	93.5

Note: Intra-regional sales were collected over the 2002–2004 period and represent data for the 2001–2003 years.

Sources: Author's calculations based on the individual annual reports of each company and Fortune, *The Fortune Global 500*, July 26, 2004.

Table 2B The 25 largest European MNEs, 2003

Rank	Company	Country	Revenues (in million of US $)	% intra-regional sales
1	BP	Britain	232,571.0	36.3
2	Royal Dutch/Shell	Britain/Netherlands	201,728.0	46.1
3	DaimlerChrysler	Germany	156,602.2	31.1
4	Total	France	118,441.4	54.8
5	Allianz	Germany	114,949.9	75.0
6	Axa	France	111,912.2	51.2
7	VW	Germany	98,636.6	71.0
8	ING	Netherlands	95,893.3	35.1
9	Siemens	Germany	80,501.0	57.0
10	Carrefour	France	79,773.8	87.0
11	Assicurazioni Generali	Italy	66,754.9	94.2
12	Nestlé	Switzerland	65,414.6	40.8
13	Royal Ahold	Netherlands	63,455.8	23.8
14	Deutsche Telekom	Germany	63,195.5	93.1
15	Peugeot	France	61,384.6	88.7
16	Metro	Germany	60,656.9	97.3
17	Aviva	Britain	59,719.4	na
18	ENI	Italy	59,304.4	80.4
19	Munich Re Group	Germany	59,082.6	72.3
20	Credit Suisse	Switzerland	58,957.1	64.5
21	HSBC Holdings	Britain	57,608.0	na
22	BNP Paribas	France	57,271.8	na
23	Vodafone	Britain	56,844.5	93.1
24	Fortis	Belgium/Netherlands	56,695.2	64.3
25	Fiat	Italy	53,499.6	74.0

Note: Intra-regional sales were collected over the 2002–2004 period and represent data for the 2001–2003 years.

Sources: Author's calculations based on the individual annual reports of each company and Fortune, *The Fortune Global 500*, July 26, 2004.

Table 2C The 25 largest Japanese MNEs, 2003

Rank	Company	Revenues (in million of US $)	% intra-regional sales
1	Toyota	153,111.0	45.2
2	Nippon Telegraph & Telephone	98,229.1	na
3	Hitachi	76,423.3	80.0
4	Honda	72,263.7	25.4
5	Sony	66,365.7	32.8
6	Matsushita Electric Industrial	66,218.4	64.9
7	Nissan Motor	65,771.1	49.7
8	Nippon Life Insurance	63,840.7	na
9	Toshiba	49,395.5	75.3
10	Dai-Ichi Mutual Life Insurance	45,065.6	na
11	Meiji Yasuda Life Insurance	44,064.0	na
12	NEC	43,440.2	82.6
13	Tokyo Electric Power	42,971.0	>90.0
14	Sumitomo Life Insurance	36,913.0	na
15	Sumitomo Mitsui Financial Group	31,450.5	93.0
16	Aeon	31,161.2	na
17	Ito-Yokado	29,332.7	66.6
18	Mitsubishi Electric	29,300.4	83.1
19	Nippon Oil	28,560.6	87.6
20	Mizuho Financial Group	28,335.2	79.2
21	Canon	27,591.7	30.3
22	Mitsui	26,385.0	78.9
23	Nippon Steel	25,902.9	82.2
24	Mazda Motors	25,816.6	65.7
25	KDDI	25,196.6	>90.0

Note: Intra-regional sales were collected over the 2002–2004 period and represent data for the 2001–2004 years.

Sources: Author's calculations based on the individual annual reports of each company and Fortune, *The Fortune Global 500*, July 26, 2004.

Table 2D The 13 largest Canadian MNEs, 2003

Rank	Company	Revenues (in million of US $)	% intra-regional sales
1	George Weston	20,834.4	100.0
2	Royal Bank of Canada	17,203.9	81.0
3	Bombardier	16,996.2	60.7
4	Magna International	15,870.0	67.7
5	Sun Life Financial	15,741.2	83.5
6	BCE	14,119.0	90.5
7	Alcan	13,652.0	41.1
8	Onex	12,352.6	65.0
9	Bank of Nova Scotia	11,960.0	71.2
10	Manulife Financial	11,887.3	71.1
11	Canadian Imperial Bank of Commerce	11,863.7	79.7
12	Power Corp of Canada	11,238.5	100.0
13	Toronto Dominion Bank	10,827.2	>74

Note: Intra-regional sales were collected over the 2002–2004 period and represent data for the 2001–2004 years.

Sources: Author's calculations based on the individual annual reports of each company and Fortune, *The Fortune Global 500*, July 26, 2004.

Table 2E The 25 largest MNEs from developing countries, 2003

Rank	Company	Country	Revenues (in million of US $)	% intra-regional sales
1	PDVSA	Venezuela	46,000.0	na
2	State Grid	China	58,348.0	na
3	Sinopec	China	55,062.0	na
4	China National Petroleum	China	47,046.9	na
5	Pemex	Mexico	49,240.1	91.7
6	Samsung Electronics	South Korea	54,400.2	na
7	Hyundai Motor	South Korea	39,100.8	81.6
8	SK	South Korea	33,768.5	na
9	Petrobras	Brazil	30,797.0	88.0
10	LG Electronics	South Korea	29,873.9	na
11	Gazprom	Russia	27,526.5	na
12	Petronas	Malaysia	25,660.9	na
13	Indian Oil	India	25,316.3	na
14	China Life Insurance	China	20,782.1	na
15	China Mobile Communications	China	20,764.7	na
16	Industrial & Commercial Bank of China	China	20,757.3	na
17	China Telecommunications	China	19,464.5	na
18	Lukoil	Russia	19,345.0	na
19	Samsung Life Insurance	South Korea	19,159.0	na
20	Korea Electric Power	South Korea	19,114.3	na
21	Sinochem	China	18,846.0	na
22	Hanwha	South Korea	16,181.9	na
23	China Construction Bank	China	15,824.8	na
24	Banco Bradesco	Brazil	15,179.5	na
25	Kookmin Bank	South Korea	15,112.4	na

Note: Intra-regional sales were collected over the 2002 period and represent data for 2001.

Sources: Author's calculations based on the individual annual reports of each company and Fortune, *The Fortune Global 500*, July 26, 2004.

Chapter 3

THE TRIAD AND INTERNATIONAL BUSINESS

Contents

Objectives of the chapter

As we noted in Chapter 1, a small number of economies account for a large portion of international investment and international trade. These triad economies—the United States, the EU(15), and Japan—are referred to collectively as the core triad. In this chapter we are going to look more closely at the "broad" triad of North America, Europe, and Asia and examine the role and impact of these regions on international business activity. We will also consider their role in both trade and FDI, and look at examples of how each member of the triad pursues target markets in other triad countries. We will also examine some of the economic and political relationships that exist between triad members and how these can have an impact on the international business community. We will also link to future chapters, such as Chapters 8 and 9, dealing with strategy and structure, respectively. In this context, we develop reasons for the need for MNEs to develop regional/triad strategies rather than "global" strategies.

The specific objectives of this chapter are to:

1 *Describe* the major reasons for FDI.
2 *Explain* the role of triad-based MNEs in worldwide FDI and trade.
3 *Relate* select examples of inter-triad MNEs business activity.
4 *Discuss* the economic interrelationships among triad members.

Boeing versus Airbus

In 1970 a European consortium consisting of Germany, France, and Great Britain (Spain later became a member) created Airbus Industrie. The objective of the consortium was to build commercial aircraft with Germany, Great Britain, and Spain taking on the job of constructing the aircraft and France assuming responsibility for assembling it. The logic of the arrangement was fairly straightforward. Given the growth of international travel, there would be a continual need for new commercial aircraft, and Airbus wanted to be a major player in this industry.

Until this time, when major air carriers such as American Airlines, Japan Airlines, and Lufthansa needed to replace aging airplanes or increase the size of their fleet, they turned to Boeing or McDonnell Douglas, the two giant American aircraft manufacturers. Cargo carriers such as FedEx and DHL also bought planes from them, and, as international air shipments continued to grow rapidly, the annual demand proved to be a boon for Boeing and McDonnell.

The initial challenge for Airbus was to capture some market share and thus establish a toehold in the industry. This, fortunately, was not a problem. The consortium had divided up the responsibility for building the aircraft among its members. In this way, each country was guaranteed some of the work and, in turn, could count on its respective government to provide financial assistance and contracts. In particular, the consortium would have to spend large amounts of money for research and development in order to build competitive, state-of-the-art craft, but by getting support from their respective governments a great deal of the initial risk would be eliminated. This, by the way, was the same approach that had been used in the United States and helped account for much of Boeing and McDonnell's success in building large aircraft. For example, much of the funding to build the giant C-5A cargo plane was provided by the US military. Then, by using this same technology, it was possible for Boeing to build its giant passenger aircraft.

Realizing that the consortium would eventually be able to build competitive craft, Boeing and McDonnell lodged complaints with the US government claiming that Airbus was being subsidized by their governments, and Washington needed to take steps to protect the US commercial aircraft manufacturing industry. As the governments on both sides met to talk and discuss these issues, Airbus started building planes. It took quite a while, but by 1990 the consortium was not only becoming well established but had back orders

for 1,100 planes and by 1997 this number had reached 2,300. In the process Airbus captured over 30 per cent of the world market. One of the major reasons for its success was that it focused on building fuel-efficient craft at competitive prices. Its wide-body, medium-range models, the A300 and A310, for example, were very reliable and the orders started flowing in from a wide number of buyers including large US carriers such as America Airlines and Northwest. During the 1990s the battle in the aircraft market also saw Boeing and McDonnell Douglas merge their operations. McDonnell could not compete effectively in this new, highly-competitive market, but when merged with Boeing it could provide the latter with a good chance to prevent Airbus from steamrolling the American aircraft manufacturing industry.

By 2001 Airbus was doing better than ever. Not only had it managed to catch up with Boeing and hold 50 per cent of the overall market, but it was in the throes of making major decisions that could result in its becoming the dominant player in the industry. The company had decided to build a giant, double-decker superjumbo jet. To be known as the A380, this plane will be capable of carrying 555 passengers, and the first craft are expected to be delivered in 2006. A host of buyers signed firm orders with the company, including Qantas, which ordered 12 of the craft, Singapore Airlines, and Air France, which each placed orders for 10. In addition Singapore Air took an option for 15 more. The Singapore deal alone was worth over $8 billion to Airbus, showing how lucrative the market for a superjumbo jet could be. In response, Boeing announced that it was going to build a smaller, faster, longer-range plane that would fly just below the speed of sound. Quite clearly the two competitors were moving in different directions.

Airbus is betting more than $12 billion that airlines will want a superjumbo jet that can carry a large number of passengers on long trips to a given region. Boeing is betting that there is a much larger demand for smaller, faster planes that can take people directly to their destination. In doing so, Boeing has ceded to Airbus a highly profitable jumbo market, wagering that the European group will not earn back its huge investment but rather end up stumbling badly. Boeing's decision to abandon the development of a larger plane (similar to what Airbus is proposing) relied heavily on follow-on studies of the giant 747. The company's engineers concluded that, except in the case of a huge

800-passenger plane, a double-deck design had to be scaled back to a single decker to satisfy technical and safety standards. One reason, according to Boeing engineers, is because a double-deck arrangement is very inefficient. Another is that, in case of evacuation, a two-level airplane can present major problems for those on board.

At this same time Airbus announced that its consortium arrangement was coming to an end and that the company would now be managed as a corporation. Today the Franco–German European Aeronautic Defense and Space Company holds 80 per cent of Airbus, and BAE Systems of Great Britain owns the remaining 20 per cent. This move effectively ended Airbus's life as an organization that operated in the world of business and politics and one in which each partner held a veto, politically motivated committees made many of the important decisions, and when things did not go well state funds could be counted on to prop up the consortium. Now with all of that behind them Airbus is working to streamline its operations and, according to the business partners, shave off about $400 million in annual expenses.

Will Airbus continue to dominate the airways? Its initial challenge is to build the A380 superjumbo. If it can do this and the demand for the huge craft does materialize, Boeing may find itself as a minor player in the industry. On the other hand, while in late 2001 Airbus was recruiting thousands of new workers to help with the project, it was having trouble finding partners to help fund the venture. A number of

European suppliers signed up but US and Japanese companies did not. For example, Airbus had offered Japanese manufacturers up to 8 per cent of the work on the A380 in return for funding but had no takers. The company also wanted to get US firms to invest and thus defuse a potential political problem that could result in the American government making it difficult for Airbus to do business in the United States. When Airbus first got started, it relied heavily on governmental support. Now that it is very successful, it no longer needs this type of help. However, the American government is unlikely to sit by and let this company dominate the industry while Boeing is forced to take a back seat. In a way, the situation is similar to that in 1970 when Airbus first got started—the main difference is that the two companies now seem to be in opposite positions.

Websites: **www.boeing.com** and **www.airbus.com**.

Sources: Adapted from Steven Greenhouse, "There's No Stopping Europe's Airbus Now," *New York Times*, June 23, 1991, Section 3, pp. 1, 6; Charles Goldsmith, "Airbus Partner Countries Are Seeking Strict Enforcement of 1992 Subsidy Pact," *Wall Street Journal*, June 17, 1997, p. B 9A; Charles Goldsmith, "After Trailing Boeing for Years, Airbus Aims for 50% of the Market," *Wall Street Journal*, March 16, 1998, pp. A 1, 8; Stuart F. Brown, "How to Build a Really, Really, Really Big Plane," *Fortune*, March 5, 2001, p. 152; Anne Marie Squeo, "Boeing Plans to Build Smaller, Faster Jet," *Wall Street Journal*, March 30, 2001, p. A 3; Daniel Michaels, "Airbus Signs Up Partners to Help Build Jumbo Jet," *Wall Street Journal*, June 21, 2001, p. A 14; Mark Odell and Victor Mallet, "Airbus Cuts Back 2003 Production Targets," *Financial Times*, August 8, 2001, p. 15; and Daniel Michaels, Zach Coleman, and Guy Chazan, "Airbus Is in Talks with Beijing on Sale of Jets," *Wall Street Journal*, August 21, 2001, p. A 12.

1. What are three reasons for the Europeans creating the Airbus consortium?

2. How will Airbus help the EU compete in the United States?

3. How will Airbus help the EU compete in Japan?

4. In what way did the Airbus consortium use a *keiretsu* approach to building the aircraft? Why do you think it opted for this approach?

INTRODUCTION

Over the last decade international business activity has increased dramatically, especially among the **triad** nations. As has already been noted in Chapter 1, foreign direct investment and trade are at an all-time high. At the same time, however, the most active economies in the international arena have remained the same: the United States, Japan, and the members of the EU(15), specially Germany, France, the UK, and Italy. During the current decade, a growing number of other countries will become increasingly prominent on the international business stage. China is moving quickly to establish itself as a major player. Others whom we will be hearing from increasingly will include Australia, Brazil, Canada, India, Mexico, the Netherlands, the Russian Federation, Singapore, South Korea, and China to

Triad
The three major trading and investment blocs in the international arena: the United States, the EU, and Japan

Table 3.1 Intra-regional FDI in the triad, 1986–2000

Year	Intra-regional outward FDI (%)		
	EU(15)	NAFTA	ASIA
2000	42.5	18.4	18.0
1999	45.7	18.2	26.2
1997	49.3	21.1	28.4
1986	35.8	30.3	20.5

Note: For an explanation of the methodology used in calculating these data on intra-regional trade and FDI stocks, see Alan M. Rugman, *The End of Globalization* (New York: Amacom, 2000), Chapter 7.

Source: OECD, *International Direct Investment Statistics Yearbook*, 2001.

name but 10. Yet despite the increase of international activity by these countries and others in emerging economies, MNEs from the triad will continue to account for most of the world's foreign direct investment and trade. For this reason, every student of international business should be familiar with the triad and be aware of its impact on world commerce.

In Chapter 1 we pointed out that two of the drivers of globalization are foreign direct investment and trade. In this chapter we want to look more closely at these drivers and the role that the triad plays in both. We begin by examining some of the main reasons for foreign direct investment in a triad context.

Much FDI is intra-regional (see Table 3.1). It has also been growing faster within the EU(15) region of the triad, rather than globally. It has, however, declined in North America as NAFTA has substituted freer trade for FDI. In Asia, there has been a recent decrease in intra-regional FDI. Japan, the largest source of FDI in the region, has only 19.1 per cent of its FDI in other Asian countries. The vast majority of Japanese FDI is in the United States and Western Europe.[1] (Table 3.1 on FDI is similar to Table 1.2 on trade.)

REASONS FOR FOREIGN DIRECT INVESTMENT

Foreign direct investment (FDI)
Equity funds invested in other nations

Foreign direct investment (FDI) is the ownership and control of foreign assets. In practice, FDI usually involves the ownership, whole or partial, of a company in a foreign country. This is called a foreign subsidiary. This equity investment can take a variety of forms. One is through the purchase of an ongoing company. For example, Solectron, the world's largest contract electronics firm, bought C-Mac Industries of Canada in order to acquire C-Mac's expertise in assembling high-end telecommunications and networking systems.[2] Rather than building this business from scratch, Solectron bought its way into the industry through FDI. Another common example of FDI is to set up a new overseas operation as either a joint venture or a totally-owned enterprise. For example, Matsushita has positioned itself to become a major competitor in the European digital industry. It has entered into a joint venture with British Telecommunications plc for the purpose of developing multimedia wireless services and products.[3] It is important to remember that FDI is different from **portfolio investment**, which entails the purchase of financial securities (especially bonds) in other firms for the purpose of realizing a financial gain when these marketable assets are sold. The objective of FDI is to provide the investing company with the opportunity to actively manage and control a foreign firm's activities, whereas the objective of portfolio investment is to achieve growth in the value of its financial holdings.[4]

Portfolio investment
The purchase of financial securities in other firms for the purpose of realizing a financial gain when these marketable assets are sold

Businesses are interested in taking an ownership position or gaining control of foreign assets for a number of reasons. In Chapter 2 we briefly discussed six of these reasons. The following section elaborates on these reasons. An Appendix in this chapter also discusses

Dunning's eclectic theory of FDI. This is an alternative to the CSA-FSA framework developed in Chapter 2 to explain FDI. Throughout the book the CSA-FSA framework is preferred and many cases ask students to identify the FSAs and CSAs of the MNEs.

Increase sales and profits

Some of the largest and best-known multinationals earn millions of dollars each year through overseas sales. Table 3.2 shows the triad firms with the largest foreign assets in 2001. In the EU, for example, companies in smaller economies need to look outside of their home borders. This helps to explain why 65.9 per cent of Royal Dutch/Shell's assets and 78.8 of BP's assets are in foreign markets, including the markets of other EU members. In addition, although Switzerland is not in the EU, nearly 60 per cent of Nestlé's assets are outside Switzerland.

The same is true of revenues. Over 50 per cent of Royal Dutch/Shell's sales originate outside its home markets (the Netherlands and the UK) and over 80 per cent of BP's sales are from outside the UK.[5] Similarly, in North America, where Canada's economy is only 10 per cent the size of the United States, companies like Thomson Corporation, have 96 per cent of its assets in foreign markets, most notably the United States.[6]

In regional terms, among firms with large foreign assets some continue to derive a considerable amount of revenues in their home region. For example, Vodafone and Vivendi derive 93.1 and 68.0 per cent of total revenues, respectively, in the European Union even

Table 3.2 The largest triad-based MNEs, 2001

Ranking foreign assets	MNE		Foreign assets (in billions of US $)	Total assets (in billions of US $)	Foreign assets as a % of total assets	Intra-regional sales as a % of total sales
1	Vodafone	EU	187.8	207.5	90.5	93.1
2	General Electric	US	180.0	495.2	36.4	59.1
3	BP	EU	111.2	141.2	78.8	36.3
4	Vivendi Universal	EU	91.1	123.2	74.0	68.0
5	Deutsche Telekom	EU	90.7	145.8	62.2	93.1
6	Exxon Mobil	US	89.4	143.2	62.5	37.5
7	Ford	US	81.2	276.5	29.4	66.7
8	General Motors	US	75.4	324.0	23.3	81.1
9	Royal Dutch/Shell	EU	73.5	111.5	65.9	46.1
10	TotalFinaElf	EU	70.0	78.5	89.2	55.6
11	Suez	EU	69.3	79.3	87.5	74.0
12	Toyota	Japan	68.4	144.8	47.2	49.2
13	Fiat	EU	48.7	89.3	54.6	73.3
14	Telefonica	EU	48.1	77.0	62.5	56.9
15	Volkswagen	EU	47.5	92.5	51.3	68.2
16	ChevronTexaco	US	44.9	77.6	57.9	43.5
17	Hutchison Whampoa	Hong Kong, China	41.0	55.3	74.1	NA
18	News Corporation	Australia	35.7	40.0	89.1	9.0
19	Honda Motor	Japan	35.3	52.1	67.7	26.9
20	E.ON	EU	34.0	87.8	38.7	80.1
21	Nestlé	Switzerland	33.1	55.8	59.2	31.6
22	RWE	EU	32.8	81.0	40.5	75.0
23	IBM	US	32.8	88.3	37.1	43.5
24	ABB	Switzerland	30.6	32.3	94.7	53.9
25	Unilever	EU	30.5	46.9	65.1	38.7

Note: EU foreign assets data include the assets of MNEs in other member countries.

Sources: Adapted from "The World's Top 100 Non-financial TNCs of the United Nations," *World Investment Report 2000* (New York: United Nations Conference on Trade and Development, 2003) and Alan M. Rugman, *The Regional Multinationals*, (Cambridge: Cambridge UP, 2005).

though over 70 per cent of their assets are abroad. Only 10 of the 25 firms with the highest assets abroad, as listed in Table 3.2, have over 50 per cent of their sales in a region other than their own.

There are also thousands of smaller firms worldwide that earn the bulk of their revenue from international customers. For an example, see the box **International Business Strategy in Action: Aflac**. SMEs also find that with the growth of large multinationals there is often a need for local suppliers; and, if they do well, there is a good chance that the MNE will extend the contract and allow them to supply other worldwide locations. So they, too, are interested in FDI because it can help them increase their sales and profits.

Foreign markets often offer more lucrative opportunities than do domestic markets. This helps to explain why Coca-Cola and IBM now earn more sales revenue and profits overseas than they do in the United States and why PepsiCo has become Mexico's largest consumer products company. In Japan, it helps to explain why 74.6 per cent of Honda's and over 70 per cent of Sony's revenues come from overseas sales.[7] It also helps account for the decision by Tesco plc, the British supermarket firm, to expand operations into Eastern Europe and Asia. And the same is true for Wal-Mart, which in recent years has expanded rapidly and now has stores on four continents and appears on the verge of becoming a major competitor in the EU thanks to its FDI in both the UK and Germany.[8] However, for most firms, including some listed above, "foreign" means in its own region; for example, Wal-Mart has 94.5 per cent in North America; Tesco has 93.6 per cent in Europe.

Enter rapidly growing markets

Some international markets are growing much faster than others, and FDI provides MNEs with the chance to take advantage of these opportunities. A good example is China. Over the past few years the Chinese economy has grown at an annual rate of around 7–9 per cent.[9] These data also suggest that, as the country continues to move toward a market-driven economy, MNEs are likely to find a huge demand for goods and services that cannot be satisfied by local firms alone. Simply put, China is a market where most multinationals want to have a presence despite the fact that there are many problems in doing business there, and few MNEs have been able to extract an adequate return on their investment.

China is not the only emerging market being targeted by multinationals. A growing number of companies are using FDI to gain a foothold in Eastern Europe by acquiring local firms or setting up joint ventures there. India has also become a large recipient of FDI, particularly in the technology sector (see Real Case in Chapter 12).

Reduce costs

An MNE can sometimes achieve substantially lower costs by going abroad than by producing at home (see the box **International Business Strategy in Action: Lafarge and Cemex: concrete multinationals**). If labor expenses are high and represent a significant portion of overall costs, an MNE may be well advised to look to other geographic areas where the goods can be produced at a much lower labor price. Surprisingly perhaps, in recent years some Canadian manufacturers have been moving operations across the border to take advantage of lower US labor unit costs.

A second important cost factor is materials. If materials are in short supply or must be conveyed a long distance, it may be less expensive to move production close to the source of supply than to import the materials.

A third critical cost factor is energy. If the domestic cost of energy for making the product is high, the company may be forced to set up operations overseas near sources of cheaper energy.

INTERNATIONAL BUSINESS STRATEGY *IN ACTION*

Aflac

The insurance industry is dominated by many well-known names: Prudential, Aetna, Northwestern, etc. Prior to 2000, few people in North America had ever heard of Aflac Inc. of Columbus, Georgia. However, the company has been the most successful insurer in Japan, with annual revenues of $9.7 billion and profits well over $650 million in 2000. Aflac is the world's leading seller of cancer insurance, which helps to pay the cost of treating the disease, and it holds 90 per cent of the Japanese market for this coverage. The Japanese subsidiary accounts for over 75 per cent of Aflac's pretax earnings and insures one out of every four Japanese.

The firm began doing business in Japan in 1974. Initially Aflac approached big Japanese insurers as potential joint-venture partners; none of them was interested. Eventually the Ministry of Finance gave the company a license to sell insurance, primarily because no Japanese insurer was in the business so that there would be no competition for local firms.

A key to Aflac's rapid growth and profitability is its system of selling through corporate agencies. The firm has set up in-house subsidiaries in Japanese corporations to handle the sale of its insurance. These subsidiaries would be illegal distributors in the United States, but they are very common in Japan. As a result, Aflac eventually ended up with over 40,000 Japanese companies offering its policies to their employees. From Hitachi to Sony, Toyota to Nissan, and Mitsui to Mitsubishi, policyholders throughout the country pay premiums of approximately $21 a month through an automatic payroll deduction plan. Moreover, once they are signed up, few Japanese drop out. In contrast to the United States, where only 25 per cent of health and accident insurance policyholders remain with the same company for a decade or more, in Japan 75 per cent of Aflac policyholders have been with them for 10 or more years.

Will Aflac be able to continue its success in the market? In many countries such as the United States, cancer insurance is declining in popularity because coverage is now provided by basic policies. In Japan, however, the first stage of cancer

treatment can cost up to $50,000. Even though the Japanese government is expected to introduce national care insurance, it has made clear that it will not be able to cover the full cost. Furthermore, about four years ago the company began to diversify its product line. Today over 30 per cent of all sales in Japan are for non-cancer-related insurance. As a result of the costs associated with cancer, Aflac's supplemental coverage remains very popular. The additional success of its new products makes Aflac find the Japanese market to be profitable.

Perhaps the biggest challenge to Aflac's Japanese market share is market deregulation. Aflac has functioned practically as a monopoly in Japan over the last 30 years. In 2001, the Japanese government allowed Nippon Life Insurance and Tokio Marine & Fire to compete in the supplementary insurance market. Aflac need not worry in the short term, since these companies' operating costs are four times its own. In the long run, however, other companies might want to wrestle this profitable market away from Aflac. The company is well aware of this and is expanding its reach by partnering with Dai-Ichi Mutual, Japan's second largest insurance company, to distribute each other's policies. In addition, a joint venture with Communicationware Corporation has seen the development of aflacdirect.com, the first company to provide insurance solely on the Internet.

Aflac has also turned to its domestic market by launching an aggressive marketing campaign featuring a mascot. The Aflac duck, as it has become known, has appeared in a series of television ads screaming Aaaaflaack to oblivious characters. This has had its desired effect, and today 95 per cent of Americans recognize the name Aflac.

Websites: www.aflac.com and www.aflac.co.jp.

Sources: Adapted from Steve Lohr, "Under the Wing of Japan, Inc., a Fledgling Enterprise Soared," *New York Times*, January 15, 1992, pp. A 1, C 5; *Forbes*, January 4, 1993, p. 167; *Fortune*, May 31, 1993, p. 218; www.reportgallery.com/aflac/japan.htm; www.oecd.org/publications/figures/money.html; and Bethany McLean, "Duck and Coverage," *Fortune*, August 13, 2001.

A fourth important factor is transportation costs. A highly price-competitive product in one country might have to retail at uncompetitive prices in another country once transportation costs are added. The box feature on Lafarge and Cemex illustrates this situation.

In recent years many firms have used all four of these reasons to justify moving assembly operations to other countries. For example, low-skill labor costs are much lower in Mexico than in the United States, Korea, Hong Kong, Taiwan, or Singapore, so Mexico has become a prime target for the manufacture of labor-intensive products. In fact, some

INTERNATIONAL BUSINESS STRATEGY *IN ACTION*

Lafarge and Cemex: concrete multinationals

Cement is extremely heavy and very costly to ship long distances. Producers must place cement plants near limestone deposits and/or a short distance from large urban areas so that materials can be shipped to their final destination. If the cement has to be shipped a long distance due to a lack of adequate resources, this is done by boat. For example, Canadian firms export cement to the United States by shipping it across the Great Lakes.

Originally, the need to be near natural resources as well as a given market created an industry of small localized cement companies. As sophisticated logistic systems allowed economies of scale to be achieved in this industry, firms began to merge with nearby rivals, eventually acquiring firms in foreign markets.

The largest of these is Lafarge, a French MNE that accounts for 10 per cent of the world's cement capacity and has operations in 75 countries. The firm is the leader in the European market and depends on it for over 50 per cent of its revenues. In North America, the firm is the third largest cement producer. Yet, it is Asia where the company is now putting its focus. All but a few countries in this region still have significant building to do for their infrastructure to meet the needs of their populations and to catch up to industrialized countries.

Lafarge is already the market leader in both the Philippines and Malaysia, but it is in China where it sees the greatest opportunity. In China, where thousands of cement manufacturers with varying degrees of efficiency and technology are scattered throughout the country, Lafarge hopes to bring its state-of-the-art technology and experience to make China one of the firm's major markets. China is presently the largest producer of cement, accounting for one-third of the world's production, and demand is expected to increase further as the country continues to modernize.

Cemex SA is Mexico's largest cement maker. It is also the third largest cement maker in the world, and in recent years the company has been much more profitable than its two larger competitors thanks to a series of well-executed strategies. These include an international expansion strategy that is very similar to Lafarge's: to look for markets with long-term economic growth potential, large and growing populations, and high pent-up demand from below average construction. Cemex's efforts have paid off. Since 1985, when Lorenzo Zambrano took over as chief executive of his family business, the firm has become Mexico's top multinational with operations in 30 countries across five continents. In 2002, Cemex was the first firm from a developing country to enter the list

Source: Corbis/Raymond Gehman

of the world's top 100 transnational firms, according to the U.N. *World Investment Report*. And, in Latin America, Cemex had the best-known construction brand in 2003.

The firm's international excursions began in 1992 with the acquisition of two Spanish cement companies. Soon after, Cemex acquired and fixed up smaller cement companies in Latin America and the Caribbean. Most recently it purchased Saraburi Cement of Thailand, a move designed to give it a base of operations in Asia. When Cemex initially embarked on this strategy, many bankers were concerned that the company would still be making most of its money in Mexico, and a devaluation of the peso would severely impact its international operations. In late 1994, when the Mexican government suddenly devalued its currency, Cemex was generating only 25 per cent of its earnings from overseas operations, and the firm was highly leveraged in dollars. However, instead of pulling back, Cemex convinced the bankers that the best strategy was to press forward and buy cement companies in Colombia and Venezuela. The decision was fortuitous. Venezuela soon devalued its own currency, but as its economy went into a tailspin Cemex sent in some of its own executives to straighten out the operation, reorganize the administrative and information system, and cut the workforce. By the end of the year Cemex had doubled the unit's annual cash flow to $200 million.

One distinct difference in Lafarge's and Cemex's strategies in developing countries is that Cemex is not entering the Chinese market, at least not yet. Although China has the characteristics that Cemex is looking for, in demographics, potential growth, and a lack of infrastructure, the country is riddled with price controls and a taxing system designed to drain profits. Whether losses in the present are warranted for future growth in China might not be relevant. Cemex is riddled with debt from all its acquisitions and might not be able to afford low levels of profits in China.

Cemex's expansion is not limited to developing markets. After its acquisition of Southdown for $2.6 billion in 2000, it became the largest cement producer in the United States. The move made sense after the United States imposed punitive antidumping tariffs on Mexican cement in 1990. Between August 2000 and July 2001, Cemex paid $29.5 million in duties which, in turn, were dispersed among US producers that claimed to be affected by the dumping.

Meanwhile in Mexico, where the firm still generates 34 per cent of its revenue, a stronger economy has resulted in higher sales and profits. As a result, Cemex is now paying down its debt and expanding operations in Europe and Asia where it is both buying and building plants; and the company estimates that by the end of the first decade of this century annual sales will be in excess of $10 billion and profits will be higher than ever.

Lafarge's and Cemex's biggest assets are their financial strength, in terms of cash flow, technology, and expertise. They compete in an industry with a sea of small, often inefficient, players. At present, these firms are snatching market share from these smaller competitors across the developing world and competing with each other in the developed world.

Websites: www.lafargecorp.com; www.cement.bluecircle.co.uk; www.holnam.com; and www.cemex.com.

Sources: Adapted from http://www.lafargecorp.com/lafarge2.nsf; www.cemnet.co.uk/news.htm; http://www.cementindia.net/; "Bagged Cement," *The Economist*, July 17, 1999; "The Cemex Way," *The Economist*, June 14, 2000; "Mexico's Cemex Wins Bet on Acquisitions," *Wall Street Journal*, April 30, 1998, p. A 14; Cemex, *Annual Report*, 2003; Lafarge, *Annual Report*, 2003; United Nations, *World Investment Report*, 2002; "Google Voted Best Brand of 2003," BBC.co.uk, February 3, 2004; and John Moody, "Mexican Cement Maker with a Worldview," *New York Times*, April 15, 2004.

US firms have even set up **twin factories**, or **maquiladoras**, which involve production operations on both sides of the border and the shipment of goods between the two countries. As a result, today US components are shipped into Mexico duty free, assembled by Mexican workers, and then re-exported to the United States or other foreign markets under favorable tariff provisions. We further discuss the maquiladora industry in Chapter 18.

Twin factories
(Also see *Maquiladoras*) Production operations set up on both sides of the US–Mexican border for the purpose of shipping goods between the two countries

Maquiladoras
(Also see *Twin factories*) Production operations set up on both sides of the US–Mexican border in a free trade zone for the purpose of shipping goods between the two countries

Gain a foothold in economic blocs

As we have noted on a number of occasions thus far, there are three major international economic blocs. MNEs that acquire a company in one of these blocs or that enter into an alliance to do business in one of these economic strongholds can obtain a number of benefits including the right to sell their output without having to be burdened by import duties or other restrictions. In the case of NAFTA, for example, the United States–Canada Free Trade Agreement of 1989 was the initial step in fashioning a giant North American market. In January 1994 this agreement was expanded to include Mexico, and in 2005 the Free Trade Agreement of the Americas (FTAA). International MNEs wanting to do business in North America are finding that it is important to gain a foothold in this region through FDI. The same is true in the EU. In 2004, the membership of this bloc has increased from 15 to 25 with the admission of Cyprus, the Czech Republic, Estonia, Hungary, Latvia, Lithuania, Malta, Poland, the Slovak Republic, and Slovenia. Bulgaria and Romania are expected to join in 2007. Turkey has also requested to join the union. Meanwhile in Asia, while Japan continues to be the major economic power, we are likely to see the rise of an "Asian bloc" that includes countries such as Australia, China, India, Indonesia, Malaysia, the Philippines, South Korea, Taiwan, and Thailand. Through the use of intra-regional trade and FDI agreements, these countries are creating a bloc that provides a balance to NAFTA and the EU. During the next two decades, it is highly likely that the super economic powers and those in the next economic tier will cooperate to create these blocs in order to stimulate their respective economies and to provide a competitive stance for firms doing business under their umbrella. This means that in Europe we are likely to see most countries including the Russian Federation (but perhaps not Switzerland) becoming members of the EU, while in the Western hemisphere most countries of North and South America join NAFTA through a more active FTAA. The final result will be three "broad" triad regions, and any company that wants to do business worldwide will have to have a presence in all three blocs. Indeed, a "global" firm is best defined as one with at least 20 per cent of its sales in each region of the triad. In 2001, only 9 of the largest 500 companies in the world fit this description.[10]

Protect domestic markets

Another reason for FDI is to protect one's domestic market. Many MNEs are now entering an international market in order to attack potential competitors and thus prevent them from expanding their operations overseas. These multinationals reason that a competitor is less likely to enter a foreign market when it is busy defending its home-market position. Similarly, sometimes an MNE will enter a foreign market in order to bring pressure on a company that has already challenged its own home market. For example, 10 days after Fuji began building its first manufacturing facility in the United States, Kodak announced its decision to open a manufacturing plant in Japan.

Sometimes the decision to go international also helps a firm to protect its position with current clients who are going international. For example, when Honda Motors set up operations in Indiana in 1989 through an Isuzu-Subaru plant in Lafayette, Nippondenso, a producer of automobile radiators and heaters, established a plant nearby. So did Mitsubishi Bank, the primary bank for Honda. In addition to the extra business it generates, this strategy helps to combat local competitors, such as Indiana manufacturers and banks, who might otherwise gain inroads and perhaps even threaten domestic business should they decide to set up operations in Japan.

Protect foreign markets

Sometimes MNEs will use FDI in order to protect their foreign markets. In the United States, for example, from 1981 to 1991 the total number of service stations had declined by over 50 per cent. British Petroleum (BP), which had a substantial presence in this market, realized that in order to protect its investment it would be necessary to make a substantial investment in order to upgrade its stations and increase its market share. The company refines and markets petroleum products and realized that if it could attract a growing number of customers to its service stations, it could profit handsomely by moving its products directly downstream to the final consumer. The company also merged with Amoco, thus assuring itself of a solid market share and, in the process, protecting its investment in this foreign market. Had it not done this, local competitors would inevitably have eroded the firm's position.

Acquire technological and managerial know-how

Still another reason for FDI is to acquire technological and managerial expertise. One way of doing this is to set up operations near those of leading competitors. This is why some US firms have moved some of their research and development facilities to Japan. With this strategy, they find it is easier to monitor the competition and to recruit scientists from local universities and competitive laboratories. Kodak is an excellent example.

The company made the decision to build an 180,000 square-foot research center in Japan, and it started cultivating leading scientists to help with recruiting. Kodak used all the same approaches that Japanese firms employ in the United States: financing research by university scientists and offering scholarships to outstanding young Japanese engineers, some of whom would later join Kodak. In addition, the company hired internationally-known scientists to help attract experienced colleagues from leading Japanese companies and to recruit young graduates from the host universities such as the Tokyo Institute of Technology. As a result, Japan is now the center of Kodak's worldwide research efforts in a number of high-technology areas.[11]

✔ Active learning check

Review your answer to Active Learning Case question 1 and make any changes you like. Then compare your answer with the one below.

1 What are three reasons for the Europeans creating the Airbus consortium?

One of the reasons for the Europeans creating the Airbus consortium was to enter a rapidly-growing market. As can be seen from the data in the case, billions of dollars will be spent on new aircraft between now and the year 2010. Singapore Airlines alone will be putting out over $8 billion for 25 A380 craft, and it is only one of a number of firms that have placed firm orders with Airbus. So there is a huge market for large craft, and the Europeans wanted to be in this lucrative market. A second reason for creating the consortium was to help build a stronger EU economy. Airbus provided thousands of jobs and billions of dollars to the member countries, and, even with its new arrangement in which it is no longer managed by governments but rather by investors, the company is continuing to provide both jobs and revenues in Europe. A third reason that Airbus was created was to protect the domestic market by making it less reliant on foreign firms such as Boeing. Given that Airbus now holds 50 per cent of the commercial aircraft market, this objective has clearly been attained.

FOREIGN DIRECT INVESTMENT AND TRADE BY TRIAD MEMBERS

As seen thus far, there are many reasons why MNEs make foreign direct investment. In addition, much of this FDI, and trade as well, is made by triad members: the United States, the EU, and Japan. The following examines these findings in more depth.

The triad's domination of FDI and trade

Over the past decade the triad has accounted for an extremely large percentage of both FDI *and* world trade. For example, triad countries make billions of dollars of investments in one another. In 2001 total US FDI was $641 billion in the EU(15) and $64 billion in Japan. In turn the EU(15) countries and Japan had total investments in the United States of $694 billion and $191 billion, respectively. EU(15) FDI in Japan was $24 billion while Japanese FDI in the EU(15) was $88 billion.[12] Quite clearly, triad countries are investing large sums of money in each other's operations.

In addition, as seen in Table 3.3a, the percentage of global FDI accounted for by the core triad countries is 76.7 per cent. Even though the amount of worldwide FDI has more than tripled over the last 10 years, the triad remained the engine of this growth.

Much the same picture holds for trade patterns in the triad as we saw for FDI; there are very strong two-way trade flows. The EU(15) conducts a large amount of annual trade with Japan and the United States, and both Japan and the United States do a great deal of trading with both the EU(15) and with each other. Table 3.3b reports the trade of the triad and shows that these three blocs accounted for 58.7 per cent of all world imports and over 52.8 per cent of all world exports in 2002. As a result of such trade (and FDI), it is clear that the triad is the major economic force in the international arena.

Table 3.3a Ten years of triad FDI

Country/regions	1993 FDI stock (in billion of US $)	% of total	2002 FDI stock (in billion of US $)	% of total
United States	559,688	26.2	1,501,415	21.9
EU(15)*	962,034	45.1	3,434,297	50.0
Japan	259,795	12.2	331,596	4.8
Triad	1,781,517	83.5	5,267,308	76.7
All others	353,102	16.5	1,599,054	23.3
World	2,134,619	100.0	6,866,362	100.0

* EU(15) numbers are outward stocks of FDI by every EU(15) member. Thus, intra-EU FDI is included.

Sources: Adapted from the United Nations, *World Investment Report 2003* (New York: United Nations Conference on Trade and Development, 2003) and United Nations, *World Investment Report 1996* (New York: United Nations Conference on Trade and Development, 1996).

Table 3.3b Ten years of triad trade

Country/regions	Exports 1993 (in billion of US $)	% of total	2002 (in billion of US $)	% of total	Imports 1993 (in billion of US $)	% of total	2002 (in billion of US $)	% of total
United States	494.4	13.1	751.8	11.3	588.2	15.8	1,132.9	17.6
EU(15)*	1,368.9	36.2	2,295.8	34.6	213.7	5.7	2,328.3	36.3
Japan	388.2	10.3	457.3	6.9	1,387.0	37.3	305.7	4.8
Triad	2,251.5	59.6	3,504.9	52.8	2,188.9	58.9	3,766.9	58.7
All others	1,526.0	40.4	3,132.0	47.2	1,529.6	41.1	2,651.7	41.3
World	3,777.5	100.0	6,636.9	100.0	3,718.5	100.0	6,418.6	100.0

* EU(15) numbers are for exports/imports of every member to/from the rest of the world. Thus, EU(15) exports and imports include intra-EU figures.

Sources: Adapted from International Monetary Fund, *Direction of Trade Statistics Yearbook, 1996* (Washington DC: IMF, 1996) and International Monetary Fund, *Direction of Trade Statistics Yearbook, 2003* (Washington DC: IMF, 2003).

Triad FDI clusters

The above data clearly show the importance of the triad in international business, but this impact extends well beyond the FDI and trade that take place among its members. Triad countries have also become major investors in poorer nations. For example, in 2002, US FDI in Latin America and the Caribbean was $16.8 billion.[13] Typically, recipients of FDI are part of an **FDI cluster**, which is a group of developing countries that are usually located in the same geographic region as the triad member and have some form of economic link to it. For example, the United States tends to be a dominant investor in Latin America, and countries such as Mexico, Brazil, and Argentina are part of its FDI cluster. Similarly, Eastern Europe is a favorite investment target for EU(15) countries and helps account for the FDI made by Germany and France in the Czech Republic and the Russian Federation. The latter is part of the EU(15) FDI cluster. And as might be expected, Japan's FDI cluster includes China, Singapore, and Thailand countries where Japanese MNEs have invested large sums of money.

Not all developing countries, however, have been successful in attracting triad investment. One reason is because much of this investment has been used by multinationals to build regional networks, often starting near their home base and then working outward. For example, 69 per cent of all FDI in Mexico comes from US firms and over 80 per cent

FDI cluster
A group of developing countries usually located in the same geographic region as the triad member and having some form of economic link to this member

of all FDI in Estonia derives from EU(15) countries.[14] The UNCTD has also found that more than half of all investment into developing countries is going to three nations: Brazil, China, and Mexico.[15] And much of this money comes from triad countries that are located in that part of the world. So Brazil and Mexico are recipients of much US FDI, and China and Singapore are favorite FDI targets for Japanese firms.

Such investment policies help reinforce our earlier comments about the triad's dominance of regional economic clusters. In the future, triad members may well continue to strengthen their FDI in specific regions, as in Europe, where the EU(15) is a major force in economic development. At the same time, these types of investment strategies by triad members may restrict trade and investment opportunities for some developing countries. This is why it is so important for non-triad countries to be linked to the triad in some way. As will be explained later in the book, by gaining linkage to the triad, a country can benefit by tapping these enormous markets as a supplier to large MNEs or by selling directly to customers in these markets.

MULTINATIONALS IN ACTION: REGIONAL BUSINESS STRATEGY

During the first decades of the new century, the triad will continue to dominate the international business scene. In particular, members will pursue market opportunities within their own triad as well as that of the other members. For example, retailing in the United States is dominated by Wal-Mart. However, the company is not content to simply sell in its home country so it has expanded within NAFTA (Canada and Mexico). It has also expanded into both Europe and Asia, but these two regions account for a mere 5.1 per cent of sales.[16] In Europe, meanwhile, Tesco is expanding rapidly across Europe where it has 94 per cent of its sales, and it is now pushing into Asia. Carrefour, the French retail giant, has more than 9,000 stores throughout Europe, where it has 87 per cent of its sales and approximately 100 more in Asia.[17] This intra-regional pattern of activity is common for triad firms. In fact, one of the best examples is provided by the automobile industry where auto makers are very much region based. For example, General Motors has 78.7 per cent of its sales in North America.[18]

Thus, a more careful analysis of international business shows that "international" expansion does not necessarily mean "global" expansion. For example, Wal-Mart has 94.5 per cent of its sales in North America (see Chapter 1, Real Case: Wal-Mart). This means that the home region of the triad is still its locus for strategy. It does not have a "global" strategy. This even confuses other professors. For example, an entire chapter in a book on global strategy is directed to learning the "lessons from Wal-Mart's globalization."[19] Yet Wal-Mart is not really a global company. Indeed, in the United Nations *World Investment Report 2001* it is reported that Wal-Mart has one of the lowest scores of any of the 100 largest MNEs. On a transnational index Wal-Mart has a "network spread index" (a measure of actual to possible FDI—of which there were a possible 187 in 1999) of under 5 per cent. Other low scores are for Woodbridge, Mitsubishi, Petróleos de Venezuela, Edison, and Nippon Oil. In contrast, many MNEs score over 30 per cent, for example, Shell, Nestlé, Unilever, TotalFina, Aventis, and ABB.

As Figure 3.1 indicates, Wal-Mart is a regional but not a global business. As of 2001, the firm had 94 per cent of its sales in its home region of North America. Europe accounted for only 5 per cent of sales and other regions for a mere 1 per cent. The locus of its business model strategy and structure is regional (see Figure 3.1).

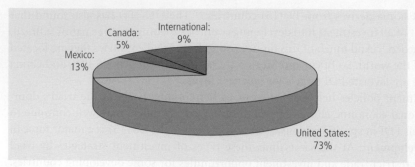

Figure 3.1 Wal-Mart's globalization: regional distribution of stores

Notes: Data are for 2004. US stores include 53 stores in Puerto Rico.

Source: Wal-Mart, *Annual Report*, 2004.

✔ Active learning check

Review your answer to Active Learning Case question 2 and make any changes you like. Then compare your answer with the one below.

2 How will Airbus help the EU compete in the United States?

Airbus will open up markets in the United States by offering alternative aircraft to those being produced by Boeing. These Airbus offerings are not only reliable but fuel efficient and, as noted in the case, are often provided at very competitive prices. As a result, Airbus has been able to tap a US market that had been previously closed to the EU because no European company could compete with Boeing and McDonnell. Now Airbus has been able to land contracts with US firms such as American Airlines, one of the largest carriers in the world. If the A380 proves successful, it will help Airbus compete ever more effectively in the United States.

The world's regional automotive industry

There are 29 automotive firms in the world's largest 500 firms.[20] Yet none of these are "global" firms, defined as having at least 20 per cent of their sales in each of the three regions of the broad "triad" of the EU, North America, and Asia. Indeed 23 of the 29 auto and auto parts firms are home-region based, with an average of 60.6 per cent of their sales as intra-regional (see Table 3.4). This includes Volvo, which is heavily dependent on the European region. There are a few special cases, two auto makers and two parts makers, with over 20 per cent of their sales in two parts of the triad and less than 50 per cent in any region. DaimlerChrysler and Honda derive more than 50 per cent of their revenue from a host region and are labeled "host-region oriented." The weighted average of intra-regional sales in the automotive sector is 60.6 per cent, just below the manufacturing sector's average of 61.8 per cent.

The automotive sector is concentrated in the three triad regions of the United States (North America), Europe, and Japan (Asia). In each of these regions, domestic producers are significantly more competitive than foreign producers. General Motors, Ford, and the Chrysler Group of DaimlerChrysler (a US company prior to the merger with Daimler Benz) each have 28.3 per cent, 21.1 per cent, and 12.9 per cent of the US market for motor vehicles. Together, the largest three domestic auto makers in the United States have 62.3 per cent of the US market. Imports account for approximately 15 per cent of the US market and do not include locally-made Japanese brands.[21]

In general, the European market is more fragmented than the North American market. In 2002, Renault had 11.3 per cent of the European market for passenger cars and light

Table 3.4 The regional nature of the motor vehicles and parts industries

	500 rank	Company	Region	Revenues (billions of US $)	% intra regional	North America % of total sales	Europe % of total sales	Asia-Pacific % of total sales
Bi-regional								
1	10	Toyota Motor	Asia-Pacific	120.8	49.2	36.6	7.7	49.2
2	58	Nissan Motor	Asia-Pacific	49.6	49.7	34.6	11.0	49.7
3	285	Bridgestone	Asia-Pacific	17.6	38.8	43.0[a]	10.1	38.8
4	342	Michelin	Europe	14.6	47.0	40.0	47.0	na
Host-region oriented								
1	7	DaimlerChrysler	Europe	136.9	29.9	60.1	29.9	na
2	41	Honda Motor	Asia-Pacific	58.9	26.9	53.9	8.1	26.9
Home-region oriented								
1	3	General Motors	North America	177.3	81.1	81.1	14.6	na
2	5	Ford Motor	North America	162.4	66.7	66.7[b]	21.9	na
3	21	Volkswagen	Europe	79.3	68.2	20.1	68.2	5.3
4	49	Fiat	Europe	51.9	73.3	13.0	73.3	na
5	112	BMW	Europe	34.4	57.3	31.7[a]	57.3	na
6	125	Renault	Europe	32.6	89.1	na	89.1	na
7	133	Hyundai Motor	Asia-Pacific	30.9	81.6	18.1	0.3	81.6
8	166	Delphi	North America	26.1	77.7	77.7	18.4	na
9	171	Mitsubishi Motors	Asia-Pacific	25.6	62.8	22.1	12.1	62.8
10	252	Denso	Asia-Pacific	19.2	73.1	20.0[a]	6.8	73.1
11	264	Johnson Controls	North America	18.4	62.9	62.9	25.6	na
12	267	Volvo	Europe	18.3	51.6	30.2	51.6	6.0
13	278	Visteon	North America	17.8	71.0	71.0[b]	15.6	na
14	296	Mazda Motor	Asia-Pacific	16.8	65.7	24.4	7.0	65.7
15	306	TRW	North America	16.4	59.3	59.3[b]	na	na
16	343	Man Group	Europe	14.6	68.7	15.6	68.7	12.7
17	352	Goodyear Tire & Rubber[c]	North America	14.1	54.1	54.1[b]	na	na
18	369	Lear	North America	13.6	58.2	58.2	31.6	na
19	381	Suzuki Motor	Asia-Pacific	13.3	68.4	13.3	14.9	68.4
20	404	Isuzu Motors	Asia	12.8	69.2	39.6	na	69.2
21	456	Magna International	North America	11.0	67.7	67.7	31.4	na
22	462	Fuji Heavy Industries	Asia	10.9	66.0	33.7	na	66.0
23	484	Dana	North America	10.5	74.8	74.8	17.4	3.2
Weighted average*				**42.3**	**60.6**			
Total				**1,226.5**				

Notes: Data are for 2001; (a) Americas; (b) US only; (c) based on the location of the selling subsidiary (i.e., exports are not included).
* Weighted intra-regional sales average is weighted according to revenues.

Sources: Author's calculations and the individual annual reports of each company.

commercial vehicles. Volkswagen and Opel (a GM subsidiary) followed with 10 per cent and 9 per cent of this market, respectively. The five largest European brands—Renault, Volkswagen, Peugeot, Fiat, and Citroen—accounted for 43.6 per cent of the European market. Ford, the fourth largest competitor in Europe, had 8.9 per cent of the market. Japanese and South Korean firms accounted for approximately 12.2 per cent and 3.1 per cent, respectively.

The Japanese market is the most consolidated of all triad markets. Toyota alone has 38.3 per cent of the automobile market.[22] Honda, the second largest Japanese auto maker, accounts for 15.6 per cent. Together, Honda, Toyota, Renault-Nissan, and Suzuki-Maruti, the four largest Japanese auto makers, have 78.4 per cent of the Japanese market. Ford, which acquired domestic Mazda, accounts for 5 per cent. General Motors, the US leader and the world's largest car manufacturer, has a mere 0.4 per cent of this market. VW, the European leader, has 1.2 per cent. Imports are a mere 4.5 per cent of the Japanese market and include imports by Japanese companies manufacturing abroad.

Excluding Japan, Toyota is the market leader in two of the six largest countries in Asia-Pacific: Malaysia and Thailand. South Korea is dominated by Hyundai, which controls 72.9 per cent of that market. Suzuki-Maruti is the leader in India, with 36.8 per cent market share. Indeed, only Australia and China have Western-based market leaders. In Australia, GM controls 22 per cent of the market, followed closely by Japan, which holds 20.6 per cent of the market. Including Japan, the top six Asian auto makers control 69.5 per cent of the Asian market. This includes Renault-Nissan (8.1 per cent) and Ford-Mazda (4.4 per cent), Japanese companies in which Western firms have a dominant share.[23]

Although the majority of the market in each of the three triad regions is controlled by home-region oriented companies, foreign companies continue to play a major role in each region. For example, Ford holds 10.9 per cent of the European market and is the fourth largest competitor. A number of foreign companies attained a competitive position by acquiring the operations of a local producer, such as GM's Opel subsidiary and others, through organic growth in foreign markets, such as Toyota and Honda in North America.

These findings counter a number of popular myths about the "archetypal global industry," many dating from the 1980s and early 1990s which saw the global expansion of Japanese firms in the industry. Common views included that a global car and a global car firm would soon evolve, that all production would shift to cheap labor regions leaving "hollow corporations" in the United States and Europe, and that sales by incumbents in the largest markets would be overtaken by more competitive foreign rivals. Yet such global car industry predictions have not come to pass for the key reason that the industry operates regionally, not globally.

The auto industry operates largely in "clusters" of localized activity within each major triad region.[24] There are networks of key suppliers, other suppliers, key distributors, other partners, and the Original Equipment Manufacturers (OEMs) assemble cars from imports of literally thousands of suppliers, all location bound. This is why of the 55 million vehicles produced each year over 90 per cent are sold where they are made.[25]

Auto firms are also strongly embedded in a range of other downstream activities and after-sales markets including financing (such as Ford Credit), insurance, maintenance and repairs (like Ford's Kwik-Fit operations), parts and accessories, and emergency rescue services (such as Ford's RESCU). These represent a substantial proportion of total revenues for the larger firms and are highly regionally specific.

Another persistent barrier to a global strategy or a global car is cultural barriers across regions. European consumers prefer performance cars with good engines while in the United States large comfortable cars are the norm. Even within NAFTA, while the United States and Canada prefer automatic transmissions, most cars in Mexico have manual transmissions. In terms of customer tastes, it is impossible to market the same car across regions, and usually all of the economies of scale for a model are achieved within each major region.

Another factor is fuel. Diesel continues to be popular in Europe but is being phased out in the United States because of its environmental implications. Rather than phase out the less expensive fuel, European auto makers are seeking ways of making it a cleaner alternative.

Each regional market in which auto makers operate has its own set of environmental regulations. In the United States, auto makers must design vehicles to conform to the

Environmental Protection Agency's (EPA) regulations and the environmental regulations of individual states. Other regulations that relate to automotive design include noise control and fuel economy. The companies' industrial processes are also heavily regulated with laws relating to water discharges, air emissions, waste management, and environmental cleanup. European and Asia-Pacific markets have different environmental laws to which auto maker's operations must comply. For instance, the European Union is making all car makers financially responsible for dismantling and recycling its own vehicles.

Finally, tariffs, ranging from 2.5 per cent in the United States to 10 per cent in some European countries to 100 per cent in some developing countries, represent another significant barrier to globalization.

Each region has a particular regulatory and competitive environment in which the major world players compete for market share. Local competitors are more adept at meeting the demands of their regional markets because they possess know-how on consumer preferences, government regulations, and market trends. While foreign companies might hire local personnel, purchase local car manufacturers, and do extensive market research, companies headquartered in that region are more capable of responding to changing circumstances of their primary market. We now discuss three of the world's largest automotive firms in more detail.

General Motors

The world's largest manufacturer of automobiles is General Motors (GM). In 2002, the company's revenues totaled $187 billion; GM accounted for nearly 15 per cent of the world's market for trucks and automobiles. General Motors produces and manufactures vehicles in all three triad markets. Nonetheless, 74.3 per cent of its sales originate in the United States, its home national market. Including Canada, Mexico, Puerto Rico, and Caribbean markets in North America, this number rises to 82.3 per cent of total sales. On the production side, its network of North American factories—which exist partly as a result of NAFTA—accounts for 65.8 per cent of production capacity. An international company, yes, but by no means a global company.

General Motors is primarily an automotive company, but it also operates communications services businesses and has a financing and insurance arm. Its automotive business is segmented geographically: GM North America, GM Europe, GM Latin America/Africa/Mid-East, and GM Asia-Pacific. Each of these regions has a set of brands it promotes. In North America, for example, these are Chevrolet, Pontiac, Saturn, etc. In Europe, GM's brands include Opel, Vauxhall, and Holden, among others. The GM Daewoo and Suzuki brands are marketed throughout Asia-Pacific.

GM is most successful in the North American market, where it holds 28 per cent of the market, compared to 8.7 per cent of the European market, and 3.4 per cent of the Asia-Pacific market. In North America, GM has a competitive advantage in that it is already well situated in the market and has a loyal consumer base. In other regions, however, it faces competition from local auto makers that know their home regions very well. In Europe, Volkswagen, BMW, and DaimlerChrysler build high-performance cars. In Asia, competitors build smaller, more fuel-efficient cars that cater to local preferences. General Motors' primary market is North America, in particular the United States. It derives most of its revenue and most of its profits from its home-region operations. GM's strategy must balance the benefit of investing in foreign regions to the benefits of investing in its home-region market. Foreign markets, though potentially profitable, do not offer the consolidated GM company sufficient incentive to switch the focus of its strategy. GM has plans to expand in China, but this is a country where rival MNEs are already active and where local Chinese producers are adept at appropriating the intellectual property of Western firms. In other words, China offers potentially high returns, but has great risks.[26]

Toyota

In 2002, two regional markets accounted for well over 80 per cent of Toyota's revenues: Asia (with Japan at 45 per cent of revenues) and North America, at 38.8 per cent of revenues. Europe was only at 8.8 per cent of revenues. In terms of units sold, the geographic distribution is similar: Asia and Oceania account for 46.2 per cent of unit sales (Japan at 38 per cent); North America for 30.8 per cent; and Europe for 15 per cent. Thus, in terms of revenue and units sold, Toyota is a bi-regional company. Market share shows a slightly different picture. Toyota holds approximately 40 per cent of the Japanese market but only 10 per cent of the North American market. Moreover, production is not as dispersed around the world; 75.9 per cent of all Toyota cars are still produced in Japan. Only 14.9 per cent are produced in North America. Other regions account for less than 10 per cent of production.

Over the last 10 years, Toyota's intra-regional percentage of sales has decreased from 57.1 per cent to 46.2 per cent. One major reason for this is the Japanese market itself, where sales decreased from 48.4 per cent of total revenues in 1993 to 38.3 per cent in 2002. In contrast, North American, European, and non-triad sales have steadily increased in importance. In 1993, Toyota derived 25.4 per cent of its sales from North America. This rose to 30.8 per cent in 2002; EU restrictions on imports of Japanese cars were one reason why Toyota historically has been unable to be successful in the European market. European sales accounted for a mere 9.9 per cent of total sales in 1993, but by 2002 Toyota almost doubled the number of units sold so that, in this year, the region accounted for 15 per cent of total sales. This is not only partly a result of more local production but also of Toyota learning to cater to the European market.

The Asian economies have been in a slump since the 1990s, and Europe has been growing slowly. This is why the North American market is very important for all Japanese manufacturers. Japanese car makers began to manufacture in the United States, the largest North American national market, in the 1980s to protect themselves from import restrictions. North America is Toyota's second largest regional market in terms of revenues. It is also highly profitable. In 2002, one-fourth of Toyota's profits originated in this region.

Toyota manufactures locally over two-thirds of the cars it sells in the United States. The company's Canadian plant also serves this regional market, and a Mexican plant in Tijuana is expected to increase local production when it opens in 2005. Local responsiveness is important. Toyota introduced its luxury models to accommodate the aging and wealthier North American baby boomers in the 1990s. Today, the company is introducing cars to target the young American customer, the demographic echo of the baby boomers. Sixty per cent of US car buyers remain loyal to the brand of their first car. It is thus imperative to service this young market.

American consumers, for their part, have been responsive to the company's reputation for quality and in particular for the lower price at which Toyota's cars are sold. In fact, during economic downturns in which consumers seek more value for their money Toyota does better in the United States. The company's cars not only are less expensive, but also consume less gasoline than American cars. The resale value is also higher for Toyota cars. One major advantage for Toyota is that it has some of the best manufacturing facilities in the world, and it combines this with excellent relationships with its suppliers. The company is so efficient that, despite the lower price of its cars, it makes an average profit of $1,000 on each car sold compared to $330 for GM.

Toyota's European operations are money losers, but the company continues to try to access this market and increase its market share from its 3.8 per cent level in 2002. To boost its image for performance in the region, the company recently began to compete in Formula One races. To protect itself from currency risk, Toyota will now produce a higher percentage of its cars within the region. That also means more local procurement. To this end, Porsche was asked to produce engines for its European models. Porsche already produces transmissions for the company. The company expects to increase its market share to 5 per cent by 2005.

Toyota is one of the most efficient companies at outsourcing production to suppliers with whom it enjoys amicable long-term, sometimes *keiretsu*-style relationships. If the auto industry is to become more like the electronics industry (as many believe may occur), vehicle brand owners (VBOs), such as Toyota, GM, and VW, will be the equivalent of original equipment manufacturers (OEMs) in the electronics industry, such as Nokia, IBM, and Microsoft, and will concentrate on designing, engineering, and marketing vehicles to be sold under their brand while others take care of manufacturing. Toyota is probably further along this outsourcing route than other triad auto makers.[27]

DaimlerChrysler

When German Daimler-Benz merged with US Chrysler, the aim of the German company was to secure a share in the large US economy-class car market. Synergies (for instance in the area of purchasing), it argued, would reduce costs across all operations. At first glance, one can argue that the merger achieved its goal. In 2002, 58.7 per cent of the company's revenues originated in North America, a trend that has remained relatively stable since 2000. These data define the firm as host-region oriented. The numbers can be deceiving though; soon after the merger the Chrysler group was plagued by management defections and decreasing profits.

Two things help explain the troubles of this merger. The first is that these companies were producing very different products. Mercedes Benz, Daimler-Benz' brand, had a competitive edge in the luxury market. Chrysler produced popular cars for the US market. Although the expensive parts of Daimler's vehicles could be used for more affordable Chrysler cars and the cheaper Chrysler parts be used on Daimler vehicles, both these moves were likely to reduce the competitive advantage on each of the markets in which the original companies operated. Chrysler cars could have become less affordable while Daimler's brand might have lost its reputation for quality. In effect, while some parts can be shared and suppliers can manufacture different products for both vehicle brands at lower prices, the benefits from the merger were limited by the different product lines of each company.

The second, and perhaps most important barrier to overcome, was the cross-cultural differences between the German and US companies. From the beginning, Daimler's management dominated the merged company, which resulted in an outflow of key US personnel from management positions and the designer ranks. The Germans tended to be bureaucratic while US managers made decisions on the spot. Many US managers left, unable to deal with the imposed management style. Capable designers went to rivals General Motors and Ford. Over time, the company has improved its cultural management of the US operations, and this is improving the company's overall position in the motor vehicle market.

DaimlerChrysler is undoubtedly a host-region based company, but a closer look at the organization shows, not a cohesive organization with a bi-regional market span, but two internal groups with individual global standings. The Mercedes Car Group, the non-commercial vehicle successor to the German part of the merger, derives 63 per cent of its revenues from the European market. The Chrysler Group, on the other hand, continues to derive over 90 per cent of its revenues from the North American market.

In terms of production, the Mercedes Group has eight production locations in Europe while the Chrysler Group has none. In the NAFTA region, the Chrysler Group has 38 production locations while the Mercedes Group has only one. This reflects two separate entities each trying to capitalize on knowledge of its home region, not a truly bi-regional or host-region oriented company.[28]

Review your answer to Active Learning Case question 3 and make any changes you like. Then compare your answer with the one below.

3 How will Airbus help the EU compete in Japan?

Japanese airlines will continually need to replace and expand their current stock of planes. US aircraft manufacturers had previously satisfied this demand. However, thanks to Airbus the EU now has an industry that can offer Japan a competitive product. Moreover, until Japan creates its own worldwide competitive aircraft industry, Airbus will be able to continue to tap this market potential.

Mergers and acquisitions

Although all three triad groups have much intra-regional trade and FDI, this does not mean that trade or FDI between them has declined. As discussed above, they also have invested large amounts of money in each other. For example, EU(15) countries have more than $700 billion of FDI in both the United States and Japan. The United States imports $232.2 billion from the EU(15) and $124.6 billion from Japan. So the three groups are closely linked in terms of both trade and FDI.[29]

Moreover, investors have poured billions of dollars into these economies, betting that they are going to profit handsomely from these investments. American investors, for example, spent more than $7 billion in the first five months of 1998 to purchase Asian properties, most of them in Japan. Part of this development was a result of the weak Japanese economy. Many companies there had no capital for expansion and were facing declining demand for their goods and services. So they were willing to unload some of their assets as well as take on foreign partners who could provide funds and growth opportunities. At the same time, the impact of Japanese deregulation was beginning to take effect. For a long time both the United States and the EU have been encouraging Japan to reduce its protectionist policies and allow greater opportunities for foreign investors. In the early 1990s the government promised to open up its markets to more foreign goods and even agreed to buy more cars, auto parts, and computer equipment from outside vendors. As the local economy began to falter and the rules and regulations that used to stymie foreign investors began to be withdrawn, the result was a rush by foreign MNEs into this marketplace.

Similarly, EU firms are very interested in buying American firms and vice versa. Some of the largest acquisitions made by EU companies in the United States in recent years include the purchase of ARCO by BP Amoco of the UK for over $27 billion, France Telecom's acquisition of NTL for $5.5 billion, and Vivendi Universal's purchase of USA Networks for $10.3 billion. At the same time, US firms have been buying EU companies. Ford Motor put out $2.72 billion to acquire Land Rover from BMW, and Cisco Systems paid $2.15 billion for Pirelli of Italy's fiber-optic operations.[30] So there is still a great deal of FDI being conducted between triad countries.

In addition to the high level of international business conducted across the triad, companies in the triad are constantly looking for new ideas from other regions that will make them more competitive. American and EU firms emulate successful Japanese business practices. In the United States, for example, the chairman of the Federal Reserve System has expressed the belief that US antitrust practices are out of date and that competitors should be allowed to acquire and merge with each other in order to protect themselves from world competition. This idea has long been popular in Japan where **keiretsus**, or business groups, which consist of a host of companies that are linked together through ownership and/or joint ventures, dominate the local environment and are able to use their combined wealth and connections to dominate world markets.[31] Today many firms including Deere & Company, Ford, IBM, and Harley-Davidson, to name but four, are copying this form of cooperation. Simply put, what happens in one part of the triad often has an effect in other parts.

Keiretsus
Groupings of Japanese firms with long-term associations and cross-shareholdings

✔ Active learning check

Review your answer to Active Learning Case question 4 and make any changes you like. Then compare your answer with the one below.

4 In what way did the Airbus consortium use a *keiretsu* approach to building the aircraft? Why do you think it opted for this approach?

A *keiretsu* is a business group, which often consists of a host of companies that are linked together through ownership and/or joint ventures. In the case of Airbus, notice how Germany, Great Britain, and Spain built the aircraft and France assembled it. This is the same approach used by *keiretsus* that coordinate their operations in such a way that each provides products and services to the group at a very low price. Another reason that the consortium undoubtedly opted for this approach is that each participant benefits because of the money pumped into its economy for doing this work. Under the new organizational arrangement the governmental role in the *keiretsu* disappears but the basic operational approach will remain, and the company will still be a *keiretsu* type of organization.

KEY POINTS

1 Foreign direct investment (FDI) is the ownership and control of foreign assets. This usually means the ownership, whole or partial, of a company in a foreign country.

2 There are a number of reasons for FDI. These include increased sales and profits, a chance to enter rapidly growing markets, reduced costs, gaining a foothold in economic unions, protecting domestic markets, protecting foreign markets, and acquiring technological and managerial know-how.

3 While there is a great amount of FDI made every year, most of it (approximately 80 per cent) occurs within or between triad countries. Much of the remaining FDI is in countries that are members of triad-based FDI clusters.

4 The triad nations dominate world trade and investments, and a great deal of this activity takes place both among and within triad countries. One of the major areas of triad trade is automobiles, which provides an excellent example of the economic interrelationships that exist among triad members.

Key terms

- triad
- foreign direct investment
- portfolio investment
- twin factories
- *maquiladoras*
- FDI cluster
- *keiretsu*

REVIEW AND DISCUSSION QUESTIONS

1 What is FDI all about? Put it in your own words.

2 What are some of the reasons for FDI? Identify and describe four.

3 Why are MNEs interested in investing in Eastern Europe?

4 How much FDI does the EU and Japan have in the United States? What conclusions can you reach based on these data?

5 How much FDI does the United States and Japan have in the EU? What conclusions can you reach based on these data?

6 How dominant are the triad countries in terms of FDI and world trade? Explain.

7 What is an FDI cluster? Why are certain countries such as Mexico and Venezuela more likely to be in the US cluster than in the EU cluster?

8 Why does Toyota choose to manufacture in the US?

9 Where is GM most successful? Why?

10 How active are US and EU firms in acquiring companies throughout the world? What accounts for this activity?

11 In what way can a *keiretsu* approach be of value to US and EU companies in becoming more competitive worldwide? Explain.

REAL CASE

Matsushita and Philips

In terms of triad-based competition, the 1980s saw the emergence of Japanese firms in the consumer electronics industry. One of the major companies was Matsushita. The firm was initially successful with color TVs, but its best-known product has been the videocassette recorder (VCR), a field it dominates by using the VHS system instead of the Sony Betamax format VCR and others produced by European and American rivals. Paradoxically, the VCR was developed in California in 1956 by a US firm, Ampex, but the product development and distribution was captured by the clever global strategy of Matsushita.

To dominate world business in VCRs Matsushita managed to make the VHS format the industry standard. The company achieved this not just by its own massive production and worldwide sales, but by licensing the VHS format to other MNEs such as Hitachi, Sharp, Mitsubishi, and even the major European-based rival, Philips. Other companies such as GE, RCA, and Zenith (which sold VCRs under their own brand names) were tied into the VHS format because of the production and process technology retained by Matsushita in its strong Japanese

home base. The company's massive global economies of scale enabled it to cut VCR prices by 50 per cent over its first five years.

In contrast, Philips was in desperate trouble by the 1980s. Built up in the interwar period of protectionism and strong government regulation, the company had developed a very highly decentralized organizational structure. Individual national country managers held the power in Philips, and they were slow to respond to the Japanese threat in the postwar period. As a result, Philips lacked economies of scale and its radios, TVs, and VCRs were too expensive compared with comparable Japanese products. Philips had more than 600 manufacturing plants across the world, all developing products for local markets. However, the challenge facing the firm was how to restructure its entire business away from locally responsive national organizations toward a more integrated and leaner manufacturer capable of reaping the necessary economies of scale through standard global production.

In essence, the Japanese changed the rules of the game in the consumer electronics business. Matsushita, as a centralized, high-quality, low-price, and innovative company, was able to beat the decentralized and nationally responsive European firm. One tactic used by European firms was to lobby their governments for protection in the form of antidumping actions and tougher customs inspection of Japanese products. But such "shelters" only bought some breathing room before MNEs such as Philips restructured and fitted their organizational capabilities to the required industry strategy.

Finally, the response of Matsushita to more protection has been to switch overseas sales from export to foreign direct investment (FDI). With FDI the firm has been able to evade European trade barriers such as antidumping actions. For example, today it manufactures in a number of European countries including the UK, where it has a major plant in Cardiff, Wales. At the same time this means that Matsushita must make its foreign subsidiaries as effective as possible by encouraging local initiatives, and this strategy can conflict with its internationally

centralized Japanese-based management culture. In short, the very government regulations that have made Philips too decentralized are now being reapplied half a century later to make Matsushita less global and more local.

Websites: www.mei.co.jp; www.panasonic.com; and www.philips.com.

Sources: Adapted from Chris Bartlett and Sumantra Ghoshal, *Managing Across Borders*, 2nd ed. (Boston, MA: Harvard Business School Press, 1998); Matsushita, *Annual Report*, 2003; Philips, *Annual Report*, 2003; www.panasonic.com; and www.philips.com.

1 What type of globalization strategy was followed by the Japanese firm Matsushita?

2 Why could the European firm Philips not compete well with its Japanese rival by the 1980s?

3 How can a government help its own firms against triad rivals?

Toys "Я" Us in Europe and Japan

Toys "Я" Us opened its first international outlet in Canada in 1984, and then it moved to parts of Europe, Hong Kong, and Singapore, where the company's "discount formula" was as popular as in the United States. The international business model applied to new markets was the same as that used by the company in the United States: the stores resembled each other, and each store had a self-service supermarket format that offered a great variety of toys sold at low prices.

By 2004, 38 per cent of Toys "Я" Us stores were located outside the United States. Yet, entering a new market has not always been easy for the company. As this case shows, cultural differences and regulations can make establishing a foreign business model very difficult.

Source: Getty Images/Tim Boyle

Toys "Я" Us in Germany

Many multinationals like to set up operations in Europe, particularly in the largest economy, Germany. Despite its economic downturn in the 1990s, this country has a very strong economy, and it greatly influences what happens in the rest of the EU.

When Toys "Я" Us decided to enter the German market, it was greeted by a partial boycott and a public relations blitz that condemned the concept of a self-service toy supermarket as being alien and wrong. Even though

the managing director of Toys "Я" Us was German, strong objections were directed against a US retailer wanting large-area sales space in Germany. The company soon learned that legal and cultural barriers could be effectively used to block foreign competition. When Toys "Я" Us applied for a construction permit in Cologne, the city fathers asked the local chamber of commerce and retailers' association how they felt about the application. The latter replied that a toy store belongs in the center of the city, not on the edge of town. Yet this is exactly where Toys "Я" Us needed to be located so that it could build a sprawling store and a parking lot that was the size of a football field. In addition, the German Toy Manufacturers Association questioned why a toy store would sell so many non-toy items.

The managing director for Toys "Я" Us refused to allow these early setbacks to thwart his efforts. He continued making the rounds of trade shows, negotiating for store sites, and presenting the company's plans to local officials; eventually he wore down the resistance. Even the competition began to realize that successful large toy stores could spark a boom in the toy market. Soon, competitors began copying some of the approaches used by Toys "Я" Us, such as piling shelves at the back of the store with baby food and diapers. Parents who come in to get diapers or baby food seldom leave without buying a toy for the child.

The German experience has taught the management that despite cultural, legal, and technical barriers, a retail company can succeed in Europe if it is patient, maintains a strong consumer-oriented marketing focus, and is nationally responsive.

By 2003 Toys "Я" Us had 48 stores in Germany. It had another 182 outlets in Europe, including 64 in the United Kingdom, 33 in France, and 32 in Spain.

Toys "Я" Us in Japan

The Japanese toy market is one of the largest, making it an attractive market for Toys "Я" Us. Yet, when the firm decided to enter this market in 1991, it had some major hurdles to overcome. Despite the rapid growth it had experienced, Japan's toy industry remained highly fragmented and locally focused. Japanese reportedly preferred personal attention from the shop owner rather than low prices. In addition to customers' habits and personal loyalties, Japan's retail structure was also bolstered by a series of laws restricting the spread of larger retail stores.

At the time, a typical Japanese toy store was less than 3,200 square feet in area. Nearly all retail shops were domestically owned and bought their toys from local wholesalers, usually for 75–80 per cent of the manufacture "suggested price." Retailers then sold the toys for the suggested price, deviating from it only rarely. Fragmented wholesalers served these shops. These wholesalers sold their products through a complex distribution system that typically involved between three and five layers of intermediaries.

The Toys "Я" Us business model clashed with traditional business structures. Its self-serve format put more attention on lower prices, minimizing personal attention to each customer, and cutting out any intermediaries from the supply process. Japan not only presented great possibilities but also involved a high risk of failure, especially if the company didn't adapt its business model.

To overcome the problems of Japanese culture and history being incompatible with the Toys "Я" Us business model, Den Fujita, who had successfully run McDonald's Japan, was enlisted as a local partner. At the time, he was the only Japanese business leader who had succeeded in bringing foreign non-luxury retail business into the restrictive Japanese market. His experience, political influence, vision, and unique understanding of both Japanese and American cultures enhanced the probability of success of Toys "Я" Us in Japan.

With the help of Fujita, a powerful opinion leader who affects government policy-making, and a younger generation that had started to realize that they were paying inflated prices for many consumer goods, many commercial restrictions were lifted, and Toys "Я" Us was able to implement a business model similar to that in the United States. As of 2003, Toys "Я" Us has 146 stores in Japan.

Websites: www.toysrus.co.uk; www.toysrus.fr; www.toysrus.de; www.toysrus.co.jp; and inc.toysrus.com.

Sources: Adapted from Ferdinand Protzman, "Greetings from Fortress Europe," *New York Times,* August 18, 1991, Section 3, pp. 1, 6; John Templeman et al., "Germany Fights Back," *Business Week,* May 31, 1993, pp. 48–51; www.toysrus.com; Paul Klebnikov, "Trouble in Toyland," *Forbes,* June 1, 1998, pp. 56–60; Michael Gestrin, Rory Knight, and Alan M. Rugman, *The Templeton Global Performance Index* (Templeton College, University of Oxford, 1998); and Debora L. Spar, *Ruling the Waves* (New York: Harcourt, 2002).

1 What are the firm-specific advantages of Toys "Я" Us?

2 What specific cultural and political barriers to entry does it face?

3 Why was Toys "Я" Us more successful in Japan than in Germany?

Endnotes

1 Ministry of Finance, *Report on External Assets and Liabilities as of Year-End 2003,* May 21, 2004.

2 Scott Morrison, "Solectron Buys C-Mac for $2.7 Bn," *Financial Times,* August 10, 2001, p. 19.

3 David Pringle, "Matsushita Looks to Go Digital in Europe," *Wall Street Journal,* May 8, 2000, Section A, p. 39 A.

4 For a discussion of an interesting combination of FDI and portfolio investment, see John Philips and Karen Woolfson, "Franco-German Banking Link-Up Ignores Sceptics," *The European,* April 12–14, 1991, p. 20.

5 United Nations, *World Investment Report 2001* (Geneva: United Nations Conference on Trade and Development, 2001).

6 United Nations, *World Investment Report 2003* (Geneva: United Nations Conference on Trade and Development, 2003) and Thomson Corporation, *Annual Report*, 2003.

7 Honda, *Annual Report*, 2002 and Sony, *Annual Report*, 2003.

8 Wal-Mart, *Annual Report*, 2001.

9 "China's Growth Hits Six-Year High," *BBC News*, January 20, 2004.

10 Alan M. Rugman, *The Regional Multinationals* (Cambridge: Cambridge UP, 2005).

11 Susan Moffat, "Picking Japan's Research Brains," *Fortune*, March 25, 1991, p. 92.

12 United Nations, *World Investment Report 2003* (New York: United Nations Conference on Trade and Development, 2003).

13 BEA, Survey of Current Business, June 2004.

14 Michael Mortimore, *DI and TNC Activities in Latin America and the Caribbean*, Presentation at the UN's ECLAC, Ottawa, Canada, June 15, 2004 and Bank of Estonia.

15 United Nations, *World Investment Report 2003* (New York: United Nations Conference on Trade and Development, 2003).

16 Wal-Mart, *Annual Report*, 2003.

17 Richard Tomlinson, "Who's Afraid of Wal-Mart?" *Fortune*, June 26, 2000, pp. 186–196; Rugman (2005); and Carrefour, *Annual Report*, 2003.

18 General Motors, *Annual Report*, 2003.

19 Vijay Govindarajan and Anil K. Gupta, *The Quest for Global Dominance* (New York: Harcourt, 2001), pp. 52–53.

20 Rugman (2005).

21 R. W. Morris, *Motor Vehicles 2000* (London: Random House, 2001).

22 F. Henderson, *Capitalizing on Global Growth*, Presentation at 2003 Tokyo Analyst Conference, October 20, 2003.

23 Henderson (2003).

24 Alan M. Rugman and Joseph D'Cruz, *Multinationals as Flagship Firms: Regional Business Networks* (Oxford: Oxford UP, 2000).

25 McKinsey Quarterly, "How Far Can It Go?" *The McKinsey Quarterly*, Special Editoin 4, 27–30.

26 Adapted from Alan M. Rugman and Cecilia Brain, "Globalization and Regional International Production," in John Ravenhill (ed.) *Global Political Economy* (Oxford: Oxford UP, 2004).

27 Adapted from Rugman and Brain (2004).

28 Rugman (2005).

29 IMF, *Direction of Trade Statistics Yearbook 2003*.

30 Marcus Walker and Anna Wilde Mathews, "As Euro Falls, US Firms Don't Pounce," *Wall Street Journal*, September 18, 2000, p. A 28.

31 For a detailed discussion of *keiretsus*, see George Ming-Hong Lai, "Knowing Who You Are Doing Business with in Japan: A Managerial View of Keiretsu and Keiretsu Business Groups," *Journal of World Business*, vol. 34, no. 4 (1999), pp. 423–448.

Additional bibliography

Agarwal, Sanjeev and Ramaswami, Sridhar N. "Choice of Foreign Market Entry Mode: Impact of Ownership, Location and Internalization Factors," *Journal of International Business Studies*, vol. 23, no. 1 (First Quarter 1992).

Andersen, Otto. "On the Internationalization Process of Firms: A Critical Analysis," *Journal of International Business Studies*, vol. 24, no. 2 (Second Quarter 1993).

Buckley, Peter J. "Problems and Developments in the Core Theory of International Business," *Journal of International Business Studies*, vol. 21, no. 4 (Fourth Quarter 1990).

Busenitz, Lowell W. "Country Institutional Profiles: Unlocking Entrepreneurial Phenomena," *Academy of Management Journal*, vol. 43, no. 5 (October 2000).

Contractor, Farok J. "Contractual and Cooperative Forms of International Business: Towards a Unified Theory of Modal Choice," *Management International Review*, vol. 30, no. 1 (First Quarter 1990).

Dunning, John H. "Explaining Changing Patterns of International Production: In Defence of the Eclectic Theory," *Oxford Bulletin of Economics and Statistics*, vol. 41, no. 4 (1979).

Dunning, John H. *International Production and the Multinational Enterprise* (London: Allen and Unwin, 1981).

Dunning, John H. "The Eclectic Paradigm of International Production: A Restatement and Some Possible Extensions," *Journal of International Business Studies*, vol. 19, no. 1 (Spring 1988).

Dunning, John H. "The Study of International Business: A Plea for a More Interdisciplinary Approach," *Journal of International Business Studies*, vol. 20, no. 3 (Fall 1989).

Dunning, John H. *Alliance Capitalism and Global Business* (London: Routledge, 1997).

Dunning, John H. "Location and the Multinational Enterprise: A Neglected Factor?" *Journal of International Business Studies*, vol. 29, no. 1 (First Quarter 1998).

Haar, Jerry. "A Comparative Analysis of the Profitability Performance of the Largest US, European and Japanese Multinational Enterprises," *Management International Review*, vol. 29, no. 3 (Third Quarter 1989).

Harrigan, Kathryn Rudie. "Strategic Alliances: Their New Role in Global Competition," *Columbia Journal of World Business*, vol. 22, no. 2 (Summer 1987).

Kim, Wi Saeng and Lyn, Esmeralda O. "FDI Theories and the Performance of Foreign Multinationals Operating in the US," *Journal of International Business Studies*, vol. 21, no. 1 (First Quarter 1990).

Kotabe, Masaaki. "A Comparative Study of US and Japanese Patent Systems," *Journal of International Business Studies*, vol. 23, no. 1 (First Quarter 1992).

Li, Jiatao and Guisinger, Stephen. "The Globalization of Service Multinationals in the 'Triad' Regions: Japan, Western Europe and North America," *Journal of International Business Studies*, vol. 23, no. 4 (Fourth Quarter 1992).

Luo, Yadong. "Toward a Cooperative View of MNC-Host Government Relations: Building Blocks and Performance Implications," *Journal of International Business Studies*, vol. 32, no. 3 (Fall 2001).

Ostry, Sylvia. "Governments & Corporations in a Shrinking World: Trade & Innovation Policies in the United States,

Europe & Japan," *Columbia Journal of World Business*, vol. 25, nos. 1, 2 (Spring/Summer 1990).

Parkhe, Arvind. "Interfirm Diversity, Organizational Learning, and Longevity in Global Strategic Alliances," *Journal of International Business Studies*, vol. 22, no. 4 (Fourth Quarter 1991).

Porter, Michael E. *The Competitive Advantage of Nations* (New York: Free Press, Macmillan, 1990).

Rugman, Alan M. "A New Theory of the Multinational Enterprise: Internationalization Versus Internalization," *Columbia Journal of World Business*, vol. 15, no. 1 (Spring 1980).

Rugman, Alan M. *Inside the Multinationals: The Economics of Internal Markets* (New York: Columbia University Press, 1981).

Rugman, Alan M. (ed.) *New Theories of the Multinational Enterprise* (London: Croom Helm and New York: St Martin's, 1982).

Rugman, Alan M. "The Comparative Performance of US and European Multinational Enterprises," *Management International Review*, vol. 23, no. 2 (1983).

Rugman, Alan M. and Boyd, Gavin (eds.) *European-American Trade and Financial Alliances* (Cheltenham: Elgar, 2005).

Rugman, Alan M. and Boyd, Gavin (eds.) *Deepening Integration in the Pacific Economies* (Cheltenham: Elgar, 1999).

Rugman, Alan M. and Verbeke, Alain. "Multinational Corporate Strategy and the Canada–US Free Trade Agreement," *Management International Review*, vol. 30, no. 3 (Third Quarter 1990).

Sullivan, Daniel and Bauerschmidt, Alan. "The Basic Concepts of International Business Strategy: A Review and Reconsideration," *Management International Review*, vol. 31, Special Issue (1991).

Vernon-Wortzel, Heidi and Wortzel, Lawrence H. "Globalizing Strategies for Multinationals from Developing Countries," *Columbia Journal of World Business*, vol. 23, no. 1 (Spring 1988).

Williamson, Oliver E. *Markets and Hierarchies* (New York: Free Press, 1975).

Yip, George. *Total Global Strategy* (Englewood Cliffs, NJ: Prentice-Hall, 1995).

APPENDIX TO CHAPTER 3

In Chapter 2 we developed the CSA-FSA framework for the study of international business. Here we examine a related approach to the study of the reasons behind the investments made by MNEs. The "eclectic" approach, first developed by John Dunning, provides a consolidation of the literature on FDI that draws on industrial organization theories, location theory, and market imperfections approaches.

Dunning's "eclectic" theory of MNEs

The eclectic theory specifies a set of three conditions that must be met if a firm is to engage in foreign operations: firm-specific advantages (FSAs), internalization advantages, and country-specific advantages (CSAs). (See Table 3A.)

Firm-specific (ownership-specific) advantages (FSA)

The firm must possess net ownership advantages vis-à-vis firms of other nationalities in serving particular (and, in practice, mainly foreign) markets. These firm-specific (or ownership) advantages largely take the form of the possession of intangible assets, which are, at least for a period of time, exclusive or specific to the firm possessing them.

Internalization advantages

A firm possessing an advantage can either use the advantage itself (internalize it) or can sell or lease the advantage to other firms. This choice is usually explained in the context of transactions costs and internalization theory (Rugman 1981). There are costs involved in use of markets and in internal coordination and control. The FDI decision depends on which option presents the best net return (revenue minus cost), when the risks associated with each alternative are taken into account. According to internalization theory, both natural and unnatural market imperfections induce internalization by MNEs. The firm

Table 3A Dunning's "eclectic" theory of international production

A. Ownership-specific (firm-specific) advantages
    Firm-specific knowledge advantages
    Management, marketing, financial skills
    Vertical integration
        Control of resources
        Control of markets
    Risk diversification

B. Internalization (by MNEs)
    To enforce property rights and overcome other transaction costs
    To reduce buyer uncertainty
    To overcome government regulations

C. Location-specific (country-specific) advantages
    National production functions
    Government controls and regulations
    Political risk; cultural values

must consider not only government-imposed regulations, but also natural barriers and other transaction costs such as the creation of buyer uncertainty.

Assuming that a firm possesses unique ownership advantages, if it is to engage in FDI it must be more beneficial for it to internalize its FSA, for example, to secure property rights over its firm-specific advantages in knowledge, rather than to sell or lease them to foreign firms. This internalization is done through an extension of its own activities rather than by externalizing them through contacts at arm's-length prices (which, in any case, may not exist) with independent firms. The management of the firm must judge that alternatives to internalization such as licensing, management contracts, franchises, technical service agreements, turnkey projects, and subcontracts are either not a feasible or the most profitable method of appropriating its firm-specific advantages.

Country-specific (location-specific) advantages (CSAs)

Assuming that the conditions stated in the two preceding sections are satisfied, if FDI is to take place it must be profitable for the enterprise to locate abroad, that is, to utilize these firm-specific advantages in conjunction with at least some factor inputs (including natural resources) outside its home country. Otherwise foreign markets would be served entirely by exports and home markets by domestic production. Therefore, the location-specific advantages of the MNE are important elements in its choice of modality for servicing foreign markets.

Relevance of the Dunning model

The net ownership, or firm-specific, advantages are required to offset the costs incurred by the MNE of operating at a distance from its home base. In the literature on the MNE, these costs are referred to, following Williamson (1975), as transaction costs. Transactions costs arise from the difficulties of communicating over large distances and of controlling many subsidiaries. Both factors come into play once production decisions are made across national boundaries. In contrast, these costs of operating internationally are not incurred by a local firm. The MNE must possess advantages that offset the disadvantages (additional costs) incurred in operating transnationally. If assets corresponding to those conferring the advantages to the MNE were available to local host-country firms, the MNE would not be able to compensate for the transaction costs of operating at a distance.

The use of the advantage in the host country is required if FDI is to take place. The cost of moving resources used in the host country must exceed the costs of controlling a subsidiary at a distance plus the costs of trade. Otherwise, the resource would be exported or moved to the home country, production would take place in the home country, and the foreign country market would be served by exports.

Sources of firm-specific advantages

The range of advantages that can lead to FDI is large but can be summarized as follows:

1 Proprietary technology due to research and development activities.
2 Managerial, marketing, or other skills specific to the organizational function of the firm.
3 Product differentiation, trademarks, or brand names.
4 Large size, reflecting scale economies.
5 Large capital requirements for plants of the minimum efficient size.

Sources of internalization advantages

The conditions that favor internalization include:

1 The high costs of making and enforcing contracts.

2 Buyer uncertainty about the value of the technology being sold.

3 A need to control the use or resale of the product.

4 Advantages to using price discrimination or cross-subsidization.

Sources of country-specific advantages

The location-specific advantages of the host country can include:

1 Natural resources.

2 Efficient and skilled relatively low-cost labor force.

3 Trade barriers restricting imports.

The first and second of these CSAs can result in FDI that leads to exports as well as to production for the local market. The third CSA will be associated with production for the local market only.

Tariff and non-tariff barriers to trade, the country's competitive environment, and government regulations also influence CSAs. Building on these CSAs, the firm makes decisions about the efficient international configuration and coordination between segments of its value chain (operations, marketing, R&D, and logistics). The skill in making such organizational decisions represents a strong, managerial firm-specific asset in itself.

In a perfect market situation, free trade would be the most efficient means of servicing markets abroad; however, given the many barriers to trade presently affecting the market, MNEs are a necessary alternative. The ability of MNEs to create internal markets enables them to bypass the barriers to trade that governments often erect.

Managers and most MNEs use strategies that build on the interactions of country-specific advantages and firm-specific advantages. They do this to position themselves in a unique strategic space. In Porter's terminology, the CSAs form the basis of the global platform from which the multinational firm derives a home-base "diamond" advantage of global competitiveness. The Porter "diamond" was discussed in Chapter 1 under "Maintaining economic competitiveness."

Part Two

THE ENVIRONMENT OF INTERNATIONAL BUSINESS

Chapter 4

INTERNATIONAL POLITICS

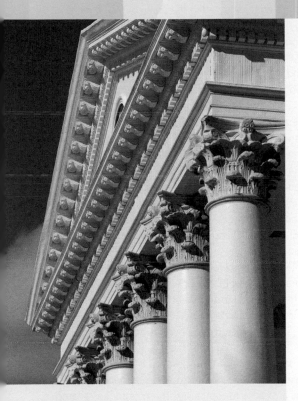

Objectives of the chapter

Politics and economics are closely linked and often affect each other. A good example is the economic changes that are sweeping Eastern Europe and Asia today. As these countries embrace open markets, their centrally-planned economies are giving way to market-driven economies. However, this latter development would have been impossible had it not been preceded by the requisite political change as reflected by more democratic governments. The purposes of this chapter are to examine the linkage between political forces and economic change and then to review some of the major forms of economic integration that are being used to create regional trade areas and common markets. In future chapters these topics will be developed in more depth.

The specific objectives of this chapter are to:

1 *Compare* and *contrast* major political and economic systems and note the linkage among them.
2 *Examine* the primary reasons for the current privatization movement and the economic impact that this movement is having on selected countries.
3 *Describe* the five major levels of economic integration and how each works.
4 *Discuss* how MNEs are using strategic planning to benefit from current worldwide economic integration efforts.
5 *Discuss* the impact of non-governmental organizations (NGOs) on international business.

Contents

How risky is investment in Russia?

When Mikhail Gorbachev began changing the economic policies of the USSR in the late 1980s, many foreign businesspeople viewed this as the beginning of new opportunities. However, by the time Gorbachev resigned in late 1991, no one seemed to know how profitable or risky an investment in Russia might be. This political situation seemed to be one of uncertainty. For example, the new union that was being created was to be called the Commonwealth of Independent States, and it was to be a loose economic and political alliance consisting of any of the former Soviet republics that wanted to join. Most of the states did, signing an agreement that called for open borders and economic cooperation but no central government. Simply put, the new political arrangement was in a state of flux.

At the same time, the Russians began to implement Western-style economic concepts. The result was devastating. Prices on many goods skyrocketed, and people found themselves paying five to ten times as much for these products. As the value of the ruble sank to around one cent, the government-owned foreign exchange bank began denying requests for withdrawals. However, no one dared to close the bank because this would have meant defaulting on nearly $85 billion of foreign debt. Meanwhile, gross national product started to decline precipitously.

In an effort to help the newly formed Russian republic, a number of prominent businesspeople and politicians called for aid in the form of grants, technological assistance, and direct investments. Additionally, the US administration urged that Russia be admitted to full membership in the International Monetary Fund (IMF) and the World Bank. This was soon done, and within the next couple of years a growing number of MNEs began to invest. Tetra Pak, a Swedish food-packing company, put $60 million into three Russian plants; Ford Motor put $150 million into a car venture and opened over 60 dealerships throughout the country; and PepsiCo and McDonald's started setting up operations.

The severe reforms that accompanied the country's turn toward a free-market economy resulted in a number of other dramatic changes, including selling most public companies to private groups, deregulating prices, promoting foreign trade, eliminating central planning, and creating a new banking system. At the same time, these changes brought about a great deal of economic uncertainty that caused social instability and problems for MNEs operating here. For example, many multinationals found that they had to pay protection money to the local mafia. In fact, overall corruption and the lack of a legal structure to protect foreign investments were instrumental in bringing about a near crash of the Russian economy in 1998. The IMF, the World Bank, and the Japanese government had to step in and provide the country with a relief loan. These efforts, however, were stopgap measures at best.

During subsequent years, the Russian economy stabilized. Many signs are cause for optimism. The country has a large middle class and there is a growing small business sector. Since 1998, the economy has been growing at an average of 6.5 per cent per year. Furthermore, the country has continued to increase its foreign currency reserves and pays its international loans on time. Yet, a number of problems continue to plague Russia. Natural resources account for 80 per cent of the country's exports, including oil and natural gas, making the economy susceptible to world price fluctuations. The banking system is weak and, after the 1998 crisis, generally distrusted. In 2004, for instance, smaller banks faced a liquidity crisis as depositors, afraid for their

Source: Getty Images/Royalty Free

savings, withdrew large sums of money. In addition, widespread corruption and government interference in the judiciary process stymies both domestic and foreign investment. A case in point is that of Yukos, one of Russia's largest oil companies, whose privatization was one of many corrupt undertakings in the transition to a market economy. Today the government is seeking to collect back taxes that are threatening to bankrupt the company. Yukos is charged with tax evasion, but critics claim the move is politically motivated and that the tools used to evade taxes were perfectly legal under Russia law when they were undertaken. Foreign investors continue to reassess their opportunities in Russia.

Websites: www.ford.com; www.imf.org; www.worldbank.org; www.tetrapak.de; www.pepsico.com; www.mcdonalds.com; www.yukos.com; www.telia.se; www.sonera.fi; and www.telecominvest.com.

Sources: Adapted from Charles Clover, "Russia Waits on Investors' Judgment," *Financial Times*, Tuesday, July 14, 1998; Martin Walker, "Investing in Russia Not for the Weak at Heart," *Europe*, March 1997; Sabrina Tavernise, "Phone Deal Raises Takes in Russia," *New York Times*, August 16, 2001, p. W 1; "Cinderella's Witching Hour," *The Economist*, July 8, 2004; "Court 'Freezes' Key Yukos Assets," **BBC.co.uk**, April 19, 2005.

1 What type of economic system now exists in Russia: market-driven, centrally-determined, or mixed?

2 Would Russia benefit by gaining admission to one of the major economic unions such as the EU? Why?

3 Is Russia a good potential investment for Western business? Explain.

INTRODUCTION

Over the past two decades, many countries have seen a dramatic change in their political systems. In the Americas, both Chile and Nicaragua have returned to democracy. The former communist countries of Eastern Europe are building, in varying degrees, free market systems. In China, meanwhile, the central government is still communist, but the nation is no longer tightly managed by Beijing. Market-driven companies have blossomed in a growing number of geographic areas (most of them in the southeastern region) lending credence to the contentions of those who hold that China will be a market-driven economy within a few decades. Whether or not this proves true, one thing is certain: political and economic changes are taking place everywhere, opening up new opportunities for MNEs.

In particular, the movement toward market-driven economies of countries that were once controlled by the USSR has affected international business. For example, Poland, Hungary, the Czech Republic, Latvia, Lithuania, and Estonia, to name but six, have all created market-driven economies. Years ago the USSR would not have permitted these satellite nations to abandon the command economy advocated by communist ideology and replace it with a free-market system. Under Mikhail Gorbachev, however, the USSR revised its political and economic thinking—and things have never been the same since.

Although this has proved to be good news for the satellite countries, Russia, as seen in this chapter's active learning case, has not been as fortunate. As a result, until MNEs feel that the government is willing to take the steps necessary to ensure that promises are kept and they are able to repatriate their funds, they are going to proceed very cautiously with their investment plans. International politics is a primary concern for these firms. This explains why Cuba has found it so difficult to attract foreign capital.

China, on the other hand, realizing that it must walk a fine line between commitment to its current political philosophy and the need to attract outside investments, has been trying very hard to balance both of these concerns. At the turn of the century, former President

Jiang Zemin noted that one of the country's primary economic objectives is to increase gross domestic product at an annual rate of 7 per cent. During the interview, the president also said that capitalists should be welcomed into the Communist Party.[1] At the same time, China encouraged foreign capital investment in order to ensure that its economic engine continues to function efficiently—this implied a change in its political ideology. One development in this direction was a government announcement that the country could no longer ensure the survival of inefficient companies. Firms now have to be able to compete with MNEs or face the risk of going under. Workers, accustomed to job security, had to accept the fact that they could be laid off and be willing to be retrained in order to find employment in this new, competitive job market.[2] These reforms have come a long way. In 2005 the private economy accounted for nearly 40 per cent of the gross product of Shanghai, China's largest urban center.[3]

These governmental decrees certainly represent a big change in the way things have been done in China for the last 50 years. The same is true worldwide. International politics and economic integration are altering the way international business is being conducted, and those nations that cannot keep up with these developments are going to find themselves falling farther and farther behind. In this chapter we will look at the major current economic and political systems and their impact on the world of international business. We will begin by examining political ideologies and economics.

Political ideologies and economics

An **ideology** is a set of integrated beliefs, theories, and doctrines that helps direct the actions of a society. Political ideology is almost always intertwined with economic philosophy. For example, the political ideology of the United States is grounded in the Constitution, which guarantees the rights of private property and the freedom of choice. This has helped lay the foundation for US capitalism. A change in this fundamental ideology would alter the economic environment of the United States. The same is true, for example, for China and the former USSR republics. Simply put, the political and economic ideologies of nations help to explain their national economic policies.

Political systems

In the extreme, there are two types of political systems: democracy and totalitarianism. **Democracy** is a system of government in which the people, either directly or through their elected officials, decide what is to be done. Good examples of democratic governments include the United States, Canada, England, and Australia. Common features of democratic governments include (1) the right to express opinions freely, (2) election of representatives for limited terms of office, (3) an independent court system that protects individual property and rights, and (4) a relatively non-political bureaucracy and defense infrastructure that ensure the continued operation of the system.

Totalitarianism is a system of government in which one individual or political party maintains complete control and either refuses to recognize other parties or suppresses them. A number of types of totalitarianism currently exist. **Communism** is an economic system in which the government owns all property and makes all decisions regarding the production and distribution of goods and services. To date, all attempts at national communism have led to totalitarianism. The best example of communism is Cuba. Another form of totalitarianism is **theocratic totalitarianism**, in which a religious group exercises total power and represses or persecutes non-orthodox factions. Iran and some of the sheikdoms of the Middle East are good examples. A third form is **secular totalitarianism**, in which the military controls the government and makes decisions that it deems to be in the best

Ideology
A set of integrated beliefs, theories, and doctrines that helps to direct the actions of a society

Democracy
A system of government in which the people, either directly or through their elected officials, decide what is to be done

Totalitarianism
A system of government in which one individual or party maintains complete control and either refuses to recognize other parties or suppresses them

Communism
A political system in which the government owns all property and makes all decisions regarding production and distribution of goods and services

Theocratic totalitarianism
A system of government in which a religious group exercises total power and represses or persecutes non-orthodox factions

Secular totalitarianism
A system of government in which the military controls everything and makes decisions that it deems to be in the best interests of the country

interests of the country. Examples of this are communist North Korea and Chile under Pinochet. Political systems typically create the infrastructure within which the economic system functions; in order to change the economic system, there often needs to be a change in the way the country is governed.

Economic systems

The three basic economic systems are capitalism, socialism, and mixed. However, for the purposes of our analysis it is more helpful to classify these systems in terms of resource allocation (market-driven versus centrally determined) and property ownership (private versus public). In a **market-driven economy**, goods and services are allocated on the basis of demand and supply. If consumers express a preference for cellular telephones, more of these products will be offered for sale. If consumers refuse to buy dot-matrix printers, these goods will cease to be offered. The US and EU nations have market-driven economies. In a **centrally-determined economy**, goods and services are allocated based on a plan formulated by a committee that decides what is to be offered. In these economies people are able to purchase only what the government determines should be sold. Cuba is the best example.

Market-driven economies are characterized by private ownership. Most of the assets of production are in the hands of privately-owned companies that compete for market share by offering the best-quality goods and services at competitive prices. Centrally-determined economies are characterized by public ownership. Most of the assets of production are in the hands of the state, and production quotas are set for each organization.

In examining economic systems, it is important to remember that, in a strict sense, most nations of the world have **mixed economies**, characterized by a combination of market-driven forces and centrally-determined planning. Mixed economies include privately-owned commercial entities as well as government-owned commercial entities. Governments in mixed economies typically own the utilities and infrastructural industries—railroads, airlines, shipping lines, and industries considered to be of economic and strategic importance—for instance, petroleum and copper. For example, the United States, a leading proponent of market-driven economic policies, provides health care and other social services to many of its citizens through government-regulated agencies, which gives it some aspects of central planning. Other democratic countries with mixed economies include Great Britain, Sweden, and Germany, all of which have even stronger social welfare systems than the United States.

Another example of the role of government in the economy is that of promoting business and ensuring that local firms gain or maintain dominance in certain market areas. The US and EU governments continually pressure the Chinese to open their doors to foreign MNEs, and the Chinese government is very active in helping its local firms do business with the West.

As a result of such developments, there has been a blurring of the differences between market-driven and centrally-determined economies. The biggest change has been the willingness of the latter to introduce free-market concepts. Examples include Russia and other Eastern European countries, which began introducing aspects of free enterprise such as allowing people to start their own businesses and to keep any profits that they make.[4] At the same time, however, many market-driven economies are increasingly adopting centrally-determined ideas, such as using business–government cooperation to fend off external competitors, or the use of political force to limit the ability of overseas firms to do business in their country. In the United States, for example, the government is frequently being urged to play a more active role in monitoring foreign business practices. An instance of this can be seen in the box **International Business Strategy in Action: Softwood lumber: not-so-free trade**. On balance, however, we are now seeing a move from central planning

Market-driven economy
An economy in which goods and services are allocated on the basis of consumer demand

Centrally-determined economy
An economy in which goods and services are allocated based on a plan formulated by a committee that decides what is to be offered

Mixed economies
Economic systems characterized by a combination of market- and centrally-driven planning

INTERNATIONAL BUSINESS STRATEGY *IN ACTION*

Softwood lumber: not-so-free trade

In 2003, both the North American Free Trade Agreement (NAFTA) and the World Trade Organization (WTO) ruled in favor of Canada on the issue of US tariffs on Canadian softwood lumber. The WTO ruling was non-binding, whereas NAFTA's ruling had to be addressed within 60 days. However, the agreement, reached in principle between the two countries is far from free trade.

The rift between producers on each side of the border is 20 years old, and in 1996 it led to an agreement: the United States–Canada Softwood Lumber Agreement (SLA), in which Canada restricted exports to the United States to 14.7 billion board feet. At that time, Canadian producers claimed such a restriction cost them $480 million annually and 11,000 jobs. When the agreement came to an end in 2001, US producers quickly lobbied their government to impose tariffs on Canadian producers. For its part, the Canadian government was hoping that the end of the SLA would lead to free trade. An investigation by the Department of Commerce determined that Canada's provincial governments were illegally subsidizing lumber production and imposed a tariff of 19.3 per cent that was later increased to 27 per cent.

At the core of the dispute are differences in the systems of production in both countries. In the United States, most harvested timber comes from private lands and is auctioned off to buyers. In Canada, provincial governments own the land and set cutting fees according to market conditions. US producers argue that government-set cutting fees are below market prices and thus constitute a 35 per cent subsidy to the Canadian industry.

Softwood lumber is one of Canada's most successful exports to the United States. In fact, Canadian producers had held a 35 per cent market share prior to the tariff, and exports to the United States had grown considerably in the 1990s, particularly as a result of the lower Canadian dollar. In addition, note the Canadian producers, the US claim ignores the extra expenses that Canadian firms have had to pay for road building, replanting, and environmental protection. As a result, the Canadians argue that the tariff is nothing more than protectionism.

The negative effects of the tariff are now being felt in both countries. The fact that US consumers are paying 10 per cent more as a direct result has so upset some industry groups that an association of US homebuilders, consumers, and contractors lobbied Washington to remove the tariff. Within a month of the tariff's enactment, 10,000 industry

Source: Getty Images/Alan Kearney

workers had been laid off, a dozen mills were shuttered, and most of the plants were operating below capacity. By 2003, Canadian producers held about one-third of the US market.

Favorable verdicts from WTO and NAFTA courts have resulted in almost no benefit to the Canadian industry. Both courts agreed that the Canadian system amounted to a subsidy to domestic producers; however, the WTO found that the subsidy was not enough to warrant retaliation from the United States, and NAFTA found that the tariffs the United States imposed were excessive and miscalculated the subsidy by not taking into consideration market conditions in Canada. An agreement in principle in 2003 proposed the elimination of the 27 per cent US tariff but reduced the amount Canadian producers can export to the United States without penalty. Canadian firms would only be able to capture 31.5 per cent (down from 33 per cent) of the US market and would have to pay $200 per each additional thousand board feet. The United States would return 52 per cent of all tariffs collected since 2001, just over $800 million, but US companies would receive the remainder. Provinces that follow the US market system, such as New Brunswick and Nova Scotia, would benefit from more market access. Perhaps the most important section of this managed trade agreement is that it prevents Canada from further pursuing resolution through the WTO or NAFTA.

Websites: www.weyerhaeuser.com; www.dfait-maeci.gc.ca; and www.wto.org.

Sources: Edward Alden, "Canada to Challenge United States Over Import Duties," *Financial Times*, August 21, 2001; Ian Jack, "US Hits Value-added Softwood," *Financial Post*, September 5, 2001; "Pettigrew Plans to Lobby Washington on Lumber," *The Toronto Star*, September 7, 2001; "Stump War," *The Economist*, August 30, 2001; "At Loggerheads," *The Economist*, May 22, 2001; Amina Ali, Sabrina Saccoccio and Justin Thomson, "Softwood Lumber Dispute," *CBC News Online*, March 2001 and updated on December 8, 2003; and "Softwood Lumber Deal Caps Canadian Exports," *CBC TV News*, July 29, 2003.

to market-driven and mixed economies. The privatization movement that is taking place worldwide provides one prominent example.

Government control of assets

Over the last decade or so, an increasing number of countries have begun moving toward **privatization**, the process of selling government assets to private buyers. To understand the reasons for, and the economic impact of, this process, it is helpful to examine both the potential benefits of government ownership and the advantages of moving to privatization.

There are six common, and sometimes interdependent, reasons for countries to control business assets, a process known as **nationalization**. These include (1) promoting economic development, such as by coordinating the assets of many businesses into one overall master plan; (2) earning profits for the national treasury; (3) preventing companies from going bankrupt and closing their doors; (4) enhancing programs that are in the national interest; (5) increasing the political or economic control of those in power; and (6) ensuring goods and services to all citizens regardless of their economic status.[5]

The opposite situation, privatization, can take two forms. The most common form is **divestiture**, in which the government sells its assets. The other is **contract management**, in which the government transfers operating responsibility of an industry without transferring the legal title and ownership. The major trend today is toward divestiture.

Some of the primary reasons for privatization are: (1) it is more efficient to have the goods and services provided by private business than by government-run companies; (2) a change in the political culture brings about a desire to sell these assets; (3) the company has been making money, and the government feels there is more to be gained by selling now than by holding on; (4) the purchase price can be used to reduce the national debt; (5) the company is losing money, and the government has to assume the losses out of the national treasury; (6) the company needs research and development funds in order to maintain a competitive stance, and it is unwilling to make this investment; and (7) international funding agencies are making assistance to the country conditional on a reduction in the size of the government.[6]

Privatization in action

Many nations have privatization programs.[7] These include countries with moderate per capita gross domestic products, such as Argentina, Brazil, Chile, Mexico, and China, as well as economically advanced nations such as the United States, Japan, Germany, and the UK. All feel that their economies can be strengthened through privatization programs.

In the case of Argentina, for example, the government has now ended the nation's phone monopoly and opened up the $10 billion market to outside investors. Previously the two

Privatization
The process of selling government assets to private buyers

Nationalization
A process by which the government takes control of business assets, sometimes with remuneration of the owners and other times without such remuneration

Divestiture
(Also see *Privatization*.) A process by which a government or business sells assets

Contract management
A process by which an organization (such as the government) transfers operating responsibility of an industry without transferring the legal title and ownership

telephone companies that monopolized all long distance and local phone services had their territories firmly established, and neither could compete with the other. Now they can. Moreover, other telephone companies also have licenses to operate throughout the country. The Argentinean government believes that, as a result of privatization in this industry, competition will increase, phone rates will drop, and service will increase sharply.[8]

In the case of the UK, privatization and deregulation have proven to be a national boon. A few years ago British Telecommunications began downsizing its operations so as to increase its competitiveness and profitability. The firm slashed 100,000 jobs, and critics said that privatization and deregulation were hurting the economy. However, just the opposite occurred. Many of the workers who were laid off began finding jobs with small telecommunications firms that were springing up throughout the country. At the same time, there was an influx of large foreign competitors such as AT&T, the giant American telecommunications company, and AB L. M. Ericsson, the Swedish telecom-equipment maker, which hired thousands of people. As a result, between 1990 and 1999 the number of jobs in the UK's telecommunications industry increased, while prices decreased and service improved sharply.[9]

Another major group of nations turning to privatization is Russia and the Eastern European countries. At the grass roots in Russia, a market economy has begun to evolve. Despite the lack of national or local laws to guide them, hundreds of small factories and service businesses are now privatizing themselves, and enterprises are pushing ahead with Russian-style versions of leveraged buyouts, employee stock ownership plans, and private spin-offs. Many are also taking their old, outmoded operations and modernizing them. A good example is the Vologda Textile Enterprise company. By significantly reducing its workforce and rebuilding the looms, the firm has found that it can sell all of the textiles it produces to buyers in the EU.[10]

Privatization is not always a popular idea, and it is often part of election debates. Yet governments continue to assess the benefits of privatization against those of state ownership. Mexico and Japan provide two recent examples. Recently the Mexican government announced that it will privatize its two national airlines, Aeroméxico and Mexicana, on the hopes that it can provide cheaper service and compete with low-cost service from the United States.[11] Despite opposition from civil servants and some political parties, Japan Post is set for a slow privatization process that is to culminate in 2017.[12]

Government–business cooperation

The fact that governments are privatizing assets does not mean they are distancing themselves from business firms. Both Japan and the EU have seen a large amount of business–government cooperation that has been extremely beneficial to the business sector in these countries.

Japan and EU assistance

Ministry of International Trade and Industry (MITI)
A Japanese ministry charged with providing information about foreign markets and with encouraging investment in select industries and, in the process, helping to direct the economy

After World War II, the Japanese government began formulating plans for regenerating its economy. In this vein, it gave responsibility for implementing the country's trade and industrial policy to the Ministry of International Trade and Industry (MITI). The initial focus of the ministry was to provide protection to Japanese companies and to assist in marketing the products of four major industries: electric power, steel, shipbuilding, and fertilizers. Incentives were created to encourage investment in these industries and to help firms export their products. In recent years, MITI's focus has been on targeting less energy-intensive industries for Japanese investment and growth. Prime examples include computers and chemicals, where MITI works cooperatively with Japanese businesses to help ensure success. The focus of MITI has changed from a proactive to a much more cooperative agency; its main role today is funding export markets for Japanese businesses.

Governments in the EU have also been very helpful in promoting businesses. One way has been to fund research consortia through research and development (R&D) support. One of the research programs that has been helped by EU governments is Research on Advanced Communications in Europe (RACE). Since the late 1980s, RACE has received billions of dollars of government money to support its efforts in developing an integrated broadband telecommunications network. Another recipient of government largesse is the European Strategic Program for R&D in Information Technology (ESPRIT II). This consortium has engaged in hundreds of projects dealing with such high-tech areas as information technologies, microelectronics, and computer-integrated manufacturing. Perhaps the best-known R&D consortium is EUREKA, a pan-European group whose main objective is to create closer cooperation between private companies and research institutes in the field of advanced technologies for the purpose of exploiting commercial opportunities. The projects that are funded bring together companies throughout the EU and involve not only large firms but also small and medium-sized enterprises. Unlike many research consortia, however, EUREKA focuses on projects whose research is now ready to be applied.[13] (See the Active Learning Case "Boeing vs. Airbus" in Chapter 3 for a closer look at government established consortia.)

The American response

The results of such governmental efforts have not been lost on Washington, which has long recognized the value of an industrial policy that provides benefits similar to those offered by MITI and EUREKA. As long ago as 1990, a special White House panel of experts from industry, academia, and the government released a list of 22 technologies that it deemed essential to US national defense and economic prosperity. Including composite materials, flexible computer-integrated manufacturing, and high-definition electronic displays, the list was intended to guide the Critical Technologies Institute, created by Congress in 1990 to conduct long-range strategic planning and to work closely with the private sector in developing important technologies.

Over the last two decades in particular, the US government has been active in supporting research consortia to help underwrite some of the costs associated with new technology development. A good example is Sematech, a consortium of 14 semiconductor manufacturing companies, which once received $100 million a year in subsidies from the US government to help shore up the chip-making equipment industry. By the mid-1990s these manufacturers were doing so well that Sematech's board voted to end federal funding, and the group is now funded entirely by private money.[14] Another consortium that has received government assistance is the National Center for Manufacturing Sciences, which has provided a host of important technology breakthroughs, including a method for hardening cutting tools by coating them with diamond film. A third has been the Microelectronics & Computer Technology Corporation, which has worked on advanced computing, software, and computer-aided design.

In the past, US administrations have supported research efforts that promoted industrial competitiveness and technological leadership. This often took one of two paths: (a) the funding of military research that could then be used to create commercially useful products; or (b) the direct funding of research efforts by American firms. The technology policy of the Bush administration is to continue the American focus on maintaining a strong, high-tech military and a world-class computer information industry.

Active learning check

Review your answer to Active Learning Case question 1 and make any changes you like. Then compare your answer with the one below.

1 What type of economic system now exists in Russia: market-driven, centrally-determined, or mixed?

A mixed system currently exists. The country is moving away from a centrally determined economy, but there is a long way to go. As can be seen from the information in the case, the transition is causing a great deal of economic upheaval. This may even result in a regression toward some of the previously employed, centrally-determined decision making. However, the country is not going to go back to the old way of doing things because it has too much committed to its current course of action. In particular, any further IMF loans or assistance from the United States, Japan, or the EU will depend on how well the country is holding the line and trying to make its market-driven economy work. So a mixed economic system will remain in place; in fact, this is really the only path the Russians can take in rescuing their economy.

ECONOMIC INTEGRATION

Economic integration
The establishment of transnational rules and regulations that enhance economic trade and co-operation among countries

Economic integration is the establishment of transnational rules and regulations that enhance economic trade and cooperation among countries. At one extreme, economic integration would result in one worldwide free trade market in which all nations had a common currency and could export anything they wanted to any other nation. At the other extreme would be a total lack of economic integration, in which nations were self-sufficient and did not trade with anyone. (The theory of these polar extremes will be discussed in Chapter 6.)

The concept of economic integration is attractive, but there are many implementation problems. In particular, it requires that the participants agree to surrender some of their national sovereignty, such as the authority to set tariffs and quotas. For example, if the United States and the EU agree to allow free trade of agricultural products, neither country can restrict the other's right to export these commodities. So although free trade may lead to lower prices, those who are unwilling to give up the right to control goods being imported into their country may well be opposed to it.

A number of regional economic efforts have been undertaken over the last 30 years to promote varying degrees of economic integration. The most successful has been the EU, although less developed countries (LDCs) have also made integration efforts.

Trade creation and trade diversion

Before examining economic integration in more depth, it is important to realize that the agreement of countries to integrate their economies will bring about a shift in business activity. This shift can result in trade creation as well as trade diversion.

Trade creation
A process in which members of an economic integration group begin to focus their efforts on those goods and services for which they have a comparative advantage and start trading more extensively with each other

Trade creation occurs when members of an economic integration group begin focusing their efforts on those goods and services for which they have a comparative advantage and start trading more extensively with each other. For example, the United States and Mexico have an agreement that allows cars to be assembled in Mexico and shipped into the United States. As a result, Mexico, a low-cost producer, supplies a large number of vehicles sold in America, and both countries prosper as a result.

Trade creation results in efficient, low-cost producers in member countries gaining market share from high-cost member producers, as well as generating increased exports. In fact, a growing number of US companies have moved some of their operations to Mexico or hired Mexican firms to be their suppliers because this is a more efficient approach than making the goods in the United States. And when efficient regional producers are able to offer lower-price and higher-quality output than their competitors, trade creation results.

Trade diversion occurs when members of an economic integration group decrease their trade with non-member countries in favor of trade with each other. One common reason is that the removal of trade barriers among member countries makes it less expensive to buy from companies within the group, and the continuation of trade barriers with non-member countries makes it more difficult for the latter to compete. Thus, trade diversion can lead to the loss of production and exports from more efficient non-member countries to less efficient member countries that are being protected by tariffs or other barriers. Quite obviously, the creation of economic integration groups is beneficial only if trade creation exceeds trade diversion. Otherwise, the economic union impedes international trade.

Trade diversion
Occurs when members of an economic integration group decrease their trade with non-member countries in favor of trade with each other

Levels of economic integration

There are five levels of economic integration, which extend from simple economic trade arrangements to full political integration characterized by a single government. The following examines each of these levels, beginning with the simplest.

Free trade area

A free trade area is an economic integration arrangement in which barriers to trade (such as tariffs) among member countries are removed. Under this arrangement, each participant will seek to gain by specializing in the production of those goods and services for which it has a comparative advantage and importing those goods and services for which it has a comparative disadvantage.

One of the best-known free trade areas is the North American Free Trade Agreement (NAFTA), which currently consists of Canada, the United States, and Mexico. The United States and Canada created this free trade area with the United States–Canadian Free Trade Agreement of 1989, and the arrangement has now been expanded to include Mexico.[15] While trade diversion can occur under free trade arrangements, NAFTA has led to a great amount of trade creation. In fact, trade among the three members of NAFTA is nearly $1 trillion annually![16]

Free trade area
An economic integration arrangement in which barriers to trade (such as tariffs) among member countries are removed

North America Free Trade Agreement (NAFTA)
A regional free trade agreement among Canada, the United States, and Mexico

Customs union

A customs union is a form of economic integration in which all tariffs between member countries are eliminated and a common trade policy toward non-member countries is established. This policy often results in a uniform external tariff structure. Under this arrangement, a country outside the union will face the same tariff on exports to any member country receiving the goods.

Under a customs union, member countries cede some of the control of their economic policies to the group at large. None of the regional integration groups in existence today has been formed for the purpose of creating a customs union; instead, many of them have sought greater integration in the form of a common market or economic union. However, because of the difficulty of attaining this high degree of integration, some countries have effectively *settled* for a customs union. The Andean Community, which will be discussed shortly, is an example.

Customs union
A form of economic integration in which all tariffs between member countries are eliminated and a common trade policy toward non-member countries is established

Common market

A common market is a form of economic integration characterized by (a) no barriers to trade among member nations, (b) a common external trade policy, and (c) mobility of factors of production among member countries. A common market allows reallocation of

Common market
A form of economic integration characterized by the elimination of trade barriers among member nations, a common external trade policy, and mobility of factors of production among member countries

production resources, such as capital, labor, and technology, based on the theory of comparative advantage. Although this may be economically disadvantageous to industries or specific businesses in some member countries, in theory it should lead to the efficient delivery of goods and services to all member countries. The best example of a successful common market is the EU, although this group has now progressed beyond a common market and is now focusing on political and financial integration.

Economic union

Economic union
A form of economic integration characterized by free movement of goods, services, and factors of production among member countries and full integration of economic policies

An **economic union** is a deep form of economic integration and is characterized by free movement of goods, services, and factors of production among member countries and full integration of economic policies. An economic union (1) unifies monetary and fiscal policy among the member nations, including the same tax rates, and (2) has a common currency (or a permanently fixed exchange rate among currencies). Additionally, most of the national economic policies of the individual countries are ceded to the group at large. There are no true economic unions in the world, but the creation of a single currency, the euro, certainly moves the EU in this direction.

Political union

Political union
An economic union in which there is full economic integration, unification of economic policies, and a single government

A **political union** goes beyond full economic integration to encompass a single government. This occurs only when countries give up their individual national powers to be united and led by one government. One successful example is the United States, which combined independent states into a political union. The EU is now also on its way to becoming a political union. The European Parliament, for example, is directly elected by citizens of the EU countries, and its Council of Ministers, which is the decision-making body of the EU, is made up of government ministers from each EU country.

Economic integration: an overall perspective

Before concluding our discussion of levels of economic integration, four points merit consideration. First, a country does not need to pursue economic integration by starting with a free trade area and then working up to a common market or an economic union. For example, Great Britain was a member of a free trade area before deciding to leave and enter the EU. Simply stated, countries will choose the appropriate level of economic integration based on their political and economic needs.

Second, economic integration in the form of free trade typically results in a winning situation for all group members, since each member can specialize in those goods and services it makes most efficiently and rely on others in the group to provide the remainder. However, when a bloc of countries imposes a tariff on non-members, this often results in a win–lose situation. Those outside the bloc face tariffs, are thus less competitive with group member companies, and lose market share and revenue within the bloc. Among group members, however, increased competition often results in greater efficiency, lower prices, and increased exports to non-member markets.

Internal economies of scale
Efficiencies brought about by lower production costs and other savings within a firm

External economies of scale
Efficiencies brought about by access to cheaper capital, highly skilled labor, and superior technology

Third, and complementary to the above, bloc members often find that their businesses are able to achieve **internal economies of scale** brought about by lower production costs and other savings. So if a company in France was only moderately efficient when producing 1,000 units a week for the French market, it is now highly efficient producing 4,000 units a week for countries throughout the EU. The elimination of tariffs and trade barriers and the opening up of new geographic markets allow the company to increase production efficiency. In addition, since factors of production in a common market are allowed to flow freely across borders, the firm may also achieve **external economies of scale** brought about by access to low-cost capital, more highly skilled labor, and superior technology. In short, in-group companies can draw on resources in member countries to help increase efficiency.

Finally, in the short run, some bloc countries may suffer because other member countries are able to achieve greater efficiency and thus dominate certain industries and markets in the bloc. The adjustment period may last as long as a decade as these less efficient countries scramble to improve their technologies, retrain their workforces, and redirect their economies to markets in the bloc where they can gain and sustain an advantage vis-à-vis other members. In the long run, however, economic integration results in all bloc countries becoming much more efficient and competitive.

Despite the logic of free trade and economic integration, many non-governmental organizations (NGOs) criticize MNEs and international institutions. We now discuss these issues. See also the box **International Business Strategy in Action: Non-governmental organizations and political power**.

Non-governmental organizations (NGOs) Private-sector groups that act to advance diverse social interests (See also *Civil society*)

Ethics, environment, MNEs, and the civil society

In December 1999, a coalition of NGOs and labor unions organized protests in Seattle that turned into riots, which hindered the launch of another round of the WTO. In July 2001, the violent riots in Genoa at the G7 Summit were another example of the work of some anti-globalization activists, mainly NGOs, attempting to prevent negotiations by world leaders.

The civil society is a group of individuals, organizations, and institutions that act outside the government and the market to advance a diverse set of interests, including opposition to global business. Demonstrations against trade and investment agreements are mainly composed of environmentalists, anti-poverty campaigners, trade unionists, and anti-capitalists that are either part of an NGO or trade union, or simply individuals that share their views.[17] The lack of a common front across these organizations has meant that, while some protestors are chanting and throwing roses, others are throwing rocks and charging at the police. The more extremist groups would like to see an end to multinationals and international trade. More moderate demonstrators would like a transformation in the rules of trade with less developed nations, debt forgiveness, and better labor and environmental standards.[18] Protestors also have different agendas. Trade unionists from developed countries are concerned about the alleged loss of jobs due to globalization, whereas human rights NGOs are much more concerned with the situation of workers in less industrialized nations.

Civil society A group of individuals, organizations, and institutions that act outside the government and the market to advance a diverse set of interests

The success of the NGOs in criticizing businesses, especially multinational enterprises (MNEs), builds on less spectacular but consistent progress in influencing the environmental agenda of international organizations. The first notable success of environmental NGOs occurred in NAFTA in 1993 when the Clinton administration inserted two side agreements on environment and labor after the first Bush administration had successfully negotiated NAFTA over the 1990–1992 period.

The UNCED Rio Summit of 1992 reflected the agenda of environmental NGOs, leading to an agreement that sets commitments but which governments have been unable to deliver on. The Kyoto Summit in 1997 resulted in the standards for reduction of greenhouse gas emissions; again, however, important economies—most notably the United States—would not meet them because of the economic and political costs of doing so.

These recent events portray the gulf between the environmental agendas of NGOs and the economic drivers of global business. How do we explain the existence of this gulf?[19] Basically, there is a traditional divide between the redistribution and equity concerns of NGOs and the economic and efficiency issues that drive business. Democratic governments in Western economies have incorporated these dual concerns in their political platforms, and, at least as part of a broader political package, voters have some say through the electoral process.

INTERNATIONAL BUSINESS STRATEGY *IN ACTION*

Non-governmental organizations and political power

When the topic of politics in the international business arena is discussed, one is likely to hear about such things as the impact of the government on international trade and the regulation of multinational enterprises (MNEs). In recent years another topic that has become more popular is the role of non-governmental organizations (NGOs) that have been gaining an increasing amount of political power.

An NGO is a non-profit organization run by volunteers with a specific mandate at a local, national, or international level. As such, NGOs take a number of different forms. Some are very large, such as the environmental group Greenpeace, the World Wildlife Fund (WWF), and Amnesty International, whereas others are smaller and less well known. NGOs' positions on international trade issues are as diverse as their mandates. For example, Oxfam, whose mandate is the long-term alleviation of poverty, suffering, and injustice, does not oppose trade itself. Indeed, it considers "fair trade" a means to achieve development in poorer countries and promotes other organizations that engage in this type of trade. The Institute for Leadership Development actively seeks to promote trade and the development of entrepreneurial skills in poorer countries. The US NGO Consumers for World Trade points out that protectionism is equivalent to a hidden tax and actively lobbies for free trade. Environmental and animal rights NGOs, on the other hand, lobby their governments and international bodies for trade rules that protect the natural environment. For example, in December 1997 at the Kyoto Summit, NGOs were instrumental in getting standards for the reduction of greenhouse gas emissions put into the agreement, even though the United States and other major economic powers refused to accept this standard because the technology was not available and the standard could not be met.

Protectionist or anti-trade, NGOs often grab the headlines. For example, the American Farm Bureau seeks to improve the financial well-being and quality of life for farmers and ranchers in the United States and opposes government policies to liberalize agricultural trade by reducing subsidies to US farmers. Yet other NGOs are more generally opposed to free trade and investment. In the 1997–1998 period, for example,

NGOs were extremely effective in defeating the Multilateral Agreement on Investment (MAI). The MAI was designed to make it illegal for signatory states to discriminate against foreign investors and to liberalize rules governing foreign domestic investment among the members of the Organization for Economic Cooperation and Development. NGOs contributed to riots in Seattle in December 1999 and violent clashes with the police in Genoa in July 2001. The NGOs influenced the Clinton administration to add two side agreements to NAFTA: setting up an environmental body in Montreal and a labor standard body in Dallas. In a nutshell, these NGOs managed to work outside the NAFTA agreement to get provisions incorporated into the overall contract. In the process, they showed that NGOs were becoming an important force in the international political arena.

Notwithstanding the variety of views emanating from NGOs, a select group is portraying MNEs as big, bad, and ugly. But is it an accurate portrayal? Starbucks, for instance, has been heavily criticized for not selling fair trade coffee, yet it directly pays farmers a price higher than that received by farmers involved in fair trading. Being the best-known brand in North America was enough to make it the target of NGOs. In general, MNEs improve the well-being of workers across the world while manufacturing goods and providing services that improve the quality of life of consumers around the world. Given its rise in popularity over the last five years, NGOs are likely to be the focus of continuing interest by both international business analysts and local voters.

Websites: www.greenpeace.org; www.oxfam.org; www.fb.org; www.cwt.org; www.starbucks.com; and www.oecd.org.

Sources: James Harding, "Activists Plan Ocean-borne Protests for WTO Meeting," *Financial Times*, September 11, 2001, p.1; Edward M. Graham, *Fighting the Wrong Enemy: Antiglobal Activists and Multinational Enterprises* (Washington, DC: Institute for International Economics, 2000); Alan M. Rugman, *The End of Globalization* (London: Random House, 2000); Sylvia Ostry, "The Multilateral Trading System," in Alan M. Rugman and Thomas Brewer (eds.), *The Oxford Handbook of International Business* (Oxford: Oxford University Press, 2000), pp. 232–258; Robert Weissman, "Why We Protest," *Washington Post*, September 10, 2003.

Complementary to the NGOs' perspective on international trade and investment is the intellectual failure of academic theory, in which the twin basic paradigms of economics and politics are found to develop explanations of today's global economy and the nature of foreign direct investment (FDI). In economics, the traditional efficiency-based neoclassical paradigm (with its associated theory of comparative advantages and the overall country gains from free trade) is unsuitable as an explanation of FDI. Despite the efforts by international business writers over the last 30 years to develop a modern theory of the multinational enterprise, most economists are unable to accept this explanation of the reasons for FDI. As a consequence, the GATT and WTO have developed institutional frameworks to deal with the "shallow" integration of tariff cuts, but have failed to deal with the "deep" integration of FDI.

Related to the out-of-date economics paradigm of free trade is the political science focus on the nation state. Despite minor modifications to nation state paradigms, such as to incorporate subnational units in decision making, there is a limited buy-in to the alternative International Political Economy (IPE) viewpoint. Indeed, there is another unfortunate parallel between economics and political science in that both sets of work on the role and power of the MNE have failed to change the out-of-date thinking of the majority of academics, despite the abundant evidence of the relevance of MNEs and the global economic and political systems of today. The NGOs have slipped into this vacuum with their view of MNEs as big, bad, and ugly. The NGO thinking is now more influential with governments in North America and Europe than is the work of serious academic scholars working on MNEs.[20]

The issue here is one of process. There is an "administrative heritage" of ideas. Today's media are poorly trained in economics, politics, and international business. Those few who have any training are usually victims of the out-of-date paradigms of traditional economics and political science, which cannot explain FDI and the MNEs. The MBAs of business schools, who are now exposed to the new thinking on MNEs, are in business rather than the media. The professional intermediaries, such as management consultants, focus on their business or government clients rather than the media, and their very skills of confidential advice and in-house retraining make them poor advocates compared to the NGOs. Finally, the civil service is basically useless in dealing publicly with anti-trade NGOs as bureaucrats attempt to support and influence ministers and other officials rather than entering into the public forum. This institutional failure of academics, consultants, and bureaucrats to prepare a credible case for initiatives such as the Multilateral Agreement on Investment (MAI) and be able to debate it publicly leaves the field open to NGOs.

During negotiations for the MAI, Canadian anti-globalization activists equated NAFTA's Chapter 11 provisions with investor protection mechanisms under MAI. Chapter 11 allows a company to sue national governments in trade matters that contravene NAFTA's principles. The provision had been used by Ethyl, an American company, to overturn a Canadian import ban on MMT, a gasoline additive that was deemed a health hazard. The Canadian Minister of the Environment could have averted litigation by banning the production of MMT as an environmental hazard, an internal matter subject to national law, but she ignored the advice of her bureaucrats and applied trade measures that came under the NAFTA. Several subsequent NAFTA Chapter 11 cases have been resolved on technical grounds with no loss of sovereignty to host nations in their environmental policies. The MAI had similar provisions to protect investors, which led to it being labeled a "NAFTA on steroids" by anti-globalization activists.

Edward Graham has exploded the myth that anti-global activists defeated the MAI.[21] Graham concludes that the draft MAI was a very weak document. In fact, the investment liberalization being negotiated in the MAI was so weak that the US business community stopped supporting it long before anti-global activists started to protest against it in Paris. There was also a lack of leadership by the US government, tepid support in the EU, and eventually hostility to the MAI by the French government of Lionel Jospin, who was dependent on left wing "green" support in his political coalition.

Perhaps what the MMT case really illustrates is the "dialogue of the deaf" taking place between trade experts and activists. The latter used the MMT case in a general assault on the MAI and on subsequent international trade and investment liberalization initiatives at the WTO and G7 summits. Graham argues that, as a consequence, the environmental

NGOs missed the boat. He states that trade negotiators were open and willing to incorporate environmental concerns into the MAI but that violent opposition to it has now closed the window for cooperation between NGOs and governments.

Any more Seattles and Genoas, with the attendant violence, however, will probably alienate the general public from the anti-capitalist agenda of the more extreme anti-global activists. This small and over-publicized section of the NGO movement, with its apparent opposition to reforming global governance mechanisms, continues to protest violently against MNEs. Eventually, the most serious NGOs, such as WWF and Oxfam, must disassociate themselves from these violent activists in order to push forward a more sensible cooperative reformist agenda for civil society.

The European Union (EU)

After World War II, Europe needed to be rebuilt and economic cooperation among these countries was paramount. One of the earliest and most successful cooperative endeavors was the 1952 creation of the European Coal and Steel Community (ECSC) for the purpose of creating a common market that would revitalize the efficiency and competitiveness of these industries. Six countries (Belgium, France, Italy, Luxembourg, the Netherlands, and West Germany) created the ECSC, and its success set the stage for the creation of what would eventually become the European Union.

Formation

The foundation of the European Union was laid in 1957 by the Treaty of Rome. The six nations that created the ECSC were the original founders of what was initially called the European Economic Community (EEC) and later the European Community (EC). By 1991 six other nations had joined the EC (United Kingdom, Denmark, Greece, Ireland, Portugal, and Spain)—and in 1995 with the admission of Austria, Finland, and Sweden, the EC was renamed the European Union. In 2004, ten new members joined the EU: Cyprus, Czech Republic, Estonia, Hungary, Latvia, Lithuania, Malta, Poland, Slovakia, and Slovenia. Today the EU is a major economic group, and a growing number of countries have applied for admission.[22] The main provisions of the founding treaty of 1957 were:

1 Formation of a free trade area among the members would be brought about by the gradual elimination of tariffs, quotas, and other trade barriers.

2 Barriers to the movement of labor, capital, and business enterprises would eventually be removed.

3 Common agricultural policies would be adopted.

4 An investment fund to channel capital from the more advanced regions of the bloc to the less advanced regions would be created.

5 A customs union characterized by a uniform tariff schedule applicable to imports from the rest of the world would be created.

Some of the countries that were not members of the initial EEC felt that the objectives of this group went beyond what they were willing to do, but they did feel that a free trade agreement would be good for their own economies. As a result, these nations formed the European Free Trade Association (EFTA), whose primary goal was to dismantle trade barriers among its members. Austria, Denmark, Norway, Portugal, Sweden, Switzerland, and the UK were the founding members. In time the distinctions between EFTA and the EC blurred, however, and some of the members (Austria, Denmark, Portugal, Sweden, and the UK) eventually joined the EC. Moreover, in 1992 EFTA signed a treaty that formally gives

European Coal and Steel Community (ECSC)
A community formed in 1952 by Belgium, France, Italy, Luxembourg, the Netherlands, and West Germany for the purpose of creating a common market that would revitalize the efficiency and competitiveness of the coal and steel industries in those countries

European Union (EU)
A treaty-based institutional framework that manages economic and political cooperation among its 25 member states: Austria, Belgium, Cyprus, Czech Republic, Denmark, Estonia, France, Finland, Germany, Greece, Hungary, Ireland, Italy, Latvia, Lithuania, Luxembourg, Malta, the Netherlands, Poland, Portugal, Slovakia, Slovenia, Spain, Sweden, and the UK

European Free Trade Association (EFTA)
A free trade area currently consisting of Iceland, Liechtenstein, Norway, and Switzerland; past members included the UK (before it joined the EU). There are now 25 member states of the EU

its members an economic association with the EU. Today EFTA members include Iceland, Liechtenstein, Norway, and Switzerland.

Growth and challenges

Over the years, the EU has made vigorous headway in pursuit of its objectives. For example, during the 1970s formal barriers to the free flow of labor and capital were gradually dismantled. The Single European Act (SEA), which effectively prevents a country from veto-ing any EU decision it deems to be in conflict with its vital interests, was enacted in the 1980s. In the past this veto power had often been used by EU members to protect their respective economic advantages, making it difficult for the group to make decisions. Now most decisions are based on a total of 321 votes allocated among the 25 members, with 72.3 per cent of votes to pass a proposal.

Other major breakthroughs are occurring in the political and financial areas. With the EC 1992 measures, the EU has transformed itself into a political, economic, and monetary superpower that can speak with one powerful voice about everything from interest rates to defense. By moving in this direction, the EU political leaders negotiated and implemented a method for ratifying two new treaties that would extend the community's powers from their present largely economic role to foreign and security policy and monetary affairs and, eventually, to defense.[23] The EU's integration is now consolidating its financial and monetary system, which will facilitate the free flow of capital. Recently, a single European currency, the euro, was introduced to replace national currencies. Closely linked to this is the establishment of a central European bank that regulates the money supply and is thus able to stabilize interest rates throughout the EU. The effect of these actions may well be the creation of a "United States of Europe."

However, the EU still faces a number of problems. One is disagreement among the members regarding the relationship that should exist between the community and the rest of the world. A second problem is the protection that countries give to their own industries, which is in direct contrast to the spirit of EU rules. A related area is the community's agriculture policies, which provide subsidies and rebates to farmers and have resulted in charges of unfair trade practices. A third problem is the disagreement among the members regarding the amount of protection that poorer countries should be given before all trade barriers are dismantled. Even if all goals are not fully attained in the next decade, the EU is going to be an increasingly powerful economic force in the international arena. A close look at the community's organizational arrangement helps to explain why.

Organization

Six major institutions manage the EU: the European Council, the Council of the European Union, the European Commission, the European Parliament, the Court of Justice, and the Court of Auditors. (See Figure 4.1.) A brief description of each of these is set out below.

The European Council is composed of the heads of state of each EU member country as well as the president of the European Commission. The Council meets at least twice a year, and each head of state is typically accompanied to these meetings by a foreign minister. The purpose of the meetings is to resolve major policy issues and to set policy direction.

The Council of the European Union is the major policy decision-making body of the EU. Decisions are conducted by the relevant ministers from each country. If the environment is on the agenda, the 25 Environment Ministers from each EU country will compose the council. This body is responsible for all final EU decisions, except for the budget.

The European Commission has 25 members who are chosen by agreement of the member governments. Each country presently has one member. When Bulgaria and Romania join the union, the number of members will be decreased, and a rotation will be introduced so

Single European Act (SEA)
An act passed by the EU that contains many measures to further integrate the member states, along economic and political dimensions, and that allows the Council of Ministers to pass most proposals by a majority vote, in contrast to the unanimous vote that was needed previously

European Council
Composed of the heads of state of each EU member country as well as the president of the European Commission. Meetings of the Council take place at least twice a year and their purpose is to resolve major policy issues and to set policy direction

Council of the European Union
The major policy decision-making body of the EU; it consists of one minister from each of the 25 member states and is one of four major institutions of the EU

European Commission
A 25-member group chosen by agreement of member governments of the EU; the Commission is the executive branch of the EU

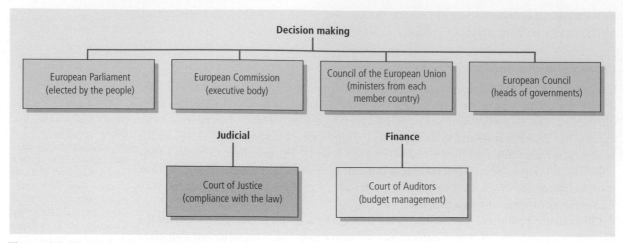

Figure 4.1 The European Union's institutions

that not all countries will have representation at a given time. The Commission, the executive branch of the EU, handles a great deal of the technical work associated with preparing decisions and regulations. The group is responsible for drafting legislation for proposal to the Council of the European Union, overseeing the implementation of EU policies, and carrying out studies on key policy issues.

European Parliament
A group of 732 representatives elected directly by voters in each member country of the EU; the Parliament serves as a watchdog on EU expenditures

Court of Justice
A court that has one judge appointed from each EU member country; this court serves as the official interpreter of EU law

Court of Auditors
A court that has one judge appointed from each EU member country; this court monitors the financial aspects of the union

The European Parliament currently has 732 members elected directly by the voters in each member country. In 2007, when representatives from Bulgaria and Romania are incorporated, this number will rise to 786. The Parliament serves as a watchdog on EU expenditures in addition to evaluating other decisions of the Council. More recently, the power of the Parliament has been expanded; it now has the right to vote on the appointment of commissioners as well as to veto matters related to the EU budget and single-market legislation.

The Court of Justice has one judge appointed from each EU member country and serves as the official interpreter of EU law. In most cases this requires the judges to rule on the meaning or application of the Treaty of Rome, based on the actions of member countries, companies, and individuals. The Court of Justice has supremacy over national law, and as a result it is increasingly being used as a court of appeal over national decisions.

The Court of Auditors has one judge appointed from each EU member country and is responsible for ensuring that revenues and expenditures are implemented lawfully in accordance to the budget.

The future

The EU is a powerful economic union. Empirical studies show that the community has created much more trade than it has diverted from the rest of the world. Moreover, this market has a greater combined gross domestic product than either of the two other triad major markets: North America and industrialized Asia. At the same time it is likely that EU-generated projects will offer major competition to other worldwide industries. For example, Airbus Industries, as seen in Chapter 3, is now a major force in the world aircraft manufacturing industry. Quite clearly, the EU promises tremendous economic gains for member countries.

Other examples of economic integration

While the EU is the most successful economic union, there are a host of others. The following briefly examines four of these.

Andean Community

The Andean Community is a customs union that was formed in 1969 with the signing of the Andean Pact by Bolivia, Chile, Colombia, Ecuador, and Peru. Today, Venezuela is a member, and Chile has withdrawn. The five members have a collective GDP of over 250 billion and 120 million inhabitants. The union is also known as Comunidad Andina (CAN) or Andean Community (Ancom). The original objectives of the CAN countries were to integrate themselves economically, to reduce internal tariffs, to create a common external tariff, and to offer special concessions to the two smallest members, Bolivia and Ecuador. Initial restrictions that curtailed foreign investment led to Chile leaving the union. These restrictions have now been removed at the CAN level, but the legislation yields to individual national governments on the matter. Except for Peru, which is slowly removing its tariffs, the Andean Community is a customs union in which goods can travel free of duty among member states.

Andean Community
An economic union consisting of Bolivia, Colombia, Ecuador, Peru, and Venezuela

Mercosur

Mercosur is a free trade group that was formed by Argentina and Brazil in 1988 to promote economic cooperation. Today the group has been expanded to include Paraguay and Uruguay, with Chile, Bolivia, and Peru as associate members. In 1995 the members agreed to a five-year program under which they hoped to perfect their free trade area and move toward a full customs union. However, things have not worked out very well in recent years. The group members have been unable to agree on a common agenda and each seems to be striking out in a different direction. For example, Argentina imposed tariffs on Brazilian televisions, shoes, and other goods; Brazil does not recognize Argentina's food-quality standards; and external tariffs are often double charged.[24] In 2004, Mercosur and the Andean Community agreed in principle to work toward a "South American Community of Nations" that will encompass 360 million people and a GDP of $1 trillion. First, however, these countries must resolve their differences.[25]

Mercosur
A free trade group that includes Argentina, Brazil, Uruguay, and Paraguay

ASEAN

The Association of Southeast Asian Nations (ASEAN) was founded in 1967 and now includes Brunei Darussalam, Cambodia, Indonesia, Laos, Malaysia, Myanmar, the Philippines, Singapore, Thailand, and Vietnam. This economic bloc is different from most others in that the primary emphasis is not on reducing trade barriers among the members, although this has been done with the agreement on the ASEAN Free Trade Area (AFTA), but rather on promoting exports to other countries. Members have been particularly successful in promoting exports to the Japanese market and to the EU. Until the late 1990s members of ASEAN experienced rapid economic growth, thanks in no small part to the efficiency and productivity of their members as well as to their impressive marketing skills.

Association of Southeast Asian Nations (ASEAN)
An economic union founded in 1967 that includes Brunei Darussalam, Cambodia, Indonesia, Laos, Malaysia, Myanmar, the Philippines, Singapore, Thailand and Vietnam; this economic bloc focuses not on reducing trade barriers among members but, rather, on promoting exports to other nations

FTAA

The Free Trade Area of the Americas (FTAA) was re-launched in Quebec City in April 2001. All the economies of North, Central, and South America, along with all Caribbean economies (except for Cuba), agreed in principle to start the FTAA in 2005. While the US Congress approved the CAFTA in July 2005, the larger FTAA is in limbo. One main problem is that Latin American countries are weary of entering the agreement if it does not involve the elimination of US agricultural subsidies. The US objective for the FTAA is to build on the framework of NAFTA, discussed in Chapters 6 and 20 in detail.

The Free Trade Area of the Americas (FTAA)
A free trade agreement of the Americas that has not yet been implemented

Active learning check

Review your answer to Active Learning Case question 2 and make any changes you like. Then compare your answer to the one below.

2 Would Russia benefit by gaining admission to one of the major economic unions such as the EU? Why?

Russia certainly would benefit by gaining admission to an economic union such as the EU. It could then take advantage of a wide variety of benefits, including free movement of goods and services across borders, trade creation, the possible development of internal economies brought about by the huge market that would then be available for Russian goods, and a strengthening of the nation's currency. Of course, admission to the EU or one of the other major economic unions is unlikely to occur, at least within the next few years as the country is not stable. However, it would offer a very big boost to the nation's economy.

ECONOMIC INTEGRATION AND STRATEGIC MANAGEMENT

How can MNEs use strategic management planning to benefit from worldwide economic integration efforts? A number of steps are proving to be helpful, particularly the use of strategic alliances, acquisitions, and the localization of business operations.

Strategic alliances and acquisitions

One of the most common ways of benefiting from economic integration is by creating a strategic alliance, often in the form of a joint venture, with other firms that can provide important forms of assistance. The following examines the use of strategic alliances and acquisitions in the telecommunications and electronics industry and acquisitions in the brewery business.

Telecommunications and electronics

Over the past decade the telecommunications industry has been expanding in terms of both products and geographic coverage. This development represents the convergence of four distinct industries: telephone, mass media (print, broadcast, and cable), consumer electronics, and computers. The result has been a growing number of products and services such as cellular phones, personal computers, and televisions that are able to interact with each other in both receiving and transmitting information. In addition, the industry has become even more competitive and complex with the advent of wireless networks. In an effort to take advantage of these developments, a number of firms in the industry are relying on strategic alliances.[26]

Strategic alliance
A business relationship in which two or more companies work together to achieve a collective advantage

A **strategic alliance** is a business relationship in which two or more companies work together to achieve a collective advantage. These alliances can take a number of forms. In some cases companies jointly conduct research or combine their efforts to market a product. In other instances they will license a firm to produce and sell a particular product in a specific market region. In the telecommunications industry, strategic alliances have been very important because of the high investment and the need to attain market penetration. A good example is provided by Concert, which is a strategic alliance composed of AT&T and British Telecommunications. Concert provides voice and data telecom services to multinational corporations and individual users through a network of distributors. It is also interested in increasing its global market presence, as seen by its recent decision to buy a 30 per cent stake in Japan Telecom.

Another example of a strategic alliance is provided by Lucent Technologies, which merged its consumer phone unit with that of Philips Electronics NV so that the two could produce a wide range of products, from corded and cordless telephones to answering machines to many types of digital cellular phones. This arrangement gave Philips's consumer phone business a strong boost while helping Lucent, which is very strong in network gear, high-tech chips, and software used in switches and phones, but which has been having trouble in the face of stiff competition from European suppliers.[27]

Yet another example is that of Microsoft and Sony, which teamed up to link personal computers and consumer electronics devices, thus moving closer together on technology standards for digital television and other consumer products. The two firms also endorsed a technology that can connect videocassette recorders, camcorders, personal computers, and other devices. Microsoft's objective in this alliance was to license the networking technology software from Sony to use with versions of an operating system that it was trying to standardize for non-personal computer (PC) products. The objective of the joint venture was to create a technology by which consumers could plug a camcorder easily to a PC or television set-top box for sending video mail over the Internet.[28]

Breweries

Not all strategic alliances and joint ventures involve giant multinationals. Many brewers have found, to their regret, that it is difficult to get customers to change brands. This is particularly true in countries such as Germany, England, and the Netherlands, where beer is popular. Customers are often fiercely loyal to local brands, and the only way of tapping into these markets is by purchasing the brewery. Major European brewers have long realized this and have not hesitated to buy operations in other countries. A good example is the purchase of La Cruz del Campo, Spain's largest brewery, by Britain's Guinness. However, the company has a long way to go before it will catch Heineken, which for years has been buying small brewers on the continent, a strategy now being emulated by large American competitors.

Localization of business operations

MNEs cannot conduct business overseas in the same way they do at home. They have to target their offerings carefully to the needs of the regional and local customer. These efforts result in the localization of business operations and typically focus on four areas: products, profits, production, and management.[29]

Localization of products

The localization of products requires the development, manufacturing, and marketing of goods best suited to the needs of the local customer and marketplace. This typically requires the modification of products that have sold well in other geographic regions. For example, in North America buyers use motorcycles primarily for leisure and sports, so they look for high horsepower output and speed. In contrast, Southeast Asians use motorcycles as a basic means of transportation, so they look for low cost and ease of maintenance; and in Australia, where shepherds use motorcycles to drive sheep, low-speed torque is more important than either high speed or ease of maintenance.[30]

MNEs commonly localize production by investing in research and development, so they can make the product that fits the specific needs of that market. This is sometimes more difficult than it appears, especially if the MNE has been successful with a product in the home market and is unwilling to change. A good example is provided by the Whirlpool

Corporation, which dominated the US market before going to Europe in the late 1980s. Believing that the giant $20 billion European appliance market with its dozens of marginally profitable companies was on the verge of consolidation, Whirlpool wanted to be one of the major players. So it bought a majority stake in a struggling appliance operation belonging to NV Philips, the Dutch electronics giant, and acquired the rest of the operation two years later for $1.1 billion. Whirlpool believed that the European market was highly regionalized because there were so many diverse consumer preferences. For example, the Swedish liked galvanized washers that could withstand salty air; the British washed their clothes more often than many others, so they wanted quieter washing machines; and so on. Stoves provided even greater examples of product diversity. However, Whirlpool believed that the market was ready for product consolidation, and therefore lent its support to a "world washer," a single machine that could be sold anywhere on the Continent. As product diversity was reduced, Whirlpool believed, the marginal producers would be driven from the market and its own share would climb. What the company found was that the European market was a lot more competitive than it realized. Sweden's AB Electrolux and Germany's Bosch-Siemens Hausgeraete GmbH proved to be excellent competitors. In particular, they revamped their factories and drove costs down sharply. They also began introducing new products that kept customers coming back. By thus appealing to local tastes, Electrolux and Bosch-Siemens managed to keep Whirlpool's profits to a minimum, while preventing it from gaining market share.[31]

Localization of profits

Localization of profits
The reinvestment of earnings in the local market

Localization of profits is the reinvestment of earnings in the local market. MNEs do this by taking their earnings and using them to expand operations, set up new plants and offices, hire more local people, and make the investment more self-sufficient. In the United States, for example, Honda started out with an initial investment of $250,000 and has gradually reinvested its US profits. Today the company has almost $2 billion in its motorcycle, auto, and engine manufacturing plants in Ohio. At the same time it has reinvested almost $200 million in Honda Canada, a manufacturing plant making Honda Civics.

Localization of production

Localization of production
The manufacturing of goods in the host market

Localization of production involves the manufacture of goods in the host market.[32] Many MNEs, upon entering a foreign market, handle this function by exporting from the home country. For a successful relationship, however, this is often only a short-run strategy and is eventually replaced by a local manufacturing base.[33] One strategy for localizing production is to increase the amount of local content in the product by making more and more of the subunits in the host country. The ultimate step, of course, is to produce the entire product locally. Honda, for example, decided back in the late 1980s to turn its Ohio auto manufacturing facility into a fully integrated, self-reliant entity. The plan involved a number of steps, including increasing the plant's production capacity so that it would be able to turn out 500,000 units annually and build them with at least 75 per cent domestic content. In the process, Honda localized its production.

The same is true for Toyota. The company increased the capacity of its Georgetown, Kentucky, plant from 380,000 units annually to 500,000 units and doubled its Corolla production to 200,000 units at its Ontario, Canada, facility. It also doubled the production capacity of its Burnaston, England, plant and increased auto production in its Thailand factory, while negotiating with the government to build an engine factory in Tianjin, China.[34]

Another way to localize production is to provide added value in operations by modifying the imported product and adapting it to local conditions and tastes. This approach is used when a product requires country-by-country (or regional) changes. Auto manufacturers, for example, take into account the terrain (unpaved roads require stronger underbody construction), the cost of gasoline (high costs often mean that the market wants smaller, more efficient cars), and which side of the road everyone drives on (right in the United States and Latin America; left in the UK and Asia).

The localization of production is often carried out in conjunction with a home country partner, which provides the plant and personnel while the MNE is responsible for the initial product and the technology needed in assembling or modifying the goods. Sometimes, however, the MNE will own the entire operation and depend on local management to help run the organization.

Localization of management

There are a number of ways for MNEs to localize management. One is by encouraging home office managers to learn the local culture and become part of the community. Research reveals that companies that staff their subsidiaries with older, mature senior managers from the home country who are fluent in the local language are often more highly productive than MNEs that staff operations with younger, less experienced managers.[35] A second way of localizing management is by delegating authority to host country managers and developing and promoting these employees wherever possible. This strategy helps to create a bond between the host and the home country management. As one MNE spokesperson put it:

> . . . we have become convinced that good communication between management and labor, as well as delegation of authority, elevate the employees' sense of participation in decision making. This, in turn, gives the employees a stronger sense of responsibility and motivation, which leads to improved productivity and maintenance of high-quality standards.[36]

 Active learning check

Review your answer to Active Learning Case question 3 and make any changes you like. Then compare your answer with the one below.

3 **Is Russia a good potential investment for Western business? Explain.**

Arguments can be made on each side. Untapped natural resources and potential consumer demand could provide billions of dollars of annual sales for investing companies. On the other hand, the economy is in terrible shape, and it is likely to take years before Russia begins to provide an acceptable return on investment for many current projects. One of the major reasons for getting in now, of course, is to try to gain a strong foothold in the market and effectively block future competition. If this should happen, those coming later would find slim pickings. However, this potential benefit is unlikely to attract many investors. Most are likely to conclude that the best strategy is to proceed with caution and wait for the current uncertainty and turmoil to settle.

KEY POINTS

1 Political ideologies and economic systems are interwoven. Democracies tend to have market-driven economies; totalitarian governments tend to have centrally-determined economies. However, few nations fit totally into one of these two paradigms. Most use a mixed economic model such as that of the United States, which is mainly a market-driven economy with some central planning, or China, which still relies on central planning but is moving to allow some degree of free enterprise.

2 Another current economic development is the trend toward privatization. Many countries are selling their state-owned enterprises. A variety of reasons can be cited for these actions.

In most cases these are economic in nature, including (a) increased efficiency, (b) reduction in government outlays, and (c) generation of funds for the national treasury.

3 Economic integration is the establishment of transnational rules and regulations that permit economic trade and cooperation among countries. Effective integration brings about trade creation, although in some cases these efforts result in trade diversion. There are five levels of regional economic trade integration: free trade areas, customs unions, common markets, economic unions, and political unions. The most successful examples have been the EU and the NAFTA. Some NGOs criticize such trade and investment agreements.

4 NGOs are an important new actor on the stage of international business, and MNEs need to take account of the civil society in their strategies.

5 Multinational enterprises use a variety of strategies to benefit from integration efforts. One is strategic alliances and acquisitions with which they are able to scale the economic wall and gain an inside position in the economic alliance or free trade area. The other is through the localization of operations by focusing on products, profits, production, and management. MNEs typically use both of these strategic approaches.

Key terms

- ideology
- democracy
- totalitarianism
- communism
- theocratic totalitarianism
- secular totalitarianism
- market-driven economy
- centrally-determined economy
- mixed economies
- privatization
- nationalization
- divestiture
- contract management
- Ministry of International Trade and Industry (MITI)
- economic integration
- trade creation
- trade diversion

- free trade area
- North American Free Trade Agreement (NAFTA)
- customs union
- common market
- economic union
- political union
- internal economies of scale
- external economies of scale
- non-governmental organizations (NGOs)
- civil society
- European Coal and Steel Community (ECSC)
- European Union (EU)
- European Free Trade Association (EFTA)

- Single European Act (SEA)
- European Council
- Council of the European Union
- European Commission
- European Parliament
- Court of Justice
- Court of Auditors
- Andean Community
- Mercosur
- Association of Southeast Asian Nations (ASEAN)
- Free Trade Area of the Americas (FTAA)
- strategic alliance
- localization of profits
- localization of production

REVIEW AND DISCUSSION QUESTIONS

1 As political systems change, economic systems follow. What does this statement mean?

2 How does a centrally-determined economy differ from a market-driven economy? Explain.

3 What are the benefits of privatization? Why will the trend toward privatization continue?

4 Why are government–business cooperative efforts beginning to increase? What benefits do they offer?

5 What is the purpose of research consortia? What is their future likely to be? Why?

6 How does trade creation differ from trade diversion? Compare and contrast the two.

7 There are five levels of economic integration. What is meant by this statement? Be complete in your answer.

8 How does the EU function? Identify and describe its organization and operation.

9 What is the purpose of the following economic alliances: the Andean Community, Mercosur, and ASEAN?

10 Some of the primary ways that MNEs use strategic planning to benefit from economic integration efforts is through strategic alliances and acquisitions. How do MNEs do this?

11 How do MNEs seek to localize their business operations? Describe three steps that they take.

REAL CASE

How environmental regulations can be used as trade barriers

With free trade areas evolving around the globe, many protected industries are now facing unwelcome competition. Free trade agreements generally include a principle of national treatment under which a country must treat all producers, domestic or foreign, equally. However, some seemingly neutral environmental regulations pose a greater burden on foreign producers than on their domestic competitors. Thus, they act as trade barriers under the disguise of environmental regulations.

For example, while environmental groups lobby for newsprint to contain a determined amount of recycled material and domestic producers of newsprint support the regulation, foreign newsprint companies, which have no recycling facilities in the host country, face a competitive disadvantage. This is what has been called a "Baptist-bootlegger" coalition. During the US prohibition era, Baptists were opposed to alcoholic consumption on moral grounds, while bootleggers actually benefited from prohibition by the sale of illegal alcoholic beverages. Today, environmental groups and domestic producers often form coalitions to promote their respective interests.

In the newsprint case, the foreign company would have two options if it were to continue to supply material from its home country. It could either open recycling plants in the host country and transport pulp from its own country to be processed there so as to meet the environmental regulations, or take the recycling material to its home country to be processed. Both alternatives would pose significant transportation costs to the foreign producer.

A similar case is presented by the Ontario Beer Can Tax. In the early 1990s the province of Ontario levied a tax of $0.10 on each aluminum beer can. The province argued that these cans were not environmentally friendly and that the tax was designed to encourage the use of re-fillable glass bottles. US producers of beer and aluminum cans contended that this was a protectionist move and that the Ontario government was singling out the competition with its beer industry since it had no similar tax for soft drinks and juice cans. Moreover, research studies found that aluminum cans and glass bottles both have the same effect on the environment, and that 80 per cent of all the cans were being recycled. They also found that the larger, heavier glass required more energy to transport than did the lighter aluminum cans.

Sources: Adapted from Alan M. Rugman, John Kirton and Julie Soloway, *Environmental Regulations and Corporate Strategy: A NAFTA Perspective* (Oxford: Oxford University Press, 1999); M. Trebilcock and R. Howse, "Trade Policy and Domestic Health and Safety Standards," *The Regulation of International Trade*, 2nd ed. (London: Routledge, 1999); Julie Soloway, "Environmental Trade Barriers in NAFTA: The MMT Fuel Additives Controversy," *Minnesota Journal of Global Trade*, vol. 8, no. 1, 1998; David Vogel and Alan M. Rugman, "Environmentally Related Trade Disputes between the United States and Canada," *The American Review of Canadian Studies*, Summer 1997, pp. 271–292.

1 How can a health and safety regulation become a trade barrier? Provide examples.

2 How can different environmental circumstances make one country's regulations inefficient in another country?

3 What are some reasons why the government might not be willing to make allowances for different countries?

REAL CASE

Embraer vs. Bombardier

Bombardier and Embraer compete in the mid-size plane market, the luxury jet market, and the military aircraft market. In 2004, both companies announced plans for bigger planes. Sixty-one per cent of all flights in the United States take off with a higher number of passengers than either of their planes normally accommodated. Indeed, analysts believe that there has historically been a lack of flexibility from the two largest players, Boeing and Airbus, in supplying this category of aircraft.

In 1942 the dreams of a budding young Quebec entrepreneur came true with the incorporation of L'Auto-Neige Bombardier, the world's first snowmobile manufacturer. Although the mechanic-turned-industrialist Joseph Armand Bombardier had great plans for his innovative transportation inventions, he could never have foreseen the course his company would take in the next 50 years. Today, Bombardier is one of the world's top manufacturers of transportation products, including trains and planes, with yearly revenues of over CDN$21.3 billion (US$16 billion) and 64,600 employees.

Bombardier's success is in no small part the responsibility of CEO Laurent Beaudoin, who in the past 30 years has followed a strategy of market entry and product improvement through acquisition, instead of relying strictly on R&D. This strategy has been exemplified by Bombardier's entry into the aerospace industry with the acquisition of Canadair in 1986.

In 1991, Bombardier took a risk on the undeveloped market of regional jets, which quickly paid off. Airlines could offer more short-haul flights at a more reasonable price at a time when airport hubs were overcrowded. Bombardier enjoyed a virtual monopoly on this airplane category until Embraer came along.

The beginnings of Embraer are very different. Founded in 1969 by a Brazilian military dictatorship, Embraer made its name building high-quality military and civilian aircraft. The planes were so expensive, however, that no one wanted to buy them, and for years the company lost millions in revenue. Then in 1994 it was privatized and given to Mauricio Botelho to turn around. He has. In 1995, the company launched a family of regional jets that were warmly received by US and European airlines. By 2004, Embraer had about half of the market; its sales reached $2.1 billion and were expected to increase by over 70 per cent in the next two years.

Because direct subsidies by governments to domestic firms are illegal at the WTO, each company has attempted to obtain WTO approval on trade sanctions against its competitor. Canada filed a complaint over Brazilian subsidies to Embraer. Brazil countered with its own complaint over Canadian subsidies to Bombardier. Both countries were successful, and today they both have a green light to impose sanctions on each other. This is unlikely to happen, however, as it would strain bilateral relations between the two nations. Instead, both countries are seeking some form of a compromise.

Both companies argue that the other has an unfair advantage. Bombardier, argues Embraer, has access to top-of-the-line technology and low-interest loans from being located in an industrialized country. Embraer, argues Bombardier, has access to cheap labor and benefits from a weak currency. The initial WTO complaint was based on low-interest loans to Embraer customers by Proex, a Brazilian agency set up to promote exports. In addition to the price of an Embraer plane being lower by about $3 million, its customers could save even more by getting one of these loans. Brazil's complaint cited subsidies from the Canadian government to three small airlines as an incentive to purchase Bombardier planes.

Now that the WTO has ruled against both countries, instead of applying punitive tariffs, Brazil and Canada are seeking to negotiate an agreement. Both have amended their subsidies. In a growing market with increased regional flights, aging planes, and expected growth in developing countries, a trade war must be averted. At stake are negotiations for the Free Trade Area of the Americas (FTAA). Indeed, the airplane dispute highlights the difficulties facing countries from the developed North and the developing South.

Websites: www.bombardier.com; www.embraer.com; and www.boeing.com.

Sources: Rita Kolselka, "Let's Make a Deal," *Forbes*, April 27, 1992, pp. 62–63; Clyde H. Farnsworth, "Bombardier Snares DeHavilland," *New York Times*, January 26, 1992, p. 12; Jonathan Wheatly, "Embraer: The Sky's the Limit," *Business Week*, January 3, 2001; and "Brazil's Embraer Hits the Stratosphere," *Business Week*, April 19, 2004.

1 How do factor conditions differ for Embraer and Bombardier?

2 How does the dispute reflect the difficulties in drafting the FTAA?

3 Why are governments involved in this trade dispute?

4 Why are Canada and Brazil hesitant to apply the punitive tariffs they were awarded?

Endnotes

1 Craig S. Smith, "Workers of the World, Invest!" *New York Times*, August 19, 2001, Section 3, p. 3.

2 For more on this, see Erik Eckholm, "Chinese President Is Optimistic About Relations with the US," *New York Times*, August 10, 2001, pp. A1, A8.

3 "Private economy yields 40% of gross product in Shanghai," *People's Daily Online*, March 9, 2005.

4 Paul Starobin and Olga Kravchenko, "Russia's Middle Class," *Business Week*, October 16, 2000, pp. 78–84.

5 R. Molz, "Privatization of Government Enterprise: The Challenge to Management," *Management International Review*, vol. 29, no. 4 (1989), pp. 29–30.

6 Ibid., pp. 32–33.

7 For excellent coverage of privatization, see Dennis J. Gayle and Jonathan N. Goodrich (eds.), *Privatization and Deregulation in Global Perspective* (New York: Quorum Books, 1990).

8 Clifford Krauss, "Argentina to Hasten End of Phone Monopoly," *New York Times*, March 11, 1998, Section C, p. 4.

9 Gautam Naik, "Telecom Deregulation in Britain Delivered a Nice Surprise: Jobs," *Wall Street Journal*, March 5, 1998, pp. A 1, A 6.

10 Michael Wines, "A Factory's Turnaround Reflects a Glimmer in Russia's Economy," *New York Times*, July 2, 2000, pp. A 1, 8.

11 "Low-cost take off," *Economist.com*, Mar 23, 2005.

12 Mayumi Negishi, "Takenaka vows to get LDP members on board for Japan Post privatization," *Japan Times*, September 29, 2004.

13 For more on the current state of EUREKA, see Caroline Mothe and Bertrand Quelin, "Creating Competencies Through Collaboration: The Case of EUREKA R&D Consortia," *European Management Journal*, December 2000, pp. 590–604.

14 Alan Goldstein, "Sematech Members Facing Dues Increase; 30% Jump to Make up for Loss of Federal Funding," *Dallas Morning News*, July 27, 1996, p. 2 F.

15 Larry Reibstein et al., "A Mexican Miracle?" *Newsweek*, May 20, 1991, pp. 42–45; and Paul Magnusson et al., "The Mexico Pact: Worth the Price?" *Business Week*, May 27, 1991, pp. 32–35.

16 United States, BEA, *Survey of Current Business*, January and April 2005.

17 "Globalization, What on Earth Is it About," *BBC.co.uk*, September 14, 2000.

18 "Who Are the Prague Protestors," *BBC.co.uk*, September 26, 2000.

19 Alan M. Rugman, *The End of Globalization* (London: Random House, 2001).

20 Sylvia Ostry, "The Multilateral Trading System," in Alan M. Rugman and Thomas Brewer (eds.), *The Oxford Handbook of International Business* (Oxford: Oxford University Press, 2001), pp. 232–258.

21 Edward M. Graham, *Fighting the Wrong Enemy: Antiglobal Activists and Multinational Enterprises* (Washington, DC: Institute for International Economics, 2000).

22 Matthew Kaminski, "Europe's Leaders Set Date for EU Enlargement," *Wall Street Journal*, June 18, 2001, p. A 15.

23 Philip Revzin, "EC Leaders Adopt 2-Year Plan to Forge Political, Monetary Unity in Europe," *Wall Street Journal*, December 17, 1990, p. A 6.

24 "A Free-Trade Tug-of-War," *Economist.com*, December 9, 2004.

25 "Fraternity of 3,300 Metres," *Economist.com*, December 9, 2004.

26 Sylvia Chan-Olmsted and Mark Jamison, "Rivalry Through Alliances: Competitive Strategy in the Global Telecommunications Market," *European Management Journal*, June 2001, pp. 317–331.

27 John J. Keller, "Lucent, Philips to Produce Phones Jointly," *Wall Street Journal*, June 18, 1997, p. A 3.

28 Don Clark and David Bank, "Microsoft, Sony to Cooperate on PCs, Devices," *Wall Street Journal*, April 8, 1998, p. B 6.

29 Hideo Sugiura, "How Honda Localizes Its Global Strategy," *Sloan Management Review*, Fall 1990, pp. 77–82.

30 Ibid., p. 78.

31 Greg Steinmetz and Carl Quintanilla, "Whirlpool Expected Easy Going in Europe, and It Got a Big Shock," *Wall Street Journal*, April 10, 1998, pp. A 1, A 6.

32 Ferdinand Protzman, "Rewriting the Contract for Germany's Vaunted Workers," *New York Times*, February 13, 1994, Section F, p. 5.

33 "Pepsi Investing $350 Million in China Plants," *New York Times*, January 27, 1994, p. C 3.

34 Brian Bremner et al., "Toyota's Crusade," *Business Week*, April 7, 1997, pp. 104–114.

35 See Robert O. Metzger and Ari Ginsberg, "Lessons from Japanese Global Acquisitions," *Journal of Business Strategy*, May/June 1989, p. 35.

36 Ibid., p. 79.

Additional bibliography

Busenitz, Lowell W. "Country Institutional Profiles: Unlocking Entrepreneurial Phenomena," *Academy of Management Journal*, vol. 43, no. 5 (October 2000).

Calingaert, Michael. "Government–Business Relations in the European Community," *California Management Review*, vol. 35, no. 2 (Winter 1993).

Dunning, John H. (ed.). *Governments, Globalization and International Business* (Oxford: Oxford University Press, 1997).

Eden, Lorraine. "The Emerging North American Investment Regime," *Transnational Corporations*, vol. 5, no. 3 (December 1996).

Eiteman, David K. "Political Risk and International Marketing," *Columbia Journal of World Business*, vol. 23, no. 4 (Winter 1988).

Geringer, J. Michael. "Strategic Determinant of Partner Selection Criteria in International Joint Ventures," *Journal of International Business Studies*, vol. 22, no. 1 (First Quarter 1991).

Gomes-Casseres, Benjamin. "Firm Ownership Preferences and Host Government Restrictions: An Integrated Approach," *Journal of International Business Studies*, vol. 21, no. 1 (First Quarter 1990).

Goodman, John B. and Loveman, Gary W. "Does Privatization Serve the Public Interest?" *Harvard Business Review*, vol. 69, no. 6 (November/December 1991).

Graham, Edward M. *Fighting the Wrong Enemy: Antiglobal Activists and Multinational Enterprises* (Washington, DC: Institute for International Economics, September 2000).

Howell, Llewellyn D. and Chaddick, Brad. "Models of Political Risk for Foreign Investment and Trade: An Assessment of Three Approaches," *Columbia Journal of World Business*, vol. 29, no. 3 (Fall 1994).

Kobrin, Stephen J. "Sovereignty @ Bay: Globalization, Multinational Enterprises, and the International Political System," in Alan M. Rugman and Thomas Brewer (eds.), *The Oxford Handbook of International Business* (Oxford: Oxford University Press, 2000), pp. 181–205.

Lieberman, Ira W. "Privatization: The Theme of the 1990s—An Overview," *Columbia Journal of World Business*, vol. 28, no. 1 (Spring 1993).

Luo, Yadong. "Toward a Cooperative View of MNC-Host Government Relations: Building Blocks and Performance Implications," *Journal of International Business Studies*, vol. 32, no. 3 (Fall 2001).

MacDonald, Kevin R. "Why Privatization Is Not Enough," *Harvard Business Review*, vol. 71, no. 3 (May/June 1993).

Moore, John. "British Privatization—Taking Capitalism to the People," *Harvard Business Review*, vol. 70, no. 1 (January/February 1992).

Ostry, Sylvia. "Governments & Corporations in a Shrinking World: Trade & Innovation Policies in the United States, Europe & Japan," *Columbia Journal of World Business*, vol. 25, nos. 1, 2 (Spring/Summer 1990).

Ostry, Sylvia. "The Multilateral Trading System," in Alan M. Rugman and Thomas Brewer (eds.), *The Oxford Handbook of International Business* (Oxford: Oxford University Press, 2000), pp. 332–358.

Ramamurti, Ravi. "Why Are Developing Countries Privatizing?" *Journal of International Business Studies*, vol. 23, no. 2 (Second Quarter 1992).

Rugman, Alan M. (ed.). *Foreign Investment and NAFTA* (Columbia, SC: University of South Carolina Press, 1994).

Rugman, Alan M. "Towards an Investment Agenda for APEC," *Transnational Corporations*, August 1997.

Rugman, Alan M. (ed.). *North American Economic and Financial Integration* (Oxford: Elsevier, 2004).

Rugman, Alan and Gestrin, Michael. "US Trade Laws as Barriers to Globalization," *The World Economy*, vol. 14, no. 3 (1991).

Rugman, Alan and Gestrin, Michael. "The Strategic Response of Multinational Enterprises to NAFTA," *Columbia Journal of World Business*, vol. 28, no. 4 (Winter 1993).

Rugman, Alan and Gestrin, Michael. "The Impact of NAFTA Upon North American Investment Patterns," *Transnational Corporations*, vol. 3, no. 1 (February 1994).

Rugman, Alan M. and Verbeke, Alain. "Multinational Corporate Strategy and the Canada–US Free Trade Agreement," *Management International Review*, vol. 30, no. 3 (Summer 1990).

Rugman, Alan M. and Verbeke, Alain. "Multinational Enterprise and National Economic Policy," in Peter J. Buckley and Mark Casson (eds.), *Multinational Enterprises in the World Economy: Essays in Honour of John Dunning* (Aldershot, UK: Edward Elgar, 1992).

Rugman, Alan M. and Verbeke, Alain. "Multinational Enterprises and Public Policy," *Journal of International Business Studies*, vol. 29, no. 1 (1998), pp. 115–136.

Safarian, A. E. *Multinational Enterprise and Public Policy* (Cheltenham: Elgar, 1993).

Sen, Amartya. *Development as Freedom* (Oxford: Oxford University Press, 1999).

Spar, Debora L. "National Policies and Domestic Politics," in Alan M. Rugman and Thomas Brewer (eds.), *The Oxford Handbook of International Business* (Oxford: Oxford University Press, 2000), pp. 206–231.

Spar, Debora L. *Ruling the Waves: Cycles of Discovery, Chaos and Wealth* (New York: Harcourt, 2001).

Trebilcock, Michael and Howse, Robert. *The Regulation of International Trade*, 2nd ed. (London: Routledge, 1999).

Weintraub, Sidney et al. *Free Trade in the Americas* (Cheltenham: Elgar, 2004).

Chapter 5

INTERNATIONAL CULTURE

Contents

Objectives of the chapter

Places and people differ. The Japanese tend to be very polite, the Australians characteristically blunt. Red means "danger" or "stop" to the British, but in Turkey it signifies death and in China, good fortune. In France getting into a "grande ecole" tends to guarantee good job prospects whereas in Saudi Arabia the wealth and status of your family is far more important.

Patterns of global diversity and the implications of these differences have been studied from a range of perspectives, by sociologists, psychologists, anthropologists, and political scientists. Here we are concerned with how cultural diversity and related differences in the behavior, norms, and expectations of particular groups of employees, managers, colleagues, or customers affect management decision making and corporate organizations. After an introduction to the kinds of business contexts in which cultural differences do matter, this chapter will describe some typologies of national cultural differences and discuss the implications of these for international managers.

The specific objectives of this chapter are to:

1 *Define* culture and explain the factors that underlie cultural differences.
2 *Show* where and why cultural differences matter to international managers.
3 *Explain* a number of frameworks that help identify important cultural differences.
4 *Examine* how firms can anticipate and cope with cultural differences.

Culture clash at Pharmacia and Upjohn

Despite all being part of the same advanced, industrialized world, Kalamazoo (Michigan, USA), Stockholm (Sweden), and Milan (Italy) are worlds apart in many important ways. Senior managers leading the merger between two pharmaceutical firms, Upjohn Company of the United States and Pharmacia AB of Sweden (with operations in Italy), came to realize how significant these differences were after the merger took place in 1995.

Swedes take off most of the month of July for their annual vacation, Italians take off most of August. Not knowing this, American executives scheduled meetings in the summer only to have to cancel many because their European counterparts were at the beach. As the more dominant American firm began to impose its way of doing things on the newly-acquired European organizations, international relationships became increasingly strained.

Neither the Swedes nor the Italians were happy with impositions such as the drug and alcohol testing policy brought in by Upjohn, or the office smoking ban. These clashed with local ways of doing things and the more informal work environment that these cultures prefer. Although Upjohn later relaxed many of these work rules, allowing some local practices and preferences to prevail, ill-feeling and a degree of resistance had already developed among European colleagues.

The additional bureaucracy and the command-and-control style imposed by the Americans created more significant problems for the 34,000 employees and managers in Pharmacia and Upjohn Company. The Swedes were used to an open, team-based style of management where responsibilities are devolved; managers are trusted and not strictly monitored or closely managed. Swedish executives also tend to build up a consensus behind big decisions, "getting everyone in the same boat" (*alla aer i baten*) rather than handing orders down the hierarchy. As a traditionally American multinational, however, Upjohn was more used to strong leadership and a centralized command-and-control structure. Its CEO, Dr. John Zabriskie, quickly created a strict reporting system, tight budget control, and frequent staffing updates, which clashed with the Swedish organization style. Swedish managers would leave meetings disgruntled, having been overruled by American executives keen to push their vision of the merged company.

The Swedes own ways of doing things had already clashed with the Italian style of management, following the takeover of Farmitalia (part of Montedison) by Pharmacia in 1993. Italians are used to a distinctive division between workers (and their strong unions) and managers. Their steeper hierarchies contrast the more egalitarian Swedes. Italians also place a high value on families and will leave work to tend to sick relatives or help with childcare, which the Swedes frown upon. The addition of the Americans from Upjohn into this mix created further cultural confusion. Communication problems, beyond the obvious language differences, became a real barrier to honest dialogue. "You go there thinking you're going to streamline the place," said American Mark H. Corrigan, Pharmacia and Upjohn vice president for clinical development, "and you leave just having added five pounds from some wonderful meals."

These differences, many of them small but important at the local level, quickly began to have an impact on the overall performance of the merged company. In the months and years following the merger unforeseen inefficiencies and added costs began to undermine the potential synergies of bringing together two such companies in the first place. At one level the problems amounted to things like canceled meetings, new organization demands (such as monthly report-writing), and a general decline in staff morale. There were also unexpected difficulties integrating the IT systems across the various parts of the merged organization. These and other changes added an estimated $200 million to the predicted costs of the restructuring, taking the total cost to $800 million. Even more seriously, for a pharmaceutical company heavily reliant on its new drugs pipeline to survive, delayed product launches and the loss of key staff (including the head of R&D at Pharmacia) had a longer-term impact. "There was probably an under-appreciation . . . of these cultural differences," says Art Atkinson, former vice president for clinical research and development.

Particular problems resulted from the restructuring of the firm's global R&D structure. Prior to the merger Upjohn owned well-known names such as Rogaine and Motrin and had annual sales of around $3.5 billion, but had a weak new product pipeline and slow sales growth compared to its larger competitors. Similar-sized Pharmacia had a more promising pipeline but weak distribution and sales in the US market, the world's largest. These amounted to a strong rationale for the merger. Together they could challenge the financial power and the larger R&D programs of their competitors. However, integrating and re-focusing the various parts of the new R&D structure became a major problem. Rather than place the R&D headquarters in the United States, Sweden, or Milan a decision was made to establish a new and neutral London-based center for the R&D function. This simply added a layer of management and a more complex matrix reporting structure, which further alienated key R&D personnel.

In 1997, after the stock price of the merged corporation had fallen significantly, CEO John Zabriskie resigned. Swede Jan Ekberg, the former head of Pharmacia, took over temporarily and began to rebuild aspects of the merged organization.

After acquiring a major part of Monsanto in 2000, Pharmacia and Upjohn became Pharmacia and was then itself acquired by the American giant Pfizer in April 2003.

This made Pfizer, according to its own Annual Report, the "number one pharmaceutical company in every region of the World."

All this proves is that going global is hard work. Not all of these problems could have been foreseen, but a real lack of awareness of cultural differences did lead to many of the organization difficulties and people problems with a real impact on the bottom line.

Websites: www.pfizer.com; and www.pfizer.com/are/investors_reports/annual_2003/review/index.htm.

Sources: R. Frank and T. M. Burton, "Pharmacia & Upjohn Faces Culture Clash; Europeans Chafe Under US Rules," *Wall Street Journal*, February 4, 1997; R. J. Thomas, "Irreconcilable Differences," *Accenture Outlook*, vol. 1, 2000; and Pfizer, Annual Report, 2003.

1. What kinds of cultural differences matter when organizations from different countries merge?

2. How well do the characteristics described in the case match the respective, stereotypical national cultures of these countries?

3. What could senior managers have done before and after the merger to alleviate some of the problems that resulted from culture clash?

4. Explain why one organization might want to impose some of its ways of doing things on another, such as an acquired firm or subsidiary.

INTRODUCTION

The number of workers employed by foreign-owned companies has grown significantly over the past 20 years as a result of the expanding activities of foreign affiliates of MNEs around the world. For many people, both employers and employees, this has brought home the realities of globalization. An estimated 53 million people globally now work for foreign companies. Companies such as Motorola, General Motors, British Petroleum, and General Electric are among the largest private-sector employers in economies such as Malaysia and Singapore.[1]

This growing multicultural workforce, part of the increasingly global patterns of exchange and interaction discussed earlier in this book, makes it more and more important to understand how people's preferences, beliefs, and values differ. Understanding international cultural differences allows us to be aware of and adapt to the differences that matter for managers.

Grande ecole
One of the "grand" or great schools considered to be the pinnacle of French higher education, highly selective and prestigious, and the main source of the country's business and political leaders

WHAT IS CULTURE?

Culture can be defined as "the sum total of the beliefs, rules, techniques, institutions, and artifacts that characterize human populations"[2] or "the collective programming of the mind."[3]

Sociologists generally talk about the socialization process, referring to the influence of parents, friends, education, and the interaction with other members of a particular society as the basis for one's culture. These influences result in learned patterns of behavior common to members of a given society.

Culture
The acquired knowledge that people use to interpret experience and to generate social behavior

Socialization
The process of enculturation, or the adoption of the behavior patterns of the surrounding culture

Table 5.1 World population percentages in terms of home region, language, and religion

Home region	%	Language	%	Religion		%
Asia	58.4	Mandarin	14.4	Christianity, including:		33%
Africa	12.4	Hindi	6.0	• Catholics	20%	
Europe	9.5	English	5.6	• Protestants	9%	
Latin America	8.4	Spanish	5.6	• Orthodox	4%	
Former Soviet bloc	5.5	Bengali	3.4	Islam		22%
North America	5.2	Russian	2.8	Hinduism		15%
Australia and New Zealand	0.6	Portuguese	2.6	Non-religious		14%
		Japanese	2.0	Buddhism		6%
		German	1.6	Chinese traditional		4%
		Korean	1.3	Primal-indigenous		3%
		French	1.3	Other		3%
		Other (approx. 200)	54.4			

Sources: **www.census.gov** and **www.adherents.com**.

As you can see, definitions of culture vary according to the focus of interest, the unit of analysis, and the disciplinary approach (psychology, anthropology, sociology, geography, etc.). This is significant in that studies of cultural differences adopt a specific definition and set of measurable criteria, which are always debatable. Research into culture and its impact in business and management studies is highly contentious and should not just be taken at face value, including the studies described below.

There is a strong consensus, however, that key elements of culture include language, religion, values, attitudes, customs, and norms of a group or society. Table 5.1 shows how the world's population is divided according to geography, language, and religion.

Language is perhaps the most important key to understanding culture in general and the specific values, beliefs, attitudes, and opinions of a particular individual or group. English is widely accepted as the language of business; many global institutions and companies have adopted English as their official language. For many firms, such as Toyota, NEC, Hitachi, and IBM Japan, English-speaking ability is a pre-requisite for promotion.[4] However, any assumption that speaking the same language removes cultural differences is dangerous—it normally just hides them. Moreover, a reliance on English by British and American managers, and a lack of other language skills, can weaken their ability to empathize with and adapt to other cultures.

Religion, linked to both regional characteristics and language, also influences business culture through a set of shared, core values. Protestants hold strong beliefs about the value of delayed gratification, saving, and investment. The sociologist Max Weber, writing in 1904, saw this Protestant work ethic as the "spirit of capitalism" during the industrial revolution.[5] Rather than spending, consuming, and enjoying life now, their religious beliefs prompted the Protestants to look to longer-term rewards (including those in the after-life). There are parallels with the Confucian and Shinto work ethics, which also view spiritual rewards as tied to hard work and commitment to the fruits of industry. Contrasting this, a more stoic attitude among some African populations partly explains their acceptance of the ways things are, because it is the "will of God" ("shauri ya Mungu").

Corporate culture
The shared values, traditions, customs, philosophy, and policies of a corporation; also, the professional atmosphere that grows from this and affects behavior and performance

At the most general level culture can refer simply to the lifestyle and behavior of a given group of people, so **corporate culture** is a term used to characterize how the managers and employees of particular companies tend to behave. But the term is also used by human resource managers and senior management in their attempts to proactively shape the kind of behavior (innovative, open, dynamic, etc.) they hope to nurture in their organizations. Promoting a distinctive corporate culture is also expected to enhance the sense of community and shared identity that underpins effective organizations.

THE IMPORTANCE OF CULTURE IN DIFFERENT BUSINESS CONTEXTS

Cross-cultural management issues arise in a range of business contexts. *Within* individual firms, for example, managers from a foreign parent company need to understand that local employees from the host country may require different organization structures and HRM procedures. In cross-border mergers and acquisitions (M&As), realizing the expected synergies very often depends on establishing structures and procedures that encompass both cultures in a balanced way. Cross-border joint ventures, alliances, or buyer-supplier relationships *between* two or more firms also require a cultural compromise. Finally, for firms to sell successfully to foreign customers requires culturally sensitive adaptations to products, services, marketing, and advertising.

Figure 5.1 outlines, at the most general level, links between business contexts and particular characteristics of individuals or groups that are influenced by social and cultural norms of a particular region. At the face-to-face level in meetings the language and behavior of different peoples vary and their mutual understanding of each other's culture will influence the effectiveness and efficiency of communication between them. This influences how well multicultural workplaces operate at all levels, from strategy setting at the senior level to plant-floor operations.

Firms also tend to have different organizational and decision-making practices depending on where they have evolved and which cultures and subcultures they encompass. For firms to build successful alliances and partnerships, or for M&A activities to succeed at the company-to-company level, there needs to be an understanding of the organizational

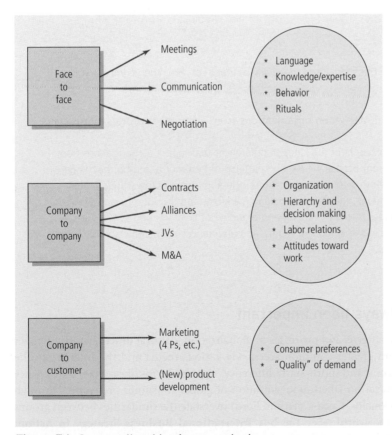

Figure 5.1 Cross-cultural business contexts

differences between them. This covers practically every element of corporate organizations from decision-making structures and systems and management-labor relationships to individual employees' attitudes toward their work and their employer.

Finally, culture influences the behavior and preferences of clients and customers. To sell successfully in a foreign market, a manager needs to adapt his/her product or service to meet the different needs of that particular group of customers. Any alteration in advertising, marketing, product or service features, after-sales support, technical back-up, documentation, etc., will be partly guided by cultural differences.

Failure to do this ends in the kinds of marketing mistakes and communication blunders that become marketing folklore. For example, Ford's low-cost truck was initially marketed as the Feira to Spanish-speaking people when this means "ugly old woman" in Spanish. The Ford Comet, a high-end car, was sold as the Caliente in Mexico, which is local slang for "prostitute." Unsurprisingly neither model did well in these markets. This reinforces the above point about the importance of language, but also demonstrates how some of the largest and most experienced companies do not appear to do the most basic cultural due diligence (their homework!) when launching products and services in foreign markets. The chapter on marketing strategy in this book examines these kinds of issues more closely.

Ethnocentrism
The belief that one's way of doing things is superior to that of others

Across all of the business contexts in Figure 5.1 ignorance of cultural differences represents a common stumbling block for international managers. Ethnocentrism, the belief that one's own way of doing things is superior to that of others, can also be a major barrier to good international management. The challenge lies in recognizing differences, combining the advantages that stem from different styles and approaches, adjusting and adapting to succeed with different people, in different partnerships, and in different markets.

 ## Active learning check

Review your answer to Active Learning Case question 1 and make any changes you like. Then compare your answer with the one below.

1 **What kinds of cultural differences matter when organizations from different countries merge?**

The definition of culture itself gives some indicators of the kinds of differences that matter. Organizations from different countries will have developed different beliefs, values, and patterns of behavior based on their underlying national culture. A wide range of differences could be important, including attitudes toward work and workplace practices, management-labor relations, the decision-making hierarchy, and division of responsibilities. Cross-border M&A often also requires changes to the marketing and branding of products and services as sales are expanded into new markets. Differences in the language, values, and preferences of customers in different countries also need to be taken into account.

Culture has always been important

Cultural convergence
The growing similarity between national cultures, including the beliefs, values, aspirations, and the preferences of consumers, partly driven by global brands, media, and common global icons

Despite the various patterns and processes of globalization, cultural differences still remain important. Even with greater common access, via various media and the Internet, to the same brands, rock icons, and sports stars, differences remain. Terms like cultural convergence or, simply, Americanization (the homogenization of global consumer preferences through the ubiquity of McDonalds, Coca-Cola, and Ford) overstate the similarities between groups of people around the world. (See the box **International Business Strategy in Action: McDonald's.**)

INTERNATIONAL BUSINESS STRATEGY *IN ACTION*

McDonald's

When José Bové, a self-proclaimed leader of France's anti-globalization movement, was sentenced for vandalizing a McDonald's restaurant in 1999, he claimed to have the backing of the French people. That might have been an overstatement, but 40,000 French people were there to show their support. It was not only the French, however; in the 1990s McDonald's restaurants were vandalized in about 50 countries. At issue is the worldwide perception that McDonald's represents a particular friendly-Ronald-McDonald type of American imperialism. Traditional lifestyles, critics say, are being eroded by McDonald's marketing practices, its value chain system, its fast-food concept, and the unhealthy food itself.

Yet, McDonald's bends over backwards to blend into local cultures. The company advertises itself to its critics as a global company owned and run by local people. Indeed, the franchise system makes it so that McDonald's Japan is run by the Japanese and Israel's McDonald's restaurants are run by Israelis. Local business owners choose their menu's offerings to fit their culture, find alternative suppliers, and create suitable marketing for their culture. An American in Saudi Arabia might seat single men with families at a McDonald's opening, but a Saudi Arabian owner would know that this is unacceptable and the restaurant will be designed to accommodate the culture.

In the land of José Bové, Asterix, a French comic-strip character who stands for individuality and ironically symbolizes local resistance to imperial forces, replaced the goofy Ronald McDonald in the company's marketing in the early 2000s. In 1999, French McDonald's went the extra mile to prove how local it was by printing advertisements making fun of US eating habits. In one ad, a large American cowboy complains that McDonald's France does not import American beef to "guarantee maximum hygienic conditions." French restaurants are more fashionably and more comfortably designed than North American ones to create an environment where customers may enjoy longer meals in accordance with French tradition. If they want, customers can order a beer from the menu.

In India, where local tastes are very different from those in America, the company crafted an entirely different menu that does not use beef or pork due to the mostly vegetarian population. The Indian Big Mac is made of lamb. In Israel, the locally-owned McDonald's purchases over 80 per cent of its ingredients from local producers, including 100 per cent kosher hamburger meat, potatoes, lettuce, buns, and milk-shake mix. There are no cheeseburgers in Israel's McDonald's because dairy cannot be eaten together with meat.

On the other hand, McDonald's does bring its own culture to its foreign operations. In China, where children's birthdays are not traditionally celebrated, a successful McDonald's marketing strategy encouraged birthday parties at their establishment. Not a bad deal for children, but still a cultural effect from a foreign multinational. More mundane things, such as combo meals, are popularized through McDonald's expansion. By promoting its carbonated beverages in India, the firm is unsettling the country's tea culture. The company's presence creates a cultural exchange, not a one-sided cultural takeover.

Beyond reactionary behavior against McDonald's cultural "impositions," McDonald's has had to suffer simply for being born in America. Just hours after the United States began bombing Afghanistan in 2001 McDonald's were vandalized in cities in Pakistan and Indonesia and Muslim clerics asked for the boycott of US products.

For activists and cultural protectors, the most frustrating thing is that their calls go unheeded. Owners of McDonald's franchises continuously remind customers that they too are locals, that their employees are locals, and that their suppliers are mainly local. In Brazil, some anti-war protestors on their way home will stop at a McDonald's for a bite to eat.

Some of McDonald's major troubles, however, are in its most established markets in the United States, Canada, and the United Kingdom. Russian and Chinese go-getters might think that a meal in McDonald's puts them in a class above, but in its two major markets of North America and Europe, where the firm derives over two-thirds of all revenue, the food is considered unhealthy. Indeed, both Canada and the UK considered imposing a tax on fatty foods on the grounds that it was damaging to people's health and it costs the health-care system a substantial amount. The tax is unlikely to be imposed because of a strong backlash from poverty groups who argue that this tax would place an uneven burden on those who depend on cheap food for their everyday survival. In the United States, the firm is being sued over claims that it misled parents about the nutritional value of its products leading their children to become obese and unhealthy. McDonald's in the UK reacted by eliminating super-sized options from their menu. A set of healthier options have now been introduced in Europe and North America as the company fends off critics in some of its friendliest markets.

Sources: David Barboza, "When Golden Arches Are Too Red, White and Blue," *New York Times*, October 14, 2001; Tony Karon, "Adieu, Ronald McDonald," *Time.com*, January 24, 2002; and Simon Romero, "War and Abuse Do Little to Harm US Brands," *New York Times*, May 9, 2004.

Cultures vary and these variations lead to real and significant differences in the ways that companies operate and people work. Moreover, *because* of globalization more and more firms are coming head-to-head with the added complexity of doing business globally, which stems from the huge amount of variety in the world that still exists (and arguably will always exist).

Before moving on to examine some typologies of global cultures, here is a word of warning. Much of this section will describe how various kinds of individual and group behavior can be linked to specific cultural groups and associate these cultural dispositions with different business styles and company structures. Acting on the basis of cultural stereotypes is highly sensitive and can be problematic. For example, at the simplest level a banker may be able to prove empirically that Pakistanis are more successful than Jamaicans at starting and running small businesses around the world. Using this insight as the basis for discriminating against Jamaicans wanting bank loans for business start-ups is not only unethical, but in most countries falls foul of race discrimination laws.

NATIONAL STEREOTYPES AND KEY DIMENSIONS OF CULTURE

Culture at two levels

There are traditionally two different approaches to looking at culture:

Psychic distance
A measure of the similarity or difference between two cultures; also commonly defined as the measurable distance between the home market and a foreign market resulting from the perception of cultural and business differences

- The psychic or psychological level, which focuses on the internalized norms, attitudes, and behavior of individuals from a particular culture (**psychic distance** is a measure of differences between groups).

- The institutional level, which looks at national (or group) culture *embodied* in institutions (government, education, and economic institutions as well as in business organizations).

In this chapter we will mainly discuss the first, culture as shared psychology, with a brief reference to national institutional differences at the end.

People who are born in, or grew up in, the same country tend to share similar cultural characteristics. Nationality and culture tend to coincide, although nations encompass a wide variety of institutions, religions, beliefs, and patterns of behavior, and distinctive subcultures can always be found within individual countries. The only way to make sense of this wide diversity is to characterize distinct cultural groups through simplified national stereotypes.

Many studies have attempted to create these stereotypes by mapping and comparing the shared characteristics of managers and employees in different countries.[6] Researchers then examine the effects of key differences on business behavior, organization, structure, and ultimately the performance of companies from different countries. The following describes the milestone studies of this kind in the management field.

Hofstede's four dimensions of culture

Geert Hofstede is a Dutch psychologist who conducted one of the earliest and best-known cultural studies in management, on IBM's operations in 70 countries around the world.[7] Getting answers to 32 statements from over 116,000 questionnaires, he mapped key cultural characteristics of these countries according to four value dimensions:

Power distance
A cultural dimension that measures the degree to which less powerful members of organizations and institutions accept the fact that power is not distributed equally

1 **Power distance** is the extent to which a culture accepts that power in organizations is distributed unequally. High power distance equates with steep organizational hierarchies, with more autocratic leadership and less employee participation in decision making (see Figure 5.2 for examples).

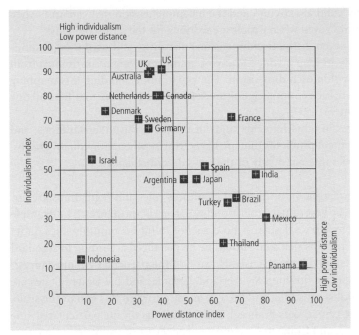

Figure 5.2 Hofstede's power distance against individualism for 20 countries

Source: Hofstede, G. (1983). The cultural relativity of organizational practices and theories, *Journal of International Business Studies*, Fall, p. 92. Copyright © Geert Hofstede.

2 **Uncertainty avoidance** is the degree to which members of a society feel uncomfortable with risk and uncertainty. High uncertainty avoidance (Japan, Argentina, France) will be reflected in the high priority placed on rituals, routines, and procedures in organizations and society in general. Countries with low uncertainty avoidance (Denmark, UK, India, US) tend to emphasize flexibility and informality rather than bureaucracy.

3 **Individualism** is the extent to which people are supposed to take care of themselves and be emotionally independent from others (see Figure 5.2 for examples).

4 **Masculinity** is the value attributed to achievement, assertiveness, and material success (Japan, Mexico, Germany, UK) as opposed to the stereotypical feminine values of relationships, modesty, caring, and the quality of life (Sweden, the Netherlands, Denmark), according to Hofstede.

Figure 5.2 illustrates some of Hofstede's findings using two of the most useful dimensions, power distance against the degree of individualism/collectivism. It reflects some general stereotypes of the countries included, with clear grouping of the UK, Australia, and US as highly individualistic and less hierarchical (small power-distance) cultures against Mexico, Thailand, and Panama at the other extreme. We will elaborate on these definitions and their practical interpretation throughout this chapter.

There are numerous problems with the methodology used by Hofstede in his most famous study, not least because the survey covered employees from just one firm, IBM. IBM's own, strong corporate culture arguably biased the cross-cultural comparisons. Although Hofstede has continued to write on culture, organizations, and management[8] it is useful to look more deeply into the work of another well-known Dutch culture guru.

Trompenaars' seven dimensions of culture

Fons Trompenaars built on Hofstede's work by expanding the framework for stereotyping and comparing different national cultures and by focusing more on the management implications of cultural differences. Using initial research involving 15,000 employees in 50 countries,

Uncertainty avoidance
The extent to which people feel threatened by ambiguous situations and have created institutions and beliefs for minimizing or avoiding those uncertainties

Individualism
The tendency of people to look after themselves and their immediate family only

Masculinity
The degree to which the dominant values of a society are success, money, and material things

Universalism
The uniform application of rules and procedures, regardless of situation, context, or individuals involved

Particularism
Judging a situation and adjusting rules and procedures according to the specific situation or individuals involved

Collectivism
The tendency of people to belong to groups who look after each other in exchange for loyalty

Neutral
A preference for unemotional, objective analysis of a situation or a decision and for limited displays of emotions and feelings in the workplace

Emotional
An acceptance of emotion and subjectivity as the bases for some decision making and a preference for explicit displays of emotions and feelings in the workplace

Specific
A tendency to limit workplace relationships and obligations, including relative status and hierarchical position, to the workplace

Diffuse
A tendency for workplace relationships and obligations, including relative status and hierarchical position, to extend into social situations and activities outside of work

Achievement oriented
Where status is earned rather than a right; recruitment and promotion opportunities tend to be more dependent on performance, as in a meritocracy

Ascription oriented
Where status is more of a right than earned; recruitment and promotion opportunities tend to be more dependent on seniority, ethnicity, gender, religion, or birth

Trompenaars explored the "cultural extremes and the incomprehension that can arise when doing business across cultures," even when people are working for the same company.[9]

Trompenaars arrived at seven distinctive dimensions of culture and used the questionnaire responses in his study to map a wide variety of countries along a continuum from one extreme to the other within each dimension. The key to understanding this mapping approach is to identify where each country or culture is positioned *relative* to others on one or more of these dimensions.

Relative positioning gives insights into the kinds of conflicts, misunderstandings, and organizational and management problems that are likely to arise when individuals, groups, or firms from these countries interact in any of the ways described above.

1 **Universalism *versus* particularism.** In universalistic cultures rules and regulations are applied in all situations, regardless of particular conditions or circumstances. The example used by Trompenaars refers to a salesman who does not fulfill his monthly sales quota because he was looking after his sick son. Should he be penalized according to standard company regulations or should he be excused because of the particular circumstances?

According to Trompenaars' findings, Switzerland, Canada, and the United States are among the most universalist. Australia and the UK are also toward this end of the scale. Germany is closer to the center, as is France, but the latter sits on the particularist side of the scale. Korea, Russia, and China are the most particularist of countries. (Note that some of the countries studied by Hofstede, like the strongly particularist Yugoslavia, no longer exist.)

2 *Individualism versus* **collectivism.** This dimension, clearly building on Hofstede, centers on whether individual rights and values are dominant or subordinate to those of the collective society.

The most individualist countries are Canada, the United States, Switzerland, and the UK. Among the most collectivist are Japan, Egypt, and India (and Nepal and Kuwait).

3 **Neutral *versus* emotional.** This reflects how much emotions are displayed in the workplace. More importantly it indicates whether emotional or subjective (rather than objective) forms of assessment are thought to be the basis for good decision making in organizations. Some organizations emphasize reports, data, and analytical decision making by managers, whereas others feel that opinions, intuition, and gut feelings are credible or valid criteria.

Predictably the most emotional countries include Italy and France and the least emotional groups (in the workplace at least) are the Japanese, Germans, Swiss, Chinese, and Indonesians.

4 **Specific *versus* diffuse.** Do work relationships (such as the hierarchical relationship between a senior manager and a subordinate) exist just in the workplace (are they specific), or do they extend into the social context outside the workplace (diffuse)? Here a telling example is whether an employee is willing to help paint a senior manager's house over a weekend. Clearly Australian bosses are likely to get a characteristically blunt answer to this request!

China, Japan, India, and Singapore display highly diffuse relationships, Australia and Netherlands, the most specific.

5 **Achievement *versus* ascription.** This dimension refers to one's status within organizations, contrasting those cultures where status, credibility, authority, and ultimately power tend to be based on merit (achieved) against those where class, gender, education, or age tend to be the defining characteristics (status is ascribed).

Countries where status tends to be ascribed include Egypt, Turkey, and Argentina (and slightly less so, Russia, Japan, and France), and those where it is achieved include Norway, Sweden, and predictably the United States, Australia, Canada, and the UK.

6 *Attitudes toward time.* Sequential (time as a sequence of events) versus synchronic (several events juggled at the same time) views of time tend to relate to punctuality for meetings and deadlines. Swedes and other northern European cultures tend to be punctual and plan according to specific timetables. Many southern European, Latin American, and Arabic cultures see punctuality and chronological precision as far less important. They also tend to naturally cope with a range of issues simultaneously, rather than one by one.

7 *Attitudes toward the environment.* This dimension reflects the emphasis a particular culture places on people's relationship with nature and the natural environment. On the one hand some cultures emphasize control and subjugation of environmental forces, whereas others emphasize the need to work with nature, in harmony with the environment. Clearly religious and philosophical differences around the world influence differences within this dimension.

Trompenaars' seven dimensions have been used in a variety of ways to gain insights into the kinds of problems that might arise in the contexts (face to face, company to company, and company to customer) outlined in Figure 5.1. In general they indicate the organizational characteristics we can expect from firms based in particular countries or dominated by certain nationalities. They are also used to measure changes in cultural values and behavior over time. Research shows that in both Japan and China, for example, achievement orientation is on the increase alongside some elements of individualism.[10]

The Japanese are moving away from a reliance on collectivism in the form of the state, large firms, and group associations and placing more value on personal responsibility and individual performance. In China there is a shift in companies toward performance-related rewards and individual initiative, built on the changing views of the growing urban elite. But there are also wider concerns regarding the social costs as well as the benefits of self-interest.

The GLOBE project's nine dimensions of culture

More recent research has built on the Hofstede and Trompenaars research. The Global Leadership and Organizational Behavior Effectiveness (GLOBE) project began in 1992 and continues today. It has involved 150 researchers collecting data on cultural values and management and leadership attributes from 18,000 managers across 62 countries in the telecommunications, food, and banking industries.[11] In the same way as Hofstede and Trompenaars before them they place countries along a standard 1 to 7 scale. The GLOBE project, however, ends up with nine key cultural dimensions:

1 *Assertiveness.* The United States, Austria, Germany, and Greece are high; Sweden, Japan, and New Zealand are low.

2 *Future orientation.* A propensity for planning, investing, delayed gratification: Singapore, Switzerland, and Netherlands are high; Russia, Argentina, and Italy are low.

3 *Gender differentiation.* The degree to which gender role differences are maximized: South Korea, Egypt, India, and China are high; Hungary, Poland, and Denmark are low.

4 *Uncertainty avoidance.* A reliance on societal norms and procedures to improve predictability, a preference for order, structure, and formality: Sweden, Switzerland, and Germany are high; Russia, Bolivia, and Greece are low.

5 *Power distance.* Russia, Thailand, and Spain are high; Denmark, Netherlands, and Israel are low.

6 *Institutional collectivism (individualism vs. collectivism).* Promoting active participation in social institutions: Sweden, South Korea, and Japan are high; Greece, Argentina, and Italy are low.

Sequential
Cultures that view time in a sequential or linear fashion; order comes from separating activities and commitments

Synchronic
Cultures that view events in parallel over time; order comes from coordinating multiple activities and commitments

7 *In-group/family collectivism.* A pride in small-group membership, family, close friends, etc.: Iran, India, and China are high; Denmark, Sweden, and New Zealand are low.

8 *Performance orientation* (much like achievement orientation). Singapore, Hong Kong, and the United States are high; Russia, Argentina, and Italy are low.

9 Humane orientation. An emphasis on fairness, altruism, and generosity: Ireland, Malaysia, and Egypt are high; Germany, Spain, France, Singapore, and Brazil are low.

Humane orientation
Cultures that emphasize helping others, charity, and people's wider social obligations

As you can see many of these dimensions match those of Hofstede and Trompenaars, and the overall GLOBE framework is very much an extension of their approach.

The GLOBE researchers have examined the human resource management implications of these cultural differences for practicing managers and looked at ways to avoid the pitfalls of ignorance and insensitivity.[12] A similar long-running study by the CRANET network has focused on European cultural differences and reports similar findings.[13]

Applying the national culture frameworks

Different styles of communication and interaction result from the cultural differences listed above. These can lead to workplace misunderstandings, poor interpersonal and intergroup relationships, inefficiency, and higher costs. Three examples provide some insights into how we can apply the above typologies.

US managers, according to all of the above studies, are highly assertive and performance oriented relative to managers from other parts of the world (they come around the mid-point on all the other dimensions). Their interaction style is characteristically direct and explicit. They tend to use facts, figures, and logic to link specific steps to measurable outcomes, and this is the main focus of workplace interaction. Greeks and Russians are less individualistic, less performance oriented, and show lower levels of uncertainty avoidance (are less driven by procedures) than the Americans. When Russian and Greek managers, employees, customers, suppliers, or public-sector officials interact with US counterparts, they may well find the American approach too direct and results focused. For them communication is likely to be more about mutual learning and an exploration of relevant issues than an explicit agreement about specific expectations and end results. Similarly, the Swedes may find the US style too aggressive and unfriendly, working against the relationship-building process that for them is a major objective of workplace interaction.

The Koreans and Japanese have highly gender-differentiated societies with males tending to dominate decision making and leading most face-to-face communication. The agenda for discussion is likely set by males, and traditional language forms differ according to whether a man is addressing a woman or an older person talking to a younger person, and vice-versa. Gender- (and age-) related roles, responsibilities, and behaviors are therefore deeply embedded in language and customs.[14] Poland and Denmark lie at the other end of the continuum on the gender-differentiation dimension. Perhaps even more than other Western managers their lack of awareness of this cultural difference runs the risk of both embarrassing female employees and offending and alienating senior Japanese male managers. This kind of clash can make negotiations and interaction of all kinds between these groups that much more difficult.

Certain kinds of human resource management techniques are inappropriate for organizations that show high power distance ratings. Companies and management consultancies in the UK, the United States, and northern European countries have developed fairly participative management systems to improve productivity, based on their characteristically low power distance and flat organizational hierarchies. Techniques such as 360-degree feedback systems for developing management-employee relationships are not likely to work, however, in Mexican, Panamanian, Thai, or Russian organizations, which have high power distance and steep hierarchies. Subordinates are uncomfortable being asked to evaluate senior managers, and managers would not see subordinates as qualified to comment on their performance. More than this, to employees in some countries this kind of consultation can give the impression that senior management do not know what they are doing! They may lose faith in senior management ability and leave!

None of the above examples means that international managers should (or ever could) entirely change their behavior to suit local values and practices. Like many of the challenges facing managers, cultural sensitivity and cross-cultural effectiveness comes from striking a balance between one's own norms, values, and principles and those of the "foreigner." The lesson for multinational firms is that **ethnocentric** corporate cultures and completely standardized HR systems do not work. The key challenge is to adapt to get the best from local differences.

Ethnocentric
A belief in the superiority of one's own ethnic group; the dominance of the home-country culture in decision making, human resource management, and overall corporate culture in a multinational firm

---

 Active learning check

Review your answer to Active Learning Case question 2 and make any changes you like. Then compare your answer with the one below.

2 How well do the characteristics described in the case match the respective, stereotypical national cultures of these countries?

According to the above frameworks they match reasonably well. The US culture is characterized as individualistic, achievement/performance oriented, and assertive. Most of these traits clash with the "feminine" (in Hofstede's characterization) values of relationships, modesty, caring, and the quality of life emphasized by the Swedes. Hofstede finds US managers less hierarchical than most cultures, which is not indicated in the Pharmacia–Upjohn case. However, as Figure 5.2 shows both countries have a low power distance, high individualism rating, relative to other countries, but the United States has slightly higher power distance (steeper management hierarchy) than Sweden. Sweden also has a relatively high uncertainty avoidance ranking, preferring order, structure, and formality, which does not stand out in the case study. Swedes are also high on institutional collectivism but low on family or small-group collectivism. The Italians are the opposite. Unlike the Americans, the Italians are not at all oriented toward achievement (Trompenaars) or performance (GLOBE). They are also more emotional than the Swedes and Americans according to Hofstede and have a relatively low future orientation (GLOBE).

"The way we do things here": the implications of cultural differences for organizations and managers

Mapping out a variety of national cultural typologies using the various dimensions of culture described above gives us some insights into the kinds of differences that exist among different groups of managers, employees, and organizations.

Two key questions about the role of the individual in a firm and the role of a firm in a society from Trompenaars' study give us a starting point to explore the management implications of cultural differences. The responses in Figure 5.3 reflect the degree of support for the particular proposition A or B for each of these questions.

Americans clearly display what has been termed (originally by the sociologist Max Weber) a mechanistic and functional view of the firm as an organization (A) and a shareholder-driven, profit-oriented view of this organization in society (although more than half the US vote in Figure 5.3 was for option B). The Japanese tend to have a more organic view of the firm, emphasizing the importance of social networks and the obligation of the firm to a wider constituency of stakeholders (although this is a characteristic of traditional Japan that has been strongly tested in the recent recessionary environment).

(1) People's role within companies

A. A company is a system designed to perform functions and tasks in an efficient way. People are hired to fulfill these functions and are paid for the tasks they perform.

B. A company is a group of people working together. The people have social relations with other people and with the organization. The functioning is dependent on these relations.

US	CAN	BEL	NL	AUS	SWE	UK	IT	GER	SIN	FRA	JAP
74	69	68	61	59	56	55	46	41	39	35	29

A ←—————————————————————————————→ B

(2) The role of companies within society

A. The only real goal of a company is making a profit

B. A company, besides making a profit, has a goal of attaining the well-being of various stakeholders, for example, employees, customers, etc.

US	AUS	CAN	UK	IT	SWE	NL	BEL	GER	FRA	SIN	JAP
40	35	34	33	28	27	26	25	24	16	11	8

A ←—————————————————————————————→ B

Figure 5.3 Excerpts from Trompenaars' cultural attitudes survey

Source: Hampden-Turner, C. and Trompenaars, F. *The Seven Cultures of Capitalism: Value Systems for Creating Wealth in the United States, Britain, Japan, Germany, France, Sweden and the Netherlands* (New York: Doubleday, 1993).

A wide range of factors within organizations are influenced directly or indirectly by the cultural predispositions of managers and employees. We know from the above studies and a wide range of other research that these factors include:

- The general relationship between employees and the organization: their roles and responsibilities, obligations, and loyalties and the link this has with life outside the workplace.
- Hierarchy, power and authority, and the accepted routes to attaining these, including factors that underpin status and credibility in different societies and organizations.
- The role of formal rules and regulations versus the informal communication, personal networks, and hidden "rules of the game."
- The accepted basis for decision making, including rationale, scientific, mechanistic, and objective versus subjective, tacit, rule of thumb, etc.
- The degree to which employees act and are treated as individuals or groups and the role of interpersonal relationships.
- Motivation and rewards systems.
- Interaction and communication mechanisms.

Work attitudes and the appropriate management of work attitudes have a significant influence on productivity and innovativeness in a company. Managers and employees who are motivated by their core social values to work hard and continually strive to improve their company's products and services and the processes by which they are produced are clearly a source of competitive advantage. It is interesting to note how social norms may

Table 5.2 Average and intra-country ranking of work goals: a seven nation comparison

Work goals	Belgium	Britain	Germany	Israel	Japan	Netherlands	United States
Opportunity to learn	5.8[a]	5.55	4.97	5.83	6.26	5.38	6.16
	7[b]	8	9	5	7	9	5
Interpersonal relations	6.34	6.33	6.43	6.67	6.39	7.19	6.08
	5	4	4	2	6	3	7
Opportunity for promotion	4.49	4.27	4.48	5.29	3.33	3.31	5.08
	10	11	10	8	11	11	10
Convenient work hours	4.71	6.11	5.71	5.53	5.46	5.59	5.25
	9	5	6	7	8	8	9
Variety	5.96	5.62	5.71	4.89	5.05	6.86	6.10
	6	7	6	11	9	4	6
Interesting work	8.25	8.02	7.26	6.75	6.38	7.59	7.41
	1	1	3	1	2	2	1
Job security	6.80	7.12	7.57	5.22	6.71	5.68	6.30
	3	3	2	10	4	7	3
Match between the people and the work	5.77	5.63	6.09	5.61	7.83	6.17	6.19
	8	6	5	6	1	6	4
Pay	7.13	7.80	7.73	6.60	6.56	5.27	6.82
	2	2	1	3	5	5	2
Working conditions	4.19	4.87	4.39	5.28	4.18	5.03	4.84
	11	9	11	9	10	10	11
Autonomy	6.56	4.69	5.66	6.00	6.89	7.61	5.79
	4	10	8	4	3	1	8

[a] First row shows average rank on a scale of 1 to 10.
[b] Second row shows ranking of work goals within each country, with a rank of 1 being *most* important and 11 being *least* important.

Source: Adapted from Itzhak Harpaz, "The Importance of Work Goals: An International Perspective," *Journal of International Business Studies*, vol. 21, no. 1, 1990, p. 81.

drive a strong work ethic despite individual dissatisfaction with workload or job responsibilities. This has been shown in several companies between US and Japanese factory workers where Japanese are found to be more loyal and aligned with company objectives but far less satisfied individually.[15]

Table 5.2 compares interview responses from sample workforces in seven countries. The resulting ranking of what it is that employees value most from their jobs shows that "interesting work" is what tends to engage most people, beyond everything else.

CROSS-CULTURAL MANAGEMENT

Three key areas capture many of the factors covered by the above typologies and cultural stereotypes, where cultural differences can make a significant difference at the company-to-company and face-to-face levels. These are organization, leadership, and communication (see Figure 5.4).

Organization

Organization styles range between organic, informal, or people oriented to systematic or mechanistic, formal, or task oriented, in keeping with some common organizational dimensions described by sociologists throughout history (such as Max Weber and Emile Durkheim). Organizations that operate very much around personal relationships and social networks contrast those that are much more functional and logical. In fact different cultures and different firms display elements of both these characteristics, but the balance

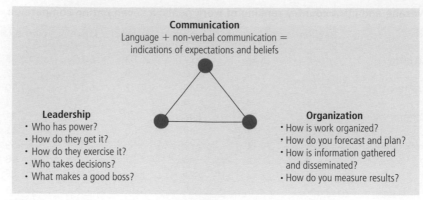

Figure 5.4 Management dimensions of culture

varies considerably and can create tensions when groups of people or firms from different ends of the spectrum interact or try to cooperate.

As an aid to predicting differences among individuals, groups, or firms, and understanding the significance of these variations, *relative* differences among countries, organizations, and groups of people are important, rather than any absolute scores. For example, family companies are characteristically directive, individual oriented but organic. Multinational firms are usually more autocratic and mechanistic. Consulting and professional services firms are often mechanistic and emphasize individual performance and rewards but may also be fairly team oriented. Entrepreneurial new ventures will usually be organic, unsystematic, and group oriented.

Leadership

Leadership styles range from individual oriented, directive, autocratic, top-down, or authoritarian to group oriented, participative, democratic, bottom-up, or egalitarian. Again, cultural groups and corporations often encompass both kinds of leadership but tend to reflect one dominant style.

Individual managers from cultures that score high on the power distance or assertiveness dimensions are likely to be viewed by those from other cultures as autocratic and directive but will tend to view others as indecisive and too compromising. They will not want to spend too much time discussing issues to achieve a consensus. If they also reflect an organic or informal (low uncertainty avoidance) culture, this will result in an instinctive or unsystematic decision-making and implementation style, and they might be viewed as an unpredictable autocrat. This contrasts the combination of high power distance and high uncertainty avoidance, which results in a more directive and mechanistic style. Such leaders prefer established formal routines and a command-and-control bureaucracy, while other managers are likely to see this as over-regulated and inflexible. The Pharmacia and Upjohn case demonstrates a range of these styles and the problems that result from the imposition of a new style of organization and leadership within a corporate merger.

Communication

Clearly, at the face-to-face level language differences can be the most prominent barrier to communication and therefore to cooperation and coordination. English speakers tend to have an advantage in many situations since English has emerged as the main language of business globally. However, this has led to complacency among some indigenous English speakers, notably the British and the North Americans. First, less effort is often made to learn other languages and their associated cultures, which normally limits a manager's understanding of foreign colleagues, workers, or customers. Second, the assumption is often made that once the language barrier is broken cultural differences are also removed, whereas these may remain, causing miscommunication and misinterpretation. As for much of this chapter on culture, preparation and awareness are the best starting points for minimizing differences that can create problems.

It is through efficient communication that two parties steer toward an understanding—a mutually-agreed basis for doing business. The signs and signals on this route to an understanding are strongly influenced by culture. Different groups have different ways of displaying approval or of showing frustration in negotiations and different ideas of what constitutes a final agreement. The Japanese do not really have an equivalent word for the English "no" and indicate disapproval in a range of non-verbal ways. The Japanese word *hai* does mean "yes" but it often means "yes, I understand what you are saying" not "yes, I agree with what you are saying." Germans place a lot of emphasis on written communications and documented evidence rather than verbal interaction, compared to the Spanish and Italians to whom verbal interaction and agreement is recognized as binding in some contexts. The Americans prefer legal contracts and have armies of lawyers to make agreements highly specified. Other, more organic business cultures tend to work toward a relationship in which trust and understanding replaces the need for legally-binding contracts. Again, awareness through preparation and anticipation of differences is the best starting point for avoiding culture clash.

Culture clash
When two cultural groups (national or corporate) meet, interact, or work together and differences in their values, beliefs, rules of behavior, or styles of communication create misunderstandings, antagonism, or other problems

The corporate response

How have MNEs responded to the challenge of managing across cultural boundaries? What kinds of organization structures, human resource management procedures, and corporate cultures have been developed to cope with the enormous differences among people and to unify this diversity toward a common purpose?

At a very general level good transnational firms develop an *awareness* and appreciation of cultural differences among their managers and employees. They also take steps to encourage *adaptation* of personal behavior or organizational practices, or products and services, to suit the changing mix of cultures within the firm, in subsidiaries and in key markets. Training programs, including a range of activities at the induction stage, when new recruits join a firm or existing personnel take up a role in a new country, are a standard way for firms to do these things. Job rotation, with a focus on developing international managers with personal experience in a variety of different countries, is also practiced by a number of firms. It is normally very difficult to assess such practices using any form of cost–benefit analysis. The costs are usually easily identifiable, but the benefits are very often intangible. For many experienced international companies, such as Shell or Nestlé, a long-term commitment to (and investment in) cultural awareness is simply accepted as a necessary part of being global.

Beyond awareness and adaptation, the best firms aim to *leverage* the diversity of cultures within their organizations and combine the best aspects of different ways of doing things. Corporate culture, a shared identity spanning culturally diverse groups of employees, provides a way to do this. Companies can usefully invest in their own socialization mechanisms, such as social events alongside regular meetings and conferences. Company magazines, intranets, and even in-house television channels for corporate communications can all support this process. These may not only improve cross-cultural awareness, but also promote shared values, symbols, and even language to help bind employees together. [16]

Here is a list of other useful strategies for managing cultural diversity distilled from a number of research studies. [17]

1 Recognize diversity. Identify and map the various national cultures and ethnic groups within the firm and use this to understand which elements of consistency and standardization can or should be promoted.

2 Build diversity issues into recruitment, HRM planning, strategy, location decisions, alliances, and partnerships. This helps avoid clashes and inefficiency and supports cultural awareness.

3 Identify where and to what degree local divisions should be encouraged or empowered to take the lead in expressing and managing diversity. Some degree of devolution of responsibility away from the center of the firm allows local divisions to identify aspects of diversity that are most important to them and their operations.

4 Encourage cross-border discussion and interaction as well as focused training. Include specific kinds/combinations of international experience for fast-track managers.

5 Aim for a cultural balance in particular areas of strategic and tactical decision making (such as brand changes for foreign markets). Ensure a (numerically) balanced pool of managers or appropriately diverse inputs into decision making.

6 Lead from the top. Aim to match the geographic diversity of the firm's businesses with a culturally mixed senior management group and board of directors (as in the case of Sony and Unilever).

 Active learning check

Review your answer to Active Learning Case question 3 and make any changes you like. Then compare your answer with the one below.

3 What could senior managers have done before and after the merger to alleviate some of the problems that resulted from culture clash?

A simple starting point would be to review the various frameworks (Hofstede, Trompenaars, and GLOBE, for example) to understand some generic differences between the national cultures involved in the merger and anticipate some of the likely problems. It would have also helped to examine the potential areas of organizational conflict with senior managers from each company and/or with managers with some experience of two or more of the countries and their ways of doing things. Some degree of cultural training or induction plus an investment in joint meetings and events to get to know each other could also have improved understanding and morale. However, the cost–benefit trade-off for these kinds of pre- and post-merger activity is difficult to precisely assess.

Multinational organization structures: imperialist or independent?

A key dilemma for international firms is the degree to which they promote or even impose a common, standardized corporate culture across the organization. Although this will create economies of scale and be more efficient in a number of respects, it will also stifle diversity and create clashes with local cultures and ways of doing things around the organization.

Firms respond to this dilemma in different ways, with different outcomes. At the simplest level we can map out a range of responses from what is termed *imperialist*, where a common culture is imposed wherever a company has a presence, to *federalist* or *independent* structures, where each national subsidiary bases its own culture on local norms and values. There are problems associated with either of these extremes and most firms try to steer a middle line, standardizing some elements across the whole organization to centralize and simplify some practices and unify employees, while allowing differentiation where necessary. This

Table 5.3 Organization types reflecting cultural predispositions

	Imperialist	Interventionist	Interactive	Independent
Organization	Ethnocentric	Ethnocentric	Geocentric	Polycentric
Structure	Steep hierarchy	Flat hierarchy	Network	Federation
Strategy	Dictated	Centrally decided	Jointly specified	Locally specified
Decision making	Centralized	Distributed	Shared	Devolved

transnational culture allows for a compromise in work styles, values, and approaches, harnessing the strengths that lie in diversity.

Table 5.3 illustrates a range of organization types. In particular, it links elements of organization structure and design with cultural orientation, for example in the relationship between headquarters and regional subsidiaries. It specifically extends the ethnocentric, polycentric, and geocentric typologies introduced by Perlmutter in the 1960s.[18]

- *Ethnocentric* firms are where top management is dominated by home-country nationals, and procedures and management styles are transferred from the head office and imposed on regional subsidiaries in place of local ways of doing things.

- *Polycentric* firms tend to act like a federation of semi-autonomous organizations with financial controls or strict reporting structures holding them together. Subsidiaries are able to reflect the local cultural norms, and headquarters appreciates the need for different organization designs, procedural norms, rewards systems, etc., as long as profits flow to the center.

- *Geocentric* firms are seen as the ideal, collaborative, and meritocratic form of global organization. (Unilever is seen as an example based on the above statement.) An equal sharing of power and responsibility between headquarters and subsidiary; senior management promoted according to ability rather than nationality; subsidiaries that share worldwide objectives with managers focusing beyond national market interests.

In the geocentric organization the *benefits* of cultural diversity, such as knowledge of local customers and business practices, are harnessed for the good of the firm as a whole. The *costs* of diversity, such as language and communication problems, different values, and attitudes toward work, are minimized. Firms moving toward this more balanced, geocentric approach have to recognize diversity and its effects and identify which elements of consistency in regulations and values should be promoted, where and when. Local divisions must identify aspects of diversity that are most important to them and their operations and take the lead in expressing and managing these differences. Discussion, interaction, cross-divisional teamwork and job rotation, support, awareness, and understanding go alongside training programs, language courses, and cultural assimilation.

Unilever is an example of a firm that has closely examined the range of cultures it encompassed and made a deliberate attempt to use cultural differences as a strength rather than a weakness for fulfilling its strategic aims. As part of a high-profile internal campaign the company described itself as a *multi-local multinational*, and this was used to explicitly inform employees of its cultural tolerance. According to a statement from a Unilever board chairman one of the firm's objectives was to "Unileverize our Indians and Indianize our Unileverians."[19]

Polycentric
Each subsidiary, division, or function reflects the culture of its host country; local managers' cultural predispositions and decision making dominate over those of home country managers in a multinational firm

Geocentric
Neither home nor host-country culture dominates decision making, human resource management, and overall corporate culture in a multinational firm

Culture-clash in cross-border M&A and JVs

The range of organization styles in Table 5.3 also reflects the range of ways multinational firms approach the management of joint ventures or of firms acquired through merger and acquisition (M&A). They can either impose their own style of management on these

INTERNATIONAL BUSINESS STRATEGY *IN ACTION*

Danone and Parmalat—going international, staying local

The dairy industry, in the main, is a local industry. Most dairy products sold at local supermarkets come from processing plants within a 500-mile radius. However, this does not mean that these firms are all small, local operations. On the contrary, there are a small number of very large MNEs in this industry that do business worldwide and target their dairy offerings to local demand. The best known of these is Nestlé, which began operations in 1904 when it opened evaporated milk factories in both Europe and the United States. Today the company is the largest dairy company in the world and has operations in 86 countries. There are a couple of other large competitors as well, although they do not compete on as broad a scale.

One of these is Danone, a French MNE whose annual revenues of euros 14.3 billion ($13.2 billion) make it one of the world's 500 largest firms. The company's product line is not as broad as Nestlé, but it is just as big as the Swiss MNE in the dairy sector. Danone has operations in 120 countries and employs over 86,000 people. However, its primary base is Europe where it generates 24 per cent of its revenues in France and another 35 per cent throughout the rest of Europe.

Danone was originally a Spanish yogurt producer that merged with the French firm Gervais in 1967. Then in 1973 the company merged with BSN, a glass manufacturer, and adopted the packaging capability of the glass system to the food business. However, the glass business was dropped in the late 1970s, and since then Danone has focused on defining its place in the dairy industry and determining how it can better address the cultural demands of its local customers. With the decision to focus most heavily in Europe and to take advantage of the expanding EU, Danone has now set up centralized purchasing and research departments in order to obtain economies of scale in food distribution across the continent. At the same time the company has been looking to gain a greater presence in other markets, including North America, and recently took a 40 per cent stake in Stonyfield Farm, an organic yogurt maker based in Londonderry, New Hampshire. Although Stonyfield will continue to operate autonomously, this firm's strong customer relations program and its expertise in marketing fast-growing organic products provides Danone the opportunity to further increase its US market share to exploit the strengths of its new acquisition.

And to ensure that it continues to focus on its main business of dairy food, Danone has sold off its grocery business and withdrawn from brewing and packaging. Today the company's efforts are being directed most heavily toward

the distribution of French-made dairy products. So in both Europe and its worldwide markets, Danone is working to answer the question: How can we develop and market French-made dairy products that meet the needs of the local market?

The other major global rival to Nestlé is the Italian MNE, Parmalat. Like Danone, Parmalat markets a wide variety of dairy products including milk, yogurt, desserts, butter, and cheese. Yet the company is best known for its development of ultra high temperature pasteurized milk (UHT) that allows milk to last up to six months without refrigeration. By specializing in the production and distribution of UHT milk across Europe, Parmalat was able to cut both production and distribution costs and to increase its profitability. At the same time, and unlike Danone, the company has been more vigorous in its international expansion. In addition to moving into France and Germany in the 1970s, the company began expanding into North and South America soon thereafter. As a result, today Parmalat earns 32 per cent of its revenues in Europe, 31 per cent in North and Central America, and another 29 per cent from South America. Australia and Asia account for the remaining 8 per cent.

Like its two other competitors, Nestlé and Danone, Parmalat carefully targets its products to the local market and seeks to acquire local companies that have established markets. For example, Parmalat has purchased Ault Dairies, one of Canada's largest operations, as well as Beatrice Foods, another major Canadian firm. Today Parmalat is that country's largest dairy firm. Parmalat also has its subsidiaries employ the company's food expertise to exploit their local markets. For example, drawing on its UHT technology, Parmalat's Australian subsidiary has been able to export milk products throughout the Asian market, and the company's Argentinean subsidiary, which specializes in UHT milk products, has been able to create export markets in Brazil and Venezuela. In addition, in catering to local tastes the company has developed a wide variety of products such as a dessert called *dulce de leche*, which it now exports to a large number of countries including the United States, the United Kingdom, Russia, Spain, Uruguay, and Venezuela.

Parmalat has, however, tended to maintain locally-known brands, rather than replacing them with its own. In the UK, for example, Parmalat owns the Loseley yogurt brand, which is well-regarded as quite an up-market brand. Similarly, consumers in Canada and Australia may be surprised to hear that their favorite brands, such as Beatrice or Pauls, were owned by Parmalat.

Danone and Parmalat are good examples of companies that sell products that are culturally influenced. In Danone's case, it has chosen to do so by staying primarily in Europe.

Parmalat, on the other hand, has been much more active in the larger international arena. Both, however, have been successful because they have been able to blend their expertise with the needs of their specific markets.

In the case of Parmalat this success now appears to have come to an end. In December 2003, with talk of fraud scandals in Italy, it was revealed that Parmalat had a reported $11 billion in debt and $5 billion in cash missing. It reached sales of $9.4 billion in 2002 and managed acquired brands in 30 different countries.

Websites: www.danone.com; www.parmalat.net; and www.nestle.com.

Sources: http://www.danone.com; http://www.parmalat.net; "A Small Town's Big Cheeses," *The Economist*, May 29, 1997; Nikhil Deogun, "Danone Groupe Scoops Up 40% Stake in Stonyfield Farm," *Wall Street Journal*, October 4, 2001, p. B 9; and Deborah Orr, "Who Gets Parmalat's Milk and Cookies?" *Forbes.com*, December 24, 2003, http://www.forbes.com/2003/12/24/cz_do_1223parmalat.html.

organizations or allow them the independence to reflect their own cultural norms and existing corporate cultures.[20]

Cultural differences often prove to be a significant post-merger barrier for managers looking to realize the synergies and added value of pooling the resources and capabilities of two companies from different parts of the world. The Pharmacia-Upjohn case above illustrates this clearly. Culture clash and its impact on the bottom line is often complex and difficult to predict. More often failure to anticipate culture clash results from the lack of awareness on the part of senior managers and deal makers driving the M&A strategy. Financial analyses that focus the due-diligence process of counting up assets and identifying cost-cutting benefits tend to miss any estimation of cultural and organizational synergy (or lack thereof). Anticipating such problems and preparing for the development of effective relationships between people from both sides of an M&A or an alliance is central to maximizing the rewards.

Daimler-Benz ran into these problems when it merged with Chrysler. A number of senior level US managers were either asked to leave or left because they were unhappy about the style of management imposed by Daimler. Among these early leavers were members of the design team responsible for the PT Cruiser and other Chrysler successes of the late 1990s. Many went to arch-rival General Motors, which is not an unusual outcome. One study showed that on average 20 per cent of a firm's top management will leave within one year of being acquired and 70 per cent will go within five years.[21]

Cultural awareness and some degree of organizational adaptation can limit the number of key people who do leave following a cross-border M&A. Understanding how to predict and mitigate the negative effects of cultural differences should be on the agenda for all managers. Despite this, in some cases an ethnocentric, imperialist approach is precisely what is needed to drive a newly-merged organization forward. When Carlos Ghosn led the partial takeover of Nissan by Renault, he imposed a very non-Japanese way of doing things on the firm. In terms of the firm within its broader economic and social context breaking *keiretsu* ties and laying off employees were radical steps to take. Internally he instituted performance-related pay and promotion and cut through a range of traditional rituals around human resource management, budget control, and decision making that were underpinned by the traditional Japanese culture of the company. These were the kinds of changes that needed to be made to reverse years of losses and indebtedness. It was also, arguably, impossible for the incumbent Japanese management to make such changes. (Chapter 17, on Japan, contains the full Nissan-Renault case.)

 Active learning check

Review your answer to Active Learning Case question 4 and make any changes you like. Then compare your answer with the one below.

4 Explain why one organization might want to impose some of its ways of doing things on another, such as an acquired firm or subsidiary.

Standardizing ways of doing things across the overall organization, to a certain extent, can be more efficient. Differences can create difficulties in communication, teamwork, motivation, or coordination, and the impact on company performance can be significant. It is important to make the distinction between the values, beliefs, and norms, plus the associated work practices and management structures that stem from the dominant national culture (the imposition can then be described as ethnocentric) or from the corporate culture. In the latter case the firm will be aiming to derive the benefits of having a shared culture that bridges the national cultural differences across the overall organization.

Cultural differences between groups of people in the one firm, or between the employees of two firms engaged in a joint venture, are not necessarily a problem. However, when they do create difficulties in terms of communication, teamwork, motivation, or coordination, the impact on company performance can be significant, despite the fact that clear cause-and-effect relationships are often difficult to identify precisely.

CULTURE EMBODIED IN NATIONAL INSTITUTIONS

The second level at which we can analyze cultural differences and their effects is at the institutional level, where national cultural characteristics are *embodied* in institutions from government agencies and governance mechanisms to the education system, economic institutions, and business organizations.

Firms engaging in cross-border joint ventures or M&A need to take account of the national context in which the new partner or acquired firm is situated. Similarly, when marketing and selling products in a new national market, these broader differences matter. A country's distinctive political, legal, and institutional context partly reflects its dominant national culture. Education systems, labor laws, environmental regulations, capital markets, and the relationships between private-sector businesses and public-sector organizations will vary accordingly.[22]

Fons Trompenaars uses his findings simply to divide various countries into subgroups reflecting shared characteristics stemming from common cultural influences (Figure 5.5).

■ *Western pluralism* emphasizes individual competitiveness, commonly represented by separate ventures competing in price-defined markets for success. Survival of the fittest is the catchphrase, and companies tend to be run as meritocracies.

■ *Command economies* are centrally-planned hierarchies with less individualism and less individual incentive. Clearly as global politics change countries are tending to move out

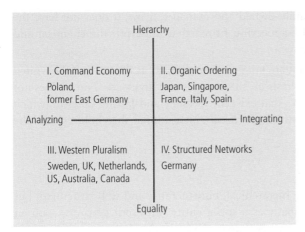

Figure 5.5 Shared characteristics stemming from common cultural influences

Source: Hampden-Turner, C. and Trompenaars, F. *The Seven Cultures of Capitalism: Value Systems for Creating Wealth in the United States, Britain, Japan, Germany, France, Sweden and the Netherlands* (New York: Doubleday, 1993).

of this category. For example, Poland is now an emerging capitalist country reflecting the characteristics of Western pluralism more than a command economy.

- *Organic ordering* refers to the family-centered hierarchies of Asia, southern Europe, and Latin America. Inter- and intra-organization interaction will be based around information sharing and collaborative competition.

- *Structured networks* reflect the more equal, structured relationships between companies and with public-sector organizations that exist in some countries.

France, with some comparisons with other Western economies and organizations, provides an example, giving a snapshot of some of the main characteristics that stem from the country's cultural distinctiveness.

France: cultural and social characteristics that create a national distinctiveness

National characteristics

- Central planning, national protectionism for domestic industry, and strong government intervention in the market (compared to other European economies) lie at the heart of the French system. Civil servants are intellectual and respected as in Japan (but not the UK) and well paid (unlike Japan).

- Communication tends to be vertical (up-across-down). Bypassing official channels is not common: uncertainty reduction tends to predominate.

- Hierarchy is important, bureaucracy respected. Clear hierarchy, divisionalization, and rules and regulations guide behavior. However, this exists alongside a respect for maverick gestures and individuals or groups that overcome the obstacles and beat the system.

- Government-to-business links are formal and informal, with the elitist groups from the *grande ecoles* bridging public and private sectors at the senior level. Ascription dominates over achievement compared to the UK or the United States, again with parallels with Japan.

- Competition occurs at school age when success determines assignment to a particular *cadre* or *echelon* inside and outside the workplace (depending on the school attended as much as individual performance).

Mittelstand
About 3.4 million small- and medium-sized firms defined as having less than 50 million euros turnover that make up the heart of the German economy

- France has a large number of family-owned and managed firms. It does not have the **Mittelstand** (small technical and engineering firms) that underpin the chemical and machine tool industries in Germany.

- Capital markets are competitive but are not as "short-termist" as the UK and the United States, with an overwhelming emphasis on share values and dividends. France does not have the strong inter-firm networks that exist in Germany and Japan (*keiretsu*), which include links between financial institutions (banks, institutional shareholders) and the companies they fund.

French organizations

Esprit de corps
The spirit of a group that makes the members want the group to succeed

- French companies also tend to be hierarchical, bureaucratic, and well structured, but there is a strong view of the company as a social entity (an **esprit de corps**) with an emphasis on obligation and loyalty rather than individual gain.

- Despite moves toward a more equal relationship, French managers continue to have a supervisory role over workers. German and Japanese managers, by comparison, tend to be more collegiate and cooperative across levels of the hierarchy, including mentoring arrangements between senior and junior managers.

- Hierarchical relationships are diffuse (in Trompenaars' terminology) rather than limited to the workplace (France ranks highest among European countries along this dimension). Companies have a responsibility toward the wider society, and managers, because of their professional status, have a role to play in society.

Gestion
The skill or practice of controlling, directing, or planning something, especially a commercial enterprise or activity

- Scientific management techniques, termed **gestion**, dominate, which parallels German zeal for quantification and measurement to guide performance improvement.

- There is a premium on technical and on-the-job training (similar to Germany and Japan). Marketing and accountancy skills are less valued than in the UK and the United States.

- A surprise to many observers is that one-fifth of the labor force is unionized. French labor law (*Code du Travail*) is comprehensive and enforced. Companies are relatively loyal to their employees compared to British or American firms, but there is not the strong social contract that exists in Japan.

KEY POINTS

1 Culture can be defined as "the sum total of the beliefs, rules, techniques, institutions, and artifacts that characterize human populations."

2 Cultural differences can have an important affect at the face-to-face or company-to-company levels and need to be taken into account in dealing with different groups of customers around the world.

3 Culture can be analyzed at two levels: the psychic distance between groups of people, and the differences in culture embodied in national institutions and socio-economic systems.

4 Hofstede, Trompenaars, and the GLOBE researchers have constructed useful frameworks for understanding broad differences between national cultures which underpin differences in the design of organizations and the behavior of managers and employees.

5 Differences in organization, leadership, and communication can be used to measure differences in groups and individuals and help managers anticipate when and why cultures may clash.

6 Company responses to the challenges of managing diversity range from the imperialist to the independent approaches.

7 Ethnocentric firms impose a common culture on all subsidiaries, polycentric firms allow subsidiaries to reflect local ways of doing things, and geocentric firms maintain a balance between center and subsidiary.

8 When in Japan, do not throw your '*meishi*'!

Key terms

- grande ecole
- culture
- socialization
- corporate culture
- ethnocentrism
- cultural convergence
- psychic distance
- power distance
- uncertainty avoidance
- individualism
- masculinity
- universalism
- particularism
- collectivism
- neutral
- emotional
- specific
- diffuse
- achievement oriented
- ascription oriented
- sequential
- synchronic
- humane orientation
- ethnocentric
- culture clash
- polycentric
- geocentric
- Mittelstand
- esprit de corps
- gestion

REVIEW AND DISCUSSION QUESTIONS

1 In your own words, what is meant by the term *culture*?

2 In what way do ethnocentrism and misconceptions about other cultures inhibit those doing business internationally?

3 Why is language so critical in understanding international culture? How can this problem be dealt with effectively?

4 Why are cultural differences an important factor when adapting products for new overseas markets?

5 Use Trompenaars' seven dimensions of culture to compare and contrast your own national stereotype to another.

6 Why are work attitudes of importance to MNEs? Cite and describe two examples.

7 What kinds of rewards systems are likely to be effective in more individualistic and achievement-oriented cultures like the United States?

8 Explain how the GLOBE project has extended the dimensions of national culture beyond the work of Hofstede and Trompenaars.

9 In the Pharmacia-Upjohn merger how did employment practices and workplace regulations differ among the Americans, the Swedes, and the Italians, and what impact did these differences have on the operational efficiency of the merged company?

10 Show with examples how managers in multinational firms could improve their employees' awareness of the important differences among cultures.

11 What are the benefits and the problems for a polycentric MNE?

12 Why is an understanding of the institutional norms, regulations, and practices of other countries important for international firms? Give examples to illustrate your answer.

13 What does the French term *gestion* mean?

REAL CASE

Do not throw your "meishi"!

Some time ago the Competitiveness Division of the Department of Trade and Industry (DTI) in the British government commissioned research on British small- and medium-sized enterprises (SMEs) that had managed to set up successful businesses in Japan, one of the toughest (though lucrative) global markets to break into for foreign firms (see Chapter 17). Numerous success stories from the study show how some firms managed to adapt to the differences in culture, society, and business practices that can act as barriers to foreign firms. But there are also numerous tales of the blunders that some managers made that undermined their efforts to establish themselves in Japan.

Meishi is Japanese for "business card," but has a deeper significance in Japan than elsewhere as a representation of the employee's allegiance to and respect for his or her company. The strong emphasis placed on loyalty and obligation between employees and their firms, lifetime employment based on a moral contract (rather than a price-based contract), and a manager's position as a member of a collective all have a strong influence on his (sometimes her) behavior when interacting with others. *Kaisha-in* literally means "company person," but it also denotes the individual as a representative of "our company" in the sense of a shared group consciousness. The company name comes first, before the individual's name on the meishi and when making introductions. The exchange of meishi also establishes relative rank within the strict corporate and social hierarchy and therefore guides the correct behavior and even form of language used for interacting. Overall for the Japanese exchanging meishi is an important symbolic ritual.

A senior technology manager from Scotland on his first assignment to Japan was attempting to establish a strategic alliance with a local firm as a starting point for marketing and selling his firm's products locally. In his first meeting he faced six senior executives from the Japanese firm, ranged across a boardroom table traditionally in order of seniority. Almost the first act of the Scottish manager was to *throw* his newly-printed meishi across the table to each of the Japanese executives in turn!

There is no way of knowing how significant this single act was in undermining this firm's market entry in Japan. It failed in its attempt to forge an alliance with this particular Japanese firm and with others, eventually leading it to abandon its attempts. What we can say for certain is that a small amount of preparation by this manager to build even a basic understanding of business etiquette in Japan would have improved this company's chances of building a successful business in Japan.

The overall study, including 30 detailed case studies of successful British firms in Japan, demonstrates very clearly that managers need to understand the cultural and social norms that underpin business practices in different countries if they are going to do business in those countries. The lesson applies to firms engaged in cross-border mergers and alliances, expanding into new markets through foreign direct investment activities, or even at the simple level, when hiring new recruits from overseas, outsourcing to foreign countries, or selling products and services abroad. Cultural awareness is critical to making business relationships work, at the face-to-face level or at the company-to-company level.

Sources: S. Collinson, *Small and Successful in Japan: A Study of 30 British Firms in the World's Most Competitive Market* (London: Avebury Press, Ashgate Publishing Group, 1996); and C. Nakane, *Japanese Society* (Tokyo: Charles E. Tuttle, 1973).

1 Explain what kinds of broad cultural differences we are likely to find between the Japanese and the British.

2 What impression do you think the Scottish engineer made on the Japanese executives?

3 What steps could the Scottish firm have taken to avoid this kind of mistake?

4 How easy is it to do a simple cost–benefit analysis on investments into improved cultural awareness among employees?

Cultural differences in international sports

One of the best examples of the impact of international culture can be found in the area of sports. Today, there is no "global" sport. Rather, professional sports are organized more on a triad than on a global basis. While sports are important to the service sector, they tend to be confined to local regions.

For example, in North America the most popular sports are baseball, football, basketball, and hockey. In particular, the first three of these are deeply embedded in the US culture. In baseball, every American child knows that Babe Ruth was a great home run hitter and that Mark McGuire, Sammy Sosa, and Barry Bonds all broke Ruth's home run record. In football, many people follow both their favorite college team as well as pro team. On a given Saturday during football season, millions of Americans sit in front of their television sets to watch college football and they do the same the next day, when the pros play. Monday Night Football always draws one of the largest audiences of the week; and whether or not they regularly watch football on TV, the Super Bowl, matching the two finalists, will typically attract one of the largest audiences of the year. Basketball is played everywhere in America and at the professional level many teams play to sold-out arenas. Everyone knows the rules of the game and the names of the great players. Even young children know that "Michael" was the greatest player in the history of the game—and no one has to tell them Michael's last name. Hockey is less popular although there is a professional hockey league in the United States and Canada and it is big business here—especially in the large cities that have franchises such as New York, Chicago, and Miami.

On the other hand, these American sports are not very popular in other geographic areas. Professional baseball is played in Canada, which has two teams that are part of Major League Baseball, and one of these teams, the Toronto Blue Jays, won the World Series in both 1992 and 1993. (One of the players was a Canadian, while the rest were all Americans.) And there is a professional baseball league in Japan. But that's about as far as the sport's international grasp extends. And while American football is played in Canada (Canadian Football League) it is not a commercially viable sport in either Europe or Asia. Basketball is played in the Olympics, but just about all of the great athletes who play against the US team are also members of the Professional Basketball Association and they make their living playing basketball in America. They simply suit up for their home country for the

Source: Getty Images/AFP/Javier Soriano

Olympics and when the games are over, they return to the United States to play for their team there. Ice hockey has some popularity in northern European countries such as Russia, Sweden, Finland, Norway, and the UK, but it accounts for but a small fraction of the popularity it enjoys in North America.

In Europe, meanwhile, professional football (soccer) is the major sport. Over 100 countries have football leagues and some Europeans view it as a global sport. Yet even this game in not a truly "global" business, although the top teams do compete in national leagues and qualify for regional and triad competitions. For example, Manchester United won the "triple" of the English football league, the FA Cup, and the European Cup in the 1998–1999 season. It then competed with a Brazilian team for an intercontinental cup in November 1999. In turn, the Brazilian team qualified through its national league and Latin American playoffs. And there is even a World Cup for which teams compete every four years. Participation is based on regional qualifications—basically from Europe, the Americas, Africa, and East Asia, but the nature of the competition is regional, not global. Even the football teams have but strong regional brand names, with only a handful (like Manchester United) having a presence in other triad markets. And even in the case of Manchester United, there is no interest in the game in the United States.

Cricket and rugby are still other examples of sports that are regional in focus. However, these games are played mainly by British Commonwealth countries and have little or no presence in the other two parts of the triad (Japan and North America).

▶

153

One sport that does seem to be global in focus is Formula One car racing. Races occur around the world including, most recently, China. A set of 10 or so international racing teams and major advertising sponsors are eager to gain global exposure through their sponsorship. But a closer look suggests that actually even Formula One car racing is a regional business. The legacy and the history of the sport are European. Races take place primarily in Europe and most of the teams are European (although they have strategic alliances with US and Japanese producers). In fact, only two of the Formula One races take place in North America (Montreal and Indianapolis). Moreover, the most popular auto race in the United States is the Indianapolis 500, and more people see this race than either of the Formula One races held in North America.

Another sport that appears to be global is that of professional tennis. However, the circuit of professional events takes place mostly in Europe. In particular, there are tournaments that are built around "grand slam" events in Australia, France, the UK, and the United States. And while the sponsors are MNEs, the organization and delivery of each of these professional events is a local responsibility. The same is true of professional golf, which has institutionalized triad rivalry in the form of the Ryder Cup, which is competed for by US and European players every two years. Although a few of the better European players also compete in some of the major US events, such as the Masters, the US Open, and PGA tournaments,

the European tour is now a solid rival to the formerly US tour and even manages to attract US players to its events. And to complete the triad emphasis, a new Asian golf tour has now been developed. However, there is no global golf business—instead, it is triad based and as it develops it becomes even less global and more regional.

What are the implications for managers of this analysis of professional sports? There are two. First, it is important to work closely with the national or local leagues since these sports are regional in focus. Second, it is important to try to gain an extension of the company's brand name into at least one other triad market. However, this has to be done through an "export" activity rather than by foreign direct investment. This is because, in the final analysis, sports are local businesses.

Source: Alan M. Rugman, *The End of Globalization* (London: Random House, 2000).

1 Why is there not a truly "global" professional sport?

2 When athletes compete in the Olympics, such as by participating as a member of the country's basketball team, why is this not an example of a global sport?

3 What do MNEs need to know if they want to sponsor professional sports events as a way of promoting their name and their products?

Endnotes

1 UNCTAD, *World Investment Report 2003*, United Nations, Geneva; http://www.unctad.org.

2 D. A. Ball and W. H. McCulloch, *International Business: The Challenge of Global Competition*, 7th ed. (Boston: Irwin McGraw-Hill, 1999), p. 258.

3 G. Hofstede, *Culture's Consequences: International Differences in Work Related Values* (Beverly Hills: Sage Publishing, 1980).

4 K. Voigt, "Japanese Firms Want English Competency," *Wall Street Journal*, June 11, 2001, p. B7B.

5 M. Weber, *The Protestant Ethic and the Spirit of Capitalism*, 2nd Roxbury ed. (London: Roxbury, 1993).

6 Many texts refer back to the work of Hall as one of the earliest authors in this field; E. T. Hall, "The Silent Language of International Business," *Harvard Business Review*, May-June, 1960, pp. 87–96.

7 G. Hofstede, "The Cultural Relativity of Organizational Practices and Theories," *Journal of International Business Studies*, Fall 1983, p. 92; G. Hofstede, *Cultures and Organizations; Software of the Mind: Intercultural Cooperation and Its Importance for Survival* (London: Harper Collins, 1983).

8 G. Hofstede, *Culture's Consequences: Comparing Values, Behaviors, Institutions and Organizations across Nations*, 2nd ed. (Thousand Oaks, CA: Sage, 2001); G. Hofstede, et al. "What Goals Do Business Leaders Pursue? A Study in Fifteen Countries," *Journal of International Business Studies*, vol. 33, no. 4, pp. 785–804.

9 F. Trompenaars, *Riding the Waves of Culture: Understanding Cultural Diversity of Business* (London: Nicholas Brealey, 1993); F. Trompenaars and C. Hampden-Turner, *Riding the Waves of Culture: Understanding Cultural Diversity in Global Business* (London: Nicholas Brealey, 1998); Fons Trompenaars and Charles Hampden-Turner also run a consultancy specializing in advice and training on cross-cultural issues. The website for the firm has some useful resources for further research: http://www.7d-culture.nl/. A similar site, with a range of tools and techniques for understanding and managing differences in European cultures is: http://www.johnmole.com.

10 C. C. Chen, "New Trends in Rewards Allocation Preferences: A Sino-US Comparison," *Academy of Management Journal*, April 1995, p. 425; Y. Ono and B. Spindle, "Japan's Long Decline Makes One Thing Rise: Individualism," *Wall Street Journal*, December 29, 2000, pp. A 1, 4.

11 M. Javidan and R. J. House, "Cultural Acumen for the Global Manager: Lessons from Project GLOBE," *Organizational Dynamics*, vol. 29, no. 4, pp. 289–305.

12 D. A. Light, "Cross-cultural Lessons in Leadership", *MIT Sloan Management Review*, Fall 2003, pp. 5–6.

13 This has involved 38 universities in annual surveys of around 7,000 organizations across Europe; C. J. Brewster and H. Harris, eds., *International Human Resource Management: Contemporary Issues in Europe* (Routledge, 1999); C. Brewster, "HRM Practices in Multinational Enterprises," in M. J. Gannon and K. Newman, *Handbook of Cross-cultural Management* (Oxford: Blackwell, 2001); J. Van Ommeren, et al, "The Cranet Survey 1999," UK Executive Report 1999, Cranfield Network on European Human Resource Management, Cranfield, Bedford.

14 C. Nakane, *Japanese Society* (Tokyo: Charles E. Tuttle, 1973).

15 J. R. Lincoln, "Employee Work Attitudes and Management Practice in the United States and Japan: Evidence from a Large Comparative Survey," *California Management Review*, Fall 1989, p. 91.

16 There are many firms that offer advice and training services to help companies improve their cultural awareness and the ability of employees to adapt to cultural diversity. A useful starting point, however, is G. Wederspahn, Do Your Employees Need Intercultural Services? (2002), http://www.grovewell.com/pub-cultural-knowledge.html.

17 Financial Times, *Managing Global Business, Mastering Management Series* (London: Pearson, 2000); M. C. Gentile, *Managerial Excellence through Diversity: Text and Cases* (Chicago: Irwin, 1996); D. A. Thomas and R. J. Ely, "Making Differences Matter: A New Paradigm for Managing Diversity," *Harvard Business Review*, September-October 1996.

18 H. V. Perlmutter, "The Tortuous Evolution of the Multinational Enterprise," *Columbia Journal of World Business*, vol. 4, no. 1, pp. 9–18.

19 Perlmutter in Bartlett and Ghoshal, 2000, p. 77; C. A. Bartlett and S. Ghoshal, *Text, Cases and Readings in Cross-Border Management*, 3rd ed. (Boston: McGraw-Hill International Editions, 2000).

20 S. Collinson, "M&A as Imperialism," in D. Angwin, ed., *Images of M&A* (Oxford: Blackwell, forthcoming).

21 J. P. Walsh, "Top Management Turnover Following Mergers and Acquisitions," *Strategic Management Journal*, vol. 9, 1988, pp. 173–183.

22 R. P. Appelbaum, W. Felstiner and V. Gessner, eds. *Rules and Networks: The Legal Culture of Global Business Transactions* (Oxford: Hart Publishing, 2001); R. Whitley, *Competing Capitalisms: Institutions and Economies* (Cheltenham: Elgar, 2002); R. Whitley, *The Multinational Firm: Organizing across Institutional and National Divides* (Oxford: Oxford University Press, 2001); R. Whitley, *Divergent Capitalisms: the Social Structuring and Change of Business Systems* (Oxford: Oxford University Press, 1999).

Additional bibliography

Ashkanasy, N. M., Trevor-Roberts, E. and Earnshaw, L. "The Anglo Cluster: Legacy of the British Empire," *Journal of World Business*, vol. 37, no. 1 (2002).

Barr, P. S. and Glynn, M. A. "Cultural Variations in Strategic Issue Interpretation: Relating Cultural Uncertainty Avoidance to Controllability in Discriminating Threat and Opportunity," *Strategic Management Journal*, vol. 25, no. 1 (2004), pp. 59–69.

Chevrier, S. "Cross-cultural Management in Multinational Project Groups," *Journal of World Business*, vol. 38, no. 2 (2003), pp. 141–150.

Collinson, S. C. *Small and Successful in Japan: A Study of 30 British Firms in the World's Most Competitive Market* (London: Ashgate Press, 1996).

Fealy, L. and Kompare, D. "When Worlds Collide: Culture Clash," *Journal of Business Strategy*, vol. 24, no. 4 (2003), pp. 9–14.

Friday, E. and Friday, S. S. "Managing Diversity Using a Strategic Planned Change Approach," *Journal of Management Development*, vol. 22, no. 10 (2003), pp. 863–881.

Ghauri, Pervez. "Negotiating with the Chinese: A Sociocultural Analysis," *Journal of World Business*, vol. 36, no. 3 (Fall 2001).

Gratchev, Mikhail V. "Making the Most of Cultural Differences," *Harvard Business Review*, vol. 79, no. 9 (October 2001).

Hampden-Turner, C. and Trompenaars, F. *The Seven Cultures of Capitalism: Value Systems for Creating Wealth in the United States, Britain, Japan, Germany, France, Sweden and the Netherlands* (New York: Doubleday, 1993).

Holden, N. J. *Cross-Cultural Management: A Knowledge Management Perspective* (London: Prentice Hall, 2002).

Kostova, T. and Roth, K. "Social Capital in Multinational Corporations & A Micro-Macro Model of its Formation," *Academy of Management Review*, vol. 28, no. 2 (2003), pp. 297–317.

Lenartowicz, Tomasz and Roth, Kendall. "Does Subculture Within a Country Matter? A Cross-cultural Study of Motivational Domains and Business Performance in Brazil," *Journal of International Business Studies*, vol. 32, no. 2 (Summer 2001).

Li, Ji, Lam, Kevin and Qian, Gongming. "Does Culture Affect Behavior and Performance of Firms? The Case of Joint Ventures in China," *Journal of International Business Studies*, vol. 32, no. 1 (Spring 2001).

Maddox, R. C. *Cross-cultural Problems in International Business: The Role of the Cultural Integration Function* (London: Quorum Books, 1993).

Marshall, R. S. and Boush, D. M. "Dynamic Decision Making: A Cross-cultural Comparison of US and Peruvian Export Managers," *Journal of International Business Studies*, vol. 32, no. 4 (2001), pp. 873–893.

Martin, J. *Cultures in Organisations: Three Perspectives* (New York: Oxford University Press, 1992).

McSweeny, B. "Hofstede's Model of National Cultural Differences and Their Consequences: A Triumph of Faith—A Failure of Analysis," *Human Relations*, vol. 55, no. 1 (2002), pp. 89–118.

Mead R. *International Management: Cross-cultural Dimensions*, 2nd ed. (Oxford: Blackwell, 1998).

Mole, J. *Mind Your Manners: Managing Business Cultures in Europe* (London: Nicholas Brealey, 1996).

Morgan, G., Kristensen, P. H. and Whitley, R., eds. *The Multinational Firm* (Oxford: Oxford University Press, 2001).

Schneider, S. C. and Barsoux, J-L. *Managing Across Cultures*, 2nd ed. (London: Prentice Hall, 2003).

Shenkar, O. "Cultural Distance Revisited: Towards a More Rigorous Conceptualisation and Measurement of Cultural Differences," *Journal of International Business Studies*, vol. 32, no. 3 (2001), pp. 519–535.

Sirmon, D. G. and Lane, P. J. "A Model of Cultural Differences and International Alliance Performance," *Journal of International Business Studies*, vol. 35, no. 4 (2004), pp. 306–320.

Sivakumar, K. and Nakata, Cheryl. "The Stampede Toward Hofstede's Framework: Avoiding the Sample Design Pit in Cross-cultural Research," *Journal of International Business Studies*, vol. 32, no. 3 (Fall 2001).

Triandis, H. C. "The Many Dimensions of Culture," *Academy of Management Executive*, vol. 18, no. 1 (2004), pp. 88–94.

Von Glinow, M-A, Shapiro, D. L. and Brett, J. M. "Can We Talk, and Should We? Managing Emotional Conflict in Multicultural Teams," *Academy of Management Review*, vol. 29, no. 4 (2004), pp. 578–593.

Chapter 6

INTERNATIONAL TRADE

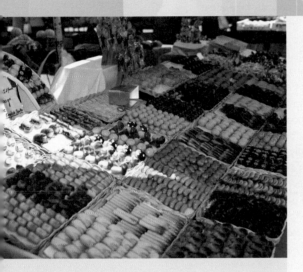

Objectives of the chapter

An understanding of international trade is critical to the study of international business. The primary objective of this chapter is to examine key economic theories that help to explain why nations trade. In addition, the role and importance of a country's barriers to trade will be studied and discussion will focus on why most nations use trade barriers despite vigorous international efforts to eliminate them.

The specific objectives of this chapter are to:

1 *Define* the term *international trade* and discuss the role of mercantilism in modern international trade.
2 *Contrast* the theories of absolute advantage and comparative advantage.
3 *Relate* the importance of international product life cycle theory to the study of international economics.
4 *Explain* some of the most commonly used barriers to trade and other economic developments that affect international economics.
5 *Discuss* some of the reasons for the tensions between the theory of free trade and the widespread practice of national trade barriers.

Contents

ACTIVE LEARNING CASE

Trade of the triad and China

Over the last three decades, new entrants into the world export market have transformed the economies of industrialized countries and the types of products they export. At the beginning of this time period, the Japanese were a growing force in the international arena. They dominated the 1980s and were able to make substantial gains at the expense of such dominant exporters as the UK and the United States. Indeed, between 1980 and 1990, both these countries lost worldwide market share to the Japanese in such industries as automotive products, office machines, telecom equipment, machinery and transport equipment, chemicals, and textiles.

In the late 1980s, however, the world economy began to see major changes. Asia, South Korea, Singapore, Taiwan, Thailand, and China were growing much more competitive in the world stage. South Korea, for example, started expanding its automotive industry, while China's market share of office and telecom equipment rose from zero to about 1 per cent of the market in 1990 to 4.5 per cent by 2000. Meanwhile, thanks to NAFTA—which decreased barriers to trade within North America—Mexico and Canada were increasing their market share of automotive products, machinery, and transport equipment. At the same time, the US economy started to turn around; 1992 marked the beginning of the longest sustained economic growth in its history, a juggernaut that didn't slow down until well into 2000. Much of this success was a result of the pounding it had taken during the 1980s from both Japanese and European firms that offered high-quality products at very competitive prices. Such competition spurred the Americans to radically restructure many of their industries; invest billions in new technology, plant, equipment, and information technology; and introduce improvement programs, such as Six Sigma, that allowed them to match the quality offerings of worldwide competitors. As a result, by the end of the 1990s, the US share of the world's export market in areas

such as automotive products, machinery and transport equipment, chemicals, and textiles was on the rise. Now the big loser was Japan, which saw its export market share decline in most of these areas.

Today the biggest threat to the export markets of industrialized countries is China. Between 1993 and 2003, China's share of the world's exports merchandise more than doubled—from 2.4 per cent to 5.8 per cent. This 3.4 per cent increase accounts for more than half of the 5.7 per cent decrease in exports by triad countries over the same period. The United States and Japan were the hardest hit with a decrease of 2.7 per cent and 3.3 per cent, respectively.

China's expansion is particularly evident in the clothing and textile markets. Today the country holds 23 per cent and 15.9 per cent of each market, respectively (see table below). More impressive, however, are China's improvements in exports of office and telecom equipment and of machinery and transport equipment, both of which require significant technology know-how.

China's share of the world's market for exports of manufactures, 1990–2003

Industry	1990	2000	2003
All manufactures	1.9	4.7	7.3
Iron and steel	1.2	3.1	2.7
Chemicals	1.3	2.1	2.5
Machinery and transport equipment	0.9	3.1	6.5
Automotive products	0.1	0.3	0.5
Office and telecom equipment	1.0	4.5	12.6
Textiles	6.9	10.5	15.9
Clothing	8.9	18.3	23.0

Note: Manufactures are a subcategory within merchandise exports. These data include intra-regional EU exports.
Source: Author's calculations based on data from World Trade Organization, *Statistics Database*.

The triad's share of merchandise world exports, 1993–2003

	1993	1995	1997	1999	2001	2003	(2003–1993)
	percentage share of world exports						
US	12.3	11.3	12.3	12.1	11.8	9.6	(2.7)
EU	14.5	14.5	14.7	14.2	14.2	14.7	0.2
Japan	9.6	8.6	7.5	7.3	6.5	6.3	(3.3)
Triad	36.4	34.4	34.6	33.7	32.6	30.7	(5.7)
Non-triad	63.6	65.6	65.4	66.3	67.4	69.3	5.7

Note: Data are calculated using world trade minus intra-regional EU trade.
Source: Author's calculations based on data from World Trade Organization, *International Trade Statistics 2004*.

The triad's share of the world's market for exports of manufactures, 1990-2003

Exports of:	EU % share of world export market			US % share of world export market			Japan % share of world export market		
	1990	2000	2003	1990	2000	2003	1990	2000	2003
All manufactures	50.3	40.5	43.4	12.1	13.8	10.8	11.5	9.6	8.1
Iron and steel	57.0	43.5	42.6	3.3	4.5	3.7	11.8	10.4	9.9
Chemicals	59.0	52.3	55.7	13.3	14.1	11.5	5.3	6.0	4.9
Machinery and transport equipment	47.7	38.6	41.5	15.1	15.7	12.2	16.7	12.6	10.9
Automotive products	53.8	46.8	51.3	10.2	11.7	9.6	20.8	15.3	14.2
Office and telecom equipment	31.1	28.0	26.4	17.3	16.0	12.1	22.4	11.3	9.7
Textiles	48.7	34.3	34.8	4.8	7.1	6.4	5.6	4.5	3.8
Clothing	37.7	24.1	26.5	2.4	4.4	2.5	0.5	0.3	0.2

Note: Manufactures are a subcategory within merchandise exports. These data include intra-regional EU exports.

Source: Author's calculations based on data from World Trade Organization, *Statistics Database*.

As can been seen in the table above, China's rise as a world exporter has decreased the share of the triad's share of world exports in manufactures. In response to China's increased competitiveness triad countries are trying to balance the need to integrate this new player into the international business arena with the negative short-term effects to their economies.

Japan's attitude toward China took a turn from protectionism when it realized that this new trade partner could help it overcome some of the problems associated with its rigid economic system. Large amounts of inexpensive, low-skill labor now allowed Japanese companies to take a portion of their manufacturing operations overseas, within its own region, while more skilled Japanese workers took care of the more specialized areas of the production process. In addition, China eased Japan's long dependence on the US economy for its industrial and consumer products.

While US and EU companies have also moved operations to Japan, the governments are reacting more aggressively to pressure from special interest groups that see China as a threat to US businesses and jobs. The United States, which runs a large trade deficit with China, has argued that the yuan is undervalued, creating an unfair advantage for Chinese producers. The United States is threatening to impose a 27.5 per cent tariff on all Chinese products. Even Japan has joined this wagon and is pressuring China to move to a more flexible exchange rate. Yet, critics argue that no one truly knows the market value of the yuan and that a fall on its price after deregulation could only worsen matters. For its part, the EU has reacted by asking China to curtail exports of textiles into the union after exports of clothing increased by 534 per cent in less than six months in 2005.

An increase in export by any nation does not necessarily mean that other countries are losing out. In terms of trade alone, any new entrant to the world exports market, other things being equal, will decrease the share of world exports of all other countries. This, however, does not mean that other countries are exporting less. They could be exporting, in value terms, a significantly higher amount as a new trade partner also means a new market to which they can export. More specifically, however, trade creates losers and winners. Triad economies are being forced to specialize. While those with most to lose pressure their governments to impose trade barriers, those with most to win –high-skilled industries—are expanding to serve the Chinese market. Further, customers' real incomes increase when they can purchase the same products at lower prices.

The data on this case help to reinforce an important principle of international trade: specialize in those products in which you can achieve an advantage. Over time, of course, competitors may erode this advantage by developing even better offerings for the export market. In this case, it is important to either counterattack by improving your own offering to win back this market share or find other markets where the country's skills and resources will allow it to compete effectively. In light of the emergence of more and more industrial countries in Asia, the growing competitiveness of Latin America, and the emerging industries of Eastern Europe and the former Soviet Union, triad managers have their work cut out for them.

Sources: "Chinese Urged to Curb EU Exports," *BBC.co.uk*, May 12, 2005; "China's Yuan under Fresh Pressure," *BBC.co.uk*, May 6, 2005; and "The Halo Effect," *The Economist*, September 30, 2004.

1. How does the process of the UK finding market niches help illustrate the theory of comparative advantage?

2. How does an EU manager's desire to buy domestic products illustrate the importance of consumer taste in international markets?

3. In what way could the EU use trade barriers to protect its markets from foreign competitors? Who can be affected by these trade barriers?

INTRODUCTION

International trade
The branch of economics concerned with the exchange of goods and services with foreign countries

International trade is the branch of economics concerned with the exchange of goods and services with foreign countries. Although this is a complex subject, we will focus on two particular areas: international trade theory and barriers to trade.

Some international economic problems cannot be solved in the short run. Consider the US balance of trade deficit. US trade with Japan and China heavily affects its overall imbalance. Moreover, this trade deficit will not be reduced by political measures alone; it will require long-run economic measures that reduce imports and increase exports. Other nations are also learning this lesson—and not just those that have negative balances. After all, most countries seem to want a continual favorable trade balance, although this is impossible, since a nation with a deficit must be matched by a nation with a surplus.[1]

International trade has become an even more important topic now that so many countries have begun to move from state-run to market-driven economies.[2] Inflation and, in many cases, unemployment are severe problems for these nations. Fortunately, enhanced international trade is one way to address a weak macroeconomy.[3] International commitment to a free market will bring prosperity to the world economic system. Since the time of Adam Smith in 1790, economists have shown that free trade is efficient and leads to maximum economic welfare. In this chapter we will discuss the economic rationale for free trade and the political impediments to it.

INTERNATIONAL TRADE THEORY

Mercantilism
A trade theory which holds that a government can improve the economic well-being of the country by encouraging exports and stifling imports to accumulate wealth in the form of precious metals

Neo mercantilism
A trade theory which holds that a government can improve the economic well-being of the country by encouraging exports and stifling imports

To understand the topic of international trade, we must be able to answer the question: Why do nations trade? One of the earliest and simplest answers to this question was provided by mercantilism, a theory that was quite popular in the 18th century, when gold was the only world currency. Mercantilism holds that a government can improve the economic well-being of the country by encouraging exports and stifling imports. The result is a positive balance of trade that leads to wealth (gold) flowing into the country.

Neo mercantilism, like mercantilism, seeks to produce a positive balance of trade but without the reliance on precious metals. Most international trade experts believe that mercantilism is a simplistic and erroneous theory, although it has had followers. For example, under President Mitterrand in the late 1970s and early 1980s, France sought to revitalize its industrial base by nationalizing key industries and banks and subsidizing exports over imports. By the mid-1980s the French government realized that the strategy was not working and began denationalizing many of its holdings.[4] More recently, China has proven to be a strong adherent of mercantilism, as reflected by the fact that it tries to have a positive balance with all of its trading partners.

A more useful explanation of why nations trade is provided by trade theories that focus on specialization of effort. The theories of absolute and comparative advantage are good examples.

Theory of absolute advantage

The theory of absolute advantage holds that nations can increase their economic well-being by specializing in the production of goods they can produce more efficiently than anyone else. A simple example can illustrate this point. Assume that two nations, North and South, are both able to produce two goods, cloth and grain. Assume further that labor is the only scarce factor of production and thus the only cost.

Theory of absolute advantage
A trade theory which holds that nations can increase their economic well-being by specializing in goods that they can produce more efficiently than anyone else

Labor cost (hours) of production for one unit

	Cloth	Grain
North	10	20
South	20	10

Thus lower labor-hours per unit of production means lower production costs and higher productivity per labor-hour. As seen by the data in the table, North has an absolute advantage in the production of cloth since the cost requires only 10 labor-hours, compared to 20 labor-hours in South. Similarly, South has an absolute advantage in the production of grain, which it produces at a cost of 10 labor-hours, compared to 20 labor-hours in North.

Both countries gain by trade. If they specialize and exchange cloth for grain at a relative price of 1:1, each country can employ its resources to produce a greater amount of goods. North can import one unit of grain in exchange for one unit of cloth, thereby paying only 10 labor-hours for one unit of grain. If North had produced the grain itself, it would have used 20 labor-hours per unit, so North gains 10 labor-hours from the trade. In the same way, South gains from trade when it imports one unit of cloth in exchange for one unit of grain. The effective cost to South for one unit of cloth is only the 10 labor-hours required to make its one unit of grain.

The theory of absolute advantage, as originally formulated, does not predict the exchange ratio between cloth and grain once trade is opened, nor does it resolve the division of the gains from trade between the two countries. Our example assumed an international price ratio of 1:1, but this ratio (P_{cloth} to P_{grain}) could lie between 2:1 (the pretrade price ratio in South) and 1:2 (the pretrade price ratio in North). To determine the relative price ratio under trade, we would have to know the total resources of each country (total labor-hours available per year), and the demand of each for both cloth and grain. In this way we could determine their relative gains from trade for each country.

Even this simple model of absolute advantage has several important implications for international trade. First, if a country has an absolute advantage in producing a product, it has the potential to gain from trade. Second, the more a country is able to specialize in the good it produces most efficiently, the greater its potential gains in national well-being. Third, the competitive market does not evenly distribute the gains from trade *within* one country. This last implication is illustrated by the following example.

Prior to trade, the grain farmers in North work 20 hours to produce one unit of grain that could be exchanged for two units of cloth. After trade, those who remain can exchange one unit of grain for only one unit of cloth. Thus, the remaining grain producers are worse off under trade. Cloth producers in North, however, work 10 hours, produce one unit of cloth, and exchange it for one unit of grain, whereas previously they received only a half unit of grain. They are better off. If grain producers in North switch to cloth production, then 20 hours of labor results in the production of two units of cloth, which they can exchange for two units of grain. Thus, international trade helps them. As long as North does not specialize completely in cloth, there will be gainers (cloth producers and grain producers who switched to cloth) and losers (those who continue as grain producers).

Because the nation as a whole benefits from trade, the gainers can compensate the losers and there will still be a surplus to be distributed in some way. If such compensation does not take place, however, the losers (continuing grain producers) would have an incentive to try to prevent the country from opening itself up to trade. Historically, this problem has continued to fuel opposition to a free trade policy that reduces barriers to trade. A good example is Japanese farmers who stand to lose their livelihood if the government opens up Japan to lower-priced agricultural imports.

A more complicated picture of the determinants and effects of trade emerges when one of the trading partners has an absolute advantage in the production of both goods. However, trade under these conditions still brings gains, as David Ricardo first demonstrated in his theory of comparative advantage.

Theory of comparative advantage

Theory of comparative advantage
A trade theory which holds that nations should produce those goods for which they have the greatest relative advantage

The **theory of comparative advantage** holds that nations should produce those goods for which they have the greatest relative advantage. In terms of the previous example of two countries, North and South, and two commodities, cloth and grain, Ricardo's model can be illustrated as follows:

Labor cost (hours) of production for one unit

	Cloth	Grain
North	50	100
South	200	200

In this example North has an absolute advantage in the production of *both* cloth and grain, so it would appear at first sight that trade would be unprofitable, or at least that incentives for exchange no longer exist. Yet trade is still advantageous to both nations, provided their *relative* costs of production differ.

Before trade, one unit of cloth in North costs (50/100) hours of grain, so one unit of cloth can be exchanged for one-half unit of grain. The price of cloth is half the price of grain. In South, one unit of cloth costs (200/200) hours of grain, or one grain unit. The price of cloth equals the price of grain. If North can import more than a half unit of grain for one unit of cloth, it will gain from trade. Similarly, if South can import one unit of cloth for less than one unit of grain, it will also gain from trade. These relative price ratios set the boundaries for trade. Trade is profitable between price ratios (price of cloth to price of grain) of 0.5 and 1. For example, at an international price ratio of two-thirds, North gains. It can import one unit of grain in return for exporting one and a half units of cloth. Because it costs only 50 hours of labor to produce the unit of cloth, its effective cost under trade for one unit of imported grain is 75 labor-hours. Under pretrade conditions it costs North 100 labor-hours to produce one unit of grain. Similarly, South gains from trade by importing one unit of cloth in exchange for two-thirds unit of grain. Prior to trade, South spent 200 labor-hours to produce the one unit of cloth. Through trade, its effective cost for one unit of cloth is $2/3 \times 200$, or 133 labor-hours—cheaper than the domestic production cost of 200 labor-hours. Assuming free trade between the two nations, North will tend to specialize in the production of cloth, and South will tend to specialize in the production of grain.

This example illustrates a general principle. There are gains from trade whenever the relative price ratios of two goods differ under international exchange from what they would be under conditions of no trade. Such domestic conditions are often referred to as *autarky*, which is a government policy of being totally self-sufficient. Research shows that free trade is superior to autarky. In particular, free trade provides greater economic output and consumption to the trade partners jointly than they can achieve by working alone. By specializing in the production of certain goods, exporting those products for which they have a comparative advantage, and importing those for which they have a comparative disadvantage, the countries end up being better off.

The general conclusions of the theory of comparative advantage are the same as those for the theory of absolute advantage. In addition, the theory of comparative advantage demonstrates that countries jointly benefit from free trade (under the assumptions of the model) even if one has an absolute advantage in the production of *both* goods. Total world efficiency and consumption increase.

As with the theory of absolute advantage discussed previously, Ricardo's theory of comparative advantage does not answer the question of the distribution of gains between the two countries, nor the distribution of gains and losses between grain producers and cloth producers within each country. No country will lose under free trade, but in theory at least all the gains could accrue to one country and to only one group within that country.

✔ Active learning check

Review your answer to Active Learning Case question 1 and make any changes you like. Then compare your answer with the one below.

1 How does the process of the UK finding market niches help illustrate the theory of comparative advantage?

The theory of comparative advantage holds that nations should produce those goods for which they have the greatest relative advantage. The finding of market niches helps illustrate this theory because it shows that the UK is picking those areas in which it has a relative advantage over the competition and exploiting its strengths in those markets. Given the rise of competitiveness in all areas of worldwide exports, few nations have been able to maintain their market share for very long. So the UK will have to continue to use this approach in order to remain one of the world's major export nations.

Factor endowment theory

In recent years more sophisticated theories have emerged that help clarify and extend our knowledge of international trade. The **factor endowment theory** holds that countries will produce and export products that use large amounts of production factors that they have in abundance, and they will import products requiring large amounts of production factors that they lack. This theory is also known as the **Heckscher–Ohlin theory** (after the two economists who first developed it). The theory is useful in extending the concept of comparative advantage by bringing into consideration the endowment and cost of production factors. The theory also helps explain why nations with relatively large labor forces, such as China, will concentrate on producing labor-intensive goods, whereas countries like the Netherlands, which has relatively more capital than labor, will specialize in capital-intensive goods.

However, the factor endowment theory has some weaknesses. One weakness is that some countries have minimum wage laws that result in high prices for relatively abundant labor. As a result, they may find it less expensive to import certain goods than to produce them internally. Another weakness is that countries like the United States export relatively more labor-intensive goods and import capital-intensive goods, an outcome that appears surprising.

Factor endowment theory
A trade theory which holds that nations will produce and export products that use large amounts of production factors that they have in abundance and will import products requiring a large amount of production factors that they lack

Heckscher–Ohlin theory
A trade theory that extends the concept of comparative advantage by bringing into consideration the endowment and cost of factors of production and helps to explain why nations with relatively large labor forces will concentrate on producing labor-intensive goods, whereas countries with relatively more capital than labor will specialize in capital-intensive goods

Leontief paradox
A finding by Wassily Leontief, a Nobel prize economist, which shows that the United States, surprisingly, exports relatively more labor-intensive goods and imports capital-intensive goods

International product life cycle (IPLC) theory
A theory of the stages of production of a product with new "know-how"; it is first produced by the parent firm, then by its foreign subsidiaries, and finally anywhere in the world where costs are the lowest; it helps explain why a product that begins as a nation's export often ends up as an import

This result, discovered by Wassily Leontief, a Nobel Prize economist, is known as the **Leontief paradox** and has been explained in terms of the quality of labor input rather than just labor-hours of work. The United States produces and exports technology-intensive products that require highly educated labor. The Leontief paradox not only shows one of the problems with factor endowment theory, but also helps us understand why no single theory can explain the role of economic factors in trade theory. Simply put, the subject is too complex to be explained with just one or two theories.

International product life cycle theory

Another theory that provides insights into international theory is Vernon's **international product life cycle (IPLC) theory**, which addresses the various stages of a good's life cycle. In particular, the theory helps explain why a product that begins as a nation's export often ends up becoming an import. The theory also focuses on market expansion and technological innovation, concepts that are relatively de-emphasized in comparative advantage theory. IPLC theory has two important tenets: (1) technology is a critical factor in creating and developing new products; and (2) market size and structure are important in determining trade patterns.

Product stages

The IPLC has three stages: new product, maturing product, and standardized product. A new product is one that is innovative or unique in some way (see Figure 6.1*a*). Initially, consumption is in the home country, price is inelastic, profits are high, and the company seeks to sell to those willing to pay a premium price. As production increases and outruns local consumption, exporting begins.

As the product enters the mature phase of its life cycle (see Figure 6.1*b*), an increasing percentage of sales are achieved through exporting. At the same time, competitors in other advanced countries will be working to develop substitute products so they can replace the initial good with one of their own. The introduction of these substitutes and the softening of demand for the original product will eventually result in the firm that developed the product now switching its strategy from production to market protection. Attention will also be focused on tapping markets in less developed countries.

As the product enters the standardized product stage (see Figure 6.1*c*), the technology becomes widely diffused and available. Production tends to shift to low-cost locations,

Figure 6.1 The international product life cycle

Source: Raymond Vernon and Louis T. Wells, Jr., *The Manager in the International Economy* (Englewood Cliffs, NJ: Prentice-Hall, 1991), p. 85.

including less developed countries and offshore locations. In many cases the product will end up being viewed as a generic, and price will be the sole determinant of demand.

Personal computers and the IPLC

In recent years a number of products have moved through the IPLC and are now in the standardized product stage. Personal computers (PCs) are a good example, despite their wide variety and the fact that some versions are in the new product and maturing product phases. For example, the early version of PCs that reached the market in the 1984 to 1991 period were in the standardized product stage by 1995 and sold primarily on the basis of price. Machines that entered the market in the 1996 to 1998 period were in the maturing stage by 1999. PCs with increased memory capability that were in the new product stage in 1999 quickly moved toward maturity, and by 2002 they were being replaced by even better machines with faster processors and more multimedia capabilities. Today, diskettes are standardized and rarely used while standard components include CD writers, DVD ROMs, DSL and wireless Internet connectors, USB ports, advanced graphics and sound, flat LCD monitors, and digital photography capabilities.

Desktop computers are increasingly being replaced by laptop models that are lighter, faster, more sophisticated, and less expensive than their predecessors. In turn, these machines are being replaced by notebooks with advanced Pentium chips, long-term battery capability, and storage capable of holding billions of bytes complete with wireless equipment and serve as a complete communications center from which the international executive can communicate anywhere in the world. These machines will first be manufactured locally and then in foreign markets. Thus, computers will continue to move through an international product life cycle.

The IPLC theory is useful in helping to explain how new technologically innovative products fit into the world trade picture. However, because new innovative products are sometimes rapidly improved, it is important to remember that one or two versions of them may be in the standardized product stage while other versions are in the maturing stage and still others are in the new product phase.

Other important considerations

Many factors beyond those we have considered greatly influence international trade theory.[5] One is government regulation. Countries often limit or restrict trade with other countries for political reasons. For example, despite the benefits of international trade, the United States has not officially traded with North Korea or Cuba for several decades. Other important factors include monetary currency valuation and consumer tastes.

Monetary currency valuation

When examining why one country trades with another, we need to consider the monetary exchange rate, which is the price of one currency stated in terms of another currency. For example, from 1995 to 1998 the value of the Japanese yen declined significantly over the value of the US dollar. As a result, many Japanese businesses found their products becoming much more competitive in the US market. Thereafter, the Japanese government announced that because the yen was again getting too strong, it wanted to weaken its value, thus ensuring that Japanese businesses could maintain their international competitiveness. Another reason why monetary currency valuation is important is because a foreign firm doing business will report its revenues and profits in home-country currency. So if a British firm sold $10 million of machinery in Canada and the value of the Canadian dollar declined against the British currency, the UK company would report less revenue (in terms of British pounds) than if the Canadian dollar had remained stable or, better yet, increased in

Monetary exchange rate
The price of one currency stated in terms of another currency

165

INTERNATIONAL BUSINESS STRATEGY *IN ACTION*

China's organic food exports

In the 1970s and 1980s, Chinese agricultural policy busied itself with finding ways to feed the country's large population. Pesticides, fungicides, antibiotics, and other aids to agriculture were not evaluated on their health and environmental effects, but on whether they were available and affordable for farmers. Organic alternatives were encouraged because they were an inexpensive alternative available to farmers.

The first organic farm, Liu Min Ying Ecological Farm, was established outside Beijing in 1982. Today, it uses organic wastes, solar energy, and other ecological approaches to sustain grain production, greenhouses, orchards, nurseries, and organic husbandry operations. It serves as a tourist attraction, and the United Nations even named it as a model to follow in 1987. By 2000, nine research groups on organic production were feeding the knowledge base required for organic farming. More than 50 bases of organic production, five organic fertilizer factories, and more than 30 processing facilities were part of the industry.

Among China's 1.3 billion people, organic farmers are still a puny minority. However, more and more are embracing this type of farming because of the premium price of 30 per cent to 50 per cent offered by buyers. At the Fuyu Farm for Returned Overseas Chinese, its 350 workers are converting 2,000 hectares into land suitable for organic soybeans, corn, or kidney beans for export to Japan, Europe, or the United States. This is just one example of what is happening in clusters across the country.

China's organic green tea was first certified by SKAL of the Netherlands in 1990, marking the beginnings of international recognition and trade. By 2001, the value of China's exports of organic products was estimated at over $25 million, an increase from $10 million in 1998. Commodities exported included tea, honey, soybeans, buckwheat, wheat, sunflower seeds, pine nuts, pumpkin seeds, walnuts, condiments, milk powder, and traditional Chinese medicines. At the time, more than 30 Chinese-based firms were engaged in the trade of organic foods. Most exports were destined to Japan and other developed countries in North America and the EU.

Two main markets for Chinese products, the United States and Japan, offer different challenges and possibilities. Japan, the closest triad market, had an organics market of $400 million in 2003. This is a tiny amount compared to the estimated

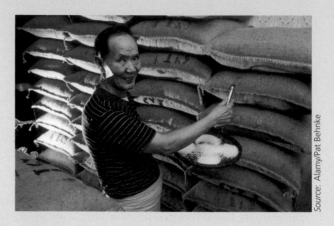

Source: Alamy/Pat Behnke

$1 trillion food market, leaving ample opportunity for the growth of organic products.

A key to success in the organics market is credibility. The Japan Agriculture Standards is the agency responsible for certifying organic products for a nation of quality-conscious customers. Chinese organic products had been able to attain certification in this country, which depends heavily on imports for food products. But in 2001, Japanese importers found pesticides in Chinese spinach that was labeled organic, and Japanese consumers and importers quickly lost confidence in Chinese organics.

Partly as a result of Japanese certification that is recognized by the United States as the National Organics Program (NOP), Chinese organic products have made their way to the US market. The value of the US organics market, estimated at $13 billion in 2003, is expected to reach $100 billion by 2010. The size of this market and its prospects has caught the attention of the domestic certification bodies in China, which are presently negotiating accreditation status with the NOP.

Sources: China, Center for Environmental Education and Communication (CEEC); China Environment and Sustainable Development Reference and Research Center (CESDRRC); adapted from Lu, Zhenhui, *Production and Market of Organic Foods in China*, 1st Gangjin International Symposium on Organic Agriculture, 2002 (November 15), Gangjin, Korea; Nao Nakanishi, "Organic Farming Set to Boom in China," *Reuters*, October 25, 2003; Claire Hope Cummings, "Japanese Consumers Hungry for More Organic Food," *New Farm*, August 8, 2003; "China to Unify Organic Food Standards," *People's Daily*, November 11, 2003; and Rudy Kortbech-Olesen, *The US Market for Organic Foods Beverages* (Geneva: United Nations Conference on Trade and Development, March 2002).

value against the pound. In mid-2005, the euro became so strong compared to the dollar that Volkswagen reported a 63 per cent decline in pre-tax profits.[6] In the next chapter we will discuss exchange rates in more detail.

Consumer tastes

International trade is not based solely on price; some people will pay more for a product even though they can buy something similar for less money. This willingness to pay more may be based on prestige, perceived quality, or a host of other physical and psychological reasons. Personal tastes dictate consumer decisions. See the box **International Business Strategy in Action: China's organic food exports**.

✔ Active learning check

Review your answer to Active Learning Case question 2 and make any changes you like. Then compare your answer with the one below.

 2 How does an EU manager's desire to buy domestic products illustrate the importance of consumer taste in international markets?

This example shows that people often buy goods based on personal preference, rather than only on such characteristics as low price, high quality, or improved productivity. Of course, this "Buy EU" focus will often come into play only when all other factors are approximately equal. The manager is unlikely to turn down a China-made product that is 30 per cent less expensive in favor of one that is made domestically. So there are limits to the effects of consumer taste on purchase decisions, though it is certainly one variable that has proven very important in international trade.

BARRIERS TO TRADE

Why do many countries produce goods and services that could be purchased more cheaply from others? One reason is trade barriers, which effectively raise the cost of these goods and make them more expensive to local buyers.

Reasons for trade barriers

One of the most common reasons for the creation of trade barriers is to encourage local production by making it more difficult for foreign firms to compete there. Another reason is to help local firms export and thus build worldwide market share by doing such things as providing them with subsidies in the form of tax breaks and low-interest loans. Other common reasons include:

1 Protect local jobs by shielding home-country business from foreign competition.
2 Encourage local production to replace imports.
3 Protect infant industries that are just getting started.
4 Reduce reliance on foreign suppliers.
5 Encourage local and foreign direct investment.
6 Reduce balance of payments problems.
7 Promote export activity.

8 Prevent foreign firms from *dumping* (selling goods below cost in order to achieve market share).

9 Promote political objectives such as refusing to trade with countries that practice apartheid or deny civil liberties to their citizens.

Commonly used barriers

A variety of trade barriers deter the free flow of international goods and services.[7] The following presents six of the most commonly used barriers.

Price-based barriers

Imported goods and services sometimes have a tariff added to their price. Quite often this is based on the value of the goods. For example, some tobacco products coming into the United States carry an ad valorem tariff (see below) of over 100 per cent, thus more than doubling their cost to US consumers. Tariffs raise revenues for the government, discourage imports, and make local goods more attractive.

Quantity limits

Quantity limits, often known as quotas, restrict the number of units that can be imported or the market share that is permitted. If the quota is set at zero, as in the case of Cuban cigars from Havana to the United States, it is called an embargo. If the annual quota is set at one million units, no more than this number can be imported during one year; once it is reached, all additional imports are turned back. In some cases a quota is established in terms of market share. For example, Canada allows foreign banks to hold no more than 16 per cent of Canadian bank deposits, and the EU limits Japanese auto imports to 10 per cent of the total market.

International price fixing

Sometimes a host of international firms will fix prices or quantities sold in an effort to control price. This is known as a cartel. A well-known example is OPEC (Organization of Petroleum Exporting Countries), which consists of Saudi Arabia, Kuwait, Iran, Iraq, and Venezuela, among others (see Table 6.1). By controlling the supply of oil it provides, OPEC

Quota
A quantity limit on imported goods

Embargo
A quota set at zero, thus preventing the importation of those products that are involved

Cartel
A group of firms that collectively agree to fix prices or quantities sold in an effort to control price

Table 6.1 Members of the Organization of Petroleum Exporting Countries (OPEC), 2004

Member country	Quotas (barrels per day)
Algeria	830,000
Indonesia	1,347,000
Iran	3,817,000
Iraq	na
Kuwait	2,087,000
Libya	1,392,000
Nigeria	2,142,000
Qatar	674,000
Saudi Arabia	8,450,000
United Arab Emirates	2,269,000
Venezuela	2,992,000
Total	26,000,000

Source: Adapted from **www.opec.org**.

seeks to control both price and profit. This practice is illegal in the United States and Europe,[8] but the basic idea of allowing competitors to cooperate for the purpose of meeting international competition is being endorsed more frequently in countries such as the United States.[9] For example, US computer firms have now created partnerships for joint research and development efforts.

Non-tariff barriers

Non-tariff barriers are rules, regulations, and bureaucratic red tape that delay or preclude the purchase of foreign goods. Examples include (1) slow processing of import permits, (2) the establishment of quality standards that exclude foreign producers, and (3) a "buy local" policy. These barriers limit imports and protect domestic sales.

Non-tariff barriers
Rules, regulations, and bureaucratic red tape that delay or preclude the purchase of foreign goods

Financial limits

There are a number of different financial limits. One of the most common is exchange controls, which restrict the flow of currency. For example, a common exchange control is to limit the currency that can be taken out of the country; for example, travelers may take up to only $3,000 per person out of the country. Another example is the use of fixed exchange rates that are quite favorable to the country. For example, dollars may be exchanged for local currency on a 1:1 basis; without exchange controls, the rate would be 1:4. These cases are particularly evident where a black market exists for foreign currency that offers an exchange rate much different from the fixed rate.

Exchange controls
Controls that restrict the flow of currency

Foreign investment controls

Foreign investment controls are limits on foreign direct investment or the transfer or remittance of funds. These controls can take a number of different forms, including (1) requiring foreign investors to take a minority ownership position (49 per cent or less), (2) limiting profit remittance (such as to 15 per cent of accumulated capital per year), and (3) prohibiting royalty payments to parent companies, thus stopping the latter from taking out capital.

Such barriers can greatly restrict international trade and investment. However, it must be realized that they are created for what governments believe are very important reasons. A close look at one of these, tariffs, helps to make this clearer.

Foreign investment controls
Limits on foreign direct investment or the transfer or remittance of funds

Tariff
A tax on goods shipped internationally

Import tariff
A tax levied on goods shipped into a country

Export tariff
A tax levied on goods sent out of a country

Transit tariff
A tax levied on goods passing through a country

Tariffs

A tariff is a tax on goods that are shipped internationally. The most common is the import tariff, which is levied on goods shipped into a country.[10] Less common is the export tariff, for goods sent out of the country, or a transit tariff for goods passing through the country. These taxes are levied on a number of bases. A specific duty is a tariff based on units, such as $1 for each item shipped into the country. So a manufacturer shipping in 1,000 pairs of shoes would pay a specific duty of $1,000. An ad valorem duty is a tariff based on a percentage of the value of the item, so a watch valued at $25 and carrying a 10 per cent duty would have a tariff of $2.50. A compound duty is a tariff consisting of both a specific and an ad valorem duty, so a suit of clothes valued at $80 that carries a specific duty of $3 and an ad valorem duty of 5 per cent would have a compound duty of $7.

Governments typically use tariffs to raise revenue and/or to protect local industry. At the same time, these taxes decrease demand for the respective product while raising the price

Specific duty
A tariff based on the number of items being shipped into a country

Ad valorem duty
A tax which is based on a percentage of the value of imported goods

Compound duty
A tariff consisting of both a specific and an ad valorem duty

Figure 6.2 Impacts of a tariff

Source: Raymond Vernon and Louis T. Wells, Jr., *The Manager in the International Economy* (Englewood Cliffs, NJ: Prentice-Hall, 1991), p. 85.

to the buyer. This is illustrated in Figure 6.2, which shows how the quantity demanded declines from Q_1 to Q_2 when a tariff drives the price of a good from P_1 to P_2 (the world price plus the tariff). This price increase allows local producers to sell Q_3Q_2 and thus take market share away from foreign firms that were exporting Q_3Q_1 into the country. However, the figure shows this is done at the price of charging the consumer more money *and* reducing the number of buyers who purchase the product. At new price P_2, there are no longer any imports.

There are numerous reasons for using tariffs, such as to protect domestic industries or firms. The US government has used them to prevent foreign companies from selling goods at lower prices in the United States than back home. US auto makers have often accused their overseas rivals of using this tactic. In the case of Japanese car manufacturers, this was a particularly troublesome area when the value of the yen rose sharply in the early 1990s. As a result, argued the US car companies, imported parts and cars had to reflect the increased value of the yen or be subjected to tariffs.[11] Others have made similar arguments. Eastman Kodak, for example, asked the US Commerce Department to impose steep tariffs on the Fuji Photo Film Company. Kodak's argument was partially based on the rising yen. However, it also reflected a concern with **dumping**, which is the selling of imported goods at a price below cost or below that in the home country. In this case Kodak argued that Fuji sold color photographic paper for less than 20 cents a square foot in the United States, while charging almost 60 cents a square foot in Japan.[12] For an example of a protectionist tariff, see the box **International Business Strategy in Action: The EU–US courier wars**.

Another reason for using tariffs is to raise government revenue. Import tariffs, for example, are a major source of revenue for less developed countries. A third reason is to reduce citizens' foreign expenditures in order to improve the country's balance of payments.

Tariffs continue to be one of the most commonly used barriers to trade, despite the fact that they often hurt low-income consumers and have a limited impact, if any, on upper-income purchasers. In recent years most industrialized countries have tried to reduce or eliminate the use of these trade barriers and to promote more free trade policies.[13] The United States is a good example. (The trade policies of the EU are discussed in Chapter 16 and those of Japan in Chapter 17.)

Dumping
The selling of imported goods at a price below cost or below that in the home country

INTERNATIONAL BUSINESS STRATEGY *IN ACTION*

The EU–US courier wars

Local businesses have many reasons for encouraging their governments to erect barriers to trade. One of the most common is when an industry is not competitive on a worldwide basis and foreign competition could bring about the bankruptcy of local firms. The US steel industry is a good example. The efficiencies of both Western European and Japanese steelmakers have brought new challenges to the American steel industry, which asked President George W. Bush to protect it from foreign imports.

Sometimes, however, local firms will seek protection from foreign competition even though they are profitable. Why? Because they don't want to give up any of their local market share— which will happen if more entrants are allowed into the industry. A good example is found in the courier wars now being fought in the United States. The three firms involved are FedEx, UPS, and DHL. The first two are American companies that collectively control 79 per cent of the US market. The other is a German company that holds 1 per cent of the market.

FedEx operates out of Memphis, Tennessee, where it has a major distribution hub and a large number of aircraft to help meet its commitment of one-day delivery. UPS's airport hub in Louisville, Kentucky, is complemented by a fleet of 150,000 trucks and 1,700 depots spread across the country. Both firms do business in Europe, where they are also profitable. Yet, despite their significant size and worldwide market coverage, both have been trying to prevent DHL from building an air fleet business in the United States to deliver packages and mail just like they do. Moreover, the two giant American firms have been receiving support from the Department of Transportation, which they have lobbied to prevent DHL from getting an air license.

One of the arguments made by FedEx and UPS is that although DHL Airways is 100 per cent US-owned, the parent company is controlled through an agreement by German owners with DHL's US subsidiary. This latter arrangement might seem a little strange, but a similar situation exists in Canada. The largest courier service in that country is Purolator, which is owned by the Canadian post office, a crown monopoly. Yet despite this monopoly, both FedEx and UPS do quite well in Canada. US law, however, does not allow foreign entities to own more than 49 per cent of the equity and 25 per cent of the voting stock of a US air carrier.

Deutsche Post circumvented these regulations by selling a controlling stake of DHL Airways to an American with large

Source: Getty Images/Business Link

stakes in DHL's international operations. Critics claimed that DHL Airways had entered into an agreement with Deutsche Post to be a captive vendor and that in practical terms Deutsche Post owned DHL. The Department of Transportation then forced DHL Airways to expand its contracts outside of DHL. To this date, however, 90 per cent of DHL Airways' business continues to be with DHL.

In 2003, DHL sought to expand its airline capacity by integrating Seattle-based Airborne's airline fleet. FedEx and UPS once again appealed to the Department of Transportation and to US politicians claiming that despite the new company being 100 per cent owned by public shareholders, it would follow the same strategy that DHL Airways always did: working under an exclusive agreement with DHL.

FedEx and UPS continue to oppose DHL's green light to build an air fleet in the United States, showing that there are many reasons for barriers to trade beyond simply wanting to reduce the amount of industry competitiveness in order to increase overall profitability. In response, DHL has sought creative ways to ensure access to air transportation for its growing business.

Websites: www.fedex.com; www.dhl.com; www.ups.com; and www.purolator.com.

Sources: "A Tricky Business," *Economist,* June 30, 2001, pp. 55–56; "Transportation Labor Urges US Government to Revoke DHL's Air Freight Forward License," *TTD News,* January 30, 2001; Gene G. Marcial, "DHL Could Help Airborne Take Off," *Business Week,* July 9, 2001; Brian O'Reilly, "They've Got Mail," *Fortune,* February 7, 2000; "A Package with Strings Attached," *Economist.com,* March 27, 2003; "Airborne Fires Back at UPS, FedEx 'Duopoly'," *Puget Sound Business Journal,* April 7, 2003.

US trade policy

Despite being a highly protectionist nation in its early years, the United States has a policy today that generally strives to lower tariffs and trade barriers through the use of multi-lateral agreements. Since the protectionist disaster of the Depression years, the United States has sought to minimize the use of tariffs. It supported the General Agreement on Tariffs and Trade (GATT), and now it supports the 1994 World Trade Organization (WTO), which exists to liberalize trade and investment. Today US tariffs average only 2 to 3 per cent ad valorem to most countries of the world.[14]

Caribbean Basin Initiative
A trade agreement that eliminates tariffs on many imports to the United States from the Caribbean and Central American regions

Foreign Sales Corporation Act
Legislation designed to allow US exporters to establish overseas affiliates and not pay taxes on the affiliates' income until the earnings are remitted to the parent company

Trade adjustment assistance
Assistance offered by the US government to US businesses and individuals harmed by competition from imports

The move away from tariffs does not mean US trade policy is completely open.[15] The US government employs a variety of approaches to promote or discourage international trade. For example, to encourage trade, there is the **North American Free Trade Agreement (NAFTA)**, which eliminates most trade restrictions (such as tariffs) among the United States, Canada, and Mexico and extends national treatment to foreign investment, and the Caribbean Basin Initiative, which eliminates tariffs on many imports from the Caribbean and Central American regions. Yet the **Trading-with-the-Enemy Act** disallows trade with countries judged to be enemies of the United States, including North Korea and Cuba. The US administration has the authority to prevent sales of goods to foreign governments when they are not deemed to be in the best interests of the United States. These goods can range from computers to chemicals to materials used for making nuclear weapons.[16]

The United States has also used negotiated agreements to limit the type or number of products entering the country. For example, a voluntary agreement with Japan restricts the number of cars imported to the United States. At the same time, exports are encouraged through legislation such as the Foreign Sales Corporation Act, which allows US exporters to establish overseas affiliates and not to pay taxes on the affiliates' income until the earnings are remitted to the parent company. The government also offers trade adjustment assistance to US businesses and individuals who are harmed by competition from imports. This aid takes such forms as loans for retooling and job counseling for those seeking alternative employment.

✔ **Active learning check**

Review your answer to Active Learning Case question 3 and make any changes you like. Then compare your answer with the one below.

3 In what way could the EU use trade barriers to protect its markets from foreign competitors? Who can be affected by these trade barriers?

The EU could take a number of steps to protect its markets from foreign competitors. Examples include establishing or increasing ad valorem tariffs, placing quantity limits on various imports, and limiting foreign direct investment. Of course, other countries could retaliate and take similar action against EU-produced goods, so the use of these trade barriers must be selective and should not be undertaken unless efforts at negotiated agreements prove fruitless.

NON-TARIFF BARRIERS TO TRADE

The economic effects of non-tariff barriers (NTBs) to trade are roughly similar to those of tariffs. They are inefficient distortions that reduce potential gains from trade. Table 6.2 lists a wide range of NTBs.

NTBs have gained prominence and importance in recent years as nations have begun resorting to them more frequently for protection. Sometimes they are not imposed by

Table 6.2 Common non-tariff barriers to trade

Specific limitation	Customs administrative rules	Government participation	Import charges
Quotas (including voluntary)	Valuation systems	Procurement policies	Import deposits
Import licenses	Antidumping rules	Export subsidies and incentives	Supplementary duties
Supplementary incentives	Tariff classifications	Countervailing duties	Import credits
Minimum import limits	Documentation needed	Domestic assistance programs	Variable levies
Embargoes	Fees	Trade-diverting	Border levies
Sectoral bilateral agreements	Disparities in quality and testing standards		
Orderly marketing agreements	Packaging, labeling, and marketing standards		

countries to interfere deliberately with trade.[17] Rather, they arise out of domestic policy and economic management. Examples include tax breaks to reduce regional income disparities or regulations designed to increase local purchasing or employment. These, in turn, result in a type of indirect export subsidy. Other NTBs are more blatant devices that restrict imports or foster exports.

Quotas

The most important NTBs are quotas that restrict imports to a particular level.[18] When a quota is imposed, domestic production generally increases and prices rise. As a result, the government usually ends up losing tariff revenues.

Historically, the GATT and WTO have prohibited import quotas except on agricultural products, as emergency measures, or when a country has short-run balance of payments problems. Countries have circumvented this regulation most notably for textiles, footwear, and automobiles by negotiating voluntary export restraint agreements that are useful in preventing retaliatory action by the importing country. In general, business would rather be protected by quotas than by tariffs. Under quotas, if future domestic demand is known, companies can determine their future production levels. Under tariffs, domestic producers must estimate the elasticity of the demand curve for imported products and the future movements in world prices, which is a more difficult challenge.

"Buy national" restrictions

"Buy national" regulations require governments to give preference to domestic producers, sometimes to the complete exclusion of foreign firms. In Europe, for example, many of the telephone, telegraph, electric utility, airline, and railroad industries are government owned and buy from national firms only, thus closing a large market to exporters. On the other hand, countries like the United States have a similarly wide range of inefficient "Buy American" regulations at the national and state levels that discriminate against foreign suppliers. During the 1970s Tokyo Round of the GATT negotiations, a mild code to open up government contracts to foreign suppliers was negotiated. Only 28 governments have agreed to the WTO's Government Procurement Agreement and these must now publicize large procurement contracts to make public the winner's bid price or the basis for selecting the winning bid.

Customs valuation

Also during the GATT Tokyo Round, considerable progress was made in the area of customs valuation for the payment of duties. In the United States, there were nine valuation systems prior to the Tokyo Round. Value for duty is now generally based on the invoice cost, and the latitude of US customs to reclassify products has been reduced.

Technical barriers

Product and process standards for health, welfare, safety, quality, size, and measurements can create trade barriers by excluding products that do not meet them. Testing and certification procedures, such as testing only in the importing country and conducting on-site plant inspections, are cumbersome, time consuming, and expensive. The costs must be borne by the exporter prior to the foreign sale. National governments have the right and duty to protect their citizens by setting standards to prevent the sale of hazardous products. But such standards can also be used to impede trade. For example, at one point Japan excluded US-made baseball bats from the market because they did not meet the country's standard. No product produced outside Japan (even products made by foreign subsidiaries of Japanese MNEs) could bear the certification stamp of the Japanese Industrial Standard (JIS) or the Japanese Agricultural Standard (JAS), and selling in Japan without the JIS or JAS logo was difficult. Similarly, at one time the new regulations for automobile safety in the United States required that bumpers be above the height practical for imported subcompact cars, thus creating a technical barrier for these car manufacturers. Today the new code on technical barriers to trade requires consultation between trading partners before a standard that impedes trade is put in place. The code also requires that testing and certification procedures treat imports and domestic goods equally and that the importing country accept certification testing conducted in the exporting country.

Antidumping legislation, subsidies, and countervailing duties

The GATT and WTO allow importing countries to protect their producers from unfair competition, such as "dumping" goods at extremely low prices in an effort to gain market share and to drive out local competition. Importing countries are allowed to impose additional duties on products that have received export subsidies or are "dumped." Before the duties are imposed, however, the country must show that its domestic industry has suffered "material" injury from dumped or subsidized imports. Although products at these artificially low prices provide consumers in the importing country with a "good buy," such competition is thought to be unfair to domestic producers who object to dumping (and also to subsidized imports that can be offset by "countervailing" duties) if the domestic market of the exporting country is closed to them. A good example is the US auto industry, which claims that some Japanese cars are cheaper in the US market than at home, while Japan continues to impede exports of US cars into Japan.

The GATT and the WTO have developed a code on countervailing duties and antidumping duties that now expedites the process of determining whether exports have been dumped or subsidized and whether the domestic industry has been injured. This subject is exceedingly complex. Here are some examples (and answers).

If the EU remits value-added taxes on exports by EU producers, is this a subsidy? (No)

If Canada subsidizes production in a specific sector in one of its depressed regions for domestic purposes, are the exports of a subsidized firm subject to countervailing action? (Yes)

If the British government subsidizes the British steel industry and its losses incurred by selling at home and abroad at prices below full cost, are its exports subject to antidumping or to countervailing duties? (Maybe, sometimes)

The problem is complex because of the difficulty in determining what material injury is and how it should be measured. This area is likely to be a point of contention for years to come.

Agricultural products

Trade in agricultural products is highly regulated by both quotas and fixed and variable tariffs. Domestic producers in most industrialized countries are often highly subsidized both directly and by artificially high domestic prices. Agricultural exports are often subsidized as well. And the EU flatly refused to discuss its Common Agricultural Policy (CAP) at the Tokyo Round. The CAP sets variable tariffs on imports to maintain high domestic prices by excluding or impeding imports. Major reforms in the CAP are now underway that will see continuing support for farmers but independently of production volumes. This is expected to improve the EU's negotiation position at the WTO. The United States is not without guilt in this area, however, since it also subsidizes the export of many agricultural products. The countries most affected by these subsidies are under-developed countries with abundant and inexpensive labor and land and thus a competitive advantage in agricultural products. Agricultural subsidies have often stalled trade talks as these countries refused to further liberalize while developed countries continued to subsidize agriculture.

Export restraints

Over the vigorous objections of countries exporting natural resources, the GATT (and WTO) rounds have moved to tighten the conditions under which exports could be restrained. In general, world tariffs increase with the level of processing; for example, import duties increase as copper is processed from concentrate to blister, to refined copper, to copper wire and bars, to copper pots and pans. This tariff structure makes upgrading of natural resources in the producing country difficult. During the Tokyo round, natural resource-producing countries were largely unsuccessful in their attempts to harmonize tariffs on a sectoral basis in order to increase their ability to upgrade prior to export. However, they did argue successfully for their right to restrict exports to induce further domestic processing.

OTHER ECONOMIC DEVELOPMENTS

In addition to the above, other economic developments warrant consideration. These include countertrade, trade in services, and free trade zones.

Countertrade

Countertrade is essentially barter trade in which the exporting firm receives payment in terms of products from the importing country. Countertrade is important to the airline industry (for example, the purchase of Boeing 747s by British Airways if Boeing uses Rolls Royce engines) and in defense (for example, the purchase of US jet fighters by Canada if some of the parts are locally sourced in Canada). Barter sometimes takes the form of a buyback in which the exporter agrees to take products that are locally produced.

Countertrade
Barter trade in which the exporting firm receives payment in products from the importing country

Countertrade tends to decrease the efficiency of world trade because it substitutes barter for the exchange of goods by the price system. For example, a US exporter of machinery to Indonesia may have to take payment in an "equivalent value" of palm oil or rattan. The exporting firm will then either have to sell these products, in which it has no expertise itself, or sell them through a broker or other firm. Some party to the trade—exporter, importer, or consumer—must bear these additional costs. Despite such obvious inefficiencies, countertrade appears likely to continue as an increasingly important factor in the international trade environment of the 21st century.

In one type of situation, however, countertrade may be beneficial. For example, if a US producer of textile machinery exports to China and agrees to take payment in the form of textile products, importers in the United States may perceive a lower risk of variability in product quality and delivery schedules (as a result of US technology and management), and the Chinese may perceive a lower risk of product failure in buying the machinery since the selling firm will not be "paid" unless the machinery performs to specifications.

Trade in services

International trade in services has received relatively little attention from governments or trade economists during trade negotiations. Reliable statistics are seldom collected. However, as high-income countries move toward a service economy, trade in services has grown and become a significant component of the current accounts of many countries.

In 2002, the United States exported goods worth $1.02 trillion and imported goods worth $1.51 trillion, which left a deficit of $490 billion on merchandise trade. In services it exported $305 billion and imported $246 billion for a trade surplus of $59 billion that partly offset its merchandise trade deficit. And, it had a deficit of $21.9 billion in the net income receipts from US FDI abroad. Thus, the net deficit on these three accounts for the United States in 2002 was $541.8 billion. Details of the US goods, services, and FDI accounts appear in Table 6.3. (The balance of payments account will be explained in the appendix of this chapter.)

Table 6.3 US balance of current account, 2002

Items	Credits (1) (in billions of US $)	Debits (2) (in billions of US $)	Balance (1) − (2)
Merchandise trade of goods and services	1,018.7	1,508.9	(490.2)
Goods, balance of payments basis	713.8	1,263.2	(549.4)
Services	304.9	245.7	59.2
Defense	12.7	23.6	(10.9)
Travel	65.1	56.2	8.9
Passenger fares	15.6	20.6	(5.0)
Other transportation	31.9	45.1	(13.2)
Royalties and license fees	47.9	19.9	28.0
Other private services	131.0	77.4	53.6
US government miscellaneous services	0.8	3.0	(2.2)
Income receipts	275.5	258.9	16.6
FDI income	272.3	250.4	21.9
Direct investment receipts/payments	175.5	71.5	103.9
Other private receipts	92.2	112.5	(20.3)
US government receipts	4.6	66.4	(61.7)
Compensation of employees	3.3	8.5	(5.3)
Unilateral current transfers, net		68.3	(68.3)
Total	1,294.2	1,836.1	(541.8)

Source: Adapted from BEA, *Survey of Current Business*, May 2004.

The flow of services across/among countries is highly regulated. Internationally traded services such as banking, investment income, insurance, media, transportation, advertising, accounting, travel, and technology licensing are subject to a host of national and international regulations for economic, social, cultural, and political reasons. In 1995, the General Agreement on Trade in Services (GATS) came into effect. It covers all services except those provided by the government and those related to air traffic. Member countries are not forced to open all their service industries but can choose those areas for which they want to guarantee access to foreigners and, within a framework, how much access they want to provide. For example, a host nation might limit the scope of a foreign bank's operation through the use of licenses or by setting a maximum number of allowable branches. As of January 2000, more than 140 WTO members started negotiating to further liberalize services.

Whatever forum is used, negotiating reductions in service trade barriers will be difficult, complex, and lengthy. The barriers are often difficult to list, much less quantify for purposes of negotiation. And the issues are often highly charged and not subject to rational analysis. For example, Canada imposes Canadian content requirements on television, radio, and print media to foster a "national cultural identity," to protect its cultural heritage, and to protect the domestic arts, theater, and movie industries. A government that reduced these trade barriers or even agreed to negotiate them would be in trouble with the (protected) Canadian media, as well as with the general public.

Free trade zones

A free trade zone is a designated area where importers can defer payment of customs duty while products are processed further (same as a foreign trade zone). Thus, the free trade zone serves as an "offshore assembly plant," employing local workers and using local financing for a tax-exempt commercial activity. The economic activity takes place in a restricted area such as an industrial park, because the land is often being supplied at a subsidized rate by a local host government that is interested in the zone's potential employment benefits.

To be effective, free trade zones must be strategically located either at or near an international port, on major shipping routes, or with easy access to a major airport. Important factors in the location include the availability of utilities, banking and telecom services, and a commercial infrastructure.

More than 400 free trade zones exist in the world today, often encompassing entire cities, such as Hong Kong and Singapore. More than two-thirds are situated in developing countries, and most of their future growth is expected to occur there.

The advantages offered by free trade zones are numerous and mutually beneficial to all stakeholders. For private firms, the zones offer three major attractions. First, the firm pays the customs duty (tariff) only when the goods are ready to market. Second, manufacturing costs are lower because no taxes are levied. Third, while in the zone the manufacturer has the opportunity to repackage the goods, grade them, and check for spoilage. Secondary benefits to firms take the form of reduced insurance premiums (since these are based on duty-free values), reduced fines for improperly marked merchandise (since the good can be inspected in a zone prior to customers' scrutiny), and added protection against theft (resulting from security measures in the bonded warehouses).

At the state and local levels, advantages can be realized in terms of commercial services. On a more global level, free trade zones enable domestic importing companies to compete more readily with foreign producers or subsidiaries of MNEs, thereby increasing participation in world trade. Favorable effects are felt on the balance of payments because more economic activity occurs and net capital outflow is reduced. Finally, the business climate is improved due to reduced bureaucracy and resultant savings to business capital, currently inaccessible because of the delay in paying duties and tariffs. A free trade zone is a step toward free trade

Free trade zone
A designated area where importers can defer payment of customs duty while further processing of products takes place (same as a foreign trade zone)

and can be an important signal by government to business that the economy is opening up. Opportunity replaces regulation, and growth of economic activity should result.

Before the establishment of more free trade zones becomes fully accepted and encouraged, governments must be convinced of their many economic benefits. Free trade zones are a vital necessity if nations are to remain competitive on an international scale. Not only will existing companies benefit from their use, but new industries will be attracted, keeping up the same benefits of world trade.

Maquiladora industry
A free trade zone that has sprung up along the US–Mexican border for the purpose of producing goods and then shipping them between the two countries

The maquiladora industry along the US–Mexican border is an excellent example of a free trade zone. The low wage rate in Mexico and the North American Free Trade Agreement (NAFTA) of 1994 make the *maquiladora* region both accessible and important to labor-intensive firms in the United States and Canada. From only 12 *maquiladora* plants in 1965, approximately 3,000 existed in 2000. The *maquiladora* industry has been so successful that only oil earns Mexico more foreign currency today.

No Mexican taxes are paid on goods processed within the *maquiladoras*. Foreign companies doing such processing can benefit from lower wages and land costs than those in the United States as they increase the value added to their products. In return, Mexico attracts foreign direct investment into permanent plants, creates jobs, and collects taxes on any final products sold to the foreign firms, or within Mexico. Even though the United States has several hundred free trade zones of its own, many near seaports or airfields, these lack the low-wage workers of their Mexican counterparts.

Canada does not have free trade zones, but the federal government allows duty drawbacks, which arguably offer many of the same advantages. Unfortunately, these drawbacks, which are repayments of customs duties, apply retroactively and involve enough paperwork to discourage all but the largest or most dedicated organizations. As such, NAFTA and the lower-wage labor in Mexico have attracted Canadian firms producing labor-intensive products. Free trade zones exist in many other parts of the world than North America, and the advantages of these zones are enjoyed by businesses worldwide.[19]

KEY POINTS

1 International economics is the branch of economics concerned with the purchase and sale of foreign goods and services. This includes consideration of areas such as international trade, balance of payments, and barriers to trade.

2 A number of international trade theories help to explain why nations trade. These include the theory of absolute advantage, the theory of comparative advantage, the factor endowment theory, the Leontief paradox, and the international product life cycle theory. While no one theory offers a complete explanation of why nations trade, they collectively provide important insights into the area. Other key considerations that offer explanations for why nations trade include monetary currency valuation and consumer tastes.

3 There are a number of barriers to trade. Some of the most common include price-based barriers, quantity limits, international price fixing, non-tariff barriers, financial limits, and foreign investment controls.

4 Although tariffs are often introduced to maintain local jobs and assist infant industries, they are inefficient. This economic inefficiency results in higher prices of imported goods for the consumers. The redistribution of resources from more efficient industry further adds to the cost of a tariff. Such costs do not occur under free trade.

5 Non-tariff barriers (NTBs) provide similar economic inefficiencies to tariffs. Unlike tariffs, however, NTBs are not imposed by nations to interfere deliberately with trade;

they arise out of domestic policy. There are several types of NTBs, including quotas, "Buy national" restrictions, technical barriers, and export restraints.

6 Countertrade is a form of barter trade in which the exporting firm receives payments in terms of products produced in the importing country. It is most pronounced in East–West trade, and although it may be beneficial to the trading partners, it increases the inefficiencies in the world trade system which in turn raises costs and decreases trade volume.

7 Services are an important but somewhat misunderstood component of trade. Despite the trade of services in the billions of dollars among high-income countries, regulation has been outside the mandate of GATT. As services increase in importance, future discussion will take place concerning whether an international organization like GATT will carry the mandate to regulate this type of trade.

8 A free trade zone is a designated area where importers can defer payment of customs duty while further processing of products takes place. In essence, it is an offshore assembly plant. The majority of these areas exist in developing countries and handle approximately 20 per cent of worldwide trade. Free trade zones are advantageous to all because they provide benefits such as increased employment and lower business costs.

Key terms

- international trade
- mercantilism
- neo mercantilism
- theory of absolute advantage
- theory of comparative advantage
- factor endowment theory
- Heckscher–Ohlin theory
- Leontief paradox
- international product life cycle (IPLC) theory
- monetary exchange rate
- quotas
- embargo
- cartel
- non-tariff barriers
- exchange controls
- foreign investment controls
- tariff
- import tariff
- export tariff
- transit tariff
- specific duty
- ad valorem duty
- compound duty
- dumping
- Caribbean Basin Initiative
- Foreign Sales Corporation Act
- trade adjustment assistance
- countertrade
- free trade zone
- *maquiladora* industry

REVIEW AND DISCUSSION QUESTIONS

1 Why is it difficult to solve international economic problems in the short run?

2 What is the supposed economic benefit of embracing mercantilism as an international trade theory? Are there many disadvantages to the use of this theory?

3 How is the theory of absolute advantage similar to that of comparative advantage? How is it different?

4 In what way does factor endowment theory help explain why nations trade? How does the Leontief paradox modify this theory?

5 If an innovating country develops a new technologically superior product, how long will it be before the country begins exporting the product? At what point will the country begin importing the product?

6 Of what value is the international product life cycle theory in helping to understand why nations trade?

7 How does each of the following trade barriers work: price-based barriers, quantity limits, international price fixing, non-tariff barriers, financial limits, and foreign investment controls?

8 What are some of the reasons for trade barriers? Identify and describe five.

9 How does the United States try to encourage exports? Identify and describe two ways.

10 Non-tariff barriers have become increasingly predominant in recent years. Describe a non-tariff barrier, and list four types, explaining how the United States does or could use such a device.

11 How does countertrade work? Is it an efficient economic concept?

12 What is a free trade zone? Is it an efficient economic concept?

13 What are two future problems and challenges that will have to be addressed by the international monetary system? Describe each.

14 What is meant by the term *balance of payments*?

15 What are the three major accounts in the balance of payments?

16 How would the following transactions be recorded in the IMF balance of payments?

a IBM in New York has sold an $8 million mainframe computer to an insurance company in Singapore and has been paid with a check drawn on a Singapore bank.

b A private investor in San Francisco has received dividends of $80,000 for stock she holds in a British firm.

c The US government has provided $60 million of food and medical supplies for Kurdish refugees in Turkey.

d The Walt Disney Company has invested $50 million in a theme park outside Paris, France.

REAL CASE

Outsourcing to China

It was not a difficult choice to make. Between 1998 and 2001, US imports of household cooking equipment from China more than doubled to $640 million, forcing National Presto to decrease the price of its pans from $49.99 to $29.99 during that period. Cheap labor—Chinese labor is six times lower than Mexican labor—accounts for this price deflation. Continuing operations in the United States and remaining price competitive was simply not feasible.

Competition on quality, which can shelter domestic manufacturing from outsourcing to developing countries, was not an alternative because Chinese products for export are just as good. When high labor intensity is tied to quality, the Chinese can outdo industrialized countries. Another factor is that the Chinese have a combination of highly skilled management and low-skilled labor, ensuring that production is efficient and that quality standards are met. This ability to produce high-quality goods is also what allows China to move from export manufacturing of Christmas decorations, toys, footwear, and clothing to household, consumer appliances, and, increasingly, the IT manufacturing sector.

National Presto, a US firm that makes high-quality pressure cookers and electric frying pans, had a difficult decision to make in the early 2000s. It could either outsource its production to China or see its market share continue to deteriorate. In 2002, the company closed plants in Mississippi and New Mexico, reducing its US workforce to less than half, and expanded its production in China. By 2003, all significant products marketed by the company were to be sourced from China.

Proponents of free trade argue that political rhetoric against trade with China is meant to appease US fears of job losses. Yet, as seen in the following table, only 2.5 per cent of all job losses in the United States in the first quarter of 2004 were the result of overseas relocation. While some argue that this percentage is undervalued because it does not take into consideration potential job gains that never materialized, others argue that given economic conditions there was no assurance that firms that created new jobs in China would have chosen to create these jobs in the United States if outsourcing to China has not been a possibility.

Like many other US, European, and Japanese companies, National Presto uses an agent in Hong Kong to subcontract production to manufacturing plants in mainland China. Larger companies like Motorola, Philips, IBM,

Outsourcing and job losses in the United States, first quarter of 2004

Reasons for job losses	Losses	% of total
Overseas relocation	4,633	2.5
Domestic relocation	9,985	5.5
Other	167,838	92.0
Total, private non-farm sector	182,456	100.0

Note: Data only covers layoffs in companies with at least 50 workers, who have filed for unemployment insurance, for at least 50 workers, and where unemployment lasted more than 30 days.
Source: US Bureau of Labor Statistics, "Extended Mass Layoffs Associated with Domestic and Overseas Relocations," June 10, 2004.

Toshiba, and GE have more control over their manufacturing plants in China. Kyocera of Japan, for example, invested $90 million in the early 2000s to construct a high-tech industrial park in Shilong Town of Dongguan City, Guangdong Province. Only 20 years ago Guangdong was dominated by paddy fields; today it is China's largest manufacturing cluster.

China has become the world's fourth largest manufacturer, after the United States, Japan, and Germany. It has outpaced Japan to become the country having the largest trade surplus with the United States. US politicians and lobby groups blame Chinese protectionist practices for the growing trade deficit between the two nations, which in 2003 was estimated at $124 billion. Among the barriers the United States claims prevent a free flow of its goods to China are import barriers, unclear legal provisions applied in a discriminate manner against US imports, limitations on foreign direct investment, and an undervalued yuan. The last one has generated the most controversy in the last few years. The Chinese yuan has been fixed at 8.28 to the dollar since 1994, a rate that critics argue to be up to 40 per cent undervalued. Yet economists do not all agree that the yuan is undervalued. Some fear that a sharp deterioration would hurt not only the Chinese economy but also those trading partners that are most heavily dependent on Chinese imports.

Sources: "Chinese Trade Reform 'Is Failing'," *BBC News*, April 1, 2004; "China Defiant on Currency Exchange," *BBC News*, September 2, 2003; Mary Hennock, "China: The World's Factory Floor," *BBC News*, November 11, 2002; www.worldbank.com; and "Kyocera to Build High-Tech Industrial Park in Dongguan", *People's Daily*, September 13, 2000.

1 Does the theory of comparative advantage apply to China's trade with industrialized countries? How?

2 How does the factor endowment theory apply to China's trade with industrialized countries?

3 Are any of the countries mentioned operating in autarky?

4 How can distribution of gains from free trade cause much of the political debate regarding trade with China?

Dumping on trade complaints

One of the biggest problems in international trade is the ability of domestic producers to lobby their home governments to erect barriers to trade. In the past, the textile, apparel, and shoe industries were able to obtain protection from cheaper imports through tariffs, quotas, and special measures. Now multilateral trade agreements under the GATT and WTO (and also regional and bilateral agreements such as NAFTA and the emerging Asian Pacific Economic Cooperation forum) outlaw such blatant instruments of protection. However, these agreements have been replaced by more subtle ones.

Prominent as a new type of protectionist device is the use of "unfair trade laws," especially antidumping (AD) and countervailing duty (CVD) actions. The economic logic of AD and CVD makes some sense. It is unfair for a foreign producer to "dump" a product in your country below its price in the home country, or below the cost of producing it. Similarly, subsidized foreign products should be offset by a countervailing duty of equivalent effect. The problem, however, lies with the administration of the trade laws, which is subject to political lobbying.

A variety of studies have found that the bureaucrats who administer AD and CVD laws are subject to capture by the home industries, who then use AD and CVD cases as harassment tools against often economically efficient foreign rival producers. For example, Rugman and Anderson (1987) found that the US administration of AD and CVD was used in a biased manner against Canadian producers, especially in resource-based industries such as softwood lumber, fishing, and agriculture. Thus, in the

Canadian–US Free Trade Agreement of 1989, and again in NAFTA, five-person binational panels of trade law experts were set up to review the decision of the US (and Canadian) trade law agencies.

In a subsequent study, Rugman and Anderson (1997) found that these binational panels were able to remand back (i.e., successfully challenge) the decision of the US agencies twice as often in cases involving Canada as in AD and CVD cases involving the rest of the world. In related work researchers have found that the EU is just as bad as the United States when it comes to taking questionable AD measures, especially against Asian countries. Indeed, one of the unresolved problems is how smaller countries can secure access to the protected markets of triad economies such as the United States and the EU. In Japan's case, there are similar arguments (including those from its triad rivals) that it has entry barriers in place preventing market access.

Website: **www.wto.org**.

Sources: Andrew D. M. Anderson, *Seeking Common Ground: Canada–US Trade Dispute Settlement Policies in the Nineties* (Boulder, CO: Westview Press, 1995); Alan M. Rugman, *Multinational Enterprises and Trade Policy* (Cheltenham: Elgar, 1996); Alan M. Rugman and Andrew D. M. Anderson, *Administered Protection in America* (London and New York: Routledge, 1987); Alan M. Rugman and Andrew D. M. Anderson, "NAFTA and the Dispute Settlement Mechanisms," *The World Economy* (December 1997), pp. 935–950; Alan M. Rugman and Michael Gestrin, "EC Anti-Dumping Laws as a Barrier to Trade," *European Management Journal*, vol. 9, no. 4 (December 1991), pp. 475–482.

1 Why are antidumping and countervailing duty measures brought and imposed?

2 What is the impact on a firm from a non-triad country if it faces an AD or CVD case in its major market?

3 What is the solution to the abusive use of AD and CVD measures by triad economies?

Endnotes

1 Asra Q. Nomani and Douglas Lavin, "US and Japan Nearing Accord in Trade Dispute," *Wall Street Journal*, March 10, 1994, p. A 3; and Richard McGregor, "Beans are on the Beijing Menu as Bush Prepares to Talk Trade," *FT.com*, February 21, 2002.

2 Douglas Harbrecht et al., "Tough Talk," *Business Week*, February 20, 1994, pp. 26–28.

3 See, for example, Dana Weschler Linden, "Dreary Days in the Dismal Science," *Forbes*, January 21, 1991, pp. 68–71.

4 Also see Steven Greenhouse, "French Shift on State-Owned Sector," *New York Times*, April 8, 1991, p. C 2.

5 For additional insights into trade theory, see Nicolas Schmitt, "New International Trade Theories and Europe 1991: Some Results Relevant for EFTA Countries," *Journal of Common Market Studies*, September 1990, pp. 53–74.

6 "Tested by the Mighty Euro," *Economist.com*, May 18, 2004.

7 See Richard W. Stevenson, "East Europe Says Barriers to Trade Hurt Its Economies," *New York Times*, January 25, 1993, pp. A 1, C 8.

8 Lucy Walker, "Sir Leon's Cartel Busters Take to the Road Again," *The European*, April 12–14, 1991, p. 25.

9 Edmund Faltermayer, "Is 'Made in the USA' Fading Away?" *Fortune*, September 24, 1990, p. 73.

10 Edward Alden and Robert Shrimsley, "EU Set to Retaliate if US Imposes Steel Tariffs," *Financial Times*, March 4, 2002.

11 See, for example, Doron P. Levin, "Honda to Hold Base Price on Accord Model," *New York Times*, September 2, 1993, p. C 3.

12 Keith Bradsher, "Kodak Is Seeking Big Tariff on Fuji," *New York Times*, September 1, 1993, pp. A 1, C 2.

13 See, for example, Robert Cohen, "Grumbling over GATT," *New York Times*, July 3, 1993, p. 13.

14 Ed Gresser, "Tariffs Biggest US Tax on the Poor," *Reuters*, September 10, 2002.

15 See, for example, Chris Adams, "Ailing Steel Industry Launches a Battle Against Imports," *Wall Street Journal*, October 1, 1998, p. B 4; and "Steel Vice," *Wall Street Journal*, October 1, 1998, p. A 22.

16 As an example, see Clyde H. Farnsworth, "US Slows Computer for Brazil," *International Herald Tribune*, April 13–14, 1991, p. 5.

17 Claude Barfield, "Nerves of Steel," *Financial Times*, March 1, 2002.

18 Sometimes these are voluntary quotas, as seen in Andrew Pollack, "Japan Takes a Pre-emptive Step on Auto Exports," *New York Times*, January 9, 1993, pp. 17, 26.

19 Anthony DePalma, "Trade Pact Is Spurring Mexican Deals in the US," *New York Times*, March 17, 1994, pp. C 1, 3.

Additional bibliography

Anderson, Andrew D. M. *Seeking Common Ground: Canada–US Trade Disputes* (Boulder, CO: Westview, 1995).

Baldauf, Artur. "Examining Determinants of Export Performance in Small Open Economies," *Journal of World Business*, vol. 35, no. 1 (Spring 2000).

Brewer, Thomas L. and Young, Stephen. *The Multinational Investment System and Multinational Enterprises* (Oxford: Oxford University Press, 2000).

Brewer, Thomas L. and Young, Stephen. "Multilateral Institutions and Policies: Their Implications for Multinational Business

Strategy," in Alan M. Rugman and Thomas L. Brewer (eds.), *The Oxford Handbook of International Business* (Oxford: Oxford University Press, 2001).

Buckley, Peter J. "Government Policy Responses to Strategic Rent Seeking Transnational Corporations," *Transnational Corporations*, vol. 5, no. 2 (August 1996).

Cavusgil, S. Tamer and Sikora, Ed. "How Multinationals Can Counter Gray Market Imports," *Columbia Journal of World Business*, vol. 23, no. 4 (Winter 1988).

Chao, Paul. "Export and Reverse Investment: Strategic Implications for Newly Industrialized Countries," *Journal of International Business Studies*, vol. 20, no. 1 (Spring 1989).

Cho, Kang Rae. "The Role of Product-Specific Factors in Intra-Firm Trade of US Manufacturing Multinational Corporations," *Journal of International Business Studies*, vol. 21, no. 2 (Second Quarter 1990).

Dichtl, Erwin, Koeglmayr, Hans-Georg and Mueller, Stefan. "International Orientation as a Precondition for Export Success," *Journal of International Business Studies*, vol. 21, no. 1 (First Quarter 1990).

Deutsch, Klaus Gunter and Speyer, Bernhard (eds.). *The World Trade Organization Millennium Round* (London: Routledge, 2001).

Dunning, John H. and Mucchielli, Jean-Louis (eds.). *Multinational Firms: The Global-Local Dilemma* (London: Routledge, 2002).

Emmerij, Louis. "Globalization, Regionalization and World Trade," *Columbia Journal of World Business*, vol. 27, no. 2 (Summer 1992).

Green, Robert T. and Kohli, Ajay K. "Export Market Identification: The Role of Economic Size and Socioeconomic Development," *Management International Review*, vol. 31, no. 1 (First Quarter 1991).

Haigh, Robert, W. "Thinking of Exporting? Export Management Companies Could Be the Answer," *Columbia Journal of World Business*, vol. 29, no. 4 (Winter 1994).

Han, C. Min and Terpstra, Vern. "Country-of-Origin Effects for Uni-national and Bi-national Products," *Journal of International Business Studies*, vol. 19, no. 2 (Summer 1988).

Hennart, Jean-François. "Some Empirical Dimensions of Countertrade," *Journal of International Business Studies*, vol. 21, no. 2 (Second Quarter 1990).

Koka, Balaji R., Prescott, John E. and Madhavan, Ravindranath. "Contagion Influence on Trade and Investment Policy: A Network Perspective," *Journal of International Business Studies*, vol. 30, no. 1 (Spring 1999).

Markusen, James R. "International Trade Theory and International Business," in Alan M. Rugman and Thomas L. Brewer (eds.), *The Oxford Handbook of International Business* (Oxford: Oxford University Press, 2001).

Miller, Janice S., Hom, Peter W. and R. Gomez-Mejia, Luis. "The High Cost of Low Wages: Does Maquiladora Compensation Reduce Turnover?" *Journal of International Business Studies*, vol. 32, no. 3 (Fall 2001).

Neale, Charles W., Shipley, David D. and Dodds, J. Colin. "The Countertrading Experience of British and Canadian

Firms," *Management International Review*, vol. 31, no. 1 (First Quarter 1991).

Ostry, Sylvia. *The Post-Cold War Trading System* (Chicago, IL: University of Chicago Press, 1997).

Ostry, Sylvia. "The Multilateral Trading System," in Alan M. Rugman and Thomas L. Brewer (eds.), *The Oxford Handbook of International Business* (Oxford: Oxford University Press, 2001).

Perry, Anne C. "The Evolution of the US International Trade Intermediary in the 1980s: A Dynamic Model," *Journal of International Business Studies*, vol. 21, no. 1 (First Quarter 1990).

Ramstetter, Eric D. "Export Performance and Foreign Affiliate Activity in Japan's Large Machinery Firms," *Transnational Corporations*, vol. 6, no. 3 (December 1997).

Robin, Donald P. and Sawyer, W. Charles. "The Ethics of Antidumping Petitions," *Journal of World Business,* vol. 33, no. 3 (Fall 1998).

Robock, Stefan H. "The Export Myopia of US Multinationals: An Overlooked Opportunity for Creating US Manufacturing Jobs," *Columbia Journal of World Business*, vol. 28, no. 2 (Summer 1993).

Ruggiero, Renato. "Foreign Direct Investment and the Multilateral Trading System," *Transnational Corporations*, vol. 5, no. 1 (April 1996).

Rugman, Alan M. *Multinational Enterprises and Trade Policy* (Cheltenham: Elgar, 1996).

Rugman, Alan M. and Anderson, Andrew. *Administered Protection in America* (London: Croom Helm and New York: Methuen, 1987).

Rugman, Alan M. and Boyd, Gavin (eds.). *The World Trade Organization in the New Global Economy* (Cheltenham: Elgar, 2001).

Rugman, Alan M. and Gestrin, Michael. "US Trade Laws as Barriers to Globalization," in Tamir Agmon and Richard Drobnick (eds.), *Small Firms in Global Competition* (New York: Oxford University Press, 1994).

Rugman, Alan M. and Verbeke, Alain. *Global Corporate Strategy and Trade Policy* (London and New York: Routledge, 1990).

Rugman, Alan M. and Verbeke, Alain. "Strategic Trade Policy Is Not Good Strategy," *Hitotsubashi Journal of Commerce and Management*, vol. 25, no. 1 (December 1990).

Rugman, Alan M. and Verbeke, Alain. "Location, Competitiveness, and the Multinational Enterprise," in Alan M. Rugman and Thomas L. Brewer (eds.), *The Oxford Handbook of International Business* (Oxford: Oxford University Press, 2001).

Sampson, Gary P. (ed.). *The Role of the World Trade Organization in Global Governance* (Tokyo, New York, Paris: United Nations University Press, 2001).

Sullivan, Daniel and Bauerschmidt, Alan. "Common Factors Underlying Barriers to Export: A Comparative Study in the European and US Paper Industry," *Management International Review*, vol. 29, no. 2 (Second Quarter 1989).

APPENDIX TO CHAPTER 6 – THE BALANCE OF PAYMENTS

How well do we keep track of the millions of transactions that take place annually among exporters and importers, international banks, and multinational companies? The bankers who tabulate the foreign exchange dealings of their own banks are only a part of the picture. How well can we account for the part of direct investment that occurs through overseas borrowing, yet affects the home country's international economic position? Even more simply, how well can we measure "international" transactions that are simply transfers of funds from the account of an importer to the account of a foreign exporter in the same bank?

The realistic answer to these questions is: not very well. National governments create elaborate accounts for the transactions between their residents and foreign residents, but it is often very difficult to obtain full and accurate information. Putting that problem aside for the moment, let us consider the methods that governments use to record each country's international transactions.

Balance of payments (BOP)

The value of all transactions between a country's residents and the rest of the world; the three broad BOP categories are the current account, capital account, and official reserves

The most widely-used measure of international economic transactions for any country is the **balance of payments (BOP)**. This record attempts to measure the full value of the transactions between residents of one country and residents of the rest of the world for some time period, typically one year. The balance of payments is a *flow* concept, in that it records flows of goods, services, and claims between countries over a period of time, rather than a stock of accumulated funds or products. It is a *value* concept, in that all the items recorded receive a monetary value, denominated in the given country's currency at the time of those transactions. *The balance of payments thus is a record of the value of all the economic transactions between residents of one country and residents of all other countries during a given time period.*

Why do we worry about measuring these transactions? We do so because if a country records a substantial imbalance between inflows and outflows of goods and services for an extended period of time, some means of financing or adjusting away the imbalance must be found. For example, if the euro zone countries record a persistent trade deficit with China for several years, there will be pressure to either devalue the euro relative to the Chinese currency, the renminbi, or for Chinese investors to place large and continuing investments into euro-denominated securities. This pressure presents both a political outcome (pressure on the Chinese government to revalue the renminbi) and an economic outcome (pressure on the euro to devalue and on European producers to lower their costs, perhaps by producing in China).

So, the importance of the balance of payments is not only macroeconomic, in the domain of government accountants, but also managerial, since an imbalance provides guidance to managers about expected government policies as well as about opportunities to take advantage of currency opportunities. Since the relatively open foreign exchange markets of many countries today leave the exchange rate substantially to supply and demand, the balance of payments is an indicator of exactly that supply and demand for a country's currency that will lead to changes in the exchange rate.

The supply and demand for a currency come from both trade flows (exports and imports) and capital flows (investments and borrowing). So, the balance of payments implications for exchange rates must include both sides of the story, the "real" flows and the financial flows.

Balance of payments accounting

There is no such thing as *the* balance of payments, since the accounts are organized in a double-entry bookkeeping system, and for every debit entry there is a credit entry of equal value. There are half a dozen BOP measures, which group some international transactions together and leave others in a second, "everything else" category. In each case the intent is to place the fundamental economic causes of transactions in the first group and leave the payments for them in the second group. In the actual accounts, the former transactions are listed "above the line," and the payments are left "below the line."

Current account

The **current account** consists of merchandise trade, services, and unilateral transfers. (See Table 6A, parts *A* and *B*.)

Merchandise trade is typically the first part of the current account. It receives more attention than any of the other accounts because this is where the imports and exports of goods are

Current account
A BOP category that consists of merchandise trade, services, and gifts (unilateral transfers)

Table 6A Balance of payments: IMF presentation

	Debits	Credits
I. Current account		
A. Goods, services, and income:		
1. Merchandise	Imports from foreign sources (acquisition of goods).	Exports to foreign destinations (provision of goods).
Trade balance		
2. Shipment and other transportation	Payments to foreigners for freight and insurance on international shipments; for ship repair, stores, and supplies; and international passenger fares.	Receipts by residents from foreigners for services provided.
3. Travel	Expenditures by residents (including internal transportation) when traveling in a foreign country.	Receipts by residents for goods and services (including internal transportation) sold to foreign travelers in reporting country.
4. Investment income	Profits of foreign direct investments in reporting country, including reinvested earnings; income paid to foreigners as interest, dividends, etc.	Profits of direct investments by residents in foreign countries, including reinvested earnings; income received by residents from abroad as interest, dividends, etc.
5. Other official	Foreign purchases by government not included elsewhere; personal expenditures of government civilian and military personnel stationed in foreign countries.	Expenditures of foreign governments for goods and services, not included elsewhere; personal expenditures of foreign civilian and military personnel stationed in reporting country.
6. Other private	Payments to foreigners for management fees, royalties, film rentals, construction, etc.	Receipts from foreigners for management fees, royalties, film rentals, construction, etc.
Goods, services, and income balance		
B. Unilateral transfers:		
1. Private	Payments in cash and kind by residents to foreigners without a quid pro quo such as charitable gifts and gifts by migrants to their families.	Receipts in cash and kind by residents from foreigners, individuals, or governments without a quid pro quo.
2. Official	Transfers by government of reporting country for pensions, reparations, and grants for economic and military aid.	Transfers received by government from foreigners in the form of goods, services, or cash as gifts or grants. Also tax receipts from non-residents.
Current account balance		

Table 6A (continued)

	Debits	Credits
II. Capital account		
C. Capital, excluding reserves:		
1. Direct investment	a. Increased investment in foreign enterprises controlled by residents, including reinvestment of earnings.	a. Decreased investment in foreign enterprises controlled by residents.
	b. Decreases in investment by residents in domestic enterprises controlled by foreigners.	b. Increases in investment in domestic enterprises by foreigners.
2. Portfolio investment	a. Increases in investment by residents in foreign securities.	a. Decreases in investments by residents in foreign securities.
	b. Decreases in investment by foreigners in domestic securities such as bonds and corporate equities.	b. Increases in investment by foreigners in domestic securities.
3. Other long-term, official	a. Loans to foreigners.	a. Foreign loan reductions.
	b. Redemption or purchase from foreigners of government securities.	b. Sales to foreigners of government securities.
4. Other long-term, private	a. Long-term loans to foreigners by resident banks and private parties.	a. Long-term loans by foreigners to resident banks or private parties.
	b. Loan repayments by residents to foreign banks or private parties.	b. Loan repayments by foreigners to residents.
5. Other short-term, official	a. Short-term loans to foreigners by central government.	a. Short-term loans to resident central government by foreigners.
	b. Purchase from foreigners of government securities, decrease in liabilities constituting reserves of foreign authorities.	b. Foreign sales of short-term resident government securities, increases in liabilities constituting reserves of foreign authorities.
6. Other short-term, private	a. Increases in short-term foreign assets held by residents.	a. Decreases in short-term foreign assets held by residents. Increase in foreign liabilities of residents.
	b. Decreases in domestic assets held by foreigners, such as bank deposits, currencies, debts to banks, and commercial claims.	b. Increase in domestic short-term assets held by foreigners or decrease in short-term domestic liabilities to foreigners.
III. Reserves		
D. Reserves:		
1. Monetary gold	Increases in holdings of gold, SDRs,	Decreases in holdings of gold,
2. Special drawing rights (SDRs)	foreign convertible currencies by	SDRs, foreign convertible currencies
3. IMF reserve position	monetary authorities; decreases in	by monetary authorities; increases
4. Foreign exchange assets	liabilities to IMF or increase in IMF assets position.	in liabilities to IMF or decrease in IMF assets position.
E. Net errors and omissions:	Net understatement of recorded debts or overstatement of recorded credits.	Net understatement of recorded debts or overstatement of recorded credits.
Balances:		
Balances on merchandise trade	*A-1 credits minus A-1 debts*	
Balance on goods, services, and income	*A-1 through A-6 credits minus A-1 through A-6 debts*	
Balance on current account	*A and B credits minus A and B debts*	

reported, and these are often the largest single component of all international transactions. In this account, sales of goods to foreigners (exports) are reported as credits because they are a source of funds or a claim against the purchasing country. Conversely, purchases of goods from overseas (imports) are recorded as debits because they use funds. This payment can be made by either reducing current claims on foreigners or increasing foreign liabilities.

Merchandise trade transactions can affect a country's BOP in a number of ways. Assume that Nissan Motor of Japan has sold General Motors in the US $600,000 worth of engines and these engines will be paid for from GM's account in a Detroit bank. In this case the imports are a debit to the current account (A-1) and a credit to the "other short-term, private" capital account (C-6b). Here is how the entry would be recorded:

		Debit	Credit
A-1	Merchandise imports	$600,000	
C-6b	Increase in domestic short-term assets held by foreigners		$600,000

The result of this purchase is that the United States has transferred currency to foreigners and thus reduced its ability to meet other claims.

Services

The services category includes many payments such as freight and insurance on international shipments (A-2); tourist travel (A-3); profits and income from overseas investment (A-4); personal expenditures by government, civilians, and military personnel overseas (A-5); and payments for management fees, royalties, film rental, and construction services (A-6). Purchases of these services are recorded as debits, while sales of these services are similar to exports and are recorded as credits. For example, extending the earlier example of Nissan and GM, assume that the US auto maker must pay $125,000 to Nissan to ship the engines to the United States. The transaction would be recorded this way:

		Debit	Credit
A-2	Shipment	$125,000	
C-6b	Other short-term private capital		$125,000

GM purchased a Japanese shipping service (a debit to the current account) and paid for this by increasing the domestic short-term assets held by foreigners (a credit to the capital account).

Unilateral transfers

Unilateral transfers are transactions that do not involve repayment or the performance of any service. Examples include the American Red Cross sending $10 million in food to refugees in Somalia; the United States paying military pensions to residents of the Philippines who served in the US army during World War II; and British workers in Kuwait shipping money home to their families in London. Here is how the American Red Cross transaction would appear in the US BOP:

		Debit	Credit
B-1	Unilateral transfers, private	$10 million	
A-1	Merchandise exports		$10 million

Capital account

Capital account items are transactions that involve claims in ownership. Direct investment (C-1) involves managerial participation in a foreign enterprise along with some account that involves degree of control. The United States classifies direct investments as those

Capital account
A category of the BOP that consists of transactions that involve financial claims

investments that give the investor more than 10 per cent ownership. Portfolio investment (C-2) is investment designed to obtain income or capital gains. For example, if Exxon shipped $20 million of equipment to an overseas subsidiary the entry would be:

		Debit	Credit
C-1	Direct investment	$20 million	
A-1	Exports		$20 million

"Other long-term" capital accounts are differentiated based on whether they are government (C-3) or private (C-4) transactions. These transactions have a maturity of over one year and involve either loans or securities. For example, Citibank may have loaned the government of Poland $50 million. "Other short-term" capital accounts are also differentiated based on whether they are governmental (C-5) or private (C-6). Typical short-term government transactions are short-term loans in the securities of other governments. Private transactions often include trade bill acceptances or other short-term claims arising from the financing of trade and movements of money by investors to take advantage of interest differentials among countries.

Official reserves

Official reserves
Funds owned by national monetary authorities that are used for bringing BOP accounts into balance

Official reserves are used for bringing BOP accounts into balance. There are four major types of reserves available to monetary authorities in meeting BOP deficits (D1 through D4 in Table 6A). These reserves are analogous to the cash or near-cash assets of a private firm. Given that billions of dollars in transactions are reported in BOP statements, it should come as no surprise that the amount of recorded debits are never equal to the amount of credits. This is why there is an entry in the reserve account for net errors and omissions. If a country's reporting system is weak or there are a large number of clandestine transactions, this discrepancy can be quite large.

US balance of payments

The official presentation of the US BOP is somewhat different from the IMF format presented in Table 6A. Because the United States plays such a dominant role in the world economy, it is important to examine the US system. Table 6B presents US international transactions for two recent years.

A number of select entries in Table 6B help to highlight the US BOP. Lines 2 and 19 show that in 2003 exports of goods and services were $496.5 billion (Line 73) less than imports. This trade deficit was greater than that in 2002 when it stood at $421.7 billion, showing that the United States continues to have trade deficit problems.

To assess the trade situation accurately, however, we need to examine the data in more depth. This information is provided in Table 6C. The table shows that although US exports are strong in areas such as capital goods and industrial supplies and materials, the country also imports a large amount of these products. In addition, the United States is a net importer of foods, feeds, and beverages, automotive vehicles and parts, consumer goods, and petroleum and products.

In the early 1980s US trade deficits were offset by large amounts of income generated by direct investments abroad. Later in the decade massive international borrowing offset these deficits. More recently the situation has improved somewhat, and dollar devaluation has helped to generate stronger demand for US exports, thus partially reducing the growth rate of its annual trade deficit. However, more concerted action will be needed if the

Table 6B US international transactions: 2002 and 2003

Line	(Credits +; debits −)	2002 (in millions of US $)	2003 (in millions of US $)
	Current account		
1	Exports of goods and services and income receipts	1,242,739	1,314,888
2	Exports of goods and services	975,940	1,020,503
3	Goods, balance of payments basis	681,833	713,122
4	Services	294,107	307,381
5	Transfers under US military agency sales contracts	11,943	12,491
6	Travel	66,728	64,509
7	Passenger fares	17,046	15,693
8	Other transportation	29,195	31,833
9	Royalties and license fees	44,219	48,227
10	Other private services	124,181	133,818
11	US government miscellaneous services	795	810
12	Income receipts	266,799	294,385
13	Income receipts on US-owned assets abroad	263,861	291,354
14	Direct investment receipts	147,291	187,522
15	Other private receipts	113,267	99,135
16	US government receipts	3,303	4,697
17	Compensation of employees	2,938	3,031
18	Imports of goods and services and income payments	(1,657,301)	(1,778,117)
19	Imports of goods and services	(1,397,675)	(1,517,011)
20	Goods, balance of payments basis	(1,164,728)	(1,260,674)
21	Services	(232,947)	(256,337)
22	Direct defense expenditures	(19,101)	(25,117)
23	Travel	(58,044)	(56,613)
24	Passenger fares	(19,969)	(20,957)
25	Other transportation	(38,407)	(44,768)
26	Royalties and license fees	(19,235)	(20,049)
27	Other private services	(75,271)	(85,829)
28	US government miscellaneous services	(2,920)	(3,004)
29	Income payments	(259,626)	(261,106)
30	Income payments on foreign-owned assets in the US	(251,246)	(252,573)
31	Direct investment payments	(46,460)	(68,657)
32	Other private payments	(128,672)	(111,874)
33	US government payments	(76,114)	(72,042)
34	Compensation of employees	(8,380)	(8,533)
35	Unilateral current transfers, net	(59,382)	(67,439)
40	US-owned assets abroad, net (increase/financial outflow (−))	(198,014)	(283,414)
55	Foreign-owned assets in the US, net (increase/financial inflow (+))	768,246	829,173
71	Balance on goods (lines 3 and 20)	(482,895)	(547,552)
72	Balance on services (lines 4 and 21)	61,160	51,044
73	Balance on goods and services (lines 2 and 19)	(421,735)	(496,508)
74	Balance on income (lines 12 and 29)	7,173	33,279
75	Unilateral current transfers, net (line 35)	(59,382)	(67,439)
76	Balance on current account (lines 1, 18, and 35 or lines 73, 74, and 75)	(473,944)	(530,668)

Sources: US Department of Commerce, *Survey of Current Business*, September 2004.

United States is to continue on this course. One way is to continue to increase US competitiveness in the international market. Another way is to get other countries to reduce their trade barriers and to make international markets more open.

When a country suffers a persistent balance of trade deficit, the nation will also suffer from a depreciating currency and will find it difficult to borrow in the international capital

Table 6C US merchandise trade, 2002 and 2003

	2002 (in billions of US $)	2003 (in billions of US $)
Exports	697	726.4
Foods, feeds, and beverages	49.6	55
Industrial supplies and materials	153.5	168.3
Capital goods, except automotive	290.4	293.6
Automotive vehicles, engines, and parts	78.9	80.7
Consumer goods, except automotive	84.4	89.9
Other	40.2	38.9
Imports	1189.6	1282
Foods, feeds, and beverages	49.7	55.8
Industrial supplies and materials, except petroleum and products	158.4	174.3
Petroleum and products	103.5	133.1
Capital goods, except automotive	283.3	295.8
Automotive vehicles, engines, and parts	203.7	210.2
Consumer goods, except automotive	308	334
Other	83	78.8

Sources: US Department of Commerce, *Survey of Current Business*, September 2004 and Bureau of Economic Analysis.

market. In this case there are only two choices available. One is to borrow from the International Monetary Fund (IMF) and be willing to accept the restrictions that the IMF puts on the country, which are designed to introduce austerity and force the country back onto the right economic track. The other approach is for the country to change its fiscal policy (tariffs and taxes), resort to exchange and trade controls, or devalue its currency. To prevent having to undertake austerity steps, the United States will have to continue working very hard to control its trade deficit.

Chapter 7

INTERNATIONAL FINANCIAL MARKETS AND INSTITUTIONS

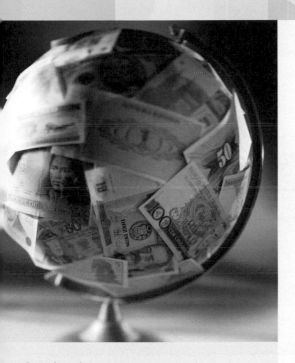

Contents

Objectives of the chapter

This chapter considers financial markets that allow firms to find sources and uses of funds outside their home countries and to deal in currencies other than the domestic one. It also considers the risks involved in operating in these markets and the tools available to deal with those risks. The main risk has to do with dealing in foreign currencies, so exchange risk and the functioning of the foreign exchange market are key elements of the discussion. For example, when a German firm borrows from a bank in dollars, because of the low interest rate, the firm faces a problem of exchange risk. The firm has to decide what to do in case the dollar rises in value relative to the euro and makes loan repayment more expensive.

The main goals of the chapter are to:

1 *Review* the basic characteristics of all the financial markets that may be available to a firm in international business.
2 *Examine* the foreign exchange market, its operation, and the main participants.
3 *Explain* the fundamental economic factors that determine the exchange rates in the absence of government intervention in the foreign exchange markets.
4 *Show* how firms can operate successfully in more than one currency without facing unacceptable levels of exchange risk.
5 *Give* insights into domestic money and capital markets that exist around the world.
6 *Describe* the functioning of the euromarkets, both short term and long term.
7 *Explain* how the international monetary system functions and how it relates to both private-sector firms and governments.
8 *Look* at a country's balance of payments and show what lessons can be drawn from it.
9 *Show* how firms can take advantage of the opportunities available in all of these markets.

ACTIVE LEARNING CASE

Barclays Bank international financial dealings

Barclays Bank, the 14th largest bank in the world (measured by capital in 2003), had a worldwide spread of branches, representative offices, and other affiliates in the early 2000s. The bank was actively involved in businesses such as corporate finance for major firms around the world, retail banking in Britain and a few other countries in Europe, and in foreign exchange dealing in London, New York, Tokyo, and other financial capitals of the world. Barclays' business was divided among the following currencies at the end of 2003:

The Barclays Group's structural currency exposures at 31st December 2003

	Net investments in overseas operations		Borrowings which hedge the net investments		Remaining structural currency exposures	
	2003	2002	**2003**	2002	**2003**	2002
Functional currency of the operation involved	**£m**	£m	**£m**	£m	**£m**	£m
US dollar	**1,448**	1,078	**1,166**	959	**282**	119
Yen	**3,063**	2,125	**2,984**	2,094	**79**	31
Euro	**4,333**	2,930	**3,520**	2,633	**813**	297
Other non-Sterling	**700**	512	**255**	164	**445**	348
Total	**9,544**	6,645	**7,925**	5,850	**1,619**	795

Growth in income and costs was constrained by foreign exchange translation movements. Approximately 56 per cent of Barclays Global Investors income was in US dollars and 31 per cent in Sterling.

These are not necessarily major concerns for a multinational bank, since Barclays has lengthy experience in using these currencies, and the bank regularly deals with foreign exchange risk. Still, some banks had encountered huge crises due to foreign exchange losses. For example, National Australia Bank lost $ US 360 million in 2003–2004 due to currency trading, and Allied Irish Banks lost more than $ US 770 million in 2002

from similar trading. Back in 1974 the entire world financial system was shaken by a pair of foreign exchange losses that caused two banks to fail (Franklin National Bank in the United States and Bankhaus Herstatt in Germany) and the entire eurocurrency system to briefly come to a halt.

Barclays is heavily involved in financial activities in more than 30 countries worldwide. This is an overstatement of the firm's

Maturity analysis of loans and advances to customers

	On demand[a] £m	Not more than three months £m	Over three months but not more than one year £m	Over one year but not more than five years £m	Over five years £m	Total £m
At 31st December 2003						
Banking business:						
United Kingdom						
Corporate lending[b]	6,108	9,298	4,596	17,138	11,796	48,936
Other lending from United Kingdom offices	2,869	6,940	6,359	12,345	66,360	94,873
Total United Kingdom	8,977	16,238	10,955	29,483	78,156	143,809
Other European Union	597	2,497	2,591	2,507	10,835	19,027
United States	–	276	253	1,745	1,299	3,573
Rest of the world	601	2,151	495	764	499	4,510
Total banking business	10,175	21,162	14,294	34,499	90,789	170,919
Total trading business	2,004	54,996	1,615	335	11	58,961
Total	12,179	76,158	15,909	34,834	90,800	229,880

	On demand[a] £m	Not more than three months £m	Over three months but not more than one year £m	Over one year but not more than five years £m	Over five years £m	Total £m
At 31st December 2003						
Banking business:						
United Kingdom						
Corporate lending[b]	8,340	7,047	5,604	14,251	10,519	45,761
Other lending from United Kingdom offices	2,416	6,693	6,135	10,919	63,976	90,139
Total United Kingdom	10,756	13,740	11,739	25,170	74,495	135,900
Other European Union	856	1,976	2,187	2,945	4,615	12,579
United States	–	768	1,227	2,451	1,692	6,138
Rest of the world	439	2,859	1,370	605	326	5,599
Total banking business	12,051	19,343	16,523	31,171	81,128	160,216
Total trading business	2,409	41,247	1,392	91	37	45,176
Total	14,460	60,590	17,915	31,262	81,165	205,392

Notes:
(a) Overdrafts are included in the "On demand" category.
(b) In the UK, finance lease receivables are included in "other lending" although some leases are to corporate customers.

global activity, since about 85 per cent of Barclays' deposits and loans are in Great Britain, the bank's country of origin. Another 10 per cent of the bank's business is in European Union countries, and about 3 per cent in the United States. This leaves only 2 per cent of Barclays' business in the remaining countries where it operates. Even with this relatively narrow exposure to risks in other countries, as the table opposite shows, Barclays has a very large exposure in US dollars.

From another perspective, Barclays had an international financial exposure through its lending activities in various countries. The table above shows this distribution of activity.

A key concern of Barclays is how to manage these overseas and foreign currency activities, especially with respect to the risk of currency losses. As an international bank, Barclays wants to operate in major financial centers, but as a prudently-managed firm, it doesn't want to take undue risk in foreign currencies or put significant amounts of assets in high-risk environments.

Website: **www.barclays.com**.

Source: Barclays, *Annual Report*, 2003.

1. What exchange risk does Barclays have at the beginning of 2004?
2. What should Barclays' expectation be about the value of the pound relative to the euro or the dollar?
3. How should Barclays deal with the risk involved in its foreign currency positions?
4. How can Barclays use the eurocurrency market in its international business, and will this help in dealing with the exchange rate problem?

INTRODUCTION

International financial markets are relevant to companies, whether or not they become directly involved in international business through exports, direct investment, and the like. Purchases of imported products or services may require payment in foreign exchange, thus involving exchange risk. A company may choose to invest in a foreign business or security, and face both different interest rates and different risks from those at home. Often companies

Exchange risk
The risk of financial loss or gain due to an unexpected change in a currency's value

Foreign exchange
Foreign-currency-denominated financial instruments, ranging from cash to bank deposits to other financial contracts payable or receivable in foreign currency

Eurocurrency
A bank deposit in any country that is denominated in a foreign currency. A yen-denominated bank deposit in Germany is a euro-yen deposit, a form of eurocurrency

find that borrowing funds abroad is less expensive than borrowing domestically, in the United States or in any other home country. The relatively unrestricted "euromarkets" generally offer better terms to borrowers (*and* lenders) than do domestic financial markets in any country. Likewise, in the 2000s, investors are discovering more and more opportunities to diversify their portfolios into holdings of foreign securities. This chapter explores the various foreign and international financial markets, including the foreign exchange market, and examines ways to utilize them for domestic and international business.

FOREIGN EXCHANGE MARKETS

Currencies, like any other products, services, or claims, can be traded for one another. The foreign exchange market is simply a mechanism through which transactions can be made between one country's currency and another's. Or, more broadly, a foreign exchange market is a market for the exchange of financial instruments denominated in different currencies. The most common location for foreign exchange transactions is a commercial bank, which agrees to "make a market" for the purchase and sale of currencies other than the local one. In the United States, hundreds of banks offer foreign exchange markets in dozens of cities. However, over 40 per cent of all foreign exchange business is done through the 10 largest banks in New York.

Foreign exchange is not simply currency printed by a foreign country's central bank; rather, it includes such items as cash, checks (or drafts), wire transfers, telephone transfers, and even contracts to sell or buy currency in the future. Foreign exchange is really any financial instrument that carries out payment from one currency to another. The most common form of foreign exchange in transactions between companies is the draft (denominated in a foreign currency). The most common form of foreign exchange in transactions between banks is the telephone or Internet transfer, generally for transactions of $1 million or more. Far down the list of instruments, in terms of the value exchanged, is actual currency, which is often exchanged by tourists and other travelers.

Exchange rate
The value of one currency in terms of another; for example, $US 1.30 / € 1

Since no currency is necessarily fixed in value relative to others, there must be some means of determining an acceptable price, or exchange rate. How many British pounds (£) should one dollar buy? How many Brazilian reals should be paid to buy a dollar? Since 1973, most of the industrialized countries have allowed their currency values to fluctuate more or less freely (depending on the time and the country), so that simple economics of supply and demand largely determine exchange rates. In graphic form, Figure 7.1 shows that the intersection of the supply curve and the demand curve for European euros (€) sets the price, or exchange rate, of euros in terms of dollars. Some of the participants in the foreign exchange market are listed below the graph; their specific activities are discussed in the following section.

The exchange rate of $1.2058 per euro is offered by one specific bank. This was the closing exchange rate quoted by Bankers Trust Company of New York for purchases of at least $1 million worth of euros on October 6, 2004. Another bank in New York may have quoted a slightly higher or slightly lower rate at the same time, and banks in San Francisco, London, or Tokyo probably quoted rates that differed even more. The rates quoted depend on each bank's interest in being involved in foreign exchange transactions and on the varying strategic positions and risks taken by the banks. Thus, the foreign exchange market among banks may be viewed as one large market or as many small markets with extensive (potential and actual) interrelations. Generally, the interbank market within any country is viewed as one market, and intercountry dealings are somewhat segmented by different rules and risks (though in the United States, the San Francisco market often offers quotations from various banks that differ noticeably from rate quotations in New York, due partly to the difference in time zones).

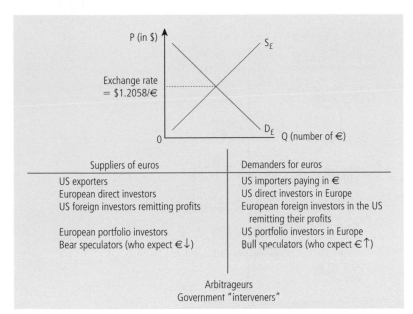

Figure 7.1 Foreign exchange market for € in New York

The differences in rate quotations may appear very small to an outsider. Euros may be quoted at $1.2055 at Citibank in New York and at $1.2060 at Bank of America in San Francisco. This difference seems small, but for every euros 1 million sold, the buyer of dollars in San Francisco receives an extra $500. Since the transactions are generally rapid, for values of $5 million to $10 million such differences may add up to a substantial gain (or cost) to the participant in the foreign exchange market.[1]

The various foreign exchange transactions just mentioned involve large commercial banks and large amounts of money. Most of the companies that do international business also utilize foreign exchange markets, but far less frequently than banks and for transactions that involve less money. Consequently, these companies' access to foreign currencies differs from that of the banks. (Specifically, banks make the market and companies pay for the use of this service.) The next section describes the various participants in the US foreign exchange market.

Foreign exchange markets in the United States

Figure 7.2 presents an overview of the foreign exchange markets operating today in the United States. This section discusses each of these markets in some detail.

The interbank market

Although the foreign exchange dealings of most managers involve a company buying from, or selling to, a bank, managers must understand the foreign exchange market among banks. This is because, as noted above, the vast majority of large-scale foreign exchange transactions are interbank, and these transactions tend to determine exchange rates, with which occasional market participants such as companies must deal.

Local and regional commercial banks may offer clients a foreign exchange service, which such banks provide on request by dealing through a larger bank, typically in a large city (such as New York, Los Angeles, or Chicago). If a local bank receives a request to buy Swiss francs (SF) for an importer in New Jersey, it will call its correspondent bank in New York (say, JP Morgan-Chase Bank) and arrange to buy the SF for, say, $0.6753/SF. Then the local bank will add on its service charge so that the importer pays $0.6853/SF. Thus, the local bank earns $0.01 per SF, or about 1.5 per cent on the transaction.

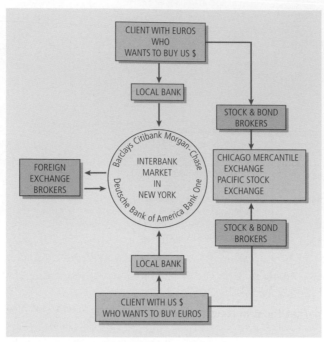

Figure 7.2 US foreign exchange markets

Source: Adapted from Robert Grosse, *St. Louis Fed Review*, March 1984, p. 91.

JP Morgan-Chase Bank, in turn, will either take the requested Swiss francs from its own holdings of that currency or enter the interbank market to buy them. Assuming that Chase does *not* have the SF on hand, one of its **foreign exchange traders** will call several other major banks (or brokerage houses, which are discussed below) and contract to buy Swiss francs from the lowest bidder.

The interbank market generally operates with large transactions only of about $1 million to $10 million exchanged for the equivalent foreign currency. On a typical day in 2004, the more than 100 members of the main association of commercial banks in foreign exchange dealings (called the Clearinghouse Interbank Payments System, or CHIPS) transacted roughly $1.3 trillion in currency trades.[2]

The brokers' market

Another facet of large-scale foreign exchange dealing in the United States is the brokers' market. About six **foreign exchange brokers** make markets for foreign currencies in New York (as well as in London and elsewhere), creating trading in many currencies similar to that in the interbank market. In this case, the key differences are that the brokers seek to match buyers and sellers on any given transaction, without taking a position[3] themselves; they deal simultaneously with many banks (and other companies); and they offer both buy and sell positions to clients (where a bank may wish to operate on only one side of the market at any particular time). Also, the brokers deal "blind," offering rate quotations without naming the potential seller/buyer until a deal has been negotiated. Brokers play a large role in the total market, arranging about half of total interbank foreign exchange transaction in the early 2000s.

Before moving on to other foreign exchange markets, let us consider an example in which the spot market is used by a tourist planning a trip to Japan. This person wants to visit Tokyo to see a friend during Christmas vacation and to do some sightseeing. She is taking $1,000 with her and has already purchased the round-trip airline ticket. Since dollars cannot be used for most purchases in Japan, she needs to buy Japanese yen. How should she do it?

Foreign exchange traders
Bankers who deal in foreign exchange, buying and selling foreign currencies on behalf of clients and/or for the bank itself; typically they deal in foreign-currency-denominated bank deposits

Foreign exchange broker
A company that provides specialized services to commercial banks in the interbank foreign exchange market, essentially functioning to unite interested buyers and sellers of foreign-currency-denominated bank deposits; brokers intermediate about half of all wholesale foreign exchange transactions in New York and London

Table 7.1 Exchange rates in the interbank market, October 14, 2004

Foreign currency exchange rates (mid)	Canada dollar	UK* sterling	Europe* euro	Switzerland franc	Japan yen
Spot rate—closing (foreign currency units per US dollar)	1.2517	1.7957	1.2393	1.2452	109.51
Forward rate—closing					
1 month outright	1.2524	1.7913	1.2390	1.2439	109.33
3 months outright	1.2535	1.7833	1.2390	1.2409	108.94
6 months outright	1.2554	1.7746	1.2395	1.2349	108.04
12 months outright	1.2586	1.7516	1.2405	1.2272	106.96
*(US dollars per foreign currency unit)	0.7989	1.7957	1.2393	0.8031	0.00913

Source: *Financial Times*, October 15, 2004.

Looking at the currency trading listing in Table 7.1, she sees that Bankers Trust is offering to sell large quantities of yen at the rate of 109.51 yen per dollar. At the "retail" level—that is, for small transactions such as this one—she can expect to receive only about 107 yen per dollar. Indeed, when she called Bank of America and Wells Fargo Bank in San Francisco, they quoted rates of 106 yen per dollar. Instead of carrying the cash with her, she wants to get traveler's checks. Upon calling the office of American Express in San Francisco, she found that yen-denominated traveler's checks were available but would cost her $1 for every 103 yen, plus a $5 service charge.

The tourist was willing to pay the extra cost to obtain the protection of traveler's checks, but one final problem arose. A friend who works in foreign exchange dealing at Wells Fargo Bank told her that the yen would probably decline in value relative to the dollar in the next few days. Since she would not leave for Tokyo for another week, she wondered whether it was worth waiting for the expected devaluation. The answer to this question is that no one knows! She can hope for a devaluation and delay purchase of the yen for a week, or ignore the potential gain or loss and buy the yen today. In such a short time period, it is probably better to ignore the few days' variability in the exchange rate—since it could be favorable or unfavorable—and just buy the yen at the most convenient time before departing for Tokyo. (One more point to confuse the matter: She could buy traveler's checks in US dollars and exchange them for yen in Japan when needed. Again, no one can be sure what the yen's value will be during her vacation time in Tokyo.)

Although this example does not offer a guaranteed way to make money from foreign exchange dealings, it does illustrate the kinds of problems that beset individuals and companies as they work with foreign currencies. Fortunately, there are some methods to help avoid the uncertainty involved in foreign exchange; they are discussed in the section below on "Protecting against Exchange Risk."

So far, our discussion has focused only on the *spot market*; that is, the market for immediate exchange of one currency for another. An additional, very large part of the US foreign exchange market is the set of instruments that allow contracting today for delivery of currency in the future. The main instruments of this type are forward contracts, foreign exchange futures contracts, and foreign currency options.

The forward foreign exchange market

The forward foreign exchange market at commercial banks in the United States offers banks, companies, and individuals the opportunity to contract *today* for a specific foreign exchange transaction in the *future*, at a fixed price (i.e., exchange rate). Forward contracts are negotiated between the offering bank and the client as to size, maturity, and price. Referring to Table 7.1, we see that Bankers Trust was offering to sell British pounds for $1.7746/£ in 180 days on October 14, 2004 (for quantities of at least $1 million).

Spot rate
The exchange rate offered on the same day as the request to buy or sell foreign currency; actual settlement (payment) may occur one or two days later

Forward rate
An exchange rate contracted today for some future date of actual currency exchange; banks offer forward rates to clients to buy or sell foreign currency in the future, guaranteeing the rate at the time of the agreement

The rationale for forward contracts in currencies is analogous to that for futures contracts in commodities; the firm can lock in a price today to eliminate uncertainty about the value of a future receipt or a payment of foreign currency. A firm may undertake such a transaction because it has made a previous contract, for example, to pay € 1 million to a supplier in three months for some needed inputs to its operations. If the firm wants to eliminate the risk that its payment in three months will change in dollar terms (i.e., that the € 1 million may cost more dollars then), it can contract with a bank to buy € 1 million three months forward, at a price established today. (From Table 7.1, we see that the price was $1.2390/ € for a contract with Bankers Trust on October 14, 2004.) Thus, firms can use forward contracts to eliminate the risk of variability in future dollar costs or revenues due to exchange rate changes. This concept, called *hedging*, and other motives for using the forward market are discussed later.

Notice that in the above example, the forward contract used for hedging is not the same thing as an insurance contract. The forward contract does fix a minimum "loss" for the firm by setting the guaranteed price of exchange in the future. Even if the dollar devalues to $1.25 per € in three months, the forward contract holder is still able to buy 1 million € for $1.2390/€. However, if the euro devalues over the next three months to, say, $1.2290/€, the forward contract holder will have an opportunity cost of the difference between the forward rate and the (eventual) future spot rate (a difference of $0.01/€, or 6.6 per cent). Thus, the forward contract insures against potential losses *and* against potential gains in foreign currency value.

Forward markets exist in any currencies and for any maturities that banks are willing to offer. Most of the forward contracts used in the United States involve exchanges of US dollars for euros, Japanese yen, British pounds, Swiss francs, and Canadian dollars. Maturities tend to be six months or less, though single-year and multiyear forward contracts are sometimes available.

The futures market in currencies

A very similar type of instrument is available on several securities exchanges in the United States and abroad. The foreign exchange futures contract is an agreement to buy or sell a fixed amount of foreign currency for delivery at a fixed future date at a fixed dollar price. The main difference between futures and forward contracts in the United States is that futures contracts have fixed sizes (about $50,000 to $100,000, depending on the currency) and pre-established maturity dates. (All are 3-, 6-, 9-, or 12-month contracts maturing on the third Wednesday of March, June, September, or December.) Also, futures contracts are available for only a few currencies (Canadian dollars, euros, Swiss francs, British pounds, Japanese yen, Mexican pesos, Australian dollars, and a few others), and only if a buyer and a seller can be found at the time.

The futures market at the Chicago Mercantile Exchange is currently very thin (i.e., few contracts are traded) except for the three-month contracts denominated in Canadian dollars, euros, Swiss francs, British pounds, and Japanese yen.

Futures contracts are more widely accessible to firms and individuals than forward contracts because of their smaller value and the margin requirements that enable brokers to obtain collateral from market participants. (However, the currently thin nature of this market does not allow participants the wide range of currencies and maturities that are available for large-scale transactions in the forward market.) The standard contracts available at the Chicago Mercantile Exchange (CME) are described in Table 7.2. Trading hours have been extended via the GLOBEX system, which permits worldwide access to CME contracts. In 2004, GLOBEX trading was available for about 19 hours per day around the world.

Foreign currency *options* are an additional instrument of the foreign exchange market in the United States; they offer participants the *right* to buy or sell foreign currency in the future rather than the obligation to do so. Foreign currency options are similar to foreign currency futures in the Unites States in that the contracts are for fixed quantities of currency to be exchanged at a fixed price in the future. The key difference is that the option may be

Table 7.2 Currency futures contract specifications* at the Chicago Mercantile Exchange

	British pound (£)	European Monetary Union (EMU) euro (€)	Japanese yen (JY)
Trading unit	£ 62,500	€ 125,000	JY12,500,00
Quotations	US$ per £	US$ per euro	US$ per yen
Minimum price fluctuation	.0002	.0001	.000001
Value of 1 point	$10.00	$12.50	$12.50
Months traded	March, June, September, December & Spot month		
Trading hours	7:20am–2:00pm (Chicago time) [+ *Globex*]		
Last day hours	7:20am–9:16am (Chicago time)		
Last day of trading	Two business days before the third Wednesday of the delivery month		
Delivery date	Third Wednesday of the delivery month		

Source: Data provided by Chicago Mercantile Exchange, August, 2004.

exercised, that is, presented for currency exchange, at *any* time between its issuance and the maturity date, or not at all.[4]

Foreign exchange arbitrage involves simultaneous contracting in two or more foreign exchange markets to buy and sell foreign currency, profiting from exchange rate differences *without* incurring exchange rate risk. Foreign exchange arbitrage may be two-way, three-way, or intertemporal and is generally undertaken by large commercial banks that can exchange large quantities of money to exploit small rate differentials.

The simplest form of exchange arbitrage is two-way arbitrage, between any two currencies and between two places. Quotations for Swiss francs in the spot market on October 14, 2004, were:

At Bankers Trust in New York: $0.7995/SF.

At Bank of America in San Francisco: $0.8007/SF.

At Lloyds Bank in London: $0.8031/SF.

An arbitrageur can buy SF in New York and simultaneously sell them in London, making a profit of $0.0036/SF, or 0.45 per cent per transaction. While the percentage gain is small, it translates to $3,600 for every 1 million SF traded, and it involves no exchange risk. By repeatedly arbitraging this price (exchange rate) differential, the arbitrageur will make a profit until the exchange rate differential drops below the transactions cost (i.e., the telephone bill, plus the arbitrageur's salary, plus other relevant costs).

Arbitrageur
A person or firm that deals in foreign exchange, buying or selling foreign currency with simultaneous contracting to exchange back to the original currency; arbitrageurs thus do not undertake exchange risk

The same two-way arbitrage may also occur in the forward market or between forward and futures markets. From the quotations here, we see that profitable arbitrage opportunities exist between the New York forward market and the Chicago futures market, as well as between the New York and San Francisco forward markets:

At Bankers Trust in New York: 108.04 yen/$ for delivery in 180 days.

At Bank of America in San Francisco: 108.94 yen/$ for delivery in 180 days.

At the Chicago Mercantile Exchange: 107.0 yen/$ for delivery on March 16, 2005.

An arbitrageur can buy yen in New York and sell them in San Francisco, both for exchange in 180 days, and earn 0.9 yen/dollar, or 0.83 per cent per transaction. Similarly, an arbitrageur can buy yen in Chicago and sell them in San Francisco, to make 1.94 yen/dollar, or 1.8 per cent per transaction. The difficulties with the latter transaction are that contracts may not be available for the desired amount or maturity date and transactions costs are higher for the intermarket exchanges. Nonetheless, both transactions may be feasible and profitable, even after costs are considered.[5]

Active learning check

Review your answer to Active Learning Case question 1 and make any changes you like. Then compare your answer with the one below.

1 What exchange risk does Barclays have at the beginning of 2004?

Barclays has exchange risk on the various assets and liabilities that were on its books at year-end 2003. These include exposures of £ 282 million in US dollars and £ 813 million in euros, among others. From the second table in the case, it appears that these exposures may be from lending to corporations in the European Union and the United States (though this is not certain, since some other activities are missing from the table). These are net asset exposures, or long positions, since Barclays will receive future cash flows in these currencies, and their values may change in terms of British pounds.

DETERMINATION OF THE EXCHANGE RATE

Exchange rates are determined by the activities of the various actors described earlier. If one could calculate the supply and demand curves for each exchange market participant and anticipate government constraints on the exchange market, exchange rate determination would be fairly simple. The composite supply and demand for foreign exchange would be as depicted in Figure 7.1

Lacking this information, the analyst can still rely on two fundamental economic relationships that underlie exchange rate determination. Note that this section considers only economic factors; government restrictions on the exchange market are ignored.

The two fundamental economic relationships are **purchasing power parity** and the **international Fisher effect**. The former posits that shifts in exchange rates will occur to offset different rates of inflation in pairs of countries, and the latter proposes that exchange rates will shift to offset interest rate differentials between countries.

Purchasing power parity
The theory of exchange rate determination that states that differences in prices of the same goods between countries will be eliminated by exchange rate changes

International Fisher effect
Theory of exchange rate determination that states that differences in nominal interest rates on similar-risk deposits will be eliminated by changes in the exchange rate

Purchasing power parity[6]

If a standard ton of polyurethane plastic costs $200 in the United States and € 190 in Germany, purchasing power parity (PPP) requires an exchange rate of $US 1.05/€. The same reasoning could be used for all products whose production processes are equivalent in two countries and that are traded between these countries. The exchange rate that comes closest to simultaneously satisfying all of these equilibrium conditions is the PPP rate—a rate that equates the internal purchasing power of the two currencies in both countries.

Assuming we begin from that exchange rate, what will happen if Germany's inflation is 5 per cent and the US inflation is 10 per cent in the following year? Purchasing power parity requires that the exchange rate adjust to eliminate this differential. Specifically, it requires that:

$$\frac{1 + \text{Infl}_{US}}{1 + \text{Infl}_{Ger}} = \frac{XR_{t+1}}{XR_t}$$

where:
$\quad$ Infl = inflation rate
$\quad$ t = time period

This means that inflation in the United States relative to inflation in Germany should be the same as the future exchange rate compared to the spot exchange rate. The relationship can also be written in a form similar to the interest parity equation by rearranging terms:

$$(1 + \text{Infl}_{US}) = (1 + \text{Infl}_{Ger})\frac{XR_{t+1}}{XR_t}$$

Purchasing power in each currency will be retained if:

$$XR_{t+1} = \frac{1.10}{1.05}(\$1.05/\text{€}) = \$1.10/\text{€, or €}0.909/\$$$

International Fisher effect

The international Fisher effect (IFE) translates Irving Fisher's reasoning about domestic interest rates to the transnational level. Fisher showed that inflation-adjusted (i.e., "real") interest rates tend to stay the same over time; as inflation rises or falls, so do **nominal** (unadjusted) **interest rates**, such that **real interest rates** remain unchanged. At the transnational level, nominal national interest rates are expected to differ only by the expected change in the national currency's price (i.e., the exchange rate). The international Fisher effect thus concludes that interest differentials between national markets will be eliminated by adjustments in the exchange rate. In terms similar to PPP, we see that:

Nominal interest rate
The actual rate of interest offered by a bank, typically given as an annual percentage rate

Real interest rate
The nominal interest rate adjusted for price changes. Domestically, this means adjusting for inflation; internationally, this means adjusting for exchange rate (currency price) changes

$$\frac{1 + i_{US}}{1 + i_{foreign}} = \frac{XR_{t+1}}{XR_t}, \text{ or } (1 + i_{US}) = (1 + i_{foreign})\frac{XR_{t+1}}{XR_t}$$

where i = the interest rate, usually on a eurocurrency deposit denominated in the given country's currency.

If the eurodollar deposit rate is 3 per cent/year and the euro-euro rate is 6 per cent/year, the euro will be expected to devalue in the coming year by:

$$\frac{1.06}{1.03} = 1.029, \text{ or } 2.9 \text{ per cent}$$

Notice that the international Fisher effect *will* operate in a free market, because investors will receive a higher return in euros otherwise. As more and more investors put their money in euros, the spot price of the euro will rise. Similarly, as US investors return their euro earnings to dollars at the end of the period (year), this increased demand for dollars will cause the euro to devalue (in the future). Thus, dollar and euro earnings will tend to be equalized.

Combined equilibrium relationships

The future exchange rate, XR_{t+1}, will be partially determined by both of the above factors (PPP and IFE), which can be viewed in a general equilibrium context as shown in Figure 7.3. This figure also demonstrates the interest parity relationship, which provides another link between current and future currency values. Remember that these relationships are *equilibrium* economic conditions, which hold only approximately since substantial uncertainty exists about future conditions. Also, if a government intervenes to prohibit the market from determining exchange rates, the relationships may diverge substantially from the equilibrium conditions. Figure 7.3 shows the main economic influences that, along with government policies and other factors, combine to determine exchange rates. Note that the expected exchange rate is in the top box, and the determinants of that rate (interest difference and inflation difference) are presented as fractions, so that they show the precise relationship between the spot exchange rate, XR_s, and the expected future rate, $E[XR_s]$.

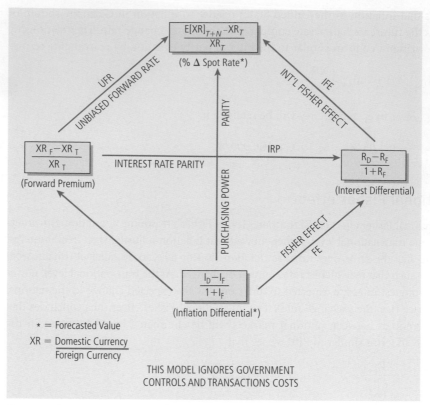

Figure 7.3 Exchange rate determination

A final caveat is in order. Despite the strong relationships among interest differentials, inflation differentials, and exchange rates, other important *economic* influences operate in international finance. Pure speculation can cause shifts in exchange rates, despite the fundamental economic conditions that have been described above. A country's balance of payments position may affect the exchange rate, even though that position also affects interest and inflation rates as well. Since the abandonment of the Bretton Woods system of fixed exchange rates, exchange rate determination has been extremely uncertain—perhaps similar to the determination of future values of stock exchange indexes.

✔ Active learning check

Review your answer to Active Learning Case question 2 and make any changes you like. Then compare your answer with the one below.

2 **What should Barclays' expectation be about the value of the pound relative to the euro or the dollar?**

Barclays can forecast the value of the euro or the dollar based on purchasing power parity, the international Fisher effect, or a chartist method, in addition to simply using the forward exchange rate. Since Barclays' business includes currency trading, the bank probably should use one or more methods for the minute-by-minute activity in the foreign exchange market, and another method or methods for its longer-term concerns such as future maturities of loans and accounting reporting periods. In sum, Barclays should forecast using the market-based tools such as IFE and PPP, as well as using additional methods such as technical forecasting or leading indicators for short periods of time such as hours or a few days.

INTERNATIONAL BUSINESS STRATEGY *IN ACTION*

The Wall Street crash of 2001

International finance affects virtually every business. Companies with overseas operations, for example, are continually concerned with the rise and fall of the currencies in the countries where they operate. Indonesia is a good example as seen by the country's currency crisis of the late 1990s that sent shock waves through the Asian business market. As a result, thousands of firms went bankrupt, the country's currency lost 80 per cent of its value, and the stock market plummeted by 60 per cent. In the aftermath, Indonesia was hit with soaring unemployment and inflation led to riots that forced the resignation of the government.

Yet the international financial markets have never suffered anything like the initial effect from the terrorist attacks on the twin towers of New York City's World Trade Center (WTC) on September 11, 2001. In addition to totally demolishing the two buildings as well as several large surrounding structures, the terrorists killed nearly 3,000 people, many of them Wall Street employees, and rocked the major international financial markets from London to Tokyo. One of the hardest hit groups was the insurers who had losses of more than $15 billion. In addition, while the important financial records of businesses in the WTC were located in safe havens such as central computer banks miles away from Ground Zero, the effect of the terrorist actions began to quickly surface.

This was reflected on Wall Street where the stock market began a sharp downturn. Within two weeks of the terrorist act, the New York Stock Exchange's (NYSE) Dow Index had lost 14 per cent of its value. Only during the Great Depression had America seen a downturn this sharp. And for the rest of the world, the financial shock was shared very quickly. And the NYSE and other major international stock exchanges saw massive sell-offs as investors headed for the sidelines, and companies seeking to raise capital in the international market put their plans on hold. Simply put, as the US economy began to slow down and focus its investment efforts on rebuilding and regenerating its own hard-hit industries, there were going to be less funds available for other things. The international finance lesson is clear: today's money markets are linked very, very closely. And a catastrophe in one geographic area can have major implications in all of the others. New York City remains a financial hub of the business world, and the effects of the September 2001 crisis have passed. Yet the financial risks that international business firms must assume will not diminish because of the large interdependency that now exists between the major centers of worldwide commerce.

Website: **www.nyse.com**.

Sources: Financial Times, September 12–30, 2001; October 1–13, 2001; and other supplemental news sources.

PROTECTING AGAINST EXCHANGE RISK

Exchange risk is a very real concern for financial managers, whether or not their firms are directly involved in international business. The fact that the prices of imported products and services often vary with the exchange rate means that a local firm's costs may depend on the exchange rate. Similarly, if any of the firm's sales are exported, its earnings may vary as foreign sales change due to exchange rate changes. Even a purely domestic firm faces these problems, since suppliers and competitors that *are* doing international business will adjust to exchange rate changes, and this will affect the domestic firm.

From this perspective, exchange risk is *not* the risk that a local currency will decrease in value (devalue) relative to the home currency. *Exchange risk is the possibility that a firm will be unable to adjust its prices and costs to exactly offset exchange rate changes.* Thus, a US importer who faces 10 per cent higher costs because of a dollar devaluation from € 0.80/US$ to € 0.72/US$ still has no exchange risk as long as the importer can raise his or her own prices by 10 per cent without lowering total sales. (This result is the microeconomic version of purchasing power parity.) The problem may be viewed as one of "passing through" cost increases to the firm's customers via higher sales prices.

Similarly, the appropriate measure of exchange risk for financial instruments is the firm's possible loss or gain in purchasing power from exchange-rate-adjusted interest rates. Investing in a US dollar account that pays 5 per cent per year is better than investing in a Swiss franc account that pays 10 per cent per year if, during the year, the franc devalues by 6 per cent.

Alternatives to minimize exchange risk

Exchange risk exists whenever the firm's prices and costs cannot be exactly adjusted to offset changes in the exchange rate. Let us now consider a group of alternatives that will allow a firm to minimize (or at least reduce) its exchange risk. These alternatives fall into four categories:

1 Risk avoidance

2 Risk adaptation

3 Risk transfer

4 Diversification

Risk avoidance

Exchange risk avoidance
An exchange risk management technique through which the firm tries to avoid operating in more than one currency

Exchange risk avoidance is the strategy of trying to avoid foreign currency transactions. A purely domestic firm can try to make all of its purchases from local suppliers of locally produced goods and make all of its sales to local buyers in competition only with other domestic firms. Obviously, this strategy is impractical, if only because all firms are affected by goods priced in foreign currency—automobiles, chemicals, steel, and so on. Also, there are very few industries that do not use imported materials, export some of their output, or compete with imported products.

Risk adaptation

Exchange risk adaptation
An exchange risk management technique through which a company adjusts its business activities to try to balance foreign-currency assets and liabilities, and inflows and outflows

Exchange risk adaptation offers a more realistic alternative for protecting the firm against exchange risk. This strategy includes all methods of "hedging" against exchange rate changes. In the extreme, exchange risk calls for protecting all liabilities denominated in foreign currency with equal-value, equal-maturity assets denominated in that foreign currency. An illustration can best clarify this point.

Assume a French firm has contracted to buy $100,000 of machinery from a foreign supplier for use in its manufacturing operations. The purchase is payable in six months in US dollars. To eliminate foreign exchange risk completely, the firm may do two things. First, it may raise its own prices to customers once the six months pass to equate euro devaluation to price increase. (Note that this does *not* involve a foreign currency hedge.) If this option is not available, which is often the case, the firm may look to its other option: obtain some equal-value *dollar asset* maturing in 180 days. This may be as simple as depositing funds in a dollar-denominated bank account for six months or as arcane as arranging a swap of the dollar liability for some other firm's euro liability. Fairly standard methods of hedging an exposed dollar liability include:

1 Obtaining a dollar-denominated financial asset (e.g., a time deposit or a CD) that matures when the liability comes due.

2 Finding a buyer for your firm's products and agreeing to receive payment in US dollars for the same value and time as the liability.

3 Finding a bank that will contract to buy euro from you and sell you dollars at a price fixed today for exchange when the liability comes due. (This is called a *forward contract*.)

4 Agreeing with another (e.g., North American) firm to exchange your dollar liability for that firm's (i.e., its French subsidiary's) euro liability.

5 Contracting for any other equal-value, equal-maturity dollar-denominated asset that will offset the exposed liability.

The firm's goal in choosing among these methods is to minimize the cost of protection against exchange rate risk.

Risk transfer

The third strategy for reducing exchange risk is exchange risk transfer. This strategy involves the use of an insurance contract or guarantee that transfers the exchange risk to the insurer or guarantor. In many countries, the central bank offers exchange risk guarantees to importers and exporters of some products according to the bank's policies. Technically, though perhaps not realistically, any firm or government agency could issue a guarantee covering exchange rate changes to a local importer, at a price that would presumably reflect the risk.

Exchange risk transfer
An exchange risk management technique through which the firm contracts with a third party to pass exchange risk onto that party, via such instruments as forward contracts, futures, and options

Diversification

The final strategy for reducing exchange risk is currency diversification. Here a firm can reduce the risk of unexpected local currency devaluations by spreading its assets and liabilities across several currencies (e.g., euros, Swiss francs, and pounds in addition to US dollars). This strategy simply means, "Don't put all of your eggs in one basket." Domestically, a firm should deal with several suppliers and a variety of customers to reduce risk through diversification. Internationally, a firm should hold assets (and liabilities) in several currencies to reduce the impact of unexpected exchange rate changes.

Currency diversification
An exchange risk management technique through which the firm places activities or assets and liabilities into multiple currencies, thus reducing the impact of exchange rate change for any one of them

The strategy that is probably most useful to the majority of firms is risk adaptation, or hedging. A key point of this section is to recognize that other alternatives may be used in many instances when hedging would be more expensive or otherwise less desirable. Nonetheless, the central problem in exchange risk management is hedging, and corporate treasurers should always be on the lookout for new instruments and techniques.

✔ Active learning check

Review your answer to Active Learning Case question 3 and make any changes you like. Then compare your answer with the one below.

③ How should Barclays deal with the risk involved in its foreign currency positions?

As an international bank, Barclays is constantly becoming involved in foreign exchange transactions. The bank needs to have a policy for its traders and its other bankers as to how much exchange risk the bank is willing to tolerate before looking for protection. The bank presumably knows more than most people about what to expect in the foreign exchange market, and it is very likely that Barclays will choose to run exchange risk without hedging because of this knowledge. Still, the bank must limit its exposure, and the usual hedging techniques for banks are forward contracts and matching loans with deposits in the same currency.

FOREIGN MONEY AND CAPITAL MARKETS

In each country the MNE enters, it will be able to obtain some degree of access to local financial markets. The MNE will generally utilize such markets to perform necessary local financial transactions and often to hedge its local asset exposure through local borrowing (or its local liability exposure through local deposits or investments). But the MNE can also utilize local financial markets to obtain additional funding (or place additional funds) for its non-local activities. A Mexican firm, for example, may choose to borrow funds through its Houston affiliate to finance its local needs in Texas *and* finance some of its needs in Mexico.

Usually national financial markets are not fully accessible to foreign firms; they are largely reserved for domestic borrowers and lenders. In these cases, use of local financial markets must be supplemented by use of the financial markets in the country of the parent company or elsewhere. Typically, such problems arise in countries that impose exchange controls, which limit the MNE's ability to put needed funds in the affiliate.

MNEs and national money markets

The advantages MNEs obtain from entering national money markets as *borrowers* of funds stem from the portfolio effect of holding liabilities in more than one (fluctuating) currency and from the local risk hedging that occurs as the MNE moves to balance local assets such as plant and equipment with local liabilities, such as local-currency borrowing. Additional benefits may occur if the local government subsidizes such loans through interest rate reduction, through tax breaks, or otherwise; a policy of this kind may be offered to attract the MNE's investment. This may lower the whole MNE's cost of capital if the subsidy does not disappear and if the interest rate remains below the comparable home-currency rate during the borrowing period.

The advantages MNEs obtain from entering national money markets as *lenders* of funds stem from the portfolio effect of holding financial instruments in more than one currency. There may also be a gain from balancing local-currency assets and liabilities if an excess of local liabilities was held previously. In addition, local financial investments may be a necessary strategy when exchange controls or profit remittance limits exist; such investments offer the firm an outlet for retained earnings that yields interest. Sometimes an exchange control policy may make the local-currency interest rates higher than those available in other currencies (after adjusting for expected exchange rate changes). In these cases, higher-than-normal profits can be earned by investing funds in local instruments, although exchange controls may limit conversion of the profits into the home-country currency, or a government-imposed exchange-rate change may wipe out the advantage.

MNEs and national capital markets

The advantages MNEs obtain from entering national capital markets as *borrowers* are similar to those obtained from entering national money markets. However, the opportunities are generally much more limited. Very few countries have substantially developed stock markets, and those that do usually restrict the issuance of shares by foreigners. A few exceptions exist, such as the United States, the United Kingdom, Germany, and France, but even they serve only the largest and most creditworthy MNEs. National bond markets, when they exist, are also very restrictive. Thus far, virtually all of the foreign bond issues have taken place in New York (called "Yankee bonds"), London, Switzerland, Germany, and Japan (called "Samurai bonds").

The eurobond market, which functions mostly outside the United States, is dominated by dollar issues, which constitute about 40 per cent of that total. In all, dollar-denominated issues account for about 36 per cent of the two types of international bonds.

The advantages MNEs obtain from entering national capital markets as *lenders* come mainly from diversification and from higher returns that may be protected by exchange controls, just as in the short-term market. Since the national capital markets are generally small, opportunities to use them are quite limited for foreign as well as domestic investors. Of course, since the main currencies of interest to MNEs and other international investors *are* those of the few large industrial countries, opportunities in those national capital markets do exist.

Foreign bond
A bond issued by a foreign company in another country's financial market

Eurobond
A bond denominated in foreign currency issued in any country's financial market; most eurobonds are issued in London or in Luxembourg (for tax reasons)

REGIONAL MONEY AND CAPITAL MARKETS

Until recently, the scope of financial markets and instruments was predominantly domestic or fully international, but not regional. In the past two decades, however, the European Union has designed both a regional monetary system (the **European Monetary Union**, or EMU) and a regional currency unit (the euro) for intergovernmental financial transactions in the Union.

The eurocurrency market

A **eurodollar** is a dollar-denominated bank deposit located outside the United States. This simple statement defines the basic instrument called the eurodollar. (Eurodollars are *not* dollars in the pockets of people who live in Europe! They are deposit liabilities of banks.) The widely discussed eurocurrency market is simply a set of bank deposits located outside the countries whose currencies are used in the deposits. Since over half of the deposits are denominated in US dollars, it is reasonably accurate to call this the eurodollar market. Notice that the eurodollar market is not limited to Europe; very large eurodollar markets exist in Tokyo, Hong Kong, Bahrain, Panama, and other cities throughout the world. For this reason, the eurodollar market is sometimes called the *international money market.*

What is the significance of the international money market? Since the eurocurrency market rivals domestic financial markets as a funding source for corporate borrowing, it plays a key role in the capital investment decisions of many firms. In addition, since this market also rivals domestic financial markets as a deposit alternative, it absorbs large amounts of savings from lenders (i.e., depositors) in many countries. In fact, the eurocurrency market complements the domestic financial markets, giving greater access to borrowing and lending to financial market participants in each country where it is permitted to function. Overall, the eurocurrency market is now the world's single most important market for international financial intermediation.

This market is completely a creation of the regulatory structures placed by national governments on banking or, more precisely, on financial intermediation. If national governments allowed banks to function without reserve requirements, interest rate restrictions, capital controls, and taxes, the eurocurrency market would involve only the transnational deposits and loans made in each country's banking system. Instead, national governments heavily regulate national financial markets in efforts to achieve various monetary policy goals. Thus, the eurocurrency market provides a very important outlet for funds flows that circumvent many of the limitations placed on domestic financial markets. Many national governments have found the impact of the eurocurrency market on their firms and banks to be favorable, so they have allowed this market to operate.[7]

Since the eurocurrency market is a creation of the regulatory structure, it may be helpful to think about the key underpinnings of the system that allow eurodollars. Essentially three conditions must be met for a eurocurrency market to exist. First, some national government must allow foreign currency deposits to be made so that, for example, depositors in London can obtain dollar-denominated time deposits there. Second, the country whose currency is being used—in this example, the United States—must allow foreign entities to own and exchange deposits in that currency. Third, there must be some reason, such as low cost or ease of use that prompts people to use this market rather than other financial markets, such as the domestic ones. The eurocurrency market has met these conditions for the past three decades, and its phenomenal growth testifies that the demand for such a market has been very large.

A wide range of countries allow foreign-currency deposits to be held in their banking systems. Many of them impose restrictions (interest rate limits, capital controls, and so on)

European Monetary Union (EMU)
The agreement among, initially, eleven of the European Union countries to eliminate their currencies and create the euro; European Union countries do not necessarily have to join the EMU

Eurodollar
A dollar-denominated bank deposit outside of the United States

207

on these as well as on local-currency deposits, so that a free market does not exist. Other countries, including most of the developed countries and many of the newly industrializing countries, allow foreign-currency deposits that are not subject to the regulations placed on domestic deposits. In such countries, participants find more favorable interest rates, greater availability of funds, and greater ease of moving funds internationally. These countries tend to be the euromarket centers.

Only a few currencies have become popular as eurocurrencies. Generally, these are the ones used widely in international trade—the US dollar, the euro, the British pound, and the Japanese yen. The governments of all the nations whose currencies are being used have consented (or, more accurately, have not objected) to allowing foreign banks, companies, and individuals to hold and use deposits denominated in those currencies. This may appear to be a trivial point, but any limitation on nonresidents' use of dollar (or other eurocurrency) deposits would quickly eliminate that currency from the euromarket. The US government's temporary freeze on Iranian assets held in US banks in 1979 caused a tremendous crisis in the eurodollar market, because other participants saw the possibility of losing use of their eurodollars at the whim of the US government. The potential problem will continue to exist, but on the whole participants in the euromarket expect that full freedom to use the (dollar-denominated) deposits will continue indefinitely.

The third condition fundamental to the success of the euromarket is that it must possess advantages that will attract participants to the market. Those advantages include the ability to carry out dollar-denominated transactions outside the United States and the availability of favorable interest rates relative to rates in the domestic market. The first advantage clearly exists, because eurodollar account owners can sell their accounts to pay for other transactions, with no need to deal directly in the United States. The second advantage also exists, primarily because lack of regulation of the euromarket allows banks to reduce their costs and pass on the savings to clients in the form of lower loan rates and higher deposit rates. Figure 7.4 shows that the eurodollar deposit interest rate has a very small spread over the comparable domestic deposit rate. (The difference in lending rates to prime borrowers essentially disappeared during the 1980s.)

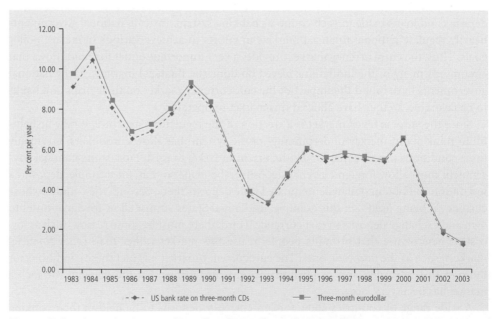

Figure 7.4 Interest rates on deposits, domestic and eurodollar

Eurocurrency interest rates

The base interest rate paid on deposits among banks in the eurocurrency market is called LIBOR, the London interbank offered rate. (Outside London, which is the center of the entire euromarket, the base rate on deposits is generally slightly higher.) LIBOR is determined by the supply and demand for funds in the euromarket for each currency. Because participating banks could default (and, infrequently, do default) on their obligations, the rate paid for eurodollar deposits is always somewhat above the domestic Treasury bill rate. Also, because domestic banks must comply with Federal Reserve requirements, they offer slightly lower deposit rates than unregulated eurobanks, as shown in Figure 7.4.

The lending rate has no name comparable to the prime rate, but it is determined as LIBOR plus some margin, or spread, charged to the borrower. Banks generally do not require compensating balances or other implicit charges in addition to the spread over LIBOR in the euromarket. This also helps reduce the cost of using the euromarket for borrowers. The total cost of borrowing in the euromarket for a prime US corporation historically was marginally below the domestic US prime rate. Because of competition among lenders in both markets, prime borrowers have been able to obtain the same rate in both markets since the early 1980s.

Interest rates on other eurocurrencies generally follow the same pattern, though when capital controls exist in a particular country (e.g., France), borrowing rates may be higher in the euromarket (which is not restricted) than in the domestic market. Figure 7.5 traces three-month eurocurrency deposit rates during the past two decades. Notice that the countries whose currencies have tended to decline relative to other currencies during this period (such as France and Great Britain) show generally higher eurocurrency deposit rates than the "strong-currency" countries (such as Germany and Japan).

Other market characteristics

Transactions in the eurodollar market generally involve $US 1 million or more, although in the past several years many deposits of $50,000 to $100,000 have been given at LIBOR, and loans of similar amounts have been offered at the analogous lending rates. The market is directly accessible to banks, which carry out about three-fourths of the total volume of transactions among themselves. Companies and individuals participate through their

LIBOR
The interest rate on large-scale foreign-currency-denominated deposits offered from one bank to another in London

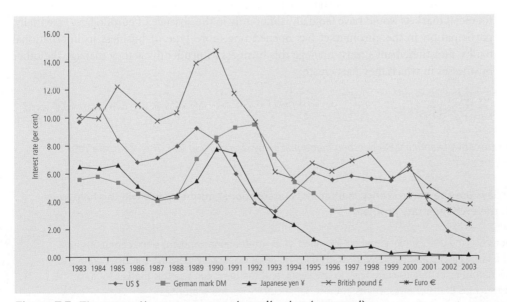

Figure 7.5 Three-month eurocurrency deposit rates (year-end)

banks, generally at interest rates slightly less favorable than those offered among banks. (Investors may also participate in the euromarket indirectly by purchasing money market funds in the United States, when the funds themselves place large portions of their pooled investments in eurodollar accounts.)

Criticisms of the euromarkets

Over the years, the eurodollar market has been criticized as contributing to worldwide inflation and creating major new risks in the international banking system. While neither claim has been proved (or disproved) conclusively, each is worth considering here.

Because the eurodollar market adds to the worldwide volume of dollar-denominated assets, it has been accused of increasing the global money supply beyond the control of the US authorities. This may be true to some extent, but a number of factors mitigate the total impact of eurodollars. First, eurodollars exist only as time deposits and certificates of deposit, never as demand deposits or cash. Hence, in the narrow definition of money that includes only cash and demand deposits, eurodollars do not even appear at all. Second, as already noted, about three-fourths of all eurodollars are interbank deposits rather than new credit to companies or individuals that may use it for capital investment and thus economic growth. The interbank transfers (sometimes called *pyramiding*) do not create any new credit, however measured. Finally, the eurodollar deposits used by companies and individuals for investment and consumption probably replace other (e.g., domestic) bank deposits that would have been used for the same purposes anyhow. That is, because the eurodollar deposits pay interest rates higher than domestic deposits, they often substitute for domestic deposits, and thus they are used for the same purposes that those deposits would have served. All in all, eurodollars probably add slightly to the total volume of economic activity worldwide because they provide a form of financial intermediation between depositors (savers) in many countries and borrowers (investors or spenders) in many countries that is more efficient than that of individual domestic financial markets.

On the issue of increased risk, it has been argued that the eurocurrency market has led to much greater extension of loans to troubled borrowers, such as the governments of less developed countries that found it virtually impossible to repay in the 1980s. Unquestionably, the eurodollar market provided the mechanism through which these governments borrowed most of the money loaned to them in the 1970s. It is not clear, however, that any other financial markets would have fared any differently in the absence of eurodollars. Essentially, participation in the euromarket has opened one more type of business to international banks, and these banks must manage this business as prudently as they manage the other businesses in which they participate.

✔ Active learning check

Review your answer to Active Learning Case question 4 and make any changes you like. Then compare your answer with the one below.

4 **How can Barclays use the eurocurrency market in its international business, and will this help in dealing with the exchange rate problem?**

Barclays can and does use the eurocurrency market for much of its international lending, since conditions in this market favor the large clients and banks with which Barclays deals extensively. Barclays can offer euro-deposits for various maturities in various currencies to its clients, and the bank can use this market to find offsetting exposures such as loans or investments in those same currencies and maturities.

Eurobonds and euroequities

Eurobonds are the long-term analogue of eurocurrencies. They are issued in countries of convenience and denominated in currencies other than the local one. With eurobonds, *taxation* of the interest income investors receive is a key concern, so most of them are issued in tax jurisdictions that do not impose taxes on such interest payments (e.g., Luxembourg). Eurobonds, like domestic US bonds, are issued by corporations and government agencies. They may be convertible into equity, and they may have fixed or floating interest rates.

Borrowers (i.e., issuers of eurobonds) utilize this market for three main reasons. First, no regulatory agency establishes rules for disclosure by issuers, so substantial red tape is avoided; however, this generally limits participation to blue-chip corporations and governments. Second, the interest rates can be marginally lower than those on domestic issues, because investors can usually avoid taxes on their interest income. Third, the issuer gains access to potential investors in many countries simultaneously because the investment banks that place the issue offer it internationally. From time to time, eurobond issue is stimulated by additional reasons, such as domestic bond market restrictions that lead issuers to seek overseas funding. In 1964, for example, the United States established capital controls that made foreign bonds less attractive to US investors (the interest equalization tax was effectively a tax on interest received by US citizens from foreign bond investments) and limited lending by US parent companies to their foreign subsidiaries. As a result, both US and foreign issuers that were trying to place dollar-denominated bonds turned to the fledgling eurobond market for their funding.

For the investor, the eurobond market offers these advantages: (1) all issues are structured to allow exemption from interest withholding tax on the income earned, and (2) the terms of eurobond issues are more varied than those of domestic bond issues. For example, eurobonds usually have shorter maturities than domestic bonds (five to eight years) and often have floating-rate interest payments.

Euroequities

Euroequities have emerged in the past decade in the London Stock Exchange as another long-term euromarket, analogous to domestic stock markets. As the name implies, euroequities are shares of publicly traded stocks traded on an exchange outside of the issuing firm's home country. They are bought and sold in shares denominated in the firm's home currency, so both company performance and exchange rate performance affect the returns on investments in euroequities.

In the United States, a market for such issues has operated for many years through an instrument called the American Depositary Receipt (ADR), which is essentially a claim on a share of stock in the foreign stock exchange intermediated by a securities broker who issues the ADR. Euroequities rival ADRs and offer the flexibility of being direct share issues by the non-local firms. The market exists primarily in London, and thus it encompasses non-British company shares. In fact, even the ADRs of British companies are now traded on the London Stock Exchange, so full global trading is possible through the exchange.

The London Stock Exchange euroequity market grew rapidly in the late 1980s. By 1989, 52 brokerage firms were making a market for euroequities issued by 707 firms. The monthly turnover during January 1989 was 278 million shares. The growing demand for these instruments (based on the firms available for investment and the tax-avoiding structure of the issues), as well as the growing supply (by firms that are blue chip and want to gain access to investors from many countries through the London Stock Exchange), makes it likely that this market will increase in importance in global equities trading.

INTERNATIONAL BUSINESS STRATEGY *IN ACTION*

AngloGold Ashanti

When it comes to international finance, one of the primary concerns of MNEs is the ability to raise capital through new stock offerings and bank loans. For many years this was a major problem for the Anglo American Corporation of South Africa (AAC), which operated gold mines in that country. During South Africa's apartheid period, trade sanctions, controls on exchange currency, and protectionism all combined to isolate AAC from outside financial markets. Unable to do business in the international arena, AAC focused on expanding its domestic operations by acquiring holdings in a variety of industries including automobiles, newspapers, and vineyards.

As apartheid came to an end, however, there was a gradual liberalization of both trade and investment. And as its opportunity to move into the international arena began to increase, the firm put its gold mining activities into a new subsidiary, AngloGold, and began restructuring its operations. Non-core businesses were sold off and the company began focusing heavily on development of its gold and uranium mines. However, its profitability and performance were handicapped by the small size of the South African economy and the fact that the Johannesburg stock market was not very influential in the worldwide financial markets. In addition, the local currency, the rand, was weak and the company needed to tie its operations to a stronger currency.

In response, AngloGold determined that it needed to link itself to the triad and expand its mining operations worldwide. As a result, the firm incorporated as a UK company and got itself listed on the London Stock Exchange. In 1998 the company was listed on the New York Stock Exchange, and today it is also listed on the Paris, Brussels, and Australian stock exchanges (although its primary listing is in London). The firm now has access to equity capital in the EU and North America, as well as Australia. In 2003 AngloGold merged with Ashanti Goldfields, so that the combined firm had mines in eight countries and a total market capitalization of about $3.5 billion in 2004. Today AngloGold Ashanti has a workforce of 62,500 and mining operations in North America, South America, Australia, and Africa. As a result of its recent

Source: Corbis/Reuters

expansion efforts, the company now accounts for 10 per cent of the world's annual gold production, and it is able to raise money for expansion operations in a number of worldwide locations.

Websites: **www.anglogold.com**; **www.londonstockexchange.com**; **www.nyse.com**; and **www.euronext.com**.

Sources: AngloGold Annual Report, 2003; company Web page.

Sometimes an MNE will lend money in the international money market. For example, if Bank of America finds that it can get a higher interest rate in Singapore than in the United States, it may deposit some money there. Similarly, if General Motors finds that there are limitations on the amount of profit that it can transfer out of a country, the company may invest in local financial instruments and thus gain interest on funds that would otherwise sit idle.

THE IMF SYSTEM

The last international financial market we will examine here may be viewed as either a very important framework for international financial dealings or as a market that is generally irrelevant to private business managers. The **international monetary system** is a financial market in which only central banks and the **International Monetary Fund** (IMF, or "the Fund") operate, so private business plays no active role in it. On the other hand, rules for international financial dealings among countries are often set at the IMF, and substantial international loan decisions are made between governments and the IMF. Thus, the rules of the game in the other international financial markets are sometimes influenced by IMF activities.

The international monetary system oversees the exchange rate regime that prevails among the major developed countries, whose currencies are used for the vast majority of international payments. The IMF negotiates with governments of debtor nations (usually less developed countries) for loans directly from the Fund and for loan conditions that are used, subsequently, as a basis for lending by private banks to these same borrowers. In addition, the IMF serves as an intermediary for emergency loans between member governments to cope with the capital flow or exchange rate crises that occur from time to time due to speculation in foreign exchange markets or other causes. All in all, the international monetary system plays an important role in determining the rules of the game for private companies and banks in some spheres of international business, so managers need to understand its functioning.

The International Monetary Fund was designed in 1944 at a conference of the Allied nations held at Bretton Woods, New Hampshire. Its general purpose was to provide a multilateral framework for avoiding international financial crises by establishing rules for national exchange rate policies and for adjustment to balance of payments disequilibria (discussed in the appendix to chapter 6). It was specifically intended to avoid the disastrous financial contraction that occurred during the 1930s. As originally negotiated, and as implemented in 1946 when the Articles of Agreement were signed by the initial 46 member countries, the IMF system required *fixed* exchange rates among member countries, with gold as the basis for currency valuation. The US dollar was initially fixed at a value of $35 per ounce of gold, and all other currencies were fixed at values expressed in both dollars and gold.

Fixed exchange rates were a fundamental base of the Bretton Woods system. Under the Articles of Agreement, each country was obligated to maintain its currency value at the initially set value (the "par" value), with a band of ±1 per cent of flexibility around the par value. If a foreign central bank demanded to sell a country's currency back to the issuer, that country was required to pay the equivalent amount of gold, US dollars, or some other acceptable currency.

To join the IMF, a country was required to make a deposit of gold (25 per cent), plus its own currency (75 per cent), such that each member country's total deposit relative to the total of IMF deposits was roughly in proportion with its share of world trade. Then each member country received the right to borrow up to 200 per cent of its initial deposit at the Fund, in any currency, to help pay for imbalances such as the one mentioned above. If a country borrowed more than its original deposit, the IMF would stipulate economic policies that the borrower had to follow to receive more financial support. (This imposition of policy demands by the IMF is called *conditionality*.)

While the IMF sought to provide assistance for nations facing balance of payments problems, its only resources were the contributions of its member countries: quotas based on each country's part in world trade, which initially constituted about $9 billion. This relatively small amount of liquidity was not sufficient to support the post–World War II economic recovery, or specifically the payments imbalances, of even the European countries.[8]

International monetary system
The arrangement between national governments/central banks that oversees the operation of official foreign exchange dealings between countries

International Monetary Fund (IMF)
The international organization founded at Bretton Woods, New Hampshire, in 1944 that includes most countries of the world and offers balance of payments support to countries in crisis along with financial advising to central banks

Ultimately, the US Marshall Plan injected the needed funding into the international financial system, and specifically into Europe, during 1948–1952.

In fact, the IMF provided very little funding to its member countries in its early years. During the Suez crisis in 1956, it loaned $1.7 billion to Great Britain, France, and India. Later, during speculative runs on the British pound (i.e., periods when speculators sold large quantities of pounds for other currencies in expectation of a devaluation of the pound) in 1961 and 1964, it extended loans to Great Britain. By the end of the 1960s, the IMF was regularly providing credit to member countries, though still not at the levels that many analysts believed necessary to stabilize the system. (The alternative view is that the IMF should not provide credit to the member countries at all; rather, these countries should be forced to adjust their economies to escape balance of payments problems.)

At the end of the 1960s, the US dollar began to be the object of speculative pressure. The problem was severe, since the dollar constituted the base for the entire system of value (through its formal link to gold at $35 per ounce). The United States was unable to devalue to stop the speculation, and later it was unwilling to continue selling its gold holdings to foreign central banks that wanted to redeem their dollars. In August 1971, President Nixon announced that the United States would no longer sell gold to foreign central banks in exchange for dollars. In December 1971, he announced a devaluation of the dollar to $38 per ounce of gold; in February 1972 it was devalued to $42 per ounce, and later that year the US declared that it would not support the dollar value at any price in gold.

These events essentially destroyed the Bretton Woods system of fixed exchange rates. Many initiatives to repair the system were presented during the following two years, but the United States would no longer accept the responsibility of providing the dollar as a fixed base for other currencies. In subsequent months, the IMF system was changed de facto to a floating exchange rate system that allowed each country to leave the value of its currency free to change with market forces or to fix that value to some other currency. Since that time, the United States has allowed the dollar to float in value relative to all other currencies, with occasional efforts by the Fed (the Federal Reserve System) to influence the dollar's relationship to particular currencies, such as the German mark and the Japanese yen.

Under the current IMF system, no limitations are set on each member country's decision to either fix its currency value relative to some other currency or allow it to fluctuate as supply and demand dictate. (Notice that it is impossible for one country to keep its currency fixed relative to all others if the others are not fixed relative to one another.) In 1976, an accord called the Jamaica Agreement altered the IMF charter to formally allow for floating exchange rates. Today, the exchange rate regimes used by each nation are substantially unrestricted, and government strategies to influence exchange rates are altered as desired.[9]

At about the same time that the link between the dollar and gold was broken, the IMF's members agreed to create a new currency that the Fund would issue when authorized to do so by a vote of the members. This currency, called the special drawing right (SDR), allows its holder to obtain (or draw) other currencies from the IMF (or from other members) when desired. SDRs have been created and issued on seven occasions to date. A total SDR of 21.4 billion existed in 2004; their total value was about $30 billion. In each instance, the SDRs were allocated to Fund members according to their quotas. This new "international money" has served to support a number of countries that encountered financial crises since 1971, allowing them to finance their imbalances, but it has not been a solution to imbalances in international financial flows. During the international debt crisis of the early 1980s, SDR use was wholly inadequate to deal with the more than $350 billion of dollar debt owed by Latin American countries to foreign lenders. Total IMF resources include member-country quotas, which totaled over $300 billion at the end of 2004—so the Fund actually has quite substantial lending power today.

Speculator
A person or firm that takes a position in foreign exchange with no hedging or protection mechanism to try to gain from expected exchange rate changes

Special drawing right (SDR)
The currency of the IMF; accounts at the IMF are denominated in SDRs, and the IMF has issued about $US 30 billion of SDRs as currency since its inception in 1969

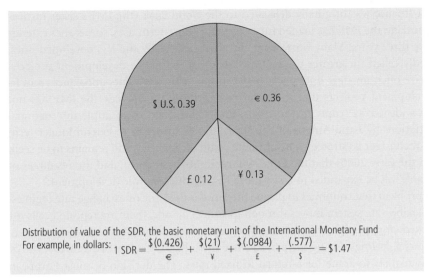

Distribution of value of the SDR, the basic monetary unit of the International Monetary Fund

For example, in dollars: $1 \text{ SDR} = \frac{\$(0.426)}{€} + \frac{\$(21)}{¥} + \frac{\$(.0984)}{£} + \frac{(.577)}{\$} = \$1.47$

Figure 7.6 Special drawing right (October 15, 2004)

During the late 20th century, SDRs became fairly widely used as a currency of denomination for private-sector financial instruments such as bonds and long-term bank loans. Because the SDR has a value based on four currencies (see Figure 7.6), it is more stable as a borrowing or lending tool than any individual currency.

When the dollar devalues relative to other widely traded currencies, so does the SDR—but only 39 per cent of the SDR's value is affected negatively. The other 61 per cent of the SDR's value is based on pounds, yen, and euros, and these currencies may rise or fall relative to the dollar in such a situation. Overall, the changes must net out over all currencies, and an instrument such as the SDR changes relatively little in value compared to any single currency. The SDR is really a "basket" of currencies whose value is generally more stable than that of any one of its components.

Just as the euro has gained wide acceptance as an instrument for denominating international financial transactions, so too the SDR promises to maintain its acceptance as a risk-reducing instrument. (The SDR has the advantage of including the US dollar in the group of currencies that determine its value, whereas the euro is based only on European currencies.) At present private-sector investors and borrowers are using a much greater volume and value of euro-denominated instruments than SDR-denominated instruments.

Unresolved problems with the IMF system

The IMF system today differs dramatically from the model established at Bretton Woods in 1944. Flexible exchange rates have been substituted for fixed ones; gold has been greatly reduced as an international monetary asset,[10] and its link to the dollar has been severed; a new reserve currency, the SDR, has been created to increase world liquidity; and, perhaps most important, the US dollar is no longer the single base for the IMF system of value. These major changes have come in response to problems and crises that have occurred during the past 60 years—yet the IMF system itself survives. While few people would argue that the IMF has led directly to greater international financial stability over its history, at least the system has been flexible enough to accommodate the various crises that have threatened it.

Several problems that remain in the system deserve note. First, there has always been an uncomfortable tension between the countries that want to utilize the IMF simply as a bank for reducing the negative impacts of balance of payments difficulties and the countries that want to utilize it to subsidize economic development. The "link" between the IMF and

World Bank
The world's largest development bank, formed along with the IMF at Bretton Woods in 1944. Its original name was the International Bank for Reconstruction and Development (IBRD). The World Bank assists developing countries with loans and economic advising for economic development

development finance was originally delegated to the **World Bank** (the IMF's sister institution). Traditionally, the IMF has loaned funds only for short-term uses, sometimes extending to two or three years. Many borrowing countries, especially the less developed ones, have repeatedly called for greater use of IMF resources to finance development projects. While there are often no clear differences between financing payments imbalances and financing development projects that may later reduce those imbalances, the IMF has not substantially widened its scope. In the 1980s, under the cloud of multiple international loan renegotiations by Latin American countries, the Fund began to extend longer-term loans and to reconsider its strategy. The ultimate result of this crisis still remains to be seen. It appears in the early 2000s that the Fund will retain its basic form, and the resources of the World Bank will be expanded to assist more heavily in economic development.

A second problem that continues to plague the Fund is the issue of exchange rate regimes. Even as the flexible rate system moves through its fourth decade, there are repeated calls for a return to fixed, or more tightly constrained, currency values. The great instability of international financial dealings during the period since the initial OPEC oil crisis of 1973–1974 has led some analysts to argue for a return to fixed rates. The decision of most European Union countries to set up a single currency, the euro, has placed a regional fixed exchange rate regime alongside of the floating rate system globally. The evidence during the entire 20th century tends to suggest that no matter what exchange rate regime prevails, if international trade relations are unstable and payments imbalances are substantial, no exchange rate regime will be able to solve the problem. Thus, this problem most likely cannot be eliminated.

On the whole, the international monetary system plays an important role in all international financial dealings by being the focal point for establishing rules on exchange rates, exchange controls, intergovernmental loans, and other official transactions. On a day-to-day basis, most international business people, especially in the triad countries, do not feel the international monetary system's impact.

MNEs AND INTERNATIONAL FINANCIAL MARKETS AND INSTITUTIONS

Whether or not a company or bank is involved in international trade, investment, or other international business, it is important that its managers understand some of the key aspects of international financial markets. The eurocurrency market may offer a low-cost borrowing opportunity, or the eurobond market may provide an outlet for selling new debt to a wider group of investors. The international monetary system establishes a framework within which governments set international financial policies that may affect many firms. The money and capital markets in foreign countries may offer opportunities to multinational firms that operate in those countries. The foreign exchange market determines the cost and availability of foreign currencies, used in business by many firms. Finally, all of these markets influence the functioning of the markets for real goods and services, the ultimate use for all financial claims.

KEY POINTS

1 Foreign exchange is any financial instrument that can be used to carry out payment from one currency to another. There are two major foreign exchange markets in the United States and the United Kingdom: interbank (including brokers) and futures/options (at stock and commodities exchanges). The most important participants in foreign exchange markets are banks—acting as traders, speculators, hedgers, and arbitrageurs. Exchange rates are determined by the activities of these five groups. The rates

are also influenced by purchasing power parity, interest rates, and technical factors such as national economic statistics and seasonal demands.

2   There are a number of international finance strategies that can be of value to firms doing business overseas. Two of the most important are strategies for managing currency exchange rate risk and strategies for financing international operations.

3   The international monetary system is a market among central banks of the countries that belong to the International Monetary Fund (IMF). The IMF's objectives include the facilitation of balanced growth of international trade, promotion of exchange stability, and the making of financial resources available to the members of the Fund. In recent years the fixed monetary system created by the IMF members in 1944 has been replaced by a managed float system. Currently the IMF faces a number of major problems, including helping third world countries to deal with their international debt crises and increasing international liquidity.

Key terms

- exchange risk
- foreign exchange
- eurocurrency
- exchange rate
- foreign exchange traders
- foreign exchange brokers
- spot rate
- forward rate
- arbitrageurs
- purchasing power parity

- international Fisher effect
- nominal interest rate
- real interest rate
- exchange risk avoidance
- exchange risk adaptation
- exchange risk transfer
- currency diversification
- foreign bond
- eurobond

- European Monetary Union (EMU)
- eurodollars
- London interbank offered rate (LIBOR)
- international monetary system
- International Monetary Fund (IMF)
- speculator
- special drawing right (SDR)
- World Bank

REVIEW AND DISCUSSION QUESTIONS

1   If your firm had a subsidiary in Japan and about 100 million yen in exposed assets (i.e., plant and equipment), how would you protect it against exchange risk?

2   If you managed the European operations of a large US-based MNE, in what market(s) would you seek long-term funding? Why?

3   Given that the euro area's inflation is about 3 per cent per year at present, while US inflation is about 2 per cent per year, what do you expect to happen to the euro/dollar exchange rate in the next few months? Why?

4   What is the difference between a eurobond and a domestic bond in the United States? Which one would you prefer to issue as a company manager? Which one would you prefer to buy as an investor? Why?

5   How can a firm such as Ajax Steel in Peoria, Illinois, utilize the eurodollar market to minimize its financing costs? This firm is a medium-size manufacturer with no foreign sales.

6   Assume that the interest rate on 12-month US dollar deposits in London is currently 2.6875 per cent per year and the rate on British pound deposits there is 4.1875 per cent per year. The spot exchange rate is US $1.93/pound. What do you expect the exchange rate to be in one year?

7   If you were offered the opportunity to establish a deposit in London-denominated euros, would you choose that rather than a deposit in British pounds or dollars? Why or why not?

8 What are the important differences between the Bretton Woods fixed-exchange-rate system and the current IMF system? How do these differences affect the MNE manager?

9 How may the International Monetary Fund affect companies' activities in international business?

10 How would you hedge the value of your export sale of € 10 million of computers to a French customer? You will be paid in 180 days in euros. On what basis would you choose among hedging methods?

REAL CASE

HSBC

What is the world's largest bank? Prior to the merger of Citicorp and Travelers in 1998, it was the Hong Kong and Shanghai Banking Corporation (HSBC). Formed in 1865 by a Scotsman in the then British Colony of Hong Kong, HSBC grew to over 10,000 bank offices in 76 countries by 2004. In the process it became the world's first truly global bank, offering a full range of financial services from retail to corporate banking to insurance and financial management. HSBC built this global business based on its strong Hong Kong base. The bank owns the Hong Kong Bank and most of the Hang Seng Bank, giving it over 40 per cent of the market in the Hong Kong Special Administrative Region of China that was created on July 1, 1997.

Perhaps less well known is that HSBC is also the owner of the former Midland Bank chain in Britain, the Marine Midland and Republic New York banks and Household Finance in the US, and the Hong Kong Bank of Canada. It has also acquired large banks in Latin America including Banco Bamerindus in Brazil and Bital in Mexico. In all these cases HSBC greatly improved the efficiency of the underperforming local banks through better systems and processes. Over recent years, HSBC has implemented a rebranding strategy of all its subsidiaries under the HSBC title and logo. This is meant to build HSBC into a global brand.

Today HSBC is well developed across the triad regions of Asia, Europe, and the Americas. It is a global bank in terms of assets, but not revenues. Its diversification strategy has helped to insulate it from the Asian financial crisis of 1997/1998. And its first-mover advantage as a truly global bank may prove hard to match by its competitors. There is constant pressure in banking to reduce costs through greater scale economies and improved information technology. HSBC is well positioned to continue as an industry leader because of its successful globalization strategy.

In retrospect, one of the world's largest banks came from one of the world's smallest economies. And it did

this despite the regulatory barriers to entry for foreign-owned firms in Europe and North America. As a result the HSBC is an example of a bank using modern management systems and market forces to win out over old-fashioned protectionism in a highly regulated worldwide industry.

Perhaps the biggest influence of HSBC and its new efficient banking methods has been on British banking. A further restructuring occurred in British banking in November 1999 when one of the country's four major banks (Lloyds, Barclays, Natwest, and HSBC) was taken over by a much smaller bank. Natwest was acquired by the Royal Bank of Scotland, only one-third the asset size of Natwest, in a drawn out and controversial takeover. Another bank, the Bank of Scotland, first bid for Natwest and the takeover efforts of both the Royal Bank of Scotland and the Bank of Scotland were defended by Natwest Chairman, Sir David Rowland, who was also President of Templeton College, University of Oxford. The takeover was successful because investors were critical of Natwest's old-style management and were supportive of the cost-cutting and new information technology methods of the Royal Bank of Scotland. After the acquisition, many Natwest branches were closed; bank buildings were turned into coffee bars, restaurants, and hotels; and a leaner, more efficient bank emerged to reclaim its place in British retail banking.

More recently the Bank of Scotland and Halifax, the largest mortgage lender in the country, finalized a merger. This has fast-forwarded Halifax into mainstream banking and greatly increased the Bank of Scotland's scope of operations. It would also allow both banks to streamline their businesses and increase their market focus. These efforts toward restructuring operations and eliminating waste are not going unnoticed by rival banks. Barclays, for example, has now begun closing some of its branches and is introducing a wide array of tools and techniques that are designed to cut costs and increase operational efficiency. It realizes that, to be a successful international operation, it must not only have wide geographic coverage but also be able to offer efficient services. In looking at these recent developments, it is clear that the steps taken by HSBC to modernize its own operations are proving to be a wake up call for British banks as well.

Websites: www.hsbc.com; www.citigroup.com; www.bankofscotland.co.uk; www.royalbankscot.co.uk; www.natwest.co.uk; and www.barclays.com.

Sources: Robert Grosse, *The Future of Global Financial Services* (Oxford: Blackwell, 2004).

1 Since HSBC does business with the People's Republic of China and has substantial holdings of Chinese yuan (renminbi) on hand, what risk does this pose for the bank?

2 How could the HSBC manage its currency exchange rate risk?

3 As the British retail banks are merged to achieve cost savings and economies, does this increase or decrease the barriers to entry for foreign banks wishing to do business in the EU?

REAL CASE

World financial crises

Throughout the 1990s, a series of financial crises rocked the world's economy. The first of these was the 1994 Mexico peso crisis. This was followed by the Asian crisis of 1997. Since then there have been the Russian crisis of 1998, the 1999 Brazilian financial crisis, and the 2001 Argentine crisis. The following examines the first two of these.

The Mexican peso crisis

In late 1994 Mexico suffered one of the worst financial crises in its history. In less than one month the Mexican peso devalued from 3.45 to the US dollar to 5.57 to the dollar, and by the end of 1995 it was trading at 6.5 to the dollar. This was accompanied by heavy inflation, unemployment, and a severe stock market crash. Some critics claimed that all of this was a result of NAFTA, but this was not so. The crisis was caused by the Mexican government itself, which had liberalized trade and financial flows but had not allowed the peso to float. Moreover, previous governments had kept the peso overvalued. As a result, in less than one year Mexico's foreign reserves were depleted by 75 per cent and the country's current account deficit was equal to 8 per cent of GDP.

Other factors also contributed to the low price of the peso. For instance, as a result of the Zapatista armed rebellion of 1996 in Chiapas, in southern Mexico, both foreign and Mexican investors took tens of millions of dollars out of the country. These developments had far-reaching consequences throughout the region. For example, many investors in other Latin American countries, fearing a similar crash, withdrew their funds from these economies and deposited them in the United States for safe keeping.

Source: Corbis/Reuters

One unexpected development of the Mexican peso crisis was the devaluation of the Canadian dollar, which was sideswiped by the Latin American currency crisis. Thanks to NAFTA, Canada and Mexico had become linked in the international currency markets. At the same time international investors began showing a preference for the US dollar against both the Mexican peso and the Canadian dollar.

Perhaps the most surprising thing about the peso crisis was how quickly the country bounded back. With the help of a $50 billion loan from the United States and other countries, a tough economic reform that saw cuts in government spending, and increases in deregulation and privatization, the Mexican economy began to revive. Hardly a year had passed when investors who were running from the region were quickly lured back by short-term interest rates of up to 40 per cent. Additionally, the stock market crash had led to underpriced shares, and investors began buying these issues and driving the prices back up. Today the financial crisis of 1995 in Mexico is a thing of the past. The country's economy is healthy and investors are back.

The Asian financial crisis

In the early 1990s, the Asian economies of South Korea, Indonesia, Taiwan, Malaysia, and Japan were being praised as economic miracles. In 1997, these countries faced one of the worst blows to their economies. The Asian crisis began in July 1997, when Thailand stopped pegging its currency to the US dollar. In two months the Thai bath had devalued by nearly 40 per cent. The effect was two-fold. First, Asian exporters to Thailand faced decreased demand for their product. Second, there was the decrease of investor confidence in the region.

Individual countries in the region faced their own sets of problems. In Malaysia, it was excessive lending to the property sector. Once foreign investment was cut short, overlending, overinvestment, and overproduction led to a downward spiral in the economy. In South Korea, the *chaebols* (large manufacturing conglomerates) that dominated the economy had invested recklessly without regard to profit. In Indonesia, President Suharto's corruption and lack of accountability led investors to flee the country. In addition, the banking system that the government there had fostered was plagued with bad loans for many unreliable projects. These loans benefited and created wealth for well-positioned individuals—in particular, members of the Suharto family, but they did nothing for the rest of the country.

Some financial observers believe that Western speculators were a major reason for the financial troubles in the region. The trend toward deregulation of the world capital markets and the free flow of capital, it was argued, contributed to the currency panic. Additionally, the relatively good health of these nations prior to 1997 made them attractive to foreign investors and lenders. Unfortunately, many of these loans were short term and

were in foreign currency. So while the economy grew, the loans presented no problem. But when trouble looked likely the foreign lenders began calling in their loans. When this happened, the value of the local currencies plummeted and the loans payable in foreign currencies created a debt crisis.

It was initially believed that the Asian economic problem would be contained in that geographic region. However, by mid-1998 the crisis was having an effect on the global economy. The cross-border interconnections of global industries and the resulting interdependence pushed the problem to other regions. Among other things, the crisis led to decreases in the prices of many commodities including oil, metals, grain, pulp, and paper.

Industrial nations came to the aid of these Asian governments. The IMF negotiated billions of dollars in bailouts. Initially, the IMF wanted these governments to decrease their budget deficit and to maintain stable interest rates. By July 1998, however, the IMF was allowing increases in deficits and lower interest rates. This helped ease some of the problems, although there was still a great deal of disagreement regarding what else needed to be done. For example, some observers argued that the government needed to continue to deregulate the country's capital markets, while others blamed the economic disaster on this deregulation.

Sources: "Crisis-ridden Indonesia to Overhaul Ailing Banking Sector," *Boston Globe on Line*, January 27, 1998, www.boston.com/dailynews/; Richard Gwyn, "Asian Flu Shows No Sign of Letting Up," *Toronto Star*, July 10, 1998; "A Crisis of Dictatorship," *Washington Post*, January 11, 1998; Raffi Anderian, "Everybody Is Going Down," *Sunday Star*, July 12, 1998; "The Downward Spiral of the Asian Tigers," BBC News, January 8, 1998.

1 How does a decrease in the value of the Mexican peso affect foreign direct investment?

2 How is trade affected by currency devaluations as a result of a financial crisis?

3 How are customers in countries undergoing a financial crisis affected by the devaluation of the peso?

Endnotes

1 Exchange rate quotations come as two-digit numbers, bid/asked, with the preceding numbers assumed. A British pound quote of 50/70 on October 14, 2004, meant an actual price of:

$ 1.7950 bid to buy one British pound.
£ 1.7970 asked for selling one British pound.

The bank is offering (bidding) to buy pounds for 1.795 dollars per pound and also offering (asking) to sell pounds for 1.797 dollars per pound. Of course, the actual transaction will involve $1 million or more, to be exchanged at those prices.

Rates are typically quoted on the **Continental basis**, as units of foreign exchange per dollar, everywhere. US banks have traditionally used the **American basis**, quoting $US per unit of foreign exchange. Clearly, whether the quote is SF 2.0 dollar or $0.50/SF, the value is the same. The *Wall Street Journal* offers both types of quotations, as shown in Table 7.2.

Another means used to distinguish the two ways of presenting an exchange rate is to call a quotation of domestic currency/foreign exchange an **indirect quote**. Conversely, a quotation of units of foreign exchange/domestic currency is called a **direct quote**. This system has more general applicability to any pair of currencies, whereas the American/Continental system relates only to rates involving the US dollar.

2 http://www.chips.org.

3 "Taking a position" means purchasing an asset (or a liability) denominated in a foreign currency without simultaneously matching it with a liability (asset) of the same value and maturity in the same currency. If a US bank buys Swiss francs, it takes a position in Swiss francs. When the bank sells those Swiss francs to a client, it eliminates the position.

4 A **foreign currency option** is a contract offering the holder the right to buy (namely, a **call option**) or sell (namely, a **put option**) a fixed amount of foreign currency for a fixed price during a fixed time period. The buyer of a call option on British pounds obtains the right to buy £31,500 at a fixed dollar price (i.e., the **exercise price**) at any time during the (typically) three-month life of the option. The seller of the same option faces a **contingent liability** in that the seller will have to deliver the British pounds at any time if the buyer chooses to exercise the option.

The market value (i.e., the price on "premium" that the buyer must pay to purchase the option) of an option depends on its exercise price, the remaining time to its expiration, the exchange rate in the spot market, and expectations about the future exchange rate. An option may sell for a price near zero, for thousands of dollars, or for anywhere in between. Notice that the buyer of a call option on British pounds may pay a small price to obtain the option but does *not* have to exercise the option if the actual exchange rate moves favorably. Thus, an option is superior to a forward contract having the same maturity and exercise price because it need *not* be used, and the cost is just its purchase price. However, the price of the option is generally higher than the expected cost of the forward contract, so the user of the option pays for the flexibility of the instrument.

5 Yet another kind of foreign exchange arbitrage involves comparing interest rates on similar investments between two currencies. Interest arbitrage is the choice of investing, say, $1 million in a euro-dollar bank deposit, versus investing the same money in pounds, depositing in a europound deposit, and contracting a forward contract to convert back to dollars. This comparison can be used for whatever currencies that may be available, and the investor benefits from taking the highest return available, with the exchange rates guaranteed through forward contracts (i.e., with no exchange risk).

6 This entire discussion refers to *relative* purchasing power parity (PPP). The stronger, absolute version refers to parity in the values of factor inputs used in the production of products whose prices reflect relative factor productivities. Relative PPP considers only *changes* in the relative price levels between countries, not the initial (absolute) levels.

7 Realistically, if any one government disallows the euromarkets, they can still function almost as effectively in other countries and currencies. At present, the US government has the most important role, since about 80 per cent of euro-deposits are denominated in US dollars.

8 See the Economic Cooperation Act of 1948 (Public Law 472, 80th Congress), US Code Congressional Service, 1948.

9 Exchange rate policies *are* constrained by the IMF if a country seeks to borrow more than its quota from the Fund. Also, a country does operate in violation of IMF rules if it imposes new exchange controls on current transactions without obtaining IMF approval; however, sanctions are seldom applied unless the country seeks to borrow as above.

10 Almost one-third of the world's monetary reserves were still being held in the form of gold at year-end 1991. See IMF *Survey*, November 8, 1993, p. 345.

Additional bibliography

Anonymous, "Euro Creates New Possibilities for Money Management," *Harvard Business Review*, vol. 77, no. 1 (January/February 1999).

Berg, David M. and Guisinger, Stephen E. "Capital Flows, Capital Controls, and International Business Risk," in Alan M. Rugman and Thomas Brewer (eds.), *The Oxford Handbook of International Business* (Oxford: Oxford University Press, 2001).

Carr, Nicholas G. "Managing in the Euro Zone," *Harvard Business Review*, vol. 77, no. 1 (January/February 1999).

Grosse, Robert. *The Future of Global Financial Services* (Oxford: Blackwell, 2004).

Huczynski, Andrzej. "International Management Behaviour," *European Management Journal*, vol. 19, no. 4 (August 2001).

Khanna, Ashok. "Equity Investment Projects in Emerging Markets," *Columbia Journal of World Business*, vol. 31, no. 2 (Summer 1996).

Kleiman, Gary and Morrissey, Elizabeth R. "African Equity Markets: Testing Latin America's Path," *Columbia Journal of World Business*, vol. 29, no. 2 (Summer 1994).

Ling-yee, Li. "Effect of Export Financing Resources and Supply-Chain Skills on Export Competitive Advantages: Implications for Superior Export Performance," *Journal of World Business*, vol. 36, no. 3 (Fall 2001).

Luehrman, Timothy A. "The Exchange Rate Exposure of a Global Competitor," *Journal of International Business Studies*, vol. 21, no. 2 (Second Quarter 1990).

Miller, Kent D. and Reuer, Jeffrey J. "Firm Strategy and Economic Exposure to Foreign Exchange Rate Movements," *Journal of International Business Studies*, vol. 29, no. 3 (Fall 1998).

Narayandas, Das. "Prepare Your Company for Global Pricing," *Sloan Management Review*, vol. 42, no. 1 (Fall 2000).

Spall, Alan. "Beyond the Currency Question," *Harvard Business Review*, vol. 77, no. 1 (January/February 1999).

Strange, Susan. *Mad Money* (Manchester: Manchester University Press, 1998).

Part Three

INTERNATIONAL BUSINESS STRATEGIES

Chapter 8

MULTINATIONAL STRATEGY

Objectives of the chapter

Multinational enterprises are businesses that are headquartered in one country but have operations in other countries. In such a complex environment, it is particularly important for these MNEs to have well-formulated strategic plans. Large MNEs do this by conducting a thorough analysis of their environments and often developing detailed, comprehensive plans for coordinating worldwide activities. These plans set forth objectives for all major divisions and units and provide for systematic follow-up and evaluation. Smaller MNEs use less sophisticated plans. However, all multinationals that conduct strategic planning go through a three-step process: formulation, implementation, and control.

Contents

The objectives of this chapter are to:

1 *Define* the term *strategic planning* and discuss the strategic orientations that affect this planning process.
2 *Explain* how strategy is formulated, giving particular emphasis to external and internal environmental assessment.
3 *Describe* how strategy is implemented, with particular attention to location, ownership decisions, and functional area implementation.
4 *Discuss* the ways in which MNEs control and evaluate their strategies.

Vodafone and the triad telecom market

Vodafone had its beginnings in 1982, when the Racal Electronics Group Board successfully bid for a private-sector UK cellular license. The Racal Telecomms Division was established with 50 employees in the rural town of Newbury and launched the first cellular network on January 1, 1985. By the end of that year, Vodafone had 19,000 subscribers. Today, London-based Vodafone is the world's largest mobile phone company with 133.4 million customers around the world.

Vodafone expanded globally through a carefully crafted "triad" strategy. From 1991 to 1998 its focus was on Europe, where it developed one of the basic ideas that it continues to use in most cases—acquire companies in association with partners and pay for it with equity. This strategy has given Vodafone access to new markets while providing it with partners who help deal with local regulatory environment agencies and provide assistance in addressing local market needs. For example, in the case of Libertel of the Netherlands, Vodafone purchased 70 per cent of the company while Dutch ING, the local partner, held the rest. Today the company has interests in companies that serve 17 European markets and holds over 50 per cent of the shares in 12 of these companies.

If we attribute to Vodafone the customers of its subsidiaries multiplied by its share of the subsidiary, Vodafone has 90.8 million customers in Europe. In total, this accounts for 71 per cent of all the customers of its wholly-owned and joint-venture subsidiaries. In geographic terms, 68 per cent of Vodafone's subscribers and 70.3 per cent of its turnover are in Europe.

To appease EU regulators during its acquisition spree, Vodafone had to divest itself of Orange, the UK's third largest wireless operator. European acquisitions could not, therefore, be the company's only growth strategy. Rather, the best strategy was to go international, gain market share in all major economies, then link together all these firms into a worldwide network. This is precisely what it has done.

In June 1999, Vodafone took a major step in implementing its worldwide strategy when it beat out Bell Atlantic for Airtouch Communications, a California-based firm. Creating Vodafone Airtouch (VA) gave the overall company a market capitalization of $154 billion and a total of 35 million wireless customers worldwide. Soon after the acquisition, VA entered into an agreement with Bell Atlantic (which was soon to merge with GTE) that gave it a 45 per cent stake in a venture called Verizon Wireless. This decision has proved to

Source: Corbis/Reuters

be a very good one; prior to the merger of Cingular and AT&T Wireless in 2004, Verizon was the largest US mobile telephone operator. Indeed, Cingular snatched AT&T Wireless from Vodafone, which was seeking to further cement its presence in the United States through a controlling interest in the company.

The US market shows relatively low penetration levels compared to Europe and Japan, where most adults have a cell phone, and has the highest potential for growth across industrialized countries. Today, Verizon has 38.9 million subscribers, of which Vodafone claims 17.3 million. This amounts to 12 per cent of Vodafone's total subscriber base.

Vodafone cemented its position in Japan in late 2001 by increasing its share of Japan Telecom to 69.7 per cent. That decision completed the firm's "triad" strategy. Today, Vodafone has 10.4 million subscribers in Japan and this amounts to 7.8 per cent of the company's total subscribers. It is a major player in the EU with holdings in Omnitel, Mannesmann, and SFR. The company is a big force in the US market through its minority of Verizon Wireless. And in Asia, where the largest market for mobile phones is in Japan, Vodafone holds operating control of Japan Telecom and also owns J-Phone, a large mobile phone operator.

Vodafone has carefully ventured into other markets. In Australia and New Zealand, it has wholly owned subsidiaries and about 4 million subscribers. In non-industrialized countries, where the risk is higher, it presently holds minority interests in most of its operations. Only in Egypt does it have more than 50 per cent ownership. In South Africa,

Kenya, and Fiji, it holds between 35 and 40 per cent. In China, the market with the largest potential growth, it holds a mere 3.3 per cent ownership of the venture. In such a huge market, however, that accounts for nearly 5 million subscribers.

Vodafone's strategy is to maximize its footprint with a common technology and offer the largest possible "roaming" wireless capability, which lends itself to overall lower costs. Perhaps surprisingly, this roaming technology is more prevalent in Europe than in the United States, mostly due to EU-wide cooperation between governmental regulatory authorities regarding common platforms.

Vodafone is not only relying on geographic diversification of acquisitions. Technology plays a major role in this industry, and Vodafone, like its competitors, purchased licenses to operate 3G technology, the next step in mobile telephony. When the industry overestimated the pace at which the technology was developed, some providers stumbled badly, but this technology is now available in urban areas in Europe and Japan and is likely to expand quickly. Mobile telephones with video and picture technology are more established in the market, but it is data transfers that mobile service providers are counting on for increased profits. This new technology is expected to reduce overall costs and,

competition permitting, might allow Vodafone to increase its revenue per subscriber.

The biggest challenge facing Vodafone will be that of coordinating all of its worldwide holdings so as to maximize shareholder value. In an effort to handle this problem, the company's head office has now abandoned the use of centralized control and opted for a decentralized type of operation. In the United States, for example, local partners and operating managers now make many of the major decisions regarding how to do business. The same is true in Europe. Vodafone is realizing that in order to manage all of these different units in worldwide markets where regulations and customer preferences are often quite different, the best approach is to create a strategic plan that recognizes and takes advantages of these differences.

Websites: www.vodafone.com; www.verizon.com; www.omnitelvodafone.it; www.mannesmann.de; www.nttdocomo.com; and www.kddi.com.

Sources: "Vodafone Moves on Japan Telecom," *Financial Times*, September 17, 2001, p. 20; Michiyo Nakamoto and Thorold Barker, "Vodafone Offer Aims to Cement Takeover," *Financial Times*, September 21, 2001, p. 25; Dan Roberts, "Vodafone Meets Forecasts," *Financial Times*, October 5, 2001, p. 20; "Vodafone's Dilemma," *Economist*, February 12, 2004; "The Shunning of 3G," *Economist*, September 18, 2003; "Vodafone Launches 3G in Europe," *BBC News*, May 4, 2004; and *Vodafone Annual Reports and Accounts*, 1999, 2000, 2004.

1 Given the competitiveness of the environment, how much opportunity exists for Vodafone in the international mobile phone market?

2 What type of generic strategy does Vodafone employ? Defend your answer.

3 What forms of ownership arrangement is Vodafone using to gain world market share? Explain.

4 On what basis would a firm like Vodafone evaluate performance? Identify and describe two.

INTRODUCTION

Strategic planning is the process of evaluating an enterprise's environment and internal strengths, identifying its basic mission and long- and short-range objectives, and implementing a plan of action for attaining these goals. Multinational enterprises (MNEs) rely heavily on this process because it provides them with both general direction and specific guidance in carrying out their activities. Without a strategic plan, these businesses would have great difficulty in planning, implementing, and evaluating operations. With strategic planning, however, research shows that many MNEs have been able to make adjustments in their approach to dealing with competitive situations and either redirect their efforts or exploit new areas of opportunity. For example, as a result of losing market share in Europe in recent years, General Motors is now cutting its European capacity in an effort to stem further losses.[1] Meanwhile, Dell Computer is expanding its international presence. In 2001 the company became the largest firm in the worldwide PC business, with a market share of

Strategic planning
The process of evaluating the enterprise's environment and its internal strengths and then identifying long- and short-range activities

13 per cent. On a different front, General Electric's strategy is to continue growing in spite of the European Commission's refusal to allow it to merge with Honeywell. Most recently, GE Medical bought Data Critical, a maker of wireless and Internet systems for communicating health-care data; GE Industrial Systems acquired the Lentronics line of multiplexers from Nortel Networks; and GE Capital purchased Heller Financial, a company in the commercial financing, equipment leasing, and real estate finance business.[2] By carefully formulating their strategic plan, these MNEs are finding that they can better cope with the ever-changing challenge of worldwide competition.[3]

STRATEGIC ORIENTATIONS

Ethnocentric predisposition
The tendency of a manager or multinational company to rely on the values and interests of the parent company in formulating and implementing the strategic plan

Before examining the strategic planning process, we must realize that MNEs have strategic predispositions toward doing things in a particular way, which help determine the specific decisions the firm will implement. There are four such predispositions: ethnocentric, polycentric, regiocentric, and geocentric. Table 8.1 lists each predisposition and its characteristics.

An MNE with an ethnocentric predisposition will rely on the values and interests of the parent company in formulating and implementing the strategic plan. Primary emphasis

Table 8.1 Typical strategic orientations of MNEs

MNE orientation	Ethnocentric	Polycentric	Regiocentric	Geocentric
Company's basic mission	Profitability	Public acceptance (legitimacy)	Both profitability and public acceptance	Both profitability and public acceptance
Type of governance	Top down	Bottom up (each local unit sets objectives)	Mutually negotiated between the region and its subsidiaries	Mutually negotiated at all levels of the organization
Strategy	Global integration	National responsiveness	Regional integration and national responsiveness	Global integration and national responsiveness
Structure	Hierarchical product divisions	Hierarchical area divisions with autonomous national units	Product and regional organization tied together through a matrix structure	A network of organizations (in some cases this includes stockholders and competitors)
Culture	Home country	Host country	Regional	Global
Technology	Mass production	Batch production	Flexible manufacturing	Flexible manufacturing
Marketing strategy	Product development is determined primarily by the needs of the home-country customers	Local product development based on local needs	Standardized within the region, but not across regions	Global products with local variations
Profit strategy	Profits are brought back to the home country	Profits are kept in the host country	Profits are redistributed within the region	Redistribution is done on a global basis
Human resource management practices	Overseas operations are managed by people from the home country	Local nationals are used in key management positions	Regional people are developed for key managerial positions anywhere in the region	The best people anywhere in the world are developed for key positions everywhere in the world

Source: Adapted from *Columbia Journal of World Business*, Summer 1985, Balaji S. Chakravarthy and Howard V. Perlmutter, "Strategic Planning for a Global Business," pp. 5–6, Copyright 1985, with permission from Elsevier Science.

will be given to profitability and the firm will try to run operations abroad the way they are run at home. Firms trying to sell the same product abroad that they sell at home use this predisposition most commonly.

An MNE with a polycentric predisposition will tailor its strategic plan to meet the needs of the local culture. If the firm is doing business in more than one culture, the overall plan will be adapted to reflect these individual needs. The basic mission of a polycentric MNE is to be accepted by the local culture and to blend into the country. Each subsidiary will decide which objectives to pursue, based on local needs. Profits will be put back into the country in the form of expansion and growth.

An MNE with a regiocentric predisposition will be interested in obtaining both profit and public acceptance (a combination of the ethnocentric and polycentric approaches) and will use a strategy that allows it to address both local and regional needs. The company will be less focused on a particular country than on a geographic region. For example, an MNE doing business in the EU will be interested in all the member nations.

An MNE with a geocentric predisposition will view operations on a global basis. The largest international corporations often use this approach. They produce global products with local variations and staff their offices with the best people they can find, regardless of country of origin. Multinationals, in the true meaning of the word, have a geocentric predisposition. However, it is possible for an MNE to have a polycentric or regiocentric predisposition if the company is moderately small or limits its operations to specific cultures or geographic regions.

The predisposition of an MNE will greatly influence its strategic planning process. For example, some MNEs are more interested in profit and/or growth than in developing a comprehensive corporate strategy that exploits their strengths.[4] Some are more interested in large-scale manufacturing that will allow them to compete on a price basis across the country or region, as opposed to developing a high degree of responsiveness to local demand and tailoring a product to these specific market niches.[5] Some prefer to sell in countries where the cultures are similar to their own so that the same basic marketing orientation can be used throughout the regions.[6] These orientations or predispositions greatly influence strategy.[7] For an example of strategic orientations, see the box **International Business Strategy in Action: Arthur Andersen, Accenture, and McKinsey.**

Polycentric predisposition
The tendency of a multinational to tailor its strategic plan to meet the needs of the local culture

Regiocentric predisposition
The tendency of a multinational to use a strategy that addresses both local and regional needs

Geocentric predisposition
The tendency of a multinational to construct its strategic plan with a global view of operations

INTERNATIONAL BUSINESS STRATEGY *IN ACTION*

Arthur Andersen, Accenture, and McKinsey

During the 1990s, some of the fastest growing global organizations were professional service firms that specialized in areas such as consulting, accounting, publishing, law, public relations, advertising, and so on. Today, more and more of these service firms are linking together their worldwide country offices in order to provide seamless service to their multinational clients. Arthur Andersen, Accenture, and McKinsey & Company, three major international consulting firms, provide good examples.

Founded in Chicago in 1913 to provide accounting services, Arthur Andersen had grown to over 85,000 employees in 84 countries by 2001. Until 1989, the firm's management and technology consulting group—Andersen Consulting Group—had complemented its audit and accounting services. However, in 1989, as part of a restructuring effort, Arthur Andersen and Andersen Consulting split and became two independent companies. The plan called for each to maintain its individual business and to cooperate under the umbrella of Andersen Worldwide. In 1997, however, Andersen Consulting sought arbitration claiming that Arthur Andersen had breached the agreement by expanding into business consulting in technology integration, strategic business planning, and business transformation. In 2000, the arbitrator ruled in favor of Andersen Consulting but also forced the consulting firm to drop the Andersen name. Today, under the name Accenture—a combination of "accent" and "future"—this company is a leader in global management and technology consulting with more than 95,000 employees in 48 countries. Arthur Andersen, on the other hand, ceased to exist after it was discovered that the company, which had been Enron's auditor since 1985, had been involved in the Enron scandal of 2001. When investigators discovered that Andersen had destroyed documents relating to the case, the reputation it had relied on was shattered and its clients departed.

In 1926, James O. McKinsey left his job as a University of Chicago accounting professor to found a company that would provide finance and budgeting services. Soon afterwards, however, McKinsey & Company came to be better known for providing advice on management and organizational issues. In the 1960s, as tariffs began to be lowered and American firms thought of ways to expand internationally, the McKinsey company provided consulting on how to expand, while expanding into Europe, Canada, and Australia itself. Today, the firm is the best known management-consultancy firm in the world, with 82 offices in 44 countries. However, it has had mixed success at running its international operations. The German subsidiary is relatively independent, for example, while the French subsidiary is not. McKinsey's core strength is its brand name built on the in-house training and management of its highly skilled people, who have been recruited from top business schools. In 2001, the firm found itself with overcapacity and had to lay off some of its most recent employees. Nevertheless, by 2004 it was estimated that the firm was using only 50 to 60 per cent of its capacity. When the IT bubble burst, McKinsey lost many of its clients. Other clients, not affected by IT, were reluctant to turn to consulting firms for advice due to the demise of one of McKinsey's largest competitors, Arthur Andersen.

In summary, consulting firms were originally designed to provide advice to managers on improving workplace efficiencies with the use of engineers and time and motion studies. But they soon began to realize that senior executives also needed advice on strategy and organization and began to offer it to their clients. The 1970s and 1980s saw the height of this type of consultancy service. In the 1990s, however, the rise of the IT sector meant that these firms themselves had to redefine their strategic focus. Today, consultancies offer accounting, legal, management, leadership training, strategic planning, operational analysis, and technology services, among others.

Consulting firms have often been deemed recession-proof because their services are needed regardless of what happens in the economy. For example, in good times, businesses need consulting assistance to help them deal with expansion, mergers, and acquisitions; in bad times, they need help in cutting back operations, trimming the workforce, and refocusing their strategy. The most recent worldwide economic slowdown, however, led to an unexpected and significant slowdown in consulting as well. In the 1990s, the market was growing by 20 per cent annually; by 2001 this growth rate had shrunk to 3 per cent. This slowdown has taken its toll. In the past, consulting firms focused their efforts on securing long-term relationships with large MNEs and other large organizations. And by drawing on their firm-specific advantages and reputation for quality, they were able to continually attract new clients. In the early 2000s, however, they have all begun to lay off junior staff, and recently hired MBAs are looking for innovative ways to get costs under control. Some critics have wondered aloud why they are having so many problems. If they are indeed experts at helping organizations solve the challenges associated with economic downturns, why do they not simply apply some of these solutions to their own current situation?

Websites: www.accenture.com and www.mckinsey.com.

Sources: Rachel Emma Silverman, "Accenture's Strong Revenue Growth Bucks Industry Slump," *Wall Street* Journal, October 12, 2001, p. B4; Andersen Worldwide 1996 Annual Report; C. A. Bartlett (1996), *McKinsey & Company: Managing Knowledge and Learning*, Harvard Business School Case No. 9-396-357; http://www.mckinsey.com; http://www/mckinsey.com/about/feet_on_the_street.html; Geoffrey Colvin, "The Consulting Slowdown," *Fortune.com*, August 21, 2001; "The Real McKinsey," *Economist.com*, January 30, 2003; and "McKinsey's Election Battle," *Economist.com*, February 27, 2003.

STRATEGY FORMULATION

Strategy formulation
The process of evaluating the enterprise's environment and its internal strengths

Strategy formulation is the process of evaluating an enterprise's environment and internal strengths. This typically begins with consideration of the external arena, since the MNE will first be interested in opportunities that can be exploited. Attention is then directed to the internal environment and the resources the organization has available, or can develop, to take advantage of these opportunities.

External environmental assessment

The analysis of the external environment involves two activities: information gathering and information assessment. These steps help to answer two key questions: What is going on in the external environment? And how will these developments affect our company?[8] One of the most common ways to do this is through competitive intelligence, which is the use of systematic techniques for obtaining and analyzing public information about competitors. These data are particularly useful in keeping MNEs alert to likely moves by the competition.[9]

Competitive intelligence
The gathering of external information on competitors and the competitive environment as part of the decision-making process

Information gathering

Information gathering is a critical phase of international strategic planning. Unfortunately, not all firms recognize this early enough. In the case of Harley-Davidson, the large US-based motorcycle manufacturer, it was not until the Japanese began dominating the motorcycle market that Harley realized its problem. A systematic analysis of the competition revealed that the major reason for Japanese success in the US market was the high quality of their products, a result of extremely efficient manufacturing techniques. Today, Harley is competitive again. It achieved renewed success because it rethought its basic business, reformulated company strategy, vastly improved product quality, and rededicated itself to its core business: heavyweight motorcycles.

There are a number of ways that MNEs conduct an environmental scan and forecast the future. Four of the most common methods include: (1) asking industry experts to discuss industry trends and make projections about the future; (2) using historical industry trends to forecast future developments; (3) asking knowledgeable managers to write scenarios describing what they foresee for the industry over the next two to three years; and (4) using computers to simulate the industry environment and generate likely future developments. Of these, expert opinion is the most commonly used.[10] The Japanese and the South Koreans provide excellent examples. Mitsubishi has more than 700 employees in New York City, where its primary objective is to gather information on American competitors and markets. All large Japanese corporations operating in the United States employ similar strategies. The same is true for large South Korean trading firms, which require their branch managers to send back information on market developments. These data are then analyzed and used to help formulate future strategies for the firms.

Such information helps MNEs to identify competitor strengths and weaknesses and to target areas for attack. This approach is particularly important when a company is delivering a product or service for many market niches around the world that are too small to be individually profitable. In such situations the MNE has to identify a series of different niches and attempt to market successfully in each of these geographic areas.[11] The information is also critical to those firms that will be coming under attack.

Information assessment

Having gathered information on the competition and the industry, MNEs then evaluate the data. One of the most common approaches is to make an overall assessment based on the five forces that determine industry competitiveness: buyers, suppliers, potential new entrants to the industry, the availability of substitute goods and services, and rivalry among the competitors. Figure 8.1 shows the connections among these forces.[12]

Bargaining power of buyers

MNEs examine the power of their buyers in order to predict the likelihood of maintaining these customers. If the firm believes buyers may be moving their business to competitors, the MNE will want to formulate a strategy for countering this move. For example, the company may offer a lower price or increase the amount of service it provides.

Figure 8.1 The five forces of industry competitiveness

Source: Adapted with the permission of The Free Press, an imprint of Simon & Schuster Adult Publishing Group, from *Competitive Advantage: Creating and Sustaining Superior Performance* by Michael E. Porter. Copyright © 1985, 1998 by Michael E. Porter.

Bargaining power of suppliers

An MNE looks at the power of the industry's suppliers to see if it can gain a competitive advantage here.[13] For example, if there are a number of suppliers in the industry, the MNE may attempt to play them off against one another in an effort to get a lower price. Or the company may move to eliminate any threat from the suppliers by acquiring one of them, thus guaranteeing itself a ready source of inputs.

New entrants

The company will examine the likelihood of new firms entering the industry and will try to determine the impact they might have on the MNE. Two typical ways that international MNEs attempt to reduce the threat of new entrants are by (1) keeping costs low and consumer loyalty high, and (2) encouraging the government to limit foreign business activity through regulation such as duties, tariffs, quotas, and other protective measures.

Threat of substitutes

The MNE looks at the availability of substitute goods and services and tries to anticipate when such offerings will reach the market. There are a number of steps the company can take to offset this competitive force, including (1) lowering prices, (2) offering similar products, and (3) increasing services to the customer.

Rivalry

The MNE examines the rivalry that exists between itself and the competition and seeks to anticipate future changes in this arrangement. Common strategies for maintaining and/or increasing market strength include (1) offering new goods and services, (2) increasing productivity and thus reducing overall costs, (3) working to differentiate current goods and services from those of the competition, (4) increasing overall quality of goods and services, and (5) targeting specific niches with a well-designed market strategy.

As the MNE examines each of these five forces, it must decide the attractiveness and unattractiveness of each. This will help decide how and where to make strategic changes. Figure 8.2 shows the five forces model applied to the semiconductor industry.

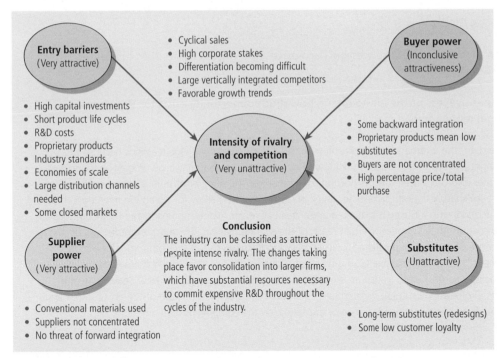

Figure 8.2 The five forces model applied to the semiconductor industry

Source. Scott Beardsley and Kinji Sakagami, *"Advanced Micro Devices: Poised for Chip Greatness,"* unpublished student paper, Sloan School of Management, MIT, 1988. Reported in Arnoldo C. Hax and Nicolas S. Majluf, *The Strategy Concept and Process: A Pragmatic Approach* (Englewood Cliffs, NJ: Prentice-Hall, 1991), p. 46.

Notice in Figure 8.2 that at the time this analysis was conducted, the suppliers in the semiconductor industry were not very powerful, so they were an attractive force for the MNE. Buyers did not have many substitute products from which to choose (an attractive development), but there was some backward integration toward purchasing their own sources of supply (an unattractive development). Overall, the attractiveness of buyer power was regarded as inconclusive. The third force, entry barriers, was quite attractive because of the high costs of getting into the industry and the short product life cycles that existed there. It was very difficult for a company to enter this market. The fourth force, substitutes, was unattractive because new products were being developed continually and customer loyalty was somewhat low. The fifth and final force, industry rivalry, was also unattractive because of the high cost of doing business, the cyclical nature of sales, and the difficulty of differentiating one's products from those of the competition.

On an overall basis, however, the industry was classified as attractive. It also appeared that the industry would see consolidation of smaller firms into larger firms that would have greater resources to commit to research and development.

MNEs operating in the semiconductor industry would use this analysis to help them increase the attractiveness of those forces that currently are not highly attractive. For example, they could work to develop state-of-the-art semiconductors that might be substituted for the competition's products, and they would attempt to maintain a technological advantage so that the substitute force would not become a problem for them. In the process, they would likely be better able to increase their power over the buyers since their products would be so high-tech that the customers could not do better by purchasing from a competitor. In summary, environmental assessment, such as that provided by an analysis of competitive forces, is used to determine MNE opportunities and threats and help identify strategies for improving market position and profitability.

✔ Active learning check

Review your answer to Active Learning Case question 1 and make any changes you like. Then compare your answer with the one below.

1 Given the competitiveness of the environment, how much opportunity exists for Vodafone in the international mobile phone market?

As seen from the case data, the international opportunities in this industry are great. One reason is because the market is going to continue growing and updating itself with new technology that may allow Vodafone to increase its revenue per subscriber and carve itself a larger portion of the market. The number of mobile phone users in the United States will increase sharply during this decade, and new technology will allow for expansion in all three triad markets. The key to success in this industry is to have a presence in all major markets, primarily the triad countries and others where the cost of mobile phones is within reach of the average person. China, for example, will be an important market because of its large population. However, newly industrialized countries offer Vodafone more stability for its investment because the average GDP is much greater than that of China's and there is less political instability. Examples include South Korea, Singapore, and Taiwan. In addition, Australia and New Zealand are important target markets. By focusing on these more affluent markets and offering both state-of-the-art products and competitive prices, Vodafone has a very good chance of outdistancing the competition.

Internal environmental assessment

The internal environmental assessment helps pinpoint MNE strengths and weaknesses. There are two specific areas that a multinational should examine in this assessment: (1) physical resources and personnel competencies, and (2) the way in which value chain analysis can be used to bring these resources together in the most synergistic and profitable manner.

Physical resources and personnel competencies

The physical resources are the assets the MNE will use to carry out its strategic plan. Many of these are reported on the balance sheet as reflected by cash, inventory, machinery, and equipment accounts. However, this does not tell the whole story. The location and disposition of these resources is also important. For example, an MNE with manufacturing plants on three continents may be in a much better position to compete worldwide than a competitor whose plants are all located in one geographic area. Location can also affect cost. In the 1980s it was possible for Japanese steelmakers to sell their products in the United States at lower prices than their US competitors. During the 1990s US firms improved their steel-producing technology and erected small minimills that were highly efficient, thus offsetting the location advantage of their foreign competitors. Today, however, European steelmakers, in particular, have sharply increased their efficiency and, along with Japanese firms, are now able to compete in the US market.[14] Between 1997 and 2003, 41 US steel firms went bankrupt, which led the industry to lobby the US government for protection from imports. In 2002, tariffs of 8–30 per cent were imposed on imports from most countries to help the US industry restructure.[15] These were removed in 2003, after complaints by other countries to the WTO.

Strategic business units (SBUs)
Operating units with their own strategic space; they produce and sell goods and services to a market segment and have a well-defined set of competitors

Another important consideration is the degree of integration that exists within the operating units of the MNE. Large companies, in particular, tend to be divided into strategic business units (SBUs). These are operating units with their own strategic space that produce and sell goods and services to a market segment and have a well-defined set of competitors.[16] SBUs are sometimes referred to as "businesses within the business." Mitsubishi, the giant Japanese conglomerate, has a host of SBUs that constitute its corporate network, including steelmaking, auto production, electronics, and banking. So when a Mitsubishi SBU that manufactures and sells consumer goods is looking for help with financing, it can turn to the banking SBU. If the bank finds that a customer needs a firm to produce a particular electronics product, it can refer the buyer to the electronics SBU.

In fact, some large MNEs use vertical integration, which is the ownership of all assets needed to produce the goods and services delivered to the customer. Many large Japanese manufacturing firms, in particular, have moved toward vertical integration by purchasing controlling interests in their suppliers.[17] The objective is to obtain control over the supply and thus ensure that the materials or goods are delivered as needed. Many US and European firms have shied away from this strategy because "captured suppliers" are often less cost-effective than independents. For example, a number of years ago *Time* magazine owned the forests for producing the paper it needed. However, the company eventually sold this resource because it found that the cost of making the paper was higher than that charged by large paper manufacturers that specialized in this product. So vertical integration may reduce costs in some instances, but it can be an ineffective strategy in others.[18] A particular problem with vertical integration is defending oneself from competitors who are less vertically integrated and are able to achieve cost efficiencies as a result. The latter rely heavily on outsourcers and employ virtual integration, which is the ownership of the core technologies and manufacturing capabilities needed to produce outputs coupled with dependence on outsourcers to provide all other needed inputs. Virtual integration allows an MNE to operate as if it were vertically integrated, but it does not require the company to own all the factors of production, as is the case with vertically integrated firms.

Personnel competencies are the abilities and talents of the people. An MNE should examine these because they reflect many of the company's strengths and weaknesses. For example, if an MNE has an outstanding R&D department, it may be able to develop high-quality, state-of-the-art products. However, if the company has no sales arm, it will sell the output to a firm that can handle the marketing and distribution. Conversely, if a company lacks a strong R&D department but has an international sales force, it may allow the competition to bring out new products and to rely on its own R&D people to reverse-engineer them—that is, to find out how they are built and develop technologies that can do the same thing—while relying on the sales force to build market share. This strategy has been used by many internationally based personal computer (PC) firms that have taken PC technology and used it to develop similar but far less expensive units that are now beginning to dominate the world market.

An understanding of what a company does well can help it decide whether the best strategy is to lead or to follow close behind and copy the leader. Not every MNE has the personnel competencies to be first in the field, and many are happy to follow because the investment risk is less and the opportunity for profit is often good.

Vertical integration
The ownership of assets involved in producing a good or service and delivering it to the final customer

Virtual integration
A networking strategy based on cooperation within and across company boundaries

Value chain analysis

A complementary approach to internal environment assessment is an examination of the firm's value chain.[19] A value chain is the way in which primary and support activities are combined to provide goods and services and increase profit margins. Figure 8.3 provides the general schema of a value chain. The primary activities in this chain include (1) inbound logistics, such as receiving, storing, materials handling, and warehouse activities; (2) operations, in which inputs are put into final product form by performing activities such as machining, assembling, testing, and packaging; (3) outbound logistics, which involve distributing the finished product to the customer; (4) marketing and sales, which are used to encourage buyers to purchase the product; and (5) service for maintaining and enhancing the value of the product after the sale through activities such as repair, product

Value chain
The way in which primary and support activities are combined in providing goods and services and increasing profit margins

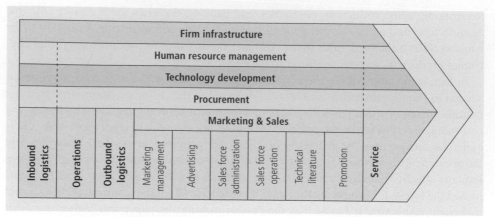

Figure 8.3 A basic value chain

Source: Adapted with the permission of The Free Press, an imprint of Simon & Schuster Adult Publishing Group, from *Competitive Advantage: Creating and Sustaining Superior Performance* by Michael E. Porter. Copyright © 1985, 1998 by Michael E. Porter.

adjustment, training, and parts supply. The support activities in the value chain consist of (1) the firm's infrastructure, which is made up of the company's general management, planning, finance, accounting, legal, government affairs, and quality management areas; (2) human resource management, which is made up of the selection, placement, appraisal, promotion, training, and development of the firm's personnel; (3) technology in the form of knowledge, research and development, and procedures that can result in improved goods and services; and (4) procurement, which involves the purchasing of raw materials, supplies, and similar goods.

MNEs can use these primary and support activities to increase the value of the goods and services they provide. As such, they form a value chain. An example is provided in Figure 8.4, which helps to explain why IBM has been so effective in the international market. The company combines the primary and support activities so as to increase the value of its products. IBM's alliance with ROLM and MCI and its strengths in software and hardware technologies have given it a solid foundation for launching successful strategies in the telecommunications industry.

Any firm can apply this idea of a value chain. For example, Makita of Japan has become a leading competitor in power tools because it was the first to use new, less expensive materials for making tool parts and to produce in a single plant standardized models that it then sold worldwide.

Analysis of the value chain can also help a company determine the type of strategy that will be most effective. In all, there are three generic strategies: cost, differentiation, and focus.

1 **Cost strategy** relies on such approaches as aggressive construction of efficient facilities, vigorous pursuit of cost reductions and overhead control, avoidance of marginal customer accounts, and cost minimization in areas like R&D, service, sales, and advertising.

2 **Differentiation strategy** is directed toward creating something that is perceived as being unique. Approaches to differentiation can take many forms, including the creation of design or brand image, improved technology or features, and increased customer service or dealer networks.

3 **Focus strategy** involves concentrating on a particular buyer group and segmenting that niche based on product line or geographic market. While low-cost and differentiation strategies are aimed at achieving objectives industrywide, a focus strategy is built around servicing a particular target market, and each functional policy is developed with this in mind.[20]

Cost strategy
A strategy that relies on low price and is achieved through approaches such as vigorous pursuit of cost reductions and overhead control, avoidance of marginal customer accounts, and cost minimization in areas such as sales and advertising

Differentiation strategy
A strategy directed toward creating something that is perceived as being unique

Focus strategy
A strategy that concentrates on a particular buyer group and segments that niche based on product line or geographic market

	Inbound logistics	Operations	Outbound logistics	Marketing & Sales	Service	
Firm infrastructure	Multidomestic presence Access to most major corporations					**Margin**
Human resource management		Lifetime employment In-house career development		All employees think in marketing terms	In-house technical training	
Technology development		Strong R&D resources	Strong software capability			
Procurement	Owns ROLM (CPE manufacturer)					
		Leading computer technology used in-house Partnership with MCI		Strong reputation for excellence Already sells to most major corporations Experienced sales force	Extensive buyer training	**Margin**
	Inbound logistics	**Operations**	**Outbound logistics**	**Marketing & Sales**	**Service**	

Figure 8.4 The value chain for IBM

Source: Reported in Arnoldo C. Hax and Nicolas S. Majluf, *The Strategy Concept and Process: A Pragmatic Approach* (Englewood Cliffs, NJ: Prentice-Hall, 1991), p. 82.

In addition, the firm will determine its competitive scope, which is the breadth of its target market within the industry. Figure 8.5 provides an example of these generic strategies as applied to the worldwide shipbuilding industry.

Competitive scope
The breadth of a firm's target market within an industry

The value chain can help an MNE create synergies within the organization's activities. For example, by combining the human resource talent of their salespeople with the expertise of their design and styling personnel, firms like PSA Peugeot-Citroën and Volkswagen have been able to increase their auto market share in Western Europe in recent years.[21] In particular, Peugeot and VW have been able to cut costs and offer a wide range of new models. Their overall success is found in their ability to manage the flow of new products, so that the offerings remain reasonably fresh without spending money on excessive investment in

		Competitive advantage	
		Cost	Differentiation
Competitive scope	Broad target	1 Korean firms that build vessels of good but not superior quality	3 Japanese firms that build high-quality vessels at premium prices
	Narrow target	2 Chinese shipbuilders that build simple, standard vessels	4 Scandinavian yards that build ice breakers, cruise ships, and other specialized vessels

Figure 8.5 Generic strategies in worldwide shipbuilding

Source: Adapted with the permission of The Free Press, an imprint of Simon & Schuster Adult Publishing Group, from *Competitive Advantage: Creating and Sustaining Superior Performance* by Michael E. Porter. Copyright © 1985, 1998 by Michael E. Porter.

updates or redesign. Firms that cannot get this aspect of the product cycle correct have been falling behind in the European market, as seen by Ford, General Motors, and, most significantly, Renault.[22] Simply put, by analyzing the ways of combining their primary and support activities, some automotive MNEs have been able to create a strategy that allows them to draw heavily on their strengths while minimizing their weaknesses.[23]

✔ Active learning check

Review your answer to Active Learning Case question 2 and make any changes you like. Then compare your answer with the one below.

2 **What type of generic strategy does Vodafone employ? Defend your answer.**

Vodafone uses a focus strategy that is geared toward identifying market niches and meeting the needs of the mobile customers in these target groups. Notice that one of the guidelines it follows in most of its acquisitions is to be the major stakeholder (or at least hold a substantial ownership position) but also to have a partner who can help the company deal with the challenges in the local market. As the case notes, the company now holds over 50 per cent of the shares in 12 of the 17 European countries in which it operates, plus 45 per cent of Verizon in the United States. Another generic strategy has been to pay for its acquisitions through equity, which saved it from the technology crash of the early 2000s. So the company targets selected markets in which there is little risk and provides innovative products at competitive prices in order to compete effectively.

Goal setting

External and internal environmental analyses provide an MNE with the information needed for setting goals. Some of these goals will be determined during the external analysis, as the company identifies opportunities it wants to exploit. Others will be finalized after the value chain analysis is complete. In either event, one of the outcomes of strategy formulation will be the identification of goals.[24]

There are two basic ways of examining the goals or objectives of international business operations. One is to review them on the basis of operating performance or functional area. Table 8.2 provides an illustration. Some of the major goals are related to profitability,

Table 8.2 Typical goals of an MNE

Profitability	Marketing	Production	Finance	Human resource management
Level of products	Total sales volume	Ratio of foreign to domestic production share	Financing of foreign affiliates—retained earnings or local borrowing	Development of managers with global orientation
Return on assets, investment, equity, sales	Market share—worldwide, region, country	Economies of scale via international production integration	Taxation—minimizing the burden globally	Management development of host-country nationals
Annual profit growth	Growth in sales volume	Quality and cost control	Optimum capital structure	
Annual earnings per share growth	Integration of country markets for marketing efficiency and effectiveness	Introduction of cost-efficient production methods	Foreign exchange management—minimizing losses from foreign fluctuations	

Source: Adapted from *International Dimensions of Management*, 2nd edition, by A. Phatak © 1989. Reprinted with permission of South-Western College Publishing, a division of Thomson Learning.

marketing, production, finance, and human resources. A second way is to examine these goals by geographic area, or on an SBU basis. For example, the European group may have a profitability goal of 16 per cent, the North American group's profitability goal may be 17 per cent, and the Pacific Rim group may aim for 18 per cent. Then there are accompanying functional goals for marketing, production, and finance. If the MNE has SBUs, each strategic business unit in these geographic locales will have its own list of goals.

This approach uses what is called a "cascading effect"—like a cascade of water rippling down the side of a hill, it reaches the bottom by moving from one level to the next. The MNE starts out by setting a profitability goal for the overall enterprise. Each geographic area or business unit is then assigned a profitability goal that, if attained, will result in the MNE reaching its overall desired profitability. The same approach is used in other key areas such as marketing, production, and finance. Within each unit, these objectives are further subdivided so that every part of the organization understands its objectives and everyone is working toward the same overall goals.

STRATEGY IMPLEMENTATION

Strategy implementation is the process of attaining goals by using the organizational structure to execute the formulated strategy properly. There are many areas of focus in this process. Three of the most important are location, ownership decisions, and functional area implementation. The box **International Business Strategy in Action: Fuji Xerox and Xerox** illustrates how these considerations can be used in gaining market entry.[25]

Strategy implementation
The process of attaining goals by using the organizational structure to execute the formulated strategy properly

Location

MNEs have greatly expanded their international presence over the past decade. Some of the areas in which they have begun to set up operations include China, the former Soviet Union, and Eastern Europe.

Location is important for a number of reasons. Local facilities often provide a cost advantage to the producer, particularly when the raw materials, parts, or labor needed to make the product can be inexpensively obtained close to the facility. Location is also important because residents may prefer locally produced goods. For example, many people in the United States like to "buy American." Some locations may also be attractive because the local government is encouraging investment through various means such as low tax rates, free land, subsidized energy and transportation rates, and low-interest loans while subjecting imported goods to tariffs, quotas, or other governmental restrictions, thereby making local manufacture more desirable. Finally, the MNE may already be doing so much business in a country that the local government will insist that it set up local operations and begin producing more of its goods there. This is a major reason why Japanese auto manufacturers began to establish operations in the United States.

Although the benefits can be great, a number of drawbacks are associated with locating operations overseas. One is an unstable political climate that can leave an MNE vulnerable to low profits and bureaucratic red tape. In Russia, for example, the government has encouraged joint ventures, but because of political and economic uncertainty many businesspeople currently regard such investments as high-risk ventures. A second drawback is the possibility of revolution or armed conflict. MNEs with operations in Kuwait lost just about all of their investment in the Gulf War, and MNEs with locales in Saudi Arabia and other Middle East countries affected by the Gulf War also withstood losses in the region. Most recently, businesses in areas targeted by international terrorists have been making

INTERNATIONAL BUSINESS STRATEGY *IN ACTION*

Fuji Xerox and Xerox

Fuji Xerox was created in 1962 as a 50/50 joint venture between Xerox and Fuji Photo Film. It is regarded as the most successful partnership between US and Japanese firms. The arrangement developed from a sales operation for Xerox products in Japan into a fully integrated organization with its own R&D and manufacturing. By 1990, Fuji Xerox revenues were $4 billion and the company had a world product mandate to supply the entire Xerox Group with the low-to-mid-range copiers that were the core of its business. Indeed, as Xerox's monopoly on large copiers began to dwindle in the 1970s, it was its Japanese partner, Fuji Xerox, that rode to the rescue with its new, high-quality smaller copiers.

In 1975, Xerox was forced by the US Federal Trade Commission to license its original core copier technology to rivals such as IBM, Kodak, Ricoh, and Canon. If it had not been for Fuji Xerox developing new copier technology, Xerox would have failed. The firm's early monopoly in the world copier business was eroded sharply by intense rivalry from Japanese competitors such as Canon and Ricoh as well as from Kodak and IBM. These rivals produced higher-quality, lower-priced, more technologically advanced, and more reliable copiers than Xerox.

When Fuji Xerox recognized the threat, its managers, acting autonomously, started R&D into new small copiers. The US head office was slow to take on board the technology and products of its Japanese partner. Loss of market share, however, especially to Canon, eventually led to ever closer degrees of cooperation between Xerox and Fuji Xerox. In particular, the high quality standards of Fuji Xerox were spread throughout the Xerox Group, and its total quality management (TQM) techniques helped Xerox regain market. In this context, Xerox was helped by a partner that was the hotbed of TQM and copier innovation in the 1970s and 1980s.

One of the reasons for success in the collaboration between Xerox and Fuji Photo Films was that the latter acted as a silent partner in the 50/50 joint venture and allowed Fuji Xerox to develop its own management cadre, who became skilled in R&D and copier technology and in the manufacturing and marketing of small copiers. Fuji Xerox also transformed itself from a marketing subsidiary into a full-line business, thus ending up being more innovative and responsive to the market than Xerox itself.

In 2004, Fuji Xerox had revenues totaling $8 billion with 14,607 employees. For its part, Xerox's revenues totaled $14.7 billion with 61,000 employees. Fuji Photo Film has revenues of $20.9 billion and 72,000 employees. Today, Fuji Photo Film owns 75 per cent of the company and Xerox the remaining 25 per cent.

Websites: www.fujixerox.co.jp; www.xerox.com; and www.fujifilm.com.

Sources: Adapted from Benjamin Gomes-Casseres and Krista McQuade, *Xerox and Fuji Xerox*, Harvard Business School Case 9-391-156; David T. Kearns and David A. Nadler, *Prophets in the Dark: How Xerox Reinvented Itself and Beat Back the Japanese* (New York: Macmillan, 1992); Benjamin Gomes-Casseres, "Group Versus Group: How Alliance Networks Compete," *Harvard Business Review*, July/August 1994, pp. 62–74; and www.hoovers.com.

plans to reduce their risks. In some cases firms are finding a way to "hedge their bets," as noted in the following example:

> Some . . . opt for locales where the cost of running a small enterprise is significantly lower than that of running a large one. In this way they spread their risk, setting up many small locations throughout the world rather than one or two large ones. Manufacturing firms are a good example. Some production firms feel that the economies of scale associated with a large-scale plant are more than offset by the potential problems that can result, should economic or political difficulties develop in the country. These firms' strategy is to spread the risk by opting for a series of small plants spread throughout a wide geographic region.[26]

Ownership

Ownership of international operations has become an important issue in recent years. Many Americans, for example, believe that the increase in foreign-owned businesses in the United States is weakening the economy. People in other countries have similar feelings about US businesses there. In truth, the real issue of ownership is whether or not the company is contributing to the overall economic good of the country where it is doing business. As one researcher noted, ". . . because the US-owned corporation is coming to have no special relationship with Americans, it makes no sense for the United States to entrust its national competitiveness to it. The interests of American-owned corporations may or may not coincide with those of the American people."[27] Countries that want to remain economically strong must be able to attract international investors who will provide jobs that allow their workers to increase their skills and build products that are demanded on the world market. In accomplishing this objective, firms often engage in strategic alliances.

Strategic alliance

Sometimes companies prefer to invest in another country and maintain 100 per cent ownership. This, however, is often very expensive and risky. Given that the MNE may not have much experience in that particular marketplace, local partners may be very helpful in dealing with all sorts of local barriers. As a result, it is becoming increasingly popular to find MNEs turning to the use of strategic partnerships. A strategic alliance or partnership is an agreement between two or more competitive MNEs for the purpose of cooperating in some manner in serving a global market.[28] The type of cooperation can be in marketing, research, or a more comprehensive manner. In recent years these partnerships have become increasingly popular,[29] although careful management of such agreements continues to be a critical area of concern.[30] An example of a strategic partnership is that of Matsushita Electric Industrial and Hitachi, Japan's two leading electronics manufacturers. These companies are now jointly developing state-of-the-art technology in three areas: smart cards, home network systems, and recyclable and energy-efficient consumer electronics. In the past, both firms have developed their own products, but now they are turning to a strategic partnership to save money and shorten development time.[31] Another example of strategic partnerships is that between IBM and NTT. Under the terms of their recent agreement, for the next decade IBM will provide outsourcing services to NTT, Japan's dominant telecommunications carrier. In turn, IBM will be able to use NTT Comware staff in outsourcing and obtaining computer service contracts with other customers in Japan.[32]

Strategic alliance or partnership
An agreement between two or more competitive multinational enterprises for the purpose of serving a global market

International joint ventures

An international joint venture (IJV) is an agreement between two or more partners to own and control an overseas business.[33] This is a special type of a strategic alliance that involves setting up a new business entity, generally involving management separate from that of the partners' own management teams. IJVs take a number of different forms[34] and offer myriad opportunities,[35] which helps explain some of the reasons for their rise in popularity in recent years. One of these reasons is government encouragement and legislation designed to make it attractive for foreign investors to bring in local partners. A second reason is the growing need for partners who know the local economy, the culture, and the political system and who can cut through red tape in getting things done—something IJVs often do very well.[36] Indeed, IJVs are often the result of two or more companies identifying the potential for "synergies," wherein each partner brings to the venture what the other partner needs but is lacking in. For example, an MNE might provide a local partner with technology know-how and an infusion of capital that, in turn, will allow the local firm to expand operations, raise market share, and begin exporting. An example is Toyota and PSA Peugeot-Citroën, which recently entered into an IJV to jointly develop and build a small, fuel-efficient car for the European market. The primary benefit for Toyota is the opportunity to expand its model line-up in Europe. The major advantage for Peugeot is that of gaining a new small car for its European product line while sharing the development costs with Toyota.[37]

International joint venture (IJV)
An agreement between two or more partners to own and control an overseas business

Unfortunately, in many cases IJVs have not worked out well. Several studies found a failure rate of 30 per cent for ventures in developed countries and 45–50 per cent in less developed countries.[38] The major reason has been the desire by foreign MNEs to control local operation, which sometimes has resulted in poor decision making and/or conflicts with the local partners. In general, joint ventures are difficult to manage and are frequently unstable.[39] This issue of joint ventures and alliances is discussed further in Chapter 20 under the flagship firm analysis of business networks.

✔ Active learning check

Review your answer to Active Learning Case question 3 and make any changes you like. Then compare your answer with the one below.

3 **What forms of ownership arrangement is Vodafone using to gain world market share? Explain.**

Vodafone uses two basic approaches. The most common is the international joint venture, which is seen by the company's decisions to acquire an ownership position in a local company but have a local partner hold the remainder of the ownership. An example is its 45 per cent stake in Verizon Wireless, which is now the largest US mobile telephone operator in America. In some cases, however, Vodafone opts for total ownership and purchases the entire company, usually when it believes it does not need a local partner. An example is Airtouch Communications, where Vodafone acquired the entire firm. In both cases, of course, the ownership arrangement is designed to help Vodafone continue to increase its market share in that geographic region.

Functional strategies

Functional strategies are used to coordinate operations and ensure that the plan is carried out properly.[40] The specific functions that are key to the success of the MNE will vary, but they typically fall into six major areas: marketing, manufacturing, finance, procurement, technology, and human resources. For purposes of analysis, they can be examined in terms of three major considerations: marketing, manufacturing, and finance.

Marketing

The marketing strategy is designed to identify consumer needs and formulate a plan of action for selling the desired goods and services to these customers.[41] Most marketing strategies are built around what is commonly known as the "four Ps" of marketing: product, price, promotion, and place. The company identifies the products that are in demand in the market niches it is pursuing. It apprises the manufacturing department of any modifications needed to meet local needs, and it determines the price at which the goods can be sold. Then the company devotes its attention to promoting the products and selling them in the local market.

Manufacturing

Designed to fit together with the marketing plan, the manufacturing strategy ensures that the right products are built and delivered in time for sale. Manufacturing also coordinates its strategy with the procurement and technology people to ensure that the desired materials are available and the products have the necessary state-of-the-art quality. If the MNE is producing goods in more than one country, it gives attention to coordinating activities where needed. For example, some firms manufacture goods in two or more countries, then assemble and sell them in other geographic regions. Japanese auto firms send car parts to the United States for assembly and then sell some of the assembled cars in Canada, Mexico, and South America. Whirlpool builds appliances worldwide with operations in Brazil, Canada, Mexico, the Netherlands, and seven other countries. Such production and assembly operations have to be coordinated carefully.[42]

Finance

Financial strategy often serves to both lead and lag the other functional strategies. In the lead position, finance limits the amounts of money that can be spent on marketing (new product development, advertising, promotion) and manufacturing (machinery, equipment, quality control) to ensure that the desired return on investment is achieved. In the lag position, the financial strategy is used to evaluate performance and provide insights into how future strategy should be changed.

Financial strategies used to be formulated and controlled out of the home office. In recent years, however, MNEs have learned that this approach can be cumbersome and, due to fluctuating currency prices, costly as well. Today's overseas units have more control over their finances than before, but they are guided by a carefully constructed budget that is in accord with the overall strategic plan. They are also held to account for financial performance in the form of return on investment, profit, capital budgeting, debt financing, and working capital management.

CONTROL AND EVALUATION

The strategy formulation and implementation processes are subject to control and evaluation. This process involves examining of the MNE's performance to determine (1) how well the organization has done and (2) what actions should be taken in light of this performance. This process is tied directly to the overall strategy in that the objectives serve as the basis for comparison and evaluation.[43] Figure 8.6 illustrates how this process works.

If the comparison and evaluation show that the strategic business unit or overseas operation is performing according to expectations, then things will continue as before. The

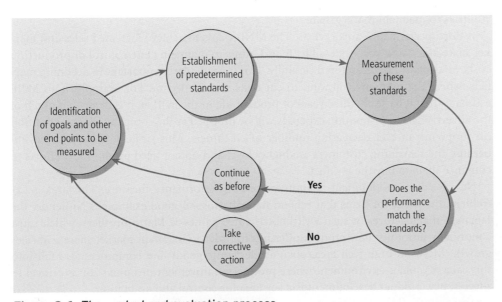

Figure 8.6 The control and evaluation process

objectives may be altered because of changes in the strategic plan, but otherwise nothing major is likely to be done. On the other hand, if there have been problems, the MNE will want to identify the causes and work to eliminate or minimize them.[44] Similarly, if the unit has performed extremely well and achieved more than forecasted, management may want to reset the objectives to a higher level because there is obviously greater market demand than was believed initially. In making these decisions, the company uses a variety of measures. Some are highly quantitative and depend on financial and productivity performance; others are more qualitative and judgmental in nature. The following discussion examines six of the most common methods of measurement used for control and evaluation purposes.

Common methods of measurement

Return on investment (ROI)
A percentage determined by dividing net income before taxes by total assets

Specific measures will vary depending on the nature of the MNE and the goals it has established. However, return on investment (ROI), which is measured by dividing net income before taxes by total assets, is a major consideration in most cases. There are a number of reasons why ROI is so popular as a control and evaluation measure: (1) it is a single comprehensive result that is influenced by everything that happens in the business; (2) it measures how well the managers in every part of the world are using the investments at their command; and (3) it allows a comparison of results among units in the same country as well as on an intercountry basis. Of course, there are shortcomings as well: (1) if one unit is selling goods to another unit, the ROI of the former is being artificially inflated; (2) the ROI in a growing market will be higher than that in markets that are just getting off the ground or are maturing, so that a comparison of the ROI performance between units can be misleading; and (3) the ROI is a short-term measure of performance that, if relied on too heavily, will not help managers develop the necessary long-term time horizons. Despite these shortcomings, however, ROI remains a major measure of performance.

Another measure is sales growth and/or market share. Units are given sales targets that usually require greater sales this year than last year. If the firm has made an estimate of the total demand, a market share figure accompanies the sales target for two reasons: (1) the MNE wants to increase its sales; and (2) the firm at least wants to maintain, if not increase, market share. If the market is judged to be declining, sales targets are lowered but the MNE still tries to maintain market share.

A third performance area is costs. The MNE wants to achieve increased sales and market share at as low a cost as possible. It also wants to maintain close control of production costs. So expenses are monitored carefully. This is particularly important in declining markets, where the company will want to cut costs as sales decline. For example, if an MNE estimates that it has only three years of product life in the market, it is likely that much of the advertising and promotion expenses will be dropped as the company focuses attention on supplying an ever-decreasing number of customers. This strategy is often successful because the remaining customers are highly loyal and do not need promotional efforts to convince them to buy the product.

New product development is another area of performance measure. This area is extremely important for firms that rely on new offerings. A good example is Nintendo, the Japanese manufacturer of such well-known video games as Mario Brothers, which must continually introduce new product offerings in order to maintain market share and sales growth. MNEs in high-tech areas such as electronic goods and computers also fall into this category. In an environment where product improvement or innovation is critical to success, new product development is a key area for control and evaluation.

MNE/host-country relations is another performance area that must be evaluated. Overseas units have to work within the cultural and legal framework of the host country. Many attempt to do this by blending into the community, hiring local managers and employees, adapting their product to the demands of that market, reinvesting part (if not all) of their profits back into the country, and working to improve the area's economic conditions. As a result, they get on well in the country and there are no problems with the government or other local groups. One thing MNEs know from long experience is that poor host-country relations can seriously endanger profits and even result in a loss of invested capital.

Finally, management performance must be considered. In rating this criterion, the MNE considers two types of measures: quantitative and qualitative. In the quantitative area, in addition to those discussed above, other common considerations include return on invested capital and cash flow. In the qualitative area, in addition to host-country relations, consideration is given to relations with the home office, the leadership qualities of the unit's managers, how well the unit is building a management team, and how well the managers of the unit have implemented the assigned strategy.

These methods of measurement are used in arriving at an overall assessment of the unit's performance. Based on the results, the MNE can then set new goals and the international strategic planning process begins anew.

✔ Active learning check

Review your answer to Active Learning Case question 4 and make any changes you like. Then compare your answer with the one below.

4 **On what basis would a firm like Vodafone evaluate performance? Identify and describe two.**

Vodafone uses a number of bases on which to evaluate performance. One is market share. Notice that the firm keeps track of how many subscribers it has by multiplying its ownership position in a venture by the venture's total subscription base. Another is overall worldwide market share. Finally, the firm evaluates its performance by its success in setting a footprint in all major markets.

KEY POINTS

1 Strategic planning is the process of determining an organization's basic mission and long-term objectives, then implementing a plan of action for attaining these goals. In carrying out their strategic plan, most MNEs tend toward one of four specific predispositions: ethnocentric, polycentric, regiocentric, and geocentric. Each was described in the chapter.

2 The international strategic planning process involves three major steps: strategy formulation, strategy implementation, and the control and evaluation of the process. Strategy formulation entails the evaluation of the enterprise's environment and the identification of long-range and short-range objectives. The analysis of the external environment typically involves information gathering and assessment, wherein consideration is given to the five forces that determine industry competitiveness: buyers, suppliers, new entrants to the industry, the availability of substitute goods and services, and rivalry among the competitors. The analysis of the internal environment involves consideration of the firm's physical resources and personnel competencies and the way

in which a value chain analysis can be used to bring these resources together in the most synergistic and profitable manner.

3 Strategy implementation is the process of attaining predetermined goals by properly executing the formulated strategy. Three of the most important areas of consideration are location, ownership decisions, and functional area implementation.

4 The control and evaluation process involves an examination of the MNE's performance to determine how well it has done and to decide what action now needs to be taken. Some of the most common measures include return on investment, sales growth, market share, costs, new product development, host-country relations, and overall management performance.

Key terms

- strategic planning
- ethnocentric predisposition
- polycentric predisposition
- regiocentric predisposition
- geocentric predisposition
- strategy formulation
- competitive intelligence
- strategic business units (SBUs)
- vertical integration
- virtual integration
- value chain
- cost strategy
- differentiation strategy
- focus strategy
- competitive scope
- strategy implementation
- strategic alliance or partnership
- international joint venture
- return on investment (ROI)

REVIEW AND DISCUSSION QUESTIONS

1 Define the term *strategic planning*.

2 In what way can the following basic predispositions affect an MNE's strategic planning: ethnocentric, polycentric, regiocentric, geocentric?

3 How will an MNE carry out an external environmental assessment? Identify and describe the two major steps involved in this process.

4 Of what practical value is an understanding of the five forces model presented in Figure 8.1? How would an MNE use this information in the strategic planning process?

5 In conducting an internal environmental assessment, why would an MNE want to identify its physical resources and personnel competencies?

6 What is a value chain? How can this chain be used in an internal environmental assessment?

7 What are the three generic strategies? When would an MNE use each? Support your answer with examples.

8 What are some typical MNE goals? Identify and briefly describe four major types.

9 One of the most important considerations when implementing a strategy is that of location. What does this statement mean?

10 When are MNEs likely to use an international joint venture? When would they opt for a strategic partnership? Defend your answer.

11 Functional strategies are used to coordinate operations and ensure that the plan is carried out properly. What are some of the most common types of functional strategies? Identify and describe three.

12 How do MNEs control and evaluate their operations? Describe the basic process. Then discuss some of the common methods of measurement.

Mountain Equipment Co-op: a small business

Outside of Canada, few people have ever heard of the Mountain Equipment Co-op (MEC), but it is one of the most successful small businesses in the world. The company currently holds 65 per cent of the Canadian market for outdoor equipment, far outdistancing all other competitive MNEs and retail brands in the country. In fact, MEC is so efficient that its products are priced lower than those of any North American competitor.

MEC was founded in 1969 when a group of outdoor enthusiasts decided to get together and purchase expensive outdoor equipment. In 1971 the organization was officially registered as a co-op and began operating under a member-elected board of directors that assumed responsibility for setting overall policy and overseeing management of all operations. Today MEC has two million members, nine stores spread across Canada, an international mail-order clientele, and a worldwide network of suppliers. For a one-time $5 fee, members are able to enjoy a wide variety of benefits from an organization that focuses heavily on four primary objectives: keeping costs down, offering affordable goods, providing high-quality merchandise, and maintaining high ethical standards.

Regarding the first of these, MEC takes a number of steps to control costs and offer affordable products. One is to use the clout of its large membership as a basis for extracting the best possible prices from suppliers, thus being able to offer low-cost products. Another is to keep the number of staff to a minimum. Some of the ways it does this is through the use of self-service in all stores and the promotion of its international mail-order business, which can be handled by a small number of personnel. In addition, the co-op minimizes overall marketing expenses by relying heavily on customer word-of-mouth and the mail-order network to help promote its products.

MEC also places a great deal of importance on the quality of goods. Its buyers and designers look not only for a low price from suppliers, but also for products that provide both functionality and durability. In addition, the co-op offers a lifetime guarantee on most of its products, regardless of whether it manufactured them, had them provided by an outsourcer, or purchased them from a large brand name company.

Co-op members are also assured that the company adheres to the highest ethical practices. MEC is an innovator in a number of areas ranging from human rights to the environment. Its stores are designed with the utmost attention to the environment, using as much natural light

Source: Getty/Melissa McManus

as possible, high efficiency HVAC (heating, ventilation, and air conditioning), low-consumption water fixtures, and recyclable materials. As an example, its Ottawa store uses only half the energy of a conventional building. In addition, the co-op gives 0.4 per cent of gross sales to environmental and conservation groups. At the same time, its retail employees are among the best paid in the country and its buyers and inspectors are charged with ensuring that all factory workers in foreign countries receive a reasonable living wage and work under safe conditions.

Some suppliers, such as Sierra Designs, Salomon, Arc Tyrex, North Face, and Patagonia, see MEC as a threat and have refused to sell to it. In many cases, however, this strategy has proven to be counterproductive, resulting in MEC designing and manufacturing these products and then successfully competing with the traditional brands that were unwilling to sell to it. In addition, the co-op's increased involvement in manufacturing has enabled it to monitor its suppliers' operations more closely.

Over the past couple of decades, MEC's strategy has been more emergent than calculated. Yet it has proven to be a successful business venture that has brought together a large group of dedicated environmentalists and other customers who need products for outdoor activities. In the process, the co-op has created a "style" and "brand" presence that appeals to outdoor enthusiasts. In fact, MEC's outdoor gear has become so popular that even urbanites, highly unlikely to go trekking or camping in the outdoors, are now becoming members. As a result, annual revenues are currently in the range of $160 million and the company is continuing to expand operations across Canada.

MEC was able to flourish as a result of the huge margins enjoyed by its competitors. This allowed the co-op to both reduce prices and maintain higher levels of environmental and labor practices than its competitors. Over the next few years, however, as competition grows and large outdoor retailers exert the same kind of pressure on suppliers that allowed it to sell at lower prices, MEC will have to switch its strategy to remain competitive. It has some advantages. For one, it has no shareholders and reinvests most of its surplus into the company. When it does choose to reimburse members, it does so by giving them merchandise credits. MEC still has to exploit to the fullest its community and environmental contributions. In the spirit of keeping advertising costs low, many members, not to mention potential members, have never heard of MEC's social policies or its charitable contributions.

Websites: www.mec.ca; www.sierra-designs.com; www.salomonsports.com; www.thenorthface.com; and www.patagonia.com.

Sources: www.mec.ca; "Mountain Equipment Co-Op Live with Socially Responsible Retail," *PR Newswire*, May 22, 2001; "One of the Greenest Commercial Buildings in the World," *Sustainable Sport Sourceline*, July 2000; and "Mountain Equipment Co-op to Stage Outdoors Skills Challenge in Celebration of its 2,000,000th Member," *Canada NewsWire*, June 16, 2004.

1 How does the Mountain Equipment Co-op use value chain analysis to increase both its membership and its revenues?

2 What is the co-op's generic strategy? Describe it.

3 How does MEC measure its performance? What are two criteria it uses to evaluate how well it is doing?

REAL CASE

Benetton

Famous for its shocking advertisements, Benetton was founded in 1955 by Luciano, Giuliana, Gilberto, and Carlo Benetton. Initially the family sold colored sweaters door-to-door in Treviso, Italy. Over time, a regional network of family, friends, and agents set up a closely monitored set of distinctive retail outlets. Over a 15-year period, Benetton built up 300 affiliated but independently owned outlets in Italy and a factory with new methods to dye and condition wool. The company was not directly involved in the retail outlets, which received high-quality products at low costs. Part of the manufacturing savings were realized by outsourcing to neighboring subcontractors.

Benetton has kept this loose network of independent production subcontractors and distribution agents but has now built up to a global network of more than 5,000 retail stores. Only a small fraction of these are flagship stores owned by the group. The great majority of its retail stores are operated by independent entrepreneurs. About 90 per cent of production still takes place in Europe, mainly in Italy, and the company is still 69.35 per cent owned by the Benetton family. Yet the wool it uses to produce its clothing line is now imported from foreign countries. The parent company raises sheep in 900,000 hectares of land in Argentina.

Benetton is one of those successful global companies that succeeded partly because their production and design concept was built on a strong home base. It expanded the marketing end of its business through closely monitored

(but not owned) independent stores, which were able to use the Benetton brand name and distinctive colors and were supported by clever international advertising.

Benetton does not advertise its clothes directly. Rather, its ads target a "lifestyle." The "United Colors of Benetton" ads are designed for a homogeneous global consumer interested in fast cars and a fast lifestyle. Benetton goes in for cutting-edge advertising that grabs public attention. This creates an image of new-age awareness, as the company's advertising ads have featured AIDS, capital punishment, inter-racial relations, high art, and "attitude." The firm also sponsors a top Formula 1 team as well as teams in rugby, basketball, and volleyball, all of which contributes to the success of its brand name. Fabrica, Benetton's Communication Research Center just outside Treviso is a mixture of philanthropy and advertising. The center sponsors 50 artists for a year and exhibits their work and publishes it in *Colors*, the company's art-focused magazine.

How well this plays out globally is uncertain. For example, Benetton had 700 retail stores in the United States in 1988, but only 150 by 1995. Is this because Benetton has too European an image to succeed in middle America? How can an Italian family firm understand the American lifestyle from its European bases? Indeed, 73 per cent of Benetton's revenue originates in the Euro area, with another 8 per cent derived from Asia and only 6 per cent from the Americas. The remaining 13 per cent originates in other regions. The firm is now looking to expand into emerging markets where potential for growth among the growing middle class is greatest.

Website: www.benetton.com.

Sources: Adapted from: *Benetton SpA: Industrial Fashion (A)*, Harvard Business School Case No. 9-685-614; *Benetton (B)*, Harvard Business School Case No. 9-685-020; INSEAD-CEDEP Case No. 01/97-4520, 1996; David Stillit, "Benetton: Italy's Smart Operator," *Corporate Finance*, June 1993 ; "Benetton's Network," *Ivey Business Quarterly*, 1997; Benetton, *Annual Report*, 2003; Peter Crush,

"CSR: Diversity Takes Central Stage," *PR Week*, April 18, 2005; "Benetton: IndiGenas Rechazan Oferta," *BBC.co.uk*, November 10, 2005; and www.benetton.com.

1 Is Benetton a multinational enterprise?

2 What are the country-specific factors that have boosted Benetton's success?

3 What are Benetton's company-specific advantages?

Endnotes

1 Tim Burt, "GM Outlines Plans to Cut European Capacity," *Financial Times*, September 27, 2001, p. 19.

2 Matt Murray, "Merger Machine: Can GE Keep Growing Through Deals?" *Wall Street Journal*, July 31, 2000, pp. C 1, 2.

3 Also see Roland Calori, Leif Melin, Tugrul Atamer and Peter Gustavsson, "Innovative International Strategies," *Journal of World Business*, vol. 35, no. 4 (Winter 2000), pp. 333–354.

4 M. A. Hitt, "The Meaning of Organizational Effectiveness: Multiple Domains and Constituencies," *Management International Review*, vol. 28, no. 2 (Second Quarter 1988), p. 28.

5 David Lei, John W. Slocum, Jr. and Robert W. Slater, "Global Strategy and Reward Systems: The Key Roles of Management Development and Corporate Culture," *Organizational Dynamics*, August 1990, p. 29.

6 See David Norburn, Sue Birley, Mark Dunn and Adrian Payne, "A Four Nation Study of the Relationship Between Marketing Effectiveness, Corporate Culture, Corporate Values, and Market Orientation," *Journal of International Business Studies*, vol. 21, no. 3 (Fall 1990), pp. 451–468.

7 For a good example, see Keith Bradsher, "Effective Today, Chrysler and Daimler-Benz Are One," *New York Times*, November 12, 1998, p. C 4; and Tim Burt, "Daimler Chief to Speak on Strategy," *FT.com*, March 4, 2002.

8 For some specific applications of these ideas, see Michael M. Robert, "Managing Your Competitor's Strategy," *Journal of Business Strategy*, March/April 1990, pp. 24–28.

9 Sometimes, of course, competitive intelligence degenerates into corporate spying, as seen in Andrew Edgecliffe-Johnson, "P&G Admits Spying on Unilever," *Financial Times*, August 31, 2001, p. 17.

10 J. E. Preble, P. A. Rau and A. Reichel, "The Environmental Scanning Practices of US Multinationals in the Late 1980s," *Management International Review*, vol. 28, no. 4 (Fourth Quarter 1988), p. 10.

11 For more on this, see R. C. Hoffman, "The General Management of Foreign Subsidiaries in the USA: An Exploratory Study," *Management International Review*, vol. 28, no. 2 (Second Quarter 1988), pp. 41–55.

12 For more on this, see Michael Porter, *The Competitive Advantage of Nations* (New York: Free Press, 1990), Chapter 2.

13 Andrew Pollack, "Nissan Plans to Buy More American Parts," *New York Times*, March 26, 1994, pp. 17, 26.

14 "A Tricky Business," *Economist*, June 30, 2001, pp. 55–56.

15 "US steel tariffs," *The Guardian*, November 11, 2003.

16 Arnoldo C. Hax and Nicolas S. Majluf, *The Strategy Concept and Process: A Pragmatic Approach* (Englewood Cliffs NJ: Prentice-Hall, 1991), p. 416.

17 Also, see Julie Pitta, "Score One for Vertical Integration," *Forbes*, January 18, 1993, pp. 88–90.

18 For an excellent discussion of this topic, see Hax and Majluf (1991) n. 16 above, Chapter 12.

19 C. K. Prahalad and Kenneth Lieberthal, "The End of Corporate Imperialism," *Harvard Business Review*, July/August 1998, pp. 69–79.

20 Hax and Majluf (1991), n. 16 above, p. 83.

21 Uta Harnischfeger, "Audi Drives Out VW's Gloom," *FT.com*, March 1, 2002.

22 "The Art of Overtaking," *Economist*, September 8, 2001, p. 68.

23 For another good example, see Seth Lubove, "Make a Better Mousetrap," *Forbes*, February 1, 1993, pp. 56–57.

24 Leslie Kaufman, "Avon's New Face," *Newsweek*, November 16, 1998, pp. 59–60.

25 Also, see W. Chan Kim and Peter Hwang, "Global Strategy and Multinationals' Entry Mode Choice," *Journal of International Business Studies*, vol. 23, no. 1 (Summer 1992), pp. 29–53.

26 Richard M. Hodgetts and Fred Luthans, *International Management*, 4th ed. (Burr Ridge, IL: McGraw/Irwin, 2000), p. 260.

27 Robert B. Reich, "Who Is Us?" *Harvard Business Review*, January/February 1990, p. 59.

28 Peter Lorange, Johan Roos and Peggy Simcic Bronn, "Building Successful Strategic Alliances," *Long Range Planning*, December 1992, pp. 10–17.

29 See Masaaki Kotabe, Hildy Teegen, Preet S. Aulakh, Maria Cecilia Coutinho de Arruda, Roberto J. Santillan-Salgado and Walter Greene, "Strategic Alliances in Emerging Latin America: A View from Brazilian, Chilean, and Mexican Companies," *Journal of World Business*, vol. 35, no. 2 (Summer 2000), pp. 114–132.

30 Mitchell Koza and Arie Lewin, "Managing Partnerships and Strategic Alliances: Raising the Odds of Success," *European Management Journal*, August 2000, pp. 146–151.

31 Miki Tanikawa, "Electronics Giants Join Forces in Japan," *Wall Street Journal*, May 24, 2001, p. W 1.

32 Robert A. Guth, "IBM Announces Deal with Japan's NTT," *Wall Street Journal*, November 1, 2000, p. 23.

33 Audrey Choi, "BMW's Chairman Plans Visit to Honda to Discuss Future of Jointly Held Rover," *Wall Street Journal*, February 18, 1994, p. A 7.

34 Hemant Merchant, "Configurations of International Joint Ventures," *Management International Review*, vol. 40, no. 2 (Second Quarter 2000), pp. 107–140.

35 Hong Liu and Kelvin Pak, "How Important Is Marketing in China Today to Sino-foreign Joint Ventures," *European Management Journal*, October 1999, pp. 546–554.

36 Gautam Naik, "AT&T, BT Form World-Wide Alliance," *Wall Street Journal*, July 27, 1998, p. A 3.

37 John Tagliabue, "Toyota and Peugeot in Pact to Produce Car for Europe," *New York Times*, June 30, 2001, p. B 2.

38 Stefan H. Robock and Kenneth Simmonds, *International Business and Multinational Enterprises*, 4th ed. (Homewood, IL: Irwin, 1989), p. 216.

39 See Sing Keow Hoon-Halbauer, "Managing Relationships Within Sino-Foreign Joint Ventures," *Journal of World Business*, vol. 34, no. 4 (Winter 1999), pp. 344–370.

40 See, for example, Caron H. St. John, Scott T. Young and Janis L. Miller, "Coordinating Manufacturing and Marketing in International Firms," *Journal of World Business*, vol. 34, no. 2 (Summer 1999), pp. 109–127.

41 Matt Marshall, "In Brazil, Coke Sells Foam as Well as Fizz," *Wall Street Journal*, July 28, 1997, p. A 12.

42 Peter Marsh, "Pressing Ahead with Plastic," *FT.com*, March 4, 2002.

43 Jeffrey E. Garten, "Opening the Doors for Business In China," *Harvard Business Review*, May/June 1998, pp. 167–175.

44 Also see John Child and Yanni Yan, "Investment and Control in International Joint Ventures: The Case of China," *Journal of World Business*, vol. 34, no. 1 (Spring 1999), pp. 3–15.

Additional bibliography

Barkeman, Harry G., Shenkar, Oded, Vermeulen, Freek and Bell, John H. J. "Working Abroad, Working with Others: How Firms Learn to Operate International Joint Ventures," *Academy of Management Journal*, vol. 40, no. 2 (April 1997).

Camuffo, Arnaldo. "Back to the Future: Benetton Transforms its Global Network," *Sloan Management Review*, vol. 43, no. 1 (Fall 2001).

Capon, Noel, Christodoulou, Chris, Farley, John U., and Hulbert, James M. "A Comparison of the Strategy and Structure of United States and Australian Corporations," *Journal of International Business Studies*, vol. 18, no. 1 (Spring 1987).

Cravens, David W., Downey, H. Kirk and Lauritano, Paul. "Global Competition in the Commercial Aircraft Industry: Positioning for Advantage by the Triad Nations," *Columbia Journal of World Business*, vol. 26, no. 4 (Winter 1992).

Dacin, M. Tina, Hitt, Michael A. and Levitas, Edward. "Selecting Partners for Successful International Alliances: Examination of US and Korean Firms," *Journal of World Business*, vol. 32, no. 1 (Spring 1997).

Davis, Peter S., Desai, Ashay B. and Francis, John D. "Mode of International Entry: An Isomorphism Perspective," *Journal of International Business Studies*, vol. 31, no. 2 (Summer 2000).

Deschamps, Jean-Philippe and Nayak, P. Ranganath. "Competing Through Products: Lessons from the Winners," *Columbia Journal of World Business*, vol. 27, no. 2 (Summer 1992).

Domke-Damonte, Darla. "Interactive Effects of International Strategy and Throughput Technology on Entry Mode for Service Firms," *Management International Review*, vol. 40, no. 1 (First Quarter 2000).

Douglas, Susan P. and Craig, C. Samuel. "Evolution of Global Marketing Strategy: Scale, Scope and Synergy," *Columbia Journal of World Business*, vol. 24, no. 3 (Fall 1989).

Douglas, Susan P. and Rhee, Dong Kee. "Examining Generic Competitive Strategy Types in US and European Markets," *Journal of International Business Studies*, vol. 20, no. 3 (Fall 1989).

Egelhoff, William G. "Great Strategy or Great Strategy Implementation—Two Ways of Competing in Global Markets," *Sloan Management Review*, vol. 34, no. 2 (Winter 1993).

Govindarajan, Vijay and Gupta, Anil K. *The Quest for Global Dominance* (San Francisco, CA: Jossey-Bass/Wiley, 2001).

Hamel, Gary and Prahalad, C. K. "Do You Really Have a Global Strategy?" *Harvard Business Review*, vol. 65, no. 4 (July/August 1985).

Hitt, Michael A., Hoskisson, Robert E., and Kim, Hicheon. "International Diversification: Effects on Innovation and Firm Performance in Product-Diversified Firms," *Academy of Management Journal*, vol. 40, no. 4 (August 1997).

Hoffmann, Werner H. and Wulf, Schaper-Rinkel. "Acquire or Ally? A Strategy Framework for Deciding Between Acquisition and Cooperation," *Management International Review*, vol. 41, no. 2 (Second Quarter 2001).

Huo, Y. Paul and McKinley, William. "Nation as a Context for Strategy: The Effects of National Characteristics on Business-Level Strategies," *Management International Review*, vol. 32, no. 2 (Second Quarter 1992).

Jones, Robert E., Jacobs, Lester W. and van Spijker, Willem. "Strategic Decision Processes in International Firms," *Management International Review*, vol. 32, no. 3 (Third Quarter 1992).

Kanter, Rosabeth Moss. "Collaborative Advantage: The Art of Alliances," *Harvard Business Review* (July/August 1994).

Kim, W. Chan and Mauborgne, Renne A. "Making Global Strategies Work," *Sloan Management Review*, vol. 34, no. 3 (Spring 1993).

Kim, W. Chan and Mauborgne, Renée A. "Effectively Conceiving and Executing Multinationals' World-wide Strategies," *Journal of International Business Studies*, vol. 24, no. 3 (Third Quarter 1993).

Kotabe, Masaaki and Omura, Glenn S. "Sourcing Strategies of European and Japanese Multinationals: A Comparison," *Journal of International Business Studies*, vol. 20, no. 1 (Spring 1989).

Merchant, Hemant. "Configurations of International Joint Ventures," *Management International Review*, vol. 40, no. 2 (Second Quarter 2000).

Merchant, Hemant. "Cooperative Strategy: Economic, Business, and Organizational Issues," *Academy of Management Review*, vol. 26, no. 2 (April 2001).

Mintzberg, Henry. "The Fall and Rise of Strategic Planning," *Harvard Business Review*, vol. 72, no. 1 (January/February 1994).

Normann, Richard and Ramirez, Rafael. "From Value Chain to Value Constellation: Designing Interactive Strategy," *Harvard Business Review*, vol. 71, no. 4 (July/August 1993).

Parkhe, Arvind. "Understanding Trust in International Alliances," *Journal of World Business*, vol. 33, no. 3 (Fall 1998).

Porter, Michael E. "The Competitive Advantage of Nations," *Harvard Business Review*, vol. 68, no. 2 (March/April 1990).

Rondinelli, Dennis. "The Struggle for Strategic Alignment in Multinational Corporations: Managing Readjustment During Global Expansion," *European Management Journal*, vol. 19, no. 4 (August 2001).

Roth, Kendall, Schweiger, David M. and Morrison, Allen J. "Global Strategy Implementation at the Business Unit Level: Operational Capabilities and Administrative Mechanisms," *Journal of International Business Studies*, vol. 24, no. 2 (Second Quarter 1993).

Rugman, Alan M. "Multinationals and Global Competitive Strategy," *International Studies of Management and Organization*, vol. 15, no. 2 (Summer 1985).

Sugiura, Hideo. "How Honda Localizes Its Global Strategy," *Sloan Management Review*, vol. 32, no. 1 (Fall 1990).

Tallman, Stephen and Li, Jiatao. "Effects of International Diversity and Product Diversity on the Performance of Multinational Firms," *Academy of Management Journal*, vol. 39, no. 1 (February 1996).

Tallman, Stephe B. and Yip, George S. "Strategy and the Multinational Enterprise," in Alan M. Rugman and Thomas Brewer (eds.), *The Oxford Handbook of International Business* (Oxford: Oxford University Press, 2001).

Thakur, Manab and Das, T. K. "Managing the Growth-Share Matrix: A Four-Nation Study in Two Industries," *Management International Review*, vol. 31, no. 2 (Second Quarter 1991).

Thomas, Howard, Pollock, Timothy and Gorman, Philip. "Global Strategic Analyses: Frameworks and Approaches," *Academy of Management Executive*, vol. 13, no. 1 (February 1999).

Chapter 9

ORGANIZING STRATEGY

Objectives of the chapter

The primary purpose of an organizing strategy is to help an enterprise implement its strategic plan. There are a number of basic organization structures from which to choose, although most MNEs tailor-make their design and sometimes use a combination of different structures. Another major area of organizing strategy is the organizational processes of decision making, communicating, and controlling. These processes are fundamental to the efficient operation of the structure, and management will need to decide how they should be carried out. This chapter examines the key elements of organizing strategy.

The specific objectives of this chapter are to:

1 *Examine* organization structures used by enterprises that are just beginning their international expansion.
2 *Describe* the international division and global structures that are used as firms increase their international presence.
3 *Analyze* the key structural variables that influence international organization designs.
4 *Review* the role of the organizational processes in ensuring that the structure is both effective and efficient.

Contents

Procter & Gamble

In 1837, William Procter, a candle maker, and his brother-in-law James Gamble, a soap maker, partnered to create a company that would manufacture and market soaps and candles from its base in Cincinnati, Ohio. When candles declined in popularity with the invention of the light bulb and production was eventually discontinued in the 1920s, soap became the basis from which the company built a successful product portfolio of cleaning products and eventually allowed Procter & Gamble to branch out into cosmetics, food, and pet products.

During P&G's first century, international expansion was an afterthought. In 1915, a Canadian plant was established, the first outside the United States. Its first overseas subsidiary was established with the purchase of Thomas Hedley & Sons Co., Ltd. in England in 1930. This coincided with the birth of P&G's brand management marketing system. Dedicated teams would work on marketing competing brands worldwide. In 1948, P&G established an overseas division to manage its growing international division, which at the time reached Asia, Europe, and Latin America. By 1963, as a result of European expansion, P&G established the European Technical Center in Belgium to serve common market subsidiaries. The Japanese market was entered in 1973 through the acquisition of the Nippon Sunhome Company, and in 1993 the Japan Headquarters and Technical Center opened in Rokko Island in Kobe City.

By 1995, sales outside the United States had reached more than 50 per cent of total sales, and a new top management team, headed by John E. Pepper, changed the organizational structure of the firm from US and International to four regional sectors: North America; Latin America; Asia; and Europe, the Middle East, and Africa. All regional sectors reported to the chief operating officer.

Today, Procter & Gamble has the workings of a global company in terms of its structure. Three interactive parts, whose subsidiaries are strategically placed around the world to best achieve cost-effectiveness, marketing and production, and design quality, are the basis of this structure. First, there are seven Market Development Organizations (MDOs) responsible for marketing products in the following regions: North America; ASEAN, India, Australia; China; Northeast Asia; Central and Eastern Europe, the Middle East, and Africa; and Western Europe and Latin America. Second, these MDOs collaborate with any one of five product-based Global Business Units (GBUs) responsible for R&D, design,

and the manufacturing processes. Third, there are Global Business Services (GBSs) located mainly in developing countries that provide accounting, human resource management, logistics, and system operations in a given region. Finally, a Corporate Functions (CF) segment oversees operations but delegates decision making to each structural unit.

In Figure 9.8, the MDOs are equivalent to marketing-based Area Profit Centers; the GBUs can be placed where the Business Profit Centers are. The GBSs, in turn, can take the place of Function Cost Centers. These three sectors interact with each other under the guidance of Corporate Functions.

This global three-axis matrix structure, however, has not resulted in an even distribution of sales across all three regions of the triad, or across P&G's seven-region segmentation. North America accounts for 55 per cent of the firm's revenues. Europe accounts for a significant 27 per cent, but no other region accounts for more than 20 per cent of sales.

The firm's most important firm-specific advantage (FSA) is its ability to market products in multiple regions. It does this through product adaptation, marketing, and packaging to the needs of customers in diverse regions and by creating successful brands. Indeed, the firm managed 13 brands with revenues of over $1 billion in 2003. Some of its most famous brands include Tide, Ariel, Pantene, and Crest.

P&G's strategy does not necessarily include developing global brands like Pringle's, its most globally diversified brand. Instead, the firm might choose locally trusted brands to channel new products to multiple regions. Blendax, a European brand, is now the portal through which P&G markets Whitestrips that are sold in North America under the Crest brand. Many successful brands were carefully picked up through acquisitions and then revamped with new marketing. Between 1980 and 2000, P&G acquired Cover Girl, Noxzema, Clarion, Oil of Olay, Blendax, Old Spice, Max Factor, and Pantene, among others. In other words, the firm finds regional brands to develop regionally.

Another firm-specific advantage is that P&G's portfolio of products allows the diffusion of R&D to different product lines in all regions. For example, a fabric detergent discovery may create improved versions of Tide and Cheer in North America, Ariel in Latin America, and Bold in Japan. It might also spill over to non-fabric cleaners such as Salvo. This, and the GBUs' ability to coordinate production across the world, translates into scale economies that are difficult to rival in the industry.

▶

P&G has gone further than most companies in creating a global structure that incorporates non-industrialized countries. For example, the GBS for the Americas is located in Costa Rica, while that in the Philippines provides services to the Asian region. Factories are located in Asia, Eastern Europe, and Latin America as well as in more developed countries. R&D, usually reserved for developed nations, has also seen its way to developing countries like China.

Website: www.pg.com.

Source: Alan Rugman, *The Regional Multinationals* (Cambridge: Cambridge University Press, 2005).

1. What type of organization structure does P&G have in place for its worldwide operations? Is this structure optimal?

2. Why does the company rely on decentralized decision making?

3. In controlling its operations, what are three areas that are paramount for the firm?

4. Why was the international division replaced by the matrix structure?

INTRODUCTION

Organizations that have decided to expand internationally do so in a number of ways. Some simply ship their goods to a foreign market and have a third party handle sales activities. If a firm's international market is a large portion of total operations, however, the enterprise may play a more active role in the distribution and sale of its products, and this requires a more complex organizational structure. Often, firms start off as exporters and then, as their foreign sales grow, develop more intricate structures that can handle their foreign operations.[1]

Major MNEs such as IBM, General Motors,[2] Mercedes, and Mitsubishi have sophisticated global structures that form the basis of their organizing strategies. Sometimes these firms will also have subsidiaries or affiliates that are integrated into the overall structure. For example, Mitsubishi has 28 core groups that are bound together by cross-ownership and other financial ties, interlocking directorates, long-term business relationships, and social and historical ties. Among these are Mitsubishi Bank, Mitsubishi Heavy Industries, Asahi Glass, Tokyo Marine and Fire Insurance, Nikon Corporation, and Kirin Brewery.[3] The Mitsubishi group obviously needs a carefully designed global structure that allows it to integrate and coordinate the activities of these many businesses. Sometimes this undertaking involves more time and effort than the formulation of the strategic plan.

ORGANIZATIONAL STRUCTURES

Multinational enterprises cannot implement their strategies without an effective structure.[4] The strategy sets out the plan of action, but the structure is critical in ensuring that the desired goals are met efficiently. A number of choices are available to an MNE when deciding on an organizational arrangement, and a number of factors can influence this choice. For example, firms that are just getting into the international arena are likely to choose a structure that differs from that of firms with established overseas operations. Conversely, companies that use their structures as worldwide sales organizations will have a different arrangement from those that locally manufacture and sell goods in various international markets. International structures will change in compliance with the strategic plan, and a structure that is proving to be unwieldy or inefficient will be scrapped in favor of one that better meets the needs of the company.[5] The following discussion examines some of the most common organizational arrangements used by MNEs.

Early organizational structures

When a company first begins international operations, such activities are typically extensions of domestic operations. The firm's primary focus continues to be the local market; international involvement is of secondary importance. International transactions are conducted on a case-by-case basis, and there is no attempt to consolidate these operations into a separate department. Under this arrangement, international sales are viewed as supplements to the income earned from home-country operations.

As international operations increase, however, the MNE will take steps to address this growth structurally. One way is by having the marketing department handle international sales. All overseas operations are coordinated through this department; if sales warrant it, some of the salespeople will handle international transactions exclusively. In this way the company develops marketing specialists who learn the specific needs and marketing techniques to employ in overseas selling.

An alternative arrangement is to create an export department. This department may report directly to the chief executive officer (CEO) (Figure 9.1, line (a)) or be a sub-department within the marketing area (Figure 9.1, line (b)). If it operates independently of the marketing department (option (a)), it is either staffed by in-house marketing people whose primary focus is on the international market or it is operated by an outside export management company that is hired to provide the company with an international arm. Whichever approach is taken, MNEs planning to increase their international presence must ensure that the export department is a full-fledged marketing department and not just a sales organization.

Another possible arrangement is the use of overseas subsidiaries (see Figure 9.2). This is often a result of individual ventures in various geographic locales in which the head of the venture is given a great deal of autonomy and reports directly to the CEO. As long as the subsidiary shows sufficient profit, it is allowed to operate free from home office interference.

As MNEs become more involved in foreign markets, the export department structure or subsidiary arrangement is generally discarded or supplemented because it cannot meet the organization's changing needs. As a result, the company will now look into joint ventures[6] and foreign direct investment, likely opting for an international division structure. To

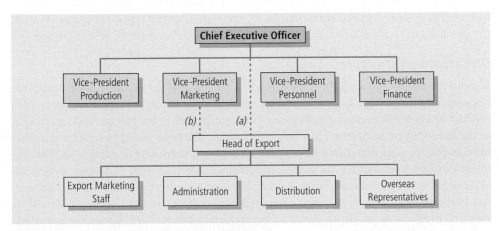

Figure 9.1 An export department structure

Figure 9.2 Use of subsidiaries during the early stages of internationalization

examine one company's international organization structure, see the box **International Business Strategy in Action: Aventis**.

The international division

International division structure
An organizational arrangement in which all international operations are centralized in one division

The **international division structure** centralizes all international operations (see Figure 9.3), an arrangement that offers a number of advantages. First, it reduces the CEO's burden of direct operation of overseas subsidiaries and domestic operations.[7] Second, it creates a management team that prioritizes overseas operations. All information, authority, and decision making related to foreign efforts is channeled to this division, so there is one central clearing point for international activities. This structure also helps the MNE to develop a cadre of internationally experienced managers.

But the international division structure also has some significant drawbacks. One is that separating operations into two categories, domestic and international, can create rivalries between the two. Second, this arrangement puts pressure on the home office to think in global terms and to allocate resources on the basis of overall market opportunity. This can be extremely difficult for a management that has been domestically focused and makes the majority of its sales in the home market. Despite these drawbacks, the international division structure remains dominant among US MNEs.

Global organizational structures

As MNEs generate more and more revenues from their overseas operations, their strategies become more global in focus and the structures used to implement them follow suit. European firms are a good example. Because their domestic markets are fairly small, these companies have traditionally had global structures. In all, there are six basic types: (1) global product, (2) global area, (3) global function, (4) matrix, (5) transnational network, and (6) mixed.

Global product structure

Global product structure
An organizational arrangement in which domestic divisions are given worldwide responsibility for product groups

A **global product structure** is an arrangement in which domestic divisions are given worldwide responsibility for product groups. Figure 9.4 provides an example. In this arrangement, each product division sells its output throughout the world. As seen in the case of Product Division C, the European group operates in a host of countries. The same would be true for the other four geographic areas noted. In each case, the manager of the product division would have internal functional support for the entire product line. All production, marketing, personnel, and finance activities associated with Product C would be under the control of this individual. In recent years, Procter & Gamble has used this arrangement to market its wide assortment of products, from paper goods to beauty care, whereas Ford Motor Company has worked to establish a single automotive operation that relies on a global product structure.[8]

INTERNATIONAL BUSINESS STRATEGY *IN ACTION*

Aventis

French Rhône-Poulenc and Hoechst of Germany recently merged to become Aventis. The merger was a result of increasing pressures within the industry to consolidate in order to achieve further economies of scale in R&D, marketing, and distribution. Today Aventis is the eighth largest pharmaceutical company in the world, with revenues totaling $20.2 billion (see the table), and the firm is now in the process of deciding the organizational structure that will best help it coordinate all of its worldwide operations. The company continues to be based in France but most of its sales, 87.2 per cent, are to foreign markets. Europe, its regional base, accounts for only 32.1 per cent of its sales. The United States and Canada alone account for a higher percentage of its sales at 38.8 per cent. The remaining 29.1 per cent of sales originate in other regions.

Source: Corbis/Vincent Kessler

World's 10 largest pharmaceutical companies, 2003

Company	Country	Revenues US$ million
1 Pfizer	United States	45,950
2 Johnson & Johnson	United States	41,862
3 GlaxoSmithKline	United Kingdom	35,059
4 Novartis	Switzerland	24,864
5 Roche Group	Switzerland	23,212
6 Merck	Germany	22,485
7 Bristol-Myers Squibb	United States	20,894
8 Aventis	France	20,162
9 Abbott Laboratories	United States	19,681
10 AstraZeneca	United Kingdom	18,849

Source: Adapted from Fortune, *The Fortune Global 500*, 2004.

Aventis has managed to become one of the major competitors in its industry through mergers and acquisitions. Back in the mid-1980s Rhône-Poulenc was the 12th largest chemical firm in the world, with 80 per cent of sales being generated in Europe. In this environment it competed with a large number of firms, including US-based giants DuPont and Dow Chemical and leading European chemical companies such as Hoechst, BASF, Ciba-Geigy, and ICI.

During this period, the chemical industry was being increasingly structured on a "triad" basis. As a result, Rhône-Poulenc decided to consolidate its successful European base and move into the American market. In the late 1980s the firm made 18 acquisitions in the United States, including Union Carbide Agrochemical Products and Stauffer Basic Chemicals. These acquisitions made the company into the seventh largest chemical manufacturer in the

world, now generating over 20 per cent of its total sales in the American market.

Managing its US operations was not easy. The takeover of Union Carbide worked pretty well because the latter's pesticide products were complementary to those of Rhône-Poulenc's herbicides and fungicides and its corporate culture was similar. However, the Stauffer acquisition proved to be more difficult because there were overlapping product lines and the US managers at Stauffer had little international experience.

To improve the efficiency of its diverse US operations, Rhône-Poulenc adapted a highly decentralized organizational structure, consolidating its American business operations into a US country group with headquarters at Princeton, New Jersey. The firm also established English as the official language of the company, even though its parent company was French. And as an intermediate step on the path toward true globalization, the firm's US regional headquarters served to create a strong American presence in the face of vigorous competition from rivals with both efficient production and effective staffing. Rhône-Poulenc's plan for the future was to create a "transnational" structure.

Websites: www.aventis.com; www.dupont.com; www.dow.com; www.hoechst.com; www.basf.com; www.ciba.com; www.novartis.com; and www.ici.com.

Sources: Rhône-Poulenc (1996) *Annual Report 1995: Rhône-Poulenc*, Courbevoie Cedex, France; Rhône-Poulenc (1997) *Annual Report 1996*: Rhône-Poulenc (1998) *Annual Report 1997: Rhône-Poulenc*, Courbevoie Cedex, France; H. Banks, "The Road from Serfdom," *Forbes*, October 21, 1996, p. 156; D. Hunter, "Reshaping Rhône-Poulenc," *Chemical Week*, vol. 156, no. 23 (1995), p. 30; D. Owen and D. Green, "Rhône-Poulenc to Focus on Pharmaceuticals Business," *Internet: FT McCarthy*, June 27, 1997, p. 1; Stephen Baker, Inka Resch, Kate Carlisle and Katharine A. Schmidt, "The Great English Divide," *Business Week*, August 13, 2001; and Alan M. Rugman, *The Regional Multinationals: MNEs and "Global" Strategic Management* (Cambridge: Cambridge University Press, 2005).

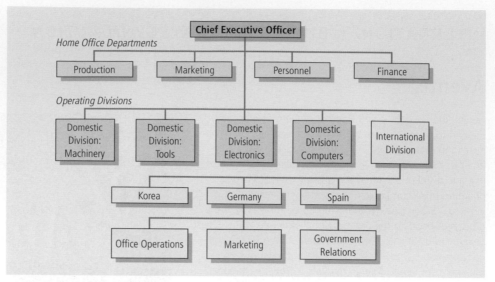

Figure 9.3 An international division structure

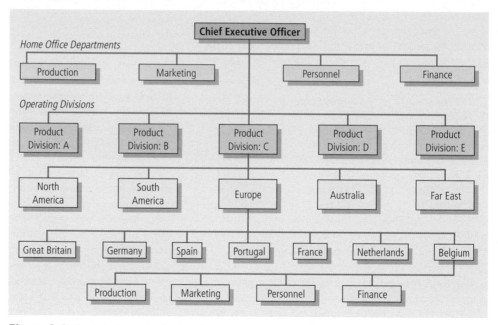

Figure 9.4 A global product structure

This arrangement employs a product division structure that relies on the "profit center" concept. Each product line is expected to generate a predetermined return on investment (ROI), and the performance of each line is measured on this profit basis. Each product line is also operated like an autonomous business, with the product division manager having a great deal of authority over how to run the operation. As long as the product line continues to generate the desired ROI, the division is usually allowed to operate unfettered by home management controls. The only major exception is budgetary constraints that are imposed by central management.

A global product division structure has several benefits. If the firm produces a large number of diverse products, the structure allows each major product line to focus on the specific needs of its customers, which would be particularly difficult to achieve if the company were trying to sell all these products out of one centralized marketing department. The structure also helps develop a cadre of experienced, well-trained managers who understand a particular product line. And it helps the company match its marketing strategy to specific customer needs. For example, a product may be in the introduction stage in some areas of the world, and in the growth, maturity, or decline stage in others. These differing life cycles require close technological and marketing coordination between the home market and the foreign market, which can best be achieved by a product division approach. The product structure also helps the organization establish and maintain the necessary link between the product development people and the customer. By continually feeding back information from the field to the home office, product division personnel ensure that new product offerings meet consumer needs.

At the same time, there are drawbacks to the product division arrangement. One is the necessity of duplicating facilities and staff personnel within each division. A second is that products that sell well are often given primary attention while those that need special handling or promotion are often sidetracked, even though this may result in the long-run loss of profit. A third is that an effective product division requires managers who are knowledgeable about the worldwide demand for their products. Most managers know the local market but do not know a lot about international markets. So it takes time to develop the necessary managerial staff to run this type of structure. A fourth shortcoming is the difficulty of coordinating the activities of different product divisions. For example, the electronics division may decide to subcontract components to a plant in Germany, and the computer division is subcontracting work to a firm in France. If the two divisions had coordinated their activities, it might have been possible to have all the work done by one company at a lower price. Finally, lack of cooperation among the various product lines can result in lost sales, given that each division may have information that can be of value to the other. However, because of the profit center concept, each product line operates independently, and communication and cooperation are downplayed, if not discouraged.

Global area structure

A **global area structure** is a polycentric (host-country-oriented) structure in which primary operational responsibility is delegated to area managers, each of whom is responsible for a specific geographic region. Figure 9.5 provides an example. Every regional division takes responsibility for all functions in its area—production, marketing, personnel, and finance. There appears to be some structural similarity between a global area and a global product arrangement; however, they operate in very different ways. With a global product arrangement, each product division is responsible for its output throughout the world. With a global area structure, on the other hand, the individual product lines are subsumed within each of the geographic areas. So the manager in charge of Belgian operations, for example, will be responsible for each of the product lines sold in that region.

Global area structure
An organizational arrangement in which primary operational responsibility is delegated to area managers, each of whom is responsible for a specific geographic region

A global area structure is commonly used by MNEs that are in mature businesses and have narrow product lines that are differentiated by geographic area. Food products are a good example:

> In the United States, soft drinks have less sugar than in South America, so the manufacturing process must be slightly different in these two locales. Similarly, in England people prefer bland soups, but in France the preference is for mildly spicy. In Turkey, Italy, Spain, and Portugal people like dark, bitter coffee; Americans prefer a milder, sweeter blend. In northern Europe, Canada, and the United States people prefer less spicy food; in the Middle East and Asia they like more heavily spiced food.[9]

The global area structure provides division managers with the autonomy to make rapid decisions that depend on local tastes and regulations; because of this, the firm can become

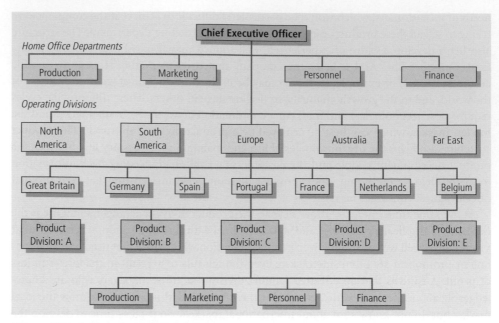

Figure 9.5 A global area structure

more "nationally responsive." Also, the company gains a wealth of experience in how to satisfy these local tastes, often building a strong competitive advantage in the process. The global area structure works well when economies of scale in production require a region-sized unit for basic production. For example, by setting up operations in the EU, a US company is able to achieve production cost advantages that would not otherwise be possible. Finally, the company can eliminate costly transportation associated with importing goods produced overseas.

If a product sells well in the United States, the company is likely to try to market it worldwide without making any modifications for local taste. Under the area structure the opposite viewpoint holds: the product must be adapted to the local tastes. But this means that the usual product emphasis in a company must be subsumed to the company's geographic orientation and the authority of the area managers. Another shortcoming with this organization structure is the expense associated with duplicating facilities. Each division has its own functional areas and is responsible for both production and marketing. Because production efficiency is often based on the amount of output, small plants are usually less efficient than large ones. Companies using a global area division structure also find it difficult to coordinate geographically dispersed divisions into the overall strategic plan. Quite often international cooperation and synergy among divisions end up being sacrificed. Finally, companies that rely heavily on R&D to develop new products often find that the global area divisions do not readily accept these offerings. This is because each group is trying to cater to the specific needs of its current market, and new products often require modification to meet those needs. Research shows that division managers prefer to sell products that have already been accepted by the market and are reluctant to take on new, untried products. Unfortunately, because most products have fairly short life cycles, this attitude is potentially dangerous to the long-term success of the MNE. The home office must continually fight such "anti-new product" drift.

Global functional structure

An organizational arrangement in which all areas of activity are built around the basic tasks of the enterprise

Global functional structure

A **global functional structure** is one built around the basic tasks of the organization. For example, in manufacturing firms, production, marketing, and finance are the three primary functions that must be carried out for the enterprise to survive. Figure 9.6 shows such an

Figure 9.6 A global functional structure

arrangement. The head of the production department is responsible for all domestic and international manufacturing. Similarly, the head of marketing is responsible for the sales of all products here and abroad. This structure is most commonly used by MNEs with a narrow product line that has reached a stable plateau of global coverage and a level of demand that does not face major changes in a competitive attack.

The advantages of the global functional structure are allowing a small group of managers to maintain control over a wide-reaching organization, little duplication of facilities, and tight, centralized control. One disadvantage is difficulty in coordinating the production and marketing areas, since each operates independently of the other. This can be particularly troublesome if the MNE has multiple product lines. A second disadvantage is that responsibility for profits rests primarily with the CEO because there is little diffusion of operating authority far down the line.

Researchers have found that the global functional arrangement is most common among raw materials extractors with heavy capital investment. Energy firms also use it. However, this is not a structure that suits many other kinds of businesses.

Matrix structure

A **matrix structure** is an organizational arrangement that blends two organizational responsibilities such as functional and product structures or regional and product structures. The functional emphasis focuses on the activities to be performed, whereas the product emphasis focuses on the good that is being produced. This structure is characterized by a dual command system that emphasizes both inputs (functions) and outputs (products), thereby facilitating development of a globally oriented management attitude. Figure 9.7 illustrates a product-region matrix.

There are three types of managers in this geocentric matrix structure: regional managers, product managers, and matrix managers. **Regional managers** are charged with business in their markets. Their operation budgets include selling any of the products made by

Matrix structure
An organizational arrangement that blends two organizational responsibilities such as functional and product structures or regional and product structures

Regional managers
In a geocentric matrix, managers charged with selling products in their geographic locale

Products \ Regions	Country A	Country B	Country C
Product 1			
Product 2			
Product 3			

Figure 9.7 Geographic matrix structure

Product managers
Managers responsible for coordinating the efforts of their people in such a way as to ensure the profitability of a particular business or product line

Resource managers
In a matrix structure, managers charged with providing people for operations

Business managers
Managers responsible for coordinating the efforts of people in a corporate organization; for example, in a matrix structure

the MNE, subject to the decision of each regional manager. Their focus is polycentric. **Product managers** are responsible for coordinating the efforts of their people in such a way as to ensure the profitability of a particular business or product line. Their attitude is ethnocentric. The matrix managers are responsible to *both* regional and product managers—they have two bosses.

With its three dimensions, the matrix design in Figure 9.8 is more complex than that in Figure 9.7. It illustrates how the matrix organizational arrangement can be used to coordinate and manage wide-reaching international operations. **Resource managers** are charged with providing the people for operations, whereas **business managers** are responsible for coordinating the efforts of these people to make profits for the product line. The resource managers are concerned with inputs, business managers with outputs. The bottom of Figure 9.8 shows functional specialists from such areas as marketing, manufacturing, and research. Individuals from each of these areas are assigned to each of the company's nine businesses. In turn, these nine profit centers operate in five different areas of the world, including the US, Europe, and Asia. Each business is run by a business board (not shown in the figure) that reports to senior-level management.

The matrix design in Figure 9.8 is sometimes referred to as a three-dimensional model because when it is drawn it has width, height, and depth. This multidimensional matrix

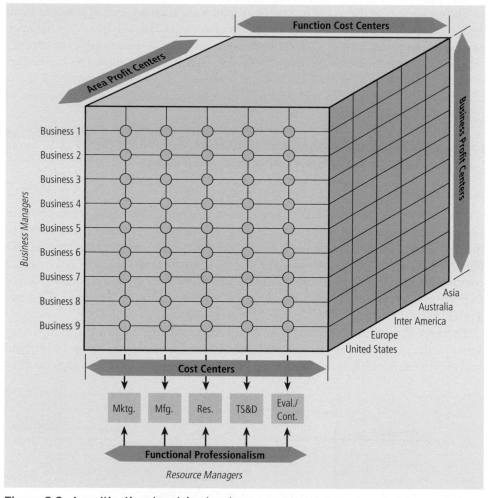

Figure 9.8 A multinational matrix structure

Source: Allan R. Janger, *Matrix Organizations of Complex Business* (New York: The Conference Board, 1979), p. 31.

INTERNATIONAL BUSINESS STRATEGY *IN ACTION*

Making matrix work

Many multinationals use matrix structures in their international operations. Some of these structures work out very well; some do not. Success can often be attributed to three important criteria: clarity, continuity, and consistency. If all three are achieved, the matrix tends to work well; if one or more are missing, the structural design is often ineffective.

Clarity refers to how well people understand what they are doing and why they are doing it. If the company's basic objectives are clear, if relationships in the structure are spelled out in direct, simple terms, and if the relevance of jobs is enunciated, there is a good chance that clarity will be achieved. A good example is NEC, the Japanese giant that decided to integrate computers and communication and to make this the focus of its business efforts. This message was clearly communicated to the personnel so that everyone in the organization understood what the company wanted to do. On the other hand, competitors like AT&T tried the same strategy but failed to clarify what they were doing. As a result, NEC has been more successful.

Continuity means that the company remains committed to the same core objectives and values. This provides a unifying theme and helps ensure that the personnel are committed. General Electric's Brazilian subsidiary is a good example of how a lack of continuity can hurt. In the 1960s the subsidiary built televisions. During the 1970s it was told to switch to large appliances. Then it was told to focus on housewares. By this time the company's dominant franchise in Brazil's

electrical products market had all but dissipated. In contrast, Unilever set up operations in Brazil and, despite volatile changes in the economy, continued to focus its efforts on the electrical products market. Today Unilever has a thriving market in that country.

Consistency relates to how well all parts of the organization are moving in accord with each other. This is often a reflection of how well managers of the various operating divisions are pursuing the same objectives. For example, Philips NV launched an international strategy for its videocassette recording system, the V2000. However, its US subsidiary did not support these efforts because it felt that Matsushita's VHS format and Sony's Beta system were too well established. Because of this, Philips was unable to build the efficiency and credibility it needed to challenge the Japanese dominance of the VCR business.

Matrix structures can be complex organizational arrangements. However, if the MNE is able to achieve clarity, continuity, and consistency, the matrix approach can be very effective.

Websites: www.nec.com; www.att.com; www.ge.com; www.unilever.com; www.sony.com; and www.philips.com.

Sources: Christopher A. Bartlett and Sumantra Ghoshal, "Matrix Management: Not a Structure, a Frame of Mind," *Harvard Business Review*, July/August 1990, pp. 138–145; Courtland L. Bovee et al., *Management* (New York: McGraw-Hill, 1993), pp. 321–323; and Richard M. Hodgetts and Fred Luthans, *International Management*, 4th ed. (Burr Ridge, IL: Irwin/McGraw, 2000), Chapter 7.

addresses three major areas: function, product, and geography. So the structure is really a combination of some of the designs discussed earlier.

One of the major advantages of the multinational matrix is that it allows management to address more than one primary area of consideration. As Figure 9.8 shows, the company is able to focus on functional, product, and geographic considerations. MNEs that need to balance a product and a global location strategy can benefit from this type of structure.[10]

A drawback to the use of the matrix structure in international operations is the complexity of the design and the use of dual command, which can result in confusion about what everyone is responsible for doing and to whom one reports on various matters. A second drawback is the large number of meetings and discussions that often result from efforts to coordinate a variety of different groups, each with its own agenda. A third is that it often takes time for managers to learn to operate in a matrix structure, and if the enterprise has rapid turnover, there is always a significant portion of the personnel who do not fully understand how to function effectively in this environment. The box **International Business Strategy in Action: Making matrix work** describes how some of these problems can be handled.

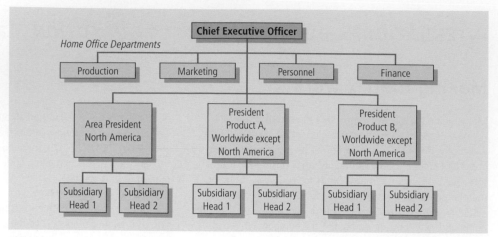

Figure 9.9 A mixed structure

Mixed structure

Mixed structure
A hybrid organization design that combines structural arrangements in a way that best meets the needs of the enterprise

A **mixed structure** is a hybrid organization design that combines structural arrangements in a way that best meets an enterprise's individual needs. Figure 9.9 provides an illustration. While pedagogically it is important to look at the models illustrated above, in practice a pure function, product, or area structure hardy ever exists. Most firms have some sort of mixed structure. Different businesses with different patterns of global demand, supply, and competition demand different management structures. Some structures might be very close to those mentioned above, but there is always some adaptation to be able to meet the needs of each specific enterprise.

Transnational network structure

Transnational network structure
An organization design that helps MNEs take advantage of global economies of scale while also being responsive to local customer demands

One of the newest forms of international organizational arrangements to emerge is the **transnational network structure**, which is designed to help MNEs take advantage of global economies of scale while also being responsive to local customer demands. This structural design combines elements of functional, product, and geographic designs, while relying on a network arrangement to link the various worldwide subsidiaries. At the center of the transnational network structure are nodes, which are units charged with coordinating product, functional, and geographic information. Different product group units and geographical area units have different structures depending on what is best for their particular operation. A good example of how the transnational network structure works is provided by NV Philips, which has operations in more than 60 countries and produces a diverse product line ranging from light bulbs to defense systems. In all, the company has six product divisions with a varying number of subsidiaries in each—and the focus of the latter varies considerably. Some specialize in manufacturing, others in sales; some are closely controlled by headquarters, others are highly autonomous.

The basic structural framework of the transnational network consists of three components: dispersed subunits, specialized operations, and interdependent relationships. *Dispersed subunits* are subsidiaries that are located anywhere in the world where they can benefit the organization. Some are designed to take advantage of low factor costs, whereas others are responsible for providing information on new technologies or consumer trends. *Specialized operations* are activities carried out by subunits that focus on particular product lines, research areas, and marketing areas, and are designed to tap specialized expertise or other resources in the company's worldwide subsidiaries. *Interdependent relationships*

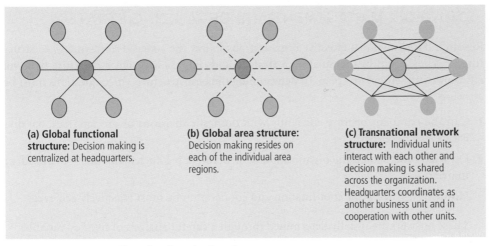

(a) **Global functional structure:** Decision making is centralized at headquarters.

(b) **Global area structure:** Decision making resides on each of the individual area regions.

(c) **Transnational network structure:** Individual units interact with each other and decision making is shared across the organization. Headquarters coordinates as another business unit and in cooperation with other units.

Figure 9.10 Transnational network structure

are used to share information and resources throughout the dispersed and specialized subunits.[11]

The transnational network structure is difficult to draw in the form of an organizational chart because it is complex and continually changing. Figure 9.10 gives a graphic scheme for the structure in comparison to the functional and area structures. The functional structure is one in which all decision making is made at headquarters, which coordinates all operations. The area, or geographic structure, is one in which each subunit acts independently from the others. That is, decision making is totally decentralized. The transnational network structure is a combination of both. Individual units interact with each other and decision making is shared across the organization. Headquarters is another business unit that coordinates the enterprise in coordination peripheral business units.

Let us now take a closer look at the transnational network structure. The peripheral circles represent the dispersed specialized subunits, each of which takes advantage of the different resources available in its environment to feed the organization. The connectors show the flows of components, know-how, labor, financial and marketing information, etc., among the different subunits. The central circle represents the headquarters, which helps to coordinate the interaction of the individual subunits using shared decision making.

✔ Active learning check

Review your answer to Active Learning Case question 1 and make any changes you like. Then compare your answer with the one below.

1 **What type of organization structure does P&G have in place for its worldwide operations? Is this structure optimal?**

P&G follows a three-axis matrix structure in which the organizational responsibilities are divided among (a) regional marketing, (b) product-based R&D and manufacturing, and (c) regional logistics. These, in turn, are overseen by the Corporate Functions department. Because of the scale and international reach of its operations, a matrix structure allows high levels of national responsiveness in the marketing of P&G's branded products, economies of scale in R&D and production to be materialized through the Global Business Units, and economies of scale in logistics through the Global Business Services. Other types of organization structures would either constrain national responsiveness in marketing or undermine the company's capacity to achieve economies of scale at a regional level.

STRATEGIC MANAGEMENT AND ORGANIZING STRATEGY

Research has shown that effective organizations follow the adage "From strategy to structure."[12] They begin by formulating a strategy and only then design a structure that will efficiently implement this plan. In determining the best structure, three questions must be answered:

1 Can the company operate efficiently with domestic divisions or are international divisions also necessary?

2 On what basis should the organization be structured: product, area, function, mixed, or matrix?

3 How can the necessary coordination and cooperation be most effectively achieved?

These answers are usually determined through a careful analysis of five key variables.

Analysis of key structural variables

There are five key variables that MNEs examine in choosing from among alternative organizational structures. In some cases one of these variables will outweigh the others, and the structure will be designed to accommodate this one. In most cases, however, there are three or four interacting variables the structure must address.

First, the MNE will evaluate the relative importance of international operations at the time and project what the situation might be within three to five years. If the company is currently doing 5 per cent of its business overseas and has an export department handling these sales, this organization structure may be adequate for now. However, if the MNE estimates that international sales will grow to 25 per cent of total revenues in five years, the company will want to consider adopting an international division structure or one of the global arrangements. Unless the firm is prepared to make this transition, it may prove difficult to handle the anticipated rapid growth.

Second, the company will take into account its past history and experience in the international arena. If the firm has done very little business abroad, it is likely to choose a simple structure that is easy to understand and control. If the company has been doing business overseas for many years, it will probably have experienced managers who can work well in a more sophisticated structure, so it may choose a mixed design or a matrix.

A third area of consideration is the company's business and product strategy. If the company offers a small number of products and there is little need to adapt them to local tastes, a global functional structure may be the best choice. On the other hand, if the products must be tailored for local markets, a global product arrangement will usually be more effective. If the company is going to be doing business in a number of diverse geographic areas, a global area structure will typically be used. For example, to improve sales growth in Europe and Asia, Coca-Cola reinforced its global area organizational arrangement by putting new managers into positions overseeing operations in these regions.[13]

A fourth influencing variable is management's philosophy of operating. If the company wants to expand rapidly and is prepared to take risks, the firm will choose a structure that is quite different from that used by an MNE that wants to expand slowly and is conservative in its risk taking. Similarly, if the home office wants to keep a tight rein on operations, it will not use the same structure as a firm that gives local subsidiaries autonomy and encourages them to make decisions about how to keep the unit competitive at the local level. French and German subsidiaries, for example, tend to be more centralized than US units. There are also differences in the way operations are controlled. For example, Japanese

MNEs like to use face-to-face informal controls, whereas US multinationals prefer budgets, financial data, and other formalized tools.

A final key variable is the enterprise's ability to adjust to organizational changes. As MNE world sales increase, there are continual modifications in the structure. For example, when the company is small, the domestic divisions dominate. As the international side of operations grows, the managers of the domestic divisions have to cede some of their authority and influence. If they are unable or unwilling to do this, the structure is affected. Similarly, if international executives begin gaining greater authority and there is a need to revamp overseas operations, their willingness to adjust to organizational changes will affect the structure. In some cases MNEs have found that overseas managers, just like their domestic counterparts, build small empires and often are unwilling to give up this power.

The ultimate choice of organization structure rests with top management. However, this group seldom tries to force such a decision on those who will be directly affected. Instead, there is a give-and-take in which the needs of the enterprise and the personnel are considered.

In recent years the increase in mergers and acquisitions has had an important impact on MNE decision making. Deutsche Telekom's T-Mobile International provides a good example. This company has an ownership position in a large number of mobile phone companies in a host of different countries, including Voice Stream (US), One2One (UK), BEN (Netherlands), max.mobil (Austria), and Radio Mobil (Czech Republic). Coordinating the operations of these holdings requires a carefully designed structure coupled with the appropriate amount of decentralized authority.[14] The result is a structure that is both efficient and humanistic. In carrying this out, companies will address the organizational processes that take place within the structure.

 Active learning check

Review your answer to Active Learning Case question 2 and make any changes you like. Then compare your answer with the one below

2 **Why was the international division replaced by the matrix structure?**

The international division is a fairly primitive type of organizational structure of an MNE. It is used at an early stage of international expansion (by P&G in the 1940s and 1950). As P&G's sales in the international market increased beyond 20 per cent or so, it turned to a more complex global organization structure, the three-axis global matrix, with which it could be nationally responsive and achieve economies of scale.

Coordination

The formal structure provides the skeletal framework within which the personnel operate. The structure is designed to answer the question: What is to be done? The organizational processes—decision making, communicating, and controlling—help make the structure work efficiently. These processes help answer the question: Who should do what, and how will they do it? These processes help put the organization structure into action.

Decision making

Decision making is the process of choosing from among alternatives. In international operations one of the primary areas of consideration is where the ultimate decision-making authority will rest on important matters. If the home office holds this control, decision

Decision making
The process of choosing from among alternatives

Table 9.1 Factors that encourage centralization or decentralization of decision making in multinational operations

Encourage centralization of decision making	Encourage decentralization of decision making
Large enterprise	Small enterprise
Large capital investment	Small capital investment
Relative importance of the unit to the MNE	Relative unimportance of the unit to the MNE
Highly competitive environment	Stable environment
Strong volume-to-unit-cost relationship	Weak volume-to-unit-cost relationship
High degree of technology	Moderate to low degree of technology
Low level of product diversification	High level of product diversification
Homogeneous product lines	Heterogeneous product lines
High interdependence between the units	Low interdependence between the units
Few highly competent managers in the host country	Many highly competent managers in the host country
High experience in international business	Low experience in international business
Small geographic distance between home office and subsidiary	Large geographic distance between home office and subsidiary

making is centralized; if the subsidiary can make many of these important decisions without having to consult the home office, decision making is decentralized. Table 9.1 provides some examples of factors that encourage both these types of decision making.[15]

Research shows that decision making in MNE subsidiaries tends to vary from country to country or culture to culture. For example, among British organizations there is a great deal of decentralized decision making. Many upper-level managers do not understand the technical nature of business operations, such as financial budgeting or cost control, so they delegate the authority for these matters to middle-level managers while they focus on strategic matters.

French and German subsidiaries tend to be fairly centralized in their decision-making approaches. French senior executives like to maintain control of operations and tend to delegate less authority than do their English counterparts. German managers are hierarchical in their approach and most important decisions are made at the top.

In Scandinavian countries like Norway, Sweden, and Denmark, operations are highly decentralized both in Scandinavian-based firms and abroad. The Scandinavians place a great deal of emphasis on the quality of work life, and they are more interested in the well-being of the worker than in maximizing profit.

The Japanese use a combination of decentralization and centralization. They make heavy use of a decision-making process called **ringi**, or decision making by consensus:

Ringi
Decision making by consensus; this process is widely used in Japan

> Under this system any changes in procedures and routines, tactics, and even strategies of a firm are originated by those directly concerned with these changes. The final decision is made at the top level after an elaborate examination of the proposal through successively higher levels in the management hierarchy and results in acceptance or rejection of a decision only through consensus at every echelon of the management structure.[16]

At the same time, top management maintains a great deal of authority over what will be discussed at lower levels. Thus, senior-level management exercises both decentralization and centralization.

US MNEs, perhaps surprisingly, tend to use fairly centralized decision making in managing their overseas operations. This is particularly true in areas such as marketing policies, financial matters, and decisions on production capacity. Ford Motor, for example, recently reduced the number of managers reporting to the CEO in order to better control operations.[17] On the other hand, Wal-Mart has been very successful in Canada by using a decentralized approach to accommodate the local market.[18] Moreover, this is the current trend worldwide as MNEs work to increase economies of scale and attain higher operational efficiency. One way in which many are doing this is through outsourcing, thus simplifying their structures and delegating the authority for some operations to their suppliers.[19]

✔ Active learning check

Review your answer to Active Learning Case question 3 and make any changes you like. Then compare your answer with the one below.

3 Why does the company rely on decentralized decision making?

The primary reason the firm relies so heavily on decentralized decision making is that the demands of the local areas are so great, it cannot make all important decisions from headquarters. This applies to the MDOs, which must market to different cultures with different languages and business environments. But it also applies to the GBSs catering directly to a given region, which must function in relevant languages and understand regionally specific logistics environments. Decision making is also delegated to the GBUs, which specialize to provide the most efficiency and innovation in each product category and to dissipate R&D knowledge across product families.

Communication

Communication is the process of transferring meanings from sender to receiver. However, the way of doing this often varies from one MNE to another. For example, US MNEs use direct communications with their subsidiaries and overseas units.[20] Directives are spelled out clearly and precisely. Meanwhile, Japanese MNEs prefer more indirect communications in which things are implied and it is up to the listener to determine what to do. The direct approach works well for Americans, whose culture encourages openness and specific communications. The indirect approach works well for the Japanese, whose culture encourages indirect and implied communications.[21] Ouchi, after conducting a series of interviews with Americans working for a Japanese bank in the US, found that this problem can be particularly disconcerting because each side is unable to understand the other's approach, as illustrated by the following:

Communication
The process of transferring meanings from sender to receiver

American managers
We have a non-stop running battle with the president. We simply cannot get him to specify a performance target for us. We have all the necessary reports and numbers, but we can't get specific targets from him. He won't tell us how large a dollar increase in loan volume or what per cent decrease in operating costs he expects us to achieve over the next month, quarter, or even year. How can we know whether we're performing well without specific targets to shoot for?

Japanese bank president
If only I could get these Americans to understand our philosophy of banking. To understand what the business means to us—how we feel we should deal with our customers and our employees. What our relationship should be to the local communities we serve. How we should deal with our competitors, and what our role should be in the world at large. If they could get that under their skin, then they could figure out for themselves what an appropriate objective would be for any situation, no matter how unusual or new, and I would never have to tell them, never have to give them a target.[22]

These types of culturally based differences can greatly affect an MNE's ability to get things done.

Another communication-based problem is nonverbal messages. In international business these take two major forms: kinesics and proxemics. Kinesics deals with the conveying of information through the use of body movement and facial expression. For example, when verbally communicating with someone in the United States, it is good manners to look the other party in the eye. However, in many other cultures, such as Arabic and Middle East, this is not done, especially if one is talking to a member of the opposite sex. Such behavior would be considered rude and disrespectful.[23]

Proxemics deals with how people use physical space to convey messages. For example, in the United States, businesspeople typically stand two to three feet away from those with whom they are communicating. However, in the Middle East and in many South American countries it is common to stand right next to the person. This often makes Americans feel very uncomfortable because this space is generally reserved only for family members and close friends. Business is not conducted at this distance. One group of authors summarized the problem this way:

> Americans often tend to be moving away in interpersonal communication with their Middle Eastern or Latin counterparts, while the latter are trying to physically close the gap. The American cannot understand why the other is standing so close; the latter cannot understand why the American is being so reserved and standing so far away; the result is a breakdown in communication.[24]

Another example of proxemics is office layout and protocol. In the United States, a large office connotes importance, as does a secretary who screens visitors and keeps away those whom the manager does not wish to see. In Japan, most managers do not have large offices; if they do, they spend little time in them since they are generally out talking to the employees and walking around the workplace. If the manager were to stay in the office all day, it would be viewed as a sign of distrust or anger at the work group. In Europe, many managers do not have walled-in offices. The bosses are out in the same large room as their people; there is no one to screen the brokers from the boss.

Every country has some unique communication patterns or behaviors.[25] These behaviors can be particularly troublesome to outsiders who are working locally and are unfamiliar with local approaches to communication. Figure 9.11 provides an interesting example in the form of epigrams that have been drawn from organization structures throughout the world.

Controlling

Controlling is the process of determining that everything goes according to plan and that performance is rewarded. It consists of three steps: (1) establishing standards, (2) comparing performance against standards, and (3) correcting deviations. Controlling is closely linked to communication since it is virtually impossible to evaluate performance and make changes without communicating information. Many of the same organizational problems discussed above also apply here.

One of the major differences between US and Japanese firms is the use of explicit versus implicit control. A major difference between US and European firms is that US MNEs tend to rely more heavily on reports and other performance-related data, whereas Europeans make heavy use of behavioral control. US multinationals compare results of a foreign unit with those of other foreign units, as well as with domestic units, in evaluating performance. European MNEs tend to be more flexible and to judge performance on an individual basis rather than simply making a comparative judgment. Other differences include:

1 Control in US MNEs relies on precise planning and budgeting that is suitable for comparison purposes. Control in European MNEs takes into consideration a high level of

Kinesics
A form of non-verbal communication that deals with conveying information through the use of body movement and facial expression

Proxemics
A form of non-verbal communication that deals with how people use physical space to convey messages

Controlling
The process of determining that everything goes according to plan

United States

Americans believe that they all have a link to the top of the organization and, if need be, can drop by and talk to the president, regardless of their position in the hierarchy.

England

In England top managers and workers communicate among themselves, but there is no communication link between the two groups.

China

In China everyone is a small cog in a giant machine. As a result, there is a massive bureaucracy, with each person directly controlling a small number of subordinates.

Norway

In Norway the chain of command runs from the top to the middle management. Those at the bottom do not receive information from their boss; instead, they get it from the chief executive officer (CEO) who violates the chain of command and comes down the line. The person to whom the CEO passes this information then conveys it to all the other workers.

Figure 9.11 Organizational epigrams

An epigram is a terse, witty statement. The organizational epigrams are designed to poke fun at the way communication flows in international organizations. Each was created by an individual with experience in the respective country. The explanation accompanying the respective epigram explains the logic behind the drawing. These epigrams illustrate that communication flows throughout the world are less efficient than the enterprise would like. They also illustrate that each country has its own unique approach to conveying information.

Source: Adapted from Simcha Ronen, *Comparative and Multinational Management.* Copyright © 1986 John Wiley & Sons, Inc. This material is used by permission of John Wiley & Sons, Inc.

company-wide understanding and agreement over what constitutes appropriate behavior and how such behavior supports the goals of the subsidiary and the parent company.

2 US multinationals do not encourage their managers to remain in overseas positions for a long period of time. As a result, they use large central staffs and centralized information gathering to carry out evaluations. European multinationals, on the other hand, encourage their managers to remain in overseas positions and rely heavily on these managers to provide input on how well the unit is doing.

3 Managers of US MNEs often report to a counterpart back in headquarters who, in turn, conveys information up the line. European multinationals have a more direct reporting channel so that the head of a foreign subsidiary reports to someone who is closer to the top of the structure.[26]

Another major difference is the way in which personnel are evaluated. In the United States and Europe, it is common to single out high performers and reward them. In Japan, however, credit is given to the entire group rather than just to one or two individuals. Singling people out for special attention is not regarded as complimentary. Rather, such attention would make individuals feel they were not regarded as team players, which would be insulting. Another important difference is the time period for personnel evaluations. Most US and European firms evaluate their people on an annual basis. However, in Japan the first major evaluation often does not occur until the employee has been with the firm for almost a decade.[27] These controlling differences greatly affect the way the structure is managed. As a result, running an overseas operation the same way as at home is often difficult.

271

✔ Active learning check

Review your answer to Active Learning Case question 4 and make any changes you like. Then compare your answer with the one below.

4 In controlling its operations, what are three areas that are paramount for the firm?

There are a number of areas P&G needs to control. One of these is profit. The company must ensure that its divisions are profitable in each market in which it operates. A second area is cost control. Presently, P&G's matrix structure is designed to be nationally responsive and decrease costs through economies of scale. A third area is innovation. One of the firm's principal competitive advantages is its ability to improve its brands against the competition; as a result, it must weigh its advances in R&D against that of the competition. A fourth area of control is the brand awareness of consumers for P&G's brands.

KEY POINTS

1. When a company first enters the international arena, it is common to find that these efforts are mere extensions of domestic operations. The MNE will typically handle foreign sales directly through its own marketing department, an export department, or an overseas subsidiary that is the result of a joint venture. As international operations become more important, however, the firm is likely to centralize these operations by adopting an international division structure. This organizational arrangement remains quite popular with many MNEs.

2. As multinationals generate increased revenues from their overseas operations, they are likely to adopt a global organizational structure. There are six basic types: global product, global area, global functional, mixed, matrix, and transnational network. Each type has specific advantages and disadvantages.

3. There are five key variables that MNEs examine in choosing from among alternative organizational structures: (a) the relative importance of international operations, (b) past history and experience in the international arena, (c) the company's business and product strategy, (d) management philosophy, and (e) the firm's ability to adjust to organizational changes.

4. The formal structure provides the skeletal framework within which the personnel operate. The organization process of decision making, communicating, and controlling make the structure work efficiently. In the decision-making process, one of the key areas of consideration is the amount of centralization or decentralization that will be used by the home office. In communicating, culturally based differences will be of major importance, including nonverbal messages. In controlling, areas of concern include explicit and implicit control and the ways in which personnel will be evaluated.

Key terms

- international division structure
- global product structure
- global area structure
- global functional structure
- matrix structure
- regional managers
- product managers
- resource managers
- business managers
- transnational network structure
- mixed structure
- decision making
- *ringi*
- communication
- kinesics
- proxemics
- controlling

REVIEW AND DISCUSSION QUESTIONS

1 How does an export department structure function? Who handles the overseas sales?

2 If a company's initial international expansion is conducted through the use of subsidiaries, how closely does it control these subsidiaries? Why?

3 Why do MNEs use an international division structure? Are there any drawbacks to this organizational arrangement?

4 How does a global product structure work? Why would an MNE opt for this arrangement? What are two drawbacks to using this structure?

5 When would an MNE use a global area structure? When would the firm reject this structural arrangement in favor of a different structure?

6 How does a global functional structure work? When would it be a popular approach? When would it be of very little value in organizing international operations?

7 When would a company opt for a mixed structure? Why? Defend your answer.

8 How does a matrix structure work? When would an MNE opt for this organizational arrangement?

9 There are five key variables MNEs examine in choosing from among alternative organizational structures. What are these five? Identify and briefly describe each.

10 Why are some overseas operations highly decentralized while others are very centralized? What factors influence this arrangement?

11 Why are US international operations more centralized than those in Sweden? Why is the US model becoming more popular among MNEs?

12 In what way is implicit versus explicit communication important in understanding how home office managements coordinate international activities?

13 What type of control techniques do US MNEs prefer? How does this preference differ from that of the Japanese? Compare and contrast the two.

REAL CASE

LVMH: organizing luxury products in the international arena

LVMH is the French-based, world-leading luxury goods group that was founded in 1987 with the merger of Louis Vuitton and Moët Hennessy. Christian Dior, Dom Pérignon, Givenchy, and Moët & Chandon are just a few of LVMH's world famous luxury brand names. In 2003, revenues for the group totaled $12 billion—putting it among the top five marketers of luxury items (including wines). LVMH has 1,592 stores across the world and currently employs about 56,000 people, most of whom work outside of France. The company generates the bulk of its sales in foreign markets; only 17 per cent of all revenues are earned in France. The United States is the company's single largest market comprising 26 per cent of revenues. It is important to note that although France earns a small fraction of LVMH's revenues, Europe as a whole

(including France) accounts for 38 per cent. Asia accounts for 29 per cent, and the remaining 7 per cent is generated mainly in Asia Pacific, Latin America, and Canada. In terms of revenues, the group's economic scope, with a balance of sales in each part of the triad, makes it a true global company.

LVMH's organizational arrangement is much more than that of a typical conglomerate. The whole organization focuses on shared costs and synergies, both backward and forward in its value chain. The five main lines of business are really strategic business units (SBUs) that are set up to market well-known, high-quality products while responding to local tastes and regulations. They are: (1) LVMH Fashion and Leather Goods; (2) Wines and Spirits; (3) Perfumes and Cosmetics; (4) Watches and Jewelry; and

Source: Corbis/Stephane Cardinale

(5) Selective Retailing. By carefully overseeing major operations from the top while allowing the individual SBUs to make the decisions that directly affect their own local markets, LVMH employs a combination of "tight and loose" control to maximize its international presence. In the process, it has become the most global retail company.

The profit margin on luxury goods is very high, so control over production, distribution, and advertising are central to profitability. LVMH ensures that production standards in its manufacturing operations are the highest. It centralizes manufacturing by using a common laboratory for cosmetics research and integrates the operations for all the branch offices in each group to ensure maximum efficiency.

Marketing is a very important part of LVMH's strategy. The company spends 11 percent of all its revenues on worldwide advertising and purchases media products in bulk to receive the best value for its money. The "Made in France" label is stressed to appeal to its home country's reputation for high-quality luxury products. The company sources only in France, Italy, and Switzerland.

The vision of a totally integrated group was and continues to be an important part of the global strategy that has positioned LVMH as an industry leader. The company walks a fine line between the exclusivity required of luxury goods and the size and scope of its operations. It might operate around the world, but its products are not accessible to all.

Websites: www.lvmh.com; www.vuitton.com; www.moet.com; www.dior.com; and www.givenchy.com.

Sources: Adapted from www.lvmh.com; LVMH, *Annual Report*, 2003; "The Sweet Smell of Success," *Business Week*, July 16, 2001; Carol Matlack, "Identity Crisis at LVMH?" *Business Week*, December 11, 2000.

1 What type of organizational structure does LVMH have?

2 What is the role of the SBUs in the organizational structure of LVMH? What problems might arise if each SBU were run independently?

3 Compare the organizational structure of LVMH with that of Procter & Gamble. Are there any similarities? How are these organizations different?

4 What are some of LVMH's FSAs that are listed in this case?

5 How would outsourcing to less developed countries affect LVMH?

REAL CASE

Command Alkon: a small software business

Based in Birmingham, Alabama, in the United States, Command Alkon is the world leader in the design and supply of computer software for the construction business. With $44 million in revenues in 2003, Command Alkon is only a small MNE but it has tremendous capabilities in technology standardization and is number one in its software in terms of market share, revenues, and distribution. Employing 350 people, it has international offices in Malaysia, the Netherlands, and Great Britain that market its products in each region through independent sales representatives. Roughly 20 per cent of the company's business is now derived outside North America.

Command Alkon is the result of a merger in December 2000 of Command Data and Alkon, two construction material software and service firms. The merger was designed to pool their R&D resources to compete more effectively in the fast-changing computer software business. Individual products were already compatible and the merger eliminated duplication of effort. The company specialized in the construction business, which was largely ignored by booming software firms, so it was able to become the largest player in a niche market. At present, it competes only with two smaller, local competitors and the systems developed in-house by customers.

Command Alkon has a purely ethnocentric strategy and organizational structure. All decisions are centralized and hierarchical micromanagement is the name of the game. The dominant culture is that of the US home office. There is no customization, no marketing department, no investment in local offices. Like most small businesses, Command Alkon is driven by its basic product or service, and it replicates its firm-specific advantage overseas.

One of the problems for small businesses is that the top management team is itself small. Often it comprises just the founder of the firm, his/her immediate family, and a few friends, so there is little managerial experience and a limited opportunity to develop international business skills, which leads to ethnocentric behavior. Indeed, most small business leaders do not have the internal resources to build an overseer business by foreign direct investment; instead, they are drawn to the export mode of foreign entry. Thus, they need an international division structure.

There are thousands of small and medium-sized businesses (SMEs) like Command Alkon. Their business strategy is not as complicated as that of MNEs; usually SMEs are in only one line of business. The international experience of SMEs is usually through licensing and/or exporting. Rarely do they engage in foreign direct investment or develop global organizational structure because the cost of doing business in foreign markets is often too high.

Websites: www.commandalkon.com and www.systechsystems.com.

Sources: www.commandalkon.com; Gilbert Nicholson, "Command Alkon Found Its Niche and Dug In," *Birmingham Business Journal*, November 2, 2001; Steven Lang, "The Merits of Specialization," *VARBusiness*, February 18, 2004.

1 Why does a small business like Command Alkon usually have little or no foreign direct investment? How does it go international?

2 What is the typical type of organizational structure for a small business like Command Alkon?

3 Why are software businesses usually ethnocentric in their organizational structure?

Endnotes

1 See, for example, Yigang Pan and Xiaolian Li, "Joint Venture Formation of Very Large Multinational Firms," *Journal of International Business Studies*, vol. 32, no. 1 (First Quarter 2000), pp. 179–189; and Tim G. Andrews and Nartnalin Chompusri, "Lessons in 'Cross-Vergence': Restructuring the Thai Subsidiary Corporation," *Journal of International Business Studies*, vol. 30, no. 3 (First Quarter 2000), pp. 77–93.

2 Brad Mitchener, "GM Takes a Gamble on Eastern Europe," *Wall Street Journal*, June 23, 1997, p. A 10.

3 William J. Holstein et al., "Mighty Mitsubishi Is on the Move," *Business Week*, September 24, 1990, p. 99.

4 Robert L. Simison, "New Data Illustrate Reshaping of Auto Parts Business," *Wall Street Journal*, September 2, 1997, p. B 4.

5 A good example is offered by Peter Siddall, Keith Willey and Jorge Tavares, "Building a Transnational Organization for BP Oil," *Long Range Planning*, February 1992, pp. 37–45.

6 For some excellent examples, see Charles H. Ferguson, "Computers and the Coming of the US Keiretsu," *Harvard Business Review*, July/August 1990, pp. 55–70; and Benjamin Gomes-Casseres, "Joint Ventures in the Face of Global Competition," *Sloan Management Review*, vol. 30, no. 3 (Spring 1989), pp. 17–26.

7 Richard M. Hodgetts and Fred Luthans, *International Management*, 4th ed. (Burr Ridge, IL: McGraw/Irwin, 2000), p. 303.

8 Joann S. Lublin, "Place vs. Product: It's Tough to Choose a Management Model," *Wall Street Journal*, June 27, 2001, pp. A 1, 4.

9 Hodgetts and Luthans (2000) n. 7 above, p. 306.

10 Yves L. Doz, Christopher A. Bartlett and C. K. Prahalad, "Global Competitive Pressures and Host Country Demands," *California Management Review*, Spring 1981, p. 66.

11 See Sumantra Ghoshal and Christopher A. Bartlett, *Managing across Borders: The Transnational Solution* (London: Random House, 1998).

12 Alfred D. Chandler, Jr., *Strategy and Structure* (Garden City, NY: Anchor Books, Doubleday, 1966).

13 Betsy McKay, "Coke Reorganization Puts Three as Contenders for No. 2 Position," *Wall Street Journal*, July 31, 2001, p. B 2.

14 William Boston, "Can Telekom Turn a David into a Goliath?" *Wall Street Journal*, June 1, 2001, pp. A 11, 13.

15 Also see Rebecca Blumenstein, "GM Is Building Plants In Developing Nations To Woo New Markets," *Wall Street Journal*, August 4, 1997, pp. A 1, 5.

16 Raghu Nath, *Comparative Management: A Regional View* (Cambridge, MA: Ballinger Publishing, 1988), p. 125.

17 Tim Burt and Nikki Tait, "Ford Refines Chain of Command in US," *Financial Times*, August 16, 2001, p. 13.

18 Bernard Simon, "Canada Warms to Wal-Mart," *New York Times*, September 1, 2001, pp. B 1, 3.

19 See, for example, "Japan Inc. on the Treadmill," *Economist*, June 9, 2001, pp. 63–64.

20 Bruce T. Lamont, V. Sambamurthy, Kimberly M. Ellis and Paul G. Simmonds, "The Influence of Organizational Structure on the Information Received by Corporate Strategists of Multinational Enterprises," *Management International Review*, vol. 40, no. 3 (Third Quarter 2000), pp. 231–232.

21 For some excellent insights into how Japanese companies function, see Noboru Yoshimura and Philip Anderson, *Inside*

the Kaisha (Boston, MA: Harvard Business School Press, 1997).

22 For an excellent contrast of American and Japanese communication problems, see William G. Ouchi, *Theory Z* (Reading, MA: Addison-Wesley Publishing, 1981), pp. 33–35.

23 Jane Whitney Gibson, Richard M. Hodgetts and Charles W. Blackwell, "Cultural Variations in Nonverbal Communication," in *Proceedings of the 55th Annual Convention of the Association for Business Communication*, 1990, p. 213.

24 Hodgetts and Luthans (2000) n. 7 above, p. 212.

25 David E. Sanger, "Tokyo's Tips For New York," *New York Times Magazine*, February 6, 1994, pp. 28–29.

26 William G. Egelhoff, "Patterns of Control in US, UK, and European Multinational Corporations," *Journal of International Business Studies*, vol. 15, no. 2 (Fall 1984), pp. 81–82.

27 Ouchi (1981) n. 22 above, p. 22.

Additional bibliography

Andersson, Ulf and Forsgren, Mats. "In Search of Centre of Excellence: Network Embeddedness and Subsidiary Roles in Multinational Corporations," *Management International Review*, vol. 40, no. 4 (Fourth Quarter 2000).

Barker, Vincent L. III. "When Things Go Wrong: Organizational Failures and Breakdown," *Academy of Management Review*, vol. 25, no. 2 (April 2000).

Bartlett, Christopher A. and Ghoshal, Sumantra. "Managing Across Borders: New Organizational Responses," *Sloan Management Review*, vol. 29, no. 1 (Fall 1987).

———. "Matrix Management: Not a Structure, a Frame of Mind," *Harvard Business Review*, vol. 68, no. 4 (July/August 1990).

———. "What Is a Global Manager?" *Harvard Business Review*, vol. 70, no. 5 (September/October 1992).

Beamish, Paul W., Karavis, Lambros, Goerzen, Anthony and Lane, Christopher. "The Relationship Between Organizational Structure and Export Performance," *Management International Review*, vol. 39, no. 1 (First Quarter 1999).

Beldona, Sam, Inkpen, Andrew C. and Phatak, Arvind. "Are Japanese Managers More Long-Term Oriented than United States Managers?" *Management International Review*, vol. 38, no. 3 (Third Quarter 1998).

Birkinshaw, Julian. *Entrepreneurship in the Global Firm* (London: Sage, 2000).

Doktor, Robert and Lie, John. "A Systems Theoretic Perspective upon International Organizational Behaviour: Some Preliminary Observations and Hypotheses," *Management International Review*, vol. 31, Special Issue (1991).

Geringer, J. Michael. "Strategic Determinants of Partner Selection Criteria in International Joint Ventures," *Journal of International Business Studies*, vol. 22, no. 1 (First Quarter 1991).

Ghoshal, Sumantra and Bartlett, Christopher A. "The Multinational Corporation as an Interorganizational Network," *Academy of Management Review*, vol. 15, no. 4 (October 1990).

Gregersen, Hal B., Morrison, Allen J. and Black, J. Stewart. "Developing Leaders for the Global Frontier," *Sloan Management Review*, vol. 40, no. 1 (Fall 1998).

Hargadon, Andrew, "Building an Innovation Factory," *Harvard Business Review*, vol. 78, no. 3 (May/June 2000).

Itaki, Masahiko. "Information-Processing Theory and the Multinational Enterprise," *Journal of International Business Studies*, vol. 22, no. 3 (Third Quarter 1991).

Jones, Gary K. and Davis, Herbert J. "National Culture and Innovation: Implications for Locating Global R&D Operations," *Management International Review*, vol. 40, no. 1 (First Quarter 2000).

Kogut, Bruce and Zander, Udo. "Knowledge of the Firm and the Evolutionary Theory of the Multinational Corporation," *Journal of International Business Studies*, vol. 24, no. 4 (Fourth Quarter 1993).

Kotova, Tatiana and Zaheer, Srilata. "Organizational Legitimacy Under Conditions of Complexity: The Case of the Multinational Enterprise," *Academy of Management Review*, vol. 24, no. 1 (October 1999).

Liker, Jeffrey K., "Japanese Automakers, U.S. Suppliers and Supply-Chain Superiority," *Sloan Management Review*, vol. 42, no. 1 (Fall 2000).

Lynn, Leonard H. "Remade in America: Transplanting & Transforming Japanese Management Systems," *Academy of Management Review*, vol. 25, no. 3 (July 2000).

Maljers, Floris A. "Inside Unilever: The Evolving Transnational Company," *Harvard Business Review*, vol. 70, no. 5 (September/October 1992).

Martinez, Jon I. and Jarillo, J. Carlos. "The Evolution of Research on Coordinating Mechanisms in Multinational Corporations," *Journal of International Business Studies*, vol. 20, no. 3 (Fall 1989).

Mills, D. Quinn. "The Decline and Rise of IBM," *Sloan Management Review*, vol. 37, no. 4 (Summer 1996).

Mintzberg, Henry, "Organigraphs: Drawing How Companies Really Work," *Harvard Business Review*, vol. 77, no. 5 (September/October 1999).

Parkhe, Arvind. "Interfirm Diversity, Organizational Learning, and Longevity in Global Strategic Alliances," *Journal of International Business Studies*, vol. 22, no. 4 (Fourth Quarter 1991).

Prahalad, C. K. and Oosterveld, Jan P. "Transforming Internal Governance," *Sloan Management Review*, vol. 40, no. 3 (Spring 1999).

Roehl, Tom. "The Evolution of a Manufacturing System at Toyota," *Academy of Management Review*, vol. 25, no. 2 (April 2000).

Rosenzweig, Philip M. and Singh, Jitendra V. "Organizational Environments and the Multinational Enterprise," *Academy of Management Review*, vol. 16, no. 2 (April 1991).

Roth, Kendall. "International Configuration and Coordination Archetypes for Medium-Sized Firms in Global Industries," *Journal of International Business Studies*, vol. 23, no. 3 (Third Quarter 1992).

Rugman, Alan M. and Verbeke, Alain. "A Note on the Transnational Solution and the Transaction Cost Theory of

Multinational Strategic Management," *Journal of International Business Studies*, vol. 23, no. 4 (Fall 1992).

Sanyal, Rajib N. "An Empirical Analysis of the Unionization of Foreign Manufacturing Firms in the US," *Journal of International Business Studies*, vol. 21, no. 1 (First Quarter 1990).

Sullivan, Daniel. "Organization in American MNCs: The Perspective of the European Regional Headquarters," *Management International Review*, vol. 32, no. 3 (Third Quarter 1992).

Westney, Eleanor D. and Zaheer, Srilata. "The Multinational Enterprise," in Alan M. Rugman and Thomas Brewer (eds.), *The Oxford Handbook of International Business* (Oxford: Oxford University Press, 2000), pp. 349–379.

Zahra, Shaker A. "The Dynamic Firm: The Role of Technology, Strategy, Organization, and Regions," *Academy of Management Review*, vol. 24, no. 4 (October 1999).

Chapter 10

PRODUCTION STRATEGY

Objectives of the chapter

Production strategy is critical to effective international operations. Most goods and services have very limited lives, so MNEs must continually provide new offerings, which can be accomplished only through a well-formulated production strategy. This chapter examines how MNEs carry out this process. In doing so, we will focus on the entire range of production strategies from research and development to manufacturing, shipment, and the final international destination. We will look at the most current approaches, including speed-to-market, concurrent engineering, and continuous cost reduction.

The specific objectives of this chapter are to:

1 *Examine* the role of research, development, and innovation in production strategy.
2 *Relate* some of the most critical steps in generating goods and services, including global sourcing, costing techniques, quality maintenance, effective materials handling, inventory control, and the proper emphasis on service.
3 *Describe* the nature and importance of international logistics in production strategy.
4 *Review* some of the major production strategies being used by MNEs, including strategic alliances and acquisitions.

Contents

The GE production process and Six Sigma

General Electric is a multibillion-dollar multinational corporation whose products range from 65 cent light bulbs to billion-dollar power plants. Based on revenues, assets, profits, and market value, the company was listed by *Fortune* magazine as number nine in the world in 2003. One reason for GE's annual revenue of more than $134 billion is its ability to manage a diverse multiproduct-line operation, handling such products as major appliances, lighting, medical diagnostic imaging equipment, motors, and commercial and military aircraft engines and engineering materials. GE also provides a range of services, including those related to electricity provision, media (GE owns NBC in the United States), and multimedia programming and distribution. Much of the company's success can be attributed to the production-related concepts it has employed over the last two decades. During the 1980s, work-out, process mapping, and best practices were GE's applied concepts.

Work-out is a training program designed to empower employees to implement their problem-solving ideas. A group of 40 to 100 people, picked by management from all ranks and functional areas, attend a three-day meeting. The first day consists of a manager leading the group in roughing out an agenda addressing areas in which productivity can be increased. Then the manager leaves and for the next $1\frac{1}{2}$ days the group breaks into teams to tackle the agenda. On the last afternoon the manager returns and one by one the team members make their proposals for improved productivity. The manager can make only three responses: agree, disagree, or ask for more information; in the latter case, an individual manager must empower a team to get the information by an agreed-upon date. These work-out sessions have proved extremely successful. In one case, a group of workers convinced management to allow their factory to bid against an outside vendor for the right to build new protective shields for grinding machines. As a result, the GE group completed the job for $16,000 versus $96,000 for the vendor.

The second method, *process mapping*, is to create a flowchart that shows all the steps, no matter how small, involved in making or doing something. The map is analyzed for ways to eliminate steps and save time and money. One work group was able to reorganize production, cut manufacturing time in half, and reduce inventory by $4 million.

The third method, *best practices*, consists of finding companies that do things better than GE does and emulating

them. GE personnel try to answer the question: What is the secret of this other company's success? Quite often the answer includes such things as getting products to market faster than anyone else, treating suppliers like partners, or having superior inventory management. As a result of best practices, GE is now keeping executives in their jobs for longer periods of time rather than rotating them quickly through new jobs; the best practices process revealed that frequent changes create problems in new product introductions. The company also learned how to use continuous improvement processes more effectively to bring a new product into the market ahead of the competition and then work on introducing new technologies. In the past the firm would try to perfect all technologies first and then introduce the final product version.

In the 1990s, the dominant production concept was Six Sigma, a name that originates from a statistical method for deriving near-perfect quality, equal to 3.4 defects per million operations. The Six Sigma process allows GE to measure how many "defects" there are in a given process and then systematically work to eliminate them to approximate "zero defects." Six Sigma recognizes three elements: the customer, the process, and the employee. The customer is the key to defining quality. GE uses the term "Delighting Customers" to generate a mentality whereby customer expectations of performance, reliability, competitive price, on-time delivery, service, clear and correct transaction processing, and other customer needs become a key factor in all processes. The second element, the process, promotes "Outside-In Thinking Quality." GE must understand the transaction life cycle from the customer's point of view and identify significant value and improvement from that same perspective. Under the banner "Leadership Commitment People," the third element of Six Sigma, the employee, requires that all personnel use their talents and energies to satisfy customers. All employees are trained in Six Sigma, including statistical tools, strategy, and techniques of Six Sigma quality. At the core of the process is a workforce mentality on customer quality expectations, defect reduction, process capability, variation (the customer reacts to the variance rather than the average results), stability of operations, and designing processes to meet customer expectations.

GE's advantage over failing conglomerates is its ability to transfer knowledge over the whole company. This can be attributed to former CEO Jack Welch, who oversaw GE's transformation from a mainly manufacturing firm to a service-oriented, knowledge-based company. He defined GE's culture by creating a workforce that can identify opportunities and implement changes.

Despite GE's firm-specific advantages (FSAs) in production, its competitive edge has not been transferred equally to other parts of the world, especially not other triad nations that have significant domestic competitors. The company derives approximately 59.8 per cent of its revenues from the United States alone. If its revenues from Canadian and Latin American operations are added in, the number rises to almost 63.7 per cent. Europe, its largest foreign regional market, accounts for only 18.5 per cent of revenues, whereas countries in the Pacific Basin account for a mere 9.1 per cent. The remaining 8.7 per cent are accounted for by other regions (3 per cent) and non-segmented US exports to other countries (5.7 per cent).

In October 2000, General Electric, as the world's largest producer of jet engines, and Honeywell, a manufacturer of aircraft electronics agreed to a $42 billion merger. The two US-based companies secured antitrust authorities' approval in the United States and Canada, but the deal came to a halt because of the European Union. This was the first time the EU blocked a merger between two American companies. The European competition commissioner claimed that such a merger would have closed the market to competitors and asked GE to divest itself of GE Capital Aviation Services by selling it to one of its main rivals. GE offered to sell the company privately, but the EU countered that a friendly transaction might not result in true divestiture. US politicians, frustrated by the European stand, threatened to retaliate if the EU did not approve the merger. Republican Senator Phil Gramm went as far as to accuse the EU of enacting policies to protect its companies. The EU rejected US government intervention in the matter and the merger did not materialize.

Website: **www.ge.com**.

Sources: Thomas A. Stewart, "GE Keeps Those Ideas Coming," *Fortune*, August 12, 1991, pp. 40–49; "The World's Super Fifty," *Forbes*, July 27, 1998, p. 118; **www.ge.com**; General Electric, *10K SEC Filing*, 2002; "EU Rejects Latest GE Offers," *BBC.co.uk*, June 29, 2001, "EU Blocks GE/Honeywell Deal," *BBC.co.uk*, July 3, 2001; "US Senators Lash Out at EU Over GE Deal," *BBC.co.uk*, June 15, 2001; and "The Fortune Global 500," *Fortune*, July 26, 2004.

1. How did General Electric use work-out to increase speed-to-market?

2. How has GE used Six Sigma to reduce cost and improve quality in consumer goods? In each case, give an example.

3. In what way could best practices help GE develop more effective international strategies? Explain.

INTRODUCTION

Production management has been responsible for many new goods and services. Examples are as varied as Palm's handhelds, Apple's iPod, Honda's hybrid cars, HP's digital cameras, eBay's Internet auctions, and five-star hotel operations at the Ritz-Carlton. The nature of production management in the MNE is similar in many respects to that in domestic firms. Both are concerned with the efficient use of labor and capital. Both are also interested in investing in research and development (R&D) and in organizing operations to generate successful new product lines and increase production and service efficiency.

Like domestic firms, MNEs need to organize their production management so they can minimize operating costs through the use of logistics and inventory control. Canon, for example, relocates production to China only if labor accounts for over 5 per cent of production costs.[1] Acer, the successful upstart from Taiwan, makes sure that computer parts with short product life cycles are shipped by air, and those with long product life cycles are shipped by sea (see Active Learning Case in Chapter 19). However, pressures from host-country governments or special interest groups can affect a multinational's decision making in these areas. For example, host governments often criticize resource-based MNEs for their backward, forward, and horizontal integration. **Backward integration**, which is the

Backward integration
The ownership of equity assets used earlier in the production cycle, such as an auto firm that acquires a steel company

ownership of equity assets used earlier in the production cycle (such as an auto firm acquiring a steel company), is criticized for doing little for employment or development in the host nation. **Forward integration**, which is the purchase of assets or facilities that move the company closer to the customer (such as a computer manufacturer that acquires a retail chain that specializes in computer sales), is criticized on the basis that MNEs use the strategy to homogenize consumer tastes to the detriment of national identities. **Horizontal integration**, which is the acquisition of firms in the same line of business (such as a computer chip manufacturer that buys a competitor), is attacked for introducing similar product lines on a worldwide basis and undercutting the existence of local firms, most of which lack the economies of scale that can be achieved by MNEs.[2]

There are similar challenges in the industrial relations area, where MNEs must take into account different labor practices and wage rates. For example, multinationals are often under pressure from host governments to use local sourcing for their supplies, hire local workers, train home-country managers and supervisors, and help improve the production environment in the host nation. These decisions can sometimes result in higher production costs, although most international auto firms, for example, use local suppliers and workers to offset this problem.

The financing of operations is another production-related challenge. The choice between local and international borrowing and the use of internally generated funds to minimize the cost of capital is complicated by foreign exchange risk, international tax laws, and government controls on capital (see Chapter 14). Additionally, MNEs need to know where they are on their production cost curves in each country, as well as globally, so as to exploit any cost advantages with an appropriate organizational structure. For example, as Toyota's worldwide market share began to stabilize, the firm found it needed to become increasingly more efficient.[3]

The above examples illustrate some of the common production-related problems facing international firms. However, experienced MNEs have learned how to deal with these challenges. In doing so, they employ a wide gamut of production strategies that address research, development, innovation, global sourcing, costing techniques, and inventory control.[4] The following sections examine each of these production strategies.

RESEARCH, DEVELOPMENT, AND INNOVATION

Production strategies do *not* begin with manufacturing. In the past many MNEs focused most heavily on this aspect of operations, failing to realize that an effective production strategy begins with new product development. This conclusion gains in importance when one considers that many of today's best-selling products and services were unavailable a short while ago. Examples include laptops, cellular phones, satellite navigation devices, DVD players, broadband DSL lines, and specialized discount stores that cater to selective product lines such as home-related goods or office supplies. Many other products and services have been greatly improved over the last decade or so. Examples include antidepressant medication, automobiles, facsimile machines, hazardous waste treatment services, home delivery food services, medical diagnostic equipment, pacemakers, personal computers, photocopiers, telephones, and televisions. MNEs have come to realize that if they are not developing new goods and services, they must be improving their current offerings. In either case the focus is on R&D and innovation.

Innovation can be broadly divided into product/service development and process development. The former refers to activities that support the creation of new products and services that customers want, or improvements to existing products/services that make more customers want them instead of those of rival firms. The latter refers to innovation activities that improve the way products/services are produced, making them quicker,

Forward integration
The purchase of assets or facilities that move the company closer to the customer, such as a computer manufacturer that acquires a retail chain that specializes in computer products

Horizontal integration
The purchase of firms in the same line of business, such as a computer chip firm that acquires a competitor

cheaper, or better quality. Continuous innovation lies at the heart of sustained competitive advantage, and managing it effectively has a strong international business component.

Most large firms are involved in all of these activities. Sony, for example, is continually coming up with new technology platforms (CDs, DVDs, minidisks, and so on) and new products based around these platforms. But it also invests in improving current product lines, with new models and new features, and it strives to make them cheaper through economies of scale and continuous improvement in manufacturing.

For us, concerned with the international strategy and organization of innovation and R&D, there are several key issues. The first is the question of how far products, services, and the processes that create them should be standardized across all locations, as opposed to customizing these to suit local markets. This lies at the heart of the "integration-responsiveness" theme that runs through this book. Despite the highly standardized nature of their products, even firms like McDonalds and Coca-Cola customize these for particular markets. Like all firms they have to manage a natural tension between country market managers who would like more customization to suit their local customer needs and head-office managers in the marketing, operations, human resource management, R&D, and strategy departments which would prefer to standardize across all markets.

A related issue is: where should firms locate different innovation-related activities? The answer to this depends on the industry and often the product or service in question. It is worth examining this by looking at the factors that influence the organization of research and development (R&D) around the firm.

MNEs tend to operate several types of R&D networks, as shown on Figure 10.1. There is an innovation hierarchy from basic, long-term, or blue-sky R&D, which is often based around finding scientific breakthroughs, to applied, near-market, or demand-led innovation.

- Blue-sky or basic R&D centers are often linked to universities or government research institutes to tap into highly specialized expertise, wherever it is in the world.

- Technical design and development centers focus on more practical, near-market R&D and may be separate or co-located with regional headquarters or major business units.

- Applied technical development and customization departments, often situated within manufacturing centers, will focus on incremental improvements to production processes or minor adaptations to products to suit local markets.

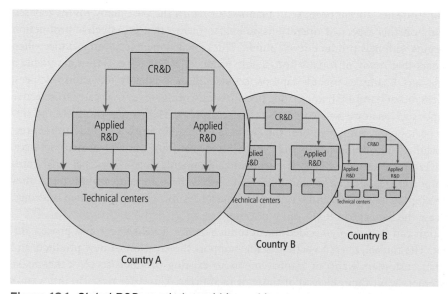

Figure 10.1 Global R&D: markets and hierarchies

Home-country-based central R&D often sets the overall R&D strategy across a firm, but funding and other resources may partly come from country market managers who will push for more applied R&D activities to adapt products and services for their markets. For a large MNE, a few key locations may have R&D units, the firm's main markets may all have one or more applied R&D centers, and production locations will have technical centers. The complexity of managing strategy and implementation up and down the innovation hierarchy and across the different country locations should not be underestimated.

In terms of both product and process development, MNEs need to prioritize country locations according to both (1) local market requirements in terms of adaptation, design and development, and engineering support and (2) local technological resources, expertise, contract companies, universities, and so on, often called the "national system of innovation."

Hewlett Packard (HP) is a good example of these kinds of structures. It has six basic R&D centers in Palo Alto, California; Cambridge, Massachusetts; Bristol, England; Grenoble, France; Haifa, Israel; and Tokyo, Japan. These explore a wide range of technologies more or less linked to its product range. Its Advanced Studies Research Labs include a subgroup doing information theory research, linking the Mathematical Science group based in Bristol with experts at the US universities Stanford and Berkeley. Grenoble specializes in business PC design and development and Israel in image and document processing, among other areas.

These centers of research excellence are linked to HP's global product divisions, mainly headquartered in the US, and its national subsidiaries around the world, which encompass most of its 85,500 employees.

The Palo Alto center pioneered HP's thermal ink-jet technology, for example. Its Consumer Products group headquartered in San Diego, California, designed, developed, and led the manufacturing of a range of imaging products using this technology. The firm's subsidiary in Singapore customizes the design and produces thermal ink-jet printers for the Japanese and Asian markets.

The R&D structure of the firm evolved a step further when the Singaporean subsidiary took the lead from San Diego for the design, development, and manufacturing of a new range of portable ink-jet printers. It had built up a range of specialist capabilities, through learning from other parts of the internal network and through local Asian technical partnerships and sub-contractors that made it the best place to lead innovation efforts in this area for the firm as a whole.[5]

The above organization structures are important because they affect how well firms leverage their R&D efforts for competitive advantage. The efficiency with which specialist knowledge inputs from experts around the firm are coordinated is paramount. For example, firms have to focus new product development (NPD) efforts at the point where technological opportunities meet market opportunities. Marketing departments and subsidiaries, distributors and retailers in country markets understand customer needs, whereas the central R&D department and technical design and development centers around the firm understand the potential of various technologies. These areas of specialist knowledge have to combine efficiently to direct NPD, and this is often done within cross-functional teams. NPD project teams are continually created and disbanded in manufacturing and service firms in response to the ever-changing technological and market opportunities they are faced with, and the strength of internal and external networks determines how well firms manage this process.[6]

Large MNEs that are good at managing knowledge networks are in a better position to leverage the scale and scope advantages that put them ahead of smaller or domestic market firms in terms of their innovativeness. They can afford large (scale) and specialist (scope) centers of excellence and can manage joint ventures with other big players to pool resources and spread the risk of R&D projects. They can then link these R&D centers to their markets around the world, prioritizing which areas of development to focus their efforts to reap the most rewards in terms of sales of new and improved products.

Global innovation management and knowledge management are seen to be increasingly important to the long-run performance of all firms. Nohria and Ghoshal use the terms *distributed innovation* and *differentiated networks* to characterize how firms should learn globally and exploit this learning globally to improve production processes and products in all markets.[7] Other studies also emphasize the internal processes, within multinational structures, that constrain or facilitate this kind of global capability.[8] See the box **International Business Strategy in Action: When the rubber hits the road** for an illustration of the importance of innovation in the tire industry.

INTERNATIONAL BUSINESS STRATEGY *IN ACTION*

When the rubber hits the road: Michelin, Ford, and Firestone

French Michelin, the world's leader in the tire industry, entered the North American market in the late1960s and has since become the second largest tire producer in the United States, accounting for 14 per cent of the market. Goodyear, the market leader, holds 17 per cent. In 2003, 35 per cent of Michelin's revenue was derived from North America. Europe remains the company's most important market, accounting for 52 per cent of sales.

Michelin's North American expansion illustrates the problem of internationalizing from one part of the triad to another. In 1969, Michelin decided to locate a new plant in Nova Scotia, Canada. The decision was based on the low degree of financial risk resulting from Canadian government tax concessions and direct grants for the project. But most important, Nova Scotia was a long way from the head offices of the giant US tire producers in Akron, Ohio. Michelin was reluctant to confront the US tire industry head on, even with its superior technology (at the time, radials, which Michelin introduced in the 1940s, lasted twice as long as the steel-belted tires made by American producers). However, Michelin overlooked the political power of stakeholders like the US government and the US tire industry—as well as their ability to influence trade with Canada.

The location in Nova Scotia was based on several country-specific advantages: Canadian financial support ($85 million in loans and grants), importing and exporting benefits (drawbacks and duty-free trade), and a lack of political risk. In addition, Michelin possessed firm-specific advantages (R&D, technology, quality control, production, marketing, management, and financing), which made production in Nova Scotia advantageous. Rather than evaluating alternative locations (Quebec, the United States), Michelin forged ahead into the Nova Scotia market without sufficient strategic planning.

The choice of Nova Scotia as the location followed from a chance airplane contact in 1967 between the president of

Source: Getty Images/AFP/Jeff Kowalsky

Michelin and a representative of Industrial Estates (IEL, the development agency for the Province of Nova Scotia), who stressed the advantages of such a location in serving both US and Canadian markets. Michelin expected to export tires from Canada to the United States. There was a very low tariff on such trade, whereas the US tariffs on imports of tires from Europe were very high.

Michelin's rapid movement into Nova Scotia resulted in retaliation from the US government and a new prohibitive tariff to protect US industry. Michelin's error came in failing to evaluate its alternatives and not anticipating any retaliation.

In February 1973, the United States imposed countervailing duties to the IEL loan of $50 million at a rate of 6 per cent, seeing the loan as an export subsidy. An appeal was heard in 1982, after which the US import tax was reduced but the damage was done. Michelin may as well have entered the US market head on, since the US competitors attacked its presence in Nova Scotia anyway. But today there are several big Michelin plants in the United States whose tires are now being used on many American cars. The Michelin experience illustrates the danger of foreign entry without a long-term triad insight.

Michelin eventually bought Uniroyal and B.F. Goodrich in 1991, some 20 years after its initial entry into North America. In one stroke, it achieved massive economies of scale by doubling its sales in North America. It also has an alliance with Goodyear to share R&D costs. Michelin is now a key supplier to original equipment manufacturers (OEMs) such as Peugeot, Citroën, Toyota, Honda, General Motors, and Ford. And it sells directly to consumers through distributors such as Sears, Wal-Mart, and FeuVert. Its global competitors include Bridgestone-Firestone and Pirelli.

Arrayed against Michelin in North America are the giant Goodyear and Japanese-owned Bridgestone-Firestone. Goodyear has a long-standing relationship with General Motors. Firestone was a supplier to Ford for 97 years until they split in May 2001 over litigation involving some 200 deaths and more than 750 accidents when the tread on Firestone tires allegedly separated on Ford Explorer SUVs. It was found subsequently in a federal study that American cars typically have underinflated tires. On the Ford Explorer, a burst tire can have fatal effects. Ford blamed Firestone and paid to replace 14 million tires on its SUVs. A lot of rubber was burned. As the reputation of Firestone suffered, both Goodyear and Michelin improved their stakes in the market.

Today, tire makers are competing on technology. Goodyear was the first to introduce a tire that runs when flat. SSTs, or self-supporting tires, can support the weight of a car even when they have been punctured. Most manufacturers have their own versions of the tire, and the technology is compatible with standard vehicles. SSTs account for 90 per cent of the run-flat tire market. In 2004, Michelin introduced the PAX system. It is superior to the SST in that its design allows for better control of the car and fuel economy. The PAX tire can also last for 200 kilometers after a puncture, twice as long as the SST. The technology has already been licensed to a number of Michelin's competitors, including Goodyear, but it is unclear whether it will be successful with consumers. For one, the PAX can be used only in vehicles with specially designed chassis and wheels. This means that consumers can only secure replacements through an authorized PAX outlet. Michelin has 1,000 PAX dealers in the United States and a mobile service to assist motorists on the road, but it is just one extra hassle for a driver with a flat. In Europe, few consumers took up the option to have PAX tires on their new Audis. When Renault offered the PAX on its Scénic minivans, most new owners insisted on having a spare tire in the car. In the United States, Michelin is hoping to capitalize on the large SUV and pick-up truck markets. SST technology cannot support these vehicles, but the PAX tire can. Honda is offering the new technology as a standard feature in its Odyssey minivan, which will give Michelin the initial boost it needs to cement the technology in the United States.

Websites: www.michelin.com; www.michelin.fr; www.goodyear.com; www.gm.com; www.sears.com; www.walmart.com; www.feuvert.fr; www.peugeot.com; www.toyota.com; www.citroen.com; www.honda.com; www.ford.com; and www.bridgestone-firestone.com.

Sources: Michelin, *Annual Report*, 2003; "Michelin: New Rubber Hits the Road," *Business Week*, August 16, 2004; "Michelin," *Business Week*, September 20, 2002; "Tyre Straits," *Economist*, August 2, 2001; Dan Ackman, "Bridgestone Says Don't Tread on Me," *Forbes.com*, May 5, 2001; Michelin, *Annual Report*, 2000; and Alan M. Rugman, Donald Lecraw and Laurence Booth, *International Business: Firm and Environment* (New York: McGraw-Hill, 1985).

Speed-to-market

One of the major manufacturing challenges facing MNEs is the speed with which they develop and get new products to market.[9] In recent years, many firms have found that a "speed-to-market" strategy can be extremely profitable. Table 10.1 provides some data to support this statement. Notice that a company that enters the market one month ahead of the competition can increase annual gross profits by $150,000 on a product that generates $25 million and $600,000 on a product that generates $100 million. Simply put, by carefully designing the product and getting it out the door fast, the company can dramatically increase profitability.

MNEs have taken a number of steps to ensure early delivery of their products. For example, Cisco Systems has outsourced the production of routers and switches to Flextronics, a contract electronics manufacturer. Flextronics receives an electronic order from Cisco, manufactures the product under the Cisco brand, and then delivers it directly to the customers.[10] BMW has combined engineering, development, and production planning in bringing new cars to market in record time.[11]

Table 10.1 The cost of arriving late to market (and still be on budget)

If the company is late to market by:					
6 months	5 months	4 months	3 months	2 months	1 month
Gross potential profit is reduced by:					
−33%	−25%	−18%	−12%	−7%	−3%
If time to market is improved profit will go up by:					
11.9%	9.3%	7.3%	5.7%	4.3%	3.1%
For revenues of $25 million, annual gross profit will increase by:					
$400,000	$350,000	$300,000	$250,000	$200,000	$150,000
For revenues of $100 million, annual gross profit will increase by:					
$1,600,000	$1,400,000	$1,200,000	$1,000,000	$800,000	$600,000

Source: Academy of Management Executive, "The New Competitors: They Think in Terms of 'Speed-to-Market'" by Joseph T. Vesey. Copyright © 1991 by Academy of Management. Reproduced with permission of Academy of Management in the format textbook via Copyright Clearance Center.

Time-to-market accelerators
Factors that help reduce bottlenecks and errors and ensure product quality and performance

Modular integrated robotized system (MIRB)
A software-based production process that relies entirely on robots

Concurrent engineering
The process of having design, engineering, and manufacturing people working together to create a product, in contrast to working in a sequential manner

The strategic emphasis is on increasing speed by developing time-to-market accelerators, which are factors that help reduce bottlenecks and errors and ensure product quality and performance. These accelerators vary from firm to firm, but they all produce the same results. For example, in 2000, Pirelli, the French tire maker, unveiled its modular integrated robotized system (MIRB), which enables the entire production system to be robotized. Small and flexible, MIRB allows smaller batches to be produced in different locations, potentially locating them next to Pirelli's industrial customers.[12]

In the past, many MNEs placed the bulk of their production attention on the manufacturing side of the operation. However, recent research shows that the best way to reduce defective products and speed delivery is by placing the greatest attention on product design and planning of operations. This is accomplished through what is known as concurrent engineering, which involves design, engineering, and manufacturing people working together to create and build the product. Concurrent engineering is useful for two reasons. First, if the product is carefully designed, fewer changes are needed later on and the good can be brought to market swiftly. Second, the costs associated with changes increase as the product gets closer to completion; that is, it is almost twice as expensive to correct a problem during production than during product design.

Once a product or service has been planned out, the MNE's attention turns to production. This strategy is focused very heavily on minimizing costs and increasing quality and productivity.

 Active learning check

Review your answer to Active Learning Case question 1 and make any changes you like. Then compare your answer with the one below.

1 How did General Electric use work-out to increase speed-to-market?

The primary way GE used work-out to increase speed-to-market was by looking for ways to eliminate production bottlenecks and streamline operations. The strategy of work-out asked the participants: How can we change the operation to get more done in less time? The workers who were familiar with the operations often had a wealth of information to share, and this was sometimes the first time anyone has asked them their opinions. They were delighted to offer suggestions and recommendations. As a result, the company produced more products in less time than ever before.

GENERATION OF GOODS AND SERVICES

Most people think of the production process as one in which physical goods are produced. However, the process can also be used in generating services, and the two are quite often interlinked.[13] For example, GM manufactures cars but also offers auto maintenance and repair services,[14] whereas Boeing both builds and services aircraft. In other cases, services are primary, such as the Hilton Corporation offering hotel accommodations, Hertz and Avis leasing cars, and CNN providing international news coverage.

Sometimes goods and/or services are provided directly by the MNE; other times the MNE has an arrangement with outside firms or suppliers (some of them being direct competitors) to assist in this process. For example, other firms make some of the Hewlett-Packard printers, but HP has its name put on the units and assumes responsibility for marketing them.[15] Service organizations follow a similar strategy. Some airlines purchase their in-flight food from companies like Marriott, and some rely on aircraft maintenance firms such as Ryder to service their craft. Many motels subcontract their food service to companies that specialize in this area, including fast-food franchisors such as McDonald's and Burger King. So there is often a mix of product/service strategies at work when generating goods and services. The following discussion examines some of the most important functions that are carried out in this process. The production of goods is emphasized most heavily because some of the areas under discussion do not lend themselves to services—although one that does is global sourcing, a primary area of consideration in production strategy.

Global sourcing

Sometimes MNEs produce all the goods and services they need. However, they often use global sourcing by calling upon those suppliers who can provide the needed output more efficiently regardless of where they are geographically located.[16]

Global sourcing
The use of suppliers anywhere in the world, chosen on the basis of their efficiency

Global sourcing has become important for a number of reasons. The most obvious one is cost. If GM wants to be price competitive in the European Union, one strategy is to build and ship cars from Detroit to Europe at a price equal to, or less than, that charged by EU competitors. Because this is not possible, GM uses overseas suppliers and assembly plants to build much of what it sells in Europe. In deciding who will provide these parts and supplies, the company uses global sourcing, as do other MNEs.

Not all global sourcing is provided by outside suppliers. Some MNEs own their own source of supply or hold an equity position in a supplier. This relationship does not guarantee that the supplier will get the MNE's business on every bid. However, if the supplier is unable to match the cost or quality performance of competitive suppliers, the MNE will eventually terminate the relationship. So there is a great deal of pressure on the supplier to develop and maintain state-of-the-art production facilities. Additionally, because the supplier works closely with the MNE, the company knows how its multinational client likes things done and is able to operate smoothly with the MNE's design and production people.

In recent years some giant MNEs have taken equity positions in a number of different suppliers. Japanese multinationals are an excellent example. These firms often have a network of parts suppliers, subcontractors, and capital equipment suppliers they can call on.

At the same time these suppliers often provide goods and services to other firms. This helps them to maintain their competitive edge by forcing them to innovate, adapt, and remain cost effective. If these suppliers are in similar or complementary industries, as in the case of NEC's suppliers, then technological innovations or revolutionary changes in manufacturing processes will be quickly accepted or copied by others. So the close proximity of the suppliers coupled with their business relationships helps to ensure that they attain and hold positions as world-class suppliers, and this advantage carries over to the customers, who gain both innovative ideas and high-quality, low-cost supplies.[17]

A good example is the leather footwear industry in Italy. Manufacturers regularly interact with leather suppliers, designers, and producers of other leather goods. As a result, the manufacturers are extremely knowledgeable about industry technology, production techniques, fashion trends, and supply sources.

These advantages also help explain why many US suppliers are going international. By setting up operations near world-class competitors, these suppliers find it easier to monitor developments, remain alert to changes in technology and production processes, and maintain state-of-the-art facilities.[18] In fact, when manufacturers expand operations to another country, it is common to find their major suppliers setting up operations nearby in order to continue serving the manufacturers. The other reason is to prevent local competitors from capturing some of this business, which often happens when the supplier attempts to compete from the home country.

When MNEs turn to global sourcing, there is typically a hierarchical order of consideration. The company gives first preference to internal sources, such as having subassemblies produced by the manufacturing department or the subsidiary that specializes in this work. However, if a review of outside sources reveals a sufficient cost/quality difference that would justify buying from an external supplier, this is what the company will do. In fact, sometimes an MNE will not attempt to make a particular part or product because it lacks the expertise to do so efficiently. The firm will simply solicit bids from outside suppliers and award the contract based on predetermined specifications (price, quality, delivery time, etc.). Over time the MNE will learn which suppliers are best at providing certain goods and services and will turn to them immediately. When this process is completed, attention will then focus on the actual manufacture of the goods.

Recently, environmentalists have reviewed the global supply chains of MNEs. They argue that all suppliers to an MNE should follow environmentally sensitive policies—in other words, be "green." The box **International Business Strategy in Action: Greening the supply chain** examines this issue.

Manufacturing of goods

MNEs face a variety of concerns in manufacturing goods and services. Primary among these are cost, quality, and efficient production systems.

Cost

Modular manufacturing
A manufacturing process that consists of modules that can be easily adapted to fit changing demand

Multinationals seek to control their costs by increasing the efficiency of their production processes. Often this means using new, improved technology such as state-of-the-art machinery and equipment. Although these purchases can be expensive, they may be the best way to raise productivity and lower costs, thus maintaining competitive advantage. A good example is provided by the automobile industry in Brazil, which is the heart of the South American automobile market. The country is host to 13 automakers, including DaimlerChrysler, Volkswagen, and Ford, which are investing over $20 billion to update Brazilian plants to modular manufacturing. Modular manufacturing allows suppliers of parts to take on some of the assembly. Dana Corporation, which has set up shop near a Chrysler factory in the city of Curitiba, is now responsible for the assembly of the Dakota's basic skeleton, which represents approximately 30 per cent of the total cost of production. Once this skeleton reaches Chrysler, it is mounted with an engine and a body. Entire assembly lines had to be rebuilt to accommodate this process. Volkswagen, Ford, and General

INTERNATIONAL BUSINESS STRATEGY *IN ACTION*

Greening the supply chain

The supply chain is an important part of the production process and overall strategy in the automobile sector, where most Tier One auto parts suppliers have adopted ISO 9000 quality standards over the last decade in order to remain key suppliers to the OEMs. Less well known is that the supply chain has also been used to introduce environmentally friendly "green" standards. This occurs through the implementation of ISO 14000.

A successful example of this is in Mexico. Despite many NGOs arguing that Mexico is a pollution haven, research by Rugman, Kirton, and Soloway shows that the use of ISO 14000 green processes has unambiguously raised Mexico's environmental standards. When both auto suppliers and assemblers have to change their engineering processes to meet ISO 14001 standards in the United States and Canada, these new manufacturing processes raise overall environmental performance in Mexico, even if the government is lagging in enforcing the standards. The "foreign-owned" firms bring in new technologies to poorer countries, including green technologies.

This also occurs in the retail/food sector. A study of the UK retail sector in 2001 found that all along the supply chain firms engage in green purchasing. This occurred across at least three sectors: grocery retailing, furniture, and building

materials. The green purchasing was helped by EU environmental regulations, which have led to basic changes in environmental management systems (EMSs) of retail companies. The EMS is closely linked to the Denning model of continuous process improvements of quality standards.

The supply chain, or Porter's value chain, typically consists of supplier management, purchasing, materials management, production scheduling, facilities planning, logistics, and consumer services.

Best practices in UK retail were B&Q (part of the Kingfisher Group) and The Body Shop. Both of these retailers require their suppliers to meet EU environmental standards.

In general, UK grocery retailers (like Sainsbury's, Safeway, and Asda) were more engaged in green purchasing than UK furniture and building material retailers, although both B&Q and The Body Shop had also developed some green capabilities.

Websites: www.kingfisher.co.uk; www.the-body-shop.com; www.sainsbury.co.uk; www.safeway.com; and www.asda.co.uk.

Sources: Linnett M. Mabuku, "Green Purchasing and Corporate Strategy: A Case Study of UK Retail Firms and their International Supply Chains," M.Sc. Dissertation, Environmental Change Institute, University of Oxford, September 2001; Alan M. Rugman, John Kirton and Julie Soloway, *Environmental Regulations and Corporate Strategy* (Oxford: Oxford University Press, 1999); Michael Porter, *Competitive Advantage* (New York: Free Press, 1985).

Motors are also developing similar assembly plants to test their efficiency for future implementation to their other factories.[19]

A second approach is to tap low-cost labor sources. A good example is the *maquiladora* industry (as discussed in Chapter 6) that has sprung up in Mexico just across the US border. Hundreds of American plants have been established in this area. Examples include TRW Inc., which has a factory where workers assemble seat belts, and Mattel, which has a plant where workers turn out Barbie-doll houses and Disney teething rings.[20] Labor costs in these facilities are less than 20 per cent of those of similar workers in the United States. Also, because this is a free trade zone, US duties are levied on the imports only to the extent of the value added in Mexico, so low wage rates in Mexico help keep down the import duty.

A third approach is the development of new methods used to cut costs.[21] For example, in the United States, it is typical for a firm to calculate selling price after a new product is developed. If the price is judged to be too high, the product is sent back to the drawing board to be reworked, or the company accepts smaller profit on the product. A different system has been introduced in Japan, where firms begin by determining the target cost of the product *before* going into design, engineering, and supplier pricing, and the latter groups then work to bring the product in at the desired price (see Figure 10.2). This unique cost-management system is helping Japanese firms cut costs and undersell competitors.[22]

A fourth method that is gaining popularity with MNEs is that of costing products not on an individual basis but as part of a portfolio of related goods. Instead of evaluating the

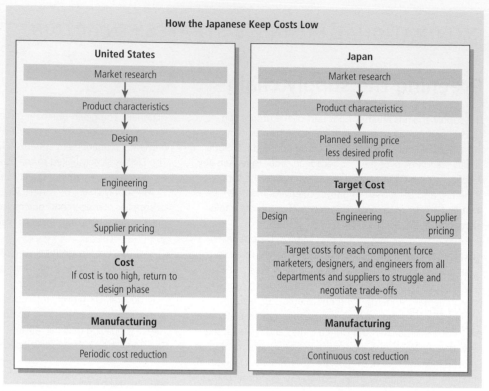

Figure 10.2 Cost reduction approaches: the United States versus Japan
Source: Ford S. Worthy, "Japan's Smart Secret Weapon," *Fortune*, August 12, 1991, p. 73.

expenses of developing one new soft drink, for example, a company looks at the costs and revenues associated with the entire line of beverages. Coca-Cola of Japan provides an example. Every year it introduces more than 1,000 new soft drinks, fruit drinks, and cold coffees into the Japanese market. Ninety per cent of them fail, but this does not stop Coke from introducing approximately one new product a month. From a cost accounting standpoint this is not a profitable strategy. However, as one Coke executive in Japan puts it, "We know that some of these . . . products will survive only a month or two, but our competitors have them, so we have to have them."[23] As a result, Japan is Coca-Cola's most profitable market and the company sells a variety of non-carbonated drinks to complement its main brand.[24]

Quality

For well over a decade, quality has been one of the major criteria for business success.[25] As the president of an international consulting firm puts it, "Products are expected to be nearly perfect."[26] Nowhere is this more clearly reflected than in the auto industry, where the Japanese have garnered a large share of the international market by using what is called kaizen, or continuous improvement.[27] A good example is Toyota Motors, which has continually worked to reduce costs and improve quality. One way Toyota has achieved this goal is partly through large R&D expenditures. Another is through meticulous design, engineering, and production processes that ensure a proper fit of all parts and overall durability of the unit.[28] In recent years US auto manufacturers have also succeeded in improving their quality, gaining market share as a result. European car makers today are also heavily focused on quality, aware that the Japanese are a major threat to their markets.[29]

Other excellent examples of MNEs that have succeeded because of a strong focus on quality include such lesser-known firms as Stanley Works, the WD-40 Co., and A. T. Cross.

Kaizen
A Japanese term that means continuous improvement

Stanley Works manufactures tape measures in Asia, then has the accuracy of samples checked by sophisticated laser computers back in New Britain, Connecticut, before selling them worldwide. Stanley has also developed a host of other high-quality products, from double-toothed saws that cut on both the upstroke and the downstroke for the Asian market, to hammers without claws for carpenters in Central Europe (who prefer to use pliers to pull out bent nails), to levels shaped like elongated trapezoids, which the French market prefers.

The WD-40 Co. of San Diego manufactures WD-40, a water-displacing lubricant that fights rust, cleans heel marks from linoleum and walls, and provides a variety of other services around the house. Car mechanics use it to loosen sticky valves and remove moisture from balky carburetors; handymen apply it to frozen locks and screws. Today the blue-and-yellow spray can is found in stores throughout the world, where it enjoys fanatical customer loyalty. WD-40 is a best-seller in Great Britain and is rapidly gaining market share throughout Europe and Asia.[30]

A. T. Cross of Providence, Rhode Island, has been manufacturing mechanical pens and pencils for almost 150 years. The units are assembled by hand and "every one of the company's hourly employees is a quality control expert who is responsible for checking the tolerances of the engraved grooves to within one ten-thousandth of an inch and for detecting nearly microscopic scratches or the slightest clotting of ink on a pen ball."[31] A. T. Cross's product quality is so high that, despite a lifetime guarantee, less than 2 per cent of its products are ever returned for repair. Today these pens and pencils are one of the most popular US-made gifts in Japan.[32]

Production systems

A **production system** is a group of related activities designed to create value. In the generation of goods and services this system includes location, layout, and material handling.

Production system
A group of related activities designed to create value

Location

Location is important because of its impact on production and distribution costs. Many MNEs have found that governments (national and local) are willing to provide tax breaks or other financial incentives to encourage them to set up operations. Accompanying considerations include the availability and cost of labor, raw materials, water, and energy as well as the development of the country's transportation and communication systems. As noted earlier, many suppliers set up operations near their major customers. So Ford has built up an integrated production network in Western Europe (see Map on Ford Fiesta production network). Ford suppliers are part of this production network so as to maintain their business relationship. Location is also important to service enterprises because they usually require face-to-face contact with their customers. Hotels and airlines are typical examples. Personal service firms such as those of accountants, lawyers, and management consultants also fall into this category.[33]

Layout

Plant layout is important because of its impact on efficiency. For example, most auto producers use an assembly line layout in which the workers remain at their station and, as the cars move past them, perform the necessary functions such as installing radios, air conditioners, interior trim, and so on. In the case of Volvo, the employees work in small teams to build an entire car and the plant is laid out to accommodate this work flow.[34] In other manufacturing settings, however, worldwide competitive firms tend to use U-shaped-cell flow lines, which are more efficient. Schonberger, an internationally known manufacturing expert, has noted that U-shaped production designs enable one person to tend several

Ford Fiesta production network

United Kingdom
Belfast: Carburetors and distributors
Dagenham: Final assembly. Body panels, engine, foundry production of casting for all engines
Enfield: Instruments, fuel and water gauges, plugs
Treforest: Spark plug insulators
Leamington: Foundry production of engine components
Basildon: Radiators, water pump assembly, engine components

Belgium
Genk: Body panels, road wheels

Germany
Wulfrath: Transmission parts, engine components
Cologne: Die-cast transaxle casing, gear engine components
Saarlouis: Final assembly. Body panels, fuel tanks, trim production

France
Bordeaux: Transmissions

Spain
Valencia: Final assembly. Body panels, engines, trim production

workstations and increase the speed at which materials can be delivered and defective parts can be reworked.[35] Finally, Maytag has chosen to combine different layouts to cater to each production line in just one factory. A traditional long conveyer belt assembly-line makes its standardized models. A second area makes more sophisticated models in smaller production cells instead of a long line. The third area makes the most sophisticated machines. In this setting, workers work as craftsmen putting together a substantial part of the machine.[36]

Layout varies widely in service organizations, although it appears to be universal in use. Most hotels, regardless of the country, have the check-in and check-out areas in the same place as such support groups as the bellhops, concierge, and cashier. In fast-food units, the food preparation area is situated so that the personnel can quickly serve both in-unit and drive-through customers. In movie theatres, the concession area is located in the lobby and the projection room at the back of the theater.

Material handling
The careful planning of when, where, and how much inventory will be available to ensure maximum production efficiency

Process mapping
A flow charting of every step that goes into producing a product

Material handling

Material handling involves the careful planning of when, where, and how much inventory will be available to ensure maximum production efficiency. Part of this is resolved through careful inventory control processes. Part of it is handled when the production layout is determined. For example, General Electric uses process mapping, a flowchart that shows every small step in producing a product. As a result, the company is able to study every part of an operation and determine those that are redundant or that can be streamlined. Consequently, the company has been able to reduce work time on some jobs by as much as 50 per cent.[37]

Inventory control

Inventory control has received a great deal of attention in recent years because a well-designed inventory strategy can have dramatic effects on the bottom line.[38] One of the most popular concepts has been just-in-time inventory (JIT for short), which is based on delivering parts and supplies just as they are needed. If this concept were carried to the extreme, it would mean that manufacturers would not need to store materials because suppliers would be delivering them just in time for shipment to the factory floor.

JIT is an important concept that has been adopted by MNEs throughout the world. However, the degree of use varies based on the product and the company's production strategy. For example, the Big Three US auto makers use JIT to keep inventory to a minimum. In Japan, firms like Toyota have taken the concept even further and apply it the same way airlines handle reservations: Supply is matched directly to demand. Dealers order directly from the factory, which means that customers can get their built-to-order car in 7 to 10 days.

One of the major problems with JIT is that its success rests heavily on the quality and reliability of the suppliers. In Japan, where MNEs often have an equity position in these companies, suppliers will go out of their way to meet partners' demands. However, in the United States and Europe, most suppliers are independent businesses that work under a contract relationship, so the bonds are often not as strong between the two parties. This helps explain why Toyota, which buys US-made parts for cars made in the United States, also keeps Japanese-made parts on hand as insurance against defective US materials.[39]

A second problem with JIT is that, although it works well in managing delivery of parts to the assembly line, few firms have been able to apply the concept to the entire production process. Most firms still manufacture and ship their output to dealers to sell, in contrast to Toyota's approach of matching supply and demand before producing.

One of the most important things to remember about JIT is that it needs strong support from the workers and the suppliers. Everyone must be operating in unison. If the workers are slow, there will be excess inventory on hand; if the supplier is late, the workers will be sitting by idly.

Demand-Flow™ Technology (DFT) is a production process that allows for flexible changes in the middle stages of production. Typically used to produce standardized assembly products, such as computers, DFT permits quick reactions to changes in demand and technology. A surge of demand for Pentium IV computers, for instance, would immediately shift inputs from other computers to be combined with Pentium IV chips to respond to demand. This virtually eliminates inventories.[40] Intermec, a company that makes bar code scanners, mobile computers, and related products, reduced inventory by 50 per cent after implementing DFT. It was also able to consolidate five different printer lines into one flexible mixed-model line, decreasing the amount of required manufacturing floor space by 20 per cent.[41]

Developing a strong service orientation

As noted earlier, many products have a service element associated with them. Sometimes this element is more important than the product itself. For example, many people will not purchase a car or home appliance unless it can be serviced easily. Service is also important

Just-in-time (JIT) inventory
The delivery of parts and supplies just as they are needed

Demand-Flow™ Technology (DFT)
A production process that is flexible to demand changes

Product-dominated businesses	Equally balanced	Service-dominated businesses
Farm produce (corn, wheat, etc.)	Aircraft manufacturing	Advertising agency
Home construction	Fast-food unit	Theater production
Auto production	TV network	Teaching

Figure 10.3 Product- and service-dominated businesses

when choosing a bank, insurance agent, lawyer, or doctor. Many of the ideas we have discussed in this section, including sourcing, cost, and quality, are also key factors in shopping for services. In addressing this area, MNEs will do two things: (1) consider whether their strategy needs to be oriented toward a product, a service, or a combination of the two; and (2) determine the ideal degree of service to provide.

Determining the product/Service balance

Some outputs lend themselves to a strong production orientation, whereas others require much more attention to service. Figure 10.3 offers an illustration. Designed more as a point of reference than as a factual source that addresses every firm in the respective industry, the figure nonetheless shows that some MNEs need to have a strong product-dominated focus whereas others benefit most from a service orientation. A good example is offered by aircraft manufacturers that must be concerned with both ends of the continuum. Olympus and Pentax, both manufacturers of flexible endoscopic equipment, provide another example. To develop their brand names in Latin America, these companies offer medical professionals the surgical training necessary to use their equipment. Because after-sale service is also an important consideration for prospective buyers, including hospitals, all major endoscope manufacturers have service stations in the region.

On the other hand, some manufactured products require far less service than they used to need. A good example is photocopiers. Manufacturers of these machines have improved product quality so substantially that many units are now sold on the basis of price. Service is no longer a major factor because everyone's product is of such high quality.

Knowing whether to sell on the basis of product or service (or a combination of the two) is critical to the success of many MNEs. A mistake at this point can result in emphasis on the wrong sales factors.

Providing the right amount of service

Once the MNE has determined the proper balance of product and service domination, it evaluates the specific type of service warranted. This is particularly important because many MNEs find that the strategy used in their own country does not work overseas. A good example is the Japanese approach to retail services.[42] The amount of personal service provided in Japan would surprise many Westerners. For example, auto dealers typically provide pick-up and delivery for repair service customers and make new car sales calls to customers' homes. In department stores, it is common to find executives and sales clerks alike lined up to bow to the first customers in the store. Japanese banks often help their customers sell or buy homes, find distributors for merchandise, and provide them with tax advice.

Although these services help Japanese companies maintain customer satisfaction, research has found that they are of little value to doing business in other countries. For example, Japanese banks in the United States have discovered that US customers want only a limited amount of quality service; they prefer quantity and efficiency in the form of a variety of different services offered at low prices. As a result, Japanese banks here offer the same types of services as do other US banks. Would they be more successful if they changed this strategy and tried to emulate the approach used back home? Given the nature of the US market, they believe this would be a mistake. The lesson is clear: When competing in terms of service, one must match the competition but not exceed it unless the customer is willing to pay for this service. In the United States, the banking customer is not willing.[43]

 ### Active learning check

Review your answer to Active Learning Case question 2 and make any changes you like. Then compare your answer with the one below.

2 How has GE used Six Sigma to reduce cost and improve quality in consumer goods? In each case, give an example.

Six Sigma allows GE to use process mapping to reduce cost by identifying those activities that can be eliminated or combined in the production process. For example, can an individual who is performing one assembly line task take on other tasks and thus reduce the number of people needed to produce the product? Can inventory be ordered and delivered in smaller amounts, thus making greater use of just-in-time? Consideration of these types of questions can help reduce cost. In improving product quality, the work group can examine how well all parts of the product fit together, examine the durability of the unit, and look for additional ways of testing the product to ensure that it measures up to quality standards.

INTERNATIONAL LOGISTICS

International logistics is the designing and managing of a system to control the flow of materials and products throughout the firm. This includes the inflow of materials, movement through the production process, and outflow to the wholesale/retail firm or final consumer. International logistics is an important area of strategic consideration because these expenses can account for 10 per cent of their total costs.[44] The material management aspect of international logistics has already been addressed. The following discussion examines three other key topics: transportation, packaging, and storage.

> **International logistics**
> The designing and managing of a system to control the flow of materials and products throughout the organization

Transportation

In examining international logistics, we focus on the primary modes of transportation: ocean and air. The others—rail, pipeline, and motor carrier—are of importance in some regions (such as the European Union), but they are not as commonly used in moving goods from an MNE's plant to their final destination. Moreover, their use is highly dependent on the infrastructure of the country—that is, the extensiveness and quality of the nation's road system and railroad network. In many non-triad countries the infrastructure is poor and the MNE's use of them is greatly limited.

Ocean shipping

International firms can choose from a fairly wide variety of ocean carriers. The three most common carriers are conventional container ships, cargo vessels, and roll-on-roll-off (RORO) vessels. **Container ships** are used to carry standardized containers that can be simply loaded onto the carrier and then unloaded at their destination, without any repackaging of the contents of the containers. **Unconventional cargo vessels** are used for shipping

> **Container ships**
> Vessels used to carry standardized containers that can be simply loaded onto a carrier and then unloaded at their destination without any repackaging of the contents of the containers

> **Unconventional cargo vessels**
> Vessels used for shipping oversized and unusual cargoes

Roll-on-roll-off (RORO) vessels
Ocean-going ferries that can carry trucks that drive onto built-in ramps and roll off at the point of debarkation

Lighter aboard ship (LASH) vessel
Barges stored on a ship and lowered at the point of destination

oversized and unusual cargoes. Roll-on-roll-off (RORO) vessels are ocean-going ferries that can carry trucks that drive onto built-in ramps and roll off at the point of debarkation. A carrier similar to the RORO is the lighter aboard ship (LASH) vessel, which consists of barges that are stored on the ship and lowered at the point of destination. These individual barges can then operate on inland waterways.

One of the major problems in planning an ocean shipping strategy is the limitations caused by the lack of ports and port services. In developing countries, for example, seaports sometimes lack the equipment necessary to load or unload container cargo, thus limiting the country's ability to export and import. In recent years a number of third world countries have been working to improve their ports so they can become more active in the international trade arena.

Air shipping

Most countries have airports that can accommodate air freight. The problem with this mode of transportation is its high cost. Thus, although international air freight has grown dramatically over the last 30 years, it still accounts for less than 1 per cent of the total volume of international shipments. It is used in trade more commonly among industrialized nations than any others, and it is usually restricted to high-value items that must reach their destination quickly.

Several developments have occurred over the past couple of decades that have helped increase the use of air shipments. These include more efficient ground facilities, larger aircraft, and better marketing of these services to shippers. In particular, the development by aircraft manufacturers of jumbo cargo jet planes and combination passenger and cargo aircraft has helped immensely.

Choice criteria

In deciding the best transportation mode to use, MNEs tend to focus on four important criteria: time, predictability, cost, and noneconomic factors.

Time

The period between departure and arrival of a carrier can vary significantly between an ocean freighter and an aircraft. So one of the questions a firm must answer is: How quickly is delivery needed? A number of factors can influence the answer. One is the perishability of the product. Exotic flowers from South America are flown to the United States because they would not survive a sea voyage. A second factor is how soon the goods are needed to replenish current stocks. Autos from Japan are brought into the United States by ship because the length of the trip does not hurt the supply of cars on hand at local dealerships.

In businesses where speed is critical, companies are now coordinating their worldwide supply chains in order to reduce the amount of time needed to get the goods through the production cycle and to the customer. Victor Fung, CEO of Li & Fung, Hong Kong's largest export trading company and an innovator in the development of supply chain management, has provided an example of how this is being done:

> Say we get an order from a European retailer to produce 10,000 garments. It's not a simple matter of our Korean office sourcing Korean products or our Indonesian office sourcing Indonesian products. For this customer we might decide to buy yarn from a Korean producer but have it woven and dyed in Taiwan. So we pick the yarn and ship it to Taiwan. The Japanese have the best zippers and buttons, but they manufacture them mostly in China. Okay, so we go to YKK, a big Japanese zipper manufacturer, and we order the right zippers from their Chinese plants. Then we determine that, because of quotas and labor conditions, the best place to make the garments is Thailand. So we ship everything there. And because the customer needs quick delivery, we may divide the order across five factories in Thailand. Effectively, we are customizing the value chain

to best meet the customer's needs. Five weeks after we have received the order, 10,000 garments arrive on the shelves in Europe, all looking like they came from one factory, with colors, for example, perfectly matched.[45]

Predictability

Although both air and water transportation are basically reliable, they are subject to the vagaries of nature. Bad weather can close an airport; inadequate seaport facilities can slow the loading and unloading of cargo. Because of the great difference in delivery time between the two modes, the choice is often obvious. If a company needs to have a package delivered tomorrow, it will come by air; if the firm wants to clear merchandise out of the warehouse today but the international customer does not need it for 90 days, it will be sent by water. However, certain carriers are more reliable than others, and the MNE will use its experience in determining which companies to choose for delivery. Reliability is particularly important for air shipments, where the difference of one day could significantly influence the salability of the product.

Cost

The expense associated with shipping is a major consideration when choosing an international transportation mode. Because air freight is significantly more costly than shipment by water, the cost must be economically justifiable. Typically, an MNE will use air shipments only when time is critical and/or the product has high value. For example, if the company has purchased expensive watches in Zurich for its specialty outlets in New York and San Francisco, the watches will be flown to the retailers. Similarly, if a London-based MNE has bought a US-made supercomputer for the home office and wants it installed immediately, the unit will be flown over from the United States. On the other hand, if the merchandise is bulky or the cost of air freight is a significant portion of the value of the product, it will be sent by water. Autos are exported by ship, as are bulk commodities and resources such as oil and coal.

Noneconomic factors

Sometimes noneconomic factors influence the choice of transportation mode. For example, in the United States all government cargo must use national flag carriers when available, so there is seldom a question of how to send these goods. Similarly, other governments own or subsidize their carriers, and there is pressure on MNEs to use these transportation modes when doing business with those countries. Such political considerations must be taken into account when formulating the transportation strategy.

Packaging

Packaging is important in ensuring that a product is shipped in a safe container and arrives undamaged. When goods are transported a long distance or to areas with climates different from the one where they are manufactured, the container can prevent spoilage or leakage. Chemicals, for example, must be carefully sealed in containers that can withstand impact and will not crack open if tipped over or dropped. Machines, such as personal computers, must have interior packing that prevents damage during transit.

Packaging is also important because of its direct effect on cost. If units must be shipped in odd-shaped containers, fewer of them can be loaded into the hold of the transport than if they are shipped in square or rectangular containers and can be loaded atop and alongside each other. The weight of the packing material is also important, especially when goods are being shipped by air and costs are based on both distance and weight.

Intermodal containers
Large metal boxes that fit on trucks, railroads, and airplanes and help reduce handling costs and theft losses by placing the merchandise in a tightly sealed, easy-to-move unit

Packaging is also important in reducing loading and unloading costs and minimizing theft and pilferage. In recent years many shippers have begun using intermodal containers, which are large metal boxes that fit on trucks, railroad trains, and airplanes and help cut handling costs and theft losses by placing the merchandise in an easy-to-move unit that is tightly sealed.

As more goods are shipped internationally, packaging will continue to be a focal point of attention. Such considerations can help an MNE maximize shipping space and minimize transportation costs.

Storage

In some cases, goods that are shipped internationally have to be stored before being moved to their final destinations. In the United States, public storage is widely available. In other countries, including Japan, warehousing facilities are in short supply. Additionally, the configuration of many warehouses is different from that in the United States. Ceilings are often lower and there is little automation for handling such common chores as loading and unloading packages or stacking containers on top of each other. In such cases, the MNE must decide whether to invest in warehouse facilities or ship goods only when needed, thus eliminating the warehouse function.

Foreign trade zones
Areas where foreign goods may be held and processed and then re-exported without incurring customs duties (same as a free trade zone)

As discussed in Chapter 6, some countries have foreign trade zones, which are areas where foreign goods may be held and processed and then re-exported without incurring customs duties (same as a free trade zone). These zones are usually found at major ports of entry (including international air terminals). Their effective use can help an MNE (1) temporarily store its goods while breaking a large shipment into smaller ones to be shipped to other locales; (2) combine small shipments into larger ones and then reship them; (3) process the goods and perform a host of value-added activities before repackaging them for the market; and (4) give those goods that will remain in the local market a "made in" status so that they can be sold as locally produced products.

An effective storage strategy can be particularly helpful in carrying out the final stages of an MNE's production plan. The strategy can also help minimize overall product cost, reduce delivery time, and increase customer satisfaction.[46]

DIFFERENT KINDS OF GLOBAL PRODUCTION SYSTEMS

Location is a key factor in deciding the global structure of firms' production systems. But it needs to be considered alongside other factors which vary considerably by industry.

Companies tend to focus on the functions and innovation activities where they have the major advantage and often outsource activities, or parts of the value chain where they add less value. This determines the "boundaries" of the firm, what activities are internalized and what are externalized or left to other firms to provide on a contract basis. Figure 10.4 shows a number of example industries and firms that have very different global production systems, determined by the functions and activities that add the most value.

Although Intel does a lot of marketing, its main competitive advantage lies in the continual development of new semiconductors, the heart of PCs and other IT and electronic devices. Product and process development are internalized and highly centralized because this suits the type of technology and product that the firm focuses on. It alone accounts for around 25 per cent of all R&D investment in the semiconductor industry. Much of its high-value manufacturing, particularly wafer production and fabrication, is done in the United States, where 75 per cent of its manufacturing workforce is based. Other production sites

Production system / Where is the value added?	Internalized (within the firm's hierarchy)	Mixed	Externalized (to other firms in the market)
R&D/technology	Example: semiconductors (Intel)		Example: telecoms (Ericsson)
Manufacturing		Example: autos (Toyota)	
Marketing			Example: clothing (Gap)

Figure 10.4 Global production systems: where is the value added?

Source: Adapted from *UNCTAD World Investment Report 2002.*

are in Israel and Ireland. Much of its labor-intensive assembly and testing takes place in Malaysia, Philippines, China, and Costa Rica, but is owned by Intel (internalized).

Ericsson also keeps much of its research, design, and development activities within the firm but not so long ago decided to let other firms make many of the components that make up its telecoms systems. In 2001 Flextronics, a $14.5 billion Singaporean firm, took over much of Ericsson's manufacturing and supply chain activities in Brazil, Malaysia, Sweden, and the UK. It externalized these activities because it decided they were not part of its core competences, and it could safely contract other firms to supply these components. (See Real Case "Flextronics" at the end of this chapter.)

Gap Inc. and other clothing firms have externalized the manufacturing function for many years now. Their focus is clothing design, marketing, branding, and real-estate management. There are enough producers in cheap labor locations (such as China, which exports more garments than any other country by far) for Gap to use the market to contract out this activity to the cheapest and/or best. Intermediaries in this industry, like Flextronics in telecoms, include Mast Industries, which works with 400 factories in 37 countries, and Li and Fung, a $5 billion Hong Kong company that connects around 700 US and European brand owners with a network of 7,500 suppliers (1.5 million workers) around the world (of which 2,000 are active at any one time).

Toyota lies in the middle of these two extremes. Because manufacturing, and particularly maintaining continuous improvement in manufacturing, is so central to its competitive advantage, Toyota is partly vertically-integrated down the supply chain. New product development (new car models and features) and process development (improving price and quality) are closely linked and involve good relationships with (and/or ownership of some) component suppliers. It cannot externalize car production because it is the source of many of its core competitive advantages.

Finally, for diversified or multi-product firms, configuring the right kind of global production system can get complicated. Philips, for example, makes semiconductors, like Intel, but also has large consumer electronics and consumer products divisions. It has to manage both technology-driven and market-driven innovation and production activities.

STRATEGIC MANAGEMENT AND PRODUCTION STRATEGY

MNEs are currently focusing on a number of areas in improving their production strategies. Three that are getting particular attention include (1) technology and design; (2) continuous improvement of operations; and (3) the use of strategic alliances and acquisitions.

Technology and production design

MNEs are now spending more money on R&D than they have in the past. For example, Aventis, Eli Lilly, AstraZeneca, and Pfizer spend over 15 per cent of their revenues in R&D. These are the backroom for the introduction of new pharmaceutical products.[47] Yet, R&D is not only developing new products, but also helping firms find alternative parts as well as production techniques.

A second current trend is the use of concurrent engineering, which was discussed earlier in the chapter. Many MNEs are now realizing that a team approach to product development, which combines the talents of research, design, and manufacturing people as well as customers and clients, results in a more successful product. Ford Motors is an excellent example. Ford put together a group called Team Taurus to develop its Taurus and Sable automobile lines. Team members were drawn from designing, engineering, and production and were brought together with customers. Collectively the group discussed how to build the new cars and replaced the sequential approach to manufacturing autos (first design the cars, then produce them, then market them) with a concurrent approach that involved addressing the design, production, and marketing issues all at the same time. The result of this strategy was a Taurus that captured a significant market niche and helped Ford close the gap between itself and the competition.[48]

Coupled with these strategies are innovative human resource development programs that are designed around the concept of empowerment, which involves giving employees greater control over their work. This strategy is particularly effective because it creates a feeling of pride and ownership in the job and makes employees feel they are important assets. The use of empowerment is not limited to the research and design areas; it is important in all phases of production, beginning with product creation. Additionally, if things go smoothly at this early stage of the production cycle, there are likely to be fewer problems later on.

Empowerment
The process of giving employees increased control over their work

Continuous improvement

Due to the success of Japanese MNEs, *kaizen* (continuous improvement) is being emulated by MNEs worldwide. No matter what the good or service is, every day the company tries to do the job better. Some consultants have referred to this strategy as "rapid inch-up,"[49] which certainly captures the essence of the concept. US firms in particular have benefited from this idea. A good example can be found in the automotive industry. In the 1980s and 1990s, Toyota and Honda were able to offset the rising value of the yen with cost saving in their factories, thus allowing them to hold the price line on many of their new cars. These innovations were exported to US plants. By the early 2000s, however, American firms had successfully fought back by imitating and improving Japanese production techniques. In 2004, four of the five most efficient auto plants in the United States were owned by GM.[50]

A large number of firms helped account for these results. One is Xerox, internationally known for its photocopiers. At the beginning of the 1980s the company was losing market share to overseas competitors. However, the firm then began implementing a production strategy for dramatically improving quality and reducing cost. Today Xerox is again a world leader in copiers.

Another example is TPG, which services Ford's Toronto factory by arranging for 800 deliveries a day from 300 parts makers. The parts arrive at 12 different stages of production within 10 minutes of scheduled time to decrease the amount of parts inventory in the plant.[51]

As discussed in an earlier section, just-in-time (JIT) is a related concept the MNEs are using to achieve continuous improvement. In the past JIT was used almost exclusively for managing inventory, but now the concept is being employed in other ways. For example,

Toyota's use of JIT helps it assemble a car in 13 labor-hours, compared to 19 to 22 labor-hours for Honda, Nissan, and Ford.

Alliances and acquisitions

Another current strategic production trend is the development of alliances and acquisitions. Many MNEs are finding they cannot compete effectively without entering into joint ventures or other alliances with MNEs that can complement their production strategy. For example, Compaq is well known for its personal computers, but many of the components in these machines are purchased from outside suppliers or are developed by these firms under an alliance agreement. When Compaq needed a hard disk drive for its first laptops, it financed Conner Peripherals, a Silicon Valley start-up with a disk drive already under way, rather than develop the machine in-house. More recently, Compaq has ventured into the market for powerful desktop workstations used primarily by scientists and engineers. Instead of going head-to-head with market leaders such as Sun Microsystems and Hewlett-Packard, the company assembled a dozen hardware and software firms, including these two computer giants, and put together an alliance aimed at defining a new technical standard for high-speed desktop computing. The objective of the alliance is to develop a standard that will suit any workstation, thus allowing customers the freedom to buy the latest, fastest machine without fear of being tied to any single manufacturer.

Compaq's approach is not unique; the Japanese *keiretsu* system has been using it for years.[52] In fact, some researchers claim that industry alliances account for more of the success of Japanese firms than does just-in-time or any other manufacturing technique. Working in unison with each other, *keiretsu* companies have been able to wield a great deal of power. Many have monthly meetings in which they exchange information and ideas. Table 10.2 provides a brief overview of six of the country's major *keiretsu* members. Looking closely at the table, we see that it illustrates how valuable cooperation among the members can be. The idea has not been lost on US firms, among others, which are now beginning to put together their own "mini-*keiretsus*." For example, Eastman Kodak has acquired a number of distributors in Japan and has taken small stakes in some 50 suppliers and customers, and IBM is investing venture capital in a host of small European computer-related firms. Motorola has not taken equity positions, but it uses a *keiretsu* approach by developing extremely close ties with suppliers.

Table 10.2 Japan's biggest business groups that regularly attend monthly council meetings

	Mitsubishi	Mitsui	Sumitomo	Fuyo	DKB	Sanwa
Financial services	Mitsubishi Bank Mitsubishi Trust & Banking Meiji Mutual Life Tokio Marine & Fire	Mitsui Taiyo Kobe Bank Mitsui Trust & Banking Mitsui Mutual Life Taisho Marine & Fire	Sumitomo Bank Sumitomo Trust & Banking Sumitomo Life Sumitomo Marine & Fire	Fuji Bank Yasuda Trust & Banking Yasuda Mutual Life Yasuda Fire & Marine	Dai-Ichi Kangyo Bank Asahi Mutual Life Taisei Fire & Marine Fukoku Mutual Life Nissan Fire & Marine Kankaku Securities Orient	Sanwa Bank Toyo Trust & Banking Nippon Life Orix
Computers, electronics and electrical equipment	Mitsubishi Electric	Toshiba	NEC	Oki Electric Industry Yokogawa Electric Hitachi*	Fujitsu Fuji Electric Yaskawa Electric Mfg. Nippon Columbia Hitachi*	Iwatsu Electric Sharp Nitto Denko Kyocera Hitachi*

Table 10.2 (Continued)

	Mitsubishi	Mitsui	Sumitomo	Fuyo	DKB	Sanwa
Cars	Mitsubishi Motors	Toyota Motor*		Nissan Motor	Isuzu Motors	Daihatsu Motor
Trading and retailing	Mitsubishi	Mitsui Mitsukoshi	Sumitomo	Marubeni	C. Itoh Nissho Iwai* Kanematsu Kawasho Seibu Dept. Store	Nissho Iwai* Nichimen Iwatani International Takashimaya
Food and beverages	Kirin Brewery	Nippon Flour Mills		Nisshin Flour Milling Sapporo Breweries Nichirei		Itoham Foods Suntory
Construction	Mitsubishi Construction	Mitsui Construction Sanki Engineering	Sumitomo Construction	Taisei	Shimizu	Toyo Construction Obayashi Sekisui House Zenitaka
Metals	Mitsubishi Steel Mfg. Mitsubishi Materials Mitsubishi Aluminum Mitsubishi Cable Industries	Japan Steel Works Mitsui Mining & Smelting	Sumitomo Metal Industries Sumitomo Metal Mining Sumitomo Electric Industries Sumitomo Light Metal Industries	NKK	Kawasaki Steel Kobe Steel* Japan Metals & Chemicals Nippon Light Metal Furukawa Furukawa Electric	Kobe Steel* Nakayama Steel Works Hitachi Metals Nisshin Steel Hitachi Cable
Real estate	Mitsubishi Estate	Mitsui Real Estate Development	Sumitomo Realty & Development	Tokyo Taternono	Tokyo Dome	
Oil and coal	Mitsubishi Oil			Tonen	Showa Shell Sekiyu	Cosmo Oil
Rubber and glass	Asahi Glass		Nippon Sheet Glass		Yokohama Rubber	Toyo Tire & Rubber
Chemicals	Mitsubishi Kasei Mitsubishi PetroChemic Mitsubishi Gas Chemical Mitsubishi Plastics Mitsubishi Kasei Poly	Mitsui Toatsu Chemicals Mitsui Petrochemical Industries	Sumitomo Chemical Sumitomo Bakelite	Showa Denko Nippon Oil & Fats Kureha Chemical Industries	Kyowa Hakko Kogyo Denki Kagaku Kogyo Nippon Zeon Asahi Denka Kogyo Sankyo Shiseido Lion	Ube Industries Tokuyoma Soda Hitachi Chemical Sekisui Chemical Kansai Paint Tanabe Seiyaku Fujisawa Pharmaceuticals
Fibers and textiles	Mitsubishi Rayon	Toray Industries		Nisshinbo Industries Toho Rayon	Asahi Chemical Industry	Unitika Teijin
Pulp and paper	Mitsubishi Paper Mills	Oji paper		Sanyo-Kokusaku Pulp	Honshu Paper	
Mining and forestry		Mitsui Mining Hokkaido Colliery & Steamship	Sumitomo Forestry Sumitomo Coal Mining			
Industrial equipment	Mitsubishi Heavy Industries Mitsubishi Kakoki	Mitsui Engineering & Shipbuilding	Sumitomo Heavy Industries	Kubota Nippon Seiko	Niigata Engineering Iseki Ebara	NTN Hitachi Zosen

	Mitsubishi	Mitsui	Sumitomo	Fuyo	DKB	Sanwa
					Kawasaki Heavy Industries Ishikawajima-Harima Heavy Industries	Shin Meiwa Industry
Cameras and optics	Nikon			Canon	Asahi Optical	Hoya
Cement		Onoda Cement	Sumitomo Cement	Nihon Cement	Chichibu Cement	Osaka Cement
Shipping and transportation	Nippon Yusen Mitsubishi Warehouse & Transportation	Mitsui OSK lines Mitsui Warehouse	Sumitomo Warehouse	Shawa line Keihin Electric Express Railway Tobu Railway	Kawasaki Kisen Shibusawa Warehouse Nippon Express*	Navix Line Hankyu Nippon Express*

* Companies affiliated with more than one group.

Source: Adapted from *Fortune*, July 15, 1991, p. 81.

 Active learning check

Review your answer to Active Learning Case question 3 and make any changes you like. Then compare your answer with the one below.

3 In what way could best practices help GE develop more effective international strategies? Explain.

Best practices could help GE develop more effective international strategies by encouraging it to identify those MNEs that are most successful and then discover how they accomplish that feat. Do these firms manage to develop more new products than do their competitors? Or are they best at getting their new goods into the marketplace quickly? Do they produce the highest-quality goods? Or are they lowest-cost producers? What accounts for their ability to achieve such an excellent performance? By asking and answering these questions, GE can gain insights into how it needs to change its own production processes in order to emulate those MNEs successfully.

KEY POINTS

1   Many of today's goods and services will be replaced during the millennium with faster, more efficient, and cheaper substitutes. For this reason, MNEs need to continually research, develop, and bring new offerings to the marketplace. One way this is being done is through the use of time-to-market accelerators. A good example is concurrent engineering.

2   The generation of goods and services entails a number of specific functions. One is obtaining materials or supplies. Many MNEs have found that global sourcing is the best strategy because it helps keep down costs while providing a number of other benefits, including ensuring an ongoing source of supply and helping the company penetrate overseas markets.

3   In the production of goods and services, MNEs focus on a number of key factors, including cost, quality, and well-designed production systems. While these three factors are often interrelated, each merits specific attention. Multinationals have also developed very effective inventory control systems that help minimize carrying costs and increase

productivity. Attention is also focused on gaining the proper balance between production and service domination. Figure 10.3 illustrates this point.

4 International logistics is the designing and managing of a system to control the flow of materials and products throughout the firm. In addition to inventory control, this involves transportation, packaging, and storing.

5 MNEs are currently focusing on a number of areas in improving their production strategies. Three approaches that have been receiving particular attention include (1) technology and design, (2) continuous improvement of operations, and (3) the use of strategic alliances and acquisitions. These approaches are helping multinationals meet new product and service challenges while keeping costs down and quality up.

Key terms

- backward integration
- forward integration
- horizontal integration
- time-to-market accelerators
- modular integrated robotized system (MIRB)
- concurrent engineering
- global sourcing
- modular manufacturing
- *kaizen*
- production system
- material handling
- process mapping
- just-in-time (JIT) inventory
- Demand-Flow™ Technology (DFT)
- international logistics
- container ships
- unconventional cargo vessels
- roll-on-roll-off (RORO) vessels
- lighter aboard ship (LASH) vessels
- intermodal containers
- foreign trade zones
- empowerment

REVIEW AND DISCUSSION QUESTIONS

1 Why are MNEs so interested in new product development? Why do they not simply focus on improving their current offerings?

2 Why is speed to market such an important production strategy? Explain.

3 What are time-to-market accelerators? In what way is concurrent engineering one of these accelerators?

4 Why do many MNEs use global sourcing? Why do they not produce all the parts and materials in-house? Be complete in your answer.

5 Why are world-class suppliers often located next to world-class manufacturers? What forms of synergy often exist between the two groups?

6 How do MNEs try to cut production costs? Identify and describe three steps.

7 In what way is the continuous reduction cost method used by Japanese manufacturers different from the periodic cost reduction method employed by many US firms? Compare and contrast the two.

8 Some MNEs use a production strategy that involves costing a portfolio of related goods rather than just costing each individually. What is the logic behind this strategy?

9 How does *kaizen* help bring about increased quality? Is this approach limited to Japanese firms or are other MNEs using it as well?

10 What types of issues does an MNE confront when it seeks to improve its production system? Identify and describe three.

11 How does JIT help an MNE control its inventory? Give two examples.

12 How is employee training an important factor in implementing JIT and DFT production processes?

13 Why would an MNE want to determine the degree to which its primary business was product-dominated and service-dominated? Explain.

14 Why are MNEs concerned with international logistics? How does this help the companies increase their competitiveness?

15 In recent years MNEs have been focusing on a number of areas in improving their production strategies. What are two of these? Identify and describe each.

REAL CASE

Flextronics

Source: Corbis/Thomas White

You wouldn't think that company rivals such as Sony and Phillips, or Ericsson, Alcatel, and Motorola, would choose to share the same factories to build competing products, but that is just what has been happening since the emergence of electronic-manufacturing service providers (EMSs). Contract manufacturing has become a sweeping trend in electronics manufacturing. Companies unknown to the public, such as Flextronics, Solectron, Sanmina-SCI, Celestica, and Jabil, among others, now make such well-known products as IBM PCs, the Microsoft Xbox video console, Web TV set-top boxes for Phillips and Sony, and portable phones for Ericsson, Alcatel, and Motorola. In 2002, EMS industry revenues were estimated at $134 billion. The two largest EMS companies, Flextronics and Solectron, account for 9.7 per cent and 9.2 per cent of this market, respectively.

Flextronics, the largest EMS, is one of the *Fortune* Global 500 companies, but most end-customers who use its products have never heard of it. Incorporated in Singapore in 1990, the company had revenues of $14.5 billion in 2004 and design, engineering, and manufacturing operations in 29 countries across the world. Though officially headquartered in Singapore, the company has strong ties to the US market and most of its customers are US companies.

Flextronics specializes in handheld electronic devices, IT infrastructure, communications infrastructure, and computer and office automation. Over the last few years it has expanded by purchasing smaller EMS contractors and factories from its customers. In 2001, Flextronics purchased half of Xerox's office equipment-making operations for $220 million. The deal came with a five-year outsourcing contract for Flextronics to manufacture Xerox products. A similar deal was accomplished in 2000 when Casio sold a Japanese factory to Flextronics.

In 2003, only 35.9 per cent of Flextronics revenues originated in its home region market of Asia. More specifically, China is the company's largest market; 18 per cent of all revenues originate there. Another 15 per cent of its sales originate in Malaysia, while Mexico and Hungary account for 12 per cent and 11 per cent, respectively. No other country accounts for more than 10 per cent of Flextronics's revenues.

Because of lower transportation costs as a percentage of total value, electronics can be transported by air, whereas cars are always transported by sea. This is one main reason why contract manufacturing has been so successful in the electronics industry, where parts might travel the world over before it is a finished product.

Flextronics has six industrial parks in low-cost regions near each large triad market. In Asia, two industrial parks in China and a network of regional manufacturing facilities supply printers, cell phones, telephone switching boards, and PDAs, among other products. In the Americas, products from its two industrial parks (one in Mexico, one in Brazil) and its network of manufacturing facilities include automotive, telecommunications, networking equipment, and hardware products, among others. In Eastern Europe, Poland and Hungary host two industrial parks that are also supported by nearby manufacturing facilities ▶

305

and that produce telecommunications infrastructure, electronics for automotives, printers, and disposable cameras, among others.

The choice of location for production facilities is determined by the quality of the labor force, the cost of producing in the country, and the proximity to a triad market. Mexico, for example, is the low-cost region in the North American market. Brazil has the best industrial capabilities among countries in South America and strong ties to large international firms from Europe and North America. China has abundant labor, high expected economic growth, and proximity to the large Japanese market where international firms like Canon, NEC, and Sony are headquartered. Eastern Europe is the low-cost production area for Western European markets. It is no surprise that the Flextronics industrial park in Poland is located near a university from which it can acquire skilled labor.

EMSs do much more than provide cost-effective manufacturing. They help in the design of products to make them easier to manufacture; they also provide logistics services, such as material procurement, inventory management, vendor management, packaging and distribution, and automation of key components of the supply chain through advanced IT. In addition, they offer after-market services such as repair and warranty services.

Today's electronic manufacturers have come a long way from the cheap labor-based contractors that used to dominate the industry. Robotic automation is now a

significant part of the production process and is handled mostly by specialists. It is their manufacturing expertise that makes for lower costs, but EMSs provide many more advantages to OEMs. They decrease the risk of manufacturing because OEMs no longer need to make large investments on a new factory to create a new product that might or might not be successful. EMSs can also purchase inputs at lower prices because they are making cell phones not only for Alcatel, but also for Motorola and Ericsson, increasing their purchasing power.

Contract manufacturing accounts for less than one-fourth of electronic manufacturing; however, there are reasons to believe that EMS companies will dominate the industry in the future. This process will redefine the role of OEMs in the electronics industry to one of design and marketing.

Sources: "Have Factory, Will Travel," *Economist*, February 10, 2000; "Let the Bad Times Roll," *Economist*, April 5, 2001; "Gadget Wars," *Economist*, May 8, 2001; Jonathan Sprague, "Invasion of the Factory Snatchers," *Fortune*, August 15, 2002; "Xerox Sells Half Its Plants for $220 Million," *BBC.co.uk*, October 2, 2001; Flextronics, *Annual Report*, 2002; and www.solectron.com.

1 Keeping in mind that Flextronics does not sell to end-customers, how does that change your interpretation of the regional sales data presented in this case?

2 What effect does the emergence of EMSs have for new entrants into the electronics industry?

3 Why should OEMs be concerned about using EMSs?

REAL CASE

Nike

One of the rules of international production strategy is: Manufacture the highest-quality product and the world is likely to beat a path to your door. A number of firms help illustrate this rule. One is Nike, the sports shoe producer. Making a wide variety of high-quality shoes, Nike catalogues more than 800 models for use in approximately 25 sports. In 1999 it had 35 per cent of the world's market for training shoes (and 45 per cent in the United States). In 2004 its sales were over $10 billion. In an effort to keep ahead of the competition, Nike updates each shoe at least every six months. Most of these ideas are generated by Nike's R&D center in Beaverton, near Portland, Oregon, where physiologists and mechanical engineers study the stresses on an athlete's feet and collaborate with stylists on new shoe ideas.

Although Nike sells its products in over 140 countries and produces in more than 50, it is really a triad MNE. Over 92 per cent of its sales are in the triad markets of the United States, the European Union, and Asia. In 2000 there was a 15 per cent growth of sales in the EU, due mainly to a new distribution facility in Belgium and a new design house in Holland. Nike is still strong in its home market, with 40 per cent of all sales in the US athletic footwear market and more than 65 per cent of the basketball footwear market. About 60 per cent of its sales are still in its US home base.

Nike's high-quality production is matched by superb marketing skills. The world might be making a path to Nike's door, but the company makes sure the world knows where it is. It spends 11 per cent of its revenue on marketing, and its "swoosh" brand is recognized the world over. The company continues to use sports stars to endorse its products. Besides American stars like Tiger Woods and Andre Agassi, it has used European soccer players like Eric Catona and cricket players in India, and has gone to China to prepare for the 2008 Olympic games in Beijing. The idea is: If you can make the "cool" guys wear your products, the rest will follow.

Perhaps the only thing Nike does not like to be remembered for is the bad publicity around its labor practices in Asia. Nike has outsourced all of its production to low-wage areas. In 2004, China produced 36 per cent of its footwear, Vietnam 24 per cent, Indonesia 22 per cent, and Thailand 16 per cent. The remainder is manufactured in other developing countries. In addition, all its apparel is produced in 35 host countries by contract manufacturers. NGOs have criticized the poor working conditions in some of its Asian factories. In 1996, such criticism led to *Life* magazine publishing a story on Pakistani children stitching Nike's soccer balls. Another famous case occurred in 1997 when a Vietnam factory, owned by a Korean sub-contractor, was found to have unsafe working conditions. NGOs in the Western world started campaigns to boycott Nike, and demonstrators protested in front of Nike's stores. Allegations of long working hours, bad ventilation, and physical abuse on a mostly young female workforce has tarnished Nike's reputation.

Nike's industry dominance was a main reason for its being severely targeted. Many of its competitors were found to have the same labor practices, but were not subjected to the same level of criticism. Nike has a corporate responsibility initiative to improve working conditions in its own factories and help influence its suppliers. Despite this, the University of Michigan ended the use of Nike products in 2001.

Website: **www.nike.com**.

Sources: Adapted from Dylan Jones, "No More Mr. Nike Guy," *Sunday Times Magazine*, August 23, 1998; David Shook, "Why Nike is Dragging its Feet," *Business Week*, March 19, 2001; Sydney H. Schanberg, "On the Playgrounds of America, Every Kid's Goal Is to Score: In Pakistan, Where Children Stitch Soccer balls for Six Cents an Hour, the Goal Is to Survive," *Life*, June 1996; Harry Dunphy, "Nike to Improve Conditions," *Associated Press*, May 12, 1998; Nike, *Annual Report*, 2000.

1 What is the key to Nike's production strategy? Explain.

2 What are the advantages of frequent design changes in Nike's sneakers?

3 Why is it important for Nike to clean up its labor practices in Asia? How would you recommend the company approach the issue?

Endnotes

1 "(Still) Made in Japan," *The Economist*, April 7, 2004.
2 Also see Emily Thornton, "Mazda Learns To Like Those Intruders," *Business Week*, September 14, 1998, p. 172.
3 Alex Taylor III, "How Toyota Copes with Hard Times," *Fortune*, January 25, 1993, pp. 78–81; and Joah Muller and Katie Kerwin, "Detroit Is Cruising for Quality," *Business Week*, September 3, 2001.
4 For a good example of these challenges, see Ferdinand Protzman, "Daimler's Quest Collides with Slump," *New York Times*, August 3, 1993, pp. C 1, C 5.
5 C. W. L. Hill, *International Business: Competing in the Global Marketplace*, 3rd ed. (New York: McGraw-Hill, 2000); and http://www.hp.com.
6 Simon C. Collinson, "Organising Knowledge to Manage R&D: A UK-Japan Company Comparison," *R&D Management*, vol. 31. no. 3, pp. 335–347.
7 Nohria, N. and Ghoshal, S. *The Differentiated Network: Organising Multinational Corporations for Value Creation* (San Francisco: Jossey-Bass, 1997).
8 Malnight, T. W. "Emerging Structural Patterns within Multinational Corporations: Toward Process-based Structures," *Academy of Management Journal*, vol. 44, no. 6 (2001); and Hansen, M. T. and Løvås, B. "How Do Multinational Companies Leverage Technological Competencies? Moving from Single to Interdependent Explanations," *Strategic Management Journal*, vol. 25, no. 8/9 (2004).
9 See Don Clark, "Intel to Ship Its Next-Generation Chip in 1995, Boosts Outlay for Production," *Wall Street Journal*, January 28, 1994, p. B 5.
10 Gene Bylinsky, "Heroes of US Manufacturing," *Fortune*, March 20, 2000.
11 Also see C. K. Prahalad and Kenneth Lieberthal, "The End of Corporate Imperialism," *Harvard Business Review*, July/August 1998, pp. 69–79.
12 Joseph T. Vesey, "The New Competitors: They Think in Terms of 'Speed-to-Market'," *Academy of Management Executive*, May 1991, pp. 23–33; and "Re-inventing the Wheel," *Economist*, April 20, 2000.
13 Saul Hansell, "Is This the Factory of the Future?" *New York Times*, July 26, 1998, Section 3, pp. 1, 12.
14 Rebecca Blumenstein, "GM Is Building Plants in Developing Nations to Woo New Markets," *Wall Street Journal*, August 4, 1997, pp. A1, 5.
15 Gene Bylinsky, "Heroes of US Manufacturing," *Fortune*, March 20, 2000.
16 Larry Holyoke, William Spindle and Neil Gross, "Doing the Unthinkable," *Business Week*, January 10, 1994, pp. 52–53; and Andrew Pollack, "Nissan Plans to Buy More American Parts," *New York Times*, March 26, 1994, pp. 17, 26.

17 Michael E. Porter, *The Competitive Advantage of Nations* (New York: Free Press, 1990), p. 103.

18 For more on this, see Earl Landesman, "Ultimatum for US Auto Suppliers: Go Global or Go Under," *Journal of European Business*, May/June 1991, pp. 39–45.

19 "The Modular T," *Economist*, September 3, 1998; and David Welch, "Why Detroit is Going to Pieces," *Business Week*, September 3, 2001.

20 Larry Reibstein et al., "A Mexican Miracle?" *Newsweek*, May 20, 1991, p. 42.

21 Ernest Beck, "Why Foreign Distillers Find It So Hard to Sell Vodka to the Russians," *Wall Street Journal*, January 15, 1998, pp. A1, 8.

22 Ford S. Worthy, "Japan's Smart Secret Weapon," *Fortune*, August 12, 1991, pp. 72–75.

23 Ibid., p. 75.

24 Suh-kyung Yoon, "Working Up a Thirst to Quench Asia," *Far Eastern Economic Review*, February 1, 2001.

25 See Louis Kraar, "Korea Goes for Quality," *Fortune*, April 13, 1994, pp. 153–159; and Gale Eisenstodt, "Sullivan's Travels," *Forbes*, March 28, 1994, pp. 75–76.

26 Erick Calonius, "Smart Moves by Quality Champs," *Fortune*, Spring/Summer 1991, p. 24.

27 See, for example, Christopher Palmeri, "A Process That Never Ends," *Forbes*, December 21, 1992, pp. 52–54.

28 "The Car Company in Front," *Economist.com*, January 27, 2005.

29 Richard A. Melcher and Stewart Toy, "On Guard, Europe," *Business Week*, December 14, 1992, pp. 54–55.

30 Louis S. Richman, "What America Makes Best," *Fortune*, Spring/Summer 1991, p. 80.

31 Ibid., p. 81.

32 Michael Shari and Pete Engardio, "The Sweet Sound of Success," *Business Week*, September 8, 1997, p. 56.

33 See Michael E. McGrath and J. Gordon Stewart, "Professional Service Firms in Europe Move Toward Integrated European Practices," *Journal of European Business*, May/June 1991, pp. 26–30.

34 Steven Prokesch, "Edges Fray on Volvo's Brave New Humanistic World," *New York Times*, July 7, 1991, p. F5.

35 Richard J. Schonberger, *Building a Chain of Customers* (New York: Free Press, 1990), pp. 50–51.

36 "A Long March," *Economist.com*, July 12, 2001.

37 Thomas A. Stewart, "GE Keeps Those Ideas Coming," *Fortune*, August 12, 1991, p. 48.

38 Lucinda Harper, "Trucks Keep Inventories Rolling Past Warehouses to Production Line," *Wall Street Journal*, February 7, 1994, p. B 3.

39 Alex Taylor III, "Why Toyota Keeps Getting Better and Better and Better," *Fortune*, November 19, 1990, p. 79.

40 Gene Bylinsky, "Heroes of U.S. Manufacturing," *Fortune*, March 20, 2000.

41 "Intermec Recognized for Its Use of Demand Flow™ Technology," *Intermec News Release*, May 21, 1997.

42 David A. Aaker, "How Will the Japanese Compete in Retail Services?" *California Management Review*, Fall 1990, pp. 54–67.

43 For still other examples of service-related problems in Japan, see Jon Woronoff, *The Japanese Management Mystique: The Reality Behind the Myth* (Chicago: Probus Publishing, 1992), pp. 120–124.

44 "A Moving Story," *Economist.com*, December 5, 2002.

45 Joan Magretta, "Fast, Global, and Entrepreneurial: Supply Chain Management, Hong Kong Style: An Interview with Victor Fung," *Harvard Business Review*, September/October 1998, pp. 105–106.

46 See, for example, Hellene S. Runtagh, "GE Tracks Transportation and Distribution Opportunities in the EC," *Journal of European Business*, September/October 1990, pp. 22–25.

47 See Alan M. Rugman and Cecilia Brain, "Regional Strategies of Multinational Pharmaceutical Firms," *Management International Review*, vol. 44 (2004/3), pp. 7–25.

48 Vesey (1991), see n. 12 above.

49 Ibid.

50 "Fighting Back," *The Economist*, September 2, 2004.

51 "A Moving Story," *Economist.com*, December 5, 2002.

52 See, "Breaking Japan's *Keiretsu*," *The Economist*, March 20, 2003.

Additional bibliography

Adler, Paul S. and Cole, Robert E. "Designed for Learning: A Tale of Two Auto Plants," *Sloan Management Review*, vol. 34, no. 3 (Spring 1993).

Beatty, Carol A. "Implementing Advanced Manufacturing Technologies: Rules of the Road," *Sloan Management Review*, vol. 33, no. 4 (Summer 1992).

Bhappu, Anita D. "The Japanese Family: An Institutional Logic for Japanese Corporate Networks and Japanese Management," *Academy of Management Review*, vol. 25, no. 2 (April 2000).

Brouthers, Lance Eliot, Werner, Steve and Matulich, Erika. "The Influence of Triad Nations' Environments on Price-Quality Product Strategies and MNC Performance," *Journal of International Business Studies*, vol. 31, no. 1 (Spring 2000).

Cantwell, John. "Innovation and Information Technology in the MNE," in Alan M. Rugman and Thomas Brewer (eds.), *The Oxford Handbook of International Business* (Oxford: Oxford University Press, 2001).

Cheng, Joseph L. C. and Bolon, Douglas S. "The Management of Multinational R&D: A Neglected Topic in International Business Research," *Journal of International Business Studies*, vol. 24, no. 1 (First Quarter 1993).

Collins, R. and Schmenner, R. "Taking Manufacturing Advantage of Europe's Single Market," *European Management Journal*, vol. 13, no. 3 (May/June 1995).

Collinson, Simon C. "Organising Knowledge to Manage R&D: A UK-Japan Company Comparison," *R&D Management*, vol. 31, no. 3 (2001).

Cusumano, Michael A. "Manufacturing Innovation: Lessons from the Japanese Auto Industry," *Sloan Management Review*, vol. 30, no. 1 (Fall 1988).

Deschamps, Jean-Philippe and Nayak, P. Ranganath. "Competing Through Products: Lessons from the Winners," *Columbia Journal of World Business*, vol. 27, no. 2 (Summer 1992).

Douglas, Susan P. and Wind, Yoram. "The Myth of Globalization," *Columbia Journal of World Business*, vol. 22, no. 4 (Winter 1987).

DuBois, Frank L., Toyne, Brian and Oliff, Michael D. "International Manufacturing Strategies of US Multinationals: A Conceptual Framework Based on a Four-Industry Study," *Journal of International Business Studies*, vol. 24, no. 2 (Second Quarter 1993).

Flaherty, M. Therese. "Global Sourcing Strategy: R&D, Manufacturing, and Marketing Interfaces," *Journal of International Business Studies*, vol. 24, no. 1 (First Quarter 1993).

Garvin, David A. "Manufacturing Strategic Planning," *California Management Review*, vol. 35, no. 4 (Summer 1993).

Ghoshal, Sumantra and Bartlett, Christopher A. "Creation, Adoption, and Diffusion of Innovations by Subsidiaries of Multinational Corporations," *Journal of International Business Studies*, vol. 19, no. 3 (Fall 1988).

Hansen, M. T. and Løvås, B. "How Do Multinational Companies Leverage Technological Competencies? Moving from Single to Interdependent Explanations," *Strategic Management Journal*, vol. 25, no. 8/9 (2004).

Hill, C. W. L. *International Business: Competing in the Global Marketplace*, 3rd ed. (New York: McGraw-Hill, 2000).

Hodgetts, Richard. *Measures of Quality and High Performance: Simple Tools and Lessons from America's Most Successful Firms* (New York: Amacom, 1998).

Julian, Scott D. and Keller, Robert T. "Multinational R&D Siting: Corporate Strategies for Success," *Columbia Journal of World Business*, vol. 26, no. 3 (Fall 1991).

Khurana, Anil. "Managing Complex Production Processes," *Sloan Management Review*, vol. 40, no. 2 (Winter 1999).

Kotabe, Masaaki. "The Relationship Between Offshore Sourcing and Innovativeness of US Multinational Firms: An Empirical Investigation," *Journal of International Business Studies*, vol. 21, no. 4 (Fourth Quarter 1990).

Kotabe, Masaaki and Murray, Janet Y. "Linking Product and Process Innovations and Modes of International Sourcing in Global Competition: A Case of Foreign Multinational Firms," *Journal of International Business Studies*, vol. 21, no. 3 (Third Quarter 1990).

Lei, David and Slocum, John W., Jr. "Global Strategy, Competence-Building and Strategic Alliances," *California Management Review*, vol. 35, no. 1 (Fall 1992).

Levy, David L. "Lean Production in an International Supply Chain," *Sloan Management Review*, vol. 38, no. 2 (Winter 1997).

Malnight, T. W. "Emerging Structural Patterns within Multinational Corporations: Toward Process-based Structures," *Academy of Management Journal*, vol. 44, no. 6 (2001).

Nohria, N. and Ghoshal, S. *The Differentiated Network: Organising Multinational Corporations for Value Creation* (San Francisco: Jossey-Bass, 1997).

Patel, Pari and Pavitt, Keith. "Large Firms in the Production of the World's Technology: An Important Case of 'Non-Globalization,'" *Journal of International Business Studies*, vol. 22, no. 1 (First Quarter 1991).

Pyke, David. "Manufacturing and Supply Chain Management in China: A Survey of State-, Collective-, and Privately-owned Enterprises," *European Management Journal*, vol. 18, no. 6 (December 2000).

Quinn, James Brian and Hilmer, Frederick G. "Strategic Outsourcing," *Sloan Management Review*, vol. 35, no. 4 (Summer 1994).

Reddy, Prasada. "New Trends in Globalization of Corporate R&D and Implications for Innovation Capability in Host Countries: A Survey from India," *World Development*, vol. 25, no. 11 (November 1997).

Rehder, Robert R. "Building Cars as if People Mattered: The Japanese Lean System vs. Volvo's Uddevalla System," *Columbia Journal of World Business*, vol. 27, no. 2 (Summer 1992).

Rondinelli, Dennis and Berry, Michael, "Multimodal Transportation, Logistics, and the Environment: Managing Interactions in a Global Economy," *European Management Journal*, vol. 18, no. 4 (August 2000).

Rondinelli, Dennis and Vastag, Gyula. "Panacea, Common Sense, or Just a Label?" *European Management Journal*, vol. 18, no. 5 (October 2000).

Rugman, Alan M. and Bennett, Jocelyn. "Technology Transfer and World Product Mandating," *Columbia Journal of World Business*, vol. 17, no. 4 (Winter 1982).

Rugman, Alan M. and Verbeke, Alain. "Subsidiary-specific Advantages in Multinational Enterprises," *Strategic Management Journal*, vol. 22, no. 3 (March 2001).

Serapio, Manuel G., Jr. "Macro-Micro Analyses of Japanese Direct R&D Investments in the US Automotive and Electronics Industries," *Management International Review*, vol. 33, no. 3 (Third Quarter 1993).

Sobek, Durward K. II, Ward, Allen C. and Liker, Jeffrey K. "Toyota's Principles of Set-Based Concurrent Engineering," *Sloan Management Review*, vol. 40, no. 2 (Winter 1999).

Swamidass, Paul M. "A Comparison of the Plant Location Strategies of Foreign and Domestic Manufacturers in the US," *Journal of International Business Studies*, vol. 21, no. 2 (Second Quarter 1990).

Swamidass, Paul M. and Kotabe, Masaaki. "Component Sourcing Strategies of Multinationals: An Empirical Study of European and Japanese Multinationals," *Journal of International Business Studies*, vol. 24, no. 1 (First Quarter 1993).

Vandermerwe, Sandra. "Increasing Returns: Competing for Customers in the Global Market," *Journal of World Business*, vol. 32, no. 4 (Winter 1997).

Yip, George S. "Global Strategy . . . In a World of Nations?" *Sloan Management Review*, vol. 31, no. 1 (Fall 1989).

Young, S. Mark. "A Framework for Successful Adoption and Performance of Japanese Manufacturing Practices in the United States," *Academy of Management Review*, vol. 17, no. 4 (October 1992).

Chapter 11

MARKETING STRATEGY

Contents

Objectives of the chapter

Every multinational has a marketing strategy designed to help identify opportunities and take advantage of them. This plan of action typically involves consideration of four primary areas: the product or service to be sold, the way in which the output will be promoted, the pricing of the good or service, and the distribution strategy to be used in getting the output to the customer. The primary purpose of this chapter is to examine the fundamentals of international marketing strategy. We will look at five major topics: market assessment, product strategy, promotion strategy, price strategy, and place strategy. We will consider such critical marketing areas as product screening, modification of goods and services in order to adapt to local needs, modified product life cycles, advertising, personal selling, and ways in which MNEs tailor-make their distribution systems.

The specific objectives of this chapter are to:

1 *Examine* the process used to conduct an international market assessment of goods and services.
2 *Study* the criteria that affect an MNE's decision to alter a good or service in order to adapt it to local market tastes.
3 *Describe* some of the ways in which MNEs use advertising and personal selling techniques to promote their products in worldwide markets.
4 *Review* some of the major factors that influence international pricing and distribution strategies.

ACTIVE LEARNING CASE

Volkswagen in the United States

During the 1960s, German-based Volkswagen AG (VW for short) held more market share in the United States than all other auto imports combined. In the 1970s, despite growing foreign competition, VW sales reached 300,000 units annually. However, the 1980s and early 1990s were not good for the company: annual sales in the US market were down to 150,000 units. In less than 10 years, market share had dropped from 3 per cent to 0.5 per cent, and VW had become a minor competitor in the North American part of the triad. Part of the problem had been that VW's American cars were competing head on with US brands that produced the traditional mid-sized car. VW could produce great cars in this range, but could not achieve the cost advantage of Japanese competitors.

In more recent years, however, Volkswagen has made a stunning comeback in America. Perhaps its biggest success story is the New Beetle, which was introduced in March 1998. The car is distinct not only because it appeals to the nostalgia of the Old Beetle, but also because of its slick European design. The New Beetle was the third largest VW seller, after the Jetta and the Passat. In addition to brisk first year sales, the Beetle was selected as the 1999 North American Car of the Year by an independent jury of 48 journalists who cover the auto industry for daily newspapers, magazines, television, radio, and the Internet. The award is a comprehensive evaluation of the year's most outstanding new car based on consumer appeal, quality, and driving characteristics. Each jury member is allowed to allot 25 votes to a small selection of finalist cars. The New Beetle garnered 292 votes, more than double the second place finisher, the Honda Odyssey, with 142 votes, and well ahead of the third place car, the Chrysler 300M, with 124 votes. Indeed, Volkswagen is back in the US market! In 2002, Volkswagen delivered over 420,000 vehicles to the United States market and accounted for approximately 10.1 percent of the passenger car import market. Including imports and domestic production, Volkswagen holds about 6.6 percent of the US passenger car market.

In its home region of Europe, where VW is the market leader, nearly 20 percent of all new cars sold are from the Volkswagen Group. This region accounts for 68 percent of VW's total revenue. North America as a whole accounts for only 20 per cent. Despite its resurgence in the United States, VW is still facing many problems. Approximately 20 per cent of VW's shares are held by the government of Lower Saxony, which prevents VW from cutting labor costs

Source: Corbis/Greg Smith

in Germany. As a result, VW is stuck paying $1,700 more to make a car in Germany than if it were manufacturing it in Eastern Europe or Portugal, limiting its ability to compete on price. This had not been a major problem when VW's reputation for quality allowed it to charge a premium, but since Mercedes-Benz and BMW started to compete in VW's market segment, the company's edge on quality diminished.

VW's problems are not new. A decade earlier the company had to reinvent itself to become competitive without reducing its labor costs. At the time, its strategy consisted of brand acquisition and manufacturing improvements. In about a decade VW purchased the Skoda, SEAT, Audi, Bently, Lamborghini, and Bugatti brands and set out to create synergies in their manufacturing processes. In the early 1990s, VW was making 30 different models using 16 floor plants. Today, the firm makes 54 models in four floor plants, with significant savings. This means that many of its cars, whether sold under the Skoda, Audi, or VW brand, share many parts. It is each brand's reputation and design that now carry the car. Inside the hood, a Skoda is very similar to a VW but the company has ensured a different market by letting Czech engineers design the Skoda. This brand-based strategy has paid off, increasing VW's market share around the world. Yet, as critics point out, the company's return on capital is lower than that of its competitors, and its brands might eventually erode each other's market share. VW continues to bargain with its union and with its major shareholder to curb labor costs in Germany or to be allowed to close plants there. However, the compromises continue to put it at a disadvantage with competitors. In addition, consumers might not take long to realize that a Skoda, which is promoted as part of the VW family, is cheaper but equivalent to a VW. Its up-market brands, such as the Lamborghini and Bently, might also suffer from a perception that many of their parts are comparable to that of VW's other brands.

In the United States, SUVs are more profitable than passenger vehicles. In 2002, VW introduced its Touareg, a very powerful SUV. It sells for $57,800 but has not been nearly as successful as expected. US and Japanese auto makers dominate the lower segments of the market, and Volvo,

Mercedes-Benz and BMW dominate the higher-end SUV market.

Websites: www.vw.com; www.gm.com; www.ford.com; and www.daimlerchrysler.com.

Sources: Alan M. Rugman, *The Regional Multinationals* (Cambridge: Cambridge University Press, 2005); Bernard Avishai, "A European Platform for Global Competition," *Harvard Business Review*, July/August 1991, pp. 103–113; www.vw.com; Christine Tierney and Joann Muller, "Another Trip Down Memory Lane," *Business Week*, July 23, 2001; Christine Tierney, Andrea Zammert, Joann Muller and Katie Kerwin, "Volkswagen," *Business Week*, July 23, 2001; "Problems with the People's Car," *The Economist*, March 14, 2002; "Higher Wages or More Job Security," *The Economist*, September 16, 2004; Michael Frank, "2005 Volkswagen Touareg V-10," *Forbes.com*, June 21, 2005.

1. How would VW use market assessment to evaluate sales potential for its cars in the United States?

2. Does VW need to modify its cars for the US market? Why or why not?

3. Would the nature of VW's products allow the company to use an identical promotional message worldwide, or would the company have to develop a country-by-country promotion strategy?

4. How would currency fluctuations affect VW's profit in the US market?

5. What type of distribution system would be most effective for VW in the United States?

INTRODUCTION

International marketing
The process of identifying the goods and services that customers outside the home country want and then providing them at the right price and place

International marketing is the process of identifying the goods and services that customers outside the home country want and then providing them at the right price and location.[1] In the international marketplace, this process is similar to that carried out at home, but with some important modifications that can adapt marketing efforts to the needs of the specific country or geographic locale.[2] For example, some MNEs are able to use the same strategy abroad as they have at home. This is particularly true in promotions where messages can carry a universal theme. Some writing implement firms advertise their pens and pencils as "the finest writing instruments in the world," a message that transcends national boundaries and can be used anywhere. Many fast-food franchises apply the same ideas because they have found that people everywhere have the same basic reasons for coming there to eat. In most cases, however, a company must tailor-make its strategy so that it appeals directly to the local customer.

These changes fall into five major areas: market assessment, product decisions, promotion strategies, pricing decisions, and place or distribution strategies. The latter four areas—product, promotion, price, and place—are often referred to as the four Ps of marketing,[3] and they constitute the heart of international marketing efforts.

INTERNATIONAL MARKET ASSESSMENT

International market assessment
An evaluation of the goods and services that the multinational can sell in the global marketplace

International marketing strategy starts with international market assessment, an evaluation of the goods and services that the MNE can sell in the global marketplace. This assessment typically involves a series of analyses aimed at pinpointing specific offerings and geographic targets. The first step is called the initial screening.

Initial screening: basic need and potential

Initial screening is the process of determining the basic need and potential of the MNE's goods and services in foreign markets. This screening answers the question: Who might be interested in buying our output? International auto manufacturers list the EU countries, North America, and Japan as potential buyers. Boeing targets the countries that will be rebuilding their air fleets in the next few decades. Kellogg's, General Mills, and Nestlé are interested in the United States and the European Union as well as any developing nations that offer potential new markets.

One way to carry out initial screening is by examining the current import policies of other countries and identifying the goods and services being purchased from abroad. A second way is by determining local production. A third is to examine the demographic changes taking place in the country that will create new, emerging markets. These cursory efforts help an MNE to target potential markets. Following the initial screening, the company begins to narrow its selection.

Second screening: financial and economic conditions

Secondary screening is used to reduce the list of market prospects by eliminating those that fail to meet financial and economic considerations. Financial considerations include inflation rates, interest rates, expected returns on investment, the buying habits of customers, and the availability of credit. These factors are important in determining whether markets that passed the initial, general screening are also financially feasible.

Economic considerations relate to a variety of market demand influences, including market indicators. Market indicators are used for measuring the relative market strengths of various geographic areas, and focus on three important areas: market size, market intensity, and market growth. Market size is the relative size of each market as a percentage of the total world market. For example, industrialized countries account for a sizable part of the market for cellular telephones, and a few nations such as the United States and Japan account for the largest percentage of this total. Nevertheless, non-industrialized countries with large populations also have a significant market size. In fact, China, the world's largest country in terms of population, is also the world's largest mobile phone market in terms of subscribers.[4] Market intensity is the "richness" of the market, or the degree of purchasing power in one country compared to others. For example, the United States and Canada are extremely rich markets for automobiles, telephones, and computers, so MNEs selling these products tend to highlight these two countries. Market growth is the annual increase in sales. For example, the market for cell phones and laptop computers in the United States will continue to grow in the years ahead, whereas the market for autos will grow much more slowly. However, given the large purchasing power in the US economy, MNEs selling these products will continue to target the United States. In recent years, other economies, such as South Korea, have become increasingly rich in terms of purchasing power, so they too are now target markets for high-tech products. Infrastructure and economic development can also influence market growth. For example, consumers in developing countries who have not yet been able to acquire a fixed line might choose instead to purchase a portable phone.

Quite often these data are analyzed through the use of quantitative techniques. Sometimes these approaches are fairly simple. Trend analysis, for example, is the estimation of future demand either by extrapolating the growth over the last three to five years and assuming that this trend will continue or by using some form of average growth rate over the recent past. A similar approach is estimation by analogy, through which forecasters predict market demand or growth based on information generated in other countries. For example,

Initial screening
The process of determining the basic need and potential of the multinational's goods and services in foreign markets

Market indicators
Indicators used for measuring the relative market strengths of various geographic areas

Market size
An economic screening consideration used in international marketing; it is the relative size of each market as a percentage of the total world market

Market intensity
The richness of a market or the degree of purchasing power in one country as compared to others

Market growth
The annual increase in sales in a particular market

Trend analysis
The estimation of future demand by either extrapolating the growth over the last three to five years and assuming that this trend will continue or by using some form of average growth rate over the recent past

Estimation by analogy
A method of forecasting market demand or market growth based on information generated in other countries, such as determining the number of refrigerators sold in the United States as a percentage of new housing starts and using this statistic in planning for the manufacture of these products in other world markets

313

if the number of refrigerators sold in the United States is 2.5 times the number of new housing starts, a US MNE that is planning to manufacture these products in the European Union will estimate demand based on the same formula. A more sophisticated approach is the use of regression analysis, a mathematical approach to forecasting that attempts to test the explanatory power of a set of independent variables. In the case of selling refrigerators in the European Union, for example, these would include economic growth, per capita income, and the number of births, in addition to other variables such as new housing starts. Another sophisticated approach is cluster analysis, a marketing approach that involves grouping data on the basis of market area, customer, and so on, based on similar variables, so that a marketing strategy can be formulated for each group. For example, US MNEs providing services in such areas as insurance, legal, financial, and management consulting know that their approaches must often vary from country to country.

Regression analysis
A mathematical approach to forecasting that attempts to test the explanatory power of a set of independent variables

Cluster analysis
A marketing approach to forecasting customer demand that involves grouping data based on market area, customer, or similar variables

Third screening: political and legal forces

The third level of screening involves taking a look at political and legal forces. A primary consideration is entry barriers in the form of import restrictions or limits on local ownership of business operations. Analysis of these barriers often results in identifying loopholes around the various restrictions or data that indicate barriers are far less extensive than initially believed.[5] For example, some MNEs have been able to sidestep legal restrictions by forming joint ventures with local firms. Production restrictions or limitations on profit remittance that restrict operating flexibility must also be considered. Government stability is an important factor in starting a successful operation; however, it is often difficult to predict. Despite the eagerness of investors to flock to the Russian market in the early 1990s, auto makers were hesitant to invest in Russia because of its uncertain political and economic environment. It was only in 1998 that Fiat made a commitment to the Russian market.[6] Another consideration is the protection offered for patents, trademarks, and copyrights. In some countries, such as China and Taiwan, pirating has been fairly common, resulting in markets being flooded with counterfeit or look-alike products.

Fourth screening: sociocultural forces

The fourth level of screening typically involves the consideration of sociocultural forces such as language, work habits, customs, religion, and values. As noted earlier, culture greatly affects the way people live, and MNEs need to examine how well their operations will fit into each particular culture. For example, although Japanese auto manufacturers have set up assembly plants in the United States, those operations are not identical to the ones in Japan because of the work habits and customs of Americans. In the United States, the work pace is less frantic and most people are unwilling to work the typical $5\frac{1}{2}$-day week, which is so common in Japan. Moreover, US managers are accustomed to going home to their families after work, whereas Japanese managers often go out for dinner and drinks and discuss business until late in the evening. MNEs will examine these sociocultural differences in determining where to locate operations.

Fifth screening: competitive environment

The fifth level of screening is typically focused on competitive forces. If three or four locations are equally attractive, an MNE will often make a final choice based on the degree of competition that exists in each locale. In some cases companies do not want to enter markets where there is strong competition. However, they will often decide to enter a competitive market because they believe the potential benefits far outweigh the drawbacks.

By going head-to-head with the competition, the company can force itself to become more efficient and effective and thus improve its own competitiveness. The MNE can take market share away from competitors and put them on the defensive, forcing them to commit more resources to defending the market under attack and thereby reducing their ability to retaliate effectively. Of course, these conditions do not always hold true, but they help illustrate why MNEs consider entering markets that are dominated by competitors.

Final selection

Before making a final selection, MNEs usually enhance their information by visiting the sites and talking to trade representatives or local officials. Such field trips are very common and can do a great deal to supplement currently available information. Sometimes these trips take the form of a trade mission; a visit sponsored by commercial officers in a country's local embassy and designed to bring together executives from MNEs that are interested in examining the benefits of doing business in the particular country.

Based on the outcome of the screenings and the supplemental data, the MNE chooses which goods and services to offer overseas.[7] The marketing strategy employed in this process revolves around what are commonly called the four Ps of marketing: product, promotion, price, and place.

 Active learning check

Review your answer to Active Learning Case question 1 and make any changes you like. Then compare your answer with the one below.

1 How would VW use market assessment to evaluate sales potential for its cars in the United States?

There are several steps VW could take. One is to look at the number of cars being imported into the country, as well as the number being built locally; this would provide important information regarding current product supply. Another would be to find out the number of auto registrations and how fast it is growing annually; this would be useful in predicting new sales potential. A third would be to examine the trend of new car sales over the last couple of years and forecast overall industry sales for the next two to three years. A fourth would be to compare the strengths offered by VW cars with those offered by the competition and evaluate how the company can position its offering for maximum market penetration.

PRODUCT STRATEGIES

Product strategies vary depending on the specific good and the customers. Some products can be manufactured and sold successfully both in the United States and abroad by using the same strategies. Other products must be modified or adapted and sold according to a specially designed strategy.[8] Figure 11.1 shows a range of possibilities. Products and services located on the left side of the continuum require little modification; those on the right must be modified to fit the market.

Little or no modification

Industrial goods and technical services are good examples of products that need little or no modification. A bulldozer, a laptop, and a photocopying machine serve the same purposes and are used the same way in the United States as they are in France or in China.[9]

Little if any modification required	Moderate amount of modification required	Extensive modification required
Heavy equipment	Automobiles	High-style comsumer goods
Electronic watches	Clothing	Cosmetics
Notebook computers	Appliances	Prepackaged foods
Chemical processes	Pharmaceuticals	Education products
Writing implements	Aircraft	Advertising
Cameras	Athletic running shoes	Packaging
Tennis rackets	Television sets	Restaurant meals
Cigarettes	Beer	Health services
		Cultural products
		Consumer distribution

Figure 11.1 Selected examples of product modification in the international arena

Alterations would be minor and would include such things as adapting the machine to the appropriate electric voltage or changing the language used for its instructions and labels. The same is true for many types of services. For example, international engineering and construction firms find that their product strategies are similar worldwide. People interested in having a dam or power plant constructed use the same basic concepts and have similar needs throughout the world. In fact, experience is the greatest selling point in convincing clients to hire an MNE in engineering or construction. For example, American firms that had experience in putting out oil well fires in the United States and cleaning up the *Exxon Valdez* oil spill in Alaska found a demand for their services in the aftermath of the 1991 Gulf War. Companies with a strong international brand image have also been able to succeed without a differentiation strategy. For example, the world-famous Scotch Chivas Regal is sold in many countries and is identical in each one. Schweppes (tonic water) and Perrier are internationally known and are also identical worldwide.

Moderate to high modification

A number of factors can compel an MNE to use moderate to high product modification. These include economics, culture, local laws, and product life cycle.

Economics

There are many examples of how economic considerations affect the decision to modify a product. For example, chewing gum packages often contain 10 to 20 sticks in the United States. But in many other countries, weak customer purchasing power necessitates packaging the gum with only five sticks. Many consumers must tote their goods home from the store, so smaller packages and containers are preferable to larger, heavier ones.

Economics is also important when the cost of a product is either too high or too low to make it attractive in another country. For example, cash registers are electronic in economically advanced countries; virtually no one uses hand-cranked machines. However, in many other countries they are too expensive and sophisticated for most retail stores and small establishments, so MNEs like National Cash Register continue to manufacture the hand-cranked versions. On the other hand, inexpensive calculators are widely used throughout the world, and many stores use handheld calculators to total customer purchases (although in some places calculations may be cross-checked for accuracy with an abacus).

Similarly, in economically advanced countries products are likely to have frills or extras, whereas only the basic model is offered in poorer countries. For example, bicycles in the United States are used for exercise and recreation and have a number of special features that make bicycle riding particularly enjoyable, whereas in many other countries they are a primary source of transportation. US bikes are built for comfort and ease of handling; elsewhere they are built for economy and ease of maintenance. As a result, manufacturers need to modify the product to fit customer needs.

Culture

A product must sometimes be adapted to different ways of doing things. Consider washing machines. The French prefer washers that load from the top, the British like front-loading units, the Germans prefer high-speed machines that take out most of the moisture in the spin-dry process, and the Italians like slower spin speeds because they prefer to hang-dry laundry in the sun. So manufacturers who sell washing machines in the European Union must produce a variety of different units.

Food is an item that often must be modified or sold differently. In fast-food franchises like McDonald's, portions of the menu are similar throughout the world while other items are designed to cater specifically to local tastes. Coffee in South American units tends to be a much stronger blend than that sold in North America. In certain parts of Europe and Asia, the food is more highly seasoned in keeping with local tastes. For products that are not modified, the marketing focus is different because of the way the item is used. Schweppes, for example, is typically served as a mixer in the United States and Britain, where drinks like gin and tonic are popular. In France, however, it is drunk without alcohol. Clearly, marketing approaches differ in these two situations. The marketing message is also important when selling hard liquors. The products remain the same, but many places have social customs that frown on excessive consumption. In these cases, MNEs such as Seagram of Canada have tailored their advertising messages along the lines of moderate drinking and the use of mixers to reduce the alcoholic content per serving.

Culture also influences purchasing decisions on the basis of style or aesthetics. Cosmetics and other beauty aids are good examples. Perfumes that sell well in Europe often have difficulty gaining market share in the United States because they do not appeal to American women. Similarly, many products that sell well in the United States, such as shampoos and deodorants, have limited market appeal elsewhere. People may not use these products, or they may find it hard to differentiate a product from local offerings. For example, Gillette has found it is difficult to develop a distinctive edge in selling toiletries because many people feel these products are all basically the same.

Convenience and comfort are other culturally driven factors that help explain the need for product modification. Early Japanese autos in the United States were designed to attack other foreign imports, specifically the VW Beetle. Researchers found that the two biggest complaints with the Beetle were the small amount of room in the back seat and the heater, which took too long to warm up the car. Aware that Americans wanted an economical car with these additional features, Japanese imports offered greater leg room for back seat passengers and a heater that was superior to the VW offering. Within a few years these imports had began to erode VW's market share. Foreign manufacturers also identified a group that wanted several convenience and comfort features. The result has been the emergence of luxury Japanese and German cars that now compete extremely well with US models in the upper end of the market.

Other culturally based reasons for product modifications include color and language. In the United States, the color black is worn for mourning, whereas in other countries white is for mourning and thus is not used for consumer goods. Similarly, most American shampoos are light-colored, whereas in some Oriental countries consumers prefer dark-colored shampoo. Language can be an important point of modification because a product may need to carry instructions about contents or use. In locations where two or more languages are spoken, such as Canada and Switzerland, this information is provided in all appropriate languages. Language is also important in conveying the right image for the product. Quite often it is difficult to replicate the message because the saying or slogan has no meaning in another language.

Local laws

Local laws can require product modification in order to meet environmental and safety requirements. For example, US emission-control laws have required Japanese and European car importers to make significant model changes before their autos can be sold in the United States. Food and pharmaceutical regulations require packaging and labeling that are often quite different from those in the home country. In Saudi Arabia, the label of any product containing animal fat or meat must clearly state the kind of animal used and the fact that no swine products are included. Brand-name protection can also require product modification. Ford found that in Mexico it had to rename its Ford Falcon because this brand name was registered to another firm. The same thing happened to Ford in the case of the Mustang in Germany.

Product life cycle

Another reason for modifying a product is to cope with its limited product life cycle (PLC). Although Ford was extremely profitable in Europe during the 1980s, those earnings had disappeared by the early 1990s because Ford did not develop new, competitive products.[10] Contrast this to Coca-Cola of Japan, which introduces an average of one new soft drink per month and has the competition scurrying to keep up. Yet Kola Real has been particularly effective in offsetting the technology and marketing of Coca-Cola to bring its own products to market in Mexico. The box **International Business Strategy in Action: Kola Real Group** describes the company's latest approach.

INTERNATIONAL BUSINESS STRATEGY *IN ACTION*

Kola Real Group

You may have heard of the cola wars in the 1980s and early 1990s, but you probably have not heard of the current Mexico cola war. Mexico is the world's second largest market for non-alcoholic drinks and an important market for the world's largest cola brands. Coca-Cola derives 11 per cent of its world sales from this market, and in 2000 it held about 70 per cent of the market for carbonated drinks. Pepsi had 15 per cent of the market, with the remaining 15 per cent dispersed among smaller competitors. Mexico was, by all accounts, a saturated market. But since 2002, when upstart Kola Real entered the market, the competitive environment has gotten tougher for the big players. Today, Coca-Cola is constantly monitoring the marketing schemes of Kola Real to prevent further erosion of its market share.

Kola Real was founded in 1988 by the Añaños family in the capital city of the province of Ayacucho, Peru. At the time, the founders were rural immigrants running from the violence

brought about by the emergence of the Shining Path guerrillas in the countryside. Once in the city, they realized that the demand for carbonated drinks was not being met by either Coca-Cola or Pepsi, which routinely discontinued deliveries because their trucks were often robbed by the guerrillas or common criminals. So Jorge Añaños, an agricultural engineer, developed a formula for a new drink. The family borrowed $30,000 and started producing it. In the early 1990s the rest of the family joined the firm to market the drink and opened a series of plants in the provinces. It was only in 1997 that the firm entered Lima, the largest market in Peru. Today, the firm has a 20 per cent market share in its domestic market.

Kola Real's first international excursion was to Venezuela in 1999. At the time, plastic containers accounted for only 3 per cent of the carbonated market. Kola Real saw an opportunity in this because the cost of plastic bottles is lower than for glass. Today, the firm has 17 per cent of the Venezuelan market. In 2001, it entered the Ecuador market because of its proximity to the northern part of Peru; today it holds 12 per cent of that market.

Kola Real was lured to the Mexican market because of its size and its high per capita consumption of carbonated beverages. It established its first plant in 2002, choosing Puebla because it is well linked to the rest of the country, the cost of land is reasonable, there is an excellent source of water, and it is not too far from Mexico City. Only two years later, the firm had captured 4 per cent of the market. A new plant is expected to open in the northern part of Mexico by 2005 and is expected to contribute to the company's goal of reaching a 10 per cent market share by 2009. Cielo, its bottled water, is presently the market leader.

A number of factors have contributed to Kola Real's success. One is that it has chosen the poorest part of the population as its market segment. When the firm started operations in Ayacucho, the city was filled with poor rural immigrants. Both the guerrillas and the Peruvian military had all but destroyed the province's economy. And this was the province that had given birth to the insurgents. There was a heightened displeasure with social injustice. Kola Real responded by providing a much cheaper product under the banner "The drink at the just price." By doing this, it not only appealed to its customers but assured them that its slogan did not use the words *cheap* or *inexpensive*, which would have undermined the quality of the product. This slogan and the accompanying low price were then exported across the nation and into the three other Latin American markets, where they were welcomed by the same lower-income population segments.

Another reason is that the firm's expenses are very austere, allowing it to offer the lowest prices in the market and still enjoy a substantial profit. Whenever possible, the firm has maintained its own distribution system. Administrative costs are kept to a minimum. Although its plants use top-of-the-line technology for production, the administrative offices are very modestly furnished. Finally, the firm relies on word of mouth to market its products.

Analysts argue that large competitors are often unable or unwilling to respond to the poorest segments of society in Latin America, relying instead on large-scale distribution to establishments servicing the middle and upper classes. Before KR entered the Mexican market, the same bottle of Coca-Cola that cost $1.00 in the United States cost $1.40 in Mexico—despite the lower per capita income. Although Kola Real may be found at Carrefour stores across Mexico, the firm relies heavily on its sales force to push the product in small establishments, which account for 80 per cent of the Mexican market and serve the chosen market segment. KR argues that by providing more personalized and fitted service to these points of sale it has increased the size of the market, not stolen a big chunk of the large players' market.

Coca-Cola is not sitting idly by. When Kola Real introduced the 2.6 liter "Big Cola" at a price of $0.75 to market to poor large families, Coca-Cola followed suit and introduced its own 2.5 liter bottle. However, it sells it for almost twice as much at $1.30. To counter KR's growing expansion, Coca-Cola began to offer discounts and incentives to many of their clients. This led to a warning from the Mexican bureau that regulates competition. Meanwhile, Kola Real recently introduced the 3.1 liter Mega Big Cola in Mexico. In the future, it is likely to introduce a larger variety of carbonated drinks.

There have always been no-frills carbonated drinks in Latin America. They have been able to succeed despite being inefficient because of the large difference between production costs and the price charged by the market leaders. Kola Real's international success was possible because it manufactured and marketed its products efficiently.

Websites: www.cocacola-femsa.com.mx; www.coca-cola.com; www.pepsico.com; and www.carrefour.com.mx.

Sources: Mario Vargas Llosa, "Los Añaños," *Caretas*, November 20, 2003; David Suarez, "Grupo Real se expande con éxito en cuatro paises," **businessperu.com.pe**, February 2004; "Cola Down Mexico Way," *The Economist*, October 9, 2003.

One of the most effective strategies has been to shorten the PLC by offering new goods and services before the demand for the old ones has dropped significantly. Figure 11.2 provides a graphic illustration. Note that there are two types of PLCs: (1) the standard PLC, which covers an extended time continuum, often four to five years, and (2) a short life cycle that lasts a much shorter time. Many companies are discovering that by shortening the PLC and offering new product adaptations they are able to capture and retain a large market share. This is typically done by offering a new product, then modifying it and bringing out a new version before the competition can effectively combat the first offering. For example, Intel first offered a Pentium processor. This was followed by the introduction of the Pentium II, Pentium III, and Pentium IV processor, all of which were faster than their predecessors. As processors get faster, they consume more energy and

Figure 11.2 Product life cycles: two different approaches

generate more heat, so for the meantime, until these issues are resolved, Intel cannot produce faster processors. As a result, more task-specific chips have been introduced. The Centrino processor now caters to wireless users and the upcoming Desktrino will cater to desktop users.[11] The video game platform market provides another example of strategic continuous innovation. Nintendo and Sony constantly introduce new products and games to capture the market,[12] always leaving the competition scurrying to keep up.[13] As long as a firm can continue such an adaptation strategy, it can outmode the old product (and those of competitors as well) and maintain market position. At some point the competition may gain the advantage by offering a product that revolutionizes the field, but as long as a product improvement strategy remains viable, the firm will continue to be the product leader. This strategy is being implemented by MNEs throughout the world.[14]

✔ Active learning check

Review your answer to Active Learning Case question 2 and make any changes you like. Then compare your answer with the one below.

2 Does VW need to modify its cars for the US market? Why or why not?

Based on the case data, it appears that VW needs to make some changes in styling and engineering. The company is convinced that Americans will buy cars that offer German engineering and quality, but in the past it has made the mistake of producing cars that look "too American." Because of this, many people bought cars from Ford, GM, and Chrysler because there were no distinctive qualities that VW could use in attracting these buyers. By modifying its cars and giving them European styling and German engineering, VW can lead from strength and exploit its market advantage.

PROMOTION

Promotion
The process of stimulating demand for a company's goods and services

Promotion is the process of stimulating demand for a company's goods and services.[15] MNEs promote their goods and services through advertising and personal selling. The specific approach used, however, will be determined by the nature of the product.

Nature of the product

In promoting a product, a company can use a variety of approaches. The choice is heavily influenced by whether the firm believes the same message can be used worldwide or needs to be adapted, and whether the product will remain the same or need to be modified. Here are four variations on this theme:

- *Identical product and identical message.* This approach is used when the MNE intends to sell the same product worldwide and believes that an identical promotional appeal can be used in all markets. A. T. Cross, for example, uses this strategy because writing instruments do not need to be adapted to local markets.

- *Identical product but different message.* This strategy is used when the product satisfies a different need in various markets. For example, in the United States many car companies tout the luxury and convenience of their products, whereas in other countries the same cars are promoted on the basis of their fuel efficiency or ability to meet basic transportation needs.

- *Modified product but same message.* This strategy is used when the market requires a different version of the product but the needs of the consumer are the same. For example, whether washing machines load from the top or the side, they provide the same function and meet the same customer needs. Similarly, in many countries the seasoning of foods differs from that of foods sold in the United States. So although the product is changed, the promotion message remains the same because the buyer's needs are the same.

- *Modified product and modified message.* When the product use and buying habits of customers are different from those in the MNE's home market, both the product and promotion message will be modified. For example, breakfast cereal companies such as Kellogg's and General Mills are developing new versions of their popular American cereals for sale in the European market. Many Europeans do not eat cereal for breakfast, however, so the promotion campaign is geared toward changing eating habits rather than getting consumers to switch product loyalty.

Advertising

Advertising is a non-personal form of promotion in which a firm attempts to persuade consumers to a particular point of view. In many cases MNEs use the same advertising message worldwide; again, because many products fill similar worldwide needs, a company can use a universal message and reduce advertising costs at the same time. However, there are times when the advertising must be adapted to the local market. Two of the most common reasons are that (1) the way in which the product is used differs from that in the home country and (2) the advertising message does not make sense if translated directly. An example of the latter is the Nike commercials that encourage the viewer to "Just do it," or Budweiser commercials that ask, "Why ask why?" These ads make sense to American viewers, but they are too culturally grounded to be used in many other countries, and would leave the viewer confused as to what the advertiser was saying. As a result, advertisers are very careful to tie their messages to buyer needs and wants. On the other hand, there are many advertisements that have been only moderately modified or carried in their entirety because they *do* make sense in other cultures. For example, Marlboro's "cowboy image" has universal appeal, and Nike's ads featuring such internationally known stars as Michael Jordan and Tiger Woods transcend national boundaries, especially after the media exposure they have received. The box **International Business Strategy in Action: IKEA in international markets** provides some examples of how this is being done.

Advertising
A non-personal form of promotion in which a firm attempts to persuade consumers to a particular point of view

IKEA in international markets

From its founding as a small, private Swedish furniture retailer in 1943, IKEA has grown to become a multinational business with 201 stores in 34 countries and annual sales of €13.6 billion. Today, Muscovites and Londoners can buy towels produced in Turkey at one of the retailer's warehouse stores.

This internationalization process is all the more remarkable in that IKEA has remained true to the basic philosophy of its founder, Ingvar Kamprad, throughout its global expansion. Kamprad redesigned the furniture industry by introducing knock-down kits that customers could take away from the store and assemble themselves, enabling the company to stock larger quantities of furniture in its warehouses. Costs were lowered because these kits were easier to transport, took up less space in IKEA's large warehouse stores, and there was no need for assembly or delivery. In turn, customers could have their furniture immediately and could transport it in their own cars, saving on delivery costs. IKEA did a lot more than just provide convenient, easy to transport products, however. First, the products are carefully designed and more stylish than bargain do-it-yourself competitors. Second, IKEA changed furniture shopping from its traditional frosty "showroom" mentality to a more "fun" place with children's playpens, nurseries, and cafés in the stores. Indeed, a trip to an IKEA store is entertainment for the entire family. IKEA also built on the fast-growing informal suburban culture by providing abundant parking.

IKEA's relaxed, informal, yet efficient image was extended to Oslo and Demark in the 1960s. It entered Switzerland in 1973, Munich in 1974. By 1980, IKEA had opened an additional 10 stores across Germany and followed this with an expansion through Western Europe that culminated with its entry into Britain in 1987. In 1990, it entered the Eastern European market with a store in Hungary; shortly after it entered Poland, the Czech Republic, and Slovakia. In 2000, it opened its first store in Moscow.

Expansion into other parts of the triad has been slower. In Asia and Oceania, IKEA opened its first store in Australia in 1975 and in Singapore in 1978. But its next expansion was in 1988, when it entered Hong Kong. Taiwan, Malaysia, and Mainland China were added in the 1990s. In North America, IKEA opened a store in 1976 in Canada and used its Canadian operations to expand into the United States in 1985. The company also has operations in the Middle East.

IKEA also brought innovation to the logistics of furniture production by setting up groups of key suppliers to produce components at low cost. It has more than 2,000 suppliers in 50 countries around the world. These subcontractors, in turn, make money by getting large-volume orders for standardized components from IKEA.

The company also has kept tight control over product design and quality to maintain its brand name and the distinctive identity of its furniture. It was able to expand rapidly because it did not have to establish expensive manufacturing facilities around Europe, but rather retained centralized control over the subcontractors.

IKEA's marketing strategy has been to build on the Swedish home-base stereotype of clean and efficient service. All furniture is well designed, modern, functional, durable, of high quality, and price competitive. Its image and brand name are well established and have survived numerous imitators. As a result, IKEA has been able to move from its Scandinavian base to being a strong regional player in Europe, and is now competing successfully in the global arena.

In particular, IKEA is a successful multinational business because it has introduced a highly differentiated product into a traditional industry and has built a globally recognized brand name for high-quality, inexpensive, and

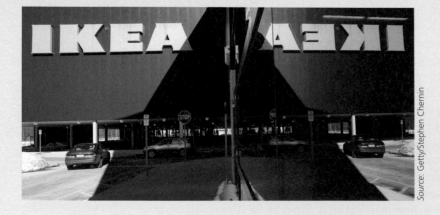

Source: Getty/Stephen Chernin

attractive furniture. It has also combined the generic strategies of differentiation, low cost, and niching and has outsourced both production and delivery components of the value chain.

Website: www.ikea.com.

Sources: Christopher A. Bartlett and Ashish Nanda, *Ingvar Kamprad and IKEA*, Harvard Business School Case 9-390-132; Joseph R. D'Cruz and Alan M. Rugman, "Developing International Competitiveness: The Five Partners Model," *Business Quarterly*, vol. 58, no. 2 (Winter 1993), pp. 60–72; James Schofield, "IKEA Wows the Russians," *BBC News*, February 22, 2002; Patric Jackson, "IKEA's Enormous Niche Market," *BBC News*, August 1, 2003; www.ikea.com; and www.hoovers.com.

As in the United States, MNEs use several media to carry their advertising messages. The three most popular are television, radio, and newspapers. Some of the major differences between the approach used in the United States and that used in other countries include government regulation of media advertising and the fact that many stations do not carry advertising, although in recent years this has been changing. In particular, the use of television advertising has been increasing in Europe, whereas in other areas of the world, such as South America and the Middle East, newspapers remain the major medium for promotion efforts. However, there are restrictions on what can be presented. Examples include: (1) some countries prohibit comparative advertising, in which firms compare their products with those of the competition; (2) some countries do not allow certain products to be advertised because they want to discourage their use (such as alcoholic beverages and cigarettes) or because they want to protect national industries from MNE competition; and (3) some countries (such as Islamic nations) censor the use of any messages considered erotic.

Comparative advertising
The comparing of similar products for the purpose of persuading customers to buy a particular one

Personal selling

Personal selling is a direct form of promotion used to persuade customers to a particular point of view. Some goods, such as industrial products or those that require explanation or description, rely heavily on personal selling. Avon, the cosmetics company, has been very successful with this approach even in countries where people are unaccustomed to buying cosmetics from a door-to-door salesperson. In Mexico, for example, Avon managed to gain acceptance by first introducing the idea of personal selling through a massive advertising campaign so that housewives became aware that the Avon salesperson was not a common door-to-door vendor but a professional trained to help clients look beautiful. Personal selling is also widely used in marketing products such as pharmaceuticals and sophisticated electronic equipment. For example, Pfizer and Upjohn use salespeople to call on doctors and other individuals who are in a position to recommend their products, and General Electric and Westinghouse salespeople use the same approach in selling overseas that they use in the United States.

Personal selling
A direct form of promotion used to persuade customers to a particular point of view

Because many international markets are so large, some MNEs have also turned to telemarketing. This approach has been very successful in the United States, and the overseas subsidiaries of such US firms as IBM, Ford, and Digital Equipment have been using telemarketing to generate new sales. European firms such as Peugeot have been adopting this approach as well.

MNEs have also focused attention on recruiting salespeople on an international basis. In some countries this work is not highly regarded, so MNEs have given these people managerial titles that command importance, such as territory manager or zone manager. Recruiting local talent is extremely important because these people are often better able to sell to local customers. If the product requires special training to sell, MNEs often bring new salespeople to the home office for training, introduce them to those who are manufacturing the products, and create a feeling of teamwork among the field staff and personnel so that the salespeople are energized to go back into the field and sell.

Active learning check

Review your answer to Active Learning Case question 3 and make any changes you like. Then compare your answer with the one below.

3 Would the nature of VW's products allow the company to use an identical promotional message worldwide, or would the company have to develop a country-by-country promotion strategy?

This answer will depend on where VW is selling its product. In less developed countries, the message would be geared toward economy and efficiency. In more developed countries, the message would focus on styling, handling, engineering, and non-economic factors as well. So VW would need to develop a series of different messages to address the wide number of market niches. No one message would appeal to everyone in the same way.

PRICING

The pricing of goods and services in the international marketplace is often influenced by factors present in home market pricing. These factors include government controls, market diversity, currency fluctuations, and price escalation forces.

Government controls

Every nation has government regulations that influence pricing practices. Some countries dictate minimum and maximum prices that can be charged to customers. Minimum prices can help protect local companies from more efficient international competitors because of a floor on price that can help ensure profit for national firms. For example, if the minimum price for a particular type of personal computer is $1,000 and local companies can produce and sell the product for $700, they will make $300 a unit. Foreign competitors may be able to produce and sell the product for $500 and make a $500 profit per unit, but the minimum price laws prevent them from driving out local competition. Without this law, overseas competitors might price the unit at $600 and then raise the price dramatically after local competitors went out of business.

Dumping
The selling of imported goods at a price below cost or below that in the home country

Governments also prohibit dumping, or the selling of imported goods at a price below cost or below the cost in the home country. The General Agreement on Tariffs and Trade (GATT) and WTO specifically prohibits this practice, which is designed to help MNEs drive out the local competition, establish a monopoly, and subsequently raise prices at will. A number of American firms have been influential in getting the US government to bring dumping charges against Japanese competitors.

Market diversity

Consumer tastes and demands vary widely in the international marketplace, resulting in MNEs having to price some of their products differently. For example, companies have found that they can charge more for goods sold overseas because of the demand. In the United States, there is a greater demand for light turkey meat than for dark turkey meat. The latter is typically sold at a lower price and is often purchased by animal food producers. However, the plump dark meat of turkey thighs has a strong market in Europe. As a result, firms like the Shenandoah Valley Poultry Company export thousands of metric tons of dark turkey meat to Europe each year.

A second factor influencing market diversity is the perceived quality of the product. For example, in the United States, German auto makers such as Mercedes found that some Americans were willing to pay a premium for German cars. In contrast, the Japanese are not willing to pay a premium for German autos, so Mercedes's pricing structure in Japan is different. More recently, Japanese luxury autos have proved to be strong competitors for Mercedes in the US market.

Another factor is the tax laws and attitudes about carrying debt. In the United States, some interest payments are tax deductible and most people have no aversion to assuming at least some debt. In many other countries, interest payments are not tax deductible and people are unaccustomed to carrying debt. In Japan, for example, little use is made of consumer credit. In pricing products, MNEs will adjust the local strategy to accommodate the impact of the tax laws and the consumer's willingness to assume debt.

Currency fluctuations

As noted in Chapter 7, when selling products overseas, MNEs often end up assuming the risks associated with currency fluctuations. This risk is particularly important when the companies have a return on investment target because this objective can become unattainable if the local currency is devalued. For example, if it costs Mercedes $30,000 to manufacture and ship a particular model to the United States, and the company sells the car to its dealer for $40,000, Mercedes is making a 33 per cent profit on the sale ($10,000/$30,000). However, if the dollar decreases in value by 10 per cent against the German mark, then the company's profit percentage will decline and the firm will have to choose between the following options: (1) increase the price of the car to the dealer to make up the loss of dollar value, (2) absorb the loss and leave the price the same, or (3) absorb part of the loss and raise the price to the dealer to make up the difference. In the mid 1980s, Mercedes absorbed the loss because price increases resulted in sharply lowered demand for the cars and even less overall profit for the company. Of course, when the value of the dollar rose against the mark during the 1990s, Mercedes profited accordingly and lowered that price in order to generate additional sales. Beginning in the late 1980s, US firms found that their products were becoming much more attractive to European buyers, thanks to the devaluation of the dollar and the accompanying rise in purchasing power of buyers on the Continent. But the strength of the dollar in the 1990s decreased the demand for US exports. Asian imports, on the other hand, became increasingly price competitive in the US market due to the devaluation of most Asian currencies in the late 1990s.[16]

Price escalation forces

A problem similar to that discussed above is price escalation forces that drive up the cost of imported goods. In the case of Mercedes, for example, if the cost of the car rose from $30,000 to $33,000, the company would want to pass this along to the dealer. In the case of MNEs that sell through a marketing channel with a series of middlemen, the effect of a price escalation can be even greater because everyone in the channel adds a percentage increase. For example, if an MNE exports and sells a consumer good for $10 to a large wholesaler and there are five additional middlemen in the channel, each of whom marks up the good by 20 per cent, as seen in Table 11.1, the final price to the consumer is $24.88. If the MNE's cost rises from $10 to $13, the final price to the consumer is now $32.35, a 30 per cent increase. So price increases by the MNE can dramatically affect what the customer pays, and as long as the company continues to export rather than manufacture locally, price will be a key marketing consideration because of its effect on consumer demand. In this

Table 11.1 The effect of MNE pricing on final consumer costs

MNE price	Price charged by each middleman				
	1	2	3	4	5
$10	$12.00	$14.40	$17.28	$20.74	$24.88
$13	$15.60	$18.72	$22.46	$26.96	$32.35

Ultimate effect of a $3 increase in MNE price: $32.35 − $24.88 = $7.47 or 30 per cent.

example it is likely that customer demand would drop substantially unless there are no effective substitutes for the product.

✔ Active learning check

Review your answer to Active Learning Case question 4 and make any changes you like. Then compare your answer with the one below.

4 How would currency fluctuations affect VW's profit in the US market?

Currency fluctuations would affect VW's profit in the US market according to the value of the German mark in relation to the dollar. If the value of the mark were to decline, VW's profit per car sold in the United States would rise because these dollars would buy more marks. Conversely, if the value of the mark increased, profit per car would decrease because these dollars would buy fewer marks.

PLACE

Distribution
The course that goods take between production and the final consumer

The importance of international logistics was discussed in Chapter 10. The focus of attention here will be on the distribution differences among countries and conditions with which MNEs must be familiar. **Distribution** is the course that goods take between production and final consumer. This course often differs on a country-by-country basis, and MNEs will spend a considerable amount of time in examining the different systems in place, the criteria to use in choosing distributors and channels, and how to employ distribution segmentation.[17]

Different distribution systems

It is often difficult to standardize a distribution system and use the same approach in every country because there are many individual differences to be considered. For example, countries such as Finland feature a predominance of general line retailers that carry a wide assortment of merchandise. In contrast, the wholesale and retail structure in Italy is characterized by a wide array of stores, many of which specialize or carry limited lines of merchandise. So in distributing goods in these two countries, MNEs need to employ different strategies.

Consumer spending habits can also negate attempts to standardize distribution. In the United States, many middlemen are geared to handling credit sales, whereas in Japan most consumer purchases are on a cash basis. In both Germany and the United States, mail-order buying has increased dramatically in recent years, whereas in Portugal and Spain the market is quite small. So the route the goods take to the consumer will vary.

The location where consumers are used to buying will also influence distribution. In economically developed countries where supermarkets have become commonplace, customers purchase a wide variety of food and other products under one roof. In most countries, however, purchases are made in smaller stores, and distribution requires the MNE or the local sales manager to deal with a large number of retailers, each of whom is selling a small amount of merchandise. In recent years, some wholesalers and retailers have been expanding their operations to other countries. Wal-Mart, the giant American retailer, has expanded into Mexico and Europe; in 1999 it bought the British supermarket chain, Asda. However, most middlemen operate exclusively within one country—another factor helping to explain why it is still difficult to standardize distribution on an international basis.

Choosing the best distribution system

MNEs use a number of criteria in creating the most efficient distribution system. One is to get the best possible distributors to carry their products. A key factor in evaluating potential distributors is the financial strength of the wholesaler or retailer, because the multinational wants to know that the distributor will be able to survive the long run. MNEs that sell goods requiring periodic maintenance and servicing will be interested in businesses that can keep sufficient inventory on hand. This is particularly important when selling products such as autos, computers, and electronic equipment. A second factor is how well connected the distributor is in terms of knowing the right people and providing assistance in handling governmental red tape. This is a key consideration for Coca-Cola when choosing overseas distributors. A third factor is the number and types of product lines the distributor carries currently so that the multinational can identify middlemen who are most likely to give its goods a strong marketing push.

In many cases, distributors have competitive products or feel that they do not need to add any new product lines. If the multinational wants to tap into this distribution system, it will have to formulate an incentive program that is designed to convince the distributor to carry its products. Some of the ways in which this is done include (1) helping to pay for local promotion campaigns of the product, (2) providing generous sales incentives, (3) conducting marketing research to identify customer niches and sales forecasts to help the distributor decide how much inventory to carry,[18] and (4) ensuring that unsold or outmoded merchandise can be returned for a full refund.

Depending on the nature of the market and the competition, the multinational may give exclusive geographic distribution to one local seller or arrange to have a number of sellers jointly selling the product. For example, auto manufacturers often have more than one dealer in a major metropolis but are willing to give exclusive geographic distribution rights to dealers in rural areas. This is in contrast to food products that can be sold in a wide variety of outlets and for which exclusivity is unnecessary. In these cases the multinational will try to get a variety of distributors to carry the product.

✔ Active learning check

Review your answer to Active Learning Case question 5 and make any changes you like. Then compare your answer with the one below.

5 **What type of distribution system would be most effective for VW in the United States?**

VW would use the same type of distribution system as that employed by other car manufacturers (i.e., auto dealerships). The big challenge would be to open new dealerships and thus increase market coverage. The market in the United States is fairly well blanketed with dealerships, but the company could look for successful dealers who would be willing to carry the VW line as well as their current offerings. Another approach is to build VWs in the United States and thus reduce the distance the product has to be transported along the distribution system. This not only reduces cost but also helps ensure faster delivery.

STRATEGIC MANAGEMENT AND MARKETING STRATEGY

Marketing strategies play a key role in helping MNEs formulate an overall plan of action. Many approaches are directly related to the major areas that have been examined in this chapter, including ongoing market assessment, new product development, and the use of effective pricing. Table 11.2 illustrates the worldwide market penetration of several MNEs to be discussed in this section.

Table 11.2 International market penetration: location of subsidiaries, holdings, and joint ventures

General Motors (US)	Clarins (French)	Daewoo (Korean)	Mitsubishi Electric (Japanese)	Royal Dutch/Shell Group (Dutch/British)	
North America					
Canada	Canada	Canada	Canada	Canada	
Mexico	Mexico	Mexico	Mexico	Mexico	
United States	United States	United States	United States	United States	
Western Europe					
Austria	Austria	Italy	Ireland	Andorra	Spain
Belgium	Belgium	Netherlands	Spain	Austria	Sweden
Denmark	France	Spain	France	Belgium	Turkey
Finland	Germany	Turkey	Germany	Denmark	United Kingdom
France	Italy	United Kingdom	Italy	Faroe Islands	
Germany	Netherlands		Sweden	Finland	
Greece	Northern Ireland		Netherlands	France	
Ireland	Portugal		United Kingdom	Germany	
Italy	Rep. of Ireland		Portugal	Gibraltar	
Netherlands	Spain			Greece	
Norway	Switzerland			Iceland	
Portugal	United Kingdom			Ireland	
Spain				Italy	
Sweden				Luxembourg	
Switzerland				Netherlands	
Turkey				Norway	
United Kingdom				Portugal	
Central and Eastern Europe					
Croatia		Russia	Czech Rep.	Albania	Romania
Czech Rep.		Uzbekistan	Russia	Belarus	Russia
Hungary				Bulgaria	Slovakia
Poland				Croatia	Slovenia
Romania				Czech Rep.	Switzerland
Russian Fed.				Estonia	Ukraine
Slovak Rep.				Hungary	Yugoslavia
Slovenia				Latvia	
				Lithuania	
				Poland	
Asia and Oceania					
Australia	Australia	Australia	Australia	Australia	Philippines
Hong Kong	Hong Kong	Bangladesh	Japan	Azerbaijan	Singapore
Indonesia	Japan	China	Singapore	Bangladesh	Solomon Islands
South Korea	Malaysia	Indonesia	China	Brunei	Sri Lanka

General Motors (US)	Clarins (French)	Daewoo (Korean)	Mitsubishi Electric (Japanese)	Royal Dutch/Shell Group (Dutch/British)	
Asia and Oceania					
New Zealand	Singapore	Japan	Hong Kong	Cambodia	Taiwan
Singapore	South Korea	Malaysia	India	China	Thailand
Thailand	Taiwan	Myanmar	Indonesia	Cook Islands	Tonga
China		Philippines	Korea	Fiji	Turkmenistan
India		Singapore	Malaysia	French Polynesia	Uzbekistan
Japan		South Korea	Philippines	Guam	Vietnam
Malaysia		Thailand	Taiwan	Hong Kong	Western Samoa
Taiwan		Vietnam	Thailand	India	
Philippines				Indonesia	
				Japan	
				Kazakhstan	
				Korea	
				Laos	
				Malaysia	
				New Caledonia	
				New Zealand	
				Niue Island	
				Pakistan	
				Papua New Guinea	
South America, Central America, and the Caribbean					
Argentina		Argentina	Argentina	Antigua	Guyana
Chile		Brazil	Brazil	Argentina	Haiti
Ecuador		El Salvador	Chile	Bahamas	Honduras
Paraguay			Colombia	Barbados	Jamaica
Venezuela				Belize	Neth. Antilles
Brazil				Bermuda	Nicaragua
Colombia				Bolivia	Panama
Mexico				Brazil	Paraguay
Uruguay				Chile	Peru
				Colombia	Puerto Rico
				Costa Rica	St Kitts
				Cuba	St Lucia
				Dominican Rep.	St Vincent
				Ecuador	Surinam
				El Salvador	Trinidad
				Falklands	Uruguay
				Guatemala	Venezuela
				Grenada	Virgin Islands UK
				Guadeloupe	
Middle East					
Bahrain	United Arab Emirates	Iran	Iran	Jordan	United Arab Emirates
Israel		Jordan	Kuwait	Oman	
Jordan		United Arab Emirates	Saudi Arabia	Saudi Arabia	
Kuwait			United Arab Emirates	Syria	
Lebanon			Lebanon		
Oman					
Qatar					

(continued)

Table 11.2 (continued)

General Motors (US)	Clarins (French)	Daewoo (Korean)	Mitsubishi Electric (Japanese)	Royal Dutch/Shell Group (Dutch/British)	
Middle East					
Saudi Arabia Syria United Arab Emirates					
Africa					
Egypt South Africa		Algeria Angola Kenya Nigeria South Africa Tunisia Egypt	Egypt South Africa	Angola Benin Botswana Burkina Faso Cameroon Cape Verde Chad Congo Congo (DR) Côte d'Ivoire Djibouti Egypt Eritrea Ethiopia Gabon Gambia Ghana Guinea Guinea-Bissau Kenya	Lesotho Mali Mauritius Morocco Mozambique Namibia Niger Nigeria Reunion Rwanda Senegal South Africa Sudan Swaziland Togo Tunisia Uganda Yemen Zimbabwe

Sources: Adapted from www.gm.com; www.shell.com/; www.mitsubishi.com/; www.clarins-financials.com/; www.daewoo.com/. All data from websites are available as of July 2005.

Ongoing market assessment

One of the major areas MNEs are continuing to pay attention to is data collection and analysis for the purpose of developing and updating market assessments. In some cases this causes multinationals to change their market approach, whereas in other cases it supports maintaining a current strategy.

Clarins

The French cosmetics firm Clarins SA is a good example of a firm that is continuing to re-fine its market strategy based on market assessment data. For more than two decades the company has been gathering feedback from customers on what they like and do not like about the firm's cosmetics. From these surveys the company has learned that women want makeup that is long-lasting, easy to choose, and easy to apply. This information has been invaluable in helping Clarins increase market share in an industry where competition is fierce. In fact, the company's growth rate in France has been more than twice the industry average, and Clarins is now achieving similar results in the US market. It is particularly interesting that this growth has been achieved despite the cost of Clarins's products. For ex-ample, one of its facial hydrating formulas sells for over $50. Aware of what up-scale cus-tomers are willing to buy, Clarins has been very successful in using market assessment information to develop and market high-quality skincare products. One marketing consultant has referred to Clarins as a "Body Shop for rich people"; certainly this target market has paid off well for the company.

Shell Oil

Shell Oil is an MNE whose market assessment has showed the importance of not making significant changes in product or delivery systems.[19] In recent years, Shell has limited its product diversification to "tightly linked and synergistic energy and chemical businesses."[20] The company has learned that it is most profitable when staying close to what it knows best. Today Shell works to balance its upstream (exploration and production), downstream (refining and marketing), and related chemical (industrial, agricultural, and petrochemical) businesses. It is also developing a strong network of service stations around the world and has learned that its ability to assess situations and react quickly is an important element in its marketing strategy.

Another approach Shell uses in improving its assessment skills is to have local operating companies simulate supply disruptions, such as dealing with a cut-off of oil from Kuwait. By evaluating these situations, the company was able to bring in alternative, preapproved crudes from other sources after Iraq invaded Kuwait in 1990 and oil from both countries was cut off.

New product development

Another marketing area that is a critical part of many MNEs' strategic management plan is that of new product development. The introduction of new products is helping these firms maintain market share and position them for future growth.

General Motors

For much of the 1980s, Ford Motor Company was the leading US auto maker in Europe. However, by the early 1990s General Motors (GM) had taken over this position, thanks to new product development and expansion.[21] In the early 2000s, overcapacity in the Western European market shifted GM's energy to cost reduction. European car makers such as VW gained market share against GM through continued product development.[22] Recently, GM has been building Opel engines in Hungary with a local partner and exporting these products to plants in Western Europe, where they are swapped for Opels to be sold in Hungary.[23] Meanwhile, the company opened a 178,000 unit capacity assembly plant in the eastern part of Germany.[24] It is also moving to increase its marketing outlets in Germany by signing up new dealers.[25]

IBM

Another example of new product development strategies is offered by IBM, which holds over three-quarters of the world market for top-of-the-line disk drives used in mainframe computers. The company recently designated this market as a top priority for the millennium. One reason for this decision is the high profit margins commanded by these disk drives, which can run as high as 60 per cent of the selling price. In an effort to stay ahead of the competition, IBM has introduced higher capacity versions of mainframe disk drives and intends to accelerate the product cycle.[26] This makes it more difficult for competitors to offer lower-priced models because by the time these models are ready for market IBM will be introducing another disk drive. Some industry analysts are predicting the advent of inexpensive disk arrays that will greatly reduce the profitability of the lucrative high end of the disk drive business. However, IBM believes that the complexity of these new drives, which integrate microelectronic controllers and software, will be sufficient to protect margins. The company is also doing well with its new PC offerings as well as other telecommunications products.[27]

Effective pricing

Some MNEs use a high-price strategy and skim the cream off the top of the market. Others employ a low-price strategy designed to penetrate and capture a larger share of the middle and lower parts of the market. Depending on the nature of the market, both strategies can be successful.

Bang & Olufsen

Bang & Olufsen is a Danish electronics company that manufactures stereo components, televisions, and video equipment.[28] The firm targets the upper end of the market, selling to style-conscious consumers who are unlikely to flinch at paying $4,000 for an audio system, $4,100 for a 28-inch color television with matching video recorder, or $5,600 for a 28-inch video system. One of the primary reasons customers buy from Bang & Olufsen is that the products are well engineered and designed. Televisions are sleek, thin, and modern-looking; stereo consoles are trim, polished, and futuristic in design. While many customers prefer to buy less stylish-looking products at one-third the price, Bang & Olufsen continues to have a steady stream of consumers who are willing to pay top dollar. Because of this, the company's worldwide sales now top the *$594 million mark*.

Wal-Mart and Cifra Inc.

In 1997, Wal-Mart acquired a controlling interest in Cifra Inc. of Mexico, the country's biggest retailer.[29] Established in 1957, Cifra was selling a wide variety of products by the 1990s, from powdered milk and canned chili to Korean television sets and videocassette recorders. Wal-Mart's acquisition fueled expansion throughout Mexico. Today, Wal-Mart has 545 stores there including department stores, warehouse retailers, clothing stores, and restaurants. One of Wal-Mart Cifra's biggest selling points is low prices. The company pushes what is called a "bodega concept": fast-moving, nonperishable goods that are sold in bulk in poor neighborhoods. By keeping gross margins in the range of 10–12 per cent and net profits at 3–5 per cent, the bodegas are able to average over $1 million per store each month. These sales are more than twice those of similar Kmart and Wal-Mart stores in the United States.

KEY POINTS

1 Marketing strategy begins with an international market assessment, the evaluation of the goods and services the MNE can sell in the global marketplace. There are a number of steps in this process, including an initial screening that is designed to determine the basic need potential of the company's goods and services, followed by additional screenings that culminate in a final selection of those outputs the company will market internationally.

2 Product strategies will vary depending on the specific good and the customer. Some products need little or no modification, and others require extensive changes. Some of the factors that influence the amount of modification include economics, culture, local laws, and the product life cycle.

3 There are a number of ways in which MNEs promote their products, although the final decision is often influenced by the nature of the product. The two major approaches

used in promotion are advertising and personal selling. Many multinationals try to use the same message worldwide because it is easier and more economical. However, this is not always possible because some messages either have no meaning in other languages or the message lacks the impact of that in other markets. Similarly, while personal selling is used in some markets, in other markets the customer is unaccustomed to this promotion approach and non-personal approaches must be used, or the customer must be educated to accept this new form.

4 Pricing in international markets is influenced by a number of factors, including government controls, market diversity, currency fluctuations, and price escalation forces.

5 Place strategy involves consideration of distribution, or the course goods will take between production and final consumer. This course often differs on a country-by-country basis, and MNEs will spend a considerable amount of time in examining the different systems in place, the criteria to use in choosing distributors and channels, and how distribution segmentation can be accomplished.

6 MNEs are using a variety of marketing strategies when formulating their strategic plans. Three of the most important strategies are ongoing market assessment, new product development, and effective pricing.

Key terms

- international marketing
- international market assessment
- initial screening
- market indicators
- market size
- market intensity
- market growth
- trend analysis
- estimation by analogy
- regression analysis
- cluster analysis
- promotion
- advertising
- comparative advertising
- personal selling
- dumping
- distribution

REVIEW AND DISCUSSION QUESTIONS

1 How does initial screening help an MNE evaluate those goods and services that might be sold in the international market? What are some ways in which this screening is carried out?

2 After an MNE has completed an initial screening of its goods and services, what other steps can it take in further refining the choice of those products to sell internationally? Briefly describe the remainder of the process.

3 Why can some goods and services be sold internationally without having to undergo much, if any, modification? Explain.

4 What factors influence the need for moderate to high modification of goods and services that have sold well in the home country and will now be marketed overseas? Identify and describe three of the most influential factors.

5 When should an MNE use the same promotion strategy overseas that it uses at home? When should it modify the approach?

6 Many MNEs find that their advertising messages can be used in overseas markets without much, if any, modification. Why is this so?

7 Why do MNEs sometimes have to modify their personal selling strategies when marketing their goods in international markets?

8 What kinds of factors influence the pricing of goods and services in the international marketplace? Identify and describe three.

9 Why do many MNEs find they cannot use the same distribution strategy overseas that they have used at home?

10 In choosing the best distribution system, what types of criteria do MNEs use? Identify and discuss three.

11 In what ways are multinationals using the following concepts to help them gain greater international market share: ongoing market assessment, new product development, and effective pricing? In each case, offer an example.

REAL CASE

Citigroup in China

The banking industry faces many barriers to globalization. Overcoming cultural differences and dealing with varying regulations and financial systems make it very difficult to establish a truly global bank. Citigroup is a leader in international banking, with 36 per cent of its income originating outside North America. Formed in 1998 by the merger of Citicorp and Travelers Group, in 2004 Citigroup had a presence in more than 100 countries around the world. Only HSBC can claim to do better.

Citibank enters a developing country with its own marketing strategy. In the first stage of development, it caters to the global customer (usually a large corporation) by providing short-term loans, cash management, and foreign exchange services. During a country's second stage of development, as demand grows in the face of a burgeoning middle class, Citibank begins to offer personal financial products.

In China, the political climate has limited Citibank's expansion plans in the Asia region. Citibank opened its first office in China in 1902 but was thrown out by the new communist government of Chairman Mao in 1949. Even after it was allowed back into the country, its business was restricted mainly to foreign currency. China's market potential, however, always attracted the bank, and when the country began to show interest in opening its borders and joining the World Trade Organization, Citibank stepped in as a key broker in negotiations with the US government. The bank's efforts are paying off. In the 1990s, the Chinese began to open their economy and make commitments for further reforms. By 2001, import tariffs had been lowered to an average of 15 per cent from 44 per cent in 1992, and they are expected to continue to decrease, averaging 9 per cent by 2006. China has also committed to the complete liberalization of its banking industry by 2006.

Deregulation is allowing Citibank to implement its emerging market strategy in China. In the initial phase, the bank marketed only to large foreign corporate clients. By 2004, it had expanded its customer base to include travelers, business people, wealthy Chinese with foreign exchange needs, and local businesses. Citibank's international network has also made it attractive to Chinese MNEs operating in other markets. Among these is Legend, a Chinese PC manufacturer that today controls over 25 per cent of the domestic market and is as yet unknown outside the mainland. Other examples include Konka (electronics), Haier (consumer appliances), and China Telecom. Local banks do not have the same level of international service.

Deregulation not only allows Citibank to open fully functional branches to cater to the wealthy and, increasingly, to the middle class, it also attracts more foreign clients. UPS and FedEx, for instance, both seek to open 100 per cent-owned delivery systems in China. Home to the largest number of mobile phone subscribers in the world and nowhere near saturation, China also expects to attract telecom service providers and product manufacturers. With 10 million PCs sold in 2001, the computer industry is also waiting to enter the market. In short, opportunities for foreign investment in China are creating a large number of MNE subsidiaries from which Citibank can draw its client pool.

Citibank's second marketing stage for emerging markets is expanding into personal banking. To some degree, Citigroup now offers consumer banking, corporate and investment banking, and insurance in the Chinese market. The bank does not yet provide a full range of consumer services to the entire population. Indeed, its banking fees are kept high for all but very large deposits to attract only the wealthier segments of the population.

In 2002, the firm was first allowed to offer foreign exchange services to Chinese nationals but is not yet allowed to offer consumer banking in yuan. In 2004, it partnered with the Shanghai Pudong Development Bank to offer credit cards that can be used in yuan and US dollar transactions. The credit card business is tricky in China because there is no credit rating agency, but by moving forward with this service, Citibank's goal is to create brand awareness that will allow it to dominate the market once it matures. The bank is likely to move consumers into mortgages, personal loans, pension funds, and other financial products in the final stage of marketing.

Although Citibank has a definite first-mover advantage in the Chinese market, it still faces competition from domestic banks. These include the Industrial and Commercial Bank of China and other large foreign competitors such as the HSBC, which also has extensive experience in the region.

Websites: www.citigroup.com; www.fedex.com; www.ups.com; www.legend.com.cn; www.konka.com; www.haier.com; www.chinatelecom.com.cn; www.icbc.com.cn; and www.hsbc.com.

Sources: Anthony Spaeth, "China's Legend in the Making," *Time.com*, May 8, 2000; "Citigroup Allowed to Build Mansion in Shanghai," *People's Daily*, December 4, 2000; Michael Shari, Brian Bremner, Heather Timmons and Becky Gaylord, "Citibank Conquers Asia," *Business Week* (international edition), February 26, 2001; "Foreign Bank Integration Accelerates in China," *The Banker*, May 3, 2004; "Citibank Business in Beijin," *China Daily*, March 26, 2004; "Another First: Citibank Wins Foreign Exchange Approval," *China Daily*, March 20, 2002.

1 How can a foreign organization such as Citibank make an initial assessment of a host-country market (such as China) in deciding how to do business there? What is involved in this process?

2 What steps can Citibank take in conducting additional screening of the Chinese market before entry? Briefly describe each step and discuss how relevant it is or is not to Citibank.

3 Based on the case facts, which of the four Ps of marketing would be relevant for Citibank's entry into China?

Brazilian soap operas: a world market

. . . I let myself get hooked on Brazilian soap operas. But those are so wild and over-the-top, the whole country stops to watch them. They're nothing like American soaps.

Paula Sharp, US Writer

When *Roque Santeiro* aired in Brazil after 10 years of censorship, São Paulo, a city comparable to New York, suddenly came to a halt. The 8:00 P.M. soap opera has become a ritual in many households; people leave anything they are doing to glue themselves to the TV. Not surprisingly, leading television stations compete heavily for this market. Indeed, soap operas are the main source of income for Brazilian TV stations, including TV Globo, Sistema Brasileiro de Televisão (SBT), and Manchete.

Fierce competition has helped Brazilian soap operas become among the very best in the world. *Roque Santeiro* revolutionized editing and launched its scriptwriter as an icon in Brazil. Period-set costumes were used for *Escrava Isaura*. And in "Torre de Babel," the shopping mall in which most of the action takes place was built for $1.1 million dollars, only to be blown to pieces as the plot developed.

Brazilian soap operas differ from their US counterparts by their running time and the structure of their plot.

While American soap operas can run for 10 years or more, Brazilian soap operas run an average of eight months and tend to have a very specific storyline and plot structure.

With a population of 172 million, Portuguese-speaking Brazil is one of the biggest markets for soap operas in the world. It is also one of the biggest producing countries, at nearly 20 soaps per year, as well as a leading exporter. Soap operas from Brazil are dubbed into foreign languages and exported to 128 countries around the world, including the United States, China, Italy, and Spanish-speaking Latin America. In Cuba, the communist government even rescheduled its electric energy rationing to allow citizens to tune into *Escrava Isaura*. Since its Brazilian premiere in 1977, *Escrava Isaura*, the story of a white slave on a Brazilian plantation, has been aired in nearly 80 countries.

Why are Brazilian soaps so successful? One reason is that audiences in other non-triad nations can identify with what is portrayed as Brazilian reality. Since their beginning in the 1960s, Brazilian soap operas have often dealt with such controversial issues as religion, the role of the state, class differences, abortion, sexuality, and racism. These issues were portrayed with due consideration to

Additional bibliography

Andersson, Ulf, Johanson, Jan and Vahne, Jan-Erik. "Organic Acquisitions in the Internationalization Process," *Management International Review*, vol. 37, Special Issue (1997).

Bonaccorsi, Andrea. "On the Relationship Between Firm Size and Export Intensity," *Journal of International Business Studies*, vol. 23, no. 4 (Fourth Quarter 1992).

Capon, Noel, Berthon, Pierre, Hulbert, James M. and Pitt, Leyland F. "Brand Custodianship: A New Primer for Senior Managers," *European Management Journal*, vol. 19, no. 3 (May 2001).

Cavusgil, S. Tamer, Zou, Shaoming and Naidu, G. M. "Product and Promotion Adaptation in Export Ventures: An Empirical Investigation," *Journal of International Business Studies*, vol. 24, no. 3 (Third Quarter 1993).

Cordell, Victor V. "Effects of Consumer Preferences for Foreign Sourced Products," *Journal of International Business Studies*, vol. 23, no. 2 (Second Quarter 1992).

Craig, C. Samuel and Douglas, Susan P. "Developing Strategies for Global Markets: An Evolutionary Perspective," *Columbia Journal of World Business*, vol. 31, no. 1 (Spring 1996).

———. "Responding to the Challenges of Global Markets: Change, Complexity, Competition and Conscience," *Columbia Journal of World Business*, vol. 31, no. 4 (Winter 1996).

Cravens, David W., Downey, H. Kirk and Lauritano, Paul. "Global Competition in the Commercial Aircraft Industry: Positioning for Advantage by the Triad Nations," *Columbia Journal of World Business*, vol. 26, no. 4 (Winter 1992).

Dominguez, Luis V. and Sequeira, Carlos G. "Determinants of LDC Exporters' Performance: A Cross-National Study," *Journal of International Business Studies*, vol. 24, no. 1 (First Quarter 1993).

Douglas, Susan P. and Craig, C. Samuel. "Evolution of Global Marketing Strategy: Scale, Scope and Synergy," *Columbia Journal of World Business*, vol. 24, no. 3 (Fall 1989).

Erramilli, M. Krishna and Rao, C. P. "Choice of Foreign Market Entry Modes by Service Firms: Role of Market Knowledge," *Management International Review*, vol. 30, no. 2 (Second Quarter 1990).

Fahy, John, Hooley, Graham, Cox, Tony, Beracs, Jozsef, Fonfara, Krysztof and Snoj, Boris. "The Development and Impact of Marketing Capabilities in Central Europe," *Journal of International Business Studies*, vol. 31, no. 1 (Spring 2000).

Hoang, Peter B. "A Causal Study of Relationships Between Firm Characteristics, International Marketing Strategies, and Export Performance," *Management International Review*, vol. 38, Special Issue (1998).

Kale, Sudhir H. and Barnes, John W. "Understanding the Domain of Cross-National Buyer-Seller Interactions," *Journal of International Business Studies*, vol. 23, no. 1 (First Quarter 1992).

Kaynak, Erdener. "A Cross Regional Comparison of Export Performance of Firms in Two Canadian Regions," *Management International Review*, vol. 32, no. 2 (Second Quarter 1992).

Kotabe, Masaaki, "Contemporary Research Trends in International Marketing: The 1990s," in Alan M. Rugman and Thomas Brewer (eds.), *The Oxford Handbook of International Business* (Oxford: Oxford University Press, 2001).

Kotabe, Masaaki and Czinkota, Michael R. "State Government Promotion of Manufacturing Exports: A Gap Analysis," *Journal of International Business Studies*, vol. 23, no. 4 (Fourth Quarter 1992).

Kotabe, Masaaki and Okoroafo, Sam C. "A Comparative Study of European and Japanese Multinational Firms' Marketing Strategies and Performance in the United States," *Management International Review*, vol. 30, no. 4 (Fourth Quarter 1990).

Kramer, Hugh E. "International Marketing: Methodological Excellence in Practice and Theory," *Management International Review*, vol. 29, no. 2 (Second Quarter 1989).

Landry, John T. "Differentiate or Die: Survival in Our Age of Killer Competition," *Harvard Business Review*, vol. 78, no. 3 (May/June 2000).

Lim, Jeen-Su, Sharkey, Thomas W. and Kim, Ken I. "Determinants of International Marketing Strategy," *Management International Review*, vol. 33, no. 2 (Second Quarter 1993).

Liouville, Jacques. "Under What Conditions Can Exports Exert a Positive Influence on Profitability?" *Management International Review*, vol. 32, no. 1 (First Quarter 1992).

Melin, Leif. "Internationalization as a Strategy Process," *Strategic Management Journal*, vol. 24, no. 3 (Third Quarter 1993).

Mitchell, Will, Shaver, J. Myles and Yeung, Bernard. "Performance Following Changes of International Presence in Domestic and Transition Industries," *Journal of International Business Studies*, vol. 24, no. 4 (Fourth Quarter 1993).

Nachum, Lilach. "The Impact of Home Countries on the Competitiveness of Advertising TNCS," *Management International Review*, vol. 41, no. 1 (Spring 2001).

Norburn, David, Birley, Sue, Dunn, Mark and Payne, Adrian. "A Four-Nation Study of the Relationship Between Marketing Effectiveness, Corporate Culture, Corporate Values, and Market Orientation," *Journal of International Business Studies*, vol. 21, no. 3 (Third Quarter 1990).

Rugman, Alan M. "The Myth of Global Strategy," *International Marketing Review*, vol. 18, no. 6 (2001), pp. 583–588.

Rugman, Alan M. and Verbeke, Alain. "Trade Policy and Global Corporate Strategy," *Journal of Global Marketing*, vol. 2, no. 3 (Spring 1989).

Ryans, Adrian B. "Strategic Market Entry Factors and Market Share Achievement in Japan," *Journal of International Business Studies*, vol. 19, no. 3 (Fall 1988).

Seringhaus, F. H. Rolf. "Comparative Marketing Behaviour of Canadian and Austrian High-Tech Exporters," *Management International Review*, vol. 33, no. 3 (Third Quarter 1993).

Walters, Peter G. P. "Patterns of Formal Planning and Performance in US Exporting Firms," *Management International Review*, vol. 33, no. 1 (First Quarter 1993).

Walters, Peter G. P. and Zhu, Mingxia. "International Marketing in Chinese Enterprises: Some Evidence from the PRC," *Management International Review*, vol. 35, no. 3 (Third Quarter 1995).

Yan, Rick. "To Reach China's Consumers, Adapt to Guo Qing," *Harvard Business Review* (September/October 1994).

Yavas, Ugur, Verhage, Bronislaw J. and Green, Robert T. "Global Consumer Segmentation Versus Local Market Orientation: Empirical Findings," *Management International Review*, vol. 32, no. 3 (Third Quarter 1992).

Chapter 12

HUMAN RESOURCE MANAGEMENT STRATEGY

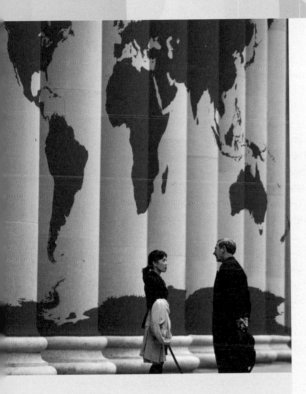

Contents

Objectives of the chapter

Human resource management strategy provides an MNE with the opportunity to truly outdistance its competition. For example, if HP develops a laser printer that is smaller, lighter, and less expensive than competitive models, other firms in the industry will attempt to reverse engineer this product to see how they can develop their own version. However, when a multinational has personnel who are carefully selected, well trained, and properly compensated, it has a pool of talent that the competition may be unable to beat. For this reason, human resource management (HRM) is a critical element of international management strategy. This chapter considers the ways in which multinationals prepare their people to take on the challenges of international business. We focus specifically on such critical areas as selection, training, managerial development, compensation, and labor relations.

The specific objectives of this chapter are to:

1. *Define* the term *international human resource management* and discuss human resource strategies in overseas operations.
2. *Describe* the screening and selection criteria often used in choosing people for overseas assignments.
3. *Relate* some of the most common types of training and development that are offered to personnel who are going overseas.
4. *Discuss* the common elements of an international compensation package.
5. *Explain* some of the typical labor relations practices used in the international arena.
6. *Describe* some of the human resource management strategies that are currently receiving a great deal of attention from MNEs.

ACTIVE LEARNING CASE

The Coca-Cola Company thinks local

The Coca-Cola Company has been operating internationally for most of its 120-year history, since it first started operations in Canada in 1906. Today the company operates in 200 countries and employs more than 400,000 people. Its human resource management (HRM) strategy helps explain a great deal of its success. It now follows a strategy of "national responsiveness" by adapting to local market conditions. For example, it transferred more than 300 professional and managerial staff from one country to another under its leadership development program, and the number of international transferees is increasing annually. One senior-level HRM manager explained Coca-Cola's strategy by noting:

> We recently concluded that our talent base needs to be multilingual and multicultural. . . . To use a sports analogy, you want to be sure that you have a lot of capable and competent *bench strength*, ready to assume broader responsibilities as they present themselves.

In preparing for the future, Coca-Cola includes a human resource recruitment forecast in its annual and long-term business strategies. It also has selection standards on which management can focus when recruiting and hiring. For example, the company likes applicants who are fluent in more than one language because they can be transferred to other geographic areas where their fluency will help them to be part of Coca-Cola's operation.

The firm also has a recruitment program that helps it identify candidates at the college level. Rather than just seeking students abroad, Coca-Cola looks for foreign students who are studying in the United States at domestic universities. The students are recruited in the United States and then provided with a year's training before they go back to their home country. Coca-Cola also has an internship program for foreign students who are interested in working for the company during school breaks, either in the United States or back home. These interns are put into groups and assigned a project that requires them to make a presentation to the operations personnel, including a discussion of what worked and what did not. The interns are then evaluated individually and management decides their future potential with the company.

Coca-Cola believes these approaches are extremely useful in helping to find talent on a global basis. Not only is the company able to develop internal sources, but its intern program provides a large number of additional individuals who would otherwise end up with other companies. Coca-Cola earns a greater portion of its income and profit overseas than it does in the United States. Its HRM strategy helps explain how, despite the success of its policies, Coke found itself facing a series of problems as it entered the millennium. During the 1980s the firm expanded its global reach and began to centralize control and encourage consolidation among all bottling partners. In the 1990s, however, the world began to change. Many national and local leaders began seeking sovereignty over their political, economic, and cultural futures. As a result, the very forces that were making the world more connected and homogeneous were also triggering a powerful desire for local autonomy and the preservation of unique cultural identity. Simply put, the world was demanding more nimbleness, responsiveness, and sensitivity from MNEs, while Coke was centralizing decision making, standardizing operating practices, and insulating itself from this changing environment. According to CEO Douglas Daft, it was going global when it should have been going local.

Today, Coca-Cola is beginning to turn things around. In particular, it has begun implementing three principles designed to make it more locally responsive. First, it is instituting a strategy of "Think local, act local" by putting more decision making in the hands of local managers. Second, it is focusing itself as a pure marketing company that pushes its brands on a regional and local basis. Third, it is working to become a model citizen by reaching out to the local communities and getting involved in civic and charitable activities. In the past, Coca-Cola succeeded because it understood and appealed to global commonalities; in the future it hopes to succeed by better understanding and appealing to local differences.

Websites: **www.cocacola.com** and **www.cokecce.com**.

Sources: Richard M. Hodgetts and Fred Luthans, "US Multinationals' Expatriate Compensation Strategies," *Compensation & Benefits Review*, January/February 1993, p. 60; Douglas Daft, "Back to Classic Coke," *Financial Times*, March 27, 2000, p. 20.

1. Does the Coca-Cola Company have a local perspective regarding the role of human resource management?

2. On what basis does Coca-Cola choose people for international assignments? Identify and describe two.

3. What type of training does Coca-Cola provide to its interns? Of what value is this training?

4. How useful is it for Coca-Cola managers to be fluent in more than one language? Why?

INTRODUCTION

International human resource management (IHRM) is the process of selecting, training, developing, and compensating personnel in overseas positions. This chapter will examine each of these activities. Before doing so, however, it is important to clarify the general nature of this overall process, which begins with selecting and hiring.

There are three basic sources of personnel talent that MNEs can tap for positions.[1] One is home-country nationals, who reside abroad but are citizens of the multinational's parent country. These individuals are typically called expatriates. An example is a US manager assigned to head an R&D department in Tokyo for IBM Japan. A second is host-country nationals, who are local people hired by the MNE. An example is a British manager working for Ford Motor Company in London. The last is third-country nationals, who are citizens of countries other than the one in which the MNE is headquartered or the one in which it has assigned them to work. An example is a French manager working for Sony in the United States.

Staffing patterns may vary depending on the length of time the MNE has been operating. Many MNEs will initially rely on home-country managers to staff their overseas units, gradually putting more host-country nationals into management positions as the firm gains experience. Another approach is to use home-country nationals in less developed countries and employ host-country nationals in more developed regions, a pattern that is fairly prevalent among US and European MNEs.[2] A third pattern is to put a new operation under the supervision of a home-country manager but turn it over to a host-country manager once it is up and running. Figure 12.1 provides an illustration of the types of managers, by nationality mix, required over the stages of internationalization. When an MNE is exporting into a foreign market, host-country nationals will handle everything. As the firm begins initial manufacture in that country, the use of expatriate managers and third-country nationals begins to increase. As the company moves through the ensuing stages of internationalization, the nationality mix of the managers in the overseas unit continues to change to meet the shifting demands of the environment.

In some cases staffing decisions are handled uniformly. For example, most Japanese MNEs rely on home-country managers to staff senior-level positions. Similarly, some European MNEs assign home-country managers to overseas units for their entire careers. US MNEs typically view overseas assignments as temporary, so it is more common to find many of these expatriates working under the supervision of host-country managers.

The size of the compensation package also plays an important role in personnel selection and placement. As the cost of sending people overseas has increased, there has been a trend toward using host-country or third-country nationals who know the local language and customs. For example, in recent years many US multinationals have hired English or Scottish managers for the top positions at subsidiaries in former British colonies such as Jamaica, India, the West Indies, and Kenya.[3]

International human resource management (IHRM)
The process of selecting, training, developing, and compensating personnel in overseas positions

Home-country nationals
Citizens of the country where the multinational resides

Expatriates
Individuals who reside abroad but are citizens of the multinational's parent country; they are citizens of the home, not the host country

Host-country nationals
Local people hired by a multinational

Third-country nationals
Citizens of countries other than the one in which the multinational is headquartered or the one in which they are assigned to work by the multinational

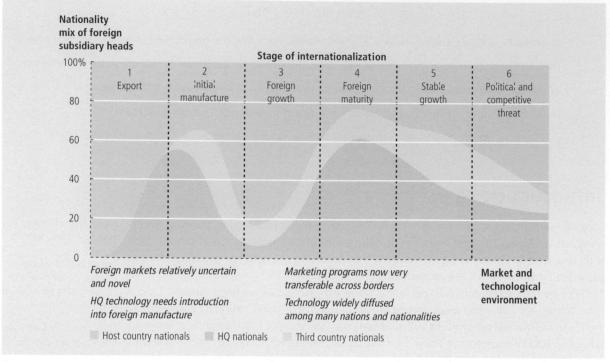

Figure 12.1 The management of multinational enterprises

Source: Reprinted from *Columbia Journal of World Business*, Summer 1973, Lawrence G. Franko, "Who Manages Multinational Enterprises?", page 33, Copyright 1973, with permission from Elsevier Science.

The above factors influence IHRM strategies and help MNEs integrate an international perspective into their human resource policies and practices.[4]

✔ Active learning check

Review your answer to Active Learning Case question 1 and make any changes you like. Then compare your answer with the one below.

1 Does the Coca-Cola Company have a local perspective regarding the role of human resource management?

The company certainly does have a local perspective regarding the HRM role. Coca-Cola is interested in recruiting people from anywhere in the world, training and developing them, and sending them to assignments around the globe. It does not confine itself to recruiting, training, developing, or promoting people from any one particular region or country. Both Americans and non-Americans have equal opportunities in the company, further reinforcing this international perspective.

SELECTION AND REPATRIATION

Two of the major human resource management challenges facing MNEs are those of selecting qualified people for overseas assignments and, in the case of home-country nationals, effectively repatriating them into the workforce upon their return. Each presents a significant challenge.

International screening criteria and selection procedures

International screening criteria are those factors used to identify the individuals regarded as most suitable for overseas assignment. Some MNEs use an extensive list, whereas others rely on only a handful of factors. A number of screening criteria are commonly used in determining whom to send overseas. These criteria focus on both individual and family considerations.

International screening criteria
Factors used to identify individuals regarded as most suitable for overseas assignments

Adaptability

One criterion is an individual's ability to adapt to cultural change.[5] Research shows that many managers are initially pleased to learn they are being sent overseas. However, within a few months many of them begin to suffer from culture shock brought on by the large number of changes to which they are subjected.[6] This often results in a decline in job satisfaction. However, as they continue their overseas assignment, satisfaction goes back up. Torbiorn, for example, reports that by the end of the first year most managers are through the cultural change phase and are beginning to adjust to their new conditions. For those who stay overseas two or more years, Torbiorn has found that satisfaction reaches new heights and continues rising.[7] Researchers have also found that men tend to adjust slightly faster than women, and that people over the age of 35 have somewhat higher levels of satisfaction after the first year.

In determining how well an individual will adapt to cultural change, MNEs examine a number of characteristics, including (1) work experiences with cultures other than one's own, (2) previous overseas travel, (3) knowledge of foreign languages (fluency is not generally necessary), (4) the ability to solve problems within different frameworks and from different perspectives, and (5) overall sensitivity to the environment.[8]

Self-reliance

Managers who are posted to overseas assignments must be self-reliant and independent because they often have to make on-the-spot decisions without consulting the home office. In determining self-reliance, MNEs evaluate the amount of field experience the individual has had, as well as experience in special projects and task forces—assignments that often require and nurture self-reliance. Consideration is also given to hobbies or avocations that require a high degree of personal independence.

Age, experience, and education

MNEs often find that young managers are eager for international assignments and want to learn more about other cultures. On the other hand, older managers have more experience and maturity to bring to the assignment. To balance the strengths of the two groups, many firms send both young and seasoned personnel to the same overseas post so that each can learn from the other.

Some MNEs believe that a college degree, preferably a graduate degree, is important for international managers. However, there is no universal agreement on this point. Multinationals that sell highly technical products tend to prefer people with science degrees. Others hold that a good education helps develop logical thinking, creative ideas, and a broad perspective of the world, so they prefer individuals with a liberal arts education. However, the best overall combination seems to be an undergraduate degree coupled with an MBA from a recognized business school.[9]

Health and family status

Expatriates must have good physical and emotional health. Those with physical problems that will limit their activities are screened from consideration. So are those judged less likely to withstand culture shock.

Multinationals also take into account a person's family situation. An unhappy family life will hurt employee productivity. One survey of US multinationals found that the primary reason for expatriate failure was the inability of the manager's spouse to adjust to a different physical or cultural environment. For this reason, some firms interview both the spouse *and* the manager before deciding whether to approve the assignment.[10]

The increasing number of dual-career families in Western countries creates a further challenge for MNEs. Equally career-minded spouses might find their careers interrupted during their spouses' overseas assignments. In fact, a study of 332 repatriates and spouses found most dissatisfaction with MNEs resulted from lack of employment support for the trailing spouse.[11]

Motivation and leadership

Another selection criterion is the individual's desire to work abroad and potential commitment to the new job. Many people who are unhappy with their position at home will consider an overseas assignment, but this is not sufficient motivation. Motivational factors include a desire for adventure, a pioneering spirit, a desire to increase one's chances for promotion, and the opportunity to improve one's economic status.[12]

Additionally, one group of researchers recently examined the factors associated with employee willingness to work overseas and concluded the following:

1 Unmarried employees are more willing than any other group to accept expat assignments.

2 Married couples without children at home or those with non-teenage children are probably the most willing to move.

3 Prior international experience seems associated with willingness to work as an expatriate.

4 Individuals most committed to their professional careers and to their employing organizations are prone to be more willing to work as expatriates.

5 Careers and attitudes of spouses will likely have a significant impact on employee willingness to move overseas.

Employee and spouse perceptions of organizational support for expats are also critical to employee willingness to work overseas.[13]

Applicants are also evaluated on the basis of their leadership potential, since most expatriates end up supervising others. Although this is a difficult factor to assess, a number of characteristics are commonly sought when making this evaluation, including maturity, emotional stability, the ability to communicate well, independence, initiative, and creativity. These characteristics are good indications of leadership potential.[14]

Selection procedures

The most common selection procedure is the interview. One international management expert has reported that extensive interviews of candidates and their spouses by senior executives still ultimately provide the best method of selection.[15] Other researchers agree. For example, 52 per cent of the US MNEs that Tung surveyed conducted interviews with both the manager and the spouse, whereas 47 per cent conducted interviews with the candidate alone. In the case of technically oriented positions, these percentages were 40 and 59 per cent. Other MNEs follow a similar pattern. Based on her research, Tung has concluded that multinationals are becoming increasingly cognizant of the importance of interviewing in effective performance abroad.[16]

Some companies also use tests to help in making the final choice of who will perform well in overseas assignments. However, this approach has not gained a great deal of support because it is expensive and many MNEs feel that tests do not improve the selection process. As a result, the candidate's domestic record and evaluations from superiors and peers, along with the interview, tend to be relied on most heavily.

Repatriation of expats

Repatriation is the process of returning home at the end of an overseas assignment. Managers are repatriated for a number of reasons. The most common one is that the pre-determined time assignment is completed. For expatriates, an overseas assignment usually lasts two to three years, although some companies are now encouraging their people to consider making the international arena a lifetime career choice. Another reason is the desire to have their children educated in the home country. The expatriate may be unhappy overseas and the company may feel there is more to be gained by bringing the person back than in trying to persuade the individual to stay on. Finally, as in any position, if a manager has performed poorly, the MNE may decide to put someone else in the position.

Readjusting

Although many expatriates look forward to returning, some find it difficult to adjust. A number of reasons can be cited. One is that the home office job lacks the high degree of authority and responsibility the expat had in the overseas job. Another is that the expat feels the company does not value international experience and the time spent overseas seems to have been wasted in terms of career progress.[17] A third reason is a change in the standard of living. While overseas, many expats have generous living allowances and benefits that they cannot match back home. An accompanying problem is the change in cultural lifestyle. For example, a person who is transferred from a cosmopolitan city such as Vienna to a small town in Middle America may find it necessary to make major adjustments, ranging from social activities to the pace of life in general. Additionally, it is common to find that those who sold their house before leaving and have been overseas from three to five years are stunned by the high price of a replacement home. Not only have they lost a great deal of equity by selling, they must also come up with a substantial down payment and much larger monthly mortgage payments. Some companies do not have plans for handling returning managers. If these individuals are assigned jobs at random, they can find their career progress jeopardized.

Recent research shows that the longer people remain overseas, the more problems they are likely to have being reabsorbed into the operations back home. In addition to the factors considered above, several factors make repatriation after longer periods difficult: (1) they may no longer be familiar to people at headquarters; (2) their old jobs may have been eliminated or drastically changed; or (3) technological advances at headquarters may have rendered their existing skills and knowledge obsolete.[18]

In many cases, it takes from 6 to 12 months before a returning manager is operating at full effectiveness. Adler reports that many expatriates have moderate to low effectiveness for the first 60 to 90 days, but they become more effective month after month as they readjust to life back home.[19]

Adjustment strategies

In recent years, MNEs have begun to address adjustment problems faced by returning expatriates. Some have now developed transition strategies that are designed to help smooth the move from foreign to domestic assignments.

One of these strategies is the repatriation agreement, which spells out how long a person will be posted overseas and sets forth the type of job he or she will be given upon returning.

Repatriation
The process of returning home at the end of an overseas assignment

Transition strategies
Strategies designed to help smooth the move from foreign to domestic assignments

Repatriation agreement
An agreement that spells out how long a person will be posted overseas and sets forth the type of job that will be given to the person upon returning

The agreement typically does not spell out a particular position or salary, but it does promise a job that is at least equal in authority and compensation to the one the person held overseas. Such an agreement relieves a great deal of the anxiety expatriates encounter because it assures them that the MNE is not going to forget them while they are gone and that there will be a place for them when they return.

A second strategy is to rent or maintain the expatriate's home during the overseas tour. Both Union Carbide and the Aluminum Company of America have such arrangements. These plans help reduce the financial burden managers face when they learn that their monthly mortgage will now be hundreds of dollars higher than when they left for a three-year tour.

A third strategy is to assign a senior executive as a sponsor for every manager posted abroad. This ensures that there is someone looking after each expatriate and ensuring that his or her performance, compensation, and career path are on track. When the expat is scheduled to return home, the sponsor begins working internally to ensure a suitable position. Companies such as IBM and Union Carbide use this form of the mentoring process, which is proving to be very effective.

A fourth strategy is to maintain ongoing communications with expatriate managers, ensuring that they are aware of what is happening in the home office. If they are scheduled to be home on leave for any extended period of time, the company works them into projects at headquarters. In this way they can maintain their visibility at headquarters and increase the likelihood that they are viewed as regular members of the management staff rather than as outsiders.

These strategies that help MNEs maintain a proactive approach in dealing with expatriate concern are becoming more widespread. For example, Tung reports that the best-managed US, European, Japanese, and Australian firms she studied had (1) mentor programs consisting of one-on-one pairing of an expatriate with a member of the home office senior management staff, (2) a separate organization unit with primary responsibility for the specific needs of expatriates, and/or (3) maintenance of constant contacts between the home office and the expatriate.[20]

✔ Active learning check

Review your answer to Active Learning Case question 2 and make any changes you like. Then compare your answer with the one below.

2 On what basis does the Coca-Cola Company choose people for international assignments? Identify and describe two.

One of the bases on which Coca-Cola chooses people is the ability to speak at least two languages fluently. A second is familiarity with at least two cultures. Both are viewed as critical for success in international assignments.

TRAINING AND DEVELOPMENT

Training
The process of altering employee behavior and attitudes in a way that increases the probability of goal attainment

Training is the process of altering employee behaviors and attitudes in a way that increases the probability of goal attainment. **Managerial development** is the process by which managers obtain the necessary skills, experiences, and attitudes they need to become or remain successful leaders. Training programs are designed to provide those who are going overseas with information and experience related to local customs, cultures, and work habits, thus helping them interact and work more effectively with local employees.[21] Development is typically used to help managers improve their leadership skills, stay up to date on the latest management developments, increase their overall effectiveness, and maintain high job satisfaction.[22]

Types of training

MNEs use several types of training and development programs.[23] These can be grouped into two general categories: standardized and tailor-made.

Standardized training programs are generic and can be used with managers anywhere in the world. Examples include programs for improving quantitative analysis or technical skills that can be used universally. Research reveals that many behaviorally oriented concepts can also be handled with a standardized program (although follow-up programs must be tailor-made to meet specific country needs). Examples include programs designed to acquaint participants with the fundamentals of communicating with, motivating, or leading people. Another form of standardized training presently offered by large MNEs addresses cultural differences on a global scale. For instance, with operations in 200 countries, managers of Colgate-Palmolive are often exposed to more than one foreign culture. To address this, the company has offered cultural diversity training to its managers.[24]

Tailor-made training programs are designed to meet the specific needs of participants and typically include a large amount of culturally based input. These programs are more commonly developed by large MNEs and by multinationals that need a working knowledge of the local country's beliefs, norms, attitudes, and work values. Quite often the input for the programs is provided by managers who are currently working in the country (or have recently worked there) and by local managers and personnel who are citizens of that country. In most cases this training is provided to expatriates before they leave for their assignment, but in some cases it is provided on-site.

Research shows that the following six types of programs are most popular:

1 Environmental briefings used to provide information about such things as geography, climate, housing, and schools.

2 Cultural orientation designed to familiarize the participants with cultural institutions and value systems of the host country.

3 Cultural assimilators using programmed learning approaches designed to provide the participants with intercultural encounters.

4 Language training.

5 Sensitivity training designed to develop attitudinal flexibility.

6 Field experience, which sends the participant to the country of assignment to undergo some of the emotional stress of living and working with people from a different culture.[25]

Typically, MNEs use a combination of the above programs, tailoring the package to fit their specific needs. A good example is provided by Underwriters Laboratories Inc., which uses a two-day, in-house program to train those personnel who will be dealing extensively with Japanese clients in the United States. The program is designed around a series of mini-lectures that cover a wide range of topics, from how to handle introductions to the proper way of exchanging gifts. It employs a variety of training techniques, including lectures, case studies, role-playing, language practice, and a short test on cultural terminology. The two-day training wraps up with a 90-minute question-and-answer period during which participants are given the opportunity to gain additional insights into how to develop effective client relationships.

Some firms extend their training focus to include families. In addition to providing language training, firms such as General Electric Medical Systems (GEMS) Group, a

Managerial development
The process by which managers obtain the necessary skills, experiences, and attitudes that they need to become or remain successful leaders

Standardized training programs
Generic programs that can be used with managers anywhere in the world

Tailor-made training programs
Programs designed to meet the specific needs of the participants, typically including a large amount of culturally based input

347

INTERNATIONAL BUSINESS STRATEGY *IN ACTION*

P&O cruise ships

Few people know that the "Princess" cruise ships, which were the "love boats" of TV fame, were at the time owned by British P&O Princess Cruises plc. The Peninsular and Orient Steam Navigation Company, known as P&O, was the sea transportation backbone of the old British Empire. In the 19th century it won British government contracts to deliver mail (post) to the Spanish peninsula and (via Africa and the Indian subcontinent) to Australia and the Far East. In the past P&O's ships have been commandeered by the British government in wartime to serve as transport vessels. As recently as the Falklands War of 1982, the large flagship *Canberra* played a central role in the British war effort.

In 2000, P&O Princess Cruises spun off from P&O and began to be traded on the New York Stock Exchange. The company retained the familiar P&O brand name as a base for its British Commonwealth cruise ships. The Princess cruise ships, acquired in 1974, were operated separately in North America.

In November 2001, P&O and Royal Caribbean agreed to a merger that would create a $6.8 billion company. With 41 ships, the new company would have dethroned Carnival Cruise Line to become the largest cruise line in the world. In 2002, however, Carnival bid for P&O in an attempt to wreck the merger of its two largest competitors. Despite the higher value of its offer, P&O management snubbed the company, arguing that the Royal Caribbean merger would create more value for shareholders in the long run and that regulatory approval for such a merger was un-likely. Carnival brought the matter to shareholders, urging them to delay voting on the Royal Caribbean merger. By August 2002, however, P&O executives had changed their minds. P&O changed its name to Carnival plc. The combined companies have revenues of $6.7 billion.

With an older population of North America "baby boomers," the growth of cruises has been striking. Occupancy is usually at 100 per cent capacity. Carnival is now the leading cruise operator along the North American West Coast to Alaska, an area that P&O previously dominated. To enter the continental Europe market, P&O purchased a major-ity stake in Germany's AIDA in 1999 and the remaining stake in 2000. It also purchased Germany's Seetours, a competing cruise line with 40 years of experience, and merged it with AIDA. Since then, AIDA has become the best-known cruise line in Germany. These brands were incorporated under the Carnival name.

Source: Alamy/Tim Gardner

Prior to the merger, P&O faced an interesting strategic challenge of integrating diverse businesses, from trucks to boat shows. In particular, it needed to link its very capital-intensive cargo ships, which require good information tech-nology and operational efficiency, with its cruise ships, which are in the leisure and entertainment business. Molding an engineering and technical culture with the marketing, sales, and service activities of the cruise ships is an interesting man-agerial challenge that P&O has tackled by providing extensive management training programs. For example, it has devel-oped a series of senior management programs at Templeton College, Oxford University, over the last 10 years that have both improved business efficiency and also moved managers into new areas of customer service, such as environmental and regulatory issues. As a result, P&O is a successful and growing business with a global mindset in its managers.

Because of stock market pressures, the P&O Steam Navigation Company has been divesting itself over the last few years of all non-core businesses. Today it specializes in logistics and transport and is a port and ferry operator. P&O operates 27 container terminals and has logistic operations in 18 countries across the triad. Approximately 58 per cent of its revenue derives from transportation and logistics originating in Europe. The remainder of its business is evenly distributed across the Americas and Australasia.

Websites: www.poprincesscruises.com and www.carnival.com.

Sources: Annual Reports of P&O; www.poprincesscruises.com; Scheherazade Daneshkhu, "Caribbean and P&O Chart Merger Course," *Financial Times*, November 21, 2001; "Carnival to Take P&O Bid Hostile," *BBC News*, January 22, 2002; and "P&O Weathers Storm in Ferry Arm," *BBC News*, August 12, 2004.

Milwaukee-based firm with expatriates in France, Japan, and Singapore, match up the family that is going overseas with another family that has been assigned to this country or geographic region. The latter family will then share many of the problems it faced during the overseas assignment and relate some of the ways these situations were resolved. It is also common to find MNEs offering cultural training to all family members, not just to the executive. This helps create a support group that will work together to deal with problems that arise during the overseas assignment. The box **International Business Strategy in Action: P&O cruise ships** details how an MNE's IHRM training is tightly related to its global expansion.

 Active learning check

Review your answer to Active Learning Case question 3 and make any changes you like. Then compare your answer with the one below.

3 **What type of training does Coca-Cola provide to its interns? Of what value is this training?**

The company puts interns into groups and assigns projects that require them to investigate or study certain areas of operations. The interns are then evaluated on the outcome. This training is useful in helping the firm identify those individuals who offer the most promise for the company.

COMPENSATION

In recent years compensation has become a primary area of IHRM attention.[26] On the one hand, multinationals want to hire the most competent people. On the other hand, they want to control costs and increase profits. Sometimes these two objectives are not compatible; it can be expensive to relocate an executive overseas. A close look at the breakdown of international compensation packages helps to make this clear.

Common elements in an international compensation package

A typical international compensation package includes base salary, benefits, and allowances. In addition, most packages address the issue of tax protection and/or tax equalization. The following examines these four elements.

Base salary

Base salary is the amount of cash compensation an individual receives in the home country. This salary is typically the benchmark against which bonuses and benefits are calculated. Survey research reveals that the salaries of expatriates are tied to their home country, so a German manager working for a US MNE and assigned to Spain will have a base salary tied to the salary structure in Germany.[27] This salary is usually paid in either home currency, local currency, or a combination of the two.

Recently, salary has become an issue when foreign firms have merged or acquired companies in other countries where salaries are significantly higher. For example, when Chrysler and Daimler-Benz merged, the Chairman and CEO of Chrysler had a salary of $1.6 million, whereas his Daimler-Benz counterpart was earning $1.1 million.[28] Moreover, a recent comparison of the base salaries of CEOs of industrial companies with annual revenues of $250 to $500 million found the following:

United States	$490,000
Brazil	$480,000
United Kingdom	$430,000
Hong Kong	$390,000
France	$360,000
Mexico	$340,000
Japan	$320,000
Germany	$300,000
South Korea	$120,000[29]

Indeed, then, base salary can present problems in the international arena.

Benefits

Benefits often make up a large portion of the compensation package. There are also a number of difficult issues that typically must be resolved, including how to handle medical coverage, what to do about social security, and how to handle the retirement package. Some of the specific issues that receive a great deal of attention are:

1 Whether or not to maintain expatriates in home-country programs, particularly if the company does not receive a tax deduction for it.

2 Whether companies have the option of enrolling expatriates in host-country benefit programs and/or making up any difference in coverage.

3 Whether host-country legislation on termination affects benefit entitlements.

4 Whether expatriates should receive home-country or host-country social security benefits.

5 Whether benefits should be maintained on a home-country or host-country basis, who is responsible for the cost, whether other benefits should be used to offset any shortfall in coverage, and whether home-country benefit programs should be exported to local nationals in foreign countries.[30]

Most US MNEs include their expatriate managers in the company's benefit program and the cost is no more than it would be back home. In cases in which a foreign government also requires contribution to a social security program, the company picks up this expense for the employee. Fortunately, in recent years a number of international agreements have been signed that eliminate requirements for dual coverage.

MNEs also provide vacation and special leave to expatriates. This often includes company-paid air fare back home for the manager and family on an annual basis, as well as emergency leave and expense payments in case of death or illness in the family.

Allowances

Cost-of-living allowance
A payment to compensate for differences in expenditures between the home country and the foreign location

Allowances are another major portion of some expatriate compensation packages. One of the most common is the **cost-of-living allowance**, which is a payment to compensate for differences in expenditures between the home country and the foreign location. Designed to provide employees with the same standard of living they enjoyed in the home country, this allowance can cover a wide variety of areas, including relocation, housing, education, and hardship.

Relocation expenses usually include moving, shipping, and storage charges associated with personal goods the expatriate is taking overseas. Related expenses can include perquisites such as cars and club memberships, which are commonly provided to senior-level managers.

Housing allowances cover a wide gamut. Some firms provide managers with a residence while overseas and pay all expenses associated with running the house. Other firms provide a predetermined amount of money each month, and the managers can make the housing choice personally. Some MNEs also help individuals sell their houses back home or rent them until their return. The company usually pays expenses associated with these activities. Other MNEs such as General Motors encourage their people to retain ownership of their homes by paying all rental management fees and reimbursing the employees for up to six months rent if the house remains unoccupied.

Education allowances for an expatriate's children are an integral part of most compensation packages. These expenses cover such things as tuition, enrollment fees, books, supplies, transportation, room, board, and school uniforms. In some cases attendance at post-secondary schools is also provided.

A hardship allowance is a special payment made to individuals who are posted to areas regarded as less desirable. For example, individuals posted to Eastern Europe, China, and some Middle East countries typically receive a hardship premium as an inducement to accept the assignment. These payments can be in the form of a lump sum ($10,000 to $25,000) or a percentage (15 to 50 per cent) of the individual's base compensation.

Hardship allowance
A special payment made to individuals posted to geographic areas regarded as less desirable

Taxation

MNEs provide tax protection and/or tax equalization for expatriates. For example, a US manager sent abroad can end up with two tax bills: one for income earned overseas and the other for US taxes on these monies. Section 911 of the US Internal Revenue System code permits a deduction of up to $70,000 on foreign earned income. For some executives, however, some US taxes might still be due. In handling these situations, most MNEs have a tax equalization program under which they withhold an amount equal to the home-country tax obligation of the manager and then pay all taxes in the host country. With tax protection, the employee pays up to the amount of taxes equal to those he or she would pay based on compensation in the home country. In this case, the employee is entitled to any difference if total taxes are less in the foreign country than in the home country. Other MNE tax considerations involve state and local tax payments and tax return preparation.[31]

The most common approach is for the MNE to determine the base salary and other extras (bonuses, etc.) the manager would make while living in the home country. The taxes on this income are then computed and compared with the total due on the expatriate's income, and the multinational pays any taxes over and above the amount that would have been due in the home country.

Current compensation trends

In terms of compensation, the MNE's objective is to ensure that expatriates do not have to pay any additional expenses as a result of living abroad. Figure 12.2 illustrates this idea. The income taxes, housing, goods and services, and reserve from the home country are protected so that the individual's out-of-pocket expenses remain the same. As we see from the figure, the overall package can be substantial. This is why there is a trend toward not sending expatriates to overseas positions unless there is a need for their specific services. In fact, the costs have become so prohibitive that firms like Dow Jones & Company, owner of the *Wall Street Journal*, have now radically revised their formula for paying allowances for housing, goods, and services.[32] In addition, MNEs are increasingly replacing permanent relocation and long-term assignments with as-needed short trips that typically last less than a year.[33]

Another trend is the creation of special incentive systems designed to keep expatriates motivated. In the process, a growing number of MNEs are now dropping bonuses or

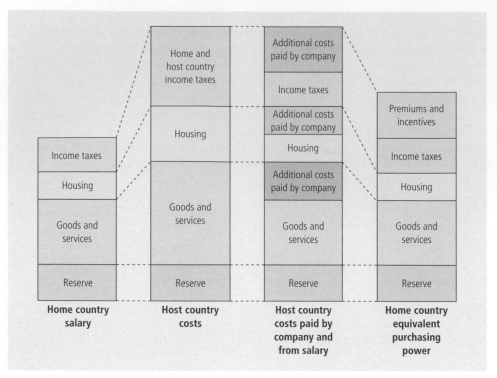

Figure 12.2 Cost of expatriate managers

Source: C. Reynolds, "Compensation of Overseas Personnel," in J. J. Famularo (ed.), *Handbook of Human Resource Administration*, 2nd ed. (New York: McGraw-Hill, 1986), p. 51. Reproduced with permission of The McGraw-Hill Companies.

premiums for overseas assignments and replacing them with lump-sum premiums. This approach has a number of benefits. One is that expatriates realize they will be given this payment just once—when they move to the international locale. So the payment tends to retain its value as an incentive. A second is that the costs to the company are less because there is only one payment and no future financial commitment.

The specific incentive program used will vary. Researchers have found that some of the factors that influence the type and amount of incentive include whether the person is moving within or between continents and where the person is being stationed. Table 12.1 provides some of the latest survey information related to these incentive practices.

Finally, it is important to realize that many companies are beginning to phase out incentive premiums. Instead, they are focusing on creating a cadre of expats who are motivated by non-financial incentives.

Table 12.1 Employer incentive practices around the world

Type of premium	Asia %	Europe %	North America %	Total %
Respondents paying for moves within continents				
Ongoing	62	46	29	42
Lump sum	21	20	25	23
None	16	27	42	32
Respondents paying for moves between continents				
Ongoing	63	54	39	49
Lump sum	24	18	30	26
None	13	21	27	22

Source: Geoffrey W. Latta, "Expatriate Incentives: Beyond Tradition," *HR Focus*, March 1998, p. S4. Reprinted by permission © *HRfocus*, March 1998. 212/244–0360. http://www.ioma.com

More companies are starting to take an entirely different approach, paying *no* premiums to expatriates regardless of where they send them. According to this philosophy, an assignment itself is its own reward. It's an opportunity for an employee to achieve personal and career growth. In some organizations, succession planning for senior-level positions requires international experience. Others view expatriate assignments as a step toward achieving globalization. Companies that subscribe to the philosophy of paying no premiums only consider cost-of-living issues, not motivational rewards, when designing pay packages.[34]

LABOR RELATIONS

One of the major challenges facing MNEs is that of orienting their strategy to meet the varying demands of organized labor around the world (see Figure 12.3). National differences in economic, political, and legal systems create a variety of labor relations systems, and the strategy that is effective in one country or region can be of little value in another country.[35]

In managing labor relations, most MNEs use a combination of centralization and decentralization, with some decisions being made at headquarters and others being handled by managers on-site.[36] Researchers have found that US MNEs tend to exercise more centralized control than European MNEs such as the British. A number of factors have been

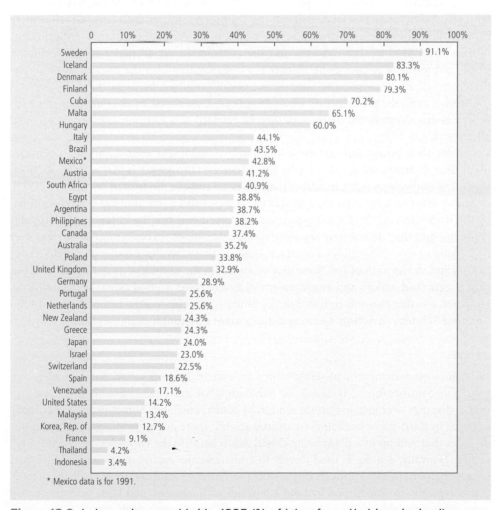

Country	%
Sweden	91.1%
Iceland	83.3%
Denmark	80.1%
Finland	79.3%
Cuba	70.2%
Malta	65.1%
Hungary	60.0%
Italy	44.1%
Brazil	43.5%
Mexico*	42.8%
Austria	41.2%
South Africa	40.9%
Egypt	38.8%
Argentina	38.7%
Philippines	38.2%
Canada	37.4%
Australia	35.2%
Poland	33.8%
United Kingdom	32.9%
Germany	28.9%
Portugal	25.6%
Netherlands	25.6%
New Zealand	24.3%
Greece	24.3%
Japan	24.0%
Israel	23.0%
Switzerland	22.5%
Spain	18.6%
Venezuela	17.1%
United States	14.2%
Malaysia	13.4%
Korea, Rep. of	12.7%
France	9.1%
Thailand	4.2%
Indonesia	3.4%

* Mexico data is for 1991.

Figure 12.3 **Labor unions worldwide, 1995 (% of labor force that is unionized)**
Source: International Labor Organization, *World Labour Report*, November 1997.

cited to explain this development: (1) US companies tend to rely heavily on formal management controls and a close reporting system is needed to support this process; (2) European companies tend to deal with labor unions at an industry level, whereas US MNEs deal at the company level; and (3) for many US firms the domestic market represents the bulk of their sales (a situation that is not true for many European MNEs) and the overseas market is managed as an extension of domestic operations.[37]

Labor relations practices

Labor relations practices vary widely. In some countries the economy is strong and unions are able to make major demands; in other countries the economy is weak and the union's ability to bargain is diminished. Similarly, some countries have strong pro-management governments whereas others are heavily union-oriented. A third factor is the willingness of unions to strike or walk out as opposed to continuing to talk with management in the hopes of resolving differences. Germany and Japan provide some interesting contrasts.

Germany

Labor unions traditionally have been strong in Germany. Although a minority of the labor force is organized, unions set the pay scale for about 90 per cent of the country's workers, with wages determined by job classifications.[38] Union membership is voluntary, but there is only one union in each major industry. This union negotiates a contract with the employers' federation for the industry, and the contract covers all major issues, including wages and terms of employment. If there is a disagreement over the interpretation or enforcement of the contract, the impasse is typically resolved between the company and the worker with the participation of a union representative or work council. If this procedure is unsuccessful, the matter can then be referred to a German labor court for final settlement.

Despite their power, unions have a much more cooperative relationship with management than do their counterparts in the United States. One reason is that workers serve on the board of directors and can ensure that the rank-and-file are treated fairly.

Strikes tend to occur after the contract has run out and a new one has yet to be ratified by the workers. As in the United States, several agreements may be in force in a particular company, and they do not have the same termination dates. So one group of workers may be striking or working without a contract while another is working under contract. On occasion, and in violation of law, there may be strikes in the middle of a contract period, but this is rare and union and management typically have a good working relationship. However, whether this will continue in the future is difficult to say; the box **International Business Strategy in Action: German management gets tough** examines this.

Japan

In Japan, union–management relationships are extremely cooperative. Social custom dictates non-confrontational behavior. So although labor agreements are often general and vague, disputes over interpretations tend to be settled amicably. Sometimes it is necessary to bring in third-party mediators or arbitrators, but there are no prolonged, acrimonious disputes that end up in a plant being closed down because the two sides cannot work together. Typically, a strike is used merely to embarrass the management and seldom lasts longer than one week. Although it is possible to resort to legal action in resolving strikes, this is typically frowned upon by both labor and management, and both sides try to stay away from using this means of bringing about solutions to their problems.[39]

INTERNATIONAL BUSINESS STRATEGY *IN ACTION*

German management gets tough

During the 1970s and 1980s, German manufacturing workers made substantial gains at the bargaining table. However, these successes are now coming back to haunt both them and their unions. In 1990, the average hourly manufacturing cost in the United States was $15 while Germany's was $22. Between 1985 and 1990, manufacturing cost in US dollars in Germany increased by 130 per cent due to the strength of German currency and a 28 per cent increase in labor costs in German currency. By 2003, average hourly manufacturing cost in Germany was at the $29.91 level, mainly as a result of the rising euro. This is much higher than in the rest of Western Europe. In Italy it is $18, in the UK $20, and in Portugal it is a mere $6.23. In the Czech Republic, labor costs in manufacturing are only $4.71 per hour. Across the Atlantic, US hourly manufacturing costs average $21.97.

Source: Corbis/Adam Woolfitt

In 1999, Volkswagen was prevented from laying off some 30,000 excess German workers by tough unions and labor laws. Job security and high wages are not the only labor disadvantages for German firms, which provide shorter labor-hour weeks, six weeks of paid vacation, and a very generous sick leave plan that promotes absenteeism. As a result, German products were having trouble finding international markets. In response, employers began looking for ways to turn things around.

In particular, companies began demanding wage concessions and started working to eliminate jobs. IBM's German subsidiary, which had almost 25,000 employees, divided itself into five companies, leaving only the 6,000 workers in the production unit working under a union contract. The remainder of the employees were not covered by the collective agreement, allowing the company to increase their work week to 40 hours. Other companies began implementing similar strategies, convinced that labor leaders would make concessions in order to ensure the long-run survival of the business. In particular, managers pointed to the fact that international competition was threatening German jobs and, unless productivity could be increased, there was a good chance that more and more local firms would go out of business. These strategies, and a decrease in the exchange rate, have led to real wage decreases and a restructuring of the labor market over the last few years.

A growing number of companies are now winning concessions from their unions. One is CED Informationstechnik GmbH, a small firm that assembles personal computers. The firm's union contract allows it to cut back the workforce when orders are weak. And since CED focuses on delivery of computers within 24 hours of receiving an order, it has no need to build inventory. Thus, the workforce size is tied directly to the amount of orders on hand, allowing CED to operate with a basic crew of only 200 people. In turn, another group of approximately 40 workers has contracts guaranteeing them at least 1,000 hours of work annually, so these people can count on approximately 20 hours a week on average— although this is all tied to work orders. The remaining 300 employees at CED work as needed and can find after a month or two of large orders that things dry up and they have no work for the next couple of months. It is a chance they have to take.

A 8.5 per cent and 18.5 per cent unemployment rate in West and East Germany, respectively, and the relocation of operations outside Germany by both domestic and foreign companies have increased the pressure on unions to accept less favorable contracts. While all of this is a big change from the days when the unions used to dictate terms, it is one that is accepted by both the workers and the CED's worker council. This attitude is reflective of a growing number of unions. In 1999, when Wacker-Chemie workers were in danger of losing their jobs because the company was losing millions of dollars, the union proactively allowed the adjustment of wages and an adjustment in workers' hours. As a result, jobs were saved and Wacker-Chemie was allowed to get back on its feet. Thanks to compromise on the part of its union, management in the chemical sector can, upon consultation with workers, decrease wages by up to 10 per cent per year, eliminate Christmas bonuses, and adjust the hours of work. In 2000, workers at Philipp Holzmann, a construction firm undergoing problems, bargained a wage decrease with the condition that workers

▶

will share the company's future gains. This new-found flexibility offers the promise of making German industry more competitive than it has been in a long time.

Websites: **www.vw.com**; **www.volkswagen.de**; **www.ibm.com**; and **www.wacker.de**.

Sources: Michael Calabrese, "Should Europe Adopt the American Economic Model?" *IntellectualCapital.com*, August 6, 1998; David Fairlamb et al., "Europe's Big Chance," *Business Week*, September 27, 1999, pp. 62–64; Jack Ewing, "This Union Leader Cuts Germany's Bosses Some Slack," *Business Week*, September 10, 2001, "Unions' Unions," *Economist*, April 27, 2000; United States, Bureau of Labor Statistics; "It's Those People All Over Again," *Economist*, August 12, 2004.

Japanese unions are most active during the spring and at the end of the year, the two periods during which bonuses are negotiated. However, these activities do not usually end up in a union–management conflict. If there is a strike, it is more likely at a time when a Japanese union is negotiating with management during industry-wide negotiations. Even here, the objective is to show that the workers are supportive of the union and not to indicate a grievance or complaint with management. In overall terms, Japanese workers tend to subordinate their interests and identities to those of the group. This cultural value helps account for a great deal of the harmony that exists between labor and management.[40]

Industrial democracy

Industrial democracy
The legally mandated right of employees to participate in significant management decisions

Unlike the United States, many countries have **industrial democracy**, which is the legally mandated right of employees to participate in significant management decisions. This authority extends into areas such as wages, bonuses, profit sharing, work rules, dismissals, and plant expansions and closings. Industrial democracy can take a number of different forms.

Forms of industrial democracy

At present there are a number of forms of industrial democracy. In some countries one form may be more prevalent than others, and it is common to find some of these forms existing simultaneously. The following describes three of the most popular forms.

Codetermination

Codetermination
A legal system that requires workers and their managers to discuss major strategic decisions before companies implement the decisions

Codetermination is a legal system that requires workers and their managers to discuss major strategic decisions before companies implement them. It has brought about worker participation on boards of directors and is quite popular in Europe, where Austria, Denmark, Holland, and Sweden have legally mandated codetermination. In many cases the workers hold one-third of the seats on the board, although it is 50 per cent in private German companies with 2,000 or more employees. On the negative side, some researchers report that many workers are unimpressed with codetermination and feel that it does not provide sufficient worker input to major decisions.

Work councils

Work councils
Groups that consist of both worker and manager representatives and are charged with dealing with matters such as improving company performance, working conditions, and job security

Work councils are groups that consist of both worker and manager representatives and are charged with dealing with such matters as improving company performance, working conditions, and job security. In some firms these councils are worker- or union-run, whereas in others a management representative chairs the group. The councils are a result of either national legislation or collective bargaining at the company–union level, and they exist throughout Europe. However, their power varies. In Germany, the Netherlands, and Italy, work councils are more powerful than they are in England, France, and Scandinavia.

Shop floor participation

Shop floor participation takes many forms, including job enrichment programs, quality circles, and various other versions of participative management. These approaches give workers an opportunity to make their voices heard and play a role in identifying and resolving problems. Shop floor participation is widely used in Scandinavian countries and has spread to other European nations and the United States over the last two decades.

Industrial democracy in action

Industrial democracy can be found in different forms throughout the United States, Europe, and Asia. The following discussion examines three examples.[41]

Germany

Industrial democracy and codetermination are both very strong in Germany, especially in the steel and auto industries. Private firms with 2,000 or more employees (in the steel industry it is 1,000 employees) must have supervisory boards (similar to a board of directors in the United States) composed of workers as well as managers. There must also be a management board responsible for daily operations to which company employees elect members.

Researchers have found that codeterminism works well in Germany. Some critics have argued that too many people are involved in the decision-making process, which slows things down, resulting in inefficiencies. However, Scholl reports that a study he conducted of both managers and work councils found no such problems.[42] In fact, the millennium is likely to see even greater efforts toward codeterminism in the unified Germany.

Denmark

Industrial democracy in Denmark gives workers the right to participate in management on both a direct and an indirect basis. The direct form maintains that employees are members of semiautonomous work groups that provide ideas on how to enhance productivity and quality and schedule work. In the indirect form, shop stewards on the floor represent fellow workers on the board of directors, and on cooperation committees that consist of both management and worker representatives. Industrial democracy works exceptionally well in Denmark, where researchers have found that cooperation committees contribute substantially to openness, coordination of effort, and a feeling of importance on the part of workers.[43]

Japan

Japan's use of industrial democracy concepts is not tied to political philosophy as in Europe; rather, it is oriented more to Japanese culture and the belief in group harmony. Moreover, Japanese industrial democracy is not as extensive as that in the West. Japanese workers are encouraged to identify and to solve job-related problems associated with quality and the flow of work. Management in turn is particularly receptive to worker ideas that will produce bottom-line results. This process is carried out in a paternalistic setting in which the company looks after the employees and the latter respond appropriately.

Unions play virtually no role in promoting industrial democracy or participative management because they are weak and, in many cases, only ceremonial. One group of researchers put it this way:

> In truth, most workers think of themselves as company employees who are simply associated with the union. Moreover, it is not uncommon to find a union strike in a company with two or three work shifts and no loss of work output. This is because, when the strikers are done picketing or

marching, they then go to work and the group coming out of the factory takes up the strike activity. In a factory with three shifts, a line employee will work a full shift, picket for a while, go home to eat and sleep, and then return to the factory for her or his shift.[44]

As a result, Japanese MNEs face the greatest challenge from industrial democracy because they are least accustomed to using the idea. On the other hand, as Japanese firms continue to expand into Europe and the United States, there will likely be a growing use of authority-sharing concepts such as codetermination, work councils, and other approaches that are becoming so common in Western firms.

STRATEGIC MANAGEMENT AND IHRM STRATEGIES

A number of HRM strategies are currently receiving attention from MNEs.[45] There are too many to address here, but three that do warrant consideration are language training, cultural adaptation, and competitive compensation.

Language training

English is the primary language of international business. However, training in the host-country language can be particularly useful because it allows managers to interact more effectively with their local colleagues and workers and communicate more directly with suppliers and customers. Another advantage is that the training allows the manager to monitor the competition more effectively. For example, in recent years a growing number of US MNEs have set up operations in Japan, including DuPont, Eastman Kodak, Hewlett-Packard, IBM, Procter & Gamble, and Rockwell International. Many of these MNE expatriate managers and R&D personnel have been given language training, which has paid off handsomely. For example, when Rockwell International entered into negotiations with a Japanese firm over royalties on a patent it holds on advanced semiconductor processing technology, the Japanese company said it had no intention of using Rockwell's patent. However, the company negotiators were able to show the Japanese an article from a Japanese newspaper in which their company had boasted about using the new technology. As a result, Rockwell now receives royalties on the use of this technology by the Japanese company.[46] In fact, thanks to language training, Rockwell was able to discover a host of patent infringements on the same technology by other Japanese firms.

Language training is useful in recruiting local talent and developing good relations with local organizations. IBM Japan, for example, hires 30 per cent of its research scientists from Japanese universities or companies. Other US firms follow a similar pattern, offering large salaries ($150,000 and up) to attract senior Japanese scientists who can help create new high-tech products. Language training also comes in handy in developing and sustaining relationships with universities and governmental agencies. In fact, Dow Chemical has created a team for just this purpose.

Another benefit of language training is the ability to monitor competition. MNEs often locate near their major competitors because new developments by these firms are most likely to be reported in local newspapers and other sources. It is often possible to learn more about what a competitor is doing through local news media than one could ever find out from an investigation conducted by MNE headquarters. Many foreign MNEs have personnel who are fluent in English, peruse the *Wall Street Journal*, *New York Times*, and US industry publications on a daily basis, then compile a thick folder on the strategies of their US competitors.

Language training is also useful in helping to learn about a country's culture and to interact socially with the people. Recent research reports that most US expatriate managers give little importance to the value of a second language. In contrast, executives from South America, Europe, and Japan place a high priority on speaking more than one language. One research study concluded by noting that "these results provide a poignant indication of national differences that promise to influence profoundly the success of US corporations."[47] Fortunately, universities in the United States are now stepping in to help out. For example, the Massachusetts Institute of Technology and other institutions of higher learning now offer courses in how to read technical Japanese and understand the Japanese research culture; this educational focus is likely to expand to other countries during the millennium. For the moment, however, language training continues to be a weak link in the development of an effective IHRM strategy for many MNEs.

 Active learning check

Review your answer to Active Learning Case question 4 and make any changes you like. Then compare your answer with the one below.

4 How useful is it for Coca-Cola managers to be fluent in more than one language? Why?

Coca-Cola's managers must be fluent in other languages because the company believes it allows them to operate effectively in at least two different cultures. This permits the company to transfer managers from one geographic region to another and to know that the managers will be able to become acculturated within a minimum time period. Moreover, because there are common languages in many regions of the world, a manager who is fluent, say, in English and Spanish could be transferred to countries throughout North America, South America, Europe, Africa, and Australia. Thus, bilingualism provides the company with a cadre of managers who can literally span the globe.

Cultural adaptation

Closely tied to language training is the need for managers to understand the culture of the country to which they are assigned. The importance of culture was discussed in Chapter 5, where it was noted that major differences exist between cultural clusters. In preparing managers for overseas positions, MNEs are now using three basic approaches. The simplest and least expensive is to design a program that provides cultural orientation by familiarizing individuals with the country's cultural institutions and value systems. This is often done through a formal training program and/or meetings with company personnel who have just returned from a posting in that country. The second is to provide individuals with language training and, if time and money permit, allow them to visit the country. Some MNEs tie this approach to a manager's assignment by setting aside the first couple of weeks on-site for orientation and acculturation. A third approach that is fairly expensive but has received high marks for its value is the use of cultural assimilators.

Cultural assimilators

A cultural assimilator is a programmed learning technique designed to expose members of one culture to some of the basic concepts, attitudes, role perceptions, customs, and values of another. Cultural assimilators are developed for pairs of cultures, such as familiarizing managers from the United States with the culture in Germany. Of course, an assimilator can be developed for expatriates who are assigned to any culture in the world, and the approach almost always takes the same format: The person being trained is asked to read a short episode of a cultural encounter and then choose an interpretation of what has

Cultural assimilator
A programmed learning technique designed to expose members of one culture to some of the basic concepts, attitudes, role perceptions, customs, and values of another culture

Table 12.2 A cultural assimilator situation

Sharon Hatfield, a school teacher in Athens, was amazed at the questions that were asked of her by Greeks whom she considered to be only casual acquaintances. When she entered or left her apartment, people would ask her where she was going or where she had been. If she stopped to talk, she was asked questions like, "How much do you make a month?" She thought the Greeks were very rude.

Page X-2

Why did the Greeks ask Sharon such "personal" questions?

1. The casual acquaintances were acting like friends do in Greece, although Sharon did not realize it.

Go to page X-3

2. The Greeks asked Sharon the questions in order to determine whether she belonged to the Greek Orthodox Church.

Go to page X-4

3. The Greeks were unhappy about the way in which she lived and they were trying to get Sharon to change her habits.

Go to page X-5

4. In Greece such questions are perfectly proper when asked of women, but improper when asked of men.

Go to page X-6

You selected 1:   The casual acquaintances were acting like friends do in Greece, although Sharon did not realize it.

Correct. It is not improper for in-group members to ask these questions of one another. Furthermore, these questions reflect the fact that friendships (even "casual" ones) tend to be more intimate in Greece than in America. As a result, friends are generally free to ask questions that would seem too personal in America.

Go to page X-1

Page X-4

You selected 2:   The Greeks asked Sharon the questions in order to determine whether she belonged to the Greek Orthodox Church.

No. This is not why the Greeks asked Sharon such questions. Remember, whether or not some information is "personal" depends on the culture. In this case the Greeks did not consider these questions too "personal." Why? Try again.

Go to page X-1

You selected 3:   The Greeks were unhappy about the way in which she lived and they were trying to get Sharon to change her habits.

No. There was no information given to lead you to believe that the Greeks were unhappy with Sharon's way of living. The episode states that the Greeks were acquaintances of Sharon.

Go to page X-1

You selected 4:   In Greece such questions are perfectly proper when asked of women, but improper when asked of men.

No. Such questions are indeed proper under certain situations. However, sex has nothing to do with it. When are these questions proper? Try to apply what you have learned about proper behavior between friends in Greece. Was Sharon regarded as a friend by these Greeks?

Go to page X-1

Source: Adapted from Fred E. Fiedler, Terence Mitchell and Harry C. Triandis (1971), "The Culture Assimilator: An Approach to Cross-Cultural Training," *Journal of Applied Psychology*, April 1971, 55, 97–98. Copyright © 1971 by the American Psychological Association. Adapted with permission.

happened and why. If the response is correct, the individual goes on to the next episode. If not, he or she is asked to reread the episode and then make another choice. Table 12.2 provides an illustration.

Cultural assimilators use critical incidents as the basis for training. These incidents are typically ones in which (1) the expatriate will be interacting with a host nation, (2) the situation may be misinterpreted or mishandled if the expatriate is not properly trained, and (3) the event is relevant to the expatriate's task or mission requirements.[48] The incidents are provided by expatriates who have served in this particular country, as well as by members of the host nation. Once they are written, they are tested on people who have had experience in this country in order to ensure that the responses are realistic and that one choice is indeed preferable to the others. Typically, 150 to 200 incidents are developed and the list is pruned to 75 to 100 incidents, which are eventually included in the assimilator booklet.

Assimilators can be expensive to create. The typical cost for developing one is approximately $50,000. However, for MNEs that are continually sending people to a particular overseas location, the cost can be spread over many trainees and the assimilator can remain intact for a number of years. A $50,000 assimilator that is used with 500 people over a five-year period costs the company only $100 per person, and the cost of revising the program is often quite small, so over the long run the assimilators can be very cost effective.

Competitive compensation

MNEs are also beginning to evaluate more carefully the cost of sending people overseas as well as to review the expense of maintaining executive talent in the international arena. The first of these concerns focuses on all expatriates. The second addresses top-level managers only.

Compensation costs vary widely because goods and services in some countries are sharply higher (or lower) than in others. For example, food, clothes, and entertainment in the United States are fairly inexpensive compared to Japan, Hong Kong, Taiwan, or Great Britain (see Table 12.3). In particular, the cost-of-living allowance for managers in Europe and Japan adds significantly to the MNE's overhead. For this reason, major MNEs, from General Motors to IBM to TRW, are looking for ways to recruit and develop local talent to staff operations and thus reduce their reliance on expatriates.

The other major area of compensation that is receiving increased attention is that of hiring and retaining top management talent. Research shows that the cost of hiring senior-level managers is extremely high, and in most cases these individuals received a substantial salary raise when they moved into their new position. Moreover, as the demand for talented executives rises, the salaries of international managers will continue to rise. This is one reason why many MNEs are now hiring people for specific locations and leaving them in place for extended periods of time. This strategy is less costly than continually moving managers from one geographic location to another.

During the millennium, HRM strategy will become an increasingly important part of the overall MNE strategic plan. Rising compensation costs are one of the major reasons for this trend.

Table 12.3 Cost of living in select cities (New York = 100), 2004

Location	Cost
Tokyo	143
Paris	130
Oslo	130
Copenhagen	129
Reykjavik	120
Geneva	118
Vienna	116
New York	100
Mumbai	46
New Delhi	45
Caracas	38

Source: Adapted from *The Economist Intelligence Unit*, June 22, 2005.

Specially designed HRM programs

Another emerging trend is specially designed HRM programs. In recent years a growing number of MNEs have begun to realize that HRM practices have to be tailor-made. This has been clearly illustrated by Sparrow and Budhwar, who compared data from 13 different countries on the basis of HRM factors. Five of these factors included the following:

1 Structural empowerment characterized by flat organization designs, wide spans of control, the use of flexible cross-functional teams, and the rewarding of individuals for productivity gains.

2 Accelerated resource development characterized by the early identification of high potential employees, the establishment of both multiple and parallel career paths, the rewarding of personnel for enhancing their skills and knowledge, and the offering of continuous training and development education.

3 Employee welfare emphasis characterized by firms offering personal family assistance, encouraging and regarding external volunteer activities, and promoting a culture that emphasizes equality in the workplace.

4 An efficiency emphasis in which employees are encouraged to monitor their own work and continually improve their performance.

5 An emphasis on long-term results such as innovation and creativity rather than just weekly and monthly short-term productivity.[49]

When Sparrow and Budhwar used these HRM approaches on a comparative country-by-country basis, they found worldwide differences in HRM practices. Table 12.4 shows the comparative results, after each of the 13 countries was categorized as being either high or low on the respective factors.

These findings reveal that countries are unique in their approach to HRM. What works well in the United States may have limited value in France. In fact, a close analysis of Table 12.4 shows that none of the 13 countries had the same profile; each was different.

Table 12.4 Human resource management practices in select countries

	Structural empowerment		Accelerated resource development		Employee welfare emphasis		Efficiency emphasis		Long-termism	
	High	Low	High	Low	High	Low	High	Low	High	Low
United States	X			X	X		X			X
Canada	X			X	X			X		X
United Kingdom	X			X		X		X		X
Italy		X		X		X		X		X
Japan		X		X	X		X		X	
India		X		X	X			X	X	
Australia	X		X			X	X		X	
Brazil	X		X		X			X	X	
Mexico	X		X		X			X		X
Argentina		X	X		X			X		X
Germany		X	X			X		X	X	
Korea		X	X			X	X		X	
France		X	X			X	X			X

Source: Adapted from *Journal of World Business*, Vol. 32, No. 3, 1997, Paul R. Sparrow and Pawan S. Budhwar, "Competition and Change: Mapping the Indiana HRM Recipe Against World-Wide Patterns," p. 233, Copyright © 1997 with permission from Elsevier Science.

This was even true in the case of Anglo nations such as the United States, Canada, Australia, and the United Kingdom, where differences in employee welfare emphasis, accelerated resource development, long efficiency orientation, and long-term vision resulted in unique HRM profiles for each. Similarly, Japan and Korea differed on two of the factors, as did Germany and France; India, which many people might feel would be more similar to an Anglo culture than to an Asian one, differed on two of the factors with both the United States and the UK, three of the factors with Canada, and all four factors with Australia.

These findings point to the fact that MNEs in the millennium will have to focus increasingly on HRM programs designed to meet the needs of local personnel. A good example is provided in Eastern Europe, where international managers are discovering that in order to effectively recruit college graduates their firms must provide training programs that give these new employees opportunities to work with a variety of tasks and help them specialize in their particular fields of interest. At the same time, the MNEs are discovering that these recruits are looking for companies that offer a good social working environment. A recent survey of more than 1,000 business and engineering students from Poland, the Czech Republic, and Hungary found that almost two-thirds of the respondents said they wanted their boss to be receptive to their ideas, 37 per cent were looking for managers who had strong industry experience, and 34 per cent wanted a boss who was a good rational decision maker. These findings indicate that multinational human resource management is now becoming much more of a two-way street: Both employees and managers need to adjust continually to emerging demands.[50]

KEY POINTS

1   International human resource management (IHRM) is the process of selecting, training, developing, and compensating personnel in overseas positions. IHRM strategies involve consideration of staffing, selecting, training, compensating, and labor relations in the international environment.

2   A number of screening criteria are used in choosing people for international assignments. These include adaptability, self-reliance, age, experience, education, health, family status, motivation, and leadership. The most common selection procedure is the interview, although some firms also use testing. In recent years MNEs have also begun formulating repatriation strategies for integrating returning managers back into the workplace at home.

3   Training and development programs are another key part of IHRM strategies. There are a wide variety of these programs, ranging from environmental briefings to language training.

4   There are a number of common parts in a typical international compensation package, including base salary, benefits, allowances, and tax protection and/or equalization. In essence, the package's objective is to ensure that the expatriate does not have to pay any additional expenses as a result of living abroad.

5   Labor relations practices vary widely in the international arena. For example, union–management relations and industrial democracy approaches are different throughout Europe, and these differ dramatically from those in Japan.

6   A number of HRM strategies are currently receiving a great deal of attention from MNEs. Three of these are language training, cultural adaptation, and competitive compensation.

Key terms

- international human resource management (IHRM)
- home-country nationals
- expatriates
- host-country nationals
- third-country nationals
- international screening criteria
- repatriation
- transition strategies
- repatriation agreement
- training
- managerial development
- standardized training programs
- tailor-made training programs
- cost-of-living allowance
- hardship allowance
- industrial democracy
- codetermination
- work councils
- cultural assimilator

REVIEW AND DISCUSSION QUESTIONS

1 Many US MNEs are accused of not focusing their efforts sufficiently on internationalization. How can they develop an international perspective among their managers? Offer three suggestions.

2 What are some of the most common screening criteria for individuals being chosen for international assignments? Identify and discuss four of them.

3 Why do MNEs tend to prefer interviews to testing when selecting people for international assignments?

4 In what way is repatriation proving to be a major problem for MNEs? How can they deal with this issue? Offer two substantive recommendations.

5 What are some of the most common forms of training and development offered to people going international or already operating there? Identify and describe three of them.

6 What are the most important parts of an international compensation package? Identify and describe three of them.

7 Why do some compensation packages have a hardship allowance?

8 In terms of compensation, why do many MNEs prefer to use a local manager rather than bring in an expatriate?

9 What are some of the primary differences in labor relation practices between Germany and Japan? Identify and discuss two of them.

10 How does industrial democracy work? Compare and contrast its use in Denmark, Germany, and Japan.

11 How are MNEs attempting to improve the language training given to their personnel being posted overseas?

12 How would an MNE use a cultural assimilator to prepare people for overseas assignments?

13 What are some of the latest trends in competitive compensation in the international arena? Identify and describe two of them.

REAL CASE

Outsourcing to India

In 1997, Computer Associates International, the world's leading business software company, announced it would invest $100 million in India over five years to establish a technology center. Indian software professionals would support and develop software for three of the company's product families. An additional $30 million would be invested to fund new Indian software ventures that were linked to Computer Associates's portfolio. At the time the deal did not cause much controversy, but over the last few years, as Western economies have slowed down and unemployment has increased, British trade unions and US politicians are campaigning to stop it—at a time when a growing number of firms, including Lloyds TSB, HSBC, Abbey, IBM, and JP Morgan, are using Indian service professionals. By 2004, India's high-tech sector was growing at 30 per cent per year and the volume of outsourcing contracts at 50 per cent per year. IT sector exports were $12 billion in 2004 and expected to number $15 billion by 2005.

The growth of the Indian IT sector is surprising because it lacked the domestic factors typically associated with the development of a competitive industry. First, local demand for software was nonexistent. Second, related and supporting industries such as telecoms or computing were highly underdeveloped. Third, the national communication infrastructure was among the worst in the world. Fourth, despite India's relatively higher level of education in relation to other countries, it was nowhere near the level of the triad countries. Finally, financial capital was in short supply.

Clearly, some general conditions help account for the time of the growth period, not least the global shortage of software programming skills relative to demand. Demand was particularly strong in the late 1990s due to fears over the Y2K or "year 2000" problem that threatened many computer operating systems and software around the world. The imbalance between supply and demand pushed up the price of software skills, globally increasing the cheap labor advantage held by Indian firms. This, coupled with strong English language skills, made Indian programmers good substitutes for more expensive Western programmers. Software engineers technically trained in the United States and Europe had developed customer links to the major customer firms (banks, telecoms, IT companies, and so on) in the West and then returned to India to establish their own ventures. New technologies enabled Indian firms to service the needs of overseas customers via satellite and the Internet.

Transportation costs are insignificant and the geography time difference can be an asset, allowing Indian firms to work through the "Western night." Finally, the Indian government had identified software as an area of potential growth in the 1970s and supported it through the 1990s, when the industry began to explode. Another important factor has been the willingness of computer firms, such as Computer Associates, to invest in the Indian market.

In the United States, fears of job losses are forcing politicians to take a stand. A US government regulation now prohibits the outsourcing of government services. This, however, has little effect on the Indian industry, which has traditionally relied on private contracts. A more direct effect could be felt if legislation is passed to prevent outsourcing; this is highly unlikely, however. Supporters of outsourcing argue that it is beneficial to customers who can now pay less for services and that the rise in wealth in India would increase bilateral trade, creating opportunities for US firms. Indeed, a recent study by McKinsey estimates that for every dollar of US outsourcing, 78 cents are value created in the United States and only 22 cents are retained by the foreign country. Britain's government is taking a different stand than the US government and outsourcing to India the modernizing of IT systems for the National Health Service. In the private sector, 28 firms in the UK outsourced more than 50,000 jobs to India between 2002 and 2003. It is no longer just IT jobs. Outsourcing of accountant services, medical services, research, and data entry to India is also growing.

Outsourcing does not always run smoothly. In the case of call centers, despite employee training in different English accents, customers have complained of problems communicating. In addition, the cultures might clash. On the other hand, many argue that Indian workers are more professional and better educated than their Western counterparts. The industry might be attracting a disproportionate number of bright minds in India because of the relatively higher standard of living enjoyed by those in the industry.

Today, Indian IT firms like Tata Consultancy Services, Infosys Technology, Wipro Technologies, and Satyam Computer Services are diversifying their portfolios and increasingly relying on e-commerce and other Internet-related businesses to cushion themselves against changes in the outsourcing market. Four factors drive this diversification: political risk from protectionists, rising wages, the rising value of the rupee, and expected competition from other nations such as China and Russia.

Websites: www.ca.com; www.wipro.com; www.infosys.com; www.tata.com; and www.satyam.com.

Sources: D. Gardner, "Bangalore-based Software Company to Use US Web Platform for E-Commerce Solutions," *Financial Times*, September 15, 2000; Zuhair Ahmed, "India Dismisses Outsourcing Fears," *BBC News*, February 9, 2004; "US Outsourcing Is 'Accelerating.'" *BBC News*, June 17, 2004; Kaushik Basu, "Outsourcing: Long-term Gains for All," *BBC News*, March 29, 2004.

1 Porter's well-known study on the competitive advantage of nations describes factors that have promoted high rates of innovation in certain industries in certain countries (Porter, 1990). These are summarized as the Porter Diamond framework showing how factor conditions, related and supporting industries, demand conditions and the strategy, structure and rivalry of other local firms can force continual improvements in productivity and new product development. How does the development of the Indian IT fit into this framework?

2 What are the threats and opportunities for Western software firms arising from this shift in the competitive landscape? How are they strategically responding to these?

3 What factors must a firm considering outsourcing take into account?

REAL CASE

Executive search firms

Commonly known as headhunters, executive search firms (ESFs) are a specialized branch of management consulting that work directly with clients, usually MNEs, to identify, evaluate, and recruit senior executives. Most *Fortune* 1,000 companies use ESFs to fill positions ranging from entry-level to CEO and board member. Worldwide ESFs are a $12 billion industry. Their fees are a percentage of the salary (including equity) the chosen candidate will receive in the first year of employment, which creates the right incentives for bargaining for high salaries by their executives. The largest firms are shown in the table below. These firms are highly competitive, particularly in North America and Europe. There are also many small local boutique firms, but these often work with the major international chains for MNE recruiting.

World's largest executive search firms, in US$ millions, 2000–2003

Executive search firm	2000 revenue	2003 revenue	% change
Hudson	n/a	1,805	n/a
Korn/Ferry International	576	351	−39.1
Heidrick & Struggles	574	318	−44.6
Spencer Stuart	345	315	−8.7
Egon Zehnder International	319	265	−16.9
Russell Reynolds Assoc.	305	229	−24.9
Ray & Berndtson	176	147	−16.5
Hever Amrop Alliance	129	113	−12.4

Note: These numbers do not include revenues from online businesses.

Source: Adapted from *FT.com*.

After several years of dot.com driven prosperity, the slowdown of the world economy hit the ESFs hard. Between 1998 and 2000, the industry had enjoyed a boom with annual growth of over 20 per cent. In the United States, growth was even higher at 31 per cent in 2000. By the first few years of the new century, however, the crash of the IT industry and the US recession reduced the number of executive spots and put a freeze on new hiring for many positions. Between 2000 and 2003, almost all ESFs were reporting losses and many headhunters were looking for work themselves. As seen in the table above, all the largest firms shrunk in size.

Korn/Ferry restructured and reduced its workforce by 20 per cent. Its largest competitor, Heidrick & Struggles, is also cutting the number of employees by 13 per cent. Ironically, this is occurring at the same time as the number of people seeking their employment services has skyrocketed. ESF revenues, however, are not dependent on the supply of executives but on the demand, which has fallen considerably.

To offset the strong dependence on the business cycle, ESFs are increasingly diversifying. Korn/Ferry and Heidrick & Struggles now offer strategic management assessments and executive development services. In 2001, a third of Egon Zehnder International's revenues came from non-search work. The company has become a consultant for private investors who want to evaluate a firm's quality of management. Like its competitors, it has entered the human resource development business by providing mid-sized MNEs with an assessment team.

Diversification has allowed these companies to stay afloat during the recession. Branching into consulting is unlikely to provide much respite for ESFs since consulting firms are also facing similar challenges.

According to Heidrick & Struggles, the economic slowdown led to a contraction of the executive search business, but has increased the number of available high-level positions. The company reported a decline of 38 per cent in the number of executive searches in third quarter 2001. Dissatisfaction with CEOs and other top-ranking managers raised the average fee per search by 12 per cent.

By 2004, things had started to turn around for ESFs, especially in financial services, real estate, security, and construction, which once again began to hire.

Websites: www.kornferry.com; www.heidrick.com; www.spencerstuart.com; www.russreyn.com; www.zehnder.com; www.hhgroup.com; www.rayberndtson.com; and www.amrophever.com.

Sources: www.kornferry.com; "The Fading Appeal of the Boardroom," *Economist*, February 8, 2001; Michael Skapinker, "Search Firms Look High and Low for Business," *FT.com*, November 14, 2001; Richard Donkin, "Korn/Ferry Is Back on Top," *FT.com*, May 14, 2001; Kathy Showalter, "Headhunting Firm Benefits from Stable Relationships," *Columbus Business First*, September 19, 2003.

1 When staffing the needs of the foreign subsidiary of a German company, what pool of candidates can the ESF choose from? Why would an international ESF be more capable of performing this task than the MNE's internal human resources department?

2 How would compensation negotiations differ for home, host, and third country candidates?

3 What types of factors would the ESF use to identify a potential candidate for an overseas assignment?

Endnotes

1 Brian O'Reilly, "Your New Global Work Force," *Fortune*, December 14, 1992, pp. 52–66.

2 Rosalie L. Tung, "Selection and Training Procedures of US, European, and Japanese Multinationals," *California Management Review*, vol. 25, no. 1 (Fall 1982), p. 59.

3 Richard M. Hodgetts and Fred Luthans, *International Management*, 4th ed. (Homewood, IL: Irwin/McGraw, 2000), p. 430.

4 Ellen Brandt, "Global HR," *Personnel Journal*, March 1991, pp. 38–44; and Stephanie Overman, "Shaping the Global Workplace," *Personnel Administrator*, October 1989, pp. 41–44.

5 Rosalie L. Tung and Edwin L. Miller, "Managing in the Twenty-first Century: The Need for Global Orientation," *Management International Review*, vol. 30, no. 1 (First Quarter 1990), pp. 5–18.

6 Indrei Ratiu, "Thinking Internationally: A Comparison of How International Executives Learn," *International Studies of Management & Organization*, Spring/Summer 1983, pp. 139–150.

7 Ingemar Torbiorn, *Living Abroad* (New York: Wiley, 1982), p. 98.

8 Hodgetts and Luthans (2000) n. 3 above, p. 434.

9 Jean E. Heller, "Criteria for Selecting an International Manager," *Personnel*, May/June 1980, p. 48.

10 Jeffrey L. Blue and Ulric Haynes, Jr., "Preparing for the Overseas Assignment," *Business Horizons*, June 1977, p. 62.

11 Michael Harvey, "Dual Career Expatriates: Expectations, Adjustments and Satisfaction with International Relocation," *Journal of International Business Studies*, vol. 28, no. 3 (Winter 1997).

12 Torbiorn (1982) n. 7 above, pp. 156–161.

13 Patricia C. Borstorff, Stanley G. Harris, Hubert S. Field and William F. Giles, "Who'll Go? A Review of Factors Associated with Employee Willingness to Work Overseas," *Human Resource Planning*, vol. 20, no. 3 (1997), p. 38.

14 See also Agis Salpukas, "From Brooklyn, Around the World, to Mobil's Top Job," *New York Times*, February 6, 1994, p. F8.

15 Heller (1980) n. 9 above, p. 53.

16 Tung (1982) n. 2 above, p. 64.

17 Gary R. Oddou and Mark E. Mendenhall, "Succession Planning for the 21st Century: How Well Are We Grooming Our Future Business Leaders?" *Business Horizons*, January/February 1991, pp. 26–34.

18 Rosalie L. Tung, "Career Issues in International Assignments," *Academy of Management Executive*, August 1988, p. 242.

19 Nancy J. Adler and Susan Bartholomew, "Academic and Professional Communities of Discourse: Generating Knowledge on Transnational Human Resource Management," *Journal of International Business Studies*, vol. 23, no. 3 (Third Quarter 1992), pp. 551–569.

20 Rosalie L. Tung, "Career Issues in International Assignments," *Academy of Management Executive*, August 1988, p. 243.

21 See, for example, J. Bernard Keys and Robert M. Fulmer, *Executive Development and Organizational Learning for Global Business* (New York: International Business Press, 1998), pp. 1–9.

22 Stephen H. Rhinesmith, John N. Williamson, David M. Ehlen and Denise S. Maxwell, "Developing Leaders for the Global Enterprise," *Training and Development Journal*, April 1989, pp. 25–34; Patricia A. Galagan, "Executive Development in a Changing World," *Training and Development Journal*, June 1990, pp. 23–35; and Madelyn R. Callahan, "Preparing the New Global Manager," *Training and Development Journal*, March 1989, pp. 29–32.

23 See Steven H. Rhinesmith, "An Agenda for Globalization," *Training and Development Journal*, February 1991, pp. 22–29; Benton Randolph, "When Going Global Isn't Enough," *Training*, August 1990, pp. 47–51; and Ronald Henkoff, "Companies That Train Best," *Fortune*, March 22, 1993, pp. 62–75.

24 "Company Culture in the Global Village," *Philips' What's Up Archive*, July 12, 1999.

25 Tung (1982) n. 2 above, p. 65.

26 See Lin P. Crandall and Mark I. Phelps, "Pay for a Global Work Force," *Personnel Journal*, February 1991, pp. 28–33.

27 Peter J. Dowling and Randall S. Schuler, *International Dimensions of Human Resource Management* (Boston, MA: PWS-Kent Publishing, 1990), p. 121.

28 Greg Steinmetz and Gregory L. White, "Chrysler Pay Draws Fire Overseas," *Wall Street Journal*, May 26, 1998, p. B 1.

29 Adam Bryant, "American Pay Rattles Foreign Partners," *New York Times*, January 17, 1999, Section 4, p. 1.

30 Dowling and Schuler (1990) n. 26 above, p. 125.

31 Ibid., p. 123.

32 Alex S. Jones, "Dow Jones Plans to Tighten Foreign Policy for Workers," *New York Times*, September 9, 1991, p. C 6.

33 "Nasty, Brutish and Short," *Economist*, December 14, 2000.

34 Geofferey W. Latta, "Expatriate Incentives: Beyond Tradition," *HR Focus*, March 1998, p. S 4.

35 A good example is workplace discrimination, which is a major issue in the US but not in many other countries. See Susan Antilla, "Workplace Discrimination? Don't Try It Around Here," *New York Times*, February 13, 1994, p. F 7.

36 See, for example, Laurie Hays, "IBM's Finance Chief, Ax in Hand, Scours Empires for Costs to Cut," *Wall Street Journal*, January 26, 1994, pp. A 1, A 6.

37 C. K. Prahalad and Y. L. Doz, *The Multinational Mission: Balancing Logical Demands and Global Vision* (New York: Free Press, 1987).

38 Ferdinand Protzman, "Rewriting the Contract for Germany's Vaunted Workers," *New York Times*, February 13, 1994, p. F 5.

39 Keith Atkinson, "State of the Unions," *Personnel Administrator*, September 1986, p. 58.

40 For additional insights into Japanese labor management practices, see Karen Lowry Miller and Larry Armstrong, "How Honda Hammered Out Its New Accord," *Business Week*, December 21, 1992, p. 86; and David E. Sanger, "Layoffs and Factory Closings: Shaking the Japanese Psyche," *New York Times*, March 3, 1993, pp. A 1, C 16.

41 For a European country comparison of labor involvement in industrial decision making, see Mark Fenton-O'Creevy, "Survey—Mastering People Management," *Ft.com*, November 26, 2001.

42 Wolfgang Scholl, "Codetermination and the Ability of Firms to Act in the Federal Republic of Germany," *International Studies of Management & Organization*, Summer 1987, pp. 27–37.

43 Reinhard Lund, "Industrial Democracy in Denmark," *International Studies of Management & Organization*, Summer 1987, pp. 27–37.

44 Hodgetts and Luthans (2000) n. 3 above, p. 504.

45 For specific examples of HRM practices throughout the world, see Michael J. Marquardt and Dean W. Engel, *Global Human Resource Development* (Englewood Cliffs, NJ: Prentice-Hall, 1993).

46 Susan Moffat, "Picking Japan's Research Brains," *Fortune*, March 25, 1991, p. 94.

47 Reported in "Report: Shortage of Executives Will Hurt US," *Omaha World Herald*, June 25, 1989, p. 1-G.

48 Fred E. Fiedler, Terence Mitchell and Harry C. Triandis, "The Culture Assimilator: An Approach to Cross-Cultural Training," *Journal of Applied Psychology*, April 1971, p. 95.

49 Paul R. Sparrow and Pawan S. Budhwar, "Competition and Change: Mapping the Indian HRM Recipe Against World-Wide Patterns," *Journal of World Business*, vol. 32, no. 3 (Fall 1997), p. 231.

50 Bodil Jones, "What Future European Recruits Want," *Management Review*, January 1998, p. 6.

Additional bibliography

Abramson, Neil R., Lane, Henry W., Nagai, Hirohisa and Takagi, Haruo. "A Comparison of Canadian and Japanese Cognitive Styles: Implications for Management Interaction," *Journal of International Business Studies*, vol. 24, no. 3 (Third Quarter 1993).

Adler, Nancy J. and Bartholomew, Susan. "Academic and Professional Communities of Discourse: Generating Knowledge on Transnational Human Resource Management," *Journal of International Business Studies*, vol. 23, no. 3 (Third Quarter 1992).

Banai, Moshe and Reisel, William D. "Expatriate Managers' Loyalty to the MNC: Myth or Reality? An Exploratory Study," *Journal of International Business Studies*, vol. 24, no. 2 (Second Quarter 1993).

Beaumont, Philip, "New Challenges for European Human Resource Management," *European Management Journal*, vol. 19, no. 4 (August 2001).

Black, J. Stewart and Gregersen, Hal B. "The Other Half of the Picture: Antecedents of Spouse Cross-Cultural Adjustment," *Journal of International Business Studies*, vol. 22, no. 3 (Third Quarter 1991).

Black, J. Stewart and Mendenhall, Mark. "Cross-Cultural Training Effectiveness: A Review and a Theoretical Framework for Future Research," *Academy of Management Review*, vol. 15, no. 1 (January 1990).

Boyacigiller, Nakiye. "The Role of Expatriates in the Management of Interdependence, Complexity and Risk in Multinational Corporations," *Journal of International Business Studies*, vol. 21, no. 3 (Third Quarter 1990).

Camuffo, Arnaldo and Costa, Giovanni. "Strategic Human Resource Management—Italian Style," *Sloan Management Review*, vol. 34, no. 2 (Winter 1993).

De Cieri, Helen and Dowling, Peter J. "Strategic International Human Resource Management: An Asia-Pacific Perspective," *Management International Review*, vol. 37, Special Issue (1997).

Ebrahimpour, Maling and Cullen, John B. "Quality Management in Japanese and American Firms Operating in the United States: A Comparative Study of Styles and Motivational Beliefs," *Management International Review*, vol. 33, no. 1 (First Quarter 1993).

Feldman, Daniel C. and Thomas, David C. "Career Management Issues Facing Expatriates," *Journal of*

International Business Studies, vol. 23, no. 2 (Second Quarter 1992).

Geringer, J. Michael and Frayne, Colette A. "Human Resource Management and International Joint Venture Control: A Parent Company Perspective," *Management International Review*, vol. 30, Special Issue (1990).

Haigh, Robert W. "Building a Strategic Alliance—The Hermosillo Experience as a Ford-Mazda Proving Ground," *Columbia Journal of World Business*, vol. 27, no. 1 (Spring 1992).

Harvey, Michael. "The Selection of Managers for Foreign Assignments: A Planning Perspective," *Columbia Journal of World Business*, vol. 31, no. 4 (Winter 1996).

———. "Dual Career Expatriates: Expectations, Adjustments and Satisfaction with International Relocation," *Journal of International Business Studies*, vol. 28, no. 3 (Fall 1997).

Jun, Sunkyu, Gentry, James W. and Hyun, Yong J. "Cultural Adaptation of Business Expatriates in the Host Marketplace," *Journal of International Business Studies*, vol. 32, no. 2 (Summer 2001).

Kayworth, Timothy. "The Global Virtual Manager: A Prescription for Success," *European Management Journal*, vol. 18, no. 2 (April 2000).

Lado, Augustine A. "Strategic Human Resource Management," *Academy of Management Review*, vol. 25, no. 3 (July 2000).

Milliman, John, Von Glinow, Mary Ann and Nathan, Maria. "Organizational Life Cycles and Strategic International Human Resource Management in Multinational Companies: Implications for Congruence Theory," *Academy of Management Review*, vol. 16, no. 2 (April 1991).

Roth, Kendall and O'Donnell, Sharon. "Foreign Subsidiary Compensation Strategy: An Agency Theory Perspective," *Academy of Management Journal*, vol. 39, no. 3 (June 1996).

Sanyal, Rajib N. "An Empirical Analysis of the Unionization of Foreign Manufacturing Firms in the US," *Journal of*

International Business Studies, vol. 21, no. 1 (First Quarter 1990).

Schuler, Randall S. and Rogovsky, Nikolai. "Understanding Compensation Practice Variations Across Firms: The Impact of National Culture," *Journal of International Business Studies*, vol. 29, no. 1 (First Quarter 1998).

Sergeant, Andrew and Frenkel, Stephen. "Managing People in China: Perceptions of Expatriate Managers," *Journal of World Business*, vol. 33, no. 1 (Spring 1998).

Shaffer, Margaret A. "Dimensions, Determinants, and Differences in the Expatriate Adjustment Process," *Journal of International Business Studies*, vol. 30, no. 3 (Fall 1999).

Shenkar, Oded and Zeira, Yoram. "Human Resources Management in International Joint Ventures: Directions for Research," *Academy of Management Review*, vol. 12, no. 3 (July 1987).

Stark, Andrew. "What's the Matter with Business Ethics?" *Harvard Business Review*, vol. 71, no. 3 (May/June 1993).

Sullivan, Jeremiah J. and Peterson, Richard B. "A Test of Theories Underlying the Japanese Lifetime Employment System," *Journal of International Business Studies*, vol. 22, no. 1 (First Quarter 1991).

Taylor, Sully, Beechler, Schon and Napier, Nancy. "Toward an Integrative Model of Strategic International Human Resource Management," *Academy of Management Review*, vol. 21, no. 4 (October 1996).

Tung, Rosalie L. "American Expatriates Abroad: From Neophytes to Cosmopolitans," *Journal of World Business*, vol. 33, no. 2 (Summer 1998).

Tung, Rosalie L. and Miller, Edwin L. "Managing in the Twenty-First Century: The Need for Global Orientation," *Management International Review*, vol. 30, no. 1 (First Quarter 1990).

Vanderbroeck, Paul. "Long-Term Human Resource Development in Multinational Organizations," *Sloan Management Review*, vol. 34, no. 1 (Fall 1992).

Chapter 13

POLITICAL RISK
AND NEGOTIATION STRATEGY

Contents

Objectives of the chapter

For international managers different countries represent different business contexts with new sources of opportunity and risk. An important management priority is to fully assess the risks as well as the potential rewards before investing in new markets. Political change represents a key source of both new opportunities and new risks. Major political changes in China and India in the early 1990s, for example, opened up these economies for foreign investors. They had always been attractive markets, but were made accessible. However, the high level of control still held by these governments over their economies, combined with the continued uncertainty regarding political change, results in a high level of political risk for investors.

Beyond these major political shifts, smaller changes in any government's policies toward foreign investors—from taxes and tariffs to profit repatriation to local input content to employment legislation to corporate governance practices—can tilt the balance between profit and loss.

This chapter examines political risk in the context of over-all country risk assessment. We look at how multinational enterprises (MNEs) try to forecast this risk, how they can understand governments' policy agendas, and how they can use negotiating tactics to minimize their political risk.

The specific objectives of this chapter are to:

1 *Examine* the nature of political risk.
2 *Understand* how to apply some of the tools and resources companies can use to measure and forecast political risk.
3 *Discuss* some of the ways that firms manage risk.
4 *Review* typical strategies and tactics used in negotiating agreements.

ACTIVE LEARNING CASE

Kodak in China: changing the rules of the game

Fewer than one Chinese household in ten owns a camera today. And that camera exposes about four rolls of film each year. If only half the people in China shot a single 36-exposure roll of film a year—a fraction of usage rates in other countries—that would swell the number of world-wide "clicks" by 25%. Each second, 500 more photos would be taken. That's the equivalent of adding another U.S. or Japan to the world photographic market. China offers more potential for photography than any other market in the world.

George Fisher (Kodak CEO), May 23, 1998 (Kodak press release at: http://www.kodak.com/US/en/corp/pressReleases/pr19980323-01.shtml).

Source: Alarry/Royalty Free

In 1997 Kodak faced growing competition in its domestic US market and was struggling with the impending techno-logical and market shift toward digital imaging, away from its traditional stronghold in film-based products. It was also losing a long-running battle with regulatory author-ities in Japan, challenging what it saw as anti-competitive practices that protected its key rival Fuji's hold on its own domestic market. At this time it had a limited presence of 600 people in the fastest-growing market, China, import-ing, distributing, and selling $250 million worth of film. It was competing head-to-head with Fuji and local manufac-turers, but falling behind; Fuji had the greater market share.

The options open to foreign investors in China then were far more restrictive than they are today. Outside-in M&As or even majority foreign-owned joint ventures were not allowed under highly-protective government regulations. Kodak needed more than a change of strategy; it needed a change in the local "rules of game." Kodak's overall aims were for exclusive rights to produce and sell locally (shut out rivals); to establish distribution, retailing, and marketing op-erations to tap into the growing consumer market in China; to establish production facilities for China and the Southeast Asian region; and to use a combination of M&A and joint ventures to tap into local film business knowledge and resources.

Surprisingly, it achieved all of these objectives. Under the direction of CEO George Fisher, who had led Motorola's developments in China, the firm engineered what is now considered to be a very successful series of M&As and joint ventures. These resulted in an investment of $1.2 billion and a massive expansion in its local production, sales, and marketing operations.

The key was an agreement with the Chinese govern-ment orchestrated from the very top, between Fisher and Prime Minister Zhu Rongji. This gave Kodak exclusive rights to the local market by placing a moratorium on other foreign investment in the industry (blocking Fuji and Agfa) and forcing all but one of the existing Chinese com-petitors to close or be acquired. Kodak was allowed to purchase majority control of three local film companies in Xiamen, Shantou, and Wuxi. Two of these had supplier relationships with Fuji, which were severed, leaving Fuji to rely on a Hong Kong company, China-Hong Kong Photo Products Holdings, to distribute its products on the main-land. Three other failing local film companies were forced to close.

The two companies formed under Chinese Company Law, Kodak (China) and Kodak (Wuxi) in Figure 13.1, are Kodak-controlled Chinese companies. The government agreement allowed Kodak a greater proportion of ownership and more management control than any other foreign company had ever been granted in China up to that point. It gained a 70 per cent share in Kodak (Wuxi), which manufactures and sells chemical products for photographic processing and an 80 per cent share of Kodak (China), which manufactures film and paper. The corporate structure adopted (a limited-liability shares company) represented a radical departure from traditional equity joint-venture structures allowed

Figure 13.2 PEST framework for country analysis

On the face of it this kind of framework may look too general and simple to guide management strategy. The general PEST overview shown above, however, is just a starting point to organize more focused analyses. Rigor can be added and accuracy improved in two ways:

1 **Add depth.** To fully understand the nature of the changes taking place within each of the categories, further tools and techniques are needed.

- Political scientists and analysts conduct formal risk assessments on political change within regions or countries. Formal rankings are published to guide investors along the same lines as insurance assessors (see related discussions later in this chapter). Such analyses also map out the key political constituencies, central and regional agencies, key ministers and bureaucrats as well as changing forms of legislation in different countries as an input into MNE strategy and implementation (for example, aiding the development of personal contacts and networks in target countries).

- Economic analyses cover everything from national-level to industry-sector or market-specific trends. Companies compiling return-on-investment (ROI) projections need to know something about productivity levels that can be expected in would-be plants, encompassing data on employees, technologies, support industries, local utilities, and so on. Any investment that relies on some element of local financing will need data on local interest-rate trends, lending conditions, and the general stability of domestic capital markets, for example.

- Social trends analyses are relevant for firms looking to market new products and services in new countries. Mapping patterns of disposable income, customer preferences, and regional differences in these requires a combination of quantitative and qualitative analyses. Statistical overviews covering demographics, buying patterns, and market research need to be complemented with insights into sociocultural norms and changing patterns of expectations if advertising messages are to be pitched correctly.

2 **Add foresight.** Arguably the most difficult challenge facing any decision maker is to predict the future. The complexity that results from the variety of factors managers need to consider when making international business decisions adds immeasurably to this uncertainty. Accurate scenario-building is central to the strategic planning and future success of any

firm and can be done using the PEST framework as a starting point. Rather than creating grandiose visions of the future, managers need to extrapolate accurately and objectively from the past and current trends across all the PEST dimensions to map out the likelihood of different futures and the implications of these for particular global strategies.

✔ Active learning check

Review your answer to Active Learning Case question 1 and make any changes you like. Then compare your answer with the one below.

1 **Why was the timing right for Kodak's market (re)entry into China?**

Kodak's success in China was partly due to the timing of its initiative. Political factors favored the unusual agreement struck with the Chinese government, adding to the economic, social, and strategic factors that led to its success. A PEST framework helps identify these factors.

Political trends in the mid to late 1990s included a strong move toward liberalization in China with specific concessions for firms making large capital investments, employing local labor and transferring particular technologies. This was associated with government-driven privatization and industry deregulation. Specifically for Kodak, the ownership regulations and the introduction of the FISC status was critical. External relations changed dramatically with a move toward WTO entry and the reciprocal moves by other dominant economies, notably the United States with Clinton's state visit in August 1998. China was seen to be politically stable with little chance of retrenchment to a central command-and-control economy.

Economic trends pointed to a strong economy growing moderate to fast (around 8 per cent GNP growth per year); large flows of inward FDI, including particularly large investments from US MNEs (GM, GE, Motorola, Coca-Cola); and strong growth of disposable income in the domestic market. On the downside, growing unemployment from denationalized industries was a destabilizing influence, and there were additional uncertainties about local capital markets, which were highly unsophisticated.

Sociocultural change in China was also dramatic, including growing income levels and growing expectations, changing consumer tastes and preferences, coupled with the rise in unemployment and reduction in state-sponsored social welfare. Capitalist entrepreneurship was on the rise, creating distinct social tensions between old and new.

Technological strengths had long existed in China, founded on a good education system and a relatively advanced science and technology infrastructure. The country had some specific weak points and gaps in its industrial capabilities that government policymakers were keen to fill through alliances with Western firms and governments, again providing opportunities for particular MNEs.

POLITICAL RISK

Risk

Danger + Opportunity

This is the Chinese character for "risk." The first symbol is the symbol for "danger," whereas the second is the symbol for "opportunity." Risk is seen as danger and opportunity combined.

Political risk
The probability that political forces will negatively affect a multinational's profit or impede the attainment of other critical business objectives

Political risk is the probability that political forces will negatively affect a firm's profit or impede the attainment of other critical business objectives. The study of political risk addresses changes in the environment that are difficult to anticipate. Common examples include the election of a government that is committed to nationalization of major industries or one that insists on reducing foreign participation in business ventures.

Most people believe that political risk is confined to third-world countries or to those with unstable governments. However, the shifting policies of triad region governments illustrate that political risk is also an issue for firms doing business in highly industrialized nations. Governments routinely protect key industries for reasons of national security, self-sufficiency, or national culture. Examples include US restrictions on foreign investment in the banking, defense, and commercial airline industries; Japanese protection of its rice producers; and France's limitations on foreign involvement in its film and media businesses. The EU and US governments have long supported their regional champions in the aerospace industry, partly for security reasons, partly to protect local firms. Most recently Airbus has spent $11 billion on building the A380 double-decker jumbo jet, one-third of which has come from European taxpayers. This may well initiate another round of trade battles, refereed by the WTO.[2]

Much of this political sparring is predictable. It is unanticipated change stemming from complexity and uncertainty that creates more dangerous kinds of risk. However, these examples indicate the pervasiveness of political risk. Given the large number of international markets in which MNEs operate, political risk is going to remain an area of concern. In dealing with this issue, effective negotiating can help to reduce and contain problem areas. This will be explained later in the chapter.

Deregulation and political risk

Overall there has been a general trend toward liberalization, deregulation, and the opening up of national borders over the past 15 to 20 years, and this has been a major driver of globalization. Table 13.1 shows the growing number of regulatory changes that have been favorable to FDI. In particular, the progressive liberalization of countries with large domestic markets and extensive privatization or denationalization programs underway, such as China, Brazil and India, has significantly changed the global economy. Huge opportunities exist for MNEs in these countries, and they have responded by investing to establish themselves in these new markets.

FDI inflows into these countries, particularly China, have grown immensely. India recorded inflows of $2.9 billion between 1991 and 1995, following the politically-led liberalization process. This compares with less than $1 billion of FDI inflows for the 20 years before 1991. In 2004 FDI into developing countries rose 48 per cent to $255 billion and accounted for an estimated 42 per cent of global FDI inflows, compared to 27 per cent in 2001–2003.[3]

Table 13.1 Changes in national regulations on FDI, 1991–2003

Item	1991	1992	1993	1994	1995	1996	1997	1998	1999	2000	2001	2002	2003
Number of countries that introduced changes in their investment regimes	35	43	57	49	64	65	76	60	63	69	71	70	82
Number of regulatory changes of which:	82	79	102	110	112	114	151	145	140	150	208	248	244
More favorable to FDI[a]	80	79	101	108	106	98	135	136	131	147	194	236	220
Less favorable to FDI[b]	2	–	1	2	6	16	16	9	9	3	14	12	24

[a] Including liberalizing changes or changes aimed at strengthening market functioning, as well as increased incentives.
[b] Including changes aimed at increasing control as well as reducing incentives.

Source: UNCTAD, *World Investment Report 2004: The Shift Towards Services* (Geneva: UNCTAD, 2004), http://unctad.org.

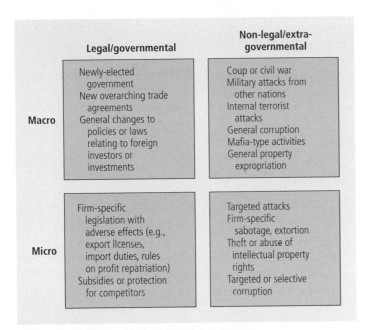

	Legal/governmental	Non-legal/extra-governmental
Macro	Newly-elected government New overarching trade agreements General changes to policies or laws relating to foreign investors or investments	Coup or civil war Military attacks from other nations Internal terrorist attacks General corruption Mafia-type activities General property expropriation
Micro	Firm-specific legislation with adverse effects (e.g., export licenses, import duties, rules on profit repatriation) Subsidies or protection for competitors	Targeted attacks Firm-specific sabotage, extortion Theft or abuse of intellectual property rights Targeted or selective corruption

Figure 13.3 Types and levels of political risk

For these giant emerging markets major political shifts led to the start of the process of integrating with the global economy and the opening up of their borders to foreign investors. Continuous, small but significant changes to their policies and legislation regarding FDI and the activities of MNEs means that ongoing assessments of political risk in these countries is of paramount importance to investors. The governments of these countries, together with their massive, complex civil service bureaucracies, maintain a strong level of control over their economies, and the direction and pace of change remains unpredictable.

The nature of political risk

We can examine political risk at two different levels, as seen in Figure 13.3.[4] Legal/governmental risks are potentially harmful to foreign businesses but are the product of, or permissible within, the existing political, economic, and legislative system. Non-legal or extra-governmental risks lie outside this system and are a violation of existing laws. Macro-level risks affect all foreign firms evenly, and micro-level risks harm individual or specific groups of firms.

Macro political risk

A macro political risk is one that affects all foreign enterprises in the same general way. Expropriation, the governmental seizure of private businesses coupled with little, if any, compensation to the owners, is an example of a macro political risk. Communist governments in Eastern Europe and China expropriated private firms following World War II. Fidel Castro did the same in Cuba from 1958 to 1959. In more recent years governments in Angola, Chile, Ethiopia, Peru, and Zimbabwe have expropriated private enterprises. In some cases this stems from indigenization laws, which require that nationals hold a majority interest in all enterprises. The privatization of a range of state-owned industries in Russia marked a turning point in that country's history. However, the corruption and racketeering that led to politically-connected individuals building massive fortunes from, for example, the oil and aluminum industries may have triggered another turning point

Macro political risk
A risk that affects all foreign enterprises in the same way

Expropriation
The governmental seizure of private businesses coupled with little, if any, compensation to their owners

Indigenization laws
Laws which require that nationals hold a majority interest in all enterprises

(see **Real Case: Yukos and the Russian oligarchs** in this chapter). The government is now considering re-nationalizing key industries.[5]

Macro political risk can also be the result of political boycotts. During the war on Iraq, following 9/11 in the United States, American consumers boycotted French imports and avoided holidaying in France because the French were unsupportive of the military invasion of Iraq.[6] In all these cases both large and small businesses feel the impact of the political decision.

Micro political risk

A micro political risk is one that affects selected sectors of the economy or specific foreign businesses. These risks are typically a result of government action in the form of industry regulation, taxes on specific types of business activity, and local content laws.

A number of factors help to determine the degree of micro political risk. One is the dominance of foreign firms or the growing competitiveness of their products in an industry. For example, small and medium-sized makers of precision tools for the electronics industry in the United States joined forces to lobby for higher tariffs on imports that compete with their products, including those made by large US firms offshore. Prompted by the growing trade deficit and job losses in manufacturing they have used the National Association of Manufacturers to push the government to defy WTO regulations and protect their particular businesses by increasing specific tariffs.[7]

The end of the global textile quota system in January 2005 drastically changed the competitive environment for countries like Kenya and Pakistan. Under this system the United States and the European Union restricted textile imports according to their country of origin. This had the effect of partly protecting these countries from direct competition with countries like India and China, because they had a guaranteed volume of exports to the big markets. Up to 60 per cent of Pakistan's annual export income comes from the textile sector, which employs more than half of the country's industrial workforce, so this change has a significant impact on its economy.[8]

This last example shows that some political risks are predictable and can be partly planned for. Others are not and tend to have a more significant effect. The changing priorities of

Table 13.2 Political risk: sources, agents, and effects

Sources of political risk	Groups that can generate political risk	Effects of political risk
Political philosophies that are changing or are in competition with each other	Current government and its various departments and agencies	Expropriation of assets (with or without compensation)
Changing economic conditions	Opposition groups in the government that are not in power but have political clout	Indigenization laws
Social unrest		Restriction of operating freedom concerning, e.g., hiring policies and product manufacturing
Armed conflict or terrorism	Organized interest groups such as teachers, students, workers, retired persons, etc.	
Rising nationalism		Cancellation or revision of contracts
Impending or recent political independence	Terrorist or anarchist groups operating in the country	Damage to property and/or personnel from terrorism, riots, etc.
Vested interests of local business groups	International organizations such as the World Bank or the United Nations	Loss of financial freedom such as the ability to repatriate profits
Competing religious groups		
Newly created international alliances	Foreign governments that have entered into international alliances with the country or that are supporting opposition to the government	Increased taxes and other financial penalties

governments, often swayed by powerful interest groups, are an important source of this kind of risk. As discussed below, governments have specific economic, social, and often military agendas, and changes in these will result in adjustments to the various levers that control trade and the activities of foreign investors.

Sources of political risk

There are a number of sources of political risk. Table 13.2 presents some important sources and their effects.

So a variety of motivations help to explain political risk. The MNE's challenge is to identify these motivations and then to decide how to manage them.

COUNTRY ANALYSIS AND POLITICAL RISK ASSESSMENT

As described above the PEST framework provides a simple way of mapping the pros and cons of foreign investment opportunities in particular countries for MNEs. There are many other analytical tools and techniques to measure the cost–benefit or risk–reward ratio for a specific investment proposition. These range from scenario planning, Delphi exercises, and multi-variant risk analyses to simple observation. The degree to which companies actually use these techniques before investing abroad varies a great deal.

Small firms, especially owner-managed firms, often move from simple exporting to engage in FDI on the basis of the owner, CEO, or senior manager seeing an opportunity when on holiday in a foreign country! Little or no rigorous risk analysis or comparison of opportunities between countries is conducted, partly because it takes time and is expensive, but often because managers are unaware of the need for analysis and/or ignorant of the tools, techniques, and information resources that can help them make these decisions.[9] Most firms, however, will conduct some level of analysis to capture the likely costs and benefits and probable risks relating to a particular overseas investment.

There are many sources of information on the PEST conditions in different country markets for use in comparative risk analysis. Country risk rating services are provided by a range of agencies that produce general reports and may conduct specific analyses on behalf of client companies. Such agencies include the Bank of America World Information Services, the Business Environment Risk Intelligence (BERI) SA, the Control Risks Information Services (CRIS), the Economist Intelligence Unit (EIU), Standard and Poor's Ratings Group, the Political Risk Services (ICRG), and Moody's Investor Services.

BERI political risk services, for example, began in 1966 using 15 variables, such as bureaucratic delays, monetary inflation, and political stability to "isolate to the degree possible the political process affecting business." It contained a weighting to emphasize certain criteria (such as political stability) over others in terms of their significance and impact. The sum of the weights was 25 and each of the 15 factors was then scored at four times its weight, so the highest possible points and lowest risk was 100. A global panel of experts (although US-based experts dominated) then assessed the score for each variable in a Delphi-style validation to help rank 40 to 50 countries according to the resulting consensus. Scores between 70 and 56 were defined as moderate risk, denoting overall stability despite the varied risk of complications that might affect day-to-day operations for businesses. Any country with a rating under 56 was considered unstable.

The FORCE Country Reports from BERI also provide a qualitative analysis of sociopolitical, economic, and financial forecasts. They include scenario analyses and so-called political, operations, and remittance/repatriation risk indices and profit opportunity recommendations (POR). The BERI risk measurement components include several categories of information, such as political factionalization, linguistic/ethnic/religious tension, coercive measures to maintain regime, mentality: nationalism, corruption, nepotism, radical left strength, dependence on outside, and so on.[10]

Online risk information resources

An increasing number of country rating and indexing schemes are available online. One of the best is the World Bank and IMF site (http://rru.worldbank.org/DoingBusiness/), which is a useful resource for off-the-shelf reports, such as *Doing Business* in country X this year. But it also allows users to create customized reports using an online database of indicators across 145 countries. This is linked to specialized topic areas covering practical guidelines for investing and managing in different countries, including Starting a Business, Hiring and Firing Workers, Enforcing Contracts, Getting Credit, and Licensing and Inspections. The World Bank's Multilateral Investment Guarantee Agency (MIGA) is also a good source (http://miga.org) as are the following sites: http://www.countryrisk.com/; http://www.economist.com/countries; http://www.worldbank.org/data/countrydata/countrydata.html.

One of the most widely-used and well-respected sources of information is the Economist Intelligence Unit (EIU) (www.eiu.com). Alongside fairly general information it has a host of interactive services, most of which are for subscribers only. Its Risk Services site (http://www.eiuresources.com/ras/default.htm) provides free snapshots of risk ratings and currently shows Iraq, Zimbabwe, and Myanmar as the riskiest propositions globally and Singapore, Spain, and Hong Kong at the top of its list. The EIU site also describes some of the indicators and the methodology underlying its Country Risk Service.

The Fraser Institute, with its very overt political view, compiles the Index of Economic Freedom (http://www.fraserinstitute.ca and http://www.freetheworld.com/). This compares 23 components across seven areas (economic structures, monetary policy, etc.) to measure the degree to which host-country institutional arrangements and policies intervene in or influence the operation of the economy. It also attempts to assess how predictable these arrangements and policies are and therefore how important they are as a source of market uncertainty.

PricewaterhouseCoopers (PwC) compiles an opacity index, which is closer to the kinds of analyses that examine non-legal activities by governments that might influence or intervene in business (http://www.opacity-index.com). This measures the impact of business, economic, legal, and ethical opacity on the cost of capital around the world.

Finally, as an indication of the importance of these kinds of analyses, the World Economic Forum (WEF) has developed a Public Institutions Index as an input for its overall annual global competitiveness ranking (http://www.weforum.org/). This index is comprised of a Contracts and Law sub-index (covering judicial independence, property rights, organized crime, favoritism in government decision making) and a Corruption sub-index (including irregular payments for imports and exports, tax collection, and public utilities). The Public Institutions Index for Africa, for example, rates Botswana top and Chad bottom of a list of 21 African countries. This ranking is one factor influencing the overall attractiveness and competitiveness of each country.

Quantifying risk vulnerability

As shown by the above risk ratings services, all risk is relative. Measuring risk therefore involves comparing options, one investment proposition against another. This means combining investment appraisal and country appraisal techniques. There are factors that may be more important for one kind of investment than another. So a production plant will have different requirements than a distribution or marketing operation, or an offshore

Table 13.3 The Weighted Country Risk Assessment Model

Weighted Country Risk Assessment Model		Country A			Country B		
	Selected Criteria	Risk (1 = High)	Importance (1 = Low)	Combined score (/25)	Risk (1 = High)	Importance (1 = Low)	Combined score (/25)
Political environment	1 Stability of the local political system	4	4	16	2	4	8
	2 Likelihood of internal conflict	5	4	20	2	4	8
	3 External threats to stability	3	3	9	3	3	9
	4 Harmful government intervention in the economic system	5	4	20	2	4	8
	5 Reliability of the country as a trading partner	3	4	12	3	4	12
	6 Policy continuity/predictability	4	5	20	2	5	10
	7 Stability of tax and tariff regime	5	4	20	3	4	12
	8 Effectiveness of public administration	4	3	12	3	3	9
	9 Prevalence of corruption	5	3	15	1	3	3
	10 Bureacratic delays	5	4	20	1	4	4
	11 Enforceability of contracts	4	4	16	2	4	8
	12 Corporate governance and ethics legislation	3	2	6	2	2	4
	13 Labor unions and labor relations	3	5	15	3	5	15
	14 Linguistic/ethnic/religious tensions	4	1	4	3	1	3
	15 Social stability	4	2	8	3	2	6
International economic environment	16 Import restrictions	2	4	8	2	4	8
	17 Export restrictions	3	5	15	3	5	15
	18 Attitudes toward foreign investors	4	3	12	3	3	9
	19 Respect for intellectual property rights (patents, brands)	4	4	16	1	4	4
	20 Restrictions on monetary transfers	3	5	15	3	5	15
	21 Revaluation of the currency during the last five years	3	2	6	2	2	4
	22 Balance of payments situation	4	2	8	4	2	8
Domestic economic environment	23 Per capita income	3	1	3	3	1	3
	24 Economic growth over the last five years	4	1	4	2	1	2
	25 Potential growth over the next three years	4	1	4	4	1	4
	26 Inflation over the past two years	3	3	9	2	3	6
	27 Accessibility of domestic capital markets to outsiders	4	4	16	4	4	16
	28 Availability of high-quality local labor force	4	5	20	4	5	20
	29 Availability of energy resources	4	4	16	4	4	16
	30 Infrastructure; transportation and communication systems	3	4	12	3	4	12
	TOTALS	113	100	377	79	100	261

Sources: The approach and the items in the table draw from prior risk assessment models and studies, including D. W. Conklin, "Analyzing and Managing Country Risks," *Ivey Business Journal*, vol. 66, no. 3 (January/February 2002), pp. 36–42; S. T. Cavusgil, "Measuring the Potential of Emerging Markets: An Indexing Approach," *Business Horizons*, vol. 40, no. 1 (1997); A. I. J. Dyck, *Country Analysis* (Boston: Harvard Business School Press, 1997); and E. Dichtl and H. G. Köglmayr, "Country Risk Ratings," *Management International Review*, vol. 26, no. 4 (1986), pp. 4–12.

IT service office, for example. Therefore different risk criteria are more or less relevant at the country level. Table 13.3 shows the Weighted Country Risk Assessment Model for combining both.

Two different country cases (A and B) are compared using 30 different criteria, 15 are political in nature and 15 are economic, although many of the latter are also directly or indirectly influenced by the governments. The Risk column gives a rating (1 is high risk; 5 is low) comparing Country A and Country B on this criteria and can represent either (1) a direct comparison (e.g., high or low current disposable income levels) or (2) a risk measure—the potential for change that would harm the investment proposed (e.g., the likelihood that disposable income levels will fall significantly in the future). So, for example, Country A is

Weighted Country Risk Assessment Model
Combines an investment project appraisal with country risk analysis

rated as more politically stable than B and has a lower likelihood of internal conflicts, more predictable policies, a more stable tax and tariff regime, and fewer (less likelihood of) bureaucratic delays. Economically the two countries are a little more similar, although Country A, for example, clearly rates higher in terms of upholding intellectual property rights, so there is less risk of breaches of copyrights, patents, or brands. They have fairly similar domestic economic environments in terms of the listed criteria, with Country A having experienced better growth in the past five years, but expecting the same growth prospects as B for the next three years. This relative country rating across the three categories is summarized by the totals at the foot of the table, 113 for Country A and 79 for Country B.

The Importance column rates each of the same 30 criteria in terms of its relevance to the kind of investment proposed. This example has been designed to reflect an overseas investment for a production facility, mainly for exports. Criteria such as export restrictions, the availability of high-quality labor, the stability of taxes and tariffs, policy continuity, bureaucratic delays, and enforceability of contracts, for example, are considered important (rating a 5 or 4). Economic growth and per capita income, for example, are considered less important. These would be important if we were considering a sales and distribution operation for consumer products, for example. As this illustration shows a country comparison, not a comparison of different types of investment, the Importance columns for Country A and Country B are identical. If we were to compare types of investment, we would change the ranking of the various criteria (between 1 and 5), but the total for this column would still need to add to 100; otherwise the weighting method would not work. We are simple changing the *relative* importance of different risk factors to suit a different type of investment proposition.

The combined score weights each country criteria according to its respective importance to the type of investment under consideration, and the combined totals provide an overall comparison of the two countries. Country A, with 377 out of a possible 500 appears to be a better option for this kind of investment than Country B with 261.

Table 13.3 presents a fairly basic example. The list of criteria can be changed and extended to far more than 30 and sub-criteria (e.g., different kinds of bureaucratic delays under item 10) can be added. The balance among political, economic, social, technological, or legal criteria can also be altered according to the investment proposition and/or the countries to be considered. We could also use a different Likert scale, such as from 1 to 10 rather than 1 to 5. The model can be extended to compare more than two country cases. For any extension of the model it is important to remember that the ratings are *relative*. For example, the above-mentioned BERI political risk ratings show Zimbabwe as riskier than Peru. We might give the former 1 for some of the political criteria in the Risk column and the latter a comparative 3 or 4. If we were to add Sweden to the comparison the rating in the Risk column would need to reflect the change, perhaps by giving Zimbabwe and Peru 1 in some categories and Sweden 5. So the rating scores are not absolute. They depend on the country comparison being made.

Note that this model only provides a summary framework for estimating relative country risk. In practice it will only reflect the intelligence that goes into the relative risk ratings. A thorough and rigorous analysis of all the factors that underlie even the limited number of 30 criteria in Table 13.3, both in terms of current and future investment conditions, is not easy. In some cases quantitative data is available, including from some of the agencies and sources listed above. For other criteria, such as political stability or the likely impact of corruption, there is no such thing as perfect information, and assumptions, estimates, and some subjective guesswork are always necessary. However, the better the expertise, information, and experience that can be leveraged to make such assessments, whether from inside or outside the firm, the more accurate the relative final scores are going to be.

What the model also helps decision makers do is identify the kinds of risks they may be able to reduce, adapt to, prepare for, or guard against prior to or following an investment. Knowing which sources of risk you can influence and which you cannot puts you in a better position to manage a market-entry strategy. Negotiating with government agencies, customs officials, or local unions; establishing alliances with local recruitment agencies or banks; or generally developing networks of local contacts and advisors can help monitor and alleviate some of these risks and is essential.

In practice, a common problem is for managers to fail to consider the full range of country risks that might affect an investment or to make uninformed assumptions in their appraisal. A project team responsible for capital budgeting in an accounting or finance department of a firm may not know a great deal about different country conditions. Project investment models and financial scenarios may be transferred with a range of built-in assumptions that can hide additional costs or risks from the appraisal. For example, differences in labor rates are a key driver for the movement of manufacturing plants and for off-shoring. Many companies build in the reduced labor cost, which make savings and resulting profits look impressive, but assume similar levels of productivity and transactions costs for the new overseas operation. The additional costs and risks may become more obvious over time, with experience, and profit can quickly turn to loss. This has happened to some of the large numbers of companies that have outsourced parts of their IT and back-office operations to India, for example.[11] So how can we build country risk analysis into our financial planning tools?

Accounting for country risk

International managers can incorporate elements of the above kinds of risk analysis into financial appraisal models when considering FDI. A five-year ROI (return on investment) or ROA (return on assets) model should take account of a range of risks as an input into financial estimates of costs and revenue. This enables a more realistic comparison between countries as locations for various kinds of investment. Although never perfect, because we have incomplete information about the past and present, and it is impossible to accurately forecast the future, this can still help decision makers build better estimations. They can develop a better understanding about the likely impact of certain events or changes on specific investment propositions; they can compare investment propositions across different country contexts; and they can revise estimates for investment returns on the basis of this kind of analysis.

Companies that try to incorporate risk estimation in financial appraisals tend to build on standard financial models at the project level. The most common work on the basis of net present value (NPV), return on investment (ROI), or internal rate of return (IRR) calculations, and these can incorporate country risks in a number of ways. A common approach is to increase the hurdle rate for return on investment at the pre-project consideration stage, which will deselect the riskiest propositions. The hurdle rate is the set rate of financial return over a period of time that covers both project costs and the cost of the capital needed for the investment. Companies or business units will often have a set rate of return below which they will not invest. A simple rule of thumb would be to increase the rate of return in line with the additional risks associated with locating the investment in a particular country, compared to another.

Also common is to adjust the cash flows of the project to reflect the potential impact of a particular event on the value of the project. So, for example, if policy changes that will lead to an increase in tax rates, import duties, or labor costs are likely, this risk needs to be built into the long-run calculation of the break-even point of an investment. There is a probability that costs will rise and net revenues will decline so this can be built into a five- or six-year forecast for an investment. The term adjusted present value (APV) is sometimes

Adjusted present value (APV)
An NPV that takes into account sources of country risk that might impact a project's expected future cash flows

used to denote an NPV that takes into account the riskiness of the project's expected future cash flows.

More sophisticated techniques for accounting for country risk have been developed. Some firms attempt to place specific probabilities on certain events taking place and calculate the direct cost implications for the project. This approach works well as an extension of the above country risk assessment model, but again relies on accurate information and intelligence to derive realistic probabilities. If political analysts estimate that there is, say, a 20 per cent chance that the government of a particular developing country will change in the next three years resulting in a radical change in policies toward foreign investors, this risk can be reflected in a higher hurdle rate or the APV and an alternative location for the investment might look more promising. This kind of approach is often termed a *sensitivity analysis* and can be combined with formal *scenario analyses*. More sophisticated real options analyses might attempt to calculate relative costs and benefits of, for example, closing a facility, moving it to another country, scaling down operations, or continuing in the face of a significant economic or political shock.

These techniques not only alert managers to relative sources of risk when comparing investment propositions, but also can help develop strategies to reduce risk. In the case of the developing country where the change of political party is likely to adversely affect foreign investors, this may lead to political lobbying by foreign firms with investments at risk. It also leads, unfortunately, to MNEs actively intervening in unethical ways in the national politics of smaller nations to secure their interests.

✔ Active learning check

Review your answer to Active Learning Case question 2 and make any changes you like. Then compare your answer with the one below.

2 **What kinds of political risk did Kodak face and how did it attempt to mitigate these risks?**

There were a range of uncertainties facing Kodak, from the macro to the micro, stemming from the ways that government agencies intervened both legally and non-legally in the operations of foreign firms in China. From the start it was clear that top-level negotiations were going to be required to secure the kind of joint venture arrangements needed to both establish a significant production operation and exclude rival Fuji from the same access. George Fisher's direct connections with the most senior political figure of the time, Zhu Rongji, could have been the key that unlocked doors all the way down the central and regional bureaucracies. This well-publicized, high-level of support also helped mitigate against discrimination and corruption at the lower levels, since the deal had the backing (and the attention) of senior officials in Beijing (and the United States). Kodak still had to make a range of payments and gestures of good citizenship to appease the powerful local constituencies in the places where it invested. In the years following the investment, various changes in policy and in the networks of power undoubtedly meant that at various levels Kodak has had to continue "smoothing the way" just like any other firm in China. Beyond these more predictable risks, there were, and always will be, highly uncertain and uncontrollable kinds of risks, such as widespread social unrest or large-scale political upheaval, which even powerful firms such as Kodak can do little to influence.

NEGOTIATION STRATEGIES

There are two key steps in developing effective negotiating strategies. First, MNE managers need to evaluate their own position and that of the other group(s) in order to determine how the interests of both can fit together. Second, they need to understand the "modus operandi" of the other groups: who has the power to make what kinds of decisions and what negotiating style are they likely to adopt.

Earlier in this chapter we discussed how widespread deregulation and liberalization were opening up emerging markets, like China and India, to foreign investors. Central and regional government agencies still maintain a strong control over these economies and the rules of engagement for foreign investors, so it is imperative that MNE managers understand (1) their political, economic, and social policy objectives; (2) their levers of power, the mechanisms by which they can influence the costs and benefits of doing business (taxes, tariffs, quotas, regulations on capital transfers, local input requirements, etc.); (3) the structures, networks, and institutional agencies through which they operate (who has the power to influence what?); and (4) their negotiation style and tactics. These represent the why's and how's of government intervention in market forces, and firms have to adapt to these to improve their chances of investment success.

Figure 13.4 depicts the interplay among (1) the elements that attract multinational firms to a particular region, which have been discussed throughout this text (central column), (2) the strategic aims of MNEs, and (3) some general policy aims of governments. MNE objectives may or may not fit with government aims and this will affect the investment decision.

Taking this a step further, the most effective negotiation strategies are those that incorporate (1) the relevant risk criteria in Table 13.3 that can be influenced through negotiation, (2) the evolving government policy priorities, and (3) the appropriate government agencies, local organizations, and key individuals who should be approached. This helps reduce the risk or increase the potential rewards from cross-border investments. If energy resources are important for a large-scale manufacturing facility, can local authorities guarantee energy supplies at a particular cost over a particular period in return for the plant being

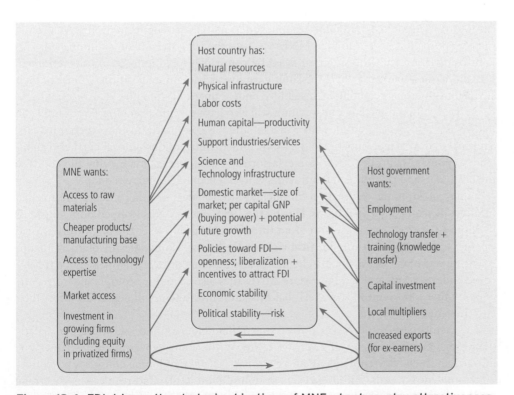

Figure 13.4 FDI drivers: the strategic objectives of MNEs, host-country attractiveness, and host-government requirements

located in their region? If labor costs are an important factor, can these be fixed for a period of time through negotiations with local trade unions?

Negotiations between MNEs and national governments or local organizations are a two-way bargaining process where each party has something the other wants. We can identify power resources or bargaining chips held by MNEs looking to invest globally on the one hand and by the governments of host countries on the other. Governments look for inflows of capital and technology, for large local employers, and for access, via MNEs, to overseas markets to boost exports and foreign exchange reserves. To get these they leverage their attractiveness, which may consist of large or growing domestic markets, natural resources, cheap or productive labor, and economic and political stability to which they may add specific incentives, such as tax breaks or higher levels of foreign ownership or profit repatriation than normally allowed.

The bargaining strength of both firms and governments is limited by the degree of competition. If other MNEs offering similar levels of capital investment, employment, or technology exist, the negotiating position of one MNE is weakened. If other regions offer cheaper labor, more economic or political stability, or better incentives to foreign investors, the negotiating position of the government is weakened.

The bargaining strengths for an MNE may come from its technology, products, services, managerial expertise, and capital. For example, when General Motors sets up a new operation in Mexico, the company invests capital, uses modern technology to build the autos, and employs managerial expertise in getting the operation off and running. When the Hilton Corporation builds a new hotel in Germany, it invests capital, employs managerial expertise, and offers a variety of world-class hospitality services to the guests. MNEs also hire local personnel, stimulate the economy, and in industries such as manufacturing, textiles, and mining help to generate exports for the country.

The bargaining strengths of the country will include such factors as large consumer markets, economic and political stability, sources of capital, tax breaks, and an appropriate labor force. The United States, for example, offers all these strengths to MNEs. As a result, the bargaining position of foreign MNEs vis-à-vis the US government is diminished. This is in comparison with the situation faced by companies looking to set up operations in least-developed countries where the latter have a weak bargaining position because of their small consumer market, political instability, and/or financial strength.

Other parties involved in a negotiation will also have specific strengths. For example, in many cases a local partner knows the market and has conducted business there for years. This makes the partner valuable to the MNE. Other contributions of local partners can include capital, a well-trained workforce, factories or retail outlets for moving the goods to the customer, and government contractors who can help to eliminate red tape.

Other parties to the transaction can include stockholders or other interest groups that monitor the company's operations. During the 1980s many MNEs stopped doing business in South Africa because of pressure from these investor groups (see the box **International Business Strategy in Action: political risk for De Beers**). Companies involved in manufacturing war material, producing chemicals, and building nuclear energy plants have also come under investor and social pressure. MNEs may also encounter complaints from partners in other joint ventures who feel that this latest investment will negatively affect their current venture.

The membership of the WTO and various trading blocs around the world, particularly the EU and NAFTA, directly affect the degree to which national governments *can* intervene in trade and FDI. Governments in emerging markets and developing countries have more direct influence over the running of the economy and the rules and regulations governing trade and investment. However, once they have joined the WTO (as China did in 2001) their use of legislation governing foreign equity participation, profit repatriation, cross-border

INTERNATIONAL BUSINESS STRATEGY *IN ACTION*

Political risk for De Beers

With an estimated $4.5 billion, Nicky Oppenheimer is the richest person in Africa, the world's poorest continent. His family still owns nearly half of De Beers and a sizable piece of Anglo American, another mining giant with interests in gold, platinum, construction, and forestry.

The De Beers name is synonymous with diamonds. Established in 1888 in Johannesburg, South Africa, it is the largest mining company in the world. It recently reported profits of $676 million on sales of $5.5 billion. But De Beers once controlled (not directly mined) about 80 per cent of the world supply of rough stones. The De Beers Groups Diamond Trading Company (DTC), formerly the Central Selling Organization (CSO), maintained a cartel for limiting supply and driving up prices. Competitors have reduced this share by challenging its single-channel distribution system and by developing other sources of diamonds outside of its control. In Canada, Australia, and Russia rival mining firms like BHP Billiton, Rio Tinto, and Alrosa have found huge deposits of lucrative stones and developed new technologies to mine them efficiently. As recently as 1998 De Beers's share was down to around 65 per cent, and today production from its own mines gives it just a 45 per cent share. Add to this its contract to sell Russian stones and its overall market share is around 55 per cent, in a global market for rough diamonds worth about $8 billion.

Yet De Beers faces a range of political risks. It is under threat from anti-globalization and ethical business groups for its involvement in civil wars in Sierra Leone, Angola, and Congo. It is also facing potentially damaging political and governance changes in South Africa, including calls to re-nationalize and/or place into "black hands" a range of natural resource-based industries including mineral mining. More worrying for the Oppenheimers is a legal campaign by activists who want reparations from firms that worked in apartheid South Africa. This is not currently being supported by South Africa's government, but this may change. De Beers has some leverage since its operations have resulted in lucrative and stable tax revenues for the South African government, as well as for Botswana, Namibia, and Tanzania.

It has been trying to cope with other sources of political risk, hindering its expansion into the end-consumer markets of the triad for some time. De Beers was banned from directly entering the US market because of an anti-trust legal ruling that sees it as a monopoly. Under the CSO, the group's market dominance had allowed it to manipulate market prices by accumulating inventory. De Beers is allowed to operate in the EU, but has faced anti-competition action, particularly in relation to its Russian and East European operations.

A major watershed occurred in 2004 as De Beers finally pleaded guilty to charges of price fixing of industrial diamonds in an Ohio court and agreed to pay a $10 million fine, thereby ending a 60-year-long lock-out of the US market. De Beers can now work directly in the largest diamond market, America. This might help it further leverage its recent partnership with luxury products firm LVMH to sell De Beers-brand diamonds.

Websites: www.debeersgroup.com; www.lvmh.com; and www.adiamondisforever.com.

Sources: "The Cartel Isn't for Ever," *Economist*, July 17, 2004; T. Buck and N. Innocenti, "De Beers Offer Set to End EU Probe," *Financial Times*, December 21, 2004; "South Africa's Cuban Missile," *Economist*, August 9, 2003; R. Smith, "Diamond's Are Not Forever," *BBC.com*, July 26, 2001; and "De Beer's Worst Friend," *Economist*, August 20, 1998.

M&A, and local content rules, as well as tax and investment incentives becomes more restricted. At this stage, though, and in the foreseeable future for such countries, a higher level of direct control over the economy and foreign relations represents a significant influence over the ever-changing opportunities and risks for investors.

Finally, individual politicians and civil servants in less-developed countries are able to use their own influence more effectively to block or to facilitate a particular MNE investment. This is partly due to the higher level of government control over the economy and individual businesses, but also because of the relative lack of legal or institutional recourse to challenge government actions. Couple this with the fact that salaries for government officials and bureaucrats in poorer countries tend to be very low and you get an insight into why corruption is so much more prevalent in developing countries, as discussed in the following section.

✔ Active learning check

Review your answer to Active Learning Case question 3 and make any changes you like. Then compare your answer with the one below.

3 **What did both sides, Kodak and the Chinese government, gain from the deal?**

Many of the clues to answering this question lie in the answers to question 1 and question 2. The timing of Kodak's investment suited the Chinese government in a number of ways. Zhu Rongji was leading a massive process of liberalization and deregulation across the economy as part of the shift toward a free-market system. In the time leading up to Kodak's entry, 300,000 firms were privatized, resulting in an increase in unemployment and some degree of social unrest. The Chinese government needed foreign firms to provide employment and new sources of income through capital investment. Their economic development plans also highlighted the need for technology transfer and training to improve China's capacity to create technology-sophisticated, higher-value manufactured products. Finally, the failure of many local firms, many of them recently privatized, had pushed local and some national banks into debt. Foreign capital was needed to maintain the pace of investment.

Kodak offered all of this. In return it wanted and gained exclusive access to produce locally, avoiding the tariff barriers; experienced local managers and engineers from the film-manufacturing sector, as well as low-cost employees; land, facilities, and infrastructure; and help with the complicated local rules and regulations, permissions, and licenses required to establish any operation in China. As a result, Kodak's market share has grown impressively since its investment and China continues to thrive (to-date).

Transparency and corruption: politically sensitive political risk

One of the most difficult aspects of foreign business for international managers is how to cope with corruption. A very large number of firms engage in bribery of various kinds, but the ethical issues are not straightforward. In many cases they argue that to opt out would simply mean they lose out to less ethically minded competitors. In other cases it is genuinely difficult to know whether such practices are simply the accepted local rules of the game. In the UK an extra payment to rail companies buys you a better seat on the train in a less crowded compartment. This is called "First Class." In India an extra payment may get you onto a train that is already overbooked (or that you are told is overbooked). The only difference is that the payment will go straight into the ticket collector's pocket, rather than the railway company. However, in many places it is accepted that workers in national industries or officials in government agencies will top-up their incomes by offering these kinds of "discretionary services."

There are very different levels of corruption, from the small scale to the very large scale. Our Indian ticket collector may make a few extra dollars each month from small-scale bribes. One estimate suggests that Mohamed Suharto, President of Indonesia from 1967 to 1998, built a personal fortune of between $15 and $35 billion through embezzlement, in a country with an average GDP per capita (an indication of average annual salaries) of $695.[12]

Governments, particularly those in previously centrally-planned economies, are directly responsible for a large volume of purchasing. The volume of government expenditure on public procurement in China jumped from $0.4 billion in 1998 to $18.7 billion in 2003, as its economy and the need for large-scale infrastructure projects grew. The international attention it has attracted in its preparations for the 2008 Olympic Games in Beijing and Expo 2010 in Shanghai has pushed the government to limit corrupt practices through policies such as the Public Procurement Act. But such activities are not confined to emerging and developing countries. Bid rigging is widespread in Japan, particularly in the construction industry. The 2003 Act Concerning Elimination and Prevention of Involvement in Bid Rigging was an attempt by the Japanese government to curb such practices, which involve collusion among powerful *keiretsu*, industry bodies, and government agencies. The amount lost due to bribery in government procurement globally is thought to be at least $400 billion.

The Berlin-based organization, Transparency International (TI), produces a number of reports each year, of which the best known is the Corruption Perceptions Index (CPI). The CPI has promoted research into, and more open discussion of, the causes and consequences of corruption. **Corruption** is defined by them as "the misuse of public power for private benefit," and each year TI has evolved the methodology to improve consensus and acceptance of the metrics that underlie the country rankings.

Corruption
The misuse of public power for private benefit

The extent of corruption is a measure of the *frequency* and *value* of corrupt payments and the resulting obstacle imposed on businesses. A composite index from 18 different data sources was used in the 2004 CPI, taken from 12 different institutions, including the World Economic Forum, the World Business Environment Survey of the World Bank, the Institute of Management Development (in Lausanne), PricewaterhouseCoopers, the Economist Intelligence Unit, and Gallup International on behalf of Transparency International. The 2004 survey shows Finland, New Zealand, and Denmark as the least corrupt economies, UK 11th, US 17th, Chile 20th, France 22nd, Japan 24th, Italy 42nd, Brazil 59th, China 71st, India, Russia (and Tanzania) 90th, Kenya and Pakistan 129th, and the most corrupt countries as Bangladesh and Haiti at 145th.

Another report is the *Bribe Payers Index* (BPI), which ranks the top 21 exporting economies in terms of how much their companies (including almost all the top MNEs) were perceived to be paying bribes abroad. Interviews were held for the 2002 survey with 835 senior managers in national and international corporations; law, accountancy, and consultancy firms; Chambers of Commerce; and other agencies in the top 15 emerging market importers (including Brazil, Indonesia, and South Korea). Australian (8.5 out of 10), Swedish (8.4), and Swiss (8.4) firms were seen to be the least frequent bribers, Chinese (3.5) and Russian (3.2) the most frequent. The UK (6.9) is significantly higher up the rankings than the Americans (5.3) and Japanese (5.3), but both the British and Americans are seen to be more likely to bribe now than they were three years ago. Other reports by TI examine other elements of corruption, including the most prominent offenders in specific countries, usefully comparing, for example, the judiciary, customs, police, local administrators, registry and permit officials, tax officials, and traffic police in various countries. Case studies and intra- or inter-regional comparisons also make up much of TI's analysis.[13]

The global corruption report by TI shows a clear correlation between corruption and income. Poorer countries (like Bangladesh) tend to have the highest incidence of corruption. In low-income, developing, and emerging markets, transparency is also more of a problem. **Transparency** reflects the *clarity* and *consistency* of policies and legislation applied in the governance of businesses and is strongly associated with corruption. There is considerable debate about the relative levels of corruptness and transparency prevalent in developing and advanced countries. The latter do tend to have more governance checks and balances and arguably more freedom of the press and leeway for interest groups to reveal and oppose corrupt practices and transparency problems.

Transparency
The *clarity* and *consistency* of policies and legislation applied in the governance of businesses

There is, however, a sociocultural dimension to such issues, and in some countries certain established, recognized, and accepted business practices are considered to be the "local rules of the game" that should simply be respected and adapted to, rather than criticized as non-Western. Again, China provides a useful illustration. One of the key obligations for China as it joins a growing range of international organizations (such as WTO) and legal treaties is to improve its transparency. In the past, import duties have been found to vary from between 10 and 20 per cent for the same product because customs officers across the country do not have a standard definition or system for categorizing product types. This has not just led to MNE managers and local importers having to engage in extended discussions with local officials regarding product categorization but significantly increases the incentive and opportunity for bribery.

Government clean-up campaigns in China have focused on the standardization of rules governing both domestic and foreign businesses. The licensing procedures for both have tended to be unregulated and very much at the discretion of local officials who are said frequently to abuse the yearly check-up system (*Nianjin*) to earn additional fees before approving licenses. However, foreign firms without the necessary *guanxi* (informal, reciprocal obligation networks) connections are subject to these and other additional charges. The more bizarre include the "spiritual civilization fee" and a "wall-cleaning fee" that can run into thousands of US dollars.[14]

Behavioral characteristics of the participants in negotiations

When it comes to the actual process of cross-border negotiations there is a range of cultural, behavioral, and tactical differences between groups that international managers need to understand if they are to negotiate effectively.

Cultural differences

Although the objective of the negotiation process may be universal (strike as good a deal as possible), the way in which the process is carried out will be greatly influenced by the cultural values and norms of the participants. Many of the following observations build on Chapter 5, which examines cultural differences between people from different countries around the world.

Commenting on the difference between Arab and US negotiators, one group of researchers noted:

> . . . [Arabs] treat deadlines as only general guidelines for wrapping up negotiations. They tend to open negotiations with an extreme initial position. However, the Arabs believe strongly in making concessions, they do so throughout the bargaining process, and they almost always reciprocate an opponent's concessions. They also seek to build a long-term relationship with their bargaining partners. For these reasons, Americans typically find it easier to negotiate with Arabs than with representatives from many other regions of the world.[15]

One of the major differences is the amount of authority that the negotiator has to approve an agreement. In some societies, such as the United States and Great Britain, negotiators are given authority to make deals or at least to express agreement on the basic arrangement that is being negotiated. This approach works well when doing business with many Western firms, as well as with Chinese negotiators. However, it is often of limited value when dealing with people from other cultures. In fact, the other parties may not have the authority to give the go-ahead on anything. For example, Japanese and Russian negotiators are often lower-level personnel who are not authorized to approve agreements. This can be frustrating to Americans who feel that they are wasting their time. The lack of face-to-face interaction with those who will be making the final decision can be unsettling. On the other hand, many foreign negotiators use this ploy because they have learned that it often leads to greater concessions from US businesspeople, who become anxious to sign a deal and thus are more flexible on terms. These are some of the issues that Dell's decision makers needed to consider when they approached potential business partners in Latin America (see **International Business Strategy in Action: Dell goes to Brazil**).

Another cultural difference in negotiating style is the objective of the negotiators. As the typologies in Chapter 5 show, American, German, and British managers, for example, tend

INTERNATIONAL BUSINESS STRATEGY *IN ACTION*

Dell goes to Brazil

In the late 1990s Dell examined the opportunities and risks of investing in Latin America. It was looking to replicate not just its direct sales activities but the whole of its "build to order" (BTO) model to serve the Latin American market.

In 1998 Dell was growing faster than most other Fortune 500 firms and was rated as the number-one performing stock in the Standard & Poors 500 for that decade. It was selling PCs globally, manufacturing in Xiamen, China; Penang, Malaysia; and Limerick, Ireland as well as the United States. However, it was only ranked the ninth PC vendor in Latin America (with 1.2 per cent market share). Despite its 20 per cent share in the United States, in the large, growing Latin American market on its doorstep, it trailed Compaq (22 per cent share and 36 per cent growth rate), IBM, HP, and several others. PCs were shipped from its manufacturing facilities in Texas with sales coming via a toll-free number, not online.

In response to this weak performance it developed a strategy to sell online, and increase Latin American sales from 80,000 units to 800,000 in five years. A major aim was to establish market leadership and to manufacture locally to avoid excessive import duties (an estimated 30 per cent) and transport and logistics costs. Not only did prospective market growth look healthy, with demand for PCs rising, but the growing use of the Internet and increasing propensity for Latin Americans to buy online suited Dell's model. Brazil was seen as the best place to locate Dell's Latin American activities. It represented the largest country market in its own right, with one-fifth of the population in the middle or upper-middle class income bracket and the recent appearance of free ISPs to encourage use of the Internet. For investing in production it had a central location, educated labor force, and government incentives for high technology FDI. Moreover, PCs produced in Brazil could be exported without tariff to other Mercosur countries, which include Argentina, Uruguay, and Paraguay.

Chile was considered as an alternative. But by comparison it had a more expensive (though on average better-educated) labor force, fewer local suppliers, a higher level of local competition (relative to the size of the domestic market), similar government incentives to invest but a higher degree of political instability and a smaller local market.

But there were also risks, many of them macro-level risks shared with any other MNE looking to invest in Brazil. These included political instability regarding FDI regulations, tariff barriers, labor regulations, and economic instability regarding inflation and possible currency devaluation. Further uncertainties would affect Dell more directly. Shipping and distribution infrastructure was weak and there were also some reasonably strong, local, low-cost PC producers that may have reacted strongly to new entrants (IBM and HP already operated at that time in Brazil). It was also difficult to assess the skill and capabilities of the local workforce not only for manufacturing, but also for sales and after-sales service, which were key elements of Dell's direct model.

In 1999 Dell opened an assembly plant in Eldorado do Sul, Brazil. In retrospect we know that both the global economic and competitive macro environment and the country-level environment in Brazil went through some turbulent changes after 1998 that would have been very difficult to predict, regardless of which of the country risk analysis techniques Dell had applied. The removal of many non-tariff import barriers in Brazil worked against the investment decision. However, market analysis shows that local competitors have done very well, regardless of Dell's investment. In 2000 Latin America's top five—Compaq, Dell, HP, IBM, and Acer—all lost market share. The firms not in the top five saw market share increase from 50 to 59 per cent, and local firms, such as Itautec and Metron from Brazil and Mexico's Alaska, performed even better. Other events, such as the 1999 currency (Real) devaluation, high interest rates, the energy crisis, and the knock-on effects of the Argentinean financial crisis in 2001, followed by a general economic slowdown, all added complexity and further uncertainty after the investment had been made.

Globally Dell's revenues have maintained remarkable growth, reaching $41.4 billion in 2004. Latin America remains a major weak spot for the firm. This is particularly important in light of forecasts which show that emerging markets overall (including these key Latin American countries) will be responsible for two-thirds of the growth in the industry in the coming years. These growing markets will add an estimated 533 million new PCs to existing markets by 2010. Dell needs to work out a better way of getting a bigger piece of this particular pie.

Website: http://www.dell.com.

Sources: K. Kraemer and J. Dedrick, *Dell Computer: Organization of a Global Production Network* (Irvine, CA: Center for Research on Information Technology and Organizations (CRITO), 2002), http://www.crito.uci.edu/GIT/publications/pdf/dell.pdf; S. Yates, "Sizing the Emerging-Nation PC Market," *Forrester Market Analysis*, 2004, http://www.forrester.com/Research/Document/Excerpt/ 0,7211,34889,00.html; Dell Company annual reports, http:// www.dell.com/downloads/global/corporate/annual/Dell2004AR.pdf; and Gartner Research, *Gartner Says Strong Notebook Sales Helped Drive Latin American PC Market to an 8 Percent Increase in 2003*, 2004, http://www4.gartner.com/press_releases/pr25feb2004b.html.

to be very practical and to focus on short-term results. Negotiators from the Far East tend to move more slowly, like to get to know the other party, and have a more long-run focus. Gift giving, social custom, and certain rituals can play an important part in negotiations and is part of the initial process of developing trust and mutual respect.[16]

Language is also a key factor. When negotiators do not speak the same language and must use interpreters, there are more chances for a misinterpretation or misunderstanding to occur. This problem also exists in written communications. Schermerhorn, for example, has found that, when documents are translated from one language to another and then translated back to check for accuracy, there are interpretation problems.[17] The original translation appears to convey the desired information, but, when another person is called in to translate the document back into the original language, some parts of it are different from that intended initially.

A related cultural problem is the use of written documents. In some countries a written document is used as a basis for establishing what is to be done. As a result, the document is detailed and factual. In Germany it will be precise and technical, in the United States it will be legalistic. In other countries, however, a written document is viewed as the basis for a general agreement and the parties then negotiate the implementation as they go along. Chinese and other Far East negotiators often view detailed contracts as a sign of distrust and believe a more open-ended agreement should be used.

Acceptance zones

Acceptance zone
An area within which a party is willing to negotiate

Each party to a negotiation will have an acceptance zone or an area within which it is willing to negotiate. For example, if Anheuser-Busch, the giant US brewer, wants to buy a brewery in Düsseldorf, Germany, the US MNE will determine three prices: the highest price it is willing to pay, the price it would like to pay, and the offer at which it will begin the bargaining. For purposes of illustration, assume that Anheuser-Busch (AB) is willing to pay up to $25 million for the company but hopes to make the acquisition for $23 million and intends to start the negotiation at $20 million.

Will AB be successful? This depends on the acceptance zone of the Düsseldorf brewer. If the company will not sell for less than $27.5 million, there will be no deal because the buyer's maximum offer is less than the seller's minimum acceptance. However, assume that the German firm will not sell for less than $21 million, would like to get $24 million, and intends to start the negotiation at $28 million. In this case the two sides should be able to strike a deal since they have overlapping zones of acceptance, as illustrated in Figure 13.5.

Notice from Figure 13.5 that, when the acceptance zones of the two parties overlap, there is common ground for negotiating. Additionally, keep in mind that, if the zones do not

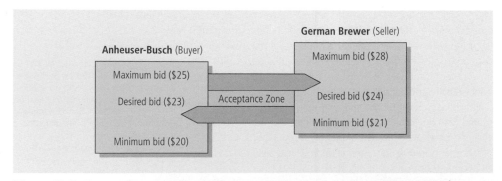

Figure 13.5 Zones of acceptance in the negotiating process (in millions of US$)

Table 13.4 Twelve examples of the differences in verbal behaviors among Japanese, US, and Brazilian negotiators

Behavior (description)	Number of times behavior was used in a 30-minute negotiating session by members of each group		
	Japanese	US	Brazilian
1 Making promises	7	8	3
2 Making threats	4	4	2
3 Making recommendations	7	4	5
4 Giving warnings	2	1	1
5 Offering rewards	1	2	2
6 Making commitments	15	13	8
7 Asking questions	20	20	22
8 Giving commands	8	6	14
9 Revealing personal information about oneself	34	36	39
10 Making a first offer	61.5	57.3	75.2
11 Granting initial concessions	6.5	7.1	9.4
12 Using the word "no"	5.7	9.0	83.4

Source: Adapted from John L. Graham (1985) "The Influence of Culture on the Process of Business Negotiations: An Exploratory Study," *Journal of International Business Studies*, Spring, p. 88. Adapted and reprinted with permission.

overlap, negotiations will not always end in a stalemate. After listening to each other the parties may agree to change their respective bids and offers, adjust the acceptance zones, and end up with common negotiating ground.

In the case of Figure 13.5 the two parties would eventually negotiate within a range of $21 million (the least amount the seller will take) and $25 million (the most the buyer will pay). It is not possible to say what the final price will be because this will depend on how willing each side is to concede ground to the other. However, whatever the final price, the seller is going to get at least the desired minimum and the buyer will not pay more than the established maximum.

Bargaining tactics

Negotiators use a range of bargaining tactics, including promises, threats, rewards, commitments, and the use of self-disclosure, in their drive for a better deal. Some of these are also linked to different cultural characteristics, as shown in Table 13.4. Keeping silent is a standard Japanese practice, when negotiating with each other as well as with foreigners. Table 13.4 shows that each group of Japanese, US, and Brazilian negotiators has a series of behaviors that make it different from the other two. For example, the Japanese like to make recommendations, the Americans make wide use of promises, and the Brazilians rely heavily on self-disclosure.[18]

These behaviors and tactics are often used in international negotiations. Effective negotiators learn how to use them and how to counteract their use by the opposition. Some examples are provided in the next section.

STRATEGIC MANAGEMENT AND POLITICAL RISK

MNEs take many steps to ensure that their strategies do not go awry because of unexpected developments. One of the most beneficial steps is the use of integrative and protective/defensive techniques.

Use of integrative and protective/defensive techniques

Integrative techniques
Strategies designed to help a multinational become a part of the host country's infrastructure

There are a variety of stratagems that MNEs employ in reducing risk. Some are collectively known as **integrative techniques**, which are designed to help the MNE become a part of the host country's infrastructure.[19] The objective of an integrative technique is to help the company blend into the environment and to become less noticeable as a "foreign" firm. One of the simplest ways is to use a name that is not identified with an overseas company and, if an acquisition is made, keep the old name in place. For example, Bridgestone is a Japanese tire company, but no one would know this based on the name of the company. Additionally, Bridgestone owns Firestone Tire & Rubber, but few Americans are aware of this fact. Similarly, Hoechst of Germany owns the Celanese Company, and most people do not know this. Nor do many people realize that almost 25 per cent of the banks in California are Japanese owned; their names provide no clues to their real owners. This tactic deflects public attention and concern that US assets are being swallowed up by overseas investors.

Another common integrative technique is to develop good relations with the host government and other political groups and to produce as much of the product as possible locally. In turn the MNE will hire and promote local personnel and use them to run a large portion of the operations. This strategy endears the company to the government and, if any action is taken against foreign firms, these firms are likely to be spared.

Protective and defensive techniques
Strategies designed to discourage a host country from interfering in multi-national operations

Protective and defensive techniques are strategies that are designed to discourage a host country from interfering in multinational operations. In contrast to integrative techniques, protective and defensive measures are aimed at fostering *non-integration* of the MNE into the local environment. A good example is conducting research and development (R&D) at other geographic locales and importing this knowledge as needed. Should the government suddenly decide to seize the firm's facilities, the company's R&D base would not be threatened.

Another protective and defensive technique is to limit the role of the local personnel to those operations that are not vital to the running of the facility. So if the government decides to take over the operation, the host-country personnel will not be able to handle things efficiently. Those with the requisite knowledge and training are overseas personnel who are sent on-site by the multinational.

A third technique is to raise as much capital as possible from the host country and local banks. When this happens, the government is reluctant to interfere in operations because this may threaten its own investment and that of the home-country banks. In a manner of speaking, this strategy co-opts the government and brings it onto the MNE's team. Any strike against the multinational is a blow against the host country.

A fourth technique is to diversify production among a number of countries. In this way, if the government seizes the MNE's facilities, only one area of production is disrupted. The company can then reallocate production and get back on stream in short order.

Combination strategies

MNEs often use a combination of integration and protective/defensive techniques to reduce and manage their political risk. Figure 13.6 provides an example of how companies can do this. In the case of the low-technology manufacturing firm (#1 in Figure 13.6), the only way to employ a protective/defensive strategy is to raise capital locally. As a result, this firm will work to integrate itself into the country and to act very much like a local firm.

An international air carrier (#2 in Figure 13.6) will use an integrative strategy by setting up local operations and by hiring people to staff the facilities, to maintain the planes, and to handle arrivals and departures. The airline will also help to generate money for the

Figure 13.6 Select examples of the use of integrative and protective/defensive techniques

country by bringing in tourists and businesspeople. At the same time the company will seldom have more than a small percentage of its planes in this locale on any one day. Additionally, the pilots will often come from other countries and be highly skilled individuals, and the top management team will be operating out of headquarters in the home country. So while the air carrier will take some steps to accommodate the country, it will also be well positioned should the country decide to seize its aircraft or to increase taxes or airport fees. Moreover, aside from facilities at the airport, the company will usually have no other fixed assets except for the planes. Therefore any crackdown on the airline might result in retaliatory action by other airlines, which would refuse to fly into the country. Such action could seriously hamper the country's economic growth. Consequently, a strategy that provides for the intermediate use of both integrative and protective/defensive techniques often works extremely well.

A high-technology R&D firm (#3 in Figure 13.6) will not put much emphasis on integrative techniques because it does not want to become integrated into the local economy. The firm may be situated where it is because the company finds that it is easier to recruit top talent to live in that region. Or other competitors may be headquartered there, and the company finds that it's easier to keep tabs on these firms by situating nearby. So while the company may hire local people to staff basic operations, personnel from other countries who live locally will handle all the R&D and other sophisticated functions. If the firm should hire local people for some of these R&D positions, the company will work to keep them loyal to the firm and not to the country. Thus if there is an attempt to seize the firm's R&D facilities, the loss will be minimized.

In the case of an oil-producing and refining company (#4 in Figure 13.6), the firm is likely to make strong use of both integrative and protective/defensive techniques. The company will need to get on well with the government since it is tapping the country's natural resources. There is likely to be a great deal of hiring of local personnel for routine jobs. The firm will also work hard to generate as much revenue as possible since the government is unlikely to interfere with the operations of a revenue-producing firm. At the same time the MNE will maintain control of the more sophisticated jobs so that these cannot be carried out by anyone else. If the company were to be taken over, local workers would be unlikely to know how to operate the machinery and equipment efficiently.

✔ Active learning check

Review your answer to Active Learning Case question 4 and make any changes you like. Then compare your answer with the one below.

4 **What are the lessons for other firms looking to enter emerging markets like China?**

A simple lesson from the Kodak case is that understanding political risk and its underlying sources can significantly increase your chances of making a successful investment in an uncertain emerging market. Kodak took the time and made the effort to understand what the risks were and how it could change some of the local rules of the game to its advantage. Kodak's success stemmed from the way it matched its power resources with the needs of the different levels of Chinese government, from senior politicians in Beijing to the more junior officials who regulated business activities at the local level. It developed an understanding of the problems facing the Chinese administration and engineered its negotiations approach to highlight how the investment could help solve some of these problems. Following this, Kodak's senior managers showed huge commitment to their investment, enduring several years of complex discussions with six provincial governments, ten city governments, five ministries and commissions, local tax authorities, and several banks and trust companies. They also had the foresight (or were co-opted) to fund a number of community projects, which earned them local support for the project and perhaps the brand. But don't forget Kodak had the local government connections, the financial muscle, and a degree of political support from the US government to achieve all of this. The majority of international firms do not, and this can make the task of successfully investing in somewhere like China even harder and far riskier.

Identifying sources of potential risk and assessing the possible impact on foreign investments of all kinds is difficult to do. Emerging and developing countries generally represent riskier markets, as well as potentially more rewarding markets for MNEs. Their rapid rate of growth, strongly interventionist policies, less mature government institutions, and evolving governance systems all create additional uncertainties for foreign investors. These add to the existing complexities of trying to cope with different economic, social, and cultural ways of doing things. International managers looking to invest in these countries need to develop an in-depth understanding of the ever-changing official, formal rules and regulations governing different kinds of investment. In addition to the country risk analysis techniques introduced here, there is no substitute for direct experience. Only by visiting and learning about the geographic, sociocultural, economic, and political context in which business takes place can managers develop a qualitative, tacit understanding about the official, formal and the unofficial, informal local rules of the game.

KEY POINTS

1 Country risk analysis examines the chances of non-market events (political, social, and economic) causing financial, strategic, or personnel losses to a firm following FDI in a specific country market.

2 A PEST analysis provides a starting point for examining and comparing political, economic, sociocultural, and technological conditions in countries that present investment opportunities. Add depth and foresight to make PEST a little more rigorous.

3 Political risk is the probability that political forces will negatively affect an MNE's profit or impede the attainment of other critical business objectives. This risk can be examined

in terms of macro and micro factors. A macro political risk is one that affects foreign enterprises in the same general way. A micro political risk is one that affects selected sectors of the economy or specific foreign businesses.

4 General trends toward liberalization and deregulation have opened up a range of emerging markets to FDI, but governments maintain a strong level of control over the economy and the activities of foreign firms. Their ever-changing policies are a source of both new opportunities and risk.

5 There are a number of sources of political risk. Among others, these include the political philosophy of the government in power, changing economic conditions, rising nationalism, social unrest, terrorism, the vested interests of local business groups, and newly created international alliances.

6 There are numerous sources of information on political risk and global rankings of various kinds showing how countries compare. Online resources provide a quick and convenient way of starting a country risk analysis.

7 When assessing risk vulnerability at the project level quantitative and qualitative information need to be combined in an analysis of both the investment proposition and the country conditions. The Weighted Country Risk Assessment Model can provide a framework for this. Information gaps and uncertainty will always remain but the process can improve FDI decision making.

8 Country risk analyses can be incorporated into financial forecasts to produce revised NPV, ROI, or IRR calculations. The adjusted present value (APV) takes into account country risk estimates.

9 Understanding the policy objectives, policy tools, institutional structures and networks, and negotiating tactics of government agencies will help foreign managers negotiate better local conditions for FDI.

10 Power resources are the bargaining chips used by companies and governments in investment negotiations.

11 Corruption is defined by Transparency International as "the misuse of public power for private benefit." It can be difficult to distinguish between corrupt practices and local rules of the game that stem from differences in local market structures and business cultures.

12 There are three key steps in developing effective negotiating strategies. First, the MNE will evaluate its own position and that of the other parties to the negotiation. Second, the firm will examine the behavioral characteristics of the other parties in order to better understand their style of negotiation. Third, the MNE will use this information to hammer out an agreement that is acceptable to both sides. Identifying the acceptance zone of the other party is an important step.

13 MNEs tend to use a combination of integrative and protective/defensive techniques in minimizing political risk.

Key terms

- country risk analysis
- PEST framework
- political risk
- macro political risk
- expropriation
- indigenization laws
- micro political risk
- Weighted Country Risk Assessment Model
- adjusted present value (APV)
- corruption
- transparency
- acceptance zone
- integrative techniques
- protective and defensive techniques

397

REVIEW AND DISCUSSION QUESTIONS

1 How can a country risk analysis help an international manager making decisions about which countries to invest in?

2 How can we make a simple PEST analysis more robust, accurate, and useful?

3 What is meant by the term *political risk*? Is there political risk in every country of the world? Explain.

4 Show, with an example, how the process of deregulation and liberalization is opening up opportunities for foreign investment in emerging markets.

5 How does macro political risk differ from micro political risk? Compare and contrast the two.

6 What are some factors that help to determine the degree of micro political risk? Identify and describe three of them.

7 What resources are available online for comparing political risk in two or more countries? Give two examples and say how their measures and rankings differ.

8 What difficulties would a manager face compiling an accurate Weighted Risk Assessment Model for two emerging market countries?

9 What is an adjusted present value calculation? Give examples of the kinds of country risks that could be incorporated into an APV calculated for a manufacturing investment in a less-developed country.

10 When predicting political risk, why will an MNE be interested in examining the economic development agenda and policies of the government?

11 Choose a well-known MNE and describe the kinds of power resources or bargaining chips it could use in FDI negotiations with a country government.

12 Why does corruption tend to be more prevalent in poorer countries?

13 Describe one method for comparing the levels of corruption to be expected in two different countries?

14 Why is improving transparency important for investors and for local populations in less-developed countries?

15 Why will an MNE be interested in the behavioral characteristics of the participants in a negotiation? How can such information help to improve its negotiating position?

16 In a negotiation, why would an MNE be interested in the acceptance zone of the other party?

17 What are some bargaining tactics that are used in international negotiating? Identify and describe three of them.

18 How do MNEs use integrative techniques in order to reduce their political risk? Describe an example.

19 How do MNEs use protective/defensive techniques in order to reduce their political risk? Describe an example.

REAL CASE

Yukos and the Russian oligarchs

Russia has been making overtures toward a free-market economy for a considerable time. During the early 1990s investment from the West was seen as a way to improve the economy. However, significant changes needed to take place to reduce political risk in Russia. Initially, five steps were recommended by outside experts: (1) change the relationship between the national government and the republics in order to set up a federal political system in which central powers are limited; (2) eliminate or slash most state subsidies, including defense spending, and create a uniform sales tax and personal and corporate income tax system; (3) establish a commercial banking system, boost interest rates, and create an independent bank that will halt current inflationary practices; (4) break up state monopolies and industrial cartels; and (5) free the price of most goods immediately and gradually add to this list those changes that must be phased in more slowly: energy, public transportation, housing, and basic consumer goods such as milk, bread, and meat.

By 1997, the private sector accounted for more than half of Russia's output. Some 18,000 industrial firms had been privatized and over 1 million new businesses were created. The old Russia, its ideology and institutions, appeared to have gone. Despite currency and interest rate problems in the late 1990s, by 2001, for the first time since the end of communism, Russia had a balanced budget, a trade surplus, reserves, and a growing economy. In 2000, the economy grew by 8 per cent.

Events since then, however, have proved to be a wake-up call to foreign investors in Russia. They illustrate that a large bureaucratic web still exists and that the small corrupt mafia is proving difficult to police. More serious than this, there have been steps toward re-nationalization and a growing level of interference by politicians in the economy. The practice of giving preferential treatment for oligarchs, the powerful individuals that span the political and business worlds, has begun to reappear. This biased system, where the state uses an administrative mechanism, rather than a market one, to distribute assets, property, and commercial opportunities to powerful individuals in return for their political support, was favored by Yeltsin. President Vladimir Putin came to power promising to end it but has recently begun to slide back into these old ways.

The turbulent history of Yukos, Russia's largest oil company, provides an interesting example. It was privatized in the 1990s along with a number of government-owned utilities and natural resources companies. These included Sibneft, the oil company in which the flamboyant Roman Abramovich had the major shareholding, and the source of the wealth with which he bought the English soccer club Chelsea. Other well-connected individuals made fortunes from the sell-offs, which were generally well below market prices. Some channeled surplus funds offshore, including the head of Yukos, Mikhail Khodorkovsky. An American investor, Kenneth Dart, who had unwisely bought stakes in Yukos's production subsidiaries, lost many millions of dollars as Mr. Khodorkovsky stripped their assets and siphoned money into offshore accounts.

Putin appears to be both trying to stem the flows of capital from these previously state-owned enterprises and trying to transfer power to his own favored oligarchs. As Mr. Khodorkovsky's political ambitions grew he was sent to jail on flimsy charges of tax evasion in 2000. The Russian state subsequently seized a large stake in Yukos, its Yuganskneftegaz subsidiary, which repre-

sented 60 per cent of its oil production capacity, apparently to pay some of Yukos's unpaid taxes. It then sold this for $9.35 billion, well below market value, to the Baikal Finance Group in December 2004. It then emerged that the Rosneft, a state-owned oil company headed by Igor Sechin, a close confidant of Mr. Putin, had bought Baikal for an undisclosed sum. So the state had taken back Khodorkovsky's prime asset by the back door. A close advisor to Putin, Andrei Illarionov, said at the time this constituted "expropriation of private property" and should take the prize for the "swindle of the year." He has since lost his job.

Around this time Putin also directed the Russian government to limit foreign firms' involvement in a range of industries for "strategic" reasons. In early 2005 the Ministry of Natural Resources stated that foreign groups and Russian companies with more than 49 per cent foreign ownership would be banned from participating in tenders to exploit oil and metals deposits. Officials argued, for example, that Siemens, the German industrial giant, should be barred from buying a stake in Power Machines engineering company, on national security grounds. It just so happens that a company controlled by one of Russia's most powerful and Putin-friendly oligarchs, Oleg Deripaska, expressed a strong interest at the same time.

Illarionov's verdict was that Russia had shifted, regrettably, to "an interventionist model of economic development, with . . . extremely incompetent intervention in economic life by state officials." While the Kremlin still argues for entry into the World Trade Organization and Russia's integration into the global economy, in practice it has been raising barriers.

Sources: "The Outspoken Silenced," Economist, January 8, 2005; "Method and Madness: Yukos, Putin and the Oligarchs," Economist, January 1, 2005; "And the Owner Is?" Economist, November 8, 2003; R. Norton and K.-L. Hubert, "The Good News About Russia," Fortune, April 14, 1997, p. 32; S. H. Hanke, "Is the Rouble Next?" Forbes, March 9, 1998, p. 64; D. Yergin and T. Gustafson, "Don't Write Off Russia—Yet," Fortune, September 28, 1998, pp. 99–102; and D. F. Cavallo, "The Immensity of Russia's Problems," Forbes, August 24, 1998, p. 263.

1 What political risks do MNEs face in Russia? Identify and describe three of them.

2 What strengths would a foreign oil or energy firm bring to the country? What Russian needs would it help to meet?

3 How could this firm employ integrative or protective/defensive techniques in the country? Identify and describe one approach that could be used for each.

Problems with ports

Ports are important. Despite the shift to services and intangibles, trade in physical goods has continued to grow significantly. Today, almost 6 billion tons of seaborne trade flows through the world's ports each year. Ports are also the location of some of the commonest types of political risk, from organized, government-connected cartels to petty corruption. Here we briefly compare and contrast the problems of two port systems in two countries separated by huge economic, political, and cultural differences as well as thousands of miles: Japan and Kenya.

Japan's ports have long been slower and more expensive than any other in the Asia region. At the end of the 1990s, when the problem was at its worst, it took three to four days to clear customs and immigration in a Japanese port and cost $36,000 to $40,000 to unload a vessel, compared to one day in most other ports and $11,000 in Singapore and $16,000 in the United States. Partly as a result of this lack of competitiveness Kobe, for example, was the third largest port in the world in 1978, in terms of container volume handled, and by 2002, it had fallen to number 27, below not just Hong Kong, Singapore, and Pusan, but even Rotterdam and Antwerp. A key reason for these problems lies in the near-monopoly power of the Japan Harbor Transportation Association (JHTA). At its height the JHTA was a cartel of 2,000 member organizations encompassing the waterfront services (stevedoring, cargo handling, and transfer documentation) across 130 ports in Japan. It was run by Chairman Takashima, the so-called king of the waterfront, 8 vice-chairmen, and 85 directors from the various port companies. The JHTA was (and continues to be) responsible for two kinds of anti-competitive practices. First, the system of prior consultations between shipping companies and the labor unions of cargo-handling companies takes place via JHTA. Foreign firms cannot select which firm handles their cargo on the basis of quality or cost; JHTA chooses for them. It also controls schedule changes, changes in berths and route calls, centrally-regulating and slowing down the entire process. There is no formal documentation, application, or appeals procedure; the system operates through informal lobbying. Second, licensing requirements for technical operators and stevedoring firms act as barriers to foreign firms (and to non-cartel Japanese firms) entering the market. Foreign firms cannot perform stevedoring or port services for themselves, or appoint third parties without the consent of JHTA.

Source: Getty Images/Pete Turner

The JHTA connects both government departments and *yakuza* (mafia-like groups in Japan) in ways that non-Japanese cannot easily understand. A US Embassy study found that 110 ex-officials from the Ministry of Transport had moved to senior management positions in waterfront companies over the previous decade. This is *amakudari* (literally, "descent from heaven"), a system of secondment or "semi-retirement" for bureaucrats common in Japan. The *yakuza* have also long had strong interests in stevedoring firms and exert an influence over all the constituencies.

Foreign pressure grew on Japan to change the anti-competitive ports practices through the 1990s. The European Commission took Japan to the World Trade Organization and US firms lobbied via their Chamber of Commerce in Tokyo. Finally in April 1997 the US Federal Maritime Committee imposed port sanctions on Japanese ships entering the US in retaliation for restrictive practices in Japanese ports. A penalty of $100,000 per US port entry by a Japanese ship from abroad was imposed. Japanese port workers subsequently went on strike and Takashima personally (side-stepping the Japanese government entirely) threatened the US administration with counter-penalties! By November the situation was diffused and US Secretary of State Madeleine Albright signed an agreement with the Japanese authorities with a package of solutions.

A sure sign of the power of cartels and the difficulties of unwinding the complex relationships between the government and the private sector in Japan (and many countries) is the fact that Japanese ports are still as costly, slow, and uncompetitive as they were in the 1990s. In January 2005 the Japanese government again promised to take measures to reduce the cost of using its main ports by 30 to 40 per cent to "arrest a dramatic drop in competitiveness."

Kenya's main port of Mombasa is a world away from Kobe or Japan. Different problems concern port users including, according to one study, security and theft; bureaucratic forwarding and clearing procedures (cost increases due to procedural delays); customs and excise harassment (leading to corruption, otherwise further delays); obsolete, poorly maintained port handling and lifting equipment (leading to further delays); high tariffs for poor service; and just plain corruption, in that order.

As with many other service operations either currently or previously owned or regulated by government agencies in less-developed countries, what they do, how they do it, and how much it costs is highly dependent on government influence. Many of Africa's problems are seen to stem from a generic "culture of corruption." Many forms of corruption exist in Kenya including petty corruption (to obtain a small service or get it done faster), corruption by harassment (where the private sector is harassed into bribing), political corruption (soliciting bribes for favors), and grand scale corruption (evading tax on a grand scale or fixing government tenders worth hundreds of millions of dollars). Political interference in Kenya's ports takes a number of forms. Particularly important are:

1 Political appointments to key management functions, resulting in unqualified and sometimes corrupt personnel in critical power positions.

2 Political undercurrents in labor recruitment; tribal affiliations and ruling political party affinity lead to biases in the recruitment of low wage labor as well as more senior posts.

3 Regular interference in tender allocations; for government-related tenders, kickbacks (bribes) are necessary to win contracts.

4 Well-connected port users have an advantage and can queue-jump or get better services or security protection, creating frustration for other port users.

Beyond these kinds of problems, small-scale corruption is rife. Port users may need to bribe petty officials to release goods or pay security guards protection money to avoid theft (which they can often be responsible for). The uncertainty for foreign managers unfamiliar with these local rules of the game is increased by the constant change in key officials and their political affiliations. Moreover, bribing the wrong person is not only a waste of money, but also can create big problems for anyone caught "playing the game" during sporadic government crack-downs.

Website: http://www.iaphworldports.org/trade/main-trade.htm.

Sources: Mariko Sanchanta, "Japanese Government to Cut Main Port Costs by Up to 40%," *Financial Times*, January 7, 2005, p. 3; Michiyo Nakamoto, "Port City Seeks to Nurture New Enterprises," *Financial Times*, April 27, 2004, p. 3; Parit Shah, *A Strategy for the Port of Mombasa*, Unpublished MBA dissertation, Warwick Business School, Coventry, 2004; US Embassy in Tokyo, *Third Report to the Leaders on the US-Japan Regulatory Reform and Competition Policy Initiative*, June 8, 2004, http://tokyo.usembassy.gov/e/p/tp-20040609-01.html; Lucy Kilalo, "10 Charged with Stealing at Port," *The Daily Nation*, March 12, 2003; A. Mutunba-lule, "Bogus Clearing Agents Have Nowhere to Hide," *Maritime Report*, *The Daily Nation*, March 20, 2000; and author's interview with Richard Neal, Head of John Swire and Sons (Japan) Ltd., March 17, 1997.

1 What are the main differences in the barriers and risks faced by foreign firms in the Japanese port system compared to Kenya's Mombasa?

2 Why is it difficult for foreign firms to challenge these unfair practices in either Kenya or Japan?

3 How could a manager looking to use these ports minimize the risk and uncertainty created by local ways of doing things?

Endnotes

1 S. Bridgewater, "Assessing Market Attractiveness," in S. Bridgewater and C. E. Egan (eds.), *International Marketing Relationships* (Basingstoke: Palgrave, 2002); K. D. Miller, "A Framework for Integrated Risk Management," *Journal of International Business* (Summer, 1992), pp. 311–331; D. Kern, "The Evaluation of Country Risk and Economic Potential," *Long Range Planning*, vol. 18, no. 3 (1985), pp. 17–25; and M. Perlitz, "Country Portfolio Analysis—Assessing Country Risk and Opportunity," *Long Range Planning*, vol. 18, no. 4 (1985), pp. 11–26.

2 D. O'Connell, "Dogfight," *The Sunday Times Newspaper*, September 19, 2004, London.

3 V. Houlder, "Record Flows to Developing World Boost Global FDI," *Financial Times*, January 12, 2005.

4 This framework partly comes from C. R. Kennedy Jr., *Managing the International Business Environment: Cases in Political and Country Risk* (New Jersey: Prentice Hall International, 1991).

5 A. Ostrovsky, "Economics Minister Hits at Putin Policy," *Financial Times*, January 12, 2005.

6 D. Brewster and A. Hill, "US Opts for Homegrown Products," *Financial Times*, April 1, 2003.

7 E. Alden, "Small Manufacturers Drive Trade Protectionism Up the US Agenda," *Financial Times*, February 1, 2005.

8   F. Bokhari, "Pakistan Weaves into a New Era," *Financial Times*, January 12, 2005; H. K. Nordas, "The Global Textile and Clothing Industry Post the Agreement on Textiles and Clothing," *World Trade Organization*, 2004, http://www.wto.org/english/res_e/booksp_e/discussion_papers5_e.pf.

9   S. C. Collinson and J. Holden, "Decision-Making and Market Orientation in the Internationalization Process of Small and Medium-Sized Enterprises," *Proceedings of the Academy of Management*, annual conference, New Orleans, 2004.

10 Details about the criteria and methodology used by BERI are available at http://www.beri.com/.

11 Mary C. Lacity and Leslie P. Willcocks, "Survey of IT Outsourcing Experiences in US and UK Organizations," *Journal of Global Information Management*, vol. 8, no. 2 (April/June 2000), pp. 5–24.

12 Transparency International, *Global Corruption Report 2004*, http://www.globalcorruptionreport.org/.

13 http://www.globalcorruptionreport.org/; http://www.transparency.org/index.html.

14 "China Moves to Standardize Regulation of Foreign Businesses," *Asian Economic News*, January 8, 2001.

15 Richard M. Hodgetts and Fred Luthans, *International Management*, 4th ed. (Burr Ridge, IL: McGraw/Hill, 2000), p. 287.

16 Nancy J. Adler, *International Dimensions of Organizational Behavior*, 2nd ed. (Boston, MA: PWS-Kent Publishing, 1991), p. 197.

17 John R. Schermerhorn, Jr., "Language Effects in Cross-Cultural Management Research: An Empirical Study and a Word of Caution," *National Academy of Management Proceedings*, 1987, pp. 102–105.

18 For additional insights into negotiating, see Brian Mark Hawrysh and Judith Lynne Zaichkowsky, "Cultural Approaches to Negotiations: Understanding the Japanese," *International Marketing Review*, vol. 7, no. 2 (1990), pp. 28–42.

19 For a good example of how Japan does this, see Andrew Pollack, "Japan Takes a Pre-emptive Step on Auto Exports," *New York Times*, January 9, 1993, pp. 17, 26; and Richard W. Stevenson, "Japanese Cars Get British Accents," *New York Times*, February 25, 1992, pp. C 1, C 14.

Additional bibliography

Alessandri, Todd M. et al. "Managing Risk and Uncertainty in Complex Capital Projects," *Quarterly Review of Economics & Finance*, vol. 44, no. 5, pp. 751–768.

Barclay, L. A. *Foreign Direct Investment in Emerging Economies: Corporate Strategies and Investment Behaviour in the Caribbean* (London and New York: Routledge, 2000).

Brett, Jeanne M. and Okumura, Tetsushi. "Inter- and Intracultural Negotiations: US and Japanese Negotiators," *Academy of Management Journal*, vol. 41, no. 5 (December 1998).

Brewer, T. "Political Risk Assessment for Foreign Direct Investment Decisions: Better Methods for Better Results," *Columbia Journal of World Business*, vol. 20, no. 3 (1981), pp. 5–11.

Brewer, Thomas L. "An Issue-Area Approach to the Analysis of MNE–Government Relations," *Journal of International Business Studies*, vol. 23, no. 2 (Second Quarter 1992).

Chakrabarti, A. "The Determinants of Foreign Direct Investment: Sensitivity Analysis of Cross-Country Regressions," *Kyklos*, Vol. 54, no. 1 (2001), pp. 89–114.

Chatterjee, Sayan et al. "Integrating Behavioural and Economic Concepts of Risk into Strategic Management: The Twain Shall Meet," *Long Range Planning*, vol. 36, no. 1 (2003), pp. 61–80.

Chi, Tailan. "Business Strategies in Transition Economies," *Academy of Management Review*, vol. 26, no. 2 (April 2001).

Cosset, Jean-Claude and Roy, Jean. "The Determinants of Country Risk Ratings," *Journal of International Business Studies*, vol. 22, no. 1 (First Quarter 1991).

Feinberg, S. E. and Gupta, A. K. "Country Risk and Network Linkages within Multinationals," *Academy of Management Conference*, New Orleans, 2004.

Fitzpatrick, M. "The Definition and Assessment of Political Risk in International Business: A Review of the Literature," *Academy of Management Review*, vol. 8, no. 2 (1983), pp. 249–254.

Gaba, V., Pan, Y. and Ungson, G. R. "Timing of Entry in International Market: An Empirical Study of US *Fortune*

500 Firms in China," *Journal of International Business Studies*, vol. 33, no. 1 (2002), pp. 39–56.

Grosse, Robert. "Restrictive Business Practices in International Service Industries: Examples from Latin America," *Transnational Corporations*, vol. 6, no. 2 (August 1997).

Henisz, W. *Politics and International Investment* (Cheltenham: Edward Elgar, 2002).

Henisz, W. and Delios, A. "Uncertainty, Imitation and Plant Location: Japanese Multinational Corporations, 1990–1996," *Administrative Science Quarterly*, Vol. 46, no. 3 (2001), pp. 444–475.

Hillman, Amy and Keim, Gerald. "International Variation in the Business–Government Interface: Institutional and Organizational Considerations," *Academy of Management Review*, vol. 20, no. 1 (January 1995).

Horrigan, Brenda D. "Debt Recovery by Foreign Investors in Post-crisis Russia," *European Business Journal*, vol. 11, no. 2 (1999).

Hoti, S. and McAleer, M. "An Empirical Assessment of Country Risk Ratings and Associated Models," *Journal of Economic Surveys*, vol. 18, no. 4 (2004), pp. 539–589.

Inkpen, Andrew C. and Beamish, Paul W. "Knowledge, Bargaining Power, and the Instability of International Joint Ventures," *Academy of Management Review*, vol. 22, no. 1 (January 1997).

Kobrin, S. "Political Risk: A Review and Reconsideration," *Journal of International Business Studies*, Vol. 10, no. 1 (1979), pp. 67–80.

Kobrin, S. "When Does Political Instability Result in Increased Investment Risk?" *Columbia Journal of World Business*, vol. 13, no. 3 (1978), pp. 113–123.

Lee, Suk Hun. "Relative Importance of Political Instability and Economic Variables on Perceived Country Creditworthiness," *Journal of International Business Studies*, vol. 24, no. 4 (Fourth Quarter 1993).

Makhija, Mona Verma. "Government Intervention in the Venezuelan Petroleum Industry: An Empirical Investigation of Political Risk," *Journal of International Business Studies*, vol. 24, no. 3 (1993).

Makhija, Mona V. and Stewart, Alice C. "The Effect of National Context on Perceptions of Risk: A Comparison of Planned versus Free-Market Managers," *Journal of International Business Studies*, vol. 33, no. 4 (2002), pp. 737–757.

Miller, Kent D. "Industry and Country Effects on Managers' Perceptions of Environmental Uncertainties," *Journal of International Business Studies*, vol. 24, no. 4 (Fourth Quarter 1993).

Mudambi, Ram and Navarra, Pietro. "Political Tradition, Political Risk and Foreign Direct Investment in Italy," *Management International Review*, vol. 43, no. 3 (2003), pp. 247–266.

Olsson, Carl. *Risk Management in Emerging Markets: How to Survive and Prosper* (London: Financial Times/Prentice Hall, 2002).

Peng, Mike W. "Controlling the Foreign Agent: Case Studies of Government–MNE Interaction in a Transition Economy," *Management International Review*, vol. 40, no. 2 (Summer 2000).

Rajan, Mahesh N. and Graham, John L. "Nobody's Grandfather Was a Merchant: Understanding the Soviet Commercial Negotiation Process and Style," *California Management Review*, vol. 33, no. 3 (Spring 1991).

Rice, Gillian and Mahmoud, Essam. "A Managerial Procedure for Political Risk Forecasting," *Management International Review*, vol. 26, no. 4 (Fourth Quarter 1986).

Reuer, Jeffrey J., Shenkar, Oded and Ragozzino, Roberto. "Mitigating Risk in International Mergers and Acquisitions: The Role of Contingent Payouts," *Journal of International Business Studies*, vol. 35, no. 1 (2004), pp. 19–33.

Rolfe, Robert J., Ricks, David A., Pointer, Martha M. and McCarthy, Mark. "Determinants of FDI Incentive Preferences of MNEs," *Journal of International Business Studies*, vol. 24, no. 2 (Second Quarter 1993).

Shi, Xinping. "Antecedents of International Business Negotiations in the China Context," *Management International Review*, vol. 41, no. 2 (Summer 2001).

Stasavage, D. "Private Investment and Political Institutions," *Economics and Politics*, vol. 14, no. 1 (2002), pp. 41–63.

Tahir, R. and Larimo, J. "Understanding the Location Strategies of the European Firms in Asian Countries," *Journal of American Academy of Business*, vol. 1, no. 2 (2004), pp. 102–110.

Yiu, D. and Makino, S. "The Choice Between Joint Venture and Wholly Owned Subsidiary: An Institutional Perspective," *Organization Science*, vol. 13, no. 5 (2002), pp. 667–683.

WWW resources

http://www.tdctrade.com
http://www.wto.org
http://www.worldbank.org/wbi/governance/govdata2001.htm
http://www.worldbank.org/data/countrydata/countrydata.html
http://rru.worldbank.org/DoingBusiness/
http://miga.org
http://www.countryrisk.com/

http://www.economist.com/countries
http://www.eiu.com
http://transparency.org
http://www.globalcorruptionreport.org/
http://www.opacity.index.com
http://www.fraserinstitute.ca
http://www.freetheworld.com/

and, between them, they control 38 per cent of Heathrow's slots.

In Europe, the UK's Office of Fair Trading and the European Commission's competition directorate examined the proposal. The loudest opposition by a competitor came from Britain's Virgin Atlantic. News of the proposal resurrected Virgin's No Way BA/AA campaign. Virgin contended that BA/AA would hold 60 per cent of all Heathrow–US service and fly 50 per cent of all passengers traveling between the US and the UK. Together, BA/AA flew 9 million passengers between the United Kingdom and the United States in 2001; the next biggest carrier flew 3.5 million. Virgin claimed that this dominance would effectively eliminate smaller airlines from the transatlantic market.

At the center of the proposal was BA's access to US market and US carriers' access to London's Heathrow. Presently, BA flies to 25 American airports but it cannot pick up passengers in one US city to fly them to another US city. If the deal with AA had gone through, BA/AA would have had total access to US and EU markets. US carriers had the opposite problem. Only two US airlines, American and United, had access to Heathrow airport. For years the US and British governments have been negotiating an "Open Skies" agreement without much progress. The proposed alliance added momentum to Open Skies. The British government had indicated that it would be willing to negotiate an Open Skies agreement if the BA/AA was granted antitrust immunity.

Though some competitors welcome deregulation of the US and UK market, they criticize the use of Open Skies as a bargaining chip for the proposed BA/AA deal. They contend that Open Skies would be irrelevant if the BA/AA agreement gives one company a virtual monopoly in the US–UK market and that competition would be better served by preventing the merger.

In 2002, the US government approved the merger of British Airways and American Airlines on condition that the merged company surrender over 200 slots in Heathrow Airport. Both airlines announced that they would not merge due to the excessive strategic cost imposed by regulators. The "final" result of the discussions and negotiations by 2005 was to leave BA and AA in the One World alliance, with code-sharing, and with occasional expansion of routes to additional pairs of US–UK cities—but not a merger of the two airlines, and not the full access that they requested and that would have virtually monopolized the UK–US air traffic. Given the continued financial losses at American Airlines during 2001–2004, some greater link(s) to BA would not be impossible in the next few years.

Websites: www.aa.com; www.british-airways.com; www.usairways.com; www.oneworldalliance.com; www.delta.com; www.nwa.com; www.airfrance.com; www.continental.com; and www.klm.com.

Sources: Adapted from Paula Dwyer et al., "Air Raid: British Air's Bold Global Push," *Business Week*, August 24,1992; Agis Salpukas, "The Big Foreign Push to Buy into US Airlines," *New York Times*, October 11, 1992; Adam Bryant, "British Air Halts Move into USAir," *New York Times*, March 8, 1994; "Predators in the Air," *Economist*, June 8, 2000; Peter Spiegel, "US Rivals Call for Hearing on Deal by BA and American," *Financial Times*, November 20, 2001; "Branson Slams BA/AA Alliance," *Virgin Atlantic News Release*, November 12, 2001; "Let Fly," *Economist*, March 8, 2001.

1. Is the BA/AA alliance going to use a polycentric, ethnocentric, or geocentric solution to handling operations?

2. If the two carriers were to complete a merger and the US dollar then weakens against the British pound as it did in 2004–2005, how will this affect the financial statements of the company?

3. If BA believed that the British pound was going to appreciate in relation to the euro, how is it likely to deal with receivables and payables?

4. Assuming that BA might choose to acquire all or part of American, United, or Delta Airlines in the United States, how could BA finance the major capital budgeting need in international markets, and what are some of the important considerations in choosing among alternative financing sources?

INTRODUCTION

Any firm with affiliates in at least two countries (even with a simple sales office abroad) needs to deal with differences in the financial environments of those countries—differences in their tax systems, their currency systems, and numerous other areas. Can you imagine trying to keep the books of a company such as Johnson & Johnson, which is required to maintain financial records according to the different accounting standards in the dozens of countries where it operates, plus records for use in internal control? Beyond the chores of recordkeeping, the firm operating at this level obtains opportunities to transfer funds (and products) between countries, utilize financial markets in each country to serve its global needs, and diversify its risks internationally. Increasing numbers of MNEs, such as Ford and General Electric, are building internal financial institutions so that they can take advantage of these opportunities around the world. This chapter explores the opportunities and problems of firms in such an environment.

National financial markets and the euromarkets were discussed in Chapter 7; here the emphasis is on using these markets to optimize the financial position of the multinational firm. The issue of transaction exchange risk was treated in Chapter 7; this chapter considers such risk in the context of a firm that does repeated international business and maintains long-term assets abroad. Finally, we consider the full set of financial issues in a firm whose subsidiaries in different countries compete for use of the available financial resources. This chapter treats the topic of multinational financial management as a whole.

The chapter is structured to cover major issues in corporate finance as they apply to the international context. Basic financial management can be divided into two broad headings: (1) choice and management of *sources* of funds and (2) choice and management of *uses* of funds. At the international level, exchange risk management must be added. Figure 14.1 depicts the topics that constitute the substance of the chapter. Overall financial management requires *control* over each type of decision depicted in the figure, especially since financial managers in each affiliate may make decisions that affect the total corporation's financial position.

In the next section, we explore aspects of the parent–subsidiary financial relationship within the MNE. Then the discussion turns to the issue of managing cash flows in the MNE. Next, we consider a more comprehensive presentation of exchange risk management than that given in Chapter 7. After that, we look at the two sides of financial management

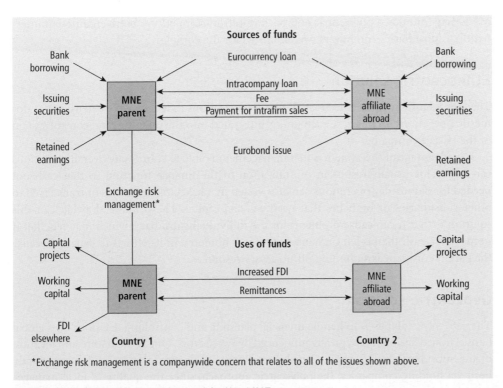

Figure 14.1 Financial management in the MNE

in the context of the MNE: namely, use of available funds (particularly for capital budgeting) and financing for the firm's short- and long-term needs. A section on control of the financial activities in a MNE follows. And finally, some strategic considerations for the firm in international finance are presented.

DETERMINING PARENT-SUBSIDIARY RELATIONSHIPS

Because finance is such an important area of operations, it is critically important that parent companies firmly establish the relationships that will exist regarding financial planning and control authority. On the one hand, each branch or subsidiary should be responsible for its own planning and control system. On the other hand, there must be some central control in order to coordinate overall operations and to ensure both efficiency and profitability. In addressing this challenge, MNEs tend to opt for one of three managerial solutions: polycentric, ethnocentric, or geocentric, just as these choices are used in other strategic areas.

Polycentric solution

Polycentric solution
A decentralized decision-making framework in which financial decisions are largely allocated to foreign affiliates, and financial evaluation of affiliates is done in comparison with other firms in that context

A polycentric solution is to treat the MNE as a holding company and to decentralize decision making to the subsidiary levels. In this arrangement financial statements are prepared according to generally accepted accounting principles in both the overseas subsidiary's and the parent's home country, and the subsidiary's performance is evaluated against that of similar domestic and foreign concerns.

The advantages of the polycentric approach are those commonly obtained with decentralization. Decisions are made on the spot by those most informed about market conditions, and international subsidiaries tend to be more flexible, motivated, efficient, and competitive. On the other hand, this solution reduces the authority of the home office, and senior corporate management often dislike this dilution of their authority. Additionally, an MNE may find that a polycentric approach results in competition between different international subsidiaries and lowers overall profits for the company.

Ethnocentric solution

Ethnocentric solution
A centralized decision-making framework in which financial decisions and control for foreign affiliates are largely integrated into home-office management

The ethnocentric solution is to treat all foreign operations as if they were extensions of domestic operations. In this case each unit is integrated into the planning and control system of the parent company.

The advantage of this system is that management is able to coordinate overall operations carefully. This usually results in centralization of the finance function so that cash not needed for day-to-day operations can be invested in marketable securities or transferred to other subsidiaries or branches that need working capital. The primary drawback of this solution is that it can cause problems for the individual subsidiary, which may feel that it needs more cash than is left on hand or that it is hindered in its efforts to expand because the parent company is siphoning off necessary resources.

Working capital
Short-term financial instruments such as bank deposits and marketable securities that can be optimized by the MNE on a global basis

Geocentric solution

Geocentric solution
A decision-making framework in which financial decisions and evaluation related to foreign affiliates are integrated for the firm on a global basis

The geocentric solution is to handle financial planning and controlling decisions on a global basis. These decisions are typically influenced by two factors. One is the nature and location of the subsidiary. For example, British investment in North America has predominantly been via holding companies, the polycentric approach, since the quality of local management largely rewards decentralization. Conversely, investment in developing countries has typically been more centralized, with the parent company maintaining close control of financial expenditures. A second influencing factor is the gains that can be achieved by co-ordinating all units in a carefully synchronized way. When an MNE's overseas units face a myriad of tax rates, financial systems, and competitive environments, it is often more efficient to centralize most of the financial control decisions because this is the best way to ensure that profit and efficiency are maximized. For example, if two subsidiaries are equally able to sell a particular product to a major customer, with centralized financial planning the parent company could ensure that the sale would be made by the unit located in the country with the lowest corporate income tax rate. Additional examples of the ways in which financial operations could be directed by using a geocentric solution are seen in the management of global cash flows.

✔ Active learning check

Review your answer to Active Learning Case question 1 and make any changes you like. Then compare your answer with the one below.

1 Is the BA/AA alliance going to use a polycentric, ethnocentric, or geocentric solution for handling operations?

The alliance is going to use a geocentric solution to handle operations. This is clear from the way in which the two air carriers are beginning to merge their operations so that they are both working in harmony. An alliance of equals, BA/AA can capitalize on their individual regional/triad strengths.

MANAGING GLOBAL CASH FLOWS

One of the key areas of international financial management is the careful handling of global cash flows. There are a number of ways in which this is done. Three of the most important ones include the prudent use of internal funds flows, the use of funds positioning, and the use of multilateral netting. The following sections examine each of these three.

Multilateral netting Payment of net amounts due only between affiliates of a MNE that have multiple transactions among the group, which can be partially netted out among them; so then only the net funds need to be transferred

Internal funds flows

When an MNE wants to expand operations or fund activities, one of the simplest ways of obtaining the needed monies is by getting them from internal sources such as working capital, which is the difference between current assets and current liabilities. For example, if General Motors' German subsidiary wants to hire more employees, it may be able to pay for this payroll increase out of the funds it generates from ongoing operations. Another way of raising money internally is by borrowing from a local bank or from the parent company. For example, an MNE's Chilean subsidiary will get a loan from the parent company or the German subsidiary and then repay the money with interest out of operations. A third way is by having the parent company increase its equity capital investment in the subsidiary. In turn the subsidiary could pay the parent dividends on the investment. These examples are illustrated in Figure 14.2 and help to show that there are many ways for multinational firms to generate internal cash for operations.

Which method is most likely to be used? The answer will depend on a number of factors, including government regulations regarding intercompany lending. For example, when tax rates are high for a profitable subsidiary, it is common to find those units willing

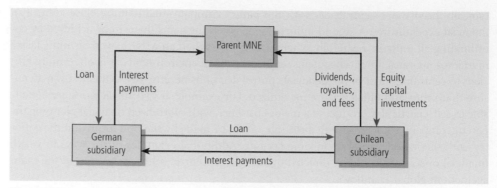

Figure 14.2 Common examples of internal sources and flows of funds

to lend money at low rates of interest to other subsidiaries in the MNE that need funds to expand into growth markets. The logic behind this strategy is quite simple: the highly profitable unit does not need to charge a high interest rate because much of this interest earning will be lost to the high local taxes. Conversely, the subsidiary that is borrowing the money needs low interest rates so as to conserve its cash for expansion purposes. By shifting the money around in this fashion, the MNE is able to support expansion efforts, to minimize taxes, and to increase the sales potential of the subsidiaries. In an effort to prevent multinationals from taking advantage of such tax loopholes, in recent years some governments have changed their tax laws and established a minimum rate that can be charged on these intercompany loans.

Another area of concern is government limits on a parent company's ability to charge subsidiaries a licensing or royalty fee for the use of technology or to assess a management fee that covers the subsidiary's fair share of corporate overhead. When there are no government restrictions in these areas, the MNE has greater freedom in drawing funds from subsidiary operations, thus providing the parent with a pool of money that can be used for other worldwide operations. The ways in which this is done are commonly referred to as funds positioning techniques.

Funds positioning techniques

Funds positioning techniques
Mechanisms such as transfer pricing, intercompany loans, and timing of payments that are used to move funds from one affiliate to another in a multinational firm

Funds positioning techniques are strategies that are used to move monies from one multinational operation to another. While there are a variety of approaches, three of the most common are transfer pricing, use of tax havens, and fronting loans.

Transfer pricing

Transfer price
The price used for an intracompany payment for shipment of products or services from one affiliate to another in an MNE; these prices can be used to reduce taxes, move funds to desired locations, and so on

A **transfer price** is an internal price that is set by a company in intrafirm trade such as the price at which the Chilean subsidiary will purchase electric motors from the German subsidiary. An initial conclusion would be that the German firm will sell the motors at the same price as it would to any outside purchaser. A second conclusion is that the Chilean subsidiary will receive a discount because it is an intrafirm transaction and the parent will not allow its subsidiaries to profit at the expense of each other. However, both of these conclusions are incorrect when a transfer pricing strategy is employed. The final price will be determined by local regulations and will be set at a level that allows the MNE to achieve certain desired goals such as to increase profit, to reduce costs, and/or to move money among the subsidiaries.

A good example is provided by a multinational that has a subsidiary located in Country A, which has a low corporate income tax and is selling goods to a subsidiary located in

Table 14.1 Shifting profits by transfer pricing

	Arm's length price		Transfer price	
	Country A	Country B	Country A	Country B
Sales	$10,000 exports	$12,000	$12,000 exports	$12,000
Costs of sales	8,000	10,000	8,000	12,000
Profit	2,000	2,000	4,000	Nil
Tax rate	800	1,000	1,600	Nil
(A: 40%, B: 50%)				
Net profit	1,200	1,000	2,400	Nil

Country B, which has a high corporate income tax. If the transfer price is set carefully, it is possible to reallocate taxable income away from the highly taxed subsidiary to the subsidiary with the low tax rate. Table 14.1 provides an example by contrasting arm's length pricing with transfer pricing. An arm's length price is the price a buyer will pay for merchandise in a market under conditions of perfect competition. As seen in the table, it cost the subsidiary in Country A $8,000 for the goods it is selling to the subsidiary in Country B. Under an arm's length price the seller is adding $2,000 for profit and selling the goods for $10,000. In turn the second subsidiary is selling these goods for $12,000. Thus both subsidiaries are making a profit of $2,000. As also seen in the table, the tax rate in Country A is 40 per cent, whereas in Country B it is 50 per cent. So the first subsidiary will have a net profit of $1,200, whereas the second subsidiary will net $1,000.

Under a transfer price arrangement, however, the objective is to maximize profits in the low tax rate country and to minimize them in the high tax rate country. In this case, as seen in Table 14.1, the first subsidiary sells the goods for $12,000, and after paying 40 per cent tax on the $4,000 profit, it ends up with a net profit of $2,400. The second subsidiary sells the goods for $12,000 and makes no profit. However, thanks to the transfer pricing strategy, the multinational's overall profit is greater than it was with arm's length pricing ($2,400 versus $2,200).

Note that taxes are not the only considerations. Import tariffs also influence the decision to use transfer pricing. If the importing country has high tariffs, the firm needs to consider whether a high or low transfer price will maximize after-tax, after-tariff profits.

One of the obvious benefits of transfer pricing is that it allows the multinational to reduce taxes. A second benefit is that the strategy lets the firm concentrate cash in specific locales such as with the first subsidiary, or to move funds away from a country facing significant exchange rate risk, or to reduce payment of import tariffs. One of the problems with transfer pricing is that the financial statements do not accurately reflect subsidiary performance because the profit margins are manipulated. A second problem is that the strategy may not encourage efficient performance by the seller in a low-tax jurisdiction, whose primary objective is to unload merchandise on the other subsidiary at a profit as high as can be justified.

In recent years countries have been rewriting their tax codes to prevent arbitrary transfer pricing. In the US, for example, the Internal Revenue Service (IRS) now asks multinationals to apply for an advanced determination ruling (ADR) before establishing a transfer pricing policy. After the firm submits the ADR request, the IRS will determine whether or not the policy is appropriate. The objective of the tax agency is to ensure that MNEs charge their overseas subsidiaries the same price for components and products as they charge independent third parties, thus effectively eliminating price manipulation for tax purposes. Because a large part (about one-third) of international trade in the early 21st century is intrafirm, transfer prices are a necessary aspect of much of international business.

Arm's length price
The price that exists or would exist on a sale of a given product or service between two unrelated companies—as contrasted with an intracompany transfer price

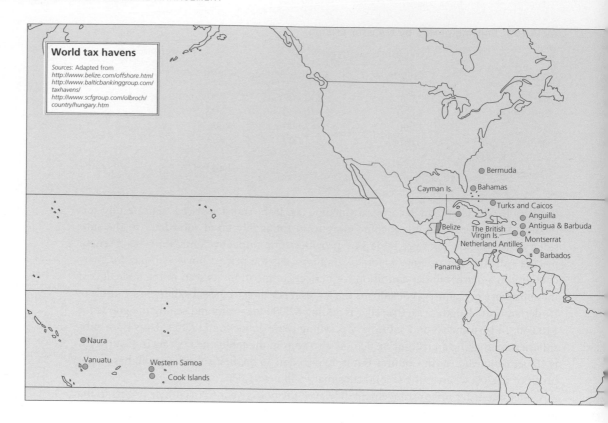

World tax havens

Sources: Adapted from
http://www.belize.com/offshore.html
http://www.balticbankinggroup.com/
taxhavens/
http://www.scfgroup.com/olbroch/
country/hungary.htm

Use of tax havens

Tax havens
Jurisdictions that offers the MNE a lower tax rate (or no tax) than in other places, so that MNEs can locate some of their business activities there and thus reduce overall tax payments

A second funds positioning technique is the use of tax havens, which are low-tax countries that are hospitable to business (see accompanying map). This strategy is typically used in conjunction with transfer pricing and involves a subsidiary selling its output at a very low cost to a subsidiary in a tax haven, which in turn sells the merchandise at a very high price to a third subsidiary.[1] Table 14.2 provides an example, which is similar to that in Table 14.1, except that the sales are now routed through a subsidiary located in a tax haven, Country B, where no tax is paid at all. The result of the example in the table is a net profit of $4,000. This is greater than that illustrated in Table 14.1, where a simple case of transfer pricing was employed. For more on the matter of tax havens, see the box **International Business Strategy in Action: Tax havens.**

Fronting loans

Fronting loan
A third-party loan in which an MNE home office deposits funds with a financial institution, which then lends to the MNE's affiliate in a country where the MNE faces political risk or currency transfer restrictions

A fronting loan is a funds positioning strategy that involves having a third party manage the loan. For example, if a US multinational decided to set up operations in China, the MNE might be concerned with the political risk that accompanies such a decision. Is it possible that the government might expropriate the subsidiary's assets, including all the cash on hand? In an effort to protect their investments, the parent company could deposit funds with a major international bank that has strong ties to China and is on good terms with the government. In turn the subsidiary would apply for a loan with this bank and the multinational company's deposit would be given to the subsidiary in the form of a loan. It is highly unlikely that the Chinese government would expropriate the subsidiary and endanger the loan or its relationship with the international bank. Thus the MNE has successfully positioned its funds.

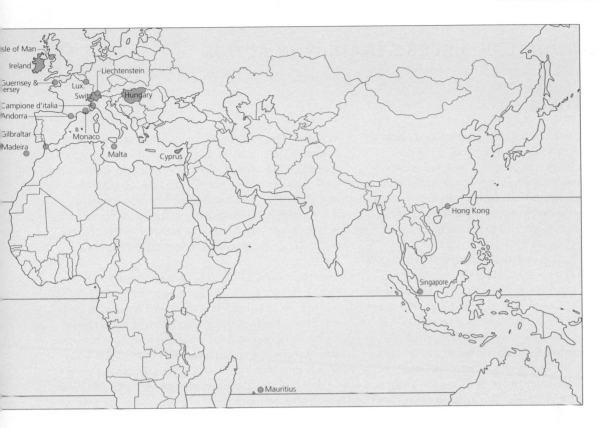

Funds positioning strategies are important in moving money around a multinational, as well as in helping the MNE to cope with political and legal roadblocks that stand in the way of such action. However, an internally operated netting process that controls the flow of funds and ensures that bills are paid promptly always complements these strategies. This process is often collectively referred to as multilateral netting.

Multilateral netting

When subsidiaries do business with each other, each may owe money to the others and in turn be owed money by them. Figure 14.3 provides an example of four subsidiaries that have both amounts due and amounts payable from each of the others. Over time, of course, these obligations will be resolved by the individual subsidiaries. In an effort to make the process more efficient, however, many multinationals have now set up clearing accounts in a certain location and assigned the manager at this location the authority to make the transfers that are necessary to pay intracompany subsidiary obligations. This process of multilateral

Clearing account
A centralized cash management bank account in which one MNE affiliate reviews payment needs among various MNE affiliates and arranges to make payments of net funds due from each affilate to others through the clearing account

Table 14.2 Transfer pricing through tax havens

	Country A subsidiary	Country B subsidiary (tax haven)	Country C subsidiary
Sales	$8,000 exports	$12,000 exports	$12,000
Costs of sales	8,000	8,000	12,000
Profit	–	–	–
Tax rate (A: 40%, B: 0%, C: 50%)	–	–	–
Net profit	0	4,000	0

INTERNATIONAL BUSINESS STRATEGY *IN ACTION*

Tax havens

What do Switzerland, the Bahamas, Monaco, and Andorra have in common? By some definition, they are all considered to be tax havens. In general, a tax haven is a country or a jurisdiction that allows individuals or corporations to set up a subsidiary and to avoid paying taxes in their country of residence, thus depriving their home governments of some tax revenues that are used to provide government services.

One of the underlying problems that led to the creation of tax havens in the first place is that there is no single international tax standard. Individual governments have different tax policies, so MNEs have an incentive to deploy their overall financial assets around their worldwide network of subsidiaries in order to minimize taxation. It would not be possible for MNEs to do this if there were a common unitary world tax system. The MNEs are reacting to the lack of a global standard in government tax policy, yet governments then blame them for using legal tax havens to reduce overall taxes paid.

Each tax haven jurisdiction has its own sets of laws on taxation and transparency. Tax havens are also sometimes accused by governments and NGOs such as Oxfam as being a means for money laundering and of hiding the proceeds of criminal activity, including political corruption, illicit arms dealing, and drug trafficking. In fact, these are serious concerns, and each of the tax haven jurisdictions has taken significant steps in recent years to reduce the possibility of being used for these purposes.

The OECD lists a number of factors used to identify a tax haven. Among these, a tax haven is a country or jurisdiction that (1) imposes no or nominal taxes and is used by foreigners to escape taxes in their own countries (this includes "ring fencing" jurisdictions that reserve preferential treatment to foreigners, thus shielding the country from tax avoidance by its own residents); (2) has laws or administrative practices that prevent the exchange of information with other governments on taxpayers benefiting from low taxation; (3) lacks transparency; (4) does not require substantial productive operations in the country, suggesting policies geared to attracting income only on a preferential tax basis. Of all these factors, only the first one is necessary for the identification of a tax haven.

In recent years, the OECD has been pressuring countries and jurisdictions to reverse what it calls harmful tax competition and lack of transparency. The United Nations, for different reasons, has been trying to curb the use of tax havens for money laundering. The EU has also challenged the use of unfair tax competition by US exporters in the World Trade Organization and won. Under US law, US exporters could set up a sales operation in an offshore tax haven and avoid paying taxes on the proceeds of this business. The British and French governments have also each targeted its own tax haven jurisdiction, the British challenging the Channel Islands and Isle of Man offshore tax havens.

Reluctantly, many of these countries have reacted to OECD pressures and reformed their policies. The Channel Islands and the Cayman Islands both have anti-money laundering legislation. Under pressure from the French government, Monaco also signed an agreement to prevent money laundering, increase transparency, and remove some tax concessions.

Yet the total eradication of tax havens will not come without confrontation. For one, tax havens and their financial institutions depend heavily on these deposits. The Bahamas, which considers itself a major international financial hub, can foresee a tremendous loss of income, especially if other countries, including Switzerland and Luxembourg, are not ready to implement the same policies. The Bahamas has argued that the OECD is using a two-tier system, cooperatively designing legislation with its member countries and then imposing this regime on smaller, less developed, non-member countries.

Switzerland, for its part, is willing to work out a tax reimbursement scheme with the EU and the US, but is not willing to increase its transparency. Though this might address the tax concerns of

Source: Getty Images/Royalty Free

OECD nations, it does little to prevent criminal activity or to address the tax concerns of poorer countries, which are estimated to lose over $50 billion a year from tax evasion. The OECD listed the Bahamas as an uncooperative tax haven, but Switzerland was not mentioned.

Another group opposing these reforms are MNEs that use tax havens. In Britain, at least one company threatened to move its operations if the government continued its

attempts to prevent the use of tax havens. Despite this type of opposition, the OECD continues to pressure for reform and expects all countries to comply by 2005.

Websites: **www.oecd.org** and **www.oxfam.org**.

Sources: OECD, *Harmful Tax Competition*, 1998; "Offshore Financial Centers Hit at OECD Tax Competition," *Financial Times*, November 21, 2001; *Oxfam, Oxfam Policy Papers—Tax Havens*, June, 2000.

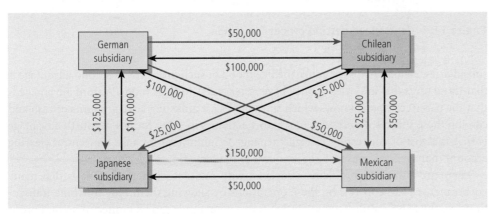

Figure 14.3 Multilateral dollar flows between subsidiaries

netting, which involves a determination of the net amount of money owed to subsidiaries through multilateral transactions, begins with a computation of the amounts owed to each. Table 14.3, which has been constructed based on the information in Figure 14.3, shows these net positions. Based on this information, those that owe money are required to transfer it to a centralized clearing account (see Figure 14.4), whereas those that are owed money are paid from this central account.

The clearing account manager is responsible for seeing that this process occurs quickly and correctly. Typically, this individual will receive monthly transaction information from all the subsidiaries and will use these data to determine the net position of each unit. The manager will then see that the necessary transfers are made. These transfers usually take place in the currency of the payer, so the German subsidiary will pay its obligation in euros, whereas the Mexican subsidiary will pay in pesos. The clearing account manager's staff will handle the process.

There are a number of reasons that multilateral netting has become popular. One advantage is that it helps the parent company to ensure that financial interactions between the units are quickly brought to completion. If bills are allowed to be outstanding for months at a time, it can result in the other units not wanting to do business with slow-paying

Table 14.3 Net cash positions of subsidiaries

Subsidiary	Total receivables	Total payables	Net positions
German	$300,000	$225,000	$75,000
Chilean	125,000	150,000	−25,000
Japanese	200,000	275,000	−75,000
Mexican	225,000	200,000	25,000

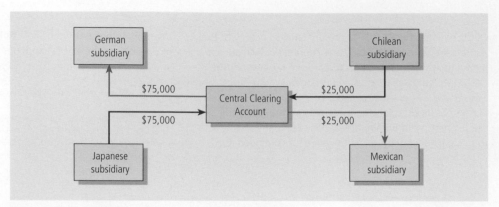

Figure 14.4 Centralized netting process in action

subsidiaries. Netting helps to reduce the likelihood of such problems. A second advantage is that those units that are owed money have faster access to their funds. A third advantage is that the parent company knows which subsidiaries are amassing large amounts of cash and can tap these sources if necessary to support activities in other locales. A fourth advantage is that the cost of converting foreign exchange is minimized because the central clearing account manager can convert large amounts at the same time.

There are also some problems associated with multilateral netting. One is that many governments place controls on these operations by allowing them only for trade transactions. So the MNE's ability to use netting for moving funds can be limited. A second problem is that in other cases governments have required that payment for imports be delayed until these goods clear customs, thus slowing down the netting process by as much as 60 to 90 days. A third is that of getting local subsidiary managers to cooperate and keep the central clearing account manager fully apprised of all transactions affecting this process. Sometimes there is a reluctance to cooperate on the part of those managers whose cash outflows are substantially larger than their inflows. Under a netting process they can no longer delay payments for three or four months while working to reverse the flow and to pay their bills out of current earnings.

Multilateral netting can help an MNE to ensure that intersubsidiary accounts are balanced, and the process is extremely useful in assisting the parent company in managing global cash flows. However, there is an inherent problem in this process that requires special attention and which netting cannot resolve: foreign exchange risk as typified by the fluctuating value of international currencies. This risk is particularly important when MNEs do business with buyers who are paying in weak currencies. In dealing with this dilemma, MNEs often formulate a foreign exchange risk management strategy.

Managing cash

Consider a multinational firm such as Nestlé (based in Switzerland) whose network of affiliates extends around the world. Each affiliate has its own customers and suppliers, as well as financial ties to the rest of the company. Viewing the company as a single unit for purposes of cash management can yield far better results than would be obtained if each affiliate managed its cash independently. For example, much less foreign exchange protection is generally needed if all of the affiliates are evaluated together than if each affiliate **hedges** its own position. The French subsidiary may have a large amount of accounts payable in euros that can be hedged simply by consolidating the German affiliate's excess cash which is also in euros. Similarly, the Canadian subsidiary may possess a large amount

Hedge
A strategy to protect the firm against risk, in this case against exchange rate risk

of Canadian dollar assets that can be hedged by having the US company contract some liabilities (e.g., by purchasing equipment or taking out loans) denominated in Canadian dollars. The whole company may coordinate its borrowing efforts through the British subsidiary, which uses the London eurocurrency market.

Centralized cash management offers five kinds of potential gains to the MNE:

1 By pooling the cash holdings of affiliates where possible, the MNE can hold a smaller total amount of cash, thus reducing its financing needs.

2 By centralizing cash management, it can have one group of people specialize in the performance of this task, thus achieving better decisions and economies of scale.

3 By reducing the amount of cash in any one affiliate, it can reduce country risks as well as financial costs.

4 As noted previously, it can net out intracompany accounts when there are multiple payables and receivables among affiliates, thus reducing the amount of money actually transferred among affiliates.

5 Its central cash management group can ensure that cash management decisions aim at corporate goals rather than the goals of individual affiliates when these might conflict.

The first kind of gain results simply from better use of the cash held by the firm. If each affiliate holds enough cash to meet its transactions needs, precautionary needs, and speculative needs (following the Keynesian categories of money demand), far more cash is likely to be held than is needed *companywide*. A domestic company centralizes the cash management function at one location (usually the home office), and an MNE can do the same. The key difference between the two is that the MNE is often restricted in its ability to shift funds among affiliates internationally; thus, less centralization is possible at the MNE level. Any reduction in cash holdings, however, enables the firm to reduce its financing needs, thus lowering costs.

The second kind of gain relates to the development of management skills. By centralizing the cash management function, even if funds are left in the affiliates for the most part, the firm can utilize the skills of a specialized group of cash managers. Gains from this group's decision making should include economies of scale in borrowing, since the group can borrow to meet the entire company's needs and then distribute funds to affiliates as required. Also, the group should develop detailed knowledge of financial opportunities worldwide, thus enabling the firm to borrow at lower cost or lower risk than firms lacking such expertise.

If the MNE reduces its total assets through centralized cash management, it also reduces both its exchange risk and its country risk in that fewer assets are at risk worldwide. The country risk does not change, but the exposure of the company to that risk decreases. Country risk may also be hedged or transferred by the decision makers in the cash management group, who have greater access to protection tools than do managers in any one affiliate.

The fourth kinds of benefits, from multilateral netting of accounts, are primarily cost savings from the reduced need to transfer funds between affiliates.

The fifth kind of gain from centralized cash management relates to business strategy. Placing the cash management function in one location, either at the home office or at a location closely monitored by the home office, makes better control possible. In this way, the firm can ensure that cash management decisions are made to meet global corporate needs rather than to improve an affiliate's position, possibly at the expense of the rest of the company. This is especially true with respect to hedging, which should be decided at the corporate level, since virtually every affiliate is likely to have assets or liabilities in another currency that are partially or totally hedged by balance sheet items of other subsidiaries.

INTERNATIONAL BUSINESS STRATEGY *IN ACTION*

News Corp

In 1952, a young Rupert Murdoch inherited the *Adelaide News*, a small, unprofitable, province-based newspaper in Australia. Upon it, Murdoch has built a world media empire that includes newspapers, magazines, books, TV networks, satellite networks, and movies. News Corp, as the holding company is now called, is a *Fortune* Global 500 firm with revenues in excess of $20 billion in 2003. Its companies include such well-known names as the Fox Network, Fox News, National Geographic cable network, *TV Guide*, and *The New York Post* in the United States; *The Sun* newspaper and *The Times* in the United Kingdom; and *The Australian* in Australia.

Over 75 per cent of News Corp's revenues originate in one market: the United States. Europe, mainly the United Kingdom, accounts for 16 per cent of its revenues. Australasia, mainly Australia, accounts for a mere 8 per cent of revenues. The United States not only accounts for the most revenues, but also is the most profitable geographic sector, accounting for 81 per cent of operating income.

Despite the predominance of the US market in the company's operations, News Corp official headquarters have remained in Adelaide, Australia, until the mid-2000s. In practice, however, the company had been managed from the United States, where Murdoch has lived since the 1970s and where he became a citizen to circumvent laws that prevented foreigners from owning US TV stations.

In the late 1990s, News Corp was criticized by the UK media because of its tax practices. The company has a complex infrastructure of loosely woven companies across the world. The group lists 800 subsidiaries of which 60 are incorporated in tax havens such as the Cayman Islands, Bermuda, the Netherlands Antilles, and the British Virgin Islands. Of all its British operations, News Publishers, incorporated in Bermuda,

was the most profitable in the 1990s, this despite the lack of any significant employees at the subsidiary, a company that seems to derive all of its income from other News Corp group companies. The company was incorporated in Australia, which has the least accountable of all accounting standards among developed nations. In the United States, News Corp lists its subsidiaries in Delaware, which does not force companies to file publicly available accounts. In 1998, News Corp's effective corporate taxes worldwide amounted to 6 per cent of pre-tax profits. This compares to 31 per cent for Disney, another competitor in the same industry. What the media has not claimed was that there was any actual wrongdoing. Murdoch's company was simply taking advantage of tax loopholes in the different jurisdictions in which it operates. Nonetheless, the lack of transparency has had some negative effect for the company, especially after the Enron scandal.

In 2004, News Corp announced that it will move its headquarters and re-incorporate in Delaware, United States. Delaware was chosen because of its business-friendly corporate laws. News Corp assured its shareholders that neither they nor the company will have to shoulder additional tax expenses. The move formalizes the company's historic dependence on the United States and is expected to provide the company with better access to capital markets. As a US company, News Corp's share will be eligible for inclusion in US-based indexes and be more attractive to investors who would rather invest in US firms.

Sources: Adapted from Alan M. Rugman, *The Regional Multinationals* (Cambridge: Cambridge University Press, 2005); Geoff Hiscock, "News Corp., Moving Home to the US," *CNN.com*, April 6, 2004; "Cable TV Boosts News Corp Profits," *BBC News*, May 6, 2004; and "News Corp Prepares to Move to the US," *BBC News*, April 6, 2004.

While centralized cash management offers obvious and potentially very large benefits, it also presents some problems. Most important, if freedom to manage cash is taken away from the affiliate manager, some of the affiliate's ability to improve its performance is also removed. The evaluation of each affiliate must recognize this point. (This idea is discussed further in the section on controls.)

Another problem with internationally centralized cash management arises when national rules restrict financial transfers into or out of some countries. Virtually all less developed countries and many developed ones limit funds outflows through exchange controls or taxation. Some countries specifically disallow international netting of payments. Because of such restrictions, international cash management today requires a great deal of knowledge about national financial constraints and often requires a decentralized strategy of funds transfers due to these constraints.

The whole idea of international funds transfer and management is a major opportunity for firms that have operations in multiple countries. Not only can transfer pricing, multilateral netting, and so on be used to move funds as needed in the firm, but other policies such as dividend remittances, payment of royalties and fees, and intracompany loans are among the many alternatives that can be used to optimize the firm's overall financial situation.

EXCHANGE RISK MANAGEMENT

We have discussed exchange risk primarily in relation to *transactions* denominated in foreign currency. In addition, exchange risk exists in the translation of financial statements and, in principle, for future, so-far unspecified activities of the firm. Three kinds of exchange risk should be differentiated: (1) transaction risk, (2) translation risk, and (3) economic risk. Each kind of risk is important to the MNE, and each leads to somewhat different conclusions for hedging strategies.

Transaction risk

When a specific contracted asset or liability is denominated in a foreign currency, it is subject to transaction risk, or the risk of an unexpected change in its home-currency value during the time to maturity. Accounts payable and receivable, loans, and bank deposits denominated in foreign currencies are examples of items that are subject to such exchange risk. Each foreign-currency transaction can be hedged (or not) with some offsetting transaction in the same currency and with the same maturity. This topic was discussed in Chapter 7, and a new example is presented at the end of this section.

Transaction risk
The risk of financial loss or gain to an MNE due to unanticipated exchange rate changes affecting future cash flows from transactions that are denominated in foreign exchange

Translation risk

Translation risk, or accounting risk, is the risk of value changes in foreign-currency assets and liabilities on the balance sheet, whether or not the transactions occur during the accounting period. For example, the plant and equipment of foreign subsidiaries is subject to valuation change even if no purchase or sale of such items takes place during the accounting period. Because balance sheet information is reported in most countries to securities regulators and in published financial statements, valuation changes in the foreign operations of multinational firms become public knowledge. Loss in the value of foreign-currency assets, regardless of its impact on company earnings, may negatively affect investors' perceptions of a firm. To avoid the appearance of weakness due to the devaluation of foreign assets, firms often try to hedge their balance sheets through financial contracts (such as forward contracts or money market hedges).

Translation risk
The risk of losses or gains on the MNE's balance sheet, due to unhedged exchange rate changes during an accounting period

A good example of this exposure for a US MNE is when the currency of a local country weakens in relation to the dollar. For example, if the Chilean peso declined by 10 per cent against the dollar, the value of the Chilean subsidiary's peso account at the local bank would also decline when translated into dollars in the consolidation process. If the company had the equivalent of $100,000 (US) on deposit, this account would now be worth $90,000 in translation and consolidation. Of course, this decline would not affect the number of pesos on deposit, and the local purchasing power of these pesos, at least in the short run, would remain the same. However, the decline would negatively affect the subsidiary's ability to purchase imports from countries with strong currencies since it would now take more pesos than before to buy these goods.

Consolidation
The translation of foreign affiliate accounts and addition to home-country accounts for the purpose of reporting complete (global) condition of a company; consolidation of foreign affiliate accounts that are denominated in other currencies necessarily produces translation risk

Balance sheet hedging
The use of financial instruments denominated in foreign currency to eliminate exchange rate (translation) risk from the balance sheet of a company

Conclusions as to the desirability of balance sheet hedging are ambiguous. On the one hand, since investor decisions may be based on valuation changes in foreign-currency assets, the firm should hedge to avoid investor preoccupation with such changes. On the other hand, since the valuation of foreign-currency assets may not affect the economic viability of the project, it would be a waste of effort for the firm to deal with such changes.

Economic risk

Economic risk
The risk of financial loss or gain to an MNE due to the effects of unanticipated exchange rate changes on future cash flows that are denominated in foreign currencies

Economic risk is the risk of unexpected changes in future cash flows from foreign operations (and from activities denominated in foreign currencies, wherever they occur). Such risk is most important to the firm, since future cash flows are the basis for the firm's value. Unfortunately for the manager, it is not possible to know with certainty the full set of future cash flows that will occur. Thus, a hedging strategy cannot be perfectly matched with such cash flows. To deal with economic risk, the firm may choose to follow a generalized strategy of hedging transactions when they are contracted and trying to balance foreign-currency assets and liabilities as they appear on the balance sheet. Or the firm may choose not to hedge at all, on the assumption that future currency fluctuation will be approximately offset by price changes in each country (i.e., that purchasing power parity will approximately hold). Despite the inherent difficulty of predicting future foreign exchange exposures, ultimately the firm should be concerned about economic (foreign exchange) risk as the key variable in exchange risk management.

Consider the economic risk involved with a subsidiary's assets. If the value of the local currency strengthens, the sale of inventory will generate larger dollar profits. However, would it be wiser to lower price, to take less profit per item, but to generate more demand? Similarly, would it be wise now to sell fixed assets such as buildings or factories and then to lease them back from the purchaser? Some US firms in Tokyo found that by the early 1990s the land and buildings that they had bought years before were now worth hundreds of times their original purchase price. Believing that the local real estate market was as high as it was going to go and feeling that it would be more advisable to sell the properties and rent them back, these firms sold their office buildings and made tremendous profits. The ensuing decline of Tokyo real estate prices showed that these firms had made very wise (lucky) decisions.[2]

Another example of economic exposure is the risk that companies take when selling to a country with a weakening currency. In this case many MNEs have sought to increase their own production efficiency, lower their costs, and continue to generate acceptable profit. Firms such as Honda, Nissan, and BMW have complemented this strategy by setting up operations in the United States, their largest international market.[3] In the process the firms have reduced their economic exposure.

In fact, all three kinds of foreign exchange risk play important parts in the management of an international firm. No single hedging strategy can cover them all, so the MNE manager must devise plans for dealing with each. Fortunately, both transaction and economic risk deal with future cash flows; thus, the management of these two kinds of risk can be combined fairly readily. For example, the firm can hedge all occasional exports denominated in foreign currencies and seek local-currency financing for the entire production of its foreign affiliates. Then, if it does not employ balance sheet hedging (as suggested earlier), it can follow a consistent and simple hedging strategy. Judging from the immense volume of material dealing with corporate foreign exchange management strategies, it is safe to say that MNEs generally do *not* follow such simple strategies. Instead, they combine some hedging with some speculation in an effort to maximize their results from foreign exchange dealings. Table 14.4 lists a range of exchange risk hedging techniques that can be used to deal with one or more of these exchange risk categories.

Table 14.4 Exchange risk hedging techniques*

To hedge an exposed liability	To hedge an exposed asset
Buy foreign exchange in the forward market	Sell foreign exchange in the forward market
Buy foreign exchange in the futures market	Sell foreign exchange in the futures market
Buy foreign exchange call options	Buy foreign exchange put options
Invest/deposit in a foreign exchange instrument	Borrow in a foreign exchange instrument
Incur accounts receivable in foreign exchange	Incur accounts payable in foreign exchange
Swap liabilities with another firm	Swap assets with another firm
Obtain any other foreign exchange asset	Obtain any other foreign exchange liability

In each instance, the hedge must produce an equal-value asset (liability) in the same currency with equal maturity to offset the exposed liability (asset).

* These techniques assume no expectation about the direction of exchange rate change. If devaluation is expected, then creation of a net liability position is attractive, and vice versa for expected revaluation.

 Active learning check

Review your answer to Active Learning Case question 2 and make any changes you like. Then compare your answer with the one below.

2 If the two carriers were to complete their merger and the US dollar then weakens against the British pound, as it did in 2004–2005, how will this affect the financial statements of the company?

This will depend on whether the two carriers continue to issue separate financial statements. If they do, AA's financials will be affected only by the amount of sterling that it has on hand. Otherwise there will be no effect, since changes in the pound do not affect the cost to AA of doing business in the United States. In the case of BA the accounts payable that are due in dollars will negatively affect the airline's financials. If the two carriers combine their statements into one, the overall effect will be a result of how these transactions net out. This would be determined based on the rules in FASB (Financial Accounting Standards Board) Statement No. 52.

An example of exchange risk management

Consider the situation faced by a US-based firm such as American Express Company (AMEX) when its subsidiary in the United Kingdom reports the purchase of £5 million of office equipment (mainly furniture and computer terminals) for the subsidiary's tourist service offices throughout that country. This equipment is to be paid for in 180 days in British pounds. The strategies for dealing with exchange risk in this transaction depend on the whole firm's position in British pounds. The problem can be analyzed as follows.

First, if American Express already has an existing asset exposure in Great Britain due to its subsidiary's ongoing activities, that position may partially or wholly cover the new transaction. In other words, if American Express-UK has a balance sheet that shows net sterling (pound) assets, typically because foreign subsidiaries have some dollar liabilities, the new account payable may partially offset that asset exposure.

Second, the same results may occur even if the British subsidiary has been operated to cover ongoing exchange risk in the United Kingdom. In the event that American Express has placed funds in euro-British pound deposits in one of its other subsidiaries (e.g., in France or Germany), the new account payable may offset the existing exposure. *Note that the exposure is still not covered unless the maturity of the existing asset matches the six-month maturity of the new liability.*

Third, American Express can look for some financial hedging technique to avoid the exchange risk. For example, some new asset such as a bank deposit or short-term security could be purchased with a maturity of 180 days and a value of £5 million. Or a forward contract could be arranged with a bank to sell dollars and buy pounds in 180 days. Through the London International Financial Futures Exchange (LIFFE) or through one of the US futures exchanges, American Express could arrange a futures contract or option contract to hedge the account payable. The alternatives are numerous, but the basic goal is to find some British pound asset that matures in 180 days, worth £5 million, to hedge the new liability that calls for a cash outflow of £5 million in 180 days.

The following table lists relevant financial information if American Express were making this hedging decision on December 28, 2004:

Spot exchange rate	$US 1.9290 / £1
180-day forward exchange rate	$US 1.9086 / £1
180-day LIBOR in pounds	4.91875% / year
180-day LIBOR in dollars	2.76625% / year
6-month sterling call option strike price	
The options cost $US 875 per contract at the CME, with £31,250 per contract.	$US 1.92 / £1
For this option, the premium is $US 0.025/pound.	
6-month sterling futures contract rate	
The futures contracts have £62,500 per contract.	$US 1.9151 / £1
Ignore commissions and other transaction costs for these instruments.	

American Express can use this information to evaluate various financial hedges for the sterling account payable.

First, the firm can use a simple forward contract to hedge the exposure. A forward contract to buy British pounds would cost about $US 7.4 million in six months, as follows:

$$£5,000,000 \times \$US\ 1.9086/£ = \$US\ 9,543,000.$$

This forward contract completely hedges the account payable, because it will result in receipt from the bank of £5 million in 180 days, which will be used to pay the supplier of office equipment.

A second alternative is to place funds now into a pound-denominated investment that matures in six months. The choice shown above is a eurosterling account that pays 4.91875 per cent per year for the six-month period. The dollar value of pounds for AMEX to buy today can be calculated by discounting the future pounds that are needed to a present value of pounds that must be deposited today to achieve that sum in six months. The calculations are as follows:

$$£5,000,000/(1.024594) = £4,879,983.$$

This first step shows that the interest earned in the eurosterling deposit for 180 days will be 2.4594 per cent and that £4,879,983 must be deposited today to reach the value needed to pay the account payable. Next, the dollars that must be used today to buy these pounds is

$$£4,879,983 \times \$US\ 1.9290/£ = \$US\ 9,413,487.$$

The hedging cost is lower for this alternative, since the funds must be paid *now* rather than in 180 days. To compare the two choices, they must be placed in the same time period. This requires discounting the forward contract value using the relevant discount rate, which would be a deposit interest rate in dollars for the same time period:

$$\$US\ 9,543,000/(1.01383125) = \$US\ 9,412,809.$$

The discount amount (1.01383125) is the implicit return to depositing funds in a eurodollar account (comparable to the europound deposit) for six months at 2.76625 per cent per year. This results in a slightly lower cost of hedging in the forward market.

A third alternative is to use a futures contract hedge in the LIFFE or the Chicago Mercantile Exchange (CME). Using the CME's quotes, we see that American Express could buy future pounds for $US 1.9151 per pound in contracts worth £62,500 per contract. Multiple contracts could be bought, so that with 80 contracts the company could obtain the needed £5 million. However, since the exchange rate is worse than the forward rate (i.e., it costs more dollars to buy the pounds), AMEX will not consider a futures hedge.[4]

Each of these financial hedges can protect American Express against foreign exchange risk. The company will want to choose the least costly hedge in this case, namely the forward market hedge. In other situations, one or another of these three alternatives will be the most beneficial to the firm. Beyond these choices, American Express should consider the possibility of structuring its business such that it could use British pound assets (e.g., accounts receivable, investments, etc.) to hedge liabilities such as this purchase of equipment.

Developing forecasting and reporting systems

The management of foreign exchange risk can be both complex and cumbersome. A multinational with 20 subsidiaries can present a formidable challenge to the parent company because so many foreign exchange risk decisions need to be made and monitored. However, there are a number of steps that MNEs typically take in creating the necessary system for managing these decisions. They may:

1 Decide the types and degrees of economic exposure that the company is willing to accept.

2 Develop the necessary expertise (in-house personnel and/or outside economists or consultants) for monitoring exchange rates and for forecasting those rates that are applicable to the identified exposures.

3 Construct a reporting system that allows the firm to identify exposed accounts, to measure this exposure, and to feed back information on what the firm is doing and the status of these decisions.

4 Include all MNE units in this reporting system so that each better understands the risks it is assuming and is aware of the actions that must be taken to deal with these risks.

5 Keep senior-level management fully apprised of what is going on in each area of responsibility so that every regional or divisional manager is able periodically to revise the exposure risk and to make those strategy changes that will help more effectively to manage the process.

As firms begin to implement these five steps, they are better able to deal with the management of foreign exchange risk.

✔ Active learning check

Review your answer to Active Learning Case question 3 and make any changes you like. Then compare your answer with the one below.

3 **If BA believed that the British pound was going to appreciate in relation to the euro, how is it likely to deal with receivables and payables?**

If BA believed that the pound was going to get stronger against the euro, and if it were owed euros, the firm would try to collect them immediately before their value declined. At the same time BA would delay payment of those obligations that were fixed in euros, for it would be getting more euros per pound after the appreciation, thus making it easier to pay those bills. The firm would lead collections and lag payables.

CAPITAL BUDGETING IN THE MULTINATIONAL ENTERPRISE

Capital project evaluation follows many of the same principles in an international firm as in a domestic firm, though additional variables and risks must be considered. Specifically, foreign projects must be evaluated for exchange risk, country risk, different financing costs, and any problems associated with the transfer of products, services, or funds due to government controls in any of the relevant countries. To see how these factors appear in the analysis, consider the following example of a food-processing plant to be constructed by a US-based company in Shapironia (a fictitious country).

The company has developed the following pro forma income statement for the proposed investment project:

Proposed Shapironia Processing Plant Pro Forma Income Statement, Typical Year (in local currency)

Sales	10,000,000
Cost of goods sold	
Local materials	1,000,000
Imported materials	2,000,000
Labor	3,000,000
Overhead expenses	600,000
Interest on loan from parent firm	400,000
Net income before tax	3,000,000
Local tax-50%	1,500,000
Net income after tax	1,500,000

Assuming the investment made by the parent firm is 4 million in local currency, the project appears to have a simple return on capital of about 38 per cent per year (1,500,000/4,000,000). As long as the firm's cost of capital is less than 38 per cent, the project is worth undertaking.[5] The normal, domestic concerns apply to this project evaluation; that is, the estimate is only as good as the forecasts of costs and sales. In addition, this foreign project faces potentially important considerations such as exchange risk, currency inconvertibility and other country risks, and preferential local borrowing opportunities. Chapter 13 provides more detailed discussion of this problem of country risk evaluation and management.

Exchange risk will affect the US dollar value of the profits earned, potentially raising or lowering them substantially. For example, if the local-currency value rises by 10 per cent in relation to the dollar, net income after tax will rise (in dollar terms) by 10 per cent, other things equal. However, if imported materials come from the United States, that cost (in local currency) will fall. Similarly, if the loan is made in dollars, interest cost (in local-currency terms) will fall. Sales, if any are exported from Shapironia, may decrease due to the exchange rate change.[6] In sum, a rise in the value of the local currency relative to the US dollar will tend to cause an increase in dollar profits from the affiliate, and such profits will tend to fall if the local currency devalues relative to the dollar.

Country risk (defined in Chapter 13) is another concern in the attempt to evaluate this project properly. If the host government decides to restrict profit remittances, then, no matter how profitable the project, the MNE will not be able to utilize its earnings elsewhere in the firm or to distribute them to shareholders. This problem is known as currency inconvertibility, regardless of whether the cause is a political decision or simply an economic reality. If discontent with the Shapironia government leads to strikes or violent confrontation between the government and opposition groups, the plant may be damaged or its production

Currency inconvertibility The inability of a firm to transfer profit from a subsidiary in a host country to other areas of the organization or to shareholders because of host government restrictions on profit remittances curtailed. Not all country risk is negative; if the government chooses to reduce corporate taxes to stimulate greater investment, the project may generate greater profitability than that shown above. In sum, country risks need to be considered when the full set of the project's financial implications is being judged.

Borrowing costs may differ in Shapironia and the United States. Thus, if the firm uses its weighted-average cost of capital in capital budgeting decisions, this project should be adjusted to account for any locally subsidized borrowing opportunity that exists. Many countries (and states or provinces within countries) offer low-interest loans to corporate investors to attract production facilities and jobs. If this is true in Shapironia and if the firm chooses to borrow some funds locally, the subsidized capital cost should be reflected in the capital budget. The project as shown uses an intracompany loan whose interest may be charged at the parent's actual cost of funds or marked up (or down) to achieve greater (or lesser) transfer of funds to the parent.

Finally, recall that the capital budget measures the project's *incremental impact* on the whole firm. Thus, if there are export sales from the parent to this new affiliate, those new sales must be counted in the evaluation. If the project replaces sales that were formerly exported to Shapironia, those lost sales must be counted. Any other intracompany impacts should also be measured in the project evaluation. This means the project should be judged in comparison with other alternatives available to the firm serving the Shapironia market. If exports from the United States offer a greater incremental profitability than the proposed plant, exports should be chosen. In summary, the incremental gains to the firm from the proposed project should be compared with the potential gains from other international business alternatives that may be available.

In contrast to domestic projects, one additional key question must be answered: Who should conduct the analysis, the parent or the foreign subsidiary? Typically, the initial analysis is done at the subsidiary or branch level and then passed up to the head office for modification and/or approval. For example, two subsidiaries may both want to build a new tire plant and sell to the same market. Without coordination, they would compete against each other and the expected profits would not materialize. So the parent corporation will make a decision that benefits the entire organization. In this latter role the parent may have to turn down a positive NPV project from one subsidiary in favor of a higher NPV project from another subsidiary. The same process applies in reverse to plant closures; the shut-down will be at the plant with the largest negative NPV. Similarly, factories or holdings that do not generate sufficient profit may be sold.

> **Weighted-average cost of capital (WACC)**
> The firm's cost of obtaining funds from the various sources available. Each source of funds is weighted (multiplied) by the percentage of total capital it provides. Thus, the WACC is W_1 (cost of using retained earnings) + W_2 (cost of bank borrowing) + W_3 (cost of other source of funds), where each cost is stated as an annual percentage rate and each W is the percentage of total capital from that source

Use of net present value

The parent company will review expenditure proposals because it has the necessary overall information to make these decisions. Moreover, such expenditure decisions will often be different from those of the subsidiary because the latter may use faulty valuation techniques or fail to address adequately the impact of political risk. In explaining why these differences occur, we must first review the basic NPV criterion. This criterion separates the financing and operating parts of the problem by discounting operating cash flows by a weighted-average cost of capital that embodies the financing decision. The NPV equation is

Equation 14.1

$$\text{NPV} = \sum_{t=0}^{T} \frac{I_t + C_t}{(1 + K_A)}$$

where

Equation 14.2

$$K_A = k_e \frac{S}{V} + k_d(1 - t_x)\frac{D}{V}$$

The definition of the terms are:

I_t = investment cash outlays in year t

C_t = cash inflows in year t

T = terminal date or end of project

K_A = weighted-average cost of capital

k_e = cost of equity capital

k_d = cost of debt financing

t_x = tax rate

D/V, S/V = debt and equity ratios, respectively

NPV = incremental net present value for the project.

In examining what determines the NPV, we must realize that disagreement between parent and subsidiary can arise because of the discount rate K_A, investment cost, and annual cash flows. Political risk can also affect all values. For example, the risk of foreign-currency controls can cause some of the future cash flows to be largely ignored by the parent. From the parent's perspective, if funds can no longer be remitted, their value is substantially reduced since they are not available for dividend payments or for reinvestment elsewhere. Conversely, once foreign exchange controls are in place, the parent will often treat blocked funds as being less valuable. From the parent's perspective, the cost of future investments in the country, financed by these blocked funds, is reduced. In both cases the subsidiary is not directly concerned with the problem of foreign exchange controls, and it will discount all cash flows that are incremental from its own perspective.

Similarly, country risk may cause the parent to increase the discount rate or required return to reflect that risk. However, if the subsidiary does not agree with that perception, it will not increase the discount rate, so its calculation of the present value of the cash inflows and NPV will be higher. Moreover, if foreign exchange controls are enforced, the local capital markets can be isolated from the international capital market. From the subsidiary's perspective, the result may be lower local real interest rates, which make local investment opportunities seem attractive. However, the parent, looking at global opportunities, may decide that it will make more sense to draw capital out of the country for reinvestment elsewhere.

Another reason that parent and local NPVs may differ is faulty application of the NPV framework. The most common errors are in incorrectly choosing t_x and K_A. The tax rate t_x is relevant in two places, the incremental tax that results from the incremental profits and the incremental tax shield that results from debt financing. Here, the errors usually come from a failure to determine the incremental tax rate. From the subsidiary's perspective the tax rate is the extra tax that it pays locally. However, the parent must also consider any incremental tax that it will pay once dividends are remitted.

In determining the discount rate K_A, several problems emerge. First, it is common that discount rates differ by several percentage points. The reason is obvious: inflation differs across different countries, and thus the inflationary premium built into the discount rate will differ. What the firm can never do is to use a discount rate from one country to evaluate cash flows denominated in another currency. The correct procedure is to calculate the real discount rate and then to "gross it up" for the inflationary expectations of the relevant country.

Additionally, debt ratios differ across subsidiaries, and the weights in Equation 14.2 may alter the cost of capital. This will inevitably occur if the multinational maximizes the use of debt financing in a country with subsidized borrowing rates. However, the debt ratio of that country is then not appropriate for determining the cost of capital since the excess debt can be carried only because that subsidiary is part of a multinational. Similarly, it is a mistake to use the local real cost of debt to determine the cost of capital. In both these examples, if the MNE uses local debt norms and local debt costs, it is negating the advantage of being a multinational. That advantage is the ability to raise debt internally where it is the cheapest. As a result, in a country with a high debt cost the firm may have very little debt, whereas in a country with subsidized interest costs it may have a large amount of debt. In both cases there is no effect on the overall cost of funds to the multinational. Hence local debt norms and interest costs will be ignored unless local regulations restrict the use of debt funds to projects within that country. In this instance, if the firm accepts a local project, it can also raise more subsidized foreign debt. If the money cannot be removed from the country by transfer pricing or whatever, then its cost is relevant in Equation 14.2.

Institutional features

Thus far the focus has been on the technical question of how to evaluate capital expenditures. However, a very important institutional factor that warrants attention is the impact of government policies such as subsidies and controls.

Government intervention can affect the profitability of a project or its financing. For example, in considering foreign investments, countries such as Australia and Canada have foreign investment review agencies, which review these investments to ensure that they benefit the local economy. As a result, foreign investment is often contingent on factors such as local employment quotas, local sourcing of components, the transfer of technology, and a degree of local ownership. This intervention can obviously complicate capital expenditure analysis. Frequently the result is to forecast specific, quantitative outcomes. For example, if technology is locally licensed, what is the possible impact of its being leaked to different countries? If the MNE has to train local middle management and to sell shares locally, how does this affect the probability of forcible divestiture at some future date? In many cases the result of local content regulations is to expropriate all the advantages possessed by the multinational. One of the particular problems here is local ownership requirements. The parent's viewpoint is dominant on the assumption that the objective of the firm is to maximize its market value, which is owned by shareholders in the home country. However, once joint ventures and significant minority shareholdings are traded locally, this solution breaks down. The problem now becomes whose market value should be maximized. The result is that while minority ownership reduces the political risk of expropriation, it restricts the multinational's freedom of action. It is, therefore, not surprising that, where political risk is lowered, minority shareholders get bought out. For example, Ford acquired its British minority shareholdings in 1961, and Shell bought out its minority US shareholdings in 1984.

However, government regulation is not all bad. Outside North America the interventionist approach of most governments creates unique opportunities for the MNE. For example, most countries provide concessionary financing that is contingent on the use of certain local resources. The British Export Credits Guarantee Department (ECGD) has some of the lowest cost money for export financing as long as the borrower uses British equipment. By structuring an investment to use British equipment, a multinational might be able to borrow $10 million at 3 per cent interest instead of at a market rate of, say, 9 per cent. In effect, this subsidized loan represents a gift by the British taxpayers. This value has to be factored into the analysis. The inclusion of subsidies also occurs in domestic capital expenditure analysis, for example with the proliferation of small business financing programs. However, in an international project, rather than being unusual, it is rare not to determine the value or cost of a particular government program. Recently government regulation of MNEs has been falling, leading to more cross-listings on the world stock exchange.

Foreign investment review agency
A government agency that reviews applications for foreign direct investment projects and approves or disapproves the projects, according to standards established by the government

INTERNATIONAL FINANCING IN THE MNE

The home office of an MNE should have available to it funding from the domestic money and capital markets, as well as from international money and capital markets. The funding sources available to a *foreign affiliate* of an MNE include debt and equity from the parent and local financing in the host country. Table 14.5 presents a view of these sources that expands on the view presented in Figure 14.1 and on the discussion in Chapter 7. The sources of credit to the MNE are divided between short- and long-term loans and between direct and intermediated provision of funds through a bank or some other financial institution.

Notice that in addition to the funding that was discussed earlier in the intrafirm context, numerous sources of external funding are available to the MNE. These sources include funding from domestic money and capital markets in each country where the firm operates, as well as funding from the euromarkets in money centers such as London, New York, and Tokyo. A large firm from Norway, for example, could seek financing in the US market through international bank loans, through bond issue, or even through issuing stock shares or American Depositary Receipts.[7]

Financial structure

Debt–equity ratio
The value of a firm's total debt divided by the value of its total equity; a higher ratio implies greater leverage, and potentially greater risk

Financial structure in a multinational enterprise is complicated by the fact that the "normal" debt–equity ratio differs from industry to industry and from country to country. For example, the average debt–equity ratio in large Japanese companies is about 2.75 to 1. In the United States, this ratio is generally far less than 1, averaging about 0.6 for non-financial industries as a whole. As a rule, the total financial structure of an MNE follows the standards of the home country financial market, since shares are usually traded there. On the other hand, a US company's affiliate in Japan may be able to operate successfully with far higher leverage than that of the parent, given local conditions in Japan. Thus, the financial structures of foreign affiliates may differ from that of the overall firm or that of the parent in particular. The only limitation is that the financial structure of the affiliate must not

Table 14.5 International sources of credit (including markets and intrafirm transfers)

Borrowing	Domestic inside the firm	Domestic market	Foreign inside the firm	Foreign market	Euromarket
Direct, short-term	Intrafirm loans, transfer pricing, royalties, fees, service charges	Commercial paper, other promissory notes, commercial credit	International intrafirm loans, international transfer pricing, dividends, royalties, fees	Commercial credit	Eurocommercial paper
Intermediated, short-term		Short-term bank loans, discounted receivables	International back-to-back loans	Short-term bank loans, discounted receivables	Euro short-term loans
Direct, long-term	Intrafirm loans, investment in affiliates	Stock issue, bond issue	International intrafirm long-term loans, FDI	Stock issue, bond issue, ADR issue	Eurobonds, Euroequity
Intermediated, long-term		Long-term bank loans	International back-to-back loans	Long-term bank loans	Euro long-term loans

Direct means borrowing from owners of wealth (e.g., investors); *intermediated* means borrowing from a financial intermediary (e.g., a bank).

cause the financial structure of the entire firm to deviate from acceptable standards in the home country.

The entire MNE may choose to meet its external financing needs by borrowing through an affiliate in a low-interest country if such funding is available and if exchange rate protection still leaves financing costs lower than those in other currencies. As already noted, since the MNE is evaluated by investors in the home country, its overall debt–equity structure must satisfy the financial community in that country. However, if the firm sells shares of an affiliate in the host country's financial market, the debt–equity position of the affiliate is an important issue.

For a wholly-owned foreign subsidiary that does not sell shares in the host country, the debt–equity ratio should be determined by overall corporate needs. If funding is available at low cost (adjusted for expected exchange rate changes), local borrowing is appropriate. If a substantial amount of assets is exposed locally, local borrowing provides a hedge to both exchange and country risks. If the local currency is expected to devalue substantially, then, even if local interest rates are high, it may make sense to borrow locally, assuming the expected postdevaluation interest costs would be lower than the home-country costs.

Local equity financing may be forced on the firm if the host government demands partial local ownership of foreign enterprises. This situation exists today in many less developed countries and in most of the formerly communist countries. In this case, the affiliate's debt–equity ratio may be skewed toward equity, especially if the parent seeks to avoid sending funds into that country. That is, financing for the affiliate would come from the local partner's equity investment plus retained earnings, and other funding would be sought only after these sources were used up.

In countries with restrictions on funds transfers, such as profit and royalty remittances, equity financing would again be sensible—using those funds that cannot be taken out of the country. That is, if funds are blocked from transfer abroad, the MNE must reinvest them locally; investing the funds in the existing operation (i.e., profit reinvestment) may offer a greater benefit than placing them in local financial instruments such as bank deposits or government securities. This strategy is widely used by multinationals, though most would prefer the freedom to take their funds out of the host country.

Finally, notice that *if* the MNE is able to lower its total borrowing costs by utilizing foreign sources of funds, it has gained an advantage relative to domestic firms that limit themselves to domestic financial markets in any country. If the MNE has a lower weighted-average cost of capital for any given capital budget, it will undertake more projects than the purely domestic firm (or will be more profitable in the same projects).

✔ Active learning check

Review your answer to Active Learning Case question 4 and make any changes you like. Then compare your answer with the one below.

4 Assuming that BA might choose to acquire all or part of American, United, or Delta Airlines in the United States, how could BA finance the major capital budgeting need in international markets, and what are some of the important considerations in choosing among alternative financing sources?

British Airways can use the eurocurrency markets in London to minimize its short-term borrowing costs, and it can also issue commercial paper in New York or London to obtain working capital. For longer-term borrowing BA could issue shares in the United States or in another money center such as Frankfort or Tokyo, as well as issuing bonds in a low-tax jurisdiction such as Luxembourg. The choices depend on interest rates, exchange rates, and currencies in which BA will have cash flows in the future.

CONTROL: IDENTIFYING OBJECTIVES, EVALUATING AFFILIATE PERFORMANCE, AND MAKING PERFORMANCE CONSISTENT WITH GOALS

Control
The fundamental function of management that involves developing profit plans for the firm and its divisions and then deciding what to do when actual operating results differ from those planned

Control is the fundamental function of management that involves developing profit plans for the firm and its divisions and then deciding what to do when actual operating results differ from those planned. For a foreign investment project, the financial control process generally begins with putting together a set of pro forma financial statements (income statement, balance sheet, cash flow report), such as the income statement shown at the beginning of this chapter. Then detailed budgets are developed for individual divisions, allocating the full capital budget to the specific purposes for which it will be used. During the time period after the creation of these plans, the firm's management observes the results and notes any deviations from the budgets. Usually, of course, actual results differ from budgeted ones. Finally, the firm develops and implements a management plan for dealing with the deviations. The process is cyclical—as each planning period ends, another begins—and new budgets and managerial contingencies may be developed.

In the multinational firm, the potential for substantial home office control over affiliates exists because major capital budgeting usually requires more resources than those available in an affiliate, and home office assistance is needed to carry out capital projects. In addition, financial reporting to the parent company provides an informational basis for controls, which may or may not be exercised, depending on the extent of the firm's decentralization. Finally, because the people assigned to manage foreign affiliates are usually well known to the home office managers, an informal, personal contact ties affiliates to the home office. All of this means that the home office has the potential to impose heavy controls on the activities of foreign affiliates.

The process described so far is substantially equivalent to the one used to evaluate and control domestic divisions in a firm. But foreign affiliates face a wide range of additional factors that may affect their performance, and these factors should be considered when setting the goals and judging the performance of affiliates. How should the managers of foreign affiliates be evaluated for their financial performance? If they are evaluated in local-currency terms, the home office must worry about hedging foreign-currency exposures and about remitting or reinvesting profits. If they are evaluated in home-currency terms, affiliate managers must deal with exchange risk and remittance policy. If they are limited in their financial dealings due to centralized cash and foreign exchange management policies but are evaluated in home-currency terms, it must be recognized that their options are limited. On another issue, if transfer prices are set to move funds to the home office, foreign profitability will look lower than it would if these prices were set to keep more funds in the affiliates. Correct evaluation of the performance of affiliate managers must take into account the constraints imposed on the affiliates.

Most managers and outside analysts agree that foreign affiliates must be evaluated in home-currency terms, since home-currency investors judge the firm as a whole. Therefore, the firm must create an evaluation scheme that produces home-currency performance measures, adjusted to account for the limitations placed on the affiliate by the home office.

STRATEGIC INTERNATIONAL FINANCE

There are a number of ways that MNEs apply the international financial concepts that have been discussed in this chapter. One way is by employing a geocentric approach that helps to coordinate subsidiary operations and ensures that there is a uniform, harmonious strategy. This approach is particularly evident in the way that some multinationals are now closing local operations in favor of overseas production and are using joint ventures and other partnership arrangements to reduce their financial risk.[8] Another approach is the manner in which financial management analysis is used in choosing sites for overseas operations. This is particularly true for foreign firms with strong currencies.

Establishing overseas operations

Because the United States is a major market for many international firms, foreign MNEs have been particularly concerned about the value of the US dollar. For example, when Ford Motor acquired Volvo's automotive business, the Swedish firm insisted on receiving the purchase price in krona.[9] This concern has also resulted in foreign firms setting up operations in the United States in order to offset the competitive impact associated with having a currency that is very strong vis-à-vis the American dollar. For example, BMW built an auto production facility in South Carolina because it found it was 20 per cent less costly to produce cars in South Carolina than to bring them in from Germany.[10] Other companies have made acquisitions in the US market in order to protect their overall profitability. For example, BASF has acquired a Mobil plastic unit for $330 million; Benckiser purchased Coty, the fragrance maker, from Pfizer for $440 million; Siemens spent $1.2 billion to purchase ROLM, a manufacturer of telecommunications equipment, from IBM; and Daimler-Benz bought Chrysler for almost $40 billion.[11]

At the same time US firms are continuing to move abroad, especially since many Asian currencies are at a low ebb and purchase prices have fallen. General Motors, for example, is now producing light trucks in China, has 16 ventures there related to producing auto components, and has opened a Buick plant in Shanghai. As of the end of 1998 the company was assembling close to 500,000 cars annually, most of which were small sedans or subcompacts.[12] At the same time Atlantic Richfield and Phillips China have invested in ventures for drilling for methane gas, IBM is expanding its investment there in the computer business, Telluride International Energy is building a power plant, and Lucent Technologies has earmarked millions of dollars to expand its Internet backbone in the country.[13] All of these moves to overseas operations give the multinational firm a reduced currency risk by diversifying the company's cash flows into additional currencies.

European and US firms are not alone in their efforts to establish overseas operations. Pacific-based MNEs are also realizing the benefits of going local, and this group is not limited to auto makers. South Korean firms such as LG Group and Samsung are now using direct investment and joint ventures to help open markets in Europe and the United States. High labor costs, runaway interest rates, and low-cost competition are battering these firms at home, and local content laws have been holding down market acceptance abroad. In an effort to circumvent these problems, LG is using alliances to widen its market share, as seen by its collaboration with Gepi of Germany and Iberna of Italy to produce refrigerators for the European market. LG designs the units in its Ireland facility, Gepi supplies the components, and Iberna assembles the finished products. Samsung has purchased Werk für Fernsehelektronik, a former East German picture tube maker, and is spending $120 million to upgrade the plant, which will be capable of turning out 1.2 million television sets annually. The company also bought an even larger German television maker, RFT, and moved its Portuguese and Spanish color television plants to England and its videocassette recorder plant from England to Spain in order to lower operational costs, to improve quality, and to increase employment. Again, the issue of concern here is that these firms are achieving a financial goal along with their strategic choices to go abroad; they are reducing exchange rate risk by diversifying their cash flows into different currencies.

Reducing financial risk

Although some of the above strategies are useful in reducing risk, there are other tactics that are also particularly useful, including mergers, acquisitions, joint ventures for new, high-risk projects, partnering with established MNEs in order to gain international market share, and cutting operating costs through new plant design.

Alliances

In recent years an increasing number of MNEs have been joining together to share the costs of high-tech projects. This sharing involves not only research and development expenses, but also the costs of manufacturing and selling the finished products.

One example is provided by Microsoft, which has entered into an alliance with Sony to link personal computers and consumer electronics devices, thus moving closer together on technology standards for digital television and other consumer products. The two firms have endorsed a technology that can connect videocassette recorders, camcorders, personal computers, and other devices.[14] Another example is GM and Isuzu, which are now extending their alliance in advanced vehicle technologies such as electric vehicles and fuel cells.[15] A third example is Kita Kyushu Coca-Cola Bottling and Sam Coca-Cola Bottling, two major bottlers in southwest Japan which have agreed to merge their operations and thus combine a somewhat fragmented distribution system into a smoother, seamless approach that should boost profitability.[16] A fourth example is Citigroup, which acquired 15 per cent equity in Taiwan's Fubon Group. This alliance will serve as a springboard for future expansion in the Asian region.[17]

Cost-cutting

Other key financial strategies include cutting costs and investing in new plant and equipment, resulting in higher productivity and lower expenses. Still another strategy is the renegotiation of labor contract agreements in high-cost areas of the world. While one strategy that is increasingly popular calls for moving production overseas to lower-cost locations, another response to this problem of high costs is to look for ways to reduce them in the existing operations.

Investment in new plant and equipment to achieve efficiencies is critical to the success of MNEs today just as it has been in the past. This is particularly true in Japan, where auto manufacturers are finding it increasingly difficult to hire new people. Worse yet, the turnover rate in some factories runs as high as 50 per cent annually. In explaining the reason for this turnover, many workers refer to the three Ks: kiken (dangerous), kitsui (difficult), and kitanai (dirty). Young people, in particular, prefer the slower-paced world of office work where people wear suits and ties, take leisurely lunch hours, and are not exhausted at the end of a long day.

In an effort to deal with this problem, Nissan Motors has built a new factory that promises to be far less stressful on the workers than anything yet. Company officials refer to it as a "dream factory" and claim that it is designed to reduce many of the pitfalls of past manufacturing plants. The latter, for example, are characterized by the traditional conveyor belt from which cars are suspended. When the car reaches the workers, the employees scramble to install parts and to complete their tasks as quickly as possible. This typically involves squatting on the floor, stretching across the seat or the hood, ducking under the car, or reaching across the top of the vehicle to install or tighten something. If the workers are unable to keep up with the line, the conveyer belt must be stopped until they finish because all cars advance in lockstep. In contrast, Nissan's new plant has done away with the conveyer belt. All cars are now placed on motor-driven dollies. These dollies can be raised or lowered so that the workers do not have to stretch or squat. Additionally, even if it takes longer than usual to complete a particular task, this creates no problem for the factory. The workers can simply scoot the dolly up to the next station as soon as they are finished.

Another difference between the Nissan plant and more conventional ones is that the work area is brightly lit with natural sunlight filtering in through skylights, compared with the poorly lit work environments in other plants. Additionally, the factory is air conditioned and the temperature is kept at 77°F (degrees Fahrenheit), in contrast to other auto plants where there is no air conditioning. Another welcome feature is the use of robots to perform the dirtiest and most difficult jobs, painting and welding. And to reduce worker exhaustion, robots carry out a large percentage of the actual assembly. A huge robot arm, for example, grabs seats from an overhead rack and swings them into the car with a flick of its mechanical wrist. Then a small robot arm bolts the seat to the floor. Nissan contends that this new plant will not only cut down on worker absenteeism and turnover, but also be 30 per cent more efficient than those of the competition.

Other Japanese manufacturers are also heavily focused on cost-cutting, but through the use of overseas production. For example, Honda and Toyota operations in the United States have been simultaneously reducing costs while increasing quality. The result is that car prices for many of their models have remained the same or dropped slightly in recent years, while the number of features have increased. This "more value for your money" concept has been influential in helping both auto makers to increase their US market share and profitability.[18] Ford has been following a similar approach through a vigorous outsourcing program and by seeking to cut $1 billion from its costs, thus boosting its return on investment from the North American market and, hopefully, helping drive up stock price as well.[19] Simply put, cost-cutting is a critical part of financial investment strategies.

KEY POINTS

1 International financial management encompasses a number of critical areas, including the management of global cash flows, foreign exchange risk management, capital expenditure analysis, and international financing. In carrying out these financial activities, MNEs can use three approaches or solutions: polycentric, ethnocentric, or geocentric.

2 There are three main areas of consideration in managing global cash flows. One is the movement of cash so that each subsidiary has the working capital needed to conduct operations. A second area is the use of funds positioning techniques that can help to reduce taxes and to deal with political and legal roadblocks that impede cash flows. A third is multilateral netting, which ensures that transactions between the subsidiaries are paid in a timely manner.

3 Foreign exchange risk management encompasses a variety of financial strategies that are designed to limit the multinational's exposure to exchange rate fluctuations. In particular, the MNE will want to reduce translation, transaction, and economic exposure. One of the most common ways of doing this is through hedging. Examples include the purchase of forward exchange contracts and the balancing of foreign currency assets with foreign currency liabilities.

4 A third major strategic financial issue is capital expenditure analysis. This entails computation and deliberation of such matters as the weighted cost of capital and the degree of political risk that is being assumed. Some of the methods of dealing with these issues were discussed with attention given to the fact that the final decision on capital expenditures is often affected by subjective considerations as well as by objective evaluations.

5   At present MNEs are taking a number of important international financial steps. Some of the primary ones include designing global foreign exchange management programs, establishing international cash management centers, and creating coordinated international borrowing programs for affiliates.

Key terms

- polycentric solution
- ethnocentric solution
- working capital
- geocentric solution
- multilateral netting
- funds positioning techniques
- transfer price
- arm's length price

- tax havens
- fronting loan
- clearing account
- hedge
- transaction risk
- translation risk
- consolidation
- balance sheet hedging

- economic risk
- currency inconvertibility
- weighted-average cost of capital
- foreign investment review agencies
- debt–equity ratio
- control

REVIEW AND DISCUSSION QUESTIONS

1   In determining parent–subsidiary relationships, how does a polycentric solution differ from an ethnocentric or geocentric solution? Compare and contrast all three.

2   What is meant by the term *working capital*, and what are two of the most common ways that parent companies can provide this capital to their subsidiaries? What are two ways in which the parent can obtain funds from the subsidiaries?

3   How can an MNE shift profits through the use of transfer pricing? Provide an example.

4   Of what value is multilateral netting in helping MNEs to manage cash flows? Give an example.

5   If a foreign country is facing high inflation, what are three financial strategies that the local multinational unit might employ? Identify and describe each.

6   Why are MNEs interested in translation and consolidation of financial statements? Of what practical value is this activity to the company?

7   Under what conditions will an MNE face translation exposure? What financial strategy might the organization use to minimize this exposure?

8   When might an MNE face transaction exposure? What is a financial strategy that the firm could use to minimize this risk?

9   What is meant by the term *economic exposure*? What is a financial strategy that an MNE could use to minimize this risk?

10 When would a multinational use a lead strategy to hedge a risk? When would a multinational use a lag strategy for this purpose? In each case, give an example. A lead strategy is a choice by an MNE to make intracompany payments (for example, from an affiliate to the home office) earlier than in an arm's length situation, to move funds out of the country of the affiliate more rapidly. A lag strategy is a choice by an MNE to make intracompany payments (for example, from an affiliate to the home office) later than in an arm's length situation, to hold funds longer in the affiliate country.

11 When might an MNE use a forward exchange contract (a contract with a bank to buy or sell foreign exchange at a future date, with the exchange rate and value fixed today)? When might the firm decide to forgo this strategy and leave a particular foreign-currency transaction unhedged?

12 What role does net present value (NPV) play in the review of capital expenditure proposals? Give an example.

13 How can country risk affect the computation of NPV? Will the risk result in the MNE wanting a higher or a lower NPV? Explain.

14 Why do parent and local subsidiaries sometimes differ in their calculation of NPV for a particular project or expenditure? How can this difference be resolved?

15 What are some of the financing alternatives available to MNEs that are not available to domestic firms? Give an example.

REAL CASE

Skandia

Information technology has transformed the financial services and insurance business into a universal product. Instead of large numbers of white-collar clerical workers toiling in large local banking and insurance halls (like Bob Cratchet in Dickens's *A Christmas Carol*) today such services can be provided on the Internet by smaller, more entrepreneurial groups and even from a home office. This is part of the new global knowledge-based economy.

Skandia is a Stockholm-based insurance and financial service company, founded some 150 years ago. In 2000, the Skandia Group had revenues of 21.7 million, six times the 1995 figure, and operations in 20 countries. In 1900 Skandia became the first non-British insurance company to enter the US market, but it incurred losses in the San Francisco earthquake of 1906 and in World War I, to the extent that its international business was largely dormant and confined to reinsurance (business accepted for another company to diversify risk).

In 1986, the Assurance and Financial Services Division (AFS) of Skandia, headed by CEO Jan Carendi, made a big push in the United States. Over the next 12 years it grew by 45 per cent per year. By 1998 the ASF Unit had sales of $3.5 billion with fewer than 2,000 employees. It sold a unit-linked variable life insurance product to independent insurance brokers. The product can be sold on the Internet. Basically, Skandia purchased mutual funds from other companies but included its own insurance package with it. Skandia was one of the first insurance companies to use such a self-directed unit trust (or mutual fund) that allowed customers to regard life insurance as being like a retirement savings plan.

To derive an ongoing competitive advantage in knowledge management, Jan Carendi transformed the ASF division of Skandia from a traditional bricks and mortar insurance company into a "clicks and mortar" virtual organization. He was one of the first to appoint a director of intellectual capital, retraining managers to be more flexible, innovative, and responsive to the consumers. While acting as a change agent, Jan Carendi traveled some 200 days a year to pull together a new "federal" model of internal management structure. One aspect of this was a group of independent fund managers; another was a new software package to manage the complex administrative structure.

By the 1980s Skandia consisted of four divisions:

1 An actuarial function, designing insurance products based on risk assessments

2 A sales and marketing group that sold directly to consumers

3 An investment management group that invested premiums

4 An administrative group that managed the customer, accounting, and regulatory paperwork

Many of the traditional insurance functions were outsourced by Carendi. The fund management and also the sales and distribution functions were outsourced. Both of these required local knowledge of regulations for mutual funds and of personal networks for sales and distribution. Instead, ASF focused on internationally mobile knowledge capabilities, using high tech and the Internet.

An overdependence on the US market, from which 60 per cent of all Skandia's revenues originate, led to a slower year in 2001. When the high-tech stocks plummeted in 2001 after the dot.com bust, Skandia's customers stopped buying. In July 2001, sales of variable annuities in the United States were halved to US$2.5 billion, down from $5.7 in the previous year. Diversification into the more stable markets of Germany, Japan, and Spain over the next few years may help to recover the company's profitability. Meanwhile, Skandia's actuaries were busy

▶

creating new, more cautious products to be ready when US investors are ready to buy again. In 2003, Prudential Financial purchased American Skandia.

The lesson is that reliance on Internet-based business on a global scale is just as risky as the old-fashioned, centuries-earlier business cycles. In those times there were speculative stock market crashes, such as the South Seas Bubble (in 1720). Today, we have seen a similar dot.com/high-tech bubble burst in 2001, with profound repercussions, even in the stodgy world of insurance.

Sources: Christopher A. Bartlett, *Skandia AFS*, HBS Case 9-396-412, Boston: Harvard Business School, 1996; "Skandia: Client Focus Brings Spectacular Rewards," *Financial Times*, June 23, 2000; Skandia, *Annual Report*, 2000.

1 Why has insurance changed from local salespeople to an Internet-provided "universal" product?

2 Why was Swedish-based Skandia so successful in the US market?

3 Was CEO Jan Carendi "Swedish" or "global" in his management style?

REAL CASE

Repsol's acquisition of YPF

In 1993 the Argentine government sold controlling ownership in the national oil company, YPF (Yacimientos Petroliferos Fiscales), through an initial public offering on the Argentine stock market and through an American Depositary Receipt (ADR) issue on the New York Stock Exchange, as well as a Global Depositary Receipt (GDR) issue on the London Stock Exchange. This was the largest privatization in Latin America at that time, bringing in to the Argentine government about $US 3 billion in the initial issue of about half of YPF's total shares.

The initial privatization was carried out in July 1993, when YPF was sold in this initial public offering to literally thousands of investors in the open market. The government hired and installed a team of managers who took YPF through a huge and painful restructuring of its business and then the public sale of the company. Once YPF began to operate in the private sector as a listed company, the government continued to sell its remaining shares over time. The privatization itself was not an example of foreign direct investment, since foreign investors only purchased small percentages of YPF shares or depositary receipts. However, in 1998, the Spanish oil company, Repsol, decided to purchase control of YPF, and did so by buying 14.99 per cent of YPF shares from the government's remaining 20 per cent stake at that time. Repsol was able to obtain controlling interest in YPF in 1999 for a price of $US 2.01 billion.

In mid-1999 Repsol raised its stake in YPF to 97.5 per cent, by making a tender offer for all the ADRs in New York and GDRs in London, along with shares in the Buenos Aires stock exchange that it did not already own. The total cost of this tender was $US 13.1 billion. These share acquisitions were financed by Repsol

borrowing in Spain and in the euromarkets, in addition to internal funding.

The net result of these purchases made Repsol the owner of almost 98 per cent of total outstanding YPF shares, with only small shareholdings outstanding to investors who failed to participate in the tender offer in 1999. The total foreign direct investment replaced portfolio investment by those investors who had purchased ADRs or GDRs back in 1993, accounting for about 40 per cent of total YPF shares. These investors probably did not reinvest their funds in Argentina once they sold their depositary receipts to Repsol, so no new investment went into Argentina at that time. Of course, the original portfolio investment in the ADRs or GDRs was an international investment, bringing new funds into Argentina to pay for the depositary receipts. Those flows were recorded in 1993, and did not appear subsequently in the 1999 FDI process. That is, the investors in New York and London who had originally purchased shares of YPF in the ADR and GDR offerings there chose to sell those shares to Repsol, thus receiving Repsol's cash, but not (necessarily) sending any funds to Argentina. All that happened was a change of foreign owners of those shares—but the new foreign owner was a direct investor rather than a portfolio, passive investor. This accounted for approximately $US 10 billion of the total direct investment by Repsol, and thus for no new money coming into the country. The shares that were purchased from shareholders in the Buenos Aires stock exchange (about $US 3 billion of the total) did likely bring new funds into Argentina, assuming that the sellers kept the funds in the country.

The purchase of the government's shareholdings in 1998 *did* imply direct financial transfers from abroad to

Argentina, as Repsol paid the government for those shares and financed the purchase with funds from abroad. This $US 2.01 billion thus *was* a transfer of funds to Argentina, different from the bulk of the investment. And as noted above, Repsol obtained the funds primarily through taking out bank loans in the eurocurrency market, denominating the loans in dollars, since YPF's earnings were mostly in dollars.

Website: www.repsolypf.com/home00.asp.

Sources: UBS Warburg, "Repsol YPF," *Global Equity Research*, January 2002; Carmen Llorente, "Repsol el Cambio Tras la Compra de YPF," *El Mundo*,

January 24, 1999; "Spanish Businesses in Argentina," *Economist*, January 3, 2002; Robert Grosse and Juan Yañes, "Carrying Out a Successful Privatization: The YPF Case," *Academy of Management Executive*, May 1998, pp. 51–63.

1 Did Repsol make a good decision in acquiring YPF in 1998–1999?

2 What is the difference between foreign direct investment and foreign portfolio investment? Is this a relevant issue in the case?

3 What are American Depositary Receipts? Were they a useful tool for YPF in selling shares to the public?

Endnotes

1 For more on tax havens, see "Gimme Shelter," *Economist*, January 7, 2000.
2 Also, see Neil Weinberg, "Rent Shokku," *Forbes*, June 7, 1993, p. 108.
3 For more on Honda, see Alex Taylor III, "How Toyota Copes with Hard Times," *Fortune*, January 25, 1993, pp. 78–81.
4 The option contract can also be used to hedge this transaction. American Express could buy 160 call options as listed in the example, for a total premium of $US 125,000. For this price, American Express would receive the right to buy pounds at the strike price of $US 1.92 per pound, a worse price than the forward and futures contracts. (Actually, options for lower strike prices are available at much higher premia.) The option does not look attractive unless American Express wants to speculate that the pound will go down in value even below the forward contract price. If this happens, by not exercising the options, AMEX could simply buy pounds in the spot market in 180 days and benefit from the lower price. The option is generally useful if the firm wants to speculate or if the original commercial contract may not be fulfilled so that the pounds may not be needed after all.
5 A full set of the measures used in capital budgeting appears in basic finance texts, such as Brealey and Myers, *Principles of Corporate Finance*, 7th ed. (McGraw-Hill, 2003).
6 However, if the local-currency price goes up due to the currency revaluation and demand is price inelastic, the total revenue received may go up even if the quantity sold declines.
7 ADRs (American Depositary Receipts) are a derivative instrument based on shares of stock in a company. The issuing company typically sells a large quantity of shares in a block to an investment bank, which in turn holds those shares in its own treasury. The investment bank then issues ADRs whose

value is based completely on the original shares, converted into US dollars, in the US market. See, for example, *http://daytrading.about.com/cs/educationtraining/a/adrs.htm*.
8 See Brian Coleman and Thomas R. King, "Euro Disney Rescue Package Wins Approval," *Wall Street Journal*, March 15, 1994, p. A 3.
9 "Ford to Pay $6.47 Billion in Volvo Deal," *Wall Street Journal*, January 29, 1999, Section A, pp. 3, 6.
10 Also, see John Templeman and James B. Treece, "BMW's Comeback," *Business Week*, February 14, 1994, pp. 42–44.
11 Keith Bradsher, "Industry's Giants Are Carving Up the World Market," *New York Times*, May 8, 1998, pp. C 1, 4; and Robyn Meredith, "A Joining of Opposites Could Help Customers," *New York Times*, May 8, 1998, p. C 4.
12 Seth Faison, "GM Opens Buick Plant in Shanghai," *New York Times*, December 18, 1998, pp. C 1, 19.
13 "Opening the Door a Crack," *New York Times*, June 30, 1998, p. A 10.
14 Don Clark and David Bank, "Microsoft, Sony to Cooperate On PCs, Devices," *Wall Street Journal*, April 8, 1998, p. B 6.
15 Lisa Schuchman and Joseph B. White, "Global Consolidations in Autos Heat Up," *Wall Street Journal*, December 21, 1998, p. A 2.
16 Nikhil Deogun, "Coca-Cola to Put Together the Merger of Two Bottlers in Japan to Lift Sales," *Wall Street Journal*, January 14, 1999, p. A 4.
17 "Citigroup and Taiwan's Fubon Group Announce a Powerful Strategic Partnership," Citigroup Press Release, May 6, 2000.
18 Valerie Reitman, "Honda Sees Performance and Profits from New Accord," *Wall Street Journal*, August 27, 1997, p. B 4.
19 Fara Warner and Joseph B. White, "Ford Plans to Reduce Costs by Another $1 Billion," *Wall Street Journal*, January 8, 1999, p. A 3.

Additional bibliography

Bowe, Michael and Dean, James W. "International Financial Management and Multinational Enterprises," in Alan M. Rugman and Thomas L. Brewer (eds.), *Oxford Handbook of International Business* (Oxford: Oxford University Press, 2001).

Clark, Terry, Kotabe, Masaaki and Rajaratnam, Dan. "Exchange Rate Pass-Through and International Pricing Strategy: A Conceptual Framework and Research Propositions," *Journal of International Business Studies*, vol. 30, no. 2 (Summer 1999).

Eden, Lorraine. "Taxes, Transfer Pricing, and the Multinational Enterprise," in Alan M. Rugman and Thomas L. Brewer (eds.), *The Oxford Handbook of International Business* (Oxford: Oxford University Press, 2001).

Egehoff, William G., Gorman, Liam and McCormick, Stephen. "How FDI Characteristics Influence Subsidiary Trade Patterns: The Case of Ireland," *Management International Review*, vol. 40, no. 3 (Fall 2000).

Eiteman, David K., Stonehill, Arthur and Moffett, Michael. *Multinational Business Finance*, 10th ed. (Englewood Cliffs, NJ: Prentice Hall, 2004).

Grosse, Robert, *The Future of Global Financial Services* (Oxford: Blackwell Publishers, 2004).

———. (with Shannon Mudd and John Mathis), "Dealing with Financial Crises in Emerging Markets," *Thunderbird International Business Review*, May/June 2002, vol. 44, no. 3, pp. 399–430.

Randoy, Trond, Oxelheim, Lars and Stonehill, Arthur. "Corporate Financial Strategies for Global Competitiveness," *European Management Journal*, vol. 19, no. 6 (December 2001).

Shapiro, Alan C. *Multinational Financial Management*, 6th ed. (New York: Wiley, 2003).

Sundaram, Anant. "Management of Exchange Rate Exposure by the Multinational Corporation," in D. Logue and J. Seward (eds.), *Handbook of Modern Finance* (New York: Warren Gorham Lamont, 2004).

Wallace, Wanda. "The Value Relevance of Accounting: The Rest of the Story," *European Management Journal*, vol. 18, no. 6 (December 2000).

Part Four

INTERNATIONAL BUSINESS STRATEGIES IN ACTION

ACTIVE LEARNING CASE

Worldwide operations and local strategies of ABB

Headquartered in Zurich, Switzerland, Asea Brown Boveri (ABB) is one of Europe's major industrial firms. Since the merger in 1987 that created it, ABB has been acquiring or taking minority positions in a large number of companies throughout the world. In recent years it has purchased Westinghouse's transmission and distribution operations and Combustion Engineering, the manufacturer of power-generation and process-automation equipment. In Mexico, ABB acquired FIP SA in 2001, an oil and gas production equipment company. The conglomerate, which currently employs 102,000 people worldwide, has annual revenues in excess of $20 billion. Fifty-five per cent of its revenues come from Europe, 25 per cent from the Americas, and 12 per cent from Asia. The remainder comes from Africa and the Middle East.

ABB operates on both local and global terms. On the one hand it attempts to maintain deep local roots wherever it operates so that it can modify both products and operations to that market. For example, managers are trained to adapt to cultural differences and to learn how to communicate effectively with local customers. At the same time the company works to be global and to make products that can be sold anywhere in the world because their technology and quality give them a worldwide appeal.

A good example of a business that demonstrates ABB's advantages is transportation. The company generates $2 billion a year in revenues from such products as subway cars, locomotives, suburban trains, trolleys, and the electrical and signaling systems that support these products. This is possible for four reasons: (1) ABB's research and development makes it a technology leader in locomotives and power electronics, enabling it to develop and build high-speed trains and rail networks throughout the world; (2) its operations are structured to take advantage of economies of scale and thus keep prices competitive; (3) it adapts to

local environments and works closely with customers so that it is viewed as a national rather than a foreign company; and (4) it works closely with companies in other countries that are favored by their own government but need assistance in financing and producing locomotive equipment for that market. As a result, ABB is able to capitalize on its technological and manufacturing expertise and develop competitive advantages in both triad and non-triad markets.

In some cases ABB has gone so far as to take an ownership position in companies located in emerging economic markets. For example, the firm purchased 76 per cent of Zamech, Poland's leading manufacturer of steam turbines, transmission gears, marine equipment, and metal castings. And it has bought into two other Polish firms that make a wide range of generating equipment and electric drives. ABB is now in the process of reorganizing these firms into profit centers, transferring its own expertise to local operations, and developing worldwide quality standards and controls for production. If all goes according to plan, ABB will soon have a thriving Polish operation that will be helping to rebuild Eastern Europe.

ABB works hard to be a "good citizen" of every country in which it operates, while also maintaining its supranational status. As a result, the company is proving that it is possible to have worldwide operations and local strategies that work harmoniously.

Website: www.abb.com.

Sources: Adapted from William Taylor, "The Logic of Global Business: An Interview with ABB's Percy Barnevik," *Harvard Business Review*, March/April 1991, pp. 91–105; Carla Rapoport, "A Tough Swede Invades the US," *Fortune*, June 29, 1992, pp. 76–79; Carol Kennedy, "ABB: Model Merger for the New Europe," *Long Range Planning*, vol. 25, no. 5 (1992), pp. 10–17; Edward L. Andrews, "ABB Will Cut 10,000 Jobs and Switch Focus to Asia," *New York Times*, October 22, 1997, p. C 2; Alan M. Rugman, *The Regional Multinationals* (Cambridge: Cambridge UP, 2005).

1 In what way does ABB's strategy incorporate Porter's four country-specific determinants and two external variables?

2 Why did ABB buy Zamech? How can the company link Zamech to its overall strategic plan?

3 How does ABB address the issues of globalization and national responsiveness? In each case, cite an example.

INTRODUCTION

Some MNEs rely on their home market to generate the research, development, design, or manufacturing needed to sell their goods in international markets. More and more, however, they are finding that they must focus on the markets where they are doing business as well as on strategies for tapping the resources of those markets and gaining sales entry. In short, multinationals can no longer rely exclusively on the competitive advantage they hold at home to provide them with a sustainable advantage overseas.

In addition, many small countries realize they must rely on export strategies to ensure the growth of their economies. Those that have been most successful with this strategy have managed to tap into markets within triad countries. Good examples are Canada and Mexico, both of which have found the United States to be a lucrative market for exports and imports. As a result, many successful business firms in these two countries have integrated themselves into the US economy, while creating what some international economists call a North American market. In the future many more MNEs are going to be following this pattern of linking into the economies of triad members.

The basic strategy these MNEs are following can be tied directly to the Porter model presented in Chapter 1, although some significant modifications of this model are in order. We will first examine Porter's ideas in more detail and then show how these ideas are serving as the basis for developing corporate strategies and international competitiveness in Canada and Mexico.

PORTER'S DIAMOND

In Chapter 1 we identified four determinants of national competitive advantage, as set forth by Porter (see Figure 15.1). We noted that these factors can be critical in helping a country build and maintain competitive advantage. We now return to Porter's "diamond" framework in more depth, examining how his findings apply specifically to triad countries and determining how the ideas can be modified and applied to nations that are not triad members.

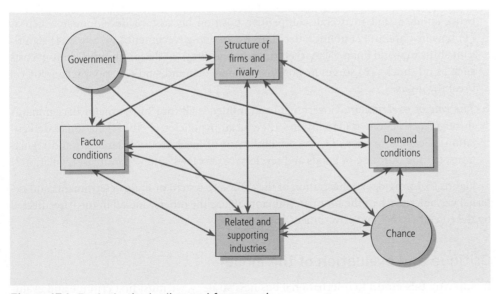

Figure 15.1 Porter's single diamond framework

Source: Adapted with the permission of The Free Press, an imprint of Simon & Schuster Adult Publishing Group, from *The Competitive Advantage of Nations* by Michael E. Porter. Copyright © 1990, 1998 by Michael E. Porter.

Determinants and external variables

Porter's "diamond" model is based on four country-specific determinants and two external variables. The determinants include:

1 *Factor conditions.* These include (1) the quantity, skills, and cost of the personnel; (2) the abundance, quality, accessibility, and cost of the nation's physical resources such as land, water, mineral deposits, timber, hydroelectric power sources, and fishing grounds; (3) the nation's stock of knowledge resources, including scientific, technical, and market knowledge that affect the quantity and quality of goods and services; (4) the amount and cost of capital resources that are available to finance industry; and (5) the type, quality, and user cost of the infrastructure, including the nation's transportation system, communications system, health-care system, and other factors that directly affect the quality of life in the country.

2 *Demand conditions.* These include (1) the composition of demand in the home market as reflected by the various market niches that exist, buyer sophistication, and how well the needs of buyers in the home market precede those of buyers in other markets; (2) the size and growth rate of the home demand; and (3) the ways in which domestic demand is internationalized and pulls a nation's products and services abroad.

3 *Related and supporting industries.* These include (1) the presence of internationally competitive supplier industries that create advantages in downstream industries through efficient, early, or rapid access to cost-effective inputs; and (2) internationally competitive related industries that can coordinate and share activities in the value chain when competing or those that involve complementary products.

4 *Firm strategy, structure, and rivalry.* These include (1) the ways in which firms are managed and choose to compete; (2) the goals that companies seek to attain as well as the motivations of their employees and managers; and (3) the amount of domestic rivalry and the creation and persistence of competitive advantage in the respective industry.

The four determinants of national advantage shape the competitive environment of industries. However, two other variables, chance and government, also play important roles:

1 *The role of chance.* Chance events can nullify the advantages of some competitors and bring about a shift in overall competitive position because of developments such as (1) new inventions, (2) political decisions by foreign governments, (3) wars, (4) significant shifts in world financial markets or exchange rates, (5) discontinuities in input costs such as oil shocks, (6) surges in world or regional demand, and (7) major technological breakthroughs.

2 *The role of government.* Government can influence all four of the major determinants through such actions as (1) subsidies, (2) education policies, (3) the regulation or deregulation of capital markets, (4) the establishment of local product standards and regulations, (5) the purchase of goods and services, (6) tax laws, and (7) antitrust regulation.[1]

Figure 15.1 provides an illustration of the complete system of these determinants and external variables. Each of the four determinants affects the others, and all in turn are affected by the role of chance and government.

Critique and evaluation of the model

In applying this model to international business strategy, we must first critique and evaluate Porter's paradigm and supporting arguments. First, the Porter model was constructed based on statistical analysis of aggregate data on export shares for 10 countries: Denmark,

Italy, Japan, Singapore, South Korea, Sweden, Switzerland, the UK, the United States, and West Germany. In addition, historical case studies were provided for four industries: the German printing press industry, the US patient monitoring equipment industry, the Italian ceramic tile industry, and the Japanese robotics industry. In each case the country is either a member of the triad or an industrialized nation. Since most countries of the world do not have the same economic strength or affluence as those studied by Porter, it is highly unlikely that his model can be applied to them without modification.

Second, the government is of critical importance in influencing a home nation's competitive advantage. For example, it can use tariffs as a direct entry barrier to penalize foreign firms, and it can employ subsidies as an indirect vehicle for penalizing foreign-based firms. Government actions such as these, however well intentioned, can backfire and end up creating a "sheltered" domestic industry that is unable to compete in the worldwide market.[2]

Third, although chance is a critical influencing factor in international business strategy, it is extremely difficult to predict and guard against. For example, until the day Saddam Hussein invaded Kuwait in 1991, the US government was predicting that there would be no invasion. In a similar vein, technological breakthroughs in computers and consumer electronics have resulted in rapid changes that, in many cases, were not predicted by market leaders.

Fourth, in the study of international business, Porter's model must be applied in terms of company-specific considerations and not in terms of national advantages. As Porter so well notes in his book, "Firms, not nations, compete in international markets."[3]

Fifth, in support of his model, Porter delineates four distinct stages of national competitive development: factor-driven, investment-driven, innovation-driven, and wealth-driven (see Figure 15.2). In the factor-driven stage, successful industries draw their advantage almost solely from the basic factors of production such as natural resources and the nation's large, inexpensive labor pool. Although successful internationally, the industries compete primarily on price. In the investment-driven stage, companies invest in modern, efficient facilities and technology and work to improve these investments through modification and alteration. In the innovation-driven stage, firms work to create new technology and methods through internal innovation and with assistance from suppliers and firms in related industries. In the wealth-driven stage, firms begin to lose their competitive advantage, rivalry ebbs, and the motivation to invest declines. As seen in Figure 15.2, Porter believes that Singapore is in the factor-driven stage, Korea is investment-driven, Japan is

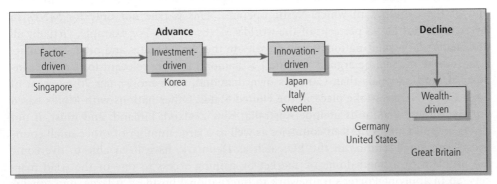

Figure 15.2 The four stages of national development and the current position of select nations

Source: Adapted with the permission of The Free Press, an imprint of Simon & Schuster Adult Publishing Group, from *The Competitive Advantage of Nations* by Michael E. Porter. Copyright © 1990, 1998 by Michael E. Porter.

innovation-driven, Germany and the United States are between innovation and wealth-driven, and Great Britain is wealth-driven. Because the stage of development greatly influences the country's competitive response, the placement of countries in Figure 15.2 is critical. So too is the logic that countries move from one stage to another, rather than spanning two or more stages because there are likely to be industries or companies in all major economies that are operating at each stage.

Sixth, Porter contends that only outward FDI is valuable in creating competitive advantage, and inbound foreign investment is never the solution to a nation's competitive problems. Moreover, foreign subsidiaries are not sources of competitive advantage, and "widespread foreign investment usually indicates that the process of competitive upgrading in an economy is *not entirely healthy* because domestic firms in many industries lack the capabilities to defend their market positions against foreign firms."[4] These statements are questionable and have already been rejected in this text. For example, Canadian-based scholars such as Safarian,[5] Rugman,[6] and Crookell[7] have all demonstrated that R&D undertaken by foreign-owned firms is not significantly different from that of Canadian-owned companies. Moreover, Rugman has found that the 20 largest US subsidiaries in Canada export virtually as much as they import (the rate of exports to sales is 25 per cent, whereas that of imports to sales is 26 per cent).[8]

Seventh, as seen in Figure 15.2, reliance on natural resources (the factor-driven stage) is viewed by Porter as insufficient to create worldwide competitive stature.[9] However, Canada, for one, has developed a number of successful megafirms that have turned the country's comparative advantage in natural resources into proprietary firm-specific advantages in resource processing and further refining—sources of sustainable advantage.[10] Moreover, case studies of the country's successful multinationals such as Alcan, Noranda, and Nova help illustrate the methods by which value added has been introduced by the managers of these resource-based companies.[11]

Eighth, the Porter model does not adequately address the role of MNEs. Researchers such as Dunning[12] have suggested including multinational activity as a third outside variable (in addition to chance and government). Certainly there is good reason to question whether MNE activity is covered in the "firm strategy, structure, and rivalry" determinant, and some researchers have raised the question of how the same rivalry determinant can both include multinationality for global industries and yet exclude it for multidomestic industries. As Dunning notes, "There is ample evidence to suggest that MNEs are influenced in their competitiveness by the configuration of the diamond in other than their home countries, and that this in turn may impinge upon the competitiveness of home countries."[13] For example, Nestlé earns 98 per cent of its sales outside Switzerland;[14] thus, the Swiss diamond of competitive advantage is less relevant than that of the countries in which Nestlé operates. This is true not only for MNEs in Switzerland but for 95 per cent of the world's MNEs as well. For example, virtually all of Canada's large multinationals rely on sales in the United States and other triad markets. Indeed, it could be argued that the US diamond is more relevant for Canada's industrial multinationals than Canada's own diamond, since more than 70 per cent of Canadian MNE sales take place in the United States. Other nations with MNEs based on small home diamonds include Australia, New Zealand, Finland, and most, if not all, Asian and Latin American countries as well as a large number of other small countries. Even small nations in the EU, such as Denmark, have been able to overcome the problem of a small domestic market by gaining access to one of the triad markets. So in applying Porter's framework to international business at large, one conclusion is irrefutable: *Different diamonds need to be constructed and analyzed for different countries.*

Active learning check

Review your answer to Active Learning Case question 1 and make any changes you like. Then compare your answer with the one below.

1 **In what way does ABB's strategy incorporate Porter's four country-specific determinants and two external variables?**

The strategy incorporates Porter's country-specific determinants as part of a well-formulated global strategy designed to tap the strengths of various markets. For example, the company draws on the factor conditions and demand conditions in Europe to support its transportation business. It also draws on supporting industries to help sustain its worldwide competitive advantage in that industry. At the same time the company's strategy, structure, and rivalry are designed to help it compete at the local level. The strategy incorporates the external variable of government by considering relations between countries as a lubricant for worldwide economic integration. It addresses the variable of chance by operating globally and thus reducing the likelihood that a war or a regional recession will have a major negative effect on operations. The firm's heavy focus on core technologies and R&D also helps minimize this chance variable.

OTHER "DIAMOND" MODELS: TWO CASE EXAMPLES

Researchers have recently begun using the Porter diamond as a basis for analyzing the international competitiveness of smaller countries. This approach builds on Porter's theme of corporate strategy and process as a source of competitive advantage for a nation.

Canada and the double diamond

Figure 15.3 illustrates how Porter's single diamond would look if it were applied to Canada's case.[15]

Two themes have recurred consistently in Canadian industrial policy: export promotion for natural resource industries and import substitution in the domestic arena. The Canadian market has always been seen as too small to support the development of economies of scale required in modern industry. Hence it has been the practice in Canada to provide the base for developing large-scale resource businesses that are designed to exploit the natural resources found in the country. Export strategies have emphasized commodity products that have been developed in isolation from major customers. In the past these strategies had been encouraged by US government policies that removed or eliminated tariffs on imports of commodities that are not produced extensively in the United States. The Canadian government's role had been to help leading Canadian-based businesses by establishing relatively low taxes on resource extraction and by subsidizing the costs of capital through grants, low-interest loans, and loan guarantees.

With respect to import substitution, the Canadian goal had been to use tariff and non-tariff measures to provide a protected environment for developing secondary industry. Under this arrangement the country's approach to business was largely focused inwardly, relying solely on the extent and quality of national resources as the basis for the creation of wealth.

By the mid-1960s, however, it had become clear that a more international focus was needed. The 1967 Canada–United States Auto Pact demonstrated that significant economic benefits would result from the elimination of tariffs on trade between the two countries

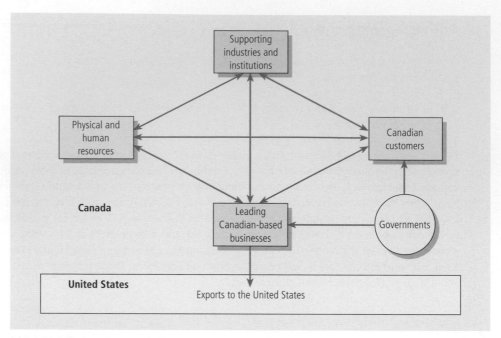

Figure 15.3 The single diamond view

Source: Adapted from Alan M. Rugman and Joseph R. D'Cruz, *Fast Forward: Improving Canada's International Competitiveness* (Toronto: Kodak Canada, 1991), p. 35.

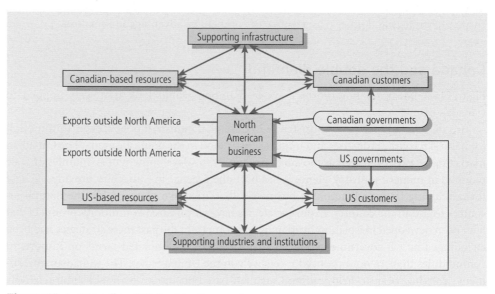

Figure 15.4 Canadian–US double diamond

Source: Adapted from Alan M. Rugman and Joseph R. D'Cruz, "The 'Double Diamond' Model of International Competitiveness: the Canadian Experience," *Management International Review*, vol. 33, Special Issue 2 (1993), p. 32.

in autos and parts. This agreement eventually became the model for the United States–Canada Free Trade Agreement.[16] In the process Canadian plants gained economies of scale by producing for the North American market as a whole rather than for the Canadian market alone. For corporate strategy, the result of North American economic integration has been the development of a Canadian–US "double diamond," which shows that the two countries are integrated for strategy purposes into a single market (see Figure 15.4).

INTERNATIONAL BUSINESS STRATEGY *IN ACTION*

Nokia and Ericsson

Based in one of the world's smallest countries, the largest producer of mobile phones is Finland's Nokia. Founded in 1865, Nokia was a major manufacturer of paper products before it transformed itself into a high-tech producer of electronic products, especially cellular phones, starting in the 1970s. By 2003, Nokia was the largest company in Finland with sales of nearly US$33 billion. Production facilities span 10 countries, and R&D is performed in 15 locations worldwide. It generates sales in 130 countries and employs some 53,000 people.

From the beginning, Nokia has pursued foreign sales. This internationalization strategy is necessary because Finland has only 3 million people and only a small share of its sales originates in its home base. So Nokia became the mobile phone leader in Scandinavia, despite competition from Ericsson of Sweden. From there it progressed to becoming the leader in Britain and then the rest of Europe, and formed strategic alliances with US distributors such as Radio Shack and US telecom companies like AT&T. The firm has also developed special phones for Chinese and Japanese users. Nokia spends a large amount on R&D, which allows it to continuously introduce new handset models. Recently, it introduced handsets with mp3 technology that allow a mobile phone to also be a portable music player.

L. M. Ericsson employs more than 105,000 people and has sales of US$14.6 billion in the 140 countries in which it operates. In 1997, Ericsson was the world's largest producer of digital mobile phones. Over 50 per cent of its sales are in Europe, 21 per cent in Asia, 13 per cent in North America, and 16 per cent in South America. Unlike Nokia, which started as a paper and rubber producer, Ericsson has always been in telecommunications, beginning in 1876 as a telephone

manufacturer. It has always been innovative; today, one in four employees works in R&D. In other areas of business it has developed telephone switches in which it competes with firms such as Canada's Nortel and France's Alcatel. Ericsson was well positioned to benefit from the telecom deregulation of the 1980s and 1990s. This has created new demand, especially for new equipment like mobile phones in areas with few local monopoly producers.

Ericsson has formed alliances with Compaq, Intel, Hewlett Packard, and Texas Instruments. These firms act as key suppliers of components and products that Ericsson uses for voice and data transmission. The company's relative weakness, compared with Nokia and Motorola, is its brand name. Ericsson has strong production technology but needs to improve on its marketing side.

Companies like Ericsson and Nokia will benefit from the alliance between AT&T and British Telecom, and that between Sprint, France Telecom, and Deutsche Telekom. Such big alliances help set standardized services to which mobile phone producers can respond efficiently. In the future, mobile phones will become even smaller, but the two producers from small countries, Nokia of Finland and Ericsson of Sweden, will become even bigger.

Websites: www.nokia.com; www.ericsson.com; www.motorola.com; www.nortelnetworks.com; www.alcatel.fr; www.att.com; www.compaq.com; www.hp.com; www.intel.com; and www.ti.com.

Sources: Annual Reports; Richard Hylton, Nick Moore and Roger Honour, "Making Money in the Tech Market," *Fortune*, May 13, 1996; Erick Schonfeld, "Hold the Phone: Motorola Is Going Nowhere Fast," *Fortune*, March 30, 1998; Caroline Daniel, "World's Most Respected Companies," *FT.com*, December 17, 2001; www.nokia.com; and www.ericsson.com.

Under this new arrangement, Canadian businesses are now in direct competition with firms operating in a diamond of their own in the United States.[17] To survive this rivalry with leading US firms, Canadian-based businesses have to develop competitive capabilities of a high order.[18] They can no longer rely on their country's home diamond and natural resource base. Innovation and cost competitiveness are equally important, and this requires strategies that are designed to access the US diamond. Now Canadian managers need a "double diamond perspective" for their strategic decisions. The double diamond is, of course, relevant for other small, open economies such as Finland and Sweden. The box **International Business Strategy in Action: Nokia and Ericsson** provides an example.

The Free Trade Agreement has also created a series of unique pressures on the Canadian subsidiaries of US multinationals, many of which were created for the purpose of overcoming Canadian tariff barriers that were designed to encourage the development of local operations. These subsidiaries are now unnecessary, and many of them are currently in direct competition with their US-based parent. If they cannot compete successfully, future business will go south of the border.[19]

Meanwhile, major Canadian companies are working to develop competitive positions in the United States as well as worldwide.[20] A good example is Nortel Networks, Canada's leading manufacturer of telecom equipment. The firm has now established a significant manufacturing and product development presence in the United States from which it sources a large part of its product line. It has two major operating centers: one outside Toronto and the other near Washington, DC. Vigorous rivalry between operations in both countries has helped Nortel Networks develop global competitiveness. Even after the tech bubble burst, Nortel was capable of successfully refocusing to remain competitive in a more modest competitive arena. It is now concentrating on voice-over-Internet protocol (VoIP), wireless, and broadband DSL equipment as well as looking into new technologies, such as multiprotocol label switching (MPLS), that reduce the cost of running large networks.[21]

Bombardier Inc. provides another example. Beginning as a Canadian manufacturer of snow-going equipment, the company has now grown into a multinational firm with interests in aviation, transportation, and financial services. In the aviation/aerospace business, Bombardier has major operations in Canada and the United States, among other locations, and manufactures corporate jets, small airliners, amphibious planes, weapons systems, and space systems. The company's transportation operations are located throughout North America and Europe and manufacture passenger trains, mass transit railcars, and engines. Its recreational products division, located primarily in North America, manufactures snowmobiles, boats, all-terrain vehicles, and small electric cars. The business/financial service operations, which are also heavily based in North America, provide business and consumer financial assistance.[22]

Other major Canadian firms are following suit, operating from a North American perspective in order to lay the groundwork for becoming globally competitive.[23] This involves viewing the United States and Canada as home-based markets and integrating the use of both "diamonds" for developing and implementing strategy. In particular, this requires:

1 developing innovative new products and services that simultaneously meet the needs of the US and Canadian customer, recognizing that close relationships with demanding US customers should set the pace and style of product development;

2 drawing on the support industries and infrastructure of both the US and Canadian diamonds, realizing that the US diamond is more likely to possess deeper and more efficient markets for such industries; and

3 making free and full use of the physical and human resources in both countries.[24]

Strategic clusters in the double diamond

The primary advantage of using the double diamond is that it forces business and government leaders to think about management strategy and public policy in a more productive way. Rather than viewing the domestic diamond as the unit of analysis, managers from smaller countries are encouraged to always be outward looking. Doing well in a double diamond is the first step toward global success.

Once a country has recognized the benefit of the double-diamond perspective, it should first identify successful and potentially viable clusters of industries within its borders and then examine their linkages and performances across the double diamond. A **strategic cluster** is a network of businesses and supporting activities located in a specific region, where the flagship firms compete globally and the supporting activities are home based, although some can be foreign owned. In addition, some of the critical business inputs and skills may come from outside the country, with their relevance and usefulness being determined by the membership of the strategic cluster. A successful strategic cluster will have

Strategic cluster
A network of businesses and supporting activities located in a specific region, where flagship firms compete globally and supporting activities are home-based

one or more large MNEs at its center. Whether these are home- or foreign-owned is irrelevant so long as they are globally competitive. They are the flagship firms on which the strategic cluster depends. Ideally, they operate on a global basis and plan their competitive strategies within the framework of global competition. A vital component of the cluster is companies with related and supporting activities, including both private- and public-sector organizations. In addition, there are think tanks, research groups, and educational institutions. Some parts of this network can even be based outside the country, but the linkages across the border and the leadership role of the nation's flagships result in world-class competitive multinationals.[25]

Currently Canada has several strategic clusters. One is the auto assembly and auto parts industry in southwestern Ontario, led by the Big Three US auto multinationals with their related and affiliated suppliers and distributors. There are linkages to various high-tech firms and research groups that span the border, as does the auto assembly industry itself. Other strategic clusters are based in banking and financial services in Toronto, advanced manufacturing and telecommunications in Toronto, forest products in western and eastern Canada, energy in Alberta, and the fisheries in Atlantic Canada. Some are led by flagship Canadian-owned multinationals such as Nortel, Nova, or Bombardier; others are led by, or include, foreign-owned firms such as IBM Canada and DuPont Canada.[26]

Many Canadian-based clusters are resource based. The challenge for managers in these clusters is to continue to add value and eliminate the commodity nature of Canada's resource industries. One way to do this is to develop a global marketing strategy that builds on the Canadian–US double diamond instead of remaining as the extractor or harvester of resources. To implement such a global strategy requires a large investment in people who will bring strong marketing skills and develop a global intelligence network to identify the different tastes and preferences of customers. This network provides a role for smaller knowledge-intensive marketing research and consulting firms to participate in the resource-based cluster. There is also the potential for collaborative ventures.

The IMD World Competitiveness Scoreboard ranks Canada as one of the most competitive countries in the world. Yet, in contrast with the United States, Canada does not fare so well. According to the IMD, the United States is the world's most competitive nation.[27] A recent study of productivity (GDP per hours worked) by Statistics Canada shows Canada trailing the United States by about 6 per cent. That is, for each hour of work, Canadians produce 94.2 per cent, in dollar terms, of their US counterparts.[28]

Further research is required to investigate Canadian-based strategic clusters and their competitive advantages in comparison with rival clusters in North America and around the world. This will require two types of work. First, the intrafirm competition of clusters in North America needs new data that do not ignore the nature of foreign ownership and whether US and Canadian FDI by sector is inbound or outbound. Instead, direct investment in North America must be regarded as "domestic" and be contrasted with "external" direct investment from Japan[29] and the European Union.[30] Similarly, trade flows between Canada and the United States must be thought of as intrafirm when they occur between components of a cluster or even between and among clusters.

This approach is so radical that many existing concepts must be rethought. For example, the level and extent of subsidies available to clusters located in the United States (for example, in the Great Lakes region) must be related to those paid by provinces in Canada (such as Ontario). Yet there is little or no published work on state or provincial subsidies; even the work on federal subsidies in either country is extremely thin.

Finally, the real sources of Canadian competitive advantage are to be discovered not only by statistical analysis but also by interviews of managers and officials—that is, by fieldwork in the strategic clusters. Such "hands-on" research is exceptionally time consuming and expensive. However, to make the task feasible a number of important strategic clusters can be selected for analysis, self-audits can be made, conferences can be held, and so on. The future success of these efforts will depend heavily on leadership by Canadian business leaders and government officials.

Mexico and the double diamond

We can also adapt the Porter diamond to analyze company strategies and international competitiveness in Mexico. The basic concepts in this framework are the same as those discussed in the Canadian diamond.

Linking to the US diamond

Mexico's linkage to the US diamond is somewhat different from Canada's. One reason is the fact that there are few home-based MNEs that have the capital to invest in the United States or Canada.[31] (Review Chapter 3 for information on how and why FDI is used by MNEs.) In fact, as seen in Table 15.1, during the 1990s Mexico's FDI in the United States increased by less than $1.5 billion and remained negligible in Canada. In contrast, by 2002 Canada had just over $2 billion invested in Mexico, whereas the United States had $58 billion there. More important, US FDI in Canada reached over $150 billion, while Canada's FDI in the United States was $92 billion. Thus, Mexico's strategy with its North American neighbors relies more heavily on trade than on FDI for outward market access, while using inward FDI to help promote internal development.

As seen in Figure 15.5, Mexico and the United States conduct over $241 billion of trade every year, while Canada and Mexico do over $4 billion of business. Mexico is the second largest trading partner of the United States, and although it has a negative trade balance with the world, it runs a positive balance with the United States. In fact, in recent years the latter has accounted for over 80 per cent of Mexico's exports *and* over 60 per cent of its imports. So Mexico is closely linked with the US economy, and its economic growth will depend heavily on participation in this North American market.[32] Figure 15.6 illustrates this idea with the US–Mexican double diamond.

Mexico is linking itself to the US diamond in a number of ways. One is by serving as a customer for outside goods. For example, Caterpillar supplies heavy equipment for road building in Mexico; Coca-Cola holds about half of the market for soft drinks in Mexico; and US soybeans dominate the Mexican oilseed market.[33]

Table 15.1 Stocks of FDI by Canada, the US, and Mexico, 1991–2002 (in millions of US $)

Year	Canada's FDI in: United States	Mexico	US FDI in: Canada	Mexico	Mexico's FDI in: Canada	United States
1991	55,353	176	70,711	12,501	—	747
1992	53,418	375	68,690	13,730	49.7	1,289
1993	52,565	413	69,922	15,221	120.4	1,244
1994	56,236	783	74,229	16,968	130.4	2,069
1995	62,975	823	83,489	16,873	144	1,850
1996	68,971	1,416	89,592	19,350	—	1,436
1997	72,140	1,555	96,626	24,050	—	1,723
1998	83,859	1,826	98,200	26,657	67	2,055
1999	90,394	1,901	119,590	37,151	64	1,999
2000	114,309	2,435	132,472	39,352	89	7,462
2001	102,127	2,062	141,781	56,554	43	7,336
2002	92,041	2,130	152,522	58,074	53	7,857

Source: Adapted from OECD (2003) *International Direct Investment Statistics Yearbook, 2003*. Data has been translated into US$ using effective exchange rates.

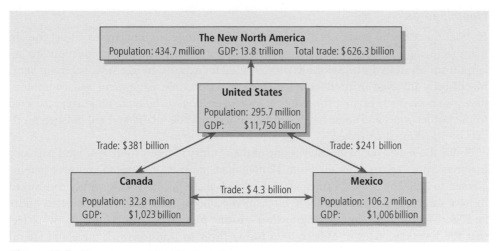

Figure 15.5 The shape of North America

Notes: Population data is for 2005, GDP data is for 2004, and trade data is for 2002.

Sources: Adapted from CIA, *The World Factbook, 2005*; IMF, *Direction of Trade Statistics Yearbook, 2003*.

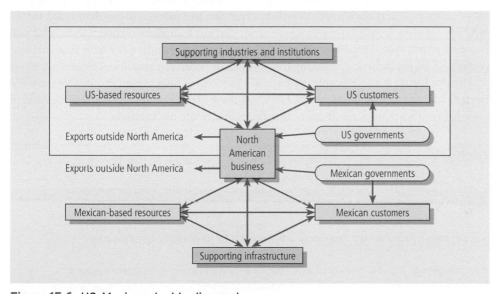

Figure 15.6 US-Mexican double diamond

Source: Richard M. Hodgetts, "Porter's Diamond Framework in a Mexican Context," *Management International Review*, vol. 33, Special Issue no. 2 (1993), p. 48.

At the same time, Mexican businesses and Mexican-based foreign subsidiaries are working to expand their links in the US market. Between 1993 and 2002, exports to the US market increased from $46 billion to almost $106 billion. Much of this output is in the form of manufactured goods, particularly automobiles. In fact, auto production in Mexico accounts for more than 450,000 workers and generates close to 1.5 million vehicles, most of which are targeted for the US market.[34] Ford, for example, is investing $1 billion in Hermosillo, Mexico, to develop a next generation of mid-sized vehicles.[35] At the same time, US firms are also investing in a wide array of non-automotive projects.[36] IBM, for example, now produces magnetic readers for computer hard-disk drives in Guadalajara and air ships them to California on a daily basis. In the entertainment industry, Mexican productions have found an eager US audience with films like *Amores Perros* and *Y Tu Mamá También*.[37]

Maquiladoras

In 1965 the Mexican government established the *maquiladora* industry to attract foreign manufacturing operations. Imported products for the *maquiladoras'* production are exempt from Mexican duties as long as they are used for exports. In recent years certain items not directly involved in production, such as transportation equipment and computers, have also been made exempt from duties. Moreover, *maquiladoras* are no longer restricted to the border zone, and some have been permitted to settle inland and sell finished products on the domestic market.

Today the *maquiladora* industry is one of the country's largest sources of hard currency earnings from exports, after oil. From 12 *maquiladora* plants in 1965, the number had increased to 2,900 by 2004.[38] Principally US-owned, these businesses are widely considered to have established a basis for more intensified economic cooperation anticipated under an FTA.[39] At the same time, their growth is creating friction because many Americans feel that the low wage rates in Mexico are causing firms to transfer work there and lay off employees back home.

What will the future hold regarding Mexico and North America? The most likely developments will be continued investment by US and Canadian firms and the establishment of worldwide competition there. Already by 2005 Mexico was manufacturing and shipping many more products back north as well as exporting to more countries than it did before NAFTA. Canada is still trying to create and nurture Canadian-owned MNEs that will compete worldwide. Mexico hopes to build these businesses internally with financial and technological investments, primarily from its North American neighbors.[40]

The double diamond examples of Canada and Mexico help explain how MNEs can use Porter's ideas to formulate strategies. However, these firms also need to address the issue of national responsiveness, the focus of the discussion in the next section.

✔ Active learning check

Review your answer to Active Learning Case question 2 and make any changes you like. Then compare your answer with the one below.

2 **Why did ABB buy Zamech? How can the company link Zamech to its overall strategic plan?**

ABB bought Zamech for a number of reasons. The company provides a springboard to the Eastern European market, which is likely to grow dramatically during the coming decade. ABB links Zamech to its overall strategic plan by using the same approach US firms are employing with Mexico. The company has purchased an equity position and is helping to set up a manufacturing operation that can provide goods for the local market as well as for other markets in both Eastern and Western Europe.

GLOBALIZATION AND CORPORATE STRATEGY

A major trend that has affected the thinking of corporate MNE strategists over the last decade or so is that of balancing a concern for "globalization" (or economic integration) with national responsiveness. Globalization can be defined as the production and distribution of products and services of a homogeneous type and quality on a worldwide basis.[41] To a large extent, MNEs have homogenized tastes and helped to spread international consumerism. For example, throughout North America, the wealthier nations of Europe, and Japan there has been a growing acceptance of standardized consumer electronic goods, automobiles, computers, calculators, and similar products. However, the goal of efficient

Globalization
The production and distribution of products and services of a homogeneous type and quality on a worldwide basis

Kodak

"You press the button, and we do the rest," was Eastman Kodak's slogan when it introduced the Kodak Brownie in 1900. The user-friendly camera put photography within reach of the average person. Today, Kodak is recycling the slogan to promote its easy-to-use digital photography cameras. But this time, Kodak no longer has a sustainable technology-based firm-specific advantage in the market. Its old FSAs in development and film have been overtaken by the digital age. Its brand name, a surviving FSA, might just give it an edge against its competitors in the digital photography market.

Kodak pioneered digital cameras in 1976, but unlike Kodak's early innovations, which mostly went unchallenged, digital photography is turning out to be a battle ground for competitors, including electronics and computer manufacturers like HP and Sony that have access to digital technology. In addition a number of upstarts have jumped into the market, including Ezonics and Vivitar, with lower quality bargain cameras.

Slowly, but surely, digital photography has become the most popular form of recording images. Consumer reaction to this new technology is yet to define the revenue generation model for producers. Traditionally, photographic companies derived revenues from selling cameras, but most importantly, from selling film and developing and printing photographs. Today, the digital camera user has a number of alternative printing methods, if he or she wants to print at all.

Consumers might choose to use one of two external printing options: take their memory chip to an Internet kiosk to have prints developed, or send their picture files over the Internet to be printed and mailed back to them. Kodak's retail network might give it a competitive advantage if consumers can be convinced to drop by and use full service or self-serve printing machines at their locations. If, however, consumers choose to do everything from home, sending photographs to a virtual kiosk that would then mail prints, upstarts might gain a hold in the better part of the market.

Kodak's brand name, however, is likely to provide a significant advantage even on the Internet. If a customer wants to develop photos, she might just try www.kodak.com. That is, if Windows will allow it. Kodak's collaboration with Microsoft became confrontational when Microsoft developed its own photo software that popped up automatically when a camera chip was inserted. The Windows software directed users to photo developers who paid fees to Microsoft. For Kodak, the consequences could be devastating. The company needs to be able to enter the web-based printing market to make up for losing profits in its traditional film business. To add insult to

Source: Getty Images/Ian Waldie

injury Microsoft teamed up with Kodak's archrival Fuji, listing it as one of the photo-developing service providers. Kodak complained to anti-trust regulators. How the battle for web-based developing will turn out is not yet known.

Another consumer alternative is to print photographs at home using a regular color printer or a more specialized photograph printer available at many computer and office supplies stores. While the concept of consumers having their own developing stations seems unlikely at the moment, CD writing was once used only by the most enthusiastic of computer users, yet it is now a standard feature in most computers sold. If something similar were to happen in the photographic industry, it would likely take revenues from traditional photographic companies to manufacturers of printer-friendly photographic paper, ink, cartridges, and toner. Will there be a spot left for Kodak to contribute in this market? The company certainly hopes so and is teaming up with computer companies such as HP and Lexmark to position itself should the market go this way. Yet, even this type of revenue generation is at risk since the European Commission began to investigate whether printer companies were illegally forcing consumers to purchase their ink, toners, and cartridges.

Perhaps the bleakest prediction for this industry is the near extinction of printing and developing revenue. Research

▶

shows that most people never print their digital photographs. Why would a consumer print his photographs if he can store them inside his computer, save them on disks, and share them with family and friends around the world at no cost or at a negligible cost? It is likely that only a select few photographs will ever make it to paper.

Other types of revenue generation include the manufacturing and selling of cameras, digital camera software and compatible computer software, and photographic printing machines. Kodak has entered all of these markets, but whether it can be successful in all of them for the long run is still being decided.

Outside the digital wars, Kodak is consistently challenged by competitors in many other of its business lines. In 1997, Kodak and Fuji participated in a price war on traditional film that threatened to make film into a commodity. In the

mid-1990s, Kodak pushed forth a case in the WTO claiming Japan's trade regulations did not allow it to enter the Japanese market. This, it claimed, allowed Fuji to reduce profit margins in the US market, effectively dumping products. The WTO dismissed all charges.

Kodak's traditional competitive advantages are being challenged by innovations that have increased the number of competitors and changed the rules of the game. Its brand name in photography now competes with other well-known brand names in the electronics industry for a market and revenue stream that are yet to be defined.

Websites: www.kodak.com; www.fujifilm.com; www.microsoft.com; www.ezonics.com; and www.vivitar.com.

Sources: Adapted from Alan M. Rugman, *The Regional Multinationals* (Cambridge: Cambridge University Press, 2005); www.kodak.com; and Kodak, *Annual Report*, 2003.

National responsiveness
The ability of MNEs to understand different consumer tastes in segmented regional markets and to respond to different national standards and regulations imposed by autonomous governments and agencies

economic performance through a universal globalization strategy has left MNEs open to the charge that they are overlooking the need to address national concerns. National responsiveness is the ability of MNEs to understand different consumer tastes in segmented regional markets and to respond to the different national standards and regulations imposed by autonomous governments and agencies. Throughout the coming years multinationals will continually have to deal with the twin goals of economic integration and national responsiveness.[42] See the box **International Business Strategy in Action: Kodak**.

Integration versus national responsiveness

To reconcile the twin issues of integration and national responsiveness, transnational MNEs can analyze them conceptually through the use of Figure 15.7, which has been adapted from Bartlett[43] and Bartlett and Ghoshal. The vertical axis measures the need for globalization, frequently called "economic integration." Movement up the axis results in a greater degree of economic integration, which generates economies of scale as a firm moves into worldwide markets, selling a single product or service. These economies are captured as a result of centralizing specific activities in the value-added chain. They also occur by reaping the benefits of increased coordination and control of geographically dispersed activities.

The horizontal axis measures the need for corporations to be nationally responsive. Companies must address local tastes and government regulations, which may result in a geographic dispersion of activities or a decentralization of coordination and control for individual firms.

On the basis of the two axes in Figure 15.7, four situations can be distinguished. Quadrants 1 and 4 are the simplest cases. In quadrant 1, the need for integration is high and the need for awareness of sovereignty is low. This focus on economies of scale leads to competitive strategies that are based on price competition. In such an environment, mergers and acquisitions often occur.

The opposite situation is represented by quadrant 4, where the need for national responsiveness is high but the integration concern is low. In this case companies adopt products to satisfy the high demands of sovereignty and to ignore economies of scale because integration is not very important.

Quadrants 2 and 3 also reflect opposing situations. Quadrant 2 incorporates those cases where the need for both integration and national responsiveness is low. Both the potential

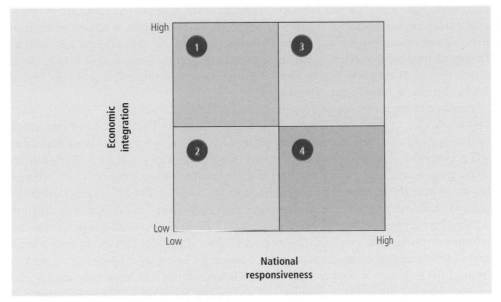

Figure 15.7 Integration and national responsiveness

Source: Reprinted by permission of Harvard Business School Press. Adapted from C. A. Bartlett, "Building and Managing the Transnational: the New Organizational Challenge," in *Competition in Global Industries,* edited by M. E. Porter, Boston, MA, 1986. Copyright © 1986 by the Harvard Business School Publishing Corporation; all rights reserved; and *Managing Across Borders: The Transnational Solution*, 2nd ed. by C. A. Bartlett and S. Ghoshal, Boston, MA, 1998. Copyright © 1998 by Harvard Business School Publishing Corporation; all rights reserved.

to obtain economies of scale and the benefits of being sensitive to sovereignty are of little value. Typical strategies in quadrant 2 are characterized by increased international standardization of products and services. This can lead to lower needs for centralized quality control and centralized strategic decision making, while simultaneously eliminating requirements to adapt activities to individual countries.

In quadrant 3 the needs for integration and national responsiveness are both high. There is a strong need for integration in production, along with higher requirements for regional adaptations in marketing. Quadrant 3 is the most challenging and the one in which many successful "transnational" MNEs operate. Using this framework, we can analyze the impact of various exogenous policy shocks and trends on different industries, firms, banks, and other private-sector institutions.

Balancing the trade-offs

MNEs in every industry apply the ideas in Figure 15.7, but they do so in a variety of ways. The following are select examples from three different industries: entertainment, personal computers, and automobiles.

Entertainment

One of the most successful entertainment firms in the world is the Walt Disney Company. Its Disneyland Paris operation in France is a good example of how integration and national responsiveness are balanced. The park offers many of the same features (integration) found in Disney's Orlando (Florida), Anaheim (California), and Tokyo operations, including amusement rides and cartoon characters such as Mickey Mouse, Goofy, and Donald Duck. The company has recently expanded its European facilities along the lines of its MGM studios near Orlando.[44] Stressing uniformity among the geographically scattered parks, this integration focus is supplemented by national responsiveness that is designed to appeal to

European visitors. English and French are the official languages of the park, and multilingual guides are conversant in Dutch, German, Spanish, and Italian. A second example of national responsiveness is found in the international emphasis the company has given its Disney characters: Pinocchio is Italian, Cinderella is French, Peter Pan is British. At its movie theater in the park, Disney shows a European history film offering (in the United States, the film is a travelogue of America).

Another example of integration/national responsiveness is offered by Sega Enterprises, best known for its Sonic the Hedgehog video game character. Using computer simulation technology like that used to train airline pilots, Sega is developing small theme parks that will provide the same thrills as a roller coaster or a trip through space. By building a series of different amusement simulators, Sega intends to offer a wide array of "rides" without having to bear the expense of physically building the facilities. The idea is captured in the term *virtual reality*, which means that participants experience the effects of a situation without literally being there.[45] "Scramble Training," a Sega simulator that is part video and part movie, provides an example. This interactive game allows eight players to enter a small space capsule and take their position as pilot trainees. The captain appears on a screen in front of the simulator and gives orders to the players, who in turn launch the capsule and swerve through space, firing missiles and competing for points. When the captain is wounded, the controls are turned over to the player with the best score, who then steers the capsule in for a landing. Sega intends to develop a host of different interactive simulators that will allow it to compete with amusement parks such as Disney. (In fact, Sega's concept is often referred to as "Disney in a Box.") The simulators are uniform in design and construction, allowing the company to employ an integration emphasis. However, the types of games will vary from country to country (national responsiveness), depending on the entertainment interests of the local populace. For example, Sega has found that Americans are very sports oriented, so there is likely to be an opportunity for players to participate in a World Series baseball simulation. In Europe, this game would have little attraction, but many players there would like to participate in the World Cup soccer finals, so the company can modify its product characteristics to meet the needs of the customer.[46]

Personal computers

Most personal computer (PC) makers compete on the bases of technology and price. They offer state-of-the-art machines and try to hold down their costs by outsourcing components and improving assembly efficiency. This strategy is particularly important in markets such as Japan, where less than 25 per cent of the population in the early 1990s owned PCs, and where local demands, such as the need to write in *kanji*, had discouraged foreign competition.

In recent years, however, US firms have been making major headway in this market, thanks to their ability to exploit both integration and national responsiveness.[47] For example, Compaq and Dell have entered this market with low-priced units that were the same as those sold elsewhere (integration) but offered sharply lower prices (national responsiveness). As a result, both firms have been able to garner market share. IBM has employed a similar strategy in addition to addressing the desire of local customers to write in *kanji*. The company has now perfected a bilingual version of Microsoft's DOS, the standard operating system that controls approximately 80 per cent of the world's PCs. This version allows these machines to prepare or search documents with Japanese characters, the Western alphabet, or both. Apple is also having very good success in Japan, thanks to its willingness to adapt to local needs. For example, the company has a Japanese management team that has helped to surmount local barriers to "buying foreign." It has also cultivated a strong network of dealers and worked to develop an image as an innovator, both of which are critical in the Japanese market. As a result of this careful balance of integration and national responsiveness, Apple and IBM alone account for almost 16 per cent of the Japanese PC market.[48]

Other US firms are also using a carefully formulated integration/national responsiveness strategy to gain market share. Microsoft has written a special version of Windows—one of the most popular PC software programs of all time—for the Japanese market. Until 1993, only 440,000 copies of the program had been sold, but when the company unveiled its new version, more than 65,000 copies were snatched up in two days. Summing up the current situation, one observer noted, "For now, American PC vendors feel the wind at their backs."[49]

Automobiles

Every car manufacturer uses economic integration by producing autos that can be made and marketed around the world. In a few cases, the Volkswagen Beetle being the best example, a car will not need to be modified for the local market.[50] Usually, however, an integration strategy is complemented by national responsiveness in the form of design, engineering, and manufacturing changes. Ford's Mondeo provides a good example. Developed for the world market, this car has uniform worldwide engineering standards with almost every specification expressed in the metric system. The company also has created uniform standards for raw materials, design, procurement, and manufacture of individual parts. Identical production tools are used at both European and US locations so that economies of scale can be maximized. At the same time, Ford has taken national responsiveness into consideration. European buyers prefer manual transmissions, whereas US buyers like automatic drive. Europeans demand cars that handle well, but this is not a priority issue with American customers. On the other hand, Americans want air-conditioned cars, and many Europeans do not. The overall cost of developing the Mondeo was $6 billion. However, initial sales in Europe were brisk and Ford believed it could maintain this momentum in the US market. It also believed it could create additional car models from the Mondeo program and thus develop a series of new offerings. If this is true, the integration and national responsiveness strategies used for the Mondeo will help smooth the way for future auto sales and help the company to recoup this enormous investment.[51]

Honda offers another example of integration and national responsiveness strategies. The firm now builds a variety of different car sizes from one production platform by bending and stretching the autos to fit the demands of the market. As a result, Honda is able to build cars in the United States that are longer and roomier, while offering smaller, more compact models of the same car in Japan. The company is now using this same approach to build sports utility vehicles for the world market.[52]

General Motors offers yet another example of integration and national responsiveness strategies. Like Ford, GM often develops cars for the European market, then introduces them into the United States. As a result, the cars are frequently identical in styling and design but have different features to accommodate local tastes. The Celta, a new subcompact offering in Brazil, has fewer features and 50 per cent fewer parts than competitive models. In collaboration with its suppliers, GM created a modular assembly plant with just-in-time supplier delivery. Efficiency costs of such an integration strategy allowed for an inexpensive subcompact for developing markets, where price and reliability are most important.[53] When the auto is made in another developing market, it will be possible to build and assemble each unit quickly because the process will have been perfected in Brazil. This integration focus is complemented by national responsiveness. In Brazil, marketing of the Celta stresses security locks and anti-theft devices, whereas in safer developing countries, the car's suspension system and handling on tough roads will receive more emphasis.

Competitiveness in the triad

From the viewpoint of MNEs, one of the most important business decisions regards the trade-off between integration and national responsiveness. Successful MNEs know they can no longer afford to ignore the latter and concentrate solely on globalization through economic integration.

In the United States

The United States experiences considerable decentralization in economic decision making. It is a country in which subnational units continue to increase in importance. This issue should not be confused with pluralism. A variety of political opinions and parties is a strength of democracy. The problem arises when the institutional structure of the nation and its businesses cannot operate in an efficient manner, relative to global competitors.

The US Constitution was designed to allow Congress to be a broker for regional and special interests. On occasion, Congress works with the Executive branch to formulate and implement a coordinated economic policy and even a social policy. Examples of social reform and government economic activity in the Kennedy–Johnson years can be contrasted with a return to more market-based principles and a somewhat reduced role for government in the Reagan years.

However, in many areas affecting the private sector today, the overwhelming characteristic of doing business in the United States is the responsiveness of governments to special interest groups and lobbies. The more decentralized the level of government, the more responsive will be the regulatory activity to the lobbyist. On occasion businesses themselves can be lobbyists, but there are many other groups, such as environmentalists and social activists, who seem to be growing in power. Examples of conflicts in business lobbying occur in the areas of administration of US trade remedy laws and in the current US debate about the possible regulation of inward foreign direct investment (FDI).

Rugman and Anderson,[54] as well as others, have demonstrated that the current administration of US countervailing duty (CVD) and antidumping (AD) laws is highly responsive to domestic producer interests and biased against foreign firms. US corporations use CVD and AD as a competitive strategy to erect entry barriers against rival firms.[55] Between 1980 and 2003, US businesses filed 1,510 AD and CVD cases against foreign competitors with the United States International Trade Commission. Thirty-seven per cent of these cases, or 559, were found to be justified after the commission investigated the complaints. Table 15.2 lists a number of selected products that were slapped with import tariffs.

Table 15.2 Products most affected by CVD and AD laws in the United States, 1980–2003

Softwood lumber	(Canada)
Minivans	(Japan)
Live cattle	(Canada)
Frozen concentrate juice	(Brazil)
Steel products	(South Korea, Russia, Germany, Japan)
All-terrain vehicles	(Japan)
Fresh tomatoes	(Mexico)
Sweaters	(South Korea)
DRAMs and DRAM modules	(South Korea)

Source: United States International Trade Commission, "Import Injury Investigations Statistics," November 2004.

Approximately 5 per cent of all cases between 1980 and 2003 are against Canada.[56] Thus, even when the US government was pursuing negotiations for free trade with Canada, individual US corporations were still using the CVD and AD laws to help restrict Canadian imports. This is a clear example of American national interests being offset by selective producer interests. There were more than 22 CVD and AD cases against Canada in the 1990s.[57] More of the same is in store in the future, although Canadian concerns about the administration of CVD and AD laws have been somewhat answered by the establishment of binational panels under the terms of the FTA and then NAFTA.

Another area of concern is inward FDI, which some congressional leaders now wish to restrict, and some Americans seem concerned with the growing amount of Japanese FDI. Some members of Congress have urged more screening of such FDI, and there is a strong "Japan-bashing" stance in US trade policy. Yet at the same time, state officials have been actively seeking Japanese FDI because they want the jobs and the tax base. This potential clash between Washington "beltway" thinking (anti-Japanese) and state-level activity (pro-Japanese) parallels Canada's experience with the regulation of FDI.

The United States seems destined in the next 10 years to repeat many of the mistakes made in Canada over the last 30 years. In 1974 the Trudeau government introduced the Foreign Investment Review Agency (FIRA), which was designed to screen FDI on economic criteria to assess whether there was a net benefit to Canada. Between 1974 and 1985, FIRA responded to Ottawa's political winds, at times rejecting as much as 30 per cent of applications but at other times (especially 1982 to 1985) approving virtually everything.[58] The administrators at FIRA and the responsible ministers made political decisions just as the US International Trade Commission and the US Commerce Department do today in US trade law cases.

In 1985, FIRA was abolished and a new agency, Investment Canada, was created with the mandate to attract FDI rather than scare it away.[59] This change in thinking about FDI came with a change in government, after the Progressive Conservatives were elected in 1984 with a mandate of job creation. Throughout the lifetime of FIRA, most provinces, especially those in Atlantic Canada, wanted FDI for jobs and taxes. The clash between the provinces that favored FDI and the central Canadian economic nationalists led to the federal government giving up many of its powers to regulate FDI by buying into the agenda of the provinces, especially their overwhelming priority about jobs. Perhaps this is some evidence of the triumph of decentralized economic power. But a paradox emerges. In Canada, the economic nationalists who have used central government power are in retreat, whereas it appears that in the United States economic nationalism is just beginning to take off. If Japan-bashing continues, then the US proponents of restrictions on FDI will have the same unhappy experience with FIRA as did Canada. Private-sector US corporate strategists will, therefore, need to respond to a large dose of economic nationalism and its associated protectionist inefficiencies.

In Eastern Europe

Another example of the use of sovereignty and the destruction of centralized economic power and values was the 1989 revolution in central Europe and the collapse of the Soviet Union in 1991. The rejection of totalitarian communist regimes by the people of countries such as Romania, Belarus, and Russia has many implications for business. The key point is that these countries are very poor, with inefficient economic and financial systems. Their economic development will probably be through FDI rather than through joint ventures. Popular wisdom to the contrary, joint ventures between poor nations and wealthy corporations rarely work. The preferable mode of international business is FDI because Western firms can then control their proprietary advantages and not risk dissipation through joint ventures.[60] Studies on joint ventures in developing countries have found a great deal of instability and failure.[61] Multinationals prefer FDI and countries such as India and Mexico, which once greatly restricted FDI, experienced inefficient economic development and eventually had to lift such regulations. This experience is relevant for Eastern Europe.

Doing business in Eastern Europe for the next five to ten years will be dominated by the need for economic efficiency. The globalization concept will overwhelm concerns about adapting products for sovereignty. It is in the EU nations that national responsiveness will be important for corporations. In the wealthy triad powers, adapting to sovereignty matters; in the developing world and in Eastern Europe, economic efficiency is what matters.

In Japan

A key explanation for the success of Japanese MNEs is that they benefit from a highly centralized home market economy. This has permitted Japan to use levers of industrial and strategic trade policies that could not be implemented successfully in the other areas of the triad.

Centralized government policy is critical to implementing effective corporate strategy.[62] The Japanese cultural, religious, social, and political system is much more centralized in nature than other triad blocs, enabling the country's MNEs to follow globalization strategies. Thus, for example, after the two OPEC oil crises of the 1970s, Japanese industry was rapidly transformed out of shipbuilding, heavy engineering, and other energy-intensive manufacturing and into computer-based manufacturing, consumer electronics, and high value-added services, including banking and finance. The government and the MNEs worked together to implement a new industrial strategy in an effective and efficient manner.

Such radical restructuring through industrial policy is unlikely to work in North America and Europe because of the decentralized nature of economic power. Attempts by the United States or Canada to implement a new industrial policy are likely to fail. Whatever government incentives and subsidies are made available will be appropriated by industries seeking shelter from competitors in the triad. To erect entry barriers against foreign competitors, companies will use the decentralized nature of the economic system. This has already occurred in the United States, with companies seeking protection from competitors through the use of CVD and AD laws. US steel, forest products, fish, and semiconductor industries, among others, have been using short-term legal remedies instead of investing in the development of sustainable, proprietary, firm-specific advantages.

What are the implications for corporate strategy of these asymmetrical developments in the triad? Japanese MNEs will continue to pursue an integration/globalization strategy, but they may face difficulties when they need to operate in the decentralized environments of North America and Europe, since marketing-type skills will become more important than production skills. Over the last decade, MNEs from Europe and North America have often abused the nature of their home country decentralized systems, and sovereignty has hindered efficient corporate development. However, MNEs from North America and Europe have a potential competitive advantage over Japanese MNEs if they can learn from their past mistakes. Awareness of sovereignty can make the former companies better equipped in the future to be more nationally responsive than their Japanese counterparts. Indeed, Japanese MNEs may become locked into a "globalization only" strategy, just as the world begins to demand much more corporate responsiveness to sovereignty.

Active learning check

Review your answer to Active Learning Case question 3 and make any changes you like. Then compare your answer with the one below.

3 How does ABB address the issues of globalization and national responsiveness? In each case, cite an example.

ABB addresses the issue of globalization by producing state-of-the-art products for worldwide markets. For example, the same high-speed trains that can carry passengers and goods through the Alps can be used for transporting people and goods across the plains of the United States or the steppes of Russia. It may be necessary to make modifications to address local geographic and climatic conditions, of course, but the basic technology and manufacturing techniques are similar. At the same time, ABB addresses national responsiveness by trying to be a local firm that is interested in the needs of that market. As a result, the company balances globalization and sovereignty—a feat that most MNEs do not accomplish very well.

KEY POINTS

1 Porter's diamond model is based on four country-specific determinants and two external variables (chance and government). This model is extremely useful in examining strategies among triad and other economically developed countries. However, when applying the model to smaller, open, trading economies, a modification is in order.

2 Canada's economic success will depend on its ability to view itself as part of the North American market and to integrate itself into this overall market. This requires the use of a "double diamond" model for corporate strategy, resulting in Canadian firms developing competitive capabilities that allow them to compete successfully with US firms in the United States. This is being done by (a) developing innovative products and services that simultaneously meet the needs of the US and Canadian customer, (b) drawing on the support industries and infrastructure of both the US and Canadian diamonds, and (c) making free and full use of the physical and human resources in both countries.

3 Mexico's economic success also depends on its ability to integrate itself into the North American market. However, this strategy is different from that of the Canadians because Mexico does not have the FDI to invest in the US market. Much of its linkage is a result of low labor costs that allow the country to produce inexpensive goods and export them into the United States. The North American Free Trade Agreement worked out with the United States and Canada in 1993 will determine part of Mexico's future economic success.

4 A major trend that has affected the thinking of corporate MNE strategists over the last ten years is balancing a concern for economic integration and globalization with that of national responsiveness. Many MNEs have focused on integration without giving sufficient attention to the sovereignty issue. However, there will have to be a reversal of this trend and MNEs will have to become much more interested in national responsiveness if they hope to succeed in overseas markets.

Key terms
- strategic cluster
- globalization
- national responsiveness

REVIEW AND DISCUSSION QUESTIONS

1 The Porter diamond is based on four country-specific determinants and two external variables. What does this statement mean? Put it in your own words.

2 Porter notes, "Firms, not individual nations, compete in international markets." How does this statement help explain some of the major challenges facing MNEs?

3 Using Figure 15.2 as your point of reference, how does the current national development of the United States differ from that of Korea? How does Great Britain's differ from that of Singapore?

4 Why does the Porter diamond need to be modified in explaining the international competitiveness of countries such as Canada and Mexico?

5 How does the double diamond, as illustrated in Figure 15.4, help explain international competitiveness in Canada?

6 How can Canadian firms view the United States and Canada as home-based markets and integrate the use of both diamonds for developing and implementing strategy? Be complete in your answer.

7 Of what value are strategic clusters in the double diamond? Explain.

8 How does the double diamond in Figure 15.6 help explain Mexico's international business strategy? Explain.

9 How important are the *maquiladoras* to the growth of the Mexican economy? In what way do these businesses link Mexico with the Canadian–US double diamond?

10 In what way are economic integration/globalization and national responsiveness important to MNE strategies?

11 In the entertainment industry, which is more important, integration or national responsiveness?

12 Based on current developments in the PC market in Japan, which is more important for US MNEs, integration or national responsiveness? Why?

13 Which is more important for US automakers doing business in Europe, integration or national responsiveness? Why?

REAL CASE

There is no global beer, only local

Beer is a good example of an industry that is not globalized. The world's largest brewery, Anheuser-Busch, still sells 90 per cent of its Budweiser brand in the United States. Heineken still generates 61 per cent of its profits within the EU. Perhaps the Belgian brewery, Interbrew, has gone the farthest in expanding from its EU base into North America through the purchase of Canada's largest brewer, Labatt, in 1993.

Beer is stubbornly local. Although Budweiser is the world's single largest beer brand, it accounts for only 3.6 per cent of world beer sales each year. Because beer is bulky and too expensive to export, it is brewed domestically; foreign producers will license their brand name products to local producers to gain a local market presence. In addition, imports of alcoholic beverages are traditionally heavily taxed. Rival domestic producers usually tie up local distribution channels. Governments also protect domestic breweries, such as in Germany, where the Reinheitsgebot purity rules have protected indigenous beer for over 400 years.

In Canada, domestic brewers were exempted from the national treatment provision of the United States–Canada Free Trade Agreement of 1989 (and later from NAFTA in 1993). The reason is that, initially, each Canadian company needed to have a brewery in each province, resulting in rather small and inefficient breweries in the low-population Atlantic Provinces. In light of such inefficiency and import protection, Labatt was taken over by the Belgian brewery, Interbrew. Molson was also doing badly by 2001.

The local, fragmented nature of the brewing industry can be offset by acquisitions. The half dozen leading world brewers are constantly attempting to increase their market share in both developed and developing countries. The world leader, Anheuser-Busch, makes Budweiser, but as already noted, most of its sales are in the United States. Belgium's Interbrew has made huge gains in the last few years, buying up such companies as Bass Brewers of the UK, Becks of Germany, Labatt in Canada, and others. Its major product line is Stella Artois. South African Breweries (SAB) was reported in late 2001 to be looking into a merger with Interbrew or Miller. The table below lists the world's largest brewers.

There are a few premium "designer" beers (high-end beers that have been developed into global brands), but they are usually produced under license. This has led to cross-licensing and distribution arrangements as well as to mergers and acquisitions. Today there is some consolidation in this segment to a few large brewers such as Heineken, Interbrew, Guinness/UDV, and Anheuser-Busch. But the premium lager segment is a minority of the total world beer market, which still has mainly local beer.

Largest worldwide brewers

Name	Volume MHL
Anheuser-Busch	150.0
Interbrew	76.2
Heineken	72.0
SAB (South African Breweries)	56.0
Ambev	56.0
Miller	53.0
Carlsberg	46.0
S&N (Scottish & Newcastle)	35.8
Asahi	35.0
Kirin	32.0

Source: Financial Times, November 29, 2001, p. 19.

Websites: www.molson.com; www.labatt.com; www.anheuser-busch.com; www.ambev.com; www.heineken.com; www.interbrew.com; www.millerbrewing.com; www.carlsberg.com; www.asahi.com; and www.kirin.com.

Sources: Adam Jones et al., "A Game of Musical Chairs Is Brewing," *Financial Times,* November 29, 2001; "Battling Brewers," *Economist,* March 16, 2000; "The Big Pitcher," *Economist,* January 18, 2001.

1 Is the production and distribution of beer nationally responsive?

2 If beer is mainly local, why are there mergers and acquisitions of beer companies?

3 In the integration/responsiveness matrix of Chapter 15, where would you position the world's largest brand name beer companies and why?

REAL CASE

IBM

In 1911, four recording and processing equipment manufacturers in the United States merged to form the Computer-Tabulating-Recording Company (C-T-R). The new company merged its Canadian operations in 1917 under the name of International Business Machines Company. This name was adopted by all the company's operations in 1924; today, most people simply recognize it as IBM.

A pioneer of the personal computer (PC), IBM is also well known for leading the way to globalization. Its operations span more than 160 countries and its research laboratories are located in six countries across the triad. Indeed, IBM is the largest of only nine global companies in the *Fortune* 500. In 2003, IBM derived 42.7 per cent of all

its revenue from the Americas, compared to 32.7 per cent from Europe, the Middle East, and Africa and 21.6 per cent from Asia-Pacific. The remaining 3 per cent of its revenue comes from its uncategorized global operations.

Production is also spread around the world. Product lines are clustered in regions that offer plentiful labor or specialized technology, depending on the nature of the product. ThinkPads are manufactured in Shenzhen, China, desktops in Guadalajara, Mexico. This reliance on developing countries allows IBM to take advantage of low labor costs while placing it inside some of the fastest-growing markets in the world.

IBM was an international company at its conception. C-T-R had brought together the international operations of all its predecessors. In the decades following its establishment, the company aggressively pursued expansion across the world. In Latin America, an office opened in Brazil in 1917. Within the next 20 years, IBM secured contracts with governments and corporations in Argentina, Mexico, Ecuador, Chile, Cuba, Uruguay, and Peru. In Asia, the company opened its first office in Bombay, India, in 1920. The Philippine market was entered in 1925, followed the next year by the first IBM equipment being installed in Osaka, Japan, for the Nippon Mutual Life Insurance Company. In China, the first IBM machines were installed at the Peking Union Medical College in 1934.

IBM's entry into the European market started when a branch of the International Time Recording Company, an IBM forerunner, opened in France in 1914. It was only in 1919 that a consolidated IBM was introduced in Europe. In the 1920s and 1930s, IBM manufacturing facilities sprang up in Germany, France, England, and Italy.

Although IBM's organizational segments are product-based, a company sales and distribution segment has a geographic focus as well as a specialized and global industry focus. Small and medium business contracts are dealt with through a global sales and distribution segment. Its foreign subsidiaries share technology, logistics, business principles, and a common source of manufacturing, but have the power to implement local strategies. In other words, they can choose their product lines and marketing strategy to respond to the needs of the local environment, including regulations, customer tastes, income levels, and the competitive environment.

In terms of production, IBM's highest commitment to globalizing production is its growing reliance on electronic manufacturing service providers. More than two-thirds of the company's Intel-based products are manufactured in worldwide factories by contract manufacturers, including Sanmina-SCI and Solectron. (See the Flextronics Case Study.)

IBM is one of only a few companies that have successfully penetrated foreign regional markets in terms of revenues and production. A main reason is that the computer, office, and electronics industry in which IBM operates is one of the most global, with average intra-regional sales of 56.2 per cent. Electronics are easy to transport and are standardized across all world regions. Seven of the nine

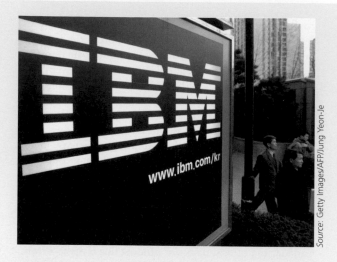

Source: Getty Images/AFP/Jung Yeon-Je

global firms are from this industry. This extra-regionality is the result of standardized components that can be transported cheaply across the world, allowing for a global supply chain.

In terms of assets, however, IBM is highly intra-regional; 62.9 per cent are in the United States. There are a number of reasons for this: (1) foreign production facilities are often owned by contract manufacturers; (2) the cost of land and equipment is higher in the United States than in many of the developing countries in which the company manufactures; and (3) the United States remains the most important market for IBM. Indeed, although IBM has over 20 per cent of its sales in each triad market, the Americas continue to account for the largest portion. It is difficult to argue that this is merely the result of a home region advantage. The United States is, after all, the largest triad economy and the largest market for technology products.

Sources: www.ibm.com; IBM, *Annual Report*, 2001; Braintrust, *The Regional Nature of Global Multinational Enterprises*, 2003; "IBM Outsourcing to Solectron, Sanmina-SCI," *Internet News*, January 7, 2003.

1 Is IBM a multinational enterprise? Is it global?

2 How does contract manufacturing fit into IBM's strategy?

3 Using the integration and national responsive matrix, in what quadrant does IBM's strategy fall?

Endnotes

1 For a detailed discussion of these variables and determinants, see Michael E. Porter, *The Competitive Advantage of Nations* (New York: Free Press, 1990), pp. 69–130.

2 Alan M. Rugman and Alain Verbeke, *Global Corporate Strategy and Trade Policy* (London and New York: Routledge, 1990).

3 Michael E. Porter, *The Competitive Advantage of Nations* (New York: Free Press, 1990), p. 33.

4 Ibid., p. 671.

5 A. E. Safarian, *Foreign Ownership of Canadian Industry* (Toronto: McGraw-Hill Inc., 1968).

6 Alan M. Rugman, *Multinationals in Canada: Theory, Performance and Economic Impact* (Boston, MA: Martinus Nijhoff, 1980).

7 Harold Crookell, *Canadian–American Trade and Investment Under the Free Trade Agreement* (Westport, CT: Quorum Books, 1990).

8 Alan M. Rugman, *Multinationals and Canada–United States Free Trade* (Columbia, SC: University of South Carolina Press, 1990).

9 See Alan M. Rugman, "Strategies for National Competitiveness," *Long Range Planning*, vol. 20, no. 3 (1987), pp. 92–97.

10 Alan M. Rugman and John McIlveen, *Megafirms: Strategies for Canada's Multinationals* (Toronto: Methuen/Nelson, 1985).

11 Ibid.

12 John H. Dunning, "Dunning on Porter." Paper presented at the Annual Meeting of the Academy of International Business, Toronto, October 1990, and published in John H. Dunning, *The Globalization of Business* (London and New York: Routledge, 1993); and John H. Dunning, "Internationalizing Porter's Diamond," *Management International Review*, vol. 33, Special Issue no. 2 (1993), pp. 7–16.

13 Ibid., 1990, p. 11.

14 United Nations, *World Investment Report* (New York: United Nations, 2000).

15 Alan M. Rugman and Joseph R. D'Cruz, *Fast Forward: Improving Canada's International Competitiveness* (Toronto: Kodak Canada, 1991); and Alan M. Rugman and Joseph R. D'Cruz, "The 'Double Diamond' Model of International Competitiveness: The Canadian Experience," *Management International Review*, vol. 33, Special Issue 2 (1993), pp. 17–40.

16 For another view of the FTA, see John N. Turner, "There Is More to Trade Than Trade: An Analysis of the US/Canada Trade Agreement 1988," *California Management Review*, Winter 1991, pp. 109–119.

17 Alan M. Rugman, "The Free Trade Agreement and the Global Economy," *Business Quarterly*, Summer 1988, pp. 13–20.

18 Alan M. Rugman and Alain Verbeke, "Strategic Responses to Free Trade," *Hitotsubashi Journal of Commerce and Management*, December 1988, pp. 69–79; and Alan M. Rugman and Alain Verbeke, "Foreign Subsidiaries and Multinational Strategic Management: An Extension and Correction of Porter's Single Diamond Framework," *Management International Review*, vol. 33, Special Issue 2 (1993), pp. 71–84.

19 See, for example, Joseph R. D'Cruz and James Fleck, *Yankee Canadians in the Global Economy* (London, Ontario: National Centre for Management Research and Development, 1987); and Alan M. Rugman and Joseph D'Cruz, *New Visions for Canadian Business: Strategies for Competing in the Global Economy* (Toronto: Kodak Canada, 1990).

20 See Doug Struck, "Canada Looks for Spot in the Big Picture," *Washington Post*, December 29, 2004.

21 "Decapitated," *The Economist*, April 29, 2004.

22 Anthony DePalma, "The Transportation Giant Up North," *New York Times*, December 26, 1998, pp. C 1, 3.

23 Doug Struck, "Canada Looks for Spot in the Big Picture," *Washington Post*, December 29, 2004.

24 Also, see Alan M. Rugman and Alain Verbeke, "Multinational Corporate Strategy and the Canada–US Free Trade Agreement," *Management International Review*, vol. 30, no. 3 (Third Quarter 1990), pp. 253–266; and Alan M. Rugman and Alain Verbeke, "How to Operationalize Porter's Diamond of International Competitiveness," *International Executive*, vol. 35, no. 4, July/August (1993), pp. 283–299.

25 For more details of this business network approach, see Joseph R. D'Cruz and Alan M. Rugman, *New Compacts of Canadian Competitiveness* (Toronto: Kodak Canada, 1992); Joseph R. D'Cruz and Alan M. Rugman, "Business Networks for International Competitiveness," *Business Quarterly*, vol. 56, no. 4 (Spring 1992), pp. 101–107; and Joseph R. D'Cruz and Alan M. Rugman, "Developing International Competitiveness: The Five Partners Model," *Business Quarterly*, vol. 58, no. 2 (Winter 1993), pp. 60–72.

26 D'Cruz and Rugman, *New Compacts of Canadian Competitiveness* (1992) n. 25 above, pp. 29–36.

27 IMD, *World Competitiveness Yearbook*, 2005.

28 John R. Baldwin, Jean-Pierre Maynard and Fanny Wong, "The Output Gap Between Canada and the United States: The Role of Productivity (1994–2002)," *Statistics Canada Analytical Papers*, January 2005.

29 Alan M. Rugman, *Japanese Direct Investment in Canada* (Ottawa: Canada–Japan Trade Council, 1990).

30 See Alan M. Rugman and F. Bill Mohri, "Trade and Investment Among Canada and the Triad," Working paper, University of Toronto, July 1991; and Alan M. Rugman (ed.), *Foreign Investment and NAFTA* (Columbia, SC: University of South Carolina Press, 1994).

31 Alan M. Rugman and Alain Verbeke, "Foreign Direct Investment in North America: Current Patterns and Future Relationships in Canada, the United States, and Mexico," Ontario Centre for International Business, Research program working paper, no. 57, November 1991, p. 4, published in Khosrow Fatemi and Dominick Salvatore (eds.), *North American Free Trade Agreement* (London: Pergamon Press, 1994).

32 Also, see "Free Trade on Trial," *Economist*, December 30, 2003.

33 Ben Juarez and Gabriel Hernandez, "Mexico's Market a Winning Bet for U.S. Soybeans," *FAS Online*, December 2000.

34 "Why Mexico Scares the UAW," *Business Week*, August 3, 1998, p. 37; and "U.S. Slowdown Adds to Mexican Auto Industry's Woes," *Forbes.com*, April 19, 2001 and www.amia.com.mx.

35 Jamie Butters, "Mexico Wins Production of Ford Futura," *Detroit Free Press*, October 7, 2003.

36 Joel Millman, "High-Tech Jobs Transfer to Mexico with Surprising Speed," *Wall Street Journal*, April 9, 1999, p. A 18.

37 "The Mexicans Are Coming!" *Economist*, October 3, 2002.

38 Alan Rugman and Alain Verbeke, "Foreign Direct Investment in North America," n. 31 above, p. 12; and Geri Smith, "Made in the Maquilas Again," *Business Week*, August 16, 2004.

39 United States International Trade Commission, *The Likely Impact on the United States of a Free Trade Agreement with Mexico*, USITC Publication 2353, February 1991, pp. 1–5.

40 Also, see *Lloyd Economic Report* (Guadalajara, Mexico), March 1994.

41 For a discussion of various definitions of globalization, see Chapter 1 of Alan M. Rugman, *The End of Globalization* (London: Random House, 2000 and New York: McGraw Hill/Amacom, 2001).

42 See Alan M. Rugman and Karl Moore, "How Global Is Globalisation," *FT Mastering Management Online*, November 2001.

43 Christopher A. Bartlett, "Building and Managing the Transnational: The New Organizational Challenge," in

M. E. Porter (ed.), *Competition in Global Industries* (Boston, MA: Harvard Business School Press, 1986), pp. 367–401; and Christopher A. Bartlett and Sumantra Ghoshal, *Managing Across Borders: The Transnational Solution* (Boston, MA: Harvard Business School Press, 1989).

44 "Disney's Euro Problem," *Miami Herald*, July 9, 1993, p. C 3.

45 Andrew Pollack, "Sega Takes Aim at Disney's World," *New York Times*, Section 3, July 4, 1993, pp. 1, 6.

46 For more on Sega, see Irene M. Kunii, "Sega: 'We're Going to Blow Them Out of the Water'," *Business Week*, December 7, 1998, p. 108.

47 Brenton R. Schlender, "US PCs Invade Japan," *Fortune*, July 12, 1993, pp. 68–73.

48 See also "PC Market Has Ups and Downs," *Asia Times*, December 5, 2001; and Apple, *Guide to Japan for Macintosh Developers*, 2000 Edition.

49 Schlender (1993) n. 47 above, p. 73.

50 Gabriella Stern, "VW's US Comeback Rides on Restyled Beetle," *Wall Street Journal*, May 6, 1997, pp. B 1–2.

51 Alex Taylor III, "Ford's $6 Billion Baby," *Fortune*, June 28, 1993, pp. 76–81.

52 Keith Naughton et al., "Can Honda Build a World Car?" *Business Week*, September 8, 1997, pp. 100–108.

53 "GM do Brasil Launches de Chevrolet Celta," *Automotive Intelligence News*, September 5, 2000.

54 Alan M. Rugman and Andrew Anderson, *Administered Protection in America* (London and New York: Routledge, 1987).

55 Rugman and Verbeke (1990) n. 2 above.

56 United States International Trade Commission, "Import Injury Investigations Statistics," November 2004.

57 International Trade Administration, *Antidumping and Countervailing Duty Cases Initiated Since January 01, 1980 Current Through January 01, 2000*, January 2000.

58 Alan M. Rugman, *Multinationals in Canada: Theory, Performance and Economic Impact* (Boston, MA: Martinus Nijhoff, 1980).

59 Alan M. Rugman and Leonard Waverman, "Foreign Ownership and Corporate Strategy," in Leonard Waverman (ed.), *Corporate Globalization Through Mergers and Acquisitions* (Calgary: University of Calgary Press, 1991), pp. 59–87.

60 Alan M. Rugman, *Inside the Multinationals: The Economics of Internal Markets* (London: Croom Helm and New York: Columbia University Press, 1981).

61 Paul W. Beamish, *Multinational Joint Ventures in Developing Countries* (London and New York: Routledge, 1989).

62 Rugman and Verbeke (1990) n. 2 above.

Additional bibliography

Akers, John F. "Ethics and Competitiveness—Putting First Things First," *Sloan Management Review*, vol. 30, no. 2 (Winter 1989).

Bartlett, Christopher and Ghoshal, Sumantra. *Managing Across Borders: The Transnational Solution* (Boston, MA: Harvard Business School Press, 1989, 1998).

Bartlett, Christopher and Ghoshal, Sumantra. *Transnational Management* (Boston, MA: Irwin, 1992).

Birkinshaw, Julian. "Strategy and Management in MNE Subsidiaries," in Alan M. Rugman and Thomas L. Brewer (eds.), *The Oxford Handbook of International Business* (Oxford: Oxford University Press, 2001).

Birkinshaw, Julian and Hood, Neil. "Characteristics of Foreign Subsidiaries in Industry Clusters," *Journal of International Business Studies*, vol. 31, no. 1 (First Quarter 2000).

Boyd, Gavin (ed.). *The Struggle for World Markets: Competition and Cooperation Between NAFTA and the EU* (Cheltenham: Elgar, 1998).

Cho, Dong-Sung and Moon, Hwy-Chang. *From Adam Smith to Michael Porter: Evolution of Competitiveness Theory* (Singapore, River's Edge, NJ: World Scientific, 2000).

Choate, Pat. "Political Advantage: Japan's Campaign for America," *Harvard Business Review*, vol. 68, no. 5 (September/October 1990).

Dickson, Peter R. and Czinkota, Michael R. "How the United States Can Be Number One Again: Resurrecting the Industrial Policy Debate," *Columbia Journal of World Business*, vol. 31, no. 3 (Fall 1996).

Dunning, John H. "Internationalizing Porter's Diamond," *Management International Review*, vol. 33, no. 2 (Second Quarter 1993).

Dunning, John H. "The Geographical Sources of Competitiveness of Firms: Some Results of a New Survey," *Transnational Corporations*, vol. 5, no. 3 (December 1996).

Kline, John M. "Trade Competitiveness and Corporate Nationality," *Columbia Journal of World Business*, vol. 24, no. 3 (Fall 1989).

Kotler, Philip. *The Marketing of Nations* (New York: The Free Press, 1997).

Kuttner, Robert. "How 'National Security' Hurts National Competitiveness," *Harvard Business Review*, vol. 69, no. 1 (January/February 1991).

Leong, Siew Meng and Tan, Chin Tiong. "Managing Across Borders: An Empirical Test of the Bartlett and Ghoshal (1989) Organizational Typology," *Journal of International Business Studies*, vol. 24, no. 3 (Third Quarter 1993).

Lodge, George C., Decker, Hans W., Tonelson, Alan, Brown, John Seely, Pennington, Hilary, Hale, David, Raduchel, William J., Shapiro, Robert J., Gilder, George and Branscomb, Lewis M. "How Real Is America's Decline?" *Harvard Business Review*, vol. 70, no. 5 (September/October 1992).

Martinez, Jon I. and Jarillo, J. Carlos. "Coordination Demands of International Strategies," *Journal of International Business Studies*, vol. 22, no. 3 (Third Quarter 1991).

Merrills, Roy. "How Northern Telecom Competes on Time," *Harvard Business Review*, vol. 67, vol. 4 (July/August 1989).

Narula, Rajneesh. "Technology, International Business and Porter's 'Diamond': Synthesizing a Dynamic Competitive Development Model," *Management International Review*, vol. 33, no. 2 (Second Quarter 1993).

Ostry, Sylvia. "Government and Corporations in a Shrinking World: Trade and Innovation Policies in the United States, Europe & Japan," *Columbia Journal of World Business*, vol. 25, nos. 1, 2 (Spring/Summer 1990).

Porter, Michael E. "The Competitive Advantage of Nations," *Harvard Business Review*, vol. 68, no. 2 (March/April 1990).

———. *On Competition* (Boston, MA: Harvard Business School Press, 1998).

Radosevich, Raymond and Kassicieh, Suleiman. "Strategic Challenges and Proposed Responses to Competitiveness Through Public-Sector Technology," *California Management Review*, vol. 35, no. 4 (Summer 1993) .

Roth, Kendall. "International Configuration and Coordination Archetypes for Medium-Sized Firms in Global Industries," *Journal of International Business Studies*, vol. 23, no. 3 (Third Quarter 1992).

Roth, Kendall and Morrison, Allen J. "An Empirical Analysis of the Integration–Responsiveness Framework in Global Industries," *Journal of International Business Studies*, vol. 21, no. 4 (Fourth Quarter 1990).

Ruhli, Edwin and Schuppisser, Stefan. "Switzerland and Its Industry in International Competition," *Columbia Journal of World Business*, vol. 29, no. 4 (Winter 1994).

Rugman, Alan M. "Diamond in the Rough," *Business Quarterly*, vol. 55, no. 3 (Winter 1991).

———. "Porter Takes the Wrong Turn," *Business Quarterly*, vol. 56, no. 3 (Winter 1992).

Rugman, Alan M. and D'Cruz, Joseph. "The Double Diamond Model of International Competitiveness: The Canadian Experience," *Management International Review*, vol. 33, no. 2 (Second Quarter 1993).

Rugman, Alan M. and Verbeke, Alain. *Research in Global Strategic Management; Vol. 4: Beyond the Three Generics* (Greenwich, CT: JAI Press, 1993).

———. "Foreign Subsidiaries and Multinational Strategic Management: An Extension and Correction of Porter's Single Diamond Framework," *Management International Review*, vol. 33, no. 2 (Second Quarter 1993).

———. "How to Operationalize Porter's Diamond of Competitive Advantage," *International Executive*, vol. 35, no. 4 (July/August 1993).

Rugman, Alan M. and Waverman, Leonard. "Foreign Ownership and Corporate Strategy," in Leonard Waverman (ed.), *Corporate Globalization Through Mergers and Acquisitions* (Calgary: University of Calgary Press, 1991) .

Scott, Bruce R. "Competitiveness: Self-Help for a Worsening Problem," *Harvard Business Review*, vol. 67, no. 4 (July/August 1989).

Smitka, Michael. "Are US Auto Exports the Growth Industry of the 1990s?" *Sloan Management Review*, vol. 35, no. 1 (Fall 1993).

Chapter 16

EUROPEAN UNION

Contents

Objectives of the chapter

The European Union (EU) is one of the world's largest markets. As a result, many MNEs are now doing business in the EU or are targeting the area in their expansion plans. This chapter examines the EU environment and reviews some of the major strategy considerations that must be addressed by companies doing business in this economic bloc.

The specific objectives of this chapter are to:

1 *Describe* the emerging single European market and the competitive status of the EU in relation to other triad members.
2 *Discuss* how firms carry out an overall strategic analysis of the EU market in terms of competitive intelligence and evaluation of location.
3 *Relate* some of the major strategy issues that must be considered when doing business in the EU, including exporting, strategic alliances and acquisitions, manufacturing considerations, marketing approaches, and management considerations.

ACTIVE LEARNING CASE

France Telecom

A good example of an organization that has become very strong in its home part of the triad is France Telecom, which has built up a major presence in the EU first through strategic alliances and more recently through acquisitions of competitors. It can now use its strong EU home base as a staging ground to enter the North American and Asian markets, as was discussed in the earlier case on Vodafone (in Chapter 8).

With $55.5 billion in revenues in 2004, the state-controlled firm is one of Europe's largest telecommunication companies. The French government recently reduced its shares of the company to just under 50 per cent, but remains its major shareholder. France Telecom has come a long way since 1995, when 75 per cent of its revenues were from fixed-line operations and foreign sales accounted for only 2 per cent of revenues. Today, the French fixed-line business accounts for less than 50 per cent of the company's revenues, and foreign sales account for over 40 per cent of total revenues.

The rise of France Telecom in the European market and its expansion into wireless and Internet are the result of a combination of R&D expenditures, alliances, and strategies. France Telecom R&D is the largest research center in Europe, employing 4,200 people and holding 7,300 patents worldwide. R&D efforts strive to facilitate human interaction through telecommunications. France Telecom has also teamed up with other companies to complement its research efforts. It is working with Ericsson to provide integrated operator services for the home. An agreement with Motorola will seek to develop "seamless mobility" services for businesses. Meanwhile, it is collaborating with Nokia to provide mobile access to home multimedia content. These types of partnerships are also used to improve the process through which services are provided. For example, France Telecom and Alcatel are working on developing a new-generation network architecture to unify fixed, wireless, and Internet media.

R&D has helped France Telecom secure a place in the European market. However, the fractured nature of the European market made strategic alliances a necessary element in France Telecom's international strategy. The EU's 25 members lack not only a common language but also a common regulatory system. Each country awards its own mobile licenses, forcing new entrants to make alliances with license holders. In addition, the previous fixed-line companies continue to own much of the local telecom infrastructure, increasing the benefits of partnering up.

Source: Getty Images/Pascal Le Segretain

In 1995, France Telecom joined Telekom and Sprint to form the Global One alliance, which was expected to serve as a springboard into the US market while protecting France Telecom's home market from competition by Telekom. In 1999, Sprint was purchased by MCI World, effectively voiding the alliance. In the same year, Deutsche Telekom also rescinded its obligations when it sought a merger with Telecom Italia. As a result, France Telecom redesigned its international strategy and began to compete directly with Deutsche Telekom in the German market by purchasing 17 per cent of E-plus, the country's third largest mobile phone operator. This marked a turning point for France Telecom's international strategy. The company now favors acquisitions over alliances.

In January 2000, France Telecom purchased the Global One alliance from its partners, an event that marked the beginning of a purchasing spree. Later that year, it bought Orange (UK) from Vodafone. Orange had a presence in 20 countries around the world, including 13 in Europe. France Telecom combined its own mobile business with that of Orange to create Europe's second largest mobile phone company. This acquisition was also a strategic move into the UK market. The firm's biggest competitor, Deutsche Telekom, had already purchased One2One in the UK. With 12.2 million active customers, Orange was the largest mobile operator in the UK, catapulting France Telecom into the big leagues.

France Telecom also purchased Equant NV and Freeserve in 2000. Equant NV was combined with Global One under the name Equant. The new company is a corporate service provider in 220 countries and has 3,700 large business

▶

471

The European Union (EU)

⬤ EU member

Year joined

Sources: *The World Factbook*, 1993–94; *The Europa World Year Book*, 1993

Finland 1995

Sweden 1995

Estonia 2004

Latvia 2004

Lithuania 2004

Ireland 1973

Denmark 1973

United Kingdom 1973

Netherlands 1967

Belgium 1967

Germany 1967

Poland 2004

Luxembourg 1967

Czech Republic 2004

Slovakia 2004

France 1967

Austria 1995

Hungary 2004

Slovenia 2004

Portugal 1986

Italy 1967

Spain 1986

Greece 1981

Malta 2004

Cyprus 2004

and is responsible for making major policy decisions for the union. The Council could now pass most proposals with a majority vote, in contrast to the unanimous vote needed previously. This opened the door for much faster progress toward both political and economic integration among member countries. Twelve of the EU15 countries have now adopted a single European currency, the euro, and have committed to a social charter, complete harmonization of social and economic policies, a common defense policy, and related measures that increase the power of the EU bureaucracy in Brussels.

Will the EU eventually bring about a **single European market (SEM)** in which the above stated goals are achieved? This will depend on the extent of progress in the area of free movement of goods and the practice of government procurement. It will also depend on whether the 10 new countries admitted in 2004, and any others that join in the future, can be harmoniously integrated.

Free movement of goods

There have been no customs duties between most EU members since March 1, 1986. Most technical, safety, and other standards and regulations for trade have now been standardized throughout the EU. However, free movement of goods has been hampered by fragmented local markets. This fragmentation has been created by exploiting language differences between countries and by setting artificially high prices for goods. With the growth of

Single European market (SEM)

A market consisting of all members of the EU, bound together by a single currency, a special charter, complete harmonization of social and economic policies, and a common defense policy discount stores, mail order houses, cross-border buying deals, and e-commerce these differences are gradually being eliminated.

The EU has also created a single currency, the euro,[4] which some believe will challenge the US dollar's dominance of international trade and finance.[5] In January 2002, the euro officially replaced individual countries' coins and bank notes in 12 of the EU15 members.[6] The 10 new entrants cannot yet join the monetary union. The common currency, originally used as a benchmark and now as the only currency, has allowed buyers to use comparative shopping in seeking the lowest prices.[7] In the process, this development has helped generate new opportunities for both EU businesses as well as for foreign MNEs doing business there.[8]

Practice of government procurement

EU government procurements account for close to 16 per cent of the union's gross domestic product (GDP).[9] In the past it has been common to find governments awarding contracts to national firms. However, with the emergence of the SEM and the Government Procurement Agreement (GPA), this is diminishing. The result will be greater efficiency, lower cost, and an economically stronger common market. On the other hand, it is important to realize that, in implementing this strategy, many companies are likely to find themselves losing business to competitors in other EU countries that can provide higher quality and service and lower cost. This development will also probably be somewhat slow in coming because of the possible negative impact of the economic growth of individual countries and the desire to favor national firms when awarding government contracts. For instance, despite the GPA, which obliges EU members to publish large tenders, in 1999 the European Commission sent "reasoned opinions" for not publishing tenders—the second stage on infringement procedures—to seven member states.[10] In 2004, a British government-commissioned study denounced the difficulties faced by British firms when competing for procurement contracts in other EU nations. Only 10 per cent of all government contracts in the EU are awarded to foreign firms, compared to 20 per cent in the private sector. It is not that the rules of government procurement are faulty but that governments evade them to favor domestic firms. For example, all contracts above a certain value must be publicly advertised but at least one government circumvented this rule by splitting the job into two smaller contracts.[11]

Meanwhile, the EU continues to try to improve cross-border access to government procurement contracts. It has sought to standardize the procurement process to overcome language barriers. For example, in 2001 the European Commission proposed a common vocabulary to be used in all public procurement notices that would standardize the procurement process and increase competition.[12]

Enlargement of the EU

The ascension of 10 members into the EU in 2004 has changed the panorama of the union and raised question about the feasibility of a truly integrated region, economically and politically. With the exception of the war on Iraq, the EU15 had been able to maintain a relatively common front in regards to foreign policy. The EU's largest members disagreed on whether or not to support a US invasion of Iraq. France and Germany opposed the war while Britain strongly supported it.[13] Despite this, the union has been able to present a unified stance on a number of other international matters, including aid to poorer nations and other wars. The inclusion of 10, mostly central European nations, into the union has added a new factor that further complicates reaching a consensus. Most of the new members are pro-American politically and aspire to their economic system, including low corporate taxation. This contrasts with the policies of Germany and France, two founding members that rely heavily on government involvement and often disagree with US foreign policy. Britain is more aligned with their views, but it stands as a less involved member in the EU when contrasted with France and Germany. Another topic of disagreement is Russia. Both Germany and France have good relations with Russia, whereas the new members see it with distrust. A common foreign policy is now less likely to emerge.

In addition, these 10 new countries have not been fully integrated into the union. The prospect of a flood of cheap labor into the EU15 nations created a negative reaction from EU15 citizens. These new members, therefore, remain outside the Schengen zone of passport-free travel for at least a couple of years and cannot work in most EU15 countries for at least another six years. Indeed, only Britain, Ireland, and Sweden have opened their borders to workers from new member nations. The 10 members have also been excluded from receiving the full amount of farm subsidies available to EU15 members. This is partly due to the expense of subsidizing farmers but also because the lower cost of producing in the new member countries would destabilize the EU15 member's agricultural industry. In addition, the EU, the US, and Japan are under increasing pressure from less developed countries to eliminate farm subsidies all together. Offering full subsidies to the 10 new members would only exacerbate the situation if the EU decided to phase out agricultural subsidies. Nonetheless, new members are finding the EU15 a welcoming market for their agricultural products; which are still competitive because of the lower costs of producing in their countries.[14] Future enlargement is likely to follow the same or even more restrictive rights for new members.

Further enlargement also threatens to increase the differences among member countries, stymieing political and economic integration. In particular, the possibility that Turkey might join the union has created a lot of tension within the EU. Turkey's mainly Islamic population is the size of all 10 new members put together, and the country has a relatively younger population that could have an impact on the political future of the aging EU. Many nationalist groups within the EU are against Turkey joining the union and, indeed, see any further enlargement as a dilution of their power within the union.[15] It is difficult to predict whether the EU25 has the potential to be as integrated politically and economically as did the EU15. For the time being, however, there is internal disagreement about further integration. In 2005, 55 per cent of French voters turned down a proposed EU constitution that would streamline EU institutions. The constitution has already been ratified by nine member countries.[16]

✔ Active learning check

Review your answer to Active Learning Case question 1 and make any changes you like. Then compare your answer with the one below.

1 Describe the stages by which France Telecom has built up a successful strategic base in the EU. What barriers to integration had to be overcome in the EU before France Telecom could buy up rival companies?

As a state-owned monopoly, France Telecom originally had a strong presence in its own market but relied heavily on fixed-line operations and had no significant international presence. Faced with deregulation, France Telecom sought to compete regionally but understood that to do so it had to have competitive products and access to international markets. Investment in R&D allowed the company to expand its product line while strategic alliances were sought to protect its market and expand into others. The Global One alliance with Telekom provided a period of competitive shelter from one of its major EU competitors. By the time this alliance was dissolved in 1999, France Telecom had the capacity to compete alone against major EU telecommunication companies and had begun to acquire companies to solidify its product line and enter new EU markets.

For France Telecom to be able to purchase rival firms, deregulation of telecommunications markets of individual countries in the EU had to occur. In addition, France Telecom acquisitions must overcome antitrust legislation in the EU.

The competitive status of the EU

The eventual emergence of an integrated EU will help greater Europe compete more effectively with the other triad members.[17] However, several EU countries are currently at a competitive disadvantage in some areas.

Productivity

High wages, salaries, and fringe benefits put some EU15 firms at a disadvantage in competing with their US and Japanese counterparts. Labor laws in all EU15 countries make it extremely difficult to fire employees once they have been employed for a year. US companies have much greater freedom and flexibility in hiring and firing their workers on short notice. This means that employees must remain productive to retain their jobs and that companies can adjust more readily to changes in demand for their product or service. Japanese firms tend to treat their workers as a fixed cost and so find the practice of firing to be unnecessary; employees are grateful to their employers and are willing to work hard to upgrade their skills and increase the company's economic performance.

With some success, EU15 firms are working to raise their productivity and match that of their major triad competitors. In 2003, EU15 hourly compensation costs for production workers in manufacturing was 9.4 per cent higher than in the United States and 19.7 per cent higher than in Japan (see Table 16.2). Over the last few years, cooperation between EU15 workers and companies to protect jobs has decreased hourly salaries.[18] Nevertheless, this decrease has been offset by the increase of the euro against the dollar. (Also, see the box **International Business Strategy in Action: German management gets tough** in Chapter 12.)

Investment spending

Investment spending in EU countries has traditionally lagged behind. Part of this can be explained by rapid increases in wages and benefits during the 1980s that were not offset by increases in productivity. As a result, EU firms found themselves without the capital to invest and had to resort to borrowing. Demands for loans resulted in higher interest rates, which also put a strain on investors. By the late 1980s EU government spending had risen to approximately 50 per cent of GDP (in contrast to about 30 per cent for the US and Japan).[19] Because of this, taxes were raised, thus limiting funds and forcing interest rates

Table 16.2 Hourly compensation costs in manufacturing, 1995–2003

Country/region	1995	2003	% change (1995–2003)
EU15	21.33	24.05	12.8
of which			
France	19.26	21.13	9.7
Germany	30.08	29.91	(0.6)
Italy	15.91	18.35	15.3
Netherlands	24.03	26.84	11.7
Portugal	5.09	6.23	22.4
Spain	12.7	14.96	17.8
United Kingdom	13.79	20.37	47.7
New EU members			
Czech Republic	2.53	4.71	86.2
United States	17.02	21.97	29.1
Japan	23.55	20.09	(14.7)

Source: US Department of Labor, Bureau of Labor Statistics, November 2004.

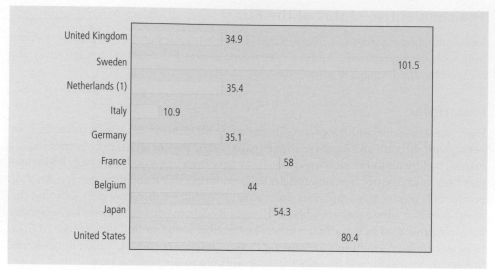

Figure 16.1 Productivity: percentage increase in output per hour, 1992–2003
Source: US Department of Labor, Bureau of Labor Statistics, February 2005.

even higher. More recently, EU economies have been doing much better, stabilizing government spending. Despite this, most European countries continue to perform below the US level in terms of both annual increases and overall productivity. (See Figure 16.1.)

Education

Another area in which EU countries have failed to maintain a competitive edge is education. While all three triad groups spend approximately 5 per cent of GDP on education, the approaches are different. In Europe, most vocational training is provided at the high school level, whereas in the United States and Japan it comes later. Moreover, in the US a higher percentage of the population attends college than in Europe or Japan. The European university curriculum is more theoretical than in either the US or Japan. European educational institutions are also more rigid and less able to adapt to the changing needs of business, and there is less interaction between European educational institutions and industry. As a result, many European students receive training that is inappropriate for the employment needs of European business and industry. This in part explains the extremely high unemployment rates in the age group under 25 in many regions of Europe. The major challenge for European countries will be to modify their education systems and make them more flexible, more practical, and better able to adapt to the changing demands of industry.

Overall evaluation

In overall terms, the EU15 has traditionally lagged behind its triad competitors. As Table 16.3 shows, in 1989 all the EU15 countries ranked in the top 22 most competitive nations in the world. By 2004 only 8 of the group were on this list. The world is becoming a more competitive place, and some EU countries are finding it hard to keep up.

What changes are likely to occur in the future? One is an increase in acquisition and mergers among EU firms and between them and companies from outside the bloc. A second change is the emergence of new technologies that will be developed in EU laboratories. A third is additional free trade agreements and other economic arrangements among European countries that are designed to make the EU a stronger, more competitive market.

Table 16.3 The world's most competitive nations, 1989 and 2005

Rank	1989	2005
1	Japan	United States
2	Switzerland	Hong Kong
3	United States	Singapore
4	Canada	Iceland
5	**Germany**	Canada
6	**Finland**	**Finland**
7	**Netherlands**	**Denmark**
8	**Sweden**	Switzerland
9	Norway	Australia
10	Australia	**Luxembourg**
11	**United Kingdom**	Taiwan
12	**Denmark**	**Ireland**
13	France	**Netherlands**
14	**Belgium/Luxembourg**	**Sweden**
15	Austria	Norway
16	Ireland	New Zealand
17	New Zealand	**Austria**
18	**Spain**	Bavaria
19	**Italy**	Chile
20	Turkey	Zhejiang
21	**Portugal**	Japan
22	**Greece**	**United Kingdom**

Sources: Adapted from IMD and World Economic Forum, *The World Competitiveness Report 1989*, and IMD, *The World Competitiveness Yearbook 2005* (**www.imd.ch**).

 Active learning check

Review your answer to Active Learning Case question 2 and make any changes you like. Then compare your answer with the one below.

2 To what extent is the triad strategy of France Telecom the same as that of Vodafone (in Chapter 8)? Are there any differences?

Both Vodafone and France Telecom have a stronger presence in the European market than in any other triad market. Acquisitions have been a major part of both their strategies to gain technology and market share in their own triad region and in other triad markets. One difference is Vodafone's continued reliance on alliances, such as its joint venture with Bell Atlantic, whereas France Telecom no longer seeks alliances but equity in competitors. Another difference is that the extent of Vodafone's international expansion is much larger than France Telecom's, including not only a strong presence in Japan but also an investment in non-triad countries.

CONDUCTING A STRATEGIC ANALYSIS

As we have seen, the EU is likely to be a very competitive market in the future. In preparing to do business in the EU, foreign MNEs must first conduct an overall strategic analysis, focusing on the competitive nature of the industry being targeted. Assuming that the enterprise intends to set up operations by FDI or alternative investments rather than merely export to the market, the analysis must also evaluate location. The following section examines both of these activities.

adding to Jaguar (bought in 1989), Aston Martin, and Land Rover.

On the face of it, the overall Ford Group, combining the core brands group and the European-centered PAG, appears to be one of the more global of the largest auto firms. It is, however, still heavily regional and primarily US-oriented. The relative lack of integration among the group companies further underlines its regional structure. Volvo is a case in point.

First produced in Gothenburg, Sweden, Volvos were initially designed to survive the rough roads and winter cold of Sweden. This emphasis on durability was eventually transformed into the concern for passenger safety upon which the company's reputation was built. Before the takeover, Volvo had made 70 per cent of its cars in Sweden but had 90 per cent of its sales abroad. The firm had developed as a high-quality niche manufacturer of safe vehicles, competing against rivals such as Saab, BMW, Audi, and Mercedes.

Volvo is listed as a "Center of Excellence for Safety" within the Ford Group and a "Center of Excellence for Telematics"

within the PAG, but this simply means that its research and product development in these areas are monitored by other group companies. Volvo's major plants are in Sweden, Belgium, and the Netherlands (operated by Nedcar), where it made 398,631 vehicles in 2002 (plus assembly units in South Africa, Thailand, and Malaysia). The company has a Swedish President and CEO and a very Swedish/North European organizational structure and culture.

The need to clearly differentiate and segment individual brands is one major factor underlying the structural separation and cultural distinctiveness of the group companies in Ford. As discussed above, customizing auto designs and marketing campaigns to regional and even national markets is still a central part of the business.

Websites: **www.volvo.com** and **www.ford.com**.

Sources: Ford, *Annual Report*, 2003; Alex Taylor III, "Volvo and Saab," *Fortune*, July 21, 1997; Christine Tierney, "Will Volvo Become Just Another Ford?," *BW Online*, December 10, 2001; and Christopher Brown-Humes, "Volvo Exceeds Earnings Forecasts," *FT.com*, February 11, 2002.

Western Europe's world market share rose from 30 to 39 per cent. An international survey reveals that US auto suppliers believed Europe promised the greatest potential for them because it is the largest single market in the world, has an industry structure that is similar to that in the United States, and offers a source of low-cost manufacturing.[23] As a result, companies like GM and Ford expanded their European presence through greater foreign direct investment and strategic alliances. Companies in a host of other industries, from computers to consumer goods, are following suit, and many are finding that regions and municipalities are prepared to provide investment incentives to encourage this activity.

Table 16.4 Comparison of investment incentives in selected EU countries based on an actual project evaluation

Source: Adapted from Maria Brindlmayer, "Comparing EC Investment Incentives and Getting the Best Deal," *Journal of European Business*, November/December 1990, p. 38.

Regional incentives

Investment incentives take a number of forms, including grants, low-interest loans, reduced land prices, and training support for personnel. For example, both Poland and Slovakia offered incentives to the South Korean auto maker Kia to lure investment for a new manufacturing plant.[24] Table 16.4, which was constructed for the purpose of evaluating a specific project, provides a general comparison of investment incentives in several major EU countries. It shows that incentives vary from country to country. Some of these incentives are available for only several years, whereas others remain in effect for a much longer time.

Typically, incentives are higher when (1) the region is economically depressed, (2) many jobs are being created, (3) the company is making a large investment, and/or (4) the investment is likely to attract other investors. Before agreeing to any contract, however, it is important that the deal be "locked in" and that any repayment of subsidies be made clear up front.

Table 16.5 Comparison of location factors: One example

	Port city X (France)	Port city Y (UK)
Labor		
Availability	More attractive	More attractive
Wages (incl. fringes)	More attractive	More attractive
Strike level	More attractive	Less attractive
Utilities		
Telephone penetration	Approximately equal	Approximately equal
Price	More attractive	More attractive
Transport		
Road access	More attractive	More attractive
Rail access	More attractive	More attractive
Air access	Approximately equal	Approximately equal
Water access	Less attractive	Less attractive
Location		
Distance from Germany	More attractive	Approximately equal
Land		
Costs/square yard	More attractive	Approximately equal
Other		
English language education	Approximately equal	More attractive

Between the two sites:
- Less attractive
- Approximately equal
- More attractive

Source: Adapted from Maria Brindlmayer, "Comparing EC Investment Incentives and Getting the Best Deal," *Journal of European Business*, November/December 1990, p. 38.

Other evaluation criteria

Although subsidies can be important incentives, most MNEs doing business in the EU consider them just one element in the evaluation process. Some of the other conditions and costs, described in Table 16.5, include operational costs such as labor, utilities, transportation, and distance from major markets. A recent survey conducted among 1,000 European companies that were not seeking financial assistance revealed that the most important location factors, in order of importance, were (1) access to customers, (2) quality of labor, (3) expansion prospects, (4) level of wage costs, (5) attractive environment, (6) access to suppliers, (7) non-financial regional assistance, (8) absence of restrictions for expansion, (9) infrastructure, (10) level of rents, and (11) public transportation.[25] Another factor often mentioned is the ease with which a company that is not doing well can withdraw. This includes laying off workers, selling facilities, and other factors involved in exiting a market. Gathering location data and the negotiating terms can take a considerable amount of time, but the results often justify the investment.

STRATEGY ISSUES

Many issues have been addressed in this book. We now focus on those that need to be considered when doing business in the European Union, including (1) an overall strategic analysis, (2) the feasibility of exporting, (3) the value of strategic acquisitions and alliances, (4) marketing considerations, (5) manufacturing approaches, and (6) management considerations. The following section briefly examines each issue.

Overall strategic analysis for the European Union

National responsiveness
The ability of MNEs to understand different consumer tastes in segmented regional markets and to respond to different national standards and regulations imposed by autonomous governments and agencies

In formulating a strategy for doing business in the EU, we should look at both the process of globalization through economic integration and the need for a firm to be **nationally responsive**.[26] This is done on the matrix in Figure 16.2. The horizontal axis represents political sovereignty and the need for a firm to be nationally responsive. We call this the "national responsiveness" axis. As a political axis, it takes into account both consumer tastes and government regulations. The vertical axis, or "integration" axis, represents globalization through economic integration. This includes the need to develop economies of scale,

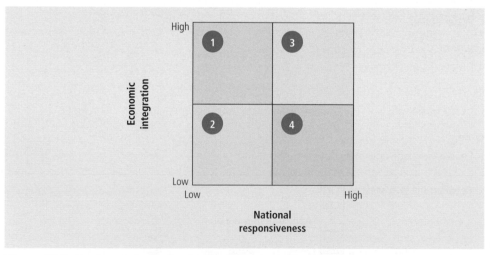

Figure 16.2 Business strategies for the EU

Source: Alan M. Rugman and Alain Verbeke, "Europe 1992 and Competitive Strategies for North American Firms," *Business Horizons*, November/December 1991, p. 77.

use a value-added strategy, and reap the benefits of greater coordination and control of geographically dispersed activities.

Quadrants 1 and 4 in Figure 16.2 present relatively simple strategy situations. Quadrant 1 requires a strategy in which the MNE does not need to be concerned with national responsiveness. The company is in a market driven by high integration and its strategy must be on achieving price competitiveness. Firms operating in this quadrant are often centralized in structure and thus can use mergers and acquisitions to benefit from high economic integration. Companies selling microcomputers frequently operate in quadrant 1.

In quadrant 4, economic integration is less important than national responsiveness, so the MNE must focus on adapting products to satisfy the specific demands of each country. In this case, integration is minimized in favor of a decentralized strategy of national responsiveness designed to appeal to select niches and target groups. Companies selling food products and designer clothes use this approach.

In quadrant 2, there is low integration and low national responsiveness. The potential of obtaining economies of scale and benefits of national or regional responsiveness are both small. MNEs operating in this quadrant are vulnerable to triad competitors. There is no advantage in centralized quality control or economies of scale and no ability to adapt activities to individual countries. MNEs selling inexpensive toys that are undifferentiated fall into this quadrant.

MNEs in quadrant 3 use a strategy of high integration and high national responsiveness characterized by strong price competitiveness and select target positioning. This is the most challenging quadrant to implement; the firm's organization structure is complex, but it is the one in which many successful triad-based adaptive multinationals operate. Auto companies fall into this quadrant.

A close look at events in the EU reveals that Brussels' administrators designed a strategy to help European firms move into quadrant 1. The plan is designed to create a natural entry barrier to outside firms and help ensure the success of local competitors. A survey of the top management of Europe's 300 largest corporations has confirmed this tendency toward integration. The survey found that European managers anticipate greater integration due to such developments as strategic partnerships, mergers, and takeovers as well as increasing economies of scale.[27] As a result, the managers expect the development of more efficient modern industries. The survey also found European managers were confident that economic integration was a viable strategy for them but would be detrimental to non-European MNEs. Only 9 per cent of the managers believed US firms would gain ground in Europe, whereas 42 per cent said US firms would lose competitive strength.

Exporting firms operate in quadrant 4. As outsiders in the EU, US firms will find it increasingly difficult to export to Europe and compete on economies of scale in the face of

---

✔ Active learning check

Review your answer to Active Learning Case question 3 and make any changes you like. Then compare your answer with the one below.

3 **In what ways will globalization and localization (sovereignty) be important issues for conducting mergers in the EU?**

Companies successfully operating in different EU countries will seek mergers to achieve some economies of scale in R&D, design, sourcing, and distribution, among others. Nevertheless, the benefits of economies of scale have to be weighed against the need to tailor-make products for customers in different markets. Globalization will therefore occur only in some sectors of the merged company.

integration by rival EU firms. Not only will costs be higher for exporters, but locally based competitors will have more access to competitive information. As a result, during the millennium many exporting firms will be switching from exporting to FDI in order to meet the new nature of competition in Europe.

Exporting

Those firms that continue to export to the EU will have to address a number of legal/ financial matters. The following sections examine some of the most important issues. (See Table 16.6.)

Table 16.6 Direction of EU15 trade, 1994-2003

Country/region	Exports to				Imports from			
	1994 (billions of euros)	% of total	2003 (billions of euros)	% of total	1994 (billions of euros)	% of total	2003 (billions of euros)	% of total
EU15*	1,023.1	61.9	1,776.1	61.5	954.7	60.1	1,644.5	59.0
Austria	39.4	2.4	63.6	2.2	30.2	1.9	48.6	1.7
Belgium/Luxembourg	93.3	5.6	168.9	5.8	86.6	5.5	159.4	5.7
Denmark	20.2	1.2	37.7	1.3	18.2	1.1	37.4	1.3
Finland	13.2	0.8	27.7	1.0	19.7	1.2	27.5	1.0
France	166.0	10.0	273.6	9.5	145.7	9.2	219.2	7.9
Germany	229.5	13.9	347.6	12.0	223.9	14.1	396.9	14.2
Greece	14.1	0.9	26.5	0.9	5.3	0.3	7.2	0.3
Ireland	16.3	1.0	36.4	1.3	21.7	1.4	64.7	2.3
Italy	96.4	5.8	175.0	6.1	97.8	6.2	145.6	5.2
Netherlands	93.1	5.6	142.9	4.9	101.5	6.4	188.7	6.8
Portugal	20.3	1.2	40.4	1.4	13.8	0.9	26.8	1.0
Spain	61.6	3.7	148.8	5.1	49.0	3.1	103.6	3.7
Sweden	33.1	2.0	57.5	2.0	35.8	2.3	55.3	2.0
United Kingdom	126.4	7.6	229.6	7.9	105.3	6.6	163.7	5.9
	—		—		—		—	
Other Western Europe	76.0	4.6	109.3	3.8	76.1	4.8	122.0	4.4
Iceland	0.8	0.1	1.8	0.1	1.1	0.1	1.9	0.1
Norway	19.9	1.2	29.3	1.0	26.6	1.7	55.2	2.0
Switzerland	55.3	3.3	78.3	2.7	48.5	3.1	64.8	2.3
	—		—		—			
Developing Europe	95.7	5.8	267.2	9.2	87.2	5.5	255.2	9.2
	—		—				—	
Total Europe	1,194.8	72.3	2,152.6	74.5	1,118.0	70.4	2,021.6	72.5
	—		—				—	
Non-European	458.6	27.7	736.1	25.5	470.2	29.6	765.0	27.5
of which	—		—		—		—	
United States	122.4	7.4	251.4	8.7	123.0	7.7	176.7	6.3
Japan	34.5	2.1	45.2	1.6	69.0	4.3	79.3	2.8
	—		—				—	
Total	1,653.4	100.0	2,888.7	100.0	1,588.2	100.0	2,786.6	100.0

* Exports and imports from and to the EU refer to intra-EU trade.

Source: IMF, *Direction of Trade Statistics Yearbook*, 2004 and 2001.

Customs duties and taxes

Goods manufactured outside the EU are subject to customs duties at the point of entry. These duties are determined by an EU-wide tariff system that establishes common rates regardless of entry point. Most duties are based on the value of the good ad valorem, which in turn depends on the stage of assembly or completion of the end product.

Product standards

Products exported to the EU must meet standards and technical regulations. Many of these are common throughout the bloc, but when they are not the product must meet the standards of the country to which it is exported. In many cases, products made in outside countries must be modified in order to gain EU entry.[28]

Conducting export operations

In recent years, many US exporters of both goods and services have consolidated their operations with those of European companies, helping them to surmount EU barriers. For example, US accounting firms typically operate through local partnerships. Other examples are management consulting firms with international operations that help address the needs of local clients and law firms with overseas offices.

Those MNEs that do choose to export to the EU must carefully select their agents and distributors. Five steps are critical to this process:

1 Examine the legal and business considerations involved in appointing foreign intermediaries and establish criteria that reflect the particular geographic market.

2 Assemble a list of potential candidates by using the various directories and consulting with other sources of information.

3 Qualify such candidates by applying certain criteria and conducting a preliminary interview.

4 Visit the proposed intermediary to obtain additional information about its resources and facilities, to get a proper feeling for the intermediary's compatibility with the organization, and to check the objectives of the agent or distributor.

5 After selecting an agent or distributor, (a) negotiate an agreement that is fair and mutually beneficial, (b) comply in good faith with the terms of the agreement, (c) continue communication between the parties, and (d) make occasional adjustments in the relationship in response to changing circumstances.[29]

Many small and intermediate MNEs will continue to export to the EU because it is too expensive for them to use any other route. Large MNEs, on the other hand, are turning more and more to strategic acquisitions and alliances.

Strategic acquisitions and alliances

Two of the most popular ways of gaining a foothold in the EU are strategic acquisitions and alliances. (See the box **International Business Strategy in Action: Kingfisher as a European retailer**.) A *Harvard Business Review* study analyzed 49 strategic alliances and concluded that the chances of success are improved if the parties keep five guidelines in mind: (1) acquisitions work better than alliances when developing core businesses; (2) alliances are effective when firms want to gain entry into new geographic markets or businesses that are tangential to the core business; (3) alliances between strong and weak companies typically do not work well; (4) alliances that last are characterized by an ability to move beyond the initially established expectations and objectives; and (5) alliances are

INTERNATIONAL BUSINESS STRATEGY *IN ACTION*

Kingfisher as a European retailer

In a study of the profitability of foreign assets, a British retailer, Kingfisher, was top of the pack. Its average return on foreign assets was 32 per cent for 1996 and 1997, well above the average of 4.78 per cent for the world's top 500 MNEs. What's more, in that period Kingfisher only had 9 per cent of its total assets in foreign markets, but by 1999 had increased this to 40 per cent.

Kingfisher leveraged its foreign assets to promote growth. Its first successful acquisition was of the French electrical retailer Darty, followed in 1998 by a merger with French do-it-yourself retailer Castorama. Kingfisher also had other operations across Europe: in Belgium, the Netherlands, and Germany. It moved into Asia with the acquisition of an electrical retail chain in Singapore in 1998, and is also in Taiwan.

Formed in 1989, Kingfisher consisted of the British Woolworth's Stores, Comet (electrical products), Superdrug, and B&Q (home improvement stores). In 1998 total sales revenues for Kingfisher were £6.4 billion (about US$10 billion). There were 2,500 stores in 13 countries, principally in Britain and France, with retail brand stores operating in chains across Britain. The CEO, Sir Geoffrey Mulcahy, has led the growth drive. He tried to consolidate Kingfisher's leading position in Britain by merging with the large supermarket chain Asda. In 1999, Asda was the third largest British supermarket chain behind Sainsbury and Tesco. However, Wal-Mart has now bought Asda.

Sir Geoffrey Mulcahy also has provided leadership in foreign expansion through patience and strategic initiative. The merger with Castorama took five years to negotiate, as did the earlier one with Darty. The French managers and workers keep their jobs because "retail is detail" and local knowledge is vital. While its foreign businesses operate autonomously, the Kingfisher group as a whole realizes logistical savings and scale economies in purchasing. Sir Geoffrey has positioned Kingfisher to ride the wave of growth through profitable international expansion.

Another popular way of doing business in the EU is through the use of strategic alliances. Experts agree that four of the most important steps include:

1 Pick a compatible partner and take the time to get to know and trust it.

2 Choose a partner with complementary products or markets, rather than one that competes directly.

3 Be patient and do not rush into a deal or expect immediate results.

4 Learn about the partner's technology and management but try not to give away your own core secrets.

In some alliances, one partner has taken advantage of the other by stealing technology or forcing the partner into a position in which it had to sell out to the other. However, this will not happen if both sides make substantive contributions to the undertaking and each realizes that it needs the other. Moreover, even when alliances have not worked out, companies have found it in their best interest to continue looking for other partners for other deals.

In 2001, Kingfisher sold its Superdrug chain and floated its Woolworth chain. It refocused in home improvement retailing under the B&Q, Screwfix, Castorama, and Brico Depot chains. Kingfisher might hold a substantial amount of its assets internationally, but most of this international expansion has remained regional. In 2005, 92.7 per cent of its stores were located in the EU25 and over 87 per cent within the EU15. This can be seen in the table below. Indeed, almost 90 per cent of the company's revenue came from the UK, Ireland, and France.

Geographic distribution of Kingfisher Stores, 2005

Country	No. of stores	% of total
UK	334	55.8
Ireland	3	0.5
France	167	27.9
Poland	25	4.2
Italy	22	3.7
Spain	4	0.7
EU25	**555**	**92.7**
Turkey	5	0.8
China	21	3.5
Taiwan	18	3.0
Total	599	100.0

Source: Kingfisher, *Annual Report*, 2005.

Websites: www.kingfisher.co.uk; www.asda.co.uk; www.j-sainsbury.co.uk; www.tesco.com; and www.walmart.com.

Sources: Michael V. Gestrin, Rory F. Knight and Alan M. Rugman, *The Templeton Global Performance Index* (Oxford: Templeton College, University of Oxford, 1998); Kingfisher, *Annual Report and Accounts*, 1997, 1998; Corporate Profile: Kingfisher; *The Times* (London), February 1, 1999, p. 44; *Financial Times*, May 18, 1988, December 12, 1989; Bernard M. Wolf, "The Role of Strategic Alliances in the European Automotive Industry," in Alan M. Rugman and Alain Verbeke (eds.), *Research in Global Management*, vol. III (Greenwich, CT: JAI Press, 1992), pp. 143–163.

more likely to be successful when both sides hold an equal amount of financial ownership. In addition, more than three-quarters of the alliances studied ended with one of the parties acquiring full control.[30]

Making strategic alliances work

It is more common to find MNEs using strategic alliances than using acquisitions. Several important steps are involved in making these arrangements work. One is that each partner must complement the other.[31] If one company is strong in R&D and the other's strengths are in manufacturing and marketing, the alliance may be ideal. On the other hand, if both are strong in R&D and weak in manufacturing and marketing, there is no synergy and the two may end up trying to steal secrets from each other and competing rather than cooperating. Second, the goals of the two groups must be carefully spelled out. Once the partners have agreed on the primary criteria such as new product development, increased market share, and return on investment, they can then decide how to commit their resources. These goals provide a basis for overall direction.

The key people from each firm must get to know each other. Building working relationships across the two firms is essential for resolving problems and issues that come up. Communication, networking, and interpersonal relationships are extremely useful in ensuring that the spirit of the alliance is kept alive.

Each group must understand how the other works so that differences can be accommodated. If one partner is responsible for making certain parts and providing them to the other, there must be a clear understanding regarding such matters as product quality and delivery time. If the partner receiving products prefers to accumulate inventory to prevent stockout problems, the other must develop a manufacturing plan that addresses this need.

The parties must hold frequent meetings and develop a trust. The successful alliance between General Electric and Snecma was a result of mutual respect and dependence. The two companies cooperated fully in developing, manufacturing, and marketing commercial jet engines. As a result, the joint venture makes one of the best-selling engines in the world.

Marketing considerations

As the EU develops toward a true economic union, internal barriers to entry and mobility barriers within the bloc will disappear. This will create both challenges and opportunities. In particular, competition is likely to increase as it becomes easier for competitors to invade each other's territories. As a result, marketing strategies in the millennium will have to reflect concern for both pricing and positioning.

Pricing

The European Commission has estimated that the price of goods and services throughout the EU will decline. Five specific developments will make this work: (1) decreasing costs of doing business, now that internal barriers and restrictions have been removed; (2) the opening up of public procurement contracts to broader competition; (3) foreign investment that will increase production capacity; (4) more rigorous enforcement of competition policy; and (5) general intensified competition brought about by economic reforms.[32]

Price will become an even more important marketing factor to the extent that EU customers develop similar tastes and are willing to accept globally standardized products. As this happens, MNEs will be able to sell the same product throughout the bloc without having to make modifications for local tastes. Unfortunately, whereas some goods can be marketed with this strategy, many will require careful positioning for select target groups.

Positioning

Some global products such as Coca-Cola, Pepsi, and Marlboro cigarettes have universal appeal, but these are more the exception than the rule. For example, in the UK the Renault is viewed as a good economy car, but in Spain it is perceived as a luxury automobile. Similarly, in Great Britain and Holland, toothpaste is viewed as a hygiene product and sells much better than in Spain and Greece, where it is marketed as a cosmetic.[33]

As a result, the marketing motto "Plan globally, act locally" will continue to be a useful dictum. A good example is provided by the EU cellular communications market, which offers tremendous opportunities but is also extremely competitive because there are so many submarkets throughout the community. As a result, the mobile communications market will likely end up being divided among a host of major competitors, each of which positions itself for a particular local or regional target group.

✔ Active learning check

Review your answer to Active Learning Case question 4 and make any changes you like. Then compare your answer with the one below.

4 **In what ways will both pricing and positioning be important for companies like France Telecom doing business in the EU?**

Companies like France Telecom must be prepared to take full advantage of the economies from EU integration. Costs must decrease in order to increase market share in the more competitive EU market. At the same time, companies must have access to markets of the EU and market their products according to both customer expectation and profit maximization.

Direct marketing

Another strategy likely to receive a great deal of attention is direct marketing. Most EU firms tailor their products to narrow markets and direct mail is only now gaining attention. Unlike the United States, where businesses have been using telemarketing and other non-traditional channels for well over a decade, this is a new approach for European consumers, and MNEs will have to surmount a number of challenges if they hope to direct-market their product, such as (1) consumers speak different languages, so a universal message or strategy will not work throughout the bloc; (2) inclusion of direct-response telephone numbers in television spots is forbidden by the privacy laws of some member states such as Germany; (3) information about potential clients is fragmented and not easily obtainable; and (4) the infrastructure for direct marketing is weak because credit cards, toll-free numbers, and computer databases are still in their infancy in Europe.[34] In addition, a high credit card fraud rate has slowed down the growth potential of e-commerce.[35] Nevertheless, direct marketing is likely to play a major role in MNE efforts to create a pan-European marketing strategy.

Manufacturing considerations

As individual country regulations are eliminated and EU members continue to standardize rules and regulations, it will be possible to produce uniform goods for the entire market. This will not come about immediately because of the time needed to change such things as electric systems so that toasters, television sets, and other home appliances can all be manufactured with the same type of plugs. However, MNEs will eventually be able to produce many products with standard parts that work in all EU countries. At the same time, manufacturers will continue producing goods that appeal to local market tastes. For example, appliance makers now manufacture self-cleaning ovens for the French because of their tradition of high-temperature cooking. However, they typically leave out this option for the German market, where food is generally cooked at lower temperatures. Some major manufacturing considerations that warrant attention by those doing business in the EU include reducing costs, building factory networks, and entering into R&D alliances.

Reducing costs

One manufacturing benefit of producing for a market with 385 million consumers is the ability to reduce cost per unit through the use of standardized components and large production runs. Under this arrangement, the cost of the components is kept to a minimum and the large production runs allow companies to spread fixed costs over more units. This means the cost per item can be sharply reduced. Moreover, economies of scale can be achieved even when production has to be tailored to local conditions. This is accomplished through the use of delayed differentiation, in which all products are manufactured in the same way for all countries or regions until as late in the assembly process as possible. In these final stages, differentiation is then used to introduce particular features or special components.

MNEs are also using outsourcing and just-in-time inventory systems to lower the cost of carrying parts and supplies. By tailoring deliveries and shipments to the production schedule, factories are able to minimize their investment in materials and work-in-process. This system is also used by large retailers such as Marks & Spencer of the United Kingdom, which employs its electronic network system to keep track of inventory at each store in England, as well as on the continent, and to replenish its outlets as needed.[36]

Another way in which costs are being controlled is by redesigning production processes, thus scrapping old, inefficient techniques in favor of more streamlined methods. This includes careful study of competitive firms in order to identify and copy their successful approaches to cost control. It also entails the elimination of red tape and the use of well-trained, highly motivated work teams.

Factory networks

MNEs in Europe are now beginning to create sophisticated networks of factories that both produce components and finished goods and provide distribution and after-sales services. For example, the Philips television factory in Bruges, Belgium, uses tubes that are supplied from a factory in Germany, transistors from France, plastics produced in Italy, and electronic components that come from another factory in Belgium.

These factory networks are also integrated with computer software packages that can operate in multiple European countries without the need for modification. Figure 16.3 provides an illustration. The software packages allow companies to make supply, production, and distribution decisions while satisfying the requirements of the different legal entities in the countries where they operate. Some specific functions they help companies to perform include forecasting, logistics planning, inventory planning, production planning, and central updating of bills of materials. The software provides each factory manager with the specific information needed and does so in the manager's own language. As a result, MNEs are able to coordinate multiple activities and thereby develop an effective pan-European manufacturing system.

Delayed differentiation
A strategy in which all products are manufactured in the same way for all countries or regions until as late in the assembly process as possible, at which time differentiation is used to introduce particular features or special components

Figure 16.3 **Pan-European manufacturing systems**

Source: Adapted from Nigel Dunham and Robin Morgan, "The Search for a Truly Pan-European Manufacturing System," *Journal of European Business*, September/October 1991, p. 44.

Research and development alliances

Another emerging manufacturing strategy is participation in cooperative R&D programs. In the EU this is taking two complementary paths. First, many companies are teaming up to share R&D expenses. Siemens and Philips have used this approach to develop computer chips, and IBM has a number of agreements with European firms for developing advanced computer technology.

Second, many firms are trying to get some of these costs funded by participating in European cooperative R&D programs. The EU is providing European industry with funding for research in such areas as information technology, biotechnology, and energy. The objective of the program is to stimulate cross-border cooperation and make Europe more productive and competitive in the world market. One of the best-known programs is the **European Research Cooperation Agency** (Eureka, for short), which was launched in 1985 and emphasizes projects in the fields of energy, medicine, biotechnology, communications, information technology, transport, new materials, robotics, production automation, lasers, and the environment.[37] This program has helped develop a European standard for high-definition television (HDTV) and has funded semiconductor research. To date, more than 2,000 organizations have participated in Eureka-related projects. Firms that are interested in participating in these cooperative programs typically do so by carrying out six steps:

European Research Cooperation Agency
A research and development alliance that emphasizes projects in the fields of energy, medicine, biotechnology, communications, information technology, transport, new materials, robotics, production automation, lasers, and the environment

1 Find out if the company is eligible for EU-funded programs.

2 Carefully study the EU rules regarding rights of ownership and dissemination of results.

3 Carefully choose the best location for a European R&D center.

4 Determine those competitors and major customers that are already participating in the program.

5 Gather recommendations from the firm's EU and local management.

6 Put together the company's application for funding.[38]

Management considerations

As more firms enter the EU, there is growing concern over their ability to manage Europeans effectively. Many firms enter the market with preconceived ideas about how to interact with their European partners or employees. Some, for example, believe that management styles that have been effective in their country will also work well in Europe. However, as the Japanese have discovered in the United States, effective management approaches must be tailor-made to meet the needs of the local situation. The primary focus must be on adjusting to cultural differences.

Adjusting to cultural differences

There are a number of differences between US and European workers. For example, Europeans are more accustomed to participating in decision making. They have a long history of worker participation programs and of holding seats on the board of directors.

Another difference is employee motivation. Researchers have found that quality of work life is extremely important in Scandinavian countries, whereas opportunities for individual achievement are of particular importance in the United Kingdom. French workers are interested in individual achievement but place strong emphasis on security. German workers place high value on both advancement and earnings.[39] Clearly, no universal list of motivators can be applied throughout the EU. These facts illustrate the importance of MNEs having a global perspective as well as having managers who are focused on the country-specific needs of the area in which they are working.

Barriers to EU market access

Throughout this book, we have explored the need for access to triad markets. Unfortunately, although the EU has become the world's largest market, some EU-based MNEs have sought to restrict access to this area. The overall trend during the postwar period has been toward an increasingly liberalized trade environment, but international managers nonetheless must know how to deal with, or at least anticipate, the use of administrative barriers in foreign markets.

The two most common trade law entry barriers are countervailing duty (CVD) laws and antidumping (AD) laws. (These were discussed earlier in Chapters 6 and 15.) While the United States uses CVD as an entry barrier (it had 90 per cent of the world's CVD cases in the 1980s), the EU uses AD. Both **countervailing duties (CVD)** and **antidumping duties (AD)** are import tariffs intended to protect domestic producers from harmful dumping and subsidization by foreign governments. However, it has been demonstrated in several studies that these laws have been "captured" and used by weak firms seeking shelter from strong competition by rival MNEs in the triad.[40]

Table 16.7 shows both the high number of AD cases that were launched and the tendency toward sectoral concentration in the use of AD by EU firms during the period from 1998 to 2002. Many AD cases were brought in the chemical, electronics, iron and steel, and other "mature" sectors that have weak firm-specific advantages (FSAs).

The use of these trade law instruments to provide shelter is by no means unique to the EU, as the earlier discussion of AD and CVD in Chapter 15 showed.[41] However, from Table 16.7 it is clear that non-EU firms in the chemical, electronics, and iron and steel sectors should probably anticipate some resistance if they plan to begin exporting to the EU market with a view to competing with domestic producers.

Figure 16.4 shows the rationale for the use of AD and CVD laws by particular firms. As with all free-market economies, the EU economy has, at any given point in time, a significant number of firms in difficulty due to the pressure of global competition. These firms

Countervailing duties (CVD)
Import tariffs intended to protect domestic producers from harmful subsidization by foreign governments

Antidumping duties (AD)
Import tariffs intended to protect domestic producers from foreign products sold at less than their cost of production or at lower prices than in their home market

Table 16.7 EU antidumping cases investigated by sector, 1998–2002

Description	1998	1999	2000	2001	2002
Chemicals and allied products	0	28	17	5	5
Textile and allied products	9	11	0	5	2
Wood and paper	0	0	0	0	0
Electronics	0	12	2	3	3
Other mechanical engineering	0	5	1	4	4
Iron and steel	19	25	7	16	5
Other metals	0	0	2	0	0
Other	5	2	1	0	4
All products listed	**25**	**45**	**29**	**33**	**23**
Of which antidumping	24	42	21	27	20
Of which antisubsidy	1	3	8	6	3

Source: Commission of the European Communities, *Twenty-First Annual Report from the Commission to the European Parliament on the Communities Anti-Dumping and Anti-Subsidy Activities*, 2002.

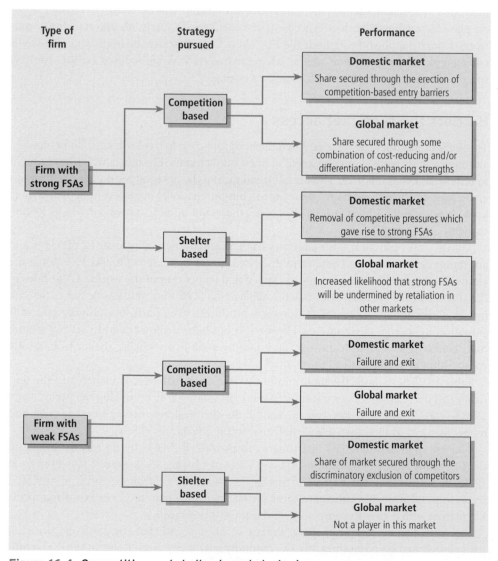

Figure 16.4 Competition and shelter-based strategies

are barely able to compete with their more efficient global rivals and find themselves on the verge of exit from the industry. If the main reason for this is international competition, and domestic administrative instruments are in place that would allow such a firm to continue operating by limiting foreign competition, the company is likely to use these instruments. Such a situation is a rare instance when it is logical for a firm to spend time and money on an activity that is not productive from a competitiveness standpoint. By using AD or CVD laws, the noncompetitive firm is able to remain in operation not by improving its firm-specific advantages but by artificially raising the price at which foreign competitors must sell in the domestic market.

The abusive use of AD and CVD is a particular problem for non-triad members and for MNEs from other parts of the triad because the administration of these trade laws is discretionary and subject to political pressures. Moreover, there is now strong evidence that the administration of these trade laws is biased in favor of domestic plaintiffs and against foreign firms.[42] The technical test of "material injury" due to the subsidies or dumped exports is routinely abused by the responsible administrative agencies in both the EU and the US.[43] This is an extremely serious problem for global business and serves to reinforce the existence of the triad at the expense of a liberalized world trade and investment system.

KEY POINTS

1   The overall objective of the EU is to create a market in which there are no economic barriers to trade between the member countries. When this is achieved, the EU will be the largest economic bloc in the world. However, there are two areas in particular in which additional progress must be made: free movement of goods and the practice of government procurement. In addition, 10 new entrants into the EU have yet to be integrated in terms of adopting the euro and are not yet allowed free movement of labor and passport-free travel. They also threaten the possibility of a unified EU25 foreign policy.

2   The current competitive status of the EU15 lags that of the United States and Japan in a number of areas, including productivity, investment spending, and education. Greater economic strides will be needed if the EU15 is to compete effectively with its triad counterparts.

3   In preparing to do business in the EU, MNEs should focus on the competitive nature of the targeted industry and the evaluation of location. Competitive intelligence gathering involves external information gathering and internal infrastructural analysis. Location evaluation entails the consideration of such factors as regional incentives, operating costs, and distance from major markets.

4   Many aspects of strategy need to be considered when doing business in the EU, including (1) an overall analysis of the environment, (2) the feasibility of exporting, (3) the value of strategic alliances and acquisitions, (4) marketing considerations, (5) manufacturing approaches, and (6) management considerations. Managers need to weigh the choices of economic integration and/or national responsiveness very carefully.

5   The EU has a large internal market. Firms located in the EU can use a new type of non-tariff barrier to entry to keep out rival firms, namely, trade remedy legislation such as countervailing duty laws (CVD) and antidumping (AD) laws. Recent research has found that the use of both CVD and AD is a "shelter" strategy designed to protect uncompetitive domestic firms. However, the more successful EU firms concentrate on the development of sustainable firm-specific advantages rather than on the use of CVD and AD laws.

Key terms

- Single European Act (SEA)
- Council of Ministers
- single European market (SEM)
- coordinated infrastructure
- market coordination infrastructure
- resource-sharing infrastructure
- autonomous infrastructure
- national responsiveness
- delayed differentiation
- European Research Cooperation Agency
- countervailing duties (CVD)
- antidumping duties (AD)

REVIEW AND DISCUSSION QUESTIONS

1 What are the ultimate objectives of the EU? Identify and describe them.

2 Will the EU bring about a single European market? What type of changes will have to take place for this to happen? Identify and describe three of them.

3 What is the competitive status of the EU15 in terms of labor productivity and investment spending? Based on your answer, what is your overall evaluation of this status?

4 How can firms doing business in the EU use competitive intelligence? Identify and describe two major steps that can be used in this process.

5 What types of regional incentives do countries offer MNEs willing to set up operations in their locales? Identify and describe two of them.

6 In addition to regional incentives, what other evaluation criteria should MNEs employ when deciding where in the EU to establish operations? Identify and describe three of them.

7 In formulating a strategy for doing business in the EU, there are two primary areas of initial consideration: national responsiveness and economic integration. What does this statement mean? Be sure to include a discussion of Figure 16.2 in your answer.

8 What do companies that want to export to the EU need to know about doing business there? Discuss five facts or strategies that would be of value to them.

9 In gaining a foothold in the EU, when is it most effective to opt for an acquisition over an alliance? When is a strategic alliance a better choice? In each case, provide an example.

10 Why will marketing strategies in the EU have to reflect a concern for pricing? A concern for positioning? Give an example of when each would be the most important consideration.

11 What is the likely future of direct marketing in the EU? Defend your answer.

12 What are three major manufacturing considerations for companies doing business in the EU? Identify and describe each.

13 How important is it for EU managers to have a global perspective? Be complete in your answer.

14 How can trade laws be used by EU firms to keep out global competitors?

15 What evidence is there that EU firms use antidumping laws?

16 The EU accepted 10 new members into the union in 2004. Are these members fully integrated?

17 How are the 10 new entrants into the union likely to affect employment in the EU15?

REAL CASE

Accor budget hotels

The largest manager of budget-priced hotels in the world is the French hotel management company Accor. In 2004, the company had 7.1 billion euros in revenue and 168,000 employees worldwide. Altogether, it manages a portfolio of 4,000 hotels in 90 countries, of which 2,000 are in the budget and economy class. In the United States, it runs all the Red Roof Inns as well as the Motel 6 chain. In Europe, it manages budget hotels such as Ibis, Formule 1, and Etape Hotels. It also runs all the Novotel, Sofitel, and Mercure hotels in the upper and medium price range.

Accor has developed international capabilities in being a major service provider to the tourist, business travel, and food business sectors. It is developing an international brand name for the group's activities in these areas. It uses B2B and B2C Internet services. There are 860,000 restaurant managers, supermarket suppliers, and other affiliated workers using its B2B services, along with another 300,000 customers/small business people using B2C.

The company began operations in 1967 and rapidly expanded its Novotel hotels across France. The acquisition of another hotel chain in 1974, Courtepailles, established Accor as a major player in the French market. During the next two years the company moved to develop a market presence in the two- and three-star hotel market segment, opening an Ibis two-star hotel in Bordeaux and acquiring the three-star Mercure hotel chain.

The first significant expansion outside France was the 1973 opening of Novotel in Warsaw, Poland. In 1976, Accor opened its first hotel in Brazil and over the next year began to rapidly develop in Latin America. In 1979, Accor entered the US market with hotels in Minneapolis and New York; in 1984 a large Novotel was erected in Broadway. To enter the affordable US hotel market, the Motel 6 chain was purchased in 1990. By acquiring Sofitel in 1980 the company entered the African market and strengthened its position in Europe. In 1986, Accor began development in Asia, including China and Thailand. In preparation for the 2008 Olympic games, Accor has entered a joint venture with the Beijing Tourism Group to manage 50 hotels by 2008.

Accor is also in the travel industry business. In France it owns Carlson Wagonlit Travel and Frantour. Acquiring international travel companies has allowed Accor to complement its international hotel expansion plans. The acquisition of Africatours in 1984 allowed Accor to control the stream of tourism in the region. In 1987, Africatours acquired Asia Tours and America Tours. In 2000, Accor purchased a 38.5 per cent stake in Go Voyages, an e-travel planner that targets the European traveler.

Growing expertise in the hospitality business has also allowed the company to diversify into other areas, including restaurants and casinos. In 2000 it operated more than 100 branches of the Courtepailles restaurants/grills and a dozen Accor casinos, mainly in France.

In December 2001, Accor agreed to purchase Compagnie Européenne de Casinos (CEC) for $233.7 million. The next month, however, the competing Groupe Partouche began acquiring CEC shares at a higher per share price. CEC has 24 casinos across Europe with the majority in France. The move comes at a time of consolidation in the casino industry. In 1996, major chains owned only 20 per cent of French casinos; by 2002 it had increased to 80 per cent. Between them Accor and CEC have a 21 per cent market share in France. France has 170 casinos with revenues totaling 1.895 billion euros and accounts for 40 per cent of the European market. Accor, Européenne de Casinos, Partouche, and Tranchant account for 45 per cent of the French market. Almost 70 per cent of Accor's revenues and profits originate in Europe. North America accounts for about a fifth of Accor's operations.

Websites: www.accorhotels.com; www.accor.com; www.fourseasons.com.

Sources: www.accorhotels.com; Raphael Minder, "Accor May Have to Rethink Casino Offer," *FT.com*, January 3, 2002; Raphael Minder, "Accor to Acquire Casino Group for E258m," *FT.com*, December 17, 2001; "Casinos on Threshold of Recomposition," *La Tribune*, January 3, 2002; "Accor Agrees Chinese JV to Manage Around 50 Hotels by 2008," *AFX Europe*, December 12, 2001; and Anaïs Jouvancy, "European E-Travel Takes Off," *Le Monde Interactif*, November 8, 2000.

1 Why did Accor concentrate on the French and European market before expanding into other regions?

2 How are acquisitions an important part of Accor's expansion strategy?

3 What are the advantages of increasingly relying on the Internet for B2B and B2C?

REAL CASE

Carrefour

Anyone observing French retail giant Carrefour over the last three decades must concede that international expansion is a key part of its strategic plan. Today, it has 6,132 stores in 29 countries. Despite this, in 2003, only 13 per cent of Carrefour's sales originated outside its European home region. Sales outside the region were evenly divided across Asia and Latin America.

In 1996, the French government introduced the "Raffarin law" to restrict the expansion of hypermarkets, with the aim of keeping the French countryside from turning into large warehouse-style retail structures. This in turn would protect the French way of life, in which local food farmers supply small local shops. For Carrefour, this meant that growth of its hypermarket business could come only from acquisitions in its local market or from expanding into foreign markets. Its success at following this strategy has varied considerably because of different competitive environments and cultural differences across regions.

In the United States, Carrefour opened three hypermarkets in Pennsylvania and closed them as a result of local competition. In its home region of Europe, however, Carrefour is the number one retailer in Spain, Portugal, and Greece, and the second largest in Italy.

Carrefour was the first Western hypermarket company to expand into the Asian market in the mid-1990s. By 2001 it was the third-largest retailer in China and had operations in Thailand and Japan. The company bet that Asian customers would be willing to move from their traditional outdoor markets to purchase at air-conditioned and "all in one roof" hypermarkets. These hypermarkets rely on local suppliers that could offer products at the same price level as those that supplied the local competition and cater to the tastes of locals. For their part, local suppliers are all too ready to enter contracts with Carrefour, which promises to put its products in shelves across the Asian region. Moreover, where local contacts are not readily available or insufficient, Carrefour's competitive advantage comes from centralized purchasing and other logistics.

Because products are offered in a comfortable environment at competitive prices, the local competition is nothing to worry about. In fact, Carrefour is more concerned about competition from other Western retailers such as Wal-Mart and Tesco. Both Tesco and Carrefour raced to open the first hypermarket in the Thai market and basically tied. Now both their hypermarkets face each other

Source: Getty Images/AFP/Omar Torres

in a busy Bangkok street. If they want to survive in the long haul, however, Western companies should always be wary of potential local or regional competitors. In Hong Kong, where Jardine Matheson and Li Ka-shing dominate the market, Carrefour was forced to close operations.

The benefits of international expansion are not clear. While Carrefour's operating margins in France were about 6 per cent in 1999, its Asian and Latin American hypermarkets, as well as some of its European operations, were losing money. In particular, the company was hit by the Asian crisis, which also contributed to a Latin American recession.

The promise of scale economies is unlikely to materialize on a global basis because in order to cater to local tastes, hypermarkets must purchase from local producers. This tying into the local economy also helps protect their investment from nationalist factions that might risk the collapsing of local suppliers with the ousting of a foreign company.

Sources: www.carrefour.com; Carrefour, *Annual Report*, 2001; "French Fusion," *Economist*, September 2, 1999; "A Hypermarket," *Economist*, April 5, 2001.

1 How can Carrefour compete with local retailers in North America?

2 How can Carrefour compete with local retailers in Asia?

3 What strategy does Carrefour need to succeed in Europe?

4 What is Carrefour's basic strategy?

5 What is Carrefour's basic structure?

Endnotes

1 "European Central Bank," *BBC.co.uk*, May 31, 2001.

2 Spyros G. Makridakis and Michelle Bainbridge, "Evolution of the Single Market," in Spyros G. Makridakis (ed.), *Single Market Europe: Opportunities and Challenges for Business* (San Francisco, CA: Jossey-Bass, 1991), p. 9.

3 Also see Trevor Merriden, "How 'Single' is the Single Market?" *Management Review*, March 1998, pp. 27–31.

4 Edmund L. Andrews, "11 Countries Tie Europe Together in One Currency," *New York Times*, January 1, 1999, pp. A 1, 8.

5 Thomas Kamm, "Emergence of Euro Embodies Challenge and Hope for Europe," *Wall Street Journal*, January 4, 1999, pp. A 1, 4.

6 Tatiana S. Boncompagni, "Europe's Retailers Prepare to Switch to the Euro, Seeking to Gain Customers," *Wall Street Journal*, November 9, 1998, p. B 13A; and "Euro Used for 75% of Payments," *BBC.co.uk*, January 8, 2002.

7 Edmund L. Andrews, "Sticker Shocks in Euro Land," *New York Times*, December 27, 1998, Section 3, pp. 1, 6.

8 Michael Hickins, "US Business Blinks at the Euro," *Management Review*, April 1998, pp. 33–37.

9 "Jobs for the Other Boys," *Economist*, November 18, 2004.

10 European Commission Spokesman's Briefing for August 9, 1999.

11 "Jobs for the Other Boys," *Economist*, November 18, 2004.

12 "New 'Common Vocabulary' Proposed for Public Procurement," *European Business News*, August 13, 2001.

13 "EU Allies Unite Against Iraq War," *BBC.co.uk*, January 22, 2003.

14 "Now That We Are All Bundled Inside, Let's Shut the Door," *Economist*, April 28, 2005.

15 "The Shape of Things to Come," *Economist*, June 23, 2005.

16 "France's EU Vote Heralds Change," *BBC.co.uk*, May 31, 2005.

17 Herbert A. Henzler, "The New Era of Euro-capitalism," *Harvard Business Review*, vol. 70, no. 4 (July/August 1992), pp. 57–68.

18 Jack Ewing, "This Union Leader Cuts Germany's Bosses Some Slack," *Business Week*, September 10, 2001.

19 US Census Bureau, *Statistical Abstract of the United States*, 2000, p. 837.

20 "GM Creates Europe-wide Management," *BBC.co.uk*, June 18, 2004.

21 Dominic Di-Natale, "Apple Begins European Adventure," *BBC.co.uk*, November 18, 2004.

22 John E. Prescott and Patrick T. Gibbons, "Europe '92 Provides New Impetus for Competitive Intelligence," *Journal of Business Strategy*, November/December 1991, pp. 20–26.

23 Earl Landesman, "Ultimatum for US Auto Suppliers: Go Global or Go Under," *Journal of European Business*, May/June 1991, pp. 39–45.

24 "Kia Gives Nod to Slovak Car Plant," *BBC.co.uk*, March 2, 2004.

25 Ibid., pp. 40–41.

26 Alan M. Rugman and Alain Verbeke, "Europe 1992 and Competitive Strategies for North American Firms," *Business Horizons*, November/December 1991, pp. 76–81.

27 Ibid., p. 78.

28 For more specifics on standards, see www.eurunion.org/legislat/standard/standard.htm.

29 Thomas F. Clasen, "An Exporter's Guide to Selecting Foreign Sales Agents and Distributors," *Journal of European Management*, November/December 1991, pp. 28–32.

30 Joel Bleeke and David Ernst, "The Way to Win in Cross-Border Alliances," *Harvard Business Review*, vol. 69, no. 6, November/December 1991, pp. 127–128.

31 See, for example, Bill Vlasic et al., "The First Global Car Colossus," *Business Week*, May 18, 1998, pp. 40–43.

32 Gianluigi Guido, "Implementing a Pan European Marketing Strategy," *Long Range Planning*, October 1991, p. 27.

33 Ibid., p. 30.

34 Ibid., pp. 31–32; and "Credit Card Boom Warning," *BBC.co.uk*, January 9, 2001.

35 "Credit Card Fraud Rises by 50%," *BBC.co.uk*, February 20, 2001.

36 Heather Ogilvie, "Electronic Ties That Bind: Marks & Spencer's Pan-European JIT Inventory System," *Journal of European Business*, September/October 1991, pp. 48–50.

37 Jean-Claude Goldenstein and Sandra Thompson, "Participating in European Cooperative R&D Programs," *Journal of European Business*, September/October 1991, p. 51.

38 Ibid., p. 52.

39 For more on this, see Richard M. Hodgetts and Fred Luthans, *International Management*, 4th ed. (Homewood, IL: Irwin/McGraw, 2000), Chapter 13.

40 The theory of shelter has been developed in Alan M. Rugman and Alain Verbeke, *Global Competitive Strategy and Trade Policy* (London: Routledge, 1990). A study on the use of EC trade law measures as a shelter strategy is by Alan M. Rugman and Michael Gestrin, "EC Anti-Dumping Laws as a Barrier to Trade," *European Management Journal*, vol. 9, no. 4 (December 1991), pp. 475–482. Related data and analysis of EC trade law cases are reported in Patrick A. Messerlin, "Anti-Dumping Regulations or Procartel Law? The EC Chemical Case," *World Economy*, vol. 13, no. 4 (December 1990), pp. 465–492.

41 For an application of the concept of shelter by the use of US trade laws, see Alan M. Rugman and Michael Gestrin, "US Trade Laws as Barriers to Globalization," *World Economy*, vol. 14, no. 3 (December 1991), pp. 335–352. For earlier data and studies of US trade law cases used as a barrier to entry against rival Canadian firms, see Alan M. Rugman and Andrew D. M. Anderson, *Administered Protection in America* (London and New York: Routledge, 1987).

42 For an excellent discussion of triad power and the use of trade laws as barriers to entry, see Sylvia Ostry, *Governments and Corporations in a Shrinking World* (New York and London: Council on Foreign Relations Press, 1990).

43 For evidence of the abuse of US trade law procedures, see Richard Boltuck and Robert Litan (eds.), *Down in the Dumps: Administration of the Unfair Trade Laws* (Washington, DC: Brookings Institute, 1991). For recent legal and economic research on this issue, see Michael J. Trebilcock and Robert C. York (eds.), *Fair Exchange: Reforming Trade Remedy Laws* (Toronto: C.D. Howe Institute and McGraw-Hill Ryerson, 1990).

Additional bibliography

Czinkota, Michael. "The EC '92 and Eastern Europe: Effects of Integration vs. Disintegration," *Columbia Journal of World Business*, vol. 26, no. 1 (Spring 1991).

Deschamps, Jean Claude. "The European Community, International Trade, and World Unity," *California Management Review*, vol. 35, no. 2 (Winter 1993).

Douglas, Susan P. and Rhee, Dong Kee. "Examining Generic Competitive Strategy Types in US and European Markets," *Journal of International Business Studies*, vol. 20, no. 3 (Fall 1989).

Dowling, Michael and Leidner, Alfred. "Technical Standards and 1992: Opportunity or Entry Barrier in the New Europe?" *Columbia Journal of World Business*, vol. 25, no. 3 (Fall 1990).

Kidd, John B. and Teramoto, Yoshiya. "The Learning Organization: The Case of the Japanese RHQs in Europe," *Management International Review*, vol. 35, Special Issue (1995).

Lawton, Thomas C. "Evaluating European Competitiveness: Measurements and Models for a Successful Business Environment," *European Business Journal*, vol. 11, no. 4 (1999).

Lowson, Robert. "Analysing the Effectiveness of European Retail Sourcing Strategies," *European Management Journal*, vol. 19, no. 5 (October 2001).

Mayrhofer, Ulrike. "Franco–British Strategic Alliances: A Contribution to the Study of Intra-European Partnerships," *European Management Journal*, vol. 20, no. 1 (February 2002).

Miller, Alan N. "British Privatization: Evaluating the Results," *Columbia Journal of World Business*, vol. 30, no. 4 (Winter 1995).

Millington, Andrew I. and Bayliss, Brian T. "The Process of Internationalisation: UK Companies in the EC," *Management International Review*, vol. 30, no. 2 (Second Quarter 1990).

Millington, Andrew I. and Bayliss, Brian T. "Non-Tariff Barriers and UK Investment in the European Community," *Journal of International Business Studies*, vol. 22, no. 4 (Fourth Quarter 1991).

Millington, Andrew and Bayliss, Brian T. "The Strategy of Internationalization and the Success of UK Transnational Manufacturing Operations in the European Union," *Management International Review*, vol. 37, no. 3 (Third Quarter 1997).

Nitsch, Detlev, Beamish, Paul and Makino, Shige. "Entry Mode and Performance of Japanese FDI in Western Europe," *Management International Review*, vol. 36, no. 1 (First Quarter 1996).

Papanastassiou, Marina and Pearce, Robert. "Technology Sourcing and the Strategic Roles of Manufacturing Subsidiaries in the UK: Local Competence and Global Competitiveness," *Management International Review*, vol. 37, no. 1 (First Quarter 1997).

Pelkmans, Jacques. "Making EU Network Markets Competitive," *Oxford Review of Economic Policy*, vol. 17, no. 3 (Autumn 2001).

Quelch, John A. and Buzzell, Robert D. "Marketing Moves Through EC Crossroads," *Sloan Management Review*, vol. 31, no. 1 (Fall 1989).

Rehder, Robert R. and Thompson, Judith Kenner. "Nissan UK: The Japanese Transplant Beachhead in Europe," *Columbia Journal of World Business*, vol. 29, no. 3 (Fall 1994).

Rugman, Alan M., Theil, Rita and Verbeke, Alain. "Entry Barriers and Bank Strategies for the Europe 1992 Financial Directives," *European Management Journal*, vol. 10, no. 3 (September 1992).

Rugman, Alan M. and Verbeke, Alain. "Environmental Change and Global Competitive Strategy in Europe," in *Research in Global Strategic Management: Volume 2: Global Competition and the European Community* (Greenwich, CT: JAI Press, 1991).

———. *Research in Global Strategic Management: Volume 2: Global Competition and the European Community* (Greenwich, CT: JAI Press, 1991).

———. "Competitive Strategies for Non-European Firms," in B. Burgenmeier and J. L. Mucchielli (eds.), *Multinationals and Europe 1992: Strategies for the Future* (London and New York: Routledge, 1991).

———. "Europe 1992 and Competitive Strategies for North American Firms," *Business Horizons*, vol. 34, no. 6 (November/December 1991).

Rugman, Alan M., Verbeke, Alain and Campbell, Alexandria. "Strategic Change in the European Flexible Manufacturing Industry," *European Management Journal*, vol. 8, no. 3 (September 1990).

Taggart, James H. "An Evaluation of the Integration-Responsiveness Framework: MNC Manufacturing Subsidiaries in the UK," *Management International Review*, vol. 37, no. 4 (Fourth Quarter 1997).

Welfens, Paul J. J. "Foreign Investment in the East European Transition," *Management International Review*, vol. 32, no. 3 (Third Quarter 1992).

Chapter 17

JAPAN

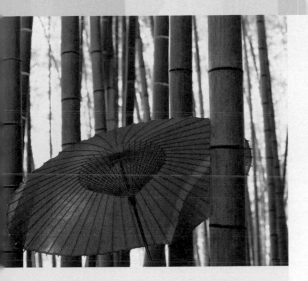

Contents

Objectives of the chapter

Japan is arguably the odd one out of the three triad regions of the world. Political, social, cultural, and economic differences underpin its unique business infrastructure and the strengths and weaknesses of its firms, relative to competitors from elsewhere. Historically it has undergone a period of unprecedented growth and internationalization and more recently recession, and this process of change helps explain this uniqueness. To understand what is so unusual about the current period for Japan, and why the ongoing corporate restructuring is so fundamental, we need to understand something of this past.

This chapter has a number of aims. By providing an overview of the key economic, political, social, and cultural characteristics of Japan we can understand more about the Japanese market and the opportunities and constraints it represents for foreign firms. We can also understand more about Japanese corporations: how and why are they different and what are the implications for collaborators and competitors?

Such insights are important for firms defending their own domestic markets against Japanese MNEs, for foreign firms breaking into the Japanese market, and for MNEs acquiring or partnering Japanese firms or recruiting Japanese employees. At a broader level, by making the links between national characteristics and corporate behavior explicit we can improve our understanding of the sources of differences between countries and help managers operate more effectively at the international level. The approach used here for Japan can be applied to other countries whose markets present opportunities or whose firms present competitive threats.[1]

The specific objectives of this chapter are to:

1 *Examine* the underlying factors—economic, political, social, and cultural—that underlie the distinctiveness of Japan, its business practices, and its corporations.
2 *Understand* why Japan is a difficult but rewarding market for foreign firms to enter.
3 *Identify* key strengths and weaknesses of Japanese firms.
4 *Explore* the ongoing changes in Japan and the implications for Japanese firms, their collaborators, and their competitors.

Doing business in Japan

Japan is the second-largest market in the world after the United States. For this and other reasons it is attractive for foreign multinational firms, large and small. It is also very different from other countries—politically, economically, and culturally—and these differences can present major challenges for market entrants.

There are a number of reasons for the imbalance in outward–inward trade and foreign direct investment in Japan. It is a tough, competitive market, characterized until recently by relatively closed interfirm business networks and a unique political, legal, and institutional infrastructure. Surveys and case studies of foreign firms in Japan reveal the difficulties many of them have faced and how they have adapted to succeed. They also reveal how things have changed over the years.

Prior to the recessionary 1990s Japan was lucrative but expensive and relatively attractive but restrictive. The major problem for foreign firms was the high basic costs of operating in Japan, including office rents, a high tax burden, staff costs (for local personnel and expatriates), materials, and other inputs. Firms also reported major recruitment problems and difficulties keeping good Japanese staff, partly because the lack of lifetime employment practices and poor social status meant that many Japanese were reluctant to work for foreign firms. Complex employment legislation and very different human resource management practices also added to the effort required to establish an effective local business.

A variety of market restrictions also faced firms, many stemming from the entrenched *keiretsu* networks, both upstream (between buyers and suppliers) and downstream (between producers, distributors, and retailers). Most Japanese firms had long-term relationships with buyers and suppliers characterized by reciprocal trust rather than short-term contractual or price-based arrangements. Breaking these ties by doing business with outsiders could affect these local relationships, so despite the potential for short-term gains, it tended to be avoided. A wide range of government-related obstacles, including binding red tape and uncertain regulations pertaining to foreigners and foreign companies, also created additional constraints for foreign firms in Japan.

In some cases these barriers to foreign entrants were the result of active protectionism, by colluding firms and their trade associations and various other coordinating agencies,

Source: Getty Images/Junko Kimura

or by the Japanese government itself. In the late 1980s and early 1990s political lobbying over alleged restrictive practices, particularly by the US administration, was at its height. In 1989, for example, the Japanese government bowed to US pressure and reformed the Large Retail Store Law to allow Toys "R" Us to open a superstore. This was a high-profile case because of the bilateral negotiations between the United States and Japan that led to the change. Toys "R" Us went on to open 64 stores up to 1995. But the Large Retail Store Law still remained to protect small retailers and indirectly supported the tied distribution networks of large *keiretsu,* creating additional barriers for foreign firms. It was again challenged in 1997 as part of another high-profile case by Kodak, against Fuji. This time the case was taken to the World Trade Organization, which ruled in favor of Fuji. Most recently, aided by further reforms to the legislation, Costco and Wal-Mart from the United States (see the Wal-Mart takes Seiyu case study later in this chapter) and Carrefour of France are aggressively challenging traditional network structures and attempting to eliminate costly local wholesalers.

More often than the direct actions of Japanese government agencies or collusion among corporate groupings, the above constraints for foreign firms in Japan simply stemmed from differences in Japanese business infrastructures, legislative mechanisms, management practices, and consumer preferences. As with any overseas market, foreign firms have to adapt or they will fail to succeed. Foreign managers have also cited competition with Japanese companies and the strictness of orders from Japanese customers in terms of quality, delivery, and after-sales service as key constraints in the past. But these are innate characteristics of doing business in Japan and two key reasons why Japanese firms themselves are so innovative. Successfully developing a business in Japan is an excellent test of a firm's competitive advantages.

More recently the continued downturn in Japan's domestic market has made it less attractive but easier to enter Japan. Government deregulation, the loosening of *keiretsu* ties, and changing consumer preferences have helped foreign investors. Foreign companies also cite falls in land prices, office rent, and utility costs as specific improvements in the Japanese business environment. Falls in distribution cost and improvement(s) in the availability of qualified personnel are also seen as important factors.

The Japanese government has taken steps to improve access for foreign firms, partly to increase consumer choice and stimulate spending and partly to expose local firms to outside competition. Policies aimed at tax reduction and favorable legal and institutional reforms, such as amendments to the Commercial Code of Japan, alongside improvements in labor market flexibility, are helping increase FDI to Japan.

There are, however, more fundamental changes taking place that are probably more important for foreign entrants. The changing economic climate of the 1990s and early 2000s, particularly the high costs of manufacturing and depressed consumer demand, has resulted in a growing preference among consumers to buy cheaper, non-Japanese products and a need for Japanese firms to buy from abroad. Long-term *keiretsu* networks have loosened considerably, opening up supplier, distribution, and retailing opportunities to foreign firms. Social and cultural changes also mean that younger Japanese are much more enthusiastic to work for non-Japanese firms, although senior, experienced managers are still relatively difficult to recruit.

More recent entrants to Japan and established foreign firms expanding their presence are a testimony to these changing conditions and the continued promise of the Japanese market. The French firm AXA Non-Life Insurance has recently set up a second operations center. Miele, the German household appliances company, which used to export via Mitsui in the late 1980s, established a subsidiary in 1992 and recently expanded its network of regional agents and opened a new showroom in Tokyo. Dyson, the British vacuum cleaner manufacturer, established Dyson Japan in 1998 and saw a 30 per cent increase in sales in 2001. It has now extended its reach to 680 retailers via mass merchandisers and department store networks.

The British retailer Tesco provides another indication of the renewed interest in Japan. In 2004 it increased its commitment to the Japanese market by acquiring the neighborhood supermarket business of Fre'c via its wholly-owned subsidiary, C Two Network Co. It had already expanded successfully to control 77 stores since its initial entry in 1994, partly by buying C Two Network in 2003. The sale of Fre'c was coordinated by the Industrial Revitalization Corporation of Japan (IRCJ), a government-affiliated body set up in mid-2003 to purchase the non-performing loans of viable but indebted companies.

Although there has been change in Japan, the key lessons from managers who have experienced this change also emphasize the continued importance of traditional Japanese practices. For newcomers they suggest the following:

- Research the culture, the market, the competition, and the relevant network affiliations.

- Understand that in Japan more than any other market "customer is king," quality is paramount, and a deep-rooted service philosophy is required.

- Be patient ("wait on the stone") and show long-term commitment; personal and corporate reputation is important and takes time to develop.

- Show sensitivity in all interaction: social gatherings are important and rituals and hierarchy have to be respected.

- Invest to adapt products, services, marketing, and management style.

- Continually innovate, stay ahead of the competition.

- Use Japan to learn, to improve, and to access other Asian markets.

Websites: http://www.jetro.go.jp/; http://www.tesco.co.uk and http://www.meti.go.jp/english/

Sources: S. C. Collinson, *Small and Successful in Japan: A Study of 30 British Firms in the World's Most Competitive Market* (London: Avebury Press, Ashgate Publishing Group, 1996); JETRO, *JETRO White Paper on Foreign Direct Investment 1995* (Tokyo: Japan External Trade Organization, 1995); JETRO *JETRO White Paper on Foreign Direct Investment 2001* (Tokyo: Japan External Trade Organization, 2001), at http://www.jetro.go.jp/ec/e/research/index.html; JETRO, *The 9th Survey on Attitudes of Foreign-Affiliated Companies toward Direct Investment in Japan* (Tokyo: Japan External Trade Organization, 2004), at http://www.jetro.go.jp/en/stats/survey/; JETRO, *Why Japan? Success Stories* (Tokyo: Japan External Trade Organization, 2004), at http://www.jetro.go.jp/en/invest/whyjapan/success_stories/; and Tesco, *Tesco Plans to Acquire Japanese Business*, Press Release, Tesco PLC, April 27, 2004, at http://www.tesco.co.uk.

1. What kinds of challenges are foreign managers likely to meet when trying to set up a subsidiary office in Japan and recruit local employees?

2. How have *keiretsu* networks limited foreign firms entering the Japanese market in the past and how is this now changing?

3. As part of the general growth of foreign direct investment into Japan, why are foreign firms increasingly able and willing to engage in mergers and acquisitions (M&A) with local firms?

4. Despite widespread changes in Japan and the restructuring of Japanese corporations, why is it still important for foreign managers to understand something of the history and the context in which Japanese businesses have evolved?

INTRODUCTION

Between 1950 and 1973 Japanese GDP grew at an unparalleled average annual rate of 8 per cent, over three times the growth rates of the United Kingdom and the United States in this period and similar to current growth rates in China. The OECD itself noted this by observing: "by the conventional measures of economic performance (income growth, inflation, unemployment) Japan has out-performed all other OECD economies since entry into the organization in 1964."[2] How did this happen?

Since 1973 until recently its average rate of growth has remained at 3 per cent per year. Then, in the last half of the 1990s the Japanese economy grew at half the OECD average (which was 2.8 per cent), and by the end of the 1990s it recorded unprecedented negative growth, shrinking by more than 2 per cent. More recently it has shown signs of recovery, but is still undergoing a period of restructuring as it comes to terms with the end of an era of continued growth.

POLITICAL, SOCIAL, AND CULTURAL CHARACTERISTICS

The 127 million people of Japan are heavily concentrated in the coastal areas and urban regions because of the mountainous nature of the country. Over half of the population lives in and around the three main metropolitan areas of Tokyo, Osaka, and Nagoya.

Up until the end of the 1980s Japan could be characterized politically, socially, and culturally as a highly stable, conservative, and homogenous country. Economic change since then has been both driven by and a driving force for change across all of these dimensions. To understand the current dynamics affecting the Japanese market, its firms, and its managers we must understand something of its political and social heritage.

A traditionally strong government role in the economy

The branches of the Japanese government are most similar to those in the United States: legislative, executive, and judicial. Legislative power is vested in the Diet, which consists of a popularly elected House of Representatives and House of Councilors. The conservative Liberal-Democratic party has been in power for most of the post-war period with the support of the powerful business and agriculture lobbies.

Executive power rests with the Cabinet, which is organized and headed by the prime minister, who is elected by the Diet. In addition to the office of the prime minister, there are 17 ministerial divisions in the executive branch. Judicial power is vested in the Supreme Court and there are eight high courts and numerous district courts throughout the country. Overall, Japan is divided into 47 prefectures. Each local political subdivision, including cities, towns, and villages, has its own executive power and operates within the scope of the national law.

Two key ministries were at the heart of Japan's post-war reconstruction, the boom years of rapid growth and, arguably, some elements of its more recent recession. The Ministry for Economy, Trade, and Industry (METI), created in 2001, is a relatively new incarnation of the long-standing Ministry of International Trade and Industry (MITI), which was established in 1951. It was responsible for leading the selective liberalization of the economy and trade particularly in the 1960s and 1970s. It used its strong control to target, promote, and coordinate specific technologies and industry groups to spearhead the national economic development program. The Ministry of Finance (MOF) was also highly influential in steering the developing and internationalizing economy via its control over prices and currency exchange in the early days of growth.

One of the more unusual systems that helped coordinate decision making and maintain the consensus among MITI, MOF, and various key flagship firms was the practice of amakudari. This involved the regular movement of senior politicians and civil servants from the public sector into private-sector companies, often as highly paid consultants.

These two ministries connected with other ministries and government agencies to influence the evolution of specific forms of business infrastructure, corporate strengths (and weaknesses), and interfirm business practices. The Ministry of Post and Telecommunications (MPT) and MITI, for example, jointly guided the development of NTT, the national telecoms carrier; its supplier group, including NEC, Fujitsu, Hitachi, and Oki; and its de-nationalization and partial break-up during the 1990s.[3]

The early 1990s saw the start of a series of restructurings in Japanese politics, following over a decade when government influence over the economy and, in particular, the strategies of the major firms became increasingly weak. Both the lead political parties and the powerful civil service bureaucracies below them were pushed to justify their roles, responsibilities, and connections with corporate Japan.

However, government in Japan still arguably plays a more important role in the economy and as an influence over corporate strategy than in other OECD countries. Agricultural and foods-related sectors, the construction industry, and financial services, for example, are still very strongly influenced by government via a number of governance mechanisms.

Distinctive cultural characteristics

Although cultural factors are often overemphasized in discussions of Japanese economic strength, there are some distinctive social and cultural elements that underlie the country's success. As described in Chapter 5 the cultural frameworks of Hofstede and Trompenaars indicate a low level of individualism and a high level of uncertainty avoidance compared with Western cultures, reflected in the high priority placed on rituals, routines, and procedures in organizations and society in general. The Japanese are relatively neutral or unemotional in the workplace and prefer more objective rather than subjective forms of decision making. They are also diffuse, in Trompenaars's terminology, with a high correlation between hierarchical relationships in the workplace and social status outside the workplace.

A strong sense of collectivism rather than individualism tends to dominate many aspects of Japanese life. Whether work-related or outside work, clubs, groups, and societies exist at

Ministry for Economy, Trade, and Industry (METI)
Superseded MITI, which was at the heart of Japan's post-war economic boom

Ministry of Finance (MOF)
Historically influential and remains a powerful force in the deregulation of the economy

Amakudari
(Literally "descent from heaven") The temporary or permanent movement of public-sector officials in Japan into private corporations as a mechanism for coordinating national policy and company strategy

all levels and people will tend to belong to several, with a distinct ranking in each according to its focus and their age and experience.

Within companies certain characteristics have strong religious roots, including honor, respect, sincerity, loyalty (*chu*), duty, obligation or responsibility (*giri*), ritual, and hierarchy. These are all central pillars of Japanese society in general and are sometimes referred to as the Japanese code. At various levels parent–child relationships characterize the hierarchical nature of inter-organizational and interpersonal links, such as government–industry, large firm–small firm, manager–employee, and so on.[4] Respect for elders, ritualistic (and highly complex) language forms and behavior, group activities, and consensus decision making are all important elements. These contrast individualism and meritocratic forms of organization and tend overall to unify the Japanese in their response to *gaijin* or outsiders.

Many of these characteristics are nurtured in the strong Japanese school system. This is characterized by a centrally-regulated curriculum (dominated by Monbusho, the Ministry of Education, Science, and Culture): conformist attitudes among pupils, teachers, and parents; high standards; and a focus on factual learning and the sciences. As a result of this educational focus Japan has double the number of scientists and engineers per head of population than the United Kingdom.

There is a significant amount of competition to get into good schools but a lack of competition between pupils once in school ("the nail that sticks out will be hammered down" is a local saying frequently used to describe this conformity). There is also a strong correlation between the level and place of education and job opportunities for school or university leavers, particularly at the top end of the business and civil service hierarchies. About 38 per cent of Japanese attend university and 75 per cent of the 480 Japanese universities are private.[5]

We get a small insight into the difficulties created for non-Japanese by the complexities of Japanese culture if we consider the *hai* dilemma. *Hai* can mean one of at least four levels of yes: recognition, but not necessarily understanding; understanding, but not necessarily acceptance and agreement; responsibility, understanding, but must consult with others and secure their agreement before acceptance; and agreement, which means understanding, agreement, and acceptance. The non-verbal signals from the speaker have to be understood to determine which yes is being meant.

Chu and *giri*

Chu, meaning loyalty, and *giri*, meaning duty, obligation, or responsibility, are often used together to denote the traditionally close, trusting relationship between managers and employees; they are also used to describe the ties between older and younger members of a family

Gaijin

A term used for non-Japanese and while not too offensive is not particularly polite; *gai* means outside or foreign, *jin* means person

Hai

Yes in Japanese does not necessarily mean "yes I agree," but "yes, I hear what you say"

✔ Active learning check

Review your answer to Active Learning Case question 1 and make any changes you like. Then compare your answer with the one below.

1 **What kinds of challenges are foreign managers likely to meet when trying to set up a subsidiary office in Japan and recruit local employees?**

One way to answer this question would be to examine the political, economic, and cultural issues in turn. Political challenges include the legislation for registering local companies, licensing, taxation, visas for foreign nationals, and employment regulations. Economic challenges include the costs of premises and business services. But there are other costs, less easy to estimate that result from the extra time and effort needed to develop customer relationships and adapt to Japanese business practices. All of the above challenges would involve a degree of cultural learning, given that they involve interaction with and an understanding of local people and organizations. Recruiting, managing, and keeping Japanese employees, however, represents one of the biggest challenges for foreign managers. Failure to adapt human resource management practices, incentive schemes, the organizational structure and hierarchy, the definition of roles and responsibilities, and decision-making systems to develop an efficient, motivated local workforce undermines many foreign firms' market-entry strategies in Japan.

ECONOMIC CHARACTERISTICS

Japan is very big and highly competitive. The unusual nature of its rapid growth in the early years stemmed from factors such as the traditional relationship between government and business, its unique capital markets (national finance and investment systems), its traditionally strong *keiretsu* groupings of firms, the role of the corporation in society, and the role of the employee in the firm. These are all linked to its unique social and cultural characteristics, leading many commentators to characterize Japan as having a different form of capitalism.

The size of the Japanese economy, combined with its productivity and the average wealth of its 127 million people make it the second largest economy in the world after the United States. Other general characteristics include its large (though declining) trade imbalance and even larger imbalance in FDI, compared to its triad counterparts (see Tables 17.1, 17.2, and 17.3).

Keiretsu
Groupings of Japanese firms with long-term associations and cross-shareholdings; each firm maintains its operational independence but coordinates strategy and often exchanges assets and resources with other firms in its group

Table 17.1 Economic and trade data for Japan

	2000	2001	2002	2003
GDP per head ($ at purchasing power parity)	25,948	26,639	26,944	28,000
GDP (% real change pa)	2.14	0.60	−0.24	2.72
Government consumption (% of GDP)	16.43	17.08	17.66	17.50
Budget balance (% of GDP)	−7.43	−6.08	−7.12	−7.42
Consumer prices (% change pa; average)	−0.67	−0.73	−0.92	−0.25
Public debt (% of GDP)	133.06	141.52	147.28	154.62
Labor costs per hour (US$)	22.27	19.61	18.83	20.49
Recorded unemployment (%)	4.72	5.03	5.38	5.26

GDP by sector	agriculture: 1.3%; industry: 29.1%; services: 69.6%
Exports	$416 billion
Main exports	motor vehicles, semiconductors, office machinery, chemicals
Main export partners	US 28.5%, China 9.6%, South Korea 6.8%, Taiwan 6.3%, Hong Kong 6.0%
Imports	$337 billion
Main imports	fuels, foodstuffs, chemicals, textiles, office machinery
Main import partners	China 18.3%, US 17.1%, South Korea 4.6%, Indonesia 4.2%, Australia 4.1%, Taiwan 4.0%

Sources: http://www.oecd.org/statsportal/;
http://www.meti.go.jp/english/statistics/index.html;
http://www.jetro.go.jp/.

Table 17.2 Japan's FDI imbalance

Direct investment flows	2001		2002		2003	
	Inward (bill. US$)	Outward (bill. US$)	Inward (bill. US$)	Outward (bill. US$)	Inward (bill. US$)	Outward (bill. US$)
Japan	6.2	38.3	9.2	32.3	6.3	28.8
United Kingdom	61.9	68.0	27.8	35.2	14.6	55.3
United States	143.9	103.7	72.4	134.8	39.9	173.8

Sources: UNCTAD, *World Investment Report*, United Nations, Geneva, 2002, at: http://www.unctad.org/en/pub/; OECD, *Recent Trends in Foreign Direct Investment in OECD Countries*, 2004, at: http://www.oecd.org/dataoecd/.

Table 17.3 Japan's FDI inflows and outflows by source and destination

Countries	FDI inflows into Japan by source (2002)	FDI outflows from Japan by destination (2002)
United States	27.7%	23.5%
North America	**33.8%**	**26.8%**
Latin America	**0.0%**	**12.6%**
Asian newly industrialized economies	1.6%	9.3%
China	0.0%	8.1%
Asia	**0.1%**	**25.3%**
France	24.9%	12.4%
United Kingdom	5.9%	6.4%
Western Europe	**68.3%**	**30.2%**
Other regions	0.0%	5.1%

Source: JETRO, *White Paper on FDI,* Japan External Trade Organization, Tokyo, 2003, at: http://www.jetro.go.jp/en/.

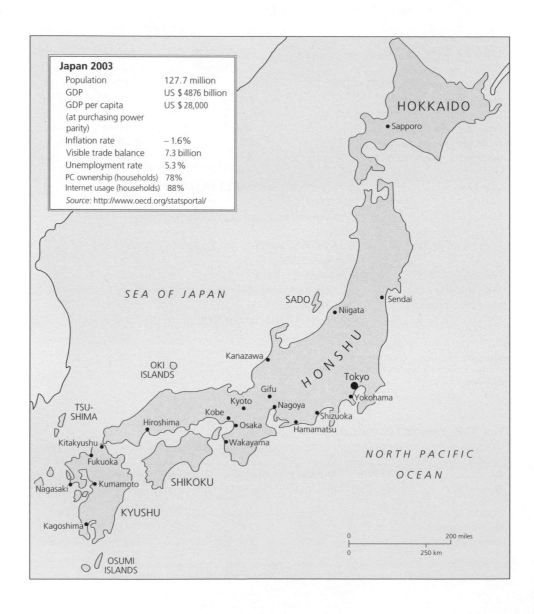

Japan 2003

Population	127.7 million
GDP	US $4876 billion
GDP per capita (at purchasing power parity)	US $28,000
Inflation rate	−1.6%
Visible trade balance	7.3 billion
Unemployment rate	5.3%
PC ownership (households)	78%
Internet usage (households)	88%

Source: http://www.oecd.org/statsportal/

Japan 2003	
Population	127.7 million
GDP	US$ 4876 billion
GDP per capita (at purchasing power parity)	US$ 28,000
Inflation rate	−1.6%
Visible trade balance	7.3 billion
Unemployment rate	5.3%
PC ownership (households)	78%
Internet usage (households)	88%

Source: http://www.oecd.org/statsportal/.

This imbalance, coupled with its trade dependence on the US market, resulted in the long-running US–Japan trade conflict during the 1980s. Japan's growth period was marked by increased exports (see Figure 17.1) and outward FDI, but for some time its domestic market remained relatively closed to competitors for a variety of reasons. More recently, linked to the domestic market recession, imports of cheaper products, particularly from China, have created a more balanced trade profile (see Figure 17.2).

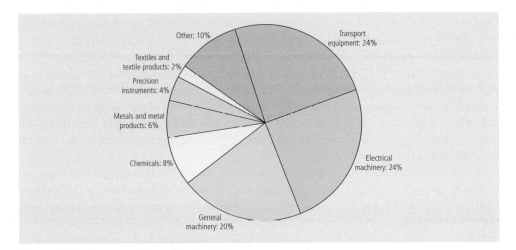

Figure 17.1 Japan: major exports (%)

Source: Japanese Ministry of Finance, at: http://www.stat.go.jp/english/data/figures/index.htm#d.

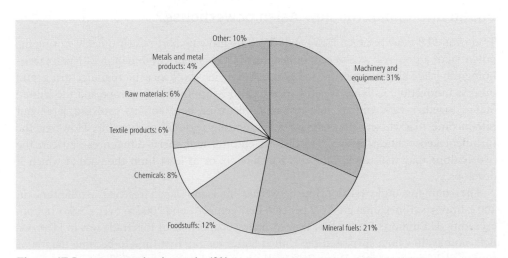

Figure 17.2 Japan: major imports (%)

Source: Japanese Ministry of Finance, at: http://www.stat.go.jp/english/data/figures/index.htm#d.

Japan is home to around a quarter of the top 100 MNEs. The kinds of sectors represented in this list of top firms, together with Japan's trade profile and sources of outward FDI, all point to a surprisingly narrow range of industry strengths. Its competitive superiority has always been limited to relatively few key sectors, as is the case for most other economies.

In the early 1990s just four industries—non-electrical machinery, electrical machinery, transport machinery, and precision machinery—accounted for 75 per cent of total Japanese exports. Three product areas—motor vehicles and parts, consumer electronics, and electronic components—were responsible for about one-third of exports. The same industry niches were responsible for the growth of foreign direct investment (primarily in production activities) and of foreign sales of Japanese firms.[6] Other data also show how the success of Japanese firms, expressed in terms of the proportion of overseas to total sales, has also been rather limited.[7] Their size, as is the case for many US firms, reflects success in their large domestic and regional markets rather than their global competitiveness.

In his book *The Competitive Advantage of Nations*, Michael Porter (1990) uses Japan to illustrate both the importance of local *rivalry* and *demanding customers* as driving forces behind the evolution of innovative, competitive firms. As shown above, Japan's strong export performance is based around relatively few industries, initially steel and shipbuilding and heavy engineering, then later capital goods production, car manufacturing, electrical engineering, and consumer electronics. In all these sectors very tough competition between many local firms battling for market share (rather than profits) pushed each competitor to develop new products, more rapidly at lower costs. The large number of firms in key industry sectors promoted this rivalry. During its rapid growth phase the country had, for example, 9 indigenous car manufacturers (whereas the United States had only three), 10 large electronics groups, and over 115 companies producing machine tools, again far more per capita than the United States.

At the same time tough markets and demanding customers at home pushed Japanese companies to cut costs and emphasize quality, personal service, and buyer-led product customization, all of which came to underlie their global competitiveness during later periods of export-driven growth. Toyota, for example, initially pioneered lean production techniques in the 1950s as a way of lowering costs to undercut local competitors, not to promote international competitiveness.[8]

Japan and China: the new Asian powerhouse?

Trade and FDI flows between Japan and China are growing particularly quickly, raising the potential of a powerful axis of economic growth in Asia. The combination of Japan's technological leadership in specific industry sectors, its excellence in manufacturing and process innovation, its large, wealthy market, and its footholds in Europe and the United States, together with China's low-cost manufacturing base and its evolving, large but low-income market, sets the stage for a very strong regional partnership. However, the turbulent geo-political history and distinct cultural and social differences between the two nations may well undermine this partnership, or at least limit the pace at which it develops.

The changing trade relationship between China and Japan reached a milestone in 2002. Imports from China grew 6.2 per cent between 2001 and 2002 to over US $61 billion, exceeding US imports for the first time. A major proportion of this trade was in IT products, and again China surpassed the United States for the first time to become the major source of IT imports into Japan. Japan also imported more motorcycles and consumer electronic products made by Chinese manufacturers. Exports from Japan to China increased

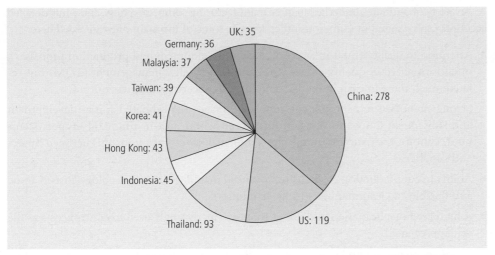

Figure 17.3 Destination of Japanese overseas business investment, 2002–2004

Note: Shows number of respondents citing each destination, multiple replies included; 175 responses also named other destinations not included in the countries shown.

Source: Compiled from data from JETRO, at: http://www.jetro.go.jp/en/.

28 per cent to US $40 billion partly due to buoyant demand for products such as automobiles. Exports to the US market are still more than twice this amount. By 2003 imports from China had grown to over US $75 billion and exports to China reached US $57 billion, leaving a deficit of almost US $18 billion.[9]

Figure 17.3 illustrates the rapid growth of Japanese business investment into China from a Japan External Trade Organization (JETRO) survey of Japanese businesses.

BUSINESS CHARACTERISTICS

Having explored some aspects of the political, social, and economic environment in which Japanese firms have evolved, we now move on to examine some of the factors underlying its economic success. This success in the 1970s and 1980s led to a fear among Western observers that the Japanese had developed an alternative model of market capitalism that would out-perform incumbent firms in the United States and Europe. High-profile articles and books on the Japanese threat fed this fear.[10] This also prompted some useful, in-depth research that sought to understand what factors underpinned this success. These include distinctive strengths in manufacturing operations, strong applied research and development (R&D), the *keiretsu* corporate networks, and domestic distribution and retailing systems that connect companies and customers.

Manufacturing strengths

The most detailed comparative studies involving Japanese manufacturers have been carried out in the auto sector looking, for example, at productivity, manufacturing efficiency, continuous process improvement, design quality, return on R&D, and new product development. The success of Japanese firms in this sector is shown by the fact that on average (up until the end of the 1980s) they produced new models of cars with only 55 per cent of the engineering hours required by US and European manufacturers, maintaining development lead times that were over 15 months shorter, and sold them at a retail price that was, on average, 30 per cent lower than competing models from the United States and Europe.[11]

A variety of attributes underlie Japanese manufacturing competitiveness, and while detailed accounts can be found in numerous other sources, some of the main ones are listed here:

■ Attention to quality (built in at every stage of development and production processes), often formalized in quality circles (QC) and total quality management (TQM) but related much more to each individual employee's concern for flawless output.

■ Strong manufacturer–component supplier linkages (coordinated initial development and subsequent innovation), again formalized within just-in-time (JIT) type systems but reliant for their success on the close, informal *keiretsu* relationships between buyers and suppliers.

■ Ability to cut production costs (using advanced manufacturing technology, just-in-time, and flexible and lean manufacturing techniques).

■ A high level of automation and use of robotics (increasingly used to control costs as the yen appreciated).

■ Higher degree of credibility and responsibility given to engineers and technical expertise.

■ *Kaizen*, or continuous improvement, and a focus at all levels on incremental productivity improvement and customer-led product development.

Strong applied R&D

Japan has traditionally spent more than the United States and most other countries on R&D as a proportion of GDP. It normally spends over 2.8 per cent and reached over 3 per cent in 2002, compared with an OECD average of 2.21 per cent.[12] Moreover, around 78 per cent comes from industry, the highest among OECD countries. Contrary to popular myth the Japanese government has always spent relatively smaller amounts on R&D compared with other advanced countries (this is partly related to the low level of defense spending).

At one time Hitachi, Toyota, Matsushita, NEC, and Fujitsu, the top five R&D spenders in Japan, spent as much (in terms of purchasing power parity) as the total R&D expenditure of the entire private sector in Britain.[13] Up until the late 1980s this R&D was predominantly applied or near-market R&D. Japan only started to catch up in terms of more basic blue-sky R&D, moving to the scientific frontiers in some technologies, in the last 15 to 20 years.

Figure 17.4 shows the high level of company spending on R&D, on a per capita basis, and a relatively slow growth rate, compared with other OECD countries. Figure 17.5, from a study of UK competitiveness by Michael Porter, shows how Japan compares with other major economies in terms of its level of output of patents. This is one indicator of national-level innovativeness, and Japan shows a very high per capita output but a relatively slow growth rate, compared with some emerging Asian countries.

Keiretsu

The renowned Japanese corporate groupings, or *keiretsu*, characterized by cross-shareholdings and regular meetings between executives, represent more or less closely tied groups of integrated businesses. There are broadly two types of *keiretsu*, the horizontal (*kinyu*) type and the vertical, manufacturing *keiretsu*.

Many of the former are descended from the pre-war *zaibatsu* conglomerates, which the allied forces attempted to break up in the late 1940s. Three of the top six are direct descendents of the pre-war *zaibatsu*: Mitsui, Mitsubishi, and Sumitomo. The remaining three, Fuyo/Fuji, Sanwa, and Dai-Ichi Kangyo are more like centralized holding companies. These top six alone directly accounted for about 5 per cent of the Japanese labor force and 16 per cent of total Japanese corporate sales in the early 1980s. But their cross-shareholding

---

Kaizen
Normally taken to mean "continuous improvement" and is associated with lean or low-cost, high-productivity manufacturing. A more accurate interpretation is "to dismantle and reassemble a process to make it better." As such *kaizen* was an early form of business process re-engineering

Kinyu
Horizontal conglomerates encompassing a wide range of diversified businesses, centered on a dominant bank and/or trading company

Zaibatsu
The pre-war antecedents of some modern-day *keiretsu* in Japan; attempts by the allied forces to break these up after World War II largely failed

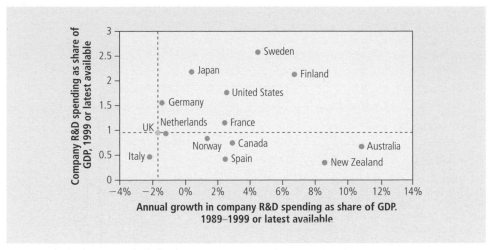

Figure 17.4 Company spending on R&D: Japan compared

Sources: M. E. Porter and C. H. M. Ketels, *UK Competitiveness: Moving to the Next Stage*, DTI Economics Paper No. 3, Department of Trade and Industry, UK Government and the Economic and Social Research Council (ESCR), 2003, at: http://www/.dti.gov.uk; and OECD, *Benchmarking Industry-Science Relationships* (Paris: OECD, 2002), at: www.oecd.org/document.

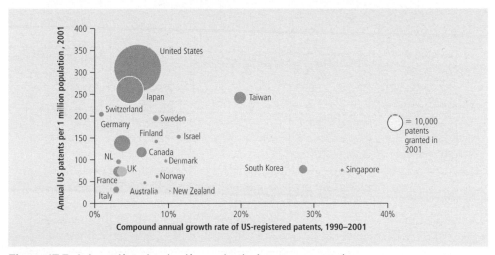

Figure 17.5 International patenting output: Japan compared

Sources: US Patent and Trademark Office, 2002; M. E. Porter and C. H. M. Ketels, *UK Competitiveness: Moving to the Next Stage*, DTI Economics Paper No. 3, Department of Trade and Industry, UK Government and the Economic and Social Research Council (ESCR), 2003, at: http://www.dti.gov.uk.

networks and their influence across and down the main corporate hierarchies in Japan was far more prevalent than these figures suggest.

The Fuyo *keiretsu* (*Fuyo-kai*) is shown in Figure 17.6, prior to its restructuring. It typifies the horizontal-type *keiretsu*, with a central bank and *sogo shosha*, or international trading company, and a diversified range of interests. These firms played a major role in bringing Japanese products to the world markets in the growth phase and underpin the global FDI network of many Japanese firms today.

Many of these Japanese banks once dominated the world rankings in asset terms, including Dai-lchi Kangyo Bank, Sumitomo Bank, Fuji Bank, and Sakura Bank. Commercial banks in Japan have always been oriented more toward corporate clients than individual customers compared with Western banks. Unlike arm's-length shareholders in the West, with short-term repayment horizons, Japanese banks and other shareholders (usually affiliated companies, suppliers, distributors, or associated companies) will have built a long-term commitment to supporting *keiretsu* member companies and their employees. As a

Sogo shosha
International trading companies that help other Japanese firms import and export products and services; they were very influential in the rapid growth era in helping local firms break into overseas markets

513

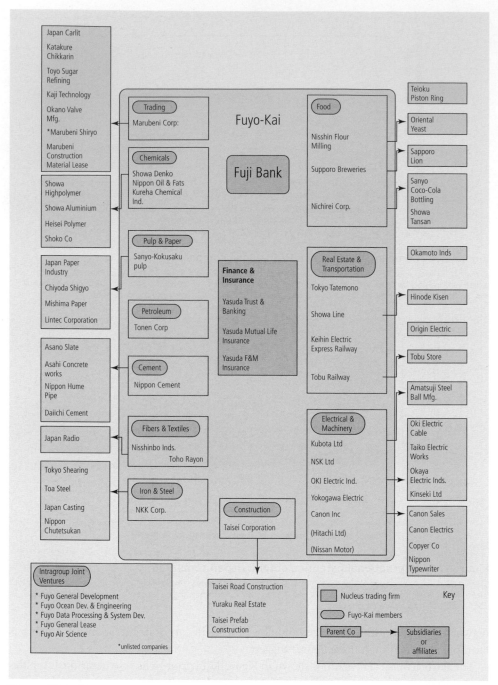

Figure 17.6 The Fuyo-*Keiretsu* group before restructuring

Source: Sir H. Cortazzi, *Modern Japan: A Concise Survey* (London: Macmillan, 1993), p. 132.

result capital markets in Japan have not traditionally emphasized return on investment (ROI) and dividends. Corporations have been much freer from the constraints and demands of shareholders and allowed to manage for long-term growth and continue *keiretsu* connections and loyalty to employees. This form of capitalism has significant benefits in a continually growing economy. But it also has weaknesses and can be an inefficient system for resource allocation as has become much more apparent in Japan's recessionary period. Subsequently, there have been fundamental changes to the structure of capital markets in Japan in recent years, as we will see below.

At one time Mitsubishi was said to be the most tightly woven *keiretsu*, based in Tokyo's business district, Marunouchi, which as a result was called Mitsubishi Village. In the mid-1990s it had over 216,000 employees in businesses ranging through the financial, manufacturing, services, and trading sectors from heavy engineering and oil to aerospace and beer. The 29 companies at the heart of the group held an average of 38 per cent of each other's shares, a high proportion even for Japanese corporate groups.[14] These companies exchanged directors, cross-financed one another, and engaged in joint investment and co-operative research projects for the benefit of the whole group. Information exchange and interfirm coordination is initiated at the most senior level and the presidents and chairmen of the 29 core firms still meet for lunch in Marunouchi on the second Friday of each month for the Mitsubishi *Kinyokai*, or Friday Club. Within the 29 core companies are an even closer-knit group which share the Mitsubishi name. The proportion of stable shareholders among this group stood at over 70 per cent in 1996 and has since fallen to about 33 per cent. The box **International Business Strategy in Action: Kirin beer goes international** describes one of the companies in the Mitsubishi group.

The newer, vertical *keiretsu* are headed by large manufacturers (Hitachi, Matsushita Electric Industrial, Toyota, and NEC, for example) and tend to belong to a particular manufacturing sector. Here the relationships are between suppliers, a flagship manufacturer and distributors and retailers, in a vertical value chain. Close information exchange, cross-shareholding, personnel exchanges, and joint ventures support excellence in supply-chain management, new product development, standardized IT and logistics, quality and service assurance, and the sharing of management best practices.

At one time Matsushita, for example, had around 500 prime contractors, or first-level suppliers, and over 6,000 smaller suppliers at lower levels of what is known as a co-prosperity pyramid or cooperative manufacturing *keiretsu*. Toyota, by comparison, once had 168 first-tier suppliers, 4,000 second-tier, and around 32,000 third-tier, according to one estimate. Small and medium-sized enterprises (SMEs) at the lower levels may rely on two or three top customers for over 50 per cent of their revenue, making them both highly cooperative (that is, willing to change component price or specifications to the buyer's requirements at short notice) and very dependent on the fortunes of manufacturers further up the hierarchy.

Mitsubishi *Kinyokai*
The Friday Club in Marunouchi, Tokyo, where the most senior managers from the 29 core firms of the Mitsubishi *keiretsu* gather each month to discuss business

Co-prosperity pyramid
A supply chain linked to a vertical, manufacturing *keiretsu*. It is hierarchical, with firms in the top tiers engaged in technology sharing, personnel exchanges, cross-shareholding, and long-term trading relationships. The further down the hierarchy a firm sits the more important price becomes and the less they are considered *keiretsu* members

✔ Active learning check

Review your answer to Active Learning Case question 2 and make any changes you like. Then compare your answer with the one below.

2 How have *keiretsu* networks limited foreign firms entering the Japanese market in the past and how is this now changing?

The degree to which *keiretsu* networks will affect foreign firms' success in the Japanese market partly depends on which industry or business they are in. In the past, foreign entrants have found it very difficult to find willing suppliers or distributors because many local firms have been tied into long-term relationships with other *keiretsu* members. Traditionally these long-term relationships have meant that foreign firms will be disadvantaged when competing against local firms, regardless of the relative price or benefits of their product or service. Consumers and corporate purchasing departments have tended to show a strong bias toward local brands and local producers. Since the recession, however, price has become more important as a selection criterion and *keiretsu* structures have loosened, providing more opportunities for foreign firms. Imported products, discount stores (by-passing the complex distribution systems), and direct sales have all become acceptable. Japanese firms of all sizes are actively seeking links with firms outside their traditional networks and outside Japan as part of their changing business strategies.

Kirin beer goes international

A kirin, a mythical eastern unicorn and a symbol of good fortune, brands Kirin's beer bottles. But its recent performance suggests that Kirin needs more than this lucky symbol if it is going to expand globally. The firm is the largest beer producer in Japan and one of the four dominant players in the industry alongside Asahi, Sapporo, and Suntory.

Kirin has been producing beer for over 130 years, with products such as Kirin Lager and Ichiban Shibori. Kirin Tanrei is Japan's leading happo-shu (low-malt) beer. Other beverages include canned coffee and tea, fruit juices, and soft drinks. Also active in floriculture and pharmaceuticals, Kirin is part of the Mitsubishi *keiretsu*.

In recent years the company has been having its share of problems. These all started back in the 1970s when Kirin held 70 per cent of the national market. At this time antitrust regulators decided to open the local market to other brewers. As a result, Asahi Beer quickly became the country's second largest brewer, and since then Asahi has continued to erode Kirin's market share with (1) better product development; (2) a successful marketing strategy with commercials aimed at young, active individuals; and (3) a distribution network that introduced what turned out to be a growing trend among beer consumers—canned beer sold in large supermarkets.

In retrospect, one of Kirin's biggest mistakes was that it was too slow in reacting to competition in a market that it long took for granted. For example, despite Asahi's tactics, Kirin continued to rely heavily on its traditional sales approach and its long-established network of "mom-and-pop" stores across the country. In truth, the company was confused regarding how to deal with competition and, as a result, made a number of mistakes. When the giant brewer decided to increase its marketing effort and create television ads directed at young people, the strategy was perceived by many viewers as a poor imitation of Asahi's own advertising strategy and the campaign flopped. As a result of such missteps by Kirin, Asahi continued to gain market share. By 2001 the company held 36 per cent of the Japanese beer market compared with Kirin's 38 per cent and in 2004 Asahi overtook Kirin reaching a 41.7 per cent share of the market for beer and happo-shu, up 1.8 percentage points from the previous year. Kirin's sales totaled $10.9 billion in 2003 and Asahi sales were $13.1 billion, although this includes a range of other products these firms sell.

Commenting on his company's inability to exploit its advantages, one of the managers in Kirin's marketing research department noted, "We are a good example of bad brand management."

Source: Getty Images/John Chiasson

Most recently, in an effort to maintain its position in the Japanese market, Kirin has been working to exploit its traditional image. Kirin Lager, Japan's oldest brew, is now being promoted as the classic Japanese premium beer, the type of beer to enjoy with family and friends. And to promote this image with its other brews as well, Kirin has begun increasing its advertising budget. Unfortunately, this new effort faces a number of challenges. The biggest one may well be that most Japanese beer drinkers admit that all beers taste the same to them—so increased advertising may not generate the desired results.

Partly in response to lack of progress in its domestic market Kirin has been expanding its international efforts. Today its products are available in 40 nations including the United States, the European Union, China, Taiwan, and a host of other Asian countries. In most instances Kirin has teamed up with a local brewer. For example, in 1998 the company entered into a partnership with Anheuser-Busch that allowed Kirin beer to be brewed in Los Angeles and then shipped to the rest of the country. By 2001 this strategy was paying off. US sales tripled within these three years.

Kirin has also been actively expanding in Asia. China (by consumption, the second largest beer market after the United States) is one of Kirin's most important foreign markets. Three subsidiaries, San Miguel, Lion Nathan, and Zhuhai Kirin, are central to its expansion in the growth markets in China. It is now the top imported beer in Taiwan. So the company is off to a good international start. Competitors, however, are also expanding internationally, creating an ongoing need for product differentiation and good brand marketing. So Kirin still has a long way to go.

One of the things that may help the company is that it is part of Mitsubishi, Japan's largest *keiretsu*. Today the Mitsubishi group has annual sales in excess of $110 billion, and there are approximately 29 core members who are bound together by cross-ownership and other financial ties. Although the members of this *keiretsu* operate independently, they can call upon one another for help. For example, when Akai Electric had financial problems, Mitsubishi Bank rescued it. When Mitsubishi Heavy Industries' shipbuilding business ran into trouble, it was able to find work at other group companies for those personnel who were laid off. And the cross-holding structure has also come in handy when warding off takeovers. For example, when Texaco bought Getty Oil, it was prepared to sell Getty's 50 per cent share of Mitsubishi Oil to Kuwait Petroleum. However, the members of the Mitsubishi group got together and outbid the Kuwaitis for Getty's shares. The group has also made important acquisitions and struck major deals in a variety of areas. Mitsubishi companies have participated in the $940 million purchase of the Pebble Beach golf course in California, won a $400 million power plant deal in Virginia, and launched a $150 million futures trading joint venture in Chicago. Overall, Mitsubishi has hundreds of interdependent companies, and they are building an empire that stretches from Asia to Europe to the United States. With their help, Kirin may be able to become a major international brewer.

Websites: www.kirin.co.jp; www.mitsubishi.com; www.asahibeer.co.jp; http://www.beverageworld.com/beverageworld/headlines/; and http://www.kirin.co.jp/english/annual2003/08source.html.

Sources: Emily Thornton, "Japan's Struggle to Restructure," *Fortune*, June 28, 1993, pp. 84–88; "Japan's Beer Wars," *Economist*, February 26, 1998; "A Right Old Brewhaha in Japan," *Economist*, February 22, 2001; and Kyodo News, "Japan Brewers' Shipments Rose Slightly in 2004," January 18, 2005, *Kyodo News International*, Tokyo.

Distribution, retailing, and customer orientation

Associated with the *keiretsu* industry groupings above are multilayered distribution and retail networks in Japan. At its height it was estimated that there was one retail outlet for every 75 people in Japan (over twice the US ratio) and over 476,000 wholesale stores. These are still organized both by region and by sector and product across Japan and tend to be geared to the large number of small retailers that serve the local markets. This "tied" system of distribution, bound by strong face-to-face ties between sellers and buyers at each level, adds substantial costs to the final product. Again, at its peak, the American Chamber of Commerce in Japan (ACCJ) found that over 48 per cent of home electronics products in Japan are sold through exclusively affiliated stores, and about 99 per cent of cars are distributed through exclusive dealerships.[15]

Many elements of this complex, high-cost distribution remain in Japan today. Ports in particular are notoriously protected and relatively slower and more expensive than in other OECD countries. The multitiered distribution hierarchy has become more simplified, however, driven by the growth in discount stores and cost-reduction measures.[16]

Until recently the strong patriotic preferences of the average Japanese consumer and, perhaps, the average Japanese middle manager responsible for company purchasing policy, provided a firm basis for the country's industrial and distribution infrastructure. Outside the luxury or branded consumer goods markets the Japanese have long had a strong preference for Japanese products.

JAPANESE CORPORATIONS

Japan is home to around 25 per cent of the top 100 multinational firms. It is not just a large economy and a large market, but a major source of global competitors. Various stereotypes underlie popular beliefs about Japanese firms that are at best inaccurate and sometimes wholly misleading.

At one extreme, during the 1970s and 1980s, Japanese firms were seen to exemplify the best of all management practices. High-profile articles and books on the Japanese threat fed a general fear about the competitive threat they posed and prompted researchers to identify what was different about Japan and its firms and how such differences might convey sustained competitive advantages.[17] At the other end of the extreme the economic and corporate failures of the period broadly from 1990 to 2003 have prompted wholesale criticism of the Japanese model.

The truth lies somewhere in between. The Japanese economy, culture, and business system underpin both relative strengths and weaknesses in Japanese companies. The former were very evident during the period of social and political stability and economic growth up to the end of the 1980s. The latter have become more apparent since then.

Very broadly speaking, two kinds of Japanese corporations have existed for some time. On the one hand those firms that have escaped the effects of the extended recession, such as Toyota, Honda, Sony, Canon, Sharp, and Toshiba, have been less dependent on the Japanese market (more internationalized) for some time. They increasingly sold products in markets outside Japan, engaged in FDI abroad, and evolved "less Japanese" styles of management well before the recessionary period. They also represent the industries in which Japan achieved its high levels of export competitiveness in the growth years, which is why we know more about them in the West.[18]

On the other hand a large number of firms, the majority of Japanese companies in fact, including firms like Nippon Steel, Sumitomo Chemical, Mitsubishi, Kajima, and Dentsu, are less geographically diversified. They have long remained more dependent on the Japanese market, Japanese suppliers, and Japanese ways of doing things.

Confirmation of this division comes from the McKinsey Global Institute study which shows that although labor productivity in Japan's top firms (such as those above) is 20 per cent higher on average than in US firms they only represent 10 per cent of the Japanese economy. The other 90 per cent of Japanese firms have an average labor productivity that is 60 per cent of US levels.[19]

Table 17.4 shows the top 40 Japanese firms (from a list of the top 500 multinational firms). It also classifies the firms according to their global distribution of sales, showing their relative dependence on their domestic (Japanese) markets. All but a very few are highly dependent on their domestic market, and only Sony and Canon are global in that they have over 20 per cent of their sales in each of the triad regions. Despite the above-mentioned variations in the structures, strategies, and management styles of Japanese firms, there are some common, distinctive characteristics of the stereotypical Japanese firm, relative to its European and American counterparts.

In one of the most extensive studies of the Japanese enterprise system, Fruin highlights high productivity, functional specialization, and manufacturing adaptability as the distinguishing hallmarks of Japanese firms. He identifies these attributes at three, connected levels: the factory, the firm, and the interfirm network.[20]

The various social, cultural, and economic characteristics above combine to create certain strengths and weaknesses in Japanese firms. From a wide range of studies[21] we can distill some of the main characteristics of the generic Japanese management style, again traditionally:

Benkyokai
Study associations or work groups for students or colleagues in companies to jointly develop particular areas of knowledge and expertise

- Effective communications internally and with outside firms (decentralized, horizontal information flows) and the use of *benkyokai* or cross-disciplinary, cross-business, and cross-functional workshops.

- Less separation of R&D, design, manufacturing, and marketing functions.

- Lifetime employment, low labor mobility, and substantial investments in training. There is also a strong emphasis on on-the-job training and job rotation within the firm.

- Managers as problem definers, not firefighters, and as educators and mentors, not disciplinarians. This is underpinned by the weak links between performance and pay and the low wage differentials between workers and managers in the age-related hierarchy.

Table 17.4 The Top 40 Japanese firms

Company	Revenues in US $ bn	F/T Sales	North America % of total	Europe % of total	Asia Pacific % of total	C
Toyota Motor	146.57	58.6	34.2	11.7	41.4^j	B
Mitsubishi	128.62	15.3	4.6^z	na	87.2	D
Mitsui	104.08	41.4	6.8^z	1.3^u	58.6^j	D
Marubeni	85.72	31.5	14.2	3.6	74.1	D
Itochu	80.65	20.9	4	1.8	92.4	D
Sumitomo	77.95	42.3	16.1	13.2	64.6	D
Hitachi	73.16	34.5	10.1	7.6	79.6	D
Honda Motor	69.17	80.1	55.7	9.4	29.8	S
Sony	63.53	70.4	28.3^z	23.6	29.6^j	G
Matsushita Electric Industrial	63.39	53.5	17.7	14.4	67.8	D
Nissan Motor	62.96	65.5	44 1	15.7	34.5^j	B
Sojitz	49.68	20.5	4.9	3.6	91.3	D
Toshiba	47.28	39.1	12.7	9.3	75.8	D
NEC	41.58	20.7	na	na	79.3^j	D
Tokyo Electric Power	41.13	<10	na	na	>90.0^j	D
Fujitsu	40.40	24.4	5.3^l	11.4	75.6^j	D
Japan Tobacco	39.20	14.8	na	6.7	85.2^j	D
Nippon Oil	36.27	2.2	0.9	0.3	98.9	D
Sumitomo Mitsui Financial Group	31.10	8.5	3.8^l	2.1	94.1	D
Ito-Yokado	30.02	36.3	33.1^z	na	63.8^j	D
Mizuho Financial Group	28.33	13.8	5.6^l	5.8	88.7	D
Mitsubishi Electric	28.05	14.1	6.6	6.2	97.7	D
Canon	27.10	74.9	32.7^l	30.3	26.8^j	G
Nippon Steel	24.80	<10	na	na	>90.0	D
Mazda Motor	24.71	60.3	31.6	22.3	39.7^j	G
KDDI	24.12	–	–	–	100	D
Mitsubishi Tokyo Financial Group	23.12	39.5	21.1^z	10.2	64.3	D
Mitsubishi Heavy Industries	22.57	11.8	6.7	2.9	90.2	D
Denso	21.72	43.7	21.7^l	13	65.1	D
Fuji Photo Film	21.70	47.8	21.2^l	14.7	52.2^j	D
East Japan Railway	21.54	0	0	0	100^j	D
Mitsubishi Motors	21.35	37.9	23.8	26.1	69.4	D
Sanyo Electric	21.25	49.5	13.4	7.4	77.2	D
JFE Holdings	20.96	<10	na	na	>90.0^j	D
Bridgestone	19.52	65.1	42.2^l	12.5	34.9^j	B
Sharp	19.13	49.3	13.7^l	14.7	63	D
Suzuki Motor	18.64	52	13.4	17	68.5	D
Daiei	16.89	<10	na	na	>90.0^j	D
Japan Airlines	16.37	<10	na	na	>90.0^j	D
Mitsubishi Chemical	16.32	15.2	na	na	93.9	D

Notes: Data are for 2003. u = United Kingdom; l = Americas; z = United States; j = Japan; D = home region oriented; S = host region oriented; B = bi-regional; G = global.

Sources: S. Collinson and A. M. Rugman, *Japanese Business Is Regional, Not Global*, Association of Japanese Business Studies Conference, Quebec, 2005.

Despite the importance of hierarchy and job titles, average CEO incomes in Japan are rarely more than 10 times the salaries of new recruits. In the US (and increasingly in the UK) there is a much bigger remuneration gap than this.

■ Strong group/team ethic, loyalty, and motivation combined with competitiveness between teams.

■ Strict formal hierarchy (based on seniority, rank and title also underpin social status) combined with strong underlying informal networks and a tendency toward consensus-based

Nemawashi
Literally means "root tying" and is a process of consultation to get agreement on a particular issue before it becomes explicit policy

Ringi
The formalized consensus process of decision making; the *ringisho* is a decision proposal circulated around company departments to be revised or approved before implementation

(*nemawashi* and *ringi*) decision making (horizontal promotion for high fliers and a lack of outsiders entering the firm at senior levels).

■ General "long-termism" with a focus on growth, employment stability, and market share rather than profits and shareholder dividends.

These are obviously generalizations, but are factors that tend to exist more or less in a wide range of Japanese firms. Overall, Japanese firms have a strong focus on human resources. A great deal of their strength (and a source of some weaknesses) lies in the employer–employee relationship and the commitment and loyalty shown by each to the other.

This overview of some of the key characteristics of the Japanese has been highly generalized, aiming to select factors that underpin significant differences in Japan relative to other countries. One of the best early books on Japanese firms and business practices called *Kaisha* ("company") by Abegglen and Stalk[22] sums up some of these distinctive characteristics as the 3 Ms:

■ *Marketing*: direct links with consumers via retailers and wholesalers and strong customer-led product development.

■ *Money*: cross-shareholding and the lack of outside pressure for short-term returns and stock price improvements.

■ *Manpower strategy*: worker involvement, loyalty, effective team working and devolvement of responsibility combined with hierarchy.

A CHANGING NATION

The past decade has seen a number of major changes in Japan's social, economic, and political structure and this change continues. The added difficulties brought about in Japan by the current period of chaotic upheaval is partly related to the unusual degree of stability and consensus that the country has experienced throughout a long high-growth era that is now over.

Starting in the early 1990s Japan has experienced its worst economic recession in the post-war period. Slower growth, reduced investment, declining property prices, and increased unemployment are all secondary effects of earlier declines in profitability, increased domestic costs, and falling domestic demand. These were masked in the late 1980s by rapid growth rates based on strong exports and cheap capital, which ended abruptly when the bubble burst and *endaka* began. The recession is linked to the fast appreciation of the yen, which partly resulted from the 1985 Plaza Accord and continued through the mid-1990s, rising 24 per cent in value between early 1993 and early 1995.

Endaka
Yen-appreciation; the growing value of the yen vis-à-vis other currencies which, among other things, made Japan a relatively expensive place to manufacture

Plaza Accord
An agreement signed by the G5 in 1985 in New York, agreeing to devalue the US dollar against the Japanese yen and the deutsche (German) mark; it triggered the bubble economy and eventual economic recession in Japan in the 1990s

Between 1990 and 2000 unemployment grew from 2.1 to 4.7 per cent; GDP growth fell from 5.1 to 1.9 per cent; motor vehicle production fell by 25 per cent; the sales of large department stores slumped by 13 per cent; and residential land prices in Tokyo dropped by 55 per cent.

Alongside this economic slump, significant social and cultural developments have resulted in an unprecedented degree of tension between traditional and modern ways of living and working. Some of the broader elements of social change include the aging population, changing diet and changing health problems, a rising crime rate (though from a very low base rate), new attitudes toward work and leisure and, among some in Japan, a perceived decline in moral values (among others, a new freedom and social openness).

Japan's social homogeneity proved to be a strength in the period of rapid economic development of the past, but may well prove increasingly to be a weakness as it becomes more international. As the country becomes less isolated from the rest of the world the individualistic, Western aspirations of the younger Japanese increasingly clash with the more conservative, group-oriented nature of the older Japanese. The latter are largely responsible for the rapid economic development of Japan in the post-war period through their hard work and their emphasis on building rather than enjoying prosperity.

Shinjinrui ("new human being") is a term that the Japanese use to describe the younger generation as well as some of the more well-traveled middle-aged citizens who are pushing at the social restrictions that emphasize education, training, and work above personal pleasure, leisure, and family. At the same time a greater degree of interaction with other countries and cultures, plus a growing number of foreigners visiting, working, and living in Japan, are forcing many Japanese to compromise what has been termed their ethnocentric view of the world.

Some of the most obvious changes are seen in the buying patterns of Japanese consumers. Beyond a long-term move to Western foods and clothing styles there has also been a growing preference for "value for money" and an increase in buying from previously frowned-upon foreign firms and discount retail stores. This is partly because of the recessionary pressure on wages but is also an indication that consumers are beginning to realize and object to the fact that Japan's consumer prices were well over the OECD average.

This change in consumer behavior, alongside the increasingly price-oriented, cost-cutting objectives of manufacturers, has challenged the multilayered distribution system that has dominated wholesale and retail networks in Japan. A flatter distribution system has begun to develop, pioneered by discount stores and direct importers, like the Daiei chain, which has experienced a boom in its own-label brands since the mid-1990s, allowing it to cut prices by using imported products, from Brazilian orange juice to Korean video tapes.

We will now examine some specific aspects of change in Japan: the restructuring of the capital markets, deregulation, and increased inward foreign direct investment and the restructuring of Japanese corporations.

Restructuring capital markets

The changing role of banks and the evolution of Japan's financial services industry have recently created instability in the corporate finance system. During the 1980s there was a general move toward using capital markets for funding investment, particularly among large manufacturing companies in Japan. These used bonds and equity for about 52 per cent of the finance they raised in 1989 compared with 27 per cent in 1980. Partly as a consequence, banking relationships became less stable with far more companies taking loans from more than one bank and changing their main lender. Loose financial discipline in the high-growth, high-investment years resulted in heavy depreciation charges, often on investments that have resulted in overcapacity rather than bringing in extra revenue.

The scale of this instability only became clear after the bubble era of the late 1980s when the collapse in property prices, which underpinned much of the private-sector borrowing, left many companies in financial difficulties. Land values in Japan's main cities fell by 50 per cent between 1990 (the peak year) and 1995. Financial problems have also been highlighted by the growing number of non-performing loans and the loan restructuring carried out by the commercial banks (like Mitsubishi in June 1994 and Daiwa in mid-1995).

In the late 1990s foreign investors took advantage of the depressed prices to buy property in Japan. US investment companies in particular invested, with 12.5 billion yen in properties sold to Goldman Sachs and 50 properties worth 20 billion yen sold to Loan Star Opportunity. Not only were property prices low, with debt-ridden financial institutions selling properties held as collateral, but government de-regulation (particularly the SPC law relating to the securitization of specified assets bill) aimed to make the real-estate market more market driven. They increased the transparency of data relating to property values, occupancy rates, and rents, and made it more difficult to use property to hide personal and corporate finances. Credit recovery, loans, and mortgage services, previously restricted to local firms, were also opened up to foreign participants, with tax laws changed to facilitate this.

Shinjinrui
The new generation of Japanese, with very different values and aspirations than their parents

Original banks	New bank groups		
IBJ		IBJ-DKB-Fuji	
Nippon Kangyo Bank	Dai-Ichi Kangyo Bank		
Dai-Ichi Bank			
Fuji Bank			
Yasuda Bank	Subsidiary of Fuji Bank		
Taiyo Bank	Taiyo Kobe Bank	Sakura Bank	Sakura-Sumitomo
Kobe Bank			
Mitsui Bank			
Sumitomo Bank			
Mitsui Trust	Mitsui-Chuo Trust		
Chuo Trust			
Hokkaido Takushoku	Acquired by Chuo Trust		
Sumitomo Trust			
Bank of Tokyo	Bank of Tokyo Mitsubishi		
Mitsubishi Bank			
Nippon Trust	Subsidiary of Mitsubishi Bank		
Mitsubishi Trust			
Sanwa Bank			
Toyo Trust	Subsidiary of Sanwa Bank		
Tokai Bank		Tokai-Asahi	
Kyowa Bank	Asahi Bank		
Saitama Bank			
Daiwa Bank	Acquires regional banks		
LTCB	Nationalized		
MCB	Nationalized		

Figure 17.7 Bank group consolidation in Japan

That conditions were getting tougher for Japanese firms is evident from the data on debt liabilities and bankruptcies. Corporate bankruptcy cases grew from about 7,000 per year in 1990 to 14,000 in 1996 and 17,000 in 2000. Levels of bankruptcy then stayed between 19,000 and 20,000 cases per year up to 2003.[23]

Figure 17.8 Declining cross-shareholding in Japan

Average proportion of shares in a company held by companies whose shares are held by this company.

Source: M. Abe and T. Hoshi, *Corporate Finance and Human Resource Management: Evidence from Changing Corporate Governance in Japan*, Dokkyo University and RIETI presentation, 2003.

Figure 17.9 Increasing foreign ownership in Japan

Foreign-owned percentage of market value of Tokyo Stock Exchange.

Source: M. Abe and T. Hoshi, *Corporate Finance and Human Resource Management: Evidence from Changing Corporate Governance in Japan*, Dokkyo University and RIETI presentation, 2003.

Average return on equity in 1997 was around 4 per cent in Japan compared with 20 per cent in the United States, a contrast that preceded the recession but had been accepted as part of the financial system. But while US companies achieve returns of around 4.5 per cent on average above cost of capital, since 1990 Japanese firms (on average) have failed to meet the growing costs of capital (i.e., they are "value destroyers" rather than "value creators").

As a result of these problems, a process of consolidation, rationalization, and mergers got underway in Japanese capital markets, partly forced on banks from government organizations, as financial deregulation continued (Figure 17.7). Disintermediation has taken place, with companies raising finance from capital markets rather than via traditional *keiretsu* cross-shareholding and bank relationships (Figure 17.8). A record 65 firms listed on Tokyo stock exchange in 1999. Private equity and venture capital also played a growing role, as did foreign investors (Figure 17.9).

Deregulation, increased M&A, and inward FDI

Although external pressure to deregulate the Japanese from European and US corporations and governments has declined, the pressure from inside Japan has grown. This, together with the changing priorities of Japanese firms and customers, has led to a significant increase in inward investment. In particular, foreign M&As, largely unheard of before the mid 1990s, have grown substantially, as shown in Figure 17.10. These are still relatively less significant than in other advanced economies (see Table 17.5).

European firms have significantly increased their investments in Japan, particularly French firms, which saw their investments in 1999 rise 51-fold over 1998 to overtake US firms as the leading foreign investors in Japan. French companies made large acquisitions in Japan's automobile, auto parts, and finance/insurance industries. Renault's 36.8 per cent stake in Nissan in March 1999 and second major investment in March 2002 has contributed to this (see **Real Case: Renault and Nissan: no pain, no gain** at the end of this chapter).

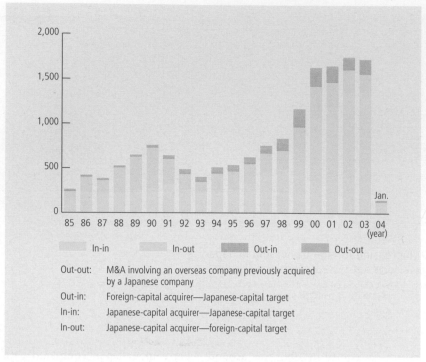

Figure 17.10 Number of Japan-related M&A transactions

Source: "M&A Integration Transforming the Corporate Landscape," *Invest Japan*, no. 4, Tokyo: Japan External Trade Organization, 2004, at: http://www.jetro.go.jp/en/invest.

Three sectors—finance, transport equipment, and telecommunications—accounted for some 90 per cent of the total value of foreign firm M&As in 1999. Large deals dominated the data for a time, including the US $6.6 billion acquisition of Japan Leasing Corp. by GE Capital and a US $1.8 billion stake in Japan Telecom by BT of the UK and AT&T of the US. There were numerous deals in excess of US $1 billion in 2000, including DaimlerChrysler's purchase of a stake in Mitsubishi Motors in October of that year. A growth in inward FDI has been driven by "out-in" M&A, foreign firms buying up local firms, such as the acquisition of Kito Corporation by the Carlyle Group and Chinon by Kodak (both cash mergers) (see **International Business Strategy in Action: Wal-Mart takes Seiyu**). By the end of 2003 the total value of inward FDI stock was up by 40 per cent on the total at the end of 2001.

Table 17.5 Out-in M&As in major developed countries and value of inward FDI (cumulative total, 1999–2003)

	(Units: no. of M&As, US$ billion)				
	Japan	Germany	US	UK	France
Number of M&As by foreign companies (Out-in M&As)	583	2,276	5,722	3,454	1,800
Out-in M&A rate (%)	10.7	36.0	15.5	25.9	37.8
Value of M&As by foreign companies (Out-in M&As)	72.9	417.3	957.1	510.0	136.1
Out-in M&A rate (%)	15.2	69.4	18.2	43.4	33.3
Value of inward FDI	42.9	324.5	890.0	301.8	236.3

Notes:

1. The out-in M&A rate indicates the proportion of the M&A market in each country accounted for by M&As where the ultimate parent company of the acquirer is foreign.

2. Figures for inward FDI indicate the cumulative net flow on a balance of payments basis.

Sources: Prepared from Thomson Financial data (as of March 18, 2004) and OECD data.

Wal-Mart takes Seiyu

The Japanese landscape is littered with the remains of foreign firms that misjudged the local market. In March 2002, Wal-Mart purchased a 6 per cent stake in Seiyu, the fourth largest supermarket chain in Japan. It retained an option to slowly increase its ownership position in the company to 66.7 per cent by 2007. In 2003, after a five-month feasibility study on opportunities in the Japanese market, it took a step in that direction by agreeing to spend $420 million to raise its stake to 34 per cent, making Wal-Mart the dominant shareholder.

To its Japanese operations, Wal-Mart brings a new management style, strategy, supplier networks, and one of the world's most formidable information and distributions systems. With $244 billion in revenues, Wal-Mart also brings the financial power to update Seiyu's ailing 400 stores. Wal-Mart hopes to repeat in Japan its successes in other "difficult" Asian markets, such as China (where it operates 18 stores) and South Korea (where it has 11). The 2001 replacement of Japan's Large-Scale Retail Store Law, which prevented large retail developments, with the more generous Large-Scale Retail Store Location Law has eased Wal-Mart's entry.

Success in Japan's retail market, however, remains anything but assured. The Always Low Prices strategy on which the company based its North American success must be adapted significantly to cater to the Japanese market. Japanese consumers insist on standards of quality that Wal-Mart is simply not used to offering in other countries. When, in the early 1990s, the Japanese retail giant Ito-Yokado stocked Wal-Mart biscuits in its stores, they were literally shunned because of their sickly taste and poor quality. Some 40 per cent of the biscuits in each packet were said to be broken. Ito-Yokado had to discontinue the product.

Further complicating Wal-Mart's strategy is the resilience of Japan's complex supply system. Carrefour, which entered Japan in 2002, is a good example. The French firm has fallen well short of its original plan to persuade all its Japanese suppliers to adopt the Carrefour direct-purchasing system. This has reflected both a lack of familiarity on the part of Japanese suppliers with such a system as well as the vice-like control over suppliers exerted by large Japanese retailers. Wal-Mart's terrifying reputation for squeezing suppliers' margins until the pips squeak—and then some more—may also make it less attractive as a partner for local firms.

Wal-Mart's success in the United States has also been based on low land prices and labor costs. The price of land in the outskirts of North American cities and suburbs has allowed the company to build large warehouse style retail stores with huge parking lots. Japanese land, however, is significantly more expensive. Despite a recession and the stagnation of the Japanese economy, Japanese labor costs are among the highest in the world. That customers demand personal service does not help either. For similar sized stores, Wal-Mart will have to hire more retail workers in a Japanese store than in the United States.

Lessons learned by Carrefour show that Wal-Mart will also have to differentiate itself from competitors. Carrefour positioned itself in the Japanese market simply as a discount retailer. With little to distinguish its product mix from those of its local rivals, the firm's stores underperformed, forcing a switch in strategy to emphasize its "Frenchness." It now offers a limited range of French products. After its initial stumble, the company now has eight stores in Japan.

The emphasis on fresh produce in Japanese cuisine means that there is high demand for perishable goods and less for the kind of processed foods that are often the staple of Western discount supermarkets. This has been cited as one reason behind the sluggish sales at the US warehouse retailer, Costco, since it entered Japan in 1999.

Another cultural consideration is that the Japanese are hesitant to purchase bulk quantities even if it would save them money. The reason for this is rather simple. While the Japanese remain among the world's wealthiest consumers with a GDP per head of US $32,000, they have on average only 33 square meters of living space per capita—45 per cent less than Americans and 14 per cent less than either the British or Germans.

To date, Wal-Mart has been finding ways to tailor its strategy to the Japanese market. The quality of its products has been raised enough to be acceptable. In renovated Seiyu stores, customers can see their sushi order prepared in front of them, as opposed to the pre-packaged variety offered in other countries. To lower land costs, Wal-Mart's stores will have two floors instead of the traditional one floor. Labor costs have been reduced by cutting 25 per cent of its workforce through voluntary retirement, saving $46 million on annual wages. It is also relying on its China-based suppliers to stock its Japanese shelves.

Other factors are adding to the company's problems, particularly from Japan's continuing economic woes and the tough competitive environment. Uniquely in the developed world, consumer prices in Japan have been falling each year since 1998. Growth has remained sluggish. Yet, that in itself ►

might make this the right moment to enter the market. By the time the country starts to grow again, Wal-Mart will have renovated stores, created new relationships with suppliers, linked all Seiyu stores to its computerized logistics system, and learned enough about the Japanese consumer. Domestic and foreign competitors, however, are also readying up. Ito-Yokado is updating its distribution system to match Wal-Mart's, and the Aeon Group is planning to have 75 Wal-Mart style super centers in Japan by the end of 2004. Wal-Mart only has one super center and only expects to build another in the foreseeable future. Its present concern is to renovate and improve the efficiency of Seiyu's supermarkets. Carrefour has fewer stores but these are entirely renovated.

Wal-Mart stumbled badly when it entered the German market and has learned its lesson. It took the firm two years to open its first super center, choosing to conduct focus groups and study local retailers instead of jumping in with a US-style mega store. Its choice of a local partner in the venture will also give it the benefit of local knowledge. In addition, this gives it a large store base, an advantage over other foreign retailers like Carrefour and Costco, which have chosen to build up stores from scratch. On the other hand, the firm has to drag with it the ailing, deteriorated, Seiyu stores for years as it slowly renovates them.

Websites: www.walmart.com; www.seiyu.co.jp; and http://www.jetro.go.jp/en/invest/whyjapan/success_stories/.

Sources: Wal-Mart, *Annual Report*, 2004; "Can Wal-Mart Woo Japan," *Business Week*, May 10, 2004; "Wal-Mart Moves to Control Seiyu," *CNN.com*, December 12, 2002; "Wal-Mart's Japanese Makeover," *International Herald Tribune*, July 19, 2004.

Overall, Japan saw 1,728 mergers and acquisitions in 2003, just under the overall total for 2002, which was a record year. Of these, foreign-based firms initiated a total of 158 M&A deals (see examples in Table 17.6), up 22.5 per cent from the previous year.[24]

Table 17.6 Main "out-in" M&A in Japan in 2002

Date	Acquired company	Industry	Acquiring company	Country of origin	Industry	Amount (US $ million)
March 2002	Nissan Motor Co., Ltd.	Transport machinery	Renault SA	France	Transport machinery	1,769
September 2002	Chugai Pharmaceutical Co., Ltd.	Pharmaceutical	Roche Holdings AG	Switzerland	Pharmaceutical	977
February 2002	Consumer credit business of Taihei	Consumer finance	CitiFinancial (Citigroup Inc.)	U.S.	Banking	796
December 2002	Seiyu	Retailing	Wal-Mart Stores Inc.	U.S.	Retailing	480*
May 2002	Loan Portfolio of Marufuku KK	Consumer finance	CitiFinancal (Citigroup Inc.)	U.S.	Banking	469
January 2002	Seiyo Food Systems Inc.	Food services	Compass Group PLC	U.K.	Food services	461
December 2002	Digital Electronics Corp.	Power distribution control systems	Schneider Electric SA	France	Industrial equipment	259
May 2002	Hokuriku Seiyaku Co., Ltd.	Pharmaceutical	Abbott Laboratories	U.S.	Pharmaceutical	252
February 2002	Showa Cabot Supermetal KK	Metals	Aizu Holdings (Cabot Corp.)	U.S.	Metals	200
April 2002	Seiko Contact Lens	Eye products	Ocular Sciences Inc.	U.S.	Eye products	169

*Includes capital increase by Wal-Mart in May.

Source: JETRO, *White Paper on FDI* (Tokyo: Japan External Trade Organization, 2003), at: http://www.jetro.go.jp/en/.

Active learning check

Review your answer to Active Learning Case question 3 and make any changes you like. Then compare your answer with the one below.

3 As part of the general growth of foreign direct investment into Japan, why are foreign firms increasingly able and willing to engage in mergers and acquisitions (M&A) with local firms?

On the one hand deregulation by the Japanese government has helped to make it easier in recent years for foreign firms to acquire Japanese firms. Changes in capital markets, some driven by the government, have promoted inflows of foreign capital to reduce the debt burden. Japanese banks are also much more interested in M&A as a means to rescue (or hand over responsibility for) failing local companies. More significant factors are, first, the growing optimism among foreign firms regarding the future prospects of the Japanese market and their confidence in M&A as a means of access. Second, the rise in M&A can be partly attributed to the changing attitudes of senior Japanese managers who see foreign firms as a means to escape their current economic problems. M&As can help drive some of the strategic changes desired by Japanese managers, such as internationalization and diversification. They can also help push through some of the necessary organizational changes, from de-linking from *keiretsu* relationships to changing internal hierarchies and reward systems.

RESTRUCTURING CORPORATIONS

The initial corporate reaction to the recession was to treat falling profits as part of a cyclical trend that companies could weather using their momentum from the previous decade. Japanese managers had little experience on how to handle the radical restructuring and downsizing that became necessary, particularly the problem of labor costs that quickly began to erode domestic manufacturing competitiveness. Labor costs per head in manufacturing were 25 per cent higher in 1992 than in 1988, in part because of the rise in white-collar employment, which expanded by a fifth between 1985 and 1992. Managers have been particularly slow in reorganizing to overcome their own office and administrative inefficiencies and this, combined with their reticence in cutting employees, resulted in the rapid collapse of corporate earnings at the start of the downturn.[25]

The impact of the corporate restructuring was clear from the series of companies announcing job losses in 2001: Toshiba cut 19,000 jobs, Fujitsu 21,000, Mitsubishi 9,500, and Nissan 21,000; even Sony asked 5,000 employees to take early retirement. Most firms cut their university recruitment programs pushing the unemployment rate for under 24 year olds to over 10 per cent. Some of the largest bankruptcies hit the economy at the start of the new decade, including Chiyoda Mutual life insurer with debts of 2,900 billion yen and the retailer Sogo in July 2001 with debts of 2,000 billion yen.

Despite rationalization, consolidation, and a significant growth of M&As in key sectors, Japanese companies are still having to restructure their operations substantially in the face of longer term pressures, including:

- more expensive capital,
- growing competition from low-cost Asian producers,
- declining prices of key manufactures, particularly electronics and autos,
- a slowing domestic economy, and
- growing inroads into the domestic economy by foreign competitors.

These developments had a knock-on effect as Japanese firms responded by restructuring internally and changing their interfirm trading relationships. The main changes are summarized below.

The decline of manufacturing and distribution *keiretsu*

Because a large proportion of Japanese SMEs are subcontractors to larger companies, within the multitiered hierarchies, recession and reorganization among the giants has had a direct effect on a large number of SMEs. Restructuring effects, coupled with the appreciation of the yen, have passed on down this hierarchy, from primary (direct) subcontractors through second-, third-, and fourth-level indirect suppliers. Mazda, for example, before being "absorbed" by Ford, attempted to cut its first-line subcontractors from 62 companies to 16, thereby passing on the responsibility for pushing down input prices to companies further down the chain. This also happened in the Renault–Nissan takeover (see **Real Case: Renault and Nissan: no pain, no gain** at the end of this chapter).

The system of cross-shareholding has become increasingly diluted through reductions in mutual equity stakes. In their drive to cut costs large manufacturing firms in Japan now avoid giving their usual suppliers a guaranteed volume of business over the long term but are encouraging them to compete with each other with a new emphasis on price as the deciding factor. More inputs are now bought from abroad so a more price-driven domestic market and freer flows of imports has evolved.

There has also been a decline in the use of exclusive agreements with single distributors or sales organizations. In the past these were the norm and in most sectors it was impossible to have multiple agreements or play distributors and retailers against each other to push up sales. Increasingly now, multiple agreements are accepted and the trader-wholesaler-retailer link need not be tied but competitive, with many players competing at each level in a "less imperfect" market.

The growth of outward FDI and off-shore manufacturing

Nearly half of all cars and machines made by Japanese-owned companies are made outside Japan. It has been overtaken by the United States as the largest producer of vehicles and by China as the largest producer of color televisions (Japan is now a net importer). A telling example of the resultant pressures was Nissan's closure of its 30-year-old Zama car plant near Tokyo in March 1995, the first Japanese car plant to be closed since World War II. Ironically, part of the plant that made 11.2 million vehicles in its lifetime was turned into a pre-delivery inspection center for Ford vehicles. Zama, with a local population of 116,000, lost 2,500 jobs, although most have been moved elsewhere within Nissan or found jobs in local service industries.

The decline of lifetime employment and changing HR management practices

Many of the changes being forced on Japanese managers are culturally taboo but economically inevitable. One of the most significant is the erosion of the lifetime employment system, which is very unlikely ever to return in its traditional form. Unemployment, traditionally very low and carrying a huge social stigma, officially grew to over 5 per cent (unofficial estimates put the peak nearer 8 per cent).

Early retirements, horizontal movement of employees, rising use of performance-related pay, and significantly reduced wage increases and bonuses at the annual wage negotiations in Japan also signified the new pressures on companies. The largest companies reduced their usual intake of university graduates to less than 20 per cent of normal levels during the early 1990s and introduced merit-based remuneration schemes. These changes also had significant knock-on effects, not least the rise in the already high rate of suicides, which went up by 35 per cent in 1998. In the long term, Japan will have an increasingly flexible labor market, with implications for all aspects of the traditional employee–employer relationship, in-house training, and company loyalty.

Diversification strategies

Diversification strategies have been the cornerstone of many corporate restructuring plans, some successful, others not.[26] NKK, Japan's second largest steelmaker, is a good example. At the beginning of 1995 its previously loss-making marine engineering division turned in an operating profit of almost 15 per cent on sales of almost $100 million (although NKK overall expects to make a loss of five times this amount). The turnaround in this particular division was due to extensive (and risky) investments into areas outside shipbuilding. These include the leisure industry, manufacturing an indoor ski slope and an artificial surfing beach (Wild Blue), using core technologies from their own test divisions. In addition to diversification within manufacturing, the changing cost structure for industrial production has, in particular, accelerated the shift toward services.

✔ **Active learning check**

Review your answer to Active Learning Case question 4 and make any changes you like. Then compare your answer with the one below.

4 **Despite widespread changes in Japan and the restructuring of Japanese corporations, why is it still important for foreign managers to understand something of the history and the context in which Japanese businesses have evolved?**

Whether competing with Japanese businesses, collaborating with them, or working for them, their current practices and their distinctive strengths and weaknesses are the result of their historical development in the political, economic, and social context of Japan. Their past is also the clue to their current restructuring, why it is necessary and why it is not a quick and simple process. Managers in firms looking to enter the Japanese market need to know about the broader context of Japan because this provides insights into the role of government agencies, the business infrastructure, *keiretsu* networks, business etiquette, the culturally-influenced preferences of customers, and the many other differences and difficulties that require adaptation. Japanese firms are a product of this unique environment and relatively few have broken away from their dependence on Japan's domestic market, and most retain elements of traditional Japanese management practices. Foreign managers will better understand the strategic options and organizational challenges they face in alliances, joint ventures, and M&A with Japanese companies if they know something of their home environment.

Examining the above changes, Michael Porter and colleagues analyzed the challenges facing Japanese managers and came up with the following guidelines for transforming the Japanese company:[27]

- *Create distinctive, long-term strategies*—rather than imitating close rivals break out of the consensus and do something different.
- *Expand the focus of operational effectiveness*—i.e., improve office-level productivity as well as plant-level efficiency.

- *Learn the role of industry strategy in structure*—among a number of strategic changes, firms should avoid getting locked into price-based rivalry.

- *Shift the goal from growth to profitability*—focusing on market share was only possible with "patient capital" (linked to *keiretsu* and traditional capital markets); shareholder pressure will push for performance-related rewards.

- *Reverse unrelated diversification*—pare down to your core competencies and let other firms do the rest.

- *Update the Japanese organizational model*—change internal practices, away from hierarchy and consensus toward meritocracy and entrepreneurship.

- *Move away from incremental change*—become more flexible and responsive to suit the new competitive environment.

Porter and his co-authors select a number of firms that they suggest epitomize what is needed in terms of the above changes. Nidec, Rohm, Murata, and Futaba Denshi are specialist firms with very good global market shares in niche areas. Between 1989 and 1998 they achieved an average 6.3 per cent return on sales, while three *sogo denki* (literally "diversified electrical") firms achieved just 0.9 per cent return over the same period.

The book discusses the strategies and organizational practices of Nidec, Rohm, Kyoden, and Shimano (the bicycle gears maker) showing how they have moved away from the constraints of the traditional Japanese corporate form. Sony, however, is praised as a global Japanese firm that has adapted successfully to the new realities with a maverick CEO, Nobuyuki Idei, devolved strategy and accountability in four market-facing divisions, stock options for executives (since 1997), and with 45 per cent of its shareholders being non-Japanese.

A final illustration of the changing views of Japanese managers came from a poll taken of 116 company presidents asked to vote for the most outstanding corporate managers for the 21st century.[28] Sony chairman and CEO Nobuyuki Idei topped the list; second was Jack Welch, former General Electric chairman and CEO; then came Hiroshi Okuda, Toyota Motors chairman; Carlos Ghosn, Nissan Motor president; and Fujio Cho, Toyota Motors president. Several deceased businessmen such as Soichiro Honda, Masaru Ibuka, and Konosuke Matsushita were praised on the grounds that they are "managers who would succeed in any era and in any country." "Creative destruction" was voted the key concept for managers in the 21st century.

CONCLUSIONS

Japan continues in a period of fundamental political, economic, and social transformation. Corporations have been forced by a drawn-out economic recession to alter radically the way they organize and invest. Foreign firms are finding, despite the depressed state of the Japanese market, there are unprecedented opportunities for alliances and takeovers involving Japanese firms and for introducing new products and services to Japanese customers. There is a new period of internationalization as Japanese firms shift investments out of Japan and attempt to reduce their dependence on local markets, while foreign imports, investment, and M&A are on the increase.

Much of this chapter has looked at the traditional way of doing business in Japan, the unique capital markets, *keiretsu*, demanding customers, lifetime employment, and the traditional strengths and weaknesses of Japanese firms. The point of this is that these are enduring facets of Japanese business and they underlie the key distinctiveness that collaborators and competitors need to understand. They also continue to strongly influence the restructuring options open to Japanese firms and the changes in the economy as a whole. Any in-depth country analysis must take account of the way that such distinctive characteristics have evolved in the past and will continue to influence *relative* business practices, markets, and competitiveness in the future.

KEY POINTS

1 The current strengths and weaknesses of Japanese firms result from their evolution in a highly-competitive but continually growing domestic economy with unique sociocultural foundations.

2 The Japanese business environment was traditionally characterized by strong inter-firm rivalry; "patient" long-term finance, partly through cross-shareholding arrangements; *keiretsu* relationships, both vertical and horizontal; complex, multitiered distribution systems; demanding customers; and strong government intervention in the early years.

3 Sociocultural factors that supported the Japanese way of doing business include ideals of obligation, loyalty, hierarchy and ritual, and a strong work ethic, linked to mainstream religion; a strong but conformist education system and "groupism" plus consensus-based decision making in general; and complex language and tacit forms of communication.

4 Japanese firms are traditionally loyal to employees, who tend not to move from company to company; hierarchical and bureaucratic but also consensus-oriented; good at integrating between functions and teamwork; good at applied R&D and training; long-termist; and close to suppliers and customers.

5 The Japanese market has traditionally been difficult for foreign investors to break into, partly because of the factors listed above and partly because of the system of governance that tends to favor local firms.

6 Japan is changing. Growing social and political heterogeneity alongside a prolonged economic recession is creating unprecedented tensions and forcing drastic corporate restructuring. *Keiretsu* families are loosening or breaking up; firms are diversifying and divesting; lifetime employment is declining; capital markets are heavily restructuring; and deregulation is the norm.

7 Changes in Japan are creating investment, M&A, and market-entry opportunities for foreign firms.

• Ministry for Economy, Trade and Industry (METI)	• *hai*	• co-prosperity pyramid
• Ministry of Finance (MOF)	• *keiretsu*	• *benkyokai*
	• *kaizen*	• *nemawashi*
• *amakudari*	• *kinyu*	• *ringi*
• *chu* and *giri*	• *zaibatsu*	• *endaka*
• *gaijin*	• *sogo shosha*	• Plaza Accord
	• Mitsubishi Kinyokai	• *shinjinrui*

REVIEW AND DISCUSSION QUESTIONS

1 List some of the factors underlying the competitive advantages of Japanese firms, developed during the rapid growth era of the 1950s, 1960s, and 1970s.

2 What kinds of social and cultural characteristics of the Japanese underlie their proficiency in manufacturing?

3 How do *keiretsu* structures promote process and product innovation in Japanese firms?

4 Why have inflows of FDI into Japan historically remained lower than FDI outflows?

5 How would a foreign firm wanting to establish a sales and marketing operation in Japan need to adapt to succeed?

6 Why is the economic recession in Japan resulting in outflows of manufacturing investment?

7 What have been the main advantages and disadvantages for many Japanese firms of relying on domestic markets rather than internationalizing?

8 How can we explain Japan's deepening trading relationship with China?

9 What has triggered the restructuring of capital markets in Japan, and what have been the effects on Japanese corporations?

10 How can an economy in recession present new opportunities for foreign investors?

11 What strategic and structural changes are many Japanese firms making in response to the changing economic and competitive environment they face?

12 Why have senior Japanese managers shown a growing admiration for some top foreign CEOs and management gurus?

REAL CASE

Renault and Nissan: no pain, no gain

In March 1999 one of Europe's biggest car makers, Renault, bought a 36.8 per cent stake in Nissan, Japan's second-largest vehicle manufacturer. It has since increased its stake to 44.4 per cent with Nissan having a reciprocal 15 per cent share in Renault. The alliance has deepened following the far-reaching changes put in place by Carlos Ghosn, installed as president and CEO of Nissan and now revered for having engineered a radical turnaround in the firm's fortunes. Although numerous alliances involving equity participation had taken place before this, notably the Ford–Mazda alliance, the Renault–Nissan case was seen to be a highly unusual foreign "rescue" of a major Japanese firm in dire straits.

Nissan had made losses in six of the seven years prior to 1999, having been hit hardest of all the major car manufacturers in Japan by the decline in domestic sales and the rise in local manufacturing costs. Factory capacity utilization had fallen to 53 per cent, and Carlos Ghosn, the new CEO of Nissan (known as "le cost-killer"), set out to cut 21,000 jobs, close five factories, and cut the number of suppliers in half. Close, *keiretsu* relationships with suppliers and distributors were traditionally seen to be a key strength of Japanese manufacturers (Nissan had formerly been part of the Fuyo *keiretsu*), supporting high-quality products, process innovation, just-in-time supply systems, and rapid, customer-led new product development. In a time of recession they represented an over-extended supplier and dealer base, undermining profitability.

Internal restructuring also took place, following Ghosn's plan to introduce stock options and bonuses based on achievement and a performance-based promotions scheme, eventually for both employees and managers.

In the case of both external and internal reorganization there are significant clashes with the traditional Japanese way of doing things. First and foremost, job losses represent an enormous problem for managers and employees alike, almost a personal admission of failure on both sides which has social as well as corporate repercussions. The ties of obligation and loyalty associated with lifetime employment are broken. Indirectly, the breakdown of *keiretsu* links with other firms has a parallel effect, also resulting in job losses and the separation of long-term associations, which include personal friendships between managers and employees in both sets of firms.

Internal changes, particularly the introduction of performance-based remuneration and reward, are also radical in the eyes of the Japanese. Lifetime employment is associated with an age-related hierarchy where salaries only grow toward the end of a manager's tenure in the firm, as a reward for long years of service. To lose this reward, either because the firm no longer needs you or because the basis of remuneration is changed, is a drastic shift in the social contract employees entered into. Moreover, losing out to fast-track younger managers who rise up the hierarchy on the basis of their ability is not expected, particularly as talented managers may themselves have had to wait their turn in the past.

The steps taken by Renault change the rules of the game in Japan. Many would say that a sharp shock to push much-needed restructuring was the only way. Renault's rescue was called for partly because of Nissan's accumulated losses, which could no longer be supported in a recession, particularly by investors who could no longer afford to ride the storm in a time when capital markets were tightening significantly. But it was also needed because of the inherent problems Japanese managers face in trying to drive such radical restructuring themselves. The senior managers responsible for six years of losses are still in charge alongside Ghosn, having "saved face" because an outsider (a *gaijin*) forced the radical steps needed to turn the company around. Without this outside shock many Japanese firms remain locked in to a certain way of doing things because forcing these kinds of changes from the inside on one's work colleagues and friends appears to be too costly. It threatens to destroy the social as well as the business fabric on which the country's impressive historic growth has been founded,

and most Japanese do not want to be responsible for this kind of destruction, however creative it might be.

The Renault–Nissan alliance is now heralded as one of the most successful in the business. In the first few years Nissan's $13 billion debt was substantially reduced, it achieved $2.3 billion profits in 2002, and its stock price went from a low of $4.50 in October 1998 to over $16 in May 2002 and over $21 in January 2005.

On reflection, it represents the combination of two very different organizations, structurally and culturally. Renault was a strongly home-region oriented firm, heavily dependent on its home economy, France. Alone it was relatively small, holding just 4.2 per cent of the global market, but vying with Volkswagen for European market leadership, which it held 10.7 per cent of in 2002. Nissan was one of the unusual bi-regional auto firms, with strong sales in the United States and a relatively good market position in countries outside the triad regions.

Together Renault and Nissan account for 9.1 per cent of global auto sales, placing them jointly among the top five companies. The table below shows the individual and combined sales of both firms. These are similar-sized firms with very different geographic footprints that complement each other well.

A similar pattern of differentiation is true for production. Nissan manufactures just over half of its vehicles in Japan with most of the rest spread fairly evenly among the United States, Mexico, and the United Kingdom. It has industrial operations in 19 countries, including manufacturing sites in Taiwan, South Africa, Thailand, Philippines, and Indonesia. Renault manufactures in 17 countries but makes over 55 per cent of its vehicles in France and most of the rest in Europe.

Driven by an alliance board, chaired by the CEO of Renault, the two firms have developed shared production facilities in Mexico, Brazil, and Spain; common engineering platforms for entry-level B segment and mid-level C segment vehicles; common power train parts and increased

The global distribution of Renault and Nissan sales, 2002

Region	Renault		Nissan		Combined Sales	
France	763,612	32%	35,800	1%	799,412	16%
Germany	227,182	9%	64,269	2%	291,451	6%
UK	215,343	9%	106,583	4%	321,926	6%
Spain	202,186	8%	56,523	2%	258,709	5%
Italy	182,352	8%	59,616	2%	241,968	5%
Western Europe	1,869,251	78%	432,017	16%	2,301,268	45%
North America	NA	NA	804,186	29%	804,186	16%
Japan	2,414	0%	773,726	28%	776,140	15%
Other	532,310	22%	725,601	27%	1,257,911	24%
World Total	2,403,975	100%	2,735,530	100%	5,139,505	100%

Source: Corporate annual reports.

533

ALLIANCE worldwide sales and production sites in 2004

The figures* represent sales in thousands of vehicles.

Renault Group
Nissan Group

Combined Renault and Nissan sales:
5,785,231 units (up 8.0% over 2003)

Renault Group sales: 2,489,401 units
Renault Samsung Motors (RSM): 85,046 (down 23.7%)
Dacia: 95,627 units (up 39.1%)

Nissan Group sales: 3,295,830 units

Renault-Nissan Alliance global market
share came to 9.6%,
of which 4.1% for Renault and 5.5% for Nissan.

(1) of which Mexico
(2) of which Russia and Turkey
(3) of which Renault Samsung Motors
  * The figures have been rounded-off.

RENAULT GROUP PLANTS

Body assembly
Argentina, Brazil, Colombia, France,
Korea (RSM), Morocco, Romania
(Dacia), Slovenia, Spain, Turkey

CKD assembly
Brazil, Chile, China, France, Malaysia,
Portugal, Romania (Dacia), Russia,
Spain, Turkey, Uruguay

NISSAN GROUP PLANTS

Body assembly
Brazil, China, Indonesia, Japan,
Mexico, Philippines, South Africa,
Spain, Taiwan, Thailand, United
Kingdom, United States

CKD assembly
Egypt, Kenya, Malaysia, Pakistan

North America 1,055
United States 1,055
Mexico

Western Europe 2,285
United Kingdom 1,812
France 473
Spain
Portugal
Morocco

Latin America(1) 450
Colombia 148
Brazil 302
Uruguay
Argentina
Chile

Central and Eastern Europe(2) 413
Russia 342
Slovenia 71
Spain
Turkey
Egypt
Pakistan

Middle East and Africa 248
Kenya 91
South Africa 157

Japan 830
Japan 3
Korea 827
Taiwan
China
China
Thailand
Indonesia
Malaysia
Philippines

Asia and Oceania(3) 503
92
411

Figure 17.11 Renault–Nissan alliance basics

Source: http://www.renault.com/qb/qroupe/alliancespl.htm.

sharing of engines and transmissions; and increasingly integrated IT, information, and communications systems.

Renault's competencies in marketing, design, and financing complement Nissan's capabilities in engineering and manufacturing processes. Synergies are enhanced through the exchange of personnel. About 50 employees from Renault have joined departments such as supplier relations, product strategy, sales and marketing, and finance in Nissan. Similarly, around 50 Nissan employees work in the areas of quality control, vehicle engineering, manufacturing, and power train in Renault. Beyond this, 250 executives from both firms are assigned to the permanent alliance structures, including cross-company teams and functional task teams, and a further 250 Nissan employees are part of the restructured European sales and marketing divisions of Renault.

Websites: **www.nissan.com.jp** and **www.renault.com**.

Sources: A. M. Rugman, *The Regional Multinationals* (Cambridge: Cambridge University Press, 2005); A. M. Rugman and S. Collinson, "The Regional Nature

of the World's Automative Sector," *European Management Journal*, vol. 22, no. 5, 2004, pp. 471–482; R. Kelts, "The Cost Killer Cometh," *J@pan Inc.*, October 2003, **www.japaninc.com**; Renault/Nissan, *Annual Report*, 2002; V. Emerson, "An Interview with Carios Ghosn, President of Nissan Motors, Ltd. and Industry Leader of the Year," *Journal of World Business*, vol. 36, 2001, pp. 3–10; A. Hamey and T. Burt, "'Killer' to Make Unkindest Cut," *Financial Times*, October 18, 1999; Pearson, *Renault Nissan Alliance 2004* booklet; and **http://www.renault.com/gb/groupe/alliances_p1.htm**.

1 What broad economic and specific corporate pressures have resulted in the need for a radical shake up of Nissan?

2 In the context of traditional Japanese employment and working practices and interfirm relationships, why are the changes being pushed by Renault's Ghosn considered radical?

3 What has accounted for Ghosn's success to date with the Nissan restructuring?

4 In what ways are the two companies better together?

REAL CASE

Canon Group

Few companies can claim to be truly global multinationals, but with sales, revenues, production, and employees distributed across the world, the Canon Group of Japan comes as close as any to fitting that title. In 2003, 69.7 per cent of Canon's revenues originated outside of Japan. The Americas accounted for 32.7 per cent of total revenues and Europe for 25.1 per cent. The remaining 11.9 per cent of revenues were generated in other areas, including other Asia-Pacific markets.

Canon develops, manufactures, and markets copiers, computer peripherals, cameras, optical products, and business information products. The company had its beginnings in 1933, when Precision Optical Instruments Laboratory was established to conduct research into cameras in Roppongi, Minato-ku, Tokyo. In 1947 the company changed its name to Canon Camera Co., and only in 1969 did the company take on the name Canon Inc. In 2003, the company had revenues totaling $29 billion with 103,000 employees.

Canon's international expansion started in 1955 with the opening of a New York branch. Initially, the company relied on sole distributors and established some in Europe and Latin America in the late 1950s and early 1960s. The

sole distributor system was abolished in 1963 to make way for company-owned subsidiaries under the direct control of the Japanese headquarters.

International expansion goes beyond marketing to include production, research, and development. Taiwan became the site of Canon's first foreign-production facility in 1970. Two years later the company opened a manufacturing plant in Germany. By 2001, the company had production facilities in all parts of the triad—Western Europe, the Asia-Pacific region, and North America. Nevertheless, the vast majority of Canon's production facilities remain in Asia, including Japan.

In 1990, R&D centers were opened in the United States, Australia, France, Thailand, and the People's Republic of China. Each R&D facility specializes in a specific product line and is coordinated by a centralized R&D lab in Japan. Together with its R&D strategy, this has made Canon one of the best world innovators and the largest holder of patents after IBM.

Canon is organized regionally. Canon U.S.A. oversees operations in the Americas. The subsidiary has its own marketing, R&D, and production facilities. Two companies oversee European operations. Together, they have two manufacturing plants in Germany and France, and R&D centers in the United Kingdom and France. Canon's operations in Asia and Oceania, excluding Japan, account for the largest number of employees in foreign countries. Regionwide activities for the Asian market are overseen by the Canon Asia Marketing Group, but marketing operations in this region are subfragmented into sub-regional or national markets. The Southeast Asia region is the responsibility of Canon Singapore. Hong Kong has its own subsidiary that is also responsible for Taiwan and part of South Korea. The mainland Chinese market is the responsibility of Canon (China) Co. Japan's home market is still very important. Nearly half of Canon's employees are still working in Japan and companywide R&D is still centralized there. Canon Australia is responsible for operations in the Oceania region.

At a time when other Japanese, and many other, large electronic companies, are struggling to remain competitive, Canon's profits are soaring. The firm has been able to remain competitive by selecting those business lines in which it can be successful given its strength in R&D and production technology. The firm abandoned the markets for personal computers, typewriters, and liquid crystal displays to concentrate on cameras, printers, and copiers.

Studies suggest that one of Canon's key competencies is its global system for new product development. In particular it has evolved a number of organizational mechanisms for linking R&D and customer requirements globally. This is partly done through alliances and joint ventures in which Canon invests over the long-term to derive the benefits of co-learning and joint resource development. Canon contributes its technological capabilities and supplier links and local partners bring expertise relating to local customer preferences, distribution, and marketing.

In 2003, Canon registered the highest number of patents after IBM. The firm spends 8 per cent of its revenue on R&D. Canon finds not only new technologies, but also new methods of manufacturing products. Canon has been re-organizing its production facilities to take advantage of its global scope, selecting suppliers and production facilities across the world to minimize costs and decrease production time. As a result product design data can now be sent to plants around the world via computer. Information is translated through an automatic translation system allowing faster communication between subsidiaries. The firm is now using simulation technology to minimize the costly process of prototype production.

In the production floor, Canon's high productivity increases have been based on cell production technology.

Here, a small number of workers have responsibility for the final assembly of the product. This type of production not only increases the amount of a product being produced per labor-hour, but also ensures quality as it is easier to backtrack the production process of a single product. It also saves floor space. Since 1998, Canon has decreased the length of its conveyor lines by 12 miles. However, the productivity increases of applying and perfecting cell technology to its operations are reaching a limit and now Canon is seeking ways of integrating automation technology into its production process.

In 2002, Canon made the unlikely decision to establish a facility in Oita, Kyushu, Japan, to produce digital cameras. CEO Fujio Mitari's explanation is that "If we switch factories each time a place with lower labor costs is found, all investment in equipment is wasted. Instead, we should use our strengths in production, and manufacture products more cheaply than they could be manufactured in location where the cost of labor is lower." Indeed, nearly 60 per cent of Canon products are still manufactured in Japan. The company's long-term plan is to reach a balance between outsourcing and Japanese production. Mitari's position is that anything for which labor costs are more than 5 per cent of production costs can be outsourced to low labor-cost areas, such as China, and anything for which labor costs are less than 5 per cent of production—typically the more advanced technologically—can be produced domestically.

Website: www.canon.com

Sources: Canon, *Annual Report, 2003*; "Hard to Copy," *Economist*, October 31, 2002; "(Still) Made in Japan," *Economist*, April 7, 2004; B. Bowonder and T. Miyake, "R&D and Business Strategy: Analysis of Practice at Canon," *International Journal of Technology Management*, vol. 13, no. 7/8, pp. 833–853; H. Perks, "Exploring Processes of Resource Exchange and Co-Creation in Strategic Partnering for New Product Development," *International Journal of Innovation Management*, vol. 8, no. 1, pp. 25, 37.

1 Explain why, over the course of Canon's internationalization process, certain functions have been moved or expanded to certain global locations.

2 Why has it been important for Canon to internationalize its R&D activities?

3 Speculate as to why Canon is so unusual in its degree of independence from Japan's domestic market, compared with most other Japanese firms.

4 How is Canon still fairly dependent on Japan as a home base?

Endnotes

1 This is a recognized approach in management theory. By examining the broader competitive environment within which firms evolve we can identify where specific differences and competitive strengths and weaknesses come from. Evolutionary theories of the firm (Peyton Young), contingency theory (Donaldson), and the theory of nationally-bound administrative heritages (Calori et al.) all follow variations of this approach. L. Donaldson, *The Contingency Theory of Organizations* (Sage Publications, 2001); R. Calori, M. Lubatkin, P. Very, and J. F. Veiga, "Modeling the Origins of Nationally-Bound Administrative Heritages: A Historical Institutional Analysis of French and British Firms," *Organization Science*, vol. 8, no. 6, pp. 681–696; and H. Peyton Young, *Individual Strategy* and *Social Structure: An Evolutionary Theory of Institutions* (Princeton, NJ: Princeton University Press, 2001).

2 OECD, *Comparative Economic Performance in OECD Nations*. (Paris: OECD, 1989), p. 66 (http://www.oecd.org).

3 M. Fransman, *Japan's Computer and Communications Industry*. (Oxford: Oxford University Press, 1995).

4 C. Nakane, *Japanese Society* (Tokyo: Charles E. Tuttle, 1973).

5 http://web-japan.org/factsheet/education/curricula.html.

6 R. D. Pearce, and M. Papanastassiou, *The Technological Competitiveness of Japanese Multinationals*. (Ann Arbor: University of Michigan Press, 1996); J. H. Dunning and J. A. Cantwell, "Japanese Direct Investment in Europe," in B. Burgenmeier and J. L. Mucchielli (eds.), *Multinationals and Europe 1992* (London: Routledge, 1991).

7 S. Collinson and A. M. Rugman, "Japanese Business Is Regional, Not Global," *Association of Japanese Business Studies Conference*, 2005, Quebec.

8 Sir H. Cortazzi, *Modern Japan: A Concise Survey*, The Japan Times (London: Macmillan Press, 1993); M. Fruin, *The Japanese Enterprise System* (Oxford: Clarendon Press, 1992); M. Fransman, *The Market and Beyond* (Cambridge: Cambridge University Press, 1990).

9 JETRO, *JETRO White Paper on Foreign Direct Investment 2003* (Tokyo: Japan External Trade Organization, 2003), at: http://www.jetro.go.jp/en/stats/statistics/2003-1.pdf.

10 L. G. Franko, *The Threat of Japanese Multinationals: How the West Can Respond* (Somerset, NY: Wiley/IRM Series on Multinationals, John Wiley and Sons, 1983); M. J. Wolf, *The Japanese Conspiracy: Their Plot to Dominate Industry Worldwide and How to Deal With It* (New York: Empire Books, 1983); W. G. Ouchi, *Theory Z: How American Business Can Meet the Japanese Challenge* (New York: Horizon Books, 1981); P. F. Drucker, "Behind Japan's Success," *Harvard Business Review*, January/February 1981; E. F. Vogel, *Japan as Number One: Lessons for America* (New York: HarperCollins, 1979).

11 M. A. Cusumano and K. Nobeoka, "Structure, Strategy and Performance in Product Development: Observations from the Auto Industry," *Research Policy*, vol. 21, 1992, pp. 265–293; J. P. Womack, D. T. Jones and D. Roos, *The Machine That Changed the World* (New York: Macmillan, 1990).

12 OECD, *Science and Technology Statistical Compendium* (2004), at: http://www.oecd.org/dataoecd/17/34/23652608.pdf.

13 M. Fransman, "The Japanese Innovation System: How It Works," *Science in Parliament*, vol. 49, no. 4, October 1992.

14 W. Dawkins, "Loosening of the Corporate Web," *Financial Times*, November 30, 1994.

15 E. Terazono, "Cheap and Cheerful," *Financial Times*, March 15, 1994; "The Emporia Strike Back," Economist, October 29, 1994.

16 JETRO, *Regulations and Domestic Costs Related to the Distribution of Imported Goods* (Tokyo: Japan External Trade Organization, 2005), at: http://www.jetro.go.jp/en/stats/survey/.

17 See note 10.

18 Collinson and Rugman (2005) n. 7 above.

19 "Survey of Japan," *Financial Times*, December 2001.

20 Fruin (1992) n. 8 above.

21 M. Aoki and R. Dore (eds.). *The Japanese Firm* (Oxford. Oxford University Press, 1994); S. Clegg and T. Kono, *Transformations of Corporate Culture: Experiences of Japanese Enterprises* (Berlin and New York: Walter de Gruyter, 1998); M. Sako, *Japanese Labour and Management in Transition: Diversity, Flexibility and Participation* (London: Routledge, 1997); J. Laage-Hellman, *Business Networks in Japan: Supplier-Customer Interaction in Product Development* (London. Routledge, 1977); E. Westney, "Japan," in A. M. Rugman and T. Brewer (eds.), *The Oxford Handbook of International Business* (Oxford: Oxford University Press, 2001); R. D. Whitley, "Eastern Asian Enterprise Structures and the Comparative Analysis of Business Organizations," *Organization Studies*, vol. 11, no. 1, pp. 47–74.

22 J. C. Abegglen and G. Stalk, Jr. *Kaisha: The Japanese Corporation* (Tokyo: Tuttle Publications, 1985).

23 The monthly report from the Teikoku databank for September 2004 lists a total of 1,119 bankruptcies and $3,481 million in liabilities. The top 15 largest cases include no less than 5 golf courses (http://www.teikoku.com/bankruptcy/2004/200409.html); M. Abe and T. Hoshi, *Corporate Finance and Human Resource Management: Evidence from Changing Corporate Governance in Japan*, Dokkyo University and RIETI presentation, 2003.

24 JETRO, "M&A Integration Transforming the Corporate Landscape," *Invest Japan*, no. 4, 2004, at: http://www.jetro.go.jp/en/invest.

25 B. R. Schlender, "Japan's White-collar Blues," *Fortune*, March 21, 1994.

26 Unsurprisingly the evidence shows, in keeping with theory, that firms pursuing related diversification strategies are doing better than those involved in unrelated diversification. T. Ushijima and Y. Fukui, "Diversification Patterns and Performance of Large Established Japanese Firms," *Working Paper*, Aoyama Gakuin University Graduate School of International Management, Tokyo 2004; H. Kim, R. E. Hoskisson and W. P. Wan, "Power Dependence, Diversification Strategy and Performance in *Keiretsu* Affiliated Firms," *Strategic Management Journal*, vol. 25, 2004, pp. 613–636.

27 M. Porter, H. Takeuchi, and M. Sakakibara, *Can Japan Compete?* (Macmillan, 2000).

28 Toyo Keizai "Japan's Most Outstanding Corporate Managers," *Toyo Keizai*, January 13, 2001.

Additional bibliography

Aoki, M. "The Japanese Firm as a System of Attributes," in M. Aoki and R. Dore (eds.), *The Japanese Firm* (Oxford: Oxford University Press, 1994), pp. 11–39.

Basu, D. R. and Miroshnik, V. *Japanese Multinational Companies.* (Elsevier, 2000).

Beechler, S. L. and Bird, A. (eds.). *Japanese Multinationals Abroad.* (Oxford: Oxford University Press, 1999).

Collinson, S. and Wilson, D. C. "Inertia in Japanese Organizations: Knowledge Management Routines and Failure to Innovate," proceedings of the *Academy of Management Annual Conference*, Seattle, US.

Delios, A. and Beamish, P. W. "Joint Venture Performance Revisited: Japanese Foreign Subsidiaries Worldwide," *Management International Review*, vol. 44, no. 1, pp. 69–92.

Dore, R. *Stock Market Capitalism: Welfare Capitalism: Japan and Germany versus the Anglo-Saxons.* (Oxford: Oxford University Press, 2000).

Dore, R. and Sako, M. *How the Japanese Learn to Work.* (London: Routledge, 1998).

Dyer, J. H. and Hatch, N. "Using Supplier Networks to Learn Faster," *MIT Sloan Management Review*, vol. 45, no. 3, pp. 57–64.

Jameson, M. et al. "Ownership Structure and Performance of Japanese Firms: Horizontal *Keiretsu*, Vertical *Keiretsu*, and Independents," *Review of Pacific Basin Financial Markets & Policies*, vol. 3, no. 4, pp. 535–537.

Kobayashi, K. *The Rise of NEC: How the World's Greatest C&C Company is Managed.* (Oxford: Blackwell, 1991).

Kotabe, M., Martin, X. and Domoto, H. "Gaining from Vertical Partnerships: Knowledge Transfer, Relationship Duration and Supplier Performance Improvement in the US and Japanese Automotive Industries," *Strategic Management Journal*, vol. 24, no. 4, pp. 293–317.

Liker, J. K., Fruin, W. M. and Adler, P. S. (eds.). *Remade in America: Transplanting and Transforming Japanese Management Systems.* (New York: Oxford University Press, 1999).

Lincoln, E. J. *Arthritic Japan: The Slow Pace of Economic Reform.* (New York: Brookings Institution Press, 2001).

McGuire, J. and Dow, S. "The Persistence and Implications of Japanese *Keiretsu* Organization," *Journal of International Business Studies*, vol. 34, no. 4, pp. 374–389.

Nobeoka, K., Dyer, J. H. and Anoop, M. "The Influence of Customer Scope on Supplier Learning and Performance in the Japanese Automobile Industry," *Journal of International Business Studies*, vol. 33, no. 4, pp. 717–737.

Nonaka, I. "Redundant, Overlapping Organization: A Japanese Approach to Managing the Innovation Process," *California Management Review*, vol. 32, no. 3, pp. 27–39.

Nonaka, I. and Takeuchi, H. *The Knowledge-Creating Company: How Japanese Companies Create the Dynamics of Innovation.* (Oxford: Oxford University Press, 1995).

Thomas III., L. G. "Are We All Global Now? Local vs. Foreign Sources of Corporate Competence: The Case of the Japanese Pharmaceutical Industry," *Strategic Management Journal*, vol. 25, no. 8/9, pp. 865–887.

Whitley, R. et al. "The Changing Japanese Multinational: Application, Adaptation and Learning in Car Manufacturing and Financial Services," *Journal of Management Studies*, vol. 40, no. 3, pp. 643–672.

WWW resources

Japanese Ministry of Economy, Trade and Industry: http://www.meti.go.jp/english/

Japan External Trade Organization: http://www.jetro.go.jp

Japanese Ministry of Finance: http://www.mof.go.jp/english/

Chapter 18

NORTH AMERICA

Contents

Objectives of the chapter

Within NAFTA, the United States, Canada, and Mexico
constitute a thriving economic bloc. More than 32 per cent
of all US trade is with Canada and Mexico; both those countries conduct well over 75 per cent of their international
trade with the United States (see Tables 18.1, 18.2, and 18.3).
Much of this textbook has focused on doing business in the
United States. This chapter will explore the other two members of NAFTA: Canada and Mexico. These countries are very
different from the United States and have distinctive business practices. Doing business in these countries requires just
as much research and attention to institutional detail as
doing business in the EU or Japan.

The specific objectives of this chapter are to:

1 *Examine* the nature of the Canadian and Mexican political and economic systems and their implications for
  business strategy.
2 *Review* the business environment with primary attention
  on the industrial, regulatory, banking and finance, and
  labor relations areas.
3 *Investigate* major economic opportunities that exist in
  Canada and Mexico and some of the ways of conducting
  business in these nations.
4 *Consider* specific institutional arrangements, namely, the
  United States–Canada Free Trade Agreement (FTA) and
  the North American Free Trade Agreement (NAFTA),
  which play an important role in shaping opportunities
  and the business environment in North America.

Table 18.1 Direction of US trade

Country/region	Exports to				Imports from			
	1993		2002		1993		2002	
	(billions of US $)	% of total	(billions of US $)	% of total	(billions of US $)	% of total	(billions of US $)	% of total
Canada	100.2	21.5	160.8	23.2	113.6	18.8	214.0	17.8
Mexico	41.6	8.9	97.5	14.1	40.7	6.8	136.1	11.3
Japan	48.0	10.3	51.4	7.4	110.4	18.3	124.6	10.4
China (incl. Hong Kong)	18.7	4.0	34.7	5.0	44.2	7.3	144.6	12.0
EU15*	102.3	22.0	144.1	20.8	109.3	18.1	232.2	19.3
All others	155.1	33.3	204.4	29.5	184.7	30.6	350.5	29.2
Total	465.9	100.0	693.0	100.0	603.0	100.0	1,202.0	100.0

* Data for the EU15 in 1993 does not include Austria, Finland, and Sweden, which joined the union in 1995.
Exports are calculated without including freight and insurance while imports include freight and insurance.

Source: Adapted from IMF, *Direction of Trade Statistics Yearbook 2000*, 2003.

Table 18.2 Direction of Canada's trade

Country/region	Exports to				Imports from			
	1993		2002		1993		2002	
	(billions of US $)	% of total	(billions of US $)	% of total	(billions of US $)	% of total	(billions of US $)	% of total
United States	114.4	81.3	221.3	87.7	87.8	65.0	139.1	62.6
EU15*	8.1	5.8	10.5	4.2	12.7	9.4	24.7	11.1
Japan	6.4	4.6	5.2	2.0	8.3	6.1	8.8	4.0
Triad	129.0	91.6	237.0	93.9	108.7	80.5	172.6	77.7
Mexico	0.6	0.4	1.5	0.6	2.7	2.0	8.1	3.6
All others	11.2	7.9	13.9	5.5	23.6	17.5	41.3	18.6
Total	140.7	100.0	252.4	100.0	134.9	100.0	222.0	100.0

* Data for the EU15 in 1993 does not include Austria, Finland, and Sweden, which joined the union in 1995.
Exports are calculated without including freight and insurance while imports include freight and insurance.

Source: Adapted from IMF, *Direction of Trade Statistics Yearbook 2000*, 2003.

Table 18.3 Direction of Mexico's trade

Country/region	Exports to				Imports from			
	1993		2002		1993		2002	
	(billions of US $)	% of total	(billions of US $)	% of total	(billions of US $)	% of total	(billions of US $)	% of total
United States	43.1	83.3	143.0	89.4	46.5	71.2	106.6	63.3
Canada	1.5	3.0	2.8	1.8	1.2	1.8	4.5	2.7
North America*	44.7	86.3	145.9	91.1	47.7	73.0	111.0	66.0
Western Hemisphere†	2.8	5.4	5.7	3.5	2.7	4.1	6.3	3.7
EU15‡	2.7	5.1	5.2	3.3	8.5	13.0	16.4	9.8
Japan	0.7	1.4	0.5	0.3	3.4	5.2	9.3	5.6
All others	0.9	1.8	2.8	1.8	3.1	4.8	25.2	15.0
Total	51.8	100.0	160.0	100.0	65.4	100.0	168.3	100.0

* Excluding Mexico.
† Excluding Mexico, Canada, and the US.
‡ EU for 1993 refers to 12 countries in the EC; EU for 2002 includes Sweden, Finland, and Austria, which joined in 1995.

Source: IMF, *Direction of Trade Statistics Yearbook 2000*, 2003.

ACTIVE LEARNING CASE

The free trade area of the Americas builds on NAFTA

The United States–Canada Free Trade Agreement (FTA) of 1989 had a dramatic effect on the strategies of many companies in both countries. One of the most common developments was a consolidation of operations, improving the efficiency of production and distribution in the more integrated market. But many inefficient Canadian plants of uneconomic size closed down.

As a result, some Canadians worry that Canada will be unable to take advantage of the benefits of free trade between the two countries, and that US business will dominate the market. Canadian unions, in particular, are strongly opposed to the FTA; they attribute plant closings and layoffs caused by the recession of 1990–1992 solely to the FTA. On the other hand, many individuals argue that these are only short-run setbacks and that in the long run the economies of both countries will benefit from free trade. They also point out that most people are relatively immobile and will continue to buy goods made in their own country. Thus, the likelihood of US firms dominating the Canadian economy is remote. In addition, they point out that the market for Canadian goods in the United States is much larger than the market for US goods in Canada. So Canadians have more to gain than to lose from the FTA.

The signing of NAFTA in 1993 has extended the FTA to include Mexico. NAFTA has helped Mexico continue to open up its markets to free trade and has helped increase its rate of economic growth. The country is also doing well in attracting outside investment by such major firms as Ford Motors, which recently announced it would invest $1 billion to build plants in Mexico. General Electric, Delphi, Mattel, Solectron, Boeing, and Johnson & Johnson are among the US companies with operations in Mexico. Foreign companies like Toyota and Volkswagen have also settled in the country to supply both the US and Mexican market.

Over the past five years triad countries have been setting up operations in Mexico to tap a growing local market. The Mexican middle and upper classes are spending more, especially on big ticket items. American autos, which often cost three times as much as they do in the United States, are a popular purchase. Moreover, although Japanese cars sell well in most places, many Mexicans prefer US-made products; Japanese are seen as lower status in Mexico. Many other retail businesses such as clothing and home appliances are seeing equal growth.

Source: Corbis/Bettmann

Talks are also under way for a Free Trade Area of the Americas (FTAA). This will build on the principles of NAFTA, which eliminated tariffs and introduced the principle of national treatment for foreign direct investment. In 2001, at the Quebec City Summit, the US government sought to renew negotiations with Latin American countries, which had not progressed very far since the Miami Summit in 1991. This was received with mixed feelings by Latin American countries, but it was agreed to launch the FTAA in 2005. Yet, nothing materialized. Brazil and Venezuela, among others, are hesitant to join the FTAA. Brazil and Venezuela want to concentrate their efforts on South American integration, not pan-American integration. Most other countries are keen to access the huge US market. Some misinformed anti-globalization groups have emerged to protest what they perceive as an imperialist move that will strengthen US multinationals at the expense of local interests. Others share in the dislike of US farm subsidies and of clauses intended to protect labor and environmental laws.

US farm subsidies hinder free trade in one of the industries in which developing countries have a competitive advantage. Not surprisingly, the US agricultural sector opposes eliminating these subsidies and counterargues (on a triad basis) that, because Japanese and EU subsidies would not be removed at the same time, they would face a competitive disadvantage. Nevertheless, whether or not the EU and Japan eliminate

▶

subsidies, the agricultural sector will be heavily hit by the entry of competitive agricultural products from developing countries.

Latin American countries are also suspicious of US-led clauses on labor and environmental protection (which the US Congress insists on). They argue that these clauses might be used more as non-tariff barriers to trade than as genuine labor and environmental protection. Still, if countries of the Americas successfully negotiate the FTAA, it will create the largest trade bloc in the world, encompassing 738 million people from Canada to Chile.

Sources: Stephen Baker, Elizabeth Weinger, and Mike Zellner, "Can Latin America Move from the Third World to the First?" *Business Week*, October 21, 1991, pp. 54–56; Louis R. Richman, "How NAFTA Will Help America," *Fortune*, April 19, 1993, pp. 95–102; John Urquhart, "Canada Pursues Latin American Trade," *Wall Street Journal*, November 7, 1997, p. A 15; Jonathan Friedland and Joseph B. White, "GM Is Leading an Investment Boom in Mexico," *Wall Street Journal*, December 24, 1998, pp. A 5–6; "FTAA Talks Enter Cyclical Stage," *BBC.co.uk*, April 6, 2001; "Brazil Skeptical of Free Trade Deal," *BBC.co.uk*, April 19, 2001; "United States Singled Out as World's Largest Polluter in Hague Conference," *CNN.com*, November 20, 2000; Christine Tierney, "Mexico to Build New Futuras," *The Detroit News*, October 7, 2003; "Loveless Brothers," *Economist.com*, January 15, 2004.

1. How did the Free Trade Agreement help the Canadian economy?
2. Will NAFTA see an increase in exports between the United States and Canada? Why or why not?
3. In what way is Mexico's economic progress creating a market for US products?
4. Will an FTAA lead to increased trade in the Americas? Why or why not?
5. Should environmental laws be included in the FTAA? Why or why not?

INTRODUCTION

In Chapter 15 we saw that governments and the various institutions through which they wield their powers are important external factors in the international business environment. This chapter focuses on institutional factors in the North American market that must be considered when looking at the Canadian and Mexican markets. The North American Free Trade Agreement (NAFTA) has not abolished all trade barriers between the United States, Canada, and Mexico. There are still major impediments to trade and investment. Furthermore, each of the partners retains its own trade laws. A legal mechanism to appeal trade decisions exists, but this is a compromise position. In contrast, EU member states cannot use trade laws against their partners. So although NAFTA is a step toward trade liberalization, business decisions should not assume that "free trade" makes Canada and Mexico identical to the United States.

CANADA

With a land area of almost 3.6 million square miles, Canada is second in size only to Russia. Divided into ten provinces and three territories (see accompanying map), Canada is so large that it encompasses four time zones. The French and British fought over the country, with control passing into British hands in 1763. Canada became a separate nation in 1867, although it did not fully repatriate its constitution until 1982. Today it remains a leading member of the British Commonwealth.

Canada's economy

Canada's 33 million people enjoy one of the highest standards of living in the world. Consumer tastes and disposable wealth are very similar to those in the United States. Gross domestic product in 2004 was about $994.1 billion in US dollars and at current exchange rates. Over the last

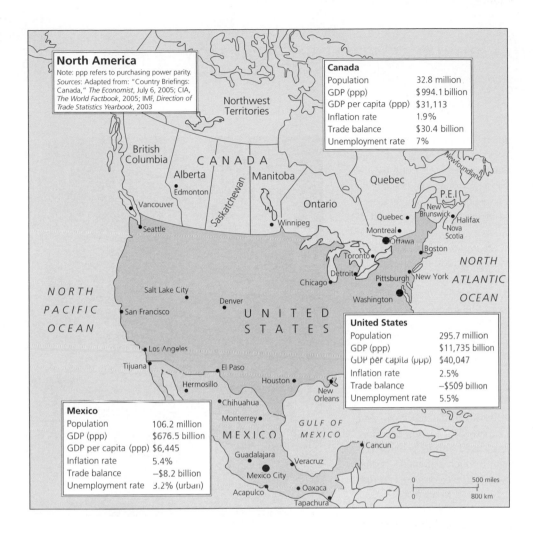

North America
Note: ppp refers to purchasing power parity.
Sources: Adapted from: "Country Briefings: Canada," *The Economist*, July 6, 2005; CIA, *The World Factbook*, 2005; IMF, *Direction of Trade Statistics Yearbook*, 2003

Canada	
Population	32.8 million
GDP (ppp)	$994.1 billion
GDP per capita (ppp)	$31,113
Inflation rate	1.9%
Trade balance	$30.4 billion
Unemployment rate	7%

United States	
Population	295.7 million
GDP (ppp)	$11,735 billion
GDP per capita (ppp)	$40,047
Inflation rate	2.5%
Trade balance	−$509 billion
Unemployment rate	5.5%

Mexico	
Population	106.2 million
GDP (ppp)	$676.5 billion
GDP per capita (ppp)	$6,445
Inflation rate	5.4%
Trade balance	−$8.2 billion
Unemployment rate	3.2% (urban)

15 years, the rate of economic growth has been in the 2 to 4 per cent range. Canada has typically had a positive balance of payments, thanks to its food, energy, and motor vehicle exports. Its primary trading partner is the United States, which provided over 62.6 per cent of Canada's imports and accounted for 87.7 per cent of the country's exports in 2002 (see Table 18.2).

Canada's economic growth historically has been based on the export of agricultural staples, especially grains, and on the production and export of natural resource products such as minerals, oil, gas, and forest products. However, major secondary industries have also emerged; Canada now ranks as one of the top 10 manufacturing nations in the world. The service industry is also expanding rapidly, especially financial services in Toronto. However, the country still faces a major productivity challenge. For each hour Canadians work, they produce 5.8 per cent less than their US neighbors.[1]

Almost 80 per cent of manufacturing activity is located in Ontario and Quebec—including the entire motor vehicle industry, which is Canada's largest segment—while Calgary has become a major high-tech center.[2] Almost one-quarter of all Canada's exports (and imports) are in autos and auto-related products. The Canada–United States Automotive Products Trade Agreement (Autopact) has encouraged this two-way trade over the last 35 years, allowing free trade in autos assembled in either country, provided there was 50 per cent value added in Canada. (Under NAFTA, the content provision rose to 62.5 per cent.) Financial institutions and other business service industries are also concentrated in central Canada.

INTERNATIONAL BUSINESS STRATEGY *IN ACTION*

Bombardier

In 1942 the dreams of a budding young Quebec entrepreneur came true with the incorporation of L'Auto-Neige Bombardier, the world's first snowmobile manufacturer. Although the mechanic-turned-industrialist Joseph Armand Bombardier had great plans for his innovative transportation inventions, he could never have foreseen the course his company would take in the next 50 years.

Today Bombardier is one of the world's top manufacturers of transportation products, with yearly revenues of over $15.8 billion and 60,000 employees. Having begun with snowmobile production, Bombardier is now among the world leaders in commuter and general transportation trains, as well as transport vehicles for industrial and military use, sailboats, motorcycles, and, more recently, smaller aircraft. This extension into numerous other industries has transformed Bombardier from a once small-town Quebec company into a global market competitor and leader with 90 per cent of its total business now conducted outside Canada.

Bombardier's success is due mostly to the industrious and timely business instincts of company CEO Laurent Beaudoin, who in the past 30 years has followed a strategy of market entry and product improvement through acquisition, instead of relying strictly on R&D. As a result, the company has managed to produce the most technically advanced, innovative, and reliable products on the market and gained substantial market share in many industries, especially with its rubber-wheeled subway car, sold to New York City in the 1980s.

This strategy has been exemplified by Bombardier's entry into the aerospace industry with the acquisition of Canadair in 1986, 12 years after diversifying into the transportation equipment business. The Canadair purchase brought the company a large pool of human resources and technical expertise, which has been applied to develop such "in-house" products as the twin-engine Challenger Business Jet. As a result, Bombardier suddenly held lead positions in numerous niche markets, which ensured ongoing relations with such manufacturing giants as Boeing and MacDonnell-Douglas. This acquisition quickly resulted in numerous contracts for CF-18 fighters from the Canadian government and contracts for Airbus components from both British Aerospace and France's Aerospatiale.

Further acquisition was a logical step for the company. By acquiring Northern Ireland's Short Brothers, Bombardier extended itself firmly into the European market as a supplier and manufacturer of aerospace technology. At the outset of the 1990s, purchases of both Learjet out of Wichita, Kansas, and Boeing's deHavilland propelled diversification into regional jets and turboprop aircraft. Finally, production of the

Source: Corbis/Keith Dannemiller

first-of-its-kind 50-passenger Canadair Regional Jet signified Bombardier's full-fledged entry into the airline industry. With the bulk of its profit already coming from this industry and the shared know-how, technology, resources, and markets of all of these companies pooled under one roof, Bombardier is ripe to become a major player in the aerospace industry through the millennium.

Over the past 10 years US and Canadian airline carriers have begun to try to improve their competitive positions through a series of alliances. For example, Air Canada has become part of Star Alliance, a collection of 15 international airlines— including United from the US—that account for 21 per cent of the global market. Similarly, prior to merging with Air Canada in 2000, Canadian Airlines had joined American Airlines and its code-sharing partners around the world in the Oneworld alliance. This is a result of a trend that is grouping the international airline business into several large alliances to compete against each other.

For the North American Airline market, this means an increase in efficiency. In 1993 US carriers were authorized to serve only 44 routes in Canada, and Canadian carriers had a mere 28 routes in the United States. A study at the time revealed that, if the skies between the two countries were allowed to open up, air traffic would double within the next few years. The study also estimated that the resulting increase in tourism and trade would generate $10.3 billion in additional economic activity. These statistics indicate why a new Open Skies agreement between the countries was enacted in 1995 that liberalized the regulatory environment for airlines in both countries. Since the establishment of Open Skies, transborder traffic has increased from 13 million passengers in 1994 to 20 million in 2000. Nonetheless, the 1995 treaty comes short of a full Open Skies agreement because of restrictions on cargo and third country rights.

Since NAFTA came into effect on January 1, 1994, there was a further incentive to liberalize trade in services such as airline travel. However, under NAFTA's restricted transportation provisions, national treatment does not apply. This means that a US airline can do business across the Canadian borders only on a point-to-point basis, from, say, New York's La Guardia to Toronto. It cannot pick up any passengers within Canada. Similarly, Air Canada can fly from Montreal to New York to Miami, but it cannot compete with US airlines on the internal New York to Miami route.

Despite the lack of national treatment, Air Canada has doubled its flights to the US and more than tripled its number of routes since the Open Skies agreement. Today, Air Canada handles over 40 per cent of the Canada–US traffic and attributes close to 3,000 new jobs to the agreement. Air travel was further eased in 1998 by a bilateral agreement to facilitate pre-clearance of customs and immigration services. This will reduce double inspections by customs and immigration officers in both countries. The large success of these agreements has led both governments to negotiate similar agreements with other countries around the globe.

Website: **www.bombardier.com**.

Sources: Adapted from Alan M. Rugman, *Foreign Investment and NAFTA* (Columbia, SC: University of South Carolina Press, 1994); **www.aircanada.ca**; Air Canada, "Air Canada President and CEO Urges U.S. AirLine CEOs Towards Further Liberalization of U.S.–Canada Market," Press Release, December 13, 2001; Canada, Ministry of Transportation, *Canada Transportation Act Review*, July 18, 2001.

The eastern and western areas of the country are more dependent on primary industries: fishing, forestry, and mining in the east; agriculture, ore, and mineral fuels in the west. The country's growth was helped by large inflows of FDI; today, 40 per cent of the primary and secondary industries are foreign owned. Yet Canada is wealthy enough now, and its economy is sufficiently mature, to have substantial outward FDI, particularly in the United States.

The United States has more FDI in Canada than in any other country, including Great Britain. Since 1988 this investment has doubled, and today it stands at about $192.4 billion. At the same time the country has invested $105.2 billion in the United States, more than in any other country.[3] We can see these relationships within individual industries. For example, many US airlines, including American, Delta, and Northwest, fly to Canada, and Air Canada and Canadian Airlines, which recently merged, among others, have US routes. So part of the US international airline strategy involves competing with Canadian carriers that are vying for the US market (see the box **International Business Strategy in Action: Bombardier**). There are many other examples of Canadian investment in the United States. Canadian Pacific has purchased the Delaware & Hudson Railway, and Bombardier Inc. bought the Learjet Corporation of Wichita, Kansas. Many other acquisitions are even larger.

✔ Active learning check

Review your answer to Active Learning Case question 1 and make any changes you like. Then compare your answer with the one below.

1 How did the Free Trade Agreement help the Canadian economy?

The Free Trade Agreement eliminates tariffs and makes it easier for efficient Canadian firms to operate competitively in the United States. At the same time, it allows efficient US firms to ship their goods into Canada without paying any tariffs and, in the process, helps drive down prices. So the FTA can help the Canadian economy by encouraging efficiency, lowering prices, and opening up new markets in the United States.

Differences in the business environment

Despite many similarities between the business environments of the United States and Canada, there are also some important differences.

Canada's industrial climate

The Canadian economy is characterized by private enterprise. However, some industries, such as broadcasting and public utilities, are government-owned or subject to substantial government regulation.[4] Over the last decade the trend has been toward privatization and deregulation. In fact, a federal government minister oversees privatization and has been responsible for selling companies that the government feels are no longer essential to meet public policy goals. Firms that have been privatized include Canadair, the deHavilland Aircraft Company, Canadian National Railway's trucking division, Fisheries Products International, and Air Canada.

Small business is a major part of the economy and accounts for almost 80 per cent of all new employment in manufacturing. The service and retail trade industries are characterized by a large number of companies that vary in size. Seventy per cent of Canadians work in service industries.

Canada's regulatory environment

Commerce and industry in Canada is regulated at every level of government: federal, provincial, and municipal. Many of these regulations are similar to those in the United States.

Competition

Competition Act
A Canadian federal law that regulates anticompetitive practices and prohibits actions that will substantially lessen or prevent competition; it is similar to US antitrust laws

Regulation of competition is under the jurisdiction of the federal Parliament. Legislation in this area was revised in the late 1980s to eliminate restrictive trade policies, stimulate production, and promote the international competitiveness of Canadian business. Although there are no price controls in Canada, there is regulation to review monopolies, acquisitions, and mergers. The regulation of anticompetitive practices is handled under the **Competition Act**, which prohibits individuals and companies from practices that will substantially lessen or prevent competition in the marketplace. The Act outlaws bid-rigging, price discrimination, or conspiring to unduly lessen competition and provides for regulation of acquisitions and mergers. If the purchase price is $400 million or more, the parties must refrain from completing the transaction for a time period ranging from 7 to 21 days. During this time the government reviews the situation and decides whether the purchase will prevent or lessen competition (using international comparisons) and thus be non-competitive in nature. A ruling is then made.

✔ Active learning check

Review your answer to Active Learning Case question 2 and make any changes you like. Then compare your answer with the one below.

2 Will NAFTA see an increase in exports between the United States and Canada? Why or why not?

In the future, US–Canada trade will increase as a result of NAFTA. Three reasons can be cited. First, the elimination of all tariffs under the FTA will encourage exports. Second, both countries are more likely to produce those goods and services for which they have a competitive advantage and to buy the others from their neighbor. Third, as the economies of the two countries grow, so will the amount of trade as each begins to adapt operations to the desires of the other and starts to tap this market further.

Exports and imports

Export permits are required for the shipment of goods having strategic value, such as uranium. They are also required to implement the provisions of various international agreements into which Canada has entered. Import documentation is also required, as well as payment of a goods and sales tax (GST).[5] The GST, which went into effect on January 1, 1991, is a value-added tax. On imports, it is collected by Canadian Customs. The tax was set at 7 per cent of the value of the goods plus any import duties.[6]

Francization in Quebec

The Canadian federal government has a bilingual policy.[7] But in the province of Quebec, French is the official language for business and education. All firms employing 50 or more people in Quebec must use French at all levels of the organization. Other regulations related to the use of French in Quebec are that (1) all product labels must be in French, and translations cannot be given greater prominence than the French portion; (2) company names and signs must be in French, but a version of the firm's name in another language may accompany the French version for use outside Quebec; and (3) all signs on the outside of stores must be in French only.[8] Moreover, all education, health services, and other services under provincial jurisdiction are delivered in French. Some exceptions to the French language and sign law policies accommodate the one-fifth of the Quebec population that speaks English. For example, McGill University and Concordia University can operate in English, and English signs can be displayed inside stores, provided they are smaller than French signs.[9]

Banking and finance

Banks in Canada offer a full range of financial services. There are six large Canadian chartered banks with extensive national branch networks that account for 90 per cent of the nation's banking industry assets. There are also many smaller (often foreign-owned) banks.[10] All these banks respond to the actions of the central bank, the Bank of Canada, a federal government institution directly responsible for the nation's monetary policy, including (1) regulating credit and currency, (2) controlling and protecting the external value of the Canadian dollar, and (3) regulating the general level of production, trade, prices, and employment, within the scope of monetary policy.

In carrying out its functions, the Bank of Canada buys and sells foreign exchange and sets the interest rate charged to commercial banks. These functions are similar to those carried out by the Federal Reserve in the United States, which helps monitor the US monetary system. The Bank of Canada is also responsible for issuing the country's notes and coins and for managing the federal debt. Canadian interest rates and its exchange rate closely follow those set in the United States, especially in relation to non-North American interest and exchange rates.

Banks operate within the confines of the Bank Act. There are two types: Schedule A and Schedule B. Schedule A banks are Canadian-owned and no shareholder has more than 10 per cent of the voting stock. Schedule B banks are closely held Canadian-owned or foreign banks. These are allowed to carry on normal banking activities. However, foreign-owned banks cannot, as a group, own more than 16 per cent of the total domestic assets of the Canadian banking system. Subsidiaries of US banks are not subject to this restriction because of the US–Canada Free Trade Agreement. In addition, Canadian banks are allowed to operate across the country.

There is also a host of specialized financial institutions that provide limited services throughout the provinces. Examples include savings banks, cooperative credit unions, loan companies, mortgage companies, and insurance companies. Investment bankers provide short-term funds to companies for acquisition or reorganization purposes.

Canada has four major stock exchanges: Toronto, Montreal, Vancouver, and Calgary. Toronto is the major exchange, accounting for approximately 95 per cent of dollar trading volume. It is also the financial center of the country.[11]

Labor relations

Canada Labor Code
A federal law that covers areas such as wages, employment practices, work safety, and conciliation of labor disputes

Labor relations are governed by both federal and provincial labor legislation. The Canada Labor Code is the federal law that covers such matters as wages, employment practices, work safety, and conciliation in the event of a labor dispute. Province governments have similar laws to cover employer–employee relations at the local level.

Unions

With the exception of farmers, domestic help, and white-collar workers, the workforce is heavily unionized. Approximately 30 per cent of the total labor force is in unions, compared to approximately 13.5 per cent in the United States.[12] In some instances the workers are free to choose or reject union membership; in other cases they must become members in order to keep their jobs. The labor–management contract determines these conditions.

As in the United States, once a union has been certified to represent the workers, management must bargain in good faith. The result of such bargaining is a labor–management agreement that determines wage rates, fringe benefits, working conditions, and management rights. Economic nationalism is a strong component of Canadian unionization, and the unions have been major opponents of the FTA, NAFTA, and other economic and political relationships with the United States.

✔ Active learning check

Review your answer to Active Learning Case question 3 and make any changes you like. Then compare your answer with the one below.

3 **In what way is Mexico's economic progress creating a market for US products?**

Mexico's progress under NAFTA will create a market for US goods in that, as the middle and upper classes in the country increase their purchasing power, they will turn more and more to the purchase of American-made goods. From cars to television sets to home appliances, Mexican consumers will be buying products sold by US MNEs. The sale of these goods will create greater interest in Mexico by US multinationals, which will mean even greater opportunities for US firms—and Mexican consumers. The elimination of tariffs under NAFTA ties Mexico into the North American triad.

Working conditions

All provinces have legislated minimum wage rates that are periodically adjusted. However, in most sectors wages and salaries are similar to US levels.

A national compulsory contributory pension plan provides retirement benefits to contributors, generally at the age of 65. This age limit varies, however, and there is growing pressure to relax mandatory retirement rules.[13] In addition, many private pension plans are in effect. Other benefits include group life insurance, medical insurance, and subsidized food and housing. Most provincial legislation limits daily or weekly working hours, with mandatory overtime pay for hours worked in excess of these limits. The government also mandates minimum annual paid vacations in almost all industries, which is typically two weeks after a year of employment and up to three or four weeks after longer employment. There are also legislated holidays, which, depending on the city and the province, usually vary between 8 and 12 days.

All provinces prohibit employment discrimination on the basis of race, religion, national origin, color, sex, age, or marital status. There are also provisions for equal pay for equal work, which vary across provinces. They are designed to prevent gender bias in pay levels. For example, Ontario has specific "pay equity" legislation that requires employers to remove gender bias in pay levels; salary adjustments were phased in, starting in 1990. Similar legislation has been enacted in a number of other provinces, including Quebec and Saskatchewan.

Investments

The **Investment Canada Act (ICA)** came into effect on June 30, 1985, and is designed to create a welcome climate for foreign investment by significantly loosening previous restrictions. At the same time, however, some regulations still remain in effect. As noted earlier, investments in certain industries are restricted. For example, a license to operate a broadcasting station can be granted only to a Canadian citizen or corporation whose stock is 80 per cent owned by Canadian citizens or Canadian-controlled corporations. Generally, non-residents cannot hold more than 25 per cent of the issued and outstanding shares of a chartered bank, a life insurance company, a sales finance firm, a loan company, or a trust company. Nor can a single non-resident together with his or her associates hold more than 10 per cent of the issued and outstanding shares of these types of companies. Limits are much less stringent in the securities industry, but the government must be kept apprised of such ownership.

Under the ICA, a non-Canadian wishing to acquire a Canadian firm must apply to the ICA for review and approval, if the assets are valued at more than $5 million or the business relates to Canada's cultural heritage or national identity. In the case of US firms buying Canadian operations, under the provisions of the Free Trade Agreement the ICA review takes place at the $150 million level. So the investment climate is much more conducive to US investors than to any others. When the ICA does conduct a review, a number of factors are considered in determining whether the investment will benefit Canada, including employment, technological benefits, and product innovation.

In addition, numerous provincial statutes place restrictions on foreigners seeking to invest in particular industries or activities. For example, in most provinces individuals have to be Canadian residents for at least a year in order to be registered securities dealers. Similarly, foreigners who are registering ownership of land must disclose their citizenship. In Alberta, British Columbia, Manitoba, Ontario, and Saskatchewan, a majority of the board of directors of corporations must be resident Canadians. However, an indirect takeover of a foreign-owned publisher will require that the firm be sold to a Canadian owner, according to the "Baie Comeau policy."

Investment Canada Act (ICA)
An act designed to create a welcome climate for foreign investment by significantly loosening previous restrictions

Canada's multinationals

It is useful to identify Canada's major companies against the background of global competition and triad power. Some larger Canadian firms like Nortel Networks and Bombardier are well known in the United States.

Table 18.4 ranks the 20 largest Canadian-owned companies in decreasing order of size measured by their sales in 2004. The largest firm is Alcan Aluminum, which had sales of over $32 billion and is widely recognized as being one of Canada's most successful multinationals. With revenues of $16.2 billion, Onex Corporation is a global conglomerate that operates in multiple industries, including sugar refining, investment, telecommunications, and automotive parts. Other well-known Canadian industrial multinationals at the top of the list are BCE, Bombardier, and Magna International.

Table 18.4 The largest Canadian-owned companies by revenues

Rank	Firm	Industry	2004 sales (in millions of Canadian $)	F/T*	2003 Intra-regional Sales
1	Alcan Aluminum	Mining	32,375	96%	38.6%
2	George Weston	Food	29,798	na	100.0%
3	Manulife Financial	Life	27,150	na	76.2%
4	Magna International	Vehicle	26,869	na	57.8%
5	Royal Bank of Canada	Banks	25,204	37%	88.3%
6	Power Corp. of Canada	Finance	24,323	50%	100.0%
7	Sun Life Financial Services of Canada	Life	21,748	62%	90.8%
8	Bombardier	High-tech	20,511	34%	54.6%
9	BCE	Telecom	19,193	2%	>98.0%
10	CIBC	Banks	16,705	21%	79.7%
11	The Bank of Nova Scotia	Banks	16,497	na	68.7%
12	Onex	High-tech	16,244	82%	54.0%
13	TD Bank	Banks	19,015	25%	73.5%
14	Petro-Canada	Energy	14,687	na	na
15	Nortel Networks	High-tech	14,260	na	59.0%
16	Bank of Montreal	Banks	13,208	30%	97%
17	Empire	Food	11,284	na	na
18	Quebecor	Publish	10,982	71%	na
19	Hydro-Quebec	Utility	10,698	na	na
20	The Thomson Corp.	Publish	10,535	na	na
Average			19,064		
Total			381,286		

* F/T refers to foreign exports and sales divided by total sales.

Sources: Adapted from "The Financial Post 500," *National Post*, June 1, 2005; Alan M. Rugman, *The Regional Multinationals* (Cambridge: Cambridge UP, 2005); individual Annual Reports.

Table 18.5 lists the 20 largest foreign-owned firms in Canada. These firms also contribute to the performance of the country, creating jobs and wealth for Canadians. However, all foreign-owned firms must be examined in terms of their relationship to their parent companies. A high degree of autonomy, or development of world-class products in Canada, is necessary for a foreign-owned firm to provide sustained benefits to the country. The Big Three auto companies have not done this. However, some energy firms, such as Imperial Oil (owned by Exxon), have a history of Canadian development, whereas others such as IBM Canada already operate divisions in Canada on a global basis. Others, such as Asea Brown Boveri (ABB), have a decentralized organizational structure with a large degree of local autonomy. These smaller but more autonomous Canadian firms (ABB is not on the list) have learned to survive within the global networks of their parent organizations, and their managers can help provide leadership to Canadians.

Another indicator of the nature of international expertise among these firms comes from the degree of their exports. Table 18.4 also reports data on the foreign sales of the largest 20 Canadian-owned firms. Exports from Canadian sales of subsidiaries in the United States and others offshore (excluding the US) are shown. According to the table, these large companies sell approximately 50 per cent of their output abroad. The foreign-owned firms in Canada (Table 18.5) also sell abroad, but information on foreign sales is not readily available. Nevertheless, the four companies that do report this information export about 65 per cent of their output.

Table 18.6 shows Canadian-based firms ranked according to overseas sales. The largest, Inco, exports virtually everything. In addition, most of The Thomson Corp. sales are outside

Table 18.5 The largest foreign-owned companies in Canada, by size

Rank	Firm	Industry	2004 sales (in millions of Canadian $)	F/T*	Ownership
1	General Motors of Canada	Vehicle	37,144	na	US (100)
2	Imperial Oil	Energy	22,408	15%	US (70)
3	DaimlerChrysler Canada	Vehicle	19,151	na	Germany (100)
4	Ford Motor Co. of Canada	Vehicle	18,127	na	US (100)
5	EnCana Corp.	Energy	15,364	65%	Widely held (55)
6	Honda Canada	Vehicle	13,300	67%	Japan (100)
7	Wal-Mart Canada	Merchant	12,500	na	US (100)
8	Shell Canada	Energy	11,228	na	Netherlands (78)
9	Husky Energy	Energy	8,440	na	Barbados (71)
10	Costco	Merchant	7,878	na	US (100)
11	Ultramar	Energy	7,113	na	US (100)
12	McKesson	Health	6,676	na	US (100)
13	Sears Canada	Merchant	6,230	na	US (54)
14	Canada Safeway	Food	5,681	na	US (100)
15	Inco	Merchant	5,565	98%	Widely held (54)
16	IBM Canada	High-tech	5,500	na	US (100)
17	Home Depot Canada	Store	5,000	na	US (100)
18	Toyota Motor	Vehicle	5,000	na	Japan (100)
19	The Great Atlantic & Pacific Co.	Food	4,435	na	US (100)
20	Gerdau Ameristeel Corp.	Steel	3,915	na	Brazil (72)
Average			11,033		
Total			220,655		

* F/T refers to foreign exports and sales divided by total sales.

Source: Adapted from "The Financial Post 500," *National Post*, June 1, 2005.

Canada, as are those for Alcan Aluminum and the Potash Corporation. For these 20 large firms, the average ratio of foreign to total sales is 70 per cent. This demonstrates the tremendous attraction of foreign markets for larger companies in a relatively small market like Canada's, providing further evidence that access to a triad market (in this case, the United States) is critical for success in a global market.

Multilateral agreement on investment (MAI)

Canada will benefit from any type of multilateral agreement on investment. An attempt to negotiate an MAI was made in Paris at the Organization for Economic Cooperation and Development (OECD) over the 1995 to 1998 period. The draft MAI was based on the lines of NAFTA. The millennium round of the WTO may take up the need for an MAI.

An MAI includes the principle of national treatment: equal access for foreign investors to the host country's market (but according to host country rules). A number of sectors are exempted from the national treatment principle. In the same spirit of the FTA and NAFTA, Canada insists on exemptions on health care, education, social services, cultural industries, and transportation. All regulations on investment are identified, as are all exemptions to the principle of national treatment. Additionally, dispute settlement mechanisms are put in place to allow individual investors (and companies) to appeal against government regulations and bureaucratic controls. The MAI helps countries harmonize their regulations, although in the areas of competition policy and tax policy not much progress can be expected (no progress was achieved in NAFTA).

Table 18.6 The largest Canadian-based firms, by degree of multinationality

Rank	Firm	Industry	2004 sales (in millions of Canadian $)	F/T*	2003 Intra-regional Sales
1	Inco	Merchant	5,565	98%	na
2	The Thomson Corp.	Publish	10,535	97%	na
3	Alcan	Mining	32,375	96%	38.6%
4	Potash Corp	Chemical	3,774	96%	na
5	Abitibi-Consolidated Inc.	Forest	5,801	86%	na
6	Teck Cominco	Mining	3,428	83%	na
7	Onex	Hi-tech	16,244	82%	na
8	Quebecor	Publish	10,982	71%	54.0%
9	Brascan	Finance	5,239	69%	na
10	Nova Chemicals	Chemical	6,856	68%	na
11	Honda	Vehicles	13,300	67%	na
12	EnCana Corp	Energy	15,364	65%	na
13	Sun Life Financial	Life	21,748	62%	90.8%
14	Alimentation Couche-Tard	Food sell	5,872	63%	na
15	Talisman Energy	Mining	5,346	55%	na
16	The Jean Coutu Group	Food sell	4,096	59%	na
17	Cascades	Forest	3,254	52%	na
18	Powercorp of Canada	Finance	24,323	50%	100.0%
19	Royal Bank of Canada	Bank	25,204	37%	88.3%
20	Canadian National Railway	Energy	6,548	37%	

Note: These data were compiled using only the top 100 Canadian companies based on revenues. The data for foreign sales are limited and companies that might otherwise be in the list might be excluded.

Sources: Adapted from "The National Post 500," *National Post*, June 1, 2005; Alan M. Rugman, *The Regional Multinationals* (Cambridge: Cambridge UP, 2005); individual Annual Reports.

The need for an MAI arises because foreign investment has become an important part of the global economy. Today, the majority of international business is not done by traded goods but through services and investments. More than 70 per cent of North Americans work in the service sector, with only 30 per cent in manufacturing. So the new agenda for international agreements is to negotiate rules for trade in services and investment.

Canada's outward stock of FDI is nearly 75 per cent in the United States, with which it already has national treatment through the FTA and NAFTA. Thus, its exporting businesses would prefer an MAI with transparent rules.

Business opportunities in Canada

North American Free Trade Agreement (NAFTA)
A regional free trade agreement between Canada, the US, and Mexico

Although the Canadian economy began to slow down during the early 1990s, the country still offers excellent investment and trade opportunities for foreign investors. This is particularly true for US firms, thanks to the US–Canada FTA of 1989 and its extension, the **North American Free Trade Agreement (NAFTA)**, which includes Mexico.[14]

United States–Canada Free Trade Agreement (FTA)
A trade agreement that eliminates most trade restrictions (such as tariffs) between these two countries and extends national treatment to foreign investment

The **United States–Canada Free Trade Agreement (FTA)** was designed to eliminate tariffs and most other trade barriers between the two countries.[15] Some of its specific provisions are:

1 All tariffs on US and Canadian goods were to be eliminated by 1998.

2 Most import and export quotas were to be eliminated by 1998.

3 Use of product standards as a trade barrier is prohibited and national treatment of testing labs and certification bodies is established.

4 Many restrictions on agricultural products, wine and distilled spirits, auto parts, and energy goods have been sharply reduced, if not totally eliminated.

5   The size of the government procurement markets that will be open to suppliers from the other country is slightly increased.

6   Travel by business visitors, investors, traders, professionals, and executives transferred within a firm is facilitated.

7   The opportunity to invest in each other's country is facilitated and encouraged through the adoption of national treatment.

8   A binational commission to resolve disagreements that may arise from the enforcement of the FTA has been established; it dealt with some 20 cases in the first three years of the Agreement.[16]

Marketing in Canada

Companies doing business in Canada need to know distribution practices and advertising and promotion channels. In many cases these are similar to those in other countries, but there are some important differences.

Distribution practices

Despite the country's vast size, sales to Canadian industries are characterized by short marketing channels with direct producer-to-user distribution. Many industries are dominated by a few large-scale enterprises that are highly concentrated geographically. It is not unusual for 90 per cent of prospective customers of an industrial product to be located in or near two or three cities.

The consumer goods market is more diffused than the industrial market, and the use of marketing intermediaries is often necessary. In many cases complete coverage of the consumer market requires representation in a number of commercial centers across the country. Firms having only one representative or distribution point typically choose Toronto. If the country is divided into two major markets, the other is often Calgary or Vancouver. If the market is divided into three areas, distributors are frequently put in Montreal, Ontario, and Vancouver.[17]

Direct selling is another growing area. This includes the sale of goods from manufacturing premises by mail, home delivery, personal selling, and other non-retail channels. Direct selling now accounts for over $1.3 billion annually in Canada.[18]

Wholesale and retail trade are also important forms of distribution. Because of the wide dispersion of customers, wholesale trade is critical. However, retail trade is even more important and accounts for more than $277 billion in sales annually.[19] Independent stores earn about 88 per cent of this, and general merchandisers, including department stores, make up the other 12 per cent.[20] Quebec and Ontario account for about 61 per cent of all retail sales, and in western Canada, British Columbia and Alberta make up approximately 24 per cent of the total.[21] Department stores and supermarkets constitute a large percentage of retail sales. However, as in the United States, they are facing increased competition from discount food stores, showroom retailing, and other forms of self-service retailing. There are also specialized markets for recreation and leisure equipment and associated services, as well as a growing demand for consumer durables. These trends are likely to continue well into the millennium.

Advertising and promotion

Media used for advertising in Canada include television, radio, newspapers, and magazines. Television and radio advertising are particularly popular because 97 per cent of all Canadian households have at least one television, and 99 per cent have at least one radio. Hundreds of private firms operate cable television and major broadcasting stations in metropolitan areas, and the country has more than 1,300 television stations and 550 cable television systems, with over 50 per cent of the population hooked into a cable system. In addition, the Canadian Broadcasting Corporation (CBC) operates two national television networks, one in English and one in French. There are 1,400 licensed AM and FM radio stations.

More than 100 daily newspapers are published in Canada and are widely used by advertisers, as are trade magazines directed at specific industries such as computers, real estate, banking, and retailing. General interest Canadian magazines such as *Reader's Digest*, *L'actualité*, and *Quest* have raised their share of net advertising expenditures in Canadian periodicals to about 30 per cent, approaching the advertising of national newspapers. Two business newspapers, *The National Post* (*Financial Post* section) and *The Globe and Mail* (*Report on Business* section), also are widely read in the business and financial community. More than 450 advertising agencies in Canada can be of assistance in developing advertising and promotion campaigns.

Exporting

One of the most popular ways of doing business in Canada is through exports. As noted earlier, Canada is the US's largest foreign market. Every year Canadians buy as much US goods as do all the member nations of the EU combined. In fact, over 20 per cent of all US exports go to Canada. In recent years the Canadian government has simplified the process for shipping goods into the country. This is particularly true for products coming from the United States, since duties have been eliminated, thanks to the FTA and NAFTA.

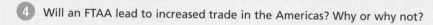

✔ Active learning check

Review your answer to Active Learning Case question 4 and make any changes you like. Then compare your answer with the one below.

4 **Will an FTAA lead to increased trade in the Americas? Why or why not?**

The Free Trade Agreement of the Americas will lead to an increase in trade in the region for three reasons. First, the elimination of all tariffs will encourage exports. Second, all countries are more likely to specialize in producing those goods and services for which they have a competitive advantage and, in turn, buy the others from their neighbor. Third, as the economies of the member countries grow, so will the amount of trade as each begins to adapt operations to the desires of the other and starts to tap this market further.

Franchising

Canada is the dominant foreign market for US franchisers. Currently more than 300 US franchise firms operate approximately 10,000 franchise units in Canada. A recent report by *Entrepreneur* magazine rated more than 1,100 US franchises, and of those in the top 10, eight indicated they were seeking to establish franchises in Canada. Thus, there is a great deal of opportunity for those who want to do business in Canada via the franchise route.

Additionally, in recent years Canadian banks have become more responsive to the needs of franchised operations. Chartered banks now offer various loans and repayment plans for franchises. In some cases they also offer payroll and cash management services. So there is considerable opportunity in international franchise operations in Canada.

MEXICO

With a land area of approximately 760,000 square miles, Mexico is equal in size to almost 25 per cent of the contiguous United States. It is the third largest nation in Latin America and has a population of over 106 million. The country is a federal democratic republic divided into 31 states and the Federal District (Mexico City). Although it endured political turmoil early in the twentieth century, the government has been stable since World War II.[22]

Mexico's economy

Mexico's economy is currently in a state of flux, brought on by new economic relations with the United States. Today Mexico has the strongest economy in Latin America. One of the primary reasons has been the economic policies of Carlos Salinas, who, after becoming president in 1988, introduced liberalization rules regarding foreign investment and privatization. These changes have dramatically improved the economy. Gross domestic product growth in 1996 was 5.1 per cent, but inflation continued to remain in the range of 25 per cent. By 2004, gross domestic growth had decreased to 2.6 per cent, but inflation had also been reduced to 6 per cent.[23] The country has also vigorously promoted exports, especially to the United States, which now counts on Mexico for 25 per cent of all imported fruit and vegetables. The *maquiladora* industry (see Chapter 15) is another growing source of economic strength for the country.[24] At the same time, Mexico has become a major region for international investment.

MNE investment

The climate for foreign investment in Mexico has grown increasingly favorable in recent years. Although there were strict controls on foreign investment during the 1970s, regulations introduced in 1989 reversed many of these restrictions. As a result, an increasing number of MNEs are investing in Mexico. Nissan invested $1 billion in a new assembly plant to produce cars for export to both the United States and Japan; Volkswagen invested $950 million to expand its plant; Sears Roebuck put $150 million into new stores and malls throughout the country, in addition to renovating older units; Wal-Mart purchased Cifra, a successful Mexican retailer; and PepsiCo expanded its snack business by purchasing a majority stake in Gamesa, Mexico's largest cookie maker.

One of the major reasons for the increase in FDI is the privatization campaign that began in 1982 and that has picked up speed since then. By 2000, the number of state-owned enterprises had decreased to 200 from 1,000 prior to 1982.[25] The government continues to play a major role in the economy, primarily through state-owned entities such as the giant oil firm Pemex, but there has been significant reduction in its ownership. These sales have been made to both foreign companies and Mexican investors.

Another reason for increased FDI has been the changes in investment laws that now permit foreigners to hold major equity positions. In the past, foreign ownership in auto parts companies had been limited to 40 per cent of equity, but a new decree now sharply reduces the number of firms subject to this law by creating exemptions based on percentages of export sales and sales to individuals. Today, approximately 80 per cent of the economy is open to full foreign ownership.[26]

Labor

Labor is relatively plentiful and inexpensive. However, MNEs report a serious shortage of skilled labor and managerial personnel, particularly at the middle and upper levels of the organization, and despite numerous engineers. Worker absenteeism in recent years has declined, but turnover remains a serious problem, even in the *maquiladora* sector.

Approximately 40 per cent of the total workforce is unionized. In industrial operations with more than 25 workers, about 80 per cent of the workforce is in unions. Union control over the members has weakened in recent years, and this trend is likely to continue. However, strikes are not uncommon.

There is a three-tier minimum wage structure in Mexico, but increases have not kept up with the cost of living. Minimum wage in US dollars in Mexico City and surrounding towns in 2005 was approximately $46.8 per day, compared to $45.4 in many other large cities and $44.1 in the rest of the country.[27]

Government regulations require that at least 90 per cent of a firm's skilled and unskilled workers be Mexican nationals, and employers must favor Mexicans over foreigners and union personnel over non-union personnel. On the other hand, these regulations are unlikely to limit investment by MNEs since the government permits hiring exceptions.

Mexico and NAFTA

In conjunction with their privatization policies, Presidents Salinas and Zedillo sought to motivate business through increased exposure to international competitive forces and access to the dynamic US market.[28] To this end, the government opened negotiations with the US and Canadian governments in Toronto on June 12, 1991, to create the North American Free Trade Agreement. This marked the first time that a less developed country had entered into an agreement with two wealthy countries to create a free trade area. NAFTA went into effect on January 1, 1994, and has had a major impact on Mexico's trade and investment.

Trade in several sectors has experienced considerable growth. In the textile and apparel sectors, quotas on Mexican products were phased out and customs duties on all textile and apparel products were eliminated. For automotive products, Mexico immediately reduced its tariffs on cars and light trucks by 50 per cent and pledged to eliminate the remaining duties over 10 years. In agriculture, tariff restrictions were lifted on a broad range of goods when NAFTA went into effect.

Mexico's investment climate has also been affected by NAFTA. In the automotive sector, all investment restrictions were eliminated. In transportation, Mexico allowed 49 per cent ownership of cars and trucking companies three years after NAFTA went into effect, 51 per cent after seven years, and 100 per cent after 10 years. The Mexican finance and insurance sectors have also been liberalized. All these changes have opened up Mexico even more to FDI and, in turn, lead to the growth of the Mexican economy and two-way flows of trade and investment with the United States.

As with the US–Canada FTA, binational panels play an important role in resolving trade disputes. Under NAFTA, panels continue to contribute toward trade disputes resolution and now also investment matters. Where investments are concerned, complainants may also take their cases to binding investor–state arbitration.

Latin American Integration Association (LAIA)
A free trade group formed to reduce intra-regional trade barriers and to promote regional economic cooperation; Argentina, Bolivia, Brazil, Chile, Colombia, Ecuador, Mexico, Paraguay, Peru, Uruguay, and Venezuela are all members

Regional trade agreements

Other developments involving Mexico as a leader in the movement toward free trade and privatization have included the efforts to create and sustain regional trade agreements based on NAFTA. One of the major regional integration efforts has been the creation of the Latin American Integration Association (LAIA), a free trade group formed in 1980 to reduce intra-regional trade barriers and promote regional economic cooperation.

Argentina, Bolivia, Brazil, Chile, Colombia, Ecuador, Mexico, Paraguay, Peru, Uruguay, and Venezuela are all members. The primary objective of LAIA is to create a Latin American common market. In recent years, its slow process toward economic integration has led some members to create sub-regional groups. For example, in the southern cone, Argentina, Brazil, Paraguay, and Uruguay have established a common market called Mercosur, which was operational by 1996. In the north, Mexico, Colombia, and Venezuela have a similar agreement, and via NAFTA Mexico is likely to be a key bridge between Latin American countries and the United States. NAFTA has a clause permitting accession of other countries. A second major integration effort is the Andean common market (Ancom), a sub-regional free trade compact designed to promote economic and social integration and cooperation.[29] Bolivia, Colombia, Ecuador, Peru, and Venezuela are all members.

In 1990, US President George Bush launched his Enterprise for the Americas, which is aimed at creating an all-American free trade area from Alaska to Argentine Antarctica. The Free Trade Area of the Americas (FTAA) that is presently being negotiated by 34 countries would achieve the main objectives of continental integration.[30] If such an idea comes to fruition, it will eliminate the need for LAIA, Ancom, and similar Latin American trade agreements. The United States is aware of the need for reducing, and then eliminating, trade barriers in the Americas if it hopes to establish a viable world market that can compete against the European Union and the Pacific Rim. The idea is also appealing to Latin American countries that see the opportunities associated with linking into the North American diamond and profiting from the economic growth it creates. This development will bring about a Western Hemisphere trading bloc and may well become a reality in the early 21st century.

Doing business in Mexico

A number of strategic approaches are being used to conduct business in Mexico. (See the box **International Business Strategy in Action: Mexico and NAFTA**.) Two primary reasons for the success of these approaches are the high quality of the workforce and the dramatic improvement in the economy over the 1990s. MNEs operating in Mexico report that the quality of the workforce is excellent. For example, senior-level executives at firms such as Caterpillar, Ford, General Electric, IBM, and Procter & Gamble all report that their Mexican workforces produce high-quality output. Moreover, a Massachusetts Institute of Technology study has named Ford's Mercury Tracer plant in Hermosillo the highest-quality assembly plant in the world. The head of IBM Mexico has stated that "for every dollar you pay a Mexican engineer, you get more from him or her than you'd get in other societies around the world."[31]

At the same time, the market for goods and services is growing rapidly. Many MNEs admit that they are not in Mexico because of the low wage rates but because of rapidly growing demand. Despite a high inflation rate and loss of purchasing power, people want to buy consumer goods and live more like their neighbors to the north. Mexicans are also expressing an interest in high-quality merchandise, with the result that US companies are now reducing their reliance on agents and dealers and are instead opening sales subsidiaries and warehouses to provide direct technical assistance. A good example is Toyota, which started a plant in 2005 to produce vans for the US market, but later in the year responded to Mexico's growing demand for vans by producing for the domestic market. With a burgeoning population of 106 million and an economy that is growing even faster, Mexico promises to be a major target area for MNEs during the millennium.[32] At the same time, these developments help Mexico link itself to the triad via the United States.

Mercosur
A sub-regional free trade group formed to promote economic cooperation; the group consists of Argentina, Brazil, Paraguay, and Uruguay

Andean common market (Ancom)
A sub-regional free trade compact designed to promote economic and social integration and cooperation; Bolivia, Colombia, Ecuador, Peru, and Venezuela are all members

Enterprise for the Americas
An idea launched by President George Bush to create a free trade area from Alaska to Argentine Antarctica

Free Trade Area of the Americas (FTAA)
A regional trade agreement that is expected to succeed NAFTA and include 34 countries across North, Central, and South America

INTERNATIONAL BUSINESS STRATEGY *IN ACTION*

Mexico and NAFTA

Many opponents of NAFTA argued that the agreement would lead to the export of US jobs to Mexico, with a resulting decline in gross national product (GNP). Economists, however, reported that the agreement would help save US jobs and that GNP would rise by $30 billion annually once the treaty was fully implemented. Recent research also found that the first five years of NAFTA had improved growth and efficiency in all three of its members. Certainly, MNEs in the motor vehicle and parts industry and the telecommunications industry agreed with the economists and have already formulated strategies to address these impending changes.

The US motor vehicle and parts industry expects to see some jobs go to Mexico. Moreover, the export of vehicles from foreign-owned factories in Mexico doubled in the three years after NAFTA. However, prior to NAFTA, Mexican government regulations forced US auto makers to buy Mexican parts, which in many cases did not meet global standards. This led Mexican subsidiaries of the auto makers to run plants at less-than-maximum efficiency levels. The government also forced the Big Three car companies to export more than they imported into Mexico. NAFTA has allowed companies to act regionally instead of on a country-by-country basis and to reorganize production more efficiently across North America. In an unexpected surge of events, some of the manufacturing previously assigned to Mexico is being brought back into the United States. For example, Ford relocated its production of Thunderbirds and Mercury Cougars from Cuautitlan to its assembly plant in Lorain, Ohio. At the same time, US auto suppliers are doing better because NAFTA requires 62.5 per cent of a vehicle's content to originate in North America. This means that foreign suppliers in Asia and Europe are losing out to regional, high-quality firms such as TRW and Dana. Thus, NAFTA is proving to be a boon to the US motor and auto parts industry.

Telecommunications is another industry in which US firms are doing very well. Annual US telecom exports to Mexico are now in excess of $2.8 billion, and Telmex, the previously state-owned phone company, is 9.1 per cent owned by SBC. In 2001, Telmex had 24.2 million phones wired in an all-digital network, up from 12 million in 1993, and US companies have supplied much of this new equipment. At the same time, some business customers in Mexico feel it is taking too long for Telmex to provide the service they need, so they are purchasing private networks that carry voice, data, and images by satellite. Scientific-Atlanta, a Georgia-based firm, is the market leader in this area and has been able to land a series of large contracts for installing communication systems, including those for Cifra, the country's largest retailer, and for the Mexican Navy. Other companies likely to benefit from the growing market include McCaw, Cantel, and Motorola. As a result, US telecom firms appear to have found a lucrative market just south of the border.

Doing business in Mexico can take a number of different forms. Four strategies have proven particularly profitable. One is to establish a wholly-owned subsidiary. This can be an expensive strategy, but it gives the company total control and allows management to make decisions quickly and efficiently. Quite often a local manager runs the subsidiary, and almost always the majority of the management team are locals. However, headquarters exercises key control.

A second approach is to become part of the *maquiladora* program. This strategy works best for firms aiming to export most of their output back to the United States. The *maquiladora* arrangement allows manufacturing, assembly, and processing plants to import materials, components, and equipment duty free, complete the work with Mexican labor, and then ship the finished products back north. Under recent changes in the arrangement, if the company wants, it can sell up to one-third of the output in Mexico and still participate in the program.

A third approach is the so-called shelter program, under which local contractors assume responsibility for all aspects of the manufacturing operation, from site selection to recruitment of personnel to running the factory. After a predetermined time, however, the US company can buy out the shelter operator at a preset price and take over the business.

A fourth approach is a joint venture with a local partner. This combines a foreign company with financial and manufacturing know-how and a local partner that knows how to market the output. A number of US firms have opted for this approach, including Ford, DuPont, and General Electric. In the latter case, GE formed a joint venture with MABE, one of Mexico's largest appliance manufacturers. Since then, the two have opened a gas range plant that now produces 800,000 units annually for the US, Canadian, and Mexican markets.

In most cases US MNEs will decide in advance which of these four strategies to implement. However, some firms have discovered that the need for such a decision is unanticipated. Take the example of Pace Foods, which went to Mexico City to film commercials for its Pace Picante Sauce. The crew did not want to carry back the jars of Pace's hot sauce that they used in the filming, so they told a local store manager to keep the jars and try to sell them. A few weeks later the company got a call from the manager. He had sold all 350 jars and wanted to know what he should do now. Today Pace has a thriving business selling products in Mexico.

Websites: www.ge.com; www.ford.com; www.pacefoods.com; and www.dupont.com.

Sources: Alan M. Rugman and John Kirton, "Multinational Enterprise Strategy and the NAFTA Trade and Environment Regime," *Journal of World Business*, vol. 33, no. 4 (December 1998), pp. 438–454; Alan M. Rugman, John Kirton and Julie Soloway, *Environmental Regulations and Corporate Strategy* (Oxford: Oxford University Press, 1999); **www.ford.com**; **www.telmex.com.mx/**; Joel Millman, "High-Tech Jobs Transfer to Mexico with Surprising Speed," *Wall Street Journal*, April 9, 1998, p. A 18; Laurie P. Cohen, "With Help From INS, US Meatpacker Taps Mexican Work Force," *Wall Street Journal*, October 15, 1998, pp. A 1, 8.

 Active learning check

Review your answer to Active Learning Case question 5 and make any changes you like. Then compare your answer with the one below.

5 **Should environmental laws be included in the FTAA? Why or why not?**

Whether environmental laws should become part of the FTAA is still up for debate. On one hand, there are issues of sovereignty. Should an international agreement set the standard for environmental laws or should the individual governments make their own laws to be responsive to their national needs? Although an environmental chapter was included in NAFTA, there is a growing concern among developing countries that environmental laws would be used as a non-tariff barrier to trade, keeping out their goods from the rich US market.

The US and Canada are pressing for the inclusion of environmental standards in the prospective FTAA. Not surprisingly, they both advocate the use of clean technology, while the developing countries may be better served by pollution vouchers or direct transfers of clean technology.

Mexico and the double diamond

To maintain its economic growth, Mexico must continue developing international competitive strength.[33] This is currently being done by linking to the US market.[34] In particular, MNEs must view this market not just as a source for export but also as part of the home market (see Figure 15.7). Specifically, this requires:

1 Developing innovative new products and services that simultaneously meet the needs of US and Mexican customers, with the recognition that close relationships with demanding US customers should set the pace and style of product development;

2 Drawing on the support industries and infrastructure of both the US and Mexican diamonds, realizing that the US diamond is more likely to possess deeper and more efficient markets for such industries; and

3 Making free and full use of the physical and human resources in both countries.[35]

To do this, Mexico is relying heavily on a series of strategic clusters. The six major ones, in order of importance, are petroleum/chemicals, automotive, housing and household, materials and metals, food and beverage, and semiconductors and computers. The two that are most internationally competitive and provide the best insights into how the Mexican double diamond is used are the petroleum and automotive clusters.

Petroleum cluster

Mexico's petroleum industry accounted for about 8 per cent of all exports in 2004. The country has the third largest proven oil reserves after Venezuela and the United States and is the world's fifth largest producer. The largest firm is state-owned Petroleos Mexicanos (Pemex), which is the world's largest crude oil producer (does not include refining) and the world's 65th largest company. Pemex has assets of nearly $49 billion, including pipelines, refineries, tankers, aircraft, and rail cars. This huge asset base helps explain why Mexico is a net exporter of energy, principally oil, natural gas, hydraulic power, nuclear and geothermal power, and coal.

The country also has strong petroleum-related industries and infrastructure. At present, 175 companies are operating about 500 basic and secondary petrochemical plants throughout the country and employing approximately 130,000 people.

Domestic demand of oil-related products in Mexico has been rising sharply, forcing Pemex to become considerably more productive. The export market for this oil is expected to remain at current levels for the foreseeable future. The United States will remain Mexico's largest customer as US conservation measures and depressed prices continue to create demand for oil imports. Moreover, although energy was excluded from NAFTA, recent discussions have centered on US access to Mexican oil through imports and increased opportunities for US technologies in the energy sector. For major US companies such as Arco, Chevron, and Phillips that are selling off some of their domestic properties and looking for exploration opportunities outside the country, Mexico is likely to prove a very attractive location. Turnkey exploration contracts are being used to integrate US expertise and improve Mexican drilling efficiency, thus reducing the cost of oil. This trend will make Mexico one of the lowest-cost producers in the world.

The commodity nature of the energy business provides little opportunity for Mexico to insulate itself from the cyclical changes of both pricing and demand in this cluster. The real opportunities lie in trying to improve efficiencies through various methods: (1) liberalizing exploration programs by allowing more efficient foreign drilling contractors to carry out turnkey operations; (2) reducing the cost base by working with the unions to rationalize jobs that are not required; (3) using foreign technologies in areas where Mexican expertise is lacking; (4) allowing greater participation of foreign firms in producing petrochemicals to expand capacity and competitiveness of commodity products to meet domestic and export demand; (5) using foreign MNEs to bring in technology to produce advanced petrochemicals for use in the US market; and (6) developing alternative, cleaner-burning fuels, such as natural gas and unleaded fuels, to reduce reliance on US imports and comply with international environmental standards.

The potential of this cluster looks promising, even though Mexican proven reserves have recently fallen slightly and the international benchmark price for crude oil has varied over $20 to $60 per barrel range. Mexico's vast unexplored areas provide long-term opportunities to continue a strong hydrocarbon-based cluster. Moreover, the proximity of the United States, with its declining proven reserves and growing dependence on imports, will provide Mexico with an export base for improving economies of scale and generating funds for reinvestment in drilling and exploration activities. Thus, Mexico's economic progress will be closely linked to the US diamond.

Automotive cluster

The global auto industry is currently undergoing worldwide restructuring. In the process, Mexico is emerging as a major car and truck producer. Since 1986 the industry has grown rapidly: total unit production in 2002 was 2 million units and accounts for 15 per cent of all exports. Eighty-five per cent of all Mexican-built cars are exported to the United States.[36] The Big Three US auto makers have been expanding their capacities in Mexico while closing plants in the United States and Canada. Today, DaimlerChrysler, Ford, and GM account for about 60 per cent of all light vehicle production. At the same time, European and Japanese firms are investing in Mexico in an effort to tap such benefits as low-cost labor, low capital cost, proximity to the world's largest auto market, growth of domestic demand, and accessibility to related support industries.

Mexico has a strong, rich resource base supporting its automotive cluster as well as an abundance of young, skilled, adaptable labor. Foreign auto firms are finding that these workers are particularly effective after they have been trained in total quality management, just-in-time inventory, and related concepts. In addition, unions in Mexico are much more cooperative with management than their counterparts to the north. As a result, this resource base is now producing some of the highest quality cars and trucks in North America, and the Hermosillo plant is widely regarded as the number one auto factory on the continent.

There are also strong supporting industries and a well-developed infrastructure in the automotive cluster. The auto parts industry has revenues of $450 million and employs over 500,000 Mexican workers, a five-fold increase since 1990.[37] Parts companies produce for both the domestic and export markets, and many are a result of FDI by US-based auto part firms. For example, GM has component plants in the country as well as financial participation with Mexican auto part companies. Ford has similar arrangements, as do Volkswagen, Nissan, and a host of other foreign firms. In fact, 30 new auto parts companies settled in Mexico between 1996 and 1998. In one instance, the decision by Volkswagen to produce the VW Beetle fueled foreign investment in auto parts to meet the increasing demand.[38]

While the boom of foreign investment in auto parts initially displaced inefficient local parts producers, a handful of efficiently run local companies have emerged to become multinational producers. For instance, with an initial $30 million investment, Mexico's Nemak has opened a plant in the Czech Republic that employs 200 people.

The primary customers for auto output in Mexico are in the local market. However, the percentage of this output that goes for export is rising every year. In particular, with the signing of NAFTA, Mexico's accessibility to the largest auto market in the world is increasing sharply. This accessibility is especially critical to the country since US protectionism is now threatening to raise import barriers. At the same time, Mexican acceptance of US cars manufactured in Mexico is at an all-time high. The same is true in the United States, where the quality reputation of Mexican assembly plants is being felt at the dealer showroom.

The market potential of the automotive cluster is extremely high. Some problems, however, will have to be dealt with if the country is to continue increasing its competitiveness.[39] Foremost among these is the need for greater technology. One major reason why Mexican autos are cost efficient is the lack of high automation and robotics. It is unlikely that this trend can continue. In addition, the shifting of more and more US and Canadian auto business to Mexico will put major pressure on NAFTA to ensure that these two countries benefit handsomely from this strategy and that other foreign producers, such as the Japanese and Europeans, do not.

Overall, Mexico's economic future is closely linked to that of the United States and North America. When analyzed in terms of the Porter diamond, some of the country's strategic clusters have already developed worldwide competitive strength. During the 1990s the petroleum and automotive clusters proved to be highly competitive.

Mexico is likely to begin making major inroads into other areas such as semiconductors and computers. Motorola already has a semiconductor plant in Mexico, and HP, IBM, Toshiba, Samsung, NEC, Phillips, and others produce computer hardware components in Mexican facilities. As in its automotive success, this is the result of favorable factor conditions, related and supporting industries, demand conditions, and the structure and rivalry of the firms. As a result, Mexico will find that it can link its diamond framework with that of the United States and become a worldwide competitor in still other areas in the process. Porter's diamond framework will prove to be a useful paradigm.[40]

KEY POINTS

1 Canada is the single largest trading partner of the United States. There has been a move toward privatization in the past few years as well as toward deregulation. As in the United States, the government attempts to promote competition, and the North American Free Trade Agreement (NAFTA) with Mexico has recognized the high degree of trade between the two countries.

2 Financial institutions are similar to those in the United States, as are labor relations practices. However, a much larger percentage of Canadian employees are unionized, and the unions have been major opponents of the FTA and the subsequent NAFTA.

3 NAFTA will eventually eliminate most trade barriers between the United States and Canada, which should help open up Canada to more economic development. At the same time, the government welcomes foreign investment, and a wide variety of incentive programs are designed to encourage such investments.

4 The approaches to doing business in Canada are similar to those in the United States, with some important regulatory differences. The chapter identified and discussed both.

5 Mexico has the strongest economy in Latin America, and its close business ties to the United States, as reflected by imports, exports, and US FDI, bode well for its future. The potential of the free trade agreement between the two countries and the growth of the *maquiladora* industry are helping Mexico link its economy to that of the United States. Mexico's petrochemical and automotive clusters are key industries in this linkage and are likely to become worldclass competitors in their respective areas.

Key terms

- Competition Act
- Canada Labor Code
- Investment Canada Act (ICA)
- North American Free Trade Agreement (NAFTA)
- United States–Canada Free Trade Agreement (FTA)
- Latin American Integration Association (LAIA)
- Mercosur
- Andean common market (Ancom)
- Enterprise for the Americas
- Free Trade Area of the Americas (FTAA)

REVIEW AND DISCUSSION QUESTIONS

1 How high is the Canadian standard of living? Of what value is this information to a company interested in doing business in Canada?

2 Is the Competition Act of any concern to US firms, given that the FTA has eliminated most trade restrictions? Explain.

3 What do companies seeking to set up businesses in Canada need to know about labor relations in that country? Identify and discuss three areas of importance.

4 What are the most important provisions of the Free Trade Agreement and how do they affect US firms doing business in Canada?

5 Are there any restrictions on foreign investments in Canada? Identify and describe two of them.

6 What should a firm seeking to enter the Canadian market know about marketing practices there? Identify and describe three practices.

7 How good are franchise opportunities in Canada? Explain.

8 Why is Mexico doing so well economically? Identify two developments that have been particularly helpful in bringing this about.

9 What is the purpose of the LAIA? Of what value is the organization to its members?

10 How might the creation of an "Enterprise for the Americas" affect the LAIA and Ancom? Give an example.

11 How is Mexico using its petroleum cluster to link itself to the North American triad?

12 How is Mexico using its automotive cluster to link itself to the North American triad?

13 Why are these linkages to the North American triad likely to be economically advantageous to Mexico? Cite two reasons.

REAL CASE

Jumex of Mexico: fruit juices for the United States

Founded in 1961, Group Jumex is the largest producer of juices and fruit nectars in Mexico. The country has a population of 105 million people and a hot climate that provides a favorable environment in which Jumex can grow. And grow it has. Today, it has six plants in Mexico and 40 distribution centers across the world that serve 20 countries in five continents.

Mexico offered other nurturing characteristics to the emerging company in the form of natural resources and market pressures. For one, Jumex has access to an incredible variety of tropical fruits from which it can develop new products. Indeed, the firm offers tamarind, guanabana, and guava nectars as well as the more commonly known mango, peach, pear, and apple.

Tropical fruits are readily available everywhere at a relatively low price, making the blending of juices in customers' homes extremely easy. Juice stands, in which the juice is made on site, are abundant throughout the country. Quality is paramount. Jumex cannot sell products with very little fruit content to Mexicans.

Jumex competes with other domestic producers at home for the juice and nectar market. It also competes with soft-drink makers, including Coca-Cola and Pepsi Cola, for the beverage market. However, Mexican consumers have recently improved the lot of the juice makers, as carbonated drinks are increasingly considered unhealthful.

Competition has made Jumex into an aggressive marketer. The firm uses all types of distribution system to maximize market share. It works with national wholesalers, regional wholesalers, supermarkets, and small convenience stores to establish a price system that allows them to benefit from selling its products.

Mobile communication was provided to the sales team so that orders could be processed immediately no matter how far away the distribution center was. This is very important because of the remoteness of many Mexican communities. Prior to this, a sales person could take two weeks before returning with paper work to put in an order. Supermarket computerized distribution systems are now integrated with that of Jumex so that their shelves can be stocked as needed.

While most firms have shifted to aluminum, Jumex has maintained the traditional tin can and created a distinct shape that stands out against the competition. A tin can is alleged to be more biodegradable than an aluminum can. To serve different markets, Jumex also packages in plastic, glass, and juice boxes.

Presently, Jumex exports only about 20 per cent of its production but it is highly successful. It has operations in Latin America and the Caribbean, North America, Europe, Asia, and Oceania. Distribution and marketing have been adapted to fit each country. In most of Latin America, because of geographic, market, and cultural similarities, the distribution system that was implemented was very similar to that found in Mexico.

Jumex has been surprisingly successful in the US market, where it is now a leading brand of fruit nectars. Part of this success can be attributed to Mexico's lower production costs and the availability of inexpensive natural resources. Another reason is the predominance of Mexican immigrants across the United States, particularly in large urban areas. Whether these are new immigrants or the children of immigrants who travel frequently to Mexico, they know the product and are familiar with the tropical fruits, creating an initial market for the product. ▶

Other Latin Americans or immigrants from tropical areas familiar with the brand or the fruits also push demand.

Another factor that has helped Jumex in developed countries is that its products are considered healthier than carbonated drinks and tend to offer more fruit content than many of its domestic competitors. However, competition in developed countries is likely to heat up in the future as Ceres, a South African juice producer, Jugos del Valle of Mexico, and new entrants from Asia compete in price, quality, and variety of fruit juices. In the healthy market sector, organic fruit juices from developing and developed countries will also offer competition.

Website: www.jumex.com.mx.

Sources: "Soft Drinks in Mexico," *Euromonitor*, June 2004; Samuel Bernal, "Jumex le saca jugo al cómputo movil," *Revista Red*, Febrero 2001; www.jumex.com.mx.

1 How has Mexico provided the environment to make Jumex into a competitive fruit and nectar producer in foreign markets?

2 What factors mentioned in this case study have contributed to Jumex's success in the US market?

3 Can you think of any other factors that may have contributed to Jumex's success in the US market?

REAL CASE

GlaxoSmithKline in the United States

Among industrialized countries, the US market for pharmaceuticals is the least regulated and thus the largest in the world. Not surprisingly, European companies like AstraZeneca, Aventis, and GlaxoSmithKline (GSK) depend more heavily on the North American market for their revenues than on Europe as a whole. Europe is a more fragmented market, with individual distribution systems and more layers of regulation, and governments are in the habit of imposing price controls. As a result, Europeans spend 60 per cent less per capita on pharmaceuticals than their American counterparts.

With $35.2 billion in revenues and 100,000 employees, GSK is one of the largest pharmaceutical companies in the world. Although incorporated in the United Kingdom, it is not surprising that GSK manages its operations in the United States. More than half of its sales originate in this host nation, a fact that is consistent with world trends—the United States accounts for nearly 50 per cent of the world market for pharmaceuticals. GSK derives 28.6 per cent of its sales from its home-market region, whereas the European market accounts for 25 per cent of the world market for pharmaceuticals.

Approximately 30 years ago, British Glaxo was a small company in the dried milk, antibiotics, respiratory drugs, and nutritional businesses. The discovery of Zantac, a drug to treat stomach ulcers, catapulted the company into the mainstream pharmaceutical market and financed its expansion into the US market. As the patent for Zantac was about to expire, Glaxo found itself in a sticky situation. Up to that point the company had relied on internal R&D, but

this had failed to develop the R&D capabilities for sustainable long-term growth. In 1995, the company merged with Wellcome, a company known for its strength in R&D and its lack of marketing capabilities. The merger was successful in that the new company now had a stream of new drugs that could be marketed using Glaxo's expertise.

By 2000, Glaxo Wellcome was disappointing investors once again. Drug prospects, at least in the short term, were below the industry average and expected revenues from some of its products never materialized. Yet the merger with SmithKline Beecham was not driven by the same urgency as the previous merger. Both companies had a reasonably stable pipeline and a balanced portfolio of drugs. According to Sir Richard Sykes, then chairman of Glaxo Wellcome, the deciphering of the human genome would transform the industry and only large companies that could afford to invest in working with this new information would succeed. Together, these two companies are immune to the near-death experience of losing a major blockbuster drug. No one drug accounts for more than 12 per cent of the company's revenues.

GSK operates in two product-based industry segments: (1) pharmaceuticals, which include prescription drugs and vaccines; and (2) consumer healthcare, which includes over-the-counter (OTC) medicines, oral care, and nutritional health care. Prescription drugs are sold mainly to wholesalers, which dispense them to the public through pharmacies. Consumer health-care products are sold through pharmacies, wholesalers, or directly to retail outlets.

The first step in the development of a drug is research and development. GSK spends $4 billion on R&D and has over 15,000 researchers in 24 R&D sites around the world. Once GSK has developed a new drug, it must obtain government approval in every individual nation where the company markets the product, a process that can differ significantly in each jurisdiction. Production and marketing are the next steps for a new drug. GSK's supply chain is divided into a primary chain and a secondary chain. The primary chain manufactures active ingredients for its products and ships them to the secondary chain, which manufactures the end product. There are 13 primary supply chain sites based in Australia, India, Ireland, Singapore, the United States, and the United Kingdom. In Europe, there are 17 secondary supply chain sites, while North America houses an additional six. The rest of the world has 32 secondary sites in 19 countries (five in the Middle East and Africa, 22 in Asia-Pacific, and five in Latin America).

Different price regulations at a national level have created some market abnormalities in each region. For instance, Canadian web-based pharmacies have sprung up to service US consumers seeking cheaper alternatives. GSK sent a heavily worded letter to Canadian wholesalers that were selling to these pharmacies and threatened to stop supplies. In Spain, GSK developed a two-price system: one lower price for products to be sold in Spain and a higher price for those to be exported to other EU member countries. The EU found this practice illegal.

Websites: www.gsk.com; www.aventis.com; and www.astrazeneca.com.

Sources: Alan M. Rugman, *The Regional Multinationals* (Cambridge: Cambridge University Press, 2005); "The Trouble with Cheap Drugs," *Economist*, January 29, 2004.

1 How is GSK's production organized?

2 Is GSK's secondary supply chain structure global, regional, or local? Why?

3 What is GSK's basic strategy?

4 Why does GSK spread R&D around the world?

5 What factors have made North America the primary market for GSK? Would the situation be different if we measured units sold? Why?

Endnotes

1 John R. Baldwin, Jean-Pierre Maynard and Fanny Wong, "The Output Gap Between Canada and the United States: The Role of Productivity (1994–2002)," *Statistics Canada Analytical Papers*, January 2005.

2 Tamsin Carlisle, "Calgary Becomes Outpost On High-Tech Frontier," *Wall Street Journal*, March 24, 1998, p. A 19.

3 US Department of Commerce, Bureau of Economic Analysis, *Survey of Current Business*, June 2005.

4 Also, see Rosanna Tamburri, "Canada Considers New Stand Against American Culture," *Wall Street Journal*, February 4, 1998, p. A18; Roger Ricklefs, "Canada Fights to Fend Off American Tastes and Tunes," *Wall Street Journal*, September 24, 1998, pp. B 1, 8.

5 Barbara Wickens, "Getting the GST of It," *Maclean's*, September 10, 1990, pp. 40–43.

6 For more on the GST, see Joseph E. Payne, Jr, "Canada's New Goods and Services Tax Has Implications for US Exporters," *Business America*, August 13, 1990, p. 12.

7 See Rosanna Tamburri, "Canadians Clash Over Cost of Diversity," *Wall Street Journal*, April 1, 1998, p. A 15.

8 For additional insights into the role of Quebec in US–Canadian economic ties, see Thane Peterson and William J. Holstein, "How a Freer Quebec Could Reshape the Continent," *Business Week*, July 9, 1990, pp. 40–43.

9 For a contrast, see Christopher J. Chipello, "Francophones Struggle Outside Quebec," *Wall Street Journal*, February 26, 1998, p. A 12.

10 Government of Canada, Department of Finance, *Canada's Banks*, August 2001 (*www.fin.gc.ca/toce/2001/bank_e.html*).

11 See *www.tse.com*.

12 Statistics Canada, *Perspectives on Labour and Income: Unionization—An Update*, 2000; and US Bureau of Labor Statistics, *Union Members Summary*, January 17, 2002.

13 E. Kaye Fulton and Nancy Wood, "A 'Reasonable Limit,'" *Maclean's*, December 17, 1990, pp. 20–21.

14 Todd Mason, "Now Tariffs Can't Fall Fast Enough," *Business Week*, October 23, 1989, p. 80.

15 *Summary of the US–Canada Free Trade Agreement* (Washington, DC: US Department of Commerce, International Trade Administration, 1988), p. 12.

16 Ibid., pp. 10–11.

17 *Marketing in Canada* (Washington, DC: US Department of Commerce), International Marketing Information Series, Overseas Business Reports, OBR 88–05, May 1988, p. 8.

18 See *http://www.dsa.ca/home.htm*.

19 Statistics Canada, *Cansim Database*, Matrix: D657192.

20 Statistics Canada, *Cansim Database*, Matrix: D657192 and D657205.

21 Ibid.

22 Also, see Stephen Baker, "Mexico: Can Zedillo Stem the Tide of Crisis?" *Business Week*, April 18, 1994, p. 60.

23 "Country Briefings: Mexico," *The Economist*, June 17, 2005.

24 Also, see Bob Ortega, "Some Mexicans Charge North in NAFTA's Wake," *Wall Street Journal*, February 22, 1994, pp. B 1, B 5.

25 "Mexico Proves a Resilient, Robust Market for U.S. Exports," *AgExporter*, January 2002.

26 Ministry of Finance and Public Credit of Mexico, *Mexico's Bimonthly Economic News*, June 13, 2000.

27 See "Labor: Minimum Daily Wages for 2005," *mexicanlaws.com*, 2005.

28 Len J. Trevino, "Strategic Responses of Mexican Managers to Economic Reform," *Business Horizons*, May/June 1998, pp. 73–80.

29 Some of the material in this section can be found in "Latin American Introduction," *ILT Latin America*, July 1991, pp. 1–13.

30 For more on the FTAA, see *www.ftaa-alca.org/*.

31 "The Business of the American Hemisphere," *Economist*, August 24, 1991, pp. 37–38.

32 Also, see Rick Wartzman, "In the Wake of NAFTA, A Family Firm Sees Business Go South," *Wall Street Journal*, February 23, 1999, pp. A 1, 10.

33 Jonathan Friedland, "Mexico Is Hit Despite Belt-Tightening," *Wall Street Journal*, September 14, 1998, p. A 27.

34 Richard M. Hodgetts, "Porter's Diamond and Framework in a Mexican Context," *Management International Review*, vol. 33, Special Issue (1993), pp. 41–54.

35 J. R. D'Cruz and Alan M. Rugman, *New Concepts for Canadian Competitiveness* (Toronto: Kodak Canada, 1992).

36 Susan Carney, "Mexico's Low Labor Costs Tempt Detroit Carmakers," *The Detroit News*, January 7, 2002.

37 Geri Smith and Elisabeth Malkin, "Mexico's Makeover," *Business Week*, December 21, 1998; and Elisabeth Malkin and Jonathan Wheatley, "Parts Shops Are Tailgating Carmakers to Latin America," *Business Week*, October 23, 2000.

38 Elisabeth Malkin and Jonathan Wheatley, "Parts Shops Are Tailgating Carmakers to Latin America," *Business Week*, October 23, 2000.

39 Elisabeth Malkin, "Holding Off Asia's Assault," *Business Week*, April 13, 1991, pp. 44–45.

40 Alan M. Rugman and Michael Gestrin, "The Strategic Response of Multinational Enterprises to NAFTA," *Columbia Journal of World Business*, vol. 28, no. 4 (1993), pp. 18–29.

Additional bibliography

Averyt, William F. "Canadian and Japanese Foreign Investment Screening," *Columbia Journal of World Business*, vol. 21, no. 4 (Winter 1986).

Batres, Robertos E. "A Mexican View of the North American Free Trade Agreement," *Columbia Journal of World Business*, vol. 26, no. 2 (Summer 1991).

Beamish, Paul W., Craig, Ron and McLellan, Kerry. "The Performance Characteristics of Canadian Versus UK Exporters in Small and Medium Sized Firms," *Management International Review*, vol. 33, no. 2 (Second Quarter 1993).

Birkinshaw, Julian and Hood, Neil. "An Empirical Study of Development Process in Foreign Owned Subsidiaries in Canada and Scotland," *Management International Review*, vol. 37, no. 4 (1997).

Crookell, Harold. "Managing Canadian Subsidiaries in a Free Trade Environment," *Sloan Management Review*, vol. 29, no. 1 (Fall 1987).

Eden, Lorraine (ed.). *Multinationals in North America* (Calgary: University of Calgary Press, 1994).

Feinberg, Susan E. "Do World Product Mandates Really Matter?" *Journal of International Business Studies*, vol. 31, no. 1 (Spring 2000).

Finnerty, Joseph E., Owers, James and Creran, Francis J. "Foreign Exchange Forecasting and Leading Economic Indicators: The US–Canadian Experience," *Management International Review*, vol. 27, no. 2 (Second Quarter 1987).

Gillispie, Kate and Teegen, Hildy J. "Market Liberalization and International Alliance Formation: The Mexican Paradigm," *Columbia Journal of World Business*, vol. 30, no. 4 (Winter 1995).

Globerman, Steven and Walker, Michael (eds.). *Assessing NAFTA: A Trinational Analysis* (Vancouver, BC: Fraser Institute, 1993).

Globerman, Steven and Shapiro, Daniel M. "The Impact of Government Policies on Foreign Direct Investment: The Canadian Experience," *Journal of International Business Studies*, vol. 30, no. 3 (Fall 1999).

Griffith, David A., Hu, Michael Y. and Ryans Jr., John K. "Process Standardization across Intra- and Inter-Cultural Relationships," *Journal of International Business Studies*, vol. 31, no. 2 (Summer 2000).

Hecht, Laurence and Morici, Peter. "Managing Risks in Mexico," *Harvard Business Review*, vol. 71, no. 4 (July/August 1993).

Hodgetts, Richard. "Porters's Diamond Framework in a Mexican Context," *Management International Review*, vol. 33, no. 2 (Second Quarter 1993).

Hufbauer, Gary C. et al. *NAFTA and the Environment* (Washington, DC: Institute for International Economics, 2000).

Hufbauer, Gary Clyde and Schott, Jeffrey J. *North American Free Trade: Issues and Recommendations* (Washington, DC: Institute for International Economics, 1992).

———. *NAFTA: An Assessment* (Washington, DC: Institute for International Economics, 1993).

Hung, G. L. "Strategic Business Alliances Between Canada and the Newly Industrialized Countries of Pacific Asia," *Management International Review*, vol. 32, no. 4 (Fourth Quarter 1992).

Janisch, H. N. "Canadian Telecommunications in a Free Trade Era," *Columbia Journal of World Business*, vol. 24, no. 1 (Spring 1989).

Kamath, Shyam J. and Tilley, J. Roderick. "Canadian International Banking and the Debt Crisis," *Columbia Journal of World Business*, vol. 22, no. 4 (Winter 1987).

Kaynak, Erdener. "A Cross Regional Comparison of Export Performance of Firms in Two Canadian Regions," *Management International Review*, vol. 32, no. 2 (Second Quarter 1992).

Kirton, John and Maclaren, Virginia (eds.). *Linking Trade, Environment and Social Cohesion* (Aldershot: Ashgate, 2002).

Martinez, Zaida L. and Ricks, David A. "Multinational Parent Companies' Influence over Human Resource Decisions of Affiliates: US Firms in Mexico," *Journal of International Business Studies*, vol. 20, no. 3 (Fall 1989).

Neale, Charles W., Shipley, David D. and Dodds, J. Colin. "The Countertrade Experience of British and Canadian Firms," *Management International Review*, vol. 31, no. 1 (First Quarter 1991).

Nichols, Nancy A. "The Monterrey Group: A Mexican Keiretsu," *Harvard Business Review*, vol. 71, no. 5 (September/October 1993).

Rugman, Alan M. *Multinationals in Canada: Theory, Performance and Economic Impact* (Boston: Martinus Nijhoff, 1980).

———. "The Role of Multinational Enterprises in US–Canadian Economic Relations," *Columbia Journal of World Business*, vol. 21, no. 2 (Summer 1986).

———. *Outward Bound: Canadian Direct Investment in the United States* (Toronto: Canadian–American Committee, and Prentice-Hall of Canada, 1987).

———. *Multinationals and Canada–United States Free Trade* (Columbia, SC: University of South Carolina Press, 1990).

——— (ed.). *North American Economic and Financial Integration* (Oxford: Elsevier, 2004).

——— (ed.). *Foreign Investment and NAFTA* (Columbia, SC: University of South Carolina Press, 1994).

Rugman, Alan M. and D'Cruz, Joseph R. "The 'Double Diamond' Model of International Competitiveness: The Canadian Experience," *Management International Review*, vol. 33, no. 2 (Second Quarter 1993).

Rugman, Alan M. and Gestrin, Michael. "The Investment Provisions of NAFTA," in Steven Globerman and Michael Walker (eds.), *Assessing NAFTA: A Trinational Analysis* (Vancouver, BC: Fraser Institute, 1993).

———. "The Strategic Response of Multinational Enterprises to NAFTA," *Columbia Journal of World Business*, vol. 28, no. 4 (Winter 1993).

Rugman, Alan M., Kirton, John and Soloway, Julie A. *Environmental Regulations and Corporate Strategy: A NAFTA Perspective* (Oxford: Oxford University Press, 1999).

Rugman, Alan M. and Verbeke, Alain. "Multinational Corporate Strategy and the Canada–US Free Trade Agreement," *Management International Review*, vol. 30, no. 3 (Third Quarter 1990).

——— (eds.). *Research in Global Strategic Management: Volume 1: International Business Research for the Twenty-First Century; Canada's New Research Agenda* (Greenwich, CT: JAI Press, 1990).

———. "Foreign Subsidiaries and Multinational Strategic Management: An Extension and Correction of Porter's Single Diamond Framework," *Management International Review*, vol. 33, no. 2 (Second Quarter 1993).

Sanderson, Susan Walsh and Hayes, Robert H. "Mexico—Opening Ahead of Eastern Europe," *Harvard Business Review*, vol. 68, no. 5 (September/October 1990).

Seringhaus, F. H. Rolf and Botschen, Guenther. "Cross-National Comparison of Export Promotion Services: The Views of Canadian and Austrian Companies," *Journal of International Business Studies*, vol. 22, no. 1 (First Quarter 1991).

Solocha, Andrew, Soskin, Mark D. and Kasoff, Mark J. "Determinants of Foreign Direct Investment: A Case of Canadian Direct Investment in the United States," *Management International Review*, vol. 30, no. 4 (Fourth Quarter 1990).

Spencer, William J. and Grindley, Peter. "SEMATECH After Five Years: High Technology Consortia and US Competitiveness," *California Management Review*, vol. 35, no. 4 (Summer 1993).

Ulgado, Francis M. "Location Characteristics of Manufacturing Investments in the US: A Comparison of American and Foreign-based Firms," *Management International Review*, vol. 36, no. 1 (1996).

Weintraub, Sydney. *NAFTA at Three* (Washington, DC: Center for Strategies on International Studies, 1997).

Willard, Kristen L. "Do Taxes Level the Playing Field? How US Tax Policy Affects the Investment Decisions of Foreign Affiliates in the United States," *Columbia Journal of World Business*, vol. 29, no. 4 (Winter 1994).

Chapter 19

EMERGING ECONOMIES

Contents

Objectives of the chapter

More than 100 nations in the world are not triad members; they lie outside North America, Europe, and Japan. An important subgroup of non-triad countries are the "emerging economies," marked by their rapid economic growth and changing involvement in the global economy. They are increasingly important for MNEs of all sizes: as growing markets whose large populations are starting to have more and more disposable income; as increasingly important sources of inputs, including products, technology, and value-adding capabilities as well as commodities and cheap labor; and as a source of competition, as non-triad firms begin to internationalize into triad markets. These developments represent many new opportunities as well as new risks for MNEs. Increased involvement in emerging market regions for managers means coping with more diversity. This includes the broad cultural, political, and economic diversity resulting from the wide range of countries outside the triad. It also includes diversity of business practices and competitors, which MNEs need to adapt to in order to survive.

The specific objectives of this chapter are to:

1 *Examine* the relative attractions, opportunities, and threats in the triad regions and emerging economies for firms looking to internationalize.

2 *Explain* how many emerging economies are becoming more integrated into the global economy and firms from these economies are internationalizing.

3 *Focus* on China as a new economic powerhouse, a major recipient of FDI, and a key source of new, emerging competitors for triad-based MNEs.

4 *Examine* the implications of changes in emerging economies for MNE managers in terms of new strategies and organization structures.

ACTIVE LEARNING CASE

Acer Taiwan goes international

In 2004 Acer Taiwan ranked as the fourth largest PC vendor in the world. The overall Acer Group of companies employed 60,000 people supporting dealers and distributors in more than 100 countries, earning revenues of US $15.6 billion. The company is one of the best-known brands in Asia, and a large player in Latin America. In the United States, where IBM, Compaq, and Dell dominate, Acer is a major competitor in the consumer electronics market. Not bad for a company no one knew just a few decades ago.

In 1976 CEO Stan Shih and some of his friends managed to pull together $25,000 and start Multitech. With seven employees, the company began developing small electronic products such as pocket calculators and games. Slowly the company began to grow by commercializing microprocessor technology and its applications. Its initial entrance into the PC market was as a supplier. Multitech began producing computers to be sold under other brand names. Then in 1986 the company launched its own brand name computer, Acer, and it began to sell in Europe and in Japan. While the firm still supplies under other brand names, Acer has become one of the best-known PC brands in the world.

How did a small company from Taiwan gain market share in an industry dominated by well-established computer manufacturers? Two key strategies underpinned its rapid international growth. First, it focused on learning: actively developing technological know-how, innovation capabilities, and later, marketing and branding expertise. It invested in engineering training, initially with the help of the Taiwanese government. In the late-1970s it founded the Microprocessor Training Center where 3,000 engineers were trained for Taiwan's information industry. It also entered into a range of subcontracting relationships and joint ventures with major multinational firms in targeted industries. One of the most prominent was its DRAM semiconductor joint venture with Texas Instruments in 1989. To acquire necessary technologies the company bought a host of firms including Counterpoint Computers, Altos, and Kangaroo Computer. It also entered into cross-licensing agreements with firms like IBM and Intel. Innovation was the constant focus. The rapid development of engineering, design, and R&D capabilities helped Acer improve both its production efficiency and its product development capabilities. In 1986 it came out with a 32-bit PC model before

IBM. In 1994 it introduced the world's first dual Intel Pentium PC, in 2001 the first Chinese Palm OS, and in 2004 a 64-bit notebook PC.

Second, Acer followed an incremental, niche strategy in order to expand internationally. Stan Shih explains this decision by noting, "It is better to be a big fish in a small pond than a small fish in a big pond." Small markets, especially in Asia, which were not yet captured by the likes of IBM and Compaq, were a driving force behind Acer's initial international success.

Acer's distribution system was also a novelty. With the product life of computer components at about three months, exporting overseas becomes a problem, but Acer built manufacturing and assembling plants all over the world. The company distributed parts with long product lives by ship, while highly volatile products like processors, PCBs, and memory were shipped by plane. This allowed for just-in-time production that Shih compared to the distribution system of a fast-food chain with perishable and non-perishable ingredients.

The success of the company also owes much to the management structure created by Shih. Unlike traditional Chinese businesses, where management is highly hierarchical and controlled by the owning family, Shih uses decentralized management. Autonomy is important Managers are encouraged to think like owners, so as to take advantage of all profit opportunities. Additionally, Acer has gone public and employees have the option of buying shares at extremely low prices.

More recently Acer has begun to shift away from manufacturing and into design, branding (in 2004 it produced a "Ferrari" notebook PC), and service-related businesses, partly following the evolution of the industries mapped out by Stan Shih's Smiling Curve in the early 1990s. He predicted that success in the combined computing, IT, consumer electronics, and telecoms industries would increasingly depend on being customer-centric, with customer-driven rather than technology-driven innovation. The firm would need to be committed to providing outstanding service and developing intellectual property such as software, rather than focusing on hardware and production activities. In 2000, Acer spun off its manufacturing operations to focus on globally marketing its brand-name products: desktop and mobile PCs, servers and storage, displays, peripherals, and e-business solutions. In December 2001

BenQ computers was also spun off by Acer (which still holds a 15 per cent stake in the firm). More recently it has become increasingly concerned by the competitive threat posed by mainland Chinese PC and electronics firms.

Websites: www.ti.com.

Sources: Willie Chien, Stan Shih, Po-Young Chu, *Business Growth Strategies for Asia Pacific* (New York: John Wiley and Sons, 2005); Daniel Lyons "Horse Power," *Forbes*, February 16, 2004, vol. 173, no. 3, p. 56; Paul Taylor, "In the CEO's Chair: Ky Lee at BenQ," *Financial Times (London)*, March 17, 2004, p. 2; Kathrin Hille, "A Head Start of Being Ethnically Chinese," *Financial Times (London)*, April 7, 2004, p. 10; Stanley Shih, "Talking About Innovation," *Far Eastern Economic Review*, October 17, 2002, vol. 165, no. 41, p. 44; Stan Shih, *Growing Global* (Taiwan: Acer Corporation Publication, 2001); Stan Shih, *Me-Too Is Not My Style* (Taiwan: Acer Corporation Publication, 1996).

1. What was the internationalization strategy of Acer and why was it successful?

2. Why did Acer form strategic alliances with IBM and Texas Instruments?

3. How should Acer cope with the rise of Chinese competitors on its doorstep?

INTRODUCTION

In Chapter 13 we examined some of the country-level risks common in emerging market countries. Although these stand out because of their rapid growth rate, they share many of the same characteristics of non-triad countries in general. Such countries are:

- growing in importance for international managers for both market-seeking investments and resource-seeking investments,

- strongly government-controlled, in that government agencies play a central role in negotiating with foreign investors and deciding the local rules of the game,

- less predictable and riskier than triad markets, which investors often underestimate in their pursuit of the high level of rewards on offer,[1] and

- the source of new competitors, as local firms move up the value chain, becoming more sophisticated and more international.

We are concerned with two broad kinds of international expansion in this chapter. First, internationalization from the triad into non-triad regions whereby established MNEs whose home base is large, mature, and includes expensive markets, expand to sell more outputs in, or buy more inputs from, cheaper emerging economies. Second, the internationalization of newer MNEs from outside the triad who are looking to both complement home-market resources with assets or capabilities from inside the triad and to sell into the much larger triad countries. For each kind of MNE these two forms of internationalization represent some major strategic threats and opportunities. Although we will briefly look at a range of emerging economies we will focus particularly on China because of its growing impact and importance in the global economy.

TRIAD FIRMS AND EMERGING ECONOMY FIRMS: WHY THE MUTUAL INTEREST?

Triad-based and non-triad-based firms will have similar objectives when exploring market-seeking investments. They both want to increase sales in each other's territories, and to do this they must customize products and services to suit these markets, establish (or buy) distribution and sales networks, and raise the profiles of their brands. In many cases they

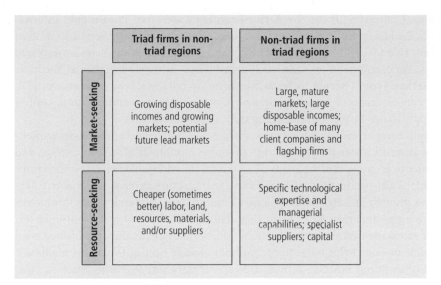

	Triad firms in non-triad regions	Non-triad firms in triad regions
Market-seeking	Growing disposable incomes and growing markets; potential future lead markets	Large, mature markets; large disposable incomes; home-base of many client companies and flagship firms
Resource-seeking	Cheaper (sometimes better) labor, land, resources, materials, and/or suppliers	Specific technological expertise and managerial capabilities; specialist suppliers; capital

Figure 19.1 What is the attraction for triad and non-triad firms investing in each other's home regions?

may also need to set up manufacturing, assembly, service, or support activities in each other's markets to avoid import duties and/or to support the needs of customers.

When exploring input-seeking investments, triad-based and non-triad-based firms may also have similar strategies, but they tend to be looking for different kinds of inputs. This is because their home regions provide each with a different set of factor endowments, as described by Porter's diamond model in Chapter 15.

Figure 19.1 provides a starting point to understand the attraction for triad firms looking to expand into emerging economies and for firms from emerging economies looking to expand into triad regions. The large markets of North America, Europe, and Japan still dominate the global economy, but they are growing slowly relative to emerging markets both large, like India, China, and Brazil, and small, like Poland or Malaysia. Triad regions also tend to be more expensive, in terms of labor costs, infrastructure, land, materials, and supporting industries, relative to non-triad regions. These represent push factors, accentuating the pull of non-triad locations. Combining these differences means that there are strong incentives for triad-based firms both to sell products, services, and other outputs into these growing markets and to source inputs, such as cheap labor or manufactured components and services, from such places.

For new MNEs evolving in non-triad regions, the main attraction of triad markets is the large, mature markets. But many firms also look to these countries to fill gaps in their assets, resources, and capabilities, from technological know-how or specialist components to brands.

FDI into emerging economies for inputs (resource-seeking) and outputs (market-seeking) takes a variety of forms. Prudential (UK), along with many other triad firms, cut many of its back-office operations in Reading, England, in 2002 and established a center in Mumbai, India. Although this resulted in around 400 redundancies in the United Kingdom, the firm was then able to take advantage of the cheaper (and, in some cases better) local Indian IT and call-center service workers that have created the local industry reviewed in the **Real Case: The Indian IT, software, and services industry** at the end of this chapter. The **Active Learning Case: Kodak in China** in Chapter 13 shows how the firm created a series of mergers and joint ventures to invest over $1 billion into China, both for producing film products more cheaply (using cheaper labor and raw materials) and for serving the growing Chinese market. The **International Business Strategy in Action: Oxford Instruments in China** box in this chapter shows how one high-tech British firm managed the process, for very

Resource-seeking FDI
MNEs invest in production-related activities to benefit from cheaper or better sources of inputs in a particular location; these can include raw materials, components, or labor and expertise

Market-seeking FDI
MNEs invest in distribution, sales, or marketing operations in order to sell products or services (outputs) in particular country markets

Korean *chaebols*
Traditionally family-dominated, diversified conglomerates. Family ownership has been reduced and many are now focused in particular business sectors, reducing their diversity. There are parallels with Japanese *sogo shosha* in terms of early government support and their relationship with dominant national banks.

similar reasons. Contrasting these, the **Active Learning Case: Acer Tawain goes international** and the **Real Case: Korean *chaebols*** charting the growth and internationalization of Korean *chaebols* Hyundai and Samsung show why and how newer MNEs have broken into triad markets. Yet in many other cases, such as for Tesco in the **International Business Strategy in Action: From Oserian to Tesco** box, firms do not see a need to engage in FDI, because they can get access to the advantages of non-triad locations and maintain control over their supply chains by buying and selling through global markets.

More generic international business reasons also exist for expanding into these markets, including risk diversification, the opportunity to extend economies of scale and scope, and the opportunity to leverage existing assets or resources for additional revenues. For example, expanding global production by establishing manufacturing plants in non-triad regions serves to diversify risk by reducing dependence on triad locations where input costs and wages are high—but may also rise further. This allows firms to reap economies-of-scale benefits across the overall production function. Similarly, extending established triad brands into new markets helps build the economies of scale needed to pay for media advertising and other brand-building activities. As sports stars and celebrities, such as Tiger Woods (for Nike) or Britney Spears (for Elizabeth Arden), develop international reputations, their images can be used to sell products around the world, and companies can earn sufficient revenues to pay for them because they are assets that can be leveraged globally.

✔ Active learning check

Review your answer to Active Learning Case question 1 and make any changes you like. Then compare your answer with the one below.

1 What was the internationalization strategy of Acer and why was it successful?

Rather than aiming to break into the triad markets directly, despite the attractions, Acer focused on building a presence in smaller local Asian markets first. In some ways it followed a pattern of gradual, step-wise internationalization. Acer built up from its relatively small home-base diamond in Taiwan and expanded production throughout Southeast Asia. It then undertook a double diamond strategy for accessing the triad markets of North America and Europe. It formed strategic alliances with the US and European MNEs and used these as a stepping-stone to FDI in these key triad markets. It also kept its production-based efficiencies of employee involvement in company growth and ongoing R&D to improve the quality of its products.

AN OVERVIEW OF EMERGING ECONOMIES, BY REGION

This growing interest between triad and non-triad regions is apparent in changing patterns of global FDI. As Table 19.1 shows, just under 70 per cent of all FDI flows into developed countries, mainly the triad. Asia, and particularly Southeast Asia, takes the major share of the remaining 30 per cent going to developing countries. Overall, though, FDI is the largest source of external finance for all developing countries and on average now amounts to about one-third of their GDP, compared with just 10 per cent in 1980. As described below, patterns of inward FDI are varied, with some countries or regions showing significant growth while others experience no growth and even decline.[2]

Given the market-seeking and resource-seeking aims of MNE investors, we can see that the varying levels of attractiveness of different non-triad investment destinations are the result of differences in market size and growth rates and the opportunities they present for firms looking for sourcing and production advantages. Opportunities for accessing these

Table 19.1 FDI inflows, by host region and economy, 1980–2003 (millions of dollars)

Region/economy	1980	1990	1995	2000	2003	2004 (estimates)
World	54,986	208,646	335,734	1,387,953	559,576	612,000
Developed countries	46,530	171,109	204,426	1,107,987	366,573	321,000
Western Europe	21,427	103,364	119,148	697,436	310,234	
European Union	21,317	96,774	114,560	671,417	295,154	165,000
North America	22,725	56,004	68,027	380,798	36,352	
United States	16,918	48,422	58,772	314,007	29,772	121,000
Japan	278	1,753	41	8,323	6,324	7,000
Other developed countries	2,377	11,741	17,251	29,752	19,986	
Developing countries	8,421	36,897	115,953	252,459	172,033	255,000
Africa, of which	400	2,427	5,392	8,728	15,033	20,000
Algeria	349	40	0	438	634	
Egypt	548	734	595	1,235	237	
Morocco	89	165	332	215	2,279	
Sudan	9	−31	12	392	1,349	
Angola	37	−335	472	879	1,415	
Chad	0	9	33	116	837	
Equatorial Guinea	0	11	65	109	1,431	
Nigeria	−739	588	1,079	930	1,200	
South Africa	−10	-78	1,241	888	762	
Latin America and the Caribbean	7,494	9,615	30,280	97,537	49,722	69,000
Argentina	678	1,836	5,609	10,418	478	
Brazil	1,910	989	4,405	32,779	10,144	16,000
Chile	287	661	2,956	4,860	2,982	6,000
Colombia	157	500	968	2,395	1,762	
Ecuador	70	126	452	720	1,555	
Peru	63	41	2,557	810	1,377	
Venezuela	80	451	985	4,701	2,531	
Bermuda	940	819	641	10,627	8,500	
Cayman Islands	20	49	50	6,922	4,600	
Mexico	2,090	2,633	9,655	16,586	10,783	18,000
Asia and the Pacific	527	24,854	80,281	146,195	107,278	166,000
Saudi Arabia	−3,192	1,864	−1,877	−1,884	208	
Azerbaijan	0	0	330	130	3,285	
Kazakhstan	0	0	964	1,283	2,068	
China	57	3,487	37,521	40,715	53,505	62,000
Hong Kong, China	710	3,275	6,213	61,939	13,561	33,000
India	79	237	2,151	2,319	4,269	6,000
Indonesia	180	1,092	4,346	−4,550	−597	
Korea, Republic of	17	759	1,249	8,572	3,752	9,000
Malaysia	934	2,611	5,815	3,788	2,474	
Pakistan	64	250	719	305	1,405	
Singapore	1,236	5,575	11,591	17,217	11,409	21,000
Taiwan Province of China	166	1,330	1,559	4,928	453	
Thailand	189	2,575	2,070	3,350	1,802	
Viet Nam	0	180	1,780	1,289	1,450	
Central and Eastern Europe	35	640	15,356	27,508	20,970	36,000
Bulgaria	0	4	90	1,002	1,419	
Croatia	0	0	114	1,089	1,713	
Czech Republic	0	72	2,568	4,984	2,583	5,000
Hungary	1	311	5,103	2,764	2,470	
Poland	10	89	3,659	9,341	4,225	5,000
Romania	0	0	419	1,037	1,566	
Russian Federation	0	0	2,065	2,714	4,144	10,000
Serbia and Montenegro	0	0	45	25	1,360	

Source: Adapted from United Nations, *World Investment Report 2004*, key data downloads at http://www.unctad.org (Geneva: United Nations Conference on Trade and Development).

Liberalization policies
Government policies that move away from planned economies toward more free-market systems; they are marked by the privatization of state-owned businesses, a lowering of tariff and non-tariff barriers, and reductions in the constraints placed on foreign firms' investments and business activities

kinds of advantages can be enhanced by government liberalization policies, which can help to reduce the limitations and constraints on foreign firms' investments and business activities. Liberalization, for many governments in emerging economies, signals a move away from a centrally-controlled or coordinated economy, toward a more free-market economy. This shift is often accompanied by the widespread privatization of state-owned firms. Again this presents opportunities for MNEs, for example, in telecoms, utilities, or energy industries to buy into newly privatized firms or establish joint ventures and alliances to access resources or the local market. India provides a clear illustration of this with FDI inflows amounting to over $2 billion between 1991 and 1995, after liberalization, compared with well below $1 billion in the two decades leading up to 1990.

Non-triad countries and regions differ, both in their initial economic attractiveness to MNEs and in the ways that governments are liberalizing parts of the economy; together these explain many of the differences we observe in regional patterns of FDI. Table 19.2 shows that, in the same time period, outflows of FDI from developing countries have grown fairly dramatically. Again Southeast Asia is responsible for the dominant share. China's stock of outward FDI has grown from $2.5 billion in 1990 to over $25 billion in 2000 and $37 billion in 2003. In addition to this, however, a significant proportion of the much larger outward flows from Hong Kong originally come from mainland China.

We will now briefly review the recent experience of each of the main non-triad regions in terms of inward FDI and look at some examples that provide insights into the drivers of FDI flows. In preparation for the discussion below about MNEs from emerging economies, we will also briefly look at some of the largest firms in these countries that are expanding within and beyond their regions.

Asia-Pacific and the Middle East

As shown in Table 19.1 above, Asia Pacific and the Middle East receives 19 per cent of global FDI flows, the most of any non-triad region. But FDI is highly concentrated, with 10 out of the 55 economies in the region (for which reliable data is available) accounting for 90 per cent of FDI. China, Hong-Kong (China) and Singapore take shares and their attractiveness has been growing steadily over the past decade.

Table 19.2 FDI from developing countries, 1980–2003 (billions of dollars)

Region/economy	FDI outflows (annual average)				FDI outward stock				
	1980–1989	1990–1994	1995–1999	2000–2003	1980	1990	1995	2000	2003
Developing economies	5.7	28.1	64.9	59.6	60.2	128.6	308.6	793.3	858.7
Africa	0.5	1.8	2.6	–	6.9	20.9	32.9	45.6	39.5
South Africa	0.2	0.7	1.9	−0.6	5.7	15.0	23.3	32.3	24.2
Latin America and the Caribbean	0.9	4.7	18.0	10.6	46.9	58.8	86.3	155.5	183.8
Brazil	0.2	0.6	1.3	0.7	38.5	41.0	44.5	51.9	54.6
Chile	–	0.4	1.5	1.8	–	0.2	2.4	11.2	13.8
Mexico	0.1	0.4	0.7	1.9	–	1.1	2.6	7.5	13.8
Asia and the Pacific	4.3	21.6	44.3	49.0	6.5	48.9	189.5	592.3	635.4
South, East, and Southeast Asia	3.7	21.6	43.6	45.8	4.5	41.0	181.8	577.8	607.5
China	0.4	2.4	2.2	3.0	–	2.5	15.8	25.8	37.0
Hong Kong, China	1.2	10.5	22.5	23.0	0.1	11.9	78.8	388.4	336.1
India	–	–	0.1	1.0	–	–	0.3	1.9	5.1
Korea, Republic of	0.4	1.5	4.3	3.4	0.1	2.3	10.2	26.8	34.5
Malaysia	0.2	0.8	2.2	1.4	0.2	2.7	11.0	21.3	29.7
Memorandum									
World	93.3	234.8	603.1	779.3	559.6	1758.2	2897.6	5983.3	8196.9

Source: UNCTAD, *World Investment Report 2004* (Geneva: United Nations Conference on Trade and Development, 2004), at: http://www.unctad.org.

We focus on China below but there are examples of events and factors elsewhere in the region that help explain these patterns of investment. Many of the countries in the region continue to liberalize their economies and privatize state-owned assets, both of which are attractive to MNEs. FDI into South Korea was driven up recently by large mergers and acquisitions (M&As) in telecoms, with Investor Group (US) buying a 40 per cent stake of Hanaro Telecom for $0.5 billion, and in finance where the Lone Star Fund (US) acquired a 51 per cent stake of the Korea Exchange Bank for $1.2 billion.

Good economic conditions and better investment climates in Singapore, Thailand, and Vietnam in 2003–2004 boosted inward investment while Indonesia experienced declining FDI because of its weakening economy. In 2003 FDI flows declined less than they might have because the successful privatization of some state assets, including Bank International Indonesia, brought in $0.6 billion of investment. Indonesia, Pakistan, India, and to some extent South Korea, are unusual in that privatization has driven inward flows of FDI in a similar way to many Latin American economies. This is much less of a driver for most of the Asia region.

FDI into India grew by 24 per cent in 2003 because of continued liberalization and because of the attractions presented by its evolving IT, software, and services industries (see **Real Case: the Indian IT, software, and services industry**).

The oil-rich countries of Bahrain, Jordan, Kuwait, Oman, and Saudi Arabia also experienced recent upturns in inward FDI, almost exclusively related to their oil industries. Less political turmoil would have resulted in larger inflows to the Middle East region in recent years.

Finally, there are two clear trends that indicate the dynamism of the Asia region. First is the growth of intra-regional investment, particularly driven by the regional giants India and China joining countries like Malaysia, South Korea, Taiwan, and Singapore as active investors. Second, FDI in services is growing rapidly and now represents over 50 per cent of FDI stock in the Asia region. Many of the high-growth economies are becoming increasingly service oriented and have developed efficient institutional and infrastructural conditions for attracting finance, telecoms, and commerce-related activities. In accordance with its commitments to the liberalization of services under its WTO accession agreement, China is opening its service industries to FDI. Restrictions on FDI in industries such as banking and finance, telecoms, logistics and distribution, transportation, and retail and wholesale trade are being removed. By 2008 these industries in China will be largely open to FDI.

Intra-regional investments
Investments in the local region rather than in other triad or non-triad regions, such as when Chinese firms invest in other Southeast Asian economies

MNEs from Asia-Pacific

The Asia-Pacific region has 32 out of the 50 largest non-financial MNEs from developing countries listed by UNCTAD (see Table 19.3). Eleven, the largest number from any country, come from Hong Kong (China). Top of the list is Hutchison Whampoa, a diversified conglomerate with over $14 billion of sales and over 150,000 employees mainly in the Asia region. Other major firms from the region include Singtel (telecoms; Singapore), Petronas (oil and petroleum; Malaysia) Samsung Electronics and LG Electronics (South Korea) and Jardine Matheson Holdings (diversified; Hong Kong). A further discussion about new multinationals from non-triad regions appears below. We also discuss the evolving future MNEs in China later in this chapter.

Central and Eastern Europe

Despite years of political and economic change, including liberalization, in the Central and Eastern European (CEE) region it still attracts a relatively small percentage (3 to 4 per cent in Table 19.1) of global FDI inflows. The importance of privatization initiatives in attracting FDI to the region is shown by the fact that a decline from a record $31 billion of inflows in 2002 to $21 billion in 2003 was almost entirely due to the end of privatization in Slovakia and the Czech Republic.

Table 19.3 The top 50 non-financial TNCs from developing economies, ranked by foreign assets, 2002[a] (millions of dollars, number of employees)

Ranking by Foreign assets	Ranking by TNI[b]	Corporation	Home economy	Industry[c]	Assets Foreign	Assets Total	Sales Foreign[e]	Sales Total	Employment Foreign	Employment Total	TNI[b] (Percent)
1	10	Hutchison Whampoa Limited	Hong Kong, China	Diversified	48,014	63,284	8,088	14,247	124,942	154,813	71.1
2	14	Singtel Ltd.	Singapore	Telecommunications	15,775[d]	19,071	3,247	5,801	9,877	21,716	61.4
3	44	Petronas – Petroliam Nasional Berhad	Malaysia	Petroleum expl./ref./distr.	13,200	46,851	6,600	21,433	4,979	25,940	26.0
4	11	Cemex S.A.	Mexico	Construction materials	12,193[d]	16,044	4,366	7,036	17,568	26,752	67.9
5	33	Samsung Electronics Co., Ltd.	Republic of Korea	Electrical & electronic equipment	11,388	51,964	28,298	47,655	28,300[f]	82,400	38.5
6	26	LG Electronics Inc.[f]	Republic of Korea	Electrical & electronic equipment	5,845	16,214	11,387	23,553	30,029	55,053	46.3
7	15	Jardine Matheson Holdings Ltd	Hong Kong, China	Diversified	5,729[d]	8,255	4,449[j]	7,398	60,000[f]	114,000	60.7
8	2	Neptune Orient Lines Ltd.[f]	Singapore	Transport and storage	4,580[d]	4,771	4,501	4,642	11,187	12,218	94.8
9	17	Citic Pacific Ltd.	Hong Kong, China	Construction	4,170	7,328	1,567	2,861	7,388	11,643	58.4
10	9	Sappi Limited	South Africa	Paper	3,733[d]	4,641	2,941	3,729	9,807[f]	17,572	71.7
11	6	Shangri-La Asia Limited	Hong Kong, China	Hotels and motels	3,663[d]	4,593	463	601	13,000[g]	16,300	78.9
12	34	Sasol Limited	South Africa	Industrial chemicals	3,623	8,960	3,687	7,114	7,107	31,150	38.4
13	3	Guangdong Investment Limited	Hong Kong, China	Diversified	3,601	3,924	815	876	5,994	6,580	92.0
14	5	Flextronics International Ltd.[k]	Singapore	Electrical & electronic equipment	3,488[d]	4,897	5,903	7,812	76,187	78,000	81.5
15	25	Capitaland Limited	Singapore	Real estate	3,165	9,403	1,114	1,823	5,111[l]	10,333[l]	48.1
16	13	City Developments Limited[m]	Singapore	Hotels	2,954[d]	6,490	806	1,278	11,001	13,940	62.5
17	50	Petroleo Brasileiro S.A. – Petrobras	Brazil	Petroleum expl./ref./distr.	2,863	32,018	1,085	22,612	2,200[f]	46,723	6.1
18	22	MTN Group Limited	South Africa	Telecommunications	2,582	3,556	729	1,991	1,970	4,192	52.1

19	21	Anglogold Limited	South Africa	Gold ores	2,301	3,964	831	1,761	30,821[g]	53,097	54.4
20	12	First Pacific Company Limited	Hong Kong, China	Electrical & electronic equipment	2,276[d]	2,313	1,892	1,892	25[f]	46,422	66.1
21	35	Companhia Vale do Rio Doce	Brazil	Mining & quarrying	2,265[f]	7,955	2,928	4,268	1,493[f]	13,973	35.9
22	31	Metalurgica Gerdau S.A.[f]	Brazil	Metal and metal products	2,089	4,093	1,340	3,136	5,977	18,995	41.7
23	27	Perez Companc	Argentina	Petroleum expl./ref./distr.	2,052	4,090	567	1,484	1,633[g]	3,255	46.2
24	39	América Móvil	Mexico	Telecommunications	2,002	10,966	1,664	5,953	6,629	14,572	30.6
25	42	Singapore Airlines Limited	Singapore	Transport and storage	1,969[h]	10,866	2,472	5,260	2,613	14,418	27.7
26	49	CLP Holdings	Hong Kong, China	Electricity, gas and water	1,905[f]	7,793	130	3,350	37[f]	4,303	9.7
27	45	Samsung Corporation	Republic of Korea	Electrical & electronic equipment	1,897[h]	6,370	5,316[l]	29,533	1,223[g]	4,105	25.9
28	29	Kulim (Malaysia) Berhad	Malaysia	Food & beverages	1,729	3,689	166	516	10,800	22,112	42.6
29	40	Keppel Corporation Limited	Singapore	Diversified	1,657	6,609	604	3,087	8,722	19,947	29.5
30	32	Naspers Limited	South Africa	Media	1,655[d]	2,498	412	1,148	1,742[f]	10,711[f]	39.5
31	20	Barloworld Ltd	South Africa	Diversified	1,596	2,569	1,984	3,409	9,973	23,192	54.5
32	41	United Microelectronics Corporation	Taiwan Province of China	Electrical & electronic equipment	1,531	9,418	1,320	2,180	1,002[f]	10,136	28.9
33	19	Fraser & Neave Limited	Singapore	Food & beverages	1,466	4,374	1,037	1,931	9,130	11,816	54.8
34	46	Hyundai Motor Company	Republic of Korea	Motor vehicles	1,461[h]	16,964	9,746	2,070	4,379[g]	50,038	21.3
35	48	Nan Ya Plastics Corporation	Taiwan Province of China	Rubber and plastics	1,403[d]	9,743	850	5,011	10,394[g]	72,174	15.3
36	36	Grupo Bimbo SA De CV	Mexico	Food	1,400	3,077	1,389	4,286	16,235	72,500	33.4
37	16	Orient Overseas International Ltd[k]	Hong Kong, China	Transport and storage	1,148	2,189	1,012	2,458	4,039	4,743	59.6
38	1	CP Pokphand Company Limited	Thailand	Food	1,086	1,107	1,542	1,542	52,976[g]	54,000	98.7
39	18	Gruma S.A. De C.V.	Mexico	Food & beverages	1,084	2,148	1,301	1,986	8,314	14,887	57.3

(continued)

Table 19.3 (continued)

Ranking by Foreign assets	TNI[b]	Corporation	Home economy	Industry[c]	Assets Foreign	Assets Total	Sales Foreign[e]	Sales Total	Employment Foreign	Employment Total	TNI[b] (Per cent)
40	38	Swire Pacific Limited	Hong Kong, China	Business services	1,000[d]	8,880	963	1,951	17,969	55,700	31.0
41	7	Savia SA De CV[f]	Mexico	Diversified	941	1,362	633	682	5,316	7,375	78.0
42	37	Grupo Imsa	Mexico	Metal and metal products	831	3,037	1,182	2,827	4,149[f]	15,800	31.8
43	8	Asia Pacific Breweries Ltd.	Singapore	Food & beverages	814	1,056	754	1,093	2,023[g]	2,624	74.4
44	24	Nampak Limited	South Africa	Rubber and plastics	782[d]	1,281	328	1,317	10,962[f]	18,062	48.9
45	23	Kumpulan Guthrie Berhad	Malaysia	Rubber and plastics	780	2,397	369	811	40,199[f]	56,143	49.9
46	4	Li & Fung Limited	Hong Kong, China	Wholesale trade	765	781	4,642	4,779	3,466	5,313	86.8
47	43	Cintra	Mexico	Air courier services	748[d]	1,937	1,169	2,969	629[f]	19,928	27.1
48	30	Advanced Semiconductor Engineering Inc	Taiwan Province of China	Computer and related activities	724[d]	3,020	990	1,317	5,340	20,401	41.8
49	28	Hong Kong And Shanghai Hotels Ltd.	Hong Kong, China	Hotels	650	2,404	135	332	3,653	5,953	43.0
50	47	San Miguel Corporation	Philippines	Food & beverages	623[d]	3,318	277	2,639	5,114[g]	27,259	16.0

[a] All data are based on the companies' annual reports unless otherwise stated.

[b] TNI, or "Transnationality Index," is calculated as the average of the following three ratios: foreign assets to total assets, foreign sales to total sales and foreign employment to total employment.

[c] Industry classification for companies follows the United States Standard Industrial Classification as used by the United States Securities and Exchange Commission (SEC).

[d] In a number of cases, companies reported only partial foreign assets. In these cases, the ratio of the partial foreign assets to the partial (total) assets was applied to total assets to calculate the total foreign assets. In all cases, the resulting figures have been sent for confirmation to the companies.

[e] Foreign sales are based on the origin of the sales. In a number of cases companies reported only sales by destination.

[f] Data were obtained from the company as a response to an UNCTAD survey.

[g] Foreign employment data were calculated by applying the share of foreign assets in total assets to total employment.

[h] Foreign assets were calculated by applying the share of foreign employment in total employment to the balance total assets.

[i] Foreign sales were calculated by applying the share of foreign assets in total assets to total sales.

[j] Data for outside Hong Kong (China) and mainland China.

[k] Data for outside Asia.

[l] Data are for September 2003.

[m] Data for outside East and Southeast Asia.

Source: UNCTAD/Erasmus University database.

Poland, the Czech Republic, and Hungary receive larger shares of FDI than other countries in the region but have experienced declines in recent years, as has the Russian Federation. These, plus five other CEE countries (Estonia, Latvia, Lithuania, Slovenia, and Slovakia) joined the EU in May 2004 and all saw FDI inflows shrink recently, but prospects look better from now on.

Some countries are attracting auto sector FDI, including Toyota-PSA's investments in the Czech Republic and PSA and Hyundai's involvement in Slovakia. Volkswagen Slovakia is already that country's largest company and biggest employer by far. Slovakia has a population of just over 5 million people, yet is expected to be producing 850,000 cars by 2007, from having no auto industry whatsoever before 1991, when VW took over Skoda's businesses in Bratislava in the Czech Republic. VW has invested around $1.3 billion in Slovakia, and Hyundai's investments are expected to total $1.5 billion eventually. But in all these cases the MNEs were attracted to the region not just because of the combination of cheap labor, good infrastructure, and proximity to Europe's large markets, but also because of the over $1 billion in subsidies and regional development loans they received to sweeten the deal.[3]

In terms of outflows of FDI from the CEE region, the Russian Federation has dominated for some time as the major source, accounting for 59 per cent of outward investment from the region in 2003. A key question for analysts is whether these capital flows represent genuine strategic investments in other parts of the world or capital flight from a politically tense Russia.

MNEs from Central and Eastern Europe

The largest MNEs in the CEE region are Russian, such as Gazprom, Lukoil, RUSAL, Norilsk Nickel, and Yukos (see the case study in Chapter 13), many of them based on the country's abundant natural resources. Others include Novoship, Primorsk Shipping, and Far Eastern Shipping (transportation; Russia); PLIVA (pharmaceuticals; Croatia); and Gorenje Gospodinjski Aparati (domestic appliances; Slovenia).

Latin America and the Caribbean

Nine per cent of global FDI went to the Latin America region in 2003, less than what went to China in that year. The lowest level of inflows since 1996 is $50 billion (Table 19.1). The three largest economies of Argentina, Brazil, and Mexico saw the steepest declines. To various degrees these economies have had a difficult decade in terms of economic growth and recession. Moreover, a spate of privatizations during the late 1990s also boosted inward FDI for these and other regional economies, but this is now over.

A number of MNEs greatly increased their involvement in Latin America during the period of privatization. An example is Endesa, the Spanish-owned electricity utility, which is the leading supplier in six countries and serves 10.5 million customers (50 per cent of its global market) in the region. Through its regional subsidiary Enersis, Endesa bought into or bought out national companies in Argentina, Brazil, Chile, Peru, Colombia, and the Dominican Republic to develop massive economies of scale in energy production, distribution, and services in the region.[4]

Regional-level, as opposed to national-level, competition has evolved in other industries, sometimes pitting home-based MNEs with foreign-owned incomers. In telecoms, for example, Mexico's America Movil and Spain's Telefonica are battling it out for regional domination, both having boosted their holdings when US telecom firms went through a divestment phase. Although it dominates the Mexican mobile telephony business, it has a long way to go to catch up with Telefonica. Telefonica Moviles, the Spanish firm's regional mobile telecom subsidiary, has a presence in 13 countries in the region, is the market leader in 7 and second in 5, and serves a total of over 40 million customers.[5]

Brazil and Mexico still received the highest amounts of FDI in 2003 and, as we would expect, one-third of all FDI into the region came from the United States. Many Latin American countries now face increased competition for US manufacturing investment from China and the Asia region. This is particularly true of Mexico, whose linkage to the North American triad via the NAFTA was discussed in Chapter 15, where the Mexico–US double diamond was explained. Between December 2000 and April 2004, the number of *maquiladora* enterprises (which accounted for almost 50 per cent of Mexico's merchandise exports) dropped from 3,703 to 2,820, with 220,000 jobs lost as a result. Combined with the decline in inward FDI this calls into question the attractiveness and competitiveness of the region in comparison to a fast-evolving Asia.[6]

MNEs from Latin America

Of the 50 largest non-financial TNCs from developing countries listed by UNCTAD (Table 19.3), 11 are from the Latin American region, 7 Mexican, three Brazilian, and one Argentinean. As with the Central and Eastern European MNEs (and contrasting those from the Asia-Pacific region) many of the largest are natural resources based. These include the largest of all, Cemex (construction materials; Mexico), Petrobras (oil and petroleum; Brazil), Companhia Vale do Rio Doce (mining; Brazil), Metalurgica Gerdau (metal products; Brazil), and Perez Companc (oil and petroleum; Argentina).

Africa

As home to most of the world's least-developed countries (LDCs), Africa has always recorded low levels of inward FDI because of its relative lack of attractiveness to MNEs. Political instability, weak infrastructure, poor labor skills, and macro-economic fragility have plagued many parts of the continent for decades. Except for Equatorial Guinea, Angola, and the Sudan, which are oil producers, the remaining 31 LDCs received less than $1 billion in 2003 (26 of them less than $200 million). The same pattern is true, however, of the 15 LDCs in the Asia-Pacific region where all but two received less than $100 million in FDI.

As shown in Table 19.1, less than 3 per cent of total global FDI normally goes to Africa, and this tends to be concentrated in resource-rich economies. Oil, diamonds, gold, and platinum in particular have been the main attraction for MNEs. Exxon Mobil, for example, expects to spend $1.7 billion for an offshore oil project in Nigeria, and the French firm Total Oil Nigeria has longer-term plans to invest $10 billion in the Nigerian oil industry before 2011. For most of Sub-Saharan Africa, however, inflows are limited, although South Africa stands out as a major recipient due to its relatively healthy economy.

FDI in telecoms and services recently overtook investment in mining and extraction in South Africa. At the same time it has extended its investments in other parts of the continent. South African firm BHP Billiton opened its second aluminum operation in Mozambique, at a cost of over $1 billion, and utilities firm Eskom has developed joint ventures with national energy firms in Tanzania, Nigeria, and Zimbabwe. Two of South Africa's telecom firms are also majority shareholders in the largest mobile telecom firm in Africa, a joint venture between Telecom S.A., VenFin, and Vodafone (35 per cent stake) with over 10 million subscribers and almost $2.5 in revenues. It competes with MTN group from South Africa, Orascom (Egypt), Orange (France Telecom), and CelTel International (the Netherlands), all of which are gradually taking market share from the fixed-line industry dominated by national telecom firms. In some industry sectors, despite the lack of inward FDI, there are growing business links between Western firms and local African firms. The Kenya cut flower industry is one example (see **International Business Strategy in Action: From Oserian to Tesco: the Kenya cut flower industry**).

INTERNATIONAL BUSINESS STRATEGY *IN ACTION*

From Oserian to Tesco: the Kenya cut flower industry

Kenya is now the leading exporter of cut flowers to Europe, with 25 per cent of the market. Yet this industry has really grown only over the last decade, with export growth accelerating rapidly in the late 1990s and continuing to grow today. How has this new-found global competitive advantage come about in one of the world's least-developed countries? The real start of the industry happened in 1994 with the formation of the Kenya Flower Council to support the operations of a number of fast-growing businesses.

In 1999 exports grew by 22 per cent, and Kenya earned $100 million in foreign exchange from sales of cut flowers abroad. Now exports are worth $180 million with some 270 million stems produced annually, 60 per cent by the top 15 farms. This amounts to nearly 10 per cent of Kenya's export earnings, more than the traditional export commodity coffee and close to exports of tea. Horticulture overall, which includes vegetables, employs about 50,000 workers directly and supports half a million people in Kenya. The average basic wage in the flower industry is around US $5,000 compared with Kenya's average GDP per capita of US $400. Most of the flower growing is in the areas of Naivasha, Thika, and Kiambu, where over 2,000 hectares are used for flower production.

Although over 30 varieties of flowers are grown in Kenya, roses make up 74 per cent of Kenya's flower exports, followed by carnations, statice, and alstromeria. The major proportion of exports go to the Dutch auction houses in Holland, but direct sales via supermarket chains, particularly in the UK, have increased dramatically.

Local factor conditions

The successful cultivation of flowers requires the following elements:

- Good physical conditions: high light intensity, abundant water, clean soil, good climate
- Appropriate seeds and planting material
- Capital for investment and working capital
- Productive labor
- Expertise in growing techniques
- Good management and organization
- Pesticides and other chemicals
- Energy for heating
- Infrastructure
- A high level of quality consciousness all along the production and post-harvesting chain

Perhaps more than any other internationally traded good, time-to-market is critical in the cut flower industry. Strict control of humidity, temperature, and air quality are essential for delivering an attractive product to the market. Growers rely heavily on the post-harvest chain of handlers, storage, and transport, and in the absence of a "cold-chain" it is not possible for equatorial producers to sell to the main northern markets.

Air freight adds significantly to the total cost and makes up by far the largest component of overall cost to African producers. Airfreight, marketing, handling in Europe, and packaging make up 50 per cent of all costs for Kenyan growers. In the Netherlands, however, transport accounts for just 14 per cent of the costs, but labor makes up 35 per cent of costs.

Although cheap labor and a good growing climate are advantageous for growing flowers, some countries have done well for some time without these local factor endowments. Holland does not have climatic, land, or labor advantages but has been a dominant player in the industry for a long time. This is partly due to the power of the Dutch auction houses, which have long overseen the international flower trade.

In Porter's terminology (in the diamond model discussed in Chapter 15) acquired factor conditions, such as the cold-transport infrastructure, plant breeding and greenhouse technologies, and production management capabilities were required before Kenya could leverage its natural endowments and the cheap labor advantage to compete in the open market. It is only in the last 10 to 15 years that these acquired factors have developed.

The Oserian Development Company

Oserian, now one of the largest privately-owned flower farms in the world, was among the first commercial exporters of cut flowers from Kenya. Although it began growing flowers in the early 1980s the company dates from 1967 and was started and is still operated and partly owned by Hans and Peter Zwager. It has about 200 hectares under cultivation next to Lake Naivasha in the Rift Valley and exports 300 million stems per year. These are mainly sold by East African Flowers (EAF) BV, through the Teleflower Auction (TFA) in Holland, to other buyers around the world; or by World Flowers in the UK, direct to Tesco. Crops include roses, spray carnations, gypsophila, chrysanthemums, statice, hypericum, euphorbia, delphinium, and perezi.

The farm employs about 5,000 people; 85 per cent are permanent employees and over 60 per cent live on the farm with their families. The facilities include three kindergartens, two primary schools, shopping centers, social halls, and a medical center.

Industry structure: Tesco and the growing power of the supermarkets

Although the Dutch auction houses have traditionally been the focal point of the world flower industry, large retailers are building direct links with growers around the world, using their purchasing power to gain better control over product price, delivery, and quality. African producers appear to be the main beneficiaries of this change in purchasing habits. Supermarkets are interested in African flowers because they are inexpensive and because growers are willing to accept a set price. To the growers the arrangement is attractive because supermarkets buy large quantities at pre-arranged prices. But in order to live up to their side of the bargain African growers must invest in optimal production methods. Often this includes investments in greenhouses, forced ventilation and heating, and, in all cases, greater attention to quality.

In 1999 Kenya's direct imports to the United Kingdom grew by 51 per cent, partly due to the establishment of direct links with Marks and Spencer and Tesco. These direct supply links have strengthened since then. In 2003 the British spent more than $2.5 billion on fresh cut flowers and indoor plants. That's an average of over $45 per person. Eighty-five per cent of all flowers sold in the UK are imported, of which about 20 per cent come from countries outside the EU. The UK imports about 15 per cent of all Kenya's flower exports, worth around $40 million each year to Kenyan farmers.

Around 23 per cent of roses sold in the UK are purchased directly from Kenya, mainly by the major supermarkets. Tesco, one of the top three supermarket chains in the world, is the UK's number one food retailer and the largest retailer of flowers and plants. Tesco has been selling houseplants for the last 19 years and flowers for the last 14 years. Sales in the last three years have shown significant growth with flowers expanding at 30 per cent per annum and

plants around 15 per cent. Tesco became an associate member of the Kenya Flower Council in early 2000 as its direct links with suppliers like Oserian began to grow. By cutting out the Dutch auction houses Tesco found that it could work directly with growers to reduce prices and improve quality and also pass on customer needs to more directly influence new developments.

Fairtrade

In 2004 Tesco and Oserian deepened their buyer–supplier alliance by opening a line of Fairtrade roses. These are grown by Oserian and one other farm in Kenya (Finlay Flowers in Kericho), which have been certified to comply with employment, social, and environmental conditions laid down in the Fairtrade agreement.

The agreement was set up in response to concerns among customers and expressed in the media about the conditions under which flowers are grown. This included the employment conditions of workers and the environmental effects on the land and particularly water availability, around, for example, Lake Naivasha. Although Fairtrade roses are slightly more expensive they represent a differentiated product designed to appeal to ethically-minded customers. Tesco does not take an additional profit as 8 per cent of the overall export price goes directly to the farms, allocated by joint management and employee committees, to improve employee conditions. This premium is expected to be worth up to $200,000 per year to the two farms involved.

Sources: C. S. Dolan, S. Jafee and R. Thoen, "Equatorial Rose: The Kenyan-European Cut Flower Supply Chain," in R. Kopiki (ed.), *Supply Chain Development in Emerging Markets* (Boston: MIT Press, 2004); Mary Hennock, "Kenya's Flower Farms Flourish," *BBC News Online*, February 14, 2002, at: http://news.bbc.co.uk/1/hi/business/1820515.stm; Chris Collinson, *The Business Costs of Ethical Supply Chain Management Report No. 2607, Natural Resources and Ethical Trade Programme* (United Kingdom: National Resource Institute, 2001), at: http://www.nri.org/NRET/2607.pdf; M. Turner, "Kenya Budget Aims to Ease Economic Crisis," *Financial Times*, June 16, 2000; Gijsbert van Liemt, "The World Cut Flower Industry: Trends and Prospects," *International Labour Organization (ILO) Working Paper*, Sectoral Activities Programme (SAP 2.80/WP.139), ILO Geneva, 1998, at: http://www.ilo.org/public/english/dialogue/sector/papers/ctflower/139e2.htm#2; Kenya Flower Council, *Fact Sheet*, June 2000, Nairobi, Kenya; Kenya Flower Council, "Flowers from Kenya Newsletter," *KFC*, June 2000, Nairobi, Kenya; further material from the KFC at: http://www.africaonline.co.ke/kfc/index.html; industry data from the Horticultural Crop Development Authority (HCDA), Nairobi; and http://www.tesco.com/corporateinfo/.

MNEs from Africa

Just 7 of the 50 largest non-financial TNCs from developing countries listed by UNCTAD (Table 19.3) are from Africa, and they are all South African. Sappi (paper products), Sasol (industrial chemicals), MTN Group (telecoms), and AngloGold (gold) are all in the top 20 in Table 19.3 and are major players in their respective sectors throughout the region.

SHIFTING PATTERNS OF COMPARATIVE AND COMPETITIVE ADVANTAGE

As we have seen from the breakdown of FDI flows above, FDI into non-triad regions tends to be concentrated in a few countries within each region. Moreover, although FDI still tends to be related to primary resources, such as oil, minerals, and agricultural commodities in many of these countries, there is a growing volume of manufacturing and service-related FDI. This is particularly true for a group of emerging markets or newly industrialized countries (NICs), which have broken the cycle of underdevelopment to achieve economic growth and wealth creation, partly through increased integration with other parts of the global economy. This group includes relatively wealthy countries like South Korea, Singapore, Hong-Kong (China), and Taiwan (China), which were together called the "four Asian Tigers" in the 1980s when they began to achieve high rates of economic growth. But there are also other growing economies, particularly in the Asia-Pacific region that appear to be moving along the same growth path. Why are these economies growing? How are they able to compete with triad firms, export, and sell in triad markets? Why are they attractive as locations for triad FDI? These are important questions as the emergence of these economies, particularly the two giant markets of China and India, is giving rise to some of the most important competitive opportunities and threats for MNEs of all types.

To understand current patterns of growth in many emerging markets we need to briefly review some of the theoretical explanations for the evolving patterns of national-level comparative and competitive advantage (we did this in Chapter 6 and some of the following summarizes our earlier description). In the original landmark study of wealth creation and national competitiveness, the economist Adam Smith stated:

> What is prudence in the conduct of every private family, can scarce be folly in that of a great kingdom. If a foreign country can supply us with a commodity cheaper than we ourselves can make it, better buy it of them with some part of the produce of our own industry, employed in a way in which we have some advantage. The general industry of the country, being always in proportion to the capital which employs it, will not thereby be diminished . . . but only left to find out the way in which it can be employed with the greatest advantage.[7]

Adam Smith's theory of absolute advantage suggested that each nation should *specialize* in producing goods it had a *natural* or *acquired* advantage in producing (and therefore could produce more efficiently than other countries). Exports of these goods would pay for the import of goods that other countries produced more efficiently. There were therefore *net gains from trade* for all countries involved. Smith also became famous for his analysis of specialization and competitive advantage at the firm level.

Over time Smith's views were extended, for example, by David Ricardo's theory of comparative advantage. A notable shift toward looking at sources of competitive advantage and regional variations in these to explain global patterns of competitiveness came in the early 1900s. Two Swedes—Eli Heckscher (in 1919) and Bertil Ohlin (in 1933)—are responsible for developing a basic model that was further refined by the American economist Paul Samuelson. The H-O or HOS model (or theory of factor endowments) takes us beyond the simple assumptions made by Ricardo about labor productivity to look at the *relative availability* of different factors of production (primarily land, labor, and capital) and therefore their *relative price* (rent, wages, and interest) in each country. These will determine the products in which a country has a comparative advantage, and in which it will therefore tend to specialize and trade.[8]

The HOS model maps out the initial conditions for regional specialization in capital-intensive or labor-intensive industries according to local factor advantages but is also a

Newly industrialized countries (NICs)
A sub-group of emerging market economies that has experienced rapid economic growth, normally accompanied by political and social change; the forerunners were the four Asian "Tiger" economies: Singapore, South Korea, Taiwan, and Hong Kong. The rapid growth, increased trade and FDI, and integration of China in the global economy suggest it is approaching this status

Theory of absolute advantage
Nations should specialize in particular industries where they have a particular advantage and trade to gain other goods and services; all countries benefit so long as protectionism is minimized

583

dynamic model, showing how economic conditions change as countries interact through trade. These theories underpin Michael Porter's diamond model (see Chapter 15). They are also incorporated into the interestingly named **Flying Geese model** by Japanese academic Kaname Akamatsu.[9]

Flying Geese model
A model suggesting that Asian countries are following Japan's historical economic transition, specializing in particular industries (steel to textiles to clothing to autos to electronics) during particular growth stages. At a particular point in time we should expect to see these industries located in different Asian countries, depending on their resource endowments, labor costs, and capabilities

Flying Geese model

The Flying Geese model (Figure 19.2) suggests that Asian economies are following similar development paths, but are at different stages along this path, following the lead "goose," Japan. Over time each country, or group, will gain and then subsequently lose specific comparative advantage in a particular industry. Japan has shifted from iron and steel to textiles to clothing to autos to electronics. The four Tiger economies—Hong Kong, South Korea, Singapore, and Taiwan—followed a similar trajectory, although quicker. Other ASEAN (Association of Southeast Asian Nations) nations such as Indonesia, Malaysia, the Philippines, and Thailand are a little further behind, but the sequence of specialization is similar. In each country the transition is marked by a shift of employment from one sector to another, within the broader move from agriculture to manufacturing and then to services. Overall, rising skills and improved technological capabilities, increased capital investment, and wage inflation (as predicted by the HOS model) drive, and are driven by, the change process.

If we look at a particular industry, the location of production activities and subsequent exports and trade flows change as different economies change their specialization (Figure 19.3). China now dominates as the world's biggest exporter of textiles and clothing, Korea has a thriving automobile sector, and Singapore and Taiwan have very successful electronics industries. These have grown to the point that Japan, now a net importer of televisions, is losing its lead in many product areas (Figure 19.4). The overall pattern of change is also in line with Vernon's international product life cycle theory described in Chapter 6.[10]

The timescale over which individual countries develop the economic conditions, resources, and capabilities to specialize in a particular industry sector appears to be shortening. Comparative advantage between nations is also therefore shifting faster than in the past (Figure 19.5). It took Toyota and Sony 30 to 35 years to evolve into leading firms in their industries, whereas Samsung (South Korea) and Acer (Taiwan) took 20 to 25 years. Firms like WIPRO, InfoSys, and TCS, which are lead firms in the Indian software industry, have achieved superior competitive positions (albeit in niche areas of customized software and IT services) in 15 to 20 years.

Figure 19.2 "Flying Geese" model: changing national-level specialization

Figure 19.3 "Flying Geese" model: the shifting location of industrial production

Figure 19.4 "Flying Geese" pattern of shifting comparative advantage

The Flying Geese model is far from perfect and has been widely criticized on a number of counts. Many studies note that the sequential transfer of industrial specialization does not follow the same pattern in each country, or that it tends to be more of a parallel process whereby emerging economies seem to develop capabilities and grow exports across several industries at the same time.[11] The example of the Indian IT and services industry (see Real Case) also demonstrates that leapfrogging is possible. Here a less developed country (LDC) has evolved competitive advantages in an advanced service sector without going through the stages depicted by the model.

For the most critical observers, the model is associated with a desire by Japan to see itself as the lead "goose" in the region from a political and perhaps military perspective (particularly given that its origins date back to the 1930s), as opposed to a useful representation of patterns of economic transformation.

There are, however, some insights we can gain into the processes affecting the changing global locations of different industries and business activities and into the changing relative

Figure 19.5 Accelerated structural transformation (Are the geese flying faster?)

competitive advantages between countries. With this in mind we need to think about the future for China—the evolving specializations of Chinese firms and the resulting competitive threats for other firms. China represents a powerful combination of cheap and well-educated labor, good infrastructure, a growing domestic market, and massive inflows of capital and technology from abroad. These are driving the rapid development of comparative and competitive advantage in a range of industries, including clothing, autos, white goods, and electronics. What we may be seeing is parallel development across these sectors, rather than sequential, stage-wise development following the lead goose (as shown in Figure 19.5).

MARKET ACCESS TO THE TRIAD

For non-triad firms the triad regions encompass by far the largest, wealthiest, and most sophisticated markets in the world. Access can be subject to complex arrangements with varying degrees of economic trade liberalization and protectionism that are inherent in the institutional and political structures of these regions. The triad represents both globalization and sovereignty dimensions. The EU is the most politically integrated, in terms of institutional structures, and the Japanese-based bloc is the least. The NAFTA is a free trade agreement, not a common market, but the NAFTA contains provisions for the accession of Latin American and Caribbean and Central American nations, and it may then evolve into stronger political linkages like the EU model.

To develop global industries, non-triad nations need both trade and investment from the triad nations and also access to the markets of at least one of the triads. This implies that the focus of business strategy for firms in a smaller, non-triad nation should be to secure inward triad investment and market access for exports to a triad bloc. This can be done by direct business contact of a double diamond type, but it is helped and reinforced by formal linkages arranged by the governments. As demonstrated in the last chapter, both Canada and Mexico have already gone this route.

In Chapter 2 we identified "clusters" of nations that are making such arrangements with triad blocs. In general, the NAFTA is the basis for a trading bloc of the Americas; the EU is the locus for Eastern European and African nations; Japan is the hub for many

Asian businesses. Some smaller, non-triad nations may attempt to open the doors to two triad markets. For example, both South Korea and Taiwan have equal trade and investment with the US and Japan. Firms from these countries need two double diamonds. Australia still has a large amount of trade with Britain and the EU, but its trade with Japan and other Asian nations is increasing rapidly. Indeed, the geographical basis of the triad serves to reinforce the dependence of neighboring nations on their dominant regional economic partner.

Later in this chapter we take a look at the Indian software and IT services industry. Within this industry there are small but significant examples of how success in one particular niche market can support triad access for firms in unrelated sectors. In March 2000 the UK's Tetley Tea Group was acquired by Tata Tea Limited. Coming more than 50 years after the end of 200 years of British colonial rule that had supported British-owned tea estates in India, this shift of power is an appropriate symbol for the 21st century. But the takeover was only made possible because of the financial success of Tata's IT division, Tata Consultancy Services (TCS). Both are part of the Tata Group, one of India's biggest publicly quoted conglomerates. Tata Tea was originally a tea estates company and is now India's second most popular tea brand with a 21 per cent share of the Indian branded teas market, 54 tea estates, and 59,000 employees. Senior management at Tata Tea said:

> We wanted to create a global brand, because the marketplace was global and in a global marketplace only global brands survive, local players get marginalised. We did not want to get marginalised, so we had to either build a global brand or acquire one.

TCS is "Asia's largest global software and services company" (according to their own PR), whose revenues have doubled every two years over the past six years. TCS is the "jewel in the crown" of the Tata conglomerate, making net profits of over $489 million in the year of the Tetley acquisition. Over 90 per cent of these revenues come from the firm's software exports, which are double those of its nearest domestic rival. TCS has 11,000 professionals in 50 countries and sells customized software, systems, consultancy services, and, increasingly, e-business products and services to a wide range of businesses partly through alliances with Western giants like Microsoft, IBM, and Netscape. The revenues and enhanced market capitalization gained from the software side provided the financial leverage to move up the value chain in the tea industry, taking over a major Western brand to enter into the UK market. A case of reverse colonization if ever there was one.[12]

CHINA

With around 1.3 billion people, China (see accompanying map) has the largest population in the world, more than Latin America and Sub-Saharan Africa combined. Although it is an ancient civilization the economy was only recently liberalized and opened up to trade and investment following Prime Minister Deng Xiaoping's reforms in 1978. Since then it has been moving from closed central planning toward an open market economy and is increasingly participating as a major player in the modern world. A particular boost came in 2001 when China joined the World Trade Organization (WTO) and began to attract record levels of FDI. **WTO accession** carried with it the commitment to phase out non-tariff barriers, provide trading rights to foreign companies, and change conditions on foreign investment, and this has been happening.[13]

The results have been impressive. GDP growth has maintained an average of 8 per cent in recent years, reminiscent of Japan's 'catching-up' period in the 1960s and 1970s. In 2004, when many analysts envisaged a slow-down, it grew at 9.5 per cent, the fastest rate for eight years (see Table 19.4). Exports and imports, as well as FDI have surged but with a positive

WTO accession
Admission to the World Trade Organization; in return for the right to access and to engage in fair trade with other national markets, the country must liberalize its own markets

South and East Asia
- ◉ Capital
- • Major city
- ⬤ Newly industrialized economies

imbalance (exports exceeding imports) resulting in growing foreign reserves and contributing in particular to the United States' massive deficit. In 2003, China's external trade reached US $851 billion, ranked fourth in the global economy, up from the fifth in 2002 (see Table 19.5). Note, though, that over 50 per cent of these exports came from

Table 19.4 China: key economic indicators

	2000	2001	2002	2003
GDP per head ($ at PPP)	3,980	4,340	4,720	5,180
GDP (% real change pa)	8.00	7.50	8.00	9.10
Government consumption (% of GDP)	13.08	13.39	13.20	12.90
Budget balance (% of GDP)	−3.62	−2.97	−2.96	−2.50
Consumer prices (% change pa; av)	0.35	0.73	−0.77	1.17
Public debt (% of GDP)	30.40	30.60	31.10	29.60
Labor costs per hour (USD)	0.59	0.69	0.80	0.92
Recorded unemployment (%)	8.20	9.30	9.75	10.10
Current-account balance/GDP	1.90	1.48	2.80	2.20
Foreign-exchange reserves (mUS$)	168,278	215,605	291,128	401,036

Source: Adapted from the Economist Intelligence Unit (http://www.economist.com/countries/China/) and National Bureau of Statistics, China (http://www.stats.gov.cn/english/).

Table 19.5 China: key trade indicators

Major exports 2003	% of total	Major imports 2003	% of total
Office machines & data-processing equipment	14.3	Electrical machinery	19.3
Apparel & clothing	11.9	Crude oil & fuels	6.5
Telecommunications products	10.3	Office machines & data-processing equipment	5.9
Electrical machinery	9.7	Machinery for particular industries	5.1
Leading markets 2003	**% of total**	**Leading suppliers 2003**	**% of total**
US	21.1	Japan	18.0
Hong Kong	17.4	EU	12.9
ASEAN	17.1	ASEAN	11.5
EU	16.5	Taiwan	12.0

Source: Adapted from the Economist Intelligence Unit (http://www.economist.com/countries/China/) and National Bureau of Statistics, China (http://www.stats.gov.cn/english/).

foreign-owned or foreign-invested firms. Overall the country is now considered to be the sixth largest economy in the world and the second largest market in purchasing power parity (PPP) terms.[14]

Although this has resulted in economic and social development nationally, with the overall reduction in poverty across the whole of China (adjusted for purchasing power, China has grown to be 70 per cent richer than India), growth has been concentrated in the industrialized East. Shanghai's economy grew at an annual rate of 13 per cent in the four years to 2005, whereas its population of around 17.5 million is rising by 500,000 a year. Average prices in the city's residential market nearly doubled between 2000 and 2004. China's national income per head in 2003 was $1,100, but some 800 million people, about 60 per cent of the population, live in the countryside on an average income of less than a dollar a day.[15]

MNE investment into China

China holds the double attraction for MNEs of a growing consumer market and an increasingly cost-effective source of inputs, particularly cheap labor. At the same time the rapid growth of the economy and the country's growing purchasing power is channeling investment into transportation, energy, utilities, communication systems, and other aspects of its infrastructure. In response to these attractions, MNEs have made a large number of investments in China. Occidental Petroleum has put over $180 million into a coal mining project. Motorola has invested $120 million to produce semiconductors and mobile phones, and General Motors has a $1.3 billion joint venture with a Shanghai automotive company to build Buick Century and Regal cars in China.[16] Dow Chemical has a $25 million joint venture in a polyurethane plant. H. J. Heinz has a majority interest in a $10 million baby-food plant. Procter & Gamble has put $10 million into a joint venture factory to produce laundry and personal care products, and Hewlett-Packard has a similar amount in an electronics joint venture. RJR Nabisco has a $9 million venture to manufacture Ritz crackers. Seagram has put up $6 million to make whiskey and wine products. Babcock and Wilcox have put $6 million into a joint venture boiler factory. Mitsubishi has invested $4.3 million in a venture to build elevators. Other firms on this growing list include Bell Telephone, DaimlerChrysler, General Bearing, Gillette, Lockheed, Pabst Brewing, Peugeot, Squibb, Volkswagen, and Xerox, to name but 10. P&G even spent $300 million in 2004 just marketing one product: Oil of Olay!

Some firms have been successful in China. Although it is not doing so well elsewhere in the world GM has generated profits for some time from its China operations. It accounts for an estimated 80 per cent of the group's Asia-Pacific operations, which made $729 million in 2004 (a fifth of the firm's $3.6 billion net profits). Sales in China, driven by the Buick Saloon and Excelle sedan, rose by 27 per cent to nearly 500,000 cars in 2004. GM has a market share of 9.3 per cent and is catching Volkswagen, the long-time market leader (although most analysts predict overcapacity problems reducing profits for all car firms in China in the coming years).[17]

As described in Chapter 13, Kodak has also done well in China, on the back of a $2 billion investment program that began in 1997. By working with the higher echelons of the central government in Beijing, Kodak managed to change the rules of the game in many ways, to gain exclusive rights to produce and sell photo-film in China. Its market share grew significantly as a result, compared with archrival Fuji, which has seen its share slip as Kodak has grown.

Others firms investing in China believe, despite losing money, that they have invested in "a foot in the door" to the most important growing region in the world. But there is a third group of firms that have failed to either break into the market or gain any return on their investments in China. Many following something of a "herd mentality" to get into China have failed to do their homework and been surprised to find how different, difficult, and risky the country is for inward investors.

Because of the evolving legislation governing foreign investment into China, there has been a noticeable shift in the mode of market entry by foreign firms. In particular M&A has become a more popular mode as opposed to joint ventures, which were more in evidence a few years ago. Table 19.6 shows a selected list of some of the larger inward foreign acquisitions in 2004. China overtook the United States in 2002 to be the largest beer market in the world, and the response can be seen here, with five of the ten listed deals involving beer companies.

This is not the first time that beer companies have rushed to enter the Chinese market, however. Between 1993 and 1996 international beer firms invested over $1 billion into the Chinese market and found that capacity far outstripped demand, prices were unsustainably low, and production plants were small-scale and inefficient. Although the local breweries were virtually bankrupt, local governments, concerned about unemployment rising, were pumping money into them, making it impossible for foreign firms to compete. Fosters, Carlsberg, Bass, and Asahi all bailed out at a loss, leaving the two largest local players, Tsingtao and Yanjing, to increase their dominance. Carlsberg alone lost $2 million

Table 19.6 · Selected inbound foreign acquisitions in China, 2004

Acquiring party	Acquired party	Deal value ($ million)	Share aquired
HSBC Holdings plc	Bank of Communications	1,747.0	19.9%
Anheuser-Busch Cos., Inc.	Harbin Brewery Group Ltd.	600.0	99.7%
Asahi-Itochu (China) Breweries Co. Ltd.	Kangshifu Food	475.0	50.0%
TESCO plc	Le Gao Shopping	260.0	50.0%
RGM International	Shandong Rizhao SSYMB Pulp & Paper Co. Ltd.	181.4	51.0%
Amazon.com, Inc.	Joyo.com Ltd.	75.0	100.0%
Heineken NV	Guangdong Brewery Holdings Ltd.	69.0	21.0%
Scottish & Newcastle plc	Chongqing Beer Group	63.0	19.5%
Interbrew SA	Zhejiang Shiliang Brewery Co. Ltd.	53.2	70.0%
International Finance Corp. (IFC)	China Minsheng Banking Corp. Ltd.	23.5	1.1%
Total 10 deals in 2004	Total value	$3,547	

between 1998 and 2000 before selling out. Breaking into the Chinese market is a difficult and risky business.[18]

Getting into China

According to folklore in China, "the mightiest dragon cannot crush the local snake";[19] in other words, local advantage can help a great deal in fending off larger and wealthier "predators." One of the primary reasons that China is becoming a focal point for multinational investment is its low labor costs. The average factory wage ($100 per month) is about 10 per cent of that in more industrialized Pacific Rim countries such as Taiwan and far lower than anywhere in the triad regions. It is more common in China for multinationals to use intermediaries in the process than elsewhere in the Pacific Rim. Among other sources, the China International Trust and Investment Corporation and the Ministry of Foreign Trade and Economic Cooperation offer such assistance. The government has a priority list of desired investments: ventures involving advanced technology, exports, or the generation of foreign exchange are given the highest priority.

In a joint venture the local partner is typically responsible for providing the land and buildings and for carrying out local marketing. The MNE is expected to contribute the equipment, technology, and capital and to be responsible for export marketing. In those cases where the multinational is manufacturing for sales in China, high-quality products, excellent service, and good promotional efforts are critical to success. Researchers have found that outstanding service and effective promotion can often make up for some lack of quality. However, price reductions and special sales terms are unlikely to offset poor quality. Similarly, while customer relations are important, they are often not enough to make up for poor quality or poor service. The Chinese want to buy the best quality available.

Additionally, much of the Chinese economy is planned or strongly influenced by central, regional, and local government agencies. Their policy agenda and decisions can have strong consequences for MNEs doing business there. There are also high-level political forces that are important to understand. For example, at the international level, China has been running a large trade surplus with the United States in recent years, and there is every reason to believe that, unless this situation is corrected, the US government will limit Chinese imports. The European Union has also been talking about limiting clothing imports from China because of the threat to local manufacturers (effectively because they are "too competitive"). These political reactions could result in a backlash against triad MNEs in China. A range of important political/economic risks must be weighed when planning a joint venture in China.

A recent survey by the US Embassy in Beijing and Gallup received 286 responses from American investors in China. About half said they had earned profits and a further half of the remaining firms were investing more in anticipation of future profits. They reported the biggest problems to be, in order of importance:

- Transparency of laws and regulations
- Cost of doing business
- Customs procedures/ export procedures
- Foreign exchange regulations/ exchange rate risk

Some key issues for foreign entrants are:

- Market-access rights from equity holdings to taxation levels vary by industry and are changing rapidly. At least three, often more, levels of government, including local, regional, and central government agencies, have a direct and strong influence over the local rules of the game and give preferential treatment to local firms and to particular kinds of foreign investors.

- Chinese tax laws and other regulations governing business practices are complex. Despite the expense it is necessary to use attorneys, accountants, and consultants familiar with Chinese requirements.

Guanxi
Denotes personalized or informal networks of relationships in China. They can be important preconditions for smoothing the way or gaining favors or advantages, particularly when both society and the economy are dominated by central government. There are parallels with the concept of social capital

- Contracting tends to based around relationships and connections (*guanxi*) rather than formal, legal documents. These are the basis of mutual trust, with due diligence on potential business partners performed by checking their network connections, as opposed to formal market mechanisms.

- Intellectual property rights (IPR) are not well-protected, legally or via any local business ethics. Investors need to carefully consider the implications of this, including the possibility of local firms getting and using key assets such as brands, patents, and business systems.

- Keeping face and being respectful is important. Group orientation and steeper hierarchies characterize Chinese organizations.[20]

- Learning the language may be important in order to provide insights into the local business culture. Too much of a willingness to do things the local way can be seen as a sign of compromise and ultimately weakness. Respect and credibility often comes from asserting one's own practices and rules of the game.

- The role of the Chinese partner in the success or failure of a joint venture or alliance cannot be overemphasized. Good partners will have the connections to overcome obstructive red tape and enable success; bad partners may have no power or knowledge to deal with obstructive bureaucrats, may violate confidentialities, and/or establish competing businesses.

- Although there is a large, cheap general labor pool, skilled managers, particularly those with marketing expertise, are difficult to find and keep. Engineers and technicians are similarly difficult to hold on to.[21]

Outward investment and the new multinationals from China

As we saw above, outflows of FDI from China have grown rapidly over the last 10 years. In 2002, the sales of Chinese companies operating overseas totaled US $77.2 billion. In 2004, more than 2,000 Chinese mainland companies were operating overseas and outward FDI totaled US $3.6 billion (excluding computer giant Lenovo), with accumulated FDI reaching US $37 billion. Private Chinese companies are stepping up their investment, but large **state-owned enterprises** (SOEs) account for the bulk of investment. In 2003, about US $2.1 billion of outward FDI came from large Chinese companies under the state-owned Asset Supervision and Administration Commission of the State Council, accounting for 73.6 per cent of the year's total. This is still, however, a tiny proportion of global FDI.[22]

State-owned enterprises (SOEs) Companies that are owned, financed, and controlled by government; privatization is the process whereby ownership and control is transferred to the private sector through sales of state-owned assets

Sinopec (China Petrochemical International) topped the list of the biggest 500 importers/exporters in China (see Table 19.7), and Hong Fu Jin Precision Industry, with $6.42 billion in exports in 2004, topped the list of the largest 200 exporters. Together the top 200 exporters reached total exports of $136 billion, 41 per cent higher than the previous year and making up 30.9 per cent of the nation's total. Companies in the fields of electronics, mechanics, and high technology increasingly feature in the top exporters and now make up over half of the 200 largest Chinese exporters. Half of the 200 largest exporters were also foreign-backed, compared to 87 in 2002. State-owned enterprises represented 35.5 per cent of the list. State-owned companies, which used to monopolize the nation's trading rights, have seen their shares dropping in recent years.[23]

INTERNATIONAL BUSINESS STRATEGY *IN ACTION*

Oxford Instruments in China

The Oxford of ancient spires and ivory towers is well known among the Chinese. The successful, high-tech spin-off Oxford Instruments (OI) is less well known, but the company is working to change this. Having sold a range of its products in China for over 10 years and experienced a 30 to 40 per cent growth in sales year after year, senior managers at OI decided it was time to invest more heavily. The company opened representative offices in Beijing and Shanghai during the last decade and employed 20 people (including two expatriates). Then, between April 2003 and August 2004 OI registered as a wholly-foreign-owned enterprise (WFOE) and established a manufacturing facility. This was a major investment for a firm with a turnover of $330 million and 1,500 staff around the world. But it was a necessary step given that over 90 per cent of OI's sales were from outside the UK, with approximately 5 per cent in China. Moreover, its managers learned a number of important lessons along the way.

A key reason for investing directly in the China market, moving to a higher level of both commitment and risk, was to get closer to the growing number of Chinese customers. OI chose to build on the strong platform of rep offices through the establishment of a repair and service center for supporting its microanalysis detector customers in China. It also wanted to provide a platform for the assembly of top-level products. To establish a business entity capable of delivering these kinds of activities it needed some outside help. One way to reduce the risks of FDI is to hire local specialists knowledgeable about the local rules of the game with the relationships and connections to help smooth the way. Another route is to hire experts who understand the international legal and regulatory conditions relating to a foreign direct investment (FDI) project. In fact, when initiating its investment plans in China, OI did both. An international law firm was hired to ensure that global regulatory standards were followed. A local sponsor was also brought in (at a significantly lower cost) to help with the submission of the investment application to government authorities.

The establishment process itself was relatively straightforward. Step one was to register the company name. Step two was the submission of a feasibility report and articles of association to show the firm would be profitable and (most important) produce good tax returns. The WFOE, Oxford Instruments (Shanghai) Co., Ltd., was then given government approval and granted a trading license around three months after the start of the process. Post-registration procedures, including securing the company "chop" (an official company seal or signature stamp) took a little longer.

Oxford Instruments (Shanghai) Co., Ltd. is formally opened by Charles Holroyd, MD of OI Analytical Ltd. (second from left).

Further development of an effective and efficient HQ–subsidiary organization structure and good working relationships between head-office management and local managers in China were seen to be key priorities in the early stages of the China venture. The UK side defined a common internal financial reporting structure and shared the group business strategy, which the senior management in China was then allowed to revise and tailor to the local context and culture. The existing OI China chief representative, a Chinese national employed by OI for five years, was named as the general manager of the new organization. The leadership of this existing member of the OI team, with experience of working both in a related industry and in an English-speaking environment, to head-up the China operation was important for creating the necessary HQ–subsidiary relationships. As with any international expansion, an overarching question for OI was (and continues to be): what business processes and decision-making responsibilities do we move to China and what do we keep in the UK?

Key constraints and challenges cited by OI include time- and resource-consuming Chinese bureaucracy at various levels including central, regional, local governments, and individual firms (one customer required 11 different VAT invoices for a single sale). It was important for OI to link the new Shanghai facility into their global IT infrastructure but the instability of the local Internet required the company to invest in alternative (and more costly) connection methods. As OI continues to grow in China the task of developing the necessary range of capable, experienced local managers in the sales and marketing functions as well as in operations will continue to be a focus.

Perhaps more significant than these problems have been OI's concerns about protecting its intellectual property rights (IPR) in China. OI's R&D assets and technological capabilities underpin its primary competitive advantage. It has had to take steps to avoid losing these to local Chinese competitors. Some formal protection and registration steps are available, and these have been taken by OI but this provides limited protection in China. More effective protection of IP is gained through placing an emphasis on the careful recruitment of staff in China and the retention of the development and some manufacturing of key technologies at home in the UK.

Many people talk about the importance of relationships in China. One interpretation is that in the process of developing relationships the Chinese are effectively performing a "credit check." In the absence of stable or reliable formal contracting rules, regulations, processes, and institutions, more emphasis is placed on interpersonal trust as the reliable basis for doing business. What rules there are in China tend not to be applied consistently. This leaves plenty of scope for influencing processes and decisions, which places even more of a premium on having the right connections.

At an early stage in the project the following light-hearted "rules" for doing business in China were presented by a speaker at a "Making it in China" session at the University of Cambridge:

Rule 1: China is a highly regulated country, in which one needs to learn, understand, and follow countless regulations.

Rule 2: China presents a chaotic and unpredictable operating environment in which anything is possible, in fact there are no rules.

Rule 3: Rules 1 and 2 are simultaneously valid.

Sources: This case has been compiled by the author from a presentation by and discussions with Daniel Ayres, project manager for the establishment of the manufacturing WFOE in Shanghai. Our sincere thanks to him and Oxford Instruments for allowing us to use the case here. http://www.oxford-instruments.com/.

Perhaps more interesting are the changes in the kinds of exports and FDI coming out of China, as indicators of its changing competitive advantage. In 1985 just 2.6 per cent of Chinese exports were categorized as high technology, whereas almost 50 per cent of exports were based on primary products or manufactured products based on natural resources. Twenty years later 25 per cent of exports are high technology and less than 10 per cent are from the latter category above. The initial boost in higher-value exports came from MNEs using China as an export base for their products. But high-technology, high-value products are increasingly exported by local Chinese firms that are moving rapidly up the learning curve.

Local Chinese firms and other firms based outside the triad are able to learn via subcontracting relationships and joint ventures with larger multinational firms. In this sense MNEs are, to a certain extent, "breeding" their future competitors through technology and capability transfer that takes place within these interfirm relationships. This may be an unintended consequence of an alliance, or it may be made explicit, through the transfer of equipment, know-how, and training; the licensing of patents or brands; and other activities that are part of the negotiated contract. Western MNEs often trade their own knowledge,

Table 19.7 China's top 10 import-export traders

1. Sinopec International Co Ltd
2. Shenzhen Hongfujin Precision Industry Co Ltd
3. Shanghai Dafeng Computer Co Ltd
4. Sinochem
5. ASUSTek Computer Co Ltd
6. China Minerals & Metals Group
7. Motorola (China) Electronics Ltd
8. PetroChina
9. Orient International (Holding) Co Ltd
10. Nokia (China) Investment Co Ltd

Sources: http://english.mofcom.gov.cn/ and http://www.chinatoday.com.cn/English/e2004/e200411/p24.htm.

technology, assets, resources, and networks in order to get access to local knowledge, technology, assets, resources, and networks as part of a market-entry or expansion strategy.

Overall, this means that China is evolving beyond its dominance as a global exporter of textiles, clothing, and toys and into areas such as autos, white goods, consumer electronics, and mobile phones (Wal-mart already imports about $15 billion in goods annually from China). In telecoms, for example, Chinese firms Huawei Technologies, Zhongxing Telecom, and Datang Telecom are but three government-backed, high-tech competitors who are quickly gaining ground against foreign equipment manufactures, including Ericsson, Lucent, Nortel, and Cisco Systems. Huawei commands the greatest market share in China for optical systems equipment, outselling all foreign competitors.[24] Although Motorola and Nokia still dominate China's mobile handset manufactures, domestic enterprises such as Bird, TCL, and Konka are chipping away the leaders' market share. In the semiconductor sector, US government analysts judge China now to be only two years or less behind US manufacturing technology and only one generation behind the commercial state of the art.[25] Zhongxing Telecom, Huge Dragon, and China's largest manufacturer of high-definition televisions, Konka, are other examples of up-and-coming local firms. Similarly in computer software, local firms Founder, Red Flag, UFSoft, Neusoft, Kingdee, and Top Group are both partnering and competing with Microsoft, Oracle, IBM, and Sun Microsystems.[26]

Lenovo, a high-profile Chinese firm, made the news in December 2004 when it bought IBM's PC business for $1.75 billion. This was a landmark deal for China, not least because of IBM's status as the archetypal American computer firm. Lenovo, originally called Legend when it was spun-off from the Chinese Academy of Sciences in the mid-1980s, makes about 30 per cent of PCs in China and is number two in laser printers. The sale gave IBM $650 million in cash, along with an 18.9 per cent stake in Lenovo worth $600 million. The merged firm will have sales of about $12 billion a year, as well as a five-year license for IBM's PC brands. Lenovo's PC operations will now be headquartered in upstate New York, rather than Beijing. Moreover, the company recently opened an R&D center in California's Silicon Valley, as a "listening post."[27]

As Chinese firms aim to move higher up the value chain, design and R&D activities will become increasingly important. This means investing overseas to acquire technologies and high-end capabilities and working with MNEs to bring R&D activities to China. The Chinese government has identified foreign R&D investments as a critical part of China's technology development strategy (originally outlined in the 2001–2005 Tenth Five-Year Plan). There are now over 300 foreign R&D centers in China. In many cases inward investors are competing for privileged access to the China market and will offer high-technology investments to gain government support for projects. GM's automotive R&D center, for example, was established in the late 1990s when global car companies were fighting to get the best joint ventures with a few, government-supported local firms. Boeing (US) and Airbus (a European consortium) were also under pressure to transfer technologies and established local training in return for access. IBM has made large R&D investments as has Microsoft, whose research lab in Beijing has developed some of the new Tablet PC technology.

China overall spends more than double the United Kingdom on R&D, and this has been growing at around 9 per cent per year in recent years, in line with GDP growth. The country has 17 million people in higher education and has established more than 60 industrial parks dedicated to Chinese graduates returning from overseas to set up businesses. Well-educated graduates and a very good science and technology infrastructure, relative to other developing and emerging countries, are important national assets for China. These are now underpinning the growth of high-tech firms, such as Beijing Yuande Bio-Medical, from Beijing Medical University; Datang Microelectronics, from Beijing's Telecoms Research Institute; and Innova Superconductor and Tsinghua Solar, both from Tsinghua University.[28]

Globalizing...	Assets	Capabilities	Connections	Reputation
Innovation and technology	Patents, licenses, IPR; specialized tools hardware, software, etc.	Low-end (maintenance) to high-end (blue-sky R&D) expertise	Strategic alliances; buyer and supplier links; R&D networks/ global capability inputs	Credibility, trust, track record, recognition
Marketing and brands	Own valued brands, logos, trademarks, awards, etc.	Brand management protection, development expertise	Formal co-branding; supplier or buyer, distribution, and retailing affiliations	Reputation for quality, price, innovation, etc.; market positioning, brand recognition; market presence

Figure 19.6 Firm-specific advantages (FSAs) for the new multinationals

Joint ventures and alliances in R&D are one way for local firms to learn from inward investors. By developing technological capabilities to improve productivity and add value in manufacturing and to develop new and better products, Chinese firms are enhancing their abilities to innovate. This follows the same path as other so-called latecomer firms who developed these kinds of capabilities through partnerships with triad MNEs (see Figure 19.5). Samsung began with subcontracting alliances with NEC and Sanyo in the 1970s, then Micron and Sharp, Intel and IBM in the 1980s. Acer had a joint venture with TI in 1989 and worked closely with Intel in 1994. Some of the major Indian software and IT services firms, Wipro, TCS, and InfoSys similarly established alliances with companies like Logica, TI, Motorola, Oracle, C.A., GE Capital Services, and Microsoft as they evolved beyond their reliance on cheap labor as a key advantage to develop their own leading products and brands. Figure 19.6 lists some of the firm-specific advantages that MNEs from China and other non-triad regions need to develop in order to successfully internationalize.

✔ Active learning check

Review your answer to Active Learning Case question 2 and make any changes you like. Then compare your answer with the one below.

2 Why did Acer form strategic alliances with IBM and Texas Instruments?

Acer was not familiar with the North American market and it was a new kid on the computer block. So it formed strategic alliances, whenever possible, with the dominant US MNEs. In doing so, Acer learned about the US triad market and how to distribute its products there. It also gained new technological capabilities for both process (manufacturing) innovation and product design and development. Acer was then able to move ahead of these once-dominant US firms once it combined its efficiency in production with its new market knowledge of the rich North American customers.

Table 19.8 lists some of the largest Chinese firms. Some of these, like Lenovo, are already in a position to acquire the outside technological assets or brands needed to internationalize. In April 2005 one of the oldest car manufacturers in the United Kingdom, MG-Rover, went into receivership. Once owned by BMW, this ailing British company had been in extended negoti-

Table 19.8 Chinese firms in the *Forbes* 2000 list, 2005

Forbes 2000 rank	Name	Category	Sales ($bil)	Profits ($bil)	Assets ($bil)	Market value ($bil)
55	PetroChina	Oil & gas operations	29.53	5.67	58.36	90.49
81	China Petroleum & Chemical	Oil & gas operations	39.16	1.94	45.32	50.09
202	China Telecom	Telecommunications services	9.12	2.04	24.85	29.92
429	Sun Hung Kai Properties	Diversified financials	2.94	0.84	20.66	24.02
592	CLP Holdings	Utilities	3.35	0.91	7.79	11.99
597	China Life Insurance	Insurance	8.59	-0.27	37.90	19.46
613	Baoshan Iron & Steel	Materials	4.07	0.52	7.43	10.34
641	Cathay Pacific Airways	Transportation	4.24	0.51	9.18	6.53
705	Swire Pacific	Diversified financials	1.95	0.69	12.46	9.94
748	China Merchants Bank	Banking	1.44	0.22	44.01	8.11
773	Citic Pacific	Conglomerates	2.86	0.50	7.33	6.45
781	Huaneng Power Intl	Utilities	2.23	0.47	6.09	13.07
941	Shanghai Pudong Dev Bk	Banking	1.14	0.15	33.64	5.46
1,090	China Minsheng Banking	Banking	0.87	0.11	29.17	4.65
1,111	PICC Property & Casualty	Insurance	4.45	0.03	8.63	5.09
1,241	Aluminum Corp of China	Materials	2.03	0.17	3.85	8.17
1,277	Hua Xia Bank	Banking	0.76	0.10	21.02	3.46
1,548	Legend Group	Technology hardware & equipment	2.59	0.13	0.87	3.56
1,583	Beijing Datang Power	Utilities	0.97	0.17	3.23	4.05
1,627	Shenzhen Development Bk	Banking	0.73	0.05	19.86	2.41
1,682	Yanzhou Coal Mining	Materials	0.77	0.15	1.56	3.95
1,735	Shanghai Automotive	Consumer durables	0.58	0.13	1.29	4.31
1,778	Jiangsu Expressway	Transportation	0.27	0.10	1.64	5.36
1,842	Guangdong Electric Power	Utilities	0.67	0.14	1.43	3.39
1,973	China Southern Airlines	Transportation	2.18	0.07	4.49	3.16

Source: http://www.forbes.com/lists/.

ations with the Shanghai Automotive Industry Corporation (SAIC) to invest in its Longbridge plant in the West Midlands. It transpired that SAIC only wanted access to some key technological assets, including the power train, engine manufacturing capabilities, and rights to the Rover 25. Once it had acquired these, to complement its manufacturing operations in China, it left the remainder of the firm to sink or swim. With high labor and manufacturing costs, a strong sterling, and general overcapacity in the auto industry, MG-Rover sank.

✔ Active learning check

Review your answer to Active Learning Case question 3 and make any changes you like. Then compare your answer with the one below.

3 **How should Acer cope with the rise of Chinese competitors on its doorstep?**

Acer has taken a step in the right direction by moving away from manufacturing, where Chinese firms have natural advantages, and into customer-oriented design, development, and services, like IBM. Acer's advantages also lie in its global distribution and marketing and its brand. These are firm-specific advantages (FSAs), which Lenovo and other Chinese firms will take some time to develop. The evolving political relationship between Taiwan and mainland China or the Peoples Republic of China is also an important factor, influencing some of the strategic options open to firms like Acer.

KEY POINTS

1 Emerging economies are increasingly important for MNEs: as growing markets; as sources of cheaper or better production inputs; and as a source of competitors in the shape of new MNEs as non-triad firms internationalize.

2 Emerging economies tend to be controlled more strongly by their governments and are less predictable and riskier than triad markets.

3 Emerging market countries need investment from, and access to, a triad bloc in order to develop global industries. Inflows and outflows of global FDI show that there is growing integration between countries inside and outside the triad.

4 Current trends such as privatization, liberalization, and legislative changes that are designed to encourage foreign direct investment (FDI) are helping emerging economies to tap their economic potential. Intra- and inter-regional trade agreements can also be helpful in creating both mini common markets and smoothing international trade.

5 FDI into Asia is concentrated in 10 fast-growing economies. There is strong intra-regional trade and FDI growth and a marked increase in the importance of service industries. Thirty-two out of the 50 largest non-financial TNCs from developing countries are from the Asia-Pacific region.

6 Despite years of liberalization the Central and Eastern European region attracts relatively small amounts of FDI. Better prospects appear to be ahead for countries that have joined the EU.

7 Latin America and the Caribbean region receive less than 10 per cent of global FDI (less than China). Intra-regional competition is strong but manufacturing exporters are losing out to China.

8 Africa receives less than 3 per cent of global FDI and remains relatively unattractive and risky for most investors. South African MNEs are expanding across the region in particular industry sectors.

9 The newly industrialized countries (NICs), a subgroup of non-triad economies, have experienced rapid economic growth and increased trade and FDI, partly by specializing in particular industries and developing comparative and competitive advantages.

10 NICs and other emerging markets in Asia are seen by some to be following the Flying Geese model of economic development. The Indian software industry appears to counter this pattern of sequential industry specialization.

11 One of the most important trends of our time is the economic development of China and its growing importance in terms of trade and FDI, as a cheap manufacturing base, as a growing market, and as a source of competitive opportunities and threats for all MNEs. Its economic growth and rising influence in the global economy may, however, be slowed or halted by social and political forces, domestic or international.

12 MNEs looking to get into the Chinese market need to be aware of its particular differences and difficulties, including changing regulations governing foreign investors; customs, tax, and foreign exchange procedures; specific cultural traits and the importance of *guanxi*; the problems with intellectual property rights; and the need to secure good partnerships and local expertise.

13 The current concern is that China and other emerging economies are increasingly competitive in manufacturing, taking investment and jobs from the triad regions. The key concern in the near future will be with their competitiveness in high-technology and knowledge-based businesses.

Key terms

- resource-seeking FDI
- market-seeking FDI
- Korean *chaebols*
- liberalization policies
- intra-regional investment
- newly industrialized countries (NICs)
- theory of absolute advantage
- Flying Geese model
- WTO accession
- *guanxi*
- state-owned enterprises (SOEs)

REVIEW AND DISCUSSION QUESTIONS

1 Why do MNE managers need to develop an understanding of changing economic conditions in non-triad regions?

2 What characteristics do we tend to associate with emerging economies that are important considerations for foreign investors?

3 How have emerging economies liberalized to encourage FDI?

4 How does inward FDI help emerging economies and their domestic industries?

5 Which non-triad regions and countries have achieved the most rapid economic growth in the last 10 to 20 years and what factors have helped their development?

6 Why does Africa receive relatively little inward FDI?

7 What insights does the Flying Geese model of economic development provide for understanding current and future trade and investment flows? What are its weaknesses as a model?

8 What indicators point to the increasing importance of China and Chinese firms in the global economy? Describe two factors that have helped its recent economic growth.

9 What guidelines must MNEs follow when doing business in China? Identify and briefly describe three specific difficulties for foreign firms breaking into the Chinese market.

10 How did Indian IT, software, and services firms evolve beyond their reliance on cheap labor to develop firm-specific advantages and internationalize?

11 Do you think China will remain a manufacturing hub? How might Chinese firms develop competitive advantages in high-technology and service industries, and what are the implications for triad-based MNEs?

REAL CASE

Korean *chaebols*: different paths for Hyundai and Samsung

Between 1970 and 2000, South Korea's GDP grew by 750 per cent. Industrial production increased at an even higher rate and grew to account for over 95 per cent of GDP in 2004. In South Korea's transition to industrialization, a transition that many other poor countries have tried to make with little success, *chaebols* played a mayor role. South Korea still maintains a healthy rate of growth, although it is not as rapid as in the boom years,

particularly since the Asian financial crisis of 1997–1998. This also marked a turning point in the role of the *chaebols* whose opaque, interdependent structures and cross-shareholdings are increasingly being questioned by South Koreans themselves, as well as by outsiders.

The four largest *chaebols* are Hyundai, Samsung, LG International, and SK. Across the world, these companies have become household names producing everything

Source: Corbis/Reuters

Chaebols had their origin in the vision of individuals. In 1946 Chung Ju Yung, who worked as a delivery boy for a rice mill in the 1930s, purchased an auto repair shop that was the early foundation of the Hyundai group. In 1947 Hyundai Engineering and Construction was established to take advantage of reconstruction contracts at the end of World War II. By 1976, Hyundai brought its country into the auto business with the introduction of the Pony.

Hyundai Automotive spun off from its conglomerate parent and merged with Kia to form one vehicle company, now the seventh largest in the world. In recent years it has experienced significant increases in overseas sales, particularly in the United States and Europe. As an indication of its standing Hyundai won top place as the most reliable car manufacturer in an influential consumer survey in the United States, joining Japanese car manufacturers in the top spots for the first time.

In 1938, Byung-Chul Lee founded Samsung and began exporting food to China, and not long after that he opened a light manufacturing business. The 1970s saw Samsung enter into the chemical and heavy manufacturing industries. In the 1980s, the company entered the aerospace and telecommunications industry. During this decade, Samsung also became a major world supplier of semiconductors.

Samsung Electronics is the largest and currently the most profitable South Korean company, with net profits of $9.5 billion on sales of over $50 billion in 2004. The 1997 Asian crisis forced Samsung to switch its focus from cheap consumer electronics to the top end of the market. The firm sold over 100 non-core businesses and let go 30 per cent of its employees, a significant step in a country with traditionally militant trades unions. The re-focusing on R&D, design, and marketing is now paying off. Driven by its four design centers in London, Tokyo, San Francisco, and Seoul, Samsung won more prizes from the Industrial Design Society of America in 2005 than any other firm. In 2004 it was world number two in mobile phones, number one in DRAM memory chips, number one in Flash memory chips, and number one in TFT-LCDs.

Contrasting the route taken by Hyundai Automotive, Samsung Electronics is still part of the Samsung *chaebol*, the largest in South Korea, with businesses ranging from shipbuilding, engineering, and chemicals to financial services, hotels, and a theme park. The conglomerate is nearly four times larger than its nearest rivals LG and SK and

from ships to autos to electronics. During the 1960s, *chaebols* prospered under a government-fostered development plan. When Park Chung Hee became South Korea's president after a military coup d'état, he instituted an import-substitution strategy that favored large local producers and provided them with cheap credit, tax breaks, and other benefits. After Park Chung Hee's death, low-interest loans continued to be made available to *chaebols* because of ties with banks. Since banks could not let a borrower the size of *chaebols* fail, credit was made available regardless of profitability, depriving the non-*chaebol* business sector from much-needed credit.

In the 1990s, the *chaebols* took on debt to finance large expansion projects. The Asian financial crisis in 1997–1998 reduced their revenues to such an extent that these companies could no longer pay their creditors. For a long time, *chaebols* managed to conceal their troubles by providing member companies with intra-conglomerate loans. In addition, foreign and domestic investors became increasingly aware of murky financial reporting practices. By the end of the crisis, Daewoo had become bankrupt.

In 1997, the IMF was called to bail out the South Korean economy after an unprecedented drop on the Korean won created a debt crisis. As part of the bailout, South Korea was to restructure its *chaebols*. Debt-to-equity ratios had to be reduced. Financial reporting had to become transparent. Most importantly, non-core businesses were to be spun off. To oversee the transformation of the *chaebol* and, in turn, the Korean economy, the Financial Supervisory Commission (FSC) was established in 1998. Although *chaebols* have reduced their debt-to-equity ratios, unreliable financial reporting continues to occur. Most importantly, many *chaebols* continue to resist selling off their non-core businesses.

Hyundai Automotive and Samsung Electronics are two of the most successful and international firms from South Korea, but they have taken different development paths to get where they are.

accounts for about one-third of the country's stock market capitalization. The group is controlled through a complicated web of shareholdings that bind its 27 subsidiaries, although over 60 per cent of Samsung Electronics shares are in the hands of foreign investors.

This opaque structure still worries minority shareholders, who have seen their returns eroded from the widespread *chaebol* practice of using profitable businesses to subsidize weaker affiliates and fund risky expansion. Samsung would arguably be in an even stronger position today had it not been called upon to bail the group out of a failed foray into the auto sector in the late 1990s, among other ill-advised diversifications.

Websites: www.daewoo.com; www.hyundai.com; www.hyundai-motor.com; www.samsung.com; and www.samsungelectronics.com.

Sources: "As Good as It gets? Special Report on Samsung Electronics," *The Economist*, January 15, 2005; C. Wright, "After the Crisis, the Fight Back," *Financial Times* (London), March 1, 2005, p. 6; A. Ward, "Hyundai Wins 'Most Reliable' Ranking in US," *Financial Times* (London), September 6, 2004, p. 15; A. Fifield, "Seoul to Clamp Down on *Chaebol*," *Financial Times* (London), March 1, 2005, p. 15; A. Fifield and J-A. Song, "SK Corp Steps Up Its Cautious Courtship," *Financial Times* (London), December 1, 2004, p. 12; Orla Ryan, "Collapse of the Korean *Chaebol*," *BBC.co.uk*, December 19, 2000; and "Hyundai's New Rescue Plan," *BBC.co.uk*, November 20, 2000.

1 Hyundai Motors is the largest non-triad auto maker. What type of obstacles does this create for Hyundai Motors that triad auto makers do not have?

2 Are Korean *chaebols* much the same as Japanese *keiretsus*? Why or why not?

3 Why and how did Korea restructure its *chaebols* after the Asian financial crisis?

The Indian IT, software, and services industry

With an average per capita GDP of $583, India is a less developed country (LDC). It has low literacy rates and high infant mortality rates. There are just five phones and two Internet users for every 100 people. Yet it also boasts one of the fastest-growing knowledge-based industries in the world.

The Indian IT software and services industry has outstripped all other industries, becoming the largest industry in India in terms of market capitalization. During the 1990s it grew an average of 50 per cent year-on-year. It is increasingly important to overall GDP and, more significantly, as a contributor to India's exports. Almost one million software professionals and a further five million people directly and indirectly are employed by the Indian software industry. India controls around 20 per cent of the global customized software market, specializing in high-quality solutions and IT services for corporate customers in the banking, finance, and insurance sectors. It is not currently a player in the market for off-the-shelf, packaged software, which is dominated by US firms.

As we know, exports provide a clear indicator of global competitive advantage. Indian software industry exports have grown from under US $5 million in 1980 to US $700 million in 1996, $2 billion in 1998, $6 billion in 2000, $8 billion in 2002, and $12 billion in 2004. The top firm, Tata Consultancy Services (TCS), a division of the Tata conglomerate, exported $1.2 billion worth of IT software and services. The number two firm, InfoSys Technologies, managed just over $1 billion, and Wipro Technologies $854 million. The top five firms earned export revenues of just under $4 billion.

However, the sources of advantage underpinning the growth rate and success of the Indian IT industry are not explained by many of the standard international business frameworks, such as Porter's diamond model. Few, if any, of the factors that led to the genesis of the industry were initially present in India. There was no local demand; related and supporting industries, such as telecoms and computing, were highly underdeveloped; the national communications infrastructure was among the worst in the world; and the main factor of production, the skills and knowledge of software programmers and IT business managers (an acquired factor endowment), were initially not home-grown.

The industry began with Indians returning from higher education, IT training, and often work experience in the United States and Europe. Many of the industry founders, such as Wipro chairman Azim Premji, Ramalinga Raju of Satyam, and S. Ramadorai of TCS were educated at US universities (although others, such as F.C. Kohli of TCS and InfoSys chairman Narayana Murthi were not). They noticed the rising demand for customized software programmers and IT expertise in the banking, insurance, financial services, and other industries in the West and saw India as a potential low-cost provider of this expertise. They returned to India and built firms to meet the software needs of the triad, primarily the United States.

Factors that were on their side were the English-language skills of the Indians, as this is the main software programming language; the time difference that allowed a 24-hour software development project cycle; new global information and communications network infrastructures; fears over the Y2K or year 2000 problem; and the low cost of labor. "Body shopping," the contracting of Indian programmers and their physical relocation to work with clients abroad, accounted for 90 per cent of industry revenues in 1989. The average cost of a software programmer in India in the late 1990s was still about one-twelfth the cost of a US or European programmer. But wage rates were relatively much lower in the early stages of the industry's growth cycle and increased at around 25 per cent per year from the mid-1990s. The cost of a programmer in China or Russia is now around 20 per cent lower than in India, and the same lack of barriers to entry will help firms based in these countries to mount a new competitive threat.

As the industry evolved, government support, particularly the development of software technology parks (the STPI network), the promotion of technical training, and subsidies to ICT infrastructure, became important. Also significant were the activities of US and European multinationals. Initially Western firms subcontracted programming and other tasks to Indian firms to exploit the cheap labor advantage. Many, like Texas Instruments, Microsoft, and Computer Associates, made substantial investments to build local operations to work within the emerging industry clusters in Bangalore and Madras. These global firms promoted innovation both as customers and as suppliers to local firms. They transferred hardware and software technology and assisted in the development of local technological capabilities through technical and management training, investment in R&D, new product and services development, and joint ventures. They also prompted and sometimes assisted in the development of local ICT infrastructure.

Perhaps the most important factor underlying the continued success of the industry is its evolution from an industry based on cheap labor and low costs to one based on value-added expertise, including specialist software and IT systems design and development capabilities.

Indian software firms have moved up the value chain, shifting the basis of their competitive advantage from just cost to a combination of cost, quality, and high-end R&D expertise.

Indian firms are also now themselves actively subcontracting to lower-cost providers in China and elsewhere as they move away from contract programming as a major source of their revenues and into e-commerce and WWW-related products and services. They are leveraging their advantages in cost and skills through joint ventures with big, established players in the computing, telecom, and consumer electronics industries. The InfoSys–Microsoft joint venture focusing on MS.Net products is an example of this, as is the Mahindra–British Telecom venture. In 2003 an estimated 230 multinational companies were engaged in R&D rather than contracting work in India. Intel, Microsoft, Cisco Systems, Samsung Electronics, Oracle, SSA Global, and others have set up R&D activities in Hyderabad, Mumbai, and Bangalore.

As a result of these developments, the industry has divided into a variety of sub-sectors. The IT software and services sector is still the largest and the key export revenue earner, but growth has slowed. A domestic software and telecom industry, with a thriving venture capital industry, has also emerged in India. This is evidence of a strong and growing industry cluster that has evolved, unusually, *after* the export success of key firms in the industry. IT enabled services (ITES) and business process outsourcing (BPO) services, including call centers, transcriptions services, and back office processing such as billing, taxation, and accounting, has been growing rapidly. Hubs of these services are Mumbai, Bangalore, Chennai, Kolkata, Hyderabad, Kochi, Ahmedabad, and Pune. Some of the key players in this market are AMX, Convergys India Services, GE Capital, Standard Chartered, Dell, Healthscribe India, EXL Services, Daksh eServices, Wipro Spectramind, and 24/7 Customer.

The development of the ITES/BPO sub-sector has brought home some of the threats as well as opportunities of living in a globally connected world for people in Europe and the United States. According to Britain's communication workers union, for example, 33 firms including Barclays, British Airways, Lloyds TSB, Prudential, and Reuters, have collectively outsourced 52,000 jobs serving UK customers to India. Norwich Union, Britain's largest insurer, has built up a workforce of 3,700 people in India and plans to double this in the near future. This is a sign of the times, and as global firms discover new ways of accessing cheaper and/or better expertise in other parts of the world, some groups of people will experience new opportunities to join and benefit from the global economy while others will feel increasingly vulnerable to the threat of new competition.

Sources: "Offshoring Pays Off for UK Companies," *The Telegraph*, January 25, 2005;" India Makes It to the Global R&D Map," *The Financial Express*, December 6, 2004; D. Gardner, "Bangalore-based Software Company to Use US Web Platform for E-Commerce Solutions," *Financial Times*, September 15, 2000; K. Merchant, "Hidden Gem Seeks Share of Limelight: Information Technology," *Financial Times*, August 9, 2000; K. Merchant and D. Gardener, "New Delhi Woos Silicon Valley Indians: IT Successes Encouraged to Invest," *Financial Times*, September 15, 2000; http://indiainfoline.com/; and http://www.indiainvest.com/.

1 How well does Porter's diamond framework explain the beginnings of the Indian IT and software services industry?

2 Why has this kind of industry not developed in other parts of the world, where triad companies also outsource IT activities (such as Barbados)?

3 What are the threats and opportunities for Western software firms arising from this shift in the competitive landscape, and how are they strategically responding to these?

Endnotes

1 D. W. Conklin, "Analyzing and Managing Country Risks," *Ivey Business Journal*, January/February 2002, vol. 66, no. 3, pp. 360–362; S. E. Feinberg, and A. K. Gupta, "Country Risk and Network Linkages within Multinationals," *Academy of Management Conference*, International Management Division, New Orleans, 2004.

2 Emerging market and developing country economies overall have grown by an average of over 6.5 per cent in recent years, which is much faster than historical trends and much faster than developed economies; "Coming into Flower," *The Economist*, October 16, 2004.

3 Robert Anderson, "Autos: Success from Nowhere at All," *Financial Times*, Special Report Slovakia, May 26, 2004, p. 3; Mark Landler, "Slovakia Vies to Create 'Detroit' of Europe," *International Herald Tribune*, April 14, 2004, p. 11; Chris Wright, "Automakers Jump into Fast Lane of Expansion," *Automotive News* (Detroit), May 3, 2004, p. 26 P.

4 http://www.endesa.com.

5 http://www.telefonica.es/accionistaseinversores/.

6 Jorge Carrillo, "*Maquiladoras*: Upgrading en el Contexto de Perdida de Competitividad?" Paper presented at the conference "La Competencia Transpacífica: Visiones sobre la Competencia Sur-Sur", Octubre 30–31, (México: Fundación Friedrich Ebert), mimeo.

7 Adam Smith, *The Wealth of Nations*, Book IV:2, Modern Library edition, 1776.

8 Among many introductory sources, see K. Fatemi (ed.), *International Trade in the 21st Century* (Pergamon, 1997); C. J. Jepma et al. *Introduction to International Economics*, (Longman, Open University of the Netherlands, 1997); C. J. Jepma and A. Rhoen (eds.), *International Trade: A Business Perspective* (Longman, Open University of the Netherlands, 1996).

9 K. Akamatsu, "Historical Patterns of Economic Growth in Developing Countries," *The Developing Economies*, 1, 1962, pp. 3–25; Kálmán Kalotay, "The European Flying Geese: New FDI Patterns for the Old Continent?" *Research in International Business and Finance*, vol. 18, no. 1, April 2004, pp. 27–49. For other analyses, at the industry and firm levels, see L. Kim, "Crisis Construction and Organizational Learning: Capability Building in Catching-up at Hyundai Motor," *Organization Science*, 9, 1998, pp. 506–521; F. J. Contractor (ed.), *Economic Transformation in Emerging Countries: The Role of Investment, Trade and Finance* (Oxford: Elsevier, 1998); Michael Hobday, *Innovation in East Asia: The Challenge to Japan* (Aldershot: Edward Elgar, 1995); Sanjaya Lall, *Learning from the Asian Tigers: Studies in Technology and Industrial Policy* (Basingstoke: Macmillan, 1996); Dosi Giovanni et al. *The Economics of Technical Change and International Trade* (Harvester Wheatsheaf, 1990); Kim Linsu, *Imitation to Innovation: The Dynamics of Korea's Technological Learning* (Boston, MA: Harvard Business School Press, 1997).

10 Vernon Raymond, "International Investment and International Trade in the Product Cycle," *Quarterly Journal of Economics*, May 1996, pp. 190–207.

11 Malcolm Dowling and Chia Tien Cheang, "Shifting Comparative Advantage in Asia: New Test of the 'Flying Geese' Model," *Journal of Asian Economics*, vol. 11, no. 4, (2000), p. 443; Edith Terry, *How Asia Got Rich: Japan, China, and the Asian Miracle* (Armonk, NY: M. E. Sharpe, 2002).

12 K. Merchant, "Hidden Gem Seeks Share of Limelight: Information Technology," *Financial Times*, August 9, 2000, *http://www.ft.com/ftsurvevs/industry/scd2b2.html; http://www.indiainfoline.com/sect/itso/ch01.html; http://www.tata.com/0_people/interviews/20001227_krishna_kumar1;* and *http://www.tata.com/tcs/index.htm.*

13 The WTO Agreement on Trade-Related Investment Measures (TRIMs) is still being implemented. It should eventually lead to the end of Chinese requirements on trade and foreign-exchange balance, local content, and export performance for foreign investors. The Chinese government is also committed to relaxing foreign investment restrictions in many important service industries, including distribution services, telecommunications, financial services, and professional services; *http://www.wto.org.*

14 *http://www.tdctrade.com/main/china.htm.*

15 "The Great Divide," *The Economist*, March 5, 2005.

16 Kathy Chen and Hilary Stout, "Boeing, GM Obtain China Agreements," *Wall Street Journal*, March 25, 1997, pp. A 3, 4.

17 "China Surprise," *The Economist*, April 2, 2005; also see Kim Woodard and Anita Qingli Wang, *Acquisitions in China: A View of the Field*, 2004, at: http://www.chinabusinessreview.com/public/0411/woodward.html.

18 Tim Clissold gives an extensive and amusing account of the local rules of the game in his book *Mr. China*, (London: Constable and Robinson, 2004). It is based around his experience as a British investor who teamed up with a Wall St. banker in China in the early 1990s. Together they invested over $400 million in a range of industries (including auto components and beer) in China and lost most of it because of the lack of legal and institutional infrastructure, fraud, and their own naivety regarding Chinese business practices.

19 This is quote from Tim Clissold's book, n. 18 above, taken from "The Battle of Ningshan" in *Journey to the West*, an unattributed sixteenth century Ming dynasty novel.

20 Among numerous how-to texts on coping with Chinese culture to "make it big" in the Chinese market, see, for example, John L. Graham and Mark N. Lam, "The Chinese Negotiation," *Harvard Business Review*, October 2003, pp. 82–91.

21 This list partly comes from discussions by the author with Alice Huang, Managing Director of Enter Consulting, a firm based in Shanghai that supports inward investors.

22 Chen Hua, "China's FDI Meets Challenges," *China Business Weekly*, April 21, 2005, http://www.chinadaily.com.cn/english/doc/2005-04/21/content_436121.htm; "Chinese Exporters Seek New Openings," *BBC.co.uk*, March 1, 2001.

23 Additional material can be found at: http://www.sinopec.com.cn; http://www.sp.com.cn; http://www.cnpc.com.cn; http://www.icbc.com.cn; http://www.chinatelecom.com.cn; http://www.sinochem.com; http://www.chinamobile.com; http://www.cofco.com.cn; http://www.abchina.com. See also United Nations, *World Investment Report 2000*, UNCTAD; http://www.unctad.org; "Pump Action," *The Economist*, June 21, 2001; and "The Giant Stirs," *The Economist*, April 5, 2001.

24 Hong Liu and Kequan Li, "Strategic Implications of Emerging Chinese Multinationals: The Haier Case Study," *European Management Journal*, vol. 20, no. 6 (2002), p. 699; Yubing Wu, "China's Refrigerator Magnate," *The McKinsey Quarterly*, no. 3 (2003), http://www.mckinseyquarterly.com/.

25 OECD, *Science, Technology and Industry Outlook, 2004: China*; http://www.oecd.org; Kathleen Walsh, *Foreign High-Tech R&D in China: Risks, Rewards and Implications for US–China Relations* (Washington, DC: Henry L. Stimson Center, 2004), at: http://www.stimson.org. See also a special issue of *R&D Management* on "Managing R&D in China," vol. 33, no. 4, September 2004.

26 In fact China's software industry is comparable in size to India's but is not export oriented. All the major firms are focused on serving local customers and foreign firms based in China.

27 Jerry Biediger et al. "Strategic Action at Lenovo," *Organizational Dynamics*, vol. 34, no. 1 (2005) pp. 89–102.

28 Ming Zeng and Peter J. Williamson, "The Hidden Dragons," *Harvard Business Review*, October 2003, pp. 92–99.

Additional bibliography

Anderson, J. and Hu, F. *The Five Myths about China and the World*, (Goldman Sachs, 2003).

Barclay, Lou Anne. *Foreign Direct Investment in Emerging Economies: The Caribbean* (London: Routledge, 2000).

Buckley, Peter, Clegg, Jeremy and Tan, Hui. "The Art of Knowledge Transfer: Secondary and Reverse Transfer in China's Telecommunications Manufacturing Industry," *Management International Review*, vol. 43, no. 2 (2003), p. 67.

Chen, Roger. "Corporate Reputation: Pricing and Competing in Chinese Markets—Strategies for Multinationals," *Journal of Business Strategy*, vol. 25, no. 6 (2004), p. 45.

Cheong, Y. R. and Xiao, G. "Global Capital Flows and the Position of China: Structural and Institutional Factors and Their Implications, in J. J. Teunissen (ed.), *China's Role in Asia and the World Economy: Fostering Stability and Growth* (The Hague, Forum on Debt and Development (FONDAD)), pp. 113–175.

Child, John. "China and International Business," in Alan M. Rugman and Thomas L. Brewer (eds.), *The Oxford Handbook of International Business* (New York: Oxford University Press, 2001).

Child, John and Tse, David K. "China's Transition and Its Implications for International Business," *Journal of International Business Studies*, vol. 32, no. 1 (Spring 2001).

De Mattos, Claudio, Sanderson, Stuart and Ghauri, Pervez. "Negotiating Alliances in Emerging Markets—Do Partners' Contributions Matter?" *Thunderbird International Business Review*, vol. 44, no. 6 (November/December 2002), p. 701.

De Meyer, Arnoud. "Technology Transfer into China: Preparing for a New Era," *European Management Journal*, vol. 19, no. 2 (April 2001).

Doh, Jonathan P., Teegen, Hildy and Mudambi, Ram. "Balancing Private and State Ownership in Emerging Markets' Telecommunications Infrastructure: Country, Industry, and Firm Influences," *Journal of International Business Studies*, vol. 35, no. 3 (May 2004), p. 232.

Doh, Jonathan P., Rodriguez, Peter, Uhlenbruck, Klaus, Collins, Jamie and Eden, Lorraine. "Coping with Corruption in Foreign Markets," *Academy of Management Executive*, vol. 17, no. 3 (2003), p. 114.

Eberhardt, Markus, McLaren, Julie, Millington, Andrew and Wilkinson, Barry. "Multiple Forces in Component Localization in China," *European Management Journal*, vol. 22, no. 3 (June 2004), p. 290.

Farrell, Diana, Remes, Jaana K. and Schulz, Heiner. "The Truth about Foreign Direct Investment in Emerging Markets," *McKinsey Quarterly*, no. 1 (2004), p. 24.

Goedhart, M. H. and Haden, P. "Emerging Markets Aren't as Risky as You Think," *McKinsey Quarterly*, Special Edition Issue 4 (2003), p. 66–74.

Gray, Kenneth R. "The Ins and Outs of Doing Business in Europe: Germany, France, Russia, and the Emerging Markets of Eastern Europe," *Thunderbird International Business Review*, vol. 47, no. 1 (January/February 2005), p. 143.

Grosse, Robert. "International Business in Latin America," in Alan M. Rugman and Thomas L. Brewer (eds.), *The Oxford Handbook of International Business* (New York: Oxford University Press, 2001).

Gupta, A. K. and Govindarajan, V. "Knowledge Flows within Multinational Corporations," *Strategic Management Journal*, vol. 21 (2000), pp. 455–472.

Isobe, Takehiko, Makino, Shige and Montgomery, David B. "Resource Commitment, Entry Timing and Market Performance of FDI in Emerging Economies: The Case of Japanese Joint Ventures in China," *Academy of Management Journal*, vol. 43, no. 3 (June 2000), p. 468.

Kumar, Sameer, Jamieson, Jacky and Sweetman, Mathew. "Software Industry in the Fastest Emerging Market: Challenges and Opportunities," *International Journal of Technology Management*, vol. 29, no. 3/4 (2005), p. 231.

Lieberthal, K. and Lieberthal, G. "The Great Transition," *Harvard Business Review*, vol. 81, no. 10 (October 2003), pp. 70–82.

London, Ted and Hart, Stuart L. "Reinventing Strategies for Emerging Markets: Beyond the Transnational Model," *Journal of International Business Studies*, vol. 35, no. 5 (September 2004), p. 350.

Luo, Yadong. "Building a Strong Foothold in an Emerging Market: A Link between Resource Commitment and Environment Conditions," *Journal of Management Studies*, vol. 41, no. 5 (July 2004), p. 749.

Luo, Yadong. "Industrial Dynamics and Managerial Networking in an Emerging Market: The Case of China," *Strategic Management Journal*, vol. 24, no. 13 (December 2003), p. 1315.

Mathews, J. A. *Dragon Multinational: A New Model for Global Growth* (New York: Oxford University Press, 2002).

Meyer, Klaus E. "Perspectives on Multinational Enterprises in Emerging Economies," *Journal of International Business Studies*, vol. 35, no. 4 (2004), p. 259.

Meyer, Klaus E. "International Research in Transitional Economies," in Alan M. Rugman and Thomas L. Brewer (eds.), *The Oxford Handbook of International Business* (New York: Oxford University Press, 2001).

Nolan, P. *Transforming China: Globalization, Transition and Development* (London: Anthem, 2004).

Nolan, P. *China and the Global Business Revolution* (Houndsmill: Palgrave, 2001).

Redding, Gordon. "The Smaller Economies of Asia and their Business Systems," in Alan M. Rugman and Thomas L. Brewer (eds.), *The Oxford Handbook of International Business*, (New York: Oxford University Press, 2001).

Williamson, P. J. and Zeng, M. "Strategies for Competing in a Changed China," *MIT Sloan Management Review*, vol. 45, no. 4 (Summer 2004), pp. 85–92.

Wyk, Jay Van. "Doing Business in South Africa," *Thunderbird International Business Review*, vol. 46, no. 4 (July/August 2004), p. 419.

Yusuf, Shahid and Evenett, Simon J. *Can East Asia Compete? Innovation for Global Markets* (Washington, DC: The World Bank and Oxford University Press, 2002).

Yizheng Shi "Technological Capabilities and International Production Strategy of Firms: The Case of FDI in China," *Journal of World Business*, vol. 36, no. 2 (2001), pp. 184–204.

Zheng Zhao, Anand, Jaideep and Mitchell, Will "A Dual Networks Perspective on Inter-Organizational Transfer of R&D Capabilities: International Joint Ventures in the Chinese Automotive Industry," *Journal of Management Studies*, vol. 42, no. 1 (2005), p. 127.

WWW resources

http://globaledge.msu.edu/ibrd/marketpot.asp
http://www.stats.gov.cn/english/index.html
http://www.tdctrade.com/
http://asnic.utexas.edu/

http://www.lanic.utexas.edu/
http://reenic.utexas.edu/
http://www.africaguide.com/
http://www.africaonline.com/

Chapter 20

ETHICS AND THE NATURAL ENVIRONMENT

Contents

Objectives of the chapter

Over the course of this text we have seen how much the world of international business has changed in the last decade. In the next decade, there will be even more changes to the field of international business. This will affect both the country factors and the strategies of multinational firms. In this chapter we explore three useful frameworks to help analyze the future of international business. First, we consider how multinational enterprises often serve as "flagship" firms at the hubs of business networks. We relate this to environmental and firm-level strategies and future trends. Second, we develop a framework to analyze trade and investment agreements. Third, we incorporate a discussion of corporate ethics and the role of NGOs into a final framework.

The specific objectives of this chapter are to:

1 *Examine* how these changing developments will create both challenges and opportunities for MNEs over the next decade.
2 *Explain* why research will continue to be of critical importance to the field of international business.
3 *Examine* three frameworks in which MNEs can cope with their changing political and economic environments.
4 *Relate* the importance of the NGOs and ethical issues to the strategies of multinational enterprises.

ACTIVE LEARNING CASE

The environment, NGOs, and MNEs

What do Microsoft, IBM, BP, The Body Shop, and Procter & Gamble have in common? They are ranked as the top five companies in the world "that best demonstrate their commitment to corporate social responsibility." That is, these are the best among companies responsive to social concerns such as the environment and labor. Furthermore, these rankings are calculated based on a survey of NGO perceptions. The top 20 firms according to NGOs are shown in the table below.

In a separate ranking of business leaders it was again found that Microsoft was number one, followed (in order) by Toyota, BP, General Electric, and IBM. This shows that there is a high correlation between the rankings by NGOs, on the one hand (groups usually critical of MNEs), and the CEOs who actually manage the MNEs. Most startling is that both surveys separately identified Microsoft as the most corporate-responsible MNE.

British Petroleum (BP) was ranked third by both NGOs and MNEs because of its success in aligning its business strategy and economic operations with the needs of the natural environment. The reasons:

1 BP makes exceptional efforts to replenish environmental resources.

2 BP develops alternative fuels and alternative energy.

3 BP communicates very well with stakeholders.

BP is the leading supplier of solar energy panels (already a $400 million business in 2004); it has made major expenditures on marine research and the environment; and it is now moving "beyond petroleum." The NGOs recognize that the oil business damages the environment, but they credit BP with accepting this responsibility to reduce the adverse effects on resources. The CEO of BP, Lord Browne, is given credit for the success of BP as a green company.

Under Lord Browne, BP has pledged to reduce the level of its own greenhouse gas emissions by 10 per cent by 2010. It was close to the goal by early 2002. BP has also invested in research initiatives to reduce carbon in fuels and to power cars with hydrogen fuel cells. BP has been an active supporter of the Kyoto protocol, believes in sustainable development, and supports codes of conduct on human rights for oil and mining groups.

Other oil companies have also invested in being green; the best example is Royal Dutch/Shell, once targeted by Greenpeace over its inappropriate disposal plans for the Brent Spar North Seas oil rig. Now NGOs rank it number

NGOs: companies that best demonstrate their commitment to corporate social responsibility

Rank 2004	Name	Country	Sector
1	Microsoft	US	IT
2	IBM	US	IT
3	BP	UK	Energy/Chemicals
4	The Body Shop	UK	Retail
5	Procter & Gamble	US	Food/Beverage
6	McDonald's	US	Media/Leisure
7	Int'l Com. of the Red Cross	Switzerland	
8	Coca-Cola	US	Food/Beverages
9	Co-operative Bank	UK	Financial
10	Nestlé	Switzerland	Food/Beverages
11	Danone	France	Food/Beverages
12	Ikea	Sweden	Retail
13	Marks & Spencer	UK	Retail
13	Sainsbury	UK	Retail
15	Royal Dutch/Shell	Netherlands/UK	Energy/Chemicals
16	Virgin	UK	Transport
17	Greenpeace	UK	
18	Médecins Sans Frontières	Switzerland	
19	BBC	UK	Media/Leisure
20	DuPont	US	Energy/Chemicals

Source: "Survey of the World's Most Respected Companies," *Financial Times/PricewaterhouseCoopers*, 2004.

15 and business executives number 6 in being an environmental leader. In contrast, Exxon Mobil is criticized by environmentalists for opposing the Kyoto protocol, and it ranks 22 by business leaders.

Another odd result is that McDonald's ranks at 6 in the NGO list for its success in recycling its packaging and reducing waste. Yet McDonald's is a number one target by anti-global activists and its restaurants have been destroyed from Seattle to London to Genoa. This would seem to indicate that protestors have a myriad of agendas. Some NGOs are just anti-business and anti-globalization and will attack any MNE, whereas other NGOs believe in sustainable development and in working with MNEs to improve the natural environment. It also indicates that many MNEs are not the problem, but the solution to environmental problems.

Websites: www.bp.com; www.the-body-shop.com; www.honda.com; www.ford.com; www.shell.com; www.greenpeace.org; www.toyota.com; www.dupont.com; www.weyerhaeuser.com; and www.mcdonalds.com.

Source: "Survey of the World's Most Respected Companies," *Financial Times/PricewaterhouseCoopers*, 2004; BP, "BP Solar Achieves New World Record for Cell Efficiency," *News Release*, March 24, 2003; www.bp.com; Kathryn Westcott, "Pressure Builds for US Climate Action," *BBC.co.uk*, February 14, 2005.

1. How have non-governmental organizations (NGOs) changed the external environment in which multinational enterprises operate? Why is BP the most successful multinational to respond to NGOs?

2. As multinational enterprises operate across the world and NGOs operate globally, why are there no "global" or "international" environmental agreements to set rules for sustainable development?

3. Where would BP be positioned in Figure 20.7? Why?

INTRODUCTION

Multinational enterprises (MNEs) are finding that one of the major challenges they face is to develop effective strategies for coping with changing environments. The international microcomputer chip industry is a good example. During the 1980s the Japanese dominated this industry, pushing out many US and European competitors to gain the majority of the world market. In the early 1990s US firms (most notably Intel) counterattacked and regained the lead. Strategic countermoves can cause successful firms to be dislodged by competitors.[1] But this is an ongoing process of triad-based attack and counterattack, and today's victor could be dislodged by the competition tomorrow. This process explains development in many industries, from autos to computers to real estate.[2] It also helps to explain why continual innovation and strategy modification are necessary for MNEs to retain their competitive advantage. In doing so, multinationals will be focusing increased attention on strategies that are designed to cope with changing environments.

DEVELOPING EFFECTIVE STRATEGIES

MNEs are supplementing or supplanting their old strategies in a number of ways in order to compete more effectively worldwide.[3] Two of the most recent developments include going where the action is and developing new business networks with governments, suppliers, customers, and competitors.

Going where the action is

One strategy that is proving increasingly important is the need to go international in order to keep up with the competition.[4] Successful multinationals have operations in the home countries of their major triad competitors. For example, IBM's strongest competitors are located in the United States, Europe, and Japan. In turn the company has facilities in all three places, to monitor the competition as well as to conduct research. Moreover, the communication network among the company's facilities allows each to share information with the others and to provide assistance. This also helps the company to maintain a strong competitive posture.[5]

Another reason for locating near major competitors is that some markets develop faster than others and the experience and knowledge that is learned here can help in other markets. For example, in the US market IBM is now trying to develop a strategy of providing the best service in the industry. In the past the company had often referred service problems to its dealers. However, now the firm is attempting to address these issues directly, ensuring a higher level of service and taking back customers who were lured away by smaller firms with better service, support, and prices. If this strategy works well, the company is likely to use it in other worldwide locations where small firms have been gaining market share.[6]

Another important aspect of a location-focused strategy is that MNEs often establish a home base for each major product line, and a multiproduct-line company will have "centers for excellence" all over the world. These centers are responsible for providing global leadership for their respective product lines. For example, Asea Brown Boveri, a Swiss firm, uses Sweden as the home base for transmission equipment. Research, development, and production are centralized in that country. Nestlé, the giant food company, has the world headquarters for its confectionery business in Great Britain because this home base is more dynamic in terms of the marketing environment and the high per capita consumption of confectionery products. At the same time Nestlé has made its Italian company, Buitoni, the world center for pasta operations. Meanwhile, Siemens has designated the United States as the world home base for medical electronics because this is where the market is most dynamic and will provide the company with the best chance of developing and maintaining state-of-the-art products.

It is also important to realize that the product line will dictate the degree of globalization. For example, food companies in Europe tend to be less international and more regional in focus. Local tastes vary widely and there are only modest gains to be achieved through large-scale operations, so European food companies tend to have an extensive local presence. The same is true for home appliances, which are often produced for regional markets. On the other hand, when European companies have become truly global, they have tended to focus on products that do not require high levels of integration on a worldwide basis.

So some companies have a need for global centers throughout the world, whereas others tend to stay in closer geographic proximity because of the nature of their product lines. Still others combine both of these approaches, as seen in the box **International Business Strategy in Action: 3M**.

✔ Active learning check

Review your answer to Active Learning Case question 1 and make any changes you like. Then compare your answer with the one below.

1 **How have non-governmental organizations (NGOs) changed the external environment in which multinational enterprises operate? Why is BP the most successful multinational to respond to NGOs?**

NGOs have captured public attention and won a lot of support in North America and Western Europe for their "green" and anti-globalization agendas. Multinational enterprises cannot afford to ignore NGOs, especially the US and EU MNEs whose home base "diamond" is threatened by NGOs who can influence government policy and regulation. BP has gained recognition as the most successful MNE because it had a responsible CEO who undertook a series of measures to make its operations more environmentally friendly.

INTERNATIONAL BUSINESS STRATEGY *IN ACTION*

3M

The 3M company is a major MNE that has over 50,000 products comprising everything from office supplies to construction and building maintenance to chemicals. It employs over 73,000 people and has operations in 60 countries. How does the firm manage such a large international operation? One way is by matching its global strategies with the needs of the local market. Some goods such as home videocassettes are standardized and are sold on the basis of price and quality. Culture and local usage are not important considerations. Other products are greatly influenced by local preferences or regulations; telecommunications is an example. Each country or region of the world has its own modifications for local application.

The company balances its global strategies and national responses on a region-by-region basis. For example, in Europe the company has set up a series of business centers to address local differences. The company also uses European management action teams (EMATs) to balance the needs of subsidiaries in responding to local expectations with the corporation's need for global direction. Today, 3M has 50 EMATs in Europe, each consisting of from 8 to 14 people, most of whom are marketing personnel. These groups are charged with bringing the firm's global plans to life by helping their execution at the local level. EMAT meetings, which usually occur quarterly, are designed to create action plans for the European subsidiaries. When the meetings are over, the members then return to their respective subsidiaries and begin executing the plans. In Asia the company uses a different approach, relying heavily on its Japanese operation to provide much of the needed direction to the subsidiaries. At the same time there are regional centers in Singapore and South Korea that help subsidiaries to address their local markets. In Latin America, meanwhile, 3M uses a macro approach, conducting business on a national rather than regional basis.

The company also carefully identifies those products that it will sell in each geographic area while following two basic strategies: (1) try to be the first in the market with new offerings because this strategy puts the competition at a disadvantage, and (2) grow new markets gradually by picking out those products that address the country's most pressing needs and focus exclusively on them. Commenting on its worldwide strategy, a company executive said:

> We don't believe in formulating a single global strategy for selling videocassettes in India and laser imagers in France and Post-it brand notes in Brazil. For each of 3M's 23 strategic business centers in each region the company's strategy is a blend of global, regional, and local companies and that will continue.

Website: **www.3m.com**.

Sources: Adapted from Harry Mammerly, "Matching Global Strategies with National Responses," *Journal of Business Strategy*, March/April 1992, pp. 8–13; Kevin Kelly, "3M Run Scared? Forget About It," *Business Week*, September 16, 1991, pp. 59, 62; James Braham, "Engineering Your Way to the Top," *Machine Design*, August 22, 1991, pp. 65–68; **www.3m.com**; 3M, *Annual Report*, 1997 and 2000.

INTERNATIONAL BUSINESS RESEARCH FRAMEWORKS

No study of international business would be complete without paying attention to the role and importance of theoretical frameworks. Much of what has been discussed in this book is based on research findings. In many cases the data were drawn from government statistics, company records, and business reports on recent developments and strategies. In other cases the information was garnered from formal studies that examined managerial behaviors among senior managers. Collectively, research provides important input for building international business theories and for formulating and implementing future strategies. As a result, it is useful to both academicians and practitioners.

Unfortunately, research can be confusing and contradictory. For example, many studies are extremely limited in focus and thus cannot be generalized to a universal setting. Similarly, when research is broadly based, it is likely that the findings cannot be generalized to specific situations. The Porter diamond, for example, helps to explain how triad nations develop competitive advantage. However, its value to non-triad nations, as explained in Chapter 15, is limited and the findings must be revised and modified in order to apply them. Despite such shortcomings, however, international business research will continue to be of critical importance to the field. Such research will allow us to test theories and to refine their practical applications.

Theories of international business

A great many theories have relevance to the study of international business. In some cases these are first constructed and then tested. A good example is Adam Smith's theory of labor specialization. Smith presented this concept over 200 years ago in his *Wealth of Nations*, and in recent years learning curve analysts have confirmed these findings. Of course, not all theories have had to wait centuries before being proven. However, this example does illustrate that international business research can be advanced through the formulation of useful theories.[7]

In other cases theories are being tested for the purpose of reconfirming earlier findings. This is particularly important in learning how well a theory stands the test of time. A good example is the theory of lifetime employment in Japan. For many years theorists have argued that lifetime employment creates a highly motivated workforce and Western organizations would be wise to copy this approach. More recent research, however, reveals that lifetime employment is less useful as a motivator than as a control tool for ensuring worker loyalty and performance. In return for guaranteed employment, workers stay with the firm for their entire career, work hard, and are compliant with management's wishes. Even unions are employer-dominated and serve more to maintain harmony within the employee ranks than to represent the workers.

Based on an analysis of empirical data collected on this topic, two researchers recently concluded, "Lifetime employment is offered within a . . . context of loyalty and benevolence based on cultural values. Its impact, however, is to increase the control of Japanese employees by managers."[8] Moreover, these researchers found that lifetime employment was not widely used by firms in tight labor markets because it was not possible to control the workers, who could easily find jobs with other companies and who derived little motivation from such guarantees.

This type of research is also important because it generates new hypotheses for testing. For example, as workers in large companies with guaranteed lifetime employment near retirement (55 to 60 years of age), will management replace them with younger people who are not given such guarantees? As the competitive environment increases, will companies stop offering these guarantees because they reduce the firms' flexibility in responding to changing conditions? Will young workers entering the Japanese workforce during this decade be motivated by such guarantees, or will they turn them down because they are unwilling to commit their career to one firm in return for job security? These types of questions will be focal points for future international business research efforts, since changing economic, cultural, and social environments are creating new conditions in which MNEs must compete. Research can help to shed light on the effect of these changes.

Practical applications of the theory

Research is also going to play an increasing role in helping to uncover how and why multinationals succeed. In particular, greater attention will be given to strategy research that is designed to explain why some firms do better than others and how these strategies are changing. For example, during the 1970s traditional international business strategy gave strong support to strategic fit, the notion that an organization must align its resources in such a way as to mesh with the environment. Auto firms had to design and build cars that were in demand, and this might mean a variety of models and accessories, depending on the number of markets being served. Similarly, electronics firms had to maintain

Strategic fit
A strategic management concept which holds that an organization must align its resources in such a way as to mesh effectively with the environment

state-of-the-art technology so as to meet consumer demand for new, high-quality, high-performance products. Today, however, successful multinationals realize that they must do much more than attempt to attain a strategic fit. The rapid pace of competitive change is requiring linkages between all segments of the business from manufacturing on down to point-of-purchase selling, and in every phase of operation there must be attention to value-added concepts.[9] So the basic strategic concepts of the past, once widely accepted, must be reconsidered and sometimes reformulated.

Other research areas likely to receive future attention will be cross-national collaborative research by individuals from two or more countries and joint efforts by international and non-international researchers. The world of international business is getting larger every day, and it is critical that research be designed not only to help explain what is happening and why it is occurring, but also to help predict future developments and thus better prepare students and practitioners for the international challenges of the 21st century.

DEVELOPING BUSINESS NETWORKS

In the future governments will become more selective in their approach to industrial policy, aware that in the past billions of dollars have been wasted by bureaucratic efforts to streamline and refocus economic efforts. This recent trend is likely to result in more government–business efforts. However, the success of international business firms will depend more heavily on the companies themselves than on the government. Some of these developments will include the forging of new business networks for competitive advantage and the development of new relationships with non-business sector groups.[10]

Forging new business networks

Increasingly, the relationship of successful MNEs with their suppliers, customers, and competitors is changing. New strategies based on trust and reciprocal support are replacing the old business–client relationship in which companies sought to dictate the terms and conditions of sales and services.

In the case of suppliers, the current trend is toward reducing this number to a small group of reliable, efficient, and highly responsive firms. These suppliers are then brought into a close working relationship with the MNE so that both sides understand the other's strategy and plans can be formulated for minimizing working problems. The multinational will detail its needs and the supplier will draw up plans that ensure timely, accurate delivery. Another trend is the increase in the amount of responsibility being given to suppliers. Previously they were charged only with manufacturing, assembly, and delivery. Now many MNEs use their network partners to develop new materials and components, to perform industrial engineering functions, and to assume liability for warranties.

In the case of customers, network linkages now involve changing the focus of the relationship from one in which sales representatives would work directly with MNE purchasing agents to one in which sellers interact more directly with their customers. D'Cruz and Rugman have explained this idea in the case of flagship firms, characterized by global competitiveness and international benchmarks.[11] In the conventional system the flagship firm and its customers maintain an arm's length relationship. However, new relationships are now being forged in which there is a direct link between the flagship firm and its most important customers (see Figure 20.1, segments 1 and 2), whereas traditional relations are maintained with some distributors to serve the firm's less important customers. At the same time, network linkages are being developed with key distributors to serve other customers better. (Again see Figure 20.1, segments 3 and 4, etc.)

Flagship firms
Multinational firms characterized by global competitiveness and international benchmarks

Figure 20.1 Network linkage and the changing shape of international distribution systems

Source: © Alan Rugman and Joseph R. D'Cruz, 2000. Reprinted from *Multinationals as Flagship Firms: Regional Business Networks* by Alan M. Rugman and Joseph R. D'Cruz (2000) by permission of Oxford University Press.

Network arrangements are also being created between international competitors in the form of joint ventures, technology transfers, and market sharing agreements such as a Japanese firm selling the product of a US firm in the Japanese market in return for a similar concession in the United States. Mazda and Ford Motor are excellent examples.

These strategic relationships among suppliers, customers, and competitors are becoming integral parts of MNE strategies, as are linkages to non-business organizations such as unions with whom multinationals are now sharing their strategies in the hope of creating a working relationship that will save jobs and ensure company profitability. Partnerships are also being fostered with universities that can help to educate and train human resources, and research institutions that can provide scientific knowledge that is useful for helping organizations to develop and maintain worldwide competitiveness. Another group that is getting increased attention is government, since this institution can be particularly helpful in supporting legislation that will encourage the upgrading of the workforce, development of state-of-the-art technology and products, exports, and the building of world-class competitors. Figure 20.2 provides an illustration of the basic structure of the five partners in an effective network. Notice how these relationships go beyond commercial transactions and involve network linkages to a wide variety of other groups. This is one of the waves of the future in international business.

Five partners
A business network consisting of five partners organizations: the flagship firm (a multinational enterprise), key suppliers, key customers, key competitors, and the non-business infrastructure

COPING WITH CHANGING ENVIRONMENTS

The international environment of the future will continue to be one of rapid change, and MNEs will have to stay abreast of a number of developments. The political and economic environments will present the greatest challenges.

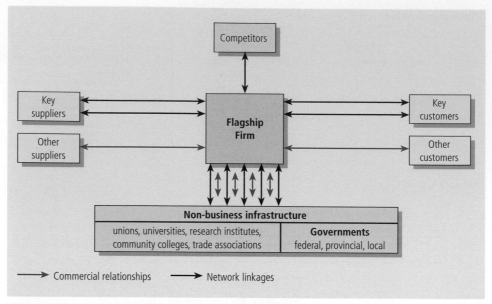

Figure 20.2 Network linkages for successful MNEs

Source: © Alan Rugman and Joseph R. D'Cruz, 2000. Reprinted from *Multinationals as Flagship Firms: Regional Business Networks* by Alan M. Rugman and Joseph R. D'Cruz (2000) by permission of Oxford University Press.

Political environment

As already seen, the political environment affects MNE activities in many ways. For example, all major triad groups have trade barriers that are designed to limit the sale of foreign goods in their countries. This in turn typically results in trade negotiations that are designed to open up these markets and/or to reduce trade deficits. Protectionism trends are particularly treacherous because they are psychological as well as legislative.[12] That is, even when trade barriers are lowered, there is a tendency for people to be protectionist and to "buy local."

Many managers say that they favor open markets, but, when questioned closely, they state strong support for protectionist strategies such as government assistance to domestic businesses and help for home-based firms that are seeking to go international.[13] In short, many businesspeople speak out for free trade but advocate policies that put foreign firms at a distinct disadvantage. The Japanese are some of the strongest supporters of free trade. However, according to the US trade representative these opinions are not translated into action. For example, Japanese telecom fees make it difficult for foreign companies to compete effectively.[14]

The ability of US firms to penetrate foreign markets will also be influenced by US government policies. The Clinton administration was more vigorous than its predecessor in pushing for open markets in Asia.[15] Its formulation of a US government trade policy toward Japan and Southeast Asia includes guidelines for negotiations for open markets in the region, coupled with US aid to US high-tech industries, among others. The administration's objective was to increase the market share of US firms in this geographic region as well as to reduce the large trade deficit that the United States is running, most noticeably with Japan and China. The latter is likely to receive particular attention, given that in recent years China has sold far more to the United States than it has purchased from them.[16]

At the same time overseas companies are lobbying their governments to negotiate greater access to the US market. For example, the governments of less industrialized countries are putting pressure on triad countries to liberalize agricultural trade. International institutions like the IMF, as well as **non-governmental organizations (NGOs)** like Oxfam, criticize the

Non-governmental organizations (NGOs)
Private-sector groups that act to advance diverse social interests (See also Civil Society)

United States, the EU, and Japan, some of the more vocal supporters of free trade, for subsidizing their agricultural and manufacturing industries to the detriment of less developed countries.

A related issue is political risk. For example, in Latin America, Venezuela and Brazil recently elected left-leaning populist governments. The effects of this on multinationals are yet to be gauged. Venezuela is a large exporter of oil and Brazil is the manufacturing hub for Latin America, a host country for VW and Mercedes-Benz, among others.[17] A recent financial crisis in Argentina that led to factories being abandoned was followed by worker occupation of these factories. These workers started producing again and sought to be legitimized by the government as owners of the factory.[18]

Hong Kong also faces an uncertain political future. The former British colony was returned to China in 1997. The Chinese government has agreed to allow the region to maintain relative autonomy and to continue functioning under its own economic and political systems for 50 years after the takeover.[19] China is now heavily investing in Hong Kong and has more total direct investment there than in any other country. At the same time two-thirds of foreign investment in China comes from Hong Kong Chinese. Yet relations between Hong Kong and China have sometimes been strained and have resulted in some Hong Kong firms diversifying their investments and moving funds to other geographic locales. Many Hong Kong businesspeople believe that relations with China will be worked out for the betterment of both sides. Certainly China needs Hong Kong and vice versa. Forty per cent of China's international trade passes through Hong Kong, and the latter provides China with a window to the West. At the same time China will eventually decide the political fate of Hong Kong.

Another country where political risk is being re-evaluated is Vietnam.[20] Relations between the United States and Vietnam are now beginning to normalize, and the country is seeking business ties with US multinationals that can provide assistance in helping to rebuild the economy. President Clinton approved a renewal of lending to Vietnam by both the International Monetary Fund and the World Bank. These funds were necessary to allow critical highway and seaport projects to begin. At the same time, Vietnam has been trying to attract billions of dollars in manufacturing investment from European and Asian companies. Now that the US trade embargo has ended, Vietnam is also trying to lure US banks, aircraft, and power plant manufacturers to help in the rebuilding effort. One major reason that Vietnam is interested in rapprochement with the United States is that it sees America as a counterbalance to Japan and the growing military might of China. As relations between the two countries continue to thaw, political risk will decline and Vietnam will become an increasingly popular area for investment opportunities.

The continuing development of free trade agreements will also work to lessen political risk. For example, the North American Free Trade Agreement (NAFTA) binds Canada, the United States, and Mexico together into an interdependent market in which each nation profits by working harmoniously with the others.[21] The same is true for members of the EU as well as for other economic unions, from those being fostered in Latin America to those in Africa and the former Soviet Union. Firms doing business in these geographic areas will find that the greatest ongoing challenge is more likely to be economic than political. There will also be further consolidation of the world's trade agreements into a triad-based system (see Table 20.1).

Economic environment

The economic environment will be replete with opportunities for MNEs. US multinationals, for example, will continue to be a dominant force in the export market, as seen by the fact that the United States has consistently ranked as the world's largest exporter over the last

Table 20.1 The world's major trade agreements

EU (25)		EFTA (4)	NAFTA (3)	ASEAN (10)	Mercosur (4)	Andean Group (5)
EU (15)	+EU (10)					
Austria	Cyprus	Iceland	Canada	Indonesia	Argentina	Bolivia
Belgium	Czech Rep.	Liechtenstein	Mexico	Malaysia	Brazil	Colombia
Denmark	Estonia	Norway	United States	Philippines	Paraguay	Ecuador
Finland	Hungary	Switzerland		Singapore	Uruguay	Peru
France	Latvia			Thailand		Venezuela
Germany	Lithuania			Brunei Darussalam		
Greece	Malta			Vietnam		
Ireland	Poland			Cambodia		
Italy	Slovakia			Laos		
Luxembourg	Slovenia			Myanmar		
Netherlands						
Portugal						
Spain						
Sweden						
UK						

OPEC (11)	Council of Arab Economic Unity (12)	CARICOM (15)	LAIA (12)	ECOWAS (15)	SADC (14)
Algeria	Egypt	Antigua and Barbuda	Argentina	Benin	Angola
Indonesia	Iraq	The Bahamas	Bolivia	Burkina Faso	Botswana
Iran	Jordan	Barbados	Brazil	Cape Verde	Dem. Rep. of Congo
Iraq	Libya	Belize	Chile	Côte d'Ivoire	
Kuwait	Mauritania	Dominica	Colombia	Gambia	Lesotho
Libya	Syria	Grenada	Ecuador	Ghana	Malawi
Nigeria	Yemen	Guyana	Mexico	Guinea	Mauritius
Qatar	United Arab Emirates	Haiti	Paraguay	Guinea- Bissau	Mozambique
Saudi Arabia	Kuwait	Jamaica	Peru	Liberia	Namibia
United Arab Emirates	Palestine	Montserrat	Uruguay	Mali	Seychelles
Venezuela	Somalia	Saint Lucia	Venezuela	Togo	South Africa
	Sudan	St Kitts and Nevis	Cuba	Niger	Swaziland
		St. Vincent and the Grenadines		Nigeria	Tanzania
		Surinam		Senegal	Zambia
		Trinidad and Tobago		Sierra Leone	Zimbabwe

Key: EU—European Union; EFTA—European Free Trade Agreement; OPEC—Organization of Petroleum Exporting Countries; NAFTA—North American Free Trade Agreement; CARICOM—Caribbean Community and Common Market; ASEAN—Association of Southeast Asian Nations; Mercosur—Mercado Comun del Sur; LAIA—Latin American Integration Association; ECOWAS—Economic Community of West African States; SADC—Southern African Development Community.

Sources: Adapted from http://europa.eu.int/abc-en.htm; www.opec.org; www.efta.int; www.caricom.org/; http://wellsfargo.com/inatl/wrldalmn/intro/other/; www.sice.oas.org/; www.aladi.org/; www.sadc-usa.net/members/default.html; www.imf.org/external/np/sec/decdo/ecowas.htm.

decade. Meanwhile Asian MNEs, except for those of Japan and Australia, will benefit from the comparatively lower cost of the labor in their home countries.

New economic opportunities will also be provided by the rise of non-triad based firms that become successful MNEs. In Mexico, for example, Anheuser-Busch owns approximately 50 per cent of Grupo Modelo, maker of Corona and the country's largest brewer. After years of unsuccessfully vying to be the market leader in Peru and losing to local Inka Cola, Coca-Cola's Peruvian bottling and distribution was transferred to its competitor. In turn, Inka Cola products are now sold in North America, mostly to immigrant South Americans, through the Coca-Cola company. As non-triad countries develop, new opportunities for telecommunication and other infrastructure companies will materialize.

New goods and services will help to create new markets. An example is Apple's iPod, an MP3 player that can store a large quantity of music. Already, firms are competing to provide ever better MP3 players to gain a share of this growing market. New PC technology is also decreasing the weight of laptops while improving their processing speed, their graphics, and their multimedia capabilities. These products lend themselves to a globalization strategy since purchasers buy them based primarily on performance characteristics and not on cultural requirements. As a result, computer industry MNEs are likely to find the millennium offering both new opportunities and new challenges. The opportunities will come in the form of emerging markets since sharp declines in PC prices tend to increase demand sharply. The major challenge will come in the form of increased competition since PC technology tends to be easy to emulate, and so the barriers to entry for new firms are often quickly surmounted.

An accompanying development is the rise of the Internet as a source of competition. Today a growing number of MNEs are becoming electronic companies, or e-corporations for short.[22] The Internet is driving down costs and helping companies reach thousands of new potential customers worldwide.[23] As a result, MNEs are now throwing out their old business models and creating new ones that will help them do business electronically with customers who in the past were not accessible to them.[24] One of the keys to this new development is the rapid rise of both businesses and households with Internet access. As recently as 2005 approximately 47 per cent of the European population and 68 per cent of those in the United States used the Internet.[25] As a result, e-commerce is now accounting for a growing percentage of GDP in these economies.[26]

Major MNEs that are finding themselves unable to compete in the ever-changing international arena are restructuring[27] and realigning markets. Examples include (1) aircraft manufacturing, where Boeing is having to scurry to meet competition from Airbus; (2) autos, where General Motors, Ford, and Chrysler are trying to stave off the onslaught of Japanese competition in their home market; and (3) household electronics, where such well-known manufacturers as Sony, Panasonic, and Goldstar are finding that the markets for products such as DVDs are becoming saturated and that Chinese manufacturers are proving themselves to be excellent competitors.

New strategies, carefully crafted to the specific market, will offer increased opportunities for MNEs. In Japan, for example, the success of firms such as Toys "Я" Us and Spiegel is a result of learning how to work within the system. As discussed in the Real Case in Chapter 3, Toys "Я" Us set up its own retail stores by teaming up with the former director of McDonald's Japan for local knowledge and investment capital. It relentlessly pursued its objective of its discounted "category killer" toys despite vigorous opposition from small, local merchants who opposed letting Toys "Я" Us into the Japanese market. Thanks to its dogged determination, the company was eventually given permission to open a large retail store and today it has over 100 stores in Japan.[28] Spiegel, famous for its mail-order business, formed a joint venture with Sumitomo Trading Company and introduced an upscale fashion catalog in Japan. The company directed its efforts at women from 20 to 40 years of age. Catalog selling proved so successful that by the mid-1990s the joint venture was generating annual sales of over $160 million. These efforts, which are characterized by strategies that are designed to circumvent problems in the distribution system rather than trying to meet them head on, are typical of those strategies that will be used in Japan and other foreign locations during the years ahead.

Business-to-business (B2B)

An example of an ethnocentric MNE is Air Liquide, the French manufacturer of industrial and medical gases. At its Paris headquarters, the vice presidents for each geographic region are all French. All regional managers in foreign offices are French and have previously worked in Paris. This allows Air Liquide to have a standardized, "global" strategy that treats the world as one integrated market. This works as the nature of the industry is B2B. The main customers of Air Liquide are other large industrial manufacturers in oil, iron and steel, and other types of chemicals. These companies depend on the gases supplied by Air Liquide. It has flagship relationships with many of those manufacturers.

The main competitors of Air Liquide are the UK-based BOC Group and Linde AG. While Air Liquide is more concentrated in the core gas business, its competitors are more diversified into the gases needed for consumers, transportation, etc.

In general, the largest number of B2B relationships would be between ethnocentric partners. Then there are clear rules of the game—both partners are in mature, standardized industries with easy-to-maintain, long-term relationships. So, B2B occurs in chemicals, autos and auto parts, oil, and other "commoditized" sectors.

TRADE AND INVESTMENT FRAMEWORKS

The tendency toward international trade liberalization has been exemplified by two recent developments, namely the North American Free Trade Agreement (NAFTA) of 1993 and the deeper integration of the European Union (EU). Both these regional triad agreements have developed from previous agreements. The principles of the 1989 United States–Canada Free Trade Agreement (FTA) are also the basis for NAFTA. Similarly, before 1995, the European Union was the European Community (EC). Albeit very different, in terms of goals and content, these two examples of trade and investment liberalization create a protected business environment for member countries, while in turn discriminating against third-country businesses.[29]

From the Canadian and Mexico perspective, the main rationale for negotiating the FTA, and subsequently NAFTA, was to secure access to the US market for both exports and FDI. Mexico also sought to create a secure economy for inward flows of FDI. In contrast, the EU's predecessor, the EC, was considered by many observers to create a "Fortress Europe" at the expense of third-country firms.[30]

Figure 20.3 classifies the different industries in the countries affected by trade liberalization in NAFTA. (It will also provide an initial framework for the EU.) The vertical axis denominates economic integration and the horizontal axis reflects the political sovereignty of nation states. The left side column therefore shows low political sovereignty in the form of national treatment. With national treatment, discrimination against foreign investors is not permitted; they are to be treated equally with domestic investors in the application of host-country laws and regulations.

Quadrant 1 refers to business sectors where there is high economic integration and low political sovereignty. But not all aspects of "free trade" agreements are here. Quadrant 2 refers to business sectors with low economic integration and low political sovereignty. These are sectors that tend to be naturally local, such as labor. Quadrant 3 refers to business sectors with combined high levels of economic integration and political sovereignty. While national treatment refers to the obligation of member states to treat all businesses

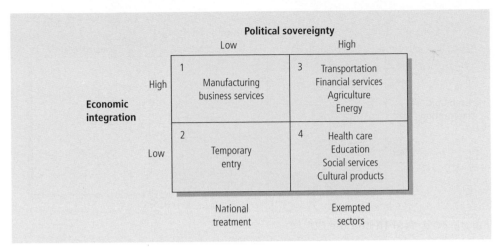

Figure 20.3 Foreign direct investment and NAFTA

from other member countries as if they were domestic businesses, this does not always apply; there are exempted sectors. Sectors in quadrant 3 are exempted from national treatment despite the efficiencies that would result from the application of national treatment. The last matrix section, quadrant 4, refers to sectors that are typically local and are exempted from national treatment.

According to the NAFTA document, national treatment in quadrant 1 applies to sectors such as manufacturing and business service. In quadrant 2 are the temporary entry permits for business service professionals (such as consultants and engineers). Exempted sectors are in quadrants 3 and 4. Those with a high level of economic integration in quadrant 3 include transportation, financial services, energy, and agriculture. Those with low levels of economic integration in quadrant 4 are health care, education, social services, and cultural products.

This framework is also a model for the Free Trade Area of the Americas (FTAA), agreed to at Quebec City in 2001, with implementation expected at 2005. It is also the model for the Asia-Pacific Economic Cooperation (APEC), although this will not be fully effective until 2015 and 2020.

Figure 20.4 shows the more complex EU matrix. The two extra quadrants in the extreme left column capture the concept of an even lower level of political sovereignty, reciprocity. The EU 1992 measures and subsequent "deepening" programs of political, social, and economic integration aim at quadrant A in everything but select sectors, such as culture. The manufacturing sector and business services are in quadrant A, which also includes banking and mutual funds, securities, insurance, transportation, broadcasting, tourism, and information services. In addition, there are harmonization laws regulating company behavior, including mergers and acquisitions, trademarks and copyrights, cross-border mergers, and accounting operations across borders. Another important objective of harmonization is the opening of public procurement. It is clear that such harmonization efforts place almost all economic sectors in quadrant A of Figure 20.4.[31] In conclusion, in contrast to NAFTA, the EU has a much deeper degree of economic, political, and social integration and a consequent loss of sovereignty for its member states.

Although both NAFTA and the EU can be analyzed in this way, many groups are opposed to such trade and investment liberalization. When they are opposed, they frequently cloak themselves in the guise of ethics, as we shall see in the box **International Business Strategy in Action: Is The Body Shop an ethical business?**

Figure 20.4 NAFTA and the EU

✓ Active learning check

Review your answer to Active Learning Case question 2 and make any changes you like. Then compare your answer with the one below.

2 As multinational enterprises operate across the world and NGOs operate globally, why are there no "global" or "international" environmental agreements to set rules for sustainable development?

The reason that there is no effective international environmental agreement is that there is no single international institution that can enforce one. The WTO deals with trade matters, not environmental issues. The United Nations deals with human rights in a political but not economic context. Further, the MNEs really do not operate globally, but are mainly "triad" based. And here, the US and EU triad blocks are often at odds on environmental, trade, and investment policies. Paradoxically, the NGOs are criticizing MNES for something that they do not do: operate globally. The more responsible NGOs, who believe in sustainable development, should lobby the respective home-based triad authorities. This is where the power is—not with "global" governance. To ensure a safe environment, NGOs need to learn the realities of triad power.

ENVIRONMENT AND MNES

Civil society
A group of individuals, organizations, and institutions that act outside the government and the market to advance a diverse set of interests

The issue of globalization has opened up a gulf between representatives of civil society such as non-governmental organizations (NGOs) on the one hand and international business such as multinationals (MNEs) on the other. Unfortunately these oppositions of opinion have become entrenched. In this section we will categorize perceptions regarding the role of international institutions and future alternatives for trade liberalization and indicate a range of more constructive responses for both MNEs and NGOs.

"Mobilizer" NGOs criticize the global trade and investment regime and believe that the major international institutions promoting free trade, such as the WTO, IMF, and World Bank, should be eliminated or fundamentally overhauled. "Technical" NGOs are relative insiders, willing to work with the mainstream international institutions in order to reduce perceived ineffectiveness or inequity in policy making. However, technical NGOs are now perceived by many national governments and business lobbies as having a common agenda with the mobilizers. This widespread perception has seriously affected the technical NGOs' capacity to achieve important objectives on their usually benevolent agendas.

INTERNATIONAL BUSINESS STRATEGY *IN ACTION*

Is The Body Shop an ethical business?

When it comes to the ethical company, The Body Shop is hailed as the prototype of the responsible firm. The company's website not only states the company's values but urges visitors to become active in the fight to end animal cruelty, to protect human rights, and to implement fair trade practices. Its founder, Anita Roddick, started the company in 1976 by opening a small store in Brighton, England, to support her family. In 1978, the opening of a small store in Brussels became its first overseas expansion. By the 1980s, the company was opening two stores per month. Today, The Body Shop has grown into a multinational enterprise with 1,900 stores in 50 countries around the world.

The company has a lengthy résumé of its social achievements. In the animal rights arena, The Body Shop joined the campaign for a ban on animal testing for cosmetic products. This was a major factor in the 1998 decision of the UK government to ban animal testing in the industry. On the environmental front, the company has publicly joined NGO causes. For example, in the 1980s, the company sponsored Greenpeace posters, joined the "Save the Whales Campaign," and started a signature petition to ask the Brazilian government to halt the burning of the Amazon forest. The company also brought attention to Shell's involvement in Nigeria. Shell's operations were blamed for severe environmental deterioration, prosecution of protestors, and bribery of state officials. More recently, the company has converted many of its operations into Ecotricity, or energy from renewal resources, and helped create an academy of business with an ethical curriculum in the University of Bath.

The company's image is tied to that of its founder. Anita Roddick has been an active participant on environmental rallies, fair trade missions, and in lobbying governments. She has also defied the cosmetics industry's portrayal of women and urged women to accept cellulite and wrinkles as a natural part of their bodies. She has stated publicly that cosmetics claiming to solve these problems do not really work, an assertion that has created a backlash from competitors. Since the company went public in 1985, she has often found herself at odds with shareholders. In fact, in 1998 shareholders pressured her to step down from the CEO chair in favor of Patrick Gournay, who oversaw a major restructuring that saw 300 job cuts, the company's withdrawal from manufacturing, and a management hiring spree to revitalize the company. In 2000, Roddick announced that she would slowly retire from managing The Body Shop to concentrate on her activism. In 2002, she and her husband resigned as co-chairs but retained seats on the board of directors. Gournay also resigned and was replaced by CEO Peter Saunders.

Another signature of The Body Shop is the "Trade not Aid" slogan. Under it, the company has sought to advance the plight of indigenous communities in third-world countries by promoting "Fair Trade." The goal is to support marginalized sectors of society to develop a livelihood within the context of sustainable development. Today, the company sources cocoa butter, babassu oil, and massagers, among other ingredients and products, from Community Trade suppliers in 26 countries, including India, Honduras, Nepal, and Mexico. In 2002–2003, the company purchased £5 million in natural products through its Community Trade Program.

In the 1990s, the company suffered a severe blow to its reputation when *Business Ethics* published an article by Jon Entine claiming that the company was the opposite of what it represented itself to be. Entine accused the company of selling drugstore quality products at a large premium by marketing cosmetics with petrochemical ingredients as natural products. In addition, the author claimed the company misrepresented the amount of its donations to charity, did not adhere to its own principles of "Fair Trade," and had itself committed unnecessary environmental damage. For instance, Entine mentions an incident in which The Body Shop went back on a contract to purchase large amounts of shea butter from suppliers in Ghana. This left the suppliers with a lot of useless stock they could not sell anywhere else. There are also alleged incidents of the company forcing low margins on suppliers in third-world countries. And, a franchisee in France claimed that The Body Shop dumped a load of plastic containers in a landfill.

Source: Getty/Time & Life Pictures/Forrest Anderson

A number of consumer groups, NGOs, and Internet websites have all jumped on the wagon. The website mcspotlight.com claims that The Body Shop sells products with ingredients that have been tested on animals, as long as the testing was not done for cosmetics, and that some of its products contain gelatin, an animal product. The same website claims that, in industrialized countries, The Body Shop pays its employees near minimum wages and is unwilling to recognize unions. The company is also accused of exaggerating the importance of its Community Trade Program and of using the Kayapo Indians of Brazil for promotions without compensating them.

The Body Shop has denied most allegations and threatened legal action to a number of news media but has only taken action against a few, including Channel 4 of England. For the company, which was built on the confidence of the "conscious customer," the consequences of this bad publicity could be devastating. Premium prices are, after all, what customers are willing to pay for that extra social responsibility.

Whether the allegations are true or not, The Body Shop can still claim to be a pioneer of corporate responsibility because it brought the issues to the table. Many companies have emulated its principles, including Boots of the UK, which has developed its own brand of environmentally friendly cosmetics to compete with The Body Shop.

Websites: www.the-body-shop.com and www.greenpeace.org.

Sources: "Body Shops Shares Slump," *BBC.co.uk*, January 12, 2001; "Body Shop Cuts Jobs," *BBC.co.uk*, May 6, 1999; "Roddick Quits to 'Smash' WTO," *BBC.co.uk*, September 17, 2000; www.the-body-shop.com; www.jonentine.com; Jon Entine, "Shattered Image: Is the Body Shop Too Good to Be True?" *Business Ethics*, September/October 1994; Sharlene Buszka, "A Case of Greenwashing: The Body Shop," in *Proceedings of the Association of Management and the International Association of Management 15th Annual Conference, Organizational Management Division*, vol. 15, no. 1 (1997), pp. 199–294; www.mcspotlight.org/; "Passion or Profit," *FT.com*, February 13, 2002; "Body Swap," *FT.com*, February 13, 2002; Alison Smith, "US Team Hopeful of Reviving Flagging Fortune," *Financial Times*, February 13, 2002, p. 20.

In addition it is difficult to see how the WTO can address the multitude of goals prescribed by the anti-global mobilizers. The WTO is an understaffed bureaucracy with little political impact. The secretariat to the General Agreement on Tariffs and Trade (GATT) has successfully acted on behalf of national governments to cut tariffs, mainly on manufactured goods. Its value lies in the improved market access it opens to previously protected markets, thereby increasing overall economic efficiency; it functions by implementing rules of fairness agreed upon by sovereign states.

Unfortunately the WTO also embodies several asymmetric elements: on the one hand it is consistently moving toward trade liberalization, but on the other, it is unable to eliminate the protectionist policies in some sectors put in place by many of its members.

Furthermore, a major structural change at the new WTO, as compared to GATT, is the increased use of trade law and litigation for dispute settlement. As the stream of disputes swell the WTO is taking on a different shape. Instead of devoting most of its resources to promoting multinational trade liberalization and non-discrimination, the WTO is forced to focus much energy and expertise on resolving bilateral trade disputes. While the WTO has been successful for 54 years in dealing with the technical tariff cuts, it is not very well equipped to deal with the new agenda of international trade and investment liberalization. Tariff cuts have allowed shallow integration across many manufacturing sectors. Today's agenda, with major implications for MNEs engaged in FDI, is one of deep integration.

Figure 20.5 contrasts the various perceived roles and outcomes of the WTO. The institutional reality is largely that of quadrant 1, while the anti-global movement has been successful in creating an image of the WTO as in quadrant 4.

The technical NGOs' perspective is usually positioned in quadrant 2. Here, an assessment of the efficiency outcomes of improved market access is often combined with a belief in the power of the WTO to actually dictate fundamental national policy choices that could favor the redistribution of wealth. The dominant picture suggested by the stakeholders hurt by free trade and investment is positioned in quadrant 3. These stakeholders typically include labor, management, and owners of non-competitive firms in import-competing sectors, which lack exports or outward FDI. Their view is that the WTO may indeed be an implementation mechanism of sovereign governments' choices, but it results in increased inequality in the international distribution of economic power and wealth.

Figure 20.5 Different perceptions of the WTO

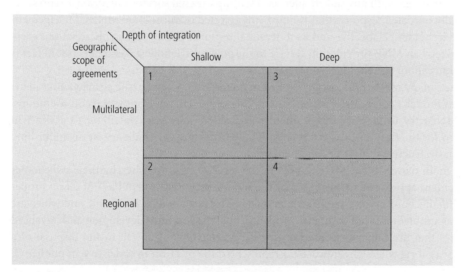

Figure 20.6 Institutional alternatives for trade and investment

Two parameters critically determine the future options for further trade and investment liberalization—the choice between bilateral or regional and multilateral negotiations and between shallow or deeper integration. These choices are represented in Figure 20.6.

Quadrant 1 represents the old, highly successful GATT process of tariffs cuts and shallow integration. Quadrant 3 represents the new agenda of the WTO in terms of deep integration, including investment liberalization. Quadrant 2 represents the old regional trade agreements with tariff cuts (the Andean pact, the Caribbean initiative, ASEAN, etc.). Quadrant 4 represents the new type of regional trade agreements, such as NAFTA. These include national treatment for foreign direct investment and also enhanced market access for services and intellectual property. Quadrant 3, with deep multilateral integration, undoubtedly constitutes an optimal situation for all nations concerned in terms of long-term wealth creation, but is at present not feasible because of constraints such as the structure of WTO and US policy preferences. Quadrant 2 represents the worst-case scenario of shallow, regional integration.

This analysis demonstrates the perverse effects that mobilizers can have on trade and investment liberalization. Poor countries and groups always benefit more from multilateral than from regional agreements. They cannot be shut out from the former, and individual nations such as the United States always have less power in multilateral than in regional cases because of the number of countries involved. The strengthening, not the weakening, of mainstream global institutions such as the WTO—so despised by the mobilizers—may well represent the fastest route for poorer countries toward achieving fundamentally higher living standards for their population.

The pattern of MNE responses

Figure 20.7 categorizes MNE responses to civil society criticisms. The vertical axis distinguishes between a strategy that differentiates between stakeholders with which a dialogue is possible and those with whom it is not, and, on the bottom, a strategy of uniform response. The horizontal axis makes a distinction between a broad stakeholder perspective on the right, whereby other goals than shareholder wealth maximization are considered relevant, and, on the left, a narrower shareholder, profit-maximizing perspective.

Quadrant 2 reflects the outdated perspective on MNEs, paradoxically adopted by most mobilizers. They view MNEs as profit maximizers, who will systematically refuse a constructive dialogue with any stakeholder representing the civil society. Quadrant 1 represents an equally outdated response that is now being rejected by most large MNEs. Management has a shareholder perspective and its differential response is usually a public-relations exercise whereby an MNE provides lip service to the goals of friendly stakeholders but in fact is not serious about stakeholder management.

In fact, many MNEs are now positioned in quadrant 3. They pursue a stakeholder management model, perhaps driven by sustainable development environmental considerations. Here MNEs try to identify those salient stakeholders that can contribute to a win-win situation for the firm and society at large. These firms face the challenge of distinguishing between destructive mobilizers and benevolent, technical NGOs.

The main danger is for MNEs to fall in the quadrant 4 trap, whereby their stakeholder management approach can be abused by mobilizers, because the firm has not set up proper screening mechanisms to establish which stakeholder demands are legitimate and which are not. This problem is faced by many companies operating in both developing and advanced countries that are unfairly accused of unethical behavior (e.g., Shell in the disposal of a North Sea oil rig where Greenpeace misrepresented the position in order to win publicity).

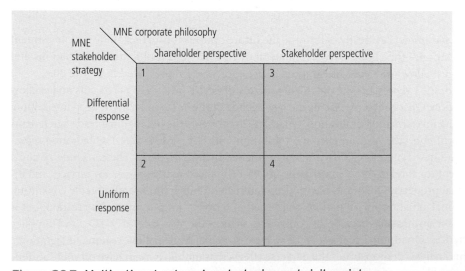

Figure 20.7 Multinational enterprise strategies and civil society

A useful alliance could take place between MNEs with a quadrant 1 viewpoint in Figure 20.7 and the technical NGOs of quadrant 2. An example of this is the idea of sustainable development, whereby MNEs are the actors making new and environmentally sensitive investments. In contrast, alliances between the protected and inefficient firms in quadrant 3 and mobilizer NGOs in quadrant 4 are not useful. Yet this was exactly the type of coalition put together in Seattle in 1999 to disrupt the WTO meetings. There, labor, mobilizer NGOs, and even technical NGOs made common cause against business and governments.

Three suggestions are offered as to how MNEs should proceed.

1 The activities of external stakeholders should be discussed at the board and top management level, and an overall strategy should be developed to deal with them. It is important to make a distinction between technical NGOs and anti-global mobilizers. Initiatives should be developed to work with the former. Clear arguments should be developed to appropriately counter the discourse of the mobilizers, and this should be combined with an effective communication strategy to reach relevant audiences.

2 Sustainable development and ethical stakeholder perspectives should be embedded within the organization and its culture.

3 The firm should not engage in a debate with mobilizers (or even technical NGOs) through a small set of public-relations people; instead all senior managers should be trained to articulate the concept of stakeholder capitalism, rather than shareholder capitalism and the contribution of the organization to the resulting wealth creation. In other words, all senior managers in the firm should engage with NGOs.

As a result of the above initiatives firms should experience a dramatic improvement both in profile and performance. The firms that will do best in future will be those that take leadership positions with respect to stakeholder management, capture the concept of values-driven rather than profit-driven capitalism, and respect their most important resource—namely, their employees. These policies will be the most effective tools at the micro-economic level against ideology-driven mobilizers.

For their part, NGOs, especially the technical ones, need to understand that anti-global rhetoric is leading to regional integration and bilateral agreements, as a politically more feasible—but ultimately less efficient—alternative to global integration. This does not benefit the objectives of civil society. Free trade and investment liberalization have not yet been achieved due to the vested interests and misperceptions of some components of civil society and affected stakeholders. We now need to recognize and correct these misperceptions as a precondition to achieving an overarching increase in world welfare and incomes.

✔ Active learning check

Review your answer to the Active Learning Case question 3 and make any changes you like. Then compare your answer with the one below.

3 **Where would BP be positioned in Figure 20.7? Why?**

BP is positioned in quadrant 3 of Figure 20.7. It is highly responsive to different stakeholder groups with whom it engages in a dialogue to pursue a differential response. As a result BP has been ranked as one of the more environmentally responsive and socially aware companies.

KEY POINTS

1   There will be an increase in the amount of international business research that is being conducted. This will come in the form of both theory testing and the practical application of information. Both academicians and practitioners will find this development helpful.

2   Multinationals, as flagship firms, are beginning to develop new business network relationships with suppliers, competitors, governments, unions, universities, and a host of other external groups. This networking relationship is proving particularly helpful in increasing productivity, profitability, and overall competitiveness.

3   The two environments that will present the greatest challenges for MNEs in the future are the political and the economic. The rising tide of protectionism will require that multinationals deal astutely with foreign governments. They will also have to weigh carefully the political risk associated with investing in countries that are now beginning to shed their central planning systems and to move toward free enterprise economies.

4   The principle of national treatment reduces political sovereignty, although some sectors are exempted in NAFTA, the FTAA, and APEC. In contrast, the EU has deep integration across political and social areas, as well as economic.

5   The interaction between MNEs and NGOs is complex but can be better understood by constructing an analytical framework.

Key terms

- strategic fit
- flagship firms
- five partners
- non-governmental organizations (NGOs)
- civil society

REVIEW AND DISCUSSION QUESTIONS

1   Why is theory testing of value to the field of international business research? What can be learned from such information?

2   In addition to theory testing, how is international business research of value to both scholars and practitioners? In your answer, give an example of how each group can benefit from such research.

3   In what ways are MNEs developing new business networks? Give two examples and then explain why these developments are likely to help the companies maintain their competitive strengths.

4   How is the political environment likely to change during the future? Give one example and relate its significance for multinationals.

5   How is the economic environment likely to change in the future? Give one example and relate its significance for multinationals.

6   How does NAFTA differ from the EU?

7   Why are NGOs opposed to MNEs? What should MNEs do?

Dell: B2C

Dell is a leader in personal computers. It competes with Acer, Compaq, IBM, HP, etc. Dell is based in Austin, Texas, and has production factories in Tennessee. It also produces in Ireland, Malaysia, Brazil, and China. But its success lies in marketing directly to consumers rather than in any technological or cost advantages associated with production.

Dell introduced the Dell Direct model, a business-to-consumer (B2C) concept, which has now been copied by major competitors. By eliminating retailers, Dell can deal directly with individual customers, offering detailed and richly configured systems. There is consumer customization, plus services and support. This method saves on inventory and introduces new technology quickly. Dell became a market leader with the first B2C direct business model.

The computer industry is at a mature stage of manufacturing. This means that there is pressure either to be extremely cost competitive or to develop value-added services that build on the computer itself. The five major computer manufacturers have responded to these market changes in different ways. IBM invented the personal computer and was perhaps the first to move strongly toward customer service. In late 2002 Hewlett-Packard and Compaq merged to try to consolidate production but also to develop the service end. This left Apple and Dell as the firms driven by low cost and technology.

In China, Dell has developed an innovative B2C concept that is allowing it to quickly increase its market share. PC manufacturers have been flocking to China because of expected growth of 20 per cent per year over the next few years. Dell entered the Chinese market in the 1990s, trailing behind IBM and Compaq. Yet, today, with 7.4 per cent of the market, Dell is the largest foreign PC market player after three local Chinese manufacturers. One way in which Dell was able to achieve this was by introducing the affordable Smart PC. Another has been to offer tailor-made PCs over the Internet. A Chinese customer virtually builds his or her desired computer and then Dell assembles and delivers it. Implementing B2C retailing has not been easy because Chinese people are not used to credit cards. To overcome this obstacle, the company has made deals with major banks to allow customers to go to a branch and make a payment that is then reported to Dell. More recently, the largest Chinese computer manufacturers started

Source: Getty Images/Business Wire

to compete aggressively in the lower end of the market, forcing Dell to move up-market where it expects to reap the benefits of a growing number of luxury-minded individuals.

Throughout the world, Dell has tried to add service value in its B2C process. It has 80 Internet sites on which more than 65,000 institutional customers do business with Dell. Through www.dell.com customers can order, price, and configure products. Dell maintains after-sale service with customers. It also brings new technology quickly to the customer. In short, Dell's B2C system allows the MNE to engage in mass customization.

▶

Websites: www.dell.com; www.dell.com.cn; www.hp.com; www.hp.com.cn; www.compaq.com; www.compaq.com.cn; www.ibm.com; www.ibm.com.cn; and www.acer.com.

Sources: www.dell.com; Bruce Einhorn, "Dell Takes a Different Tack in China," *BW Online*, December 3, 2001; Scott Morrison, "Stronger Consumer Demand for PCs Lifts Dell," *FT.com*, February 15, 2002; "Dell Halts Sales of Low-End PCs in China," *Reuters*, August 16, 2004.

1 What is meant by B2C? How does Dell achieve B2C?

2 Why is Dell so successful in China?

3 Is B2C a viable strategy in the mature, competitive computer industry of today?

REAL CASE

Merck

Merck is a US-based firm deriving 63.4 per cent of its revenues from its home national market. That Merck derives most of its profits from the United States is no surprise. This is the case for most large pharmaceutical companies. After all, the United States is the largest market, and it has the least price regulation among all industrialized countries.

Most of Merck's research is conducted in North America, where the company has six research facilities (five in the United States and one in Canada). Yet, despite the dominance of the North American region, the company also has five R&D facilities in Europe and one in Japan.

Ray Gilmartin, Chairman of Merck, stands by the motto, "Medicine is for the people. It is not for the profits. The profits follow." This is why the company stood aside while the pharmaceutical industry restructured through a wave of mergers in the late 1990s.

At the time, Merck faced the same problems plaguing the entire industry: (1) the patent expiry of some of its most important drugs; (2) competition from generic companies; (3) increased price regulation by national and sub-national governments; (4) increase costs of developing a drug; and most importantly (5) a slowdown in the number of successful new products that it develops. Yet, while competitors rushed to buy rivals to increase overall R&D expending, Merck chose to go at it alone. It will rely, it said, on the strength of its research force. This strength is undisputed. Between 1996 and 2000, the company patented 1,933 new compounds, the highest in the industry. That this is done with a lower R&D budget than that of other large pharmaceuticals only increases the reputation of Merck as a research-oriented company. The benefit of such a vision is that the company can lure some of the best scientists, or, at the very least, some of the more dedicated to their research. Merck's relationship with the investment

community is not as rosy. Analysts do not see that research-oriented activity necessarily translates into shareholder value creation. Only time will tell if it does. In this industry, however, time can be a decade.

The company has also had to take a different stance in poorer countries where the cost of medication is prohibitive for many patients. In 2001, together with other large pharmaceutical companies, Merck launched a lawsuit against the South African government. At the time, the country was switching to generic drugs to combat AIDS, which was affecting 10 per cent of its population. Drug costs were often higher than salaries, and, like Brazil, the country had to decide to either honor the patents of large MNEs to produce its own or to import it from countries that already legalized generics and produced them at a fraction of the cost. Throughout the world, protestors rose up against the lawsuit, forcing pharmaceutical companies to justify letting 250,000 people die every year. Merck was the quickest to realize the public relations hole which it had dug, and it acted to broker an agreement between the industry and developing countries. Merck no longer makes a profit from selling HIV drugs in the poorest of countries. Others in the industry complain that this inhibits future research, but Merck was quick to point out that as long as pharmaceuticals can continue to make significant profits in the developed world, research will continue at the same pace.

1 What are some of Merck's FSAs?

2 What are some of Merck's CSAs?

3 Given that Merck derives over 80 per cent of its sales in the United States, why has it opened research facilities in the other two regions of the triad?

Endnotes

1 See, for example, Dean Takahashi, "How the Competition Got Ahead of Intel in Making Cheap Chips," *Wall Street Journal,* February 12, 1998, pp. A 1, 11.

2 Jeanne B. Pinder, "Japan's New York Realty Investing Plunges," *New York Times,* March 19, 1993, p. C 10.

3 Shaker A. Zahra, "The Changing Rules of Global Competitiveness in the 21st Century," *Academy of Management Executive,* vol. 13, no. 1 (February 1999), pp. 36–42.

4 Also, see James B. Treece et al., "New Worlds to Conquer," *Business Week,* February 28, 1994, pp. 50–52.

5 Also see Howard Thomas, Timothy Pollock and Philip Gorman, "Global Strategic Analyses: Frameworks and Approaches," *Academy of Management Executive,* February 1999, pp. 70–82.

6 Also, see David Kirkpatrick, "Why the Internet Is Boosting IBM's Mainframe Sales," *Fortune,* January 11, 1999, pp. 148–149.

7 Otto Andersen, "On the Internationalization Process of Firms: A Critical Analysis," *Journal of International Business Studies,* vol. 24, no. 2 (Second Quarter 1993), pp. 209–231; and Sumantra Ghoshal and Nitin Nohria, "Horses for Courses: Organizational Forms for Multinational Corporations," *Sloan Management Review,* Winter 1993, pp. 23–35.

8 Jeremiah J. Sullivan and Richard B. Peterson, "A Test of Theories Underlying the Japanese Lifetime Employment System," *Journal of International Business Studies,* vol. 22, no. 1 (First Quarter 1991), p. 79.

9 Richard M. Hodgetts, "A Conversation with Michael E. Porter," *Organizational Dynamics,* Summer 1999, pp. 25–26.

10 Joseph R. D'Cruz and Alan M. Rugman, *Multinationals as Flagship Firms: Regional Business Networks* (Oxford: Oxford University Press, 2000). This book is based on earlier work such as: Alan M. Rugman and Joseph R. D'Cruz, *New Compacts for Canadian Competitiveness* (Toronto: Kodak Canada, 1992), p. 31; and Joseph R. D'Cruz and Alan M. Rugman, "Business Networks for International Competitiveness," *Business Quarterly,* vol. 56, no. 4 (Spring 1992), pp. 101–107.

11 D'Cruz and Rugman (2000) n. 10 above.

12 For an example of this psychological reaction, see David E. Sanger, "64 per cent of Japanese Say US Relations Are 'Unfriendly,'" *New York Times,* July 6, 1993, pp. A 1, A 6.

13 For more on this, see Rosabeth Moss Kanter, "Transcending Business Boundaries: 12,000 World Managers View Change," *Harvard Business Review,* vol. 69, no. 3 (May/June 1991), pp. 151–164.

14 "US Targets Trade Partners" *BBC.co.uk,* April 3, 2002.

15 See, for example, Keith Bradsher, "US Upset with Japan on Chip Pact," *New York Times,* March 4, 1993, pp. C 1, C 2.

16 "China 'Too Slow' to Open Markets," *BBC.co.uk,* December 19, 2003.

17 Rob Hugh-Jones, "Analysis: Rice's Latin American Tour," *BBC.co.uk,* April 20, 2005.

18 Alicia Jrapko, "Workers Seize Control of 150 Plants," *Worker's World,* May 8, 2003.

19 "Country Profiles: Regions and Territories: Hong Kong," *BBC.co.uk,* May 25, 2005.

20 Mark Landler, "Back to Vietnam, This Time to Build," *New York Times,* September 13, 1998, Section 3, pp. 1, 11.

21 See "Mexico: A Market that Is Ready for Services," *New York Times,* July 21, 1993, pp. C 10–C 15; and Bob Graham, "Free Trade Means Fair Trade," *Miami Herald,* July 22, 1993, p. 21 A.

22 Gary Hamel and Jeff Sampler, "The E-Corporation," *Fortune,* December 7, 1998, pp. 80–92.

23 R. Duane Ireland and Michael A. Hitt, "Achieving and Maintaining Strategic Competitiveness in the 21st Century: The Role of Strategic Leadership," *Academy of Management Executive,* February 1999, pp. 43–57.

24 Heather Green and Linda Himelstein, "Throw Out Your Old Business Model," *Business Week E-Biz,* March 22, 1999, pp. EB 22–23.

25 *www.internetworldstats.com.*

26 Robert D. Hof, Gary McWilliams and Gabrielle Savers, "The 'Click Here' Economy," *Business Week,* June 22, 1998, pp. 122–128.

27 Claude H. Deutsch, "Digital Polish for Factory Floors," *New York Times,* March 22, 1999, pp. C 1, 7.

28 Debora L. Spar, *Ruling the Waves: Cycles of Discovery, Chaos and Wealth* (New York: Harcourt, 2001).

29 Alan M. Rugman and Alain Verbeke, "Corporate Strategy After the Free Trade Agreement and Europe 1992," in John Longair (ed.), *Proceedings: Regional Integration in the World Economy: Europe and North America* (Ottawa: Conference Board of Canada, March 1990).

30 See Gerard Curzon, "Ten Reasons to Fear Fortress Europe," Mimeo. Graduate Institute of International Studies, Geneva, 1989 and B. Burgenmeir and J. L. Mucchielli, *Multinational and Europe 1992* (London: Routledge, 1990) for an overview.

31 Rugman and Verbeke (1990) n. 29 above.

Additional bibliography

Bhagwati, J. *In Defense of Globalization* (Oxford: Oxford University Press, 2004).

Brewer, Thomas L. and Young, Stephen. *The Multilateral Investment System and Multinational Enterprise* (Oxford: Oxford University Press, 1998).

Clarkson, Max B. E. "A Stakeholder Framework for Analyzing and Evaluating Corporate Social Performance," *Academy of Management Review,* vol. 20, no. 1 (January 1995).

D'Cruz, Joseph R. and Rugman, Alan M. "Developing International Competitiveness: The Five Partners Model," *Business Quarterly* (Winter 1993).

D'Cruz, Joseph R. and Rugman, Alan M. "Business Network Theory and the Canadian Telecommunications Industry," *International Business Review,* vol. 3, no. 3 (1994).

Doyle, Frank P. "People-Power: The Global Human Resource Challenge for the '90s," *Columbia Journal of World Business,* vol. 25, nos. 1, 2 (Spring/Summer 1990).

Dunning, John H. *Multinational Enterprises and the Global Economy* (Reading, UK: Addison-Wesley, 1993).

Dunning, John H. *The Globalization of Business: The Challenge of the 1990s* (London and New York: Routledge, 1993).

Egelhoff, William G. "Information-Processing Theory and the Multinational Enterprise," *Journal of International Business*, vol. 22, no. 3 (Third Quarter 1991).

Emmerij, Louis. "Globalization, Regionalization and World Trade," *Columbia Journal of World Business*, vol. 27, no. 2 (Summer 1992).

Ghoshal, Sumantra and Bartlett, Christopher A. "The Multinational Corporation as an Interorganizational Network," *Academy of Management Review*, vol. 15, no. 4 (October 1990).

Giddens, A. *Runaway World: How Globalization is Reshaping Our Lives* (London: Profile Books, 1998).

Gray, J. *False Dawn: The Delusions of Global Capitalism* (London: Granata Books, 1998).

Guntz, Hugh P. and Jalland, R. Michael. "Managerial Careers and Business Strategies," *Academy of Management Review*, vol. 21, no. 3 (July 1996).

Kim, W. Chan and Mauborgne, Renée A. "Effectively Conceiving and Executing Multinationals' Worldwide Strategies," *Journal of International Business Studies*, vol. 24, no. 3 (Third Quarter 1993).

Kirton, John J., Daniels, Joseph P. and Freytag, Andreas (eds.). *Guiding Global Order: G8 Governance in the 21st Century* (Aldershot: Ashgate, 2001).

Kogut, Bruce. "Methodological Contributions in International Business Research and the Direction of Academic Research Activity," in Alan M. Rugman and Thomas Brewer (eds.), *The Oxford Handbook of International Business* (Oxford: Oxford University Press, 2001).

Martinez, Jon I. and Jarillo, J. Carlos. "Coordination Demands of International Strategies," *Journal of International Business Studies*, vol. 22, no. 3 (Third Quarter 1991).

Miller, Kent D. "Industry and Country Effects of Managers' Perceptions of Environmental Uncertainties," *Journal of International Business Studies*, vol. 24, no. 4 (Fourth Quarter 1993).

Morrison, Allen J. and Inkpen, Andrew C. "An Analysis of Significant Contributions to the International Business Literature," *Journal of International Business Studies*, vol. 22, no. 1 (First Quarter 1991).

Nehrt, Chad. "Maintaining a First Mover Advantage When Environmental Regulations Differ Between Countries," *Academy of Management Review*, vol. 23, no. 1 (January 1998).

Ohmae, Kenichi. "Managing in a Borderless World," *Harvard Business Review*, vol. 67, no. 3 (May/June 1989).

Rosenzweig, Philip M. and Singh, Jitendra V. "Organizational Environments and the Multinational Enterprise," *Academy of Management Review*, vol. 16, no. 2 (April 1991).

Rugman, Alan M. "Multinationals and Trade in Services: A Transaction Cost Approach," *Weltwirtschaftliches Archiv*, vol. 123, no. 4 (December 1987).

Rugman, A. M. *The End of Globalization* (London: Random House, 2000). (Also published in 2001 by AMACOM/McGraw Hill.)

Rugman, Alan M. and D'Cruz, Joseph R. "A Theory of Business Networks," in Lorraine Eden (ed.), *Multinationals in North America* (Alberta: University of Calgary Press, 1993).

Rugman, Alan M. and D'Cruz, Joseph R. *Multinationals as Flagship Firms: Regional Business Networks* (Oxford: Oxford University Press, 2000, paper, 2002).

Rugman, Alan M., Kirton, John and Soloway, Julie. *Environmental Regulations and Corporate Strategy* (Oxford: Oxford University Press, 1999).

Rugman, Alan M. and Verbeke, Alain. *Research in Global Strategic Management: Volume 3: Corporate Response to Global Change* (Greenwich, CT: JAI Press, 1992).

Rugman, Alan M. and Verbeke, Alain. *Research in Global Strategic Management: Volume 4: Beyond the Three Generics* (Greenwich, CT: JAI Press, 1993).

Rugman, Alan M. and Verbeke, Alain. "Corporate Strategies and Environmental Regulations: An Organizing Framework," *Strategic Management Journal*, vol. 19, Special Issue (April 1998).

Rugman, Alan M. and Verbeke, Alain. "Six Cases of Corporate Strategic Response to Environmental Regulations," *European Management Journal*, vol. 18, no. 4 (August 2000), pp. 377–385.

Rugman, Alan M. and Verbeke, Alain. "Towards a Theory of Multinational Enterprises and the Civil Society," in A. Ghobadian, et al. (eds.), *Strategy and Performance, Achieving Competitive Advantage in the Global Marketplace* (Basingstoke, Hampshire: Palgrave Macmillan, 2004).

Shan, Weijian. "Environmental Risks and Joint Venture Sharing Arrangements," *Journal of International Business Studies*, vol. 22, no. 4 (Fourth Quarter 1991).

Stiglitz, J. E. *Globalization and its Discontents* (New York: Norton, 2002).

Vandermerwe, Sandra and Oliff, Michael D. "Corporate Challenges for an Age of Reconsumption," *Columbia Journal of World Business*, vol. 26, no. 3 (Fall 1991).

Westcott, William F., II. "Environmental Technology Cooperation: A Quid Pro Quo for Transnational Corporations and Developing Countries," *Columbia Journal of World Business*, vol. 27, no. 3 (Fall/Winter 1992).

Wright, Richard W. *International Entrepreneurship: Globalization of Emerging Business: Volume 7: Research in Global Strategic Management* (Oxford: Elsevier/JAI Press, 1999).

Yip, George S. "Global Strategy . . . In a World of Nations?" *Sloan Management Review*, vol. 31, no. 1 (Fall 1989).

Zahra, Shaker A. "The Changing Rules of Global Competitiveness in the 21st Century," *Academy of Management Executive*, vol. 13, no. 1 (February 1999).

Glossary

Acceptance zone. An area within which a party is willing to negotiate.

Achievement oriented. Where status is earned rather than a right. Recruitment and promotion opportunities tend to be more dependent on performance, as in a meritocracy.

Ad valorem duty. A tax that is based on a percentage of the value of imported goods.

Adjusted present value (APV). An NPV that takes into account sources of country risk that might impact a project's expected future cash flows.

Advertising. A non-personal form of promotion in which a firm attempts to persuade consumers of a particular point of view.

Amakudari. (Literally "descent from heaven") The temporary or permanent movement of public-sector officials in Japan into private corporations as a mechanism for coordinating national policy and company strategy.

Andean common market (Ancom). A sub-regional free trade compact designed to promote economic and social integration and cooperation; Bolivia, Colombia, Ecuador, Peru, and Venezuela are all members.

Andean Community. An economic union consisting of Bolivia, Colombia, Ecuador, Peru, and Venezuela.

Antidumping duties (AD). Import tariffs intended to protect domestic producers from foreign products sold at less than their cost of production or at lower prices than in their home market.

Arbitrageur. A person or firm that deals in foreign exchange, buying or selling foreign currency with simultaneous contracting to exchange back to the original currency. Arbitrageurs thus do not undertake exchange risk.

Arm's length price. The price that exists or would exist on a sale of a given product or service between two unrelated companies—as contrasted with an intra-company transfer price.

Ascription oriented. Where status is more of a right than earned. Recruitment and promotion opportunities tend to be more dependent on seniority, ethnicity, gender, religion, or birth.

Association of Southeast Asian Nations (ASEAN). An economic union founded in 1967 that includes Brunei Darussalam, Cambodia, Indonesia, Laos, Malaysia, Myanmar, the Philippines, Singapore, Thailand, and Vietnam; this economic bloc focuses not on reducing trade barriers among members but, rather, on promoting exports to other nations.

Autonomous infrastructure. An infrastructure used by multinationals that compete in dissimilar national markets and do not share resources.

Backward integration. The ownership of equity assets used earlier in the production cycle, such as an auto firm that acquires a steel company.

Balance sheet hedging. The use of financial instruments denominated in foreign currency to eliminate exchange rate (translation) risk from the balance sheet of a company.

Basic mission. The reason that a firm is in existence.

Benkyokai. Study associations or work groups for students or colleagues in companies to jointly develop particular areas of knowledge and expertise.

Business managers. Managers responsible for coordinating the efforts of people in a corporate organization; for example, in a matrix structure.

Canada Labor Code. A federal law that covers areas such as wages, employment practices, work safety, and conciliation of labor disputes.

Caribbean Basin Initiative. A trade agreement that eliminates tariffs on many imports to the United States from the Caribbean and Central American regions.

Cartel. A group of firms that collectively agree to fix prices or quantities sold in an effort to control price.

Centrally-determined economy. An economy in which goods and services are allocated based on a plan formulated by a committee that decides what is to be offered.

Chu, meaning loyalty and **giri,** meaning duty, obligation, or responsibility. These terms are often used together to denote the traditionally close, trusting relationship between managers and employees. They are also used to describe the ties between older and younger members of a family.

Civil society. A group of individuals, organizations, and institutions that act outside the government and the market to advance a diverse set of interests.

Clearing account. A centralized cash management bank account in which one MNE affiliate reviews payment needs among various MNE affiliates and arranges to make payments of net funds due from each affiliate to others through the clearing account.

Cluster analysis. A marketing approach to forecasting customer demand that involves grouping data based on market area, customer, or similar variables.

Codetermination. A legal system that requires workers and their managers to discuss major strategic decisions before companies implement the decisions.

Collectivism. The tendency of people to belong to groups who look after each other in exchange for loyalty.

Common market. A form of economic integration characterized by the elimination of trade barriers among member nations, a common external trade policy, and mobility of factors of production among member countries.

Communication. The process of transferring meanings from sender to receiver.

Communism. A political system in which the government owns all property and makes all decisions regarding production and distribution of goods and services.

Comparative advertising. The comparing of similar products for the purpose of persuading customers to buy a particular one.

Competition Act. A Canadian federal law that regulates anticompetitive practices and prohibits actions that will substantially lessen or prevent competition; it is similar to US antitrust laws.

Competitive intelligence. The gathering of external information on competitors and the competitive environment as part of the decision-making process.

Competitive scope. The breadth of a firm's target market within an industry.

Compound duty. A tariff consisting of both a specific and an ad valorem duty.

Concurrent engineering. The process of having design, engineering, and manufacturing people working together to create a product, in contrast to working in a sequential manner.

Consolidation. The translation of foreign affiliate accounts and addition to home-country accounts for the purpose of reporting complete (global) condition of a company. Consolidation of foreign affiliate accounts that are denominated in other currencies necessarily produces translation risk.

Container ships. Vessels used to carry standardized containers that can be simply loaded onto a carrier and then unloaded at their destination without any repackaging of the contents of the containers.

Contract management. A process by which an organization (such as the government) transfers operating responsibility of an industry without transferring the legal title and ownership.

Control. The fundamental function of management that involves developing profit plans for the firm and its divisions and then deciding what to do when actual operating results differ from those planned.

Controlling. The process of determining that everything goes according to plan.

Coordinated infrastructure. An infrastructure used when there is a high degree of similarity among national markets and business units share resources in an effort to help each other raise overall sales.

Co-prosperity pyramid. A supply chain linked to a vertical, manufacturing *keiretsu*. It is hierarchical, with firms in the top tiers engaged in technology sharing, personnel exchanges, cross-shareholding, and long-term trading relationships. The further down the hierarchy a firm sits the more important price becomes and the less they are considered *keiretsu* members.

Corporate culture. The shared values, traditions, customs, philosophy, and policies of a corporation; also, the professional atmosphere that grows from this and affects behavior and performance.

Corruption. The misuse of public power for private benefit.

Cost strategy. A strategy that relies on low price and is achieved through approaches such as vigorous pursuit of cost reductions and overhead control, avoidance of marginal customer accounts, and cost minimization in areas such as sales and advertising.

Cost-of-living allowance. A payment to compensate for differences in expenditures between the home country and the foreign location.

Council of Ministers. The major policy decision-making body of the EU and one of its major institutions, consisting of one minister from each of the 12 member states.

Council of the European Union. The major policy decision-making body of the EU; it consists of one minister from each of the 25 member states and is one of four major institutions of the EU.

Countertrade. Barter trade in which the exporting firm receives payment in products from the importing country.

Countervailing duties (CVD). Import tariffs intended to protect domestic producers from harmful subsidization by foreign governments.

Country risk analysis. Examines the chances of non-market events (political, social, and economic) causing financial, strategic, or personnel losses to a firm following FDI in a specific country market.

Country-specific advantages (CSAs). Strengths or benefits specific to a country that result from its competitive environment, labor force, geographic location, government policies, industrial clusters, etc.

Court of Auditors. A court that has one judge appointed from each EU member country; this court monitors the financial aspects of the union.

Court of Justice. A court that has one judge appointed from each EU member country; this court serves as the official interpreter of EU law.

Cultural assimilator. A programmed learning technique designed to expose members of one culture to some of the basic concepts, attitudes, role perceptions, customs, and values of another culture.

Cultural convergence. The growing similarity between national cultures, including the beliefs, values, aspirations, and the preferences of consumers, partly driven by global brands, media, and common global icons.

Culture. The acquired knowledge that people use to interpret experience and to generate social behavior.

Culture clash. When two cultural groups (national or corporate) meet, interact, or work together and differences in their values, beliefs, rules of behavior, or styles of communication create misunderstandings, antagonism, or other problems.

Currency diversification. An exchange risk management technique through which the firm places activities or assets and liabilities into multiple currencies, thus reducing the impact of exchange rate change for any one of them.

Currency inconvertibility. The inability of a firm to transfer profit from a subsidiary in a host country to other areas of the organization or to shareholders because of host government restrictions on profit remittances.

Customs union. A form of economic integration in which all tariffs between member countries are eliminated and a common trade policy toward non-member countries is established.

Debt–equity ratio. The value of a firm's total debt divided by the value of its total equity. A higher ratio implies greater leverage, and potentially greater risk.

Decision making. The process of choosing from among alternatives.

Delayed differentiation. A strategy in which all products are manufactured in the same way for all countries or regions until as late in the assembly process as possible, at which time differentiation is used to introduce particular features or special components.

Demand-Flow™ Technology (DFT). A production process that is flexible to demand changes.

Democracy. A system of government in which the people, either directly or through their elected officials, decide what is to be done.

Differentiation strategy. A strategy directed toward creating something that is perceived as being unique.

Diffuse. A tendency for workplace relationships and obligations, including relative status and hierarchical position, to extend into social situations and activities outside of work.

Distribution. The course that goods take between production and the final consumer.

Divestiture. (Also see *Privatization.*) A process by which a government or business sells assets.

Dumping. The selling of imported goods at a price below cost or below that in the home country.

Economic integration. The establishment of transnational rules and regulations that enhance economic trade and cooperation among countries.

Economic risk. The risk of financial loss or gain to an MNE due to the effects of unanticipated exchange rate changes on future cash flows that are denominated in foreign currencies.

Economic union. A form of economic integration characterized by free movement of goods, services, and factors of production among member countries and full integration of economic policies.

Embargo. A quota set at zero, thus preventing the importation of those products that are involved.

Emotional. An acceptance of emotion and subjectivity as the bases for some decision making and a preference for explicit displays of emotions and feelings in the workplace.

Empowerment. The process of giving employees increased control over their work.

Endaka. Yen-appreciation; the growing value of the yen vis-à-vis other currencies which, among other things, made Japan a relatively expensive place to manufacture.

Enterprise for the Americas. An idea launched by President George Bush to create a free trade area from Alaska to Argentine Antarctica.

Esprit de corps. The spirit of a group that makes the members want the group to succeed.

Estimation by analogy. A method of forecasting market demand or market growth based on information generated in other countries, such as determining the number of refrigerators sold in the United States as a percentage of new housing starts and using this statistic in planning for the manufacture of these products in other world markets.

Ethnocentric. A belief in the superiority of one's own ethnic group. The dominance of the home-country culture in decision making, human resource management, and overall corporate culture in a multinational firm.

Ethnocentric predisposition. The tendency of a manager or multinational company to rely on the values and interests of the parent company in formulating and implementing the strategic plan.

Ethnocentric solution. A centralized decision-making framework in which financial decisions and control for foreign affiliates are largely integrated into home-office management.

Ethnocentrism. The belief that one's way of doing things is superior to that of others.

Eurobond. A bond denominated in foreign currency issued in any country's financial market. Most eurobonds are issued in London or in Luxembourg (for tax reasons).

Eurocurrency. A bank deposit in any country, which is denominated in a foreign currency. A yen-denominated bank deposit in Germany is a euro-yen deposit, a form of eurocurrency.

Eurodollar. A dollar-denominated bank deposit outside of the United States.

European Coal and Steel Community (ECSC). A community formed in 1952 by Belgium, France, Italy, Luxembourg, the Netherlands, and West Germany for the purpose of creating a common market that would revitalize the efficiency and competitiveness of the coal and steel industries in those countries.

European Commission. A 25-member group chosen by agreement of member governments of the EU; the Commission is the executive branch of the EU.

European Council. Composed of the heads of state of each EU member country as well as the president of the European Commission. Meetings of the Council take place at least twice a year and their purpose is to resolve major policy issues and to set policy direction.

European Free Trade Association (EFTA). A free trade area currently consisting of Iceland, Liechtenstein, Norway, and Switzerland; past members included the UK (before it joined the EU).

European Monetary Union (EMU). The agreement among, initially, 11 of the European Union countries to eliminate their currencies and create the euro. European Union countries do not necessarily have to join the EMU.

European Parliament. A group of 732 representatives elected directly by voters in each member country of the EU; the Parliament serves as a watchdog on EU expenditures.

European Research Cooperation Agency. A research and development alliance that emphasizes projects in the fields of energy, medicine, biotechnology, communications, information technology, transport, new materials, robotics, production automation, lasers, and the environment.

European Union (EU). A treaty-based institutional framework that manages economic and political cooperation among its 25 member states: Austria, Belgium, Cyprus, Czech Republic, Denmark, Estonia, Finland, France, Germany, Greece, Hungary, Ireland, Italy, Latvia, Lithuania, Luxembourg, Malta, the Netherlands, Poland, Portugal, Slovakia, Slovenia, Spain, Sweden, and the United Kingdom.

Exchange controls. Controls that restrict the flow of currency.

Exchange rate. The value of one currency in terms of another. For example, $US 1.30 / € 1.

Exchange risk. The risk of financial loss or gain due to an unexpected change in a currency's value.

Exchange risk adaptation. An exchange risk management technique through which a company adjusts its business activities to try to balance foreign-currency assets and liabilities, and inflows and outflows.

Exchange risk avoidance. An exchange risk management technique through which the firm tries to avoid operating in more than one currency.

Exchange risk transfer. An exchange risk management technique through which the firm contracts with a third party to pass exchange risk onto that party, via such instruments as forward contracts, futures, and options.

Expatriates. Individuals who reside abroad but are citizens of the multinational's parent country; they are citizens of the home, not the host country.

Export tariff. A tax levied on goods sent out of a country.

Exports. Goods and services produced by a firm in one country and then sent to another country.

Expropriation. The governmental seizure of private businesses coupled with little, if any, compensation to their owners.

External economies of scale. Efficiencies brought about by access to cheaper capital, highly skilled labor, and superior technology.

Factor conditions. Land, labor, and capital.

Factor endowment theory. A trade theory which holds that nations will produce and export products that use large amounts of production factors that they have in abundance and will import products requiring a large amount of production factors that they lack.

FDI cluster. A group of developing countries usually located in the same geographic region as a triad member and having some form of economic link to this member.

Firm-specific advantages (FSAs). Strengths or benefits specific to a firm and a result of contributions that can be made by its personnel, technology, and/or equipment.

Five partners. A business network consisting of five partner organizations: the flagship firm (a multinational enterprise), key suppliers, key customers, key competitors, and the non-business infrastructure.

Flagship firms. Multinational firms characterized by global competitiveness and international benchmarks.

Flying Geese model. A model suggesting that Asian countries are following Japan's historical economic transition, specializing in particular industries (steel to textiles to clothing to autos to electronics) during particular growth stages. At a particular point in time we should expect to see these industries located in different Asian countries, depending on their resource endowments, labor costs, and capabilities.

Focus strategy. A strategy that concentrates on a particular buyer group and segments that niche based on product line or geographic market.

Foreign bond. A bond issued by a foreign company in another country's financial market. In Japan, these are called "Samurai bonds."

Foreign direct investment (FDI). Equity funds invested in other nations.

Foreign exchange. Foreign-currency-denominated financial instruments, ranging from cash to bank deposits to other financial contracts payable or receivable in foreign currency.

Foreign exchange broker. A company that providers specialized services to commercial banks in the interbank foreign exchange market, essentially functioning to unite interested buyers and sellers of foreign-currency-denominated bank deposits. Brokers intermediate about half of all wholesale foreign exchange transactions in New York and London.

Foreign exchange traders. Bankers who deal in foreign exchange, buying and selling foreign currencies on behalf of clients and/or for the bank itself. Typically they deal in foreign-currency-denominated bank deposits.

Foreign investment controls. Limits on foreign direct investment or the transfer or remittance of funds.

Foreign investment review agency. A government agency that reviews applications for foreign direct investment projects and approves or disapproves the projects, according to standards established by the government.

Foreign Sales Corporation Act. Legislation designed to allow US exporters to establish overseas affiliates and not pay taxes on the affiliates' income until the earnings are remitted to the parent company.

Foreign trade zones. Areas where foreign goods may be held and processed and then re-exported without incurring customs duties (same as a free trade zone).

Forward integration. The purchase of assets or facilities that move the company closer to the customer, such as a computer manufacturer that acquires a retail chain which specializes in computer products.

Forward rate. An exchange rate contracted today for some future date of actual currency exchange. Banks offer forward rates to clients to buy or sell foreign currency in the future, guaranteeing the rate at the time of the agreement.

Free trade area. An economic integration arrangement in which barriers to trade (such as tariffs) among member countries are removed.

Free Trade Area of the Americas (FTAA). A regional trade agreement that is expected to succeed NAFTA and include 34 countries across North, Central, and South America.

Free trade zone. A designated area where importers can defer payment of customs duty while further processing of products takes place (same as a foreign trade zone).

Fronting loan. A third-party loan in which an MNE home office deposits funds with a financial institution, which then lends to the MNE's affiliate in a country where the MNE faces political risk or currency transfer restrictions.

Funds positioning techniques. Mechanisms such as transfer pricing, intercompany loans, and timing of payments that are used to move funds from one affiliate to another in a multinational firm.

Gaijin. A term used for non-Japanese and while not too offensive is not particularly polite. *Gai* means outside or foreign, *jin* means person.

General Agreement on Tariffs and Trade (GATT). A major trade organization that has been established to negotiate trade concessions among member countries.

Geocentric. Neither home nor host country culture dominates decision making, human resource management, and overall corporate culture in a multinational firm.

Geocentric predisposition. The tendency of a multinational to construct its strategic plan with a global view of operations.

Geocentric solution. A decision-making framework in which financial decisions and evaluation related to foreign affiliates are integrated for the firm on a global basis.

Gestion. The skill or practice of controlling, directing, or planning something, especially a commercial enterprise or activity.

Global area structure. An organizational arrangement in which primary operational responsibility is delegated to area managers, each of whom is responsible for a specific geographic region.

Global functional structure. An organizational arrangement in which all areas of activity are built around the basic tasks of the enterprise.

Global product structure. An organizational arrangement in which domestic divisions are given worldwide responsibility for product groups.

Global sourcing. The use of suppliers anywhere in the world, chosen on the basis of their efficiency.

Globalization. The production and distribution of products and services of a homogeneous type and quality on a worldwide basis.

Grande Ecole. One of the "grand" or great schools considered to be the pinnacle of French higher education, highly selective and prestigious and the main source of the country's business and political leaders.

Guanxi. Personalized or informal networks of relationships in China. They can be important preconditions for smoothing the way or gaining favors or advantages, particularly when both society and the economy are dominated by central government. There are parallels with the concept of social capital.

Hai. "Yes" in Japanese does not necessarily mean "yes I agree," but "yes, I hear what you say."

Hardship allowance. A special payment made to individuals posted to geographic areas regarded as less desirable.

Heckscher–Ohlin theory. A trade theory that extends the concept of comparative advantage by bringing into consideration the endowment and cost of factors of production and helps to explain why nations with relatively large labor forces will concentrate on producing labor-intensive goods, whereas countries with relatively more capital than labor will specialize in capital-intensive goods.

Hedge. A strategy to protect the firm against risk, in this case against exchange rate risk.

Home-country nationals. Citizens of the country where the multinational resides.

Horizontal integration. The purchase of firms in the same line of business, such as a computer chip firm that acquires a competitor.

Host-country nationals. Local people hired by a multinational.

Humane orientation. Cultures that emphasize helping others, charity, and peoples' wider social obligations.

Ideology. A set of integrated beliefs, theories, and doctrines that helps to direct the actions of a society.

Import tariff. A tax levied on goods shipped into a country.

Imports. Goods and services produced in one country and brought in by another country.

Indigenization laws. Laws which require that nationals hold a majority interest in all enterprises.

Individualism. The tendency of people to look after themselves and their immediate family only.

Industrial democracy. The legally mandated right of employees to participate in significant management decisions.

Initial screening. The process of determining the basic need potential of the multinational's goods and services in foreign markets.

Integrative techniques. Strategies designed to help a multinational become a part of the host country's infrastructure.

Intermodal containers. Large metal boxes that fit on trucks, railroads, and airplanes and help reduce handling costs and theft losses by placing the merchandise in a tightly sealed, easy-to-move unit.

Internal economies of scale. Efficiencies brought about by lower production costs and other savings within a firm.

International business. The study of transactions taking place across national borders for the purpose of satisfying the needs of individuals and organizations.

International division structure. An organizational arrangement in which all international operations are centralized in one division.

International Fisher effect. Theory of exchange rate determination that states that differences in nominal interest rates on similar-risk deposits will be eliminated by changes in the exchange rate.

International human resource management (IHRM). The process of selecting, training, developing, and compensating personnel in overseas positions.

International joint venture (IJV). An agreement between two or more partners to own and control an overseas business.

International logistics. The designing and managing of a system to control the flow of materials and products throughout the organization.

International market assessment. An evaluation of the goods and services that the multinational can sell in the global marketplace.

International marketing. The process of identifying the goods and services that customers outside the home country want and then providing them at the right price and place.

International Monetary Fund (IMF). The international organization founded at Bretton Woods, New Hampshire, in 1994 that includes most countries of the world and offers balance of payments support to countries in crisis along with financial advising to Central Banks.

International monetary system. The arrangement between national governments/central banks that oversees the operation of official foreign exchange dealings between countries. The central organization in the system today is the International Monetary Fund.

International product life cycle (IPLC) theory. A theory of the stages of production of a product with new "know-how"; it is first produced by the parent firm, then by its foreign subsidiaries, and finally anywhere in the world where costs are the lowest; it helps explain why a product that begins as a nation's export often ends up as an import.

International screening criteria. Factors used to identify individuals regarded as most suitable for overseas assignments.

International trade. The exchange of goods and services across international borders.

Internationalization. The process by which a company enters a foreign market.

Intra-regional investments. Investments in the local region rather than in other triad or non-triad regions, such as when Chinese firms invest in other Southeast Asian economies.

Investment Canada Act (ICA). An act designed to create a welcome climate for foreign investment by significantly loosening previous restrictions.

Just-in-time (JIT) inventory. The delivery of parts and supplies just as they are needed.

Kaizen. Normally taken to mean "continuous improvement" and is associated with lean or low-cost, high-productivity manufacturing. A more accurate interpretation is "to dismantle and re-assemble a process to make it better." As such *kaizen* was an early form of business process re-engineering.

Keiretsu. Groupings of Japanese firms with long-term associations and cross-shareholdings. Each firm maintains its operational independence but coordinates strategy and often exchanges assets and resources with other firms in its group.

Kinesics. A form of non-verbal communication that deals with conveying information through the use of body movement and facial expression.

Kinyu keiretsu. Horizontal conglomerates encompassing a wide range of diversified businesses, centered on a dominant bank and/or trading company.

Korean *chaebols.* Traditionally family-dominated, diversified conglomerates. Family ownership has been reduced and many are now focused in particular business sectors, reducing their diversity. There are parallels with Japanese *sogo shosha* in terms of early government support and their relationship with dominant national banks.

Latin American Integration Association (LAIA). A free trade group formed to reduce intra-regional trade barriers and to promote regional economic cooperation. Argentina, Bolivia, Brazil, Chile, Colombia, Ecuador, Mexico, Paraguay, Peru, Uruguay, and Venezuela are all members.

Leontief paradox. A finding by Wassily Leontief, a Nobel prize economist, which shows that the United States, surprisingly, exports relatively more labor-intensive goods and imports capital-intensive goods.

Liberalization policies. Government policies that move away from planned economics toward more free-market systems. They are marked by the privatization of state-owned businesses, a lowering of tariff and non-tariff barriers, and reductions in the constraints placed on foreign firms' investments and business activities.

LIBOR. The London Inter-Bank Offered Rate is the interest rate on large-scale foreign-currency-denominated deposits offered from one bank to another in London.

License. A contractual arrangement in which one firm (the licensor) provides access to some of its patents, trademarks, or technology to another firm in exchange for a fee or royalty.

Licensee. A firm given access to some of the patents, trademarks, or technology of another firm in exchange for a fee or royalty.

Licensor. A company that provides access to some of its patents, trademarks, or technology to another firm in exchange for a fee or royalty.

Lighter aboard ship (LASH) vessel. Barges stored on a ship and lowered at the point of destination.

Localization of production. The manufacturing of goods in the host market.

Localization of profits. The reinvestment of earnings in the local market.

Macro political risk. A risk that affects all foreign enterprises in the same way.

Managerial development. The process by which managers obtain the necessary skills, experiences, and attitudes that they need to become or remain successful leaders.

Maquiladora industry. A free trade zone that has sprung up along the US–Mexican border for the purpose of producing goods and then shipping them between the two countries.

Maquiladoras. (Also see *Twin factories.*) Production operations set up on both sides of the US–Mexican border in a free trade zone for the purpose of shipping goods between the two countries.

Market coordination infrastructure. An infrastructure used by firms that compete in similar national markets but do little resource sharing among their businesses.

Market growth. The annual increase in sales in a particular market.

Market indicators. Indicators used for measuring the relative market strengths of various geographic areas.

Market intensity. The richness of a market or the degree of purchasing power in one country as compared to others.

Market size. An economic screening consideration used in international marketing; it is the relative size of each market as a percentage of the total world market.

Market-driven economy. An economy in which goods and services are allocated on the basis of consumer demand.

Market-seeking FDI. MNEs invest in distribution, sales, or marketing operations in order to sell products or services (outputs) in particular country markets.

Masculinity. The degree to which the dominant values of a society are success, money, and material things.

Material handling. The careful planning of when, where, and how much inventory will be available to ensure maximum production efficiency.

Matrix structure. An organizational arrangement that blends two organizational responsibilities such as functional and product structures or regional and product structures.

Mercantilism. A trade theory which holds that a government can improve the economic well-being of the country by encouraging exports and stifling imports to accumulate wealth in the form of precious metals.

Mercosur. A subregional free trade group formed to promote economic cooperation; the group consists of Argentina, Brazil, Paraguay, and Uruguay.

Micro political risk. A risk that affects selected sectors of the economy or specific foreign businesses.

Ministry for Economy, Trade and Industry (METI). Superseded MITI, which was at the heart of Japan's post-war economic boom.

Ministry of Finance (MOF). A historically influential Japanese ministry that remains a powerful force in the deregulation of the economy.

Ministry of International Trade and Industry (MITI). A Japanese ministry charged with providing information about foreign markets and with encouraging investment in select industries and, in the process, helping to direct the economy.

Mitsubishi *Kinyokai.* The Friday Club in Marunouchi, Tokyo, where the most senior managers from the 29 core firms of the Mitsubishi *keiretsu* gather each month to discuss business.

Mittelstand. About 3.4 million small- and medium-sized firms defined as having less than 50 million euros turnover that make up the heart of the German economy.

Mixed economies. Economic systems characterized by a combination of market and centrally driven planning.

Mixed structure. A hybrid organization design that combines structural arrangements in a way that best meets the needs of the enterprise.

Modular integrated robotized system (MIRS). A software-based production process that relies entirely on robots.

Modular manufacturing. A manufacturing process that consists of modules that can be easily adapted to fit changing demand.

Monetary exchange rate. The price of one currency stated in terms of another currency.

Multilateral netting. Payment of net amounts due only between affiliates of a MNE that have multiple transactions among the group, which can be partially netted out among them, so then only the net funds need to be transferred.

Multinational enterprises (MNEs). A company headquartered in one country but having operations in other countries.

National responsiveness. The ability of MNEs to understand different consumer tastes in segmented regional markets and to respond to different national standards and regulations imposed by autonomous governments and agencies.

Nationalization. A process by which the government takes control of business assets, sometimes with remuneration of the owners and other times without such remuneration.

Nemawashi. Literally means "root-tying" and is a process of consultation to get agreement on a particular issue before it becomes explicit policy.

Neo mercantilism. A trade theory which holds that a government can improve the economic well-being of the country by encouraging exports and stifling imports.

Neutral. A preference for unemotional, objective analysis of a situation or a decision and for limited displays of emotions and feelings in the workplace.

Newly industrialized countries (NICs). A sub-group of emerging market economies that has experienced rapid economic growth, normally accompanied by political and social change. The forerunners were the four Asian "Tiger" economies: Singapore, South Korea, Taiwan, and Hong-Kong. The rapid growth, increased trade and FDI, and integration of China in the global economy suggest it is approaching this status.

Nominal interest rate. The actual rate of interest offered by a bank, typically given as an annual percentage rate.

Non-governmental organizations (NGOs). (Also see *Civil society*.) Private-sector groups that act to advance diverse social interests.

Non-tariff barriers. Rules, regulations, and bureaucratic red tape that delay or preclude the purchase of foreign goods.

North American Free Trade Agreement (NAFTA). A regional free trade agreement between Canada, the United States, and Mexico.

Organization for Economic Cooperation and Development (OECD). A group of 30 relatively wealthy member countries that facilitates a forum for the discussion of economic, social, and governance issues across the world.

Particularism. Judging a situation and adjusting rules and procedures according to the specific of the situation or individuals involved.

Personal selling. A direct form of promotion used to persuade customers of a particular point of view.

PEST framework. Examines the political, economic, sociocultural, and technological conditions in particular country markets.

Plaza Accord. An agreement signed by the G5 in 1985 in New York agreeing to devalue the US dollar against the Japanese yen and the Deutsche (German) mark. It triggered the bubble economy and eventual economic recession in Japan in the 1990s.

Political risk. The probability that political forces will negatively affect a multinational's profit or impede the attainment of other critical business objectives.

Political union. An economic union in which there is full economic integration, unification of economic policies, and a single government.

Polycentric. Each subsidiary, division, or function reflects the culture of its host country. Local managers' cultural predispositions and decision making dominate over those of home-country managers in a multinational firm.

Polycentric predisposition. The tendency of a multinational to tailor its strategic plan to meet the needs of the local culture.

Polycentric solution. A decentralized decision-making framework in which financial decisions are largely allocated to foreign affiliates, and financial evaluation of affiliates is done in comparison with other firms in that context.

Portfolio investment. The purchase of financial securities in other firms for the purpose of realizing a financial gain when these marketable assets are sold.

Power distance. A cultural dimension that measures the degree to which less powerful members of organizations and institutions accept the fact that power is not distributed equally.

Privatization. The process of selling government assets to private buyers.

Process mapping. A flow charting of every step that goes into producing a product.

Product managers. Managers responsible for coordinating the efforts of their people in such a way as to ensure the profitability of a particular business or product line.

Production system. A group of related activities designed to create value.

Promotion. The process of stimulating demand for a company's goods and services.

Protective and defensive techniques. Strategies designed to discourage a host country from interfering in multinational operations.

Proxemics. A form of non-verbal communication that deals with how people use physical space to convey messages.

Psychic distance. A measure of the similarity or difference between two cultures. Also commonly defined as the measurable distance between the home market and a foreign market resulting from the perception of cultural and business differences.

Purchasing power parity. The theory of exchange rate determination that states that differences in prices of the same goods between countries will be eliminated by exchange rate changes.

Quota. A quantity limit on imported goods.

Real interest rate. The nominal interest rate adjusted for price changes. Domestically, this means adjusting for inflation. Internationally, this means adjusting for exchange rate (currency price) changes.

Regiocentric predisposition. The tendency of a multinational to use a strategy that addresses both local and regional needs.

Regional managers. In a geocentric matrix, managers charged with selling products in their geographic locale.

Regression analysis. A mathematical approach to forecasting that attempts to test the explanatory power of a set of independent variables.

Repatriation. The process of returning home at the end of an overseas assignment.

Repatriation agreement. An agreement that spells out how long a person will be posted overseas and sets forth the type of job that will be given to the person upon returning.

Resource managers. In a matrix structure, managers charged with providing people for operations.

Resource-seeking FDI. MNEs invest in production-related activities to benefit from cheaper or better sources of inputs in a particular location; these can include raw materials, components, or labor and expertise.

Resource-sharing infrastructure. An infrastructure used by firms that compete in dissimilar national markets but share resources such as R&D efforts and manufacturing information.

Return on investment (ROI). A percentage determined by dividing net income before taxes by total assets.

Ringi. The formalized consensus process of decision making. The *ringisho* is a decision proposal that is circulated around company departments to be revised or approved before implementation.

Roll-on-roll-off (RORO) vessels. Ocean-going ferries that can carry trucks that drive onto built-in ramps and roll off at the point of debarkation.

Secular totalitarianism. A system of government in which the military controls everything and makes decisions that it deems to be in the best interests of the country.

Sequential. Cultures that view time in a sequential or linear fashion. Order comes from separating activities and commitments.

Shinjinrui. The new generation Japanese, with very different values and aspirations than their parents.

Single European Act (SEA). An Act passed by the EU that contains many measures to further integrate the member states, along economic and political dimensions, and that allows the Council of Ministers to pass most proposals by a majority vote, in contrast to the unanimous vote needed previously.

Single European market (SEM). A market consisting of all members of the EU, bound together by a single currency, a special charter, complete harmonization of social and economic policies, and a common defense policy.

Small- and medium-sized enterprises (SMEs). The definition of SMEs varies according to the nation. In the US, SMEs are companies with up to 500 employees. In the EU, SMEs have between 11 and 200 employees and sales of under US $40 billion. In Japan, SMEs in industry have up to 300 employees while those in wholesale and retail have up to 150 and 50 employees, respectively. Developing countries use the World Bank benchmark of 11 to 150 employees and sales of under US $5 billion.

Socialization. The process of enculturation, or the adoption of the behavior patterns of the surrounding culture.

Sogo shosha. International trading companies that help other Japanese firms import and export products and services. They were very influential in the rapid growth era in helping local firms break into overseas markets.

Special drawing right (SDR). The currency of the IMF. Accounts at the IMF are denominated in SDRs, and the IMF has issued about $ US 30 billion of SDRs as currency since its inception in 1969.

Specific. A tendency to limit workplace relationships and obligations, including relative status and hierarchical position, to the workplace.

Specific duty. A tariff based on the number of items being shipped into a country.

Speculator. A person or firm that takes a position in foreign exchange with no hedging or protection mechanism. The person would take this action to try to gain from expected exchange rate changes.

Spot rate. The exchange rate offered on the same day as the request to buy or sell foreign currency. Actual settlement (payment) may occur one or two days later.

Standardized training programs. Generic programs that can be used with managers anywhere in the world.

State-owned enterprises (SOEs). Companies that are owned, financed, and controlled by government. Privatization is the process whereby ownership and control is transferred to the private sector through sales of state-owned assets.

Strategic alliance. A business relationship in which two or more companies work together to achieve a collective advantage.

Strategic business units (SBUs). Operating units with their own strategic space; they produce and sell goods and services to a market segment and have a well-defined set of competitors.

Strategic cluster. A network of businesses and supporting activities located in a specific region, where flagship firms compete globally and supporting activities are home based.

Strategic fit. A strategic management concept which holds that an organization must align its resources in such a way as to mesh effectively with the environment.

Strategic management. Managerial actions that include strategy formulation, strategy implementation, evaluation, and control and encompass a wide range of activities, including environmental analysis of external and internal conditions and evaluation of organizational strengths and weaknesses.

Strategic planning. The process of evaluating the enterprise's environment and its internal strengths and then identifying long- and short-range activities.

Strategy formulation. The process of evaluating the enterprise's environment and its internal strengths.

Strategy implementation. The process of attaining goals by using the organizational structure to execute the formulated strategy properly.

Synchronic. Cultures that view events in parallel over time. Order comes from coordinating multiple activities and commitments.

Tailor-made training programs. Programs designed to meet the specific needs of the participants, typically including a large amount of culturally based input.

Tariff. A tax on goods shipped internationally.

Tax havens. Jurisdictions that offers the MNE a lower tax rate (or no tax) than in other places, so that MNEs can locate some of their business activities there and thus reduce overall tax payments.

Theocratic totalitarianism. A system of government in which a religious group exercises total power and represses or persecutes non-orthodox factions.

Theory of absolute advantage. A trade theory which holds that nations can increase their economic well-being by specializing in goods that they can produce more efficiently than anyone else.

Theory of comparative advantage. A trade theory which holds that nations should produce those goods for which they have the greatest relative advantage.

Third-country nationals. Citizens of countries other than the one in which the multinational is headquartered or the one in which they are assigned to work by the multinational.

Time-to-market accelerators. Factors that help reduce bottlenecks and errors and ensure product quality and performance.

Totalitarianism. A system of government in which one individual or party maintains complete control and either refuses to recognize other parties or suppresses them.

Trade adjustment assistance. Assistance offered by the US government to US businesses and individuals harmed by competition from imports.

Trade creation. A process in which members of an economic integration group begin to focus their efforts on those goods and services for which they have a comparative advantage and start trading more extensively with each other.

Trade diversion. Occurs when members of an economic integration group decrease their trade with non-member countries in favor of trade with each other.

Training. The process of altering employee behavior and attitudes in a way that increases the probability of goal attainment.

Transaction risk. The risk of financial loss or gain to an MNE due to unanticipated exchange rate changes affecting future cash flows from transactions that are denominated in foreign exchange.

Transfer price. The price used for an intra-company payment for shipment of products or services from one affiliate to another in an MNE. These prices can be used to reduce taxes, move funds to desired locations, etc.

Transit tariff. A tax levied on goods passing through a country.

Transition strategies. Strategies designed to help smooth the move from foreign to domestic assignments.

Translation risk. The risk of losses or gains on the MNE's balance sheet, due to unhedged exchange rate changes during an accounting period.

Transnational network structure. An organization design that helps MNEs take advantage of global economies of scale while also being responsive to local customer demands .

Transparency. The *clarity* and *consistency* of policies and legislation applied in the governance of businesses.

Trend analysis. The estimation of future demand by either extrapolating the growth over the last three to five years and assuming that this trend will continue or by using some form of average growth rate over the recent past.

Triad. The three major trading and investment blocs in the international arena: the United States, the EU, and Japan.

Twin factories. (Also see *Maquiladoras.*) Production operations set up on both sides of the US–Mexican border for the purpose of shipping goods between the two countries.

Uncertainty avoidance. The extent to which people feel threatened by ambiguous situations and have created institutions and beliefs for minimizing or avoiding those uncertainties.

Unconventional cargo vessels. Vessels used for shipping oversized and unusual cargoes.

United States–Canada Free Trade Agreement (FTA). A trade agreement that eliminates most trade restrictions (such as tariffs) between these two countries and extends national treatment to foreign investment.

Universalism. The uniform application of rules and procedures, regardless of situation, context, or individuals involved.

Value chain. The way in which primary and support activities are combined in providing goods and services and increasing profit margins.

Vertical integration. The ownership of assets involved in producing a good or service and delivering it to the final customer.

Virtual integration. A networking strategy based on cooperation within and across company boundaries.

Weighted Country Risk Assessment Model. Combines an investment project appraisal with country risk analysis.

Weighted-average cost of capital (WACC). The firm's cost of obtaining funds from the various sources available. Each source of funds is weighted (multiplied) by the percentage of total capital it provides. Thus, the WACC is W_1 (cost of using retained earnings) + W_2 (cost of bank borrowing) + W_3 (cost of other source of funds), where each cost is stated as an annual percentage rate and each W is the percentage of total capital from that source.

Work councils. Groups that consist of both worker and manager representatives and are charged with dealing with matters such as improving company performance, working conditions, and job security.

Working capital. Short-term financial instruments such as bank deposits and marketable securities that can be optimized by the MNE on a global basis.

World Bank. The world's largest development bank, formed along with the IMF at Bretton Woods in 1944. Its original name was the International Bank for Reconstruction and Development (IBRD). The World Bank assists developing countries with loans and economic advising for economic development.

World Trade Organization (WTO). An international organization that deals with the rules of trade among member countries. One of its most important functions is to act as a dispute-settlement mechanism.

WTO accession. Admission to the World Trade Organization; in return for the right to access and to engage in fair trade with other national markets, the country must liberalize its own markets.

Zaibatsu. The pre-war antecedents of some modern-day *keiretsu* in Japan. Attempts by the allied forces to break these up after World War II largely failed.

Indexes

COMPANY INDEX

NAME INDEX